Cultural History
of Reading

Cultural History of Reading

Volume 1
World Literature

Edited by
GABRIELLE WATLING

GREENWOOD PRESS
Westport, Connecticut • London

Library of Congress Cataloging-in-Publication Data

Cultural history of reading.
    p. cm.
 Includes bibliographical references and index.
 ISBN 978–0–313–33744–4 (set : alk. paper) — ISBN 978–0–313–33745–1 (v.1 : alk. paper) —
ISBN 978–0–313–33746–8 (v.2 : alk. paper)
 1. Books and reading—Social aspects—History. 2. Books and reading—Social aspects—United
States—History. I. Watling, Gabrielle. II. Quay, Sara E.
 Z1003.C89 2009
 028'.9—dc22   2008019927

British Library Cataloguing in Publication Data is available.

Library of Congress Catalog Card Number: 2008019927
ISBN: 978–0–313–33744–4 (set)
      978–0–313–33745–1 (vol. 1)
      978–0–313–33746–8 (vol. 2)

First published in 2009

Greenwood Press, 88 Post Road West, Westport, CT 06881
An imprint of Greenwood Publishing Group, Inc.
www.greenwood.com

Printed in the United States of America

∞™

The paper used in this book complies with the
Permanent Paper Standard issued by the National
Information Standards Organization (Z39.48-1984).

10 9 8 7 6 5 4 3 2 1

The publisher has done its best to make sure the instructions and/or recipes in this book are correct. However, users should apply judgment and experience when preparing recipes, especially parents and teachers working with young people. The publisher accepts no responsibility for the outcome of any recipe included in this volume.

Contents

Preface

Cultural History of Reading explores what people have read and why they have read it, at different times and in different places in America and around the world. Written in two volumes, the project links key cultural changes and events to the reading material of the period. In doing so, it offers students and teachers a lens through which to better understand the way that culture shapes, and is shaped by, the act of reading.

The set is divided into two volumes, one focused on reading throughout the world, the other focused specifically on reading in the United States. While Volume One explores reading in different regions of the world, Volume Two looks at reading in different periods of American history.

Both volumes trace reading trends through an exploration of types of texts as well as specific examples of books, magazines, and political treatises that were influential and/or widely read. The chapters use a similar organizational framework based on the types of texts readers read. Whereas Volume Two explores reading patterns in the United States from the early colonial period to the present day, Volume One examines reading as a global phenomenon, and includes chapters on the non-U.S. Americas (Canada, Latin America, and the Caribbean), Europe and Britain, Asia and the Pacific, South Asia and the Indian Sub-Continent, and Africa and the Middle East.

Though different genres were popular at different times and in different regions, students and teachers will find common categories across chapters and volumes, including political texts, religious texts, historical texts, domestic texts, and creative texts such as fiction, poetry, and drama. As a result, they can explore the ways in which readers have engaged with a specific type of text over time, as well as tracing the general cultural history of reading within particular regions and time frames. Specific books, too, were important to readers at different times and in different regions. Such significant works—and their effects—can be explored across chapters and even volumes, as in the cases of the Bible, Harriet Beecher Stowe's *Uncle Tom's Cabin*, or the Harry Potter books.

Chapters also include a "Timeline of Events" and an "Introduction to the Region/Time Period" that point out major events of the time or region that would have influenced what and how people read. An overview of "Reading Trends and Practices" traces key trends in reading practices, including the development of lending libraries, the rise of the novel, and the impact of technology. The book also explores the relationship between popular reading materials and cultural change. Finally, each chapter includes a full reference section, including a list of "Recommended Readings," which highlight key sources that can be used for further study of a particular subject.

It is our hope that *Cultural History of Reading* sheds light on the complex and often fascinating relationship between what people read and why they read it.

Sara E. Quay, PhD
Gabrielle Watling, PhD
Endicott College 2008

PART 1
The Americas

CHAPTER 1

Canada

Diana Chlebek

TIMELINE

1969   Official Languages Act passed
1970   October Crisis; Royal Commission on Status of Women Report
                Québec referendum on sovereignty defeated
1977   Charter of the French Language adopted in Québec (*Charte de la langue française*)
1980   "O Canada" officially adopted as national anthem
1982   Repatriation of Constitution, Charter of Rights
1995   Québec referendum on sovereignty narrowly defeated
1996   Human Rights Act
1999   Nunavut established

INTRODUCTION TO THE NATION

Canada is the second-largest country in the world and is also one of the most sparsely populated. With a citizenry that has been built of immigrants from every part of the globe, this is a nation that is known as a highly literate model of multicultural society.

Canada was once contested by England and France, historically two of Europe's greatest powers, and this historical legacy is reflected both in the nation's official bilingual policy and in the rich repository of its Anglophone and Francophone literatures. Canada's original inhabitants, often collectively called the First Nations, are the native Indian peoples and the Inuit peoples. The former are the larger group, and the latter have semi-autonomous status in the country's newest territory, Nunavut, which lies in the far north and was created in 1999. Canada's government is a confederation with a parliamentary democracy; the country has long been an influential member of the British Commonwealth of Nations, and Queen Elizabeth II is still Canada's ceremonial head of state. Canadian prime ministers, who are elected by democratic process, govern the nation from its capital, Ottawa. Toronto and Montréal (located in the province of Québec) are the country's largest cities and are also its most important centers of publishing and media production.

The Canadian nation emerged from a conglomerate of colonial and indigenous interests. Significant shaping influences came from competition for Canada's abundant natural resources, most notably the fur trade. Occupying groups, all of which had a stake in the fur-producing territories, waged battles long and short over control of the lucrative trade. The famous "French and Indian War" was fought largely over the fur trade. Furthermore, Canada became a key player in other people's wars. In 1812, Canadian territory played a role in one of the major wars between Britain and the United States. But Canadians desired their own independence as well, and in 1837, Britain granted Canada "responsible government." Canada's borders and possessions took recognizable shape in 1849 with the signing of the Oregon Treaty. This act ceded Vancouver Island, and later British Columbia, to Canada. By 1949, all ten provinces and two territories had officially come under Canadian control.

However, Canada has long struggled with its dual language identity. Although recognized as one of the world's most successful multicultural nations, the battle over French-speaking citizens' secession from English-speaking Canada (that is, Québec's secession from the rest of the nation) has tugged at Canada's self-identity. In 1969, Canada became officially bilingual, but in 1995, the nation voted in a referendum to decide whether Québec would gain sovereignty from the rest of Canada. The referendum was defeated by a slim margin, and in 2006, the

Canadian House of Commons passed a bill stating that Québec was its own nation within "a united Canada."

Today, Canada is a key nation in the global economy; a member of NATO and NAFTA, Canada has supported efforts for peace and development throughout the world. Canada was the first developed nation to recognize indigenous rights to territory, and in 1999 the Nunavut Territory officially separated from the Northwest Territories to become a culturally autonomous zone.

Given its active and influential aboriginal culture, its colonial history, and its political inheritance, Canada is considered a "post-colonial" nation in literary and cultural terms. That is, its cultural output is often read in terms of the various struggles for autonomy that characterize colonial experience. Canadians themselves are aware of the raft of sociopolitical issues that are negotiated daily in their country. They understand that Canada is a product of contested territorial and cultural claims, and they view their country's cultural artifacts through these social and political lenses.

READING TRENDS AND PRACTICES

Despite the country's long history, publishing in the modern sense did not develop in Canada until well into the nineteenth century. Small populations and a large geographical area made publishing on a risk-venture basis very difficult. In addition there was no copyright protection for books originating in the colonies, or for those imported from England and the United States; thus, the pirating of books in Canada was a common practice. Literary publishing was undertaken at the author's expense or on a subscription basis, so many domestic authors published their books abroad. Literary magazines were ephemeral and their pages usually replete with material reprinted from foreign magazines. *The Literary Garland* (1831–1851), which published many domestic authors, was a notable exception. All in all there was a somewhat limited range and quantity of book material available to Canadian readers in the earlier decades of the nineteenth

The *Ottawa Citizen* is an English-language daily newspaper published for the readership of Canada's capital city, Ottawa. The paper was first published in 1845, and currently has a circulation of 141,540. [Courtesy of Hossein Derakhshan]

Rustic bookstore on Prince Edward Island.
[Courtesy of Nigel Beale, www.nigelbeale.com]

century. Newspapers were far more abundant, but since they were financed primarily through political patronage, their existence could be precarious. After the middle of the century, advances in printing technology and substantial growth in the nation's transportation systems markedly improved conditions for the publishing and distribution of books. In 1867, after Confederation, public school systems expanded throughout the country; the literacy rate in the country quickly rose, and Canada began to develop a substantial readership.

After U.S. copyright legislation halted the reprint industry in Canada at the end of the nineteenth century, several domestic publishing houses were established, a number of which were determined to publish Canadian writing. The publishing industry grew considerably in the country throughout the first half of the twentieth century, and by the 1950s, four large companies were specializing in Canadian literature: Clarke & Irwin, Macmillan, McClelland & Stewart, and Ryerson. With the development of a truly Canadian literature in the 1950s and 1960s, the appearance of many of the greatest authors in Canada's history, the development of a booming economy, and a greatly expanded readership, this era proved to be a golden age for publishers, authors and readers. Small alternative publishers appeared in every major Canadian city.

In addition to the plethora of major humanities journals and literary periodicals, dozens of little magazines covered various aspects of creative writing, book reviewing, and literary criticism. In addition, through the recommendation of the 1951 report of the Royal Commission on Development in the Arts, Letters and Sciences (dubbed the "Massey Commission Report"), the Canada Council was established. This body provided funding for publishers, grant money and prizes to authors, and support for many types of reading and book programs.

However, in the 1970s, the country was hit by economic recession, and this ebullience soon vanished. As book sales declined and government funding diminished, several large publishing firms closed down. In 1972 a Royal Commission report on the state of publishing in Canada recommended a more organized and systematic federal program of support to encourage the publication of Canadian authors. Today, Canada has more than three hundred publishers; English-Canadian book publishing is centered in Toronto, and French Canadian publishing is based in Montréal. Authors receive federal assistance through grants and are regularly recognized through awards and prizes, such as the annual Governor General's Award. Funding provided by the federal Book Publishing Industry Development Program helps to buffer publishers of Canadian books against the competition posed by foreign-owned publishers. Readers have free access to books in Canada through one of the best public library systems in the world. The

National Library of Canada scrupulously collects and conserves every book published in Canada, provides information about books and authors on its website, and organizes book-related events such as exhibits, lectures, and reading programs. Thus, both reading and print cultures in Canada receive a substantial amount of government support and encouragement. Even though French and English cultures in Canada remain sharply distinct, the bodies of seminal literary texts associated with each culture have become established through a process of development that is somewhat similar.

For both anglophone and francophone societies in Canada's early history, most of the creative literature that was circulated and read was produced in Europe and imported into the colonies. During a large part of the nineteenth century, when the country was gradually developing a mass reading public, the most popular and influential literature in both English Canada and Québec was imported or, when written by native authors, was largely derivative of European and British sources. For both cultures the twentieth century witnessed the development of readily distinguishable Canadian and Québécois traditions of literature. The developmental stages of both anglophone and francophone literary traditions followed similar trajectories: periods of domination by a few seminal figures, the expression of avid nationalism in the 1960s, and finally several periods when writers explored the diversity of their cultures with greater individuation and artistic experimentation.

POLITICAL AND HISTORICAL TEXTS

Canada's First Nations were the descendants of Asian hunters who penetrated the North American continent by a vanished land bridge over the Bering Strait over twelve thousand years ago, just at the end of the last ice age. The first Europeans to arrive in Canada were Icelanders, led by Leif Ericson around one thousand C.E., but the colonies they established in Greenland and Newfoundland were short-lived. In 1497 John Cabot explored the coast of Newfoundland, and Martin Frobisher reached Baffin Island in 1576 in his search for the Northwest Passage. Attempts by Europeans to establish settlements in Canada began in 1535–1536, when Jacques Cartier and his company of explorers wintered over in Stadacona (later Québec). By the early seventeenth century, both the French and the English were vying to establish colonies in the country; the most successful were the French settlements of Port Royal, founded in Acadia (now Nova Scotia) in 1605, and Samuel de Champlain's Habitation at Québec, established in 1608.

The rivalry between the French and the English for the fur trade and for imperial control of North America eventually erupted into the Seven Years' War (1756–1763). The conflict ended in 1759 when the British commander, James Wolfe, defeated the French leader, the Marquis de Montcalm, on the Plains of Abraham and captured the city of Québec. The terms of the Treaty of Paris, which settled the war in 1763, ensured Britain's domination over most of the continent. By this time French Canadians were already a vigorous community; an important document created several years after the settlement of the English-French conflict ensured the consolidation and survival of a distinct French settlement within North America. This agreement, the Québec Act, was drawn up in 1775 and was intended to ensure the loyalty of the French subjects by granting them special status.

The Act enlarged the boundaries of the Province of Québec to include several territories such as Labrador and, most significantly, the Indian territory south of the Great Lakes, between the Mississippi and Ohio rivers. The Québec colony was to be administered by a governor and seventeen to twenty-three appointed councilors. The Québec Act can be interpreted in a number of ways. It was partly an attempt to deal more equitably with the British colony's French Catholics, to ensure their loyalty in the event of troubles with the American colonies. In fact it maintained the survival of the old regime society in North America. The Act returned to the Québec economy its traditional links with the fishing and fur trades. However, the American colonists viewed the Indian territory as theirs by right; when Québec acquired this land, American outrage made the Québec Act one of the Intolerable Acts that contributed to the outbreak of the American Revolution. Moreover, the Act's entrenchment of the *seigneurial* system seriously eroded the living standards of Québec's habitant population; this decline would persist well into the twentieth century. Finally, the Act was also to become the historical-legal basis upon which Québec would stake its claim for special status several centuries later when Canada was framing its economic, cultural, and political policies and finalizing its constitution. The Act would thus be the first in a series of political documents that would dramatically shape the development of Canada, establishing its uniqueness within the North American sphere.

After the American Revolution, waves of Loyalists immigrated into Canada, settling in the areas of Upper Canada (now Ontario) and in the Maritimes, where a new province, New Brunswick, was created to accommodate them. Later, non-Loyalist Americans came to Canada seeking cheap land. This migration was halted by the War of 1812, during which the Americans attacked the British North American colonies and were repulsed. The colonies that existed in British North America, including the area of the former New France, ruled with a governor and a group of oligarchic magnates who jealously guarded their economic and political privileges; any assemblies that were permitted to exist had limited suffrage and restricted powers. The situation bred such discontent among the populace that by 1837 open rebellion broke out in Upper Canada (later Ontario), led by the journalist William Lyon Mackenzie, and in Lower Canada (later Québec), led by the politician Louis-Joseph Papineau. The rebels were defeated, but these revolts so disturbed the British parliament that a liberal reformer, Lord John George Durham, was sent from England to investigate the causes of the "Canada problem." His observations and recommendations resulted in an official document that would be the initial step in Canada's progress toward becoming a self-governing continental nation.

The so-called Durham Report, officially known as the *Report on the Affairs of British North America*, was completed in January 1839, and was officially presented to the Colonial Office in February 1839. Durham proposed such reforms as the creation of municipal governments and a supreme court. His two main recommendations—responsible government and the union of Upper and Lower Canada—emerged from an analysis of the causes of the rebellions. He criticized the defective constitutional system in Upper Canada, where power was monopolized by the Family Compact, a corrupt group of wealthy men who manipulated political appointments. This compact blocked economic and social development in a potentially wealthy colony, thereby causing the discontent that led to the rebellion. His solution, based on advice from colonial reformers, was a system in which the executive would be drawn from the majority party in the assembly.

In Lower Canada, Durham described the problems as racially, not politically, based. He found "two nations warring in the bosom of a single state" (*Report on the Affairs of British North America* 7). To ensure harmony and progress, he recommended assimilating the French Canadians, whom he called "a people with no literature and no history" (*Report on the Affairs of British North America* 112), through a legislative union of the Canadas, in which an English-speaking majority would dominate. Durham's report was condemned by Upper Canada's Tory elite, but Montréal Tories supported the union, largely because they saw it as a way to overcome French Canadian opposition to their plans for economic development. French Canadians were opposed to the union and reaffirmed their determination to defend their nationality. The British government accepted the recommendation for a union of the Canadas, and issued an Act of Union. However, responsible government was not formally implemented until 1847. Although controversial in its direct influence in the creation of the Province of Canada, the emergence of a party system, and the strengthening of local self-government, the Durham Report is generally believed to have played an important role in the development of Canadian autonomy. A fascinating aspect of Durham's assessment and solutions was the contrasting ways in which these were interpreted by opposing factions in Canada.

Durham's report had taken into account the recent British experience with the American Revolution; England's failure with the American colonies was to profoundly influence the subsequent history of Canada. In particular, the report's recommendation of the unification of Upper and Lower Canada was a spur for the national drive to unite all the British North American colonies. An important advance toward this goal happened when all the colonies became self-governing by 1855. Over the next dozen years conferences were held in various parts of the country about the possibilities of unification. The terms of the Confederation were outlined in a text that became the most significant political document in Canada's history, the British North America Act of July 1, 1867.

The British North America Act (later renamed the Constitution Act of 1867) was a statute enacted by the British parliament providing for Confederation of the Province of Canada (Ontario and Québec), Nova Scotia, and New Brunswick into a federal state with a parliamentary system modeled on that of Britain. Other territories and provinces were added to the union in later years. The Act does not contain the entire Constitution of Canada. Complementing its text are British and Canadian statutes having constitutional effect, and certain unwritten principles known as "the conventions of the constitution." Conventions such as the power vested in the Crown to dissolve Parliament and call a general election are usually exercised on the advice of the Prime Minister. The Act created a unique fusion of British and American constitutional influences: the monarchy, represented by a governor-general; a bicameral legislature, consisting of an elected House of Commons and an appointed Senate; and political federalism. In contrast with American federalism, all powers not explicitly granted to the Canadian provinces resided with the federal government, though provincial jurisdiction included direct taxation, control of provincial public lands, the communications infrastructure, education, and the administration of justice.

Confederation did not resolve the struggle between centralist and decentralist powers within the country. To this day, the federal government has kept control of matters such as foreign policy, defense, banking, and currency; the provinces have retained firm jurisdiction over the areas of education, property, civil rights, and policing. However, as the federal government gradually concerns itself with more areas, disputes between the central government and the provinces have increased concerning their respective areas of authority. Moreover, the Anglo-French conflict in Canada was not solved by the act of union; instead it would become an escalating problem over succeeding decades.

Canada's involvement in World War I became another source of Anglo-French conflict in the nation. When thousands of French Canadian men refused to be

Maclean's Magazine

Maclean's magazine is Canada's only weekly news magazine, and has been published since 1905. *Maclean's* covered the major events in Canadian history, politics, entertainment, and involvement in world affairs throughout the twentieth century and into the twenty-first. The magazine began a French language edition in 1961. It ran until 1975, when it was taken over by another publication, *L'actualité*. The magazine is widely read in Canada, and it is especially noted for its ranking of Canadian universities according to undergraduate experience and its annual list of Canada's top one hundred employers.

drafted for compulsory service in a war that they perceived as a British imperialist conflict, the resulting conscription crisis that erupted almost split the nation apart. The interwar years were a period of rapid development for the country. Canada's international prominence was boosted by its entry into the British Commonwealth of Nations in 1917 after World War I. It also attained dominion status of virtual independence through the 1931 British Statute of Westminster, a British law that clarified the powers of Canada's parliament and those of the other Dominions. The Statute granted the former colonies full legal freedom, except in those areas where they chose to remain subordinate.

On the domestic front, the country cultivated national cohesion and pride through the implementation of numerous federal enterprises in banking, commerce, and transportation, such as the creation of the Bank of Canada, the Canadian Broadcasting Company, and Trans-Canada Airlines. Many French Canadians perceived these achievements as anglophone aspects of nationalism that threatened the survival of French Canada. Québec nationalism grew in tandem with anglophone federalism. Similarly, after World War II, most of Canada enjoyed a post-war economic boom while Québec was bogged down in economic and social stagnation.

Linguistic barriers, an antiquated education system dominated by the Catholic Church, regressive fiscal policies, and the corrupt practices of Québec's political leaders stymied progress for its French Canadian population. In 1960, demands by the Québécois for reforms in church-state relations and electoral laws finally led to the election of a progressive Liberal party government that launched what was dubbed a "Quiet Revolution" to modernize Québec. The impulse toward reform in the province also intensified feelings of French Canadian nationalism, leading to the formation of separatist political parties such as the Parti Québécois. However in addition to these legitimate groups that espoused sovereignty for the province, there also arose terrorist organizations such as the Front de libération du Québec (FLQ), a revolutionary movement that used propaganda and extreme violence to promote the emergence of an independent, socialist Québec.

In response to the growing unrest in Québec, the federal government created a Royal Commission on Bilingualism and Biculturalism in 1963. It was charged with investigating the existing state of bilingualism and biculturalism in Canada and with recommending ways of ensuring greater recognition of the cultural dualism in the country. The report of the Commission was issued over the years of 1967–1970, and the group's cochairmen, André Laurendau and A. Davidson Dunton, assumed responsibility for the authorship. The Report of the Royal Commission on Bilingualism and Biculturalism (1967–1970) had a profound effect on provincial policies affecting education, government employment, and cultural development, and its recommendations were quickly implemented across the country. Most significantly, the Report laid the foundation for functional bilingualism throughout Canada and for increased diversity. An incidental result of the report was the advent of official multiculturalism, which provided authoritative sanction for recognizing the fact that many cultures are represent-ed in the Canadian mosaic, and that these cultures are all entitled to acknowledgement by public policy. Therefore the Report profoundly affected educational practices by expanding both the range of languages that students could be taught and the extent of literature that would be accessible to them. Ultimately, these effects would have a great impact on both the reading and publishing cultures of the nation.

After the election of a francophone, Pierre Elliott Trudeau, as Prime Minister of Canada, the most important part of the Commission's Report was enacted. In 1969 the federal government issued the Official Languages Act of Canada, a document that had a most resounding effect on the country. As a federal statute, the Act declares French and English to be the official languages of Canada; under the Act all federal institutions must provide their services in English or French at the customer's choice. It also created the office of Commissioner of Official Languages to oversee its imple-mentation. All federal parties endorsed the Act but it was met with mixed public com-prehension and acceptance. In June 1987 the Conservative government introduced an amended Official Languages Act to promote official language minority rights. The bill prepared the way for a bilingual federal civil service and for the encouragement of the French language and culture in Canada. Its designers hoped it would ultimately begin a new relationship between the English and the French in the nation.

The federal government's investigation and assessment of Canadian francopho-nes' rights spurred official inquiries about the status of other minority rights in the country. In 1970 the Royal Commission on the Status of Women was released. The Report's 167 recommendations continue to influence the public agenda to this day. Most notably, many of the Commission's public hearings were broadcast on CBC radio and roused the women across the nation to a common cause. The Commission received federal funding for a conference as a follow-up to the report's recommendations; out of that meeting emerged the National Action Committee on the Status of Women, an umbrella organization of women's groups that has grown to represent millions of Canadian women. The heightened concern over human rights in the 1960s also served to awaken consciousness over ethnic and racial rights among Canada's First Nations populations and among citizens who were immigrants and descendants of immigrants from countries across the globe.

However, francophones' fears for the survival of their culture and language were not allayed. In 1970 the terrorist FLQ committed a violent kidnapping and murder in Québec. The federal government immediately suspended civil liber-ties in the country with the War Measures Act and over five hundred persons were arrested in Québec in an event that came to be known as the October Crisis. Many Canadians were shocked, but Québécois were especially outraged and support for separatism soared in the province. In 1977, the incidents of the 1970 crisis and concerns about French language rights spurred the creation and passage of a crucial document that was enacted by the pro-separatist government in Québec—Bill 101, the Charter of the French Language ("Charte de la langue française"). It made French the official language of the state and the courts in the province of Québec, as well as making it the normal and habitual language of the workplace, of instruction, of communications, of commerce, and of busi-ness. Education in French became compulsory for immigrants, even those from other Canadian provinces, unless a reciprocal agreement existed between Québec and that province (the so-called Québec clause). This language legisla-tion was significantly modified following a series of court rulings that changed its content and reduced its scope. In 1980, the Supreme Court of Canada sup-ported a judgment of the Québec Superior Court that struck down the section of the Charter that declared French the language of the legislature and courts.

In 1984, it was ruled that the Canadian Charter of Rights and Freedoms limited the bill's power to regulate the language of instruction. In the same year, the Court ruled that the compulsory and exclusive use of French on public commercial signs was contrary to the right of freedom of speech. Eventually the party leadership succeeded in blunting the most radical of nationalist views regarding Québec's language policies with the original bill. Ultimately, Bill 101 can be read as one of the most significant statements about the divisiveness between Canada's populations.

The dramatic political events of the 1960s and 1970s sparked a continuing debate in the country over the status of minorities in Canada and acted as an important prelude to one of the most crucial documents in Canada's development as a nation. In the early 1980s, the federal government began initiatives to reform the Canadian Constitution in response to the ongoing Québec Referendum campaign for that province's separation from Canada. A first important step was the *patriation* of Canada's original constitution, whereby the document was amended to end the British parliament's sole preserve of amending the Canadian constitution. Queen Elizabeth II issued a proclamation making Canada fully independent and recognizing the new Constitution Act, which included the Canadian Charter of Rights and Freedoms. The document ensures every law that is inconsistent with the Constitution is, to the extent of the inconsistency, of no force and effect. The Constitution is thus the supreme law of Canada. With the Act comes a new dimension, a new yardstick of reconciliation between the individual and the community and their respective rights. This dimension, like the balance of the Constitution, remains to be interpreted and applied by the court. The object of the Charter of Rights is to protect the citizen against the State and to protect minorities against parliamentary majorities. The Canadian Charter is comprehensive and covers fundamental, democratic, mobility, legal, equality, and linguistic rights. The equality between men and women is also expressly protected by a particular section of the Charter. By placing the civil rights and liberties above the reach of federal or provincial legislatures, the Charter is an extremely important document for the protection of Canadians from the abuses of government. Many of the country's legislators deemed the Charter's advent as the nation's most important event since the adoption of federalism in 1867. Many rulings based upon the document have been landmark decisions for the country.

TEXTS OF SOCIAL CRITIQUE AND CULTURAL ANALYSIS

In the decades following World War II, texts of social critique and cultural analysis became increasingly important for Canadian readers as they sought to comprehend the forces that were shaping their country into a more complex and multicultural society. In the 1940s, while the rest of Canada optimistically enjoyed increasing advantages in economy, education, and social advantages, Québec's citizens were struggling with a much lower standard of living and with a cultural repression imposed by a reactionary provincial government and the conservative Catholic Church. In 1948, the Québécois artist Paul-Émile Borduas led a group of avant-garde artists and writers in the launching of a manifesto in pamphlet form called "Le Refus global." This critique challenged the traditional values of Québec, especially those promulgated by the Catholic Church, which Borduas's group perceived as a block to the progress and modernization of Québec society. The protest was also directed against government-run education and the conventionality of society in general. It argued for "resplendent anarchy" for artists, who must be liberated from such suffocating influences in order to create. Church and political authorities in the province were incensed by these anarchistic views and had Borduas removed from his post at the École du Meuble, where he had been teaching since 1937. The Québec press echoed the views of the government and most newspaper or magazine articles published at the time condemned the manifesto. The *Refus* not only voiced an important stance for artists, but is also often considered a precursor of Québec's Quiet Revolution of the 1960s.

> **Le Journal de Montréal**
>
> *Le Journal de Montréal* is the largest French-language newspaper in Canada, and has the largest circulation of any French-language newspaper in North America.

Twenty years later, when Québec was undergoing its social transformation and leaning toward separation from the rest of Canada, another protest for Québécois liberation appeared in a very different form. Pierre Vallières' *Nègres blancs d'Amérique* (*White Niggers of America*) is part autobiography and part manifesto. It was written in a New York prison, with Vallières awaiting extradition to Canada to face charges of manslaughter. It outlines the making of Québécois militancy and the emergence of the Front de libération du Québec. The work dramatizes his impoverished, frustrated childhood as the son of working-class parents in a tough Québécois neighborhood, his various and checkered careers, and his conversion to Marxism and FLQ involvement. For Vallières, Québec's working class shows the traits of a colonized people; "white niggers" denotes a condition of being that he thought could be altered only through violent revolution. When it appeared in English translation in 1971, the work was proclaimed as a way for Canadians to know the terrorist enemy. Even today, readers find the book a powerful literary testament of the oppression faced by generations of French Canadians who were overcome by conquest, colonization, class exploitation, and a repressive church.

The inequities inherent in Canadian society were also revealed by John Porter in his 1968 work, *The Vertical Mosaic: An Analysis of Social Class and Power in Canada*. Porter used the image of the "vertical mosaic" to convey the concept that Canada is a mosaic of different ethnic, language, regional, and religious groupings, unequal in status and power. This was opposed to the American "melting pot" ideology, which discourages immigrants and their descendants from maintaining close ties with their countries and cultures of origin, and instead encourages them to assimilate into the American way of life. Many Canadians pointed with pride to the alternative Canadian policy of *encouraging* immigrants and their descendants to maintain important aspects of their ancestral cultures. Porter contended that in income, occupation, and education, this supposedly beneficial policy worked to the advantage of some ethnic groups and to the disadvantage of others, so that those of British origin enjoyed better incomes, education, and health than others, particularly those of eastern and southern European origin. Native Indian and Inuit people were the most disadvantaged. According to Porter, this vertical arrangement also applied to power and influence in decision-making. In the bureaucratic, economic, and political spheres, those of British origin are overrepresented among the elite. The work was well-received by social scientists at the time as a highly insightful analysis, and it inspired students and scholars for more than a decade.

CREATIVE TEXTS

In the tradition of English Canadian literature, the earliest texts that impacted reading culture were often works of fiction that sought to record regional experience and use literature to shape their own culture, particularly through humor. An early Canadian best-seller in this genre was Thomas Chandler Haliburton's novel *The Clockmaker* (1836), which uses satire about its central character, the aptly named Sam Slick, as a social critique of politics and social mores. By the early twentieth century, the literary talent of two Canadian regionalist writers had begun to acquire an international reputation. The economist and novelist Stephen Leacock became famous at home and abroad as a comic writer in the Dickensian tradition, based on his lampooning of narrow social attitudes. His most popular and enduring work is *Sunshine Sketches of a Little Town* (1912), which is a series of vignettes that dramatizes the comedy of day-to-day life in small-town Canada by scrutinizing the foibles and pretensions of the citizenry of the fictional Mariposa, Ontario.

One of the novelists of this period has maintained a reputation as Canada's best-selling author. Lucy Maud Montgomery's *Anne of Green Gables* appeared in 1908 and, a century later, continues to be the nation's most renowned work of fiction abroad. The book is usually described as fiction for children or adolescents, yet the tale of Anne's development as an imaginative, spontaneous, and sensitive child-heroine continues to appeal to a wide category of readers, thus ensuring its status as a classic of Canadian literature. Set in Nova Scotia, the work tells the story of Anne Shirley, who is rescued from an orphanage and sent to live at Green Gables. Here she finds ample "scope for the imagination" (*Anne of Green Gables* 32) and wins over her adoptive parents, Matthew and Marilla Cuthbert, who had expected a boy orphan to help them on their farm. In Avonlea she gains the town's affection, despite her foibles and misadventures. Montgomery extends the scope of her narrative to encompass social critique by placing the story of Anne's poignant and sometimes comic passage from childhood into adolescence against the backdrop of the smug, puritanical community life of Avonlea. The novel has gone through numerous editions, has been translated into at least 15 languages, and has twice been made into a film. A musical version of the story has played annually in Charlottetown, Prince Edward Island, since 1965.

The interwar years in the development of the Canadian novel brought to readers' attention several writers who focused on social issues that were preoccupying the nation. The problems of urban life were the main theme of Morley Callaghan's *Such Is My Beloved* (1934), which is the tale of an idealistic young Catholic priest's failure to help two prostitutes he befriends. When Stephen Dowling's rich, sanctimonious parishioners and his bishop condemn his friendship with the girls, he is driven mad by his despair over the dreadful future they face. The novel ends on a note of some hope when Stephen is consoled by his realization of the purely Christian love he bears for them and for humanity. The work had a somewhat sensational impact on readers when it appeared because of its frank assessment of the uneasy relationship between sacred and profane love. In this period of the nation's social history, when most Canadians strongly embraced traditional beliefs about religion, family life, and sexuality, Callaghan's novel helped to reorient the public's considerations about what he once described as the difficulties of being a Christian.

A decade later in 1945, Hugh MacLennan's novel *Two Solitudes* focused on Canada's most troubling legacy: the conflict between English and French Canadians. MacLennan examines the tense relationship between the two cultures within a historical framework set in the interwar years from World War I to 1939. The English Canadian portion is set in Montréal where characters such as Huntley McQueen, a Presbyterian businessman from Ontario, represent the WASP economic interests that collaborate with Québec's regressive political machine to retard progress for the francophone population. The French Canadian portion takes place in the parish of Saint-Marc-des-Érables, which is dominated by the medieval Catholicism of its priest, Father Beaubien, and by Athanase Tallard, a powerful but tragic figure ostracized by his church for trying to industrialize the village. Tallard's son, Paul, who represents the "new" Québec, is at home in both languages but alienated from both cultures. He sets off on a quest for his own identity by traveling abroad, seeking a more enlightened education, and by joining forces with an English-Canadian lover, Heather Methuen, who is a rebel in her own right. At the story's end, as Paul struggles to write a novel that will define his own Canadian experience, he and Heather plan together to make a new Canada that will work. The book endures as a popular Canadian classic for its astute observations that illuminate the cultural debate that has racked the nation for many years. It has been translated into French, among other languages.

With the publication in 1959 of Mordecai Richler's *The Apprenticeship of Duddy Kravitz,* Canadian novelists embarked on an exploration of cultural themes with attitudes and techniques that betrayed a more sardonic bite, presaging the social rebellion of the next decade. With cruel clarity Richler presents the story of Duddy Kravitz, a brash Jewish Montréal youth determined to "make it" at all costs. He follows up his grandfather's maxim that a man is nothing without land by scheming to acquire a lakeshore property in the Laurentians. He succeeds in the venture at the cost of exploiting and destroying those he loves. Richler's raw satire of Montréal's Jewish and WASP middle-class gentility immediately resonated with readers. The author's bold stance on portraying his minority community the way he wanted was highly admired. This perspective became a trademark of Richler's fictional style. The novel was made into a film in 1974 and staged as a play in 1984.

When interest in minority rights began to engage the country during the 1970s and 1980s, Canadian novelists focused on themes that drew public attention to the grievances of various ethnic cultures that had been obscured by the glare of the French-English conflict. In his work *The Temptations of Big Bear* (1973), Rudy Wiebe uses his own Mennonite roots to help him convey the Native people's understanding of the spiritual relationship of human beings to the land. Set in Canada's West during the last decades of the nineteenth century, Wiebe focuses on the story of Big Bear, the Plains Cree chief who opposed the signing of the Indian treaties. By using multiple narrative viewpoints, backed with much documentary material, the author successfully presented to his predominantly non-Native audience the Native perspective on the tragic historical clash between political power exercised by whites and the religious vision that centered the lives of First Nations people. Wiebe's book became a landmark in the national consciousness by giving the public a basis for understanding the activism of the First Nations as they struggled for the cause of Native rights throughout the 1970s and 1980s.

Women novelists attained major stature during these decades, especially for their attention to feminist issues and the social problems that had an impact on women. Laurence Margaret's *The Stone Angel* (1964), the debut novel in her series about stifling life in Canada's Manawaka, was one of the earliest works to explore the deep psychological frustrations of Canadian women whose hopes and expressions of self-identity were being stifled by their restrictive roles in marriage and family life. Later works by women writers, such as Alice Munro's *Lives of Girls and Women* (1971), Carol Shields' *The Stone Diaries* (1993), and much of Margaret Atwood's fiction also explored the trajectories of women's lives. These novels used innovative narrative techniques in a way that resonated with their readers and gained their authors critical acclaim. Margaret Atwood's work *The Handmaid's Tale* (1985) was an especially powerful outcry against female oppression. Using the form of a futuristic fantasy, Atwood portrays a world in which a male fundamentalist, theocratic junta rules over Gilead, a territory formerly known as Maine. A large majority of the female population is sterile, and fertile women are forced into surrogate motherhood as "handmaids" to privileged but barren couples. In this police state, women are also victims of a right-wing feminism that supports male authority in return for certain privileges. Most of the story is rendered through a transcription of tapes made by Offred, an escaped handmaiden who relates her experiences growing up in the old society, being retrained for the new one, and temporarily belonging to one of its Commanders. Her story also records her internal resistance to a state that reduces human beings to objects. Probably Atwood's most popular work, *The Handmaid's Tale* has won wide critical acclaim both as a brilliant allegorical protest against patriarchy and as a prescient chronicle that holds a dark and disturbing mirror up to the present.

Many immigrant writers have made notable contributions to the tradition of the English Canadian novel. These include older authors such as Czech-born Josef Svorecky, whose award-winning work *The Engineer of Human Souls* (1977, trans. 1984) was widely read, as well as newer writers such as Rohinton Mistry, whose works, such as the popular and critically acclaimed *A Fine Balance* (1995), are often set in his native India and are examinations of a humanity beset by social and political repression. The Sri Lankan-born author Michael Ondaatje is probably Canada's best-known immigrant writer. His novel *The English Patient* (1992) won critical recognition in both Canada and international literary circles. The novel is structured as a double narrative in which a tale of present time is set in Tuscany at the end of World War II in a semi-ruined villa, where a young Canadian nurse tends a mysterious English man. The second tale is presented through a series of sustained flashbacks and recounts the patient's affair with the wife of one of his fellow explorers. In the novel, Ondaatje uses highly evocative poetic prose and numerous allusions to other artistic works to transform his novel into allegory about the ruins of mid-twentieth-century European civilization, the demise of colonialism, and the complex nature of race. The novel won the Man Booker prize in 1992 and was made into an Oscar-winning film in 1996. Ondaatje's novels, along with the recent prose works of other national authors, have been instrumental in presenting the Canadian experience as increasingly complex and multifaceted. Both at home and abroad, such books have transformed the general public's sense of Canadian fiction.

One of the most successful novels in the tradition of French literature was one of the earliest written in the twentieth century, when Québécois fiction began to flourish. Louis Hémon, who was from France, wrote *Maria Chapdelaine* (1914) after spending only two years in rural Québec. The novel relates the story of a young girl, Maria, who lives with her family on a farm in the northern wilderness of Québec, on the very edge of survival. Following the deaths of her mother and lover, François Paradis, Maria must choose between two suitors: Lorenzo Surprenant, who tempts her with the riches of America and Europe, and Gagnon, a neighbor who represents the enduring aspects of his Québécois heritage through his fidelity to French language and culture, his support of the Catholic Church, and his love of the land. Maria rejects the temptations of a comfortable life in America with Lorenzo and unselfishly accepts Gagnon, thereby ensuring the survival of family and community and affirming the traditional values of rural French Canada. The work's simple portrayal of the devotion of francophone Québécois to images of their rural, Catholic past ensured that the novel became an instant bestseller throughout Canada and abroad. It has been translated into over twenty languages, has sold millions of copies, and has been filmed three times.

During the years of World War II, French Canada was cut off from France and both its literary culture and book trade came of age. The war pushed both the nation and Québec to open up to the world. During the 1940s French Canadian novelists explored new directions in themes and techniques by presenting protagonists with more depth of characterization in more complex settings. Out of this period emerged a classic work of fiction that won awards and fame across the globe—Gabrielle Roy's *Bonheur d'occasion* (*The Tin Flute*, 1945). The novel, set in a Montréal slum on the eve of World War II, focuses on the gritty existence of members of the Lacasse family who, like their neighbors, perceive the war as a form of economic salvation. The daughter, Florentine Lacasse, a dime-store waitress, is seduced by Jean Lévesque, a successful but selfish engineer. After becoming pregnant, Florentine marries Emmanuel Létourneau, an idealistic soldier. Her long-suffering and patient mother, Rose-Anna, bears yet another child just as her husband goes to enlist in the war. Florentine's young brother Daniel is dying of leukemia in a hospital; surrounded by new toys, he experiences material comfort for the first time. Roy's skillfully ironic and sympathetic work of social observation made her a major Canadian novelist and marked a turning point in the portrayal of Québec society.

The new nationalism that emerged in Québec in the 1960s was echoed in the thematic content of the novels written over the following decades. The experimental structures and daring narrative techniques of these works reflected the new sense of artistic freedom that writers experienced as the stifling traditional values were peeled away from Québécois culture. This emerging identity was fueled by the acceptance among French Canadian readers of the new novels that the community was producing.

One of the most prominent and complex fictional expressions of liberation to emerge at this time was the 1965 novel *Prochain episode* (*Next Episode*), written by Hubert Aquin, who was incarcerated for his revolutionary activities. This reflexive work describes a jailed separatist distracting himself by writing an allegorical thriller about attempted political assassination. The psychological mystery develops into a suspenseful confession with suicidal overtones as the individual quest for revolution collapses. Once the narrator confronts his enemy and double H. de Heutz, he does not have the will to murder the man, who is a fellow art-lover. Throughout the narrative there flits the shadowy presence of the beautiful K, possibly a double agent, who is an allegorical symbol for the protagonist's long-lost love, the Québec nation. In many ways the novel is an eerie presage of the violent events during the October Crisis of 1970 in Québec. The work won great critical praise and made Aquin into a literary icon for the radical separatist movement.

During the same year, there appeared another dark fictional vision of Québec in Marie-Claire Blais's *Une Saison dans la vie d'Emmanuel* (*A Season in the Life of Emmanuel*). Her novel chronicles one year in the life of a family consisting of an exhausted mother, a violent and indifferent father, their sixteen offspring, and a grandmother who represents power and endurance. Blais uses multiple viewpoints to narrate events surrounding the winter birth of Emmanuel, who is the family's last-born sixteenth child. Emmanuel's brother, Jean Le Maigre, is an adolescent friar who becomes the victim of a pedophile priest; his autobiographical manuscripts frame the narrative of the novel. In this rural Québécois nightmare, the deaths of Emmanuel's siblings from cold and hunger become an allegory for the insulation and ignorance in which the province has shrouded itself. Blais's terse narrative, which strips away all illusions about the traditional Québécois values espoused by Hémon's *Maria Chapdelaine*, was translated into a dozen languages and won many national and international awards.

Roch Carrier's 1968 novel *La Guerre, Yes Sir!* is his most famous novel and is set in rural Québec during World War I. The narrative focuses on the brutal events surrounding the wake and funeral of the war hero Corriveau. Corriveau's friend Bérubé beats his bride Molly, a Newfoundland prostitute, while his officers, the "English" soldiers who deliver the corpse, are attacked by the villagers. Other vignettes reflect violence literally and linguistically: one villager, Joseph, chops off his hand to avoid conscription, while another villager, Amélie, emotionally abuses both her deserter husband and her draft-dodging lover. The violent events connected with the Conscription Crisis that occurred in this era are used by Carrier as an allegory for the tragic fear and hatred that beset English-French relations. This highly popular work was adapted for the stage in both French and English Canada.

Several acclaimed collections of poetry were published in early Canadian literature at the end of the nineteenth century, especially those produced by the so-called Confederation Group of poets, who rendered the beauty and reality of the Canadian landscape in natural language. A collection of the works of one of the group's best-known poets, *The Poems of Archibald Lampman* (1900), best exemplifies the innovative techniques and the broad thematic treatment of the group's poetry. However, it was the poets of the twentieth century—writers such as Edwin John Pratt, Irving Layton and P. K. Page—who gained broad international recognition for Canadian literature. Among the most notable collections is Al Purdy's *Collected Poems, 1956–1986*. Purdy's career spanned nearly the entire century from 1918 to 2000, and his *Collected Poems* contains his most memorable poetry, especially those pieces that speak to the 1960s social movements that set him wandering the country, reading his poems to large audiences. The oral patterns in his poetry that resulted from the close relationship he had with his audiences at his reading performances also made his work more accessible and comprehensible to his wider reading public. Purdy's work has received critical praise for the way in which it exemplifies a close artistic contact between experience and writing.

The work of a younger poet, Leonard Cohen, has also gained both wide national and international recognition. His collection *The Spice-Box of Earth* (1961) established his reputation as a lyric poet; with rich and evocative language, the work highlights Cohen's best love poetry but also covers many darker themes, such as victimization, loss and cruelty. The pieces deal with self-conscious topics such as the role of the poet and the inheritance of a Jewish tradition. The book continues to be his most popular volume of verse.

Early Canadian drama was mostly derivative or consisted of dramatic sketches that were not meant for the stage. Up until the mid-twentieth century, there were few memorable Canadian plays in performance. After the 1950s there was a heightened interest in drama in the nation when modern Canadian professional theater was established, especially the founding of the Stratford Shakespearean Festival in Stratford, Ontario. From the 1930s, the Canadian Broadcasting Corporation hired playwrights to write broadcast scripts, often for the dramatization of popular Canadian fiction; radio thus aided the evolution of professional theatre.

The most notable Canadian dramas have been written in the last several decades by acclaimed playwrights such as James Reaney, George Ryga, and David French. Ryga's 1967 play *The Ecstasy of Rita Joe* was the work that made him famous. As in much of his best dramatic work, the play pleads the case of oppressed minorities by presenting the story of a young First Nations woman torn between the traditional ways of her people and the contemporary Canadian urban world. Rita's tragic life history is revealed through her courtroom trial, which is the predominant frame for the narrative. The play's resounding debut success onstage drew the attention of the general public to the plight and exploitation of many Native people who come to the city.

David French's 1972 play *Leaving Home* explores a social problem that has become endemic in Canada during the late twentieth century—the uprooting of a Maritimes family in search of better economic prospects in the heartless and alien urban setting of Toronto. In French's drama, archetypal family conflicts are explored when the father, Jacob Mercer, refuses to relax his paternal authority by not allowing his two elder sons to leave home and seek their own fortune in the city. The play's theme resonated deeply with Canadian audiences and French's work continued to influence English Canadian drama for several decades.

Like much of his drama, James Reaney's landmark trilogy *The Donnellys* (1975–1977) is part history and part fantasy. In the work he combines unusual theatrical techniques with archival research, poetry, and elements of romance, melodrama, mime, and myth to tell the central stories and legends of Ontario, specifically the mysterious murder of an Irish immigrant family in 1880. Reaney's dramatic treatment of the tragic history exemplifies the great imagination that he has brought to Canadian drama.

Modern drama in French Canada has often been used effectively to give an aesthetic dimension to the lives of the destitute, despairing, and down-trodden in francophone society. The playwright, Michel Tremblay, is an acclaimed and popular exponent of such realism in the theatre. His work *Les Belles-soeurs* (*The Sisters-in-Law*, 1968) dramatizes the portrayal of a party of women in a poor, working-class district of Montréal. The drama's protagonist, Germaine Lauzon, has recruited family members, friends, and neighbors to help her paste into a book the million supermarket trading stamps that she has won. As she dreams of the items she can acquire with the stamps, the all-women cast speaks frankly about their tedious lives and daily frustrations. The play ends in an uproar when the women steal the stamps and leave Germaine crying over her lost happiness. Tremblay's play was highly innovative in its use of Québécois street slang, known as "joual," which gave an anti-establishment approach to its depiction of French Canadian working-class life. As a comic but pessimistic portrayal of the women's downtrodden existence, the play operates as a true metaphor for national alienation of the oppressed in Québec. With its raw language and unabashed presentation of the ugly, the drama became a turning-point in the recent history of Québec theatre. The play also achieved a center-stage presence across Canada through Tremblay's work.

CONCLUSION

Reading culture continues to thrive across Canada because of the rich heritage of literature that Canadians have cherished throughout their country's history and because they have consistently supported governments that seek to nourish print culture. Unlike their U.S. neighbors, Canadian readers expect that their national literature will have a political or social dimension. Given that their country has been so influenced by the French/English split, Canadians are sensitive to issues of political and cultural identity. Moreover, especially with the recognition of Nunavut in the late twentieth century, Canadians now recognize that their national identity goes beyond the multicultural to the post-colonial. And finally, as a nation with many cultural faces, Canadians also look for literary evidence of a strong national identity to offset the overwhelming influence of the U.S. culture industries. Therefore, government programs that encourage authorship and that ensure that domestic publishing remains a vital enterprise provide Canadians with access to the information, pleasure, and enlightenment in books and in literature that will make them better citizens of their country and more responsible inhabitants of their world.

RECOMMENDED READING

Atwood, Margaret. *Strange Things: The Malevolent North in Canadian Literature*. New York: Oxford University Press, 1996.

Frye, Northrop. *The Bush Garden: Essays on the Canadian Imagination*. Toronto: House of Anansi, 1995.

Howells, Coral Ann, ed. *The Cambridge Companion to Margaret Atwood*. New York: Cambridge University Press, 2006.

Meindl, Dieter. *North American Encounters: Essays in U.S. and English and French Canadian Literature and Culture*. Hamburg: Lit Verlag, 2003.

Moses, Daniel David and Terry Goldie, eds. *An Anthology of Canadian Native Literature in English*. New York: Oxford University Press, 1998.

New, W.H. *A History of Canadian Literature*. Montreal: McGill–Queens University Press, 2003.

Silvera, Makeda, ed. *The Other Woman: Women of Colour (Color) in Contemporary Canadian Literature*. Toronto: Sister Vision Press, 1995.

Stouck, David. *Major Canadian Authors: A Critical Introduction to Canadian Literature in English*. Omaha: University of Nebraska Press, 1988.

Sugars, Cynthia, ed. *Home-Work: Postcolonialism, Pedagogy, and Canadian Literature*. Ottawa: University of Ottawa Press, 2004.

PRIMARY SOURCES

Aquin, Hubert. *Next Episode* (originally published in French as *Prochain episode*). Toronto: McClelland & Stewart, 2001.

Atwood, Margaret. *The Handmaid's Tale*. New York: Anchor, 1998.

Bill 101, Charter of the French Language (*Charte de la langue française*). 1977.

Blais, Marie-Claire. *A Season in the Life of Emmanuel* (originally published in French as *Une Saison dans la vie d'Emmanuel*). Toronto: New Canadian Library, 1992.

Borduas, Paul-Émile. *Refus global*. Montréal: Parti pris, 1977.

Callaghan, Morley. *Such is My Beloved*. Toronto: McClelland & Stewart, 1957.

Canadian Charter of Rights and Freedoms. April 17, 1982.

Carrier, Roch. *La Guerre, Yes Sir!* Translated by Sheila Fischman. Toronto: House of Anansi, 1998.

Cohen, Leonard. *The Spice-Box of Earth*. New York: Viking, 1968.

Durham, John George Lambton, Earl of. *Report on the Affairs of British North America*. 1839.

French, David. *Leaving Home*. Toronto: House of Anansi, 2002.

Haliburton, Thomas Chandler. *The Clockmaker*. Lennox, MA: Hard Press, 2006.

Hémon, Louis. *Maria Chapdelaine*. Translated by W.H. Blake. Toronto: Dundurn, 2007.

Lampman, Archibald. *The Poems of Archibald Lampman*. Toronto: University of Toronto Press, 1975.

Laurence, Margaret. *The Stone Angel*. Toronto: McClelland & Stewart, 1998.

Leacock, Stephen. *Sunshine Sketches of a Little Town*. Toronto: McClelland & Stewart, 1947.

MacLennan, Hugh. *Two Solitudes*. Montréal: McGill-Queen's University Press, 2007.

Massey Commission Report (Royal Commission on National Development in the Arts, Letters and Sciences), 1951.

Mistry, Rohinton. *A Fine Balance*. New York: Vintage, 2001.

Montgomery, Lucy Maud. *Anne of Green Gables*. New York: G.P. Putnam's Sons, 2008.
Munro, Alice. *Lives of Girls and Women*. New York: Vintage, 2001.
Official Languages Act. 1969.
Ondaatje, Michael. *The English Patient*. Toronto: McClelland & Stewart, 2006.
Porter, John. *The Vertical Mosaic*. Toronto: Univ. of Toronto Press, 1967.
Purdy, Al. *Beyond Remembering: The Collected Poems of Al Purdy*. Madeira Park, BC: Harbour Publishing, 2000.
Québec Act. 1774.
Report of the Royal Commission on Bilingualism and Biculturalism. 1967–1970.
Richler, Mordecai. *The Apprenticeship of Duddy Kravitz*. Toronto: McClelland & Stewart, 2006.
Roy, Gabrielle. *The Tin Flute* (originally published in French as *Bonheur d'occasion*). Toronto: New Canadian Library, 1989.
Ryga, George. *The Ecstasy of Rita Joe and Other Plays*. General Publishing Co. Ltd., 1980.
Shields, Carol. *The Stone Diaries*. New York: Penguin, 2005.
Tremblay, Michel. *Les Belles-soeurs*. Vancouver, B.C: Talonbooks Ltd., 1993.
Vallières, Pierre. *White Niggers of America: The Precocious Autobiography of a Quebec Terrorist* (originally published in French as *Nègres blancs d'Amérique*). New York: Monthly Review Press, 1971.
Wiebe, Rudy. *The Temptations of Big Bear*. Athens, OH: Swallow Press, 2000.

SECONDARY SOURCES

Balthazar, Louis. *French-Canadian Civilization*. East Lansing: Michigan State University Press, 1996.
Canadian Parliament. House of Commons; Standing Committee on Canadian Heritage. *The Challenge of Change: A Consideration of the Canadian Book Industry*. Ottawa: The Committee, 2000.
Dorland, Michael, ed. *The Cultural Industries in Canada: Problems, Policies and Prospects*. Toronto: J. Lorimer & Co., 1996.
Gundy, H. Pearson. *Book Publishing and Publishers in Canada before 1900*. Toronto: Bibliographical Society of Canada, 1965.
Jones, Raymond E. & Jon C. Stott. *Canadian Children's Books: a Critical Guide to Authors and Illustrators*. New York: Oxford University Press, 2000.
Kroller, Eva-Marie, ed. *The Cambridge Companion to Canadian Literature*. New York: Cambridge University Press, 2004.
Litt, Paul. *The Muses, the Masses, and the Massey Commission*. Toronto: University of Toronto Press, c1992.
Lockhart Fleming, Patricia, and Yvan Lamonde, eds. *History of the Book in Canada*. Toronto: University of Toronto Press, 2004.
Morton, Desmond. *A Short History of Canada*. Toronto: McClelland & Stewart, 2006.
Moss, John, ed. *The Canadian Novel: a Critical Anthology*. Toronto: N.C. Press, 1980–.
Parker, George L. *The Beginnings of the Book Trade in Canada*. Toronto; Buffalo: University of Toronto Press, 1985.
Shek, Ben-Zion. *French-Canadian & Québécois Novels*. New York: Oxford University Press, 1991.
Weiss, Jonathan and Jane Moss. *French-Canadian Literature*. Washington, D.C.: The Association for Canadian Studies in the United States, 1996.
Whiteman, Bruce. *Lasting Impressions: A Short History of English Publishing in Québec*. Montréal: Véhicule Press, 1994.

CHAPTER 2

Mexico, Central and South America, and the Caribbean

Sergio Inestrosa; translated by James L. Citron

Where the readers are . . .
It doesn't make sense to make enemies with people just because they don't share our exact
literary tastes when, in truth, most people aren't even interested in books.
—Andrew Lang, qtd. in Borges, Textos cautivos, *1986*

TIMELINE

1325	Aztecs occupy Tenochtitlán (later México City)
1350	Rapid Inca expansion in Andean South America
1492	Columbus makes landfall in the Bahamas on October 12
1507	A German cartographer publishes a map of the New World, using the name "America" in honor of Amerigo Vespucci
1519–22	Cortez arrives in México, conquers Montezuma and Tenochtitlán
1524	Council of the Indies established to help administer the new colonies
1530	Portugal begins to colonize Brazil
1532	Pizarro captures Atahualpa, ending the Incan Empire
1535	Antonio de Mendoza becomes first Spanish viceroy
1536	Pedro de Mendoza establishes Buenos Aires
1540	Pedro de Valdivia begins the conquest of Chile
1610	First Jesuit missions established in Paraguay, Argentina, and Brazil
1700s	Gold and diamonds discovered in Brazil
1759	Charles III of Spain accelerates modernization of royal bureaucracy, deeply affecting entrenched *criollo* elite in Spanish America and leading to revolts
1767	Jesuits expelled from Spanish America
1776	The Viceroyalty of La Plata is created, with its capital at Buenos Aires
1780–81	Indian revolt led by Túpac Amaru in Upper Peru
1781	Comuero Revolt in Colombia

1804	Haiti declares independence from France
1810	Hidalgo's "Grito de Dolores" in México
1811	Venezuela and Paraguay declare independence from Spain
1816	Argentina declares independence from Spain
1818	Chile declares independence after Spanish defeat at the Battle of Maipú
1846–48	United States defeats México and annexes the northern half of the country with the Treaty of Guadalupe Hidalgo
1862–67	French occupation of México until Benito Juárez and his liberal forces defeat, and then execute, Archduke Maximillian
1870s	Mass European emigration to Latin America; increased foreign investment, railway building, industrialization, organized labor, and the rise of positivist philosophy
1873	Dominican Republic declares independence from Spain
1876–1911	Dictator Porfirio Díaz rules México (except 1880–84)
1879–84	Chile defeats Peru and Bolivia in the War of the Pacific
1898	Cuba wins independence from Spain
1899	Brazil finalizes independence from Portugal
1903	Theodore Roosevelt intervenes to assist Panamanian independence from Colombia
1910–20	Bloody phase of the Mexican Revolution
1911–13	Francisco Madero replaces Porfirio Díaz as president of México
1917	México's revolutionary leaders author a new constitution
1927–33	Augusto César Sandino and his guerrillas successfully defy U.S. Marines in Nicaragua
1929	Ecuador becomes the first Latin American nation to grant women the right to vote
1946	Juan Perón elected president of Argentina.
1950	María Eva Duarte de Perón ("Evita") conducts successful "Rainbow Tour" of Europe to increase support for the regime of her husband, Argentinean president Juan Perón
1954	CIA overthrows constitutional government of Jacobo Arbenz in Guatemala
1956	U.S.-supported dictator Anastasio Somoza assassinated in Nicaragua
1959	Cuban Revolution; Cuban revolutionary government begins 1967
1960	Brasilia officially becomes Brazil's capital
1964–85	Military rule in Brazil
1967	Gabriel García Márquez publishes *Cien años de soledad* (*One Hundred Years of Solitude*)
1970–73	Democratically elected Chilean president Salvador Allende is overthrown in a U.S.-backed coup, dies mysteriously, and is succeeded by Augusto Pinochet
1974–76	Isabel Perón, third wife of Juan Perón, serves as Argentina and Latin America's first female president
1976–83	"Dirty War" in Argentina
1977	United States and Panama sign a new treaty providing for Panamanian control of the canal in 1999
1979	Sandinista (FSLN) Revolution takes power in Nicaragua
1994	EZLN (Zapatista) revolutionaries launch attacks in México's southern state of Chiapas

| 2000 | México elects Vicente Fox (PAN), ending the PRI's seventy-one-year domination of the presidency |
| 2008 | Fidel Castro resigns as leader of Cuban government |

INTRODUCTION TO THE REGION

Before 1492, when Christopher Columbus first set foot on American soil, the region that is known today as Latin America consisted of over a hundred different indigenous groups. Most of these groups had their own languages, and they all had their own customs, religions, and traditions. In the early sixteenth century, Spanish and Portuguese explorers began to colonize the region. By the end of the century the conquest had been completed, bringing with it the Spanish and Portuguese languages and the Catholic religion. The conquest also resulted in the formation of the *mestizo* race. For the next three hundred years, most of the region fell under Spanish rule and was organized into four vice-royalties. These were located in what are now México, Central America, Peru, Argentina, and the Dominican Republic, while the Portuguese colonized Brazil. During this period slavery was a common practice in the region, most notably in the Caribbean and Brazil, with the majority of slaves coming from Africa. At the beginning of the nineteenth century, the independence movement began to take form and quickly spread throughout the region. Today the region consists of twenty-two individual countries. This chapter will focus on Spanish-speaking North America (i.e. México), Central America, South America, the Caribbean, and Portuguese-speaking Brazil.

READING TRENDS AND PRACTICES

Summarizing in one chapter the cultural history of reading in Latin America presents a number of challenges. The first is the sheer size and diversity of this region, which spans three continents. More importantly the oral tradition, which has been passed down by the region's indigenous ancestors, continues to play a more important role than written texts, even today when so many languages are being replaced by Spanish and Portuguese. In Latin America attending school simply to learn to read and write has been a privilege enjoyed by a decidedly small minority of the population, leading to widespread illiteracy. As a result, reading and writing have taken a back seat to radio and, more recently, television, both of which play a much larger role in defining the region's cultural identity than written texts.

However, Latin American writers played significant roles in the development of global literary styles, especially in the twentieth century. These writers were motivated by a general desire to break with the past and launch a search for the new, even though it was unknown. Furthermore, events in the early twentieth century—World War I had just ended, and the Spanish Civil War was about to about to begin—allowed for creative change and experimentation, which found a willing readership within the Latin American elite. Vicente Huidobro in Chile, Jorge Luis Borges and Roberto Artl in Argentina, Xavier Villaurrutia in México, and Mário de Andrade in Brazil are some of the writers who made up the Latin American avant-garde movement that was the direct precursor to what would later come to be known as the Latin American "boom." Another group of avant-garde writers moved into political protest literature. Some of these writers included Nicanor Parra, César Vallejo in Peru, Juan Gelman and Alfonsina Storni in Argentina, Miguel Angel Asturias in Guatemala, Ernesto Cardenal in Nicaragua, and the most famous Latin American poet, Pablo Neruda of Chile.

Mural of Pablo Neruda's life and work in Bellavista, Santiago, Chile. [Courtesy of Seton R. Droppers]

Latin Americans have a taste for melodrama and scandal, a passion for sports, and a biting sense of humor. So although the cultural history of reading and the history of literature were once one and the same, since the emergence of the newspapers—especially sports newspapers and tabloids—they, as well as comic books, political cartoons, radio shows, and soap operas, have played a larger role in the region's daily reality than have literary texts or magazines. Yet despite all of the above phenomena, it would be a mistake to imply that Latin Americans do not love the written word; after all, some of the world's finest writers have come from the region and have been on the forefront of many literary movements. Throughout this chapter, we will treat Latin America as an entity rather than a fragmented group of countries. We will also examine the cultural impact of texts in an historic perspective, since a text that may not have been popular in its day may have become popular later, while, at the same time, the relative popularity of a text when it first emerges can impact generations of writers to come.

PRE-COLUMBIAN AND EARLY COLONIAL TEXTS

Because written language was virtually unknown in pre-Columbian cultures, it is difficult to access the majority of these cultures' narratives, which were passed down from generation to generation either informally or by a community's official story-teller. It was not until the colonial period that a few indigenous groups, with the assistance of Spanish priests, tried to write down some of their traditions and legends. Such was the case of *Popol Vuh*, which captured the Quiché people's view of the universe, and with the book of *Chilam Balam*, which recorded the traditions and memories of the Cakchiquel people. Yet in truth these books were intended to help the colonizing Spaniards, especially priests looking to understand the cultures of those they hoped to convert, rather than the indigenous peoples themselves, who were illiterate and already knew all they needed to about their own heritage.

Over time these books, along with works such as the poems of the king Netzahualcoyotl from Texcoco, México, and other collections of Quechua poetry, have come to be regarded as part of the pre-Columbian cultural tradition and have reinforced a sense of pride within—and admiration for—these peoples. For example, Netzahualcoyotl's writings during the final years of Aztec domination foreshadow the pending ruin and destruction of Aztec civilization. Twentieth-century ministries of education have turned these works into textbooks from which to teach pre-Columbian history in schools.

However, few texts could have had a greater impact on Latin Americans' social, political, and cultural lives than Christopher Columbus's journal entries. Although the indigenous people themselves neither read nor were aware of these texts' existence, they were the ones who paid the price of the conquest and who suffered the direct consequences of the euphoria and greed that these texts unleashed in Europe. The interest in these texts and the news of the discovery of the New World grew from Columbus's almost naïve description of an earthly paradise inhabited by mild-mannered, gentle people who lived on a continent of unsurpassed beauty. These tales awakened greed across Europe as explorers took off on adventures of conquest and, later, colonization. It can be further argued that Columbus's diaries had a direct and fundamental impact on the development of Latin America because these texts, which were hardly literary, served as the catalyst for the *Reyes Católicos* to support future expeditions and for a large number of explorers and clergymen to join the conquest; from there a new race, a new culture, and a New World emerged.

The conquest was both a military and a religious endeavor. Many explorers took off for America—some motivated by dreams of wealth and fame and others by the thought of converting those strange people to the "real religion." The two main players in this wave of explorers were Hernán Cortés on the military side, and Fray Bartolomé de las Casas on the religious side. Bartolomé de las Casas fought for the rights of the Indians—both their right to resist religious conversion, and their right to occupy their lands. Cortés, on the other hand, saw this as a unique opportunity to install a new culture in these lands and collect his share of the reward the crown had promised for his services.

The conquest began with Santo Domingo, the cultural center of the region. There the monks established the first schools and convents and wrote the first textbooks. With the exploration of the continent, the island of Hispaniola soon decreased in importance. The indigenous people narrated their accounts of the conquest to the monks, who then translated them to Spanish. The primary impact of these texts was on the Spanish crown, rather than on the colonies. In these accounts we hear the anguish of the Indians: the uncertainty created by the conquest, the moral and physical cost of defeat, and the collapse of their world, their values, and their cultures. But these indigenous accounts that the Spaniards captured in codices, such as that by Bernardo de Sahagun, were less important for the relatively small impact they had on the indigenous people than for how they flamed the fires of legal and theological disputes in the European courts. *The True History of the Conquest of New Spain*, by Bernal Díaz del Castillo, is one of the books that not only had great success, but also created huge disputes in Spain between those who championed the rights of the Indian and those who defended Spain's right to exploit the resources of the new territories. This book continues to be key to understanding the conquest. It constitutes one of the most passionate chronicles of the

Bernal Diaz del Castillo was a conquistador under Cortez who wrote an influential account of Mexican society called *Historia verdadera de la Conquista de la Nueva España*.

Spanish conquest and is one of the most widely read sources for those studying its history.

Ironically, readings from this period profoundly impacted the indigenous people's lives but escaped their notice completely. They did not read Spanish, and in fact many still do not read Spanish; their daily survival is of far greater concern to them than schooling and education. On the other hand, the indigenous people readily embraced theater, which the Spaniards also brought to the New World in an attempt to convert them to Catholicism. In large part because of the indigenous peoples' natural tendency toward oral traditions and celebrations, the reglious plays adapted for the colonial era were very popular during this period. These depictions of biblical stories such as the nativity, at times in the European languages and at times in indigenous ones, enjoyed enormous popularity and typically culminated in mass baptisms of Indians. Attendance was so heavy that the stages were known to collapse, eventually prompting the colonizers to construct "open chapels" in order to attract audiences. This type of construction can still be found in the Yucatan Peninsula of México.

It is important to mention here that in 1502, the Spanish crown proclaimed a law that restricted publication of books in Spain to those that dealt with Catholicism; subsequently, in 1531, King Charles I prohibited the introduction of romance novels to the New World. In 1558 King Phillip II issued a decree calling for the death penalty for those who published or introduced forbidden books to the colonies. Nonetheless, a number of significant texts emerged between the middle of the sixteenth century and the beginning of the nineteenth century.

One of the most notable texts that emerged from early Latin American discourse was Sor Juana Inés de la Cruz's *Response to Sor Filotea*. Sor Juana, a Mexican nun, is a unique case, not just for her literary contributions, but also for what she represented as an intellectual woman of the seventeenth century who defended women's rights to study and to think for themselves—rights that were unheard of in her day. The only way for her to develop her intellectual passion was to seek refuge in the convent and dedicate her life to the pursuit of knowledge. She has been called the first feminist in the Americas. Although the concept of feminism was unheard of in this era, she stood out as someone who knew how to intelligently defend a woman's right to learn and seek knowledge as she demonstrated in *Response to Sor Filotea.* "Sor Filotea" was a pseudonym taken by the bishop of Puebla, who could not argue publicly with a nun. Some of Sor Juana's poems were, and continue to be, quoted at all levels of society and are even parodied on popular television programs.

ETHNOGRAPHIC TEXTS

Garcilaso de la Vega (1501–1536) is an important literary figure, and much of today's knowledge of Incan culture comes from him. He was born in Peru to a Spanish father and an Incan mother, and he immigrated to Spain when he was quite young. Thanks to his work, *Comentarios Reales de los Incas,* Spain gained access to a much more direct and rich view of Incan culture and history than it would otherwise have known. These days this work is frequently consulted by experts on pre-Columbian cultures and is an important source of information about the Incan past. Although it is no longer a popular text, it can be found in select anthologies of Latin American literature.

Although not strictly ethnographic, *La Araucana* (published in three parts between 1569 and 1589) by Alonso de Ercilla, the first epic poem written in the Americas, captures a colonial view of Indian practices and customs, specifically during wartime. *La Araucana* describes the defense that the Araucano Indians in Chile mounted against their Spanish conquerors. It is the first text of literary importance written in America by a Spaniard—and not just any Spaniard, but an educated and enlightened one who was well aware of the role the Spaniards were playing in history. Despite his belief in the fight he was carrying out, he was also able to recognize and capture in writing the strength and courage of the Araucano warriors. This book continues to be read in high school classrooms and is considered a classic by literary scholars.

El Lazarillo de los Ciegos Caminantes (1773) is primarily a tourist's guide to life in Latin American cities such as Lima, Buenos Aires, and México City, and to situations that European travelers could come across when visiting the colonies. This text, written by a Spaniard under the pseudonym "Concolorcorvo," made two noteworthy contributions to the history of reading. The first was to argue that nomadic cultures, such as the gauchos who lived an itinerant lifestyle in the countryside of South America, were incapable of developing a culture or wealth. The second was to denounce the relaxed lifestyle of Latin American natives as irresponsible and potentially destructive, and to assert the superiority of the Spaniards and their right to colonize. Although this work enjoyed great popularity at the end of the colonial era, it has disappeared from bookstores and is virtually unknown today.

CREATIVE TEXTS

In 1816 Mexican journalist and liberal writer Fernández de Lizardi wrote *El Periquillo Sarmiento* (*The Mangy Parrot*), a picaresque novel, which became one of the most popular books of the era. What made it so popular and keeps it popular to this day is that the protagonist is not an elite, upper-class hero, but a lower-class rogue who is always dreaming up ingenious ways to survive in the diverse metropolis of México City. The characters in this novel are social parasites in a corrupt, racist, and elitist society. Although the novel reinforces the European democratic ideals of the day—that hard work pays off and is the only way to move up the social ladder—it still set the tone for what became a tradition in Latin American

Martín Fierro was a legendary gaucho from Argentina who was made famous in an epic poem of the same name by José Hernández.

literary consumption: the love of local, recognizable, and accessible themes over elite settings, characters, or concepts.

For example, in the middle of the nineteenth century, gaucho poetry became one of Argentine literature's most popular and characteristic forms. Contrary to its name, it was written by educated city dwellers, but it is still genuinely popular. For the Argentinean poet, Jorge Luis Borges, the practice has an historic explanation: during the wars in that area, urban soldiers intermixed with rural soldiers and identified with them, giving rise to this popular genre. José Hernández' *Martín Fierro* is a sad poem that enjoyed great popularity from its first publication. True or false, gauchos who knew how to read found within the words and rhythm of *Martín Fierro* a poetic version of their own lives, and they embraced it as their own. According to Borges, within seven years of its initial appearance in 1872 it went through eleven editions in Argentina and Uruguay, selling a record-setting 48,000 copies. Many consider *Martín Fierro* to be the premier work of gaucho literature and the quintessential Argentine book, in much the same way that *Don Quixote* is the quintessential Spanish book.

Another literary form, the sentimental novel, which gave rise to radio novels and then soap operas, continues to be enormously popular today. Books of this genre differ in setting and period but share a specific romantic theme, that of a love gone bad because of one partner's social position or race. These works reinforce traditional values—just as soap operas do today—by melodramatically depicting a nostalgic longing for the stability of days past. Most of these books have women's names: *Cecilia Valdés* (1882), by Cuban writer Cirilo Villaverde, *María* (1867), by the Colombian author Jorge Isaac, *Clemencia* (1869) by Ignacio Altamirano from México, and *Amalia* (1844) by Argentine author José Marmol. Although these works were read primarily by the educated elite, their melodramatic portrayal of women as passive, "good" wives and mothers, in charge of the domestic sphere but excluded from the public domain, holds great appeal across all social classes in Latin America to this day. This phenomenon can be seen in the way these novels gradually gave way to the *radionovela* and then to the *telenovela* or soap opera, which still dominates today.

Much of the reading material produced in Central America from the end of the nineteenth century well into the twentieth century can be considered *costumbrista*—that is, depicting the daily customs and habits of rural life. Writers such as Salvador Salazar Arrué (1899–1975) and Napoleón Rodríguez Ruiz show a marked tendency in this direction in their descriptions of simple, gentle, and humble people from the countryside. These texts stand out for the simplicity both of their characters and of their depictions of rural life in Central America. The beauty of this movement is that it recorded the traditions, legends, and rhythms of rural life and, in so doing, elevated the standing of *campesinos* and established a legitimacy and permanence for them in the literary realm.

In Colombia, the stories of Tomás Carrasquilla (1858–1940) were well known and popular for the way they recounted stories gathered from the people. In one a man makes fun of the devil, and in another the main character is a disabled schoolteacher called "El Tullido," who is said to be based on a teacher the author had as a child. In the Dominican Republic the book *Cuentos frágiles* (1908), by Fabio Fiallo gained great popularity for the romanticism it depicted. *Por el Cibao* by Tulio M. Cestero (1877–1955) also gained popularity, especially because it describes the living conditions of the campesinos in the Dominican Republic. In Cuba the book *La tierra adentro* (1906), by Jesús Castellanos was also quite popular for its costumbrista flavor.

Another key element of these texts is that they are quite plausible and realistic. They all aim to capture the colloquial way of speaking, which makes them especially popular because people see themselves in the ways these characters speak, dress, and act. These books were often enlisted as textbooks in basic education programs, as they helped maintain popular traditions.

Another type of realism can be found in books that view nature as a permanent threat. Such is the case of the stories of Horacio Quiroga (1878–1937), where nature is depicted as barbaric and destructive. Quiroga's *Cuentos de la Selva* (1919), Rómulo Gallegos' *Doña Bárbara* (1929), Ricardo Güiraldes' *Don Segundo Sombra* (1926), and José Eustasio Rivera's *La Vorágine* (1924) are the best-known examples of this type of work, where natural forces destroy communities and individuals. These books were the first Latin American novels and stories to be read in Europe and the United States. They present a deterministic view of the relationship between humans and nature, where humans are no match for the destruction and havoc that nature can wreak. This genre gained great popularity among Latin American readers for its depiction of the dominance of nature over humanity—a theme that has great resonance in a region where the idea that people are subject to larger forces has been heavily reinforced by indigenous faiths.

This type of realism was extended by leftist thinkers and has two forms. The first is the intellectual political essay that was linked to the international directives of the Communist Party of the USSR. The most dramatic case in Latin America is that of Juan Carlos Mariátegui (1894–1930), founder of the Peruvian Communist Party, who brought together a group of intellectuals to work for the magazine *Amauta*. From there they brought to light the working conditions of laborers and attacked "Yankee" imperialism. This type of realism also includes novels of the form known as protest literature, which has continued to develop in Latin America. Its impact has been strongest at the peak of leftist political movements in Peru, Colombia, Bolivia, Uruguay, Chile, and Central America.

Brazil also had a significant Social Realist movement, its most important representative being Joaquim Maria Machado de Assis (1839–1908), who wrote several best-selling novels during the nineteenth century. His most famous works are *A Mão e a Luva* (*The Hand and the Glove*, 1874) and *Ressurreição* (1872). His novels were generally pessimistic about the future of Brazilian society, although they are famous for their biting humor. Perhaps the novel that best demonstrates his style is *Memórias Póstumas de Brás Cubas* (*Posthumous Memories of Bras Cubas*, 1881), which ridicules Rio de Janiero society in the words of a dead man who claims to be speaking from beyond the grave.

The other form of social realism is the Indian narrative, which demonstrates how hard life is in indigenous mountain villages. Many books have addressed indigenous life, traditions, and culture. Some, such as *Huasipungo* (1934) by the Ecuadorian writer Jorge Icaza, *Los Hombres de Maíz* (1967) and *Torotumbo* (1971) by Guatemalan Miguel Angel Asturias, and *La Patria del Criollo* (1970) by Severo Martínez Pelaez in Guatemala, have stirred up heated academic debate, with no consensus being reached on whether indigenous people's interests are best served by westernizing or preserving their separate cultural identity. In contrast, Jesús Castellanos (1878–1912) and Mariano Brull (1891–1956) were Cuban voices who began to introduce what may have been the most important topic of the Caribbean: the struggle of the black population in the Caribbean to gain the same rights as the majority.

Politics has always played a major role in the generation of creative works in Latin America. The Mexican Revolution, for example, was a defining moment in Mexican history, and its impact was felt throughout the Americas. The Mexican Revolution, the first social revolution of the twentieth century, involved significant changes to the political, social, and economic life of the country. With time, the social gains from the Revolution have been eroded. Nonetheless, the Revolution was the most important event in México in the twentieth century, and its influence was especially felt in education and culture. The Revolution inspired significant artistic, literary, and cultural gains and generated a cultural crusade that encompassed film, education, the news media, and literature. Mexican muralism, for example, cannot be understood without first understanding the social, political, economic, and cultural goals of the Mexican Revolution. Among the most-read novels on the Mexican Revolution, two that cover both the military side and the revolutionary process itself are *Los de Abajo* (*The Underdogs*, 1915) by Mariano Azuela and *El águila y la serpiente* (*The Eagle and the Serpent*, 1928), by Martín Luis Guzmán. Both are key to understanding this period of México's history and are unusually popular in a country where so few people are literate.

Once the armed revolts had ended and the country had achieved a certain level of political stability, México began to change from a largely rural society to one in which cities were growing in size at a disproportionate rate. The novel that best reflects this atmosphere of change is *La Región Más Transparente* (*Where the Air is Clear*, 1959), by Carlos Fuentes. Although the book never achieved the popularity of *Los de Abajo*, it has been central to understanding this period of transition in a country that is still in search of its own identity. The revolution's promises of social change were never realized, and instead a new social and political force called bureaucracy was born and became the nation's guiding force.

Literary critics point to modernism as the movement that marked Latin American literature's coming of age. Until the rise of modernism, Latin America's literary contributions remained primarily at the regional level. As the works of the modernist writers gained acceptance from European writers and literary critics, Latin America began to emerge for the first time as a legitimate contributor to international cultural literacy. The list of world-renowned Latin American modernist writers is extensive and includes Rubén Darío, José Martí, Julián del Casal, Leopoldo Lugones, Ramón López Velarde, Amado Nervo, Horacio Quiroga, Macedonio Fernández, Froilán Turcios, Mário de Andrade, José Enrique Rodo, and Julio Herrera, most of whom wrote between the late nineteenth and early twentieth centuries.

Best-selling Brazilian modernist Mário de Andrade (1893–1945) was representative of this literary trend. He rejected the European literary conventions and instead championed Brazilian folklore, music, and colloquial languages. He was a major figure in Brazil's avant-garde movement and has had an enormous impact on Brazilian literature, even into the twenty-first century. His readers were mostly fellow members of the modernist movement, but he was and still is widely read in Brazil's school and university system. His great novel, *Macunaíma* (1928), connects with South American traditions of so-called Magic Realism and fuses Brazilian Indian folk themes with modern urban settings and contexts. The mixing of the local and native with the urban and urbane signalled a shift in Latin American cultural perceptions and established Brazil as a significant contributor to twentieth-century literary development.

Poetry was not modernism's claim to fame, but some of the poems still roll off people's tongues today thanks to music. Such is the case of *Simple Verses* by José Martí, which was turned into the popular song "Guantanamera" and immortalized by the Cuban singer Celia Cruz. The works of poets such as Martí, Darío, and Lugones paved the way for future generations of Latin American writers, making such deep inroads that later writers from the region found their works accepted much more quickly and eagerly. In this sense then, the impact and reach of modernist writers went far beyond their era, impacting later literary generations not just in Latin America, but also in Europe, and especially in Spain.

But regardless of when it was written, poetry has always been important in Latin American culture. In Nicaragua, for example, it is said that if one lifts up a rock, one will find a poet, and Chile is known as the land of poets. It is not surprising then that two of the greatest Latin American poets have been Rubén Darío (1867–1916) of Nicaragua and Pablo Neruda (1904–1973) of Chile. Rubén Darío's famous collection of poems, *Azul* . . . , was published in 1888, but Neruda is probably Latin America's best-known poet, especially for his small work *Veinte Poemas de Amor y Una Canción Desesperada* (1924), which has been translated into many languages and read worldwide.

Although reading was never fully embraced by all social classes, Latin American music certainly was. No discussion of popular culture is complete without mentioning poetry set to music or turned into songs. In the case of some genres, Latin American music started as an imitation of foreign styles. Such was the case with Spanish Rock, which began by mimicking U.S. models, but later came into its own in Latin America. Mexican ranchera music, Latin American folk music with its marked indigenous influence, and, of course, Argentine tango and Brazilian *bossa nova*, are all decidedly Latin American genres in their own right and are vital expressions of Latin America's lively musical interests. Cuba is often cited as the birthplace of Latin American rhythms. Much of Latin America's diverse musical offerings were written by such poets as Violeta Parra and Mario Benedeti or singer-composers with a poetic style such as Ricardo Arjona, Silvio Rodríguez, Augustín Lara, José Alfredo Jiménez, and more recently, the ever-popular singer and songwriter Juan Gabriel.

Afro-Caribbean culture—most notably Afro-Cuban culture—first began to appear in the region's literature in the early part of the nineteenth century as part of an antislavery effort. Black and mulatto culture began to appear as a nostalgic yearning for Africa and its natural beauty. This nostalgia was then transformed into a political movement. One of the most representative books of this movement is *Message to the People: The Course of African Philosophy* by Marcus Garvey of Jamaica. The book *Ansi parla l'oncle* (1928), by Jean Price-Mars, marked the start of the appearance of black culture in Caribbean literature, providing legitimacy for topics such as voodoo and other African traditions in the Caribbean, especially in Haiti. Cuban writer Alejo Carpentier (1904–80) later named this tradition "Magic Realism" and described it in beautiful detail in his book, *El reino de este mundo.*

Perhaps the most important writer in the black and mulatto tradition is Nicolás Guillén (1902–1989), the Cuban poet best known for giving voice to poor mulattos and black Cubans. In Puerto Rico, that voice was provided by the poet Luis Palés Matos (1898–1959), who represented the topic of Afro-Caribbean culture and set it to music. In the Dominican Republic, it was Manuel Cabral who brought the rich traditions of the black population alive with his poetry.

Black and mulatto populations in the Caribbean also played a significant role in the evolution of music and dance, and new rhythms such as son, salsa, mambo, reggae and, more recently, reggaeton have had significant influence in other countries. These rhythms were heavily influenced by the slaves' African heritage and by such Caribbean cultural concepts as voodoo and "Santería."

In January of 1959, Fidel Castro took power in Cuba, an event that had repercussions throughout Latin America. The Cuban Revolution created new social conditions on the island, including a literacy campaign that reduced illiteracy in Cuba to levels unheard of in other parts of the region. The Revolution also improved social services for the majority of Cubans, especially in the areas of medicine and education. To this day, Cuba's health care system enjoys an outstanding reputation. The literacy campaign is one of the major achievements of Cuba's socialist revolution, and it introduced many opportunities for Cubans who today have the highest level of education in Latin America. The revolution also created conditions for the publication and dissemination of a large number of books, especially by Russian authors. Another effect of the Revolution was the creation of an international prize for the best novellas and works of poetry and theater, under the umbrella of *La Casa de las Américas.*

The list of well-known writers in Cuba is lengthy. Some of these writers celebrated the Revolution, while other popular writers such as Severo Sarduy, Guillermo Cabrera Infante, and Reynaldo Arenas, to name just a few, chose to go into exile. Those who chose to stay in Cuba include Alejo Carpentier, Nicolás Guillén, and José Lezama Lima, widely regarded throughout Latin America as the master of the new narrative. A similar phenomenon occurred with musicians. Some, such as Celia Cruz, Pérez Prado, and Amaury Pérez, fled the country, while others such as Silvio Rodríguez and Pablo Milanés stayed to support the Revolution.

As well as celebrating Latin American traditions and social themes, Latin American writers have used creative forms to speak to readers' political interests and to communicate their opinions on the region's peculiar political leaders. The novel, *El señor presidente* (*Mr. President*, 1946), by Miguel Ángel Asturias, is one of many texts that criticize the military regimes that have threatened to destroy Latin America. This novel, which earned the Guatemalan author the Nobel Prize for Literature, follows in the tradition of taking on Latin American dictators. This was started by José Domingo Sarmiento during the nineteenth century in Argentina and continued by such writers as Gabriel García Márquez, Eduardo Galeano, Mario Benedetti, Mario Vargas Llosa, Carlos Fuentes, and more recently, Isabel Allende. The dictator's prominent role in Latin American literature is largely due to the prevalence of military dictatorships in the region.

Of all the Latin American writers who have tackled the theme of the Latin American dictator, Gabriel García Márquez is the best known in the United States. Winner of the Nobel Prize for Literature in 1982, author of numerous books and newspaper articles, and a tireless champion of indepent film, García Márquez has lived in México City since the 1970s. Yet it would be wrong to suggest that García

Márquez has only written books about dictators. In fact, dictatorships are only one of the many themes he has undertaken and one that many critics do not count among his most significant contributions. Gabriel García Márquez's narratives can be read or reread from the perspective of the longstanding battle between liberals and conservatives that is eating away at his native Colombia. His novels are extraordinarily popular worldwide and are required reading for anyone interested in the cultural history of reading in Latin America. Although almost all of his books have been bestsellers, his novel *Cien años de soledad* (1967; published in English as *One Hundred Years of Solitude*) is the most widely read and translated. As mentioned above, García Márquez has also addressed the figure of the dictator in his book, *El otoño del patriarca* (1975), published in English as *The Autumn of the Patriarch.*

Perhaps the area where García Márquez has had the most impact has been the point of view of his narrations—all of which are told in the style of *Realismo mágico*—which is a direct descendent of the "Lo real maravilloso" genre of Cuban writer Alejo Carpentier. Magic Realism, as this style has come to be known, has had a notable impact on Latin American fiction. Although García Márquez is perhaps the most famous of the Magic Realist novelists, other authors have had great critical and popular success writing in this style as well. Amongst the most widely read in this genre are Chilean author Isabel Allende, with her best-selling work *La Casa de los espíritus* (*The House of the Spirits,* 1982), and Mexican author Laura Esquivel, with her book *Como agua para chocolate* (1989), published in English as *Like Water for Chocolate.* Along with *One Hundred Years of Solitude*, these novels have enjoyed huge international success and both *The House of the Spirits* and *Como agua para chocolate* were made into movies.

NEWSPAPERS AND MAGAZINES

A noteworthy development in the seventeenth century was the birth of the newspaper, and with it political criticism and enlightenment. According to Pedro Henríquez Ureña, "The first newspapers appeared in the seventeenth century. Before 1600, broadsides containing news from Europe were printed in the capitals of the two viceroyalties" (34). The first newspaper in México, the *Gaceta de México*, appeared in 1667, but it was published very irregularly and was eventually replaced by others such as the *Mercurio de México* and later *El Diario de México*, which lasted until 1817. Another newspaper, *El Pensador Mexicano*, was established in 1812 by the liberal writer José Joaquín Fernández de Lizardi, who used the paper to champion the independence movement. In Lima, *La Gaceta de Lima* was first published in 1743. It was published regularly until 1767 and then reappeared sporadically. But the first true daily newspaper in the region was *El Diario Erudito Económico y Comercial de Lima.*

Newspapers covered the increasingly certain dawning of independence and were avidly read by the educated class. Newspapers, posters, and comic books all offered the population the opportunity to express criticism of the crown and to offer proposals for change in a society that was looking for a way out of the social, religious, and political unrest that plagued it. At the same time, the colonial Spanish government continued to use these same media as an official form of communication.

As one would expect, the Spanish crown reacted with force to the growing political unrest in the colonies. It expelled the Jesuit priests for having agitated the colonial elite, suppressed several indigenous uprisings such as that of Túpac Amaru in

Peru, and censored Inca Garcilaso de la Vega's *Comentarios Reales de los Incas*, which it considered a subversive book that encouraged pride in indigenous heritage.

Nonetheless change was occurring in other parts of the world, most notably in the United States and France where revolutions had toppled a colonial regime and a monarchy, respectively. It was not long before news of these events started reaching the colonies through books such as Montesquieu's *The Spirit of Laws* (1748) and Rousseau's *Social Contract* (1762). These ideas of change were picked up by newspapers and helped further the fight for independence. Another important factor in this call for change was the cultural life that had been developing in the colonies. In cities such as Lima, for example, cultural life was thriving in theaters, cafes, and bull fighting arenas, all of which provided a perfect backdrop for the exchange and display of ideas for political change.

In the Caribbean, most notably in Cuba at the beginning of the nineteenth century, Spanish power remained intact. Nonetheless many creoles (descendants of Spaniards who were born in the Americas) created academic societies to disseminate ideas of liberty that were rising to prominence in the rest of the region, following the examples of the United States and France. The first Cuban newspaper was published in Havana in 1790, and the first Puerto Rican newspaper was published in 1806, demonstrating the strides being made to popularize and promote the concepts of freedom and progress in the region. As a side note, it is worth observing that in 1804 Haiti became the first country to gain independence from France—a decade before any country under Spanish rule achieved the same.

In 1830 the magazine *Bimestre Cubana* was founded in Cuba. This publication served as a platform for countless writers, and its influence extended throughout the Caribbean. Many authors shared their passion for rural customs in Cuba, the Dominican Republic, and Puerto Rico. This group of writers also opposed U.S. annexation of Cuba. Under the umbrella of this magazine, José Antonio Saco (1797–1879) wrote his *Historia de la esclavitud* (*History of Slavery*), which gained a solid reputation among those who opposed slavery both in the Caribbean and throughout the continent.

Another important factor that helped to consolidate the sense of patriotism was the foundation of the magazine, *La revista de la Habana*, which served as the daily record of those, including José Martí, who wanted to see Cuba gain its independence from Spain. This magazine had great influence in Puerto Rico and the Dominican Republic. It is also important to bear in mid that Puerto Rico failed to gain independence from Spain and eventually became a U.S. territory. The Dominican Republic declared independence in 1873, and Cuba gained its independence in 1898.

The Latin American avant-garde movement was the work of a diverse group of writers who, by publishing their works mainly in literary journals and magaines, converted magazines into an accepted cultural form. Almost all of these writers were educated in Europe under the influence of different "-isms," such as Existentialism, Dadaism, Futurism, and Cubism. Two famous early-twentieth-century examples from Argentina were the magazine *Proa y Martín Fierro* and, later, the renowned magazine *Sur*, which is essential reading for those interested in understanding the discourse surrounding modern Latin American culture. In México, the magazine of the era was *Contemporáneos*, which brought together the group of writers of the same name. Uruguay's *Alfar* and Chile's *Mondrágora* both fulfilled this role. But it should be emphasized that even magazines were a cultural form utilized by the educated class rather than the average citizen.

Two magazines emerged in Cuba: *Avance*, which provided a forum for the black poetic and cultural movement, and *Ultra*, an academic journal that published research on the Afro-Caribbean population. Another noteworthy publication is the *Diccionario de Afro-cubanismos*, which explained African concepts such as *Santería* to Cuban audiences. In Puerto Rico, the magazine *Poliedro* represented Afro-Caribbean culture.

Irony and dark humor have been a constant in Mexican culture. Although humor and irony are qualities that define Latin Americans, as can be seen in the prevalence of comic books and cartoons, humor in México has always had a uniquely dark tone that Mexicans have developed as a way to deal with often-unpleasant realities while undermining the traditional order of things. For example, the oft-repeated expression, "Poor México, so far from God and so close to the United States," reflects that cynical wit as a way of dealing with the irreversible fate of geography. *Sálvase Quien Pueda, Instrucciones Para Vivir en México,* and *México y Otros Lugares* are three compilations of articles by Jorge Ibargüengoitia that were originally published in the newspaper *Excélsior*. Few Mexican writers have made use of irony like Ibargüengoitia. His widely read weekly column reflected a biting critique of Mexican traditions and culture.

EDUCATIONAL TEXTS

The reader may be surprised by the inclusion of a grammar book as part of *Cultural History of Reading*, but *Gramática de la lengua castellana, destinada al uso de los americanos,* or *Spanish Grammar Intended for the Use of Americans* by Andrés Bello (1847) is an essential part of Latin American culture, basic to understanding the richness of the Spanish language in Latin America. Bello himself wrote in the prologue that it was not his intention to write for Spaniards; his lessons, he said, were directed toward his brothers and sisters in Latin America. This book has been and continues to be an indispensable reference for those who speak and teach Spanish, and it is one of the most widely recognized books in Latin American academic circles. Despite the fact that Spanish grammar books are not read by the masses, this book in particular is known, respected, and admired throughout the continent.

POLITICAL TEXTS

The first half of the nineteenth century in Latin America was characterized by a marked dichotomy between modern European civilization and the traditional, less-developed life of gauchos and peasants. This era of premodernism was best expressed in Argentina, perhaps because of the sense of emptiness created by the expansive plains of the Argentinean prairies. Argentine intellectuals were among those who most reflected on the imposing immensity of the natural environment. The sense of emptiness was aggravated by the lack of cultural traditions upon which to seize and by the political chaos that had resulted from independence. This political confusion provided fertile ground for military dictatorships to take hold, ostensibly to protect the interests of the landowners, thus closing the country off to foreign investors and to immigration. In fact, military governments remained the norm in Latin America until the end of the twentieth century.

In Argentina, confronting the dictatorship of the landowner Juan Manuel Rosas (1793–1877) was Domingo F. Sarmiento (1811–1888), who criticized the backwardness of the country and, by extension, all of Latin America, in his essay *Facundo*. The character of Facundo is a gaucho—an Argentine cowboy—impulsive in his fight to tame the wilderness. Civilization, on the other hand, meant the rule of law, social norms, schooling, investment in infrastructure, and development. Democracy is in direct opposition to dictatorship, the fundamental form of barbarism. For Sarmiento, civilizing Argentina meant Europeanizing it—permiting immigration, investing in public infrastructure such as railroads, and putting an end to the isolationist policies of the day. Sarmiento advocated pursuing the course set by European nations, especially France, and, to a certain extent, the United States. *Facundo* is one of the most influential texts in the history of Latin American culture. In it, Sarmiento depicted the region's historical reality as a struggle between civilization and barbarism; this framework has served as a lens through which to interpret much of Latin America's social and cultural reality to this day.

The year 1968 turned out to be pivotal for many of the world's countries, and this was certainly the case for México. With the international press corps assembled in México City to cover the Olympic Games, the government of Gustavo Díaz Ordaz took over the National University and then violently suppressed the resulting uprising of students, who protested the occupation and demanded that the university be returned to its autonomous state. The book that best recounts these tragic events and serves as a reference for understanding what happened during the period is Elena Poniatowska's 1968 history, *La Noche de Tlatelolco* (published in English as *Massacre in México*). The book documents the events of October 2 and provides multiple testimonies about the student massacre.

Another glimpse into urban life comes from commentaries and critiques of daily life that appeared in various media sources. Without a doubt, México's best chronicler is Carlos Monsiváis (b. 1938). Monsiváis's biting critiques focus on daily life in Mexican society. His texts are a historiography of the routine, a record of life's daily thoughts. They are a mirror into which Mexicans can peer to see multiple images of their own faces. He has achieved such popularity that he is regularly mimicked on a comic television program. His book, *Amor Perdido* (the title of which echoes a popular Mexican song), launched his career as a social, political, cultural, and entertainment critic. This text has been read by a variety of audiences, from high school students to academics, politicians, university students, and housewives, and is another highlight in the history of reading in Latin America.

COMIC BOOKS

Another type of social observation can be found in political cartoons and comic books. Both are extremely popular in Latin America and form a fundamental part of the culture. *Mafalda*, by Argentine cartoonist Quino (b. 1932), and such comic books as *500 Years Screwed but Christian*, *The Never Ending Conquest of México*, and *Hitler for Masochists*, all by Mexican cartoonist Rius (b. 1934), are just a few examples of this type of political humor. Cartoons have also been used in educational campaigns to educate the population about health topics or to teach history. Much of this work has been directed toward young audiences, resulting in ever more comic books for children. All of today's newspapers employ cartoonists and comic books have been widely published since the middle of the twentieth century. Some are foreign, such as *Batman*, *Superman*, and *Archie*, but others are homegrown, such as the Argentinean magazine *Humor*. México and Argentina have produced an especially wide variety of comic strips. Apart from *Mafalda*, some of the best known are *Boogie el Aceitoso*, *La Familia Burrón*, *Memín Pinguín*, and *Los Supermachos*. The popularity of comics can be attributed to the appeal of both humor and visual arts throughout the region, as well as to widespread illiteracy.

Another use of humor is as a teaching tool. Just after the Nicaraguan revolution in 1979, a book was published teaching history through comics, building on the success of an earlier work published in México, *Historia de México para niños*.

LIBERATION THEOLOGY TEXTS

During the 1970s and 1980s, both Central and South America experienced great political and military turmoil. Paraguay, Uruguay, Argentina, Brazil, Chile, Peru, Nicaragua, Guatemala, Honduras, and El Salvador suffered, to varying degrees, civil wars and political repression resulting in thousands of deaths. As a result of this misery and political oppression, revolutionary movements sprang up via the region's religious networks, and religious leaders began calling for change. In many cases, broad social awareness was being awakened by political and social consciousness-raising activities that used the Latin American Bible and readings by Liberation Theologists, such as Gustavo Gutiérrez and Leonardo Boff, who popularized the reading of the Bible within the Christian Base Communities of the Catholic Church.

For the first time in the history of Catholicism, parishioners, meeting in Catholic Base Communities, began to read directly from biblical texts whose interpretation had traditionally been the privileged domain of priests. The most famous figure from this movement in Latin America was Archbishop Oscar A. Romero of El Salvador, who was assassinated while officiating a mass in 1980.

Throughout Latin America, Catholic Base Communities became the place where readings and social interpretations of the Bible occurred. The poet Ernesto Cardenal, who developed an especially active Catholic Base Community on the island of Solentiname on Lake Nicaragua, further represents the role these communities played. Cardenal's community produced poetry and music, and used Biblical readings to inspire political reflection. Many of the songs of the group Palacaguinas, and of the singer-songwriter Carlos Mejía Godoy (b. 1943), had ties to this community during the Sandinista revolution.

With the notable exception of the Sandinistas in Nicaragua, who triumphed in July of 1979, none of the revolutionary movements in Latin America succeeded in the goal of taking power from the ruling *juntas*. Yet under the influence of these movements, a good deal of literature, poetry, theater, novels, and music recorded the hope that the revolution awakened in the oppressed masses.

> **Anti-Neoliberalism: Voices from the Jungle**
>
> On January 1, 1994, the same day that the North American Free Trade Agreement went into effect between the governments of Canada, the United States, and México, a small group of indigenous people in the Lacandon Jungle in Chiapas issued a call to arms against México's neoliberal government. From that morning, the Zapatista movement has been a constant presence in México's political life. Its leader, Sub-commander Marcos, has been a key player on the political stage and has awakened the national conscience with his writings from the jungle. His texts have been published primarily by the newspaper *La Jornada* and have resonated not just at the national level, but internationally as well. Many Mexicans regularly read his communications, and many academics and political and social leaders have reacted to his texts, which have now become part of México's cultural history. His latest work is a novel, co-authored with Paco Ignacio Taibo II, with the loaded title *The Uncomfortable Dead*.

FILM AND TELEVISION

Though reading and writing have enjoyed less popularity in Latin America, film and, to an even greater extent, television are indisputably popular. The Mexican film industry peaked during the 1950s and 1960s when stars such as María Felix, Emilio "el Indio" Fernández, Pedro Infante, Sara García, and Jorge Negrete graced the screens. Mexican film is experiencing a resurgence today with such acclaimed productions as *Amores Perros*, *La Ley de Herodes*, and *Todo el Poder*. The same has happened in Argentina, where films such as *La Historia Oficial* and *Nueve Reynas* enjoy international prestige. Cubans have a similar passion for cinema. Even before the Revolution, many writers, including Guillermo Cabrera Infante (1929–2005), started their writing careers as film critics for newspapers and magazines. In fact, Cuban cinema has long been regarded as among the best in Latin America. One example is the multi-award winning 1994 film, *Fresa y Chocolate*, about a young but sophisticated gay man who falls in love with a young and radical, but prejudiced, straight man. Cuba and México have typically enjoyed excellent relations, and these have spread to the realm of cinema, as can be seen in such joint productions as *Who the Hell is Juliette?*

Nonetheless, television is the undisputed winner in the contest for Latin Americans' free time. Statistics show that Latin Americans watch between three and five hours of television a day. Popular forms include soap operas, sports, game shows, reality shows, and comedy programs. Among this last group, one show that made a name for itself through its characters, the popularity of its stories, its longevity, and the impact it had not only in México but throughout Latin America is *El Chavo del Ocho*, which has been viewed by millions. A production of México's Televisa network, this program from the 1970s depicted life in a México City *vecindad*—a building where multiple families each occupy a one-room apartment. The characters showed humor in the face of economic adversity, and a positive attitude toward life. Televisa later sold these comic episodes throughout Latin America, taking advantage of the widespread appeal of Mexican humor. Today the program lives on as a cartoon series. Other television programs have come close to it, but no book will ever have the impact that this program and its characters had on the Latin American market.

CONCLUSION

As the reader will have gathered, there is no denying the role that written texts have had on the cultural development of Latin America and the Caribbean, despite the region's high illiteracy rates, low rates of literary production, and high average rates of television consumption. However, in some Latin American countries, reading is on the rise. Populations are growing, and more children are attending school, creating more potential readers not just of textbooks, but of narratives, poetry, and other genres. Furthermore, a small but significant number of Latin American writers have received international acclaim, including five winners of the Nobel Prize for Literature. The era of modernism, when José Martí and Rubén Darío defined Latin American literature, is but a distant memory. Latin America is no longer just a continent of poor illiterate people, of so-called third-world countries, of military dictatorships, and of people willing to risk their lives fleeing to the United States. For the first time ever, democratic governments are common. As a result, the economies of these nations are improving, and the high birth rates are declining, however slightly. Living conditions have also improved slightly in some countries. Today, women presidents head the governments of both Chile and Argentina, and Nicaragua and Panama have also recently had women presidents— while the United States struggles to come to terms with this possibility.

The educational level of the population is also rising. And although an alarming number of students still drop out of school—among them a high percentage of women, indigenous people, and those in the poorest regions—more professional and graduate degrees are being conferred by Latin American universities than ever before, impacting the labor market in significant ways. In this context, the future of reading in this part of the continent looks more promising. Although reading is facing more competition than ever from television and video games, we are optimistic that it will continue to play a significant role in the region's future.

ACKNOWLEDGMENTS

The author acknowledges the feedback and suggestions that Claudia Oxman of the Universidad de Buenos Aires has provided for this chapter.

RECOMMENDED READING

Anderson-Imbert, Enrique. *Spanish-American Literature: A History.* Trans. John W. Falconieri. Detroit: Wayne State University Press, 1963.

Fernández Moreno, César, ed. *América Latina en su literatura, Siglo XXI.* México: Unesco, 1972.

Foster, David W. ed. *Handbook of Latin American Literature.* New York: Garland Publishing, Inc., 1987.

González Echeverría, Roberto and Enrique Pupo-Walker, eds. *The Cambridge History of Latin America Literature* (Vols. I and II). Cambridge, UK: Cambridge University Press, 1996.

Henríquez Ureña, Pedro. *A Concise History of Latin American Culture.* New York: Frederick A. Praeger, 1966.

PRIMARY SOURCES

Allende, Isabel. *The House of the Spirits.* New York: Dial Press Trade Paperback, 2005.

Altamirano, Ignacio Manuel. *Clemencia. Cuentos de invierno.* México, D.F. México: Porrua, 2005.

Andrade, Mário de. *Macunaíma.* New York: Random House, 1984.

Asturias, Miguel Ángel. *The President.* Trans. Frances Partridge. Long Grove, IL: Waveland Press, 1997.

———. *Torotumbo.* Barcelona, Spain: Plaza & Jánes S.A., 1972.

Azuela, Mariano. *Los de abajo.* Stockcero.com: Stockcero, 2007.

Bello, Andres. *Gramática de la lengua Casteliana.* U.S.A.: Lectorum Pubns. Inc., 2001.

Bimestre Cubana. La Habana, Cuba 1831–present (Cuarta etapa).

Borges, Jorge Luis. "El Martín Fierro." In *Obras en colaboración.* 5th edition. Barcelona, Spain: Emecé editors, 1997.

Carpentier, Alejo. *El Reino De Este Mundo.* Barcelona, Spain: Editorial Seix Barral, 1983.

Carrasquilla, Tomás. *Cuentos Tomás Carrasquilla.* Bogotá D.C. Colombia: PanAmericana Editorial, Ltda., 1997.

Castellanos, Jesús. *Poemas, Viejos Y Nuevos.* Librero Editor, 1926.

Cestero, Tulio M. *La Sangre: Una Vida Bajo la Tirania.* Santo Domingo, Dominican Republic: Editora De Santo Domingo, 1975.

Columbus, Christopher. *The Four Voyages: Being His Own Log-Book, Letters and Dispatches with Connecting Narratives.* Trans. J.M. Cohen. New York: Penguin Classics, 1992.

"Concolorcorvo." *El Lazarillo De Ciegos Caminantes.* Miami, FL: Stockcero, 2005.

de la Cruz, Sor Juana Ines. *Poems, Protest, and a Dream: Selected Writings.* Trans. Margaret Sayers Peden. New York: Penguin Classics, 1997.

Darío, Rubén. *Azul . . . .* Madrid, Spain: Edaf S.A., 2003.

The Destruction of the Jaguar: Poems from the Books of Chilam Balam. Trans. Christopher Sawyer-Laucanno. San Francisco, CA: City Lights Books, 1987.

Diario Comercial de Lima. Founded in 1839.

El Diario Erudito Económico. Established in 1764.

El Diario de México. Printed until 1817.

de Ercilla, Alonso. *La Araucana.* Trans. Louis Carrera. Pittsburgh, PA: RoseDog Books, 2006.

Díaz del Castillo, Bernal. *Historia verdadera de la conquista de la Nueva Espana/True Story of the Conquest of The New Spain.* México D.F, México: Grupo Editorial Tomo, 2007.

Esquivel, Laura. *Like Water for Chocolate.* London, UK: Trans-World, 1996.

Excélsior. Founded by Rafael Alducin in 1903.

Fernadez de Lizardi, Jose Joaquin. *The Mangy Parrot: The Life and Times of Periquillo Sarniento, Written by Himself for His Children.* Trans. David L. Frye. Indianapolis, IN: Hackett Publishing Company, 2004.

———. *El Periquillo Sarmiento.* México D.F., México: Editorial Porrua; Octava Edicion, 1967.

Fiallo, Fabio. *Obras completas.* Santo Domingo, Dominican Republic: Editora de Santo Domingo, 1980.

Flores Medina, Antonio. *Historia De Mexico Para Niños/ Mexican History for Children.* Tlalnepantla, México: Ediciones Euromexico S.A. De C.V., 2003.

Fontanarrosa, Roberto. *Todo Boogie el Aceitoso.* De La Flor, 1999.

Fuentes, Carlos. *La Región Más Transparente.* Buenos Aires, Argentina: Aguilar, Altea, Taurus, Alfaguara, S.A. de C., 2000.

La Gaceta de Lima. 1743.

La Gaceta de México. Appeared for a very short time in 1767.

Gallegos, Rómulo. *Doña Bárbara.* Ediciones Norte, 2007.

García Márquez, Gabriel. *The Autumn of the Patriarch.* Trans. Gregory Rabassa. New York: Harper Perennial Modern Classics, 2006.

———. *One Hundred Years of Solitude.* (First published in 1967 as *Cien años de soledad.*) New York: Harper Perennial Modern Classics, 2006.

Garibay K, Angela Ma. *Poesia Nahuatl. Three Volumes. I: Romances de lose Senores de la Neuva Espana Manuscrito de Juan Bautista de Pomar Tezcoco, 1582. II & III: Contares Mexicanos manuscrito de la biblioteca Nacional de Mexico. 1964–68.* México D.F., México: Universida Nacional Autonoma de México, 1964.

Garvey, Marcus. *Selected Writings and Speeches of Marcus Garvey.* Ed. Bob Blaisdell. Mineola, NY: Dover Publications, 2005.

Güiraldes, Ricardo. *Don Segundo Sombra/Mr. Second Shadow.* Spain: Jorge A. Mestas Ediciones, 2004.

Guzmán, Martín Luis. *The Eagle and the Serpent.* Gloucester, MA: Peter Smith Publisher, 1969.

Ibargüengoitia, Jorge. *Olvida usted su equipaje? (Obras de Jorge Ibargüengoitia).* México D.F., México: Joaquin Mortiz, 1997.

Icaza, Jorge. *Huasipungo.* Madrid, Spain: Catedra, 2006.

El Inca Garcilaso de la Vega. *Comentarios Reales.* Casavaria.com: Linkgua US, 2006.

Isaacs, Jorge. *María.* Turtleback Books, 2003.

La Jornada. Established in 1984 by Carlos Payán Velver.

Machado De Assis, Joaquim Maria. *Hand and the Glove* (first published as *A Mão e a Luva*). Trans. A.I. Bagby. Lexington, KY: University Press of Kentucky, 1982.

———. *The Posthumous Memoirs of Bras Cubas.* Trans. Gregory Rabassa. New York: Oxford University Press, 1997.

———. *Ressurreição.* New York: Luso-Brazilian Books, 2006.

Marmol, Jose. *Amalia.* New York: Houghton Mifflin Company, 1949.

Martí, José. *Simple Verses/Versos Sencillos.* Topeka, KS: Tandem Library, 1999.

Martínez Pelaez, Severo. *La Patria Del Criollo: Ensayo De Interpretacion De LA Realidad Colonial Guatema.* México D.F., México: Fondo De Cultura Economica USA, 1997.

Memin Pinguin. Comic strip, 1943–present.

El Mercurio de México. Established 1789.

Monsiváis, Carlos. *Amor perdido.* México D.F., México: Ediciones ERA, 2007.

Neruda, Pablo. *Veinte Poemas de Amor y Una Canción Desesperada / Twenty Poems and A Desperate Song.* Madrid, Spain: Edaf S.A., 2003.

El Pensador Mexicano. Established in 1812.

Poniatowska, Elena. *Massacre in Mexico.* (First published in Mexico as *La noche de Tlatelolco,* 1968). Trans. Helen R. Lane. St. Louis, MO: University of Missouri Press, 1992.

Popol Vuh: The Definitive Edition of the Mayan Book of the Dawn of Life and the Glories of Gods and Kings. Trans. Dennis Tedlock. Clearwater, FL: Touchstone, 1996.

Quino. *Mafalda.* México D.F., México: Editorial Nueva Imagen, 1977.

Quiroga, Horacio. *Cuentos de la selva.* Casavaria.com: Linkgua S.L., 2007.

Revista Alfar, Montevideo, Uruguay, 1929–1955 (segunda etapa).

Revista Amauta, Lima, Perú, 1926–1930.

Revista Avance, Argentina 1927–1930.

Revista Avance, La Habana Cuba, 1927–1930.

Revista Contemporáneos, Ciudad de Mexico, Mexico, 1929–1931.

Revista Mandrágora, Santiago, Chile, 1938–1943.

Revista Poliedro, Puerto Rico. August 1926–December 1926.

Revista Sur, Buenos Aires, Argentina.

Revista Ultra, La Habana, Cuba, 1937–1946.

Rius. *Todo Rius/All Rius.* Grijalbo Mondadori S.A., 2006.

Rivera, José Eustasio. *La voragine.* Madrid, Spain: Catedra, 2006.

Saco, José Antonio. *Historia de la esclavitud.* Madrid, Spain: Ediciones Jucar, 1974.

Sarmiento, Domingo F. *Facundo: Or, Civilization and Barbarism.* Trans. Mary Peabody Mann. New York: Penguin Classics, 1998.

Taibo, Paco Ignacio II and Subcomandante Marcos. *The Uncomfortable Dead (What's Missing Is Missing).* Trans. Carlos Lopez. New York: Akashic Books, 2006.

Vargas, Gabriel. *La Familia Burrón.* México D.F., México: Editorial Porrua, 2002.

Villaverde, Cirilo. *Cecilia Valdes or El Angel Hill.* Ed. Sibylle Fischer, and trans. Helen Lane. New York: Oxford University Press, 2005.

SECONDARY SOURCES

Agosin, Marjorie, ed. *Landscapes of a New Land: Short Fiction by Latin American Women Writers.* Buffalo, NY: White Pine Press, 1989.

Caceres Romero, Adolfo, ed. *Poesia Quechua Del Tawantinsuyu.* Buenos Aires, Argentina: Ediciones del Sol S.R.L., 2000.

Foster, David William. *From Mafalda to Los Supermachos: Latin American Graphic Humor as Popular Culture.* Boulder, CO: Lynne Reinner Pub., 1989.

Franco, Jean. *Spanish American Literature since Independence (A Literary History of Spain).* New York: Barnes and Noble, 1973.

Jackson, Richard L. *Black Writers in Latin America.* Albuquerque, NM: University of New México Press, 1979.

CHAPTER 3

The Latin American Diaspora

Molly Metherd

TIMELINE

1979–88	Civil wars in many Central American nations including Nicaragua, Guatamala, and El Salvador lead to increased U.S.immigration from these regions
1980	The Mariel Boatlift: over 125,000 Cubans allowed to leave Cuba in boats for the United States
1992	North American Free Trade Agreement (NAFTA), a regional trade agreement between the governments of Canada, the United States, and Mexico, is signed
1994	California Proposition 187, a ballot initiative designed to deny undocumented immigrants social services including education and health care, passed; the proposition was ultimately deemed unconstitutional by the California Supreme Court
2006	U.S. House of Representatives passes HR 4437, which makes it a felony to be in the United States illegally or to help anyone who does not have proper documentation; the bill incites massive protests throughout the United States; the bill is stalled in the Senate
2006	President George Bush signs the Border Security Act, which directs the construction of a seven hundred-mile-long fence along most of the United States-Mexico Border

INTRODUCTION TO THE PERIOD AND THE PEOPLE

The Latin American Diaspora in the United States is made up of peoples from many countries who have left their homelands for a variety of reasons. Immigrants from Mexico make up, by far, the largest percentage of this group, followed by Puerto Ricans, Cubans, Dominicans, and Central Americans. Latin Americans have sought refuge in the United States from government persecution, violent revolutions and civil wars, and economic hardship. Some have immigrated permanently, others relocated temporarily to wait out tumultuous times at home, and a third group regularly moves back and forth between jobs in the United States and extended family in their home countries. Consequently, the cultures, histories, motivations, and experiences of people within the Latin American Diaspora to the United States tend to vary widely.

Throughout the twentieth century, Mexicans have emigrated to the United States for political and economic reasons. Millions of Mexicans crossed the border into the United States during the Mexican Revolution of 1910 to 1924, fleeing violence and poverty. These immigrants settled in border towns, where they found Spanish-speaking agricultural communities that had been in the region since before the Treaty of Guadalupe Hidalgo of 1848, which made the residents U.S. citizens. The war refugees viewed themselves as exiles, waiting to return to their country once the war ended. Although many did return, others stayed in their new land.

They were joined in the next decades by immigrants seeking employment in the United States. Hundreds of thousands of immigrants found seasonal employment picking crops as a part of a guest-worker plan known as the Bracero program. Some came to the United States for a season and then returned to Mexico, while others traveled around the United States following the picking seasons. Although the Bracero program ended in 1964, many still cross the border to work in the fields, while other immigrants find wage-labor employment in the restaurant and construction industries. First- and second-generation Mexican Americans have greatly expanded the range and scope of their employment opportunities.

The 1980s were a tumultuous time for many Central American republics, and the United States saw a sharp rise in immigration from El Salvador, Guatemala, and Nicaragua during this decade. Immigrants from Central America and Mexico typically have settled and formed thriving communities throughout the southwestern United States. The 2000 census, however, shows that Hispanic immigration now reaches throughout the United States.

Puerto Ricans have primarily immigrated to New York City. Because Puerto Ricans are U.S. citizens, they can easily move between the island and mainland United States. In fact, the daily flight between San Juan, Puerto Rico, and John F. Kennedy airport in New York is known as *la guagua aerea*, or "the flying bus," because it is always packed with people "commuting" between these two locales. Puerto Ricans living in New York call themselves *Nuyoricans*, and they have formed a close-knit community. The Nuyorican community in New York has been joined by many immigrants from the Dominican Republic.

Cubans did not settle in the United States in large numbers until the Cuban Revolution of 1959. Following the revolution, Fidel Castro's new communist government nationalized all industry and private property, and many middle- and upper-class landowners fled the country. They formed an exile community in Miami, Florida, where they still await the end of Castro's government. This community has become an economic and political force in the state of Florida.

READING TRENDS AND PRACTICES

While there has been a long history of reading among these peoples, the history is not always easy to document. Some people choose to read in their native Spanish, while others learn English quickly and seek out newspapers, novels, and other texts in English. Even among the large group of English speakers, who are often second- and third-generation Latinos living in the United States, some find themselves identifying more with other Latino authors and their texts, while others gravitate toward readings on general topics. Much of what we do know about the composition, publication, and distribution of Spanish-language texts in the United States is indebted to the work of Nicolás Kanellos and many scholars who have participated in the Recovering the U.S. Hispanic Literary Heritage Project.

The first groups of Spanish-speaking readers and writers were the early conquistadors and missionaries arriving from Mexico and the Caribbean. These sixteenth-century explorers of the territory that is now the United States wrote diaries, chronicles, and letters recounting their journeys, such as *La relación* (1542) by Alvar Núñez Cabeza de Vaca and *La Florida*, an epic poem by Friar Alonso de Escobedo. However, these texts were written and published for readers in Spain, rather than for any New World readership.

By the middle of the sixteenth century, the Hispanic settlers in the New World had begun producing texts for their own readers, and opened schools, universities, libraries, government archives, and courts to North America, thereby creating a literate reading public. As people began to move north from Mexico into what is now the Southwestern United States, they carried some of these reading materials, many of which were religious texts, with them. As communities became more established in the northern regions, ships from Mexico delivered pamphlets, broadsides and books.

In the early 1800s, Mexican residents of the current U.S. Southwest began printing their own texts. As early as 1813, a Spanish-language printing press was publishing broadsides in Texas encouraging citizens to join the insurgents fighting

This Chicano teen and his friends represent the new readership in the United States—young, bilingual, and associated mainly with the news and issues generated by the growing Latino community in the United States. [Courtesy Danny Lyon, South El Paso, Texas, July 1972]

against Spanish rule. In 1834, Spanish-speaking residents of the current state of New Mexico and California also acquired presses. These presses were vital for the survival of the Spanish language and culture in the Southwest, for they fostered a literate public. They allowed communities to disseminate news, to document their histories, and to have a voice to express themselves through various types of publication.

The newspaper was the most important form of text for Spanish-language readers in the nineteenth century. Newspapers printed local and national news and also had a section dedicated to news from the homeland. These periodicals, such as *La Voz del Pueblo* (*The Voice of the People*; Santa Fe, New Mexico); *La Lucha* (*The Struggle*; El Paso, Texas); *La Crónica* (*The Chronicle*; Laredo, Texas), also printed opinion pieces, poetry, and fiction. Local and regional newspapers helped to promote both a sense of cultural community among the Spanish-speaking immigrants from different Latin American countries and the Spanish language in the United States. Newspapers also proved to be particularly important tools of protest for the Spanish-speaking residents of the current southwestern United States when, in accordance with the 1848 Treaty of Guadalupe Hidalgo, Mexico ceded over one-third of its territory to the United States. At this time there were approximately seventy-five thousand Spanish-speakers inhabiting the region. By far the largest population was in New Mexico (60,000), followed by California (7,500), Texas (5,000), Arizona (1,500), and Colorado (1,000). The treaty directed that these residents would become citizens of the United States and that they would be afforded all rights of such citizenship. As more and more Anglo-Americans moved west, newspapers became particularly important vehicles for cultural preservation as well as forums to protest injustices against the Spanish-speaking peoples of the Southwest. Many of these newspapers also published books in Spanish by local authors, imported Spanish-language texts from writers in Latin America, and translations of English-language texts to be purchased via mail.

The newspaper was also the most important reading material for immigrants from the Caribbean, many of whom were fleeing Spanish colonial rule and who settled on the East Coast of the United States in Tampa, Philadelphia, and particularly in New York. In New York, Spanish-speakers found an active Spanish-language publishing industry already established by immigrants from Spain. This industry evolved to serve the exile populations from the Caribbean who produced and distributed political, commercial, and religious texts, Spanish translations of creative works in English, and fiction and poetry by exiled and immigrant writers such as José Martí and José María Heredia. Newspapers, essays, political tracts, pamphlets, and novels by exiles from the Caribbean served to unite and educate this community. Readers seeking camaraderie and intellectual exchange could join the *Sociedad Literaria Hispano Americana de Nuevo York* (Spanish American Literary Society of New York), established by Cuban Martí, Colombian Santiago Pérez Triana, and publisher Nestor Ponce de León. This literary society sponsored readings by local and visiting authors and discussions of the latest literature.

In the twentieth century, several geo-political events served to fuel immigration to the United States from Latin America. The Spanish-American War of 1898, which the United States fought against Spain to gain influence and control of the Caribbean, led to fifty years of U.S. intervention in Cuban politics and the establishment of Puerto Rico as a commonwealth of the United States. In 1917 Woodrow Wilson signed the Jones Act, which made all residents of Puerto Rico U.S. citizens. Millions of Puerto Ricans immigrated to the United States and to New York in particular, in search of jobs. A number of these new emigrants published autobiographies and personal sketches of their experiences in New York or worked as journalists, like Jésus Colón, who wrote columns, essays and creative work documenting the inequalities and injustices experienced by their fellow Puerto Ricans.

The Mexican Revolution of 1910–1920 also brought millions of exiles and political refugees to the United States and to the U.S. Southwest. Many of these exiles set up newspapers supporting their causes and worked to create a *Mexico de afuera* (a Mexico abroad). Novels of the revolution were particularly popular among Spanish-speaking readers in the United States during this time, and these would often appear in newspapers in serial form.

A third important event that prompted large scale emigration from Latin America to the United States was the Cuban Revolution in 1959, which brought Fidel Castro to power. Castro's government nationalized industry and dissolved the relationship between the largest Caribbean nation and the United States. It also provoked hundreds of thousands of exiles to flee to Miami and southern Florida in 1959 and 1960, as well as two secondary waves of immigration. Today, two-thirds of Cubans in the United States reside in the Miami-Dade region of Florida. This community was initially united in its opposition to the revolution and to Castro. They organized anti-Castro newspapers and other publications. Subsequent generations have modified and diversified the political stance of this population somewhat, but many remain steadfastly loyal to overthrowing Castro's government.

Although most communities with a significant number of Spanish-speakers had a daily or weekly magazine and could purchase books via mail, until very recently acquiring Spanish-language books was slow and expensive, and the selections were often limited. While small groups of intellectuals and academics in the United States might have access to texts through University libraries and specialty book stores, the average reader would have to specially order foreign-language texts through bookstores in major cities or through booklists sponsored by distributors of Spanish-language texts. If readers preferred to read texts by Latin Americans in English, it often took three, five or even ten years for translations of major novels to appear in U.S. bookstores.

The U.S. book market has been shaped by language and colonial history rather than by geographical proximity. U.S. publishers were closely tied to Britain, while the Spanish American market was connected to Spain. Consequently, a reader living in San Antonio, Texas would find it much easier to find the work of a British novelist at her local bookstore than a book by a Mexican writer living just across the border. The Old World/New World relationship altered somewhat in mid-century when World War II made it more difficult to import books from Europe to the Americas. The publishing houses began to look to their American counterparts for titles, so more texts were translated. Another important shift in reception occurred in the 1960s with the Latin American Literary Boom, and the academic attention and media frenzy that accompanied it. The rise of the Latin American novel led to the import of larger numbers of Spanish-language texts and initiated many more translations of Spanish American texts into English.

Readers became aware of a whole group of Latinos writing in the United States as a result of the Chicano Civil Rights Movement in the early 1960s. This movement fostered an ethnic nationalism and a growing interest in texts written by and about Chicanos. The United Farmworkers Union led by César Chávez, the emergence of *El Teatro Campesino* led by Luis Valdez, and the student meeting in Denver that established the manifesto, the *Plan Espíritual de Atzlán*, all helped to shape a new Chicano identity. Small independent publishing houses like Quinto Sol, Bilingual Review Press, and Arte Público Press were created to encourage Chicano writers and to construct a Chicano canon. Puerto Ricans living in New York also began to identify themselves as *Nuyorican*s and publish poetry and prose that explored their urban identities. Such projects were clearly successful, as a little more than a decade later an explosion of Latino writing began (what some have referred to as a Latino boom). Authors like Sandra Cisneros, Oscar Hijuelos, Ana Castillo, Richard Rodriquez, Helen María Viramontes, Gary Soto, and more recently, Dagoberto Gilb, Cristina García, Junot Díaz, and Julia Álvarez, have received acclaim from a wide range of academic and mainstream readers.

While major publishing houses have embraced Latino writers in English, U.S. publishers are also beginning to take interest in Spanish-language texts. According to the 2000 census, there are over thirty-seven million Hispanics living in the United States with a purchasing power of $580 billion a year (although it is important to note that certainly not all of these Hispanics choose to read in Spanish). Publishing houses are reaching out to Spanish-language audiences in the United States. This data demonstrates that national audiences are no longer clearly defined by language. The success of Mexican author Laura Esquivel's novel *Como agua para chocolate* (*Like Water For Chocolate*, 1989), which sold over 150,000 copies in Spanish in the United States in the first two years of publication, demonstrated to publishers the potential US market for Spanish-language texts. Major U.S. publishing houses like Vintage and Penguin are forming strategic partnerships with Spanish-language publishers or opening Spanish-language publishing offices of their own. Nearly two hundred publishers in the United States and Puerto Rico now publish Spanish titles. This doesn't include sales by publishing houses such as Santillana Publishing USA, Grupo Editorial Planeta, and Fondo de Cultura Economica, which import the bulk of their products for US distribution. The number of Spanish-language titles available in the United States has jumped from five thousand in 2001 to over thirty thousand in 2003.

Because the industry has responded to the rapid population changes in the United States, readers today have more access to Spanish-language books and works by Latinos. In the United States, major book chains like Borders, Barnes and Noble, Ingram, and Baker and Taylor are expanding their Spanish-language offerings. Borders opened a bilingual bookstore in Pico Rivera, California and stores like Target, K-Mart, and Costco have begun to sell Spanish-language books. Both Amazon and Barnes and Noble have launched online Spanish-language boutiques to allow customers to access their over five million Spanish-language texts more easily. The boutiques offer chat rooms, interviews with authors, ideas for book clubs and reading groups, and links to other relevant web sites. And there are bilingual sites like the Mosaico Book Club that sell Spanish-language books online. The most popular categories of books for this community are adult fiction—including translations of U.S. bestsellers and novels by major Latin American authors—self help/spirituality, and children's books.

Moreover, public and academic libraries throughout the United States are expanding their Spanish-language collections and working to hire bilingual librarians. The Association of American Publishers established 2003 as the Year of Publishing Hispanic Voices and named May as Latino Books Month. The Association of American Publishers also initiated the Get Caught Reading/*Ajá leyendo* campaign. Together, these actions are designed to promote English- and Spanish-language texts written by Latinos and to encourage reading for Spanish-language speakers.

NEWSPAPERS AND MAGAZINES

A real, documented history of reading in the Latin American Diaspora in the United States really begins with the first newspapers at the beginning of the nineteenth century. The first Spanish-language newspaper was *El Misisipí*, published in New Orleans in 1808. In fact, as many as twenty-five hundred different daily and weekly Spanish-language periodicals were issued between 1808 and 1960 (Kanellos, *Herencia* 3). These newspapers served different communities in the diaspora: long time residents of the current American Southwest who became U.S. citizens after 1848 with the Treaty of Guadalupe Hidalgo, exile communities fleeing to the United States until they could return to a more politically stable homeland, and immigrants escaping from civil wars, revolutions, or economic crises moving permanently to the United States. In such periodicals, these different communities of readers could find local and national news, community events, and

El Nuevo Herald is a widely read daily Spanish-language newspaper, published in Miami. The paper began life in 1976 as a supplement to the *Miami Herald*. [Courtesy of Jenny Romney]

politics and news of the homeland, as well as essays, stories, poetry, and serialized novels by local writers and major figures in the Hispanic world. Readers in most Spanish-language newspapers would find *crónicas*, satirical weekly columns usually written under pseudonyms that commented on the local issues and social norms of the community. The periodicals were also the publishers of literature at the time. These newspapers helped to construct a cultural identity for their readers as well as to create a sense of community.

A number of these periodicals were dailies like *La Prensa* (San Antonio); *La Opinión, El Heraldo de México, El Clamor Público* (Los Angeles); and *La Prensa* and *El Diario de Nueva York* (New York). These dailies had wide distribution systems including newspaper stands, home delivery, and mail, and they had correspondents writing from posts in major U.S. cities. The primary audiences for these newspapers were new immigrants looking for news of the homeland and bound by ethnic solidarity. The newspapers explored the experience of exile and promoted ethnic and linguistic unity. These periodicals often became tools for the dissemination of revolutionary ideas and for political organization.

Recent arrivals to New York from Cuba, the Dominican Republic, and Puerto Rico would find Spanish-language newspapers like *El Mensajero Semanal* (*The Weekly Messenger*), *El Mercurio de Nueva York* (*The New York Mercury*) and *Las Novedades* (*The News*). Another important newspaper of the early twentieth century was *Gráfico*, first published in New York in 1927. This periodical was written primarily by writers and artists who were associated with Spanish-language theater in the city. Readers of *Gráfico* would find poetry, short stories, essays, theater news and reviews, crónicas, and photographs and illustrations. Essayists, including the Puerto Rican Jesús Cólon, wrote to unite their readers with an intense Hispanic nationalism, to maintain the language and cultural traditions of the Latin communities, and to defend the civil rights of immigrants and residents of Spanish Harlem.

Most small towns in the Southwest had a Spanish-language weekly periodical. These were much smaller operations with more limited distributions. These weeklies reported on local and national politics, entertainment, and community affairs but also had political and cultural commentary and creative works. Community members could air their grievances and counter the accounts of the local communities in the Anglo-American newspapers. These newspapers also became a unifying, oppositional voice against the encroaching Anglo-Americans, defenders of the rights of their readers, and a force against cultural and linguistic assimilation.

Today there are at least six hundred bilingual or Spanish-language newspapers and magazines published in the United States. Cities with large Latino populations may have several newspapers with circulations of over fifty thousand. According to the 2006 State of the News Media report by the Project for Excellence in Journalism, in 2004 *La Opinión* in Los Angeles reported circulation of 125,000, while *El Nuevo Herald* in Miami reported 88,977 and *El Diario* in New York reported circulation at 50,105.

In addition to local and national newspapers, Spanish-speaking immigrants of the Latin American Diaspora could chose from a number of magazines to read about news and culture. For example, in the literary magazine *Revista Ilustrada*, published by Camilo Padilla, readers in the Southwest could find creative works including poetry, essays, historical articles, woodblock prints, and photographs. The monthly magazine was first published in 1907 in El Paso, Texas, and was published under changing names and from different cities until Padilla's death in 1933. In the first decades of the century, a number of English-language literary magazines were appearing in English in the Southwest. However, these publications usually omitted works by Mexican Americans, and many of the works published in them often included negative, stereotyped representations of local communities. *Revista Ilustrada* worked to combat such stereotypes and to promote creative works in Spanish throughout the Southwest. The magazine included works by local, Mexican, and Latin American authors. It also published works by New Mexican women. Readers could also purchase books via mail from the Revista bookstore. These titles included books by regional authors, imported books from Latin American authors, and works of world literature, including novels by Hugo, Dumas, Verne and Cervantes (Meléndez, 255).

New York also had several Spanish-language cultural magazines that published literature, illustrations, and commentary in the late nineteenth century. These included *Ambas Americas: Revista de Educación, Bibliografía y Agricultura* (*Two Americas: Review of Education, Bibliography and Agriculture*) and *La Revista Illustrada de Nuevo York* (*The Illustrated Review of New York*). Both of the magazines were transnational in scope, publishing works by authors in New York and Latin America and promoting a pan-Hispanic perspective.

In the twentieth century, a number of small literary magazines, many coming out of U.S. universities, published creative works in Spanish and English. The most important of these was the *Revista Chicano-Riqueño*, which later became *The Americas Review*. Latino readers also have a much wider variety of mainstream magazines in Spanish, English, and bi-lingual editions. The magazines with the highest circulation are *People en Español, Hispanic, Latina, Hispanic Business,* and *Selecciones,* a Spanish-language version of *Reader's Digest*. Each of these magazines has a circulation of over 300,000 per issue, and *People en Español*'s circulation topped 450,000 in 2005.

ETHNOGRAPHIES

From the 1930s through the 1950s, readers expressed a new interest in local, native cultures in the United States, and a number of creative writers and scholars began to explore the Spanish-speaking regions of the country. Several women in New Mexico published personal narratives, ethnographies, and social histories of the region. These narratives often emphasized the Spanish colonial past, while glossing over the Mexican and Indian histories of the community. Nina Otero-Warren, an activist and political leader, wrote *Old Spain in Our Southwest* (1936) while Aurora Lucero-White Lea wrote *Literary Folklore of the Hispanic Southwest* (1953). Several authors combined personal memories with recipes and descriptions of local life. For example, in 1939 Cleófilas Jaramillo published *The Genuine New Mexico Tasty Recipes: Old and Quaint Formulas for the Preparation of Seventy-Five Delicious Spanish Dishes,* and ten years later, in 1949, Fabiola Cabeza de Baca wrote *The Good Life: New Mexico Traditions and Food.* Jaramillo and Cabeza de Baca also published ethnographies, including Jaramillo's *Romance of a Little Village Girl* (1955) and Cabeza de Baca's *We Fed Them Cactus* (1954). These texts received new attention in the 1970s when they were rediscovered by Chicano scholars and activists.

In Texas during the same period of the 1930s through the 1950s, two Chicano anthropologists and literary scholars were also documenting the cultures of the Texas-Mexican border. Jovita Gonzalez depicted the folklore of the Texas-Mexico border region in her works. Although she wrote two novels that were published posthumously in 1996, during her life she published stories in several collections including "The Bullet-Swallower" in *Puro Mexicano* (1935) and "Among My People" in *Tone the Bell Easy* (1932), as well as a number of essays in local journals including *Southwest Review, LULAC News and Texas Folklore,* and *Folklore Publications.* Gonzalez, with her husband Edmundo E. Mireles, also published two sets of Spanish textbooks, *Mi libro espanol* (1941) and *El espanol elemental* (1949).

Another folklorist, writer, and scholar working and writing about the Texas-Mexico border region is Américo Paredes. During his long career, Paredes published over sixty essays on the south-Texas region, paying particular attention to the music, jokes, riddles, and legends of the border communities. His best-known work is his 1958 text *With a Pistol in His Hand,* which explores the *corrido* border tradition, the Mexican American male hero, and the myth of Gregorio Cortez. *With a Pistol in His Hand* was very well received at the time of publication, and it became an important text for Chicano activists in the 1970s.

CREATIVE TEXTS

Spanish-language book publishing and distribution in the nineteenth century was primarily centered in New York, but was also taking place in New Orleans and Philadelphia. Many of the authors publishing at the time were exiles who had fled to the United States to escape from Spanish colonial rule. These political figures and authors found a freedom of expression that was otherwise unavailable to them in their home countries. Readers would have access to Spanish-language books printed by New York publishers like Lanuza, Mendía and Co, and Imprenta Española. These houses printed books of poetry, novels, pamphlets, and political essays, many of which were nationalist texts that denounced colonial rule and slavery. They published these texts for readers within their exile communities and smuggled them into their homelands for distribution there.

Readers also had access to creative works by local authors and well-known writers and poets throughout Latin American in their daily and weekly newspapers. Newspapers published essays, poems, short stories, and serialized novels. For example, *Las aventuras de Joaquín Murrieta* (published in English as *Life and Adventures of the Celebrated Bandit Joaquín Murrieta: His Exploits in the State of California*), a novel based on the life of a notorious bandit, was published in 1881 in *La Gaceta* (*The Gazette*) in Santa Barbara. Mariano Azuela's novel *Los de abajo* (*The Underdogs*), one of the central texts in the Mexican canon, was first serialized in 1915 in the newspaper *El Paso del Norte* in El Paso, Texas.

Early in the twentieth century, Spanish-speaking readers began to have more access to books published in the United States. A number of newspapers, including *La Prensa*, which began in San Antonio in 1913, and *La Opinión* first published in Los Angeles in 1926, also opened publishing houses. Presses like Casa Editorial Lozano in San Antonio (started in 1917), *El Heraldo de Mexico* (*The Herald of Mexico*, from Los Angeles), and Hispanic Publishers in New York (cofounded by Puerto Rican author Jesús Colón), published religious books, political propaganda, how-to-books, history, novels, and poetry. The most popular novels were novels of the Mexican Revolution and sentimental novels, many of which were published by Casa Editorial Lozano.

One important novel that dealt more with issues of Hispanic identity in the United States was María Amparo Ruiz de Burton's novel *The Squatter and the Don* (1885), published under the pseudonym C. Loyal. This novel is a romance written in English and set in California. It sentimentally depicts the life of *Californios* or Spanish-speaking residents of the current state of California who became U.S. citizens in 1848 with the Treaty of Guadalupe Hidalgo. The novel tells the story of two young lovers: Mercedes, the daughter of a Californio family, and Clarence, the son of a squatter. It is a critique of the harsh treatment of the Californio families who lost their land and their status under U.S. rule.

A second important work is Daniel Venegas's novel *Las aventuras de Don Chipote, o Cuando los pericos mamen* (published in English as *The Adventures of Don Chipote, or When Parrots Breast Feed*, 1928). In this humorous novel, Don Chipote leaves his family and life as a sharecropper in Mexico to come to the United States. There he becomes a manual laborer and encounters all sorts of trials working for a railroad company; after a series of mishaps in Los Angeles, Don Chipote is ultimately deported back to his life in Mexico. The novel is interesting because it is written in the Spanish of the region. In the past two decades, the Recovering the U.S. Hispanic Literary Heritage has republished these two novels, among others, and there has been much scholarly interest in the two texts.

The Civil Rights movement and the work of César Chavez and the United Farmworkers Union in the 1960s fostered a pride among Mexican Americans who united under the term *Chicanos*. In the epic poem "Yo Soy Joaquín," Rodolfo "Corky" Gonzalez takes readers on a journey through Mexican and Mexican American history, promotes Atzlán as the mythic homeland of Chicanos, and shapes a contemporary Chicano identity. Gonzalez published the bilingual pamphlet of the poem, and it was passed around by hand in communities and read at rallies, quickly becoming a central text in an emerging Chicano canon.

In 1967, Tonatiuh/Quinto Sol Publications began to publish the works of Chicano authors. The goal of this publishing house was to find authors whose forms and techniques reflected the social, political, and economic realities of the Chicano community and confronted Anglo-American stereotypes. As a result of this and other such projects, Latino readers in English and in Spanish had more access to texts that explored their identity and culture. For example, in 1971 Quinto Sol published Tomás Rivera's novel *Y no se lo tragó la tierra* (*And the Earth Did Not Devour Him*), a novel that unites the multiple narrations of Mexican and Mexican American migrant farm workers, and in so doing works to create a coherent community voice speaking out against social injustice. Through Quinto Sol, readers were also introduced to the works of Rolando Hinojosa-Smith, who wrote in English and in Spanish about the Texas-Mexican borderlands in the *Estampas del valle y otras obras* (*Sketches of the Valley and Other Works*, 1973) and other texts, and Rudolfo Anaya, author of *Bless Me, Ultima* (1972). Both Rivera and Hinojosa wrote in the language of working-class inhabitants of the border regions. Quinto Sol's efforts to create a Chicano canon was assisted and later sustained by other publishing houses that emerged around this time, including Arte Público Press and Bilingual Review Press.

Around the same time, readers began to hear more about the Puerto Rican experience in urban Manhattan through the work of a group of poets, novelists, and playwrights. The autobiographical form was prevalent among a number of prose writers. Most important is Piri Thomas, who draws from earlier autobiographies by Puerto Ricans in New York like Bernardo Vega and Jesús Colón, in his autobiography *Down These Mean Streets* (1967), which explores his life as a black Puerto Rican in inner-city New York. Poetry was also vital to the emerging Nuyorican voice. Poets like Miguel Algarín, Miguel Piñero, Tato Laviera, and Pietro Pietri lived in Spanish Harlem and wrote about their experiences there. Readers could not only read about the urban Nuyorican experience through this poetry, but they could also hear these poets perform their work at the Nuyorican Poets Café. These authors wrote of the urban, working-class Puerto Ricans and helped to construct a new Puerto Rican identity.

Initially, most of the works by Chicano and Nuyorican authors were deemed too "exotic" for the larger U.S. publishing houses. With the best-selling success of Sandra Cisneros's *The House on Mango Street* (1989) and the Pulitzer Prize for Cuban American Oscar Hijuelos's novel *The Mambo Kings Play Songs of Love* (1989), publishers began to recognize the rapidly growing market for English-language Chicano and Latino texts and began to reposition these works from exotic to mainstream. Starting in the 1980s, a new group of Chicano and Latino writers emerged including Cisneros and Hijuelos, as well as Ana Castillo, Richard Rodriquez, Helen María Viramontes, and Gary Soto. They were joined in the 1990s by Domincan American authors Julia Alvarez and Junot Díaz and Cuban American Cristina García, among others.

A large number of the novels, short stories, and poetry published by Chicanos, Dominican Americans, Puerto Ricans, and Cuban Americans in the last three decades have been in English. Many of these writers were born in the United States and drew from their own experiences as second- or third-generation Latinos. Readers of these texts will find a range of characters and themes. Some depict rural life, while others focus on urban experiences. Many of these authors introduce questions of language and identity and of living on a literal or figurative border between two cultures. Prominent themes in these works include explorations of family life, language, history, and memory, and many have child or young adult narrators.

Julia Alvarez, Pat Mora, Isabel Allende, Gloria Anzaldúa, and Cristina García are among many other well-known authors who have written books for children and young adults in Spanish and in English. A number of the children's books retell myths and legends from Latin America. Most of these books incorporate many Spanish words in their English texts. Many are also published in bilingual format or are translated into both languages. The young adult fiction often explores the issues of identity and of growing up within two cultures.

CONCLUSION

As both the chapter on the Latin American readership and this chapter indicate, Latino/as have long revered writers and writing, even if educational barriers have prevented individuals from the act of reading. But as Latin Americans became established as the largest minority in the United States, the combination of publishing and educational opportunities has resulted in a significant diasporic readership. Newspapers probably represent the most widely read documents within the Latino communities, but these readers have continued to read the classics from their original countries, as well as following the careers of authors who remain in Central and South America. However, Latin American readers have also fostered new writing styles, which have emerged from the hybridization of cultures in the United States. And the entrepreneurship that has emerged within the Latino communities has ensured that Latino/a authors, writers, journalists, essayists, commentators, web designers, and bloggers have developed alongside the "mainstream" publishing industry in the United States.

RECOMMENDED READING

García, James E. "Newspapers and Periodicals." *Encyclopedia of Latino Popular Culture.* Edited by Cordelia Chávez Candelaria. Westport, Conn: Greenwood Press, 2004.

Gómez-Quiñones, Juan. *Roots of Chicano Politics 1600–1940.* Albuquerque: U of New Mexico P, 1994.

Gutiérrez, Ramón, et al., eds. *Recovering the U.S. Hispanic Literary Heritage.* Vols. I–VI. Houston: Arte Público Press, 1993–2006.

Gutiérrez-Witt, Laura. "Cultural Continuity in the Face of Change: Hispanic Printers in Texas." *Recovering the U.S. Hispanic Literary Heritage, Vol II.* Eds. Ramón Gutiérrez and Genaro Padilla. Houston: Arte Público Press, 1996.

Kanellos, Nicolás. *Hispanic Literature of the United States: A Comprehensive Reference.* Greenwood, CT: Greenwood Publishing, 2003.

———. "A Socio-Historic Study of Hispanic Newspapers in the United States." Ramón Gutiérrez and Genaro Padilla, editors. *Recovering the U.S. Hispanic Literary Heritage.* Houston: Arte Público Press, 1993.

Kiser, Karin N. "Spanish-Language Publishing in the U.S. Nears Critical Mass." *Publishers Weekly* 247, no. 38 (2000): 47. Expanded Academic ASAP, Infotrac 14 June 2004.

Lopez, Adriana and Carmen Ospina. "Mass Merchandising Books in Spanish." *Críticas Magazine.* 1 January, 2005. http://www.criticasmagazine.com.

Pitt, Leonard. *The Decline of the Californios: A Social History of the Spanish-Speaking Californians, 1846–1890.* Berkeley: University of California P, 1966.

Rinn, Miriam. "Latinos Break into Mainstream Publishing." *Hispanic Outlook in Higher Education,* 1 December 1994.

Rostegno, Irene. *Fifty Years of Looking South: The Promotion and Reception of Latin American Literature in the United States.* Diss. U of Texas at Austin. Ann Arbor: UMI, 1984.

Project for Excellence in Journalism. "2006 State of the Media Report: An Annual Report on American Journalism," 12 October 2006. http://www.stateofthemedia.com/2006.

PRIMARY SOURCES

Ambas Americas: Revista de Educación, Bibliografía y Agricultura [magazine: *Two Americas: Review of Education, Bibliography and Agriculture*]. New York, nineteenth century.

Amparo Ruiz De Burton, Maria. *The Squatter and the Don.* Houston: Arte Publico Press, 1997.

Anaya, Rudolfo. *Bless Me, Ultima.* Boston: Grand Central Publishing, 1999.

Azuela, Mariano. *The Underdogs.* Fairfield, IA.: First World Library—Literary Society, 2004.

Cabeza de Baca, Fabiola. *Good Life: New Mexico Traditions and Food.* Santa Fe: Museum of New Mexico Press, 2005.

———. *We Fed them Cactus.* Santa Fe: University of New Mexico Press, 1994.

Cisneros, Sandra. *The House on Mango Street.* New York: McGraw Hill College, 1984.

De Escobedo, Friar Alonso. *La Florida.* The entire poem is no longer available in print; however, an excerpt is available in *Nicolas Kanellos* (Editor), *Herencia: The Anthology of Hispanic Literature of the United States.* New York: Oxford University Press, 2003.

Delegates to the Youth and Liberation Conference, Denver, CO. 1969. *El Plan Espiritual de Aztlán.* Full text available at: http://www.umich.edu/~mechaum/Aztlan.html

El Clamor Público [newspaper: *The Public Cry*]. Los Angeles, 1855–1859.

El Diario de Nueva York [newspaper]. New York, 1947–1963.

El Diario [newspaper]. New York, 1963–present.

El Heraldo de México [newspaper].

El Mensajero Semanal [newspaper: *The Weekly Messenger*]. United States, nineteenth century.

El Mercurio de Nueva York [newspaper: *The New York Mercury*].

El Misisipí [newspaper]. New Orleans, 1808–end date unknown.

El Nuevo Herald [newspaper]. Miami, 1987–present.

Esquivel, Laura. *Like Water for Chocolate: A Novel in Monthly Installments with Recipes, Romances, and Home Remedies (Como agua para chocolate).* New York: Anchor Reprints, 1995.

Gonzales, Jovita. "The Bullet-Swallower." In *Puro Mexicano.* Edited by Frank Dobie. Dallas: Southern Methodist Univ. Press, 1935.

————. "Among My People." In *Tone the Bell Easy*. Edited by Frank Dobie. Dallas: Southern Methodist Univ. Press, 1932.

————. *El español elemental*. Austin: W.S. Benson and Co., 1949.

Gonzales, Jovita, and E. E. Mireles. *Mi libro español*. Austin: W.S. Benson and Co., 1941.

Gráfico [newspaper]. New York, 1927–end date unknown.

Hijuelos, Oscar. *The Mambo Kings Play Songs of Love*. New York: Harper Perennial Modern Classics, 2005.

Hinojosa, Rolando. *Estampas del valle y otras obras* (*Sketches of the valley and other works*). Editorial Justa, 1977.

Hispanic [magazine]. 1987–present.

Hispanic Business [magazine]. 1979–present.

Jaramillo, Cleófilas. *The Genuine New Mexico Tasty Recipes: Old and Quaint Formulas for the Preparation of Seventy-Five Delicious Spanish Dishes*. Layton, UT: Gibbs-Smith, Publisher, 1981.

————. *Romance of a Little Village Girl*. Santa Fe: University of New Mexico Press, 2000.

Núñez Cabeza de Vaca, Alvar. *Chronicle of the Narvaez Expedition* [also known as *La relación*]. *Harold Augenbraum* (Editor), *Fanny Bandelier* (Translator). New York: Penguin Classics, 2002.

La Voz del Pueblo [newspaper: *The Voice of the People*]. Santa Fe, New Mexico, 1888–1890.

La Lucha [newspaper: *The Struggle*]. El Paso, Texas, dates unknown.

La Crónica [newspaper: *The Chronicle*]. Laredo, Texas, 1890–1914 and later, but end date not known.

La Prensa [newspaper]. San Antonio, 1913–1959.

La Opinión [newspaper]. Los Angeles, 1926–present.

Las Novedades [newspaper: *The News*].

La Revista Illustrada de Nuevo York [magazine: *The Illustrated Review of New York*]. nineteenth century.

Latina [magazine]. 1996–present.

Lucero-White Lea, Aurora. *Literary Folklore of the Hispanic Southwest*. San Antonio: Naylor Co., 1953.

Otero-Warren, Nina. *Old Spain in Our Southwest*. Santa Fe: Sunstone Press, 2006.

Paredes, Américo. *With a Pistol in His Hand*. Austin: Univ. of Texas Press, 1958.

Paz, Ireneo. *Life and Adventures of the Celebrated Bandit Joaquin Murrieta: His Exploits in the State of California*. Introduction by *Luis Leal*. Translated by *Frances P. Belle*. Houston: Arte Publico Press, 2002.

People en Español [magazine]. 1996–present.

Revista Chicano-Riqueño [magazine, later published as *The Americas Review*]. 1972–1999.

Revista Ilustrada [magazine]. El Paso, 1907–1933.

Rivera, Tomas. *And the Earth Did Not Devour Him/Y No Se Lo Trago la Tierra*. Translated by Evangelina Vigil-Pinon. Topeka: Topeka Bindery, 1999.

Selecciones [magazine: Spanish-language edition of *Reader's Digest*]. 1921–present.

Southwest Review [literary journal; started as *Texas Review*]. Southern Methodist University: 1915–present.

Thomas, Piri. *Down These Mean Streets*. New York: Vintage, 1997.

Venegas, Daniel. *The Adventures of Don Chipote, or When Parrots Breast Feed*. Houston: Arte Publico Press, 2000.

SECONDARY SOURCES

Kanellos, Nicolás, ed. *Herencia. The Anthology of Hispanic Literature in the United States*. New York: Oxford UP, 2002.

Meléndez, Gabriel. "Spanish-Language Journalism in the Southwest: History and Discursive Practice." *Recovering the U.S. Hispanic Literary Heritage, Vol II*. Edited by Ramón Gutiérrez and Genaro Padilla. Houston: Arte Público Press, 1996.

PART 2
Europe and Britain

CHAPTER 4

Ancient Greece and Rome

Hannah Platts

But when he [bishop Ambrose] was reading, his eyes travelled [sic] across the pages and his heart searched out the meaning, but his voice and his tongue stayed still. Often we would be there . . . and we would see him reading silently. He always read like that. And having sat for a long time in silence . . . we would go away, guessing that, because he had so little leisure to refresh his mind, he was taking a rest from the clamour [sic] of other people's affairs and did not want to be distracted . . . . A more legitimate reason for his reading silently could perhaps have been that he needed to spare his voice, which was all too liable to go hoarse.
—*Augustine,* Confessions, *VI. 3.3*

TIMELINE: GREECE

(Athens provides us with much of our source material for Greek history, thus giving a slightly imbalanced picture of ancient Greece.)

800–750 B.C.E.	Development of Greek alphabet created on Phoenician models, widely diffused throughout the Greek world
621 B.C.E.	Draco promulgates Athens's first written laws
594 B.C.E.	Solon, archon at Athens, institutes a new law code and social and political reforms
560–10 B.C.E.	Tyranny at Athens: initially under Pisistratus and then under his son Hippias
508 B.C.E.	Social and political reforms of Cleisthenes at Athens after Hippias' expulsion (**510** B.C.E.)
490 B.C.E.	First Persian expedition to mainland Greece; Battle of Marathon
480 B.C.E.	Great Persian expedition by land to Greece; battles of Artemisium, Salamis and Thermopylae; Athens sacked by Persia
479 B.C.E.	Battles of Plataea and Mycale between Persia and Greece

461–51 B.C.E.	First Peloponnesian War between Sparta and Athens
451 B.C.E.	Five-year truce between Athens and Sparta; Pericles' citizenship law
449 B.C.E.	'Peace of Kallias' ends hostilities between Athens and Persia
445 B.C.E.	Thirty Years Peace agreement between Athens and Sparta
431–04 B.C.E.	Second Peloponnesian War between Athens and Sparta
411 B.C.E.	Oligarchic revolution of the 400 at Athens
410 B.C.E.	Athenian democracy restored
404 B.C.E.	Capitulation of Athens to Sparta; installation of the regime of the Thirty at Athens
403 B.C.E.	Fall of the Thirty; democracy restored at Athens
371–62 B.C.E.	Greek world dominated by Thebes following Theban victory over Sparta at the Battle of Leuctra (371 B.C.E.)
359 B.C.E.	Philip II becomes king of Macedon
357 B.C.E.	War between Athens and Philip
346 B.C.E.	Philip and Athens make peace
338 B.C.E.	Philip defeats Athens and Thebes at Chaeronea, ending Greek independence
336 B.C.E.	Accession of Alexander (son of Philip II) to Macedonian kingship
334 B.C.E.	Alexander crosses into Asia; Battle of Granicus; conquest of Asia Minor
331 B.C.E.	Foundation of Alexandria; Alexander defeats Darius (King of Persia) at battle of Gaugamela, takes Mesopotamia, and enters Babylon, Persepolis, and Pasargadae
323 B.C.E.	Death of Alexander at 32 years old; Period of "the Successors" for Alexander's throne
311 B.C.E.	Peace between "the Successors" that recognizes in effect the division of empire between Antigonos (Asia), Cassandros (Macedon/Greece), Lysimachos (Thrace), Ptolemy (Egypt), and Seleukos (the Eastern satrapies)
301 B.C.E.	Battle of Ipsos destroys power of Antigonos and son Demetrios (Antigonos killed)
279 B.C.E.	Invasion of Greece and Macedon by Gauls.
276 B.C.E.	Antigonos Gonatas, son of Demetrios, defeats Gauls and becomes king of Macedon
263–41 B.C.E.	Eumenes, ruler of Pergamum, founds independent power in Asia Minor.
214–167 B.C.E.	Three wars between Macedon and Rome; Battle of Pydna ends Macedonian kingdom
209 B.C.E.	Attalus I of Pergamum allies with Rome against Philip V of Macedon
196 B.C.E.	Rome declares the freedom of the Greeks at the Isthmus of Corinth
194 B.C.E.	Romans evacuate Greece
148 B.C.E.	Fourth Macedonian War; Macedonia becomes Roman province
133 B.C.E.	Attalus III of Pergamum bequeaths kingdom to Rome
129 B.C.E.	The former kingdom of Pergamum becomes a province of Asia
86 B.C.E.	Sulla in the East captures Athens and Greece

ROME

(Early Rome's events and dates are uncertain. Rome began on the fringes of Etruscan culture and grew.)

753 B.C.E.	Traditional date of the foundation of Rome
509 B.C.E.	Traditional date for the foundation of the Roman Republic
390 B.C.E.	Gauls sack Rome
327–290 B.C.E.	Series of Samnite Wars between Rome and Samnites in the central Apennines
264–41 B.C.E.	First Punic war between Rome and Carthage, which Rome wins.
218–01 B.C.E.	Second Punic War; Rome wins and Carthage becomes a dependent of Rome
202–191 B.C.E.	Roman conquest of Cisalpine Gaul
200–146 B.C.E.	Rome conquers Greece; Greek culture influences Rome
149–46 B.C.E.	Third Punic War: Carthage destroyed, Africa becomes Roman province
91–88 B.C.E.	Social War in Italy concerning issue of full Roman citizenship
87 B.C.E.	Sulla appointed dictator of Rome, passes Sullan reforms
73–71 B.C.E.	Slave revolt of Spartacus
66–63 B.C.E.	Pompey's reorganization of the East; end of Seleucid monarchy
58–49 B.C.E.	Julius Caesar's campaigns in Gaul
49–45 B.C.E.	Civil war between Caesar and Pompey
47–44 B.C.E.	Dictatorship of Caesar in Rome. (**March 15, 44** B.C.E.: Caesar murdered)
42 B.C.E.	Defeat of Caesar's assassins at battle of Philippi; Brutus and Cassius commit suicide
31–30 B.C.E.	Octavian defeats Antony at Battle of Actium, Egypt; Egypt annexed by Rome
27 B.C.E.	"Restoration of Republic"; Octavian assumes title *Augustus*
14 C.E.	Augustus dies
14–37 C.E.	Reign of Tiberius
37–41 C.E.	Reign of Caligula; Caligula murdered by Praetorian Guards
41–54 C.E.	Reign of Claudius, Caligula's uncle; Claudius poisoned by his wife, Agrippina
54–68 C.E.	Reign of Agrippina's son (and Claudius' adoptive son), Nero
68 C.E.	Nero forced to commit suicide
69 C.E.	"Year of the Four Emperors": Galba, Otho, Vitellius, and Vespasian
69–79 C.E.	Reign of Vespasian
79–81 C.E.	Reign of Titus (son of Vespasian)
81–96 C.E.	Reign of Domitian; Campaigns of Agricola in Britain
96–98 C.E.	Reign of Nerva
98–117 C.E.	Reign of Trajan, under whom the Roman Empire reaches its peak
117–138 C.E.	Reign of Hadrian
138–161 C.E.	Reign of Antoninus Pius
161–180 C.E.	Reign of Marcus Aurelius
180–192 C.E.	Reign of Commodus

193–211 C.E.	Reign of Septimius Severus
212–17 C.E.	Reign of Caracalla (**212** C.E.: *Constitutio Antoniniana* gives citizenship to all in the empire)
218–22 C.E.	Reign of Elagabalus
222–35 C.E.	Reign of Alexander Severus
235–84 C.E.	Period of military upheaval with many emperors; Problems with bureaucracy, the economy, and on the frontiers
284–306 C.E.	Reign of Diocletian, who founds the tetrarchy that divides the empire
306–37 C.E.	Reign of Constantine the Great, who reunites the Roman Empire
312 C.E.	Christianity declared official state religion at Rome
324 C.E.	Foundation of Constantinople; Seat of Roman Empire moved to Constantinople
340 C.E.	Rome splits again into two empires under Constantine's sons
360–63 C.E.	Reign of Julian the Apostate
378–95 C.E.	Reign of Theodosius the Great
395 C.E.	Empire divided by Theodosius' sons
410 C.E.	Sack of Rome by Alaric the Visigoth; Rome formally renounces Britain
476 C.E.	End of the Roman Empire in the West

INTRODUCTION TO THE PERIOD AND REGION: GREECE

Although the literature examined in this chapter begins with Homer and dates to c. 750 B.C.E., a history of Greece should arguably begin with pre-historical Greece, giving us an insight into the start of her development prior to the period commonly known as the dark ages, which ran from 1100 to 800 B.C.E.

The history of early Greece begins on the island of Crete with Minoan civilization, named after King Minos who, according to legend, was the son of Zeus. Here excavations have uncovered a series of palace complexes, which have been dated to c. 2000 B.C.E. The largest of these was discovered at Knossos in 1900 C.E. by the English archaeologist Arthur Evans. Little is known for certain about who lived in these buildings or indeed their function; although Evans suggested they belonged to Minoan kings, later theories argue that they acted as religious centers on the island. Irrespective of these debates, however, it is important to note that clay tablets from excavations on Crete are inscribed with both hieroglyphic script and a later script that scholars have termed Linear A. Analysis of these tablets shows they are records for goods stored in the palace complexes on the island, and are therefore one of the earliest examples of writing and recording in the Greek world. These palaces were destroyed c. 1600 B.C.E. Although they were rebuilt on a grander scale with wall frescoes in the palaces, particularly at Knossos, in c. 1425 B.C.E. the Minoan palaces were again destroyed and abandoned.

The following civilization to inhabit Crete, the Mycenaeans, were different and employed a written script, now called Linear B, which analysis has revealed to be a rather different language from that of the island's previous occupants. Exactly how this island was reinhabited by the Mycenaeans has been subject to significant discussion. Suggestions have been made that either the Minoan settlements were destroyed by fire and resettled sometime later, or that the Minoan palaces were destroyed through conflict and then resettled by their conquerors. Whichever argument is more accurate, it was the Mycenaeans who became the first known civilization of mainland Greece.

Archaeology has demonstrated that during the thirteenth century B.C.E., mainland Greece was relatively densely populated. By c. 1200 B.C.E., however, the situation had changed dramatically. Sites on mainland Greece and Crete were destroyed, and the so-called Dark Ages began around 1100 B.C.E. During this period, the number of populated areas and their population density decreased in many areas of the Greek world. In addition to reduced populations, excavation has suggested that material possessions were significantly fewer in this period and that Linear B disappeared and was not replaced by another form of writing. Quite how "Dark" this period was for its inhabitants is open to debate and, increasingly, recent archaeological excavations highlight the subjective nature of this term. What is clear, however, is that from 1100 to 800 B.C.E. the Greek world underwent significant change. One significant development was the migration of people from within and outside Greece—initially eastwards, and then south and south-eastwards.

After the dark ages, the successive periods of Greek history are often divided into the following sections: The Archaic Age, from 620 to 480 B.C.E., in which order and formality were apparently brought to Greek culture; The Classical Age, between 480 and 336 B.C.E., during which the culmination of Greece's cultural achievement occurred; and The Hellenistic Age, between 336 and 31 B.C.E., during which the Greek world was split between a number of monarchical states. This period ends with the Greek world being subsumed into the expanding Roman Empire. This introduction will consider Greek history up to the death of Alexander in 323 B.C.E., and the subsequent division of his kingdom, since this division symbolises a serious shift from a relatively cohesive empire to the division of mainland Greece into kingdoms ruled by separate kings.

As Hesiod's writings indicate, the ancient Greek world began to emerge in the eighth century B.C.E. During this period Greece's population increased considerably, encouraging not only the resettlement of regions previously abandoned during the dark ages but also a revival in metalwork and pottery. Furthermore, this era witnessed the emergence of the *polis* (loosely translated as "citizen-state"). This was a political and social unit that drew not only on the activities and individuals within city walls but also on those that occurred in the surrounding countryside. It was a development that allowed the inhabitants of each *polis* to define themselves as members of elementary political communities (for example, as either Spartan or Athenian) under the general umbrella of "being Greek." This identification was at the heart of daily life and Greek identity in ancient Greece for many centuries.

One should not underestimate the importance of the *polis* system for understanding Greek history and for examining Greek identity in terms of the contact between the Greek and the non-Greek world. The system also aids in understanding the interaction between the inhabitants of the different *poleis* of ancient Greece. In 490 B.C.E., the Greek world faced a significant threat from the barbarian world in the East: the Persian Empire, under Cyrus the Great. A number of Greek *poleis,* though by no means all, joined military forces against the threat and managed to defeat the Persian forces at the Battle of Marathon. Ten years later, at the battles of Salamis (480 B.C.E.) and Plataea (479 B.C.E.) the Greeks were again victorious over the Persian Empire, who were led this time by King Xerxes. Greece's success over the Persian invasion has often been perceived as a demonstration of a Greek identity and cultural unity, or a "common Greekness," against foreign invasion. This notion is belied, however, not only by the fact that only thirty to forty out of about seven hundred Greek *poleis* fought together against the

Persians, but also by the subsequent fighting between many *poleis* for sole domination over the Greek world following the end of the barbarian threat.

The main instigators of conflict in the Greek world during the fifth century B.C.E. were Athens and Sparta. The first Peloponnesian war, between these states and their respective allied *poleis* from around the Greek world, was fought between 461 to 451 B.C.E. and culminated with the signing of the Thirty Year Peace in 446 B.C.E. The peace did not last however, and the Second Peloponnesian War, again between Sparta and her allies and Athens and her allies, broke out in 431 B.C.E. This protracted war, interspersed with brief spells of peace, finally ended in 404 B.C.E. It spelled the decline in power of two of the Greek world's most important *poleis*, Athens and Sparta, during the first half of the fourth century B.C.E.

In 371 B.C.E., Sparta was defeated by the *polis* of Thebes at the battle of Leuctra, which enabled Thebes, albeit briefly, to become the dominating power of the Greek world. By 362 B.C.E., Theban supremacy had ended with the death of her leader, Epaminondas, and it would appear that no other Greek state was able to take Thebes' place at the head of the Greek *poleis*. Instead, under the rule of its new king Philip II (who took the Macedonian throne in 359 B.C.E.), Macedonian power expanded and consolidated, first throughout Macedon and into the surrounding area and then into Greece. By 356–352 B.C.E., Philip II achieved hegemony of central Greece. In the Battle of Chaeronea in 338 B.C.E., Philip's destruction of Athenian and allied troops demonstrated the end of the independent citizen-state and the end of the Greek world as it had been known.

Philip's ambitions for further expansion of Macedonia did not stop there. Only two years after his destruction of Athens and her allies, he turned his attention to Persia. Although his expansionist ambitions were thwarted by his death, his son Alexander the Great took on responsibility for the empire. Once Alexander had subdued uprisings in Thebes and Macedonia, he invaded Persia. Alexander managed to expand his empire into Egypt, Asia Minor, Babylon, Susa, Persepolis, and finally into India at the Battle of Hydaspes during the years 336–323 B.C.E. by using a mixture of diplomacy and aggression. He returned to central Persia in 325 B.C.E. and died in 323 B.C.E. at Babylon.

With the death of Alexander, the Greek world was thrown into disarray. Power struggles broke out between Alexander's successors, made up of both familial descendants and his serving officers. Attempts to control Alexander's empire as a single unit failed, and the empire was eventually divided into three major kingdoms: Macedonia under the Antigonids, Egypt under the Ptolemies, and the Seleucid Kingdom in the East. These kingdoms never combined again to form a united Greek world, either as it had been before the rise of Macedon in the fourth century B.C.E. or as it had later become under Alexander. Instead, these kingdoms ruled separately at first; later they were, one by one, subsumed into the expanding Roman Empire. The last of the Hellenistic kingdoms to be annexed into the Roman Empire was Egypt, which fell in 31 B.C.E. at the Battle of Actium.

ROME

The early history of Rome is shrouded in legend, and trying to decipher Rome's historical past from the seamless mix of fact and myth that comprises early Roman history is almost impossible. Our literary sources for Rome's early history only begin to be written, at first in Greek, from the late fourth or early third century B.C.E. Compositions in Latin then follow, first in c. 180 B.C.E. with the poetry of

Ennius, and then in 149 B.C.E. with the first prose history of Rome in Latin, by Cato. The subject matter for much of this Greek and Latin literature considers the period from Rome's foundation up to the contemporary times of each individual author. Given that the traditional date from literature for Rome's foundation is 753 B.C.E. however, the problems of accurately recording Rome's early years become apparent, because all our literary sources write on Rome's foundation centuries after the event, and therefore often relied on inaccurate and fragmentary evidence from which they aimed to construct a coherent narrative of events.

Archaeology has suggested that the first settlement on the hills around Rome occurred in c. 1000 B.C.E. As already mentioned, the traditional date of Rome's founding in literature was 753 B.C.E., and although the accuracy of this date can be challenged, some archaeological finds of pottery from Rome's Esquiline Hill can be dated to around the seventh century B.C.E. The fact that some of the pottery finds from this period originate from the Greek world, for example, from Euboea and Corinth, suggests that from relatively early on in Rome's history there was contact between Rome and the wider world.

From the eighth century to the sixth century B.C.E., Rome was ruled by "kings." Almost nothing is known for certain about the early monarchs of ancient Rome, and once again, much of Rome's early monarchical history is confused with myth and fiction. However, in archaeological terms, this period provides evidence for Rome's development and expansion. For example, in the years 616–579 B.C.E., traditionally associated with King Tarquin I, the first architectural developments of the city of Rome emerged. These included the paving of the Roman Forum and the building of temples and sanctuaries.

Rome's monarchical period ended in the early sixth century B.C.E. The traditional date for the collapse of Rome's age of kings and the start of the Roman Republic is 509 B.C.E.; according to myth, it occurred following the rape of Lucretia by the son of Rome's then king, Tarquin the Proud. The ensuing power struggle resulted in the creation of the Roman Republic under the control of elite aristocrats, who depicted themselves as the protectors of the empire and her people from those who might seek political power for themselves. This republican ideology of Rome underpinned the self-perpetuated aristocratic position of supremacy. This is nowhere more evident than during the conflict of the patrician and plebeian orders in Rome's mid-republic, when the lower orders of Roman society began to rebel against their subjugated position under the patrician elite.

Rome's republican period witnessed considerable expansion of the area of the empire. Initial growth began into the surrounding area of Latium and then progressed further into Italy as Rome defeated the remaining tribes, including the Etruscans to the north of Rome and the Samnites to the south-east of Rome and Latium. Rome's growth did not end with her expansion into Italy, however. During the third century B.C.E., Rome's interests extended beyond Italy's shores; by the end of her Republican period, Rome's supremacy had spread into the surrounding Mediterranean region giving her domination over areas of Spain, North Africa, Macedon, Greece, Judaea, and Syria, among other important powers.

By the last century of the Republic, Rome had become a significant military power. The political situation at home had seen Rome's upper classes compete for positions of increased power via election to magistracies in Rome's political system (the *cursus honorum*). Furthermore, Rome's late republic also witnessed a rise in power of a handful of individuals, for example Crassus, Pompey, and Caesar, who as military generals had commanded large numbers of troops in Rome's wars of expansion. Following victories abroad, these generals had successfully maintained the loyalty of their legions through the distribution of military *spolia*, or booty.

Roman emperor Julius Caesar, who has inspired readers in works from his own time, from Shakespeare's Renaissance, and from modern depictions and histories.

Soon, the struggle for supremacy in Rome was being fought between Pompey and Caesar. As these warlords vied for sole domination, they utilized the inherent threat their military might posed by refusing to relinquish command of their personal armies. These struggles led to civil war in Rome, which resulted in Caesar's assumption of a ten-year dictatorship in 46 B.C.E. Only two years later however, on March 15, 44 B.C.E., Julius Caesar was assassinated and Rome was once again flung into a period of significant internal conflict.

The ensuing period between the murder of Caesar and the rise of Rome's *principate* under her emperors was characterized by Roman bloodshed. The initial conflict arose between the assassins and the supporters of Caesar. However, once Caesar's assassins (Brutus and Cassius) had been forced to commit suicide after their defeat at the Battle of Philippi in Greece, Caesar's leading supporters (Octavian, Marc Antony, and Lepidus) soon turned on each other. Although Lepidus disappeared into political insignificance and ended his life peacefully in Africa, the struggles that followed in the late 30s B.C.E. resulted in civil war, with Octavian on one side and Marc Antony, allied with the Egyptian queen Cleopatra, on the other.

Octavian's victory over Marc Antony and Cleopatra at the battle of Actium in 31 B.C.E. is a defining point of Roman history. Not only did this enable the annexation of Egypt into the Roman Empire, but it also spelled the collapse of Rome's republic and the birth of a new political system in ancient Rome: the principate, where Rome was ruled under the sole power of an emperor and his imperial family. Octavian, renamed Augustus in 27 B.C.E., became the first emperor of Rome. He clearly had to maintain a careful balance between a position of sole power in Rome and accusations of tyranny. After Augustus died and his imperial power passed on to his adopted son, Tiberius, and then further down the line of the Julio-Claudians, the people of Rome became more accepting of imperial rule.

However, it would be wrong to assume that the position of emperor was passed on through family lines entirely without problems after Augustus. In 68–69 C.E., following the enforced suicide of the emperor Nero (the last of the Julio-Claudian line), Rome once again found itself facing civil war to decide sole power in Rome. This was the year of the four emperors, which ended in the seizing of power by a military general called Vespasian, who could claim no connections with the previous family of emperors. Again a ruling dynasty was begun (called the Flavian dynasty), allowing Rome's political system to survive in a relatively stable period of imperial control.

This political system of Rome under imperial control continued to the end of the fifth century C.E. However, the face of the Roman Empire had changed dramatically since Augustus' rule. Following the conversion of the emperor Constantine to Christianity in 312 C.E., Rome's traditional pagan religions had undergone a significant change in fortunes. By the end of the fourth century C.E., pagan worship had been outlawed in the empire. Moreover this period also saw the permanent division of the Roman Empire into the East and the West, which were ruled by different emperors. Never again was the Roman Empire to be ruled as a united whole. Furthermore, the capital of the western half of the empire was moved from Rome to Ravenna, while Constantinople was made the capital of the eastern half of the empire. Rome's empire in the east survived more successfully. Indeed, a reduced Byzantine state was maintained until 1453 C.E., when Ottoman Turks sacked Constantinople. Rome's empire in the west, however, was not so fortunate and found herself continuously under threat of invasion from the barbaric tribes of the Vandals, the Goths, and the Alamanni, among others, during the fourth and fifth centuries C.E. Rome herself was invaded by the Goths, led by Alaric in 410 C.E., a defeat that was to prove highly symbolic of Rome's declining power at this time. Only about sixty years later, in 476 C.E., the deposition of Romulus Augustus, the Emperor of the western empire, marked the end of Roman power in the West.

READING TRENDS AND PRACTICES

The key to understanding the history and culture of reading in ancient Greece and Rome is to consider the dominance of the Mediterranean Sea upon these regions. For the peoples of Greece and Rome, whose coastlines bordered it, the influence of the sea was all-pervasive: vital trade routes developed and the dissemination of religious practices, customs, alphabets, languages, and artistic styles between Greece and Rome was common. These demonstrations of cultural interaction between Greece and Rome help to emphasize the role played by the Mediterranean in facilitating the movement of ideas across her waters, a crucial factor when examining the development of reading in these ancient cultures.

An investigation into reading in Greece and Rome presents us with questions that appear, perhaps, irrelevant to studies of reading in more recent cultures. For us to gain a fuller picture of reading in the ancient world, we cannot merely examine the authors being read and the types of literature that existed two thousand or more years ago. We must also enquire who was doing the reading as well as where and why people read. We cannot even assume, necessarily, that the documents that Greeks or Romans read resembled the books that we read today or indeed that the basic process of silent reading was the most common method of reading in the ancient world.

At the outset, we must consider the varying formats of texts in antiquity. The extant evidence from written documents of the ancient world comprises an extensive corpus of material. It is not solely made up of examples of poetry and prose from authors such as Herodotus or Livy as one might at first think, but can be seen to include examples of monumental inscriptions, edicts, private letters, and even tax returns and graffiti. This chapter will examine the longer documents of poetry or prose that were copied, and later printed and produced in book form throughout the centuries, because these are the literary works that will provide us with

much of our understanding of the types of literature people read in Greece and
Rome. These are not the only examples of literature that existed in the ancient
world and neither are they our only extant examples. This chapter discusses some
of the most important texts read by people in ancient Greece and Rome. Due to
constraints of space, it does not consider examples of inscriptional material, later
Roman literature, or Christian literature.

Books, as we perceive them today, did not provide the original format of literature in the ancient world. Initially they were produced on papyrus scrolls that
required unrolling and re-rolling in order to be read. Finds of a blank sheet of
papyrus in a tomb that has been dated to c. 3000 B.C.E. and the earliest papyrus
texts that date to c. 2450 B.C.E. demonstrate the long-standing use of papyrus in
writing prior to its employment by the Greeks and Romans. The average scroll
measured between six and eight yards in length and its text was arranged in
columns. Line length depended on the type of text written, but could contain
twenty or more letters without word breaks. Aids to the reader, such as spaces and
punctuation, were rare at first; they only became more common in the first century
B.C.E. Text was read from left to right. The size of scrolls was such that reading
might require the help of a slave making the physical process of reading different
from today.

A significant innovation was the replacement of writing tablets, made of thin
wooden panels fastened together at one side, with parchment, which was used to
make an early form of book called a codex. Evidence from Roman authors such
as Martial demonstrates that parchment codices were used for classical literature
from the first century C.E.;
however, the dominant medium for secular literary material
remained the papyrus scroll
until the fourth century C.E. It
was the adoption of the codex
by Christian authors, due to
their more compact size and
easier format for quicker referencing, which increased the use
of the codex format in the
production of texts.

Over recent years, research
has taken place into how reading was undertaken in the
ancient world (see Gavrilov,
"Techniques of Reading in
Classical Antiquity" in *CQ* 47,
no. 1, 1997). Sources such as
the extract at the start of this
chapter from Augustine have
encouraged some to believe
that reading in antiquity only
ever involved people reading
aloud, and that Augustine commented on Ambrose's silent
reading because it was a novel
occurrence to which he was
unaccustomed. Although today

Papyrus

Papyrus was the most widely employed material
for writing in the Graeco-Roman world. It was
made from a marsh plant (*Cyperus papyrus*) found
mainly in the damp conditions of the Nile Delta.
To make a piece of papyrus, the triangular stem of
the plant was cut into sections measuring approximately 14 in. in length. From these, the outer
skin was removed and the white pith inside sliced
lengthways into thin strips. These strips were
placed vertically side-by-side and slightly overlapping each other on a hard surface and then on top
of these was put another layer of strips, this time
horizontally parallel. The layered strips were then
pressed together in presses so that the strips were
stuck to each other by the plant's juices, which
acted like a glue. The sheet that was produced was
then dried and its surface rubbed smooth with a
rounded object, perhaps a seashell or a stone to
make it ready for writing on. To make a scroll
(which measured approx. 6–8 yards) sheets were
then glued together with the horizontal fibers
together on one side of the scroll and the vertical
fibers together on the other. Generally texts were
written firstly in lines following the fibers of the
papyrus and parallel to the long sides of the scroll.
Scrolls were then often re-used with text being
written across the fibers on the back of the scroll.

this concept of only reading aloud in antiquity is less widely held, it highlights a crucial question about which members of society were actually able to read. Today, in most developed countries, literacy levels are high due to the accessibility of education and because reading material is readily available in public libraries and bookshops. However, it is difficult to determine accurate literacy levels in antiquity. Not only do we lack statistical evidence, but we know that there were numerous levels of literacy, ranging from those who had the very basic skills necessary for reading short messages, right up to those who were able to read complex literary papyri. For the purposes of this chapter, we are concerned with those who had the high literacy levels required for reading substantial literary texts as opposed to those with basic or functional literacy.

It is generally accepted that the widespread nature of literacy today was not experienced in the ancient world, but rather that the reading of literary works was a pursuit reserved for elite members of society who had the financial security to support this pastime. The act of reading itself was not necessarily indicative of social status. Indeed, in antiquity (and especially in Rome), slaves performed much of the reading and writing. Many factors made the reading of literary texts the preserve of the elites of Greece and Rome. The elites had the ability to finance higher levels of education, and access to reading materials. They also had the economic wherewithal to pay for either well-educated slaves, who could read aloud to a master and act as a scribe, or slaves who worked in the fields, mines and elsewhere, thus maintaining the master's wealth and providing him with both the financial and temporal opportunities to spend his time reading. It was a consequence of constraints such as these, then, that meant that literary pursuits were restricted to the wealthy members of ancient society; it furthermore ensured that the pastime of reading was generally associated with an individual's attempts to display social standing and erudition.

This connection of reading with individual displays of status presents an interesting insight into the culture of reading in antiquity, enabling us to understand more clearly how, why, and where acts of reading took place in the ancient world. Although evidence for reading silently has been gathered from ancient sources to show that silent reading was not unknown, as had previously been believed, Augustine's comment on Ambrose does suggest both his surprise and his lack of familiarity with this style of reading. Combining this with comments within ancient literature, which recount numerous examples of people reading texts aloud in public places such as bath-houses, libraries, and philosophical schools, we can begin to understand the particularly public characteristic of ancient reading. Thus the association of reading in antiquity with personal display is further emphasized not only by the fact that it often occurred aloud, but also because it frequently took place before audiences of friends, patrons or students in public.

When we consider the public nature of reading and literary culture in the ancient world, not only should we examine literacy levels in antiquity (and consequently the widespread nature of reading) but we should consider other factors that encouraged the spread of literary culture in the ancient world. In ancient Greece, oral tradition has a lengthier history than written texts. Our earliest example of written Greek literature is found in Homer's poetry, which is dated, albeit approximately, to the second half of the eighth century B.C.E. Most scholars believe, however, that the stories from Homer existed orally and were passed down for centuries before being written down and formalized in literature around 750 B.C.E. Without these stories' initial popular retelling via oral tradition, the success of the spread of ancient literature and the examples of ancient literary culture that remain extant might have been adversely affected.

Turning to Latin literature, we must remember that the Latin alphabet—a predecessor of our own—was itself derived and adapted from the Greek alphabet. Given that the first examples of Greek literature appeared about five hundred years before the first example of Latin literature in 240 B.C.E. from Livius Andronicus, the influence of Greek literature on the development of Latin literature is clear. That Livius Andronicus was himself Greek, and produced Latin versions of both a Greek comedy and a Greek tragedy, further emphasizes the indebtedness of Latin language and literature to ancient Greece.

A final factor affecting literary culture in the Greek and Roman worlds was the role that imperialism and conquest played in spreading contact with books and literature throughout the Mediterranean. The first libraries of the ancient world were found in the Near East; however, it is not until the Greek world that we find examples of libraries with books on a multitude of subjects accessible to readers with varying interests. The development of the library, which was open to selected members of the public, was brought about by two events: the creation by Aristotle of a large personal library and, perhaps more importantly, the development of the library at Alexandria by the Ptolemies. When Rome conquered Egypt the emperors maintained the Library, although membership was now granted to men distinguished through government service rather than learning. As Rome increased contact with other cultures of the ancient world through conquest, such as Greece and Asia Minor, her library resources further increased. Victory on the battlefield meant booty. This in turn gave successful generals a quick way to develop their own libraries, as is demonstrated by the libraries of Aemilius Paulus, Sulla, and Lucullus. In addition to Roman libraries developed from plunder, many were put together by men devoted to learning and literature, such as Cicero and Varro; these consisted mainly of Greek texts but did also hold some Latin works. These libraries owned by individuals were then opened up to friends and contemporaries for personal research.

EPIC

As peoples of different Greek city-states (*poleis*) and different cultures came into contact, their traditions, stories, and myths spread and mixed. Inevitably, these stories and traditions found their way into the early oral culture of the Greek world and were later recorded in early Greek literature. The first examples of storytelling and literature from the ancient Greek world can be found in Homer's two epic poems, the *Odyssey* and the *Iliad*. Although difficult to date these texts accurately, most scholars believe that the original oral transmissions were first recorded in c. 750 B.C.E. In addition to queries regarding the dating of these texts, a significant question also remains concerning Homer's identity. After all, throughout the works, he neither tells us who he is or where he is from, or indeed the audience for whom he is writing. Consequently, there are on-going discussions as to whether Homer was an individual or a group of poets who recorded the poems passed down to them in their culture. Some have also asked whether the *Iliad* and the *Odyssey* were the work of the same poet(s). Such enquiries clearly demonstrate the level of mystery surrounding these texts, their composition, and their recording, and because the arguments surrounding these questions are too complex and lengthy to discuss here, it remains convenient to use the shorthand "Homer" in reference to both poems.

Although today the term "epic" is often employed to describe blockbuster Hollywood films, in antiquity, it referred to poems that followed certain rules and conventions. They were composed in a specific meter called *dactylic hexameter*, consisting of lengthy and flowing lines, and often used specific formal features such as elaborate speeches, Homeric epithets, and extended similes. More importantly, ancient epic texts were generally long works dealing with specific grand themes of historical or cosmic importance.

The first epic poem, the *Iliad*, is a long narrative consisting of over 15,600 lines that records some of

---

The Library and *Mouseion* at Alexandria

Alexandria's library and *Mouseion* were benefactors of philosophy and the arts of the Hellenistic world. The resources and the opportunity for intellectual endeavor in this cultural center attracted scholars from all over the ancient world, who brought prestige to the Ptolemies. The Ptolemies aimed to own a copy of every book ever produced. In this vein, they even impounded books arriving on ships at the harbor of Alexandria. It is estimated that their holdings in Alexandria contained around 500,000 papyrus rolls. In time other Hellenistic kingdoms developed their own similar—and competing—cultural centers, such as those at Antioch and Pergamum, further demonstrating the importance of literary and philosophical culture in the ancient world. The library probably continued until around 270 C.E., when significant fighting in Alexandria laid waste to the Palace at Alexandria and probably the Library as well.

---

the episodes from the Trojan War. The war itself was fought between the Trojans and the Greeks, following the abduction of Helen of Troy by the Greek prince Paris, but the *Iliad* only records an episode from the end of the 10-year conflict. The story considers the withdrawal from combat by the Greek hero, Achilles, who has been insulted by the Greek King Agamemnon. This, in turn, has disastrous consequences for Greece's armies. Finally, Achilles' close friend Patroclus persuades him that he might fight in Achilles' place, wearing his armor, and so defeat the Trojans. In the event Hector, the Trojan prince, kills Patroclus. Enraged by Patroclus' death, Achilles fights and kills Hector, and proceeds to mistreat his body. In the last book of the poem, Priam—Hector's father and the Trojan King—visits the Greek encampment and begs Achilles to return Hector's body. Achilles is moved by pity and he hands over the body of Hector. The poem ends with Hector's burial and the Trojans mourning his death and waiting for the inevitable destruction of their city at the hands of the Greeks.

The *Odyssey* is a slightly shorter poem, set in the aftermath of the Trojan War, and focuses on the journey and homecoming of its eponymous hero, Odysseus. It tells the story of his travels in strange and foreign lands, fighting mythical monsters such as Polyphemus the Cyclops, Scylla, and Charybdis, and meeting exotic beings such as Circe and the Sirens, all of whom try to prevent him from reaching home and reasserting his authority on his kingdom and family. Although most of the poem depicts Odysseus' eventful journey, the narrative occasionally examines life for those whom Odysseus left behind when he went to fight in the Trojan War. Thus, we see his wife struggling against the unwanted interest of suitors who, believing Odysseus to be missing, and presumably dead, are trying to gain her affections and thus control Odysseus' kingdom. The end of the story brings Odysseus' return, the defeat of his wife's suitors, and the reassertion of his authority over his kingdom.

Both of these texts were highly influential in the ancient world, and their importance for understanding the history of reading in antiquity should not be underestimated. Homer was undoubtedly the most admired poet of the Hellenic world; as such, these poems played a vital role in the education of children of the elite and in the literature of later authors from both Greece and Rome. The continued employment of the Homeric poems throughout antiquity helped them maintain

A first-century C.E. marble relief depicting Nike and Apollo from ancient Greek myth.

an unrivalled position of supremacy in the ancient literary tradition and copies of the texts were regarded as the most prized possessions of learned men.

The second Greek author of epic poetry was Hesiod. Again, significant debate concerning the date of his writing has arisen. It is generally accepted that his two poems were composed about a generation after Homer. Unlike Homer's works, we get some biographical information concerning the author from his writing. He tells us his name, that he lived below Mount Helikon, and some detail on his family history, all of which means that we know more about Hesiod than we know about Homer. His two epic poems are entitled *Theogony* and *Works and Days*. Today, the latter is arguably the more studied of his works. It is the shorter of the two and consists of advice, especially on the subject of animal husbandry and morality. A central theme in the advice given in *Works and Days* is the virtue and necessity of labor and piety, which Hesiod says will be rewarded by the gods. This poem is addressed to his brother, Perses, and to local lords whom Hesiod accuses of corruption.

His other text, *Theogony* ("the birth of the gods"), is about one thousand lines in length and covers the origins and genealogies of the gods. This work names hundreds of gods—although not all are considered in depth—and examines the establishment of Zeus as the divine ruler over them all. It contributed to, and developed an understanding of, a complex pantheon of Greek deities. Given the divine subject matter of this text, it is likely that in antiquity, at least, this was the more important of his works.

Although both poems are significantly shorter than Homer's, and their style is thought to be less fluent, Hesiod and Homer were generally regarded together, even in ancient times, as the founding figures of Greek epic poetry. Their joint influence and perceived importance in ancient literature, as observed in antiquity, is highlighted by the later historian of the Greek world Herodotus when he says, "I think that Hesiod and Homer lived no more than four hundred years before my time, and they were the ones who created the gods' family trees for the Greek world, gave them their names, assigned them honors and areas of expertise, and told us what they looked like" (2.53).

Given the indebtedness of the Roman world to Greek culture, it is perhaps not surprising that the genre of epic plays a similarly important role in the development of ancient Roman literature. That Livius Andronicus, the first author to write in Latin, produced a version of the *Odyssey* in Latin highlights the importance of epic for the Roman world. Yet it is with Virgil's *Aeneid* that we find the most influential example of the epic tradition from Rome. Although this

> **Mount Vesuvius**
>
> Vesuvius is an active volcano located in Southern Italy in the region of the Bay of Naples. It last erupted in 1944, and it is estimated to erupt on a fifty-year cycle, which if accurate would mean an eruption is again imminent. Its most famous eruption was in 79 C.E., when a cataclysmic blast destroyed numerous ancient cities of Italy and killed thousands of inhabitants. The lava and mud released in the eruption covered and destroyed many cities of the region, such as Pompeii, Herculaneum and Stabiae. Following the eruption, many of the cities were abandoned and forgotten until they were rediscovered centuries later and excavated in the hope of revealing the treasures, secrets, and history of a past civilization.

text remained unfinished at its author's death in 19 B.C.E., it is clear that Virgil intended the work to be Rome's equivalent to the poems of Homer.

The published text comprised twelve books, in which Virgil narrates the fall of Troy and the flight of the conflict's survivors and their leader, Aeneas. After time spent in Carthage, they are destined to move on and settle in Italy, where Aeneas' descendants are later to found the city of Rome and her empire. Virgil wrote following a period of one of Rome's bloodiest civil wars, where Romans were pitted against each other in support of powerful individuals who sought sole control of Rome and her empire. Ultimately it was Octavian, later called Augustus, who was successful in the quest for sole power and presented himself as the bringer of internal peace and prosperity to Rome. Yet this text was not about Augustus but rather Rome's recent past from a mythologizing viewpoint, which, through the language, events, and people employed in the work, echoed the poems of Homer.

The question of to what degree Virgil was an "Augustan" poet and a supporter of Augustus' regime is often raised. Both sides of this complex argument are often poorly examined, because throughout the celebrations of Rome's greatness in the work are often interspersed tragic images of conflict, violence, and loss. Regardless of, or perhaps because of, the potential for multiple readings of the work, the success of Virgil's *Aeneid* was immediately recognized, giving its author significant renown. It soon became established as a piece of canonical literature and remains regarded as such today. Like Homer, the text became a cornerstone of the Latin curriculum, with Roman children studying Virgil for his exemplary command of the Latin language so that they might imitate his written style.

POETRY

Although today we have a fairly fixed understanding of the term "poetry," in the ancient Greek world, poetry was further subdivided into genre groups depending on form and meter. The earliest style of poetry for which we have examples is that of hexameter poetry as discussed above. Yet there were numerous other genres of poetry in existence contemporaneously, such as iambic, elegiac, and melic (also called lyric) poetry. Unfortunately, our evidence for these other poetic styles remains in papyrus fragments or preserved in later quotations from only a few dozen poets out of the probable hundreds who would have composed poetry. The extant examples of these poetic styles date from the middle of the seventh century to the early fifth century B.C.E.

The specific genre of poetic style employed in ancient Greece depended on the occasion and context of the performance—for example, whether the poem was to be performed in the public sphere of the city or in the rather smaller group sphere of the symposium, and whether it was to be performed by a group (i.e. chorally) or by an individual (i.e. monody). The public poetic contests were civic festivals, which often contained athletic and musical contests. Evidence from vase painting and literary remains suggests that a private poetry contest often followed a banquet and was the preserve of a small group of elite diners who, under the direction of a "master of revels," partook of drinking wine mixed with water and playing drinking games. The different contexts of the poems' performance reflected the varying subject matter and values of the poems. Thus poetry for the small group of the symposium often expressed elite values, but poetry for the public sphere was often more egalitarian in the ideas that it espoused.

Some poets composed in several genres. Archilochus of Paros provides an example of this, for he wrote both iambic recitation and elegiac poetry. The dating of his work to the mid-seventh century B.C.E. provides us with perhaps our earliest example of a composer of multi-genre poetry. The subject matter of his poetry ranged from the serious to the light-hearted to the obscene and the aggressive, and his poetic skills earned him comparisons with Homer even in antiquity. Today however, due to the fragmentary nature of his poetry, it is often difficult to be sure of the dramatic context, or indeed the title, of specific poems.

In addition to iambic recitation and musically accompanied elegiac poetry evidenced by the poems of Archilochus, we have examples of another form of Greek poetry called melic (or lyric) poetry. Melic poetry was either sung by individuals at symposiums or other small gatherings, as demonstrated by Sappho's poems, or sung by choirs as large festivals, as is shown by songs from Pindar.

Possibly our most famous example of melic monody poetry comes from the female poet Sappho, who came from the island of Lesbos and was writing around the late seventh and early sixth century B.C.E. As with most Greek poetry, when considering Sappho's work we are looking at fragments, which makes identification of poem or song titles problematic. Thus, here we must consider the general subject matter of her work rather than specific titles. As one of the few female writers preserved for us from antiquity, her poetic skill was renowned even in antiquity when she was hailed as "the tenth muse." Most of her poetry was written for performance by individuals and much of it referred to love between women and girls, which in turn has encouraged speculation about her own sexual preferences. Other subject matters considered in her poetry were hymns to deities and the voicing of personal worries such as her concerns for the safety of her brother. Only a small amount of her work was written for choral performance for example her *epithalamia*, which were written for performance at weddings.

Unfortunately, we know little about the biographical details of Sappho's life. It is likely that she was married, although the only family to feature in her works were her brother and her daughter. We know she spent a period of time in exile on Sicily, perhaps as a result of her family's or her husband's family's involvement in political struggles on Lesbos.

The final Greek poet for consideration is Pindar, who wrote melic poetry generally for choral performance. He was probably born around 518 B.C.E. and his last dateable composition is from about 446 B.C.E. In antiquity he was regarded by many as one of the poets who made up the nine poets of the lyric canon. His work was divided into seventeen books, which included hymns, processional songs (*prosodia*—two books), maiden-songs (*parthenia*—three books), and victory songs (*epinicia*—four books). Of these, only the choral victory songs survive intact; the rest of the poems are fragmentary. His choral victory songs, *epinicia,* were written for the celebration of victories in Pan-Hellenic athletics festivals and were probably his most important work. The victory song was generally performed at the festival immediately after the victory or soon after the victor returned to his native city. It followed a specific structure, which included the honoring of the god of the games, praise for the victor and his family, his ancestors, and his generosity, as well as a mentioning of any previous victories. Beyond this, Pindar was able to be flexible in what he included in his victory poems in terms of either the poetic forms he employed or the visual images he portrayed.

Arguably the most important poet from ancient Rome, apart from Virgil, is the late republican poet Gaius Valerius Catullus, who came from a propertied family from Verona but spent much of his life in Rome. We cannot be entirely sure of his dates, however it is likely that he was born around 84 B.C.E. and died around 54 B.C.E.; at least, there is no further record of his poems after 55 B.C.E. The period in which he composed his poetry was one of significant social change for poets in Roman society. Previously poets were of low status, but by the late republic, there was a significant shift in attitude toward poets and their poetry. This was called the Neoteric movement and it embraced Hellenistic culture, taking it as an important model for life, which in turn affected styles of writing. The poets in this movement, including Catullus about whom we know the most, regarded the profession of poetry seriously, believing that writing poetry was a befitting activity for the upper classes to undertake. On his death, Catullus left a corpus of 114 poems, the subject matter of which was varied and considered the daily lives of people with whom he mixed in the aristocratic circles of Rome. He is probably best known for the mocking style of his poems that lampooned his contemporaries, for example his poem 39 on Egnatius, whom he ridiculed for brushing his teeth in urine. However it was not always men who figured in his poetry. He wrote a series of twelve poems addressing a married woman called Lesbia whom he initially depicts as being beautiful and self-confident. On becoming her lover, however, he soon realized her duplicity and unfaithfulness as she took on a multitude of partners. His misery at her behavior leads to both confusion and vitriolic criticism of her in his works as can be seen in poem 85 where he writes, "I hate and yet love. You may wonder how I manage it. I don't know, but feel it happen and am in torment." This tortured style of love poetry found no precedent in the light-hearted Hellenistic models and is often regarded today as Catullus' most significant poetic achievement. However, in antiquity greater regard was probably given to his most ambitious work, his 64th poem, entitled "Wedding of Peleus and Thetis," which employed the hexameter style of epic poetry but was only four hundred lines in length. The work followed the wedding celebrations of the Argonaut Peleus and the nymph Thetis, which is tinged with an undercurrent of sadness because the child of the marriage, Achilles, was fated to die young at the battle of Troy. It is perhaps the vibrant descriptions employed in this work that encouraged its author to become regarded in antiquity as one of the greatest poets of the Roman republic.

The last Roman poet for consideration is the Augustan poet Quintus Horatius Flaccus, who lived between 65 and 8 B.C.E. The numerous poems that he composed were grouped together under the general titles *Satires, Epodes,* and *Odes,* and all contained a variety of poems on both public and private subjects. His *Epodes* was a volume of seventeen poems containing examples of his earliest work, written prior to his acceptance into the literary circle of Maecenas (who was himself a close friend of the soon to be emperor, Augustus) as well as poems written later celebrating Horace's friendship with Maecenas. Thus, both *Epodes* 1 and 9 praise Maecenas' participation in the Battle of Actium, which saw Rome defeat Egypt. His praise of his patron is further continued in his *Satires* where he demonstrates his gratitude for Maecenas' gift of a Sabine estate. However, we would be wrong to believe that Horace's poetry was merely effusive praise for his patron. Throughout his poetry, he is careful to depict the client-patron relationship between himself and Maecenas as based on merit, not just patronage and servility. Given that Horace wrote in a period when Rome was moving toward imperial rule under Augustus, and remembering his relationship with Augustus' friend Maecenas, it is unsurprising that some examples of Horace's poetry on more public matters spoke most positively of Augustus. Thus, *Odes* III.5 suggests that Augustus will be viewed as a god when he has successfully defeated Britain and Parthia, thus avenging Rome's earlier losses at the hands of the Parthians in 53 B.C.E., and his earlier *Odes* I.2 celebrates Augustus' defeat of Antony and Cleopatra.

A number of his *Odes* show Horace as a love poet, speaking of women and boys as is demonstrated in *Ode* I.5 where he writes of a man's love for a young boy. Other examples of his poetry present him as being equally concerned with pleasure and leisure, as his *Ode* III.28 on wine highlights. Furthermore, some of his *Satires* and *Epodes* contained attacks on people in Roman society; however, these are often relatively generalized criticisms, which are careful not to attack men of eminence. This was particularly important because he lacked the necessary personal protection offered by high social standing and esteemed ancestry, thus making him potentially vulnerable to vitriolic attacks by contemporaries of higher social status.

HISTORY

The origins of historical writing in the Greek world have generally been seen to start with the work of Herodotus entitled *Histories*. Furthermore, his text is our earliest surviving example of Greek prose. Born in the Greek city of Halicarnassus in Asia Minor around 484 B.C.E., it is likely that he came from a fairly prominent family. Ancient sources suggest that he was exiled from Halicarnassus, and spent time on the island of Samos and also in Athens. It is also assumed from the detailed material covered in his *Histories* that he spent significant amounts of time traveling both in Egypt and the Near East, although he doesn't specifically say this in his work. The approximate dates for the composition of his text, ascertained from events described in his work, are c. 442/1 B.C.E. to c. 425 B.C.E.

The text is nine books long and its theme is set out in its first sentence, where he says, "This is the account of Herodotus of Halicarnassus, undertaken so that the achievements of men should not be obliterated by time and the great and marvelous works of both Greeks and barbarians should not be without fame, and not least the reason why they fought one another." (Herodotus, *Histories*, Bk I. 1) The ultimate reason for this work, then, is to provide an account of the wars between Greece and Persia, which culminated in the military expedition of the Persian King, Xerxes, to Greece in 480 B.C.E. This episode is described at the end of the work. To gain insight into the significance of this conflict between the West and the East, however, the preceding chapters of the work aim to set up the nature of the conflict and where and when it started. As such, the work starts by examining the early struggles between the Greeks settled in Asia Minor and the nearby Persian kingdom of Lydia, as well as examining Persian power and monarchy.

This investigation into the history of the conflict between Greece and Persia is only one of the many important themes of Herodotus' work. Throughout his work, the stories and people he met on his various travels play an important role in his *Histories*. Thus he tells of the rise and fall of important cities such as Sparta as well as relating stories of famous individuals and the ethnographies, customs, and geographies of foreign peoples and places such as Egypt. The depth of investigation and insight into other non-Greek cultures gives to Herodotus' text the feeling of a complete history, rather than an account purely interested in a specific conflict. This helped him to be regarded by some from antiquity, such as Cicero, as "the father of history." Ironically however, it was Herodotus' uniquely global interest in matters both Greek and non-Greek that encouraged vitriolic criticism from other authors of the ancient world. He was defamed as a *barbarophile* (barbarian lover) by the second century C.E. Greek author Plutarch because he investigates the successes of both Greeks and Persians alike. Herodotus' *Histories* is further criticized by Plutarch as an account filled with "malice" against the Greeks, because it is not purely celebratory in his account of their achievements against the barbaric Persians.

The second Greek historian to be considered is Thucydides who lived from c. 460 to c. 400 B.C.E. and wrote *The History of the Peloponnesian War,* an historical account of the war between Athens and Sparta that occurred between 431 and 404 B.C.E. His account of this conflict, although incomplete, comprises eight books that can be divided into five parts: (1) an introduction, (2) the ten years war, (3) the unstable peace, (4) the Sicilian War, (5) a part of the Decelean war.

Although Thucydides was writing around the same time as Herodotus and was of the same generation, at the outset of his work he presented himself as a rival of Herodotus, saying "Thucydides of Athens wrote the history of the war . . . beginning as soon as war broke out and believing that it would be a great war and more worthy of record than any preceding one." (Thucydides, *History of the Peloponnesian War*, BK I. 1) Thus not only does he comment that his war is the most important to date, but he also claims his closeness to the events due to being contemporaneous with them. His work certainly demonstrates some clear differences between his style and Herodotus'. Not only does he restrict his text to a highly chronological consideration of politics and war but, throughout his work, we see his obsession with methodology. In his attempts to record accurately the events of the war, he criticizes the lack of critical attention paid by some to sources and eye-witness accounts, and takes significant care in trying to correlate the often varied accounts of events presented by different people. Moreover, when his attempts at accuracy fail, for example in his recording of speeches, Thucydides admits the problems he faces by highlighting the difficulties of being exact when recording speeches from memory.

Thucydides was not without his limitations, however. Not only was his work incomplete, but there is evidence to suggest that his historical recording was often swayed by his own personal beliefs and biases. Thus, for example, the character of Pericles is portrayed in a highly positive manner but that of Cleon appears at the very least to be rather selective. Yet even with such flaws in mind, the perception that Thucydides was a foundational figure in ancient historical investigation has been held by many. That Thucydides' account of the Peloponnesian War was highly regarded in antiquity is perhaps best demonstrated by the fact that many fourth century historians, such as Xenophon, chose to start their histories where Thucydides ended.

Only a small proportion of the works from Roman historians have survived today. Titus Livius (Livy) who was born in Patavium (modern day Padua) and lived from 59 B.C.E. to 17 C.E., provides us with a text that is both the first example of annalistic historical writing from Rome that has survived in any quantity and the last great annalistic history written during the Roman Republic. As the title of his work, *Books from the Foundation of the City* (*Ab urbe condita libri*), suggests, Livy's history covered the history of Rome from the founding of the city to 9 B.C.E. Unfortunately, however, only books I–X and XXI–XLV survive, and indeed books XVI and XVIII–XLV themselves have significant gaps in their narrative. The work in total comprised 142 books and probably took about forty years to write. It is interesting to note the uneven coverage of events; although book I concerns the 250-year regal period of Rome, book V takes us to the sack of Rome by Gaul in 390 B.C.E. and by book XXI, the subject matter is the Punic war with Hannibal in 218 B.C.E.

Like the example set by Thucydides, Livy concentrated his investigations upon Roman affairs both at home and abroad—for example, the conquest and destruction of cities, the expansion of empire and capture of kings, and domestic concerns such as the struggles between different groups of society. Rather than sifting through original documents when composing the work, he often relied on the literary and historical sources of his predecessors, adapting and adding to what had already been written. His awareness of the difficulties that faced his investigations, particularly concerning the early years of his work where the separation of myth from history was especially problematic, is demonstrated in the preface to the work where he referred to the events he was recording as being "more pleasing poetic fictions than reliable records of historical events." Furthermore, at the start of his work he outlines how it should be seen when he invites the reader to critically evaluate the events of Rome's past and the actions of her people, so that the reader might employ the lessons learned from it in present day:

> My wish is that each reader will pay the closest attention to the following: how men lived, what their moral principles were, under what leaders and by what measures at home and abroad our empire was won and extended: then let him follow in his mind how as discipline broke down bit by bit, morality at first foundered . . . and then began to topple headlong in ruin . . . . The special and salutary benefit of the study of history is to behold evidence of every sort of behavior set forth as on a splendid memorial; from it you may select for yourself and for your country what to emulate [and] . . . what to avoid. (*Books from the Foundation of the City*, Preface 1, 9–10)

A study of Livy's work quickly highlights the idealized manner in which he viewed Rome's past. His presentation of Rome's glory, the dignity of her leaders, and her virtuous behavior in conflict clouds his judgment and gives Rome a past more glorious than reality. Although he produced a dramatic, if not totally accurate, insight into Rome's history and brought to life important figures from both her history and myths, it was the size of the tome that caused difficulty for its survival. Not only was it abridged by the latter years of the first century C.E., but it soon disappeared from use altogether. It is perhaps this last point that explains the fragmentary nature of the text today.

Livy's importance in antiquity for the cultural history of reading is not merely the text that he produced but also the considerable influence he had on later historians. Livy's historical texts proved to be of fundamental importance to the later work of Cornelius Tacitus, who was arguably the most important historian of Rome's Principate. Tacitus was born c. 56 C.E. in Gaul and died after 118 C.E. in Rome having had a successful political career under the emperors Vespasian, Titus, and Domitian. Among his many works was an annalistic history recording the reign of the first emperors of Rome from Augustus to Nero called *Ab excessu divi Augusti* ("From the decease of the deified Augustus"). The more commonly employed title for this work, *Annales of Imperial Rome* actually dates from the sixteenth century. This work originally consisted of either sixteen or eighteen books in total and was further subdivided into smaller groups, each examining one of the emperors. Thus six books examined Tiberius' reign, six books were devoted to Caligula and Claudius' reigns, and the final six (or possibly four books) recorded Nero's reign. Again, various sections of the accounts have been lost over time: most of book V has been lost, all of books VII–X, the first half of XI, and everything from the middle of book XVI to the end. The loss of the end section of the work makes it impossible for us to know exactly how many books the work comprised.

Tacitus' *Annales* highlights his particular concern with the virtues and vices of the dawning of the Principate and its emperors. Following Livy's example of structuring historical investigations, Tacitus' work is a year-by-year (annalistic) enquiry into the first years of imperial rule. His cynical and vivid portraits of the Julio-Claudian emperors' violent and depraved behavior, his use of innuendo and pessimistic interpretations of imperial behavior, and his criticisms of the cowardice of many members of the senatorial elite do much to undermine his claims of impartiality early in his text. Throughout the work, therefore, stories abound of the crimes committed by the emperors against members of their families and the people of Rome, such as Nero's numerous attempts to murder his mother, his burning of Rome, and the subsequent persecution of the Christians, and Tiberius' treasons trials and violence against the senate as his paranoia spiraled out of control. The Roman world that Tacitus presents is not one of total despair, however, for there are some figures of dignity and virtue in the melée of Roman immorality. An example of one such character is Thrasea Paetus, a senator who strives to maintain traditions of senatorial independence against Nero's increasing dominance and tyranny. Furthermore, although Tacitus' *Annales* bemoaned the collapse of Rome's republican regime and the loss of freedom that the move to the Principate signaled for many, it ultimately demonstrated an understanding of the necessity for single-man rule in Rome.

BIOGRAPHY

The Latin text entitled *De Vita Caesarum* (The Lives of the Twelve Caesars) is often read in conjunction with Tacitus' *Annales*. Written by Gaius Suetonius Tranquillus, a slightly younger contemporary of Tacitus, this text is a collection of twelve biographies of the Roman emperors from Caesar to Domitian. It provides us with one of the earliest surviving examples of the biographical tradition from ancient Rome. Tranquillus experienced a fairly successful political career in Rome and held a number of important posts in imperial administration during the reigns of the emperors Trajan and Hadrian, although we hear nothing of his political career from 122 C.E. to his death around 130 C.E.

Although there are similarities between the traditions of history and biography, the differences between the two styles must be noted. History generally focused upon military and political exploits and was perceived to be a more prestigious form of writing, whereas biography focused on the life (both public and private), tastes, and actions of specific individuals. For example, Suetonius' twelve biographies depicted both the public actions and private lives of Rome's emperors. The first six lives, from Caesar to Nero, are more detailed than the last half of his work. This imbalance demonstrates, perhaps, a realization of the potential entertainment the immoral exploits of the family of the Julio-Claudians might have presented to his readers. Certainly, the lascivious detail that he employed to discuss the sexual predilections of emperors such as Caligula and Nero, (although it is difficult to ascertain its accuracy), makes for some vivid and shocking accounts of an emperor's lifestyle. The lack of accuracy in the twelve biographies is further emphasized by his description of the physical appearance and his characterization of each emperor, which often depends on each specific emperor's popularity. Thus, Suetonius describes the rather unpopular Nero as malodorous with a protuberant belly and weak spindly legs, while the emperor Augustus enjoys a more positive presentation of character and appearance and is described by Suetonius as handsome.

As the first imperial biography in Latin, Suetonius' *De Vita Caesarum* provided the most successful example for the later set of imperial biographies, the so-called *Historia Augusta*, the reliability and authorship of which are highly questionable. Thus, although the reliability of Suetonius as a source for the reigns of the emperors from Caesar to Domitian might be questioned today, the biographical style it employed was to become influential in later ancient texts.

While Suetonius provides us with a Latin example of biography, undoubtedly the greatest biographer of the ancient world was a contemporary of both Suetonius and Tacitus called L. Mestrius Plutarchus. Born before 50 C.E. in Chaeronea near Delphi in Greece, he lived there for much of his life until he died after 120 C.E. Toward the end of his life, he received numerous honors from the emperors Trajan and Hadrian that highlighted his elite status.

Although he wrote many different works, his series of biographies entitled *Parallel Lives* was his greatest achievement. Its importance has been perceived almost continuously from antiquity to today. The form these biographies took was to compare the life of a distinguished Greek with that of a distinguished Roman from the Republic; for example he paired the lives of Demosthenes and Cicero in one book, and in another he paired the life of Alexander the Great with that of Julius Caesar. Today twenty-three paired lives remain, nineteen of which have "comparisons" attached that draw formal comparisons between the two men they present. At the outset of his biography of the life of Alexander the Great, Plutarch identifies his aims of the work as being to record the virtues or vices of eminent men rather than to provide a chronological history of events. Thus in the work he draws attention to the characters and education of his subjects and anecdotal tales of significant episodes in their lives, rather than analyzing the period in which they lived.

The influence of Plutarch's biographies has been immense. By the fourth century C.E., his *Lives* was perceived to be a "classic" tome, and a few centuries later during the Byzantine period it was popularly employed as an educational text. Moreover, from information and insight contained in his *Lives*, many authors of more recent centuries have developed their understanding of the ancient Roman and Greek worlds. One such example of the influence of Plutarch can be found in the plots of Shakespeare's *Julius Caesar*, or his *Antony and Cleopatra*, which are heavily reliant on Plutarch's biographical accounts.

DRAMATIC TEXTS

In the Greek world, dramatic texts were produced in the genres of tragedy, comedy, and satire, although there is little complete evidence for the genre of the satire play. Of the three tragic poets—Aeschylus, Sophocles, and Euripides—many regard Aeschylus as a primitive example of a tragedian playwright, leading the way to Sophocles who reached the heights of tragic writing with a quality that was not fully maintained by Euripides. Sophocles wrote more than 120 plays for performance at competitions connected with the festivals celebrating the god Dionysus. He celebrated at least twenty victories and apparently never came lower than second place in the other competitions in which his plays were performed. Only seven of his plays survive today, however they continue to be performed on a regular basis.

Arguably, Sophocles' supreme work can be found in his play *Antigone*. We lack reliable evidence for when this play was written, although the date of 441 B.C.E. has been suggested. Furthermore, there is evidence to suggest that when it was performed it was the winning play of the competition. The theme of this play revolves around piety and conflict, with the main character, Antigone, vowing on numerous occasions throughout the play to bury the body of her brother after his death in the civil war of Thebes. When banned by the tyrant and leader of the city, Creon, from fulfilling what she perceives to be her duty and condemned to death, tragedy ensues. Both Antigone and Creon believe themselves to be doing what the gods require of them. The poignant irony of this play becomes clear at the end of the play when Antigone dies questioning the strength of her belief, and Creon confronts his misinterpretation of what the gods required of him only after Antigone and his wife and son are dead.

The tradition of tragedy in Roman drama was upheld by authors such as Ennius, however the only surviving examples of Roman tragedy come from the author Seneca the Younger, who was the Emperor Nero's tutor until forced to commit suicide in 65 C.E. We are not sure exactly when Seneca wrote his plays, nor are we sure that they were performed on stage, because it has been suggested that Seneca's tragedies were composed rather as recitation-dramas. Whether or not this is the case, Seneca's works did retain some of the traditions of Greek tragedy. As with the examples of Greek tragedy, Seneca's plays are mythological in subject matter and concerned with the important characters of Greek myths such as Medea and Thyestes. Though they are generally shorter than Greek tragedies, they retain some of the typical Greek tragic conventions such as using a limited number of actors and the use of choruses and messengers.

Perhaps one of the main areas of difference between Seneca's plays and the examples of Greek tragedy is that he did not adapt individual Greek tragedies. Rather, he drew on the whole corpus of tragic plays from the Greek world as well as employing further dramatic techniques from Roman poetry. His plays were generally divided into five acts, with the first act providing the prologue to the rest of the play. Each act was then divided by choral odes.

His final play, *Thyestes,* highlights well the dark nature of Senecan tragedy. In the play, Atreus, who is the father of Agamemnon and Menelaus, is established as king of Mycenae and consequently banishes his brother Thyestes. During the play Atreus decides to destroy his brother, although the reasons for this are not made clear. In order to carry out his plan, Atreus invites his brother to return to Mycenae and become joint ruler. Once Thyestes has arrived, Atreus pollutes the temple (which is part of the Palace of Mycenae) by murdering two of Thyestes' sons as though they were sacrifices, despite the bad omens sent by the gods. The two boys are then cooked and served to their father, who, at the end, is told what he is eating.

It is the powerful and monstrous characters such as this that proved to be the greatest legacy of Senecan tragedy and ensured that their importance was not restricted to the Roman world. Rather, their influence was wielded throughout the Renaissance in the theatres of Elizabethan England, as well as in France and Italy in the characters of playwrights such as Christopher Marlowe and Ben Jonson.

The arrival of the genre of comedy in the ancient Greek world was a later tradition in Greek drama. The bulk of our evidence for this style of dramatic play can be found in the numerous plays written by the greatest poet of the tradition of Old Attic Comedy, Aristophanes, who was producing his texts during the latter half of the fifth century B.C.E. As the name "Old Attic Comedy" suggests, a slightly different tradition followed, known as "New Attic Comedy," whose best-known exponent is the author Menander, who wrote in the very different Greek world of the fourth century.

Aristophanes was born between 460 and 450 B.C.E. and died shortly before 386 B.C.E. He was a prolific comic poet. Although only eleven of his plays survive, we have titles for another thirty-two and thousands of fragments from other plays. The first play he wrote was entitled *The Banqueters* and is dated to 427 B.C.E., although this play no longer survives. The first extant example of his dramatic texts can be found in his play *The Acharnians,* which was presented in 425 B.C.E. His last play can be dated to 388 B.C.E. and was a second play of the title *Plutus* (a first play of this title was produced in 408 B.C.E., although this no longer survives today). As with the tragic genre, comedies were acted in competitions connected with Dionysiac festivals. Initially, the festival with which comedies were connected was the City Dionysia. Later on the festival called the Lenaea held a prominent place in the history of the genre. Similar to tragedy, Aristophanes' comedies followed regular plot patterns. They were comprised of an *agon* (confrontation between two sides), a *parabasis* (a mid-play interlude where the actors address the audience directly) and a conclusion with festivities and often an emphasis on excessive sex and drinking.

Perhaps the funniest of Aristophanes' plays was *Lysistrata,* which was performed in 411 B.C.E. and produced by Callistratus for the festival of Lenaea, which occurred every January. The play's plot follows the protagonist, a woman called Lysistrata, who forges a plan with other Athenian women to force the men of Athens to end the Peloponnesian War. In order to make the men give up the war with Sparta, the women seize the Athenian Acropolis, which held the economic heart of the city as well as being of huge political and religious significance. In addition to causing disruption to the functioning of the city and the war effort, the women refuse to have sex with the men of Athens until peace with Sparta has been reached. The irritation of the disruption to the city's functioning and the discomfort that enforced celibacy brought gives the play a light-hearted humor, even though the darker subject matter of war provides the backdrop to the play as a whole.

The comic genre develops fairly early in Rome's literary history with the plays of Titus Maccius Plautus written between c. 205 and 184 B.C.E. Twenty-one of his plays are extant, and we know that more were written. These comedies are the earliest surviving examples of the genre from ancient Roman literature. The plays are modeled on Greek comedies, nearly all of which were from the tradition of New Comedy composed by playwrights such as Menander, who lived about one hundred years earlier. Unfortunately, the Greek originals for Plautus' plays no longer survive, although a discovery of a section of Plautus' *Bacchides* together with the

Menandrian model on which Plautus' play was based (called the *Twice-deceiver*), has enabled us to examine how Plautus adapted Menander's Greek play to suit a Roman audience. The changes he made to the Greek model include increased musical content and development of the stock-characters such as the parasite, or "sponger." Furthermore, like the Greek plays on which they are based, Plautus' plays are written in verse and were performed at religious festivals. However, unlike their Greek predecessors, which were performed on permanent theatres in the city, these Roman comedies were performed on temporary stages erected for the occasion.

Plautus' play *Miles Gloriosus* was based on a Greek play called *The Braggart*. Although the characters of the play speak Latin, they have Greek names and are meant to be Greek. The play is set in Ephesus, a Greek city on the coast of Asia Minor. As with all Greek and Roman drama, all characters, whether male or female, were played by men who wore masks specific to the character that they played. The play begins with the braggart soldier called Pyrgopolynices (fighter of many fortresses) entering the stage with three companions and the popularly employed stock character of a parasite. Next enters the clever slave of the soldier called Palaestrio (wrestler) who delivers the play's prologue, explaining how he became the slave of Pyrgopolynices. Previously he had been the slave of an Athenian called Pleusicles (sailor), whose girlfriend, Philocomasium, was kidnapped from Athens and taken by the soldier. When he tried to tell his master, Palaestrio was sized by pirates and sold, by chance to the same solider. Palaestrio secretly manages to send a message to his previous master saying where both he and Philocomasium can now be found, and Pleusicles (his master) comes to find them. On arrival in Ephesus, Pleusicles stays in the house of an old man called Periplectomenus (entangler), who happens to live next door to the soldier, and visits are made between the houses by the two lovers, without Pyrgopolynices knowing. Trouble occurs when the lovers are seen kissing by another slave of the soldier. To try and explain the situation Periplectomenus and Palaestrio concoct the story that Pleusicles was actually kissing the twin-sister of Philocomasium who had recently arrived from Athens with her boyfriend. Further schemes ensue increasing the comic situation of the play, and the play concludes with Pleusicles, in disguise, managing to escort Philocomasium to a ship and leaving with her while the soldier is left having learned a serious lesson about himself and his treatment of others.

The plays of Plautus retained their popularity and were performed in Rome until the time of Horace, and they continued to be read by later generations as is attested by the discovery of a sixth-century manuscript. They also continued to be popular in Renaissance Italy and throughout Europe until well into the seventeenth century, thus helping to develop the European comic tradition.

THE NOVEL

The birth of extended fiction in prose form in the ancient world is particularly difficult to track given the large gaps in our evidence, and thus in our understanding of its development. Although there are some examples of Greek fiction, these are relative late-comers to the Greek literary tradition, because the examples that survive have all been dated to the first and second century C.E.

The tradition of the Roman novel starts with Petronius' *Satyricon*. The author of the work has generally been understood to be Petronius, the "arbiter of taste" from Nero's court, who was forced to commit suicide in 65 C.E. A portion of the work survives, however we have only books fourteen through sixteen of what has been suggested to be a work of perhaps twenty-four books when written. The extant section of the work is set in Southern Italy, and its plot revolves around the escapades of a homosexual couple. The main character and narrator, Encolpius—one of the couple—is infatuated with a young boy called Giton who accompanies Encolpius on his travels but continually deserts him. The only complete major event of the story is the *Cena Trimalchionis* (The Dinner of Trimalchio), which centers on a raucous and decadent dinner party hosted by the wealthy freedman, Trimalchio, which ends with the host rehearsing his own funeral and saying to his guests, "Pretend I am dead. Say something nice" (78). This part of the novel has proven the most popular section of the work; other partial scenes appear to depict the sexual antics and quarrels of the main protagonists. The scene of Trimalchio's feast highlights the important element of satire within this novel, which is suggested by the title as well as emphasizing the farcical nature of the story's plot.

PHILOSOPHY

Plato lived between c. 429 and 347 B.C.E. and was descended from an influential Athenian family. Having spurned marriage and the familial duty of producing male heirs to the family line, Plato founded a philosophical school in Athens called the *Academy* and spent his time in debate and investigation, through which he produced large numbers of written philosophical works. Beyond this, we know little about the biographical details of Plato's life.

All his texts are written in the form of dialogues in which Plato himself does not figure. This is an interesting technique, which separates him from the ideas expounded in his works and aims to force the reader to form his or her own opinions on the arguments presented. His works are generally divided into three periods: the early period, which includes the *Apology, Crito, Euthyphro, Protagoras,* and *Gorgias;* the middle period, which includes the *Symposium, Phaedo, Republic,* and *Phaedrus;* and the late period, which includes the *Sophist, Statesman, Timaeus,* and *Laws.* In his early examples, Plato focuses his dialogues on discussions of political and ethical ideas, which he places in the mouth of Socrates, who had had an important influence on Plato's philosophical ideals.

The *Republic,* from his middle period of work, was made up of ten books. Its Greek title was actually *On the State,* which was then translated into Latin as *Res Publica* giving us the English title *Republic.* The text describes a society governed by an intellectual elite, the "Guardians," trained in mathematics and philosophy. It is presumed that, because of its training, this governing elite could resolve problems faced both on mundane and more complex levels. This work argues that an individual's soul bears a similar structure to that of the state. It suggests that justice in the state is found when its three sections (its rulers, ruler's aids, and the citizenry) work together under the guidance of the governing elite. Similarly, justice in the individual is found when the three parts of a person's soul work harmoniously. In the *Republic,* each individual's justice revolves around identification of his or her own interests as far as possible in relation to the common interest of the state.

The philosophical influence of Plato throughout antiquity was immense. His works had a profound impact in the continuation of the Greek philosophical movement following his death, as well as in the development of philosophical thought in the Roman world. One example of Roman philosophy can be found in the philosophical texts of Cicero written during the first century B.C.E. Marcus

Tullius Cicero was born in Arpinum in 106 B.C.E. and died in 43 B.C.E. He was a prolific writer of correspondence, oratorical speeches, works on rhetoric, poems, and philosophy and examples of many of these have survived to today. His *De re publica* follows the form of a dialogue between Scipio Aemilianus, Gaius Laeius, and others, and is loosely based on the ideas put forward by Plato. We have only sections of the six books this work comprised, however the fragments give us an important insight into the ideas developed in the work. In it, Cicero examines the notion of the ideal State, in which he favors a mixture of the three constitutional systems of democracy, oligarchy, and monarchy. The experiences of the political upheavals of the late republic influence the arguments put forward in this work. This is arguably his most ambitious literary work and was closely followed by the related text of *De legibus*. Cicero's influence on European thought and philosophy of later centuries is significant; though he did not develop original philosophical ideas, his skill and importance lay in his articulate rewriting of Greek philosophy into Latin, which allowed Rome her own claims to the philosophical learning that had been regarded as so fundamental to Greek culture.

CONCLUSION

Given the fragile nature of our literary sources, it is unsurprising that many literary texts from the ancient world no longer survive. Those that do survive today are often rather fragmentary with sections, if not whole chapters, missing as has been demonstrated in many of the works discussed above. Moreover, it is not merely the particularly delicate nature of the written sources from Greece and Rome, nor the destruction of texts due to disaster or war, that has led to significant obstacles in salvaging literature from these ancient cultures. In many cases, the survival of literature from antiquity also relied upon judgments of its literary merit and relevance by individuals in later centuries. Thus while some (especially Christian texts, but also pagan works such as Virgil's *Aeneid*) were continuously recopied, others deemed less important were not. Just as clothing or hairstyles go in and out of fashion, the same might be said of literature, and it was the changing trends in literature that affected what examples make up the body of ancient literature that remains to us today. The texts surviving to date, which provide us with our corpus of ancient literature, are by no means an exhaustive list of the literature that existed in antiquity. It is worth noting that frequently in extant texts, ancient authors give us tantalizing hints of titles of works that have not survived from the ancient world. Furthermore, if we are fortunate, we can sometimes glean an insight into these lost texts and their subject matters from brief discussions in the works of other authors. In addition to these insights from existing texts, improvements in archaeological techniques have increased our abilities to find and read fragments of texts, such as the reading of fragments of carbonized texts found in the Villa of Papyri at Herculaneum. Thus there are always possibilities that new examples of Greek or Roman literature, as yet unknown or unread, might come to light and develop further our collection of literature from the ancient world.

It is perhaps surprising, given that so many literary works from antiquity have previously been lost, that copies of all the works discussed in this chapter are today available in print to varying extents. Published copies of all the above works can be obtained either in translation, in their original ancient language with commentaries, or both, as is the case with the *Loeb Classical Library* editions of the texts where the original language is printed alongside the translation. As well as

The Villa of Papyrii

The Villa of Papyrii was a luxurious residence situated outside Herculaneum on the Bay of Naples. By the time of its destruction in 79 C.E. following the eruption of Vesuvius, the residence had numerous rooms and internal and external gardens. Unearthed in the villa remains were over eighteen hundred carbonized scrolls of papyrus found in a room believed to be a library of the residence. Among these scrolls were found examples of Greek and Roman literature. In addition to these scrolls were uncovered a number of statues, herms and busts of important scholars and authors from the Greek and Roman world. Although names for possible owners of this villa have been proposed, the evidence behind these suggestions remains circumstantial given the incomplete nature of the excavations. A life-size reconstruction of the villa can be found in Malibu, USA. It was built by John Paul Getty, the oil tycoon and classical enthusiast.

different editions of translations and commentaries in English, many of which can be found in bookshops worldwide, all of the texts examined above have been published, at some point, as editions with either translations or commentaries in European languages such as German and Italian. All of these texts remain especially popular as they are often taught in schools and universities, thus encouraging frequent retranslation and publication. As well as being available as new copies from bookshops, many of the texts can be found in second-hand bookshops, markets, and public libraries. Moreover, copies of all the texts examined are available from libraries of schools and universities that run courses on the ancient world.

Technological advancements have resulted in a wide range of texts from antiquity being made available, either as translations or commentaries, on the Internet. Through classical websites such as the Perseus Project, perhaps the most comprehensive Internet resource for the ancient Western world, translations into English of the most popular works of ancient literature have been made available for study. Of the works discussed above, only those by Sappho, Petronius, and Catullus are not yet posted on the Perseus Project in either their original language or as translations. This online classical resource is, however, often updated, with new works and authors regularly being added to the existing database. As a method of encouraging people's contact with the literature of the ancient world, however, online publication of ancient literature is not without its problems. The most significant of these issues concerns copyrights and the replication of material on the Internet; avoiding copyright infringement results in many translations online being rather old-fashioned English translations, sometimes dating back to the early twentieth century and before. Thus, although the versions of classical texts produced online increases the availability of ancient texts, they do not necessarily encourage access to the freshest and most comprehensible translations.

Developments in television and film since the early twentieth century have further encouraged the adaptation of numerous texts for film and DVD. Examples of the films made for cinema can be seen in *Satyricon* (dir. Fellini, 1968), which depicts Petronius' *Satyrica* as a spectacular, if rather shocking, visual fantasy of Roman decadence; *O Brother, Where Art Thou* (dir. the Cohen Brothers, 2001), which was loosely based on Homer's *Odyssey* and set in deep south America in the 1930s; and *Troy* (dir. Wolfgang Peterson, 2004), a retelling of Homer's *Iliad* set in ancient Greece. Most recently, the film *300* (dir. Zack Snyder, 2006) focuses on the specific event of the Battle of Thermopylae as recorded by Herodotus in his history of the Persian Wars. There is even an example of a Broadway musical and film, *A Funny Thing Happened on the Way to the Forum* (dir. Richard Lester, 1966), which draws extensively on Plautus' *Miles Gloriosus*.

RECOMMENDED READING

Boardman, John, Jasper Griffin, and Oswyn Murray, eds. *The Roman World*. Oxford, UK: Oxford UP, 1986.

————. *The Greek World*. Oxford, UK: Oxford UP, 1986.

Boyd, Clarence. *Public Libraries and Literary Culture in Ancient Rome*. Chicago, IL: University of Chicago Press, 1915.

Casson, Lionel. *Libraries in the Ancient World*. New Haven, CT: Yale UP, 2001.

Easterling, Pat and Bernard Knox, eds. *The Cambridge History of Classical Literature: Volume I, Greek Literature*. Cambridge, UK: Cambridge UP, 1985.

Gavrilov, Alexander. "Techniques of Reading in Classical Antiquity." *Classical Quarterly* 47.1 (1997): 56–73.

Harrison, Stephen, ed. *A Companion to Latin Literature*. Oxford: Blackwell, 2005.

Kenney, E.J., ed. *The Cambridge History of Classical Literature: Volume II, Roman Literature*. Cambridge, UK: Cambridge UP, 1982.

Rutherford, Richard. *Classical Literatures: A Concise History*. Malden, MA: Blackwell, 2005.

Taplin, Oliver, ed. *Literature in the Greek World*. Oxford, UK: Oxford UP, 2000.

Taplin, Oliver, ed. *Literature in the Roman World*. Oxford, UK: Oxford UP, 2000.

PRIMARY SOURCES

Archilochos, Sappho, Alkman: Three Lyric Poets of the Late Greek Bronze Age. Translated by Guy Davenport. Berkeley, CA: U California UP, 1980.

Aristophanes. *Lysistrata, The Acharnians, The Clouds*. Translated by Alan Sommerstein. London: Penguin, 1973.

Catullus. *Carmen LXIV: A Prothalamion for Peleus and Thetis*. Translated by Charles Dennis. London: Burns, Oates and Washbourne, 1925.

Catullus. *The Complete Poems*. Translated by Guy Lee. Oxford, UK: Oxford UP, 1998.

Cicero. *De re publica: Selections*. Edited by James Zetzel. Cambridge, UK: Cambridge UP, 1995.

Herodotus. *Histories*. Translated by Aubrey De Selincourt. London: Penguin, 1996.

Hesiod. *Theogony, Works and Days, Testimonia*. Vol. 1. Edited and translated by Glenn Most. Loeb Classical Library. Cambridge, MA: Harvard UP, 2007.

Homer. *The Iliad*. Translated by Robert Fagles. London: Penguin, 1992.

————. *The Odyssey*. Translated by Robert Fagles. London: Penguin, 2004.

Horace. *Odes and Epodes*. Edited and translated by Niall Rudd. Loeb Classical Library. Cambridge, MA: Harvard UP, 2004.

————. *Satires*. Edited and translated by Henry Fairclough. Loeb Classical Library. Cambridge, MA: Harvard UP, 1929.

Livy. *Ab Urbe Condita*: bks 1–45, vol. I–XIV. Translated by Robert Forster. Loeb Classical Library. Cambridge, MA: Harvard UP, 1948–1959.

Petronius. *Satyricon*. Translated by John Sullivan. London: Penguin, 1965.

Pindar. *Olympian Odes & Pythian Odes*. Edited and translated by William Race. Loeb Classical Library. Cambridge, MA: Harvard UP, 1997.

————. *Nemean Odes, Isthmian Odes & Fragments*. Edited and translated by William Race. Loeb Classical Library. Cambridge, MA: Harvard UP, 1997.

Plato. *The Republic*. Translated by Henry Lee. London: Penguin, 1974.

Plautus. *Miles Gloriosus*. Mason Hammond, Arthur Mack, Walter Moskalew eds. Revised, Mason Hammond. Cambridge, MA: Harvard UP, 1997.

Plutarch. *Parallel Lives*, vols, I–XI. Translated by Bernadotte Perrin. Loeb Classical Library. Cambridge, MA: Harvard UP, 1914–1926.

Sappho. *Greek Lyric: Sappho and Alcaeus*, vol. I. Translated by David Campbell. Loeb Classical Library. Cambridge, MA: Harvard UP, 1928.

Seneca. *Four Tragedies and Octavia*. Translated by Edward Watling. London: Penguin, 1966.

Sophocles. *The Theban Plays*. Translated by Edward Watling. London: Penguin, 1973.
Suetonius. *The Twelve Caesars*. Translated by Robert Graves, revised, Michael Grant. London: Penguin, 1957.
Tacitus. *The Annals of Imperial Rome*. Translated by Michael Grant. London: Penguin, 1956.
Thucydides. *History of the Peloponnesian War*. Translated by Rex Warner. London: Penguin, 1974.
Virgil. *The Aeneid*. Translated by Robert Fagles. London: Penguin, 2007.

GREEK AND LATIN TEXTS AND TRANSLATIONS ON THE INTERNET

Perseus Project website*: http://www.perseus.tufts.edu.*

CHAPTER 5

Establishment of Christianity

Tiffany Yecke Brooks

TIMELINE

INTRODUCTION TO THE PERIOD

As the world unknowingly crossed the line that would later be deemed the divider of ancient times from the Common Era, the Roman Empire was reaching its apex. Culturally, some of the greatest writings of western antiquity were being composed by Lucan, Tacitus, Virgil, and both Pliny the Elder and his nephew, Pliny the Younger. Meanwhile, on the political front, the edges of the empire continued to expand. By 15 C.E., the empire contained approximately five million people within its borders and the armies continued to march onward, invading and conquering as they went.

These martial victories were not necessarily celebrated by the conquered peoples, however; although incorporation into the empire assured Roman protection and infrastructure, such benefits did not guarantee an improvement in lifestyle. Boudicca, the Celtic warrior Queen, led a famous and bloody rebellion against the Romans in the British Isles in 60–61 C.E. And when the Roman general (and later emperor) Titus destroyed Jerusalem in 70 C.E., the Jews were scattered throughout the empire, moving westward into Europe and deeper into the Middle East in large numbers. A few pockets of Jews remained and continued the battle for autonomy that their Maccabean ancestors had successfully waged from 164 to 63 B.C.E. They suffered a major blow in 73 C.E. when the Romans breached their stronghold at Masada after several months of siege, and discovered a mass suicide of 936 of the 943 Jews taking shelter there—two women and five children were the only survivors.

The political situation at the nerve center of the Roman Empire was shaky as well. A succession of mentally unstable emperors assumed control, including Caligula (whose appetite for perverse and extreme sexual excesses was legendary, and who sought to make his horse Incitatus a Senator, consul, or priest, depending on the source), and Nero (who famously set fire to Rome and blamed it on the new upstart religious band of Christ-followers). Others of similarly depraved and deranged mindsets would follow in subsequent centuries. Meanwhile, natural disasters ranging from Vesuvius to various plagues besieged the empire.

As Christianity began to take root and spread among the people, so did the fear of its growing power; but state-sanctioned persecutions did little to ebb Christianity's advance. In fact, the steadfast belief and peaceful embrace of death by many Christian believers even helped to spread the faith in some places. By some estimates, as many as fifteen million of the fifty-five million residents of the Roman Empire were Christians by the early fourth century, at the commencement of the last of the great persecutions enacted by Diocletian. As the Roman Empire began its decline, Christianity continued to prosper. In 359 C.E. the capital was transferred from Rome to Constantinople—a move that acted as a catalyst for ushering in the Byzantine era. Julian the Apostate, the last pagan emperor of Rome, attempted to reinstate the old religions during his reign from 361 to 363 C.E., but the momentum was now on the side of the Christians. The transfer of power, along with repeated attacks on Rome by various Germanic tribes, caused the population of the once-imperial city to dwindle to less than one hundred thousand people by the year 500 C.E. Christianity now held the preeminent spot in the Mediterranean, and well into Europe and the Middle East—a largely unchallenged position it would enjoy until the rise of Islam in the seventh century.

READING TRENDS AND PRACTICES

The first few centuries of the Common Era are perhaps most easily defined by the tensions contained therein. There were socio-political tensions occurring both on the borders of the expanding Roman domain and at the empire's heart. There were religious tensions occurring between the polytheistic religions of antiquity, the rebellious Jewish "zealots" in the eastern provinces, the newly emerging and rapidly spreading sect of Christianity, and the myriad mystery cults that bore similarities to all three. One of the subtler but ultimately most timely tensions, however, was the literary and historiographical one that was occurring between the various factions. The great question was, whose culture would eventually reign supreme?

For an era with such low literacy rates and such limited means of textual dissemination, it is a wonder that any debate took place at all, let alone one that raged so fiercely for several centuries. The old adage is certainly true to a point: History is written by the winner. However, there was no traditional battle and certainly no clear winner in the cultural struggles that define late antiquity. Though Christianity eventually emerged victorious over paganism, the road to establishing orthodoxy within that faith was by no means an easy one. Various letters, copied multiple times with little supervision (and subsequently, often altered or even forged) were the primary texts used to instruct the earliest Christian churches. Ascetic colonies and copy houses developed in the third and fourth centuries, but even then the body of texts being duplicated was by no means uniform from region to region, even after the Council of Hippo in 393 C.E. established the familiar twenty-seven book canon of the New Testament.

It is for these reasons—and many others—that any discussion of "common" literature of the time is sure to miss documents that were key in some areas while focusing on ones that were hardly known in others. The texts outlined in this section have been chosen for one of the following reasons: 1) archaeology and textual records provide ample evidence that they were widely disseminated throughout the Mediterranean and Europe; 2) the ideas or stories contained within the text are representative of commonly held ideas of the era; 3) the ideas or stories contained within the text had significance in later philosophy, doctrine, politics, science, or art; or 4) the work is representative of the kind of texts that were popularly consumed, though the content may have varied greatly.

The classification of these documents is difficult as well, as many texts had multiple purposes, such as to promote doctrine through the presentation of history, to disguise Christian teaching by presenting it in a creative and seemingly innocuous form, or to send church-wide instruction in personal correspondence. That the categorical lines are more often blurred than not demonstrates that the authors and readers alike clearly did not hold to the same concepts of genre as their modern counterparts; therefore, the works have been grouped into general categories that are perhaps more debatable than they are set. However, this lack of a clear literary taxonomy (at least among Christian texts) demonstrates that the religious beliefs of the writers were inseparable from their daily lives, education, and understanding of the world.

The politics of the era were ever-changing as battles were won and lost and peoples were conquered. Hellenism, the adoption of classical Greek beliefs and practices for the sake of social and political betterment, was a powerful force. The Romans encouraged it, as they believed association with Greece's Golden Age added to their own legitimacy as a cultural force and world power. The Roman Empire hoped to make an especially strong impression on the Jewish nation when it concluded the two hundred years of battles in Israel by sacking Jerusalem in 70 C.E. and destroying the Temple. The intent had been to assimilate the people fully into Roman control, but the effect was rather the development of strict and uncompromising sects that submitted to Roman rule only so far as it stayed out of religious observance—a precedent that was followed later by the Christians.

Among the emerging group of Christians, the first century of the era is marked by an outpouring of religious works intended to spread the word of the new faith, and to evangelize the masses by presenting the story of Christ's life, death, resurrection, teachings, and miracles. By the second and third centuries, most religious writings were either philosophical examinations of these texts, or forgeries that carried a specific theological agenda and purported to be of the earliest group of documents.

No fewer than a dozen (and almost certainly more) Gospels were circulating by the end of the second century, each bearing its own theological agenda. As various interpretive theories and heterodox varieties of belief (usually referred to as "heresies") arose, each one wanted a life story of Jesus that espoused its unique Christology. One of the most prevalent heterodox strains was Gnosticism, which maintained that secret knowledge was required to achieve harmony with the multiple sub-gods governing the universe. As Christianity developed its own theological doctrines further, the meditations and observations of various church leaders began to be composed, and were in turn consumed by the faithful. As some of these works began to be revered by certain churches, there arose a desire for distinction between the commentaries on holy writings and the actual holy writings themselves. This led to the difficult question of inspiration, and ultimately to an established canon.

And of course, Christianity was not the only religion generating literature around this time. Jewish writing had flourished in the centuries preceding the fall of Jerusalem, and scribal communities and sects were producing and reproducing texts that ranged from scriptural exegesis to community rules to enigmatic keys recording the whereabouts of wealth hidden from the Roman authorities. The Dead Sea Scrolls collection, ranging in age from the second century B.C.E. to the first century C.E., are perhaps the most famous examples of these kinds of texts.

Paganism was still the dominant faith for several generations, and many of the classically trained Latin philosophers were producing treatises of their own. Some of these directly addressed the new upstart religion; more never mention it. Scientific theories were also being composed in the non-Christian world that would prove to have lasting effects on Western medicine, astronomy, cartography, and navigation, as well as mathematical advances in the Middle East.

Most of these developments were taking place in the great centers of learning in North Africa and Asia Minor, where classical learning still abounded but was somewhat removed from the struggles of Rome. The increasing presence of the Germanic tribes and the receding borders of conquered lands spelled trouble for the empire. As the prosperous era of imperial expansion and relative peace came to a close toward the end of the second century, several emperors found a scapegoat in the burgeoning religion centered around the Jewish carpenter from Galilee—a common practice that only increased in severity as time went on. The resulting persecutions, which ranged from imprisonment to unspeakably cruel and horrifically creative means of execution and torture, did not succeed in killing off the new faith. Instead, such efforts only seemed to empower the believers, and stimulate even more proselytizing and conversion through treatises, letters, and books.

As Christianity began to develop an ever-growing following, traveling preachers and evangelizers began to develop their own means of spreading the Gospel and enlightening the masses as to the proper understanding and worship of God. Popular messages were often copied and sent to other churches that did not have the benefit of hearing the delivery first-hand, and also offered encouragement to Christians facing persecution. Scripted prayers helped believers by providing a template for worship and allowing the speakers to feel connected to their brothers and sisters in the faith, hundreds of miles away, who were offering up the same words and often suffering the same trials. But the common experiences and texts were not enough to combat other challenges that geographical separation was posing on the church.

Questions of liturgical practice, proper execution of rites, appropriate handling of those who denied Christ under legal duress but wished to repent, and basic administration plagued many young church bodies that longed for precedent and instruction. One means of determining proper religious practice and instruction was in studying the correspondence of the important figures in the early Church. At the time of their composition, the letters were generally directed toward one specific church and its issues, but with the understanding that copies of the Epistle were to be shared with other bodies of Christians. Colossians 4:16 is a clear example of this kind of textual exchange, as the church at Colossae is specifically instructed to make sure that the letter reaches the church in Laodecia, and that one of their letters is shared with the believers in Colossae. Letter-writing seems to have been an important means of communication in the early church, and compositions of particular theological importance were held in high esteem and cherished by Christians hungry for advice, encouragement, and personal greetings. Diaries and memoirs were also a popular form of written expression, though because these were often intended only as private musings, they were copied and distributed with far less regularity. Nevertheless, the personal insights that such documents grant modern scholars are important windows into the intricacies of the culture and psychology of the people.

As Christianity began to penetrate the more distant areas of Europe, pilgrimages began to arise as a means of reconnecting to the Holy Lands, as well as learning from the more established churches with close historical ties to the apostolic tradition. These travel narratives are important documents for several reasons. For their contemporary audiences, they were more than just entertaining accounts of recreational travel. Many of the early pilgrimage records consist largely of reports sent back home—usually somewhere in western Europe—with detailed descriptions of observances of the religious calendar and liturgical practices from the major Christian centers: Constantinople, Jerusalem, and Rome. Sometimes these writings focus on differences in traditions; at other times they may praise the younger church's consistency with the practices of the older ones. Shrines and churches began to be established on supposed holy sites of scripture, which prompted pilgrimages to increase. There eventually developed a kind of religious nostalgia for the Biblical lands—a sentiment that helped in large part to fuel the Crusades in the Middle Ages.

Creative expression also abounded, though it began to take different forms from many of the classical works of antiquity. Holy day liturgy seems to have filled the void created by the rejection of bawdy dramatic festivals, while narratives of spiritual visions and adventures were considered entertaining stories by some, sacred texts by others, and dangerous teachings by many of the church fathers. Other creative forms appear to be secret forms of religious expression during especially bad periods of persecution.

It was not until 313 C.E. that Christianity finally found a sympathetic ear with the Emperor Constantine, who granted it protection under the law and effectively put an end to the pursuit of its followers. With the reign of Emperor Theodosius at the end of the fourth century, Christianity was endorsed by the Roman government and became the official religion of the empire. Yet even as Rome was crumbling, its newly endorsed faith was spreading to the farthest reaches of the known world. Internal conflicts existed within the church that would later result in splits and schisms, but the religion was now established broadly and securely, with its own written history and the texts to bear testimony to its development.

POLITICAL TEXTS

Flavius Josephus' voluminous chronicles of the history of the Jewish people, *The Jewish Wars* (c. 75–79), are often criticized for exhibiting his Roman patronage, but it would be unfair to evaluate all of his works in this light, as he consistently defends his Jewish heritage and history. *The Jewish Wars,* Josephus' first major work, is an examination of the Maccabean revolts beginning in 175 B.C.E. against the Roman campaigns in the region, and ending with the invaders' destruction of Jerusalem in 70 C.E. He describes numerous sieges, such as the famous Jewish stand at Masada, which resulted in mass suicide rather than surrender to the Romans. Such death-before-defeat agreements were commonplace among Jewish groups who viewed subjugation to the pagan conquerors as a compromise of their religious obligations. A major theme of *The Jewish Wars* is the honorable and principled nature of Jewish citizens, and the unlikelihood of any further combat from their ranks.

Extremely popular among Romans and some Christians, Josephus was extremely unpopular among Jews, who considered him a traitor. Nevertheless, he authored a number of other important works including *The Antiquities of the Jews*, which was completed in 93 C.E. and outlines the history of the Jewish culture and faith from the creation of the world to the Roman era. *The Antiquities* was an especially well-received text among early Christians.

Also popular among early Christians was the heroic account of Polycarp's Christian spirit in the face of Roman persecution, known as the *Martyrdom of Polycarp* (second half of second century). As Bishop of Smyrna in Asia Minor, Polycarp was generally considered more of a community leader than a theological doctor, though several of his writings carried great importance among the young churches. His letter to the church at Philippi is still read in some Christian services in Asia today.

Perhaps Polycarp's most significant contribution to the developing church, however, was the example he set with his death. Recorded by his followers in Smyrna in epistolary form addressed specifically to the Church at Philomelium, and generally to believers throughout the world, this document gives a detailed account of the bishop's initial desire to hide from his persecutors, the heavenly vision that moves him to gladly accept his

Flavius Josephus, author of *The Jewish Wars,* was criticized for accepting Roman patronage, although his chronicles consistently defend his own Jewish heritage.

fate, and the love he shows toward his persecutors. The year of the event seems to be 155 C.E., when Polycarp was eighty-six years old, yet the elderly man is said to have demonstrated incredible strength and vivacity first in willingly surrendering himself to his pursuers and then in unflinchingly facing his death in the arena. Early in the narrative, one man who was to face his martyrdom is reported to have lost heart and recanted his faith in Christ before the crowd—an act that the authors of the letter condemn. The letter was clearly intended not only to memorialize Polycarp, but also to urge other Christians to follow the martyr's example of civil disobedience in the face of the Roman policies.

RELIGIOUS/PHILOSOPHICAL TEXTS

Gospels (accounts of the life of Christ) were among the very earliest Christian texts to have been written. A wide variety of Gospels were in existence, but the four canonical ones of the New Testament—*Matthew, Mark, Luke,* and *John*—also seem to have been the most commonly studied and widely read. However, the countless volumes of modern scholarship that have been dedicated to establishing exacts dates, influences, and even the exact identities of the four Gospel authors is overwhelming, and the most popular theories are always shifting.

The third canonical Gospel (85–90 C.E.) is an especially interesting text for several reasons. First, some scholars believe that it was written by a physician named Luke who was a traveling companion of Paul, though others believe the author did not know the apostle at all. Both schools of thought, however, generally agree that Luke was either Greek or perhaps a Hellenized Jew. The precise date of the text is difficult to determine, as is the meaning of its dedication to a patron named Theophilus. This is enigmatic because the name Theophilus means "lover of God," and there are varying schools of thought on whether this addressee is an actual individual or an allegory for all believers. For our purposes, though, what matters is that the Gospel did ultimately end up in the hands of a broad readership.

Luke begins his narrative with a brief synopsis of the events leading up to the birth of Jesus (an element excluded in many other texts), and pays special attention to Jesus' healings and the experiences of the poor and pariahed, before concluding with the longest post-Resurrection account of the canonical Gospels. Its companion text, *The Acts of the Apostles* (similarly dedicated to the mysterious "Theophilus"), narrates the evangelistic efforts of the disciples, the conversion and travels of Paul, and the establishment and growth of the earliest churches. Both *Luke* and *Acts* were universally accepted by the Council of Hippo.

Also approved by an overwhelming majority at the Council, *The Book of Hebrews* (unknown, late first century) is thought to have originated before the destruction of the Jewish Temple in 70 C.E., and was generally attributed to Paul from the fifth century onward. But before that point, and subsequently in the late Renaissance, serious questions arose about its supposed Pauline origin. In modern scholarship, such a notion has now been almost universally rejected. Several other authors have been suggested in Paul's place, with the two most likely being his former traveling companion Barnabus, a theory first put forward by Tertullian around 200 C.E.; or Apollos, who is mentioned several times in other canonical books (Acts 18:24, I Corinthians 1:12, 3:4–6, 22), and was suggested by Martin Luther. There are several self-referential passages in the text of Hebrews, but none that serve to elucidate the mystery. Whatever the case, the enigma surrounding the attribution of the work in no way diminishes the power of its message. The writer encourages his readers—mostly Jewish Christians who may be questioning their conversion—to draw on the strength of the patriarchs and Godly heroes of the Jewish faith, while looking toward the new covenant established through Jesus as the promised Messiah.

Within a century of the earliest Christian accounts of Christ's life and teachings, a new kind of writing began to emerge. Infancy Gospels were popular texts among the early Christians. These stories, which purported to fill in the holes of Jesus' childhood left out of the most mainstream Gospel narratives, were often filled with fantastic (and even bizarre) incidents that often read more like peccadillo tales than religious writings. In the *Infancy Gospel of Thomas* (anonymous, mid second century), for example, the activities of the Christ-child range from helping Joseph in the carpentry shop to hitting ignorant school teachers, turning playmates into pigs, and even killing (though eventually resurrecting) another boy.

The most popular of the Gospel prequels, however, was the *Protevangelium of James*. This text, which provides an explanation of the Immaculate Conception that left Mary without the mark of original sin, thus enabling her to bear the baby Jesus without passing original sin on to him, was an important document in the development of the veneration of the Virgin. It makes a case for her perpetual chastity and a harsh example of the midwife who dares to question the chaste birth. It embellishes the nativity elements of Gospels such as Matthew and Luke by adding back stories for the wise men and dramatizes Herod's decree to kill all infant boys. The *Protevangelium of James* was more widely received in eastern churches than western ones, though its prevalence throughout the Christian world can be attested to by the fact that it was a common source of inspiration for medieval artists.

The life of Christ was a popular subject for many early Christian writers. The *Diatessaron* (c. 175 C.E.), composed by the second-century philosopher, scholar, and Christian apologist Tatian, was a single narrative compilation of the life of Christ, and is thought to have been the first translation of any canonical works into Syriac. It seems to have been the only widely read Gospel text in Syria through the fourth century, and was eventually translated into Latin, Armenian, and Arabic. Early in the fifth century, the Bishop of Edessa finally ordered that all churches must have an individual copy of each of the four Gospels, but the *Diatessaron* remained the more popular text for several more decades.

Even as these texts about Jesus were being composed and consumed by the faithful, differing ideas about worship and the nature of Christ began circulating. The sharp

A 10th century icon of Luke working on his gospel.

rise in the number and popularity of heterodox sects in the second century was an obvious cause of concern among mainstream churches. The Gnostics, Marcionites, and Arians, among many others, were growing in strength and infiltrating orthodox churches with their interpretations, teachings, and literature. Irenaeus was a leader of the Smyrna church following the martyrdom of Polycarp, and wrote extensively on the growing problem of distorted Christian beliefs. Several of his personal letters to Christians who had joined heterodox groups have been found, but his most significant work was his volume *Against Heresies*, also called *The Detection and Overthrow of False Knowledge* (mid second century). This treatise was designed to caution other church leaders against erroneous teachings and was sought among many second- and third-century churches. It was considered essential reading for bishops and other leaders. Until archaeological finds in the twentieth century shed new light on the movement, *Against Heresies* was the primary source of our modern understanding of Gnosticism.

Others looked outside of the exclusive realm of Christianity for their inspiration. Origen's works are uniquely suited for their cultural context, as his main goal was to reconcile Greek philosophy with Christian teachings. In *On First Principles* (mid second century), Origen explains his theory that Christianity is not just a system of beliefs, but is actually the organizing force behind the universe, and has been the major point toward which all of human history has heretofore been angled. He was particularly interested in the notion of the Logos, which was a philosophical theory of perfection and infinite creation that was espoused by the Neo-Platonist and Stoics. Origen believed that this theory was put into physical form in the body of Christ.

He produced voluminous amounts of writings, many of which focused on discrediting of heterodox beliefs. His most important work on this subject, *Against Celsus*, was a popular text among later church leaders for combating false teachers. *Hexapla* is still often studied for its importance in historical textual reception and criticism, and the school he established in Alexandria produced countless intellectuals, theologians, church leaders, and Christian martyrs. The extent of Origen's theological influence was unmatched until Augustine, and his three-pronged approach to understanding scripture by literal, ethical, and allegorical means continued to influence Biblical scholarship through the medieval period.

As it grew in popularity and spread throughout the Mediterranean region, Christianity still faced fierce opposition. Though it now only exists in fragments—many of which, ironically, are preserved only in later Christian texts aiming to combat and refute Porphyry's assertions—the fifteen-volume treatise entitled *Against the Christians* (late third century), was a fierce defense of paganism and systematic deconstruction of the Christian faith. Porphyry questions Jesus' silence in his trial and dismisses it as cowardice, and elsewhere accuses Christ's followers of being a fractured, misled group of people with a fairly brutal disposition.

Porphyry also composed several important philosophical texts, including *The Introduction to Categories*, which reexamines Aristotelian logic in a Neo-Platonist light, and one called *The Cave of the Nymphs*.

Once their faith was granted legal status and protection, Christian leaders recognized the need to take stock of their religion's widespread and geographically diverse development. Called by the Emperor Constantine in an effort to set certain points of unifying orthodoxy and combat the growth of several heterodox branches, the Council of Nicaea was the first gathering of church leaders from throughout Christendom. The two major issues at-hand were the nature of the Trinity and the rise of Arianism, which claimed that Jesus was a being separate from and inferior to God. The resulting Nicene Creed (325 C.E.), which is still a part of the regular liturgy of many modern Christian churches, was a comprehensive but concise statement of

Early Readings in Vegetarianism

Following the example set by the classical philosopher Pythagoras, the Syrian Neo-Platonist Porphyry was a fierce proponent of animal rights for ethical reasons. He wrote two works on the subject, *On Abstinence* and the *On the Impropriety of Killing Living Beings for Food*, the latter of which enjoyed a fairly widespread readership and is still often featured in modern vegetarian propaganda.

beliefs made all the more significant by the fact that it was the first wide-spread effort to establish a uniform and concrete assertion of Christian doctrine among the regionally distinct congregations.

The most prolific writer of the early church and a champion of orthodox beliefs, Augustine of Hippo took on almost every religious issue of his day, as well as introducing doctrines that would incite theological debate for fifteen hundred years. He was named the Bishop of Hippo in 396 C.E., and his theological grasp is evident in his meticulously detailed sermons and letters on such varied topics as faith, conversion, marriage, widowhood, heresies, grace, sin, baptism, free will, Christ's teachings, the Psalms, and the nature of the soul. Augustine also authored a number of theological books, the most significant of which are *Confessions* (c. 397–398 C.E.), a highly emotional work in which he examines and acknowledges the presence of God in his own soul; and his magnum opus, *The City of God* (c. 413–c. 428 C.E.), which was begun in the early fifth century and completed around 428 C.E.

The City of God embraces a number of themes, including pagan accusations that the adoption of Christianity resulted in the fall of the Roman Empire. Augustine combats such claims by establishing the case of Christianity's role in mankind's destiny from the beginning, and God's presence in the historical and intellectual development of human history. The philosophies presented in this work are profound, and all of Augustine's writings quickly gained a loyal readership and awe-struck following as they spread beyond North Africa to Asia Minor and Europe, where they became foundational texts for much medieval theology.

ORATIONS

If Augustine was the pen of the growing church, John of Antioch (late fourth century) was the mouthpiece of it. The influence and importance of the sermons of John cannot be overestimated. His dynamic presentation is attested to by the appellation by which he is better known: "Chrysostom," which means "golden-mouthed." He longed to evangelize the Gothic tribes and even had part of the Bible translated into their language. His uncompromising theology resulted in his appointment to the Patriarchate of Constantinople in 398 C.E., but his unabashed attacks against governmental corruption earned him an unjust accusation of treason and eventual exile. Even after his banishment, he never ceased composing the homilies that were so dear to him.

It was for these sermons that Chrysostom was most famous. He often preached about the importance of active Christianity, and insisted that all Christian members of society needed to be useful. His speeches condemning wasteful, greedy, and immoral priests were especially resonant in certain circles, but it was his sermons on mercy, grace, forgiveness, humility, and holy praise that were the most popularly received and disseminated. Regarded by the Eastern Orthodox faith as one of the four Great Doctors of the Church, many of Chrysostom's writings were incorporated into Orthodox liturgy and essential study, and remained so through to modernity.

On the edges of the known world, Christianity was taking root as well. Patrick (late fifth century) is a notable figure because he is the first known Christian to evangelize the British Isles—an effort not otherwise widely attempted until the late sixth century outreach under Pope Gregory the Great—and his life reads more like an adventure tale than a journey of faith. At sixteen, he was abducted from the west coast of Britain by pirates while tending his sheep near the coast and was sold into slavery in Ireland. After six years of bondage to a cruel master who was also a Druid priest, Patrick met an angel in a dream who urged him to escape and preach the Christian faith to the Celtic people.

In his *Confessio,* Patrick writes of his days as a shepherd boy in which he would recite prayers, which helped to create a rhetorical link between himself and the psalmist David. Patrick continued to compose throughout his life, and many of the resulting prayers are not only worship aides, but also poems of great artistic merit that reflect devotion as well as chronicle his life. The prayer commonly known as "St. Patrick's Breast-Plate" is traditionally regarded to have been written as a celebration of the growth of

> **Saint Patrick's Biographers**
>
> It is interesting to note that Patrick had two early biographers in the seventh century, Celtic priests named Muirchú and Tírechán, who composed books about the saint and his writings.

Christianity against Druidism. Many of Patrick's other prayers take the form of blessings that have become an important tradition in Irish Christianity.

INSTRUCTIONAL/EDUCATIONAL TEXTS

Even as the religion was spreading, and in many cases factionalizing, early Christians sought direction in how to correctly and appropriately express their religion. Though written in letter form, *I Timothy* (unknown, late first c.) was composed to answer such questions by serving as a guide for how to properly administer a church and conduct worship. Included in the canonical Christian New Testament, it is addressed to Paul's former traveling companion, a Greek Christian named Timothy, who is now shepherding the church at Ephesus in Asia Minor. The letter contains precise details about the criteria for selecting church leaders, the expected cultural behavior of women in worship settings, praying for governmental leaders, and replacing materialism with Godly contentment. It was traditionally ascribed to Paul and often read alongside *Titus,* also a traditional Pauline Epistle with a similar theme. Because of stylistic and vocabulary choices, however, modern scholarship generally holds that *I Timothy* may have been the product of an unknown author and not Paul himself.

A similarly themed document called the *Didache* (unknown, c. 100 C.E.), also known as *The Teaching of the Twelve Apostle to the Nations,* is a detailed instruction manual that lays out precisely how Christians were to conduct their lives and their liturgical practices. It includes directions for proper fasting, praying, and administration of the Eucharist, as well as offering advice on how to distinguish between and appropriately handle traveling preachers and false prophets. The *Didache* is one of the earliest noncanonical documents in existence and reveals a great deal about the practices of the earliest Christians. The extent of its readership is not clear, however, as many of its instructions seem to have been disregarded by—or were not common practice in—other roughly contemporary churches, and it was not even known to modern scholarship until 1873, when a copy of it was uncovered in Constantinople among the copious holdings of the Patriarchal Library.

The history of Christianity became a popular subject in late antiquity. Eusebius, a versatile theologian who was appointed Bishop of Caesarea Palestine around 313 C.E., was a respected leader who figured prominently at the Council of Nicaea in 325 C.E., and a prolific author who composed copious apologies, exegetical works, treatises, letters, and sermons. It is his historical study, however, that earned him the nickname the "Father of Church History."

Though the reign of Diocletian had ushered in some of the worst persecutions—Eusebius himself was even imprisoned for a short time—many theologians were recognizing that the era of the primitive Church was fading away and that efforts must be taken to preserve what was left of their practices and traditions. Eusebius reacted by authoring *The History of the Church* (early fourth century), a compendium of ecclesiastical records of the early church that remains a seminal text for Christian historians.

Yet despite its detailed records, it is certainly not a comprehensive nor objective study of the development of the faith. For example, the *History of the Church* is focused almost exclusively on the development of the Christian faith in the east and seems to indicate that Eusebius' knowledge of the western branch of the faith was very limited. He knew very little Latin, a fact that probably limited his access to the texts of western church leaders who wrote in that language. He also glosses over a number of early—and very important—controversies and doctrinal debates. Nevertheless, the text was broadly studied in late antiquity and has remained an important piece of historical and historiographical literature ever since.

The interest in history is also evident in the writings of Gregory of Tours. Born to a powerful family in what is now France, Gregory's life exhibits some of the major shifts that took place during the fourth and fifth centuries with regard to the place of Christianity in society; his family's prominence was bolstered by the presence of several Christian leaders, including an uncle who was Bishop of Clermont, and to whom Gregory was sent to live. Gregory later became a bishop himself and was canonized after his death. Nevertheless, he often mourned his lack of a secular education and viewed his exclusively Christian schooling as something of a handicap. He never swayed from strict orthodoxy, however, and adhered to the belief that the history of mankind was actually the history of God's interaction with the world.

The *History of the Franks* (c. 575–c. 595 C.E.) is a ten-volume work composed over two decades, which chronicles the creation of the world to Gregory's own day. The first book is an ambitious account stretching from the Garden of Eden to the arrival of the Frankish tribes in Gaul. The subsequent books are detailed, almost year-by-year summaries of the political and social changes that were taking place in the country. Although the writing is always matter-of-fact, and almost journalistic in its reporting, Gregory of Tours always manages to remind the reader of the presence of the supernatural in the unfolding events and developing story.

SCIENTIFIC TEXTS

Though political and religious changes often get the most attention during this era, scientific knowledge was continuing to prosper as well. Claudius Ptolemaeus was a member of the powerful Greek Ptolemy dynasty that controlled much of Egypt following the conquests of Alexander the Great in the fourth century B.C.E., but his interests lay in science and mathematics rather than politics. He authored a number of works on astronomy and geography, including the *Tetrabiblios,* which was a treatise on the observation and interpretation of celestial movements, and *Geography,* which was a seminal work on the issue of cartography, topography, and land study through the Age of Discovery in the sixteenth century. His works were studied as far abroad as the Middle East and India.

Ptolemaeus' most important work, however, was the *Almagest* (mid second century), also called the *Mathematical Syntaxis* or *The Great Treatise*), in which he compiled ancient observations of the heavens with his own studies to make a compendium of astronomical knowledge. The *Almagest* makes detailed observations of the solar system that includes tracing the paths of the planets, moon, and sun. His theory of the spherical construction of the universe, which maintains a geocentric system around which various celestial bodies are suspended on crystal spheres, was the accepted model for nearly fourteen hundred years, until Copernicus' 1543 theory of a heliocentric universe gained wide-spread acceptance. Other of Ptolemaeus' ideas did not gain such a popular following, such as his theory that the earth was spherical and that cartographers must adjust projections accordingly.

Medical science was also making advances; healing was regarded as both a science and an art among the Greeks of antiquity, and by the time he was twenty, Galen had studied the practice extensively enough to work as an attendant in one of the temples of his hometown, Pergamum, which was dedicated to Asclepius, the Greek god of healing. He later gained experience in triage treatment when he served as a physician to gladiators in training.

Through his study of wounds and experiments on live animals, Galen was able to gain a detailed knowledge of the body and its hidden workings. His most comprehensive work, *On the Usefulness of the Parts of the Human Body* (mid-late second century), consisted of seventeen volumes and theorized on the workings of the brain, heart, liver, and the *pneuma*—or essence of life—that medieval Christian readers would equate to the notion of a soul. Most importantly to the acceptance and longevity of his work, however, was his assertion that life was the obvious result of a single, design-minded creative entity.

Because much of his experimentation and composition was conducted in Rome, his writings were primarily in Latin, which helped to establish it as the language of science. Galen's works were considered an essential part of the medical canon until well into the sixteenth century.

CREATIVE TEXTS

Healing was an art with practical applications, which many of the early Christian creative writings had as well. Language crafting coupled with moral messages to produce a number of simultaneously beautiful and didactic texts. In the middle of the second century, for example, the brother of a Roman bishop composed a lengthy work that describes a series of visions in which he receives instruction from several characters, including the shepherd of the title. Hermas (the author) is presented with a list of twelve commandments for Christian living, as well as instruction from various angelic beings, who often present their messages to him in the form of parables. At times the work seems allegorical, as one of the angels takes the form of a backwards-aging woman, who says that she represents the Church, and eventually appears as the radiant bride of Christ.

The book deals with several themes, the most basic being the issue of repentance for baptized believers and whether salvation can be lost and regained. *The Shepherd of Hermas* (mid second century) also takes a harsh stance on those Christians who have outwardly committed to the faith but still question the teachings of the Church or the veracity of Christian claims, or who continue to find the temptations of the world alluring.

The Codex Sinaiticus, which dates from the fourth century, incorporates this book into its version of the New Testament canon, and it seems to have had a number of supporters for its inclusion at Hippo. Eventually, however, its authorship resulted in its elimination; it was clearly the work of a later convert rather than one of Christ's original companions, and its theology was not universally accepted. Nevertheless, the text maintained its popularity and was read well into the fifth century. Even as it passed from being accepted as theological literature, it still seems to have been read by many early Christians as a kind of spiritual or moral entertainment.

Other creative works enjoyed less attention from the church authorities, but greater popularity among the laypeople. Even though it was considered early on to be a work of fiction originating in Asia Minor, the unusual book, *The Acts of Paul and Thecla* (c. 180–190 C.E.), was accepted by many churches as a powerful testimony to the persistence of faith. It even resulted in veneration of Thecla in certain areas. It tells of a female follower of Paul who rejects her former life in order to travel with the apostle. Paul is not enthusiastic about Thecla's company, and despite her pleadings he declines to baptize her. Later, she is sentenced to death for refusing the sexual advances of a powerful but lascivious man. Thecla survives multiple execution attempts and finally, because of Paul's denial of her request, baptizes herself in a barrel full of water and carnivorous sea animals. In the end she is blessed by Paul and encouraged to preach to the nations.

The popularity of the text was considered dangerous by several church fathers because it depicted a woman preaching, baptizing, and at one point, even wearing men's clothes. Despite—or perhaps because of—these unconventional elements, *The Acts of Paul and Thecla* enjoyed wide reception well into the Middle Ages.

The heterodox sects had their own creative output. *The Hymn of the Pearl* (late second century), for example, a lyric story of a prince's quest to retrieve a pearl from the clutches of an Egyptian dragon, is an interesting intersection between folk traditions and Christian mysticism. On the surface it reads like a compact epic with little theological value. But the text itself—which appears as part of the *Acts of Thomas*, a third-century Gnostic book that seems to have lifted the *Hymn* from an unknown second-century work—addresses such themes as the awakening of the soul from its temporary, earthly blindness in order to recognize its duality, which is very much in line with Gnostic teachings.

In an interesting bridge between Christian and pagan writings, a series of works emerged in the mid-fourth century by a Roman noblewoman and Christian convert named Proba. Her poems—only one of which is extant—were written in the style known as *centos*. Centos were an art form that functioned as something of a patchwork quilt of classic epics, wherein passages would be lifted from context and rearranged to tell a completely new story. The technique was not a new one, but it has been proposed by a number of scholars that Proba's compositions may have stemmed from the decree in 362 C.E. by Julian the Apostate, that Christians would no longer be allowed to teach classical writings to students.

Proba's most famous cento, often referred to as *Cento Virgilianus* (mid fourth century) because it consists of 694 lines of Virgil's writings, may have been written as a means of smuggling a Christian message through to her readers in the form of the classical texts otherwise forbidden to them. The *Cento Virgilianus* forms a kind of Christian history of the world. It begins with God's creation of the world and man, and proceeds through various Biblical narratives until it concludes with the resurrection and ascension of Christ.

Roughly contemporary with Proba's work is the *Cento Nuptualis* (mid fourth century), by the Gaullic poet Ausonius. His text relied on the battle scenes of the

Iliad to give a graphic and violent recounting of sexual conquest on a couple's wedding night. Ausonius is said to have become a Christian late in life, a conversion that was apparently made rather grudgingly, and only because religious trends of the empire continued to shift in that direction.

One aspect of the centos that makes them so potentially interesting is that they are a two-fold revelation of commonly read literature of the time. In one aspect, they show creative retellings of themes important at the time of their arrangement. But they also demonstrate that many older, classical works were still very much part of the common cultural literacy, as the potency of the cento depended a great deal on the reader's or hearer's recognition of and appreciation for the original source of the repackaged lines.

> **Ausonius and the Victorians**
>
> Many of Ausonius' works were so bawdy or explicit that they were often left untranslated by Victorian publishers of Latin volumes, because it was feared that they could morally corrupt the school boys who might encounter the verses in their study.

TRAVEL NARRATIVES

The first Christian pilgrim of note was Helena, the mother of Emperor Constantine, who was a devout Christian and probably very influential in her son's conversion. Her travels were compiled in a document by Eusebius, *Travels of Helena* (c. 335 C.E.). Helena's pilgrimage to the Middle East in c. 320 C.E. was driven by her intense desire to worship in the same place as Christ and to make such an opportunity available to other Christians. As a result, much of her trip was dedicated not only to benevolence to the poor and sick, but also to the location and identification of sacred sites. Many of the locations she deemed as noteworthy are still standard stopping points on modern religious tours of the Holy Lands. Her system of finding and naming sites was rather haphazard—local tradition combined with her belief in spiritual guidance led her to "find" many sacred sites, including the cave in Bethlehem where Christ was born and placed in a manger; the Via Dolorosa—that is, the winding pathway through the city streets through which Jesus and Simon of Cyrene were forced to carry the cross; Golgotha, where the crucifixion was said to have taken place; and even the True Cross itself, which was to be of such fame and abundance at the height of the medieval relic craze. Following Helena's death in c. 330 C.E., Constantine began construction of many of the famous basilicas built upon the holy sites, such as the Church of the Holy Sepulcher, based upon his mother's instructions.

Helena's journeys were recorded in narrative form by several authors, but the earliest and most significant was Eusebius' in his *Life of Constantine,* which was written around 340 C.E. and was testament to the importance that was already being placed upon her pilgrimage in the years immediately following her visit.

Not long after Helena's journey to the Holy Lands, there is another recorded account of a pilgrimage from the West, in what is commonly referred to as simply *Itinerary of an Anonymous Pilgrim of Bordeaux* (c. 333 C.E.). This document, which records a journey taken in c. 333 C.E., is a straight-forward text originating in the Gallic city of Bordeaux, from whence the manuscript derives its name. The traveler writes of his journeys to Constantinople via Milan and the ancient city of Sirmium in the Balkans, then of his further travels to Jerusalem and the surrounding country. It is here that he observes the early stages of the church construction decreed as a result of Helena's pilgrimage, before returning home through Heraclea (a Greek colony in northwest Turkey) and Rome. The traveler's intended audience is not specified, but as his itinerary was recorded by him in a journal-like form at the time of the trip rather than being recounted at a later date, it is actually the earliest extant record of a Christian pilgrimage even though it post-dates Helena's visit by roughly ten to fifteen years.

Roughly between 381 and 384 C.E., a Spanish nun named Egeria also underwent a pilgrimage and recorded her experiences in a series of letters that she composed for her sisters back home, which have collectively come to be known as *Travels of Egeria, a Spanish Nun*. Though only part of her writings survive, and these in the form of an eleventh-century manuscript copy of an unknown source, her words certainly had a broader audience than just the women of her cloister. A seventh-century letter by a Galician monk mentions Egeria's letters and her conduct as worthy of approbation, and indicates that her audience had expanded at least to other regions of the Iberian Peninsula.

Though her writings are sometimes rather difficult to follow—they read more like transcribed casual speech than polished compositions—her enthusiasm and reverent awe are both charming and admirable. Her writings were obviously composed with great care and received with equal enthusiasm. Her desire to share the practices of her beloved religion with those at the farthest reaches of Christianity's borders is evident. She fills her descriptions of her climb of Mt. Sinai with vivid detail, and notes with interest the efforts to identify and preserve various holy places. She also makes special efforts to visit shrines dedicated to early Christian women of note, such as Thecla.

Perhaps most significant of Egeria's recorded observations, however, are her meticulously detailed recountings of liturgical practices of Christian worship services in the major geographical centers of the faith. Because Egeria's stay is so lengthy, she has the opportunity to take part in several Christian observances of special feasts, and to record the rituals of such major celebrations as Epiphany. She also takes interest in the study of baptism candidates who are preparing for their Easter morning immersion.

Probably within the year following Egeria's return to Spain, two more female pilgrims undertook to record their own travels to the Holy Lands. The journey of a wealthy widow named Paula and her daughter Eustochium is outlined in a letter the women penned to a friend named Marcella, who remained back home in Rome. Their trip included not only the now-traditional pilgrim stops in Israel and Turkey, but also visits to shrines in North Africa, and ended with them taking up permanent residence in Bethlehem. There they acted as patronesses to the great translator Jerome, as he labored to produce the Latin Vulgate version of the Bible from existing Hebrew and Greek manuscripts. In fact, it is Jerome to whom we are in debt for preserving the text of Paula and Eustochium's letter, known as *Travels of Paula and Eustochium* (c. 404 C.E.), in his own collected *Epistolae*.

From her writings, we learn that Paula is especially struck by the poverty in Bethlehem as opposed to the opulence of Rome. Jerome also records the willingness with which the mother and daughter undertake the study of Biblical texts and the language of Hebrew so that they might participate more fully in singing the psalms, as well as have an active hand in Jerome's translation efforts.

PERSONAL TEXTS

Of the canonical epistles, *I Thessalonians* was written c. 49–51 C.E., and is one of Paul's earliest canonical letters. Addressed to a demographically diverse church of both Jewish and gentile converts in the booming Macedonian city of Thessalonica, the Epistle contains a message of support and comfort to the Christians, especially in light of what seems to have been local persecutions. Paul also employs some eschatological language to remind his readers about the Second Coming of Christ, and to encourage them to vigilance and faithful living.

Another Pauline Epistle, *II Corinthians,* was written around 55 C.E., and addresses the infiltration of nonorthodox teachers who are diluting and manipulating Paul's message. He confronts these detractors generally, while specifically attacking those who have falsely accused him of pilfering benevolence gifts for the impoverished Christians in Jerusalem. Paul urges the church to discipline the troublemakers and also exhorts them to humility, prayer, generosity, and hope.

Romans, which most scholars agree was also composed by Paul between 55 and 58 C.E., is intended for the predominantly gentile church in Rome. It addresses basic doctrinal points of the Gospel of Christ, as well as questions of salvation—especially those concerning the small but significant Jewish sector of the assembly.

Philemon is an intriguing letter from c. 60 C.E. that is a short text and perhaps the most personal of all of Paul's preserved writings. Its intended recipient is a wealthy Christian by the name of Philemon who is living in Colossae in Asia Minor. Some time earlier, a slave named Onesimus from Philemon's household ran away, studied under Paul, and converted to the Christian faith. Onesimus is now returning to Philemon and bearing the letter from Paul, which asks that he be received mercifully and as a brother in Christ.

Paul was not the only letter-writer to have his words added to the canon, though. *I Peter* was widely accepted by the early church fathers as being from the pen of Jesus' disciple Peter. Modern scholarship has called into question its artistic use of Greek, which some feel to be beyond the grasp of a fisherman-turned-itinerant-preacher; and although some scholars maintain that the influence of Hellenism was pervasive enough throughout the Mediterranean to affect the speech and writing of the laboring classes, others believe that *I Peter* is from an unknown source in the very late first or early second century. The letter is intriguing in that it seems to indicate a familiarity with several of Paul's Epistles, and has a consistent message with them in advocating courage in the face of persecutions, reminding the readers of the wonder of God's grace, and urging them to persevere with their holy living.

Several canonical texts are preserved in the Christian New Testament without clear attribution. This is due, in large part, to the fact that the original authors were not seeking personal glory in having their names attached to their writings. Rather, they sought to communicate with churches in order to instruct, encourage, and evangelize in a variety of ways. *Jude* is one such enigmatic text, for which the proposed dates of composition range from 65 to 80 C.E. Some theologians believe that the author is the same man described as the brother of Jesus in Matthew 13:55 and Mark 6:3. Other scholars have questioned this claim, however, as there does not seem to be any direct evidence for such an assertion. The letter, which is one of the shortest works of the canonical New Testament, contains references to stories not mentioned in the Hebrew scriptures, but which do appear in apocryphal literature. As a result of its mysterious composition and content, *Jude* was almost not included in the canon. It barely managed to garner enough support at Hippo because it seems to be addressed to Christians at large, and it takes an orthodox stance against heterodox teachers.

Letters from popular religious figures were not limited to the earliest generation of Christians, although these epistles are not part of the Christian canon. *I Clement* is thought to have originated in Rome, and was sent to the church at Corinth between 95 and 96 C.E. Purportedly from Clement, the leader of the Roman church, it addresses a change in leadership in the Corinthian church that was considered potentially problematic. The letter insists that the situation must be rectified and that the instigators be disciplined. The letter seems to have been received with solemnity, regarded with authority, and was treated like scripture by many Christians even after it failed to be deemed canonical at the Council of Hippo.

In an interesting trend that arose about a century after the composition of the works that would eventually form the Christian New Testament, some correspondence was actually forged to create an air of authority. The letter *III Corinthians* was also addressed to the notoriously troubled church at Corinth, as were the two canonical letters to the same congregation. Appearing in the apocryphal *Acts of Paul*, and ostensibly written by that text's title figure, the book and contained epistle were actually created in the late second century, and may have originally been independent documents brought together to form the complete text. The letter takes up some of the same concerns as do the two canonical letters—gluttony, drunkenness, and selfish behavior during fellowship meals, rampant sexual immorality, and heretical teachings. The main focus of *III Corinthians* is on a literal interpretation of the physical reality of Christ's crucifixion and the resurrection of the body, and it appears to have been read as an authentic piece of correspondence in Asia Minor until it failed to gain acceptance into the canon because of the obvious impossibility of it having been written by Paul.

Another attempt at forgery, the *Letters of Paul and Seneca* seem to be a fourth-century attempt to assert the legitimacy of Christianity by claiming that it held the attention of the great Roman minds of the first century. This collection of correspondence consists of fourteen written exchanges between the scholar and politician Seneca and the apostle Paul. "Seneca" claims to have read Paul's writings to the Emperor Nero, and that both men were profoundly impressed by the truths contained therein. The choice of characters seems especially odd, considering Nero's famed persecutions of the early church, but the writings were a popular text of study in monasteries from late antiquity through the Middle Ages.

One of the most touching and deeply personal sets of writings we have from the early Christian period was originally part of a widely disseminated text that told the story of two female martyrs and their courage in the face of death. *The Martyrdom of Perpetua* (early third century) is a work in twenty-one parts that is the obvious amalgamation of several authors, but the authenticity of which is generally confirmed by modern scholars.

The story is set in Carthage during one of the many waves of persecutions that swept the Mediterranean, including North Africa, during the late second and early third centuries. The book of the *Martyrdom* was compiled soon afterward by at least one editor, who provides commentary that bookends the work and contains both exposition and a detailed narration of the violent deaths of Perpetua and a number of other Christians. The internal sections are thought to be the actual prison writings of Perpetua (sections 3–10) and another victim, a man named Saturus (sections 11–13). The words of Perpetua are an intimate look at her hopes, fears, and beliefs as she awaits her death. She has been separated from her entire family, including being disowned by her Roman father and rejected by her unbelieving husband. She is forced to surrender her child and submit herself to imprisonment and eventual death in the arena by wild animals and armed men.

These writings are particularly poignant in light of many other martyrdom accounts, which by modern standards seem overly embellished and generally feature protagonists too perfect to seem real. Perpetua does not shy away from admitting that she is worried and scared, but she nevertheless outlines her religious convictions and asserts her faith. She demonstrates humanity packaged in absolute grace. When her own writings conclude and the editor again takes up the narration to tell the reader of the story's conclusion, he makes careful note of how Perpetua, before entering the arena, requested a hairpin so that she could make herself presentable in what she felt was her greatest moment.

The Martyrdom of Perpetua, which circulated throughout the Mediterranean region for several centuries, is the first extant example of writing by a Christian woman. It has attracted renewed attention in recent decades by feminist scholars interested in the broad readership and religious significance assigned to such a work.

CONCLUSION

The Byzantine Empire had expanded to its largest size by the middle of the sixth century, encompassing the majority of the Mediterranean basin and firmly planting Christianity and the Latin language as the unifying elements in an otherwise factional and diverse region. Constantinople was now the recognized political center of the Christian world, but even as it was an important hegemonic presence, the empire's position was precarious. Rome had already fallen to the various Germanic tribes that had threatened invasion for decades, and a new threat loomed in the sands to the south and east.

By the middle of the seventh century, wars with the Persian Empire caused the Byzantines' boundaries to shrink; and just as Christianity had usurped pagan and native religions in the previous centuries, its hard-fought battle for supremacy in the region was challenged by another up-start faith. As Islam took root in the Middle East and began its expansion up and out from the Arabian Peninsula, many former Christian areas were converted to the new religion. By the middle of the eighth century, Islam had even taken root in Europe, with most of the Iberian Peninsula falling under the control of the Umayyad Caliphate.

The Library at Alexandria also disappeared from the scholastic landscape during this time. Having previously faced destruction at the hands of Caesar in 48 B.C.E. as outlined in Plutarch's *Lives,* it seems to have undergone another pillaging during the Roman emperor Aurelian's attack on the city in c. 272 C.E. In a fit of religious fervor in 391 C.E., the Christian Emperor Theodosius I ordered that all pagan temples and centers of worship in Alexandria be disbanded, and the library, though not itself a religious structure, seems to have suffered because of the content of some of its holdings. Finally, when the Arab invasions swept through northern Egypt in the 640s, the library's remaining contents were again threatened. History does not make clear whether the wanton destruction of the library, later reported to have occurred in this last raid, was an actual historical event, or if it was merely a sensationalized account of the city's fall that would serve as propaganda for eager medieval crusaders. Whatever the case, the library had a turbulent past reflecting the various political and martial power shifts in the region. By the dawn of the eighth century the library was obsolete, if not obliterated.

Meanwhile, the western edges of Europe had their own violent reality with which to contend. The Anglo-Saxons who swept into Britain from Germany and Denmark beginning in the fourth century were to face their own invasions from the north, as the Viking raids began in the eighth century. As Europe slipped into what would later be termed the Dark Ages, the literary, architectural, and technological advances that had flourished in earlier centuries slowed. Literacy, while never widespread, was now almost the exclusive realm of the Church. The abundance of early Christian texts that had once persisted across the Mediterranean were now cloistered in monasteries or, because of their noncanonical status, simply slipped into oblivion, as their words were forgotten or literally wiped clean from the page by economically minded scholars seeking to reuse pages of valuable velum. Many of the traditions remained, however, and would emerge again in medieval art and vernacular spirituality.

RECOMMENDED READING

Clark, Elizabeth. *Ascetic Piety and Women's Faith: Essays on Late Ancient Christianity.* New York: Edwin Mellen Press, 1986.

Clark, Gillian. *Women in Late Antiquity: Pagan and Christian Lifestyles.* New York: Oxford University Press, 1994.

Ehrman, Bart D. *Lost Christianities: The Battles for Scripture and Faiths We Never Knew.* New York: Oxford University Press, 2003.

———. *Lost Scriptures: Books that Did Not Make It into the New Testament.* New York: Oxford University Press, 2003.

Krueger, Derek. *Writing and Holiness: The Practice of Authorship in the Early Christian East.* Philadelphia: University of Pennsylvania Press, 2004.

McGill, Scott. *Virgil Recomposed: The Mythological and Secular Centos in Antiquity.* Philadelphia: American Philological Association, 2005.

Moynahan, Brian. *The Faith: A History of Christianity.* New York: Doubleday, 2002.

Wright, Neil. *History and Literature in Late Antiquity and the Early Medieval West: Studies in Intertextuality.* Variorum Press, 1995.

PRIMARY SOURCES

It should be noted that some works, such as the Nicene Creed, may be found in many books of Christian liturgy. Further, some texts, such as the prayers of Saint Patrick, are usually printed individually rather than in a compendium or collection. Other texts, such as the *Itinerary of an Anonymous Pilgrim of Bordeaux, The Travels of Paula and Eusotchium,* and *Cento Nuptualis* have fallen out of print, but enjoy a new life in fairly reliable translation on several websites dedicated to early Christian writings or texts from late antiquity.

Readers should also note that some of the editions listed here have maintained the original Latinate version of the title, even though the text itself has been translated into English, or an editor has opted to use a slightly different version of the title than what is most common. In such cases, the title of the work as it is discussed above is enclosed in parenthesis but listed first for ease of reference. The title of the work as it appears in the printed version of the primary document referenced for this work follows.

The Acts of the Apostles. NRSV Harper Study Bible ed. Grand Rapids: Zondervan, 1991.

(*The Acts of Paul and Thecla*) *The Acts of Thecla. Lost Scriptures: Books that Did Not Make It into the New Testament.* Edited by Bart D. Ehrman. New York: Oxford UP, 2003.

Augustine of Hippo. *The City of God.* Translated by Henry Bettenson. New York: Penguin Classics, 2003.

Didache. Loeb Classical Library: the Apostolic Fathers, I: I Clement. II Clement. Ignatius. Polycarp. Didache. Translated by Bart D. Ehrman. Cambridge: Harvard UP, 2003.

Egeria. *Egeria: Diary of a Pilgrimage.* Edited by George E. Gingras. Westminster, MD: Newman P, 1970.

Eusebius. *Eusebius: the Church History.* Edited by Paul L. Maier. Grand Rapids, MI: Kregel Publications, 2007.

———. *Life of Constantine.* Translated by Averil Cameron and Stuart Hall. New York: Oxford UP, 1999.

First Peter. NRSV Harper Study Bible ed. Grand Rapids, MI: Zondervan, 1991.

First Thessalonians. NRSV Harper Study Bible ed. Grand Rapids, MI: Zondervan, 1991.

First Timothy. NRSV Harper Study Bible ed. Grand Rapids, MI: Zondervan, 1991.

Galen. *On the Natural Facilities.* Whitefish, MT: Kessinger, 2004.

The Gospel of Luke. NRSV Harper Study Bible ed. Grand Rapids, MI: Zondervan, 1991.

Gregory of Tours. *A History of the Franks.* Trans. Lewis Thorpe. New York: Penguin Classics, 1976.

Hebrews. NRSV Harper Study Bible ed. Grand Rapids, MI: Zondervan, 1991.

"The Hymn of the Pearl." *Lost Scriptures: Books that Did Not Make It into the New Testament.* Edited by Bart D. Ehrman. New York: Oxford UP, 2003.

Irenaeus. *Against Heresies.* Whitefish, MT: Kessinger, 2004.

John Chrysostom. *The Divine Liturgy of St. John Chrysostom: the Greek Text with the English Translation.* Translated by C. C. Canellopoulos. Whitefish, MT: Kessinger, 2007.

Josephus, Flavius. *The Jewish Wars.* Translated by G. A. Williamson. New York: Penguin Classics, 1984.

Jude. NRSV Harper Study Bible ed. Grand Rapids, MI: Zondervan, 1991.

(*I Clement*) *The Letter of First Clement. Lost Scriptures: Books that Did Not Make It into the New Testament.* Edited by Bart D. Ehrman. New York: Oxford UP, 2003.

"Letters of Paul and Seneca." *Lost Scriptures: Books that Did Not Make It into the New Testament.* Edited by Bart D. Ehrman. New York: Oxford UP, 2003.

(*On First Principles*) *De Principiis.* Whitefish, MT: Kessinger, 2003. Origen. Translated by G.W. Butterworth. Gloucester: Peter Smith, 1985.

Origen. *On First Principles.* Translated by G.W. Butterworth. Gloucester: Peter Smith, 1985.

Perpetua. "The Mothers: The Diary of Perpetua." *The Fathers of the Church, Expanded Edition.* Edited by Mike Aquilina. Huntington: Our Sunday Visitor, 2006.

Philemon. NRSV Harper Study Bible ed. Grand Rapids, MI: Zondervan, 1991.

Polycarp. *Martyrdom of Polycarp. Loeb Classical Library: the Apostolic Fathers, I: I Clement. II Clement. Ignatius. Polycarp. Didache.* Translated by Bart D. Ehrman. Cambridge: Harvard UP, 2003.

Porphyry. *Against the Christians.* Edited by R. Joseph Hoffman. Amherst: Prometheus Books, 1994.

Proba, Faltonia. *The Golden Bough, the Oaken Cross: the Virginlian Cento of Faltonia Betitia Proba.* Translated by Elizabeth A. Clark. Otterup, Denmark: Scholars P, 1981.

"*The Proto-Gospel of James.*" *Lost Scriptures: Books that Did Not Make It into the New Testament.* Edited by Bart D. Ehrman. New York: Oxford UP, 2003.

Ptolemaeus, Claudius. *Ptolemy's "Almagest."* Translated by G. J. Toomer. Princeton: Princeton UP, 1998.

Romans. NRSV Harper Study Bible ed. Grand Rapids, MI: Zondervan, 1991.

(*II Corinthians*) *Second Corinthians.* NRSV Harper Study Bible ed. Grand Rapids, MI: Zondervan, 1991.

"*Shepherd* of Hermas." *Lost Scriptures: Books that Did Not Make It into the New Testament.* Edited by Bart D. Ehrman. New York: Oxford UP, 2003.

Tatian. *The Earliest Life of Christ Ever Compiled From the Four Gospels: Being the Diatessaron of Tatian.* Translated by J. Hamlyn Hill. Piscataway: Gorgias, 2003.

"The Third Letter to the Corinthians." *Lost Scriptures: Books that Did Not Make It into the New Testament.* Edited by Bart D. Ehrman. New York: Oxford UP, 2003.

CHAPTER 6

Medieval Period

K. Sarah-Jane Murray and Emily Rodgers

TIMELINE

751	St. Boniface anoints Pepin of Heristal a divinely sanctioned king
c. 787	Viking raids on England begin
800	Charlemagne is crowned Holy Roman Emperor
871–99	Reign of King Alfred the Great of England
936	Coronation of Otto the Great of Germany
962	Otto the Great is named emperor in Rome
1050–1200	First agricultural revolution of Europe: invention of the heavy plow, adoption of the three-field system of crop rotation
1066	Norman Conquest of England by William I "The Conqueror" (Battle of Hastings)
1095–1221	Crusades
1122	Concordat of Worms (in Germany)
1152	Future King Henry II of England marries Eleanor of Aquitaine; Frederick I of Germany claims the title of "Holy Roman Emperor"
1164	Constitutions of Clarendon
1170	Murder of Thomas Beckett in Canterbury Cathedral
1189	Coronation of Richard the Lionhearted in England
1198	Innocent III becomes pope
1212	Spanish Reconquest
1215	Fourth Lateran Council; Magna Carta
1226	Coronation of Louis IX (St. Louis) in France
1244	Jerusalem lost by the West (until 1917)
1252	Papacy approves torture for religious disobedience
1282	"Sicilian Vespers" Revolt
1305	Papacy moves from Rome to Avignon ("Babylonian Captivity")
1315	Devastating famine spreads throughout Europe
c. 1337–1453	Hundred Years' War

1347–48	Black Death appears
1358	Peasant uprisings in France ("Jacqueries")
1362	English adopted by law courts and Parliament in England
1378	The Great Schism, resulting in two popes: Urban VI in Rome, Clement VII in France.
1381	People's uprising in England
1409	Council of Pisa results in three popes
1417	Council of Constance ends the Great Schism
1431	The English burn Joan of Arc at Agincourt

INTRODUCTION TO THE PERIOD

The Middle Ages played a crucial role in shaping the cultural history of reading in Britain and Europe. Although often synonymous with war, plague, and generally poor conditions of living, this period in western European history by no means constitutes a "Dark Age" devoid of cultural production. Medieval readers and writers viewed themselves as inheritors and transmitters of the culture and knowledge disseminated by the classical world, and participated actively in the transmission of ancient learning to future generations (a process known as *translatio studii*). At the same time, they cultivated, and took to a new level, the themes and ideals nursed during the early Christian period.

No one ever imagined Rome would fall. Yet, by 410 C.E. Alaric, king of the Visigoths, had sacked the imperial city. This event marked the end of the *Pax Romana* (Roman Peace), and signaled the beginning of economic decline and political uncertainty throughout Europe. Barbarian hordes raged across the Continent; amid the chaos, major libraries were destroyed, along with their precious books. Literacy was in jeopardy. And yet, against all odds, it survived—thanks to the dedicated efforts of medieval scribes and scholars. Indeed, the history of reading is intrinsically linked to the history of writing. At first glance, this statement seems utterly obvious: without books or written records, there can be no act of reading. Nonetheless, this simple truth encapsulates the greatest gift bestowed by medieval readers on their successors. By copying by hand the (often damaged) manuscripts and papyri they themselves read, and by creating detailed commentaries and translations, medieval scribes and scholars ensured the survival of literacy, and of a culture of reading, in western Europe prior to the development of the printing press.

In *How the Irish Saved Civilization,* Thomas Cahill documents the fascinating part Ireland played in this process of preservation. After the fall of Rome, scholars fled to this small island sanctuary off the coast of Britain, taking their books with them. Ireland had never been conquered by the Romans, and would remain, at least until the time of the Vikings, of little interest to continental invaders. Following St. Patrick's conversion of the Irish to Christianity (c. 432 C.E.), monasteries became the cultural and economic centers of the island. As they grew in strength and size, they came to include schools of classical learning, vernacular poetics, and law. Students flocked from Britain and the rest of Europe in order to read the classics and study theology at centers such as Armagh, Clonmacnoise, and Monasterboice. Furthermore, Latin and Roman writing came to Ireland with Christianity, provoking a transition from oral to textual culture. At the same time that the Irish were creating lavish Gospel books such as the *Book of Durrow* and the *Book of Kells,* they were also beginning to record in writing vernacular tales from their pagan past. Most notable, and popular, were the *imramma* (rowings about)—stories of great sea voyages, such as the *Voyage of Mael Duin* or the *Voyage of Bran Mac Febal*—which may in turn have inspired the widely read Christian and Latin-language *Voyage of St. Brendan.*

The Irish monastic movement gained momentum and, through the work of dedicated missionaries, spread throughout the European continent. St. Columba left Ireland in 563 C.E. to settle on the Scottish island of Iona. He was followed by countless other men and women, who traveled to France, Germany, Italy, Switzerland, Norway, and more. Of all these holy people, St. Columbanus is particularly interesting. After arriving in Gaul, he established monastic centers at Fontaines, Annegray, and Luxeuil. Due to political pressures, he moved on to Switzerland; there he left behind one of his most cherished disciples, who went on to found the monastery of St. Gall. After traveling on to Italy, Columbanus found-ed the abbey of Bobbio, a great center of spirituality and learning. More than one hundred monasteries in continental Europe can be traced back to Columbanus and his many disciples. Most of these establishments included active *scriptoria* and libraries, where monks copied the Bible, the writings of the church fathers, and the works of classical authorities. This pan-European network of monasteries played an important part in setting up the infrastructure that would later fuel the great Carolingian Revival.

Meanwhile, in Britain, libraries were flourishing at centers such as Canterbury, York, Wearmouth, and Jarrow. In *Medieval Foundations of the Western Intellectual Tradition*, Marcia Colish describes the set of circumstances that led to this dynamic culture of reading (63–65). During the fourth and fifth centuries, Roman troops had pulled out of England, leaving the country vulner-able to the invasions of the Angles, Saxons, and Jutes. The settlers were soon evangelized by Irish missionary efforts from the north and then the south, by Roman missionaries such as St. Augustine (d. 604 C.E.), the "Apostle to the English," who was sent to Britain by Pope Gregory the Great in 597 C.E. St. Augustine was influential in spreading the monastic rule of St. Benedict of Nursia. Theodore of Tarsus (c. 602–690 C.E.) succeeded Augustine as archbish-op of Canterbury in 669 C.E., and founded many monastic schools, where stu-dents learned to read both Greek and Latin.

By the eighth century, Anglo-Saxon England had become the cultural center of Europe. L.D. Reynolds and N.G. Wilson note in their book, *Scribes and Scholars*, that the writings of Aldhelm (c. 639–709 C.E.) and Bede (c. 672–735 C.E.) give us a good idea of the books that were circulating at this time (79). Readers pos-sessed a second-hand knowledge of many classical authors through the writings of Macrobius and Isidore; to these we can add direct knowledge of Virgil, Lucan, Persius, Juvenal, Cicero, Ovid, and Eutropius. Other surviving manuscripts attest to the popularity of Pliny's *Natural History,* the writings of Justinus, and Servius's *Commentary* on the *Æneid* (*Scribes and Scholars* 81). In sum, medieval readers exhibited a great thirst for the classics. Yet, in his *Ecclesiastical History of the English People,* Bede also states that he undertook a full translation of the Bible into Old English, signaling an important (albeit not yet widespread) shift toward reading in the vernacular.

Anglo-Saxon missionaries (e.g., Willibord and Boniface) now followed the Irish to the Continent. "With them, the Anglo-Saxons brought a [new] script, books, a liberal intellectual outlook, and the recognition that a well-stocked and well-balanced library was the basis of ecclesiastical education" (*Scribes and Scholars* 81). Books containing Christian and pagan texts were imported from Britain, while others, such as Calcidius's Latin translation of Plato's *Timaeus,* were rediscovered and copied on the Continent.

In the ninth century another shift occurred, as the Continent—and especially the Holy Roman Empire established by Charlemagne (Charles the Great)—asserted itself as the center of learning and book production. Wars, invasions, and disputes over succession had jeopardized the Frankish kingdom since its establishment by Clovis (c. 466–511 C.E.). In 732 C.E., Charles Martel (Charles the Hammer) defeated Islamic invaders at the battle of Poitiers; in turn, Charles's son, Pepin the Short, proclaimed the union of church and state, thereby solidifying the relationship between political and religious spheres. Under Pepin and his son, Charlemagne, the Frankish monarchy closely supported (and was supported by) the papacy. In the year 800 C.E., on Christmas day, Charlemagne was crowned Holy Roman Emperor by the Pope. Taking the spread of Christianity as his principle charge, Charlemagne conquered an immense empire—from the Ebro and the Apennines to the Eider River, and from the Atlantic to the Elbe and the Raab. Thanks to the foundation of new monasteries and dioceses, Charlemagne established a basis of religious unity in Europe that remained in place until the Reformation.

The administration of such an empire increased the demand for priests and functionaries. In response, Charlemagne launched a widespread educational program. He also encouraged the revival of classical learning, attested to by the production of numerous textbooks on the liberal arts, especially the more literary arts of Boethius's *trivium*—grammar, rhetoric, and dialectic. Numerous teaching tools were also developed: glossaries, dictionaries, commentaries, handbooks on spelling, compilations, and summaries of the great encyclopedists (Isidore, Boethius, Cassiodorus, and Martianus Capella). Under the leadership of Alcuin of York (c. 735–804 C.E.), chosen by Charlemagne to head up the Palace School, new scripts were developed to facilitate the copying of manuscripts (see *Scribes and Scholars*, 84–85). In fact, the compact "Carolingian Minuscule" is still used today as the basis for the Times New Roman font.

What, then, did the educated elite read in Carolingian Europe? The Bible and the writings of the church fathers continued to enjoy immense popularity. A list surviving in a Berlin manuscript (Diez B. 66) provides us with a partial list of the other authors and books in Charlemagne's court library (*Scribes and Scholars* 86): Lucan, Statius's *Thebaid,* Terence, Juvenal, Tibullus, Horace (the *Ars poetica*), Claudian, Martial, Cicero's speeches, and Sallust. To this list other works can be added that were widely copied by the mid-ninth century: Livy, Columella, the Elder Seneca, the Younger Pliny, Caesar's *Gallic War,* the *Ad Herennium,* Macrobius's commentary on the *Dream of Scipio,* Martial, Ovid's *Heroides* and *Amores,* Vitruvius, and Vegetius (*Scribes and Scholars* 87). In addition, stories of saints' lives (commonly referred to as *Lives*), often composed to increase the notoriety of local pilgrimage destinations and generate revenues, were well-received by Carolingian readers.

The manuscripts copied by the Carolingians set the stage for a dynamic culture of reading during the Renaissance of the twelfth century (see Charles H. Haskins's *Renaissance of the Twelfth Century*). By this time, education had gradually passed from the monasteries to the cathedral schools (e.g., Chartres, Orléans), and, in the second half of the twelfth century, to the universities (e.g., Paris, Bologna). Classical authors—especially Virgil, Ovid, Horace, Lucan, Priscian, Juvenal, Persius, Cicero, Seneca, and Sallust—remained popular, and were read with great attention. At the same time, education took on a new role: "to cater for the specialized needs of a complex society with a professional interest in law and medicine, rhetoric and logic. The exciting new books for this age were Euclid and Ptolemy, the Digest, and such works of the Aristotelian and medical corpus as were rapidly becoming available" (*Scribes and Scholars* 98).

The enthusiasm for antique themes and subjects infiltrated the courts of France and northern Europe. This led to the emergence of vernacular translation-adaptations, such as the Old French *Romance of Eneas* (a reworking of Virgil's *Æneid*), and Benoît de Sainte-Maure's pseudo-historical account of the Trojan War, the *Romance of Troy*. The demand for Ovid was also high. Several vernacular courtly Ovidian poems were composed at this time: *Piramus et Tisbé, Narcissus,* and *Philomena.* (The latter is often attributed to Chrétien de Troyes.) By the thirteenth century, these had been integrated into the immense, and extraordinarily popular, *Moralized Ovid.* This compilation of tales from the *Metamorphoses* attests to the medieval Christian audience's tendency to read classical literature as allegory: within the collection, the translation of each classical fable is followed by a Christian lesson (or "moral"). The flowering of vernacular literature in twelfth-century Europe attests to the relative peacefulness and economic prosperity of the age. In Anglo-Norman England, King Henry II and his French wife, Eleanor of Aquitaine, were both generous patrons of the arts (Marie de France dedicates her *Lais* to King Henry); in France Eleanor's daughter, Marie of Champagne, supported the endeavors of authors such as Chrétien de Troyes, inventor of the popular and influential Arthurian romance. Rulers such as these encouraged the development of a court-centered literature, which sheds light on the values of the twelfth-century ruling class.

It is important to remember that much early vernacular literature was composed to be performed aloud and in public, often by professional *jongleurs* (literally, "jugglers" of words). Oral tales of love and death, like the famous *Tristan* legends, had been spreading throughout western Europe for some time, as had the lyric poetry of the troubadours. What sets the twelfth century apart on the Continent and in England is that people began to *write* prolifically in the vernacular. Possibly inspired by their reading of Plato's *Timaeus,* twelfth-century men of letters were keenly aware of the precarious conditions in which learning and history had survived for centuries. Thus European nations, led by the Britons and the French, set about recording their cultural histories. In Britain, Geoffrey of Monmouth composed the *History of the Kings of Britain,* a pseudo-historical work, written in Latin, which traces the origins of the British nation back to the fall of Troy. Around the same time, in France, the oldest surviving manuscript of the popular (oral) eleventh-century *Song of Roland* was copied, commemorating forever the brave actions of Charlemagne's soldiers against the Saracens.

But this widespread enthusiasm for writing and storytelling must not be confused with an open dissemination of knowledge and learning. Education—and, therefore, the ability to read—remained the privilege of a select few. Although the vernacular took precedence in the world of the courts, Latin remained the learned language of theology and philosophy, reserved for those training for the priesthood or for careers in the universities. In addition, manuscripts—copied on vellum (calf's skin) or parchment (sheep's skin)—were extraordinarily costly. Even medieval students in the cathedral schools and universities would have taken their notes on wax tablets, and committed them to memory before resetting the tablet for use again the next day.

Reading, throughout the Middle Ages, impacted the ideas of the educated elite. Thus it molded and shaped the faces of nations through their rulers and religious leaders. Books did not, however, reach populations on a widespread scale (as they would during the Enlightenment and modern era). To be sure, the rediscovery of Aristotle, through contact with the Arabic world, profoundly shook up the cultural landscape of thirteenth-century Europe. But the scholastic method, adopted by Thomas Aquinas in his *Summa Theologica,* was of little immediate concern to the common farmer, for example. Nonetheless, later medieval theologians like Thomas Aquinas (1224–1274) and Bonaventure (c. 1221–1274) exerted a lasting and primordial influence, felt even today, on the articulation of Catholic doctrine. Furthermore, the growing popularity of the vernacular, which now provided a means to critique social norms and values—as evidenced, for example, by the success of Dante's *Divine Comedy* (c. 1308–1321) and Chaucer's *Canterbury Tales* (c. 1386–1400)—placed the late Middle Ages on the doorstep of modernity.

READING TRENDS AND PRACTICES

The following texts have been chosen because they offer us a unique glimpse into the history of medieval Britain and the European continent. The list is by no means exhaustive. Rather, it will allow us to consider the influence of certain works on the fields of education, politics, religion, philosophy, theology, travel writing, and literature. Each of these books, in its own way, shaped the practices of reading during the Middle Ages, and contributed significantly to the formation of cultural identity in pre-Renaissance Europe.

EDUCATIONAL TEXTS

Plato's *Timaeus* (360 B.C.E.), translated into Latin by Calcidius (fourth to fifth centuries C.E.), was one of the most widely read classical works in medieval Europe. More than one hundred and eighty manuscripts of the *Timaeus,* dating back as early as the ninth century, have come down to us, making it a medieval "best-seller." (The great classical rhetorician, Cicero, also made a partial translation of the *Timaeus.* Augustine read it, but it was less popular than the work of Calcidius, which includes a detailed commentary.) For centuries the *Timaeus* was the only dialogue by Plato available in the West, and the many notes inscribed in the margins of manuscripts containing the dialogue confirm that it fascinated medieval readers.

Much of the *Timaeus* centers on a technical speech made by the physicist Timaeus to three interlocutors: Socrates, Hermocrates, and Critias. Timaeus methodically discusses the origins of the universe, the nature of time, and the creation of humankind. It has been suggested that medieval readers paid particular attention to the "Myth of Atlantis," which prefaces the cosmographical discussion (Murray). In the opening pages of the *Timaeus,* Critias narrates the story of the lost civilization of Atlantis, which, thousands of years ago, rose up out of the Atlantic and sought to conquer the entire European continent. Athens fought bravely against the tyrants, and won the war. But in the midst of the night, an enormous tidal wave swept over the island, killing all of the soldiers—Atlantians and Athenians alike. As Atlantis sank to the bottom of the ocean, the memory of Greece's heroic military action was lost. Fortunately, Egyptian priests kept written records of the story of Atlantis within their temples. Thousands of years after the disaster, Critias's ancestor, the great law-giver Solon, traveled to Egypt, heard the story, and carried it back to Greece, thereby restoring the cultural memory of his compatriots. Plato's message—which Calcidius sought to preserve through his translation—is clear: without writing, without the knowledge of our past, we are only children.

The *Timaeus* exerted considerable influence in medieval Europe. As Augustine of Hippo pointed out in his *City of God,* Plato presented the Christian West with a philosophical vision in tune with Christianity, predicated on the immortality of the soul and even a sort of trinity of Gods. Furthermore, it is likely that the *Timaeus* inspired the fervor with which scribes and writers engaged in the process of preserving the knowledge of the past. Medieval readers understood that their civilizations would suffer the fate of Atlantis (or Greece) if they did not record their histories in writing. The link between the *Timaeus* and the rise of national histories is attested by a manuscript now preserved at the Oxford Bodleian library. Here, the *Timaeus* has been bound to the oldest surviving copy of the *Song of Roland,* the great nationalist, eleventh-century epic poem composed in Old French.

Martianus Capella's *Marriage of Mercury and Philology* (*De nuptiis Mercurii et Philologiae*; fl. 430 C.E.) was another popular fixture of the medieval school curriculum, and an important source for the study of the liberal arts during the Middle Ages. The work belongs to a group of encyclopedic books of late antiquity—such as Marcobius's *Commentary on Cicero's Dream of Scipio,* Servius's *Commentary on the Æneid,* and Boethius's *Consolation of Philosophy*—which allowed for the transfer of ancient learning and letters to medieval Europe. Martianus's book is significant in that it provides us with an idea of the themes and topics discussed by medieval students in the schools.

The *Marriage of Mercury and Philology* is a *prosimetrum,* or "Menippean satire": it is composed in both verse and prose. Martianus divides his treatise into nine books, a number that perhaps alludes to the nine Muses. In the first two books, the elderly narrator tells his son the story of Mercury's decision to wed Philology, a studious earth maiden. During the wedding feast, Philology receives seven gifts, each representing one of the liberal arts personified as a maiden: grammar, dialectic, and rhetoric (the literary arts making up the *trivium*); and geometry, arithmetic, astronomy, and harmony, or music (the scientific arts of the *quadrivium*). The following seven books are each given over to one of the arts, who makes a speech about her discipline. The unity of the *Marriage* is ensured, at the end of the ninth book, by a return to the story: Harmony, humming a lullaby, accompanies the newlyweds as they retire to the marriage chamber.

The influence of Martianus Capella's narrative treatise was considerable. He is cited by Gregory of Tours, translated and glossed by Remigius of Auxerre, and adapted or copied by countless compilers. In his *Metalogicon,* John of Salisbury declares Martianus to be the "equal of Virgil." In the early thirteenth-century *Battle of the Seven Arts* by Henri d'Andeli, Martianus even figures as a defender of grammar against the rise of Aristotelian logic.

In the *Metalogicon* (1159 C.E.), John of Salisbury defends the study of the *trivium* (see Martianus Capella, above) against the attacks of a probably fictitious character, Cornificius, and his followers. One of the most notable characteristics of the book is John's success at outlining, for the first time in the West, a program for integrating Aristotle's *Organon* into the school curriculum. Throughout the Middle Ages, the *Metalogicon* was a popular handbook for the study of philosophy and logic.

The *Metalogicon* is also unique in its testimony about the routine of students at the cathedral school of Chartres. Based on the second-hand information he received from his own teachers, John provides a detailed account of what it was like to study under the famous school teacher, or *magister,* Bernard of Chartres. In book one, chapter twenty-four, John describes Bernard's method. Every day, students would present from memory something of yesterday's lesson. In this way, Bernard stressed the continuity of the learning process: "each day became the disciple of the predecessor." Much of the lesson was then given over to a detailed reading of the classics: pupils would read and systematically explain (or "gloss") the structure and content of ancient works. This practice of close reading was common throughout Europe during the eleventh and twelfth centuries, a fact attested to today by the numerous notes and comments that fill the margins of medieval manuscripts. Finally, students would progress to the exercise of imitation, whereby they imitated the style of the author they were studying, and produced their own texts. Bernard took this part of their training very seriously indeed: John notes that he would not hesitate to flog students who did not pay attention.

John also leaves us a record of his own studies with several famous twelfth-century teachers in book two of the *Metalogicon*. He recounts how, as a young man, he traveled to Gaul to study under Peter Abelard, "the Peripatetic of Palais." Under Abelard's guidance, John acquainted himself with basic logic. He went on to further his knowledge of dialectic under Alberic, and eventually fell under the tutelage of William of Soissons.

Few writings have impacted the intellectual tradition of Europe as much as the Aristotelian corpus (rediscovered in the twelfth to thirteenth centuries). And yet, until the twelfth century, medieval readers had very little knowledge of Aristotle. What they did know was transmitted through commentaries and compilations. Five commentaries on Aristotle's works by Boethius (480–c. 524 C.E.) were particularly influential, as were his translations of the six books of Aristotelian logic known as the *Organon*.

In the tenth century, the knights of the Spanish *Reconquista* (Reconquest) began a lengthy struggle to free the Iberian Peninsula from Muslim invaders, who had settled there more than three hundred years earlier. Although Grenada would remain under Muslim control until 1492, much of Spain had been reclaimed by Christian armies by the beginning of the twelfth century. As they explored the libraries in Toledo, Lisbon, Segovia, and Cordoba, Christian scholars must have been struck with surprise and awe. Arabic translations and commentaries of important Greek works, entirely lost to the rest of western Europe, lined the shelves: Ptolemy's *Almagest,* Galen's *On the Art of Healing* and *On Anatomical Procedures,* Euclid's *Elements of Geometry,* Archimedes' work on engineering, and—most impressive—the entire corpus of Aristotelian philosophy: *On the Philosophy of Being,* the *Metaphysics,* the *Physics, On the Heavens, On the Soul,* the *Nicomachean Ethics,* the *Politics,* and more. As Richard Rubenstein notes in his book *Aristotle's Children,* "taken together, these books represent the most important documentary discovery (or "rediscovery") in Western intellectual history. One historian [Robert Fossier] calls the recovery of Aristotle's works 'a turning point in the history of Western thought . . . paralleled only by the later impact of Newtonian science and Darwinism'" (16–17).

After centuries dominated by Neoplatonic thought, with its emphasis on the unstable, imperfect, and transient nature of the material world, the recovery of Aristotle sent shock waves throughout western Europe. Aristotle's books on natural science, ethics, aesthetics, and politics spawned a new interest in the natural world, and led to the popularization of mathematics, medicine, and the natural sciences. At the same time, Aristotle challenged the traditionally Christian outlook of the West: although the philosopher does make room for a godlike "Un-Moved Mover" in his universe, "his writings have nothing to say about God the Creator or the Redeemer, and pay little attention to our sinfulness or its consequences in the afterlife . . . . [Nonetheless,] the Aristotelian corpus, troubling though it might be, represented the most comprehensive, accurate, and well-integrated and satisfying account of the natural world that medieval readers had ever encountered" (*Aristotle's Children* 79–80).

Over the next two centuries, three major approaches to Aristotle prevailed, impeding or allowing for the progress of scientific and philosophical inquiry. The first possibility was to reject Aristotle as pagan and sacrilegious, and, indeed, some church authorities declared his works to be too dangerous for consumption in the schools. (The writings of orthodox Muslims, such as al-Ghazali's *Incoherence of the Philosophers,* brought an end to the study of Aristotle in the Arabic world; and Jewish rabbis denounced Maimonedes' commentary on Aristotle, *The Guide to the Perplexed,* as heretical. It was later burned by the Inquisition.) Others, following the lead of the eleventh-century Persian thinker Avicenna (Ibn Sina), sought to spiritualize Aristotle. In so doing, they portrayed the great classical master as lacking in Christian wisdom, and updated his writings so that they "fit" into the Christian worldview. A third option was to explore how faith and reason might interact and inform one another (a dialogue that built upon issues already raised by St. Anselm of Canterbury). This fostered a dynamic debate, which continues even today. "A new demand for understanding—a demand to "know" the truths of religion in addition to believing them—drew students from all across the Latin world to cities such as Paris, Bologna, and Oxford, where pioneer thinkers such as Abelard were creating a new fusion of philosophy and religion that they called theology" (*Aristotle's Children* 101). The application of Aristotelian reasoning to questions of theology achieves its most famous and influential form during the thirteenth century, in Thomas Aquinas's *Summa Theologica.*

PHILOSOPHICAL AND THEOLOGICAL TEXTS

Numerous significant theological and philosophical treatises were also composed during the period; not least among them were the writings of St. Anselm of Canterbury (c. 1033–1109). St Anselm was born in Aosta to a noble and devout family. Recognized as the father of scholasticism, he is most famous for his ontological proof of God's existence in the *Proslogion,* as well as his explanation of the doctrine of atonement in *Why God Became Man* (*Cur Deus Homo*). He became Archbishop of Canterbury in 1093 and held that office until his death on April 21, 1109. Due to the great influence of his writings, Anselm was consecrated Doctor of the Church in 1720 by Pope Clement XI.

Anselm's treatise on *Why God Became Man* (completed in 1098) closely examines the meaning of the crucifixion, and bears witness to an important shift in religious sensibility in Britain and Europe during the eleventh century. In *The Making of the Middle Ages,* R.W. Southern explains Anselm's influence as follows: "Anselm . . . prepared a theoretical justification for the new feeling about the humanity of the Savior. His words on this subject had a decisive importance and marked a break with an age-long tradition" (234). Until the end of the eleventh century, theologians emphasized that sin caused man to withdraw from the service of God and press himself into obedience to the Devil. Southern compares it to the process of a vassal who passes from one liege-lord to another (a process known in feudal custom as *diffidatio*). This set in motion a war between the Devil and God for the soul of man, in which man was a static bystander. When God became man, and was subjected to death, the Devil was tricked: Christ had committed no act of *diffidatio,* so his death was unwarranted. Thus, as Southern says, the crucifixion brought to terms a longstanding "drama enacted between heaven and hell" (234).

Anselm challenged this common assumption, insisting upon Christ's humanity. He summarizes this major argument of *Why God Became Man* in the short and very beautiful *Meditation on Human Redemption*. Man had sinned, and man had to atone for that sin. Such an act could only be accomplished by a new man, devoid of original sin. By becoming man, God made an enormous sacrifice, thereby demonstrating his great love for humanity (see John 3:16). By the end of the eleventh century, images of the crucifixion in art, sculpture, and manuscripts had changed dramatically. Far from representing the serene Godhead typically found in early (sixth- through tenth-century) images, "the dying figure was stripped of its garments, the arms sagged with the weight of the body, the head hung on one side, the eyes were closed, the blood ran down the cross" (*Making of the Middle Ages* 237). From this point forward, a renewed interest arose in the humanity of Christ. And thus, "the Devil slipped out of the drama and left God and Man face to face" (*Making of the Middle Ages* 236).

Anselm also challenged philosophers with his ontological argument for the existence of God. Anselm believed, as St. Thomas Aquinas would, that faith and reason could work together to allow human beings to understand their place in the world, as well as their relationship to God. He captures this idea in two of his most famous mottos: "faith seeking understanding" and "I believe so that I may understand." It is important to note that the *Proslogion* is addressed to a community of believers; it is not an evangelical work aimed at converting non-Christians. Taking as his point of departure the idea that God is "that than which nothing greater can be thought," Anselm argued that what exists in reality is greater than what is only in the mind. Ergo, because "God is that than which nothing greater can be thought," he must exist in reality. (No brief summary can do justice to the subtlety of Anselm's argument. Readers are referred to the *Proslogion* for the detailed exposition.) Anselm answered his first major critic, a monk named Gaunilo, by including Gaunilo's letter, as well as his own response, alongside the *Proslogion*. In so doing, Anselm set up the standards for lively, yet correct, debates about matters of philosophy and theology.

Anselm's claims sparked heated conversations not only during the Middle Ages (for example, Thomas Aquinas and his followers rejected the ontological argument), but also for centuries to come. This can be seen, for example, in the writings of Descartes, Kant, and Hegel.

Let us turn now to the Cistercian St. Bernard of Clairvaux (1090–1153). Although St. Bernard is best known today for his mystical treatise *On Loving God* and the *Sermons on the Song of Songs,* his popular *In Praise of the New Knighthood* (*De laude novae militae*) provides us with an interesting look at the formation of the Knights Templar and the enthusiasm with which medieval Europe embraced the crusades. St. Bernard sent the work in the form of a letter to Hugues de Payens, the founder of the Knights Templar, in 1127. His goals were to dispel the apparent conflicts between the chivalrous life and monastic charity. Of particular interest to us here are chapters one through five.

In chapter one, Bernard identifies "a new kind of knighthood and one unknown to the ages gone by," which "ceaselessly wages a twofold war against flesh and blood and against a spiritual army of evil in the heavens." The purpose of knighthood, according to Bernard (who, we might add, preached in favor of the crusades), must not be limited to defending one's lands and serving one's liege-lord. The soldier must above all serve God, and become a "soldier of Christ" (*miles Christi*), whose "soul is protected by the armor of faith just as his body is protected by armor of steel." The new knighthood thus combines the physical attributes of traditional soldiers with the unwavering faith of the monastic orders. In the second chapter, Bernard questions the typical knights of his day, who dress up their horses in silk and spend their time being concerned with the trifles of this world.

(Chrétien de Troyes identifies a similar lack of purpose among the knights of King Arthur's fictional court in his last romance, *Perceval,* or *The Story of the Grail* [c. 1189].) Bernard then exalts the charge of the *miles Christi,* who need not fear death, for "the Knights of Christ may safely fight the battles of their Lord, fearing neither sin if they smite the enemy, nor danger at their own death; as to inflict death or to die for Christ is no sin, but rather, an abundant claim to glory" (ch. 3).

Chapter four describes in detail the discipline to which the brotherhood of Christian soldiers must adhere on a daily basis, at all times emphasizing how they must differ from the "knights of the world." This code strongly resembles a monastic rule. The knights "come and go at the bidding of their superior. They wear what he gives them, and do not presume to wear or to eat anything from another source. Thus, they shun every excess in clothing and food and content themselves with what is necessary." The *miles Christi* must remain celibate, and, upon joining the order, he must give up all personal property so as "to keep the unity of the Spirit in the bond of peace." He shuns idleness and, when not on duty, applies himself to the repair of his armor and torn clothing. Above all, the knights are considered to be equals, no matter what their parentage: "deference is shown to merit rather than to noble blood." They are exemplars of charity, "rival[ing] one another in mutual consideration, and they carry one another's burdens, thus fulfilling the law of Christ." Their charge, revealed in chapter five, is to reinforce the Christian presence in Jerusalem, where the recent events "have shaken the world." The knights' residence, Bernard notes, must be in the holy temple itself, for "what could be more profitable and pleasant to behold than seeing such a multitude coming to reinforce the few?"

No survey of medieval theological and philosophical readings can fail to recognize the importance of St. Thomas Aquinas (c. 1225–1274). A doctor of the church and a prolific author, Thomas is best known for his encyclopedic *Summa Theologica* (c. 1266–1273), itself an extraordinary example of medieval scholasticism.

Thomas was born into a noble Italian family in 1224 or 1225. Against the will of his parents, he joined the Dominican order (a mendicant order) in 1244. Thomas's parents, horrified that their son would not at least consent to joining the prestigious Benedictine monastery of Monte Cassino, kidnapped him and held him captive for close to a year, giving him only the Bible to read. According to one notorious story, they even tempted him with a naked woman. However, Thomas's faith was only strengthened by this period of captivity, and, ultimately, his parents relented. The Dominicans sent him to study at the university in Paris, an exciting intellectual hub, where scholars were rediscovering Aristotle and exploring how his philosophy (especially logic) could be reconciled with Christian revelation. Thomas's *Summa* exemplifies the application of Aristotelian logic to questions of faith; he worked on it until about three months before his death, when he had a vision of God that caused him to view everything he had written as dry straw. He refused to write any more.

In introducing the *Summa,* Thomas explains that his purpose is to instruct beginners in theology (a fact that never fails to intimidate modern students approaching the *Summa* for the first time). With this in mind, he divides the work into three major parts. The first part (*prima pars*) deals at length with sacred doctrine: especially God's existence, the Blessed Trinity, the Creation, the angels, the six days, man, and the government of creatures. The second part is so detailed as to merit being further divided into two parts. The first part of the second part (*prima secundae* partis) discusses the major issues of man's last end, human acts, the passions, habits, vices and sin, law, and grace. In the second part of the second part (*secunda secundae partis*), Thomas turns to a discussion of faith, hope, charity, prudence, justice, fortitude, temperance, and the acts that pertain to certain men.

The third part (*tertia pars*), meanwhile, focuses on Christ, conducting the reader toward his or her "ultimate end" (defined by Thomas himself in the *Compendium of Theology* as "the vision of God in His essence"). Here, Thomas's topics are the Incarnation, the life of Christ, the sacraments (including baptism, confirmation, and the holy eucharist), and the idea of penance. Thomas did not complete his treatise on penance, which he began shortly before his death, and the remainder of the *Summa*, known as the supplement to the third part (*supplementum tertia partis*), was probably compiled by his friend Fra Rainaldo da Piperno. The materials for the supplement were gathered in large part from Thomas's commentary on the fourth book of the *Sentences* by Peter Lombard and, quite possibly, from reports composed by Thomas's students. The supplement discusses the topics of extreme unction, the holy orders, matrimony, and the resurrection. It also includes two appendices on: (1) The quality of souls who die with original sin only, and of those in purgatory; and (2) two additional articles on purgatory.

Each of the parts of the *Summa* is divided into specific "questions," themselves divided into "articles," which carry the reader systematically and carefully through Thomas's exposition. For this reason, the architecture of the *Summa Theologica* has often been compared to that of the great medieval cathedrals, with each question and article—indeed, each sentence—serving as a building block for the gigantesque and awe-inspiring edifice Thomas constructs. To have an idea of the magnitude of the *Summa*, one can begin by considering the sheer volume of questions Thomas engages: 119 in the *prima pars*, 114 in the *prima secundae partis*, 189 in the *secunda secundae partis*, and ninety in the *tertia pars*. A remaining ninety-nine questions are addressed in the *supplementum* (to which we must add the two appendices).

One cannot hope even to begin to grasp the contribution Thomas Aquinas made to Western thought without delving into the structure of the *Summa*. Let us consider briefly, then, the first question, on "The Nature and Extent of Sacred Doctrine." In order to establish the importance and nature of theological inquiry, Thomas expounds upon ten distinct, yet closely related, articles: (1) "Whether, besides philosophy, any further doctrine is required"; (2) "Whether sacred doctrine is a science"; (3) "Whether sacred doctrine is one science"; (4) "Whether sacred doctrine is a practical science"; (5) "Whether sacred doctrine is nobler than other sciences"; (6) "Whether this doctrine is the same as wisdom"; (7) "Whether God is the object of this science"; (8) "Whether sacred doctrine is a matter of argument"; (9) "Whether Holy Scripture should use metaphors"; and (10) "Whether in Holy Scripture a word may have several senses." A detailed look at these articles affords us a general understanding of the systematic way in which Thomas approaches each question of the *Summa*. Thus, the title of an article serves to ask a specific question. Then, Thomas always begins a section with the word *videtur* ("it seems that"), where he presents arguments for what often turns out to be the wrong answer to the query. In other words, Thomas begins by presenting the claims his adversaries might make. This section is followed by the *sed contra* ("but on the contrary"), which offers counter-claims to the *videtur*. Thomas then moves into his *responsio* ("response"), where he develops a sound response to the question he posed at the beginning of the article. Each article concludes with a clear refutation of the arguments introduced in the *videtur* section. Throughout his inquiry, Thomas draws upon examples from the scriptures, the church fathers, and even classical authors.

The *Summa* mimics disputations Thomas would have held in the classroom. One can imagine that he would engage his students with a question, such as "Whether Holy Scripture should use metaphors." The students would provide the *videtur* and *sed contra*, and Thomas, ultimately, would provide the *responsio*. His students, in turn, would refute the arguments they initially presented in the *videtur*. The meticulous and logical approach Thomas cultivates throughout the *Summa* incites his readers to consider all aspects of a question—and to let go of any preconceived ideas they might have as they begin the inquiry. For Thomas Aquinas, the application of logic could only strengthen and illumine matters of faith, directing us toward the truth and, ultimately, "the vision of God in His essence." His theology is celebrated by numerous vernacular authors, including Dante Alighieri, who introduces his readers to Thomas in the sphere of the sun (*Divine Comedy, Paradiso* X–XII).

POLITICAL AND PSEUDO-HISTORICAL TEXTS

Like Thomas Aquinas, the Venerable Bede (c. 673–735 C.E.) left behind him an impressive body of writings. He entered the twin monastery of Wearmouth-Jarrow in Northumbria by age seven, and remained there for the duration of his life. In an autobiographical note, Bede describes his passion for writing and teaching: "amid the observance of the discipline of the Rule [of St. Benedict] and the daily task of singing in the church," he writes, "it has always been my delight to learn or to teach or to write" (*Ecclesiastical History*, book 5, chapter 24). Bede's works were widely read and copied throughout the Middle Ages; today, they survive in hundreds of manuscripts. Among these, the *Ecclesiastical History of the English People* (*Historia Ecclesiastica Gentis Anglorum*, c. 731 C.E.) is the most famous.

As the title suggests, the *Ecclesiastical History* provides an extensive overview of the history of England, focusing on the conversion of its inhabitants to Christianity (with notable attention paid to St. Augustine and his followers). Bede prefaces this discussion with an introduction, at the beginning of book one, to the island of Britain and her inhabitants. He writes: "Britain, an island in the ocean, formerly called Albion, is situated in the northwest, opposite the coasts of Germany, France, and Spain, which form the greatest part of Europe, though at a considerable distance from them." He comments on the richness of the land, full of grain, trees, cattle, vines, and waterfowls; the rivers, meanwhile, abound in fish (particularly salmon and eels). Bede groups the inhabitants according to their five languages: English, British, Irish, Pictish, and Latin—noting, however, that the Latin tongue has become most common, due to the study of the scriptures. He then begins to describe the early cycles of immigration and invasion, beginning with the Britons (from whom the land derives its name) and followed by the Picts (from Scythia), the Irish, the Romans (who subsequently withdraw their legions from Britain after the Goths' sack of Rome in 410 C.E.), and finally the English (or Angles), who brought peace to the island and promoted the spread of Christianity.

Bede's *Ecclesiastical History* affords us detailed accounts of the church conflicts that plagued Britain throughout the so-called Dark Ages. It also contains several mentions of historical references that have subsequently been linked to legendary materials, such as the battle at Mount Baden, of Arthurian fame. The *History* is also notable in that it provides significant information about the earliest English poet, Cædmon (died c. 680), a lay brother who was a herdsman at the monastery of Streonæshalch (Whitby Abbey). After falling asleep one night out in the fields, Cædmon had a miraculous dream that inspired him to compose a nine-line hymn praising God as Creator of heaven and earth. This poem is one of the earliest attested examples of Old English.

The oldest surviving example of Old French, meanwhile, is contained in the Strasbourg Oaths, a political document that records the oaths of allegiance made by two grandsons of Charlemagne, Charles the Bald and Louis the German, in 842 C.E. Upon Charles's request, the Frankish historian Nithard (died c. 843–844 C.E.) wrote a history of the years 841 to 843 C.E. in Latin. Nithard included the text of the Oaths, taking care to preserve the languages in which they had been originally delivered orally: German and Old French. An Old French religious poem, the Cantilena of St. Eulalia, also survives from around the same period (c. 879–881 C.E.), marking the beginning of the acceptance of the vernacular as a literary medium in the French-speaking world. Nonetheless, surviving texts in Old French from prior to the twelfth century—such as the *Life of St. Alexis* and the *Song of Roland*—are few.

The *Song of Roland* (*Chanson de Roland*, c. 1090–1100) is the most famous surviving Old French epic. The oldest copy dates from the mid-twelfth century, and is preserved in MS Digby 23 of the Bodleian Library (Oxford University). The *Roland* celebrates the courage of Charlemagne's rear guard, led by the count Roland, his friend Olivier, and the archbishop Turpin, who were massacred at Roncevaux in a savage and treacherous attack by the Saracens. Although the poem is based on an historical event, described by Einhard in his *Vita Karoli*, the author of the *Roland* takes certain liberties with his source. Thus, in Einhard, the Frankish rear guard is attacked by the Basques at Roncevaux as the men return from Spain. In the *Roland*, however, they succumb to the treachery of the Saracens; the poem thus establishes a binary opposition between the noble and Christian Franks, and the treacherous infidels. The eponymous hero of the *Song of Roland* will stop at nothing—even death— to defend Charlemagne's Christian empire, and when Roland dies, his soul is carried away to heaven by angels. In this way, the *Roland* attests to, and participates in, the celebration of French national identity, and also bears witness to western Europe's dedication to upholding Christianity against the growing threat of Islam. Interestingly, in the thirteenth or fourteenth century, the *Song of Roland* of Digby 23 was bound together with a copy of Calcidius's Latin translation of Plato's *Timaeus*. Read together, the two parts of this manuscript attest to the humanist spirit of the age: whereas the *Timaeus*, placed at the beginning of the codex, underlines the importance of recording our history and identity in writing, the *Roland* actualizes this teaching (see Murray, *From Plato to Lancelot*).

The work of Geoffrey of Monmouth offers another example of pseudo-historical narrative. Geoffrey drew from the writings of Bede, Gildas (*On the Ruin of Britain*) and Nennius (*History of the Britons*), as well as early Welsh sources, in order to compose his *History of the Kings of Britain* (c. 1137). His work also incorporates knowledge handed down in the Briton oral tradition. In the dedication, he comments that he will relate an account of the kings of Britain just as they "were also celebrated by many people in a pleasant manner and by heart, as if they had been written."

Rather than writing a work filled with florid language, Geoffrey desired to fascinate his readers with the history itself. He was a master storyteller, and although some of his accounts appear to be products of his own creation, he succeeded in fashioning a historical narrative that was quickly and widely received by the people of the Middle Ages. Although his readers may have been mesmerized by the stories of Arthur and Merlin, his nationalistic undertones were perhaps even more appealing. By opening his history with the story of Brutus, the great-grandson of Aeneas, and tracing his line through Arthur up to the more modern kings, Geoffrey establishes Britain as a power rivaling those on the European continent. His account of the defeat of Rome is particularly significant when viewed in this light. Like other readers and writers of his time, Geoffrey was acutely sensitive to the relevance of ancient authority and its impact on the medieval mind.

Completed exactly half a century prior to the coronation of Richard the Lionhearted, Geoffrey's work further orients British history around the central event of Christ's coming. He states explicitly in his dedication that he wishes to provide an account of the kings who came before the Incarnation, as well as those who came after it. More than merely providing a nationalistic account of the Arthurian legend (though it was the most comprehensive Arthurian chronicle of its time), Geoffrey's *History* establishes British history within the meta-narrative of Christianity. Throughout the text there are references to the biblio-historical events that occur simultaneously with those Geoffrey documents in Britain. This correlation becomes particularly evident when he depicts Arthur as a distinctly Christian king who carries the image of the Virgin Mary on his shield into battle. The influence of Geoffrey of Monmouth was far-reaching; in addition to popularizing the subject of the mythical king Arthur, he is the first to hint at the treason of Mordred and his liaison with Guinevere (although one must wait until Chrétien de Troyes for the introduction of the adulterous affair between Guinevere and Lancelot).

Around 1155 Wace completed his *Roman de Brut,* a translation of the *History of the Kings of Britain* into Old French verse. Wace builds upon the tradition of writing an epic in the vernacular, which had begun with the *Song of Roland, Le Roman d'Enéas* (c. 1150) and the other early religious works mentioned above. (Five years before writing the *Roman de Brut,* he had in fact composed the *Roman de Rou,* another pseudo-historical narrative tracing the history of France back to Troy.) By presenting his work as a "romance" rather than a "history" Wace deliberately reclaims the imagination for the genre of history. Rather than adhering strictly to Geoffrey's Latin text, he edits some themes and inserts others in an effort to legitimize the role of the Normans as inheritors of the British throne. His introduction of the Round Table, previously absent from the Arthurian legend presented by Geoffrey, emphasizes equality as the basis of British rule, advances the program of his own writings, and gives birth to one of the most famous and popular of medieval motifs. This motif continues to appear in later articulation of the Arthurian legends, from Thomas Malory, to Alfred Tennyson, and even to T.H. White.

It would be remiss, in this discussion of history, not to make mention of arguably the most famous historical document to survive from medieval England: the Magna Carta. In early 1215, discontented English barons challenged King John (1167–1216) for his infringement of their liberties, and a brief civil war ensued. By mid-June, a precarious peace was established as a result of the signing of the *Magna Carta* (*Great Charter*) at Runnymede. Composed in Latin, it was both a resurrection of and a reaction against the charter instituted by John's father, Henry II. Though it is difficult to claim that the Magna Carta was veritable as a constitutional or legislative document, the transformation it underwent during the interval between its original conception and 1225, when it was genuinely granted by the Crown (then Henry III), provides a textual description of the relationship between the church, the baronetcy, and the monarchy in early thirteenth-century Britain.

The original charter comprises sixty-three clauses that do not follow any obvious logical order. The most notable of its dictates include the establishment of freedom for the church, the remittance of all unjust fines and *amercements* (punishments), the removal of *scutage* and other excessive taxes, and the standardization of measurements. It might be said that the voice of Pope Innocent and of the barons can be heard more strongly in the document than that of the king. John had little choice but to accept their demands, establishing the Magna Carta as a record of the imperial limitations of this time rather than a legitimate constitution. Several major revisions took place before its final acceptance by Henry III. Among these were the partition of all clauses dealing with royal forests into a separate Charter of the Forests, and the deletion of the clauses restricting taxation. Though the monarchy successfully reclaimed some of his power before the document was finalized, the Magna Carta still remains a testament to the increasing capacity of the church and of the British nation to legally resist an erratic government.

HAGIOGRAPHIC TEXTS

Much medieval narrative was devoted to religious themes, and those mentioned in this section constitute but a meager sampling of works read with great attention and fervor during the period in question. Before delving into some of the most popular hagiographical works (i.e., biographies of saints), we will begin with one of the most influential medieval treatises on religious life: the *Rule* of St. Benedict.

In his *Dialogues,* St. Gregory the Great notes that St. Benedict of Nursia (c. 480–547 C.E.), who founded the great monastery of Monte Cassino in Italy, "wrote a Rule for monks that is remarkable for its discretion and its clarity of language" (Book 11, ch. 36). The best surviving copy is preserved in a ninth-century manuscript of the abbey of St. Gall (Codex San Gallensis 914) in Switzerland, founded by Irish monks in the sixth century. Benedict's *Rule* contains a prologue and seventy-three chapters, dealing with a great variety of topics. On one hand, he carefully teaches and expounds upon what he considers to be the greatest Christian virtues—such as humility (see especially ch. 7, which outlines the twelve steps of humility, presented as rungs on a ladder leading to heaven), silence (see ch. 6), and obedience. The prologue makes explicit the main tenets of religious life: one must renounce one's own will, submitting to the "strong and noble weapons of obedience" (Prol. 3). Benedict goes on to explain that he wishes to form "a school for the Lord's service" (Prol. 45), where the pupils will learn the way to salvation.

On the other hand, though, Benedict also includes specific information on how daily life is to be organized in the monastery. The monastic day revolves around the eight canonical hours and is organized into regular periods of prayer, sleep, spiritual reading, and manual labor (sometimes replaced with intellectual work or teaching). The monks devote themselves to each of the tasks at hand, so "that in all things God may be glorified" (ch. 57). Certain activities can occur simultaneously. Thus, Benedict prescribes reading aloud during meals (see ch. 38). He also carefully regulates the type and amount of food adherents to the Rule receive: two meals a day, each composed of two cooked dishes. Each monk is also allotted a pound of bread a day and a ration of wine. The consumption of meat is reserved solely for the sick and the weak (see chs. 39 and 40).

The popularity of the *Rule,* which led to its adoption in numerous religious houses and endures to our own age, was no doubt due to the emphasis Benedict placed on moderation. Although Benedictines do not maintain any personal possessions, they are provided with sufficient food, drink, and clothing by their abbot (see ch. 33), and are encouraged to refrain from overly excessive fasting and vigil.

The ascetic life was the subject of many Latin and vernacular stories during the Middle Ages, and the *Life of St. Alexis* (*Vie de saint Alexis,* c. 1140) provides us with a representative example of hagiographical narrative. According to the Old French text, Alexis's parents, who had trouble conceiving a child, prayed to God that he might bless them with a son. When Alexis is born, his father Eufemien has great plans for him. He imagines

The Magdalene Reading, Rogier van der Weyden, 1445.

that he will serve the emperor and become a rich and powerful citizen of Rome. Alexis, however, has other plans: he desires only to serve God. When his parents arrange for him to marry a suitable young woman, he goes through with the ceremony but refuses to consummate their union in the marriage chamber, explaining to his young spouse that there can be no true happiness in *this* world. Before leaving his wife, however, Alexis entrusts to her his ring and his sword, thereby signifying the solidity of their union. Later in his life, Alexis returns to Rome, but is so changed in appearance from his ascetic life that no one recognizes him. He lives as a stranger under the stairs in his father's own home.

When Alexis's family discovers the holy man's dead body, he is clutching a letter detailing the account of his life; it is read aloud in front of the Pope, and Alexis's parents lament the loss of their son. But his bride, who has remained in Rome at his parents' home, waiting for him, finally understands the lesson Alexis attempted to impart to her on their wedding night: she henceforth commits to taking her vows and devoting the rest of her earthly life to God's service. The Alexis legends attest to the extraordinary reading and rewriting of hagiographical narrative during (especially) the eleventh, twelfth, and thirteenth centuries. The Old French *Vie de saint Alexis* is itself the translation of an earlier Latin *Vita* (itself derived from a Syriac *Life*). Alexis's story was so popular, indeed, that it resulted in the composition of other vernacular versions of the legend, including a Middle-High German account, according to which Alexis performs a miracle when his bride dies and is laid to rest beside him: the saint's body rolls over and holds her in his arms, embracing her in death. The *Life of Saint Alexis* engages the Augustinian theme of the "city of man" versus the "city of God." It was read with great fervor in religious circles, and may even have served as a model for young women in the religious orders who, like Alexis's bride, were to reserve themselves for their heavenly spouse. To this end the Alexis story was included in the famous *St. Alban's Psalter*

Byzantine mosaic of Saint John Chrysostom (Hagia Sophia, Istanbul, Turkey).

(Hildesheim, Dombibliothek MS St Godehard 1) belonging to the anchoress and prioress Christina of Markyate.

Few stories captured the imagination of medieval readers more than the legends surrounding St. Brendan the Navigator. The historical St. Brendan was born in County Kerry (in southwestern Ireland) in the late fifth century, but it is his mythical voyage through the Atlantic ocean to paradise that interests us here. The earliest account is provided in the Latin *Navigatio sancti Brendani* (or *Voyage of St. Brendan*), composed by an Irish monk living on the Continent in the late seventh or early eighth century. This text is not a typical saint's *Life* (as is, for example, the *Life of St. Alexis*), in that it does not provide much information on Brendan's birth and death. Rather, it is more of an adventure-quest, which constitutes a sort of chapter of Brendan's life.

Upon hearing the account of Barinthius's (or Barrind's) journey into the West, Brendan sets sail with a group of monks. Their circular seven-year journey—a pilgrimage in the truest sense of the term—from and back to Ireland takes the monks via many extraordinary islands, including an island full of giant sheep, hell (which closely resembles a volcano), a rock where they encounter Judas (who benefits from a day of rest on Christian feast days and the sabbath) and paradise (presented as an island far out in the Atlantic and surrounded by dense fog). Most notable, though, is the annual encounter with the great fish, or whale, Jasconius (deriving its name from the Old Irish í asc, "fish"): every Easter, Brendan and his fellow travelers land on the beast's back to celebrate the Mass. Scholars have pointed out that Brendan's pilgrimage bears remarkable resemblance to the Celtic *immrama* (tales of sea-journeys to the otherworld) and *echtrai* (tales about journeys to the otherworld but not necessarily undertaken by sea). With the visit to heaven and hell, it also provides an important precursor to Dante Alighieri's quest for paradise in the *Divine Comedy*.

Brendan's story had such an impact on the medieval imagination that a number of medieval and early modern maps include "St. Brendan's Isle" (which bears a certain resemblance to the mythical Hy-Brasil) or Brendan's whale-island in their depiction of the western Atlantic. To this day, the people of St. Malo in Brittany remember Brendan as one of their own, and the village of St. Brandon on the Dingle Peninsula—right at the foot of a mountain named after the saint—claims to be his birth-place. In Scotland, the Orkneys, Greenland, and Iceland, place names refer back to visits (real or legendary) made there by the historical St. Brendan during the sixth century. And as Denis O'Donaghue notes in his *Lives and Legends of Saint Brendan*, in England a little oratory standing at the point where the rivers Avon and Severn meet in the Bristol Channel still bears St. Brendan's name, "to remind the Bristol mariners that once upon a time the great sailor-saint . . . had blessed the seaward approach of their city of Bristol" (214).

In the twelfth century, the *Navigatio* was translated into Old French by an Anglo-Norman poet named Benedeit. Following Benedeit's translation, the story made its way into at least seventeen European languages, including German, Catalan, Occitan, Venetian, and even Old Norse.

CREATIVE TEXTS

St. Brendan's *Voyage*, particularly in the twelfth-century version by Benedeit, can also be labeled a creative work. Benedeit "translates" from his Latin source in order to compose his Old French poem but, in so doing, he adapts the content for his courtly audience (the Anglo-Norman court of King Henry I). In truth, many of the works in the present section also bear religious preoccupations as their central theme, so that the divide between hagiography (e.g., the stories of Brendan and Alexis), epic (e.g., *Roland*), and romance (e.g., Marie de France and Chrétien de Troyes) is less rigid than the modern reader may expect. Nonetheless, a common thread running through all of the works in this section is the establishment and development of vernacular literary (and poetic) traditions.

As our mention of Benedeit's *Voyage* above suggests, the Anglo-Norman court of King Henry I was an important literary center in the early twelfth century. (In addition to Benedeit's *Voyage*, for example, Philippe de Thaün composed there his influential *Bestiaire* or "Bestiary," a vernacular adaptation of the second-century *Physiologus*.) The patronage of the arts grew to new heights under King Henry II and his wife, Eleanor of Aquitaine. By the time of their marriage in 1152, the twelfth-century Renaissance was well underway (see introduction to the present chapter); Geoffrey of Monmouth had composed his *History of the Kings of Britain* (c. 1137); the Old French *Roman d'Enéas*—a translation of the *Aeneid*—had appeared (c. 1150); and classical motifs and themes permeated Old French and Anglo-Norman literary traditions. However, it was also around the same time that a female poetess (to whom Claude Fauchet attributed the name "Marie de France" in 1581) composed a collection of *Lais* (c. 1160–1165) that took as their central matter not the illustrious past of Greece and Rome, but the Celtic, and primarily oral, traditions of the western Atlantic seaboard.

Marie's twelve *Lais* have been preserved in five manuscripts; the best of these is British Library Harley 978, which contains the complete collection. It is Marie's prologue to the *Lais* that is of particular interest to us here. In the opening lines, Marie explains that she first intended to translate a good story from Latin into Old French; but, she adds, so many people had already done that. Her mind then turns to the *Lais* she had heard in Britain and Brittany. By translating them into Old French, and, ultimately, by providing them a written, material form (through the manuscripts that have survived), Marie illustrates the importance of preserving cultural memory—a central theme of Plato's *Timaeus* (see above, "Educational"). It is important to note, however, that Marie does not view the task she sets herself as being divorced from the classical and Mediterranean-centered process of *translatio*, in which the authors of poems like the *Enéas* engaged. She explains, rather, taking Priscian—a Latin grammarian—as her witness, that the ancients wrote obscurely so that we, the moderns, would "gloss the letter" (*gloser la lettre*) of their texts and reveal the meaning with which they had invested them. For Marie, the modern (i.e., medieval) poet is above all other things a glossator, who applies the knowledge gleaned from both a careful reading of classical works, and by listening attentively to the oral traditions of the Celtic West, to the composition of new works in the vernacular.

Marie's *Lais* are full of marvelous creatures, including a mysterious speaking white hind in *Guigemar*, a werewolf in *Bisclaveret*, and even a healing weasel in *Eliduc*. The stories often deal of the love of men and women outside of marriage—an idea predicated on the "refined love" (*fin' amors*) of which the Provençal troubadours sang, and which was labeled courtly love (*amour courtois*) by Gaston Paris in 1883. Thus, *Laüstic* recounts the secret love affair of a married lady and a neighboring knight, while in *Eliduc*, the eponymous hero brings back to his country a young woman who believes Eliduc will marry her, despite the fact that his wife is waiting patiently for him at home. Although scholars have been at pains to determine why Marie at times rewards the lovers and at other times appears to punish them, an important underlying theme of the *Lais* is furnished by the Christian ethical and moral framework Marie provides in her prologue. There she tells her readers that assiduous study will help them "guard against vice." Furthermore, the story of *Eliduc* is steeped in Bernardian theology (see St. Bernard of Clairvaux, in "Philosophical/Theological"), especially the "Four Degrees of Love" (*On Loving God*, ch. 15). In this way, Marie's *Lais* disprove Jean Bodel's claim, in the *Song of the Saxons* (*Chanson des saisnes*, c. 1200) that the "matter of Britain and Brittany" is simply "vain and pleasing." Indeed, provided we learn to "gloss the letter," Marie's Celtic stories reveal themselves to be as "learned and wise" as the myths inherited from Greco-Roman antiquity.

Around the same time as Marie de France was composing her *Lais* in Anglo-Norman England, Chrétien de Troyes had begun writing his *Arthurian Romances* in France, at the court of Eleanor of Aquitaine's daughter, Marie de Champagne. For the first of these, *Erec et Enide* (c. 1165–1170), Chrétien drew heavily on both Martianus Capella's *De nuptiis* and an ancient tale of Welsh provenance—Gereint and Enid—now preserved in the *Mabinogi*. Chrétien composed four other romances, each dealing with a story related to life at the court of the legendary King Arthur: *Cligés* (c. 1170–1175); *Le Chevalier de la Charrette* (*The Knight of the Cart*) or *Lancelot* (c. 1180); *Yvain* (c. 1180) or *Le Chevalier au Lion* (*The*

Knight with the Lion); and *Le Conte du Graal* (*The Story of the Grail*) or *Perceval* (c. 1190).

Most notably, Chrétien contributed two lasting motifs to the Arthurian corpus. In *The Knight of the Cart,* he provides the earliest surviving account of Lancelot's adulterous love for Queen Guinevere. Here, Arthur, who appears only at the beginning and end of the romance, is presented as a bumbling fool, who allows his wife to be abducted by the evil Meleagant. Ironically, it is only because of Lancelot's great love for Guinevere that he, in turn, manages to save her from the clutches of her abductor. Even Gauvain (Gawain), reputed to be the greatest knight at Arthur's court, fails in his quest. Although Lancelot and Guinevere do spend a night together in the kingdom of Gorre, it is nonetheless important to note that Chrétien makes no mention of their ever having sex together (and it is, we might add, the evil Meleagant who jumps to this conclusion when he sees blood on the queen's sheets, caused by a fresh wound of Lancelot's that reopens when he lies down next to his lady). In any case, the *Knight of the Cart* ends with Lancelot and Guinevere's return to court, where they must continue to live out their lives in sad separation: she, as Arthur's queen, and he as his knight.

Chrétien's second-greatest contribution to the Arthurian legends was his articulation of the Grail quest in *Perceval,* his fifth and final romance, composed under the patronage of Philippe of Flanders. (Chrétien probably passed into Philippe's service after the death of Marie de Champagne's husband, Henri, in 1182.) In this book, Chrétien tells the story of the young and naïve Perceval, who has been raised by his mother in a forest, far from society. One day, he sees knights in the wood—he mistakes them for demons, angels, and then even God—and resolves to go to Arthur's court to be knighted himself. When his mother realizes that she can no longer shelter Perceval from the harsh realities of courtly society, she offers him very brief instruction on how to treat ladies and the importance of going to church. She falls down on the doorstep—apparently fainting, but actually dead—and the extraordinarily self-centered Perceval, who apparently feels no need to check on his mother's well-being, steps over her prostate body and rides off, without looking back. Perceval's adventures over the course of Chrétien's romance can be qualified as a "Bildungsroman," that is, the story of the formation of his character. When he fails to ask the right questions (or, in fact, any questions at all) during the Grail procession he witnesses at a mysterious castle, Perceval is condemned to become the "Wretched" and to seek out the Grail and the bleeding lance that accompanied it in the procession. After many adventures, he comes across a group of penitents in the forest on Easter Friday and makes his way to a hermit, to whom he confesses his sins. The book last speaks of Perceval on Easter Sunday, when he takes communion with the hermit. Although Perceval may not have found a physical, material, Grail, he has found God and forgiveness—a fitting ending indeed for Perceval's quest.

But the story then turns to the adventures of Gawain, and abruptly cuts off in mid-sentence. This has led scholars to conjecture that Chrétien died before completing his final masterpiece. However, others contend that the open-endedness of *The Quest for the Grail* was intended by the author. Whatever the case may be, subsequent authors saw themselves authorized, got to work, and wrote an impressive number of sequels, including the immense *Prose Lancelot* and *Vulgate Cycle,* upon which Thomas Mallory later based his influential *Morte d'Arthur* (c. 1450–1470), the great English epic about King Arthur. Mallory added some of his own material to the legends (e.g., the story of Gareth), and the *Morte d'Arthur* remains the best-known work of English-language Arthurian literature today. It inspired, in turn, other rewritings, such as Tennyson's nineteenth-century *Idylls of the King* and T.H. White's twentieth-century *The Once and Future King.*

Equally popular and widespread were the pan-European legends associated with Tristan, a knight of the Round Table, and Iseult (or Isolde), the wife of King Mark of Cornwall. The basic storyline common to all of the versions is as follows: Tristan, nephew of King Mark, is sent to bring Iseult from Ireland to marry his uncle. However, during the sea journey, the wind subsides, the boat progresses very slowly, and the travelers become thirsty. Tristan and Iseult inadvertently consume a love potion made by Iseult's mother, which she had disguised as a bottle of wine, to be drunk on Iseult's wedding night. Tristan and Iseult fall hopelessly in love.

The earliest surviving accounts of Tristan and Iseult's love affair are divided into two categories. On one hand, the courtly branch includes the Anglo-Norman version by Thomas of Britain (c. 1170), and the German *Tristan* by Gottfried von Strassburg (c. 1210). The common branch refers to the work of the Old French poet Béroul (c. 1190), and the German Eilhart von Oberge (c. 1170). In the preface to *Cligés*, Chrétien de Troyes claims to have composed a story about "King Mark and Iseult the Blond," and Marie de France provides her own, very short contribution to the Tristan legends in her *lai* of *Chevrefoil* (c. 1165). It is, however, the later *Prose Tristan* (c. 1240) that provided the inspiration for Thomas Mallory's first and second "Boke of Syr Trystrams de Lyones" in the *Morte d'Arthur.*

The story follows a slightly different course with every retelling. In all variations Iseult marries Mark, but she and Tristan remain passionately in love because of the potion they consumed. (And in this way, according to the twelfth-century doctrine of intentionality, articulated by Peter Abelard, Tristan and Iseult are absolved from sin.) The king's men attempt to catch the lovers and reveal them to Mark, but, for the most part, Tristan uses his great wit to escape their plots. In Béroul's version the love potion wears off after three years, inciting the characters to renounce their adulterous affair, although they still cannot refrain from loving one another. Béroul thus introduces a morally ambiguous dimension into the story, as the lovers are now free to act according to their conscience.

In the *Prose Tristan* and Thomas Mallory's *Morte d'Arthur,* the story culminates when Tristan—who has married another princess, also named Iseult—is wounded by a poisoned weapon. Only his true love, Iseult of Ireland, can heal him. Tristan sends for her: if she returns on the ship, the sailors will fly white flags; if she does not, the sails will be black. As Tristan lies dying, his wife spies the ship on the horizon. She sees the white sails but cannot bring herself to reveal the truth, and tells Tristan the sails are black. He immediately dies. Iseult of Ireland arrives shortly thereafter and out of grief she falls dead over Tristan's body. In a remarkable climactic scene, Eilhart recounts how King Mark discovers the truth: "A short time later, King Mark learned the story of how Tristan died, as well as his wife the queen, and about their mutual love that had bound them together. And now he was told the truth, that it was because of a drink that, against their wishes, they loved each other so much. Then he lamented ever more that he had not known this in time, while they were still in life" (vv. 9464–9476). Together with the messenger who revealed the truth to him, King Mark brings the bodies of Tristan and Iseult across the sea. He buries them with great honor and plants a rosebush and grapevine on their tombs.

The legends of *Tristan and Iseult* have analogues in early Welsh and Irish literatures. Most significantly, versions have survived in nearly every European vernacular, including French, English (*Sir Tristem* [c. 1300]), Scandinavian (*Af Tristram ok Ísodd* and *Tristrams kvœði*), Dutch, Spanish (the fourteenth-century *Carta enviada por Hiseo la Brunda a Tristá* by the Arcipreste de Hita, and the fifteenth-century *Respuesta de Tristán*), Czech (thirteenth c.), Italian (*Cantari di Tristano* and *Tristano Veneto*), and Belarusian (*Povest Trychane* [c. 1560]). In some versions, the lovers even have children: the eponymous hero of the late medieval *Ysaie le Triste* (*Ysaie the Sad*) is their son.

Most of the creative works discussed above originated in the twelfth century, and can all be qualified as courtly (that is, destined to oral performance in front of a court audience). But the thirteenth and fourteenth centuries saw the rise of encyclopedic, and learned, vernacular narratives, such as Jean de Meun's continuation of Guillaume de Lorris's courtly dream vision, the *Roman de la Rose,* and an anonymous fourteenth-century friar's translation and allegorization of Ovid's *Metamorphoses,* the *Ovide moralisé.* The best-known of these *summa,* and undoubtedly the most influential, was the *Comedia* (*Comedy,* c. 1308–1321), by the Italian poet Dante Alighieri. (Dante did not originally entitle his work the *Divine Comedy;* it was not until a later date that scribes and editors added the epithet "Divine" to the title.)

Dante's poem is divided into three canticles: *Inferno* (*Hell*), *Purgatorio* (*Purgatory*), and *Paradiso* (*Paradise*). The second and third canticles contain thirty-three poems each (significant in medieval numerology as the age of Christ when he died), whereas hell—a place where the sinners have lost the good of the intellect and have, through the choices they made in life, chosen to live far from God—contains thirty-four. All together, then, the entire *Comedy* contains one hundred cantos, the perfect square of the number ten, itself the number of perfection, order, and completion.

It is impossible to do justice to the complexity of Dante's masterpiece, which draws upon classical and medieval sources (notably Virgil, Boethius, Macrobius, Plato, Ovid, Augustine, Thomas Aquinas, Bonaventure, and more), and engages in a fervent satire of the morals of Dante's time and the political strife that so characterized life in thirteenth- and fourteenth-century Florence (especially the wars between the Guelph and Ghibelline factions). The poem begins in a dark wood—a *locus horridus*—where Dante has lost the "true path" and encounters three terrifying beasts. The darkness of the wood signifies Dante's spiritual slumber; he has moved away from the light that shines down from the top of the mountain. The beasts, meanwhile—a leopard, she-wolf, and a lion—recall the passage from Jeremiah (5:6): "Wherefore a lion out of the wood hath slain them, a wolf in the evening hath spoiled them, a leopard watcheth for their cities: every one that shall go out thence shall be taken, because their transgressions are multiplied, their rebellions strengthened." Summoned by a lady in heaven, Beatrice (whose name signifies "blessed" and who personifies a young girl Dante loved from afar in his youth), the classical poet Virgil appears to lead Dante back to the "true path," that "way of the righteous" of which Psalm 1 speaks. On his journey through hell, Dante encounters a slew of pagan poets (e.g., Homer, Aristotle, and Ovid) in Limbo, and then a series of mythical and historical figures who have succumbed to one of the seven deadly sins and never repented during their lifetime. Each condemned soul is subjet to a *contrapasso,* a fitting form of punishment for their respective sins. Thus in the circle of the lustful (canto five) the pilgrim meets Paolo and Francesca, who succumbed to their illicit love-affair after reading of Lancelot and Guinevere (probably in the *Prose Lancelot*), and who are now buffeted around in a perpetual whirlwind, symbolic of their inordinate desires in life; in canto nineteen, we meet the pope Nicolas III, a simonist who is half-buried upside down, like money in a great purse, and whose feet are set afire (he announces boldly that he is waiting for the current pope, Boniface); and so on, until we reach the innermost circle of hell, where Satan is frozen in a great lake of ice and endlessly munches on the heads of the traitors Judas, Brutus, and Cassius.

In the second canticle, Virgil leads Dante up Mount Purgatory, through seven terraces—each one representing deadly sin: pride, envy, wrath, sloth, avarice and prodigality, gluttony and lust. As he climbs the mountain, Dante is himself purged of sin and prepares to encounter Beatrice herself, who will guide him through paradise. Virgil, meanwhile, disappears, and we are left to understand that the four pagan virtues (prudence, temperance, fortitude, and justice) are not sufficient for admittance into paradise. Only the believer, who recognizes and embodies the three theological virtues (faith, hope, and charity) can complete the journey. After passing through the earthly paradise, a beautiful garden reminiscent of Eden, Dante is purified and ready to rise to the stars in the company of Beatrice.

Dante's *Paradiso* is carefully based on the Platonic division of the universe into ten spheres: the Moon, Mercury, Venus, the Sun, Mars, Jupiter, Saturn, the Fixed Stars, the Primum Mobile, and the Empyrean. In the sphere of the Sun, the pilgrim encounters such notable figures as St. Thomas Aquinas and St. Bonaventure—the writings of whom profoundly influenced Dante's work. Indeed, as the *Comedy* unfolds, it becomes clear that it represents what Bonaventure would describe as a "journey of the mind toward God." And, when Dante's journey culminates in the beatific vision, it effectively embodies the principle articulated by Thomas Aquinas in chapter 104 of the *Compendium of Theology*: that "the ultimate end of the intellectual creature is the vision of God in His essence." Interestingly, Beatrice ascends into the vision in canto thirty-one, leaving Dante in the capable hands of St. Bernard of Clairvaux, as he contemplates the "love that moves the sun and the other stars" (canto thirty-three).

Dante's work had precursors in the Celtic and Latin traditions (e.g., the *Visions* of Tnugdal and Adomnán; Marie de France's *Espurgatoire seint Patriz;* St. Brendan's *Voyage;* Macrobius's *Commentary on Scipio's Dream*). Furthermore, the *Comedy* clearly attests to how its author read and implemented classical works, such as Virgil's *Aeneid*. Although the *Comedy* was not the only allegorical vision of heaven and hell described by medieval authors, it was probably the most influential.

About half a century later, though, William Langland completed another very popular allegorical work: the *Piers Plowman* or *Visio Willelmi de Petro Ploughman* (*William's Vision of Piers Plowman*, c. 1360–1399), a Middle English narrative poem composed in unrhymed alliterative verse. The poem, divided into sections known as "passus" (step), articulates, like Dante's *Comedy,* the quest for the Christian life. (At the same time, like the *Comedy*, it offers a poignant social satire.) The poem begins when the narrator, Will, falls asleep—a sign of spiritual dullness—in the Malvern Hills (in Worcestershire). Will dreams of a tall tower where truth dwells (God, or heaven), set on a hill, and a dungeon of wrong (the Devil, or hell), in a deep valley far below. In between the two lies a "fair field full of folk," representing the world of living men. The narrator describes all of the different classes of people he observes there, until a lady representing the holy church rebukes him for falling asleep and explains the meaning of his vision. There follows a series of Macrobian visions, during which other allegorical characters appear (such as Conscience, Liar, and Reason). Conscience attempts to convince mankind to reject the seven deadly sins and commit instead to seeking out St. Truth. Piers, a simple plowman, appears and offers himself as a guide; because he is simple and has common sense and a clean conscience, Piers knows the way. In the last section of Langland's poem, Will, aided by Thought, Wit, and Study, goes in search of three allegorical characters: Dowell ("Do-Well"), Dobet ("Do-Better"), and Dobest ("Do-Best").

Piers Plowman was an extraordinarily popular tale throughout the later Middle Ages and well beyond, and it enjoyed success among a wide readership—from literate city tradesmen to country gentry, and even more learned (Latinate) readers. It survives in over fifty manuscripts. Its popularity in its own time is well attested by John Ball's letter to the men of Essex in the Peasant's Revolt of 1381, in which he admonishes them to "do welle and bettere." Thomas Usk also references Langland's poem, in his late fourteenth-century *Testament of Love* (c. 1385). *Piers Plowman* also significantly influenced future English authors, such as Spenser, Milton, and John Bunyan.

Like Dante and William Langland, Geoffrey Chaucer centered his best-known work, the *Canterbury Tales* (c. 1386–1400), on the theme of pilgrimage. Set along the medieval pilgrimage route from Southwark to Canterbury, the story begins in a tavern, where a group of pilgrims is assembling to make their way to the tomb of St. Thomas Beckett. In the prologue, the narrator acquaints the reader with the "condicioun," the "degree," and the "array" of each of the pilgrims, drawing upon the conventions of physiognomy. Thus, the rowdy Miller has all the appearances of a rather dubious Celt: red hair, a wart (with red hair growing out of it) on his nose, etc. One senses already the licentiousness of another character, the infamous Wife of Bath, who wears red stockings (like a prostitute) and has spent the greater part of her adult life marrying men younger than she and traveling around like a professional pilgrim—she has been to Jerusalem, Santiago de Compostela, and a number of other exotic locations. With witty humor, Chaucer also points out the shortcomings of his Prioress: instead of promoting charity (*caritas*), she wears a brooch engraved with a quote from Virgil and celebrating *eros:* "Amor vincit omnia." The Host proposes to the company that they hold a storytelling competition on the way to Canterbury; whoever tells the best tale will receive a dinner paid for by the group. The Knight—a gentle fellow who, of all the pilgrims, appears to be the most reasonable—is selected to tell the first story, and he proceeds with a tale that Chaucer extracted primarily from Statius's *Thebaid,* which is full of Boethian resonances. (In addition to Classical sources, Chaucer draws throughout the *Canterbury Tales* on the work of his contemporaries, such as Boccaccio's *Decameron.*)

One by one, the pilgrims make their offering, sometimes interrupted by squabbles of a less-than-amicable nature. The genre of the tales, and the rhyme schemes in which they are composed, is as varied as the pilgrims themselves. Following the Knight's tale of romance and courtly love are the *fabliaux* of the Miller, the Reeve, and the Cook. The Man of Law's Tale is of a more religious bent, but we return to the genre of fabliaux with the tale of the infamous Wife of Bath. Other genres include the Breton lai, the beast fable, and the sermon.

The last of the pilgrims to speak is the Parson. As the travelers come near Canterbury, the Host entreats him to "knytte up wel a greet mateere," that is, to close the game. Chaucer accomplishes much more than that, however, with this final monologue. Rather than telling a fable (as so many of his companions have), the Parson speaks of the glorious pilgrimage that culminates in the heavenly Jerusalem; he also offers a homily about the three steps of penitence and the seven deadly sins, reminding us of the true meaning of the pilgrimage in which the reader and Chaucer's characters have been participating. Chaucer then concludes the *Canterbury Tales* with a retraction that doubles as a personal confession. Just as the pilgrimage itself is a physical outworking of an inner transformation, the process of writing this book serves as a means of purification for its author. To emphasize the theme of penitence and forgiveness, Chaucer situates the journey during the season of Lent and Easter, indicating to his readers that even fables and tales can communicate themes of eternal significance. Along with the *Canterbury Tales,* Geoffrey Chaucer's other works—including the *Book of the Duchess,* the *Legend of*

Good Women, the *Parliament of Fowls,* and a translation of Guillaume de Lorris and Jean de Meun's famous dream vision, the *Roman de la Rose*—have rightly earned him fame as the most-loved and most-widely read English poet of the Middle Ages.

CONCLUSION

The texts summarized above provide only a brief sampling of medieval masterpieces. Readers who wish to gain a more thorough understanding of the materials should refer to the primary texts themselves before turning to other foundational works, such as Hugh of St. Victor's *Didascalicon,* John Gower's *Confessio Amantis,* John of Garland's commentaries on Ovid's *Metamorphoses,* the pilgrim's guide to Santiago (along with Rome and Jerusalem, one of the three great Christian pilgrimage sites of the Middle Ages), Giovanni Bocaccio's *Decameron,* and Christine de Pisan's *Cité des Dames* (City of Ladies), to name but a few. Readers would do well, also, to take into closer consideration than has been possible here the rich manuscript evidence that enables us to account more adequately for what kinds of books and texts were specifically used by medieval readers for learning, public display, or personal devotion. One thinks, for example, of the impressive Moralized Bibles that became so popular in the thirteenth and fourteenth centuries, or the beautiful Books of Hours produced for so many noble men and women (see Eamon Duffy's *Marking the Hours: English People and their Prayers,* 1240–1570), of which the classic example is the *Très Riches Heures* written and illuminated for the French duke Jean de Berry at the beginning of the fifteenth century.

What is clear from the pages that precede is that the richness of the medieval Latin and vernacular traditions of writing and reading leave no doubt that the period extending from the fall of Rome to the late fifteenth century was far from a "Dark Age" devoid of cultural production. Although oral storytelling traditions continued to flourish throughout medieval Europe, these centuries were also foundational in affirming the culture of the book, and of reading, in learned and court circles alike. Clearly, medieval readers were conscious of what Benoît de Sainte-Maure tells us so eloquently in his mid-twelfth-century *Roman de Troie* (Romance of Troy): without books, and, consequently, without readers, "we should live [not only as children as the *Timaeus* suggests, but] as beasts."

RECOMMENDED READING

Baranski, Zygmunt and Martin McLaughlin, eds. *Italy's Three Crowns: Reading Petrarch, Dante, Bocaccio.* Oxford, United Kingdom: Bodleian Library, 2007.

Bloch, Howard. *The Anonymous Marie de France.* Chicago: U Chicago P, 2006.

Brown, Michelle P. *Understanding Illuminated Manuscripts: A Guide to Technical Terms.* Los Angeles: Getty Museum, 2004.

Cahill, Thomas. *Mysteries of the Middle Ages: The Rise of Feminism, Science, and Art from the Cults of Catholic Europe.* New York: N.A. Talese, 2006.

Curtius, E.R. *European Literature and the Latin Middle Ages.* Princeton, NJ: Princeton UP, 1991.

Duggan, Joseph. *The Romances of Chrétien de Troyes.* New Haven, Conn.: Yale UP, 2001.

Echard, SIân and Stephen Partridge. *The Book Unbound: Editing and Reading Medieval Manuscripts and Texts.* Toronto: U Toronto P, 2004.

Fleming, John V. *An Introduction to Franciscan Literature of the Middle Ages.* Chicago: Franciscan Herald Press, 1977.

————. *Reason and the Lover*. Princeton, NJ: Princeton UP, 1984.

————. *The Roman de la Rose: A Study in Allegory and Iconography*. Princeton, NJ: Princeton UP, 1969.

Huot, Sylvia. *From Song to Book*. Ithaca, NY: Cornell UP, 1987.

Jacoff, Rachel, ed. *The Cambridge Companion to Dante*. Cambridge, United Kingdom: Cambridge UP, 2007.

Jeffrey, David Lyle. *Chaucer and Scriptural Tradition*. Ottawa: U Ottawa P, 1979.

Jordan, William C. *Europe in the High Middle Ages*. London: Penguin, 2004.

Kelly, Douglas. *The Conspiracy of Allusion: Description, Rewriting, and Authorship from Macrobius to Medieval Romance*. Leiden: Brill, 1999.

Lacy, Norris J. and Joan Tasker Grimbert. *A Companion to Chrétien de Troyes*. Cambridge, United Kingdom: D.S. Brewer, 2005.

Lerer, Seth, ed. *The Yale Companion to Chaucer*. New Haven, Conn.: Yale UP, 2007.

Lewis, C.S. *The Disgarded Image: An Introduction to Medieval and Renaissance Literature*. Cambridge, United Kingdom: Cambridge UP, 1964.

Mazzota, Giuseppe. *Dante, Poet of the Desert: History and Allegory in the Divine Comedy*. Princeton, NJ: Princeton UP, 1987.

Meehan, Bernard. *The Book of Durrow: a Medieval Masterpiece at Trinity College Dublin*. Dublin: Townhouse, 1996.

————. *The Book of Kells: an Illustrated Introduction to the Manuscript in Trinity College Dublin*. New York: Thames and Hudson, 1994.

Murray, K. Sarah-Jane. *From Plato to Lancelot: A Preface to Chrétien de Troyes*. Syracuse, NY: Syracuse UP, 2008.

Reydam-Schils, Gretchen, ed. *Plato's* Timaeus *as Cultural Icon*. Notre Dame, IN: U Notre Dame P, 2003.

Southern, Richard W. *St. Anselm: A Portrait in a Landscape*. Cambridge, United Kingdom: Cambridge UP, 1992.

————. *Scholastic Humanism and the Unification of Europe*. 3 vols. Cambridge, MA: Blackwell, 1997.

————. *Western Society and the Church in the Middle Ages*. London: Penguin, 1990.

Tennyson, Alfred E. *Idylls of the King*. London: Penguin, 1959.

Wetherbee, Winthrop. *Platonism and Poetry in the Twelfth Century. The Literary Influence of the School of Chartres*. Princeton, NJ: Princeton UP, 1972.

Whalen, Logan. *Marie de France and the Poetics of Memory*. Washington, D.C.: Catholic U of America P, 2008.

White, T.H. *Once and Future King*. New York: Ace, 1996.

PRIMARY SOURCES

Alighieri, Dante. *The Divine Comedy*, Book 1: *Inferno*. Edited and translated by Anthony Esolen. New York: Modern Library, 2002.

————. *The Divine Comedy*, Book 2: *Purgatory*. Edited and translated by Anthony Esolen. New York: Modern Library, 2003.

————. *The Divine Comedy*, Book 3: *Paradise*. Edited and translated by Anthony Esolen. New York: Modern Library, 2004.

Alighieri, Dante. *The Divine Comedy, Part 3: Paradiso*. Introduction by Barbara Reynolds. Translated by Dorothy L. Sayers. New York: Penguin Classics, 1962.

Al-Ghazali. *Incoherence of the Philosophers*. Edited and translated by Michael E. Marmura. Provo, UT: Brigham Young UP, 1997.

Anselm. *St. Anselm of Canterbury: The Major Works*. Translated by Brian Davis and Gill Evans. New York: Oxford UP, 1998.

Aristotle. *The Complete Works of Aristotle: The Revised Oxford Translation*. Translated by J. Barnes. Oxford, United Kingdom: Oxford UP, 1995.

Augustine. *City of God*. Translated by Garry Willis. New York: Viking, 1999.

Bede. *Ecclesiastical History of the English People*. Loeb Classical Library. Cambridge, MA: Harvard UP, 2007.

Benedict. *The Rule of St. Benedict.* Translated by Timothy Fry. New York: Vintage, 1998.

Benoît de Sainte-Maure. *Le Roman de Troie: Extraits du manuscrit de Milan.* Edited and translated by Emmanuelle Baumgartner and Françoise Vieillard. Paris: Livre de Poche, 1998.

———. *Le roman de Troie.* Edited by Léopold Constans and Edmond Faral. Paris: Champion, 1922.

Bernard of Clairvaux. *Selected Works.* Translated by G.R. Evans. New York: Pauline Press, 1987.

Béroul. *The Romance of Tristan with the Tale of Tristan's Madness.* Translated by Alan S. Fedrick. London: Penguin, 1978.

Bible moraliseé: Codex Vindobonensis 2554, Vienna, Österreichischen Nationalbibliothek. With a commentary and translation by Gerald B. Guest. London: Harvey Miller, 1995.

Bocaccio, Giovanni. *Decameron.* Translated by Mark Musa and Peter Bonanello, with an introduction by Thomas G. Bergin. New York: Signet Classics, 2002.

Boethius. *The Consolation of Philosophy.* Translated by Victor Ernest Watts. London: Penguin, 1976.

Book of Durrow. See Bernard Meehan (under "recommended reading").

Book of Kells. See Bernard Meehan (under "recommended reading").

Bowers, John M. *Chaucer and Langland: The Antagonistic Tradition.* Notre Dame, IN: U Notre Dame P, 2007.

Calcidius. *Timaeus.* Edited by J.H. Waszink. London: Warburg Institute, 1962.

La Chanson de Roland. Edited by Joseph Duggan et al. 3 vols. Turnhout: Brepols, 2005.

Chaucer, Geoffrey. *The Canterbury Tales.* Translated by Nevill Coghill. London: Penguin, 1977.

———. *The Riverside Chaucer.* Edited by Larry D. Benson. Oxford, United Kingdom: Oxford UP, 1988.

Chesterton, G.K. *Saint Thomas Aquinas: The Dumb Ox.* New York: Image, 1974.

Chrétien de Troyes. *Arthurian Romances.* Translated by William Kibler. London: Penguin, 1991.

———. *Le roman de Perceval ou le conte du graal.* Tübingen: Niemeyer, 1993. (see also Chrétien de Troyes, *Arthurian Romances*)

Christine de Pisan. *The Treasure of the City of Ladies.* Translated by Sarah Lawrence. London: Penguin, 2003.

Cicero. *Rhetorica ad Herennium.* Edited and translated by Harry Caplan. Cambridge, MA: Harvard UP, 1954.

Enéas: A Twelfth-Century Romance. Translated by John A. Yunck. New York: Columbia UP, 1974.

Euclid. *The Elements of Geometry, Containing the Whole Twelve Books.* Translated by George Phillips. Whitefish, MT: Kessinger, 2007.

Galen. *Galen On Anatomical Procedures: Translation of the Surviving Books with Introduction and Notes.* Translated by Charles J. Singer. Oxford, United Kingdom: Oxford UP, 1998.

———. *Opera omnia.* Edited by Kal G. Kühn and Friedrich W. Assmann. Leipzig: C. Cnobloch, 1821–33.

Geoffrey of Monmouth. *History of the Kings of Britain.* Translated by Lewis G.M. Thorpe. London: Penguin, 1973.

Gottfried von Strassburg. *Tristan with the Surviving Fragments of the Tristan of Thomas.* Translated by A.T. Hatto. London: Penguin, 1960.

Gregory the Great. *Dialogues.* New York: Fathers of the Church, 1959.

Gower, John. *Confessio Amantis.* Edited by Russell A. Peck and translated by Andrew Galloway. Kalamazoo, MI: Medieval Institute Publications, 2000.

Henri d'Andeli. *Bataille des sept arts.* Edited by Achille Jubinal. Paris: Edouard Pannier, 1938.

Horace. *Satires, Epistles, and Ars Poetica.* Edited and translated by H. Rushton Fairclough. Cambridge, MA: Harvard UP, 1929.

Hugh of St. Victor. *The Didascalicon of Hugh of St. Victor: A Guide to the Arts.* Translated by Jerome Taylor. New York: Columbia UP, 1991.

John of Garland. *The Integumenta on the Metamorphoses of Ovid by John Garland: First Edited with Introduction and Translation.* Chicago: U Chicago P, 1929.

John of Salisbury. *Metalogicon.* Translated by Daniel D. McGarry. Berkeley, CA: U of California P, 1955.

Julius Caesar. *The Battle for Gaul.* Translated by Anne and T.P. Wiseman. Boston: D.R. Godine, 1980.

Lives and Legends of St. Brendan the Voyager. Ed. and trans. Denis O'Donaghue. Felinfach: Llanerch, 1994. Rpt. of *Brendaniana: St. Brendan the Voyager in Story and Legend,* 1893.

Macrobius. *Commentary on Scipio's Dream.* Translated by William H. Stahl. New York: Columbia UP, 1952.

Maimonides. *The Guide for the Perplexed.* Translated by M. Friedländer. New York: Dover, 2000.

Marie de France. *Lais.* Translated by Glyn Burgess and Keith Busby. London: Penguin, 1999.

Martianus Capella. *Martianus Capella and the Seven Liberal Arts.* Translated by William H. Stahl. New York: Columbia UP, 1977.

Narcisus et Dané. Edited and translated by Penny Eley. Liverpool, United Kingdom: Department of French of the University of Liverpool, 2002. Also available online at http://www.liv.ac.uk/soclas/los/narcisus.pdf.

Ovid. *Heroides, Amores.* Edited and translated by G.P. Goold and Grant Showerman. Loeb Classical Library. Cambridge, MA: Harvard UP, 1914.

———. *Metamorphoses.* Edited and translated by Frank J. Miller. 2 vols. Cambridge: Harvard UP, 1999.

Ovide moralisé. Poème du commencement du quatorzième siècle. Edited by Cornelius de Boer. 5 vols. Amsterdam: Johannes Muller, 1915–38.

The Pilgrim's Guide to Santiago. Translated by William Melczer. New York: Italica, 1993.

Piramus et Tisbé. Edited and translated by Penny Eley. Liverpool, United Kingdom: Department of French of the University of Liverpool, 2001. Also available online at http://www.liv.ac.uk/soclas/los/piramus.pdf.

Plato. *Timaeus.* Translated by H.D.P. Lee. London: Penguin, 1971.

Pliny. *Natural History.* Edited by H. Rackham. Loeb Classical Library. Cambridge, MA: Harvard UP, 1938–63.

Ptolemy. *Almagest.* Translated by G.J. Toomer and with a foreword by Owen Gingerich. Princeton, NJ: Princeton UP, 1998.

Le Roman d'Enéas. Edited and translated by Aimé Petit. Paris: Livre de Poche, 1997.

Servius. *Servius' Commentary on Book Four of Virgil's Aeneid: An Annotated Translation.* Edited and translated by Christopher Michael McDonough; Richard E Prior; Mark Stansbury. Wauconda, IL: Bolchazy-Carducci, 2002.

The Song of Roland. Translated by Glyn Burgess. London: Penguin, 2003.

Statius. *Thebaid.* Edited and translated by P. Papinius Statius and D.R. Shackleton Bailey. Cambridge, MA: Harvard UP, 2003.

Thomas Aquinas. *Summa Theologica.* 61 vols. Cambridge, United Kingdom: Cambridge UP, 2004.

Thomas Malory. *Le Morte d'Arthur.* Translated by Janet Cowan and John Lawlor. 2 vols. London: Penguin, 1970.

Three Ovidian Tales of Love. Edited and translated by Raymond Cormier. New York: Garland, 1986.

Tristan et Yseult. Les premières versions européennes. Edited and translated by Christiane Marchello-Nizia et al. Bibliothèque de la Pléiade. Paris: Gallimard, 1995.

La Vie De Saint Alexis: The Old French Text and Its Translation into English and Modern French. Edited and Translated by Guy R. Mermier. New York: Edwin Mellen, 1995.

The Voyage of Bran Son of Febal to the Land of the Living. An Old Irish Saga. Edited and translated by Kuno Meyer. London: D. Nutt, 1895–97.

The Voyage of Mael Duin's Curragh. Translated by Patricia Aakhus. Santa Cruz, CA: Story Line, 1997.

The Voyage of St. Brendan. Representative Versions of the Legend in English Translation. Translated by W.R.J. Barron and Glyn Burgess. Exeter, United Kingdom: Exeter UP, 2002.

Timaeus MS Digby 23; available online at http://image.ox.ac.uk/list?collection=bodleian

Wace. *Wace's Roman de Brut: A History of the British.* Translated by Judith Weiss. Exeter, United Kingdom: University of Exeter Press, 2002.

William Langland. *Piers Plowman: Piers the Plowman.* Translated by J.F. Goodridge. London: Penguin, 1968.

SECONDARY SOURCES

Cahill, Thomas. *How the Irish Saved Civilization.* New York: Bantam Doubleday Dell, 1996.

Colish, Marcia. *Medieval Foundations of the Western Intellectual Tradition.* New Haven, CT: Yale UP, 1997.

Duffy, Eamon. *Marking the Hours: English People and their Prayers, 1240–1570.* New Haven, Conn.: Yale UP, 2006.

Haskins, Charles H. *Renaissance of the Twelfth Century.* 1927. Cambridge, MA: Harvard UP, 2005.

Reynolds, L.D. and N.G. Wilson. *Scribes and Scholars: A Guide to the Transmission of Greek and Latin Literature.* New York: Oxford UP, 1991.

Rubenstein, Richard. *Aristotle's Children.* Orlando, FL: Harcourt, 2003.

Southern, R.W. *The Making of the Middle Ages.* New Haven, CT: Yale UP, 1961.

CHAPTER 7

The Renaissance

Carme Font Paz and Joan Curbet

TIMELINE

1517	Martin Luther publishes his "95 Theses" against Catholic practice
1519	Death of Leonardo da Vinci; Charles V, archduke of Austria and king of Spain, elected Holy Roman Emperor
1534	Henry VIII of England breaks with Rome, becomes head of English church
1541	John Calvin assumes civil leadership of Geneva, Switzerland
1545	First session of the Council of Trent held in Trent, Italy
1556	Beginning of the reign of Philip II of Spain
1558	Elizabeth I becomes queen of England
1560s	French Wars of Religion: Protestant minority in conflict with the Catholic majority
1563	Last session of the Council of Trent
1571	John of Austria smashes the Ottoman fleet at Battle of Lepanto
1572	Massacre of St Bartholomew: eight thousand Protestants die in Paris, France
1588	English fleet defeats Spanish armada off the south coast of England
1598	Henry IV, first Bourbon king of France, grants equal rights to Protestants
1603	Death of Queen Elizabeth I of England
1606	Foundation of the Virginia Company in England
1609	Galileo Galilei confirms that the earth is not the center of the universe
1610	Beginning of the reign of Louis XIII of France
1616	Death of Shakespeare and Cervantes
1618	Beginning of Thirty Years' War, involving almost all of Europe except Britain
1624	Cardinal Richelieu becomes first minister in France
1625	Charles I accedes to the English throne
1627	Catholics besiege Huguenots in La Rochelle, on the western coast of France

1628	Petition of Right, England; Parliament curtails king's powers
1629	Charles I tries to rule Britain without Parliament
1642	Beginning of the civil war in England, Scotland, and Ireland, lasting until 1651
1643	Beginning of the reign of Louis XIV of France
1648	The treaty of Westphalia ends the Thirty Years' War
1649	Charles I of England and Scotland is executed
1650	Beginning of the British Interregnum, lasting until 1660
1660	Restoration of Charles II of England
1678	"Popish Plot" to overthrow Charles II of England
1679	The "Habeas Corpus" Act in England ensures that there can be no imprisonment without a court appearance first
1682	Beginning of the reign of Peter the Great of Russia
1688	Revolution in England against James II, bringing William of Orange to the throne
1689	Grand Alliance of the Habsburgs, the Dutch, and the English against France
1697	Treaty of Ryswick between France and the Grand Alliance

INTRODUCTION TO THE PERIOD

In many ways the sixteenth and seventeenth centuries brought about the beginning of Western modernity, in terms of cultural mentality and political development. The first great break with the European medieval past came through the Reformation, in its many forms: first in the Germanic context, through the impact of Luther's writings in the late 1510s and all through the 1520s, and then through the spread of Calvinism from Geneva, from 1541 onward. The solid development of Protestant thought establishes the major cultural divide cutting across Europe from the mid-sixteenth century onward. In the case of England, the initial break with the Catholic Church and the spread of the Reformation under Edward VI led to a complex situation in terms of religious definition. This situation would eventually be solved by the inclusive approach taken by the church under Elizabeth I that guaranteed a Protestant state church, but with a doctrinal basis that was more ambiguous than in the other Protestant states.

The main reason for dissension between the major European states, therefore, was the new religious divide. But there was another major point of conflict in the struggle for the domination of the sea routes and the colonial expansion over the New World: during most of the sixteenth century, external pressure was put on Europe by the Ottoman Empire, a serious menace that would only be overcome by the Spanish fleet in the battle of Lepanto, in 1571. This military triumph signalled the culmination of the Spanish sea power, which would receive its first serious setback almost two decades later, in 1588, when the "Invincible Armada" was defeated by the British navy. This would open the way for unrest and rebellion in the territories controlled by Spain in northern Europe (Flanders and the Low Countries), and would eventually lead to the gradual disintegration of the Spanish Empire all through the seventeenth century.

At the turn of the century, in political terms, the major Catholic powers of southern Europe were evolving toward forms of absolutist monarchic rule. This was the case in Spain, in spite of the gradual decline of its imperial power, and especially in France, under the rule of Louis XIII (from 1610 onward) and then of Louis XIV (from 1643 onward). The control established by Cardinal Richelieu (under Louis XIII) over the French nobility would eventually situate the institutional framework of the state under the direct control of the monarchy and its administrative system. The firm union between the crown and the church also legitimized this strictly pyramidal hierarchy. In this way the European states were divided into, on the one hand, systems that allowed or encouraged the participation of the bourgeoisie in the political arena (the Protestant countries) and on the other hand, rigidly structured and quasi-feudal states in the east (Russia) and the south (Spain and France).

The defeat of the Spanish Armada in 1588 also gave further strength to England's colonial project, which was institutionally strengthened through the initiative of the East India and Virginia companies, starting in 1606. But the major historical changes taking place in England in the seventeenth century came about as a result of the civil war, from the initial rebellion of the parliament against Charles I, to his beheading in 1649. The further, short-lived development of the Commonwealth and the Protectorate (led by Oliver Cromwell) would eventually end in the Restoration of the monarchy in 1660. In the long run, however, the civil war and its aftermath left a lasting legacy in the limitation of the powers of the monarchy and the furthering of the new political and social leadership of the emerging middle classes. Seen from this perspective, the civil unrest and institutional changes taking place in England in the seventeenth century can be seen as the blueprint for the transformations that would affect Europe in the following centuries.

READING TRENDS AND PRACTICES

On May 15, 1513, from his temporary residence in Bologna, where he was working as a private educator for the sons of Giovanni Battista Boerio, Erasmus of Rotterdam wrote a letter to the Venetian printer Aldo Manutio. In the letter, the humanist and polygraphist (still some years away from becoming the world-famous beacon of humanistic and biblical studies he would turn into) introduces himself to the printer for the first time, praises him for the work he is doing and the fame he is achieving, and tells him that he is sending him two Greek tragedies that he has recently translated into Latin, to have them printed in Venice. Then Erasmus concentrates on the kind of book he would like to see printed by Manutio:

> I should consider my labours immortalized if they should come out printed in your types, particularly the smaller types, the most beautiful of all. This will result in the volume being very small, and the business being concluded at little expense. If you think it convenient to undertake the affair, I will supply you with a corrected copy, which I'll send by the bearer. (Huizinga 208)

Soon before this, and in the same letter, Erasmus has already referred to the "splendid types" by which Aldo is casting new light "on Greek and Latin literature." Erasmus is thinking not only of the work that Aldo had done in the last decade of the fifteenth century, in his edition of the complete works of Aristotle in Greek, but specifically of his editions of the Latin classics in a new, small type and format: not in quarto (double-folded sheets of paper, which would allow for four printed sides) but in the octavo format (four-folded sheets, which reduced the size of the book by half), and in the new kind of small typed letter that Aldo had introduced in 1501. This new type was a more stylized version of the round, clear, and harmonious type in which humanistic works had been printed in the late fifteenth century; it fully preserved its clarity and its legibility, but the letters now appeared in a slightly sloped hand, inclining softly toward the right side. This was the *littera cursiva,* the type that we still call "italics" in English.

The small volume in littera cursiva introduced by Aldo Manutio was a stroke of genius, both in aesthetic and in commercial terms. It first appeared in 1501, at the precise moment when the net of international relations between the European humanists was beginning to have strong influence beyond academic or courtly circles and was starting to seriously alter the intellectual life of Europe. Several of the monarchs rising to the throne in the first and second decades of the sixteenth century had received a fully humanistic education, had been trained widely in the use and practice of the *bonae litterae,* and had every intention of furthering their presence in educative circles, both in the existing universities and academies and, where necessary, through the foundation and endowment of new centers of study. This meant a significant increase in the size of the target audience that printers such as Aldo Manutio (or others such as Estienne in France or the Froben family in Germany) were looking for. This audience consisted of well-informed, urbane readers who had a taste for Latin poetry and history, a strong curiosity about new renditions of the Greek classics, and who could appreciate the aesthetic value of a pocket-size edition in *cursiva* that was clear and reader-friendly.

What were the implications of being a humanistic reader at the start of the sixteenth century? That peculiar situation is perhaps better defined by the paradoxes it entails. A humanistic reader had full knowledge of belonging to an intellectual elite, but was also interested in the expansion of that elite. These readers had a strong interest in the cultural past, but kept an eye on its practical applicability in the present. Above all, these readers had a good appreciation of classical literature (almost exclusively Latin), but did not see a contradiction between that taste and the practice of Christianity. Contrary to the neo-paganizing strands of thought that had occasionally appeared among the Italian humanists of the fifteenth century, the spiritual tendencies of early sixteenth-century humanistic scholarship was resolutely Christian, and it was purposefully oriented toward a renovation of the church and its practices, based on a return to the very essentials of Christianity.

Above all then, humanistic reading involved a sense of participation in a common cultural enterprise: the project of doing away with the rusty traditions of university scholasticism and medieval logic and theology, through the clarity and elegance of style and thought of the classics, to a renovation of culture and religious belief in the present. In the writings of Erasmus of Rotterdam, John Colet, and Elio Antonio de Nebrija, we trace over and over again a constant sense of engagement with the *barbari* (barbarians), who are always identified as grammar teachers, university dons, and practitioners of late medieval scholasticism. The main problem presented by the barbari is, precisely, their lack of ability in the practice of reading and the mastery of letters: their Latin is rough and inelegant, reduced to *formulae;* their knowledge of the classics is scanty; their knowledge of theology does not reach beyond Thomas Aquinas. What is needed at the beginning of the sixteenth century, then, is a twofold model of recuperation of texts: on the one hand, a renewed accessibility to Greek literature, either in new Latin translations or in the original (which, as yet, was but the preserve of a few); on the other, a recovery of the Fathers of the Church, the early writers who, in the first centuries of Christianity, had framed the essentials of doctrine in terms that were still informed by the easy practice of latinity and (it was supposed) by the spirit of the original Christian communities.

To read better, then, is to *become* better: ideally, the practice of the *bonae litterae* was to lead to a new spirit of toleration, intellectual honesty, and renewed Christianity. During the first two decades of the sixteenth century, before the crisis of the Reformation became apparent, there was a visible sense of intellectual optimism in the humanist community, where the confidence in the transforming and renovating power of letters and of reading was confidently projected toward the future. And for this purpose, the knowledge of classical letters was as valid as that of Christianity; indeed, the basis of a truly ethical behavior could be found in each. As Erasmus himself put it in one of his Colloquia, "nothing must be called profane if it involves a holy and profitable doctrine, useful for the improvement of customs." There was, therefore, a solid continuity between the study of the classics and the practice of Christianity, and this continuity must be based as well on a common approach to reading. Just as there could be no solid knowledge of the classics without a return to the sources, there could be no good knowledge of Christianity without a return to its sources. This implied, above all, a recovery and revision of the Bible, not in the Latin Vulgate version that had become the stronghold of early modern culture, but rather in the purity and simplicity of the original texts in Hebrew (Old Testament) and Greek (New Testament).

Thus we have come to the crux of all the battles for readership in the sixteenth and seventeenth centuries: the struggle for a renewed access to scripture, and for the possibility of opening up the Bible to acts of reading and interpretation beyond the institutional control of the Catholic Church. It goes without saying that, for the humanists of the 1510s and 1520s, such an access need not be, and should not be, seen as an act of dissent against official doctrine. What it represented was, above all, the basis of a spiritual renovation that would shake the foundations of the church from within and lead it to a serious spiritual renovation, away from a world of ceremonialism, ritual, and political power, and toward a spirit of true austerity and piety. Erasmus himself put it thus, in a long passage that is worth quoting in its entirety:

> The equipment for that journey is simple and at everyone's disposal. This philosophy is accessible to everyone. Christ desires that his mysteries shall be spread as widely as possible. I should wish that all good wives read the Gospel and Paul's epistles; that they were translated into all languages, that out of these the husbandman sang while ploughing, the weaver at his loom; that with such stories the traveller should beguile his wayfaring . . . . What is the philosophy of Christ, which he himself calls *Renascentia*, but the instauration of nature created good? Moreover, though no-one has taught us so absolutely and effectively as Christ, yet also in pagan books much may be found that is in accordance with it. (*The Praise of Folly and Other Writings*, 304)

The quest for renewed access to the original texts of classic literature was only part of the humanist project. The other part, and the most significant at the beginning of the sixteenth century, was the recovery of the biblical texts in their original purity. Of course, only a few of the intellectuals eager for a renewed understanding of the Bible had the capacity to read these texts in the original: John Colet, dean of biblical studies at St Paul's Cathedral, used to lecture on the Pauline Epistles by basing himself on the Latin texts of the Vulgate, and Cardinal Jiménez de Cisneros used to complain of the very basic knowledge of Latin widespread in the Spanish universities. In fact, prestigious printing presses at this time were fully incorporating the Greek alphabet into their production, thus contributing directly to the distribution and accessibility of Hellenistic texts in the original language. But the presence of Greek studies in the European university curricula of the period was still scant: a chair of Greek was instituted at the University of Alcalá de Henares around 1513; the first chair of Greek in

Hans Holbein the Younger's portrait of Erasmus, the prolific Renaissance philosopher.

Oxford was established in 1517; the trilingual college of Basle (Greek, Latin, and Hebrew) was opened in Basle in 1519, and the Collège Royal in Paris (which was later to become the *Collège de France*) was inaugurated in 1530, with a full curriculum in Greek and Hebrew languages. Still by then, the number of students who received a full exposure to Greek in Europe was exclusively limited to those who were educated in one of the few universities where it was taught; and yet, the language was perceived as one of the indispensable tools in the renovation of studies, for it was through Greek that one could gain access to the original version of the Gospels.

The strong alliance between the printing press and humanism brought about two of the most important—and controversial—editorial ventures of the early sixteenth century: the publication of two new versions of Biblical texts, made newly accessible, respectively, in bilingual and multilingual versions. Perhaps the most anticipated one was the *Novum Organum* published by Erasmus in 1516 through the printing house of Froben, at Basle. It contained the fully revised Greek text of the New Testament, with annotations in Latin, and an accompanying Latin translation that Erasmus offered to the reader as an alternative to the Vulgate. The new Latin text had been put, as Erasmus stated, "by the side of the Greek text, so that the reader could readily compare the two, the translation being so made that it was our first study to preserve, as far as was possible, the integrity of the Latin without any injury to the simplicity of the apostolic language" (quoted in Hall 71). More ambitious, and far more important from the viewpoint of the progress of scholarship, was the multilingual version of scripture known as the Complutensian Bible, edited by cardinal Jiménez de Cisneros in Alcalá de Henares. The Complutensian Bible was a massive, revolutionary set of six volumes, published between 1514 and 1517, the last of which appeared shortly after the cardinal's death. It was also a spectacular feat of printing, brought about by the house of Guillén de Brocar. Each of the wide, capacious folio pages was divided into several columns, which offered the same text in parallel versions—Latin, Greek, and Hebrew—to allow for a full and detailed comparison. To these texts were added the canonical Targum (Aramaic) and Septuagint (Koiné Greek) versions of the Old Testament. Of course, the ideal reader for the Complutensian Bible would be the erudite, multilingual scholars who could spend the necessary time and effort for the comparison of the various texts, and who could then proceed to their own editions or commentaries of biblical and patristic texts.

The *Novum Organum* (New Instrument) by Erasmus, as its title indicated, was meant to have a far more practical use. Essentially, it was offered as a more purified, more accessible version of the Gospels that could act as an alternative to the Vulgate for the educated reader. But, at different levels, both versions were equally engaged in the process of what Erasmus had called the renascentia, or rebirth, of Christian life, one which could only come from a new, unrestricted access to the foundational texts of Christianity.

Beyond the strenuous efforts in biblical scholarship, it was above all in the field of education that the reading practices of humanism were to have lasting effects. The development of humanism from the mid-thirteenth century onward had established a basic canon of Latin authors (Cicero, Virgil, Horace, Ovid) that could be taught and offered to students as essential, referential models of writing. Humanism also brought about a renewed interest in rhetoric and dialectic, putting them both at the basis of any educational program. In a practical sense, all the educational practices of the sixteenth century were fully informed by these two developments. To have access to schooling in sixteenth-century Europe meant having access to basic training in Latin rhetoric and composition. This does not imply, of course, that true erudition ever ventured outside the elite circles of humanist intellectuals; literacy in itself was to be, throughout Europe, restricted to the aristocracy and the emerging middle classes (though, as we shall see later, in very different proportions on both sides of the Reformation). However, even the short periods of study that the sons of wealthy or well-to-do tradesmen spent in obscure grammar-schools must have exposed them, however briefly, to select samples of classical literature, and they must have acquired some kind of familiarity with the procedures and practices of verbal art.

To be a student in a grammar school meant, above all, to become a reader of Latin literature. These enforced reading practices were not necessarily enjoyable or even pleasant to young boys (girls not being admitted to public education at this time) of the emerging middle classes who, in many cases, did not expect to reach the university. In most cases, what their parents expected them to obtain from a grammar school was simply a solid alphabetization, a basic training in reading and a sufficient polish of culture. The teaching of Latin was conducted through painstaking reading, copying, and assimilation of the best models of writing. Vocabulary and grammatical turns would be introduced as well, through set texts. As a result, the process of reading and comprehension would inevitably involve a lengthy and monotonous effort on the part of the student.

It is possible to reconstruct, in general terms, the archetypal functioning of class work in the schools, judging from the recommendations of the textbooks and the surviving documentation from student notebooks and memoirs. In the schools located in urban centers, which were always better endowed and could hire several teachers, children would not be grouped by age, but rather by their levels of skill at Latin. In rural or poorer schools, all students would be gathered in the same room, regardless of their expertise in Latin. At the beginning of the day, some *sententiae* from Ovid or from Horace would introduce the vocabulary and the grammar that had to be learned. These sententiae would then be repeated and/or copied until they were assimilated, and the students would be evaluated to see if they had memorized the text correctly. In most cases (and very especially in the case of verse), the texts had to be learned verbatim. New sententiae would be included in the afternoon sessions, complementing those that had been introduced in the morning, and the day would end with a general revision of all the material that had been introduced during the day.

On the higher levels, when the students had acquired enough mastery of the basic structures, the reading sessions would go on to include lengthier fragments extracted from the *Aeneid,* the *Georgics,* and the *Metamorphoses.* Historical and political material would be introduced as well, mostly coming from Cicero's orations. In going through all these texts, the teacher would present the material as containing lessons of lasting ethical or moral value, as worthy of being applied in the sixteenth century as they had been in Augustan Rome. Quite obviously, the efficiency of this model would depend very much on the capacity of the teacher to communicate his enthusiasm for the texts at hand and to make them come alive before his pupils. The eloquence of the ancients, in itself, would rarely appeal in a first reading to children who would never use Latin in their everyday lives. A resourceful teacher would be able to mobilize the interest of his class by tracing historical parallelisms with present-day reality; by showing them how to play with their newly-acquired verbal toys; and by awakening their curiosity through the commentary on mythological episodes.

The children of the aristocracy would be exposed to the same process, often under more exacting or demanding programs, but with the great advantage of receiving a personalized training. From the early sixteenth and all through the seventeenth century, the figure of the private tutor would become popular among the more exclusive social circles, and even the upper middle classes would, in time, integrate it in their domestic world.

The young sons of noblemen or magistrates were expected to play an active part in society, either in politics or law, and the acquisition of rhetorical skills was considered indispensable. In the sixteenth century, the prevailing models for such a task would be Cicero's *Rhetoric,* Quintilian's *Institutione Oratoriae,* and the pseudo-ciceronian *Rhetorica ad Herennium.* Most of the manuals in vernacular languages more or less followed these models of reference, ensuring the wide popularity of Ciceronian practice. True humanistic learning, in consequence, was designed to accumulate knowledge for the purposes of practical application; to enable the scholar to turn, whenever necessary, from *verba* to *res,* from the text to reality. All the situations or sententiae contained in the texts cast new light on the various areas of actual life. None of them should be lost or forgotten. From the very beginning, the educational innovators of the sixteenth century (Erasmus, John Colet, Guarino) encouraged the active participation of the student in the process of learning, through the practice of compiling, selecting, and structuring all the brief fragments or sentences that could be useful to him at any given moment. All these quotations could be copied on the back of the textbooks, in their empty final pages, or indicated in the margins of the pages. But it soon became far more practical (in the case of those who intended to make a career in letters, law, or politics) to dedicate one or several separate notebooks to the collection of these fragmentas, where they would be gathered under separated headings and sub-headings, each of which could spread over several pages. These were called "commonplace books," in reference to their function as storehouses of *loci classici.* In actual practice, though, these capacious collections, sometimes gathered over the course of several years, were seen as very practical instruments, furnishing the raw material from which the public orators, poets, or lawyers could proceed to build their own discourses.

A true humanistic reading of the classics would always be undertaken with pen in hand. Even as adults, readers would underline, mark out, or memorize the most significant moral concepts of Herodotus, or the most curious descriptions of animals and plants in Pliny. Having finished a daily reading, or sometimes while still engaged in it, readers would copy out the most relevant of these fragments into commonplace books, placing them in the section or sub-section that corresponded thematically to it. Erasmus, one of the most enthusiastic theoreticians of this method, lamented in his *De Duplici Copia Verborum ac Rerum* (1512) about not having had the advantage of learning to read in this way when he was a young man: "I just wish that I myself, when young, had followed the advice I am about to give: I see now how much my efforts would have benefited!" (quoted in Moss 107). Later on, in his *De Rhetorica* (1519), Philip Melanchton would insist on the need for subdividing all forms of knowledge in a practical way while reading:

> Some things pertain to nature, such as life, death, physical appearance; others to fortune, such as wealth, forebears, preferments; others are in our own powers, such as vices and virtues . . . . Accordingly, anyone wishing to make correct judgements about anything related to human life must refer to everything that comes his way to these constituents "sets" of things. (in Moss, 119)

Even through the conflicts and tensions brought about by the various religious schisms and controversies throughout Europe, this central trend of humanistic education kept solidifying and establishing traditions of teaching, learning, and reading that would last well through the following century. Collections of *exempla* such as Theodor Zwinger's *Theatrum Vitae Humanae* (1565) or moral compilations such as Nicholas Ling's *Wit's Commonwealth* (1597, a collection that, notoriously, included fragments of vernacular writings by Thomas More and others) were, each in its own fashion, printed *thesauri* that tried to complement and facilitate (not substitute) the individual task of compiling commonplace books.

Under the aegis of humanism, then, the practice of good reading is seen as a necessary first step for writing, acting, and living. The poetry of this period bears the signs of such an approach in its tendency to the practice of *imitatio,* which had become firmly set in the minds of all practicing poets during the years of their education. Writing was, to a certain extent, a way of reorganizing in a new and creative form the materials that had been assimilated during the process of reading. The term *inventio,* which defined the initial moment of composition, did not imply a notion of creativity. In Ciceronian fashion, *invenire* (discovering) refers to finding the topics and the elements that are to become part of the composition. Most of these topics belonged to the series of commonplaces that would have been gathered from the canon of classics shared by most European readers. The subsequent steps of *dispositio* (organization of the text) and *elocutio* (the turning of the topics into verbal shape) could only take place if the point of departure was assured enough. This, of course, necessarily meant that Renaissance poetry became a highly allusive art, an act of communication involving a net of complicities based on the recognition of the topics treated by the poet, and of the new accent that could be given to the commonplaces being voiced. The Spanish poet, Fray Luis de León, begins his *Ode on the Solitary Life* (*Vida Retirada*), composed in 1560, by phrasing the desire to have a quiet life, running away from worldly noise and following the hidden path of wisdom.

The late-sixteenth-century reader would recognize these lines, of course, as a clever rehearsal of the beginning of Horace's second *Epode* ("Beatus ille qui procul negotiis/ ut prisca gens mortalium," etc.), evoking the wisdom that lies in withdrawing from political and active life. And yet, this recognition would not detract from the appreciation of the poetry, but would contribute actively to it. Ideally, the reader would be able to compare the hexameters of the original poem with the fluent, harmonious development of the Spanish *lira* (a stanzaic form combining heptasyllabic and pentasyllabic lines), and would take pleasure in the subtle enjambments and the new directions into which the poet, with the help of many more commonplaces, led this topic. Imitatio was anything but servile copy; it was an assimilation of the verbal and textual tradition of the past, in order to turn it into new shapes, and to adapt it to a different intention.

Love poetry was one of the territories where this became most evident. There, classical *topoi* (from Greek rehtoric, plural of *topos*, the standard method of constructing an argument) were put to the service of a rhetoric of seduction or of melancholy to create the impression of a personal perspective (which may not necessary coincide with the poet's own sentimental situation). A reader trained in the humanist tradition taking up a copy of Edmund Spenser's carefully organized edition of his *Amoretti/Epithalamion* sequence, published in 1595, would probably be very able to identify the textual source for sonnet XVIII, and, thanks to it, would be better able to understand the emotional plight of the speaker. In the sonnet, Spenser compares himself to Arion, the musician who was saved from drowning by a dolphin, and laments that his beloved will not save him in the same way.

The source here is a passage from the first book of Pliny's *Naturalis Historia* (1:23), in which the fate of Arion, a Persian musician who was thrown into the sea, is described. But the dolphin, seduced by Arion's music and who readily saves him from death in Pliny's text, has become a strange and wild beast in Spenser's sonnet, where the "rude musick" (i.e. the poetry) of the speaker cannot appeal to his beloved, or elicit any kind response from her. Here, as in all humanistic poetry, the pleasure of the reading experience depends very much on the collaborative work of the reader, who is able to identify the referential, intertextual game being played.

All this may give the impression of a strong bookish, almost erudite flavor in the transmission and reception of the poetry of the period. It would be wrong, however, to see Renaissance poetry as being only an intellectual game, deprived of contact with reality or everyday life. Precisely because the humanists saw reading as preparation for experience, writing was also logically seen as a means of intervention in life, as having a performative function with a practical effect on the audience. That function could be personal (as part of a strategy of seduction), or political (as part of a program of personal promotion), or it could combine both aspects (in courtly circles, where the language of love could often be read in terms of a coded political intervention). But, most of all, the clearest sign of the vitality of the reading of poetry during the sixteenth century lies in the strong oral projection that this poetry retains. For virtually all poets, publication and printing was only the final part of a process that took place through the circulation and transmission of their work in manuscript form. In university circles, courtly environments, and exclusive coteries, handwritten copies of lyrical poems, meant to be read or recited in groups, established the lyrical identities of the poets long before they were collected in printed anthologies or neatly ordered sonnet sequences. It is no coincidence that a sonnet sequence such as William Shakespeare's, written as late as the last decade of the sixteenth century (and only published in the early seventeenth century), should remind its main addressee that his fame would remain alive only so long as men could breathe or eyes could see (Sonnet 18). Shakespeare's own lines can only exist as such as long as they can be "seen" (perceived visually as black marks on a white page) and also "breathed" (read aloud). Renaissance poetry thus incorporated into itself a full consciousness of the essential orality through which it would always be experienced, even if it was read in solitude.

THEOLOGICAL TEXTS (AFTER THE REFORMATION)

It is possible to see the foundational moment of the Reformation as the result of an individual act of reading. As an Augustinian monk and lecturer on theology in Wittenberg, Martin Luther had been lecturing extensively on the first chapter of St. Paul's *Epistle to the Romans* for years before he presented his ninety-five polemical "theses" (1517). It was his reading and interpretation of that biblical text, and especially of the meaning of *iustificatio* (righteousness) that would give rise to the first manifestations of what would later be called a "Protestant" doctrine. The first chapter of Paul's *Epistle* had become for Luther the source of an obsession, a constant reminder of his own inability to feel worthy in the presence of God. He deeply internalized the text until, at his most critical moment of crisis (the moment of sudden revelation that, according to Protestant tradition, took place in the tower of the Augustinian convent in Wittenberg), it seemed to open itself to him:

> Though I lived as a monk without reproach, I felt that I was a sinner before God with an extremely disturbed conscience. I could not believe that He was placated by my satisfaction . . . . I beat importunately upon Paul at that place, most ardently desiring to know what St. Paul wanted. At last, by the mercy of God, meditating day and night . . . I began to understand that the "righteousness" of God is that by which the righteous lives by a gift of God, namely by faith." (*Selections from his Writings* 11)

Even though Luther is not specific about the exact moment of this transformation, this has to be taken as a true turning point in the cultural history of the West. Moreover, it is highly representative of the new approaches to the reading of the Bible that would be promoted in the Reformed countries. Here the reader is not in full, detached control of his reading experience. On the contrary, he passionately absorbs the letter of the text, debates it within itself, sees himself through it, and finally, in a sudden revelation, the text not only becomes fully intelligible, but seems to speak and address itself to him personally. It is not that there is a free interpretation of scripture (as Catholic propaganda would put it later), but rather that the believer integrates scripture within the self, metabolizes it, and confronts it seriously, in a close, intimate experience that must inevitably change his perception of that self.

Initially, the main reason for Luther's translation of the Bible into German was to guarantee an intimate encounter with the sacred text, and to situate that encounter away from the control of any institutional structure. Such a purpose could be seen as fully coincident with the main goal of the humanists: the promotion of a form of reading that could bring about a renovation of faith by a new, purified, and generalized access to the texts. This is indeed the motivation that Luther expressly admits, for instance, in the preface to his translation of the Psalms (1524): "Of old, in the dark times, what a treasure would it have been held to be, if a man could have rightly understood one Psalm, and could have read it or heard it in simple German! Today, however, blessed are the eyes that see what we see and the ears that hear what we hear" (*Selections from his Writings* 41).

No gesture could be more humanist than Luther's reference to the medieval past as the "dark times" where scripture was zealously kept away from men of good faith. But it would be a mistake to see the union of Reformers and humanists as more than a tacit, strategic alliance at the beginning of the sixteenth century. The strong dissension between Luther and the humanist reformers became evident as soon as the Catholic Church began to respond to his bold pronouncements. Luther was explicitly excommunicated in 1520 and, in April 1521, he was forced to defend his positions at the Diet of Worms, where he refused to recant before the emissaries of the Pope. Luther was only able to escape from the city because he enjoyed the Emperor's special protection. In the immediately following years, he would proceed to further the elimination of icons in the areas under his influence, and to introduce the practice of Mass (including the Eucharist) in German. These would soon become the most immediate signs of identification of the Reformed churches. Very soon, these religious changes began to show their potential for revolutionary action, even beyond the intention of their founder. Between 1524 and 1525, the Peasants' Revolt in Germany, which was in itself a powerful popular uprising against the privileges of the nobility, justified most of its claims by quoting the very text of scripture. Luther initially tried to stop the rebellion, to no avail, and in only a matter of months he came to write very aggressively against what he saw as the "criminal hordes" of the revolutionaries. After the forces of the peasants were categorically and violently crushed by the imperial army in Frankenhausen in 1525, Luther clearly began to distance himself from further attempts to produce politically subversive readings of Biblical texts.

From that moment onward, free interpretation of scripture was anything but favored by Protestantism. Most of the early crises within the Reformation, and among its leaders, came out of dissension as to the exact interpretation of terminology or phrases extracted from the New Testament. To give just one representative example, the break between Luther and Ulrich Zwingli came out of their disagreement on the exact meaning of the phrase "hoc est corpus meum" (Matt 26:26), by which Christ consecrates the bread in the last supper. Was it to be read as proclaiming the transubstantiation of the bread (Luther) or as a purely metaphoric expression (Zwingli)? As a result of contentions such as this, the nascent Reformation began to suffer from strong internal divisions.

In the 1520s, scholars such as Zwingli and Oecolampadius began to argue in favor of a more figural, metaphoric understanding of the sacraments, and of the words that Christ had used referring to them in scripture. As Zwingli himself put it, "in dealing with signs, sacraments, pictures, parables and interpretations, one should, and one must, understand the words figuratively and not understand the words literally." As a response to this, Luther published one treatise centering exclusively on the words "this is my body," further widening the gap between reformation groups. In the heated environment of the mid-to-late 1520s, as the political upheavals within the German-Spanish Empire increased in frequency and violence, interpretive differences such as this were bound to end in tragedy. In 1531, Zwingli himself died in the war between reformed and Catholic cantons in Switzerland, and Oecolampadius was killed at the hands of the Catholic faction in Basle. Different forms of reading could imply different vital and spiritual choices, and provide sufficient cause for living and dying.

In the face of such a dramatic process of doctrinal dispersion, the various churches of the Reformation tried to ensure doctrinal unity by finding a middle way: on the one hand, promoting the direct reading of Scripture, and on the other, ensuring that such reading was complemented by the use of interpretive guidebooks and theological primers. Most often these books would take the form of catechisms; long series of questions and answers divided into thematic areas, which could be used both for teaching purposes or to clarify doubts in communal readings of the Bible. In a moment of religious upheaval and controversy, the Catechism could guarantee a quick and easy clarification of doctrinal aspects. An English Zwinglian primer by George Joyes, the *Hortulus Animae* (1530) could summarize the central iconoclastic perspective of the Reformation, encouraging the believer to abandon the worship of images, in the following way:

The Question:
For as the myche, then: As God is the spirite and may not be ymagined of other wittes, howe shall we knowe hym?
The Answer:
Faityhe and truste fynde hym, when we are in perel, and shewe hym unto us, and yet this faythe to fynde hym must he geve us: for if we . . . gete us a faithe of owre owne fashioninge whereby we beleve and truste in any other thinge then God, then make we an idole. (Quoted in Sinfield 10)

Luther himself published his *Lesser Catechism (Kleiner Cathechismus)* in 1529; the Catholic Church responded by publishing its own counter-catechisms, meant to provide sets of arguments and positions that could assert its own religious model in the new religious debates. As early as 1529, trying to prevent the spread of Lutheranism in Britain, Thomas More published his massive *Dialogue Concerning Heresies,* a text where the humanistic form of the *colloquium* (in this case, between the scholar "Morus" and a young anti-Catholic student) was sometimes weakened to reproduce, in the brief form of questions and answers, the basic contents of the new heresy:

I pray you, quod he, that our lord was born of a virgyn how know you?
Mary, quod he, by scripture.
Howe know you, quod I, the ye shoulde byliue the scrypture?
Mary, quod he, by faith.
Why, quod he, what doth faith tell you therin?
Faith, quod he, telleth me that hoy scrypture is thynges of trouth wryten by the secrete techyng of god.
And wheby know you, quod I, that ye sholde byleve God?
Wherby, quod he? This is a strange question! Euery man quod he, may well wete that. (More 131)

The intention of this dialogue is exactly the opposite of what we find in Luther's *Kleiner Katechismus* and its epigones. More's main aim is to force the reformed positions into a *reductio ad absurdum,* a recognition of the dangers of abandoning the ancient scholarship and traditions of the church, and to remain alone with one's own conscience as a tool for the reading of scripture. For traditionalists such as More, it was above all the belief on an unmediated, direct interaction between the self and the sacred text (the solitary encounter with *sola scriptura*), without any support of gloss or interpretation, that had to be counteracted. And yet, most of the great reformed leaders did not recommend the unmediated access to *sola scriptura,* as it is evident in the most important of the several catechisms of the sixteenth century, such as John Calvin's *Institutes of Christian Religion.* In spite of its bulk, Calvin's text would prove perhaps the most modern of all the Reformed doctrinal *summae,* thanks to its capacity for ordered, clear, and detached exposition. But it is especially important to see the *Institutes* as a guide to be read *alongside* scripture, never substituting for it, and never meant to be left in the hands of the reader for open interpretation. The success of the *Institutes,* and the proliferation of smaller, more practical Calvinist catechisms between 1559 and the end of the century, show the usefulness of this model, and also the intense concern of the various reformed churches to ensure a full control, or supervision, over the reading of scripture carried out among the faithful.

Thus, in all the geographical areas of the Reformation, the spectacular increase of the production and circulation of printed books was a formidable weapon of indoctrination: catechisms, guidebooks, sermons, and vernacular versions of the Bible were distributed quickly and widely among the newly emerging religious communities by itinerant booksellers, who multiplied in response to the increasing demand. The collections and compilations of sermons also became popular among the literate middle classes, as they could furnish occasions for family reading or for recitation and commentary in small rural communities. The most popular sermons often were the most didactic, such as those produced by Calvin himself, which were far less weighty with doctrinal matter than his theological work. In his prologue to Calvin's *Vingt-Deux Sermons* (1554), Jacques Roux had felt compelled to specify that their author, "when pronouncing his sermons, only wanted to guide the fold that God had put under his protection, and not to pronounce homilies for his own satisfaction, so that they could later be offered to the eyes of all" (Calvin XXXV 524). Roux's distinction here between the original "pronunciation" of the sermons as a direct service to the fold and their subsequent appearance in "the eyes of all" (that is, in printed form and for all to read), still shows an implicit trust in the written word against the secondary status of the printed page. And yet Calvin's sermons would, no less than his *Institutes,* become essential instruments of indoctrination in their various editions, and contribute to the new demand for spiritual literature.

On the other hand, and just as the use and reading of newly printed material increased, some of the manuscript culture that had been preserved in monasteries tended to fall into disregard or be directly destroyed. The various stages of the Peasants' Revolt in Germany involved the destruction of several monastic libraries, sometimes against the will of the leaders of the Reformation. In England, as well, the Edwardian secularization brought about the destruction of rich bibliographic collections. The university library of Oxford was sacked by Edward's emissaries in 1550, and most of its contents were either sold or burned. The enormous losses in terms of manuscripts were, to a certain extent, contained by the building of new libraries and collections, encouraged by the new necessities of the reformed countries. Luther himself encouraged the building of several *Stadtbibliotheken* throughout the reformed areas in Germany; many of the collections housed there were to be based on the older collections of manuscripts, alongside the newly printed material. In the completion of these libraries can be perceived, once more, the intellectual affinities that had initially linked the interests of humanists and Protestants. There was an insistence on ensuring an availability of the fathers of the church (Gregory, Jerome, Cyprian, etc.) and to guarantee easy access to the new translations of scripture, both in Latin and in the vernacular. The emergence and progress of the grammar schools, which are described in the previous section, was particularly sustained in the countries of the Reformation, leading to a spectacular increase in the number of literate citizens.

In the case of England, and apart from the primers and catechisms discussed above, two books were published in the mid-to-late sixteenth century that epitomized the new, reformed ideology, and which became referential models for most subsequent English prose and verse. The first is the *Book of Common Prayer,* first authorized in 1549. Through its several subsequent editions, the *Book of Common Prayer* gave shape to the liturgical life of the new Anglican church, and to the beliefs of the lay people. The prayers for the dead (still included in the first version) soon disappeared, and the wording of some of the main prayers kept reflecting, even in their phrasing, the influence of Luther's German versions of the Psalms or of the Gospel. By the end of the century, the *Book* had become the most influential and widely circulated printed text in English, and for many, their main or only reading matter. The use of the *Book* in church or in the domestic environment ensured that its language became familiar, and that it kept inhabiting an intermediate and vital space between the printed page and oral performance.

A 1641 engraving from John Foxe's *Ecclesiasticall Histories* shows the martyrdom of Alexander Gouch and Driver's wife.

The other key text in this period is John Foxe's *Acts and Monuments of these Latter and Perilous Dayes* (1563), a martyriological tract specifically aimed toward the new readership. As a collection of exemplary, saintly lives, it offered enough anecdotal and narrative matter to ensure a good reception. It was widely reprinted until the end of the century, and it probably did more than any other text to consolidate the emerging consciousness of a distinctively Anglican identity, and to extend the perception of Roman Catholicism as a clearly defined political enemy. Doubtless, the majority of the book's audience would have heard it read as part of household routine, rather than read it themselves. Throughout the cultural space of the Reformation, and in spite of the increase in literacy, it was the continuity of the practice of reading aloud that ensured a greater longevity for the most influential and well-distributed texts.

A function very similar to that of the Prayer Book in England was performed by the German hymnals and Psalters, which started to appear in the 1520s, and which were steadily spread through Reformed territories in the following decades. Most of these collections were directly based upon Luther's version of the Psalms. In several areas, the very act of singing them in the vernacular was perceived as a sign of identity of the new creed. In 1576, a Czech catholic, Vaclav Sturm, saw the Lutheran hymn book as a dangerous instrument: "Everyone, noblemen, villains, poor and rich men alike, have it at home. Since they use it to sing in all their meetings and at home, those who can only read a bit use the book of Hymns as if it was a tool for preaching, and they comment upon the canticles" (Gilmont 1990: 19–20).

This is a very interesting instance of the active, instrumental use of a book by semi-literate readers. The text would in these cases be used only as a prop or reminder of the specific texts of the hymns, and these would then become the object of commentary and discussion among the community. No doubt a large section of the newly reformed population had only a limited or partial access to the practice of reading at first; even among the churches that were most concerned with the need for a direct access to scripture, the expansion of literacy would be slow and halting. The use of hymnals and Psalters would thus meet two needs: on the one hand, they would ensure a growing familiarity of the believers with the vernacular text of the prayers and Psalms; on the other, they would often substitute the Bible itself as basic reading matter, thus preventing the spread of radical or uncontrolled interpretations of scripture, which Luther himself had been wary of in the last years of his life.

By the second half of the sixteenth century, the practice of individual readings of the Bible was far more widespread in the areas of Europe where Calvinism had progressed the most. Even there, however, the new religious authorities had become very alert to the potential danger that an unrestricted access to scripture could entail. John Calvin himself had complained repeatedly of the continued printing of theological texts all over Europe, which allowed for an uncontrolled spread of "the absurd fantasies of those who confuse everything." The multiple editions of Calvin's *Institutes,* in various formats, complete or abridged, were meant to be a safeguard against deviant or extravagant readings, and to ensure a certain continuity of doctrine wherever they were read. Among those who learned their doctrine from various versions of this source were Sir Philip Sidney, Joseph Scaliger, and Edmund Spenser.

After the initial expansion of the sixteenth century, the gradual union between Reformed doctrines and the modern nation-states in the north of England and in Britain directly contributed to guaranteeing that scripture would reach an even greater number of people. The work done through grammar schools and local parishes initially affected the members of the emerging middle classes, to an extent that would have been unthinkable in Catholic countries. It is nevertheless certain that the real breakthrough in the expansion of literacy in Germany and in Britain would take place in the seventeenth century. In Germany, the work of Philip Jakob Spener and of the pietist brothers in the second half of the seventeenth century would be especially important. Working mostly from Frankfurt, Spener instituted several *collegia pietatis,* which acted as meeting grounds for the reading and commentary of scripture. His own work, *Pia Desideria* (1675), would prove a useful and popular practical primer in Lutheran doctrine. The true culmination of this process would emerge from the work of Hermann Francke, who in the 1690s became the founder of the *Deutsche Schule* (oriented to the spread of literacy among the poor and the middle classes) and of the *Paedagogium,* specifically designed to teach the children of the aristocracy. In England, the enormous expansion of literacy in the seventeenth century came from two complementary phenomena: the development of Puritanism among the middle classes, before and during the years of the civil war, and the explosion of grammar schools throughout Britian, especially in rural areas.

At the beginning of the seventeenth century, and all through the areas of influence of the Reformation, the *ars praedicandi* (i.e. the rhetorical art of preaching) had reached new heights in the voices of humanist preachers. Very often, their sermons would come to live a double life, in oral performance and in print. The learned reader could enjoy the linguistic and literary virtuosity of sermons composed by humanists such as Richard Hooker or John Donne through solitary reading. These printed versions of the sermons generated a renewed appreciation of the punning, verbal gaming, and dramatic structure in the text. We can safely assume that the solitary act of reading them would have sent one directly back to the Bible, as each sermon was constructed as a commentary or elaboration on the set text from the New Testament that corresponded, liturgically, to the day in which it had been delivered. As Richard Hooker himself repeatedly emphasized, it was the word of God in the Bible that legitimized all meanings and interpretations, and not the other way around. Ultimately, and beyond all commentary and interpretation, the very text of the Bible could acquire an invigorating, life-giving force, as this passage by Hooker makes clear: "The very letter of the word of Christ giveth us plain security that these mysteries do as nails fasten us to his very Cross, that by them we draw out, as touching efficacy, force and virtue, even as the blood of his gored side; in the wounds of our Redeemer we dip our tongues, we are dyed red within and without" (Hooker 1978, II: 361).

The passionate celebration of even the word "Christ" suggests a powerful, dense, even sensorial experience, but one that is brought about not by contemplation of the cross or by interpretation of the sacred text, but rather by a direct access to the "very letter" of the text. It is only by receiving the "security" given by the word (not, let us note, by speculating upon its meaning) that the believer can have access to the effective grace brought by the sacrifice of Christ, and can be filled by it. An example like this, by no means unusual, may help to explain why Biblical language would become the common basis for all the literature written, in later centuries, in the Reformed countries. This was already visible in the seventeenth century, when the poetic language of Angelus Silesius (in German) and George Herbert (in English) proceeded from a deep, pervasive impregnation of colloquial language by the verbal structures of scripture, through its daily reading and use. Along with the spread of literacy, it was this impregnation that, more than anything else (certainly more than the much-invoked but rarely applied "free interpretation" of the Bible), was to be the most lasting legacy of the Reformation in the history of reading.

ORTHODOX TEXTS: THE COUNTER-REFORMATION

If the Reformation can be said to have its origins in individual acts of reading, the Counter-Reformation must inevitably be seen as an attempt to control reading, to supervise it, to frame it within a solid institutional structure. The consequences of this attempt in the individual lives of readers through the seventeenth century and beyond would be far-reaching, and would ultimately contribute to define very different forms of cultural identity, on both sides of the Reformation, all through Europe and in the Americas.

The celebration of the Council of Trent (1545–1563) was meant not only to oppose the expansion of Protestantism and to reaffirm the unity of Catholic dogmatisms, but to vindicate and recover the role of the Church itself as the source and mediator of any interpretation of doctrine, against the Reformed insistence on *sola scriptura*. Pope Paul III, in his convocation of the council of 1542, had established as its main aim the clarification of "whatever pertains to the purity and truth of the Christian religion, whatever pertains to the restoration of good morals . . . [and] whatever pertains to the peace, unity and harmony of Christians among themselves, whether they be princes or people" (Pelikan 275).

This was a euphemism that subtly relegated, from the outset, all kinds of reformed creeds to the category of "heretical." Only nine years after the convocation, the council stated that its procedure was based on working "from Sacred Scripture, the apostolic traditions, the holy and proved councils, the constitutions and authorities of the supreme pontiffs and the holy father, and the consensus of the Catholic church." Scriptural interpretation as mediated only by the church councils was the ideal for which Thomas More had fought so relentlessly and in his time as Lord Chancellor, under Henry VIII.

Still, the philological work that had been done inside the Church itself during the sixteenth century had inevitable consequences: there could be no way back to a situation of rigid scholastic thought based on the text of the *Vulgata*, now long perceived as corrupt. The efforts of Cardinal Cisneros, of Erasmus, and of Lorenzo Valla before them, had involved an acceptance of the need for a revised text of the Latin Bible, one that could be proclaimed anew as the basis for the magisterial function of the church. The version that was intended to be definitive (the "Sistine" Bible) was published in 1592, under Pope Clement VIII, as a final culmination of the Council, and after an exhaustive work of revision that had taken years, reaching up until the very last minute. It is important to point out, though, that the Council of Trent did not explicitly ban the individual reading of scripture (which, anyway, could not be directly controlled). Instead it managed to reach beyond the matter of prohibition by concentrating on aspects of creed and interpretation, and by ensuring its direct control over these aspects. As a result of this, the functions of the Congregation for the Doctrine of Faith, the Inquisition, were reinforced and reimplemented, both during and after the Council. It was especially important to guarantee doctrinal unity in the territories that were politically linked to the Papacy. What is explicitly prohibited is the translation of the Bible into the vernacular. This is the reason why, in the Catholic countries, the literary use of the Biblical language will always be strongly reduced, in contrast with the German and Anglo-Saxon traditions.

In France and in Spain, more than in Italy, the development of the Inquisition as a machinery of ideological control had immediate effects on the actual practice of reading—not only on matters of choice and availability of books, but also on the actual interpretation of the act of reading itself. Humanism, being above all a practice of reading and reinterpretation, was bound to suffer in the new context. Already in 1566, López Pinciano described, in a private letter, the new anxieties overcoming those who based their lives on the practice of the *bonae litterae* (education based on reading great books):

> Worst of all is the fact that they would like no one to develop any affection for the *litterae humaniores*, because of the great danger that, as they say, lies within them, since, just as a humanist is used to correct a fragment by Cicero, he will as well emendate another from the Scriptures . . . . These follies and others like these have got me worried, so much so that I hesitate to continue my work. (Alcalá 297)

The *Indexes* were also guides on how to read, or how to approach, the heterodox works that were allowed to circulate. For example, here are some inquisitorial remarks on how to read the translations of the *Novum Organum* by Francis Bacon, or rather by Franciscus Verulam, as he is named in the *Novus Index Librorum Prohibitorum* from 1632: "Read with caution, since the author [Bacon] . . . seems to think that all concepts generated by human understanding are erroneous, full of vice, and that their falseness denotes the weakness of the mind, and thus he attributes to himself the task of reconstructing all forms of human knowledge" (*Novus Index Librorum Prohibitorum* 365–366).

This passage must be seen, in itself, as symptomatic of the long history of difficulties that empiricism and the various other forms of the "new science" were
going to suffer in Spain, a history that has continued, with small alterations, on
until the twenty-first century. This institutional effort for the control of reading
was complemented, all through the area of influence of the Counter-Reformation,
by a renewed insistence on the role of iconography (so as to counteract the
iconoclasm of Lutheranism). Just as the letter of scripture was being contained and
kept away from the laypeople, their visual imagination was being encouraged and
reinforced within religious practice. Already Ignatius of Loyola, in the anti-
Lutheran *Spiritual Exercices* (1526), had insisted particularly on the role of the
visual in worship, encouraging the worshipper to build "imaginative pictures" of
Christ or of the sacred family. The new focus on the cult of Mary, and especially
on the theme of the *Mater Dolorosa*, gave rise to the richest and most expansive
forms of iconography; Marian brotherhoods proliferated throughout the southern
regions of Spain, extending the cult among the lower *strata* of society. In Seville,
the worship of the patrons of the city, Saint Rufina and Saint Justina, was intensely
renewed. Some fragments of their clothes and even bits of their fingers were
exhibited in the Cathedral, and offered to be kissed or worshipped during
Christmas and Easter. The legend of their torture at the hands of the Romans, and
of their having received the *stigmata* or wounds of Christ on their hands and feet,
was popularized in the form of oral storytelling and of ballads. The *beatas* operated in the limits or fringes of fully established religious practice. They did not attach
a particular importance to scholarship or writing; and the firm rooting of their
work in popular culture—which directly contributed to their empowerment—also
implied a relativism of the importance of written culture in their areas of influence.
The lack of material authored by the *beatas* stands in stark contrast with the
abundance of writings by Teresa de Jesús, the renowned mystic and reformer of
the Discalced (barefoot) Carmelite order, a contrast that becomes even more significant if we take into account the fact that Teresa herself was accused of *beatería*
and underwent the scrutiny of the Inquisition. Sixteen years after her death, her
works received the following description in a survey carried out, at the behest of
Rome, by father Francesco da Pisa:

> These books contain the doctrine of an unlettered woman, who did not always heed the
> opinions of learned men and confessors, but acted according to her own thinking . . . .
> Therefore, it seems that these books by Teresa should be gathered up, and not reprint-
> ed or translated into other languages, since there are many other books from which one
> can safely and profitably learn of the spiritual path. (Weber 161–162)

And yet, precisely because of the strong sensorial and plastic nature of Teresa's
mystical experiences, her written work would in the end be fully assimilated, and
recommended as reading matter by the Spanish Church: Teresa would thus be
absorbed, especially through her canonization in 1622, into the official discourse
of the Counter-Reformation.

ESSAYS

In the later decades of the sixteenth century, and all through the seventeenth,
the influence of inquisitorial thought and of the Baroque aesthetics would determine the main reading practices of Catholicism within the paradigms of religious
control that we have just described. And yet, in the meantime, some of the forms

of reading that had originated under the aegis of humanism, and which had established themselves firmly on the continent, were stabilizing and slowly leading to approaches that would, in time, prove essential in the creation of the modern forms of relation between reader and text. One of these modifications becomes very evident in the work of Michel de Montaigne, which offers itself to the reader as a series of "attempts," or *Essais* (comprising three *Livres* published in progressively enriched editions between 1580 and 1595) rather than as completed, finally finished, systematic discourses. The description that Montaigne makes of his own passion for his library is particularly relevant here:

> When at home, I little more frequent my library, from where I at once survey all the concerns of my family . . . . There I turn over a book, and then another, of various subjects, without method or design. One while I meditate; another I record, and dictate as I walk to and fro, such whimsies as these I here present you . . . . It is here that I am in my kingdom, and there I endeavour to make myself absolute monarch, and to sequester this corner from all society. (Rabinowitz and Kaplan 99)

Montaigne's representation of himself as a reader (if we see it in the context of the second half of the sixteenth century) is a distinctively continental one, unaffected by the religious changes and pressures of the Reformation, and offering a moderate but clear vindication of reading as a source of pleasure. We can hear the echoes of Francesco Petrarca's description of his friendly dialogue with the classics, written two centuries before. Montaigne also sees private reading as a process that is formative and constitutive of his personality, and at the same time as a source of continuous enjoyment and relish. And yet there is a new, unmistakably modern accent here that links reading and the company of books with the domestic environment and personal property (the library is the place from which the speaking self can "survey all the concerns of [his] family": a distinctly middle-class perspective, in which reading is part of the patriarchal control over the household). Finally, this text is also representative of the tone and mood of a radically new genre, one to which Montaigne himself was to give its definitive name: the genre of the literary essay (*essai*), an offspring of the humanistic tradition, which was born of the commentaries and meditations that are produced by the very experience of reading. And yet, Montaigne's most important contribution to the history of reading lies beyond this self-consciously literary perspective. It lies in his address to the reader as an intellectual equal, as one who shares his fundamental skepticism and his taste for a relaxed, pleasing, speculative exchange. Montaigne's *Essais* are the first step toward the acknowledgment of a cultured bourgeois audience for the writer. It is not at all strange that the new genre he introduced should have flourished not in France, but in early eighteenth-century England.

CREATIVE TEXTS

Most of the literature of this period, however, still incorporated into itself a full consciousness of the orality through which it would be communicated and experienced, even when it was read by a single individual; of course, this was even more obvious in the domain of lyric poetry. The French poets of La Pléiade, for instance, sought to establish a contemporary canon that could compare to Latin and Greek literature, but they never forgot the fact that poetry was above all a verbal art, one that could only be fully tasted in the act of reading it aloud. Pierre Ronsard began in this way one of the sonnets he addressed to Hélène de Surgères (published in 1578). Ronsard imagines his beloved as "singing" his poems in the distant future, when she will be old. The female addressee, at the end of her life, is still imagined "singing" the lines that were addressed to her when she was young. Even in poetry that involves (or simulates) a close interpersonal relationship, the act of reading verse maintains its full oral quality. Ronsard knew very well that, whenever a reader took up a piece of poetry to read it in solitude, he or she would pronounce the lines in solitude, or at least would imagine the sound of the words while gazing at the pages. This does not prevent the poet from imagining the act of reading as the transformation of the printed words into voice, even if the voice is the reader's own, reciting to him or herself. The very act of reading from paper, even in solitude, is pregnant with orality, even if it is only in an imagined, individual transition to voice from paper. In a sonnet addressed to himself, the poet-dramatist, Lope de Vega, complains of the little success of the "leaves" he has written, and laments seeing them ripped to pieces, because of an excess of fury. Lope de Vega often refers to his own sonnets as "papeles," papers or manuscripts, that can be rewritten, answered, or torn up by addressees.

This poem refers to leaves (isolated leaves, pages: certainly not a book) that have been successively adored and despised, and lie now destroyed in the poet's hands. In this case, the poems have fully completed their vital cycle by being written and then read, presumably aloud, without ever reaching print. Lope de Vega is among the poets who made better use of the interpenetration of the oral and written words. A great part of his production in verse took precisely the quintessential form of the octosyllabic Hispanic ballad, and he uses it to broadcast the poet's own private life, by simply putting him, his lovers and rivals, in archetypical plots and patterns (the pastoral solitude of a spurned lover, rivalries between Moorish knights, etc.) that had already been widely used in the tradition. This is part of the phenomenon defined as the *Romancero Nuevo* (the new ballads): a fashion for imitations of popular narratives in verse, authored and newly written by well-known poets, but which, in many cases, could easily be mistaken for popular ballads. Several of the best examples from this tendency were in fact eventually set to music, and some of them survived in purely oral form for centuries. Ballads originally written by Lope de Vega were documented as part of the repertoire of itinerant and blind singers in several rural areas of Castile, at the beginning of the twentieth century.

In itself, this intersection of the oral and the written shows that medieval forms of song and lyric remained fully alive at a popular level, even while being gradually influenced by the fiction that circulated in print. Some of the most dramatic episodes from printed romances and chivalry books gradually adopted the form of ballads, and were popularized in exclusively oral form among communities and social groups where access to books was limited or nonexistent. Characters such as Lancelot or Guinevere, or figures from the Hispanic post-Arthurian saga, *Amadís de Gaula,* came to be the protagonists of whole cycles of ballads, sometimes grafted onto motifs or narrative structures that had predated them for decades. Thus oral and written culture could interweave, both equally becoming spaces of fictional entertainment. It is characteristic of this scenario that the protagonist in Miguel de Cervantes's novel, *Don Quixote de la Mancha* (1605–15), who starts his first journey under a madness contracted through the influence of the printed word (his wide collection of chivalric romances), should shift to imagine himself as a character in a popular ballad as soon as he receives his first beating, and to sing the ballad he is evoking while lying helpless and beaten on the ground. In the very realistic Castilian world of Don Quixote, reading books or singing ballads are complementary ways of having access to the worlds of fiction. In later chapters of this same novel, when Don Quixote rides in the company of his squire, Sancho Panza, the text becomes a rich interaction and interpenetration, in the form of dialogue, between the literary voice of Don Quixote and the popular accents of Sancho Panza, who (despite being very able to write and read well) incorporates into the text a vast repertoire of popular sayings, ballads, and forms of oral storytelling.

MORAL AND STYLE MANUALS

In France the early seventeenth century saw the emergence of two developments that acted as a renewal within the traditions of religious literature and of its reception; both of them must be seen as configurations generated by the dominant paradigm of the Counter-Reformation. Chronologically, the first of them is the extraordinary success of the *Introduction à la Vie Dévote* (1609), by François de Sales, written directly in the vernacular and addressing very explicitly an audience that covers the newly emerging and wealthy middle class (the "bourgeois gentilhommes" who would be later satirized by Molière). This simple and elegant manual was reprinted constantly through the seventeenth century. By the end of the century, it would be a common feature in most literate and semi-literate households. Its quick and lasting influence is easy to understand if we consider its integration of Christianity in everyday life and its promotion of a simple, gentle acceptance of the difficulties of life as part of a practical disciplining of the self, oriented toward a full harmony with the designs of God. This perspective was promoted by the Catholic authorities as a gentle, attractive antidote against the lasting influence of Huguenot/Calvinist thinking in French culture: an influence that was far from extinguished. This reappearance occurred through the adoption, in French monastic culture, of trends of thought that duplicated the Protestant insistence on the importance of grace and the helplessness of man's action against the will of God. The most important of these is the influence of Jansenism, which reached an extraordinary strength through the direct influence of the monastery of Port-Royal, which came to be one of the key intellectual centers of seventeenth-century France.

Jansenism (the adaptation of the doctrines of the French theologian Jansenius) put a major emphasis on the salvific importance of divine grace, to such an extent that it reduced dramatically the participation of people in their own salvations. Some of its central theses were condemned by the French church in 1649 as being suspicious of heresy (that is, of covert Protestantism), but by that time the intellectual rigor of the movement had already influenced the main forms of literary expression in French. Thinkers such as Blaise Pascal, poets, and dramatists such as Pierre de Boileau and Jean Racine had assumed some of its main tenets and, above all, had assimilated its intellectual habits. These habits were, in themselves, essential in the history of writing and reading in French. For (just as happened in the case of Calvinism in the Reformed countries), Jansenism tended to express itself in a rational, detached style of argument, which allowed and encouraged the use of reason and deduction in theological and intellectual speculation. The radical theologian Blaise Pascal, whose sister was a nun in Port-Royal, started his career as a mathematician; and in 1660, a group of Jansenists produced the *Grammaire Générale et Raisonnée*, a key development in the prehistory of linguistics, and a text that promotes purely rational and deductive criteria as guidelines for establishing the correct grammatical usage. With the influence of Jansenism, therefore, we have very much come to the intellectual atmosphere of the Enlightenment, and especially of its main habits of reading: the disregard of intuition and of received knowledge, and the assertion of a rational and deductive basis as a starting point for any serious intellectual discussion.

CHANGES IN THE PHILOSOPHOPHY
OF READING AND RHETORIC

From the beginning of the Jacobean period, the main attempt of the Church of England was its consolidation as a cohesive political body, with the king as its head. In the long run, it was precisely this attempt, together with the control of doctrine by the ecclesiastical authorities, that would become one of the major causes of the civil war. In the first two decades of the century, the key doctrinal emphasis was put on the Book of Common Prayer, which, with minor alterations introduced in 1604, remained basically the same version that was approved in 1662, under Elizabeth I. The 1604 edition included the following injunction:

> And all Priests and deacons shall be bound to say daily the Morning and Evening Prayer, either privately or openly, except they be let by preaching, studying of divinity, or by some other urgent cause. And the Curate that ministereth in every Parish-church and chapel . . . shall say the same in the Parish-Church or chapel where he ministereth,and shall cause a Bell to be tolled thereunto a convenient time before he begin, that the people may come to hear God's word. (Preface to the 1604 *Book of Common Prayer*)

This emphasis on prayer, both individual and personal, became in this period the basis of devotional practice. The worshipping subject was seen, in basic Protestant fashion, as entirely depending on God, and the desire or longing for grace, freely given by God without any apparent merit on the part of the human subject. Several passages in John Donne's *Holy Sonnets* had to be read as explorations of the paradoxical nature of God's love, seen, in strict coherence with the Augustinian and Lutheran tradition, as an unpredictable and uncontrollable force. Occasionally, Donne inverted the approach taken by profane Petrarchan poets, presenting the human aspiration to divine grace in terms of physical desire, as he does in "Batter My Heart, Three-Personed God." Thus Donne's language, in his religious verse, is far from tending toward idealization and abstraction. It forces the reader to confront the paradoxes of grace through the use of a language that tends, in strict Protestant fashion, to individualize that experience, and to describe it in terms of material, intense reality.

The relationship between the Protestant worshipper and God was seen as purely personal, independent from any mediatory or external intervention. In the work of another priest and poet, George Herbert, the soul is always solitary and individualized, and it has to examine for itself the progress of its relation with the transcendent, without any external intervention (as in the original perspective adopted by Luther). As a result, Herbert draws a detailed picture of his own subjective religiosity, from an initial state of doubt and fear, on to the joyful reception of grace. Herbert's lyric does not rely so much on complex visual elements, nor does it try to move through an accumulation of imagery; instead, it appeals to the intelligence of the reader, who has to follow the development of the metaphor he is using—usually only one per poem, though slowly explored, and presented with a sense of deep but restrained emotion. In one of his moments of despair, the poet dedicated several lines simply to wishing that he was a tree or a flower, or some form of simpler life, in the most direct and transparent language (see "Affliction (1)").

One of the most interesting features of Herbert's poetry is his vindication of a simple, nonrhetorical style, which is entirely coherent with the iconoclasm of the Anglican church. If Herbert's mastery of metaphysical conceits is so extremely clever, it is because he knows that their expressive validity is limited. They are only tools in the expression of something that is inexpressible: the feeling of grace and of trust in the might of God. Herbert is aware of the limits of language, and actually formulates, in some occasions, a poetics of "plainness." The feeling of faith has to be conveyed directly and austerely, without relying on an abundance of images. This is most clearly expressed in his sonnet "Jordan," when he wishes to be simply able to say the plain words, "My Lord, my King." This absence of overt rhetorical features, in poetry as in preaching, will be defined from within the Church as the "Anglican plain style": the language of naked, direct devotional impulse, suspicious of the excesses of rhetoric or iconography.

But beyond the scope of the Protestant approaches to texts and their consumption, there was already a significant, powerful new tendency in pre-civil war England in the forms of reading and writing; a tendency that situates itself, very self-consciously, on the margins of the main traditions of humanism. This tendency was clearly placed in the context of the early manifestations of the "New Science" (and therefore in a development that parallels the spread of Cartesianism in continental Europe) of the beginnings of the empirical tradition, which required a simplification and clarification of the forms of writing and reading. Francis Bacon was one of the first humanists to question the legacy of humanism, insofar as it had involved an excessive "delight in the manner of style and phrase," an excessive concentration on form at the expense of content:

> The admiration of ancient authors, the hate for schoolmen, the exact study of languages and the efficiency of preaching did bring in an affectionate study of eloquence and "copie" of speech, which then began to flourish. This grew speedily to an excess, for men began to hunt more after words than content, and more after the choiceness of the phrase, and the round and elegant composition of the sentence . . . than after the weight of the matter, worth of subject, soundness of argument, life of invention and depth of judgment. (*The Advancement of Learning* 70–71)

Here content, subject, and judgment begin to matter more than subtlety of form or argument. These are the initial requirements for an abandonment of "copie" (the Erasmian *copia*) in favor of a simplified, direct prose. Bacon is one of the first unambiguous examples of a new breed of readers, who value the practical and performative use of language above anything else. This does not indicate, of course, a disregard of basic humanistic training (indeed Bacon, like most scholars of his time, takes it for granted as the starting point of all valid knowledge): what it shows is a new emphasis on favor of legibility, accessibility, and clarity, all in favor of the practical uses of reading. Even such a demanding educative program as the one framed by John Milton in his *Of Education* (1644) shows signs of this Baconian tendency: although the classics are to be used in every level of a young man's education, the selection of texts must be geared toward application in every sphere of life. The study of Caesar's *Gallic Wars* must directly lead to a practical understanding of strategic thinking in the context of war. Reading Pliny will lead to the development of a sense of curiosity for nature. And not only this, for Milton, the practice of reading must be complemented by a direct interaction with manufacturers, peasants, and all those who are involved in actual, material production of goods:

> To set forward all these proceedings . . . they [the students] may procure, as oft as shall be needful, the helpful experiences of hunters, fowlers, fishermen, shepherds, gardeners, apothecaries; and, in the other sciences, architects, engineers, mariners, anatomists; who doubtless would be ready some for reward, and some to favor such a hopeful seminary. (*The Riverside Milton* 983)

The renewed emphasis on practicality and factuality could easily converge with the Protestant emphasis on self-analysis, and on the discussion of the analysis between self and the world. And, as a result of this convergence, some practices of diary and auto-biographical writing came to incorporate an insistent approach to external reality. It was not only scripture but also nature that could speak to the self, and that could offer itself to being interpreted and read in its interrelation to human life and its multiple affairs. As Robert Boyle put it in his own *Occasional Reflections* (1665):

> The world is the great Book, not so much of Nature, as of the God of Nature . . . crowded with instructive lessons, if we had but the Skill, and would take the pains, to extract and pick them out: the Creatures are the Aegyptian Hieroglyphics, that under the rude forms of birds, and beasts, conceal the true secrets of Knowledge and of Piety. (Hunter 202–03)

It is no coincidence that Robert Boyle was one of the founders of the Royal Society, from its very origins during the civil war itself on to its official founding in 1660, under the direct patronage of the monarchy. Only seven years after the foundation of the Royal Society, the divine Thomas Sprat clearly saw that one of its most beneficent effects was a cleansing, or simplification, of language: in its short history, its scientists had already been careful to uphold:

> A constant Resolution to reject all the amplifications, digressions, and swellings of style: to return back to the primitive purity, and shortness, when men deliver'd so many *things* almost in an equal number of *words*. They have exacted from all their members, a close, naked, natural way of speaking; positive expressions; clear senses; a native easiness: bring-ing all things as near the Mathematical plainness, as they can: and preferring the language of Artisans, Countrymen and Merchants, before that of Wits or Scholars. (*History of the Royal Society of London*, 1667)

Here, Sprat celebrates precisely the kind of simplification and streamlining of style that will allow for the spread and development of an informed, active read-ing middle class in England, and which will make possible, among other develop-ments, the rise of the novel in the eighteenth century. For, after all, the language of *Robinson Crusoe* and *Moll Flanders* was to be that of "artisans, countrymen and merchants," subtly adapted by Daniel Defoe to the genre of autobiographical, exemplary narratives.

The other key element in this development is the unstoppable spread of read-ing for religious and moral purposes. The spread of the literature of the self, that had begun its development at the beginning of the century, reached its apogee after the English Civil War. The long road to the war was paved by the growth in polemical discussion, itself a result of the growing gap between the Stuart monar-chy and the English middle classes that were already, by the beginning of the century, notably literate. The Revolution was a moment of outburst of the power-ful forces that had been engendered by the development of the many traditions of radical Protestantism since the beginning of the century. Popular movements such as those of Levellers and Diggers emerged, to a great extent, as the direct result of new forms of reading the scripture. The period seemed to confirm the original reservations that Calvin and Luther had had more than a century before, when fearing that an excessive openness in the Protestant approach to the Bible could generate endless and unpredictable doctrinal standpoints. The extraordinary upsurge of religious leaflets, libels, chapbooks, and doctrinal tracts of various kinds led to an increased attempt, on the part of the Church of England, to control all sorts of political publications.

It is in this context that we must understand the polemical concern with the freedom of the press in the 1640s. Initially, the English Revolution led radical groups to expect a more tolerant, open approach to the circulation of contrast-ing religious viewpoints. The reality would, of course, prove different in the long-term development of the revolutionary process into the Protectorate. The Act, passed by Parliament in 1643, banned the publication of any text that was not directly authorized by Parliament. The Act motivated the appearance of such an impassioned defense of literature as John Milton's *Areopagitica*. Some of the passages of the tract would become very popular in later centuries, par-ticularly its humanistic identification with books of rational thought: "Who kills a man kills a reasonable creature, God's image; but he who destroys a good book, kills reason itself, kills the image of God, as it were in the eye. Many a man lives a burden to the earth; but a good book is the precious lifeblood of a master spirit, embalmend and treasured up on purpose to a life beyond life" (Milton 1998: 999).

Milton's vibrant defense of books, however, has to be strongly qualified. *Areopagitica* is a tract written specifically against the licensing Act of 1643, and a text that opposes preprint censorship, but not any censorship or prohibition undertaken *after* the publication of an immoral or dangerous book. Milton him-self would, in later years, act as a censor for the Protectorate. Modern scholarship has been able to establish, however, that Milton's tracts (and not only *Areopagitica*) were appreciated in the radical revolutionary circles, where they directly contributed to the justification of the new forms of heterodox, heretic, and unconventional religious thought.

WOMEN'S TEXTS

It was precisely in the revolutionary environment where the access that women had to scripture, and the integration of Biblical language in their individual experi-ence, could lead to the creation of new (though marginal) forms of female author-ity. Testimonial or autobiographical narratives, which were abundant among radical groups during and after the civil war, could also be adapted and appropriated by women in unexpected directions. The second half of the seventeenth century saw an enormous upsurge of women's writing in English. Before 1650, only eighty texts written by women appeared in print, whereas the 1650s alone saw the publi-cation of nearly 130 works, by more than seventy women authors. The greater number of these were religious and testimonial writings inscribed in different radi-cal Protestant traditions. And it must be pointed out that, among them, the largest single body of texts was produced by Quaker authors. These modes of autobio-graphical narration became especially important in the Restoration, when the links between the different Quaker communities, in England and abroad, had to be strategically reinforced. These testimonials were written from a subjective perspec-tive, presented as the result of an intense spiritual experience; at the same time, they fulfilled a precise function within the larger community: the individual response to the Holy Spirit was meant to be projected outward, retold, and reenacted for the benefit of others. Narratives of the journey to the encounter with God were meant to encourage fellow believers on the same path. Works such as *A Short Relation of their Sufferings* (1562), coauthored by Katharine Evans and Sarah Cheevers, oper-ate at two different and complementary levels: as accounts of subjective experiences and as products for religious consumption, meant to strengthen the ideology and the practices of the community they addressed.

Inside revolutionary England, the work of radical female preachers such as the Fifth-Monarchist, Anna Trapnel, became possible through the interaction between their direct oral performance and the written circulation (which must have begun in manuscript form) of their sayings. The very text authorized by Trapnel (*The Cry of a Stone,* 1654) acknowledges the marks of this interaction:

> Though I fail in an orderly penning those things, yet not in the true Relation of as much as I remember, and what is expedient to be written. I could not have related so much from the shallow memory I have naturally, but though often relating these things, they became as a written book, spread often before me and after which I write. (34)

For Trapnel, the actual writing of a book is a direct result of the work of her preaching; that initial oral work acts as a palimpsest for the final written text. This indicates as well the presence of two kinds of subsequent audiences for religious works such as hers: an initial audience for her oral preaching, and another one that would read the text either in private or aloud, to a far larger community guaranteed by the circulation of print.

Another case in point in the later seventeenth century is, for instance, the testimonial written by Agnes Beaumont (*A Narrative of the Persecution of Agnes Beaumont* 1652–1720), a member of John Bunyan's independent church. Beaumont was accused and then declared innocent of the death of her father, and described her ordeals in her book. This text presents itself as an exemplary narrative, in which the author-narrator makes her experience available to other members of her church and presents her own trials as exemplary of Christian behavior in time of need. Literary strategies such as these were clearly more available to women in the context of radical, dissenting groups. The fact that these groups became marginalized and dispersed in the Restoration must not make us forget their importance in the history of reading and writing practices.

AUTOBIOGRAPHICAL TEXTS

These examples are not only representative of the new forms of women's reading and writing in the second half of the seventeenth century, but especially of the ease with which gender barriers could be superseded in radical Protestant and dissenter contexts. It is clear that these circles were primarily responsible for the renewed attention to, and the circulation in print of, spiritual autobiographies, and it is clear as well that the success of such texts and their diffusion went well beyond the communities to which they were originally addressed. To mention just one canonical and representative example, John Bunyan's *Grace Abounding to the Chief of Sinners,* which for him was essentially a means of continuing to preach to his community from his prison in Bedford, was published in 1666 and reached seven editions some twenty years later, by 1688. Bunyan's vibrant account of his trials by faith could thus become an exemplary narrative in itself, and one that could affect readers of many Protestant denominations. *Grace Abounding* combines a sense of deep intimacy with a radical contemporaneity, which is evident from the very beginning of the text:

> In this relation of the merciful working of God upon my soul it will not be amiss if, in the first place, I do, in a few words, give you a hint of my pedigree and manner of bringing up, that thereby the goodness and bounty of God towards me may be the more advanced and magnified before the sons of men. (Bunyan 16)

In this way, despite its strong individual accent (and despite the text's lack of a very strong and precise contextualization), readers know that the speaking voice is that of an immediate contemporary, and are inevitably led to compare their spiritual troubles with Bunyan's own. Several other texts of a similar nature were published in the second half of the seventeenth century, some notably less successful than Bunyan's. But these were equally significant in their attempts to generate exemplary literature for a readership that required a sense of a personal identification and contextual proximity with its spiritual referents, and that had a strong perception of the presence of the spiritual in material and ordinary circumstances. Texts such as Lodowick Muggleton's *Acts of the Witnesses* (1699), Reverend Richard Baxter's *Reliquiae Baxterianae* (1696) or the Quaker George Fox's *Journal* (a text that was not directly authorized by its author, but which was published in response to the demands of those who knew him) all testify to the importance of this new and powerful trend. The enthusiastic demands for these texts would, in time, lead to significant developments in literary history. There was only a short step from genuine autobiographies to false ones, and from these to the novel, the great literary innovation of the eighteenth century.

TRANSITIONAL TEXTS

The process of renewal of the habits of reading that started at the beginning of the sixteenth century had prevailed and asserted itself in the long run. The great poems of the Restoration, and the various responses to them, show clear evidence of the persistence of the methods of reading and interpretation that humanism had introduced, as well as their dramatic consequences. In Andrew Marvell's poetical dedication to Milton's *Paradise Lost* (in its 1674 edition), for instance, there is a clear indication of the dangers involved in the reinterpretation and rereading of the Bible, which had begun with the *translatio studii*, and which could be seen as culminating in Milton's greatest poem. When Marvell first read *Paradise Lost*, he was awestruck by the greatness of the poet, and (as he put it in his dedication to the 1674 edition) feared that the consequences of Milton's poetic effort might ruin the sacred truths inherited from ancient times.

Only two centuries before, these lines would have been written very differently, if at all; they would certainly not have involved such a sense of anxiety at the demystifying power of poetry and literature. Marvell was writing after one hundred and fifty years of Reformation, after the turmoil of the English Civil War, after the early years of the Restoration. In the latter half of the seventeenth century, it was clear that the very act of reading and rereading the Bible could lead to ruin, and to more than ruin—that the sacred text, the basis of a common culture, could easily be desacralized in the hands of poets and scholars. In spite of the intentions of the original humanists, this would remain one of the lasting legacies of the translatio studii, and one that would lead directly to the Enlightenment. The act of reading itself, even when coated in purely philological intentions, could never be seen as endowed with the original innocence it once had.

One final example will make this point even clearer, and will leave us just at the threshold of the eighteenth century. At the root of the translatio studii there had always been a sense of implicit continuity between the past and the present, a sense of implicit similarity between cultures that were distant in time: a sense, in brief, that the past could help readers interpret the events of the present. John Dryden's dedication of his version of Virgil's *Aeneid* (1697) is full of this awareness of the continuities of the past in the present, or, rather, of the suggestion that the present may be better read, and interpreted, through an analysis of the conflicts of the past:

The Commonwealth had received a deadly wound in the former civil wars betwixt Marius and Scylla. The Commons, while the first prevailed, had almost shaken off the yoke of the nobility, and Marius and Cynna, like the Captains of the Mob, under the specious pretence of the Public good, and of doing Justice on the oppressors of their liberty, revenged themselves, without form of Law. (*The Works of John Dryden*, V: *Poems 1697* 278).

A passage like this obtains its strength from the constant hint of a translatio that the reader is implicitly invited to make between the conflicts of classical Rome and those of contemporary (late seventeenth century) England, a parallelism that is never explicitly drawn by the author, but which will quickly be understood by the humanistically trained reader. Dryden has no need to insist upon the continuities between the Roman and the English commons, or between the disasters that were visited on two or three occassions in one century upon the people of Rome and those that have visited the English through the political crises of the seventeenth century. By the time when that paragraph was written, it had become commonplace to trace moral and political links between ancient history and contemporary culture. This tendency to active translatio would become, in time, one of the springboards for the main traditions of reading in the eighteenth century and afterward.

CONCLUSION

By the middle of the seventeenth century, it was evident that the humanistic project of a general, widespread renewal of European society through a return to classical culture had essentially failed. The rate of translations and editions of the classics in this period, as contrasted between reformed and unreformed countries, was significant. Between 1500 and 1700 there was a steady decline in the number of editions from Greek and Latin classics in Spain and France (slightly above one hundred new editions in Spain, nearly one hundred and fifty in France), while there were 122 new editions of Greek classics alone (excluding the ones from Latin) in England during the same period. The great period of translation of Greek and Latin Classics in Spain and France was, without a doubt, the first half of the sixteenth century; from the early seventeenth century onward, scholars and students in both countries had to rely increasingly on translations from the previous century. A simple survey of the number of writer-scholars who were proficient in both Greek and Latin in the early seventeenth century on both sides of the Reformation is also significant: in England, the first half of the seventeenth century gives us names of writer-scholars such as Ben Jonson, Francis Bacon, Thomas Browne, and the young John Milton, all of them proficient in Greek; in the same period, in Spain, only Francisco de Quevedo can be quoted as a good Hellenist, and recent scholarship on his works has questioned even that. Thanks to the influence of the Counter-Reformation, the teaching of Greek in the Spanish universities declined all through the seventeenth century, with disastrous consequences. In the University of Valladolid the subject remained untaught from 1591 onward. It was entirely abandoned in the universities of Santiago and Sevilla, and even the chair of Greek in the university of Alcalá de Henares (the very site of production of the Complutensian Bible) was left empty after 1698.

Throughout this period, however, and in spite of the decline in classical studies and the general advance of the new languages of empiricism and science in Europe (and especially in England), some of the old ideals by which humanism had consolidated itself as a reading practice remained alive in intellectual circles. For practically all the European intellectuals of the seventeenth century, a good basis in Latin and a good knowledge of rhetoric and history remained as the basis for all forms of intellectual progress. When Pierre-Daniel Huet prepared his series of editions of the Greek and Latin classics for the French prince in the 1670s, taking them as the best basis for any educative process, or when Marc-Antoine Muret lectured on the need of reading Tacitus for a better understanding of present times, they were following on the footsteps of the early modern humanists. They were still affirming the need to sustain any process of self-fashioning on a good rhetorical and ethical basis, and on the assimilation of classical culture as the key to personal and social improvement. Perhaps the best rendition of such a perspective was given by the Spanish poet Francisco de Quevedo, in his sonnet on the art of reading in solitude. Speaking from a very Counter-Reformist perspective, under the strong consciousness of the fragility of life and the proximity of death, the poet still asserts the validity of the experience of reading in the face of the devastations of time, but still he asserts that there are hours that count for the best: the hours that are spent in study and reading, which can make one wiser.

Erasmus, Cisneros, or More could not have said it better, or more memorably. The simple but sincere desire for personal improvement through active reading remained, all through the cultural crises of the seventeenth century and beyond, one of the basic ethical and cultural values of the West.

RECOMMENDED READING

Chartier, Roger. *The Order of Books: Readers, Authors and Literature in Europe.* Stanford, CA: Stanford University Press, 1994.

Chartier, Roger and Arthur Goldhammer. *Inscription and Erasure: Literature and Written Culture from the Eleventh to the Eighteenth Centuries.* Philadelphia, PA: University of Pennsylvania Press, 2007.

Ferguson, Wallace. *The Renaissance in Historical Thought.* Toronto: University of Toronto Press, 2005.

Finkelstein, David. *A Book History Reader.* London and New York: Routledge, 2006.

Grafton, Anthony. *Defenders of the Book: the Traditions of Scholarship in an Age of Science.* Cambridge, MA: Harvard University Press, 2003.

Grafton, Anthony, and Lisa Blair, eds. *The Transmission of Culture in Renaissance Europe, 1450–1800.* Philadelphia, PA: University of Pennsylvania Press, 1998.

Kraye, Jill, ed. *The Cambridge Companion to Renaissance Humanism.* Cambridge, UK: Cambridge University Press, 1996.

PRIMARY SOURCES

Bacon, Francis. *The Advancement of Learning.* London: Scholarly Press, 1973.

————. *Novum Organum: True Directions Concerning the Interpretation of Nature.* 1620. Whitefish, MT: Kessinger Publishing, 2004.

Beaumont, Agnes. *A Narrative of the Persecutions of Agnes Beaumont.* 1760. Edited by Vera J. Camden. East Lansing, MI: Colleagues Press, 2002.

The Book of Common Prayer. 1549, 1559, 1604 & 1662. New York, NY: Church Publishing, 2001.

Bunyan, John. *Grace Abounding to the Chief of Sinners.* Edited by W.R. Owens. London: Penguin, 1987.

Calvin, John. *Opera Quae Extant Omnia.* Vol. 35. Berlin: Hengstenberg, 1887.

Ceasar, Julius. *The Gallic Wars.* 50–40 BCE. New York, NY: Oxford University Press, 1999.

Cervantes, Miguel. *Don Quixote.* 1605. Translated and edited by John Rutherford. Roberto Gonzalez Echevarria (Introduction). New York, NY: Penguin, 2003.

Donne, John. *Complete Poems.* Edited by H.W. Garrod. Oxford, UK: Oxford University Press, 1967.

Dryden, John. *The Works of John Dryden,* V: *Poems 1697.* Los Angeles, CA: University of California Press, 1988.

Erasmus. *The Praise of Folly and Other Writings.* London and New York: Norton and Co., 1989.

Evans, Katherine and Sarah Cheevers. *A Short Relation of their Sufferings.* 1562. Not currently available.

Foxe, John. *Acts and Monuments of these Latter and Perilous Days.* 1563. New Kensington, PA: Whittaker House Paperback, 1981.

Grammaire Générale et Raisonnée. 1660. Paris: Republications Paulet, 1969. No longer in print.

Herbert, George. *Herbert: The Complete English Works.* New York, NY: Everyman, 1995.

Hooker, Richard. *The Works of Richard Hooker* I–IV. Edited by W. Speed Hill. Cambridge, Massachusetts: 1977–81.

Horace. *The Complete Odes and Epodes.* 30s BCE. Translated by David West. New York, NY: Oxford World Classics, 2000.

Ignatious of Loyola. *Spritiual Exercises.* 1526. Not currently available.

León, Fray Luis de. *Poesías.* Edited by Oreste Macrí. Barcelona: Crítica, 1982.

Luther, Martin. *Selections from His Writings.* Edited by John Dillenberger. New York, NY: Doubleday, 1961.

Milton, John. *The Riverside Milton.* Edited by Roy Flannagan. New York: Houghton Mifflin, 1998.

Montalvo, Garci Rodríguez de. *Amadis de Gaula.* Vols. 1 & 2. 1508. Madrid: Catedra, 2006.

Montaigne, Michel de. *Essais.* 1580–95. Paris: Impr. nationale editions, 1998.

More, Sir Thomas. *Complete Works VI.* Edited by Thomas Lawler, Germain Marc-Hadour and Richard Marius. New Haven, CT: Yale University Press, 1981.

Novus Index Librorum Prohibitorum. Sevilla: Francisco de Lyra, 1632. Not currently available.

Pliny. *Naturalis Historia.* 77 CE. Edited by Joyce Irene Whalley. London: Victoria and Albert Museum, 1982.

Quevedo, Francisco de. *Obras Poéticas.* Edited by José Manuel Blecua. Madrid: Castalia, 1969.

Ronsard, Jean de. *Oeuvres Complètes II.* Edited by Gustave Cohen. Paris: Gallimard, 1950.

———. *Oeuvres Complètes I.* Edited by Cérard, Ménager and Simonin. Paris: Gallimard, 1993.

Sales, Françoise de. *Introduction à la Vie Devoté.* 1609. Paris: Editions du Seuil, 1995.

Shakespeare, William. *Sonnets.* Edited by Stanley Wells. Oxford: Clarendon Press, 1985.

Spenser, Edmund and Kenneth J. Larsen. *Edmund Spenser's Amoretti and Epithalamion: A Critical Edition.* Phoenix, AZ: MRTS, 1997.

Spener, Jacob. *Pia Desideria.* 1675. Edited by Theodore G. Tappert. Eugene, OR: Wipf & Stock Publishers, 2002.

Sprat, Thomas. *History of the Royal Society of London.* 1667. Not currently available.

St. Paul. *Epistle to the Romans.* Edited by Griffith Thomas. Grand Rapids, MI: Wm. B. Eerdmans Publishing Co., 1946.

Trapnel, Anna. *The Cry of a Stone.* 1654. Edited by Hilary Hinds. Phoenix, AZ: MRTS, 2000.

Vega, Lope de. *Obras Poéticas.* Edited by José Manuel Blecua. Barcelona: Planeta, 1983.

SECONDARY SOURCES

Alcalá, Ángel, ed. *Inquisición Española y Mentalidad Inquisitorial.* Barcelona: Ariel, 1984.

Gilmont, Jean-François. *La Réforme et le Livre: L'Europe de l'Imprimé (1517–1750).* Paris: Cerf, 1990.

Huizinga, Johann. *Erasmus and the Age of Reformation.* Princeton, NJ: Princeton University Press, 1984.

Hunter, J. Paul. *Before Novels: the Cultural Contexts of Eighteenth-Century English Fiction.* New York, NY: W.W. Norton, 1994.

Moss, Ann. *Printed Commonplace-Books and the Structuring of Renaissance Thought.* New York, NY: Oxford University Press, 1996.

Pelikan, Jaroslav. *The Christian Tradition: A History of the Development of Doctrine. Volume 4: Reformation of Church and Dogma (1300–1700) (The Christian Tradition: A History of the Development of Christian Doctrine).* Chicago: University of Chicago Press, 1984.

Rabinowitz, Harold, and Rob Kaplan, eds. *A Passion for Books.* New York: Three Rivers Press, 1999.

Sinfield, Alan. *Literature in Protestant England.* London: Croon Helm, 1983.

Weber, Alison. *Teresa of Avila and the Rhetoric of Femininity.* Princeton, NJ: Princeton University Press, 1990.

CHAPTER 8

The Enlightenment

Gabrielle Watling

TIMELINE

1791   Paine's *Rights of Man* is published
1792   Mary Wollstonecraft's *Vindication of the Rights of Women* is published
1793   Post-revolution Terror in France
1798   Many British radicals flee to America after the Sedition Act in Britain

INTRODUCTION TO THE PERIOD

Like the Renaissance before it, the Enlightenment represented a major turning point in European history. Whereas previous historical movements and/or revolutions were generated by wars of succession or expansion, or religious chauvinism, the Renaissance and the Enlightenment were chiefly the result of major developments in science, which were extrapolated to politics and, most significantly, philosophy. The Enlightenment in particular represents a dividing line between broad acceptance of church and monarchical doctrine on the one hand, and the emergence of antidoctrinal ideas based on the existence of individual reason, an orderly Christian God, and the rise of "Natural Philosophy" on the other. In terms of scientific progress, the Enlightenment saw major advancements in mathematics, engineering, and technology, as empirical methodologies replaced inductive assumption as the dominant form of establishing "truth."

The Enlightenment was an era of rapid change and expansion. The eighteenth century witnessed the consolidation of several European empires. The British extended their interests and administrative control of North America; began operating, albeit through a private trading company, in India; claimed Australia and New Zealand for George III, and by the end of the eighteenth century, had annexed the South African cape. The Netherlands, Spain, Portugal, and France, to a lesser extent, had all secured or begun securing colonial holdings in Asia, South America, and Africa. In fact, the merging of European rationality and native tribal customs in colonial locations became a trope for the era's philosophical, narrative, aesthetic, and social developments. The "noble savage" became a symbol of the "natural" human condition for philosophers such as Jean-Jacques Rousseau. African, Asian, and North American figures began appearing in domestic decor and in the art of the period. Furthermore, experiences in the colonies pushed European imaginations beyond Western religious, scientific, and social traditions, and provided both a catalyst for and a contradiction to scientific rationality.

The eighteenth century was also a time of profound political change. European politics had certainly never been stable, but some political traditions had endured during the medieval era and the Renaissance. However, the events of the late seventeenth century, which had a profoundly destabilizing effect on European politics, were largely religious at base. Charles II's restoration of the monarchy in Britain, although not initially controversial, became so with the ascent of his son, James II, whose sole ambition as British monarch was to restore the primacy of the Roman Catholic Church. In the one hundred and fifty years or so after the reign of Henry VIII, founder of the Protestant Church of England, the British had largely come to associate Catholicism with the suppression of individual rights *à la* the Spanish Inquisition. Furthermore, the English Civil War had ensured that the powers of the British monarch were now much weaker, and a great deal more authority had been given to the elected parliament. When James II fled to Ireland in 1689, his Protestant daughter and son-in-law, Mary and William of Orange, became joint monarchs of Great Britain, at the expense of his Catholic son.

As Catholic fortunes fell in Britain, scientific thinking and the establishment of empirical research and analysis rose. Catholicism, with its emphasis on faith in church doctrine, fostered a culture of *a priori* acceptance of the veracity of Biblical narratives, dogma, hierarchy, social roles, and miracles. The Catholic doctrine was fundamentally conservative and required an adherence to church authority that discouraged analysis of the world and its constituent parts beyond official church explanation. Therefore, as Catholic influence retreated, secular methods of inquiry started to sprout. Perhaps the most important figure in the promulgation of scientific and empirical analysis was Sir Isaac Newton. Among other important discoveries, Newton established that the motion of objects on Earth and of celestial bodies is governed by the same set of natural laws, thereby casting further doubt on the concept of the earth's centrality in the universe. Moreover, Newton's rational, scientific applications of mathematical and mechanical principles emerged as viable alternatives to traditional religious explanations for natural phenomena. In fact, later generations of religious thinkers adopted Newton's discoveries as evidence of "Natural Religion," a hugely popular concept during the Enlightenment.

On the "Continent" (a collective term used to refer primarily to France, Spain, the Netherlands, and Germany), religious persecution was also fueling changes in both political philosophy and practice. Whereas the British were reinforcing their Protestant identity, and conversely persecuting Catholics, Spain was persecuting Protestants, especially in the Netherlands. However, as philosophical change moved across Europe, the Netherlands became a haven for Protestant thinkers escaping Catholic persecution, and it was here that Protestant presses published some of the first of the Enlightenment's "radical" political and social treatises. Although the Enlightenment is usually associated with profound growth in scientific and philosophical ideas in Britain and France, the Netherlands played a key role in fostering the first political documents of the era.

Whereas Britain, France, and the Netherlands all enjoyed significant advances during the period, Spain and Germany struggled to make the same connection with the new intellectual trends. Spain had dominated the western European continent during the Renaissance and into the seventeenth century. The Spanish colonial network was powerful, and colonial possessions enriched Spain's economy beyond those of its European neighbors. The plundering of South America's gold, gems, and spices helped to maintain Spain's domination of the Netherlands and other parts of Europe, and ensured the almost military strength of the Spanish Church. However, a long period of domestic war, centering on the War of Spanish Succession, dominated the early years of the eighteenth century. Given its domestic difficulties and its reluctance to challenge Catholic doctrine, which had helped support Spanish dominance of Europe for so long, Spain has never been considered a primary contributor to, or beneficiary of, Enlightenment ideologies.

Germany, like many European "countries" at the time, was not a sovereign nation, but rather a collection of "duchies" that were almost feudal in their economic and social structure. The region was called Prussia, and it was made up of federated states such as Silesia, Bavaria, and Westphalia. Whereas academic discovery dominated Britain and France during the eighteenth century, Prussia, under the "Soldier King," Frederick William I (r. 1713–1740), concentrated on expansion and consolidation of its member states under an efficient bureaucracy and disciplined standing army. Although Fredrick William's son, Frederick II ("Frederick the Great"—r. 1740–1786), was more interested in philosophy and the arts than his stern father, he too was focused on Prussia's military strength and the expansion of his administration's reach. The combination of a martial ideology and an emerging sense of cultural cohesion in the late eighteenth century meant that Germany had a very different Enlightenment experience from Britain and France. Unlike those countries, Germany was slow to grasp the material, intellectual, and ideological changes brought about by the Enlightenment. Instead, the Prussian focus was on the recognition of a shared cultural identity based on language, customs, beliefs, and narratives. Therefore, the German Enlightenment experience was less reflective and intellectual, and more a passionate call for unity and patriotic self-recognition. In fact, it could be argued that Germany, because of its unique social, political, and economic structure, skipped the Enlightenment as such and went straight from late feudalism to Romanticism.

In its final years, the Enlightenment became the age of the Revolution. Although the Enlightenment's key philosophers—Locke, Rousseau, Voltaire— would have despaired at the collapse of "rational society" into revolution, the combination of the widespread philosophical endorsement of individual freedom and the continuation of "old regime" style politics in Europe and colonial America resulted in spectacular, and ostensibly successful, efforts to establish the promised liberties of the age on both an individual and a national scale. Across the Atlantic, the American-born colonists were chaffing under Britain's economic and legislative control. In an effort to enact the freedoms and self-determinations that the Enlightenment had made popular, and in particular to wrest economic control from the British, the Americans revolted in 1776. American victory over the British gave heart to radical thinkers in Europe and helped to provide philosophical justification for revolution in France, especially as France itself had played a major role in helping the Americans throw off the colonial yoke.

Back in Europe, the *"Ancien Régime"* that had operated in France since the fourteenth century had become increasingly oppressive, indulgent, and wasteful over the course of the eighteenth century. For the Parisian bourgeoisie, Marie Antoinette came to symbolize every excess of the French ruling classes. Furthermore, France had been supporting the American revolutionaries against the British, and this act of international bravado eventually drained the French economy. The French people perceived that they were paying the cost of the nation's generosity, and when bread prices rose beyond the reach of the average citizen in 1789, Parisians rose up against the monarchy. The ineffectual French king Louis XVI, his hated Austrian wife, and the aristocracy that supported them were overthrown, to the delight of the Revolution's many supporters. Soon after, France became a republic under a revolutionary "Assembly." However, much against the spirit of the preceding philosophical Enlightenment, the aftermath of the French Revolution under the Assembly reduced Paris to a city of fear, oppression, and persecution, symbolized by the guillotine. The Revolution's staunchest allies turned on one another and on the *citoyens*, regardless of their affiliation with the hated aristocracy, in an attempt to enforce the Revolution's original ideals. In France, at least, the eighteenth century ended in a series of bloody counter-revolutions, reprisals, and persecutions that came to be known as "the Terror."

READING TRENDS AND PRACTICES

Not surprisingly, this era is rich in texts. The explosion in scientific thought, the need to record complex ideas, experiments, and observations, and the development of improved writing and publishing technologies all helped to make the Enlightenment a heavily documented period in European history. However, as Robert Darnton has famously argued, the texts that we in the twenty-first century recognize as representative of Enlightenment thought and discussion, from chic *salon* to Grub Street coffee house, were very likely outnumbered by the multitude of illegal, unofficial, and underground publications that emerged alongside legalized commercial printing and bookselling. But given the working definition of "read" texts—texts that were widely read and distributed, as well as texts that were influential enough to spur significant changes in thought and policy—the traditionally recognized scientific and philosophical texts that emerged from the Enlightenment will also be included in this subsection.

Roy Porter maintains that the Enlightenment was the age of the book. Whereas "books" had been produced for many thousands of years prior to the eighteenth century, they were, until the Enlightenment, inaccessible to most. Texts of all descriptions were mostly unique. Book production and reproduction was an expensive and highly skilled operation that could be undertaken only by those who were both literate and not required for more pressing community duties such as food production. These individuals belonged to the ecclesiastical classes, and as book production occurred in-house, the various monasteries, churches, convents, and ecclesiastical communities retained control of which books were produced, as well as their storage, distribution, and consumption. Furthermore, most noncclesiastical citizens (in fact, most citizens) were illiterate and had no need of books or reading. The relaxation of church control and the rise of the educated, literate, middle-class consumer in the early eighteenth century therefore changed the significance and trajectory of the book enormously.

In a relatively short period, books evolved from laboriously produced, highly prized, and jealously guarded works of art into a wide variety of forms, from the respectable scientific or educational treatise to the cheaply produced pamphlet or hastily edited magazine on rough paper with smudged type. The idea of the book was no longer tethered to the idea of intellectual or spiritual authority. In much the same way that the Internet has allowed anyone with access to a computer the ability to "publish" in the twenty-first century, the boom in inexpensive printing technologies and presses allowed a huge segment of eighteenth-century European citizenry to circulate their views on paper. And, not unlike the Internet, the publishing field in the eighteenth century was awash with material—some of it important and world shaping, some of it writing for writing's sake, all of it intended to make the writer, or more likely, the publisher and seller, wealthy, influential, and more socially significant. And, given that the Enlightenment included such disparate writers as Newton, Pope, Voltaire, Lady Mary Wortley Montagu, and the Marquis de Sade, author of *La Philosophie dans le boudoir*, it could be argued that the only consistent characteristic of the Enlightenment was books and reading. The Enlightenment is just as famous for the birth of European intellectualism as it is for the so-called hack—the under-paid and undernourished writer of under-recognized gossip broadsheets, overly sentimentalized or sensationalized plays and novels, and extreme political tracts and radical social theories. And because these materials were cheaper than books to produce and distribute, they perhaps constituted the bulk of what was read during the European Enlightenment. This subsection will therefore recognize both the major, socially significant texts and the lesser, but more widely consumed, popular texts that established this period as "the age of the book."

The eighteenth century is represented in the historical imagination as a period of rapid social change. Indeed, it contained two world-changing revolutions that led to the collapse of the French monarchy and the birth of the American nation, saw the emergence of the middle class and a true market economy, and supported the rise of the British parliamentary system. France's absolute monarch, Louis XIV— the so-called Sun King—may have symbolized the beginning of the century, but Josiah Wedgwood, enlightened middle-class entrepreneur and factory owner, symbolized its end. In between, the people of Europe changed as well. Families that had served as feudal farm workers to the aristocracy began to move toward the cities and work in the emerging industrial economy. Capital, and social influence, began to drain from the rural squiredom to the metropolitan middle-class entrepreneurs. The middle classes were quick to see the potential of scientific technology for manufacturing the raw materials that Europe's imperial outposts were starting to deliver. As the fortunes of the middle class rose, their desire for the trappings of social legitimacy also rose. They could now afford to educate themselves and their children. The need for educational and cultural resources merged with improvements in printing and bookmaking technologies, and a whole new world of published materials was born.

However, the rewards of social mobility and economic improvement were not restricted to the middle classes. Improvements in European literacy paralleled the proliferation of the printed word. The availability of printed materials meant that general familiarity with writing and documentation increased. Furthermore, the rise of commerce as the medium of production, supply, and exchange meant that more daily business required writing and documentation in the form of deeds, contracts, bills of sale, commercial agreements, and invoices. The modernization and stratification of the new commercial workplace required the involvement of many individuals, some of whom were expected to deal with the documentation of the new commerce. Therefore, even those whose lack of finances and assets disbarred them from membership in the middle classes became somewhat literate. Workplace literacy generated social and recreational literacy, which led to profound shifts in patterns of literature availability and consumption. As Roy Porter puts it, "market forces—affluence, leisure, the fast-developing book trade—led to high culture becoming available, if not to the masses, at least to the many" (*English Society in the Eighteenth Century* 229). In fact, Porter goes on to argue, bourgeois interests in literature, performance, and ideas gained so much momentum in the eighteenth century that public tastes replaced court preferences as the primary influence on new cultural trends. Perhaps because Georges I (r. 1714–1727) and II (r. 1727–1760) were commonly known as "Dunce the First" and "Dunce the Second," and the Hanoverians were generally more famous for their cultivation of roses than their familiarity with literature and philosophy, "the new audience [for literature and theater] was broadly middle-class and middle-brow. To please them, drama shed the Frenchified gentlemanly taste of the Restoration . . . . Satire gave way to gentle and humorous comedy, sentiment replaced cynicism; morals and happy endings were wanted" (Porter, *English Society in the Eighteenth Century* 231).

CREATIVE TEXTS

The changing cultural patterns of the period can be observed in the shift, in the early eighteenth century, from elite, "literary" treatments of contemporary themes using classical styles, to the middle-class embrace of the sentimental novel of morals and social lessons by the end of the century. The transformation of reading into a popular and everyday activity helped to simultaneously stimulate the generation of creative fiction as we know it today. Roy Porter cites James Lackington, a London bookseller whom Porter credits with the creation of the commercial book industry, who observed in 1792,

> The sale of books in general has increased prodigiously within the last twenty years . . . . I suppose that more than four times the number of books are sold now than were sold twenty years since. The poorer sort of farmers, and even the poor country people in general, who before that period spent their evenings in relating stories of witches, ghosts, hobgoblins etc., now shorten the winter nights by hearing their sons and daughters read tales,

romances etc,. and on entering their houses you may see *Tom Jones* [a popular romance by Henry Fielding], *Roderick Random* [a similar novel by Tobias Smollet], and other entertaining books stuck up in their bacon racks. (*English Society in the Eighteenth Century* 236)

At the beginning of the century though, Alexander Pope's satires, mock epics, and epic literary battles with intellectual rivals and Grub Street upstarts characterized that symbolic cultural engine of the Enlightenment, the literary salon. The early Enlightenment was, after all, an age of neo-classical tastes, perhaps generated by the three primary phenomena of the period: the rebirth of scientific discovery; the concomitant accumulation of capital, and the growing pretension to culture among those who were accumulating that capital. Alexander Pope was a major proponent of the neo-classical aesthetic. He wrote countless "Odes," Epistles," and "Imitations," as well as translations of Homer, essays, and, perhaps most famously, mock epics. "The Rape of the Lock," which was first published in Linot's *Miscellanies* in 1712, appeared in its final and enlarged form in 1714. In Pope's characteristic mock epic language, "The Rape of the Lock" amplifies the trivial story of Belinda, a young society belle, and the theft of a lock of her hair by "the Baron" during a genteel game of cards. Pope uses all the standard classical epic conventions; the narrator describes Belinda's *toilette* in the same language that Virgil uses to describe the preparation of the hero for battle in the *Aeneid*. Belinda's dressing table is her "Altar" upon which "Each Silver Vase in mystic Order [is] laid" (1.122). Later, among her society friends, the poem sends Belinda into "battle" (in the form of a hand of *Ombre*, a popular card game among the *beau monde*), and describes how the Baron manages to cut off one of her prized locks with a pair of borrowed scissors after a particularly contentious hand. Pope wrote the poem to heal a breach between two prominent London families, and the success of the original two-canto version spurred him to expand the piece to five cantos and add illustrations and a "moral." The final version was tremendously popular among eighteenth-century readers, and helped to position Pope among Britain's fashionable "literati."

The success of "The Rape of the Lock" allowed Pope to continue writing and accruing status among the social elite. But as the world of literary patronage and paid writers grew, individual jostling for recognition and preferment among the hacks, "scribblers," and self-identified "wits" intensified. Pope attracted (and perhaps cultivated) a host of literary enemies with whom he carried on published battles. However, this open warfare between literary competitors did more than just provide the combatants with a forum for venting spleen; it also provided a live showcase for their literary talents. The reading public, particularly the coffee house crowd, was delighted with each fresh attack, written as they were in a variety of creative classical styles. The literary battles raised insult, parody, and put-down to an art, and Pope emerged from the period as the master of the poisoned pen. He published the first three-volume version of *The Dunciad* anonymously in 1728. The final version, published in 1743, describes the reign of "Dulness" in mock-epic style. Pope's enemies are enlisted as the various purveyors of Dulness in all its forms. The playwright Colley Cibber, one of Pope's chief targets, was enthroned as the "King of Dulness." After the coronation, a competition tests the ability of literary critics to stay awake while the poetry of two poets is read aloud. Not only the critics, but the spectators and everyone present at the event, falls asleep. *The Dunciad* was emblematic of the sharp wit and combative nature of the literary field at the salon level. This adversarial approach to literary production and circulation was not restricted to Britain, but was more representative of the British experience during the early Enlightenment than the experience of any other European literary field.

However, when Queen Anne died without an heir in 1714, the taste for court-sponsored sharp wit and high culture in Britain began to dissipate. It was replaced, over the course of the century, by more middle-brow and middle-class fashions and sympathies. The newly prosperous bourgeoisie comprised the primary market for published materials and controlled the printing and publishing industries. The first novel to find favor with British readers of the period was *Robinson Crusoe*, which, perhaps not coincidentally, is also considered the first novel written in English. Its author, Daniel Defoe, was the son of a London butcher, and his emergence into literature and politics perfectly demonstrates the rise of the literate class from among Britain's working and merchant classes. *Robinson Crusoe* first appeared as a published novel in 1719, but Defoe had written several other tracts and pamphlets before the publication of *Crusoe*. Perhaps because of the "novelty" of its form, and the popularity of its story (exploration and travel, encounters with exotic peoples, and challenges to the idea of a compassionate God), the novel became an immediate success and has been in continual publication to the present day. Its influence was so great that another of the Enlightenment's key authors, Jean-Jacques Rousseau, announced in his educational treatise, *Émile,* that *Robinson Crusoe* should be the only book allowed to boys under the age of twelve. This was because Crusoe "on his island, alone, deprived of the assistance of all the arts, providing nevertheless for his subsistence" (Book III, 147) would teach young readers independence of spirit. The book itself was also emblematic of the growing European imperial project. In fact, Crusoe himself enacts an allegory of colonial mastery, first through his intellectual and physical ownership of "exotic" space, and later through his domination and exploitation of Friday, the displaced native. Furthermore, Ian Watt famously characterized Crusoe as a symbol of the emerging bourgeois individual, a description that also helps to explain the success of the novel among those other emerging bourgeois individuals, the newly literate eighteenth century readers.

However, if *Robinson Crusoe*'s appeal was built on its accessibility for the eighteenth century reading public and its broad potential for reader identification, then Jean-Baptiste de Boyer Marquis d'Argens' *Thérèse Philosophe* satisfied an even more fundamental desire for the bourgeois reader. The Enlightenment's obsession with scientific reason and empirical rationality had loosened religion's grip on eighteenth-century society. This shift not only led to the possibility of major scientific discoveries, but also to a greater and more open appreciation for the more corporeal human pleasures. *Thérèse Philosophe* was an illustrated pornographic narrative that was illegally printed, distributed, and sold; it was, Robert Darnton might argue, the most widely read book in France during the Enlightenment. The novel combined two important themes of the period: sex and the expansion of religious philosophy. *Thérèse Philosophe* has no difficulty arriving at a doctrinal justification for sex between unmarried men and women, and in fact posits sexual fulfillment as a physical, as well as a spiritual imperative. However, the readership of the time would not have considered *Thérèse Philosophe* "pornographic" as such; the category did not exist in the French intellectual imagination. As Darnton points out, "Frenchmen [sic] in the eighteenth century did not normally think in such terms, nor did they distinguish a genre of 'pure' pornography from erotic fiction, anticlerical tracts, and other varieties of 'philosophical books'" (*The Forbidden Best-Sellers of Pre-Revolutionary France* 87). So *Thérèse Philosophe,* erotic illustrations, salacious narrative, rich description and all, was, for its huge French readership, emblematic of a broad challenge to the values and standards of the Ancien Régime. It was not a challenge to sexual morality specifically, but to all established social ideology and expectation. This is perhaps why the novel, although illegal, was so widely taken up: if discovered with a copy, the reader could be thought daring and socially rebellious, but not sexually obsessed or morally perverted, as later cultural critics might imagine.

In fact, nothing was sacred for the Enlightenment's (British) philosophers or (French) *philosophes*. Each scientific, philosophical, or intellectual discovery diminished the hold of the old institutions, and none suffered more from the challenge to blind faith than the church. However, given that Britain had banished the Roman Catholic church in the sixteenth century under Henry VIII, and the Netherlands overtly celebrated its Protestantism after gaining independence from Spain in 1648, the symbol of diminished influence and power became the French Catholic church. Although never in danger of separating from Rome, the French experienced and/or participated in an Enlightenment backlash against centuries of church domination, oppression, and insistence on political, social, and intellectual obedience to Catholic doctrine. One of the church's most vocal critics was Voltaire, perhaps the most popular of the French *philosophes* and arguably the symbol of the Enlightenment in the contemporary imagination. Voltaire was born François-Marie Arouet, the son of a minor government official in Paris. His bourgeois location allowed

CANDIDE,

O U

L'OPTIMISME,

TRADUIT DE L'ALLEMAND

D E

MR. LE DOCTEUR RALPH.

MDCCLIX.

The frontispiece of Voltaire's Enlightenment bestseller, *Candide*, or *Optimism.*

him a perfect vantage point from which to criticize the institutions that had hitherto suppressed social, intellectual, and scientific development. By the time he published *Candide* in 1758, he was a celebrity within the beau monde, and had established influential friendships across Europe. He was therefore in a position to prescribe and/or condemn specific ideas and positions within the philosophical field. *Candide*, for example, not only satirized the church, but many of the period's popular *philosophes* and philosophical trends as well. In particular, Voltaire targeted Liebnitz's optimism.

Candide was written in response to the fashionable, "quasi-philosophy" of optimism that had settled over western Europe. The so-called Lisbon earthquake in Portugal, which reportedly killed thirty thousand people in six minutes, seriously shook the notion that optimism was a benevolent force that could generate harmony and good fortune. Voltaire's own satire on the cult of optimism informs the adventures of Candide, an illegitimate but intellectually curious vagabond who roams the world in search of his lost love, Cunegonde. He is accompanied by his tutor, Dr. Pangloss, the target of the novel's sharpest satire. Against all evidence to the contrary, Pangloss continually insists that "all is for the best in the best of all possible worlds." Voltaire uses the backdrop of the Lisbon disaster and, following that, a montage of human cruelty and self-destructiveness to demonstrate that the Liebnitzian belief in optimism was misplaced, dangerous, and absurd given the realities of the time. The story also challenged the notion that humans have a "God-given . . . dignity" (Mason, *Voltaire: A Biography* 10). Instead, the novel suggests that humans are cruel, vain, foolish, and unpredictable. Furthermore, as Mason argues, *Candide* reveals how "readily prone [humans are] to finding 'lessons' in disasters because any system of order to which we may appeal seems better than no system at all" (11). In the end, once Candide is reunited with Cunegonde, he gives up his travels and "get[s] on with [his] gardening" (Mason 11), an act that has come to represent the Enlightenment endorsement of the emerging middle-class focus on self-interest and self-enrichment.

Goethe in the Roman Campagna (1786) by Johann Heinrich Wilhelm Tischbein. Städelsches Kunstinstitut, Frankfurt.

Although influential, celebrated, and wealthy, Voltaire spent much of his life escaping the authorities. He and his household regularly crossed into Switzerland from France because his publications incurred the wrath of Versailles or the Catholic Church, which was a powerful enemy. *Candide* was therefore published anonymously. But knowing that he had written a bestseller, Voltaire conspired with his Genevan publishers, brothers Gabriel and Philibert Cramer, to deliver copies of the book to Geneva, Paris, London, Liège, and Amsterdam for simultaneous publication and sale. In February 1759, *Candide* appeared in bookstores throughout western Europe. Pearson notes that the authorities were "duly taken by surprise and quickly overwhelmed" (267). Although they confiscated as many copies as they could find and destroyed as many presses as were printing *Candide* at the time, they were "powerless to stem the tide. By 10 March Voltaire calculated that some 6,000 copies had already been sold, and it was likely that this had risen to 20,000 after a further fortnight" (Pearson 267). The English translation sold as many copies, and *Candide* became one of the most widely read books of the period. Not only did *Candide* increase Voltaire's wealth and prestige, it became a symbol of Enlightenment ideals and opposition to Catholic authority.

Whereas *Candide* offered a wry, ironic, and detached view of social politics during the eighteenth century, the most-read Prussian novel of the day reflected the deep Romantic anxiety that characterized fashionable German intellectuals of the period. Johann Wolfgang Goethe's 1774 bestseller, *The Sorrows of Young Werther*, was a huge success and consequently came to represent the so-called *Sturm und Drang* (storm and stress) movement. The novel was so popular with the European readership that young men began dressing like the novel's tragic hero, and literary legend has long reported that "Werther-style" suicides rose exponentially in the wake of the book's publication. The novel consists of letters between Werther, a lovelorn youth, and his best friend Wilhelm on the topic of Lotte, the object of Werther's emotional obsession. Lotte is an idealized figure of the German imagination—maternal, domestic, and associated with the beloved German peasant tradition. However, Lotte is unattainable, as she is engaged to Albert, whom she later marries. In her sensible compassion for the young man, Lotte grants him a final visit after her marriage. During the visit, Werther recites a section of *Ossian* (at that time, believed to be an ancient German folktale), and the experience moves them both to such an extent that they kiss. At this point, it becomes clear to Werther that he has only one option. He borrows a pair of pistols from Lotte's husband and shoots himself. The combination of obsessive love with the idealized and domesticated German maiden, the stirring recitation of a "classic" German folktale, and the cult of tragic but noble suicide that emerged after the book became so popular greatly impacted a European readership that was quickly becoming mesmerized by notions of liberty, passion, and romance. In fact, *Werther* signaled a break from the scientific rationality and world-weary irony that characterized a number of British and French texts of the time, and perhaps indicated that Europe's readers were ready for material that spoke to emotionalism once again.

> ### The Sorrows of Young Enlightenment Readers
>
> *The Sorrows of Young Werther* was as popular with Napoleon Bonaparte as it was with young male eighteenth-century readers. In fact Napoleon himself wrote dramatic prose that mimicked Werther's own declarations of love for Lotte, and later, as an adult, carried a copy of Goethe's classic with him on his military campaigns. The adulation that followed Goethe's classic came to be known as "Werther-Fieber" (or Werther-fever), which hit a peak in the 1770s. One of the most notable characteristics of Werther-Fieber was the wearing of yellow trousers, blue jackets and open-necked shirts, which Werther himself wears in the novel.

PHILOSOPHICAL TEXTS

Of course, most of the creative works that were so widely read during the period could not have been written without the influence of the philosophical movement that characterizes the Enlightenment. The *philosophe* was an Enlightenment invention. The world had certainly witnessed philosophers and philosophy before the eighteenth century, but these were individuals whose works traveled a very narrow path, which usually ran from one monastic library to another. Philosophy in the eighteenth century was a full-time obsession, and the proud label *philosophe* was as much a social goal as it was an intellectual recognition.

France's pension system, linked to various official cultural centers such as the *Académie Française*, was designed to protect and foster literary and academic talent through a patronage system. However, the explosion of thought and ideas that occurred in the eighteenth century was accompanied by a concomitant and exponential rise in the number of authors, especially in France. The patronage system, open only to "young men with the right style, the perfect pitch of bon ton" (Darnton *The Literary Underground* 6), excluded many, and although eighteenth-century Europe was awash in pamphlets, poetry, stage scripts, treatises, novels, and philosophical tracts, it was also awash in "a record crop of potential *philosophes*, far more than could be absorbed under the archaic system of protections" (Darnton *The Literary Underground* 19). Eager young writers, inspired by Voltaire and

Montesquieu, flocked to Paris hoping to join the ranks of *le monde,* only to discover that the very movement that called for an end to aristocratic privilege and social preferment was closed to the "multitude of versifiers and would-be authors" who flooded into Paris from the provinces (Mercier qtd. in Darnton *The Literary Underground* 17). The inference that can be drawn from this situation is that everyone was writing and/or reading during the Enlightenment, but the handful of philosophes who enjoyed literary preferment (above the thousands who fell by the wayside) have perhaps erroneously come to represent that great leap in social literacy. Therefore, the list of texts chosen to represent the period in this subsection perhaps more closely represents history's version of the Enlightenment's reading practices. As Darnton points out via a document discovered by chance, which lists a collection of texts available to French readers during the period,

> if one measures [the list] against the view of the philosophic movement that has been passed on piously from textbook to textbook, one cannot avoid feeling uncomfortable: most of those titles are completely unfamiliar [and] perhaps the Enlightenment was a more down-to-earth affair than the rarified climate of opinion described by textbook writers. (*The Literary Underground* 2)

Although the Voltaires, Montesquieus, and Wollstonecrafts (whose works were widely read, censored, and/or banned during the eighteenth century) have survived into the twenty-first century, they must share space in any examination of the period's reading habits with *Venus in the Cloister or the Nun in a Nightgown, Inquiry on the Origin of Oriental Despotism,* and *Margot the Campfollower.* These are all titles that appear on Darnton's chance-discovered list, none of which have survived into this century.

POLITICAL, EDUCATION, AND SOCIAL PHILOSOPHY TEXTS

More than any other advance in knowledge, eighteenth-century Europeans gave the world a new vision of what it meant to be human. Isaac Newton had begun this repositioning of mankind in the universe with his scientific observations about the nature of physical movement, force, mathematics, and the planets. Once Europe had absorbed the implications of Newton's findings—that humans, and not God, were responsible for the existence and elimination of evil in the world— theories of social and individual behavior, political models designed to produce "rational men," and treatises on the role and elements of education began to appear throughout the Continent. Every scientific and technological advance further distanced humans and human societies from the religious mysticisms and superstitions of the earlier centuries. Rationality, empirical fact, and the pursuit of natural virtue (social models that would produce virtuous citizens) dominated philosophical thinking. Political philosophy dominated the trend. Now that church and monarch no longer controlled thought and the administration of state authority, thinkers could muse on alternative political systems and roles for citizens. In fact, the notion of the "citizen"—an independent, engaged, and active participant in the social and political life of the community—emerged at this time. The pursuit of freedom and liberty (usually from church and/or state oppression) also characterized the philosophies of the period. Although not every citizen read the philosophers, most citizens at least grasped the fundamentals of the philosophies that were appearing in every conceivable binding.

John Locke's *Two Treatises of Government* first appeared in 1689, a year after the so-called Glorious Revolution in Britain. His timing was perfect. While James II was trying to revive both monarchical and Catholic authority, Locke was describing the elements of rationality. Locke believed in the rights of property owners and the educated. These were the men, Locke argued, who embodied human virtue. Thus he was mostly read by the propertied and educated. But his views on social rationality, which were heavily imbued with his views on education, were taken to heart across the social spectrum. One reason that his philosophies were so popular was that he supported innate rationality over external authority. That is, humans should be educated to recognize and obey natural virtue, not a monarch who has simply been thrust into power on the basis of birth. Locke's ideas may have had broad appeal, and helped to establish the atmosphere of ideological change that characterized the period, but in the final analysis, Locke's poorer readers could only benefit from his ideas if they influenced change at the parliamentary level. They themselves did not have access to the educational resources that Locke advocated.

Montesquieu's *L'Esprit des lois* became one of the great documents of political philosophy during the French Enlightenment, but its primary influence was on the American Revolutionaries. *L'Esprit des lois* was initially published anonymously, as Montesquieu was well known to the government censors. But *L'Esprit* was so rapidly picked up by French readers that the book was quickly translated into other languages. The first English edition appeared in 1750, two years after its first French publication, and by 1751 it had been added to the notorious *Index Librorum Prohibitorum* (List of Prohibited Books) maintained by the Catholic Church. The reasons for the book's censorship were clear. Montesquieu advocated liberty and rights for the individual, ideas that went on to inform the United States Declaration of Independence, the Bill of Rights, and the Constitution. Furthermore, Montesquieu's book argued for the separation of the legislative, executive, and judicial branches of government, so as to avoid concentrating power in a single authoritative body. Given that the French monarchy *was* that single authoritative body—Louis XIV once famously announced "I am the state"—those who were invested in maintaining the political status quo were keen to stop these ideas gaining any traction in the public sphere. Of course, ironically, by 1789 these were the only ideas that the public was interested in.

Jean-Jacques Rousseau was a Swiss *philosophe* who wrote a number of widely read treatises on society, education, and the law. His 1762 publication *The Social Contract* famously began with the line "Man is born free; and is everywhere in chains." Rousseau argues that the "general will" of the people should be the governing authority of a nation. According to *Du Contrat Social,* a truly free and virtuous people are not ruled by masters, but rule themselves by designing laws that are maintained and enacted through the "general will." His goal was to convince the people of France in particular, to return to a more primitive and pristine state, and live in a state of social agreement and mutual governance. Rousseau was something of a Romantic idealist, less radical in his approach to social foundations than Montesquieu. Because he was part of Denis Diderot's *Encyclopédie* group, he had connections with the fashionable publishing circles in Paris. His books and treatises therefore sold well, and he gathered a following in the salons and among the intelligentsia. He influenced the growing Romanticism movement, which had its earliest political victories with the American Revolution of 1776 and the French Revolution of 1789.

As with many of the *philosophes,* Rousseau's concerns were not limited to social laws. He was also very interested in the links between education and social cohesion. In fact, his 1762 treatise on education, *Émile: or, On Education,* contained a popularized version of *The Social Contract,* which is where most French readers would have encountered his political tract. As Darnton points out, *Émile* "was incontestably a best-seller" (*The Forbidden Best-Sellers* xviii) in pre-revolutionary France. It was read by aristocrat and bourgeois alike, and it fueled the late-Enlightenment obsession with "natural goodness." The tract is a semi-fictional narration of the life of a young boy, Émile, and his tutor, a thinly disguised Rousseau. Rousseau argues in *Émile* that it is possible to produce good citizens in an inevitably corrupt society. His educational philosophies deal first with the young child, then with the adolescent Émile, and then with Sophie, Émile's ideal domestic partner. Among other observations, Rousseau advocates raising children as close to nature as possible, avoiding overprotective behaviors such as swaddling, and reviving natural practices such as breastfeeding. *Émile* had a marked impact on parental behaviors and child-rearing practices after its publication. In particular, aristocratic and wealthy bourgeois women began adopting (at least the appearance of) "natural" concepts. Children spent more time outdoors (in artificially constructed "forests" on private estates, or in miniaturized, working "dairies" in private gardens). Mothers themselves began dressing as milkmaids and stylized peasant girls, in line with Rousseau's beliefs that the open air and countryside were superior to the library and the city street. But these affectations aside, Rousseau's ideas helped to refocus attention on the value of manual work (as opposed to effete "cultured" pursuits) and the lives of the marginalized rural and working classes. This recognition and validation helped to stir resentment among these classes toward the monarchy and aristocracy, who were perceived as wasteful, decadent, and unsympathetic to the realities of life for ordinary French people.

While French readers were pondering Rousseau's exhortations, British readers were grappling with Thomas Paine's *The Rights of Man,* which first appeared in 1791. Written in response to Edmund Burke's *Reflections on the Revolution in France,* in which Burke condemns the Revolution and predicts its disastrous outcome, *The Rights of Man* uses the spectacular success of the American Revolution to argue for modern democracy. Paine wrote for the common reader and not for the educated aristocrat. The core of his argument was that every man had equal rights, and that these rights should not be determined by birth, rank, or economic position. His powerful arguments for individual rights sold abundantly in a number of languages. Along with his earlier pamphlet, *Common Sense,* Paine established both his fame and his infamy. *Common Sense* was written and published in the United States, after Paine left his native England for America in 1774. Having raised both the admiration and ire of the Americans, Paine returned to England in 1787. His sense of timing—he arrived in America two years before the outbreak of the Revolution, and returned to Britain two years before the French Revolution—meant that he was perfectly situated to analyze the impact and implications of both of the eighteenth century's most significant events. As with many of the Enlightenment's political documents, *The Rights of Man* was widely read. Fruchtman describes the document as an American "bestseller [that sold] well into the hundreds of thousands [and was o]ften reprinted in England" (VII). But broad consumption also often generated strong negative responses, especially from those in power. Although Thomas Jefferson hailed Paine as a great thinker and supporter of freedom, Paine made many enemies in Britain and France. He was jailed in Paris for a year during the post-Revolutionary "Terror," and in his absence was convicted of treason in England. Moreover, Paine never made a penny from his writings. Paine's example perfectly demonstrates that wide publication, broad public consumption, and great political fame do not always guarantee an author an easy life.

Political revolution was not the only major change that occurred during the eighteenth century. Revolutions based on race and gender also threatened to over-turn the status quo. In the Caribbean colonies, Toussaint L'Overture led a string of slave rebellions against colonial masters. And in Europe, women began to take part in public dissent. Women were active during the French Revolution and published many pamphlets supporting the overthrow of the monarchy and protesting governmental food pricing and distribution policies. Olympe de Gouges, a playwright and journalist during the French Revolution, wrote *Declaration of the Rights of Women and the Citizen* (*Déclaration des Droits de la Femme et de la Citoyenne*) as a call for equality between the sexes. But perhaps the most celebrated expression of women's rights was Mary Wollstonecraft's *A Vindication of the Rights of Woman*, which was published in 1792. Wollstonecraft wrote the *Vindication* in response to claims in a report to the French National Assembly that women only needed training in domestic skills. The *Vindication* argues that women deserve the same education as men, and that women are vital to the health and growth of society. The *Vindication* was well-reviewed and received when it first appeared, but perhaps the greatest evidence of its public reception came in the form of references in novels published after the book's appearance. Mary Hays, a novelist, and Mary Robinson, an actress and writer, both from the late eighteenth century, included references to the *Vindication* in their novels. But readership does not always translate into acceptance. Many who read the *Vindication* were shocked by its ideas.

Wollstonecraft's husband, the political philosopher William Godwin, published her life story after her death. But what he thought was a memoir of love and respect inadvertently scandalized readers. Godwin revealed that his wife had had two illegitimate children, had lived with men without the blessing of marriage, and had attempted suicide. Wollstonecraft's ideals survived her biography however, and even Jane Austen echoed some of her ideas on the importance of women for the stability of society in *Pride and Prejudice* early in the following century.

ENCYCLOPEDIAS AND DICTIONARIES

Encyclopedias were not an invention of the Enlightenment, but, because they found their first committed readership in this period, they are primarily associated with the eighteenth century. Prior to the Age of Reason and its atmosphere of intellectual curiosity, encyclopedias were considered highly dangerous texts. The intellectual tradition had belonged in the monasteries, and knowledge was owned by the church. Moreover, European monarchs had been traditionally uninterested in academic pursuits. Fighting off intrigues, conducting foreign wars, and setting standards of style and amusement were the roles of the European monarch. Therefore, the distribution of knowledge by secular editors, without church endorsement and often in contradiction to Biblical doctrine, was considered improper at best and blasphemous at worst. Nevertheless, by the middle of the eighteenth century several encyclopedias had been compiled, one going back as far as the Sumerian civilization in Mesopotamia. Attempts at the universal indexation of knowledge had also occurred in China, ancient Greece, and medieval Europe (under strict church control). But during the eighteenth century, a brazen, self-aware, and hugely intricate attempt to consolidate all known experience, concept, and idea was launched in Paris. Philipp Blom argues in his history of Denis Diderot and Jean d'Alambert's groundbreaking *Encyclopédie* that the growing independent middle classes in eighteenth-century Europe were

> no longer content to leave exploration, debate, and discovery to a handful of scholars while limiting their reading to works of edifying piety and classical legends; and in a world of scholarship that became more complex and more detailed with every passing day, works of synthesis were in strong demand. (*Enlightening the World* xxii)

That is, the eighteenth century was ripe for the production, sale, and consumption of the comprehensive—and secular—reference book. While government and church authorities had tried to close off free thought and expression in reaction to the era's explosion of discovery and knowledge, Enlightenment readers themselves consumed as much of the new knowledge as they could. As Blom points out, "Between 1674 and 1750 alone, more than thirty [reference books] were published in English, German, French, Italian, more than in the previous two hundred years" (xxii). Encyclopedia projects flourished under these conditions. They were largely forbidden, because both secular and church authorities considered knowledge and its distribution to be their domain. But small groups of committed, radicalized, and ideologically motivated men persisted, mostly to the completion and publication stages. In fact, one such project, Zedler's *Universal Lexicon*, was so committed to comprehensive inclusion that German booksellers opposed it on the grounds that it would make all other books redundant.

Diderot and d'Alambert's *Encyclopédie* began as a translation of another successful encyclopedic enterprise, Ephraim Chambers' *Cyclopaedia: or, An Universal Dictionary of Arts and Sciences* [sic], which first appeared in 1728. But the *Encyclopédie* soon emerged as a project in its own right, and that project, according to literary historians, changed all aspects of book writing, production, distribution, and reception.

According to Blom, the *Encyclopédie* was beset with problems from the moment of its conception. As the alphabetization of entries in reference books had only just been adopted as standard practice, the entire project had to be meticulously planned from the first to the last entry before a single article could be written. Earlier reference volumes could be planned thematically, volume by volume. But alphabetization required that the project organizers know exactly how many, and which, entries would appear in the finished series beforehand. Logistics aside, the ideological issues surrounding a number of the entries made any public definition, description, explanation, or analysis of them politically problematic. For example, the entry on theology was hotly contested. The Jesuits, a powerful order of monks, were incensed that they were not asked to contribute the article. They therefore launched a prolonged attack on the *Encyclopédie,* accusing its editors of plagiarism, blasphemy, and inconsistency in order to discredit the project. In fact, Blom argues that the Jesuits "decided there were two options: to destroy [the *Encyclopédie*] altogether, or to weaken it so much that they could eventually take it over" (83). Clearly the project struck fear into the hearts of French social and religious conservatives before it even appeared in print.

The long process of building and publishing the *Encyclopédie,* volume by volume, took about twenty-five years, from 1747 to 1766. During that time, Diderot and d'Alambert faced censure, exile, imprisonment, debt, conflict, and slander. But toward the end of the process, their fortunes experienced a turnabout. Blom reveals that, after years of avoiding recognition and compiling their mammoth work in near secrecy, Diderot and d'Alambert emerged as celebrated literary rebels who had not only fought off, but had effectively nullified the Catholic

Church's condemnation and the Paris *Parlement*'s opposition. In fact, the Encylopedists became darlings of the fashionable Paris salons, and were widely perceived as "the only faction standing for progress and openness, for a spirit of inquiry and criticism" (Blom 268).

Nobody has ever argued that the *Encyclopédie* was politically neutral. Diderot and d'Alambert gathered around them a group of writers who shared their radical political views, and many, if not most, of the series' articles contained distinct anti-monarchical, anti-Catholic sentiments. The readership for the *Encyclopédie*, therefore, was already connected to the age's spirit of ideological, political, and religious freedom. Because the *Encyclopédie* encouraged revolutionary thought (one of its most controversial maneuvers was to classify religion under the heading of philosophy, and not as the transcendent source of all truth and knowledge), it became a prime documentary source for France's building revolutionary movement. It was not published for public purchase, however. Its buyers had committed to a subscription (a sales technique that ensured funding for a project before the project commenced). Given that the subscriber was being asked to commit to a significant outlay over a long period, for a set of thirty-seven volumes that were officially banned, the Encyclopedists were forced to become sharp business and advertising specialists as well. However, as word spread and the Encyclopedists weathered political storm after political storm, the project gained powerful friends, which helped to circulate its status and raise its profile as a desirable and necessary tool for understanding the era's rapid change. Given that the project had attracted the support of learned people across Europe, including Voltaire, Montesquieu, Catherine the Great of Russia, Jean-Jacques Rousseau, and the intellectual aristocrat de Jaucourt, it is not surprising that the *Encyclopédie* became one of the most talked-about and read documents of the era. In fact Robert Darnton explains that, although the first four volumes of the *Encyclopédie* were "luxurious folio publications ordinary readers could not afford," later, cheaper, quarto editions of the volumes made the *Encyclopédie* "the biggest best seller of the century" (*The Business of Enlightenment* 6).

The same public thirst for knowledge and self-education that had propelled Diderot and d'Alambert's *Encyclopédie* was to energize the other great reference book of the Enlightenment, Samuel Johnson's *Dictionary of the English Language*, which was first published in 1755. But unlike the *Encyclopédie*, which employed a variety of contributors, the *Dictionary* was largely Johnson's sole effort. His student, Garrick, and his great friend, Boswell, helped with copying and administrative tasks, but the document's almost forty-three thousand entries were written by Johnson alone. Again, like the *Encyclopédie*, Johnson's work appealed to Britain's up-and-coming middle-class readers. Johnson himself was the embodiment of the successful middle-class professional, whose time had come during this period. He symbolized the professional writer—a figure that did not exist before the eighteenth century in Britain. Henry Hitchings says of the *Dictionary's* readership,

> Johnson's [achievement] chimed not only with the growth of the British press, which buttressed the idea of national identity, but also with the contemporary growth of the middle-classes, and with their emerging self-consciousness . . . . The *Dictionary* was not a success with the *bon ton* [the aristocracy], but it appealed to the newly affluent and the upwardly mobile. Its creator, like them, was a self-made man. (225)

However, Hitchings also points out that ownership of a major reference work such as the *Dictionary* (and, for that matter, the *Encyclopédie*) might not have equated with readership of the document. Owning the *Dictionary* might have been a means of conveying a level of intellectual and high culture grandeur that was not actually commensurate with the owner's experience and education. Or, as Hitchings argues, "It is the self-made and the self-aggrandizing who tend to surround themselves with artifacts designed to attest to their respectability and seriousness. The *Dictionary* succeeded thanks in no small part to the shift from Restoration elitism [in the previous century] to a more middle-class Britain, characterized by a mercantile consciousness [in the eighteenth century]" (225–226). The experience of Johnson's *Dictionary* reminds us once again that any analysis of readership in the European eighteenth century has to be aware of the difference between reading and owning. Documents from the eighteenth and nineteenth centuries reveal that although Europe's bourgeoisie were now legitimate consumers of print, they worked on "two sets of books" as it were. There were the public books, leather-bound and gold stamped, never opened perhaps, but ostentatiously displayed in one's library or parlor, and there were the private books, cheaply produced paper-bound copies, read voraciously in dark corners, but never considered "literature" in the contemporary sense. However, books in any shape or binding were always more expensive than the staple reading product of the Enlightenment. Whereas a book needed at least some planning and industrial investment for publication, "ephemera"—magazines, pamphlets, newspapers, and broadsheets—required very little in the way of printing technology, and were therefore produced, and read, in huge numbers.

Johnson's *Dictionary*

Samuel Johnson's *Dictionary of the English Language* was not the first English dictionary published, but it was the first to find an audience with the public and the first to be recognized as a comprehensive examination and explanation of the English language. It was reprinted five times in its one hundred-year reign as the most significant document of its type, and was only supplanted in English libraries and private homes by the first *Oxford English Dictionary*, which was first published (after another massive research and writing effort) in 1857.

MAGAZINES, JOURNALS, NEWSPAPERS, AND PAMPHLETS

The *Encyclopédie* and Johnson's *Dictionary* may have represented the grand narratives of the era, but it was the minutia of the publishing world—magazines, journals, newspapers, and especially pamphlets—that sold in greatest numbers, were read by the most people, and more closely represented the era's reading tastes. Easy to find, buy, read, pass on to the next reader, and replace with the next issue, these ephemeral publications not only satisfied the public's thirst for published entertainment and news, but they helped to advance print culture through rapidly developing methods of commercial production, marketing, distribution, and replication. Magazines and newspapers had the advantage of being able to stimulate their own consumption, as well as the consumption of other salable goods, such as fashion, household innovations, books, and leisure goods. Roy Porter points out that the emergence of "provincial presses" throughout Britain meant that

> almost every district got its own paper . . . . A successful provincial paper, such as the *Salisbury Journal,* would have a weekly sale running to a few thousand (a flourishing Paris newspaper during the Revolution could not expect to sell more). Its readership was

probably five to ten times that number . . . . Provincial newspapers publicized local events, carried a welter of local commercial advertisements, and conveyed military, political and financial intelligence from London . . . to say nothing of the latest fashions. Contemporaries believed that, of all the media, newspapers shaped opinion the most. "The mass of every people must be barbarous where there is no printing and consequently knowledge is not generally diffused," remarked Dr Johnson: "Knowledge is diffused among our people by the news-papers." (*English Society in the Eighteenth Century* 234)

As well as daily and weekly newspapers, eighteenth-century readers could keep up with literary fashions and the changing standards of social behavior through the popular magazines of the time. The model was established by Richard Steele's *Tatler*, which was followed by *The Spectator*, which Steele compiled with his friend, Joseph Addison. Neither magazine was published after 1714, but many similar magazines followed the trend. Porter observes that "[b]y 1800, 250 periodicals had seen the light of day, including the *Matrimonial Magazine*, the *Marconi*, the *Sentimental Magazine*, and the *Westminster*" (*English Society in the Eighteenth Century* 235). Another major periodical was the *Gentleman's Magazine*. These magazines invited regular readers—those who aspired to, but were not born into the cultured classes—to partake of the sorts of topics, ideas, fashions, and affectations demonstrated by the beau monde. Those in the provinces could fashion dresses and pants after the styles worn in London and Paris. Those without formal education could bring themselves up to speed on the current philosophical debates. *Gentleman's Magazine*, in particular, carried parliamentary gossip and political intrigue from London. For not only did the eighteenth century witness the birth of popular literacy, it also saw the rise of the popular politician. Politics had been restricted to the very well-connected in centuries past. But now, a half-century after the English Civil War and the dilution of monarchical powers in Britain, elected office was open, if not to anyone, at least to a much broader cross-section of men. The rising commercial middle classes were becoming politically organized, and the dissolution of the Licensing Act in 1695 meant that publishing was opened to anyone with an opinion, an axe to grind, or a political campaign to float.

The nexus of a more liberated press, an explosion in philosophical thought, a reformed political system, and the emergence of the nonclerical public persona meant that, as Porter puts it, "printing became a free market, and nothing stood in the way of any bold writer or bookseller willing to run the risk of post-publication prosecution" (*The Creation of the Modern World* 73). Pamphlets were the chosen medium of expression, and the reading public consumed them voraciously. The average pamphlet sold for pennies and promised the reader political scandal, philosophical reflections on current events, accounts of riots and other social uprisings from provincial towns and other counties, pornography, and slanderous satire of public figures. Pamphlets educated the self-made, gave the poor access to worlds from which they had traditionally been barred, linked the city and countryside, provided a voice for those who had neither the means nor the status to be publicly heard, and provided a cheap means of self-promotion or—which is more likely—enemy degradation.

In France, censorship was much more strongly enforced. The Revolution that would loosen the monarchical grip on France did not occur until the end of the century, and for most of the era, the French labored under the enlightened absolutism established by Louis XIV, the so-called Sun King. And after the Revolution, censorship under the Terror was even more far-reaching and brutal than during the pre-revolutionary period. Pamphlets were common before 1789 and were known as *occasionnels, feuilles volantes*, or *pièces fugitives*. Darnton argues that they did not generally contain personal slander; however, research has revealed that Marie Antoinette, Louis XVI's hated Austrian queen, was mercilessly slandered in both text and heavily pornographic images by a mountain of such *libelles*. Despite the efforts of the Royal Censors, pamphlets that showed the queen in a variety of obscene poses proliferated around Paris, much to the delight of the common people.

CONCLUSION

The Enlightenment has been called the age of the book, but it could just as easily be called the age of the reader. Reading emerged as a common social practice throughout Europe at this time. As Europe settled, consolidated, and won or lost its colonies, reading and reading materials were exported to, generated in, and exported back from places other than Europe. However, the Enlightenment could just as easily be called the age of the book buyer, as the age of the reader. As many historians have pointed out, the book emerged as the bridge between the accumulation of wealth through commercial trade and the accumulation of social legitimacy through education. Newly wealthy industrialists, middle-class merchants, trades-people, and emerging professionals began to amass libraries that resembled those of the aristocrats to whose positions they aspired. Therefore, book sales did not always reflect readership trends during, and for a long time after, the eighteenth century.

Heavy censorship also accompanied the rise of the book trade. The very people who were enticing the bourgeoisie to read were the those whose books were appearing on lists of banned publications. And so a variety of legitimate and illegal book trades appeared. High street booksellers in Britain, France, the Netherlands, and Germany stocked their shelves with uncontroversial and expensively bound scientific tracts, lives of the Saints, and orthodox Christian philosophies. But these same booksellers sold sentimental novels (which were mostly read by young women), pornographic "philosophical" novels, as they were known in France, and outright-banned books, which at any given moment might include *Candide, The Social Contract, Gulliver's Travels, Tom Jones,* or *The Rights of Man.* Furthermore, a flourishing pamphlet industry produced an enormous amount of material that was by its very nature outside the mainstream, ineligible for public legal sale or possession. The pamphlets were designed to appear, sell, and circulate, and then to disappear to make room for the next set of scandalous allegations, roughly drawn parodies of royalty or

> **The Public Library**
>
> Libraries had been the sole province and privilege of monasteries, convents, religious orders, and high-ranking church officials until the eighteenth century. The sheer volume of secular publication and the rise of "biblio-capitalism" led to the invention of the circulating library. In Britain, citizens subscribed to libraries for a small fee, and enjoyed access to a larger number of books and periodicals than they could possibly buy themselves. The libraries were mostly devoted to popular sentimental and gothic novels, but also offered access to educational materials that most, especially women, could not access otherwise. The popularity of the circulating library also lead to the "abridgement" trend. Classical works, long "serious," novels and reference books were compressed especially for popular distribution and inclusion in the library offerings.

the aristocracy, blasphemous polemics, or satires on government. Ironically, most of what we in the twenty-first century have come to associate with eighteenth-century readership began life as just such a pamphlet or illegal publication. Therefore, the heavy and expensive texts that lined the walls of upwardly mobile middle-class libraries never represented the era's reading tastes. In a foreshadowing of our own reading habits, most of what was read in the Enlightenment was light, scandalous, amusing, or forbidden.

NOTE ON AVAILABILITY OF TEXTS

All texts mentioned or cited in this sub-section are currently commercially available, with the exception of *Venus in the Cloister or the Nun in a Nightgown*, *Inquiry on the Origin of Oriental Despotism*, *Margot the Campfollower*, and *Universal Lexicon*, none of which can be found on any of the usual trade sites. Although these texts might be available in European libraries or academic collections, it is unlikely they would be represented in American public or academic libraries. Although there was a copy of *Chambers's Encyclopædia: A Dictionary of Universal Knowledge for the People* available on Amazon.com, this was a single antique copy; the text, although available for individual sale, is not in print and not commercially available. The *Tatler*, *The Spectator*, and the *Gentleman's Magazine* all ceased publication within the eighteenth century. Extant copies very likely exist in private collections, within Britain's national libraries, and in major University libraries.

RECOMMENDED READING

Bate, W. Jackson. *Samuel Johnson*. Orlando, FL: Harcourt Brace, 1977.
Davies, Norman. *Europe: A History*. New York: Oxford University Press, 1996.
Gay, Peter. *The Enlightenment: The Science of Freedom*. New York: Norton, 1996.
Israel, Jonathan I. *Radical Enlightenment: Philosophy and the Making of Modernity 1650–1750*. New York: Oxford University Press, 2002.
Jacob, Margaret C. *The Enlightenment: A Brief History with Documents*. Boston: Bedford St. Martins, 2001.
Manguel, Alberto. *A History of Reading*. London: HarperCollins, 1996.
Poplawski, Paul. *English Literature in Context*. Cambridge, UK: Cambridge University Press, 2008.
Porter, Roy. *The Enlightenment*. 2nd edition. New York: Palgrave, 2001.
Reddick, Allen. *The Making of Johnson's Dictionary 1746–1773*. New York: Cambridge University Press, 1996.
Scharma, Simon. *Citizens: A Chronicle of the French Revolution*. New York: Alfred A. Knopf, 1989.
———. *A History of Britain Vol. II: The Wars of the British, 1603–1776*. New York: Talk Miramax Books, 2001.
Soll, Jacob. *Publishing* The Prince: *History, Reading and the Birth of Political Criticism*. Ann Arbor: The University of Michigan Press, 2005.
Treglown, Jeremy and Bridget Bennett. *Grub Street and the Ivory Tower*. Oxford: Clarendon Press, 1998.

PRIMARY SOURCES

Austen, Jane. *Pride and Prejudice*. New York: Bantam, 1983.
Burke, Edmund. *Reflections on the Revolution in France*. New York: Oxford University Press, 1999.

Chambers, Ephraim. *Chambers's Encyclopædia: A Dictionary of Universal Knowledge for the people*. London: J. B. Lippincott & Co, 1870.

De Boyer, Jean-Baptiste (Marquis d'Argens). *Thérèse philosophe ou mémoires pour servir à l'histoire*. Paris: Actes Sud, 1992.

Defoe, Daniel. *Robinson Crusoe*. New York: Modern Library, 2001.

De Gouges, Olympe. *Déclaration des Droits de la Femme et de la Citoyenne*. Paris: Mille et une nuits, 2003.

Diderot, Denis and Jean le Rond d'Alambert. *L'Encyclopédie Diderot et Alembert*. French & European Pubns, 1985.

Fielding, Henry. *Tom Jones*. New York: Modern Library, 2002.

Goethe, Johann Wolfgang. *The Sorrows of Young Werther*. New York: Modern Library, 2005.

Johnson, Samuel. *A Dictionary of the English Language: in Which the Words are Deduced from their Originals, and Illustrated in Their Different Significations by Examples from the Best Writers*. Classic Books, N.D.

Locke, John. *Two Treatises of Government*. Whitefish, MT: Kessinger Publishing, 2004.

Montesquieu, Charles-Louis. *The Spirit of Laws* (*L'Esprit des lois*). Amherst, NY: Prometheus Books, 2002.

Newton, Isaac. *Newton's Philosophy of Nature: Selections from His Writings*. Edited by H. S. Thayer. Mineola, NY: Dover, 2005.

Paine, Thomas. *Common Sense, Rights of Man, and Other Essential Writings of Thomas Paine*. New York: Signet, 2003.

Pope, Alexander. *The Dunciad*. Whitefish, MT: Kessinger Publishing, 2004.

———. *The Rape of the Lock*. Boston: Bedford St. Martin's, 1998.

Rousseau, Jean-Jacques. *Émile*. London: Everyman, 1984.

———. *"The Social Contract" and Other Later Political Writings*. Edited by Victor Gourevitch. Cambridge: Cambridge U. Press, 1997.

Sade, Marquis de. *La Philosophie dans le boudoir*. Bookking International, Classiques Francais, 1997.

Swift, Jonathan. *Gulliver's Travels*. New York: Penguin, 1999.

Voltaire, Francois. *Candide: Or, Optimism*. Translated by Theo Cuffe. New York: Penguin, 2005.

Wolstonecraft, Mary. *A Vindication of the Rights of Woman*. New York: Penguin, 2004.

SECONDARY SOURCES

Blom, Philipp. *Enlightening the World: Encyclopédie, the Book that Changed the Course of History*. New York: Palgrave, 2005.

Darnton, Robert. *The Business of Enlightenment*. Cambridge, MA: Belknap/Harvard. 1979.

———. *The Forbidden Best-Sellers of Pre-Revolutionary France*. New York: Norton, 1996.

———. *The Literary Underground of the Old Regime*. Cambridge, MA: Harvard University Press, 1982.

Fruchtman, Jack. "Forward." *Common Sense, The Rights of Man and other Essential Writings of Thomas Paine*. New York: Signet, 2003.

Hitchings, Henry. *Defining [the World]: The Extraordinary Story of Dr Johnson's Dictionary*. New York: Picador, 2006.

Mason, Hayden. *Voltaire: A Biography*. Baltimore: Johns Hopkins University Press, 1981.

Pearson, Roger. *Voltaire Almighty: A Life in Pursuit of Freedom*. New York: Bloomsbury, 2005.

Porter, Roy. *English Society in the Eighteenth Century*. London: Penguin, 1990.

———. *The Creation of the Modern World*. New York: Norton, 2001.

CHAPTER 9

Romanticism and the Nineteenth Century

Diana Chlebek

TIMELINE

1803–05	War of the Third Coalition
1804	Napoleon crowned emperor and Code Napoleon introduced
1805	Battles of Trafalgar and Austerlitz
1806	Holy Roman Empire disbanded
1807	British slave trade abolished
1813	Battle of Leipzig
1814	Napoleon exiled to Elba; Congress of Vienna convenes
1815	Napoleon's defeat at Battle of Waterloo, and exile to St. Helena
1819	Karlsbad Decrees
1821–29	Greek war of independence; ends with liberation of Greece from Turkey
1830	Revolutions in France, Belgium, and Poland
1832	First Reform Act in Great Britain
1833	Great Britain outlaws slavery in its colonies
1834	New Poor Law created in Great Britain
1837	Queen Victoria begins reign in Great Britain
1838	People's Charter created in Great Britain
1846	Corn Laws repealed in Great Britain
1848	Revolutions in France, Italy, Austria, and Germany; Second Republic declared in France
1852	Louis Napoleon establishes the Second Empire in France
1853–56	Crimean War
1864	War over Schleswig-Holstein between Prussia and Austria; First International Working Men's Association established
1866	Austro-Prussian War
1867	Creation of the Austro-Hungarian monarchy; Second Reform Act in Great Britain

1870	Franco-Prussian War (ends 1871); Third Republic declared in France
1871	German Empire proclaimed; Paris Commune
1873	Dreikaiserbund, or Three Emperors' League
1876	Queen Victoria proclaimed Empress of India
1878	Congress of Berlin
1879	Dual Alliance formed
1882	Triple Alliance formed
1884	Third Reform Act in Great Britain
1890	Bismarck dismissed as German Chancellor
1894–1906	Dreyfus Affair in France
1901	Death of Queen Victoria

INTRODUCTION TO THE PERIOD

The nineteenth century, in many ways, represented the culmination and implementation of the concepts launched during the eighteenth century. The eighteenth century was the Age of Reason: a period of scientific advances, the birth of self-aware technologies, and experimentation with concepts of social organization and human freedom. And as the century ended with two spectacular attempts to gain, ratify, and codify freedom, it comes as no surprise that one of the following century's earliest movements, Romanticism, would be an attempt to translate individual human freedom into literary form. However, of the two revolutionary events that closed the eighteenth century—the American and French Revolutions—only the first was a success in terms of the enshrinement of its ideals. The French Revolution collapsed into the "Terror," and most of its ideals were lost, along with its staunchest allies, to the guillotine.

However, the combination of new political freedoms and major technological advances in the eighteenth century gave rise to the nineteenth century's greatest and most enduring invention—the commercial middle class (known as the *bourgeoisie* in France). Technologies that turned raw materials from the colonies into mass-produced retail goods were being harnessed, shaped, and exploited by the entrepreneurial middle classes, who had bided their time behind the entrenched aristocracy for centuries. Once the opportunities for speculation emerged, on the back of the Continent's various colonial enterprises, the middle classes became their own masters and launched a "revolution" that had only a commercial link to theories of freedom. The Industrial Revolution invented the European middle class, and announced the beginning of the aristocracy's slow decline into social and economic irrelevance. If the powdered wig and the carefully manicured aristocratic estate symbolized the eighteenth century, then the factory owner, his demure wife, marriageable daughter, and ambitious son symbolized the nineteenth century.

The European monarchies and their aristocratic courts remained arbiters of style, but their moral influence on society fell away, replaced by the notion that material gain was as effective an indicator of individual worth as *noblesse oblige,* or service to the church. Political gains put propertied middle-class men in control of town councils and national legislatures alike. Middle-class anxieties about appearing low-born and newly rich resulted in extravagant displays of piety and morality. However, the apparent moral restraints that characterized the factory owner during the day were often reversed at night, when wealthy men sought out the very lascivious pleasures that they promised to stamp out as respectable politicians. These were the same men who financed exploration and settlement of colonial possessions, and established productive plantations in Southeast Asia or the Caribbean, or huge mining operations in Canada, Australia, and Africa. The middle classes set up and maintained the operations that produced, transported, and manufactured the millions of tons of raw materials from the colonies into finished goods for sale to the (also recently invented) working classes, and in some cases, back to the colonized subjects themselves. Of course, industrialization did not emerge at the same rate throughout Europe. Britain pioneered the commercial and industrial systems that launched the phenomenon. But all the major European nations established, or expanded, their colonial holdings during the nineteenth century.

The century began with a series of bloody and potentially continent-destabilizing wars. Other disruptions came in the form of social revolutions, uprisings, and squabbles over borders, colonial possessions, and the building of new nation-states. Despite these struggles, however, the nineteenth century has come to be viewed as one hundred years of prosperity and progress. Britain's great symbol of nineteenth century stability and achievement was Queen Victoria. However, it was the Romantics—those modern, rebellious, radical, and fearfully nostalgic intellectuals—who characterized the beginning of the new nineteenth century. They eloquently demanded a return to rural folk traditions, the reembrace of nature (as opposed to the new urban, industrial world), the recognition of human feeling, and a rejection of "reason," which by the opening of the nineteenth century had morphed into economic pragmatism. But Romanticism was not an evangelical movement, and the already clannish Romantics did not make it out of their own generation. Although of huge cultural significance, they hardly made a dent in the relentless commercial machinery that was overtaking western Europe.

France reappointed its monarchy, albeit in a reduced political role. Nineteenth-century French society was transformed politically, economically, and socially by a succession of mostly conservative regimes, which were divided by several dramatic revolutions whereby liberal idealists struggled to democratize the country. French print and reading culture helped to shape, and were themselves molded by, a brew of ideas, emotions, and material circumstances that nourished these changes. After the French Revolution, when the country experimented with constitutional government, Napoleon I introduced some legal and social reforms but also retained the conservative influence of the Catholic Church. His downfall was followed by the restoration of the Bourbon monarchy, whose conservative politics pushed the country into the July Revolution of 1830 and the establishment of the so-called bourgeois regime of Louis-Philippe. Liberal reaction against his corrupt government again forced the country into revolution in 1848–1849, resulting in the government of the Second Republic lead by Louis Napoleon. Louis Napoleon eventually became Napoleon III and headed France's Second Empire, which lasted until the country's defeat in the Franco-Prussian War of 1870–1871. In 1871 the socialist uprising of the Paris Commune was savagely repressed and, in the same year, the conservative Third Republic was confirmed. This regime would last through France's emergence into the twentieth century. Throughout the century, France underwent the processes of democratization and industrial revolution, but at a more gradual pace than that of England. The growth of capitalism after the 1830s swelled the ranks of the bourgeoisie and strengthened this class's political and social power, but it also produced a new force in French society—that of the urban proletariat. For much of the era, the country's lowest classes remained in dire circumstances, especially in the cities. However in the last decades of the century, more enlightened governments improved the lot of the urban proletariat by introducing greater educational reforms and rehabilitating the slum-ridden areas of large cities such as Paris.

Prussia and Italy both achieved nation status during this period through unification of their many duchies and principalities. In the early 1800s, German society was mainly agrarian, virtually pre-industrial, and organized around strictly defined class levels. The fettered class system and the lack of a capital city hampered the intellectual and aesthetic development of German citizenry. The aftermath of Napoleon's defeat of Austria and Prussia, and the consequent imposition of the Code Napoleon, helped to introduce various economic and political reforms that democratized German society. This was particularly achieved through the liberation of the peasants from serfdom and the breakdown of the guild system that had hampered the development of an industrial-based economy. Consequent social and material improvements gradually moved the country toward unification, and Prussia began to take a leadership position among the German states. A sense of nationhood soon began to reveal itself in German print culture, especially through the literary and intellectual movement of Romanticism.

The key characteristic of the period was organization: of industry, of politics, of wealth, of colonies, and of peoples. The winners were those who embraced industrial and commercial opportunities. The losers were those who resisted social and economic change (the aristocracy); those who didn't have the resources to buy into commercial opportunities, instead becoming cogs in the new industrial machinery (the working classes); and, of course, those whose resources were seized and whose labor was exploited for industrial gain (the colonized).

READING TRENDS AND PRACTICES

The transformation of the reading cultures in Britain and Europe during the nineteenth century sprang from economic, social, and technological effects wrought by two significant historical phenomena that had already occurred or begun in the late eighteenth century: the French Revolution and the Industrial Revolution. Revolutionary changes in France had started to affect people's thinking about class and had advanced ideas of democratization and liberalism that soon spread rapidly through print culture. Authors of creative works, particularly those who followed the precepts of the Romantic movement, quickly realized and exploited literature's potential to change society and politics. Moreover, the Industrial Revolution sparked economic and technological advances that fueled a burgeoning publishing industry, which exploded with cheaper books and more diverse forms of printed matter, including affordable newspapers, journals, and reviews. Because industrialization increased European societies' demands for a more skilled and professionalized workforce, many nations in this era improved their education systems and literacy rates quickly improved in their populations. Furthermore, as schooling was extended to wider constituencies within these societies, reading audiences became more highly diversified. Women, children, and especially the working classes swelled the reading audiences, especially when standards of living substantially improved in Britain and the western European countries after mid-century. An increasingly commercialized publishing industry responded to the new reading market by producing a huge variety of popular informational and literary subject matter, especially in new formats, such as serialized fiction.

Within a couple of decades of the start of Queen Victoria's reign, Britain's advanced economy, relatively democratic political structure, and stable society had begun to positively transform British reading culture so that a truly cohesive relationship developed between writers, their audiences, and the publishing world, which facilitated the huge growth of a literature industry. The First Reform Bill of 1832 would give further impetus to the steadily growing literacy rate, because the British middle class wanted suffrage to be practiced by an electorate that was literate and informed (and hence responsible), rather than by an illiterate and ignorant (and hence potentially volatile) rabble.

The invention of advanced printing technologies, such as steam and roller presses, and the availability of cheaper printing materials lowered publishing costs dramatically, so that a wave of affordable books of diverse types began to flood the reading market: informational and instructional books of all types, religious and inspirational books, and reprints of popular and classic literature. For the first time in British society, even a family of modest means could afford to maintain a small collection of reading material.

Up until mid-century, the reading and print cultures of France were molded by a consistent cultural viewpoint that privileged classical standards and internal values. A reader's choice of texts was used to define that individual's social position, especially when the traditional indicators of class began to erode with the dwindling of the aristocracy and the ascension of bourgeois wealth, power, and status in French society. Throughout the era, censorship also became a critical factor in determining what was published and read in France. The predominantly conservative and insecure regimes of the period were vigilant both of journalistic critiques that they perceived as challenging the legitimacy of their governments and of literary works that would undermine the nation's moral fiber.

Throughout the early part of the nineteenth century, German culture was rooted in two major central European areas: the Austrian Empire, under the Hapsburg dynasty, and the Prussian kingdom, which was under the rule of the Hohenzollerns. The changes in German reading culture that occurred in the era's first decades are linked to several important factors affecting German society and literature, such as the struggle against a feudal political order and a philosophical and aesthetic reaction against the dictates of French classical literary forms and Enlightenment thought. In addition, German society had to struggle against the repression of native and nationalist expression and traditions. Thus the establishment of German as the primary language of print culture would become emblematic of the society's break with the previous regimes that were often foreign-dominated.

The pre-Romantic *Sturm und Drang* (Storm and Stress) aesthetic movement of the late 1700s, dominated by the influential author Wolfgang Goethe, laid the groundwork for the new writing styles and ideas of Romanticism that engaged German authors and their audiences until the mid-nineteenth century. Educational reforms in the early 1800s had made German universities strong institutions of learning, and they began to play important roles in the growth of a national cultural consciousness through the teaching and writing of famous authors affiliated with them. The playwright, Gotthold Ephraim Lessing, formulated a dramatic genre that would more expressly render the concerns of both the growing German middle class and the common folk. The philosopher and poet Johann Gottfried Herder promoted the revival of folklore to stimulate a new awareness of the German language and a sense of nationhood in society. These authors stressed the need for writers to communicate directly and intensely with their audiences, emphasizing the importance of freedom of expression and immediacy of emotional response to phenomena and literature. Such aesthetic ideas would dominate the direction of German Romanticism.

By using both the aspect of emotional appeal and the political agenda of nationalistic struggle as important elements in their works, German Romantic poets played a crucial role by rallying their countrymen during the 1812–1815

German Wars of Liberation that ended in Napoleon's defeat. Unfortunately, in the war's aftermath, progress toward democratization and free expression in German society was stymied by the reactionary policies of Prussian and Austrian rulers, who convened with Russian leaders in a "Holy Alliance" at Vienna in 1815. These conservatives issued the Karlsbad Decrees of 1819, which imposed stringent press censorship and monitoring at universities, which were forced to dismiss professors suspected of political activity. Violent public reaction against these measures and other repressive actions by the government erupted in the 1848 Revolutions that quickly spread across Europe.

The urban middle class in most of the European countries became a predominant force that influenced reading trends; soon writers of both literary and nonliterary works responded to these bourgeois tastes by either reinforcing them through pedestrian genre publications or by reacting to them with texts inspired by various intellectual and aesthetic schools of "-isms." These included Realism, Positivism, Darwinism, Socialism, Naturalism, and Symbolism, all of which struck reading audiences of the time as highly radical. Indeed, nineteenth-century societies experienced a veritable reading revolution, at the core of which was a huge audience of unprecedented diversity, size, and rate of growth. The scenario of this cultural phenomenon was played out in the cultures of England, France, and Germany with particularly dramatic results that eventually spread throughout the rest of Europe.

CREATIVE TEXTS

The opening years of the nineteenth century were a dramatic period for Britain on many levels. From the country's involvement in campaigns to defeat Napoleon Bonaparte to the passing of the Great Reform Bill in the English parliament, the period was one of great reactions to the revolutions abroad in Europe and to the effects of the Industrial Revolution at home. Both the reading and the print cultures of the Romantic period in England were greatly affected by the political, economic, and industrial transformations that occurred in the country at the time.

From the beginning of this movement, although writers did not designate themselves "Romantic," intellectuals such as William Wordsworth and Samuel Taylor Coleridge were very aware that they were writing in a highly politicized social and cultural milieu, and they regarded themselves as active agents in their relationship to the upheaval of historical events occurring around them. In addition to this new role for the writer, Wordsworth's "Preface" to their joint collection of poems, *Lyrical Ballads* (1798), also envisioned an enhanced relationship between author and audience, specifically one that was more personal and more direct. The volume of poetry itself, published in four successive editions, is a landmark of English Romanticism that signals the beginning of a new age in English literature. The first edition contained twenty-three poems that were mostly narrative and personal in form, and which dealt with the theme of common folk who can feel deeply.

Wordsworth wrote nineteen of the volume's pieces, and Coleridge was responsible for four. But future editions would include many more poems and supplementary materials, such as a preface and an essay on poetic diction. The significant parts of the work include Coleridge's "Rime of the Ancient Mariner," which opened the collection and dwelt on supernatural elements. This was followed by a group of Wordsworth's poems that delight in nature's powers and focus on the human instincts of ordinary folk, and finally the long concluding meditative poem,

"Lines Written a Few Miles Above Tintern Abbey," which dwells on the circumstances of its composition and was Wordsworth's expression of his faith in nature and humanity. Included was an "Advertisement" by Wordsworth that stated his ideas about poetic diction and attacked the overwrought language of many modern writers.

The very important "Preface" by Wordsworth to the second edition of 1800 expanded on his crucial aesthetic concepts about poetry, poetic language, and subject matter, all of which inspired the collection. He stressed that the language of poetry should be a selection of diction really spoken in society. Wordsworth also focused on the psychological interest of the poems, which he proposed should "trace the primary laws of our nature" and illustrate "the manner in which we associate ideas in a state of excitement" (preface to the *Lyrical Ballads*). The significance of the collection lay in its influence in beginning a "Romantic" transformation in the way readers read literature, particularly poetry. With its new focus on humble subjects and colloquial, direct poetic language, and its combined use of both personal and narrative forms, the collection challenged preconceived notions of literary and social values. In all these ways, but especially in its introduction to the reader of a new poetic world and a new democratic community of the imagination, *Lyrical Ballads* was a break with eighteenth-century reading culture and a veritable Romantic Revolution in literature.

Later generations of English Romantics such as Percy Bysshe Shelley would urge the role of political activist for the writer. Indeed Lord George Gordon Byron, who was of this generation, achieved a cult status among his many readers and admirers in England and throughout Europe when he acted out the drama of his own works—such as *Childe Harold's Pilgrimage* (1812–1818)—by fighting for liberal causes in Europe, such as the Greek War of Independence, in which he died in 1824. *Childe Harold's Pilgrimage,* the most famous of Byron's poems, made him famous throughout England and Europe and contributed to a cult of Byronism that developed around him, his poetry, and his scandalous life. The work consists of four cantos that draw directly on the poet's travels in Europe and the Near East. Its originality resides in the way Byron successfully joins together different traditional forms in the poem, combining travelogue, topographical meditations, and, especially, dramatization through the character Harold, who expresses the essence of the poet's own tormented psyche. Like Byron himself, Childe Harold is a melancholy self-exile and bitter outcast, who expiates the sins of his scandalous life by his wanderings abroad and his philosophical contemplations among the historic sites of Europe. Thus the work uses landscape, art, architecture, and history to symbolize the poet's travails, but also as consolations for his suffering. In Canto IV, although the poet agonizes over the ruins of Roman civilization as symbols of humankind's destructiveness, he is also spiritually and aesthetically uplifted by these artifacts, which are evidence of humanity's creative and inventive genius. With its focus on the association of history and literature, its depiction of Promethean defiance through the figure of Harold, and its Romantic expression of revolt against the tyrants and spoilers of the era, *Childe Harold's Pilgrimage* became hugely popular and culturally influential among readers and writers of late European Romanticism. Byron and Byronism embodied a new and darker figure of the public artist, providing models of poetic sensibility, cynicism, and despair that reverberate throughout nineteenth-century literature.

An outgrowth of the contemporary interest in history was the literary re-creation of an idealized past for the country. Historical romances became the focus of a national reading craze as the public devoured the *Waverley* novels (1814–1832) of Sir Walter Scott, who was widely imitated not only in England but throughout

Europe. With *Waverley,* Scott invented the historical novel based on historical sources. The novelist published this work anonymously (and most of the succeeding historical novels that he wrote) because, fearing for the successful reputation that he had already established as a poet, he thought that the novel might not be successful with the public. He did not acknowledge authorship of his fictional works until 1827, but by then *Waverley* had made publishing history with its phenomenal sales.

The novel is a vivid human drama that focuses on Scotland during the eighteenth century when the country was making a transition from a feudal era into the modern world. Scott's use of exotic setting, sublime landscapes, and local color in his fiction would have an enormous effect on the manner in which later British and European writers would approach rural themes. The novel's complicated plot describes the adventures of Edward Waverley, a young English commissioned officer, who becomes involved in the Jacobite causes in Scotland during the Rebellion of 1745. After being arrested for fomenting mutiny in his own army through the ruses of the Highland chieftain Fergus MacIvor, he is rescued through the intervention of Rose, who is one of Edward's romantic interests and also the daughter of a family friend. Edward, who views the rebellions of the Scottish clans in a romantic fashion, impulsively joins the Jacobite forces at the battle of Prestonpans. Here the English are defeated and Edward saves the life of an English officer and family friend, who secures a pardon for him. The novel ends with Edward's marriage to Rose and the execution of MacIvor.

What made Scott's fiction unique, popular, and also significant as literature was his use of a very ordinary man, rather than a politically powerful hero, to relate great historical events. By using a viewpoint that shows the subjective, personal, and social implications of surviving earth-shaking events that one can't control or understand, Scott renders the sense of important events of historical change in a way that is at once accessible and meaningful to the reader. In bridging the movements of Romanticism and realism in its form and outlook, Scott's work was invaluable in its influences on British and European authors, reading culture and tastes, and the development of literary genres throughout the century.

The expanded audience of women readers correspondingly elicited more writing by women. A number of celebrated female authors chose male pen names so that their works would be more marketable, and also because of the questionable respectability of writing as an activity for genteel women. The Brontë sisters, Emily and Charlotte, both focused on questionable aspects of passionate love in their respective novels *Wuthering Heights* (1847) and *Jane Eyre* (1847). They also raised some red flags regarding accepted customs and legal issues in connection with marriage and sexual relations in British society.

George Eliot, who also used a male pen name, won the respect and sympathy of both female and male British readers through novels such as *Middlemarch* (1874–1876), which focused on the rights and place of women in contemporary society. The work is a masterpiece not only for its technical virtuosity as a piece of fiction, but also for its clarity in representing her moral and aesthetic aims. In all of her fiction, Eliot strove to show human beings as they really are, hoping to elicit sympathy from her readers

---

The Rise of Popular Literature

The vogue for historical romance and other adventure stories filtered down to the level of mass popular literature. The presence of chapbooks, hawked about the streets of urban centers such as London, indicated that a mass reading public for literature was taking root in the early decades of the nineteenth century.

to enable people of all classes to treat each other with justice and compassion. *Middlemarch* was the most celebrated book of its era for its probing exploration and exposure of the condition of England at a time when certainties of an older moral and social order were continuously being shattered.

By the time Eliot wrote *Middlemarch,* the scientific concepts of Darwin's theory of evolution and Comte's positivism had spread throughout English intellectual circles, Karl Marx's political ideas were attracting radical groups in Britain, and various social and political reforms were causing upheavals in the Victorian class system. The plot of the novel is complex, but basically focuses on life in the provincial town of Middlemarch in the years of turmoil before the passage of Britain's first Reform Bill. Both the workaday world of the town as well as the aims, talents, and ideas of its exceptional citizens are all explored through the prism of several marriages and relationships of Middlemarch's inhabitants. The heroine, Dorothea Brooke, becomes trapped in an unhappy marriage to Casaubon, an elderly pedant whose monumental and somewhat absurd scholarly project Dorothea first admires, but later despises. She is sustained by her friendship with Casaubon's nephew, Will Ladislaw, whom Casaubon detests and suspects has feelings for Dorothea. Other unhappy marital unions also appear in the novel, such as the marriage between Doctor Tertius Lydgate and the mayor's daughter, Rosamund Vincy, whose frivolousness, selfishness, and extravagance lead her husband to frustration and professional ruin. Rosamund's brother, Fred Vincy, is another unstable character who is fortunately redeemed by the love of his steadfast and practical childhood sweetheart, Mary Garth. After Casaubon dies, Dorothea and Ladislaw confess their love to one another but soon discover that her dead husband's will stipulates that she will forfeit her fortune if she marries Ladislaw. Dorothea renounces her inheritance, and the young couple marry.

Through the stories of her characters, Eliot analyzes the social and political turmoil of the era. She contrasts the conservative, "Tory" attitudes of those who represent the fossilized prejudices of the past with the growing demand for reform espoused by the younger, forward-thinking townspeople. Dorothea becomes a forum for many of Eliot's own ideas. The heroine shares her author's opinions about the rights and place of women in contemporary society, but she also demonstrates how the heart can be pulled in different directions. With intellectual and creative abilities that matched or superseded those of her male colleagues, and with a woman's psychological acumen about human relationships, Eliot held a unique place in the patriarchal culture of Victorian England. With these dual endowments of her mind and heart, Eliot's fiction became for many English readers both an influential articulation of the anxieties and confusions of mid-nineteenth-century society, and a uniquely sympathetic exploration of its will and spirit.

As mass readership grew and more information became available, especially through the daily and weekly serial publication of newspaper and magazine, the public at large became more aware of unjust material and social conditions suffered by the lowest classes in the country. Thomas Carlyle's work *Past and Present* (1843), which analyzed the effects of industrialization on society, opened with a chapter called "The Condition of England Question." This was later adapted into the name of a genre of social fiction in British literature: the "Condition of England" novel.

Charles Dickens's groundbreaking and tremendously popular 1837 work, *Oliver Twist,* combined the suspense–raising format of the serialized novel with a unique, narrative focus on a child's consciousness in the aim of raising public awareness about the horrors of the English workhouse and the inhumanity of the nation's Poor Laws. Dickens's impact on the culture and society of the Victorian era can

Charles Dickens's popular character, Oliver Twist, asking for more. [Courtesy of Library of Congress]

hardly be exaggerated. *Oliver Twist* stands out as his first serious engagement in exploring the effects of institutions upon people, especially the working-class children who were among the most vulnerable groups in early-nineteenth-century British society. *Oliver Twist* was the first British novel to focus on the character of a child and also to give the English pauper child a voice; it thus maintains a special status in the history of British literature and culture. The work was serialized in the magazine *Bentley's Miscellany,* over the two-year period of 1837 to 1838, when the dire effects of the New Poor Law Amendment Act of 1835 were eliciting the most vociferous protests from the poor and their supporters.

The plot is based on the story of Oliver Twist, a child of unknown parentage, who is born in a workhouse and brought up under cruel conditions of deprivation. In London, Oliver falls in with a gang of child thieves headed by Fagin, a devious old criminal who tries to convert Oliver into a thief. The novel guides Oliver through danger and rescue, killing off the villains who have threatened him in the process. Eventually, Oliver is reunited with his only living relative, a kindly aunt; receives his inheritance, which was hidden from him after his parents' deaths; and finally is adopted by the kindly Mr. Brownlow. When he was criticized for glamorizing crime in his novel, Dickens attempted to dissociate his work from the Newgate crime fiction that was a staple of working-class reading. Yet many of the more violent elements in the novel are certainly incidents that Dickens would have observed and noted in his days as a law clerk and through his familiarity with London's underworld. Among Dickens's greatest accomplishments in this novel, and throughout his fiction, is his ability to marry elements of popular street fiction with narrative material that had a clear social purpose and a moral tone that would appeal to more "respectable" middle-class readers. He was thus the first British novelist to forge a true mass market for his fiction. He was especially effective in exploiting the resources of weekly serialization to grip the attention of his Victorian readers, who waited impatiently for the suspenseful plots and unforgettable characters of his novels. It is through that popularity, and the immense status that he held with his public as a force for social good, that Dickens wielded his greatest influence on Victorian culture. As an author of conscience, he became and remains one of the most emulated writers throughout Western society.

The works of Thomas Hardy, one of the last great Victorian writers, played a key role in the

Elizabeth Gaskell

Through works such as *North and South* (1855), which dealt with labor unrest in rural England, Mary Gaskell, a protégée of Charles Dickens, enhanced the use of the novel as a tool for raising social consciousness in the Victorian reading public.

Threatened innocence: Joseph Syddall's 1891 illustration for Thomas Hardy's scandalous novel *Tess of the d'Urbervilles.*

evolution of British reading culture. Victorian readers were shocked and fascinated by his novels, particularly *Tess of the D'Urbervilles* (1891) and *Jude the Obscure* (1894–1895), which shed light on the brutal realities of emotional and sexual relations between men and women in rural Victorian England. These works gave British readers a modern and realistic assessment of the vanishing agrarian world that Victorian commerce and greed were destroying.

Tess of the D'Urbervilles focuses on the story of Tess Durbeyfield, who is the daughter of a poor English villager whose head is turned by the discovery of his noble lineage. Tess is seduced by a cunning young man of means, Alec D'Urberville. She has an illegitimate child, Sorrow, who dies when Tess refuses to ask her seducer for aid. Tess perseveres and eventually meets and marries Angel Clare, a minister's son. Their marriage falls apart when Angel learns of her previous disgrace. Despite revelations of his own questionable past, he cannot forgive Tess for her "sin," and he abandons her for a life in Brazil. Tess embarks on a life of impoverishment and hardship until she is reacquainted with Alec, who has become a preacher and pursues her until she is forced to accept his protection by becoming his mistress. When Angel returns from Brazil to find Tess with Alec, she becomes distraught and murders Alec to liberate herself. After a short period of concealment with Angel, she is captured at Stonehenge, tried and hung.

The question of immorality in *Tess of the D'Urbervilles* revolved around the issue of the subtitle that Hardy added: *A*

Thomas Hardy

Up until the period of his later fiction, Thomas Hardy's work had never been socially or critically censured. The condemnation of *Tess of the D'Urbervilles* and *Jude the Obscure* as immoral and pessimistic became so hostile that Hardy gave up his career as a novelist and turned permanently to the writing of poetry.

Pure Woman Faithfully Presented. The idea of describing an adulterous murderess as "pure" shocked the public and enraged the novelist's critics, but it was thus that Hardy attacked the double standards of sexual behavior for men and women in Victorian society. The subtitle also underscores the depiction of Tess as a character who grows in strength through a sense of herself. In this manner the author imbues Tess's story with both a moral thrust and a poignant sense of tragedy, as he did with so many of his rural heroines and heroes.

Hardy was influenced by the ideas of Darwin and Mill. Thus his fiction reflects his concern about the vulnerability of the rural poor; at the same time, it very realistically and grimly depicts a vanishing way of life in an England that was blinded by smugness and materialism. Above all, *Tess of the D'Urbervilles* shows Hardy as a writer whose work prefigured the transformation of cultural expectations for women, and on this basis his influence on English literary writing survived well into the twentieth century. As a writer who impelled his readers both to look back to the past and, at the same time, to anticipate modern attitudes about sexuality and morality, Hardy was surely a fitting author to bridge the literary threshold between the nineteenth and twentieth centuries.

Like most of the French literary movements throughout the century, Romanticism was radical in nature, although some of its writers were conservative aristocrats. Two writers of the French nobility produced texts that were particularly important for cultural renewal in the country's early decades. François-René Chateaubriand's works stressed aristocratic ideals, such as nobility of sentiment. His historical and polemical 1802 text, *Le Génie du Christianisme* (*The Genius of Christianity*), was both influential and popular in the early years of the era; it accorded with Napoleon's restoration of the Catholic Church in the country, and its emotional plea for the place of religion in French cultural life caught the mood of the time. This historical survey of religion is the work of the foremost voice of the first generation of the French Romantic writers. It is not a factual history, but is rather a text of apologetics that functions as a tribute to the regenerative power of the Christian faith and to its ability to reconcile and repair what past revolutions had broken. Chateaubriand proposes that man's desire for the absolute is infinite and that only religion fulfills that need. And Christianity, with its power to satisfy the imagination and the emotions, has inspired beautiful works of art and has contributed to civilization and progress. As examples of the genius bequeathed by Christianity to humankind, the author calls to witness the great religious poetry of past eras such as Dante's *Divine Comedy* and Milton's *Paradise Lost.*

To support his argument, Chateaubriand includes a chapter of his own creative work called "René," which describes the anguish and wanderings of the prototypical Romantic hero who suffers from *le mal du siècle* (sickness of the century), a form of world-weariness that other Romantic authors had described in their works, especially Goethe in his *Die Leiden des jungen Werther* (*The Sorrows of Young Werther,* 1774). To relieve his sorrows about his personal life and his existential despair about the ruination of Europe by its destructive history, René finds consolation in the beauties of the North American natural wilderness. He furthermore finds an outlet for his depressed state of mind through the narration of his troublesome life to an American native, Chactas.

The Genius of Christianity, and especially its chapter "René," were hugely popular and influential in France, the rest of Europe, and America in establishing a new aesthetic for the Romantic movement, complete with literary models. Chateaubriand's work caught the new mood in France of the country's return to religious faith based on emotional appeals. Chateaubriand's text also works as part of the country's process of national stock-taking after the traumas of the French Revolution. Through the popular narrative text of "René," French readers avidly participated in the Romantic author's interest in the turbulence of human feeling, as well as the new vision of dynamism and self-division of the human mind as it was portrayed through the Romantic temperament.

> **Madame de Staël**
>
> Mme. Germaine de Staël's *On Germany* (*De l'Allemagne* 1807) was a critical treatise of observations on the relations between social conditions and literature. It also popularized German Romanticism in France. Napoleon's regime censored the text and forced the writer into exile because the government regarded the work as unpatriotic and too pro-German.

The works of Victor Hugo were widely read and influential in France and throughout Europe and Britain during both the era of the Romantic movement and the later period of realism in literature. Hugo's Romantic play, *Hernani*, caused a sensation and physical remonstration when it appeared in 1830 because it so deliberately and blatantly broke the rules of classical French theatre with its provocative choice of subject matter and unorthodox treatment of dramatic form and language. Eventually the play won popular acceptance and established Romanticism as the dominant form of aesthetic expression of the time. The appearance and staging of Hugo's Romantic verse drama established him as both the major Romantic dramatist and the leader of the French Romantic school in the period of France's July Monarchy.

Set in an imagined sixteenth-century Spain, the plot focuses on the conflict between honor and passion that emerges from the rivalry for Doña Sol between an outlawed noble (Hernani), the king of Spain, and Don Ruy Gomez, a grandee who follows the values of old Spain. On the night of the play's first performance at the *Comédie-Française*, a physical battle broke out between Hugo's followers and the defenders of classical principles. The latter felt that Hugo had deliberately broken the rules of drama in his piece by fusing comedy and tragedy, by focusing too much on the specificity of time, place, and the tribulations of an historic individual, and above all, by flaunting the unorthodox use of conversational French and run-on lines of verse, all of which were considered unacceptable infractions of language and form for French drama at the time.

The conflict was actually less a quarrel about theatre than a clash of generations and aesthetic systems. In his famous preface to *Cromwell* (1827), one of his earlier plays, Hugo had underscored the need for new language, new genres, and new subjects in literature to mirror the interests of contemporary audiences. He proposed the models of foreign playwrights, especially Shakespeare, to forge a type of French Romantic drama that would be flexible enough to represent the widest possible range of actions and emotions experienced in the personality struggles of individuals involved in the grand conflicts of "anecdotal" history. Hugo's play, and the ideas he proposed about new forms, idioms, and subjects for the new Romantic era, were all important for the ascension of the Romantic avant-garde to aesthetic dominance. *Hernani,* and the aesthetic concepts that fueled Hugo's creation of the play, underscored the advance of a modern notion that each century must have its own prophets of creative and discursive texts to reconstruct its stories and histories in a language appropriate to its time.

Whereas Hugo's play appealed to French intellectuals, newspapers such as Paris's *La Presse* aimed for a broad appeal. In 1836 *La Presse* scooped a first in French publishing history by printing in its pages the first serialized novel, or *roman-feuilleton*. The venture was very successful and created a publishing trend that was instrumental in expanding readership and improving literacy in the country. Historical romances became popular in France when Sir Walter Scott's translated works were introduced abundantly in cheap book formats, often sold as street literature (*livres de colportage*). Newspaper and journal publishers quickly capitalized on the craze for this genre by serializing the works of writers such as Alexandre Dumas (père) whose novels, *Les Trois Mousquetaires* (*The Three Musketeers,* 1844) and *Le Comte de Monte-Cristo* (*The Count of Monte Cristo,* 1844–1845), remained widely read throughout most of the century. Eugène Sue's serialized and very popular fictional chronicles of life in Paris, *Les Mystères de Paris* (*The Mysteries of Paris,* 1842–1843) also whetted the French reader's appetite for fiction that focused on realistic details and local color.

The success of such novels inspired the novelist Honoré de Balzac to produce his ambitious and prodigious fictional masterwork, *La Comédie humaine* (*The Human Comedy*), which he wrote over a nineteen-year period (1828–1848). However, rather than presenting romances, Balzac determined that this cycle of ninety-five fictional works would portray in realistic detail the material, historical, and psychological nuances of all French life of the era. Among the individual novels in the *Comédie,* the narrative *Old Goriot* (1834) proved especially popular with the readers of Restoration France. With his monumental cycle of ninety novels, Balzac was instrumental in establishing the traditional form of the realistic novel, which became the dominant literary genre in the nineteenth century. Balzac's aim in this project was to record societal observations with minute attention to the description and domestic background of his characters, emphasizing the details of occupations and class distinctions. The cycle covers almost the complete range of human activity in Restoration France in terms of geography, social levels, and lifestyle through its three major parts: *Études de moeurs* (*Studies of Customs*), *Études philosophiques* (*Philosophic Studies*) and *Études analytiques* (*Analytic Studies*). The *Studies of Customs* are further divided into six sections of "scenes" that overlap in their coverage of what Balzac designated as spheres of life: private, provincial, Parisian, political, military, and country.

Much of Balzac's originality resides in the ingenious creative transference to his fiction of his obsessive examination of virtually all spheres of French life: the contrast between provincial and metropolitan manners and customs; the commercial spheres of banking, publishing, and industrial enterprise; the worlds of art, literature, and high culture; politics and partisan intrigue; romantic love in all its aspects; and the intricate social relations and scandals among the aristocracy and the *haute bourgeoisie.* These topics provided material largely unknown, or unexplored, by earlier writers of French fiction. Central to Balzac's whole project of representing all of French society through his fiction was his conviction that humanity's outer appearance and environment reveal its inner reality. As a central organizing theme for his work he focuses on an idea from the writings of the nineteenth century scientist, Geoffroy de Saint-Hillaire, who described the natural world as an arrangement of variations of types of plants and animals that derived from a prototype, a kind of pre-Darwinian principle. Thus, Balzac presents the actions of the *Comedy's* characters as variations of the same striving will to possess and climb in French restoration society; that "will" is symbolically represented by money. In such works as *Le Père Goriot* (*Old Goriot,* 1834), the driving will is twisted into Goriot's monomaniacal obsessions of excessive paternal love, or into the strivings of upward social mobility of the ambitious young provincial poet-hero, Rastignac, or in the purely evil desire for power sought by the arch-criminal, Vautrin.

Old Goriot is also the source of one of Balzac's greatest innovative novelistic techniques—that of the device of characters who reappear from novel to novel and thus give a sense of density and multidimensionality to the all-encompassing world of the *Comedy*. In one of the other great novels of the cycle, *Illusions perdues* (*Lost Illusions*, 1837–1843), the characters become part of a changing era that has special reverberations for the author and reader alike, because Balzac describes the evolutions of the printing, publishing, and authorship cultures in the early decades of nineteenth-century France. The stories of two upwardly mobile young provincials—David Séchard, a publisher, and Lucien de Rubempré, an aristocratic poet turned journalist—are intertwined in the novel. Balzac describes how quickly and effectively the money-nexus of Restoration France corrupts their ambitions and dashes their hopes. The theme of compromise for commercial gain becomes the central motif of the book, which shows how the profession of authorship itself devolves into dishonest hack journalism as it becomes implicated in the era's immoral political and social schemes, which focus purely on expediency and self-interest.

As serialized works, Balzac's novels were quite popular and widely distributed, and his fiction was the first to be published in a French daily paper. Thus the *Comedy* itself is partially a function of the economics of publishing in France. It is also a totally unique literary construct, a monumental edifice of writing that is constructed as a model of the very society that it unmasks. Its individual novels provide diverse perspectives as points of entry into the labyrinth of Restoration France. It is as much for this accomplishment of totally re-creating his century as for his techniques of realistic writing that Balzac's work stands as a unique model of narrative creativity for the world of literature.

From the start of the Second Empire to the century's end, the extent of published material, especially in newspaper and journal formats, became voluminous. The size of the mass reading audience swelled as well. Reading material became more affordable and more accessible than ever before in French history. Printing and paper costs fell sharply, cheap book binding became feasible, and the government's investment in better national rail and road systems facilitated the rapid transport of consumer goods to all parts of France. Almost every French reader could follow the daily events of the country in a source such as *Le Petit Journal* (1863), which became one of the most affordable and popular papers available, offering wide reporting of events, opinions, and scandalous news, especially from Paris. Two writers of the era provided grist for the tabloid mills when their literary works were deemed to test the limits of moral norms in French reading culture. Charles Baudelaire's collection of poems, *Les Fleurs du mal* (*The Flowers of Evil*, 1857), and Gustave Flaubert's novel, *Madame Bovary* (1857), were deemed offensive to public morality and both writers were brought to trial in 1857.

The poems of Baudelaire's *Flowers of Evil* first appeared as a group of eighteen pieces in the journal *Revue des Deux Mondes*, in 1855. That selection, which focused on the theme of premonition of the physical decomposition that lies in wait for the syphilitic lover, was prefaced by a cautionary note from the journal's editor. When a separate edition of *Flowers of Evil*, expanded to 101 poems, appeared in 1857, the book was seized by the French police, and Baudelaire and his publishers were prosecuted for offenses against morality and religion. The author was fined three hundred francs and was ordered to reissue the book minus six condemned poems. Eventually the verdict was quashed in 1949 and the six poems were reinstated.

One of the reasons for the swift prosecution of Baudelaire's work may have been the authorities' desire to avenge the recent acquittal of the case against Flaubert's *Madame Bovary* earlier that year. The trials only increased public interest and sales of both books. Baudelaire's condemned poems especially piqued readers' curiosity. It was in the spirit of protest against such moral and cultural strictures of bourgeois French society that Baudelaire had composed the poetry of his collection. As a writer who was deeply concerned with the relationship between humanity, morality, and art, he believed his aim as an artist was to see and communicate to his contemporaries the truth about themselves. He also wished to bring his clarity of vision into a world polluted by hypocrisy, conformism, and self-interest, all aspects of bourgeois society and politics in France's Second Empire. Thus the images of his pieces center on the community of the dispossessed in the modern city: the prostitutes, drug addicts, beggars, and other social outcasts who were not previously subject matter for poetry, especially in the literature of French Romanticism. Furthermore, Baudelaire's artistic persona implicates not only himself but also his readers in the rendering of this new perception of art and life, as he indicates in his collection's preface, "To the Reader." The poetic exploration of modern life involves the discovery of correspondences in its discontinuities, and this results in exposing the beauty in ugliness and evil, and vice versa.

In addition to the shocking subject matter of the collection, Baudelaire's innovations in poetic technique, especially his verbal experimentation in verse, jarred the conservative tastes of his reading audience. Baudelaire was not only a pivotal writer for his time but also exerted a crucial influence on the aesthetics of the twentieth century. Both his poetry and the controversy surrounding it created a new sensibility toward literature—a new way of seeing and feeling its effects—that would dominate Europe's artistic life for generations.

Flaubert's *Madame Bovary* piqued the interest of the French reading public because it was one of two major creative works in mid-nineteenth-century France that was prosecuted by the authorities on grounds of immorality. It was serialized in 1856 in the *Revue de Paris*; upon its appearance in book form in 1857, the volume was seized by police and Flaubert, his editor, and his printer were charged with publishing a morally offensive book. The novel is based on the very simple story of a sentimental and slightly vulgar Norman bourgeois heroine, Emma Bovary, whose dreams of glamour and love begin to exclude her husband, a prosaic rural doctor. As she tries to base her life on ideas of passion and romance that she has gathered from popular romances, she becomes involved in two adulterous affairs, falling victim to exploitative men. She becomes embroiled in debt, eventually commits suicide by swallowing arsenic, and leaves behind an impoverished husband and child.

When the prosecution objected to the nihilistic quality of the novel and to its devastatingly negative account of marriage and adultery, Flaubert's defense attorney countered that Emma's story was a moral warning, not a model to be followed. This argument won a dismissal of charges. The process of the trial not only made the novel hugely popular, but also underscored the brilliance of Flaubert's novelistic technique and the validity of his aesthetic concept. Flaubert stressed the necessity of accuracy of observation and documentation in literary writing and also emphasized that the author should take an impersonal stance vis-à-vis his characters and their actions. To this end, he strove for perfect accuracy in the diction of his narrative descriptions and invented a form of narration called *le style indirect libre*. This technique entailed the reporting of the speech and thoughts of the fictional characters by using images, memories, and vocabulary typical of the protagonists.

Flaubert's innovative form of storytelling, in which readers share the perceptions of the characters in fiction and yet are forced to maintain a critical distance from them, was disconcerting for those in the public who saw themselves as the arbiters of society's morality and the guardians of good taste in literature. The brilliance of Flaubert's concept of the visible, unobtrusive, ironic, and yet analytic authorial presence was that it even more pointedly reinforced *Madame Bovary*'s strength as a tale of hypocrisy, stupidity, and cruelty spreading through society at large. Flaubert's work shows how the artist's reworking of language in a literary text gives it the power to undermine the sense of stability in a society's perceptions and values. It is through this aesthetic achievement that *Madame Bovary* wielded its greatest influence on both the writers of Flaubert's era and those of many future generations. The fact that Flaubert was acquitted and Baudelaire received only light punishment, along with the avid reporting of their sensational trials and the consequent phenomenal sales of their books, all mark a significant turning point in the history of France's reading culture. These events signify the public's acknowledgment that French society would tolerate almost unlimited creative freedom for its writers.

In the last decades of the century, French literary authors experimented with a diversity of new forms of writing. Some focused on exploring aspects of society from the vantage point of recent ground-breaking concepts about human behavior that had been discovered through the psychological and biological scientific research of this era. Influenced by Claude Bernard's treatise on scientific experimentation, *Introduction à la médecine expérimentale* (*Introduction to Experimental Medicine*, 1869), the novelist Émile Zola wrote his own treatise, *The Experimental Novel* (*Le Roman expérimental* 1880), which theorized on the application of Bernard's scientific method to novel writing. Zola's experimentation with his fictional work resulted in a vast cycle of twenty novels on the social life of the Second Empire, *Les Rougon-Macquart* (*The Rougon-Macquarts*, 1871–1893). This monumental series covers the natural and scientific history of the extended Rougon-Macquart family over several generations during France's Second Empire.

Zola organized the novels within the structure of his historical cycle by four groups of psychological types according to class levels: working-class people, shopkeepers and the business class, the class of the bourgeoisie and professionals, and finally the class of high society. Areas of social deviancy such as alcoholism, prostitution, and psychopathic violence also came under his impartial scrutiny. The uniqueness of Zola's fictional treatment of these groups is that he attempted to model his analysis after a scientific method that he described in *The Experimental Novel*. Under the influence of the scientist Claude Bernard and the method outlined in his scientific text, *An Introduction to Experimental Medicine,* Zola proposed that he would use minute and impersonal observation and documentation and a scientific method he designated as "Naturalist" (for its similarity to investigation in the natural sciences) to trace the effects of heredity and environment on the actions of his characters. He had undoubtedly read the works of Darwin. To what extent his novels strictly applied such a method is debated even today, but the power of his descriptions of proletarian characters and movements in his novels remains unsurpassed. Zola was driven by an outraged sense that literature had strayed from its main responsibility of telling the truth about the modern French state and especially about the misdeeds of France's Second Empire.

Of the series, the novel *Germinal* (1885), with its depiction of mining strikes in northern France, resonated the strongest with the reading public. By this time Marx and Engels's *Communist Manifesto* had been translated into French and its ideas had proved attractive to numerous socialists in the nation. Zola's *Germinal* thus tapped into one of the greatest fears that haunted French society in the waning years of the century, that of the specter of radical class struggle and the revolt of the country's proletariat. The Rougon-Macquart cycle ventured into a social landscape hitherto unexplored by French writers. Zola's documentary realism about the verities of the conflicts between the bourgeoisie and the ill-fated, working-class life in an industrial context transformed this novel into a modern epic of poetical and mythical proportions, which drew more readers to socialism than any radical political manifesto or pamphlet. Zola, like other writers before him who focused on the substrata of French society, was often accused of immorality for his unvarnished descriptions of explicit subject matter, such as sexuality. It was probably in this sense that his influence on the reading and writing cultures of Europe was the greatest. He played a very significant role in clearing the way for the frank and honest discussion of problems that had previously been banned from polite society, and in doing so, he conferred the poetry of tragedy on the most economically and socially deprived sections of his society.

A new aesthetic movement in poetry—symbolism—also intrigued French readers, almost as much as the scandalous lives of its practitioners. Works by Paul Verlaine, and especially, Arthur Rimbaud, with his collection *Une saison en enfer* (*A Season in Hell*, 1873), all struck an appreciative emotional chord with poetry readers in the country. The engagement of the personal sensibilities of French readers to such a degree in connection with avant-garde literature was surprising, because this audience's literary tastes had been predominantly formed by a conservative educational system and guided by the narrow classical standards imposed by literary critics and reviewers. The public's easier acceptance of both unorthodox forms of literature and unsettling subject matters signaled that French readers were more disposed than ever before to explore the modern cultural terrain of the next century with the help of their writers.

In both the early and later periods of German Romanticism, authors sought to build a consciousness in their audiences of what German literature could become. In order to free German writing from the constraints of classical (and mainly French-derived) forms, they sought to give more direct expression to sentiment in their works. In addition, they explored the substrata of German mythology, folklore, and tradition to find native-based themes and subject matter. Finally, to embrace both those aesthetic aims, German writers developed a form of fantasy literature that tapped a vein of original legends and folktales from a tradition that was specifically "Germanic."

Ernst Theodor Amadeus Hoffman, a writer of the second generation of German Romanticism, developed a particularly eerie strain of this fantastic narrative. His collections of short stories, *Fantasiestücke in Callots Manier* (*Fantastic Pieces in the Manner of Callot*, 1814–1815), became well-known and imitated throughout Europe, initiating a reading craze for German tales of terror. With the publication of the four volumes of this short story collection, Hoffmann quickly established an international reputation as a master of fantastic narrative and of the tale of terror. His fiction uses the genre of the *Märchen* (adult fairy tale) to frame the Romantic obsession with "otherness" and show how the realm of irrational, mysterious, and supernatural forces intrudes on everyday reality to create havoc that the author cannot resolve. The stories of the *Fantastic Pieces* were influenced by the grotesque style of the seventeenth-century artist, Callot, and also by the publication of Jacob and Wilhelm Grimm's collection of folktales, *Kinder-und Hausmärchen* (*Domestic and Children's Fairy Tales*, 1812–1815).

The simple tales of folk culture were transmuted by Hoffmann into complex narratives that probe the imagination and psyche of artistic individuals who are in conflict with the modern materialistic and philistine values of early-nineteenth-century society. Such is the theme of a masterpiece that represents Hoffmann's worldview in the *Fantastic Pieces*, "Der Goldne Topf" ("The Golden Pot"). The tale describes how a young poet, Anselmus, who resides in the contemporary middle-class society of Dresden, becomes involved in a struggle between the forces of good and evil over the possession of the "magic pot," which is a symbol of the imagination. Hoffmann uses the motif of the *doppelgänger*, or double, in the tale to highlight the darker alter-ego of otherwise normal people, and to illustrate the menacing influence upon daily life of an inner world that is shaped by fear, suspicion, and madness, and which represents the psyche's subconscious parts.

This characterization was also used in Hoffmann's more sinister tale, "Der Sandmann" ("The Sandman," 1816), which became the focus of a famous study by the twentieth-century psychologist Sigmund Freud in his work, *Das Unheimlich* (*The Uncanny*, 1919), an exploration of aesthetics, obsessive imagination, and the repetition compulsion. The fertile imagination, extraordinary inventiveness, and fearless exploration of the dualism and dark side of the human psyche that are all exemplified in Hoffmann's prose fiction had an immense impact on the reading culture and literature of his time, both in Europe and abroad. In addition, his tales also inspired innovations in the other arts such as music, opera, and ballet and anticipated many of the narrative strategies and themes of later imaginative writing in the twentieth century.

The agenda of building a sense of nationhood and a national consciousness of German tradition and heritage through the collection of original folk oral narrative became the foundation for research by Jacob Joseph and Wilhelm Grimm, two philologists and folklore specialists. Jacob Joseph and Wilhelm Grimm were part of the second movement of German Romantic writers, and their interests in literature were more philological and national than those of previous Romantic authors. Like many writers of their own generation, they aimed to re-create the German nation out of a glorified and mystified past, and their project of collecting folklore had the specific goals of uncovering and preserving in print the genius of local color, what they called the *naturpoesie* of the common people. They felt that this precious national heritage was threatened by the urbanization and industrialization that was encroaching upon German rural society in the early 1800s. The Grimms scoured the German countryside and collected oral folk narratives from the informants of various regions. Their life-long project produced several collections, most notably *Domestic and Children's Fairy Tales* (*Kinder– und Hausmärchen* 1812–1814), which became one of the most popular books for Germans of all ages. The work was first issued in 1814 as a first edition consisting of two volumes that included several dozen fables, legends, jokes, anecdotes, and other lore. It was eventually expanded to a collection of over two hundred tales for the 1857 edition. It was widely translated both in Europe and abroad, and it soon became the model for folklore collections in many countries.

The tales depict a world of threatening wilderness and savage animals to which children are abandoned at times of great famine and poverty. The stories also focus on themes of bereavement, loss, and the dissolution of the family, especially through the abuses that children and young folk suffer from

The Brothers Grimm

The Grimm brothers also used their training in language to produce both the best German dictionary and German grammar of the nineteenth century: *The German Dictionary* (*Deutsches Wörterbuch*, begun in 1852) and *German Grammar* (*Deutsche Grammatik* 1819–1837). They hoped to establish a form of standardized German that could be used as the common idiom and that could also be taught throughout the German school system. These projects were also driven by the Grimms' desire to give Germans a sense of national unity by guiding them toward a shared language.

wicked stepmothers, neglectful parents, and the cruel rivalries of siblings. There is a solid reality behind the poverty depicted in the tales, which can be verified by the historical accounts about disease, starvation, hard work by children, and beggary that were the hardships of German society in the late 1700s, when only half of the nation's children survived to adulthood. One of the collection's best-known tales, "Hänsel und Gretel," depicts all of these grim circumstances, including the shocking practice of *himmeln lassen* (deliberately exposing children to die) in times of economic stress. Like most of the collection's stories, the tale is narrated in straightforward language, using formulaic repetitions and a simple structure of tableaux, all of which make the story easy to remember and retell in an oral culture. Yet the Grimms' reworking of the tale also vividly depicts the basic urges of the children, such as their unbearable hunger, as well as their intense emotions of fear and anxiety. Coloring the whole retelling is the Romantic notion of "otherworldliness," with a magic world featuring a witch, a cottage made of candy, and talking animals that act as saviors for the children, all of which have the aspects of a dream existence.

The Grimms provided scholarly notes about the typology and variants of the tales. However some contemporary reviewers and critics of the collection disputed the authenticity of the tales, pointing out that the Grimms used several informants and mediators who were literate townspeople and thus were misrepresented as "pure" voices of common rural folk. Nonetheless, the collection stands out as the authoritative source of fairy and folktales in Europe. Not only were the Grimms sympathetic and imaginative writers about children in their refashioning of the stories, they also contributed to a cultural and historical sense of national consciousness that helped to eventually unify their country. The Grimms' precious legacy of their *Märchen* to humanity lies in the power of these simple yet eternal tales to psychologically grip both the popular and literary imagination.

In the 1840s German literature had settled into a complacent apolitical mode, often designated as the "Biedermeier" period; writing focused on the private domestic sphere of the middle class and promoted inner security, abstinence from passion, and mediocre tastes. By the 1850s and 1860s, German authors again became increasingly politically and socially conscious and followed the trends of realistic writing that had taken a foothold across Europe and Britain. However, unlike other European authors such as Balzac and Dickens, who used realism to depict alienated characters and social disorder, the German writers of this period generally avoided any critique of the status quo in their works and instead narrowed their fictional explorations of contemporary society to what they designated as "Poetic Realism." Thus the major novelists of this era, such as Theodor Sturm, Gottfried Keller, and especially Gustav Freytag, focused on narratives of personal development (*Bildungsroman*) that portrayed heroes who grew toward moral maturity and integration within society. These novelists were very popular with the German middle class, which greatly admired their works for upholding bourgeois moral, political, and social values.

By the 1870s, Germany had achieved leadership in its economic, industrial, and technological development. With its strong material advantages, it easily conquered France in the Franco-Prussian War of 1870. In 1871, the German Chancellor Bismarck successfully completed the unification of Germany, and Wilhelm I was declared emperor. In the following years, Germany's strength as a world power was consolidated when it acquired colonial interests in Africa, the Pacific, and China. As the end of the century approached, the echelons of society changed dramatically. As educational opportunities expanded, the organization and levels of social orders shifted drastically. A large work force of upwardly mobile workers filled the ranks of a petty white-collar class. The wealthy and powerful bourgeoisie continued to take credit for what it regarded as its own achievements, particularly Germany's rapid economic growth and its prestige in scholarship, culture, and technological expertise. Women also gained advances in Germany's golden age of the bourgeois at the century's end, as they became more educated and moved into jobs as secretaries or typists and into professional positions. However hostility to female emancipation remained deep-rooted in German society, especially in sexual morality. The "woman question" in Germany remained largely unresolved as the century closed. Such transformations and divisions in German society came under the scrutiny of a number of authors who were influenced by both the Realist and the Naturalist schools of aesthetics and writing, especially through Nietzschean philosophy and the novels of Emile Zola. Gerhart Hauptmann's plays, such as *Die Weber* (*The Weavers,* 1892), used Naturalist themes such as biological fatalism, tabooed subjects of alcoholism, sexuality, and violence, and above all, shocking dramatic techniques such as crude speech and explicit references to bodily functions, to outrage bourgeois audiences with harsh and undeniable truths about their hypocritical society.

However, the works of Theodor Fontane were the most masterful at shaking his reading audience out of their bourgeois complacency. His novel about a socially and emotionally broken adulteress, *Effi Briest* (1895), made his readers confront the social erosion and the system of false values upon which the nation's prosperity and progress were being built. A number of features in Fontane's novels indicate that he is already a modern writer. Unlike many of his peers in the literary world, who wrote about the exemplary character-building aspects of bourgeois life in late-nineteenth-century Germany, Fontane's chronicles of middle-class life in the Bismarckian era focus on social criticism and use subtle psychological observation. Both in form and in subject matter, *Effi Briest,* like much of his later fiction, closely approaches the conventions of the realistic social novels that were written in England, France, and Russia in the latter part of the nineteenth century. The novel deals with the tragic life of Effi, a young bourgeois, who lives in the rural town of Kessin in late-nineteenth-century Germany. Misled by her own naïve ambition, she marries a Prussian nobleman who is an officer employed as a civil servant. He is twice her age and dedicates most of his time to the activities of Bismarck's inner circle, particularly its agenda to build a militarily strong, industrially advanced Germany. When she becomes frustrated by her husband's neglect and subsequently disillusioned by her marriage, Effi commits adultery with Crampas, an officer in her neighborhood. The affair is only discovered six years later by her husband, who nonetheless blindly follows the strict dictates of Prussian moral convention by killing Crampas in a duel and shunning his wife, "for the sake of an idea, a concept," as he states (*Effi Briest* 175). Effi, forced to live in seclusion by her husband and family, resigns herself to her sad fate and dies of tuberculosis soon after her family relents and allows her to return home. Using a multiplicity of perspectives rendered through a highly nuanced depiction of conversational language and social ritual, Fontane enables his readers to enter the minds of his characters. Such narrative techniques allow him to extend his thematic focus beyond a mundane treatment of courtship and marriage and to open up the topics of the nature of female sexuality and the social costs attendant upon the restricted sphere of female experience in the late nineteenth century. *Effi Briest* was not popular with German audiences of the time because the author suggests the repressive and patriarchal society that was shaped by the influence of Bismarck's political regime is implicated in Effi's tragedy. However in the twentieth century, the subtle irony and penetrating social and psychological criticism of Fontane's fiction would gain a wide appreciation and would exert a considerable influence on modern writers such as Thomas Mann. Twentieth-century culture and historic events would function as even more brutal agents of change for Germany, forcing its citizens to examine more closely than ever before the terms of their homeland's success and the compromises in their society's moral outlook.

POLITICAL TEXTS

For British readers, the works of several philosophers and historians of the period became significant and popular sources of reflection on the meaning of recent past events. They were object lessons for what was often perceived as England's precarious social and spiritual state. Such analyses were a specialty of the social critic Thomas Carlyle; in particular, his works *The French Revolution* (1837) and *Past and Present* (1843) were widely read and very influential on later thinkers and politicians who determined the direction of the country.

There were many dissenting views in England, in particular, about the political and social turmoil in Europe and its effects upon British society. There was an equally vigorous public discussion about the economic and social consequences of industrialization and technological changes for the country, often framed as the "Condition of England" question. In the early decades of the century, as the publishing industry exploded and middle-class readership greatly expanded, print media—especially the journal and the review—became very popular forums for the staging of such crucial debates. Numerous journals sprang into existence to support various political factions. The two most popular (and partisan) were the Whig-oriented *Edinburgh Review* (1802–1929) and the Tory rival created to oppose it, *Blackwood's Magazine* (1817–1980.) Both mass readership and literacy rates grew rapidly as the British mass public became eager to learn about exciting events in the country and follow current opinions and ideas.

By the 1860s, England had become an economic and industrial powerhouse among Western countries. It had acquired numerous colonial possessions in Africa and Asia, and its cultural and intellectual horizons had broadened substantially. Percolating through Victorian society were new ideas and opinions from print sources from Britain and abroad, such as those published in Karl Marx and Friedrich Engels's *Kommunistisches Manifest* (*The Communist Manifesto,* 1848). The basic concepts of Marxist theory that were presented in the *Manifesto* were issued in 1848 by a group called the Communist League. The manifesto itself was written as a type of party platform for an international conference of workingmen in London. The document outlined the history of the labor movement, gave a critical overview of existing socialist texts, and explained the basic ideas of communism. Marx and Engels began their analysis with the materialistic interpretation of history and, using John Stuart Mill's labor theory of value, they predicted an inevitable class struggle, the triumph of the working classes, and the eventual establishment of a Communist state. Marx would expand his ideas about Marxist theory in his extensive work *Das Kapital* (*Das Capital,* 1867–1894). What distinguishes this text from other contemporary works that sympathize with the misery of the urban poor is the author's total lack of nostalgia for pre-industrial times.

Marx played an important role in late-nineteenth-century British and European political thinking and also influenced authors such as William Morris and George Bernard Shaw in England, and Jean Jaurès, a French novelist and socialist. In the twentieth century, Marxist ideas had an especially strong impact on the works of the German dramatist Bertolt Brecht, and on Jean-Paul Sartre, a French philosopher and writer who was an exponent of Existentialist thinking. From the time of its original appearance, the *Manifesto* went through about 544 editions and was translated into thirty-five languages, and after 1917, new editions and translations of the work made it a global bestseller.

The same year, the social philosopher and economist, John Stuart Mill, published his challenge to the Victorian moral and social ethos, *On Liberty,* which argued for daring reforms that would substantially expand political and social freedoms in society, especially for women. His political essay is the most succinct and best expression of liberalism in the nineteenth century. Written primarily as a challenge to the tide of reaction that followed the revolutions of 1848, Mill's text summarized the faith of a liberal in the progress of humanity through freedom of thought and stressed his faith in the ultimate triumph of liberalism. He proposed that liberalism was a universal creed, not limited to class interests but applicable to all humankind. In clearly stated, logical terms he laid out the ideals of liberty, freedom of speech, liberty of association, and popular education. He lashed out against both individual and social tyranny. Mill's essay was a source of inspiration to many of his contemporaries in Victorian society who supported his ideals. Mill's liberalism also included the advocacy of sexual equality, particularly with regard to the nineteenth-century marriage contract, a position that he outlined in another of his famous works, "On the Subjection of Women" (1869). Partly because of the eminence of his publications, in 1865 he was elected to the English parliament; there he championed radical causes such as women's suffrage.

Mill's 1869 pamphlet, "On the Subjection of Women," laid out the issues of a debate that would engage English writers and their readers through the end of the century and far beyond: that of gender equality. These works all helped to liberate Victorian writing from social and moral restrictions that hindered frank and open discussions about the nature of marriage, gender relations, and sexuality in contemporary society. However, the threat of censorship constantly loomed over such texts and worked to stifle debate.

By the early 1830s in Germany, a period of polemical and politicized writing arose in reaction to the repressive policies of the Metternich government that held power during this era. These works emanated from an organization of young writers who designated themselves "Young Germany," and who aimed to establish a liberal German government. One of the group's most famous members, the poet Heinrich Heine, was an accomplished journalist and social critic who wrote very popular and scathing exposés about the German homeland, such as his prose poem, "Die Harzreise" ("A Journey Through the Harz Mountains," 1826), which mirrored the public's disgust with the government and its conduct of the country.

Politically, the German state started the process of unification with the formation of the Zollverein in 1834. Divisions still existed through the states and society, and political debates permeated daily life, especially in the expanding market of newspapers in the late 1840s. With the introduction of the telegraph and news agencies such as Reuters, rapid reporting of daily events and opinions to a national reading audience became possible. The news media facilitated wide public awareness about the civil unrest caused by the economic depression of the 1840s, when masses of poverty-stricken unemployed roamed the country. During the years of the worst disturbances in 1844, 1846, and 1847, political groups were able to rapidly disseminate their political messages about the dire state of the country through pamphlets and their own newspapers published with the rapid technology and cheap printing materials that were now available to anyone. The radical paper *Rheinische Zeitung,* edited by Karl Marx, was one such news forum that played a major role in spreading the public debate over the causes of, and solutions to, the boiling social crisis. In 1848, Karl Marx and Friedrich Engels published *The Communist Manifesto,* their seminal critique of the bourgeois class. Just a few weeks later, a full-scale revolution erupted in the German states and spread quickly throughout the country, lasting through 1849. Revolutions broke out in other European countries at the same time; the message of Marx and Engels reverberated throughout the German states, on the Continent, and abroad. In the aftermath, Metternich was dismissed, and some steps were taken toward constitutional government. German industrialization advanced rapidly throughout the rest of the century, and a more powerful and wealthier middle class evolved that profited from the burgeoning industrial economy.

Agricultural workers and artisans fared less well and sought work in cities, so that there was a major population shift from the countryside to urban areas. Political groups still argued over issues of liberalization of the government, but conservative business interests increasingly held sway. In 1862, a conservative politician, Otto von Bismarck, became prime minister of Prussia and became instrumental in forging the modern German state, especially with his designation of a constitution in 1867.

NEWSPAPERS AND JOURNALS

With the appearance in London of *The Daily Telegraph,* by mid-century even the lowest classes could afford a daily paper. The paper began publication in 1855, after the stamp tax was abolished. It was a leader in journalism and marketing, becoming the first penny daily newspaper in London, and it was thus very affordable for all levels of English society. It positioned itself between quality papers such as *The Times,* the *Chronicle,* and the *Post,* which typically appealed to the Victorian upper-middle classes, and the mass-circulation Sunday papers that catered to the lower classes and built their popularity on thrilling reports and fiction. Although the *Telegraph* also depended on sensational crime and personal stories for its popularity, it built its circulation on a new type of reporting, that of human interest. It soon gained a large following as a family newspaper so that within a few years it surpassed *The Times* in circulation and had twice the readers of the more established "quality" paper.

There was an increase in the diversity and number of venues where readers could access publications such as books and newspapers. Earlier in the century, subscription libraries had been popular with middle-class readers and lasted until mid-century, when books became cheap enough so that families could stock their own libraries. Religious groups and mechanics' institutes offered working-class families both reading instruction and access to their institutional libraries. As printing technologies improved, publishers were able to make the formats of their publications more attractive. Not only books but newspapers and magazines became more profusely illustrated to extend their appeal to a greater range of readers.

Among these publications, *Punch* became a landmark illustrated weekly that combined visual appeal, shrewd wit, and timely commentary on issues of the day. It was founded by John Mayhew, a celebrated Victorian author, who enlisted the support of Mark Lemon and Joseph Stirling Coyne to become the paper's first editors. *Punch* was modeled along the lines of Philipon's Paris publication *Le Charivari.* Among the famous writers for *Punch* were Mayhew, Thackeray, and Hood, who were associated with its iconoclastic and humanitarian attitudes. Cartoons and satirical drawings were the mainstay of *Punch,* and a number of influential illustrators filled the magazines with memorable images of the British Lion, John Bull, Father Time, and countless Englishmen and -women depicted as representative, comic types. Even Queen Victoria herself was included in the cartoons, albeit in a somewhat dignified manner. Some of the more famous illustrators included Richard Doyle, John Leech, Hablot Browne (best known as "Phiz," the illustrator of numerous novels by Charles Dickens), and Sir John Tenniel (renowned for his illustrations to Lewis Carroll's *Alice* books.) As an affordable paper whose graphic material appealed to many levels of English society, *Punch* both reflected and shaped the views of Victorians toward their capital city, their nation in its domestic and foreign character, and their fashions, family lives, manners, occupations, and beliefs.

By 1830 the popularity of Romantic works had begun to create a growing market for all types of reading matter—books, journals, and newspapers. The rate of literacy in France had been improving since the regime of Napoleon I, who had introduced educational reforms. The surge of growth in newspapers gave a strong impetus to the democratization of the press throughout the country; daily and weekly papers became a cheap and rapid channel of disseminating news and opinions, keeping French people from every social rank abreast of current events, ideas, and popular trends. Books and other print formats were widely available in subscription libraries (*cabinets de lecture*) or as cheap street literature. Journals and newspapers had their various constituencies, such as fashionable Paris readers, various scholarly circles, and the mass popular market.

The illustrated satirical paper, *Le Charivari* (Paris: 1832–1937), was a particular favorite of the French middle class for its bold lampooning of well-known personalities, such as corrupt politicians or other rogues who had alienated the public. Founded by the publisher Charles Philipon in 1832, it was notorious for its subversive treatment of life under France's July Monarchy and Second Empire; however it was less political than its rivals, such as the radical paper *La Caricature*. When the French government banned political caricature in 1835, *Charivari* began publishing satires of everyday life. The paper featured material that ruthlessly exposed political corruption and social opportunism, and it was probably best-known for featuring the caricatures of Daumier. The artist's "Robert Macaire" series lampooned the foibles of France's middle class through the fictional character Macaire, who—with his toadyism, greed, dishonesty, and social pretensions—embodied the worst tendencies of the *nouveaux riches.* Daumier also mocked the country's national leaders, especially the "bourgeois monarch," Louis-Philippe, whose stupidity and large girth were embodied in Daumier's caricature of him as a pear. The leader henceforth had to suffer the French public's ridiculous and ignominious designation of himself as "la Poire" (the Pear). *Charivari* was also well-known outside France, especially in England, where it had imitators such as *Punch.*

CHILDREN'S TEXTS

Reforms in education laws not only improved literacy rates at all class levels, but also expanded the diversity of the English reading audience, so that women and children readers became new marketing targets for British publishers. Children's books of a didactic and moral nature had been profitable for publishers such as John Newbery since the mid-eighteenth century. As the mass audience began to demand more entertainment in their reading matter, nineteenth-century publishers began to produce juvenile books and periodicals that increasingly appealed to the child's imagination, both in their fantastic subject matter and through their lavishly illustrated formats. With the 1865 publication of Lewis Carroll's much-beloved *Alice's Adventures in Wonderland* and its 1871 sequel, *Through the Looking Glass,* the golden age of fantasy literature for children reached its full flower in the Victorian era.

Germany's rapid industrialization and economic growth were linked to advances in education and huge improvements in literacy. As technology-based industries and factories became more crucial for commercial growth, reforms of the German school system were introduced at all levels. Child-centered learning had been pioneered in the 1830s by Friedrich Froëbel, who had developed his prototype of the German kindergarten, and German manufacturers and publishers supported the new focus on juvenile interests by manufacturing toys and books that especially appealed to the child's imagination. More books were published that matched children's reading abilities and that could comprehend the child's psychological state of mind. Heinrich Hoffmann's *Struwwelpeter* (*Slovenly Peter,* 1845), written originally as a collection of didactic cautionary tales about the consequences of naughty juvenile antics, actually became a popular classic because of its quirky stories and wild illustrations of grotesquely exaggerated punishments. It ended up glamorizing badly behaved children and thus, ironically, became a source of entertainment and humor for children.

SCIENTIFIC TEXTS

In 1859, after careful consideration, Charles Darwin, an English naturalist, published what many called the most important and influential work of the century: a scientific treatise entitled *On the Origin of Species by Means of Natural Selection.* Darwin and Alfred R. Wallace, another famous naturalist, arrived at similar theoretical ideas on evolution at about the same time. The first edition of Darwin's book, around 1,250 copies, sold out on the first day, a stupendous publishing event at the time. Darwin proposed that because offspring can vary from parents and, because nature tolerates only the "survival of the fittest," the principle of natural selection explains the evolution of a high species from a low one.

In the nineteenth century, a significant corollary of Darwinism was Social Darwinism, which advocated the notion that the doctrine of physical science should be utilized not just for animal history, but, with a change of form, could be applied to human history. Therefore a scientific idea could support the notion that those nations that are strongest should prevail over the "weaker" nations, and that in certain tendencies the strongest tended to be the best. This idea was highly controversial because it violated Christian belief in the divine creation of humanity and the uniqueness of human attributes. It was highly influential in Victorian culture because it was used to support many different, often opposing, political and moral positions that were debated in the press and by many Victorian authors. The work set off a firestorm of opposition and would collapse some of the most cherished cultural, religious, and scientific beliefs both in the Victorian world and throughout nineteenth-century Europe.

PHILOSOPHICAL TEXTS

By mid-century and the beginning of the Second Empire, as more authors followed the precepts of the movement of realism in their writing, both reviewers and the members of France's predominantly bourgeois mass reading public became uneasy with what they saw as a moral trespass in the new mode of literature. Some of the conservative reaction to the perceived immorality in texts of this period sprang from the cultural shockwaves produced during this era by provocative new concepts. Some of these controversial ideas appeared in the recently published texts of social philosopher, Auguste Comte, whose treatise, *Course in Positive Philosophy* (1830–1842), proposed the exclusion of religion from the study of human problems. His work was instrumental in establishing and spreading the philosophical system of positivism throughout Europe, Britain, and abroad. His work outlines the development of human knowledge of the world in three stages, progressing from a religious stage, whereby phenomena are explained as actions of supernatural forces; to the metaphysical stage, during which people attribute such effects to abstract but poorly understood causes; and finally to a scientific phase, when people gain positive knowledge and understanding of natural events through observation and experimentation, ceasing to speculate about the ultimate causes of phenomena and seeking instead simply to make use of them. Comte proposed that the sciences must free themselves of nonrational concerns. Thus positivism denies the validity of any way of knowing other than the scientific and derives rules for human conduct from the scientific method. Comte's positivism was responsible for an intellectual sea-change in the later nineteenth century throughout the Western societies. His philosophical system helped to accomplish that era's movement from a social order based on religious faith to one grounded in rationalism and a scientific understanding of the world.

In line with the theme of controversy, Pierre-Joseph Proudhon's polemical book *On Property* (1840) also shocked middle-class readers with its vehement critique of capitalism and its advocacy of working-class interests. Such texts added fuel to the public outcry against literary works that many readers perceived had passed the borders of decency in their realistic portrayal of the problems of French society.

On the other hand, the works of the first wave of German Romantic writers, such as Novalis—and especially his lyrical work "Hymnen an die Nacht" ("Hymns to the Night," 1800)—were infused with the spiritualism, mysticism, and philosophical ideas that predominated in the German intellectual and cultural climate of political and social resistance so typical of this early period. Novalis, the pen name of Friedrich von Hardenberg, was a German novelist, philosopher, and poet and was most renowned as one of the founders of the first German Romantic movement, along with Ludwig Tieck and the Schlegel brothers, Friedrich and Wilhelm. Novalis's literary work and philosophical ideas about the nature of creativity and aesthetics simultaneously shaped and reflected the ideas and the spirit of the times; they were highly influential in intellectual and artistic circles throughout Germany and Europe. Novalis also became famous and influential for his mystical and intensely lyrical poetry, which is exemplified in his "Hymns to the Night," a lyrical piece consisting of six short hymnal poems, some of which are prose poems and some of which are written in rhyming verse. The work, which was first published in *Das Athenäum,* the leading journal of the early German Romantic movement, is Novalis's reckoning with death after the demise of both his brother and his betrothed, Sophie von Kühn. The poem focuses on the poet's lyrical reflections on love and especially on his attempt to contact his beloved Sophie, who has left the natural world for a higher realm. The work describes his journey from earth-bound existence to ethereal spirituality, which the poet learns can only be reached by those prepared to embrace darkness and death as positive values. The third part of the work describes a famous vision of Novalis at Sophie's grave, seeing her transformed into a kind of astral body. Symbolically, the scene signifies the elevation of the poet and his love into God's higher realm and specifically into Christ's company.

The central theme of the work is very much aligned with the major concepts of the early German Romantic school, the idea that Enlightenment thinking and scientific rationality have destroyed the sympathetic bond between the individual and nature, a link that once existed in the "golden age" of the human past. Also underlying much of the poet's anguish in the work over the loss of his love is the Romantic idea that language is an inadequate and finite medium, both to express the poet's true depth of feeling and to represent the infinite realm where he tries to contact his beloved. The poet argues that the ideal past world can be regained in the human mind by a great intellectual leap to a higher reality and by the replacement of mental habits of calculating rationality with greater feeling for the ineffable in all forms, symbolized by the motifs of dreams, shadows, and the subterranean—all aspects of the night. With his promulgation of a belief in the transforming powers of the subjective imagination and literature's ability to enrich, expand, and transform reality, Novalis exerted a huge influence on numerous generations of European and British writers throughout the nineteenth century and well into the twentieth century.

CONCLUSION

Britain and the countries of Europe entered the turn of the century having experienced both numerous advances and regressions in their quest for power and knowledge. The censorship imposed by repressive political regimes and the cultural restraints exercised by reactionary moral forces had been especially problematic for the expansive development of reading cultures within these nations. By way of contrast, new areas of scientific inquiry, more liberal social attitudes, stupendous economic growth, and numerous technological innovations all worked to open up the wider fields of knowledge and more enticing realms of creativity that print culture made available to its mass audiences for their enlightenment and enjoyment. Nonetheless, poised on the brink of the twentieth century, both the readers and writers of these societies were confronted by a question that would haunt their cultures for decades to come: would the wisdom that they had inherited from the intellectual and literary resources of their own century stand up to the challenges of the modern era that loomed ahead?

RECOMMENDED READING

Allen, James Smith. *In the Public Eye: a History of Reading in Modern France, 1800–1914*. Princeton, N.J.: Princeton University Press, 1991.
———. *Popular French Romanticism: Authors, Readers, and Books in the 19th Century*. Syracuse, N.Y.: Syracuse University Press, c. 1981.
Becker, George J., ed. *Documents of Modern Literary Realism*. Princeton, N.J.: Princeton University Press, 1967.
Berger, Stefan, ed. *A Companion to Nineteenth-Century Europe, 1789–1914*. Malden, MA: Blackwell Pub., 2006.
Blackbourn, David. *The Long Nineteenth Century: a History of Germany, 1780–1918*. New York: Oxford University Press, 1998.
Blanning, T.C.W., ed. *The Nineteenth Century: Europe, 1789–1914*. Oxford; New York: Oxford University Press, 2000.

Coward, David. *A History of French Literature: From Chanson de Geste to Cinema*. Oxford; Malden, MA: Blackwell Pub., 2002.

Cruickshank, John. *French Literature and its Background*. Vols. 4 & 5. London; New York: Oxford U.P., 1968–1970.

David, Deirdre, ed. *The Cambridge Companion to the Victorian Novel*. New York: Cambridge University Press, 2001.

Deane, Bradley. *The Making of the Victorian Novelist: Anxieties of Authorship in the Mass Market*. New York: Routledge, 2003.

Flint, Kate. *The Woman Reader, 1837–1914*. New York: Oxford University Press, 1993.

Hohendahl, Peter Uwe. *Building a National Literature: the Case of Germany, 1830–1870*. Translated by Renate Baron Franciscono. Ithaca: Cornell University Press, 1989.

Jordan, John O. and Robert L. Patten, eds. *Literature in the Marketplace: Nineteenth Century British Publishing and Reading Practices*. New York: Cambridge University Press, 1995.

Murray, Christopher John, ed. *Encyclopedia of the Romantic Era, 1760–1850*. 2 Vols. New York: Fitzroy Dearborn, 2004.

Raimond, Jean and J.R. Watson, eds. *A Handbook to English Romanticism*. New York: St. Martin's Press, 1992.

Vincent, David. *Literacy and Popular Culture: England, 1750–1914*. Cambridge: Cambridge University Press, 1989.

PRIMARY SOURCES

Balzac, Honoré de. *The Human Comedy and Other Short Novels* (originally published in French as *La Comédie humaine*, 1829–1848). BiblioBazaar, 2006.

Baudelaire, Charles. *Flowers of Evil* (originally published in French as *Fleurs du mal* 1857). Wesleyan, 2006.

Bronte, Charlotte. *Jane Eyre*. New York: Penguin Classics, 2006.

Bronte, Emily. *Wuthering Heights*. New York: Penguin Popular Classics, 2007.

Byron, Lord George Gordon. *Childe Harold's Pilgrimage*. BiblioBazaar, 2006.

Carlyle, Thomas. *Past and Present*. Teddington, U.K.: Echo Library, 2002.

Carroll, Lewis. *Alice's Adventures in Wonderland and Through the Looking Glass*. New York; Signet Classics, 2000.

Le Charivari. Paris: 1832–1937.

Chateaubriand, François René de. *The Genius of Christianity* (originally published in French as *Le Génie du Christianisme*, 1802). Translated by Charles I. Whitefish, MT: Kessinger Publishing, 2006.

Comte, Auguste. *Course in Positive Philosophy* (originally published in French as *Cours de philosophie positive*, 1830–42). Currently available as *Introduction to Positive Philosophy*. Indianapolis, IN: Hackett Pub Co Inc, 1988.

The Daily Telegraph. 1855–.

Darwin, Charles. *The Origin of Species by Means of Natural Selection*. Mineola, NY: Dover Publications, 2006.

Dickens, Charles. *Oliver Twist*. Mineola, NY: Dover Publications, 2002.

Dumas, Alexandre (père). *The Count of Monte Cristo* (originally published in French as *Le Comte de Monte-Cristo*, 1844–1845). New York: Modern Library Classics, 2002.

———. *The Three Musketeers* (originally published in French as *Les Trois Mousquetaires*, 1844). New York: Penguin Classics, 2007.

Eliot, George. *Middlemarch*. New York: Penguin Classics, 1994.

Flaubert, Gustave. *Madame Bovary*. New York: Penguin Classics, 2002.

Fontane, Theodor. *Effi Briest*. New York: Penguin Classics, 2001.

Gaskell, Elizabeth. *North and South*. New York: Penguin Classics, 1996.

Goethe, Johann Wolfgang von. *The Sorrows of Young Werther* (originally published in German as *Die Leiden des jungen Werther*, 1774). New York: Modern Library Classics, 2005.

Grimm, Jacob and Willhelm Grimm. *The Complete Grimm's Fairy Tales.* New York: Pantheon, 1974.

Hardy, Thomas. *Jude the Obscure.* New York: Penguin Classics, 1998.

———. *Tess of the D'Urbervilles.* New York: Penguin Classics, 2003.

Hauptmann, Gerhart. *The Weavers* (originally published in German as *Die Weber,* 1892). *Three Plays: The Weavers, Hannele, the Beaver Coat.* Translated by Horst Frenz. Long Grove, IL: Waveland Press, 1990.

Heine, Heinrich. *A Journey Through the Harz Mountains* (originally published in German as *Harzreise,* 1826). *The Harz Journey and Selected Prose.* Translated by Ritchie Robertson. New York: Penguin Classics, 2007.

Hoffmann, Ernst Theodor Amadeus. *Fantastic Pieces in the Manner of Callot* (originally published in German as *Fantasiestücke in Callots Manier,* 1814–1815). Not currently available in English.

Hoffmann, Heinrich. *Slovenly Peter* (originally published in German as *Struwwelpeter,* 1845). *Struwwelpeter in English Translation.* Mineola, NY: Dover Publications, 1995.

Hugo, Victor-Marie. "Hernani" (originally published in French as *Hernani,* 1830). *Victor Hugo: Four Plays-Hermani, Marion de Lorme, Lucrece Borgia and Ruy Blas.* Translated by Claude Schumacher. London: A&C Black, 2004.

Marx, Karl. *Capital* (originally published in German as *Das Kapital,* 1867). New York: Penguin Classics, 1993.

Marx, Karl and Friedrich Engels. *Communist Manifesto* (originally published in German as *Kommunistisches Manifest,* 1848). New York: Penguin Classics, 2002.

Mill, John Stuart. *On Liberty.* New York: Penguin Classics, 1982.

Novalis. *Hymns to the Night* (originally published in German as *Hymnen an die Nacht,* 1800). McPherson, 1988.

Punch, or The London Charivari 1841–1992; 1996–.

Rimbaud, Arthur. *A Season in Hell* (originally published in French as *Une Saison en enfer,* 1873). New York: Modern Library Classics, 2005.

Scott, Sir Walter. *Waverley.* New York: Penguin Popular Classics, 1994.

Staël, Madame de. *On Germany* (originally published in French as *De l'Allemagne,* 1810). Not currently available in English.

Sue, Eugène. *The Mysteries of Paris* (originally published in French as *Les Mystères de Paris,* 1842–43). IndyPublish.com, 2006.

Wordsworth, William and Samuel Taylor Coleridge. *Lyrical Ballads, with a Few Other Poems.* Dodo Press, 2007.

Zola, Émile. *The Rougon-Macquarts* (originally published in French as *Les Rougon-Macquart* 1871–93). Only available in French. *Les Rougon-Macquart (Oeuvres Completes, volume 4).* Paris: Cercle du Precieux, 1967.

CHAPTER 10

Modernism

Malin Lidström Brock

TIMELINE

1914–19	World War I
1917	The Russian Revolution
1918	The Weimar Republic is formed
1919	Treaty of Versailles
1921	British women gain the right to vote; the Anglo-Irish Treaty
1922	A fascist coup d'état takes place in Italy
1923–25	French and Belgian troops occupy the Ruhr
1929	The New York stock exchange crashes
1933	The Nazi Party comes to power in Germany
1934	The Union of Soviet Writers is founded
1936–38	The Spanish Civil War
1938	The Munich Agreement
1939–45	World War II
1941	United States joins the Allied Powers in World War II
1942	The Nazis set up extermination camps
1944	Allied troops land on the beaches of Normandy, France
1945	The Battle of Berlin; World War II ends

INTRODUCTION TO THE PERIOD

European history and experience between 1914 and 1945 were characterized by wars and revolutions. The assassination in Sarajevo of Archduke Franz Ferdinand, the future heir to the Austro-Hungarian throne, led to the outbreak of World War I. Various international alliances forced all the major European powers to become involved in the conflict. New inventions such as the machine gun, the tank and the U-boat contributed to unprecedented death tolls, which were increased by a world-wide influenza epidemic in 1918. More than fifty million people died as a direct or indirect result of the conflict. The war ended with the victory of the Entente Powers, led by France, Russia, the UK, Italy, and, later, the United States, over the Central Powers, which included the Austro-Hungarian, German, and Ottoman Empires.

Revolution in 1917 and an ensuing civil war prevented Russia from participating in the final stages of World War I. The civil war resulted in an implementation of communism as a form of state rule and the formation of the Union of Soviet Socialist Republics (USSR). Vladimir Ilyich Lenin became the Soviet Union's first head of government. He was succeeded by Josef Stalin, whose power over the Communist Party gradually increased to full control over the country and its people. Stalin's dictatorship lasted until his death in 1953. During the 1930s, he introduced nationwide programs to effectively industrialize and modernize the country. Stalin also initiated campaigns to repress political dissent. The result was the nation-wide creation of labor camps, in which millions of soviets lost their lives.

World War I transformed Europe politically, physically, socially, economically, and especially technologically. Politically, the German, Austro-Hungarian, and Ottoman Empires had disintegrated. Poland gained independence and Yugoslavia and Czechoslovakia emerged as entirely new nations. In Germany, a revolution in 1918 resulted in the forming of the Weimar Republic. The Anglo-Irish Treaty established Ireland as a dominion within the British Empire and brought an end to the Irish War of Independence. National, economic, and political unrest characterized the interwar years. A coup d'état in Italy gave power to the fascist leader Benito Mussolini. Another coup d'état initiated the Spanish Civil War. The war ended with the formation of an authoritarian regime governed by the fascist General Francisco Franco, who ruled Spain until his death in 1978.

Meanwhile, Germany found it increasingly difficult to pay its war debts. When payments ceased, French and Belgian armies occupied the Ruhr. This brought Germany's industrial production to a complete halt. The result was an economic inflation that was exacerbated by the crash of the New York stock exchange. The social and economic turbulence in Germany left the political field open for Adolf Hitler and the NSDAP, better known as the German Nazi Party. In 1933, Hitler became Chancellor of Germany. Shortly thereafter, he gave his party totalitarian powers and proclaimed himself Führer, or leader of the German Reich. In 1939, Hitler broke the Munich Agreement with the UK by invading Poland. In response, the British declared war on Germany, and World War II had begun.

The three major Axis Powers (Germany, Italy, and Japan) successfully fought the Allied Powers until 1941, when the United States joined the Allied forces. By then Germany, which had a secret nonaggression pact with the Soviet Union, had successfully invaded nearly all of Europe. The agreement with the Soviet Union came to an end in 1941, when German troops entered soviet territory. In 1944, Allied troops landed on the beaches of Normandy. One year later, the soviet army entered Berlin. The deadliest conflict in human history was finally over. The systematic genocide of Europe's Jewish population—later referred to as the Holocaust—and other targeted groups resulted in the organized deaths of millions of people, mainly in concentration camps. In total, more than sixty million people died as a result of the conflicts.

READING TRENDS AND PRACTICES

The violent events of the first half of the twentieth century were felt at all levels of society. These events also affected the production and consumption of books and other printed material. In larger numbers than ever before, people turned to newspapers, magazines, and various printed sources for information about current affairs. In 1914 a series of actions escalated to what soon became known as The Great War (and later World War I). In the war-diary *The Storm of Steel* (1920), German author Ernst Jünger described the general feeling of elation that immediately followed the war declaration.

The optimism among soldiers soon abated. On the European continent, battles were fought mainly in trenches and the war was recorded by participants on all sides. Extensive propaganda machines aimed to boost the morale of soldiers and to create fear among the civil population. To pass the time, soldiers turned to writing. Some of this writing ended up in so-called trench magazines, such as *The Wipers Times*, which were produced and printed on the front (1916–1918; "Wipers" referred to Ypres, a town on one of the main battlefronts in France). Writing also became a means to make sense of the fighting. It has been estimated that thousands of poems were written every day by soldiers and their relatives. British poet Rupert Brooke's collection *1914* (1916) contains some of the most famous poems from the period.

World War I ended in 1918. Peace between the Entente and Central powers was established with the *Treaty of Versailles* (1919). Meanwhile, writers struggled to make sense of the recent events. The war was treated satirically by Czech writer Jaroslav Hašek, while German author Erich Maria Remarques's novel *All Quiet on the Western Front* (1929) became a classic account of war's meaninglessness. In contrast, French author Marcel Proust produced a nostalgic account of life before the war in his seven-volume novel, *In Search of Lost Time* (also published in English as *Remembrance of Things Past*, 1913–1927).

The general intellectual climate was pessimistic. Several critiques of civilization appeared in the period between the two World Wars. In *The Decline of the West* (1918–1923), German mathematician Oswald Spengler argued that Western civilization was approaching its own destruction. The decline of civilization was also the subject of American poet T. S. Eliot's poem, *The Waste Land* (1922), and Czech author Karel Čapek's play *R.U.R.* (1921). The German journal *Die Weltbühne* (1905–1933) became an important forum for an emerging German pacifist movement. Meanwhile, Russian revolutionary Vladimir Ilyich Lenin blamed the war on the capitalist system and its rivalries over markets, goods, and investments. Lenin's *The April Theses* (1917) also provided the ideological groundwork for the Bolsheviks, who initiated the Russian revolution in 1917.

In the early period of the Soviet Union, writers such as soviet poet Vladimir Mayakovsky, who expressed sympathy with the Bolsheviks, experienced an unusual degree of artistic freedom. Yet, many members of the Communist Party viewed formal experimentation as typical of decadent, bourgeois art. In 1932 socialist realism, which purported to further the goals of socialism and communism, was proclaimed as the guiding principle for all writing. Two years later, the Union of Soviet Writers was founded. The aim of the union was to control the literary output of authors. Soviet newspapers, films, and radio focused on socialist achievements and the evils of capitalism. Writers who strayed from the instructions were severely punished, often by being sent to Stalin's labor camps. Some writers left the Soviet Union to live and work in exile. Others protested by writing and distributing their work secretly. One such author was Michail Bulgakov, the soviet author whose novel *The Master and Margarita* (1941) was not published in the Soviet Union until 1973.

The everyday life of women underwent drastic changes during the first half of the twentieth century. Due to a shortage of male workers, many women entered the workforce during and after World War I. Women in Norway and

World War I forced Europe into the modern world. After the horrors of the war, readers looked to art and literature to "make sense" of the new post-technological human condition.

Denmark had achieved suffrage in 1915. British women won the right to vote in 1921, in direct recognition of their contribution to the war effort. Many young women of the period cropped their hair and wore shorter skirts. Soviet diplomat and author Alexandra Kollontai advocated free love in her novels, while Scottish author Marie Carmichael Stopes campaigned for women's rights and became a pioneer in family planning through her controversial sex manual, *Married Love* (1918).

In the UK, the cookbook market had long been dominated by Victorian author Isabella Mary Beeton. British author Hilda Leyel's popular cookbook *The Gentle Art of Cookery* (1921) introduced the British to a lighter and more Continental type of cooking. British author Jan Struther began a popular series of newspaper columns in 1937, featuring a fictional housewife. The columns were later published in book form as *Mrs. Miniver* (1939).

The 1920s saw economic upswings punctuated by dramatic recessions. It was also a time of expansion, new developments, and changes in the class system. A new type of self-made man emerged, modeled after his American counterpart. British author John Galsworthy described the new business-man in novels such as *The Forsyte Saga* series. Etiquette books were produced to facilitate the social mobility of the middle class, which also favored middlebrow novels by British authors such as Mary Webb, Rosamund Lehmann, and Nancy Mitford. The middlebrow genre was parodied by British author Stella Gibbons in *Cold Comfort Farm* (1932), which became a bestseller in its own right. Meanwhile, British crime author Agatha Christie's books, such as the groundbreaking *The Murder of Roger Ackroyd* (1926), gained a world-wide audience. In Germany, concern about the new reading habits of women, teenagers, and the working class resulted in new legislation, which aimed to protect young people from the perceived indecency of so-called pulp fiction.

Throughout the first half of the twentieth century, children's literature typically communicated traditional values. French author Antoine de Saint-Exupéry had a background as a fighter pilot. This influenced his philosophical and idealistic children's book *The Little Prince* (1943). Series of novels aimed at young readers proliferated. Most series were clearly marketed for either boys or girls. However, the most prolific children's author of the era was British writer Enid Blyton, whose books appealed to both sexes. *Five on a Treasure Island* (1942) was the first in a popular mystery series by Blyton. In France and Belgium, comics magazines such as *Spirou Magazine* (1938–) became popular among young readers and teenagers.

Developments in science, philosophy, the social sciences, literature, and art mirrored a shift in the consciousness of European intellectuals. British author D. H. Lawrence's *Lady Chatterley's Lover* (1928) was banned in the UK and the United States because of its sexually explicit content. Members of the intellectual Bloomsbury group criticized the Victorian values of the previous generation. In the biography *Eminent Victorians* (1918), British author Lytton Strachey offered a satirical and irreverent view of its heroic subjects. Human sexuality also dominated the works of Austrian psychologist Sigmund Freud. *Beyond the Pleasure Principle* (1920) marked a turning point in Freud's psychoanalytic theory by its identification of the human death drive. In *The Archetypes and the Collective Unconscious* (1934–1954), Swiss psychiatrist Carl Gustav Jung presented an alternative to Freudian psychoanalysis, based on mythology and mysticism. German authors Hermann Hesse and Thomas Mann found inspiration for their novels in both Jungian and Freudian psychological theories. In *The Trial* (1925), Czech author Franz Kafka described a surreal bureaucratic state apparatus and its effects on the human psyche.

As Europe lit up after the Great War, authors and artists from all over the world flocked to the Continent's major capitals. France became a second home for many American writers, such as Ernest Hemingway and Gertrude Stein. A relatively stable German economy contributed to making Berlin the most culturally and intellectually sophisticated city of the decade, yet conservative critics referred to the German capital as decadent and socially disruptive. Brothels and nude ballets were very popular, and sensationalist and pornographic magazines flourished. German playwright Bertolt Brecht's musical theatre *The Threepenny Opera* (1928) became immensely popular. The play emphasized what many intellectuals saw as the hypocrisy of conventional morality in the face of working-class deprivation. In Vienna, Austrian playwright and critic Karl Kraus expressed a similar opinion in his newspaper *Die Fackel* (1899–1936), which targeted corruption, hypocrisy and all forms of brutality.

The New York stock exchange crash in 1929 initiated an alarming, world-wide economic downturn. It became known as the Great Depression and also affected Europe. The Depression contributed to the end of Berlin as Europe's intellectual capital and to the decline of the Weimar Republic. In *General Theory of Employment, Interest, and Money* (1936), influential British economist John Maynard Keynes offered a macroeconomic perspective on the events. Fierce conflicts, including strikes and lockouts, characterized the labor market between the wars.

The UK experienced unrest in its overseas colonies, particularly in India where Indian lawyer Mahatma Gandhi became the leader of the Indian Independence Movement. In her memoir *Out of Africa* (1937), Danish author Karen Blixen offered a personal perspective on changes in colonial life in Kenya. In Spain, violent struggles between Republicans and fascist Nationalists led to the outbreak of the Spanish Civil War in 1936. The so-called International Brigades, which consisted of American and European volunteers, fought on the side of the Republicans. In *Homage to Catalonia* (1938), British author George Orwell described his experiences as a volunteer in Spain. The war ended in 1939 with the victory of the fascists led by General Francisco Franco.

In 1933 Adolf Hitler, leader of the German Nazi Party (NSDAP), became Chancellor of Germany and officially banned a number of Jewish and left-wing German authors such as Thomas Mann, Sigmund Freud, and Bertolt Brecht. That same year, Nazi youth groups began burning books by authors they considered degenerate. Hitler had already described his political and ideological vision in *Mein Kampf* (1925–1926). In an attempt to appease the Nazis, British Prime Minister Neville Chamberlain signed *The Munich Agreement* (1938), which meant the surrender of an important part of Czechoslovakia to Germany.

The political rise of NSDAP caused many intellectuals to consider leaving Germany and Austria. In 1939 the Nazis occupied Poland. As a consequence, the UK declared war on Germany. The declaration resulted in a massive wave of emigration from continental Europe, mainly to the UK and the United States. This event became known as the Great Sea Change. Among those leaving for the United States was German physicist Albert Einstein, whose groundbreaking theories on relativity were published as papers in 1905 and later in book form as *Relativity: The Special and General Theory* (1917).

During the war newspapers, publishers, and radio channels in the occupied areas were forced to submit to strict censorship, or shut down. Possession of foreign or subversive reading was severely punished. Despite the dangers, a small group of university students in Munich, calling itself the *White Rose*, secretly wrote, printed, and distributed a total of six leaflets in which they criticized Hitler and the Nazis. The group was discovered and its founding members executed. Switzerland, Portugal, and Sweden remained neutral during the war. However, in the allegorical novel *Ride This Night!* (1941), Swedish author and critic Vilhelm Moberg protested against what he saw as the Swedish government's complacency toward German demands.

The Nazis ruled by terror and fear. Millions of people from all over Europe were sent to German-controlled labor and extermination camps. The impact of World War II on European intellectual life was profound. As the war ended, members of the so-called Frankfurt School, a loosely associated group of European thinkers, philosophized about the failure of Enlightenment beliefs, exemplified most horrifically by the Holocaust. French Algerian author Albert Camus described human existence as absurd, while French author and philosopher Jean-

Paul Sartre's treatise *Being and Nothingness* (1943) dealt with questions regarding human freedom.

European reading habits in the first half of the twentieth century were affected positively by an increase in state education and higher living standards. Specialization among publishers became more frequent, especially in areas such as educational books. Wars and economic recessions resulted in temporary reductions in sales, but also created a huge demand for both instructive and light reading. Apart from censorship, the most serious threat for publishers in Europe was the shortage of paper during war time. In many countries, book clubs were formed to satisfy readers' demands for affordable reading material. Members undertook to regularly buy, at a reduced price, books selected by the club. Book tokens, which could be exchanged for books in selected book stores, also appeared in the interwar years. Public and commercial libraries were very popular. In 1938, the British *Booklovers' Library*, which was situated in Boots Chemist stores, had thirty-eight million borrowings and over one million subscribers during World War II. The century also saw the emergence of a popular mass culture, which was disseminated through books, newspapers, and magazines, and facilitated by technical advances in film, radio, and television.

CREATIVE TEXTS

The novel entered a highly experimental period in the first half of the twentieth century, as authors reacted to the dramatic world events that took place around them. General readers often found modernist novels demanding both in form and content. French author Marcel Proust's seven-volume series of novels *In Search of Lost Time* (1913–1927, also published as *Remembrance of Things Past*), deals with a recapture of an idyllic past before World War I. The most famous passage in the novel describes how the narrator's memory of childhood is triggered by biting into a Madeleine, a shell-shaped biscuit. The memories are recounted in a style referred to as "stream-of-consciousness," an interior monologue that traces the character's fragmented thoughts and feelings. Other practitioners of this style, which is typical of modernist writing, include Irish author James Joyce and British author Virginia Woolf. *In Search of Lost Time* had a profound influence on subsequent experimental writing, although readers were sometimes put off by its more than three thousand pages. American scholar Harold Bloom has called Proust's work the best example of the modernist novel. Several stage and film adaptations have appeared, among them the films *Swann in Love* (1984), starring Jeremy Irons, and *Time Regained* (1999). References to the novel appear in Italian author Umberto Eco's novel *Foucault's Pendulum* (1988). *In Search of Lost Time* has also been parodied in a *Monthy Python's Flying Circus* sketch called "The All-England Summarise Proust Competition," where competitors are asked to summarize the seven books in fifteen seconds.

Apart from memory, other themes explored in Proust's novel are art, music, and homosexuality. Sexuality is also a prominent topic in British author D. H. Lawrence's novel *Lady Chatterley's Lover* (1928), which describes the taboo relationship between a frustrated, married, upper-class woman and the local gamekeeper. The novel, which includes several explicit sex scenes, also challenged the notion of the separation between the classes. *Lady Chatterley's Lover* was privately printed in Florence in 1928. The novel was not published in the United States until 1959 and appeared in the UK in 1960, where it sold two hundred thousand copies on its first day of publication. Penguin Books, the novel's publisher, went on trial under the British Obscene Publications Act of 1959, but was found not guilty. The verdict meant greater freedom for the publication of sexually explicit material in the UK, and *Lady Chatterley's Lover* became a symbol for the sexual revolution of the 1960s. Other twentieth-century novels that were suppressed because of their sexual content include Joyce's *Ulysses* (1922) and British author Radclyffe Hall's *Well of Loneliness* (1928). The Penguin trial is mentioned in British poet Philip Larkin's poem "Annus Mirabilis." The novel has been dramatized on stage and several film adaptations have appeared. In 2006, French director Pascale Farran filmed a French-language version of "John Thomas and Lady Jane," Lawrence's second version of the Chatterley story.

In the Soviet Union, authors were also censored, mainly for failing to adhere to the socialist realism stipulated by the state. Soviet author Michail Bulgakov's novel *The Master and Margarita* (1940–1941) takes place in Moscow and Jerusalem. It includes characters such as Satan, a failed author known as the Master, and his lover, Margarita. The story is defined by so-called magic realism, where supernatural elements appear in an otherwise realistic story. Bulgakov's novel is widely considered a satire of the Soviet Union, including the effects of its literary bureaucracy on art. Themes include the responsibility of truth and the need for spiritual freedom in a totalitarian state. *The Master and Margarita* was completed by Bulgakov's wife after the author died in 1940. The first unabridged version was published in the Soviet Union in 1973. The book is sometimes described as the greatest Russian novel of the twentieth century. It has provided inspiration for British author Salman Rushdie's novel *The Satanic Verses* (1988), the Rolling Stones' song "Sympathy for the Devil" and the film *The Rocky Horror Picture Show*. An opera based on the book appeared in 1989. *The Master and Margarita* has also been filmed numerous times and several adaptations have appeared on stage.

Like Bulgakov's characters, the main protagonist in Czech author Franz Kafka's novel *The Trial* (1925) cannot accept reality as it is presented to him. *The Trial's* nightmare vision of modern society can be interpreted as an effect of the shock and horror felt by Europeans after World War I. In Kafka's novel, these feelings express themselves as an absurd and surreal chain of events that begins with the arrest of the main character, Josef K, for reasons that no one cares to explain to him. The novel reads like a mystery, but unlike traditional mysteries, it remains unsolved. As the novel progresses, it becomes clear that Josef K is no longer in control of his fate. He is sentenced to death without ever being told of the charges leading to his execution. French philosopher Jean-Paul Sartre has compared Josef K's feelings to that of a Jew in a world defined by anti-Semitism. Colombian scholar Guillermo Sánchez Trujillo has suggested that Kafka based much of his book on Russian author Fyodor Dostoyevsky's novel *Crime and Punishment* (1866). *The Trial* has come to symbolize the small man's futile struggle against an absurd bureaucracy and modern man's sense of being trapped by events beyond his comprehension. References to *The Trial* are made in French author Albert Camus's novel *The Plague* (1947). Several films based on the novel have appeared. The Woody Allen film *Shadows and Fog* (1992) is loosely based on the book.

Alienation and anxiety are also apparent in the more lighthearted literature of the era. In British author Stella Gibbons's novel *Cold Comfort Farm* (1932), social anxiety is expressed in the comic meeting between the upper-middle-class flapper Flora and her rural relatives. Gibbons's novel both satirizes and constitutes an example of the so-called middlebrow novel, aimed primarily at a middle-class, female readership. Marked by contradictions, *Cold Comfort Farm* communicates snobbism and bohemianism, as well as daring and conventionality, through its plot. The pretty, urbane heroine Flora visits distant relatives in the country side, and proceeds to solve each family member's personal problem through her level-headed common sense. The book shares its nostalgia for a largely imaginary aristocratic past with popular novels by British authors such as Mary Webb and Nancy Mitford. The middlebrow novel dominated the British female book market between the 1920s and the 1950s, and renegotiated questions regarding gender, class, and home in and through its plot. *Cold Comfort Farm* has been filmed for television twice and was turned into a stage play in 1992.

The economic crisis of the 1930s, the rise of fascism, and the Spanish Civil War coincided with a return to a more serious mode in fiction. German author Erich Maria Remarques's *All Quiet on the Western Front* (1929) has been called the most representative novel dealing with World War I. The title echoes the understated, brief style that characterized official communiqués from the front. *All Quiet on the Western Front* describes German soldier Paul Bäumer's gradual realization that the war is pointless. Unlike previously romanticized and heroic accounts of war, Remarques focuses on the monotony and brutality of the fighting, and the role chance plays in events. The story realistically describes the use of poison gas, machine guns and tanks, which facilitated the impersonal killing. Nature offers the only temporary relief from the horror. The book caused a great deal of controversy on its publication. The Nazis considered the author unpatriotic and copies of the book were burnt publicly. As a consequence, Remarques emigrated to Switzerland and later to the United States. Unlike other World War I books that have become popular among English-speaking readers, *All Quiet on the Western Front* deals uniquely with the experience of German soldiers. The novel's title has become a catch-phrase for a lack of action during war. The 1930 film adaptation of *All Quiet on the Western Front* received Academy Awards for Best picture and Best Director. A play based on the book appeared on stage in 2006.

During World War II, novels sometimes functioned as veiled expressions of political opinion. Swedish author and critic Vilhelm Moberg's novel *Ride This Night!* (1941) was written in response to the German invasion of Denmark and Norway. The allegorical story takes place in seventeenth-century Sweden. It focuses on a group of local farmers who must accept life under the rule of the foreign invaders and traces their response to the situation. *Ride This Night!* illustrates a belief in the futility of individual courage and the need for joint action against the powers of evil. After the blitzkrieg attack and invasion of Sweden's Scandinavian neighbors, Moberg became increasingly critical of what he saw as the Swedish government's acquiescence to Nazi demands. In particular, he criticized the government's decision to allow the transportation through Sweden of German troops to occupied Norway and for providing the Germans with Swedish iron ore. As a consequence, the book was banned in Nazi Germany. Through *Ride This Night!* Moberg became a crusader for human rights in the eyes of his fellow countrymen and a symbol of grassroots-resistance against the Nazis. In 1942, the dramatic adaptation of the novel premiered. The same year, a popular film based on the book also appeared.

The 1930s is often referred to as the golden age of British crime writing. The most popular mystery writer was British author Agatha Christie, whose book *The Murder of Roger Ackroyd* (1926) has a novel plot twist that had a significant impact on the genre of mystery writing. The book concerns two murders and is narrated by a Dr. Sheppard, but includes Christie's famous Belgian detective, Hercule Poirot. Dr. Sheppard's sister also plays a part in events, which later inspired Christie to create her other famous amateur detective, Miss Jane

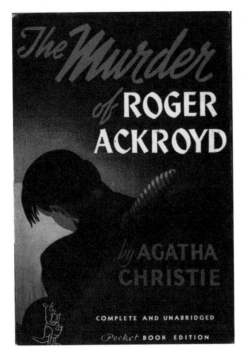

Agatha Christie's first mystery novel, *The Murder of Roger Ackroyd*, introduced readers to the modern genre and turned Christie into one of the most widely read authors of all time. [Courtesy of numberstumper]

Marple. Christie's mysteries share many of their characteristics with the female middlebrow novel. Typically, her books are set in large country houses or quiet villages among the upper-middle-classes, although Christie also drew inspiration from her travels in the Middle East, where some of her stories take place. Unlike the American hardboiled detective fiction, which relied on action and characterization, Christie's books are puzzle mysteries with logical plotting and tidy solutions. Other mystery writers in the same tradition include British authors Dorothy L. Sayers and Margery Allingham. Christie has been listed as the best-selling fiction author of all time; it is estimated that her work has sold a billion copies in English, and another billion in more than forty-five languages. She wrote over eighty novels and more than a dozen plays, including *The Mousetrap*, which opened in London in 1952. It is now the longest continuously running play in theatrical history. Christie's books have also been adapted numerous times for film and television.

Much of the poetry produced in the first years of World War I aimed to convince readers that the fighting had a noble purpose. British poet Rupert Brooke became known for his idealistic war sonnets, collected in *1914 & Other Poems* (1916). These poems deal primarily with heroic death. Brooke's short life added to his reputation as a symbol of his generation. The opening lines from the patriotic poem "The Soldier," which describes a young soldier dead in a foreign field, are still familiar to most British people. Other war poets also idealized the war effort. Canadian poet John McRae's poem "In Flanders Field" may be as well-known as Brooke's poems about World War I. Others, such as British poet Wilfred Owen in the poem "Dulce Et Decoum Est," made ironic use of the heroic rhetoric to describe the horrors of the war. After the war, most European poets found it difficult to glorify warfare in their writing.

In 1919, French poet Paul Valéry drew attention to the absence of any fixed reference system for living and thinking after World War I. Moreover, American T.S. Eliot, who lived and wrote mainly in the UK, belonged to a group of modernist literary giants who came to fame in an age characterized by anxiety about existence, culture, and destiny. His long poem *The Waste Land* (1922) both exemplifies and articulates a fragmentary state of human existence. Although the poem lacks a narrative structure, it still manages to convey both the cultural legacy of modern poetry and its decline. Much of the text consists of literary allusions to earlier literature, in both form and content. The poem contains several voices, yet the accompanying footnotes suggest one central consciousness. *The Waste Land* is dedicated to American poet Ezra Pound, who helped revise the poem before publication. It is generally considered the most famous modernist poem and many of its phrases have become familiar even to those who have not read it. These include the poem's opening line: "April is the cruelest month." Eliot's poem has inspired, among others, American authors Stephen King and Tim Powers. The poem's closing line is quoted at the end of the dystopian science fiction film *The Children of Men* (2006).

In the first half of the twentieth century, technology became an increasingly important part of daily life. In Czech author and playwright Karel Čapek's drama *R.U.R.* (*Rossum's Universal Robots*, 1921), the ethics and possibly nightmarish future of such dependence was investigated. The play takes place in a robot factory and describes a world-wide robot revolt, which results in the extinction of humankind, with the exception of one man. He is assigned to create new robots, but fails in his task. The play ends on a positive note, as two robots fall in love. Through the success of the play in both the UK and the United States, the word "robot" entered the English language. Čapek is seen as the forerunner of so-called hardcore science fiction, which deals with technology rather than space travel. His play provided inspiration for later science fiction, such as British author Aldous Huxley's novel *Brave New World* (1932) and American author Isaac Asimov's short story collection *I, Robot* (1950).

An overtly political theatre also developed in Europe at this time, expressed in the work and theories developed by German playwright Bertolt Brecht. His musical play *The Threepenny Opera* (1928) was inspired by a 1728 satiric opera by English poet John Gay. Brecht's play begins with the marriage between the anti-heroic thief, Mack the Knife, and Polly Peachum. It is followed by Mack's arrest and impending hanging, which is interrupted by the Queen at the last minute. The play is a socialist critique of contemporary society and invites the audience to ask who the real criminals in society are. *The Threepenny Opera* relies on a theatrical device known as *Verfremdungseffekt*. This is an alienation technique developed by Brecht that aims to distance the audience from responding emotionally to the performance. Instead, the audience is meant to be made aware that they are watching a play. Characters in Brecht's plays typically represent opposing sides of an argument on which the audience is invited to reflect. In *The Threepenny Opera*, projections, unnatural stage lighting, and the abrupt use of song are used to create the desired effect. Later playwrights, but also filmmakers such as Lars von Trier, Rainer Maria Fassbinder and Ingmar Bergman, made use of Brecht's

---

Futurist Poetry

Futurism was an international arts movement, whose adherents expressed a fascination with speed, technology, and violence. The first futurist manifesto, written by Italian poet and editor Filippo Tommaso Marinetti, was published in the French newspaper *Le Figaro* in 1909. Futurist poets aimed to increase the expressivity of language through a variety of visual and sonic techniques. Central to futurism's philosophy was the destruction of past culture and conventions, which would allow new forms of art, more suitable to modern life. By composing poems with nonsense words in various typefaces positioned freely across the page, Marinetti hoped to increase the expressivity of language and create a more primitive, and thereby more authentic, form of communication. Other futurist writers included British poet Mina Loy, Italian poet Aldo Palazzaschi, and Russian poet Vladimir Mayakovsky. In the period between the two World Wars, the aesthetic message of the movement blended with the political message of Italian fascism and soviet communism. Increasingly, futurists came to believe that all manifestations of the old society had to be overthrown. Although futurist poetry continued to flourish in Italy, in the Soviet Union it was later condemned as bourgeois and replaced by socialist realism. In Germany, Hitler viewed futurism as a degenerate art form.

Penguin Paperbacks

In 1935, the British publicist Allen Lane launched the first Penguin paperbacks, a format already existing on the European continent. The paperback format quickly revolutionized the British and American book businesses. Within twelve months, Penguin had sold over three million books. Early paperbacks included works by American author Ernest Hemingway, French biographer André Maurois, and British mystery author Agatha Christie. Genre was indicated by the book cover's color. Lane also came up with the idea of book sales outside traditional bookshops, in places such as railway stations and chain stores. In 1937 the first Penguincubator, a book-dispensing machine, was introduced at Charring Cross station in London. Shortly before World War II, books that discussed the European conflict achieved record-breaking sales. During the war, Penguin also started the Armed Forces Book Club, which brought books to soldiers in combat. Over the years, Penguin has published controversial titles, such as *Lady Chatterley's Lover* (1960), *The Satanic Verses* (1988), and *Stupid White Men* (2002). Throughout the latter half of the twentieth century, the company continued to expand, mainly through new imprints and the acquisition of smaller publishing companies such as Frederick Warne.

Verfremdungseffekt in their work. *The Threepenny Opera* was a success when it premiered in Berlin in 1920. Within four years, it saw over 130 productions all over Europe. The score was written by German composer Kurt Weill. The opening song was translated into English as "Mack the Knife" and became a swing standard made famous by American big band performer Bobby Darin. The play has also been filmed and turned into at least seven off-Broadway productions.

CHILDREN'S AND YOUNG ADULT TEXTS

Between the two wars, comics—or *bandes désinées*, as they are called in Francophone countries—first gained popularity in Europe. These comics were typically published in newspapers, but also appeared as monthly magazines. The Belgian weekly comics magazine *Spirou Magazine* (1938–) became one of the most popular and long-lasting. Originally, the magazine included only two home-produced series and half a dozen American comics, such as "Superman" and "Red Ryder." During World War II, the importation of American comics was no longer possible, which gave more French and Belgian artists the opportunity to venture into the business. In 1943, a publication stop was decreed by the occupying Germans, which was not lifted until the end of World War II. As the publication of *Spirou Magazine* resumed in 1946, a host of new locally produced series was introduced to its pages. Over the years, now-famous comics such as *Spirou and Fantasio, Lucky Luke, Gaston,* and *Les Schtroumpfs* (*The Smurfs* in the United States) made their first appearance in the magazine. Together with *Tintin* (1946), *Spirou Magazine* became one of the most successful magazines after the war. It is still published in magazine form, whereas the majority of other existing comics are published in albums of about forty to fifty pages. Unlike the word *comics*, the name *bandes désinées* or BD—which is French for "drawn strips"—does not specify content, and subject matter can sometimes be quite serious. However, the magazine's readers consist mainly of children and adolescents. Characters from the comics, such as Marsipulami from *Spirou and Fantasio*, have reappeared in their own series, television cartoons, and videogames.

Serialized novels were also popular among young readers. The most prolific children's author of the century was British author Enid Blyton, whose eight hundred books have sold more than four hundred million copies. This makes her the fifth-most popular author in the world. One of her most-loved mystery series of twenty-one books begins with *Five on a Treasure Island* (1942). The *Famous Five* books describe the adventures of four children and a dog. The children regularly stumble upon and solve mysteries in the English countryside when they are on holiday from their respective boarding schools. Picnics, bicycle trips, smugglers, and secret passages feature frequently in the stories. Blyton's books communicate traditional values through their stories, and not surprisingly, late-twentieth-century critics have referred to her books as sexist and conservative. Blyton stopped writing the series in 1963, but more books in the series have been written by other authors in both French and German. The books were instantly popular and remain so today, particularly in the UK, Australia, New Zealand, France, and India.

Unlike Blyton, French aviator and author Antoine de Saint-Exupéry's children's book *The Little Prince* (1943) offers an idealistic, yet also quite critical, account of human behavior. The book's narrator, who appears to be Saint-Exupéry himself, ends up stranded in the desert with his plane, where he meets a young extra-terrestrial prince. In their conversations, the prince presents his view of the world, which is that of a child, by contrasting it with six grown-up characters that he has met in space. The glorification of the prince's childlike innocence has been interpreted as a commentary on what Saint-Exupéry viewed as the world's spiritual decay. Similarities between the prince and the narrator suggest that the book is an allegorical description of introspection, wherein two halves of the same person meet and learn from each other. The book was written during World War II, but there are no direct references to the war. Instead, *The Little Prince* aims for a more general, apolitical analysis of the world. The book became immediately popular upon publication and is one of the most widely translated French books of the twentieth century. It has sold more than fifty million copies worldwide and been turned into an animated series.

BIOGRAPHICAL AND AUTOBIOGRAPHICAL TEXTS

Biography lost much of its scientific status in the twentieth century, as authors began to question its objectivity. No longer perceived as a branch of history, critics began to pay more attention to the genre's literary qualities. British author and biographer Lytton Strachey's popular group biography *Eminent Victorians* (1918) portrayed iconic Victorians such as Florence Nightingale and General Gordon with irony and irreverence. Strachey's satirical treatment of his subjects provided a refreshing perspective on a generation that had previously been treated with somber reverence. The biography revived and renewed the genre as a whole through its innovative style, which brought attention to the biographer as a defining presence in the story. Indirectly, it criticized the idealizing formula of biographical writing of the previous century.

Like biography, autobiography allowed writers to adopt a personal perspective on history and current events. *The Storm of Steel* (1920) is based on German soldier Ernst Jünger's diary, written during World War I. The book describes Jünger's experiences of fighting against the French and English, and is often considered a glorification of warfare. As a young man, Jünger enlisted on the day Germany declared war, and he participated in some of the bloodiest battles of modern time, among them the battles at Somme, Cambrais, and Passchendaele. Jünger does not analyze the war or ponder its outcome. Instead, he presents a day-by-day account of the often confusing and uncertain experiences and duties of a German infantryman. The 1924 revision of the memoirs was influenced by Jünger's nationalism.

Later revisions played down the more blood-thirsty aspects of the text. Adolf Hitler famously received a signed copy of the book. Even though Jünger initially welcomed Hitler's ascent to power, he never became a member of the Nazi Party and ended up distancing himself from Nazism. The memoirs have been admired by writers such as Argentinean author Jorge Luis Borges, German playwright Bertolt Brecht, and French author André Gide, who considered *The Storm of Steel* the most honest war book he had ever read.

War is also the subject of *Homage to Catalonia* (1938), British author and journalist George Orwell's account of his experience of the Spanish Civil War. Orwell went to Spain as a volunteer for the republican side of the conflict. After being seriously wounded in 1937, he returned to the UK. There he wrote *Homage to Catalonia*, which describes his experiences but also explains the defeat of the socialist republicans and the nationalist victory. In particular, Orwell draws attention to the infighting among the various socialist, Communist, and anarchist groups that made up the Republican side and contributed to their losses. Although the book sold few copies when first published, it has since been described as the greatest literary work written on the Spanish Civil War in any language. Other writers who reported and wrote about the war include American authors Martha Gellhorn, Ernest Hemingway, and John Dos Passos. Ken Loach's film *Land and Freedom,* which appeared in 1995, closely resembles Orwell's book.

War plays a more peripheral role in *Out of Africa* (1937), Danish author Karen Blixen's memoir of her life as a coffee farmer in Kenya between 1914 and 1931. Together with her largely absent husband, Blixen was one of many Europeans who settled in Kenya as farmers. By 1930, nearly thirty thousand white farmers lived in the area, which was already home to the Kikuyu tribe, most of whom lived as itinerant farmers on white settlers' estates. Blixen's description of life in Africa resembles a utopian ideal, which is spoiled by war, financial difficulties, and the tragic death of her lover, British adventurer Denys Finch-Hatton. The book ends with her leaving Kenya, after helping to relocate the native Kikuyu who live on her estate. The aristocratic Blixen compares the Kikuyu's dignified behavior with that of European nobility, behavior that she finds lacking among the mainly middle-class settlers of Kenya. She identifies this lack of manners as the main reason for the troubles that occur in the colony. Blixen wrote *Out of Africa* in both English and Danish. It was published under her pen name, Isak Dinesen, and became an instant best-seller. At the time of her death in 1962, she was the best known Danish author of the twentieth century. In 1985, *Out of Africa* was made into a movie starring Meryl Streep, who won an Academy Award as Best Actress for her role as Blixen.

DOMESTIC TEXTS

In the early years of the twentieth century, lack of information about sexuality meant that couples had little or no control over their fertility and would sometimes end up in unconsummated marriages. The personal experience of such a marriage led British doctor Marie Carmichael Stopes to write her controversial book *Married Love* (1918). The book celebrates marriage and argues that it should be an equal relationship between husband and wife. In particular, the book draws attention to women's sexuality and sexual desire. Sexual intercourse is described in detail, which shocked some contemporary readers.

The church, the press, and many male doctors called the book obscene and immoral. Yet, *Married Love* was an immediate success among general readers. The book sold two thousand copies in just two weeks and had to be reprinted six times during its first year of publication. *Married Love* made only a brief mention of contraception, but the subject prompted so many letter inquiries that Stopes later wrote a second book on birth control. In 1921, she opened the first family planning clinic in the UK. The clinic offered free service to married women and collected data on various forms of contraception. From the 1920s onward, more clinics opened throughout the country. These clinics ended up having a great impact on private life in the twentieth century. The average number of children in British families decreased from six, during the Victorian period, to two after the 1920s.

In the years after World War I, people were eager to enjoy life. The idea that food could be pleasurable grew in a culture that was released from the restrictions of the war years. At the same time, servants were gradually disappearing from upper-middle-class households. As a result, a whole generation of middle-class women had to learn how to cook. A number of stylish cookbooks were produced to show them how, but also to point out the pleasure that could be gained from cooking. British author Hilda Leyel's cookbook *The Gentle Art of Cookery* (1921) fulfilled both purposes. The book is unusually detailed in its instructions and contains many innovative recipes. One section focuses on edible flowers used in food, which reveals Leyel's interest in herbs. In 1927, Leyel founded the Herb Society in the UK and opened the first of many Culpepers shops, which sold culinary and aromatic herbs, and other herbal products. The shops are still in existence all over the UK. As travel became more affordable, food from other countries was introduced to the British. Such food was often considered both exotic and bohemian. This is suggested by some of the chapter titles in *The Gentle Art of Cookery,* such as "Arabian Nights." Cookbooks of the interwar years appear quite modern. *The Gentle Art of Cookery* contains recipes normally associated with the 1980s, such as polenta and raspberry vinegar, and it assigns six whole chapters to vegetables, pulses, and grains. The culinary culture that flourished in the interwar years was interrupted by the outbreak of World War II, when food-control measures severely restricted the use of ingredients and encouraged cheap substitutions. Leyel's cookbook nevertheless provided inspiration for post-war British cookbook authors such as Elizabeth David.

World War II also affected the writing of British author Jan Struthers, whose columns about fictional British housewife Mrs. Caroline Miniver first appeared in *The Times* in 1937. Mrs. Miniver became so popular among readers that they wrote her letters, despite Struthers' insistence that the character was fictional. The columns,

> **Mrs. Miniver**
>
> Jan Struthers' bestseller *Mrs. Miniver,* with its tales of an ordinary British family affected by war, is rumored to have hastened U.S. entry into World War II. This reportedly caused British Prime Minister Winston Churchill to proclaim that *Mrs. Miniver* had done more for the Allies than a flotilla of battleships.

which appeared every few weeks in *The Times'* Court Page, were turned into a book, *Mrs. Miniver* (1939), shortly after the outbreak of World War II. By then, the subject matters in the columns had taken on a darker note, marked by wartime directives and restrictions. The book became especially well-liked in the United States, which was still neutral in the conflict. It was also turned into a very popular film in 1942.

NEWSPAPERS AND MAGAZINES

The newspaper and magazine market flourished during World War I. Yet, the papers and magazines produced at home were remarkably different from those written by the soldiers themselves. Hundreds of so-called trench newspapers were published by individual unions and battalions on both sides of the conflict. *The Wipers Times* (1916–1918) was one of the most popular British papers. It took its name from the town of Ypres in France, where a printing press had been salvaged by soldiers fighting in the region and the newspaper was first produced. Papers such as *The Wipers Times* were written strictly by and for soldiers, and contained poetry, in-jokes and comments on events that could sometimes be understood only by those in active combat. They also contained a surprising amount of subversive satire, which indirectly criticized the war and the authorities in charge. Together, these two aspects of the newspapers brought the soldiers together in a communal sense and highlighted their separateness from other groups, including friends and relatives back home. The first fifteen issues of *The Wipers Times* were published in book form in 1918. In 1930, all issues were published in one volume.

In the interwar years, magazines often functioned as arenas for social and political commentary. Around 1918, the German weekly magazine *Die Schaubühne* changed its name to *Die Weltbühne* (1905–1933). The magazine, which traditionally focused on art, politics and business, became a forum for left-democratic and pacifist intellectuals of the Weimar Republic. Regular contributors included German journalist and critic Kurt Tucholsky, who for a short while was editor-in-chief of the magazine. *Die Weltbühne* criticized antidemocratic tendencies in the military, in the justice system, and among the old pro-monarchist elites. It also denounced the political murders of pacifists such as Rosa Luxemburg. Tucholsky, who eventually became the magazine's Paris correspondent, warned against the emerging and populist Nazi party eleven years before it came to power. The magazine also exposed the secret German rearmament in violation of the *Treaty of Versailles*. In 1927, the leadership of the magazine was passed on to German pacifist Carl von Ossietzky who, after Hitler's rise to power, was imprisoned in a concentration camp. His imprisonment meant the end for *Die Weltbühne*. Ossietzky was awarded the Nobel Peace Prize in 1935, shortly before his death.

Newspapers and magazines also functioned as vehicles for more personal observations on the human condition. The Austrian newspaper *Die Fackel* (1899–1936) was the brain-child of influential Austrian author, critic, and journalist Karl Kraus, who after 1911 became its sole contributor. Kraus's newspaper attacked all forms of hypocrisy and corruption, but also psychoanalytic theory and populist journalism. The newspaper became staunchly antiwar during World War I and editions were repeatedly confiscated by censors. For thirty-seven years, and in more than four hundred issues, Kraus analyzed and criticized cultural, social, and political life. Public lectures held by Kraus in the 1920s drew huge crowds and were regularly frequented by the Viennese intelligentsia. The contemporary German critic Walter Benjamin referred to him as the most powerful opinion maker of his time.

SCIENTIFIC AND ECONOMIC TEXTS

In the early twentieth century, Germany dominated Europe's chemical and electrical industries. The country's imperial and expansionist ambitions also contributed to the high standard of its technical education. In 1905, German scientist Albert Einstein achieved his doctorate and published five papers in the prestigious journal *Annalen der Physik*. The papers were to change the scientific understanding of the physical world. In these papers, Einstein introduced his special theory of relativity, which showed that the speed of light is always constant, but that time and velocity are relative to the position of the observer. This theory led to the realization that the spatial dimensions of an object depend on the velocity of whoever measures it, and that space and time are not separate and regular. The papers also presented the now famous equation $E=mc^2$, which states an equivalence between energy (E) and mass (m) in direct proportion to the square of the speed of light in a vacuum (c^2). During World War I, Einstein worked on a general theory of relativity, which was published in 1916. The year after, the two theories were published in book form as *Relativity: the Special and General Theory* (1917). In 1919, his theories were proven correct. As a result, Einstein became an overnight celebrity and his name entered popular culture. He received the Nobel Prize for Physics in 1921. In 1933, he left Germany for the United States, where he helped set up the Manhattan Project in an effort to stop Hitler from developing the atomic bomb.

The 1930s also experienced an economic recession that came to be known as the Great Depression. In 1936, British economist John Maynard Keynes published his now-classic book *General Theory of Employment, Interest, and Money* (1936), which, in its attempt to explain the Depression, also introduced many of the key concepts that came to characterize the new field of macroeconomics. In his book, Keynes offered suggestions on how to influence the economy of a whole nation. In particular, he became famous for advocating interventionist government policy to alleviate the negative effects of recessions and depressions. The book advocated an active economic policy, whereby governments needed to stimulate demand in times of high unemployment. Keynes's economic theories became immensely influential and their effects have sometimes been referred to as a Keynesian revolution. He is generally accredited with inspiring U.S. President Franklin Delano Roosevelt to develop his New Deal in the 1930s. Keynes's theories were not seriously questioned until the 1970s.

PSYCHOLOGY TEXTS

Psychology had developed as a separate and popular area of study in the nineteenth century. As a consequence, twentieth-century culture was familiar with terms like "the unconscious," "dream symbolism," and "sexual repression." Many of these expressions were coined by Austrian psychoanalyst Sigmund Freud. The public's fascination with Freud's method of psychoanalysis, and his theories concerning the mind, meant that previously taboo subjects could now be openly discussed in society. In the aftermath of World War I, Freud completed the study *Beyond the Pleasure Principle* (1920), which examined the human instincts. In particular, Freud was interested in those instincts that seemed to contradict his earlier conclusions regarding the human drive toward pleasure. The book contains two case studies, which provided Freud with examples of what he identified as the human death drive, that is, a desire for absolute satisfaction and calm, which can be achieved only in death. The discovery of this self-destructive drive radically changed Freud's subsequent theories on the human psyche. In later works, he also identified an aggressive instinct in society, which closely resembles the human death drive.

Freud's psychoanalysis became tremendously influential in the twentieth century, but was also challenged by former colleagues and competitors. One such former colleague, Swiss psychotherapist Carl Gustav Jung, presented an alternative to

Freud's psychoanalysis in his book *The Archetypes and the Collective Unconscious* (1936). In the book, Jung parted ways with Freud over the concept of the human consciousness. Unlike Freud, he argued for the existence of a three-layered psyche, which includes a collective unconscious populated by a number of archetypes, that is, certain universal mental predispositions shared by all humans and not grounded in history or experience. Rather, argued Jung, these archetypes appear spontaneously in the mind, often as dreams, and can also be found described in art, religion and mythology. Some of the most important archetypes are the Shadow, which personifies shameful and hidden aspects of the self, and the Anima/Animus, the male and female objects of desire. After World War II, Jung was accused of collaboration with the Nazis. He defended himself by arguing that acquiescence to Nazi demands was made to save psychology as a discipline. Jung's theories influenced writers such as German author Hermann Hesse, but he was also ridiculed in Irish author James Joyce's novel *Finnegan's Wake* (1939). His theories became particularly popular in the 1960s, when recreational drugs were used in attempts to reach the collective unconscious. Jung's theories have sometimes been called pseudoscientific. Other critics have pointed out that the popularity of the occult and the pan-Germanic in 1930s Germanic Europe offers a problematic context to Jung's theories.

PHILOSOPHICAL TEXTS

An acute need developed in the 1920s to understand and reconcile with the apparently irrational and horrendous consequences of World War I. One of the most discussed texts of the time was German mathematician Oswald Spengler's ambitious two-volume study *The Decline of the West* (1918–1923). Spengler's work offers a comparative theory of the rise and decline of cultures, focusing especially, but not exclusively, on Western culture, which he claims is in its final stages of decline and destruction. Modern civilization, he argues, is characterized by irrationality and a breakdown of social norms. Such thoughts offered comfort to the Germans who had experienced the humiliation of defeat in World War I, but also to other Europeans who suffered under the conditions of the inflation and other socioeconomic upheavals. These breakdowns, Spengler explained, were part of larger historical processes. The book was translated into several languages and was a huge success. Although it was criticized by some historians, it introduced the so-called social cycle theory, which argues that history is repeating itself and does not involve any social progress. *The Decline of the West* also inspired American authors of the so-called beat generation, Finnish philosopher Georg Henrik von Wright, and German architect Ludwig Mies van der Rohe.

Spengler shared many of his antidemocratic and pro-authoritarian views of society with the Nazis. When their systematic genocide became public knowledge, it brought about an existential crisis among European intellectuals. In *Being and Nothingness* (1943), French philosopher Jean-Paul Sartre offered an analysis of the nature of existence from the point of view of human consciousness. For Sartre, existence is the same as constantly transcending one's present circumstances. Human freedom is defined as intentional and active, yet always situational—that is, arising from a particular space and time. Sartre later attempted to formulate an ethics to complement his theory of consciousness. His aim was to bridge the difference between an individual freedom and collective, social, and political liberation. Sartre's theories were inspired by some of the great thinkers of the twentieth century, such as German philosopher Martin Heidegger, and challenged the reader to confront questions regarding freedom, responsibility, and action. *Being and Nothingness* had a profound and direct influence on Sartre's contemporaries and later generations of intellectuals, from the drama of Irish playwright Samuel Beckett to the American beat poets of the 1950s.

POLITICAL TEXTS

The Russian Revolution began with the February revolt in 1917, when Tsar Nicholas II was forced to abdicate in favor of a provisional government consisting of liberals and socialists. A month after the transfer of power, Vladimir Ilyich Lenin returned to Russia from his exile and presented the government with his *April Theses* (1917). The "theses" consisted of short notes, which outlined Lenin's ideas for a Russia governed exclusively by the proletariat. In them, he suggests various social changes, such as the abolition of the police and the army, which would begin Russia's transition to socialism. Lenin also voiced opposition to World War I with the motivation that it was a war fought for the interests of the bourgeoisie. His theses were part of a power struggle within the Bolshevik quarters, against a more moderate political line, which argued that World War I was justified and favored a provisional government that included liberals. *The April Theses* laid the foundation for the Bolsheviks' ascendancy to power in the October Revolution in 1917, when power was seized from the provisional government by force. Five years later, the Union of Soviet Socialist Republics (USSR) was formed.

In his two-volume autobiography *Mein Kampf* (1925–1926), German Chancellor Adolf Hitler presented his future plans for Germany and the underlying ideology for his propositions. The book describes his plan for Germany's foreign policy, which included an intentional breach of the *Treaty of Versailles* (1919). In the book, Hitler also expressed a desire to form alliances with the UK and Italy to overthrow the Soviet Union, with the aim to provide the German people with more *lebensraum,* or living space. Although the book offers insight into Hitler's strategic thinking, it is best known for its account of his racist ideology. *Mein Kampf* argues the supremacy of "Aryans", or white Europeans, while claiming the existence of a Jewish conspiracy to dilute the purity of the races. The struggle for world domination is described as a racial and cultural battle between Aryans and non-Aryans. The book sold well before World War II, and during the war *Mein Kampf* became extremely popular among Nazis and the general German population. Since the end of World War II, the government of Bavaria, which owns the copyright to the book, has not allowed any printing of *Mein Kampf* in Germany. In Austria, possession of the book is illegal.

Although World War I had effectively ended with the armistice in 1918, peace was officially declared with the *Treaty of Versailles* (1919). The treaty was signed in Versailles, France, by the heads of the Allied and the Central Powers and set out the conditions imposed on the German Empire, which had lost the war. The treaty stipulated that Germany must part with a certain amount of territory to its neighbors, give up all its overseas colonies, and restrict the size of its military. Germany was not invited to discuss the treaty and issued a protest, but later agreed to the conditions. The country was ordered to pay a heavy war debt, which contributed significantly to the German economic inflation in the 1920s. For this reason, it has sometimes been argued that the treaty also contributed, however indirectly, to Hitler's ascent to power. The treaty was considered unsatisfactory by all participants, as conflicting interests resulted in too many compromises.

When Hitler came to power in 1933, he promised improved economic conditions and immediately overthrew the *Treaty of Versaillies* by deliberately rebuilding Germany's military forces. In 1938 Germany annexed Austria and was expected to claim the Sudetenland, an area of Czechoslovakia with a large German population. In an effort to appease Hitler, Russia, France, Italy, and the UK invited the German Chancellor to a conference where the terms for what became known as *The Munich Agreement* (1938) were negotiated. The agreement gave Germany control over the Sudetenland in Czechoslovakia, on the condition that Hitler would not claim more of Europe. Hitler and British Prime Minister Neville Chamberlain also signed a separate agreement, which stipulated that Germany and the UK would solve all future conflicts peacefully. On Chamberlain's return to the UK, he waved the agreement between Britain and Germany and uttered the famous, but erroneous words: "peace in our time." One year later, Hitler broke the agreement by occupying the rest of Czechoslovakia, followed by the occupation of Poland, which started World War II in Europe.

Not all Germans were in favor of the Nazis. In 1942, Germany experienced heavy losses in the battle of Stalingrad. As a consequence, many civilians were critical of Hitler's war strategy, believing that he merely used German soldiers as cannon-fodder for the country's war machine. Such sentiments could not be expressed openly, because the Nazis severely punished all critics. However, in a series of six anonymous leaflets signed "The White Rose," a group of students from the University of Munich began calling for active opposition to Hitler's regime. The White Rose pamphlet campaign lasted for a year before the students and their philosophy professor were arrested and executed. The Nazis were shocked to discover that the dissidents were well-educated, middle-class Germans, who appealed to their own class by quoting Plato, Schiller, and Goethe in their pamphlets. Spin-off groups were also formed in Hamburg, where members were also arrested and executed. After the original group had been disseminated, one leaflet was smuggled to Sweden and eventually found its way to the UK. The leaflet was reprinted and more than ten thousand copies were dropped over Germany by the Allied air forces. German author Thomas Mann later said that the White Rose leaflets offered him new hope for a better future. Several films and books about the group have appeared. In 2005, a German film focused on Sophie Scholl, the younger of the two Scholl siblings who were part of the original Munich group. The film was based on newly discovered documents from Scholl's interrogations by the Gestapo.

CONCLUSION

Reading practices in the first half of the twentieth century reflect the central and important role the printed word had as a means of information and communication. In times of social and political instability all writing was taken very seriously by the totalitarian regimes in Europe, and reading could have serious, even deadly, consequences for individuals when various forms of censorship were implemented. In an attempt to understand the social, political, cultural, and economic changes that characterize the period, people turned to all kinds of reading material, from published novels to secretly distributed leaflets. For many, reading also offered a much-needed form of escapism from current events.

RECOMMENDED READING

Benoit, Annick and Guy Fontaine. *History of European Literature*. Translated by Michael Wooff. London: Routledge, 2000.

Bloom, Clive. *Bestsellers: Popular Fiction Since 1900*. London: Palgrave Macmillan, 2002.

Epic Revisionism: Russian History and Literature as Stalinist Propaganda. Edited by Kevin M.F. Platt and David Brandenberger. Madison, WI: University Of Wisconsin Press, 2006.

The Holocaust and the Book: Destruction and Preservation. Edited by Jonathan Rose. Boston: University Of Massachusetts Press, 2001.

Humble, Nicola. *The Feminine Middlebrow Novel 1920s to 1950s: Class, Domesticity and Bohemianism*. Oxford: Oxford University Press, 2001.

Lottman, Herbert R. *The Left Bank: Writers, Artists and Politics from the Popular Front to the Cold War*. Chicago: University Of Chicago Press, 1998.

Paris, Michael. *Over the Top: The Great War and Juvenile Literature in Britain*. Westport, CT: Praeger Publishers, 2004.

Reuveni, Gideon. *Reading Germany: Literature and Consumer Culture in Germany Before 1933*. Oxford: Berghahn Book, 2006.

Stites, Richard. *Russian Popular Culture: Entertainment and Society Since 1900*. Cambridge: Cambridge University Press, 1992.

Turner, Catherine. *Marketing Modernism Between the Two World Wars*. Boston: University Of Massachusetts, 2003.

PRIMARY SOURCES

Blyton, Enid. *Five on a Treasure Island*. London: Hodder Children's Books, 2001. First published in 1942. Available in print.

Brecht, Bertolt. *The Threepenny Opera*. Translated by John Willett and Ralph Manheim. New York: Penguin Classics, 2007. First published in German as *Die Dreigroschenoper* in 1928.

Brooke, Rupert. *1914 & Other Poems*. New York: Penguin Classics, 1999. First published in 1916.

Bulgakov, Mikhail. *The Master and Margarita*. First published (censored) in Russian as Мастер и Маргарита in 1966–1967. Available in print in English.

Čapek, Karel. *R.U.R./Rossum's Universal Robots*. Translated by Claudia Novack-Jones. New York: Penguin Classics, 2004. First published in Czech as *R.U.R./Rossumovi univerzální roboti* in 1921.

Christie, Agatha. *The Murder of Roger Ackroyd*. New York: Black Dog & Leventhal, 2006. First published in 1926.

Die Fackel. First published in 1899–1936. Excerpts available in English in *In These Great Times: A Karl Kraus Reader*. Edited by Harry Zohn. Translated by Joseph Fabry and Max Knight. Chicago, IL: University of Chicago Press, 1990. Out of print in English. All thirty-seven volumes available in German at The Austrian Academy Corpus: Fackel Gate. http://corpus1.aac.ac.at/fackel/.

Dinesen, Isak. *Out of Africa*. New York: Random House, 2002. First published in 1937.

Einstein, Albert. *Relativity: The Special and General Theory*. Translated by Robert L. Lawson. New York: Henry Holt, 1920. First published in German as *Über die spezielle und die allgemeine relativitätstheorie* in 1917. Available in print in English.

Eliot, T.S. *The Waste Land*. New York: W.W. Norton, 2000. First published in 1922.

Freud, Sigmund. *Beyond the Pleasure Principle*. Translated by James Strachey. New York: W.W. Norton, 1990. First published in German as *Jenseits des Lustprinzips* in 1920.

Gibbons, Stella. *Cold Comfort Farm*. London: Penguin Classics, 2006. First published in 1932.

Hitler, Adolf. *Mein Kampf*. Translated by Ralph Manheim. Boston: Houghton Mifflin, 2001. First published in German as *Mein Kampf* in 1925–1926.

Jung, C.G. *Archetypes and the Collective Unconscious*. Translated by R.F.C. Hull. Princeton, NJ: Princeton University Press, 1981. First published in German as *Archetypen und das kollektive Unbewusste* in 1936.

Jünger, Ernst. *Storm of Steel*. Translated by Michael Hoffman. New York: Penguin Classics, 2004. First published in German as *In Stahlgewittern* in 1920. Available in print in English.

Keynes, John Maynard. *General Theory of Employment, Interest, and Money.* New York: Palgrave Macmillan, 2007. First published in 1936. Available in print.

Lawrence, D.H. *Lady Chatterley's Lover.* New York: Penguin, 2006. First published (privately) in 1928.

Lenin, Vladimir. *The April Theses.* Moscow: Progress Publishers, 1970. First published in Russian as апрельские тезисы in 1917. Out of print in English. Available in English at the Marxist Internet Archive, 2007. http://www.marxists.org/archive/lenin/works/1917/apr/04.htm.

Leyel, Hilda. *The Gentle Art of Cookery.* London: Kegan Paul, 2005. First published in 1921.

Moberg, Vilhelm. *Ride This Night!* Translated by Henry Alexander. Garden City, NY: Doubleday, Doran and Company, Inc. 1943. First published in Swedish as *Rid i natt!* in 1941. Out of print in English. Available in the Library of Congress, Washington DC, USA.

"The Munich Agreement" aka "Agreement between Germany, Great Britain, France and Italy Concluded in Munich on September 29, 1938." First published in German as *Das Münchener Abkommen* in 1938. Available in English at The Avalon Project, 1996. http://www.yale.edu/lawweb/avalon/imt/munich1.htm.

Orwell, George. *Homage to Catalonia.* New York: Penguin Classics, 2000. First published in 1938.

Proust, Marcel. *In Search of Lost Time.* 7 Vols. Translated by Lydia Davis et al. London: Penguin, 2003. First published in French as *À la Recherche du Temps Perdu* in 1913–1927.

Remarque, Erich Maria. *All Quiet on the Western Front.* Translated by Brian O. Murdoch. London: Vintage Classics, 2007. First published in German as *Im Westen nichts Neues* in 1929. Available in print in English.

Saint-Exupéry, Antoine de. *The Little Prince.* Translated by Richard Howard. New York: Harvest Books, 2000. First published in French as *Le petit prince* in 1943.

Sartre, Jean-Paul. *Being and Nothingness: An Essay on Phenomenological Ontology.* Translated by Hazel E. Barnes. London: Routledge, 2003. First published in French as *L'Être et le néant* in 1943.

Spengler, Oswald. *The Decline of the West.* Translated by Charles Francis Atkinson. New York: A. Knopf, 1934. Out of print but available in the Library of Congress, Washington DC, USA. First published in German as *Untergang des Abendlandes* in 1918–1923. An abridged version in English is also available: *The Decline Of The West: An Abridged Edition.* Translated by Charles Francs Atkinson. Oxford: Oxford University Press 1991.

Spirou Magazine. Amsterdam: Jean Dupuis, 1938–. First published in French as *Le Journal de Spirou* in 1938. Not available in print in English.

Stope, Marie. *Married Love: A New Contribution to the Solution of Sex Difficulties.* Oxford: Oxford World's Classics, 2004. First published in 1918.

Strachey, Lytton. *Eminent Victorians.* Oxford: Oxford World's Classics, 2003. First published in 1918. Available in print.

Struther, Jan. *Mrs. Miniver.* London: Virago, 1989. First published in 1939. Available in print.

Treaty of Versailles or *Treaty of Peace with Germany.* Washington DC: Govt. print. off., 1919. First published in French as *Conditions de Paix* in 1919. Available in English in the Library of Congress, Washington DC, USA.

Die Weltbühne: Vollständiger Nachdruck der Jahrgänge 1918–1933. Königstein: Athenäum Verlag, 1987. First published in 1905–1933. Not available in print in English.

The White Rose Leaflets. First published in German as *Flugblatt I–IV der Weissen Rosein* in 1942–1943. Available in English e-text at The White Rose Society. http://www.whiterosesociety.org/WRS_pamphlets_home.html.

The Wipers Times: The Complete Series of the Famous Wartime Trench Newspaper. Edited by Malcolm Brown. London: Little Books, 2006. First published in 1916–1918. Available in print.

SECONDARY SOURCES

"About Penguin: Company History," Penguin.uk.http://www.penguin.co.uk/static/ packages/uk/aboutus/history.html (accessed January 2, 2007).

Agatha Christie: The Official Agatha Christie Website. http://uk.agathachristie.com (accessed January 2, 2007).

Bloom, Harold. *How to Read and Why.* New York: Scribner, 2000.

Bodek, Richard. *Proletarian Performance in Weimar Berlin: Agitprop, Chorus and Brecht.* Columbia, SC: Camden House, 1998.

Canetti, Elias. *The Torch in My Ear.* Translated by Joachim Neugroschel. London: Granta Book, 1999.

Grahame, Robert Maxtone. "Preliminary Notes to the Internet Edition," *Mrs. Miniver.* http://digital.library.upenn.edu/women/struther/miniver/miniver.html (accessed December 29, 2006).

Humble, Nicola. "The Evolution of Cookbooks," *Waitrose Food Illustrated.* http://www. waitrose.com/food_drink/wfi/foodpeople/specialists/0511065.asp1 (accessed January 2007).

The Kurt Weill Foundation: The Threepenny Opera. http://www.threepennyopera.org/ (accessed January 4, 2007).

Leslie, Esther. "Walter Benjamin." *The Literary Encyclopedia, The Literary Dictionary Company.* http://www.litencyc.com/php/speople.php?rec=true&UID=357 (accessed January 4, 2007).

McCallum-Stewart, Esther. "Feature Articles: Satirical Magazines of the First World War: *Punch* and the *Wipers Times.*" *First World War.Com.* http://www.first worldwar.com/features/satirical.htm (accessed January 4, 2007).

Noll, Richard. *The Jung Cult: Origins of a Charismatic Movement.* New York: Touchstone, 1997.

"On This Day 10 November, 1960: Lady Chatterley's Lover sold out." BBC News. 10 November, 2006. http://news.bbc.co.uk/onthisday/hi/dates/stories/november/10/ newsid_2965000/2965194.stm. (accessed January 2, 2007).

Peterson, Klaus. "The Harmful Publications (Young Persons) Act of 1926. Literary Censorship and the Politics of Morality in the Weimar Republic." *German Studies Review* 15, no. 3. (October, 1992), 505–523.

Poetry of the First World War: A Casebook. Edited by Dominic Hibberd. Basingstoke and London: Macmillan, 1990.

Rudd, David. *Enid Blyton and the Mystery of Children's Literature.* London: Palgrave Macmillan, 2000.

Sartre, Jean-Paul. *Anti-Semite and Jew: An Exploration of the Etymology of Hate.* Translated by George J. Becker. New York: Schocken Books, 1995.

The Threat of Pandemic Influenza: Are We Ready? Workshop Summary (2005). Edited by Stacey L. Knobler, Alison Mack, Adel Mahmoud, Stanley M. Lemon. Washington, D.C.: The National Academic Press, 2007. p. 7. http://www.nap.edu/openbook. php?isbn=0309095042&page=7 (accessed September 2, 2007).

Trujillo, Guillermo Sánchez. *Crimen Y Castigo De Franz Kafka, Ànatomia de el Proceso.* Medellín: Libros En Red, 2004.

Valéry, Paul. "The Crisis of the Mind," In *The Collected Works of Paul Valéry: History and Politics.* Vol. 10. Translated by Denise Folliot and Jackson Mathews. Edited by Jackson Mathews. (Princeton, NJ: Princeton University Press, 1962), 23–36.

CHAPTER 11

Post-Modernism

Malin Lidström Brock

TIMELINE

1945	World War II ends
1951	The European Coal and Steel Community (ECSC) is founded
1954–62	The Algerian War of Independence
1956	The Hungarian Revolution
1961	The Berlin Wall is erected
1965–72	Peak period of immigration from the Caribbean, India, Pakistan, and Zimbabwe to the UK
1968	Troops from the Eastern Bloc countries invade Czechoslovakia; student protests in Paris
1979	Margaret Thatcher elected Prime Minister of Britain
1980	The trade union federation Solidarity is established in Poland
1982	Britain goes to war with Argentina over the Falkland Islands/Las Malvinas
1989	The Berlin Wall is torn down
1990	Collapse of the Soviet Union and the Eastern Bloc
1990	Reunification of East and West Germany
1991–95 (–2001)	War in former Yugoslavia
1992	The term "European Union" (EU) is introduced
1999	Introduction of the Euro as the basic unit of currency in the majority of EU-member nations
2004–07	Terrorist attacks in Madrid, London, and Glasgow
2007	The EU celebrates fifty years

INTRODUCTION TO THE PERIOD

Europe after World War II underwent fundamental changes in all areas of society. A sharp political and ideological division of the European continent gradually gave way to the idea of a new, pan-European identity. World Wars I and II had ended western Europe's dominant position on the world stage in favor of two ideologically opposed super powers, the Soviet Union (USSR) and the United States. Liberation negotiations in the aftermath of World War II took place at the Yalta Conference in 1945. Several Eastern and Central European countries were annexed by the Soviet Union as a result of the Conference agreements, effectively dividing the European continent into eastern and western zones.

In the decades following the peace declaration, political and ideological tensions between the world's two super powers increased. The reverberations were felt all over Europe. National revolts against the Communist governments in Hungary and Czechoslovakia were crushed by soviet and Eastern Bloc military troops. In Poland an anti-Communist trade union federation, *Solidarity,* inspired a social protest movement. The political tensions between the Eastern Bloc and the Western allies did not diminish until the 1980s, when General Secretary of the Soviet Union Mikhail Gorbachev initiated a series of reforms to save the crumbling soviet economy. Gorbachev's democratization reforms ultimately led to the dissolution of the USSR and its control over Eastern Europe.

Social and economic developments within and across national borders helped to modernize Europe. World War II had left countries in ruins. Two decades later, the economic prosperity in many countries exceeded that of pre-war years. National health services, social security systems, and central control of the economy were some of the reforms implemented throughout Europe. Greater prosperity resulted in what is generally referred to as a consumer culture. However, in the 1960s students in Europe protested against the values associated with consumerism. At the end of the century, similar youth protests were voiced against economic globalization. The period after World War II experienced an influx of immigrants from former European colonies, which revived the national economies, but also resulted in ethnic and cultural tensions. Rapid changes in areas such as communications technology also altered the social reality of contemporary Europe.

The desire to promote peace and democracy revived pre-war discussions of a unified Europe. The European Coal and Steel Community (ECSC) was formed as a result. By pooling economic resources in a common market, the member nations of ECSC hoped to avoid previous economic mistakes. They also wished to assert their combined presence on the world market. The ECSC eventually developed into the European Union (EU). The EU single market allowed for the free flow of goods, services, people, and money, mainly through the abolition of systematic border controls between member states. A single European currency, the Euro, was also introduced. In the twenty-first century, the Czech Republic, Poland, and other countries of the former Eastern Bloc have been accepted as new members of the EU. The expanded EU has effectively ended the political and ideological division of Europe into East and West, a division that was first initiated at the Yalta Conference.

READING TRENDS AND PRACTICES

"After Auschwitz—no more poetry," wrote Theodore W. Adorno in 1967. His words were not prophetic, but expressed the feelings shared by millions of Europeans when the atrocities performed in the Nazi concentration camps during World War II became known. Europe lay in ruins, structurally and morally, and a sense of disillusionment marked much of its literary production. In the decades after the war, literature took on a new urgency as writers and readers struggled to understand the causes of the war and its aftereffects. A large number of small- and medium-sized publishing houses assured the diversity of the book market, and the uncertain political climate encouraged the popularity of nonfiction and theoretical books that promised to throw new light on current events. For example, Viktor E. Frankl's *Man's Search for Meaning* (1946) became one of the most widely read eyewitness accounts of the Nazi concentration camps. American journalist William Shirer's *The Rise and Fall of The Third Reich* (1960) offered the first comprehensive history of Nazi Germany in English, and Irish playwright Samuel Beckett's absurd drama, *Waiting for Godot* (1949), focused on the meaninglessness of existence in a world of human suffering.

The strained relationship between the United States and the Soviet Union dominated the second half of the twentieth century. In the aftermath of World War II, several countries in Eastern Europe were annexed by the Soviet Union, and a wall was eventually erected in Berlin, which cut the city in half. In an effort to build unity among the American allies, American President John F. Kennedy visited Berlin, where he uttered the famous words, *"Ich Bin Ein Berliner"* (1963). Increasingly suspicious of one another, the two super powers escalated their respective nuclear weapon arsenals. This geopolitical, economic, and ideological struggle became known as the Cold War and provided inspiration for several apocalyptic, nuclear war novels, such as British author Nevil Shute's *On the Beach* (1957). Despite the destruction caused by the war, western Europe experienced unprecedented material prosperity in the fifteen years after peace had been declared. Due to the political tensions, the espionage novel also experienced a wave of popularity. British author Ian Fleming's *Casino Royale* (1953) was the first in a series of James Bond novels. It introduced a new type of hero, whose refined taste in luxury consumer goods mirrored the desires of the increasingly affluent middle classes. In stark contrast, fellow countrymen John Le Carré and Frederick Forsyth portrayed the unglamorous side of international espionage, fraught with treacherous double-crossings. The Cold War continued to inspire writers of popular literature until Mikhail Gorbachev came to power in 1985. His democratization reforms led to the end of the Cold War and the dissolution of the Soviet Union.

In Eastern Europe, the production of literature came under strict ideological control after 1945 and restrictions were not lifted until the 1980s. Polish writer Czesław Miłosz defected to France where he wrote *The Captive Mind* (1953), which described the situation for intellectuals in totalitarian states. Soviet author Alexander Solzhenitsyn's monumental three-volume account of Stalin's work camps, *The Gulag Archipelago* (1973), was published in the West to great acclaim. As a result, Solzhenitsyn was stripped of his soviet citizenship and expatriated to West Germany. Ironically, the ideological pressure on intellectuals in Eastern Europe often contributed to their radicalism. Czech author Milan Kundera's early work was decidedly Marxist, but his expulsion from the Communist party resulted in an openly antitotalitarian stance. Among intellectuals in western Europe, the idea of communism dominated the debate during the decades immediately after the war. British author George Orwell offered a critique of the totalitarian state in the classic novel *1984* (1948), while the eventual merits of communism were discussed in *Les Temps Modernes* (1945), the most influential journal in postwar France.

In 1949, French philosopher Simone de Beauvoir wrote *The Second Sex* (1949), a study of women's condition in society. The book influenced the emerging women's movements in both Europe and the United States. After the war, rising numbers of women entered the formal economy as new opportunities for education and professional careers became available to both sexes. In 1945, *Elle* magazine was launched in France, aimed specifically at the modern female consumer. Gradually, lifestyle magazines were developed to attract young male readers. In the 1980s, *i-D* (1980) became one of the most influential British magazines. The majority of European countries had already granted women the right to vote, but women in France (1945), the Balkans (1945), Switzerland (1971), and Liechtenstein (1984) had to wait until the second half of the century for that same right. A new awareness of women's status in society informed the novel *Manrape* (1975), in which Finnish author Märta Tikkanen identified the patriarchal structures that sanctioned male sexual violence. British author Fay Weldon commented on the pressure on women to be beautiful in the satiric novel *The Life and Loves of a She-Devil* (1983). However, in the twenty-first century, such messages have become less popular. British stylists Trinny Woodall and Susannah Constantine's style guide *What Not to Wear* (2002) has topped the best-seller lists in recent years. Meanwhile, British author Helen Fielding's novel *Bridget Jones's Diary* (1996) revived the traditional romance genre.

World War II led to a so-called brain drain in Europe as scientists fled from the occupied areas and Britain to the United States. A rise in the school-leaving age and rapid growth in university enrollment characterized western Europe after the war, but the Continent still lost the lead to the United States in both nuclear research and astrophysics. The British novelist C. P. Snow held a controversial lecture at Cambridge in 1959 where he argued that the two cultures in society, science and the humanities, had become separated, with very little contact between them. He considered this breakdown of communication between the sciences and the humanities a major hindrance to solving the world's problems. The lecture sparked a heated public debate. However, the gap between the two cultures was somewhat ameliorated later in the twentieth century with the appearance of popular science books such as Stephen Hawking's *A Brief History of Time* (1988).

A distinctive youth culture, inspired by American popular culture, emerged after the war. Françoise Sagan's female protagonist in *Bonjour Tristesse* (1953) exemplified the bored but rebellious teenager, who also appeared in music and film. The importance of self-development took the place of collective values in children's books, which were designed for readers at every stage of development. Swedish children's author Astrid Lindgren's *Pippi Longstocking* (1944) introduced an anarchic and independent girl as the main protagonist. In the 1960s and 1970s, social realism entered children's books and literature aimed at young readers. Norwegian author Jostein Gaarder's *Sophie's World* (1994) was a sophisticated philosophical story that turned into a best-seller.

Despite growing prosperity, social mobility was limited for the European working classes. Political awareness characterized the male British authors known as "the angry young men." John Osborne's controversial play *Look Back in Anger* (1956) burst onto the London stage, challenging the establishment. Newly arrived immigrants were another group who found social mobility difficult. An active period of European de-colonization of Africa and Asia took place after World War II, beginning with the independence of India from the UK in 1947. The violent de-colonization of Algeria involved the troubled repatriation of French settlers. At the height of economic prosperity in the 1950s and 1960s, western Europe initially encouraged immigration from places such as Turkey, North Africa, Pakistan, and the West Indies. By the 1970s, many of these immigrants and their children faced unemployment, poverty, and inadequate housing and schooling. They also became the object of xenophobic attacks from far-right movements. In the twenty-first century, fiction that described the immigrant experience firsthand entered the best-seller lists, such as French author Faïza Guène's novel *Kiffe Kiffe Tomorrow* (2004).

The 1960s were marked by social unrest. Young people demonstrated in the streets against the capitalist system, the Vietnam War, and established society. In May 1968, Parisian students initiated a series of strikes, which soon spread to include more than two million workers. When the people of Prague took to the streets in protest against the socialist government in the spring of 1968, soviet and Eastern Bloc troops invaded Czechoslovakia. A decade later, protests took the form of terrorism by various resistance and national liberation movements in, among other countries, Ireland, the UK, Spain, and Germany. In West Germany, the jailing of members of the left-wing terrorist group the Red Army Faction resulted in split sympathies among the German press. The journalist Ulrike Meinhof, later a founding member of the Bader-Meinhof terrorist cell, argued in the members' defense while more conservative newspapers condemned the group's actions. German author Heinrich Böll's novel *The Lost Honor of Katharina Blum* (1974) described the West German government's aggressive response to terrorism. In Sweden, the critique against governmental complacency and social inequality informed Maj Sjöwall and Per Wahlöö's crime novel *The Laughing Policeman* (1968).

The consumption of newspapers varied greatly from country to country. In Scandinavia, the consumption of daily newspapers was the highest in the world. Until the dissolution of the Soviet Union in the 1980s, the Eastern European press was heavily censored by the state, which explained its lack of readership. In the twenty-first century, the Belarus government was still criticized by human-rights groups for suppressing freedom of speech and denying the political opposition access to state-owned media. The post-war period in Britain was marked by the emergence of tabloid newspapers, such as Rupert Murdoch's *The Sun* (1969). Free newspapers were also introduced, and *The Big Issue* (1991) was sold by homeless people in the streets. Europe's first online daily newspapers appeared in the 1990s. At the end of the twentieth century, illiteracy still prevailed among the poorest segments in Europe, such as the Roma in Central and Eastern Europe.

The social awareness of the 1960s also resulted in new interpretations of Europe's past. Historians abandoned studies of national and political history in favor of social, economic, and cultural descriptions of events. *The Peasants of Languedoc* (1966), by the French historian Emmanuel Le Roy Ladurie, was a pioneering work of so-called total history. Fiction also became more self-conscious. The plot in Italian author Umberto Eco's medieval mystery *The Name of the Rose* (1980) centered on the very process of reading. This exploration of literature's own literariness was interpreted by critics as an example of postmodernism. The term described a dramatic change in thinking and was popularized by French philosopher Jean-François Lyotard's *The Postmodern Condition* (1979). It was first used to explain modern architecture, but soon came to describe European post-war politics.

World War II was perceived by politicians in Europe as a warning against national rivalries. It also brought home the realization that the United States and the Soviet Union were the new world powers. In an effort to strengthen the European identity and economic market, The European Coal and Steel Community (ECSC) was created, which eventually led to the establishment of the European Union (EU). In 2005, the people of France and the Netherlands voted against the proposed *EU Constitution* (2004), which caused several other member-states to postpone their ratification plans. The constitution itself temporarily entered the best-seller lists. Among the events that complicated the idea of a unified Europe, the war in former Yugoslavia (1991–1995) must be considered the most serious. With the fall of the Berlin Wall in 1989, communism gradually lost its grip on Eastern and Central Europe, which enabled ethnic and national conflicts to resurface in the area. The effects of the war on ordinary people's lives were described in Croatian author Slavenka Drakulić's essay collection *Balkan Express* (1992). At the beginning of the twenty-first century, the environment and the expansion of the EU became increasingly important issues for Europeans. Turkey's future membership came under particular scrutiny and highlighted the cultural and religious divides that existed within the EU's borders. Opinions on the Iraq War (2003–) divided individual Europeans and governments. Muslim terrorists detonated explosives on commuter trains in Madrid in 2004 and in London in 2005.

The European book market experienced dramatic changes during the second half of the twentieth century. Paperback sales expanded into the millions, and independent publishing houses were incorporated into multinational conglomerates, which increased the pressure on book sales. Best-sellers became the priority for both publishers and booksellers. With the emergence of electronic mass media, new marketing strategies exploited the potential links among different media. The success of J. K. Rowling's first Harry Potter book, *Harry Potter and the Philosopher's Stone* (1997), illustrated this trend. Popular food programs on television generated a new interest in celebrity cookbooks, such as Jamie Oliver's *The Naked Chef* (1999). To ensure the diversity of the book market, many European countries introduced so-called fixed book prices. Despite this effort, the availability of books outside larger cities was often limited to the latest best-selling popular fiction by authors such as Dan Brown and Catherine Cookson. The emergence of so-called Internet bookstores in the 2000s was a further threat to independent booksellers, but broadened the market for consumers.

CREATIVE TEXTS

The political tensions between the Soviet Union and the West inspired novelists in the decades that followed the end of World War II. British author George Orwell's satirical science fiction novel *1984* (1948) takes place in a dystopian future where a totalitarian state, "Oceania," enforces complete control over its inhabitants through the Party, which uses propaganda and fear to ensure conformity. Individuals are under constant surveillance by selected Party members, who answer to the mysterious head of government, the omnipotent "Big Brother." The main protagonist, Winston Smith, meets and falls illegally in love with Julia (her last name is never given), but they are caught by the Thought Police and forced to endure interrogation and torture. *1984* has often been interpreted as a critique of Stalin's Soviet Union and used as anti-Communist propaganda. It has also been read as a critique of the British Imperial rule in Burma and other forms of authoritarian rule. The novel was an instant best-seller, and the title has entered Western culture as an often-used metaphor for the totalitarian state. It also introduced a number of popular concepts, such as Big Brother, which is commonly used to describe attempts by a government to increase surveillance, and the Thought Police, which has come to refer to a real or imagined enforcement of ideological correctness. The novel has been adapted for television, film, radio broadcasts, and, in 2005, an opera. A reality television show, which was named *Big Brother* after the all-seeing leader in Orwell's novel, was first produced in the Netherlands in 1999 and subsequently exported to other European countries and the United States. The premise of the show is that contestants have to spend a certain amount of time in a specially designed house, under twenty-four-hour surveillance.

The Cold War theme continued to capture a significant European readership throughout the next three decades. If *1984* offered readers a bleak image of a brutally regulated society, British author Nevil Shute's *On the Beach* (1957) crystallized Western fears about escalating nuclear tensions between the Soviet Union and the West. In Shute's novel, the world has experienced a nuclear war, and only a few pockets of people in the Southern Hemisphere are still alive. A small group of people in Melbourne, Australia, try to cope with the knowledge that they have only a few weeks or months to live before they, too, will die of the slowly spreading nuclear contamination. Faced with certain death, the characters choose to spend their last time as normally as possible. *On the Beach* effectively captured the feeling of doomsday that permeated much of Western culture in the aftermath of World War II. The novel, which was a best-seller, played a role in influencing U.S. public opinion against atmospheric testing of nuclear weapons. Similar opinions were also formed in Europe. In April 1958, British protesters marched from Aldermaston to Trafalgar Square in London to demonstrate against nuclear power. The popularity of the marches culminated in 1962, with over fifty thousand participants. That year, thirty thousand demonstrators also walked from Holbaek to Copenhagen, despite the fact that Denmark did not have any nuclear weapons.

The political tensions that epitomized the Cold War also contributed to the popularity of the espionage novel. British author Ian Fleming's *Casino Royale* (1953) was the first in a series of James Bond novels and takes place at a glamorous casino on the French Riviera. Bond (also known as Agent 007) is assigned to break Russian spy Le Chiffre's bank at the baccarat tables, but things soon take a more violent turn. The combination of suspense and glamour contributed to the success of the James Bond books and, later, to the popularity of the films. In the decades after the war, middle-class readers coveted the same luxury goods that were part of the agent's lifestyle. Yet, Fleming's 007 was a more troubled character than the one who later appeared on the big screen. He was a womanizer with a tendency to depression, who drank and smoked excessively and was frequently advised by his superiors to cut back. John F. Kennedy helped popularize the series by announcing that they were among his favorite books. After Fleming's death in 1964, further Bond novels were written by, among others, British authors Kingsley Amis (as Robert Markham) and John Gardner.

The fall of the Berlin Wall meant that James Bond found himself without his traditional enemies. They were replaced by villains in the form of international terrorists and megalomaniac media moguls. The films based on the novels brought the character 007 to the attention of a worldwide mass audience. The Bond character has also appeared in a TV series, a comic strip, and several spin-off books, such as the Young Bond series (2004–). A film remake of *Casino Royale* appeared in 2006.

Unlike Fleming, who used political events as a backdrop to Bond's action adventures, Swedish authors Maj Sjöwall and Per Wahlöö critically explored the current social and political climate and its effects on the individual. Their crime novel *The Laughing Policeman* (1968) is one of a series of popular books that focuses on a team of police investigators in Stockholm. The book begins with an attack on a bus by what appears to be a random madman with a machine gun. The series is noteworthy for how the characters change over the books. Team leader Beck gets divorced, while other characters leave the force or die on duty. In the last two novels, Beck contemplates quitting the force and joining the Marxist-Leninist party. He feels his work as a policeman is contributing to the increasing violence, rather than preventing it. Sjöwall and Wahlöö used the crime novel to comment on the changing Swedish welfare state of the 1960s and 1970s, and the series was meant as a barometer of the increasingly harsh social and economic climate. An American film based on the book appeared in 1973. Like later Swedish made-for-television movies based on the series, the American adaptation kept the crime story elements but omitted the social critique. It also changed the location from Stockholm to San Francisco. The novels are considered modern classics of the genre and represent an abandonment of the traditional whodunit format in favor of the modern police procedural.

The historical whodunit nevertheless experienced a revival in the 1980s, due largely to the Italian author Umberto Eco's medieval mystery *The Name of the Rose* (1980). The book is a classic murder mystery set in an abbey in fourteenth-century Italy. The central character, William of Baskerville, is aided by his young companion, Adso of Melk, in trying to solve the murders of several of the abbey's residents. In the process, they go in search of a mysterious book that is somehow connected with the killings. *The Name of the Rose* can be read on several levels: as a straightforward murder mystery, as an example of the scholastic method (a popular medieval method of learning that involves both logic analysis and philology), and as an introduction to Eco's own discipline, semiotics, or the study of signs. Eco makes a number of references to historical characters and other works of fiction. The closer William and Adso come to solving the mystery, the more they must focus on the meaning of texts and how to read them. This multilayered, self-conscious exploration of the reading process was interpreted by contemporary critics as an example of postmodern literature. The highly erudite novel became a surprise best-seller upon its publication. It coincided with a renewed interest in the Middle Ages, both in Europe and the United States, and followed in the footsteps of popular nonfiction books by writers such as the American historian Barbara Tuchman. The novel was made into a popular film in 1986. It also paved the way for later historical mysteries, such as those written by British author Iain Pears and American author Dan Brown.

In the politically volatile 1960s and 1970s, European writers increasingly used the novel to criticize social inequality and governmental misuse of power. Social realism became the preferred literary mode. In *The Lost Honor of Katharina Blum* (1974), Heinrich Böll, one of West Germany's most popular authors, attacked both the West German government and the tabloid press. The novel tells the story of Katharina Blum, who meets and spends the night with a man who turns out to be a wanted bank robber. As a consequence, she is interrogated aggressively by the police, who treat her as a terrorist. The local tabloid *Zeitung* is soon on to the story and hounds Blum, her friends and family for newsworthy information. One journalist in particular, Werner Tötges, publishes increasingly wild articles, which threaten to ruin Blum's life. Desperate, she shoots Tötges. The novel critiqued the methods used by an increasingly merciless tabloid press, which did not hesitate to fabricate news to sell more issues. European criticism of the sensationalist press culminated in 1997 with the death of Princess Diana, who was chased by so-called *paparazzi* moments before her car crashed in a Paris tunnel. Böll is one of Germany's most widely read authors; like *The Lost Honor of Katharina Blum*, his other novels dealt mostly with the lives of ordinary Germans after World War II. In particular, he attacked the materialistic values that he saw dominating post-war Western society. Böll won the Nobel Prize for Literature in 1972.

With the emergence of women's movements in the 1960s, novelists also began to explore women's condition in society. In Finland-Swedish author Märta Tikkanen's novel *Manrape* (1975), the divorced protagonist Tova Randers meets a stranger, who later rapes her. Instead of reporting the assault, she decides to rape her male attacker in an act of retaliation. The novel's original Finland-Swedish title, which translates as "Men Can't Be Raped," expresses more accurately the dilemma that faces Randers. She is torn between a will to adhere to traditional notions of femininity and the desire to step outside the female role through acts of rape, humiliation, and revenge. The novel can be read as a discussion of 1970s feminist strategies and ideologies in fictional form. It caused a scandal when it was first published in Finland, which was not ready to read about such subjects as rape and divorce. As a consequence, Tikkanen found herself ostracized by the Finnish cultural establishment. In the other Nordic countries, reactions were more positive and *Manrape* is now considered a Scandinavian feminist classic. The novel has been back in print in Swedish since 2004.

Female readers were drawn to novelists who dealt critically with subjects pertaining especially to women's lives. The popularity of British author Fay Weldon's *The Life and Loves of a She-Devil* (1983) was due largely to her humorous exploration of the myths by which women are described in modern society. The novel is a satirical critique of romance fiction, yet relies on many of the genre's formulaic images. It traces the personal remake of the large and ugly housewife Ruth into a copy of the woman who has seduced her husband, the successful and beautiful romance author Mary Fisher. Through the novel, Weldon explores female stereotypes and the limited choices available for women who wish to escape them. Ruth is an example of the monstrous female, unable to live up to the image of the happy housewife but equally unsuitable for the role of seductress. The ambivalent ending suggests that Weldon sees both women characters as victims of a society that limits women's perception of themselves. The novel can also be read as a critique of the increasing popularity of cosmetic surgery in the 1980s. It anticipated later popular studies of public images of women, such as American author Naomi Wolf's *The Beauty Myth* (1991). *The Life and Loves of a She-Devil* became an international best-seller, was adapted into a hugely popular television mini-series by the BBC, and was later turned into a Hollywood film.

Despite feminist criticism, the romance novel continued to thrive, and it experienced a new popularity with the emergence of so-called chick-lit in the mid-1990s. An early example of the chick-lit genre was British author Helen Fielding's hugely popular novel *Bridget Jones's Diary* (1996). Based loosely on Jane Austen's *Pride and Prejudice,* the book describes Bridget Jones's romantic entanglements with two men: her boss, Daniel Cleaver, and Mark Darcy, who is a successful human-rights lawyer. Fielding's novel, which was first published in diary form in the British newspaper *The Independent,* provided the blueprint for later books in the same genre. It featured a hip female protagonist in an urban setting and was written for and marketed to single, working women in their twenties and thirties. The story typically focused on weight issues, love, and the differences between the sexes, and was told in a humorous manner. Fielding's book and its sequel were also made into two very successful films. In the wake of the novel's popularity, the word "singleton" became a trendy and positive self-description of young career women without romantic partners.

In a review of French-Algerian author Faïza Guène's debut novel *Kiffe Kiffe Tomorrow* (2004), *Elle* magazine referred to its heroine as "a Bridget Jones teenager of the [French] suburbs." Guène belongs to a line of successful new writers with an immigrant background. Her novel tells the story of fifteen-year-old Doria, a French Moroccan girl growing up in a run-down high-rise estate north of Paris. As would be expected of a teenager, much of Doria's time is spent thinking about boys. Unlike other depictions of female life in the suburbs, *Kiffe Kiffe Tomorrow* is characterized by love and humor. Guène's use of slang expressions caused some reviewers to argue that the French language was in danger of depletion. Other critics celebrated the nineteen-year-old author's ability to offer her readers a unique insight into the world of a young second-generation immigrant girl. The novel has also been praised for giving a more positive view of life in *la banlieue*. The word strictly means "the suburbs," but since the 1970s, for many people in France it conjures up images of unemployment, crumbling tower blocks, gang violence, and in 2005, riots, shootings, and death. Guène's success has been interpreted by many critics as a departure from stereotypical and negative views of the descendants of Algerian expatriates, so-called *pieds-noirs*.

The *Richard and Judy* Effect

In 2004, the magazine-style program *Richard and Judy* on British Channel Four launched a television book club. The result was a reshaping of British book sales and publishing. During the ten-minute weekly book club section of the program, presenters Judy Finnegan and Richard Madeley discuss books with celebrity readers. When the show featured Irish author Joseph O'Connor's novel *Star of the Sea* (2003), the book's sales went up 1,200 percent. In the book trade, this phenomenon has became known as the *Richard and Judy* Effect, and British publishers are increasingly taking the show into account when choosing among submitted manuscripts. The selected titles have included both challenging literary novels and lighter reads. Some readers buy the entire set of *Richard and Judy* seasonal selections, and the program was said to be responsible for one in fifty books sold in the UK in 2005.

DRAMA

Irish playwright Samuel Beckett's absurdist drama *Waiting for Godot* (1949) effectively captured the feeling of meaninglessness that permeated the period immediately after World War II. The play, which Beckett wrote in French, opened in 1953 in the Theatre Babylone in Paris. It focuses on two tramps, Vladimir and Estragon, who meet by chance under a tree and discover that they are both waiting for a Monsieur Godot. The two tramps quarrel, eat, contemplate suicide, and try to sleep, but above all, they wait for Godot, who never arrives. The play has been called the quintessential play of the late twentieth century, mainly because of its influence on later playwrights such as British author Tom Stoppard, but also because of its tragicomic description of the human condition. Like other absurdist plays, the stoical yet ultimately meaningless wait in *Waiting for Godot* affected the public deeply. It seemed to offer a more honest response to life after World War II than the traditional belief in a rationally ordered universe. The play has been viewed as an existentialist commentary on humanity, and Godot has frequently been interpreted as God. Beckett himself refused to categorize or explain his play, which he translated into English in 1954. *Waiting for Godot* has since entered into the realm of popular myths by which modern man defines himself.

Beckett's absurdist play contrasted dramatically with the realist British theatre that emerged in the 1950s. British playwright John Osborne's so-called kitchen sink-drama *Look Back in Anger* (1956) first appeared at London's Royal Court Theatre. *Look Back in Anger* was set in contemporary Britain and addressed issues such as free love, abortion, and the social and political condition of post-war Britain. Frustrated by the class-bound nature of society and his own unfulfilled ambitions, the rebellious and misogynist working-class character Jimmy Porter takes out his feelings on his pregnant, upper-middle-class wife Alison. Her passive acceptance of the abuse causes him to embark upon an affair with another woman. The affair indirectly contributes to Alison's miscarriage. The play takes place in a squalid one-room flat in the Midlands, which shocked many contemporary theatre critics, who also objected to Jimmy's left-wing sympathies and loudmouthed ranting. Other critics were more enthusiastic and identified Osbourne as part of a new generation of playwrights and authors: "the angry young men." The phrase came to represent a new movement in 1950s British theatre and literature and included radical authors and playwrights such as Kingsley Amis, Alan Sillitoe, and Harold Pinter. In a predominantly realist style, they criticized the establishment and spoke on behalf of the dispossessed young, who felt increasingly unhappy with the situation in conservative Britain. Their work also paved the way for the socially aware literature of the 1960s. *Look Back in Anger* was adapted for film in 1958.

> ### Theatre of the Absurd
>
> Absurdist theatre first became popular in the 1950s. The term was coined by the critic and scholar Martin Esslin in 1962 to describe the work of playwrights such as Samuel Beckett, Eugène Ionesco, Jean Genet, Arthur Adamov, and Harold Pinter. The moral crisis that followed World War II, and the trauma of living under threat of nuclear annihilation, resulted in a belief that human existence is essentially meaningless and therefore absurd. Absurdist plays are antirealistic, seeking to produce an allegorical, mythological vision of the world. Language and logic are viewed with distrust. Often, the public initially reacted with incomprehension and rejection. Some critics have argued that the antitheatre devices of absurdist theatre were aimed at shocking European audiences, in particular, out of their complacent existence and restoring in them a new sense of cosmic wonder. The roots of absurdist theatre can be traced back to Greek drama and the surrealist movement of the 1920s.

TEXTS FOR CHILDREN AND YOUNG ADULTS

The influence of child-centered education and new insights in children's psychology were visible in children's literature after World War II. Swedish author Astrid Lindgren's *Pippi Longstocking* (1945) is the first book in a series of four. It introduced readers to an antiauthoritarian girl-protagonist and a narrator who spoke from the point of view of a child. Pippi is a financially independent nine-year-old who lives by herself in a big house, accompanied only by a monkey and a horse. Her two best friends, Tommy and Annika, are considerably more conformist. It is Pippi who must save them from adult laws and introduce them to the freedom of anarchic behavior. Through *Pippi Longstocking,* Astrid Lindgren established her reputation as a popular children's book author around the world. The books are an early exploration of perceived gender roles and acceptable social behavior. For this reason, they have always been surrounded by a certain amount of controversy, although most people today read them simply as amusing children's stories. In the mid-1990s, a Swedish social commentator argued that the stories had a highly detrimental effect on schoolchildren and could seriously harm their social development. The books are considered classics among children's literature and have been translated into more than sixty languages. A Swedish television series based on the books was created in the 1970s, and an American feature film appeared in 1988.

Independence also characterizes the female protagonist in French author Françoise Sagan's debut novel *Bonjour Tristesse.* (1954). The seventeen-year-old girl Cécile personified the image of the new teenager, which appeared in European popular culture after World War II, inspired mainly by American film and music.

Cécile spends lazy summer days on the French Riviera with her father and his latest girlfriend, Elsa. Anne, a beautiful and intelligent friend of the family, appears unexpectedly and profoundly disturbs the peacefulness of the trio. In an attempt to break up this new group installation, Cécile convinces Cyril, a young man she has met on the beach, to initiate a secret affair with Elsa. As a result, her father's interest in Elsa is renewed, and the two lovers are discovered by Anna, who leaves the house in such a state that she crashes her car and dies. The father and daughter's amoral lifestyle upset contemporary French critics. Sagan was only eighteen when she started writing the book that made her famous both in France and abroad. The novel was an instant best-seller, and in 1957 it was made into a film. Meanwhile, the author and her fictional characters became symbols for a generation of disillusioned and rebellious teenagers, similar in some ways to the characters of American author J. D. Salinger.

The social realism that dominated literature production in the 1970s also influenced literature aimed at young readers. Authors began to address sensitive subjects such as death, divorce, and sexuality in their work. Norwegian author Jostein Gaarder chose a highly original approach to discuss existential questions in *Sophie's World* (1991), a sophisticated philosophical story that turned into a surprise best-seller. Gaarder's book is both a novel for young readers and an introduction to the history of Western philosophy from the pre-Socratic Greeks to Jean-Paul Sartre. Sophie Amundsen is a fourteen-year-old Norwegian girl, who receives a series of mysterious letters that ask a set of questions about existence and the meaning of life. The sender is the enigmatic philosopher Alberto Knox, and the letters are part of his correspondence course in philosophy. The genre-crossing *Sophie's World* became a European publishing phenomenon, selling particularly well in Germany, France, and the UK. It has been translated into more than fifty-three languages, and in 1995 it was among the best-selling books in the world. *Sophie's World* spawned a movie, a musical, a board game, and a CD-ROM. Gaarder received high critical acclaim for approaching difficult issues in a book aimed at young readers.

The popularity of children's books reached an unprecedented high with Joanne K. Rowling's *Harry Potter and the Philosopher's Stone* (1997). The first book in a series of seven volumes introduces the reader to the young Harry Potter, who lives under the reluctant care of his relatives, the Durselys. Shortly before his eleventh birthday, Harry receives a letter offering him a place at Hogwarts School of Witchcraft and Wizardy. Gradually, Harry discovers his real identity as the orphan of two famous wizards. At Hogwarts, he befriends two other students, Hermione Granger and Ron Weasley, who help Harry in his struggle against evil, personified by the wizard Voldemort, who killed Harry's parents. The series is targeted at young readers but has attained a following of devoted fans of all ages, unparalleled by other children's books. The books have been praised for encouraging children to read, but also received criticism from Christian groups that have denounced the books for promoting witchcraft. The series' success can be ascribed largely to the emergence of the Internet as a global community of communications and commerce. *Harry Potter and the Philosopher's Stone* was first published by Bloomsbury, a relatively small, independent publisher in the United Kingdom. Initial sales were based on positive reviews and word-of-mouth. By 2005, sales of the latest volume exceeded 275 millions copies. Later installments of the series have received much wider publicity than is standard for new books, and sales have relied largely on worldwide distribution by Internet bookstores. Advance orders of new volumes and midnight release parties at bookstores have also kept up the public's interest. The involvement of a global media conglomerate in the creation of a Harry Potter franchise has coincided with several films based on the books. The films, in their turn, have generated computer games and other branded merchandise. The series has also generated several spin-off books, which describe J. K. Rowling's fictional world in further detail.

POLITICAL TEXTS

In the essay collection *The Captive Mind* (1953), the Polish author Czesław Miłosz reflects on the situation for intellectuals in totalitarian states. Miłosz describes the seductiveness of Stalinist ideology on authors in Poland and the Baltic countries, but he also stresses its morally and intellectually corrupting features. In particular, he criticizes the readiness to accept totalitarian terror for the sake of a hypothetical better future. He also describes the survival skills developed by dissident intellectuals living under oppression. The book is an analysis of the life of the mind under all intellectually oppressive dictatorships, not just Stalinist communism, yet it upset many intellectuals, who resented Europe's dependence upon American help and had placed their hope in Stalin and the Far Left. Other critics were uncomfortable with Miłosz's refusal to take sides in the ideological war that characterized the 1950s. By 1953, Miłosz found it impossible to remain in Poland; he moved with this family to France, where he stayed until 1960, before emigrating to the United States. *The Captive Mind* is considered a classic post-World War II text and is still widely read in many central and eastern European schools and universities. Czesław Miłosz won the Nobel prize in Literature in 1980.

Unlike *The Captive Mind*, the focus of Croatian journalist Slavenka Drakulić's *Balkan Express: Fragments from the Other Side of War* (1992) is about ordinary people. In eighteen short personal essays, Drakulić conveys the shattering effects of the war in former Yugoslavia on the Balkan population. She interviews a young man who has joined the Croatian Guards, reports from the battle front, visits her exiled daughter in Vienna, and ponders the effects of the war on the next generation. In particular, Drakulić tries to understand why a pluralistic nation of apolitical men and women of her own generation has become so obsessed with ethnicity that it has resulted in a violent conflict. She proposes a number of reasons, most of which relate to Tito's dictatorial rule of Yugoslavia until 1980, and points to a lack of democratic tradition in the region. With *Balkan Express,* Drakulić brought the conflict closer to the readers, from the abstract view of war as a battle of ideas, to its daily tragic consequences. The Yugoslav conflicts in the west of the region ended in 1995, but continued in the east and south parts until 2001. Feeling increasingly unsafe in her home country, Drakulić moved to Sweden in the early 1990s.

TREATIES AND SPEECHES

With the end of the Cold War, European politics came to be defined by the establishment of the European Union (1992), an intergovernmental alliance of European states. The unique structure of the EU resembles that of a confederation, but it also gives its member-states national sovereignty in a number of areas. Despite becoming a popular text amongst European readers, the *European Constitution* (2004) was voted down in France and the Netherlands in 2005, which caused other states to halt their ratification procedures. More than one million titles relating to the *Constitution* were also sold in the months leading up to voting day. Guides and explanatory notes to the full text were the most popular titles. The subtitle to the *EU Constitution* was "Bringing Europe Closer to its Citizens," yet the treaty was criticized by many readers for its dense, bureaucratic language and length.

On June 26, 1963, John F. Kennedy gave one of the most memorable speeches of the Cold War. It ended with the famous words "*Ich Bin Ein Berliner.*" The phrase, which translates as "I am a citizen of Berlin," stressed American support for West Germany shortly after the erection of the Berlin Wall by the Soviet Union. It was also a reference to the Latin phrase "Civis Romanus sum" ("I am a Roman citizen"), which identified the speaker as a free man. In the speech, Kennedy pointed out that no democratic state had ever had to put up a wall to prevent its people from leaving. The Berlin Wall was erected in 1961 by the soviet state in an attempt to prevent citizens of East Germany escaping to the West via the city. The wall was guarded by soldiers with machine guns and effectively cut the city in half. Nearly two hundred people were killed trying to cross from East to West Berlin. In Germany, Kennedy's speech is considered a landmark in the country's postwar history. The phrase itself is often referred to humorously in popular culture, because it has been argued (mistakenly) that the correct translation of the phrase is "I am a sausage," and in other translations, "I am a doughnut."

DOMESTIC TEXTS

British celebrity chef Jamie Oliver came to the public's attention through the popular television cooking show *The Naked Chef.* The humorous title referred to the state of the ingredients, fresh and unprocessed, and not the chef himself. The show resulted in a cookbook of the same name in 1999, followed by other books based on Oliver's later shows. Like the food cooked on the television show, the recipes in *The Naked Chef* are unpretentious and simple. They make generous use of fresh herbs and pasta, two ingredients strongly associated with Oliver's cooking. *The Naked Chef* contributed to the prodigious burst of new interest in the cookbook genre, which has become a mainstay in the publishing world. Sales in cookbooks have increased at a steady five percent a year since 1996, which makes it the strongest segment in the international book market. This boom is explained partly by the international success of food television—*The Naked Chef* has been exported to over 45 countries—and partly by an increase in health and nutrition awareness. Large, full-color photographs and an emphasis on regional and seasonal specialties help explain why cookbooks are often considered leisure reading. Oliver's book has been translated into twenty-one languages.

Like the *Naked Chef,* the book *What Not to Wear* (2002) began as a British television show. It is the first of three best-selling style guides by British authors Trinny Woodall and Susannah Constantine. In each makeover program of *What Not to Wear,* presenters Woodall and Constantine confronted their guests with a harsh evaluation of their fashion sense. Each guest then received style advice and a makeover, which included a new and more flattering wardrobe. The success of the first series resulted in the first *What Not to Wear* book, which is organized into separate chapters, each of which deals with a different part of a woman's body, such as her legs, arms, and hips. The authors stress that knowing "what not to wear" is the first step in achieving a real sense of style. Subsequent books have focused on fashion for different occasions and lifestyles. An American version of the television show has also been launched. The huge success of the *What Not to Wear* television shows and books coincided with the popularity of the American sitcom *Sex and the City,* where the characters' luxury fashion outfits were given as much consideration as the story line. *What Not to Wear* is the latest in a long tradition of style guides for women. It differs from its predecessors mainly by its focus on keeping up with the current fashion (as opposed to building a capsule wardrobe of classic pieces) and the way its message has been adapted to fit different media.

NEWSPAPERS & MAGAZINES

The most influential post-World War II journal in France was *Les Temps Modernes* (1945–). The journal was founded by French philosophers Jean-Paul Sartre, Simone de Beauvoir, and Maurice Merleau-Ponty and immediately became an arena for French intellectual debate. From the very beginning, the idea of communism dominated the discussions. The journal's content was often controversial and most issues sold out quickly. In 1949, it carried two extracts from de Beauvoir's book *The Second Sex*—"The Lesbian" and "Woman's Sexual Initiation," which caused a scandal, but did not diminish the popularity of the publication. In 1960 *Les Temps Modernes* published *Manifesto 121,* a document protesting against the Algerian War and signed by many of France's leading intellectuals, among them Sartre, Beauvoir, and the entire journal staff. As a result, the August and October issues were confiscated by the police, followed by searches and arrests at the journal's headquarters. Political discussions dominated the content in the 1960s and 1970s. An article in 1968, written by the journal's editorial committee, denounced the USSR for its intervention in Czechoslovakia. Other issues focused on French colonialism in Africa and the Israeli-Palestinian conflict. French thinker and actor Francis Jeanson became the managing director of *Les Temps Modernes* in 1951. He was followed by French filmmaker Claude Lanzmann.

Unlike *Les Temps Modernes,* which attracted well-educated, mostly male readers, *Elle* magazine (1945–) targeted the average, middle-class, female reader. Inspired by American women's magazines such as *Harper's Bazaar* and *Vogue,* Russian-born Hélène Gordon-Lazareff identified a gap in the French magazine market after World War II. The meager war years had made European women long for flair and fashion. Unlike previous women's magazines, *Elle* did not offer dictatorial fashion decrees, but cheerful advice and conspiratorial guidance. The publication's focus was fashion, arts, politics, and culture. *Elle* was the first European magazine to write about plastic surgery, unwanted pregnancies, and time management for women. It was also the first magazine to feature younger, more natural-looking women, like Brigitte Bardot, on its pages. In 1983 an American edition was launched. In the twenty-first century, there were thirty-six editions of the magazine throughout the world, which reached twenty-one million readers every month. This makes *Elle* the largest fashion magazine in the world. Offshoot magazines include *Elle Décor* (with nineteen editions), *Elle Girl* (nine editions) and *Elle Cuisine* (five editions). The magazine has also spawned sixteen web-editions.

Meanwhile, the newspaper business is dominated by *The Sun* (1969–). This British tabloid newspaper has the highest circulation of any daily English-language newspaper in the world: around 3,200,000 copies a day. *The Sun* is published both in the United Kingdom and Ireland. The paper was launched in 1964, but experienced a relaunch in 1969, when it was sold to Australian multinational media proprietor Rupert Murdoch, who popularized the editorial content and introduced the so-called page-three girl, a nude glamour photograph on page three of every issue. Feminists have long denounced the paper as sexist, and since its relaunch, the newspaper has also been called jingoistic and sensational. It supported both the Falkland and the Iraqi Wars, and takes a skeptical position toward the EU. In 1989, the paper

Issues of the French women's magazines, *Elle* and *Marie Claire* on sale in Paris. [Courtesy of Vanessa Berry]

published an article on the Hillsborough football stadium disaster in Sheffield, where ninety-six people died. The paper claimed falsely that Liverpool football fans were to blame. As a consequence, the paper still sells poorly in Liverpool. Traditional readers of *The Sun* are working-class conservatives, who read the paper for its popular take on news and politics, but also for its celebrity coverage and strong focus on sports. The profitability of *The Sun* helped Murdoch to launch the *Sky* satellite television channels and, in 1993, begin a price war between the British newspaper *The Times* (owned by Murdoch's company *News Corporation*) and its competitors *The Daily Telegraph* and *The Guardian*. *The Sun* is considered one of the most successful, profitable, and influential tabloids in the world.

In contrast, one of the most influential fashion publications of the twentieth century began as a small fanzine, dedicated to London street fashion. The periodical *i-D* (1980–) is a trend-setting British style magazine that focuses on fashion, music, art, and youth culture. The magazine was founded by British art director and publisher Terry Jones and explored the style of the 1980s punk era, a scene that was largely ignored by mainstream fashion. In the process, it also documented key moments in the explosion of global popular culture. The result was a magazine that blurs the distinction between art and fashion. In particular, the magazine became known for its groundbreaking photography and typography. Photographers such as Juergen Teller, Corinne Day, and Ellen von Unwerth pioneered a hybrid style of documentary/fashion photography that spoke directly to young readers. In contrast to the glamorous images that dominated traditional fashion photography, *i-D*'s fashion spreads were unconventional and confrontational, often including androgynous-looking models that questioned the gender stereotyping found in mainstream media. The magazine also pioneered a style of photography called "the straight up," where models, often punk and New Wave youth found on English streets, were simply asked to stand against a nearby blank wall. In the 1980s and 1990s, *i-D* had a significant impact on the cutting-edge of high fashion, art, and culture. It also set the template for a new type of publication, the style magazine, which was read by young people of both sexes.

Unlike conventional magazines, *The Big Issue* (1991–) is sold in the streets by homeless people. It is Europe's first street paper and was launched in the UK in September 1991. Initially a monthly magazine, it is now published weekly. More than 250,000 issues are sold across the UK each week by over six thousand vendors. Today, the magazine can also be found in other European cities, South Africa, and Australia. It offers a mixture of feature articles, celebrity interviews, current affairs, and news. It also includes contributions by and about homeless people and functions as a campaigning paper. The original financial backing came from *The Body Shop Foundation*. The principle of *The Big Issue* is based on a philosophy of self-help, and the selling of the magazine gives homeless people a chance to earn their own living. Vendors buy the magazine from *The Big Issue* and sell it at a fifty percent profit. The price was £1.50 per copy in 2007. The vast majority of vendors are men, most between the ages of twenty-five and thirty-five. *The Big Issue* has also developed writing workshops, vendor support teams, training and education departments, and housing teams, in addition to producing the magazine itself.

HISTORY TEXTS

The Rise and Fall of the Third Reich (1960) was the first definitive history of Nazi Germany in English. American author and journalist William L. Shirer described the gradual rise of the Nazis and Hitler's ascent to power, the unfolding of the war, the holocaust, and the German defeat in 1945. On more than 1,200 pages, he offered a detailed account of events and suggested reasons for the war. Information about Hitler's background, his upbringing in Vienna, and the final days in the bunker fascinated contemporary readers, and the accounts of the genocide of the Jews—substantiated by eyewitness reports—gave new insights into the horrors of the concentration camps and the decisions that preceded them. Much of the book is based on the 485 tons of documents captured from the confidential archives of the German government. Other sources include the diaries of the German propaganda minister Joseph Goebbels, confidential speeches, conference reports, transcripts of tapped telephone conversations, and Shirer's own recollections of working as a journalist during the war. The book was an instant best-seller upon publication both in

---

Samizdat

The word comes from the Russian *sam* (self) and *izadatel-stvo* (publishing) and is a play on the word *Gosizdat* (State Publishing House). Samizdat refers to illegal literature, which began to circulate in the USSR and other Eastern Bloc countries after Stalin's death in 1953. Under communism, literature was a state-controlled instrument for soviet propaganda. The government's monopoly on printing presses meant that samizdat publications had to be photocopied or made of carbon copies of typewritten sheets. These were passed by hand from reader to reader. Originally a product of the intelligentsia of Moscow and Leningrad, samizdat literature was soon produced and distributed throughout the constituent republics of the Soviet Union. In Poland, underground publications became more numerous than elsewhere. A distinct underground literary culture grew out of samizdat, which included writing by soviet authors such as Michail Bulgakov and nonfiction texts that criticized the soviet government. A related phenomenon was *tamizdat* (there published), which referred to manuscripts that had been printed abroad and then smuggled back into the Eastern Bloc. Samizdat disappeared with the fall of the USSR in the early 1990s.

Reading Alexander Solzhenitsyn's *One Day in the Life of Ivan Denisovitch*, which detailed the horrors of government oppression of Soviet citizens.

western Europe and the United States. Shirer also popularized a quotation from philosopher George Santayana in the epigraph to the book: "Those who cannot remember the past are condemned to repeat it." *The Rise and Fall of the Third Reich* is considered a classic of modern history and has never been out of print since its first publication.

Unlike Shirer and other traditional historians, the French *Annales*-school was a loose group of historians all working on similar topics who, by using a similar methodology, were committed to broadening the range of their discipline. In particular, they challenged the dominance of political and diplomatic history and favored social, economic, and cultural narratives of events, so-called total history. The result was often a focus on ordinary people, traditionally left out of official histories. *The Peasants of Languedoc* (1966), by French historian Emmanuel Le Roy Ladurie, was a groundbreaking work of total history. The book describes life among ordinary people in a province in the south of France, from the Renaissance to the Enlightenment. In some ways the protagonist of this study is the agrarian cycle, whose movements over time Ladurie traces and interprets. Yet, the narrative remains close to the people affected by the cycle and includes details of everyday life for struggling peasants. The volume combines elements of human geography, historical demography, economic history, and folk culture. Many of the Annales historians introduced or further developed new approaches to history, such as comparative history, the history of mentalities, and quantitative history. Through his work, Ladurie contributed to breaking down the barriers between disciplines, in particular geography; social sciences such as anthropology, economics, and psychology; and linguistics. His focus on mentalities and cultural history also anticipated the work of later scholars such as French philosopher Michel Foucault, who was interested in the changing significance of language.

The soviet author Aleksandr Solzhenitsyn's novel, *One Day in the Life of Ivan Denisovitch* (1962) and memoir *The Gulag Archipelago* (1973) also focus on the plights of ordinary men and women. The three volumes of *The Gulag Archipelago* describe Solzhenitsyn's experiences as a prisoner in Stalin's infamous prison camps (known by the acronym gulag) and caused a sensation upon its publication in the West. Millions of readers were shocked to learn about the conditions in the labor camps and the corruption of the soviet legal system. The books reinforced growing anti-Communist sentiments in western Europe and added pressure on the soviet government to reveal the truth about the camps. Solzhenitsyn spent eight years in the gulag. During this time, he recorded accounts from more than two hundred fellow prisoners, which make up a substantial part of the memoirs. The "archipelago" refers to the vast spread of camps, from the Bering Sea to the Bosporus Strait. *The Gulag Archipelago* was Solzhenitsyn's attempt to produce a literary and historical record of the soviet regime's use of terror against its own people. A copy of the first volume was confiscated in the Soviet Union by the secret police, the KGB, but was finally published in Paris. Upon publication of the memoirs, Solzhenitsyn was arrested and charged with treason. As a result, he was exiled from the Soviet Union. This meant that he could finally take possession of his Nobel Prize in Literature, awarded in 1970.

PHILOSOPHICAL TEXTS

The dramatic social, political, and economic changes that took place in the aftermath of World War II had a profound influence on contemporary thinkers. Austrian neurologist and psychiatrist Viktor E. Frankl's *Man's Search for Meaning* (1946) is among the most influential works of psychiatric literature since the work of Sigmund Freud. Frankl's experiences in the German concentration camps during World War II provided him with the basis for the development of a new school of psychotherapy: logotherapy. *Man's Search for Meaning* begins with an account of Frankl's five-year imprisonment in Auschwitz and other concentration camps and focuses on his struggle during this time to find reasons to live. The second part of the book describes the methods of logotherapy. Unlike Freud, Viktor E. Frankl did not identify sexuality as the prime motivating force of human life, but argued instead that humans are always motivated by the will to find a meaning and a purpose with life, even in concentration camps. Whereas Freudian psychoanalysis requires introspection and self-reflection of its patients, one of the primary aims of logotherapy is to enable patients to view their life in a broader perspective. Frankl's focus on the human search for meaning made his school of psychotherapy compatible with Western religion to a higher degree than psychoanalysis. *Man's Search for Meaning* was voted one of the ten most influential books of our time by the American Library of Congress in 1991, and it has been translated into thirty languages. More than 145 books have been written about Frankl and logotherapy, and Frankl himself received twenty-eight honorary degrees.

Like Frankl, French existentialist philosopher Simone de Beauvoir emphasized the human capacity for choice. Yet, she also argued that women occupied a less favorable position in society than men, which in actuality limited their choices. Her book *The Second Sex* (1949) was a groundbreaking feminist and existentialist study of women's inequality. Beauvoir defined women as the "other" in relation to the male subject or self. The other, she explained, is not a complement, but a projection of everything that the self rejects and cannot be: it is passive and immanent. Yet this position, she continues, is not a fact, but a social construction. The book offers a critical analysis of biological, psychological, and materialistic historical theories on women's situation and character, and traces images of women through myths and literature. In *The Second Sex*, Beauvoir pioneered the idea of women's oppression in society and openly discussed women's sexuality and sexual problems, four years before American biologist Alfred C. Kinsey's famous study *Sexual*

Behavior in the Human Female (1953). She also argued for the legalization of abortion and birth control. The book caused a scandal upon publication and was added to the Vatican's Index of Forbidden Books. Beauvoir was called "frustrated" and "abnormal" by many contemporary male critics. Despite criticism, *The Second Sex* became an international best-seller and contributed significantly to the development of feminist theory. It also inspired women's movements both in France and internationally. The book was quickly translated into several languages, and Beauvoir became the most widely read feminist author in the world. In Japan, *The Second Sex* topped the best-seller list for over a year. The axiom "One is not born a woman, rather, one becomes one," is the most quoted sentence from the book. Despite its popularity the English translation remains incomplete and, in some places, inaccurate. Critics have pointed out that it misrepresents many of Beauvoir's ideas and arguments.

The technological advancements and the computerization of society in the 1970s also resulted in new theories of knowledge and communication. In *The Postmodern Condition: A Report on Knowledge* (1979), French philosopher Jean-François Lyotard developed a fundamentally different understanding of knowledge than the one that had dominated since the Enlightenment. In particular, he argued that the so-called meta-narratives, total philosophies of history and humanity (like Marxism), had lost their credibility. Instead, Lyotard believed that the speed of modern society meant that each situation developed its own narrative, which operated like an ever-changing language game. Scientific knowledge, he insisted, was subservient to narrative knowledge. Historical progress is an illusion. In this multiple-narrative society, the development of rules of ethics and other forms of legitimization depend entirely on open access to information. Lyotard's definition of the postmodern became immensely influential, and it was embraced by other thinkers who sought to deconstruct universal claims on objectivity, unity, and truth. Postmodern thinkers, such as French philosopher Jacques Derrida, emphasized the multiplicity of meanings and focused their critique not just on the written word but on all cultural phenomena, such as science, technology, art, and politics. The translation of Lyotard's work into English in 1984 further globalized the postmodern debate. Some critics continued to dismiss Lyotard's theories as relativist, nihilist, and politically unviable.

SCIENTIFIC TEXTS

With *A Brief History of Time* (1988), Stephen Hawking, British professor of theoretical physics, attempted to fill the gap between the average person's understanding of the universe and the highly specialized knowledge of scientists. What do we know about the universe, and how do we know it? What is the nature of time? Is the universe infinite? Questions such as these serve as introduction to an account of the great theories of cosmos, from Aristotle to quantum mechanics. In the process, Hawking also writes about black holes, string theory, the big bang, time, and the possibility of a universe comprising several dimensions. To simplify the content and make it more accessible to the average reader, the book includes illustrations, diagrams, and models. There is also a noticeable absence of mathematical equations. *A Brief History of Time* was a landmark book that became a worldwide success and remained on the *London Sunday Times* best-seller list for a record-breaking 237 weeks. It was an early example of the popular science genre, which, in the twenty-first century, appeared regularly on the best-seller lists. Despite the high sales figures of *A Brief History of Time*, it has sometimes been referred to as an example of the "unread best-seller," that is, a book bought for its popularity but never read by its owner.

CONCLUSION

Reading practices in Europe since the mid-1900s mirror the social, economic, and political changes of the period. In the aftermath of World War II, reading became a means to make sense of past events and the uncertainty of the future. As the Cold War came to an end, people's reading choices revealed a new political engagement with a quickly changing society. The new roles that women, children, and immigrants came to occupy in European societies were debated, questioned, and confirmed in literature. Lifestyle books and popular magazines reflected the type of leisure pursuits that Europeans enjoyed as prosperity rose and consumerism increased. Technological developments, such as the Internet and digital printing, gave European readers unprecedented access to written information. Since the late 1990s, newspapers are increasingly read and published on the Internet, and books are frequently published electronically or as audiobooks. It remains to be seen what effects these trends will have on future European reading preferences.

AVAILABILITY OF SOURCES

All primary sources are commercially available in English except for Märta Tikkanen, *Manrape,* which is out of print in English.

RECOMMENDED READING

Barker, Adele Marie, ed. *Consuming Russia: Popular Culture, Sex, and Society Since Gorbachev.* Durham, NC: Duke University Press, 1999.

Bartram, Graham, ed. *The Cambridge Companion to the Modern German Novel.* Cambridge, UK: Cambridge University Press, 2004.

Best, Victoria. *An Introduction to Twentieth Century French Literature.* London: Gerald Duckworth & Company, 2002.

Bloom, Clive. *Bestsellers: Popular Fiction Since 1900.* London: Palgrave Macmillan, 2002.

Burns, Bob. *German Cultural Studies: An Introduction.* Oxford, UK: Oxford University Press, 1995.

Christopher, D. *British Culture: An Introduction.* London: Routledge, 1999.

Godsland, Shelley, and Nickianne Moody, eds. *Reading the Popular in Contemporary Spanish Fiction.* Newark, DE: University Of Delaware Press, 2004.

Head, Dominic. *The Cambridge Introduction to Modern British Fiction, 1950–2000.* Cambridge, UK: Cambridge University Press, 2002.

Hewitt, Nicholas, ed. *The Cambridge Companion to Modern French Culture.* Cambridge, UK: Cambridge University Press, 2003.

Houe, Poul. *Documentarism in Scandinavian Literature.* Amsterdam: Rodopi, 1997.

Kelly, Mare, ed. *The Media in Europe: The Euromedia Handbook.* London: Sage Publications, 2004.

Moliterno, Gino. *Encyclopedia of Contemporary Italian Culture.* London: Routledge, 2000.

Sutherland, John. *Reading the Decades: Fifty Years of British History Through the Nation's Bestsellers.* London: BBC Books, 2002.

Travers, Martin. *An Introduction to Modern European Literature: From Romanticism to Postmodernism.* London: Palgrave Macmillan, 1997.

Whelehan, Imelda, ed. *The Feminist Bestseller: From* Sex and the Single Girl *to* Sex and the City. London: Palgrave Macmillan, 2005.

Zuck, Virpi, ed. *Dictionary of Scandinavian Literature.* Westport, CT: Greenwood Press, 1990.

PRIMARY SOURCES

Beckett, Samuel. *Waiting for Godot: A Tragicomedy in Two Acts.* Translated by Samuel Beckett. London: Faber & Faber, 1998. First published in French as *En attendant Godot* in 1949.

The Big Issue. London: The Big Issue Co. Ltd., 1991–.

Böll, Heinrich. *The Lost Honor of Katharina Blum: or How Violence Develops and Where It Can Lead.* Translated by Leila Vennewitz. London: Penguin Classics, 1994. First published in German as *Die verlorene ehre der Katharina Blum* in 1974.

Constantine, Susannah and Trinny Woodall. *What Not To Wear.* London: Weidenfeld & Nicholson, 2003.

de Beauvoir, Simone. *The Second Sex.* Translated by H. M. Parshley. London: Vintage, 1989. First published in French as *Le Deuxième Sexe* in 1949.

Drakulić, Slavenka. *Balkan Express: Fragments from the Other Side of the War.* New York: Perennial, 1994.

Eco, Umberto. *The Name of the Rose.* Translated by William Weaver. New York: Vintage Classics, 2004. First published in Italian as *Il nome della rosa* in 1980.

Elle. Paris: Hachette Filipacchi, 1945–.

Fielding, Helen. *Bridget Jones's Diary.* New York: Penguin, 2001.

Fleming, Ian. *Casino Royale.* New York: Penguin, 2002. First published in 1953.

Frankl, Viktor E. *Man's Search for Meaning.* Translated by Ilse Lasch. London: Rider, 2004. First published in German as *. . . trotzdem Ja zum Leben sagen. Ein Psychologe erlebt das Konzentrationslager* in 1946.

Gaarder, Jostein. *Sophie's World: a Novel about the History of Philosophy.* Translated by Paulette Moller. New York: Farrar, Straus and Giroux, 2007. First published in Norwegian as *Sofies verden* in 1994.

Guène, Faïza. *Kiffe Kiffe Tomorrow.* Translated by Sarah Adams. London: Chatto & Windus, 2006.

Hawking, Stephen. *A Brief History of Time.* New York: Bantam, 1998. First published in 1988.

I-D Magazine. London: Levelprint Ltd., 1980–.

Kennedy, J. F. *"Ich Bin Ein Berliner." The World's Great Speeches. 4th ed.* Edited by Lewis Copeland, Lawrence W. Lamm, Stephen J. McKenna. Mineola, NY: Dover Publications, 2007. Speech delivered on June 26, 1963 in Berlin, West Germany.

Le Roy Ladurie, Emmanuel. *The Peasants of Languedoc.* Translated by John Day. Urbana & Chicago: University of Illinois Press, 1977. First published in French as *Les Paysans de Languedoc* in 1966.

Les Temps Modernes. Paris: Gallimard, 1985–. First issue published in 1945.

Lindgren, Astrid. *Pippi Longstocking.* Translated by Louis S. Granzman. London: Puffin, 2005. First published in Swedish as *Pippi Långstrump* in 1944.

Lyotard, François. *The Postmodern Condition: A Report on Knowledge.* Translated by G. Bennington. Manchester, UK: Manchester University Press, 1984. First published in French as *La Condition postmoderne: Rapport sur le savoir* in 1979.

Miłosz, Czesław. *The Captive Mind.* Translated by Jane Zielonko. London: Penguin, 2001. First published in Polish as *Zniewolony umysł* in 1953.

Oliver, Jamie. *The Naked Chef.* London: Penguin, 2001.

Orwell, George. *1984.* London: Secker & Warburg, 2003. First published in 1948.

Osborne, John. *Look Back in Anger.* New York: Penguin, 1982. First published in 1956.

Rowling, J. K. *Harry Potter and the Philosopher's Stone.* London: Bloomsbury, 1997.

Sagan, Françoise. *Bonjour Tristesse.* Translated by Irene Ash. London: Penguin, 1998. First published in French as *Bonjour Tristesse* in 1954.

Shirer, William L. *The Rise and Fall of the Third Reich.* New York: Simon & Schuster, 1990. First published in 1960.

Shute, Neville. *On the Beach.* Thirsk, North Yorkshire: House of Stratus, 2002. First published in 1957.

Sjöwall, Maj and Per Wahlöö. *The Laughing Policeman.* Trans. Lois Roth. London: Orion, 2002. First published in Swedish as *Den skrattande polisen: roman om ett brott* in 1968.

Solzhenitsyn, Aleksandr Isaevich. *The Gulag Archipelago: 1918–1956.* Translated by Thomas P. Whitney. London: Harper Perennial Modern Classic, 2002. First published in Russian as *Архипелаг ? ГУПАГ* in 1973.

The Sun. London: News International Ltd., 1969–.

Tikkanen, Märta. *Manrape.* Translated by A. Weir. London: Virago Press, 1978. First published in Finland-Swedish as *Män kan inte våldtas* in 1975.

Treaty Establishing a Constitution for Europe (TCE) [The EU Constitution]. Stationery Office Books, 2005.

Weldon, Fay. *The Life and Loves of a She-Devil.* London: Trafalgar Square, 1995. First published in 1983.

SECONDARY SOURCES

Adorno, Theodor W. "Cultural Criticism and Society." Translated by Samuel and Shierry Weber. *Prisms* 1967. Cambridge, MA: MIT Press, 1981.

"The Big Issue: A Publishing Phenomenon." http://www.bigissue.com/bigissue.html (accessed December 11, 2005).

Bjöl, Erling. *Vår Tids Kulturhistoria. Del 3: Sköna Nya Värld.* Translated by Erik Holm. Stockholm: Bonniers 1979.

Bonvoisin, Samra-Martine. *La Presse Féminine.* Paris: Presses Universitaires de France, 1996.

Butler-Bowdon, Tom. *50 Self-Help Classics: 50 Inspirational Books To Transform Your Life.* Boston: Nicholas Brealey Publishing, 2003.

Cantor, Norman F. *Inventing the Middle Ages: The Lives, Works, and Ideas of the Greatest Medievalists of the Twentieth Century.* New York: William Morrow And Company Inc., 1991.

Cointreau, Edouard. "Cookbook-Boom," *Gourmand World Cookbook Awards 2006.* http://www.cookbookfair.com/html/cookbook-boom.html (accessed April 2, 2006).

Day, Julia. "Newspaper Sales Decline Across the Board," *The Guardian.* 15 July 2005. http://media.guardian.co.uk (accessed April 2, 2006).

Emery, David. "JFK: 'I am a Jelly Doughnut.'" *About.com: Urban Legend and Folklore 2007.* http://urbanlegends.about.com/cs/historical/a/jfk_berliner.htm (accessed July 9, 2007).

"Harry Potter," Wikipedia contributors. *Wikipedia: The Free Encyclopedia.* http://en.wikipedia.org/w/index.php?title=Harry_Potter&oldid=46312381 (accessed February 22, 2006).

Jones, Terry and Tricia. *SMILE i-D: Fashion and Style. 20 Years of i-D Magazine.* London: i-D, 2000.

Lappin, Elena. "Reading Richard and Judy," *The Spectator.* March 2006: Issue 120. pp. 66–68.

Meri, Tiina. "Pippi Longstocking: Swedish Rebel and Feminist Role Model," *The Swedish Institute/Sweden.se: The Official Gateway to Sweden* 2006. http://www.sweden.se/templates/cs/Article____11230.aspx (accessed February 27, 2006).

Pollock, Robert L. "All Those Words: And so Little Time to Read Them," *The Wall Street Journal* August 10, 2001. http://www.opinionjournal.com/taste/?id=95000946. (accessed May 7, 2006).

Pringle, Colombe. *Telles qu'Elle: cinquante ans d'histoire des femmes à travers le journal ELLE.* Paris: Bernard Grasset, 1995.

Richard, Arsène and Ronald Pabst. "France: More than One Million Books about EU Constitution Sold," *Democracy International.* May 6, 2006. http://www.democracy-international.org/bestseller.html (accessed December 12, 2006).

"samizdat." *Encyclopædia Britannica.* 2007. *Encyclopædia Britannica Online.* http://www.britannica.com/eb/article-9065214 (accessed September 1, 2007).

"Viktor E. Frankl: Life And Work," *Viktor Frankl Institute: The Official Website of the Viktor Frankl Institute Vienna.* http://logotherapy.univie.ac.at/e/lifeandwork.html (accessed February 20, 2006).

CHAPTER 12

A Note on the Soviet Union and Post-Soviet Russia

Ksanna Mazhurina

TIMELINE

1917	Bolshevik Revolution; Czar Nicholas abdicates
1918	The Bolsheviks under Lenin move the capitol to Moscow
1918	Establishment of the Russian Soviet Socialist Republic; establishment of the economic policy of "wartime communism"
1918–22	Russian Civil War (between the Bolshevik Red Army and anti-Bolshevik forces, known as the White Army)
1921	First Communist Party purge
1922	Belorussia, the Ukraine, and Transcaucasia (present-day Georgia, Azerbaijan, and Armenia) join Russia, and the Union of Soviet Socialist Republics (USSR) is established
1922–34	Rise of Stalin; first Five-Year Plan; industrialization and collectivization of agriculture
1924	The Union of Soviet Socialist Republics (USSR) is established
1937	The Soviet Union becomes the second-largest industrial nation in the world
1936–53	Millions die under Stalinist purges
1941	World War II: Germany invades Russia, despite the signing of a nonaggression pact
1945	World War II ends; USSR shares the control of post-war Europe with Britain, France, and the United States; Russia occupies much of central and eastern Europe and forms Eastern (Soviet) Bloc by controlling Bulgaria, Czechoslovakia, East Germany, Hungary, Poland, Romania, and Albania; USSR becomes one of the two superpowers and the world's largest country in terms of geography; Cold War between USSR and the United States begins
1949	USSR enters the atomic age and explodes a nuclear device; the nuclear arms race between USSR and the United States begins
1953	Stalin dies; Nikita Khrushchev becomes First Secretary

1957	The Soviet Union launches the first artificial satellite, *Sputnik*, into outer space
1961	Soviets beat the United States into space with the first manned space flight (and with the first woman astronaut in 1963)
1962	The Cuban Missile Crisis; The United States and USSR come close to nuclear war
1964	The Sino-Soviet split widens
1969	Major border clashes between USSR and China
1972	Nixon visits USSR; arms limitation process begins
1979–89	USSR at war in Afghanistan
1980	Moscow hosts Summer Olympics, which are boycotted by the United States, Canada, West Germany, and Japan because of the war in Afghanistan
1985–91	Mikhail Gorbachev initiates "perestroika"—the policy of economic reforms—and "glasnost"—the policy of maximal publicity, openness, and transparency; strict Communist policy starts to weaken
1991	The Soviet Union disintegrates; fourteen former member republics become independent nations; Boris Yeltsin becomes the first post-soviet-era President of Russia
1994–2000	Instability in the northern Caucasian provinces
1994	Russian novelist and historian, Aleksandr Solzhenitsyn, the Nobel Prize-winning author whose books chronicled the horros of the Soviet gulag system, returns to Russia from exile
1998	Russia's stock market collapses; Russian rocket puts the first section of the International Space Station into orbit
1999	Under a free-market economy, organized crime becomes entrenched in Russia; the Second Chechen War (follows the Russian apartment bombing in Moscow and Volgodonsk and instability in the Dagestan region)
2000	Vladimir Putin becomes President
2002	Moscow theater hostage crisis
2004	Putin wins re-election; Beslan kindergarten hostage crisis
2006	Journalist Anna Politkovskaya assassinated in Moscow; news sources describe her death as a "contract killing"
2007	Russian submersible performs the first ever manned descent to the seabed under the geographic north pole, in connection with Russian territorial claim

READING TRENDS AND PRACTICES
IN THE SOVIET UNION (USSR)

The history of reading in Russia—always a literature-centered country—in the twentieth and twenty-first centuries is probably, more than anywhere else, connected to the political history of the region. However, in Russia the reading public emerged significantly later than in the rest of Europe. In fact, the first studies on reading were undertaken at the beginning of nineteenth century, almost simultaneously with the shaping of the reader.

In the beginning of the twentieth century, when the Bolsheviks came to power,

The St. Petersburg Library

The Imperial Public Library in St. Petersburg initiated public opinion polls soon after it was established in 1795, and its first report was presented in 1817.

the Russian way of life changed dramatically. Now reading was regarded not only as a form of enlightenment and public education, but also as a means for revolutionary propaganda and ideological training to find an ideological target. Later, under the soviets, reading preferences in the USSR and some Eastern European countries were shaped by official ideology, without regard to popular tastes. The reading "map" of that period can be categorized into three different forms of reading:

A. Mandatory/required reading. This category included the works of revolutionary and Communist leaders such as Lenin and Stalin, Communist Party Congress papers, and more. All party members had a mandatory subscription to *Pravda* (*The Truth*), the leading newspaper in the Soviet Union, and the official mouthpiece of the Central Committee of the Communist Party. The circulation and publication of state-controlled literature, newspapers, books, and other literature was substantial, and these documents were read and studied countrywide.

B. Unofficial reading. The category covers voluntary reading, given what people could find to read within the limitations of the tightly controlled book market. Bookstores and libraries operated under rigid censorship. The state was always aware of library activity, because it was recognized that library use could reveal both illegal reading *and* reading density of approved materials. Therefore, every book and transaction at the library was observed by the party. Statistics that were acquired in the 1970s from the largest library in soviet-era Russia—Lenin's Library, in Moscow—indicate that the most popular reader requests were for "big novels" and/or war novels (World War II was the major event of the second half of the century). Readers apparently yearned for the big picture, which would reveal the whole of the twentieth century, and thereby offer the individual a frame of reference for his or her own life. Readers craved any explanation of what had happened, of what had been witnessed: the civil war between the Bolshevik Red Army and anti-Bolshevik forces (known as the White Army), World War II, the disasters of the postwar period, and the ordeals of the Stalin era. Of great popularity were Petr Proskurin's *Destiny* (*Sud'ba*, 1972), and Anatoly Ivanov's *All Shadows Vanish at Noon* (*Teni Ischezayut v Poden'*, 1963) and *Eternal Call* (*Vechny Zov*, 1970, 1976). There was also a huge demand for "simple" anthropology. This was reflected in the popularity for such monthly magazines as *Rabotnitsa* (*Working Woman*) and *Krestyanka* (*Country Woman*), the readers of which were rural and urban men and women who came from a wide variety of occupations and professions. The magazines gave details and knowledge of simple, everyday life—in contrast to the previous publications, which were highly political and full of propaganda.

At the same time, there was also interest in adventure novels and science fiction, such as the works of James Fenimore Cooper, Mayne Raid, and Alexandre Dumas—anything that could offer an alternative worldview to the official soviet doctrine, as found in official soviet literature. But by the beginning of the 1970s, science fiction, as well as contemporary foreign writing, became the subject of a "book deficit": the short supply of popular titles from the "actual reading" category. People would stand in long lines in bookshops and would register on long waiting lists in libraries. The book deficit resulted in a new phenomenon—book value, not in terms of the official retail price, which was comparatively cheap, but in the cost according to the book's ownership status.

During the soviet era, culture was the one and only way to demonstrate one's place in society. One could not buy a factory or own a business, but one could try to collect a good home library, and thus demonstrate one's position in terms of connections and social position. Rare and deficit books on a bookshelf at that time were a clear symbol of individual status and success. Cheap retail prices and short supplies meant that one had to use a variety of strategies to find a good book.

These included legal means, such as participating in collecting waste paper in exchange for a book certificate, and less-legal means, such as jumping queues and registration lists, or illegally bribing shop personnel.

Limited book titles brought about similarities in home libraries throughout the country; their content reflected not a genuine reader's preference, but the reader's ability to actually get deficit books. That is, one was reduced to what was commonly available, rather than what one might prefer to read and collect, and so the household library was made up of just one list of book titles with limited variations. The most common items were *The Collection of World Myths,* the poetry collections of Marina Tsvetaeva, the classic medieval works of Michel de Montaigne, the short stories of Akutagawa Ryunosuke (a Japanese writer), *The Ides of March* by Thornton Wilder, and *Le Petit Prince (The Little Prince)* by Antoine de Saint-Exupéry. This same set of books could be found at a philologist's home, a nuclear physicist's home, or a restaurant manager's home. Indeed, the restaurant manager's library would be more abundant, because he could establish connections through his customers, source and buy the books, and demonstrate his social status.

Another consequence of the book deficit was the cult book genre of the 1970s and 1980s. Members of the same generation would pick an "author-hero" to whom they could relate. The 1960s generation flocked to books by Ernest Hemingway, young readers in the 1970s adopted *The Glass Bead Game* by Hermann Hesse, and readers in the 1980s celebrated Julio Cortazar's *Hopscotch* and the writings of Jorge Luis Borges.

C. Underground literature and the phenomenon of samizdat. The word *samizdat* is formed from *sam* (Russian: *сам,* "self, by oneself") and *izdat* (Russian: *издат,* shortened *издательство, izdatel'stvo,* "publisher"), thus, *self-published.* Self-published and self-distributed literature has a long history, but samizdat was a unique phenomenon in the post-Stalin Soviet Union and other countries with similar socioeconomic systems. Samizdat literature was either banned by the government or restricted in its distribution (i.e. limited to library archives), due to its anti-Soviet content. Finally, samizdat could also be prohibited foreign writings that were printed abroad and then smuggled back into the USSR. A copy of forbidden literature or a periodical would be duplicated using carbon paper, either by hand or on a typewriter. Later on, when professional and semiprofessional copying machines became more available, people who had legal use of the technology would use them illegally to duplicate the forbidden documents. Soviet Russia did not have a supply of copiers that could be used for private purposes. Therefore, any illegal reading material would have to be duplicated for distribution using technology owned and controlled by the state, which made the production of samizdat literature a crime on two different levels.

The emergence of samizdat was connected with the deep crises of Communist ideology that followed the denunciation of Stalin's cult of personality. However, the so-called Khrushchev thaw of the late 1950s and early 1960s saw a decline and relaxation of censorship. After Khrushchev's dismissal in 1964, and the end of the thaw, many talented writers and artists either left the country or went underground and thus became part of the samizdat movement. By the mid 1960s, samizdat stopped manifesting as occasional, individual texts that circulated underground and became a mass phenomenon. By the 1970s, the vast majority of the population was aware of, or was a reader of, samizdat. Young people at the end of the 1970s and the beginning of the 1980s got their first access to samizdat literature in high school. However, people were persecuted if they dealt with the politically motivated distribution of samizdat or collected considerable quantities of samizdat literature in their homes (what came to be known as "samizdat libraries"). They were charged according to the notorious article 190-1 of the Criminal Codes of the Soviet Union, which defined punishment for various forms of "dissemination of false information discrediting the soviet country."

Despite official government condemnation, there were several samizdat libraries in the USSR. Some of them were named after the city or town where they were first located (Odessa Library, Leningrad Archive) or by a collector's last name (Markov's Library). Samizdat libraries, therefore, became significant elements of social, cultural, and political life in the Soviet Union. For example, the Odessa Library had more than five hundred samizdat texts, and had branches in all major cities: Moscow, Leningrad, Novosibirsk, and others.

Samizdat attracted a very broad and heterogeneous readership, from the most radical, underground opposition leaders and dissidents, to the general public. The content was similarly diverse: from political texts, protesting Communist rule, to rare fiction that was the subject of book deficit (especially in the 1970s). With very few exceptions, one could get a photocopy of a deficit text for an "overnight-read" (i.e. the copy had to be returned by the morning, for the next reader in line), or one could purchase a samizdat copy of a deficit text for a high price. A striking example would be Mikhail Bulgakov's novel, *The Master and Margarita* (*Master I Margarita*), a satire of life in the Soviet Union in the 1930s. The novel featured Yeshua Ha-Nozri (Jesus of Nazareth) and the Devil as the protagonists, and magic and witchcraft as basic elements of the plot. *The Master and Margarita* was banned in secular, Communist Russia. Written at the end of the 1930s, the novel was finally published in Russia in 1966, but it was controlled by strict censorship laws and produced as a limited edition in small numbers. Not surprisingly, reader demand for the novel was huge, and hundreds of illegal copies were distributed among the people.

Besides political and fictional writings, samizdat literature also included texts for everyday life: books on the raw-food diet, eroticism, astrology, jazz, occultism, and the martial arts were a few examples of nonpolitical, subversive samizdat books. Basically, samizdat and book deficit were two phenomena of the same origin: they both arose from a limited public access to information. All that changed in 1985, with the emergence of Mikhail Gorbachev, the last soviet-era head of state.

READING TRENDS AND PRACTICES IN POST-SOVIET RUSSIA

Perestroika and *glasnost*—the two main strategies of Gorbachev's policy—combined to finally lift media censorship and limitation. In 1991 the Soviet Union dissolved, following a failed coup d'état by conservative Communist elements opposed to Gorbachev's reforms, and Boris Yeltsin was elected president of the Russian Republic. The new Russian Press Law was adopted in 1990, and censorship ended.

Newly established private publishing houses mushroomed all over the country to quench the book deficit of the previous decades. Writings that had been banned under the soviets were published in monthly literary magazines. These periodicals were called "thick journals" (*tolstyi jurnal*) due to their substantial size. The circulation, as well as the social influence, of these thick journals increased rapidly. Other periodicals—weekly and daily newspapers—experienced an unprecedented rise in sales too; people were hungry for information, especially at the end of the 1980s and the beginning of the 1990s, when something new happened every day and even every hour.

The cat character, Béhémot, from the hugely popular but difficult-to-obtain novel, *The Master and Margarita*, in the city of Kiev, Ukraine. A single copy of the book could be handed around between readers for many years.

However, the lifting of censorship was not without its downside. The rapid creation of an unregulated free market meant that many books that appeared for sale were very badly written and included illegal, violent, racist, and exploitative content. Books that appeared in the late 1980s and early 1990s might have sated the "reading hunger" of the previous decades, with a wider variety of titles and greater intellectual breadth, but that same reading hunger was exploited by those who saw only profit in the newly opened Russian book market.

Another unforeseen offshoot of censorship's collapse in the new Russia was that, now that all the previously banned books had been published, publishers and readers were no longer motivated to collect them at the same rate. The old guidelines had vanished. Anyone could publish—and read—anything. Readers no longer desired the forbidden text and were instead trying to make sense of the enormity of the freedom they had been given. As a result, Russian readers lost interest in "serious" literature and turned instead to "easy-reading," mass-market texts. First, foreign detective stories became the focus; then humorous crime fiction (such as that by Polish author, Joanna Chmielewska) was particularly favored; then, as organized crime became established in post-soviet Russia, Russian detective stories, by authors such as Aleksandra Marinina, and Russian "ironic" crime fiction, characterized by the novels of Darya Dontsova, became popular.

As the book deficit was no longer a problem, books were desacralized in Russia. After a centuries-long tradition of literacy and literary engagement, the country was no longer literature-focused—at least, not to the same extent. Books were transformed from cult items to everyday commodities. This is evidenced by the fact that when books were first published in paperback at the end of the 1980s, as a cheap substitute for hardcover titles, they did not sell well. This was the case especially in the provinces, where one might imagine that there would be more demand for cheaper books. The publishing houses had misjudged the reading public, who still saw books as a substantial investment and something to be passed down through the family. Paperbacks were simply too common to be taken seriously. In a country where individuals were not supposed to own property, land, or businesses, books had been a substantial possession that could be collected and cherished. However, once book production and marketing became a cost-controlled, privately run enterprise, the book lost its revered status. The paperback became a disposable possession—something that was lightweight, easy to read, and easy to throw away.

Statistics reveal a great deal about reading patterns in the country after the soviet era. Generally speaking, reading habits switched to the easy-reading genres in the 1990s. In 2005, a leading Moscow sociological center researched reading in Russia. The results revealed that, in terms of sales, 79% of those polled said that they did not buy books or magazines; 79% did not use libraries at all, and 34% had no books at home. Of the respondents who did read, 11% preferred crime/detective fiction/thrillers. The remaining readers favored romantic novels and science fiction/fantasy. As further evidence that the physical book had lost its cultural appeal in Russia, 12% of readers revealed that they preferred to read books on the Internet.

CONCLUSION

The anecdotal and statistical evidence agree that the typical reader in Russia today is different from the traditional reader. The reasons for this shift in reading habits and culture are clear. The first reason is the appearance of profit in the Russian book industry. As soon as the book became a commodity, hardcover, serious literature became expensive, and traditional readers, poor in this new Russia, could no longer afford their preferred materials. Moreover, only twenty percent of the available published titles reach the provincial market. Therefore, it is not economically feasible for publishers to bring books to poor regions, or to open bookstores in small towns. In today's Russia, there is one bookstore for every sixty thousand potential book buyers; this compares to one store for every ten to fifteen thousand in Europe. As far as libraries are concerned, there used to be a law that the government provided one copy of a published text to a library at a fifty-percent discount. In 2002, that law was suspended, and seventy-five percent of libraries were crossed off the book delivery lists.

Along with these financial constraints, there was huge pressure on an individual's free time, and this is the second major reason why reading habits have changed so markedly. Low income in today's Russia means that the majority of the population is too busy surviving to have time to read. And if there isn't a need to survive, then there is a necessity to improve one's professional skills. Therefore, in order to maximize the value of individual free time, another new reading habit has merged with the need to continually improve or maintain professional and social positions. Self-improvement and self-help books are a booming new sector of the total publishing industry in Russia. And this phenomenon leads to the third reason for changes in reading patterns—the pragmatization of reading. That is, reading is becoming a working tool, not an aesthetic phenomenon. Self-improvement reading is now so widespread that there is a book to cover any aspect of an individual's life. Health and illnesses, food and recipes, image and fashion, home-improvement and DIY books, pets and gardening, foreign-language textbooks, dictionaries and encyclopedias, business guides, and even DIY psychoanalysis texts are commonly available and increasingly top the best-seller lists.

It is clear now that future generations are not going to place the same importance on nonpractical books and reading that soviet-era generations did. New economic systems, changes in time and work management, and changes in social and cultural needs have already altered the ways that Russians get and process their information. Furthermore, the implementation of new technologies (such as the Internet) also "steal" free time from reading (online games, chatting, general web-surfing). On the other hand, online reading has become a substantial part of today's reading map. But as an article called "Who Reads Today and Why?" by M. M. Samohina puts it, "Only those who really *love* to read will keep on reading. And by reading I do not mean time spent exclusively with books by Leo Tolstoy, Boris Pasternak or Johan Huizinga. I mean that if a person *loves* to read, say, love novels, he or she will go on reading in opposition to watching soap operas on TV" (338).

Perhaps the growth of technology in the everyday lives of Russians will, somewhat paradoxically, help to restore reading to its previous position of prominence in the country's culture. Ru-Net (the Russian Internet) has all the elements of the book realm: literary criticism, bookstores, libraries, books, poems, and dramas. The most famous and voluminous of the Russian literary sites is probably Maxim Moshkov's Online Library (www.lib.ru), where one can find writings of various Russian and foreign writers from Abe Kobo to Emile Zola. The literary magazine *Druzhba Narodov* conducted a research exercise in 2005 that analyzed a single day's activity at Maxim Moshkov's Online Library. The results showed that online reader preferences are different from those of offline readers: the most poplar request was for science fiction, then classical literature, and then contemporary writings. Though one might think it is not convenient to read texts from a computer screen, it has its advantages—entire bodies of work can be downloaded with a single mouse click, for free. Thus, one can save money, time, and space on home bookshelves.

In general, the way reading has been transformed from an old soviet pattern to a contemporary Russian one highlights and reflects the pivotal phenomena in Soviet Union/Russian history. The state has dissociated itself from the book realm, and is keeping itself aloof from social and cultural realms as well. As a result, one can see a number of consequences for Russian society and culture: the library crisis, the lack of incentive for regular citizens to read, the drop in educational standards and social expectations of education, and the collapse of the *intelligentsia*. Formerly, the intelligentsia played a leading and influential role for the mass reader—through schools, the mass media, and literary criticism. This role has now been left vacant, and Russians are observing an erosion of culture in today's society. The future consequences of this erosion have yet to be seen in their full perspective.

RECOMMENDED READING

Kelly, Catriona. "Kul'turnost' in the Soviet Union: Ideal and Reality." In *Reinterpreting Russia*. Edited by Geoffrey Hosking and Robert Service. Oxford: Oxford University Press, 1999.
———. *Refining Russia: Gender, Manners and Morals from Catherine to Yeltsin*. Oxford: Oxford University Press, 2000.

Lovell, Stephen. *The Russian Reading Revolution: Print Culture in the Soviet and Post-Soviet Eras.* New York: St. Martin's Press, 2000.

Olcott, Anthony. *Russian Pulp: The Detektiv and the Russian Way of Crime.* Lanham, MD: Rowman and Littlefield, 2001.

Zavisca, Jane. "The Status of Cultural Omnivorism: A Case Study of Reading in Russia." *Social Forces* 84.2 (December 2005): 1233–55.

PRIMARY SOURCES

Akutagawa, Ryunosuke. *Rashomon and Seventeen Other Stories.* Translated by Jay Rubin. New York: Penguin Classics, 2006.

Bulgakov, Mikhail. *The Master and Margarita.* Surrey, U.K.: Oneworld Classics, 2008.

Chmielewska, Joanna. *Two Heads and One Leg.* Ekaterinburg: Faktoria, 1998.

Cortazar, Julio. *Hopscotch.* New York: Pantheon, 1987.

Dontsova, Darya. *Dentists Can Cry Too.* Moscow: EKSMO, 2000.

Hesse, Herman. *The Glass Bead Game.* Translated by Richard Winston and Clara Winston. New York: Picador, 2002.

Ivanov, Anatoly. *All Shadows Vanish at Noon.* Moscow: EKSMO-Press, 1999. First published in Russian as *Teni Ischezayut v Poden'*, 1963.

———.*Eternal Call* (*Vechny Zov,* 1970, 1976). Moscow: AST, 2000.

Krestyanka (*Country Woman*). Moscow.

Marinina, Aleksandra. *Men's Games.* Moscow: EKSMO-Press, 1998.

Montaigne, Michel de. *The Complete Works.* New York: Everyman, 2003.

Pravda. Moscow, 1921–1991.

Proskurin, Petr. *Destiny* (*Sud'ba,* 19). Moscow: EKSMO-Press, 1999.

Rabotnitsa (*Working Woman*). Moscow.

Saint-Exupéry, Antoine de. *The Little Prince* (*Le Petit Prince*). Translated by Richard Howard. Fort Washington, PA: Harvest Books, 2000.

Tsvetaeva, Marina. *In the Inmost Hour of the Soul: Selected Poems of Marina Tsvetaeva.* Translated by Nina Kossman. Clifton, NJ: Humana Press, 1989.

———.*Selected Poems.* Translated by Elaine Feinstein. New York: Penguin Classics, 1994.

Wilder, Thornton. *The Ides of March.* New York: Harper Perennial, 2003.

SECONDARY SOURCES

Alekseev, Vyacheslav, Alla Kuznetsova, and Leonid Ashkinazi. "Literature and the Internet." *Druzhba Narodov,* Moscow 10 (2002): 194–206.

Dubin, Boris and Natalia Igrunova. "Obryv Svyazi" ("The Ties are Torn"). *Druzhba Narodov,* Moscow 1 (2003): 187–219.

Igrunov, Vyacheslav. *The Anthology of Samizdat.* Moscow: IGPI 1.1 (2005): 8–16.

Melentieva, Yulia. "From the Nation of Readers Towards the Nation of Viewers. The Evolution of Reading and How to Study It." *Library Issues,* Moscow 10 (2006): 2–6.

Nesterov, Anton. "Translation or 'Mother tongue'?" *New Literature Review,* Moscow 1 (2002): 314–18.

Samohina, Margarita. "Who Reads Today and Why?" *New Literature Review,* Moscow 5 (2001): 327–40.

Stelmakh, Valeriya. "Who Needs Libraries in Russia?" *New Literature Review,* Moscow 5 (2005): 327–37.

Vaneev, Alexei. "Stanovlenie peterburgskoi shkoly bibliotekovedenia" ["The Formation of Library Science in St. Petersburg"]. *Istoria bibliotek* [*The History of Libraries*] 5 (2004): 23–30.

Yakovleva, Elena. "Tell Me What You Are Reading and I'll Tell You About Tomorrow's Russia. A Review of the 2005 Statistics." *Rossijskaya Gazeta* (July 27, 2005).

PART 3
Asia and the Pacific

Imperial China

Evan Lampe

TIMELINE

1750 C.E.	Chinese population reaches three hundred million
1764 C.E.	Writer Cao Xueqin dies, leaving his *The Story of the Stone* unfinished
1787 C.E.	The Four Treasuries project, commissioned by the Qianlong Emperor, is completed
1800 C.E.	Beginning of the opium trade
1839 C.E.	Opium War begins

INTRODUCTION TO THE PERIOD

When Li Yü was born in 1611, the Ming Empire had long passed its peak of power and stability. But it was not yet clear that those entering life in the early decades of the seventeenth century would undergo the destruction of their world at the hands of foreign invaders. Li Yü did not come from a distinguished family of scholar officials—the type that ran the Chinese Empire and protected the Confucian tradition since the tenth century. His father was a physician, and as long as anyone in his clan could remember, no one had passed the all-important civil service exams and become an official of the empire. This did not prevent Li Yü, or millions of others not from gentry families, from attempting the exams with the hope of meeting the emperor in Beijing after successfully proving their mastery of the Chinese classics. Li Yü only passed the lowest-level examinations. This gave him some local prestige but not power or national recognition. In 1644, about the time that he gave up on the examination system, the Ming Empire fell due to internal rebellions and Manchu conquerors. It was at this time that Li Yü took up a career in writing fiction. By all accounts, Chinese fiction has one of its most glorious periods in the century around Li Yü's life. Some of the greatest and most commonly read novels came from this period. Li Yü would not build on his training in the Confucian classics to write his stories. Instead, he would tap into popular desires by writing poetry, drama, and pornographic stories. In his famous novel, *Carnal Prayer Mat* (*Rouputuan*), Li Yü thumbed his nose at Confucian morality and the popular religious traditions of the day. He reached success as a writer for popular genres despite his earlier goals of Confucian conformity through the exam system. In this way, Li Yü's life reflects one of the most important characteristics of reading in Imperial China: the bifurcation of reading materials into those reflecting the official orthodoxy and those catering to the interest of the popular audience. From the earliest days of writing in China, these two traditions stood side by side. Despite efforts by the scholarly elite to saturate popular literature and drama with Confucian values, this division would remain until the Confucian tradition was almost shattered in the early twentieth century.

The first writing emerged in China in the middle of the second millennium B.C.E. in the Yellow River Valley. As in other regions, writing developed in China to solve practical problems of government administration. This early Chinese writing appeared on "oracle bones," turtle shells that seers used to predict events for the leaders of the early Shang State. Kings would pose specific questions, which would be written onto the turtle shells. After being placed in a fire, the shells would crack. Seers interpreted these cracks. The Zhou State, following the Shang, was honored by Confucian scholars for centuries as a golden age of wisdom and peace. The major texts from this era are collectively known as the Confucian Classics and are made up of the *Classic of Rituals*, the *Classic of Poetry*, the *Book of Changes*, the *Book of History*, and the *Spring and Autumn Annals*. We cannot know how often they were read in the lengthy Zhou period, but we know that they were the core of classical education for over a thousand years beginning in the tenth century C.E. Their content does suggest a rather broad readership. The *Book of Poetry*, for instance, draws on a variety of perspectives of the lives of aristocrats and commoners, including women.

Confucius drew heavily on these texts and probably edited most of them into the forms in which we know them today. But he was only one of many scholars active in the late Zhou. From this period of intense debate over the nature of government and social order emerged the major Chinese traditions of Confucianism, Legalism, and Daoism. At issue was the lack of unity in China and the best means to bring an end to the infighting between Chinese states. All of these traditions dealt with the practical concerns of running a state, and the intellectuals who pioneered these schools were primarily interested in converting governments to their position. Some, such as Confucius, brought their message directly to kings. Confucius and his followers argued that kings should rule through benevolence and proper ritual and that a harmonious state would be reflected in a harmonious and well-ordered society. Daoists argued that the state should not directly manipulate society and should not take actions that countered a seemingly natural order. Legalists believed that both of these views were naïve. They argued that a king could succeed only by promoting service through reward and punishment, without mercy, disobedience, and disorder. The ultimately successful Qin Kingdom followed the Legalist approach and unified China in 221 B.C.E. Thus the first Chinese Empire was formed.

In the early imperial age, this division between popular reading and official reading continued and came into sharper focus due to the expansion in extant popular literature. Because of the tyrannical nature of its rule and heavy Legalistic policies, the Qin Empire collapsed not long after the first emperor, Qin Shihuang, died. The Han Empire emerged in its wake and attempted a synthesis of Confucian and Legalist policies. Literacy remained an important tool for running the state. The Han philosopher, Dong Zhongshu, attempted to complete this synthesis of political thought. Dong Zhongshu argued that the emperor had a duty to sustain the imperial order through proper rule and goodness. Leaders could know of the will of heaven by properly interpreting cosmological, natural, and social occurrences. In Dong's imperial order, an important job of the official class was to perform this interpretation. Although revised by later Chinese empires, this basic understanding of the nature of imperial rule as contingent on the will of heaven and proper rule endured.

History writing has its origin in the Zhou period with the *Book of History*. Scholars continued this tradition but, as with philosophy in general, it was directed to serve the state. Histories, such as the history of Sima Qian, completed in the first century B.C.E., revealed the errors of previous states; in effect, they worked to justify the rule of the current rulers by claiming that the old leaders lost the will of heaven. Ban Gu and his sister, Ban Zhao, later wrote the first complete history of the Han Empire in the first century C.E. Chinese historiography, although highly politically, followed rules of evidence and logic, making the Han historians similar to the Greek historians Herodotus and Thucydides.

During the Han Empire, and the three centuries of disunity that followed its collapse, the Buddhist tradition filtered into China from India. The Silk Road, connecting China and western Eurasia, became a conduit for the transmission of religious texts. For much of Imperial China, Buddhism lacked official approval. It was nevertheless extremely popular among the Chinese people, including the reading public. Disunity aided Buddhism's spread because there was not a strong imperial ideology to prevent it. By addressing questions such as the fate of one's spirit after death, Buddhism ran counter to the secular Confucian tradition. By the

> **Ban Zhao**
>
> Ban Zhao (32–102) was China's first major female writer. She helped her brother Ban Gu complete the *Hanshu*, a history of the early Han Empire. She also made major contributions to China's gender politics. In her *Precepts for Women* (*Nujie*), Ban Zhao argued that women were inferior to men and should accept a life of duty to marriage and men. Hierarchy was the key to harmony in marriage as well as society. Ban Zhao's instructions would lay the foundation of Confucian gender relations for almost two thousand years. We cannot know how many women read *Precepts for Women* but it, along with other guides to married life, suggest some degree of female literacy. Nevertheless, marriage guides ensured that women in Imperial China would have less social freedom than their ancestors.

time the Sui Empire reunified China in the sixth century, Chinese Buddhists had formed sects addressing the needs of various groups. For example, the Pure Land School argued that believers could receive salvation from the Buddha by simply calling for his aid. Such popular traditions could be spread without the requirement that practitioners could read. Buddhist sutras and philosophical investigations were still popular reading in Imperial China.

The literate public in the early imperial period consumed literature as well as Buddhist sutras. Some of these stories, which exist today in the form of anthologies, may have been shared with the illiterate public through oral readings. These stories were generally in short form. More popular than short stories was poetry, and poets experienced a golden age during the Tang Empire. The most important of these poets, Li Bo, wrote almost two thousand poems that survived, but this reflects only a fraction of his voluminous work. These poems explored nature as well as the noumenal, suggesting the influence of nonsecular thought on Chinese popular writing.

The Late Imperial period, the thousand years from the founding of the Song Empire to the collapse of the Qing Empire in 1911, is partially defined by three important elements. First, during this period the Chinese experienced several foreign invasions and long periods of foreign rule by pastoral people from North and Central Asia. It was only during the Ming Empire (1376–1644) that the Chinese did not experience some form of foreign rule. Second, this period saw the codification of the Confucian imperial orthodoxy, known as Neo-Confucianism. This multilayered tradition dominated Chinese philosophy until the nineteenth century. Third, in this entire period most of the administration of the empire was staffed by Chinese who successfully completed a series of competitive examinations. This civil service examination system enforced the Neo-Confucian tradition, but it also expanded learning by offering power and prestige to any Chinese who could prove their intellectual erudition in the exams. Thanks to the examination system, Imperial China became a limited meritocracy. It was limited because education still required resources that were beyond the reach of much of the peasant class.

Confucianism was an important part of the ruling ideology after the Han Empire, but it was not fully instituted as the official orthodoxy until the Song Empire. During Han rule, Confucianism was simply one part of an eclectic imperial ideology that included Legalism. In the long period of disunity that followed the collapse of the Han Empire, few states could live up to the Confucian ideals. Throughout much of the Tang Empire, Buddhism was much more influential than Confucianism. The endurance of the Chinese aristocracy prevented the emergence of a ruling elite of cultured and educated sages, a Confucian ideal. In the eighth century, an increased interest in Confucianism as a method of ruling the empire began with the work of the philosopher Han Yu. Han Yu attacked the popular Buddhist creed and, in so doing, supported a Confucian alternative.

Many other thinkers maintained an interest in Confucianism after Han Yu. The philosopher Zhu Xi confided this thinking in the eleventh century. Modern historians have labeled the creed that emerged as Neo-Confucianism. Neo-Confucianism represented a revival of the traditional Confucian values of rule by educated sages, human goodness reinforced by proper ritual, and government by benevolence. Zhu Xi and other Confucian scholars could not remain unaffected by the questions posed by Buddhists such as, "What is reality and humanity?" In addressing these concerns, the Neo-Confucian tradition became a synthesis. Neo-Confucians honored a tradition of investigation and Reason. In so doing, they found wisdom in objective investigation of texts instead of in mysticism. Specifically, Zhu Xi canonized the "four books": the *Analects* of Confucius, the *Mencius*, the *Great Learning*, and *The Doctrine of the Mean*. The latter two were actually subsections of the *Book of Rites*. Despite answering metaphysical questions, Neo-Confucianism remained as worldly as ancient Confucianism. Advocates honored government service, family life, and public morality. As such, Neo-Confucianism became idealized as an imperial orthodoxy. The primary means of spreading Neo-Confucianism would prove to be the civil service examination system.

Artist's impression of Ban Zhao (班昭 45–116 C.E.), the first female Chinese historian.

READING TRENDS AND PRACTICES

The civil service examination system, which reached maturity in the Song Empire, had its origins in an earlier era. During the Han and Tang Empires most recruitment into imperial service was done by individual recommendation or tapping into the aristocracy. Still, there were always some openings in the bureaucracy for professionals recruited through competitive examinations. The Tang established an imperial university for training candidates for public service. This is not particularly remarkable. But what was impressive for a pre-modern society was the almost complete replacement of nepotism and aristocratic preference with merit-based competitive examinations in the eleventh century.

In the system's maturity, there were three levels of examinations. The first took place on the district or prefecture level. Successful candidates would be awarded a degree and were qualified to take the provincial level exams. Graduates of the provincial exams could take the highest-level examinations in the capital. Graduates of this examination could qualify for highly prestigious government service, although lower-level graduates could look forward to careers as teachers or local bureaucrats. Only a small fraction of individuals attending the local exams earned the highest degree. During the Ming and Qing eras, fewer than one hundred candidates earned the highest degree per year. Of those who earned the lowest-level degree (a not insignificant task) only one percent could expect to pass the metropolitan examinations. This meant that many qualified candidates failed due to inevitably capricious evaluators.

One important result of the examination system was the expansion of literacy and learning in China. Because anyone who hoped to become a member of the elite class of scholar-officials had to prove erudition in poetry, calligraphy, Confucian philosophy, and history, those seeking degrees began to study early in their lives. And because there was no boundary based on lineage, any family with means could provide sons with the necessary education. Many communities established schools and academies for the education of young men, in preparation for the exams.

As in earlier periods of Chinese history, this official learning coexisted alongside a vibrant popular tradition. It was during the Ming period that we see a major development in Chinese fiction with the expansion of novel writing and reading. These novels dealt with many themes but most tapped into popular religion, storytelling, and myth-making. *The Journey to the West* by Wu Chengen told a highly mythologized version of the story of a monk's transcontinental voyage to India in search of Buddhist texts. Another novel, *Water Margin,* examines the lives and adventures of a gang of uncommon bandits. This novel was extremely popular among Chinese, particularly those who appreciated the social divisions in Imperial Chinese society. Another novel, *The Golden Lotus,* was semi-pornographic and, like the works of Li Yu, challenged Confucian morality. Many of the writers of popular literature were not necessarily bitter toward the Confucian orthodoxy. In fact, some of them were trained to be scholar-officials and were well-versed in Neo-Confucian thought. Their careers show that the bifurcation of the uses of the written word in Imperial China was as important within individuals as it was in society at large.

Intellectuals, trained to think in terms of government service and the public welfare, sometimes looked upon popular beliefs with concern. Popular religion and Buddhism did not fit comfortably into a Neo-Confucian worldview. At times, the empire took actions to incorporate popular beliefs into the imperial creed. The Manchu Qing were sympathetic to Buddhism. They even incorporated the goddess of the sea, Mazu, into the imperial pantheon in an effort to attract Chinese from the maritime south of the empire. Much more common, however, was an effort to spread Confucian values to the people. Because most Chinese were illiterate, it would not be enough simply to introduce them to the Confucian classics and hope that they found them appealing. Officials were forced to work with popular traditions, literature, opera, and gender politics to "Confucianize" the people. Zhu Xi wrote a guide to family rituals that taught proper relations between members of families. Other guides trained children in the proper respect due to parents. Even popular novels commonly held Confucian warnings, urging the reader not to make the same mistakes that the people in the story did. The effort to bring orthodox learning with popular trends never completely succeeded but, thanks to the efforts of these disseminators of Confucianism, the Chinese population was more familiar with the orthodox tradition in the Qing than in earlier periods.

Most people in late Imperial China considered education, which meant education in the Confucian tradition, to be the major means to power and prestige. Indeed, without a strong aristocracy as in medieval Europe education was indispensable for ambitious men. The examinations were arranged so that examiners did not know the names of candidates and could not even recognize their handwriting. A son of a prestigious family had no guarantee of inheriting his family's position. But social mobility was by no means universal. Poor peasants could not afford to send their children to academies, where they would spend long hours memorizing the Confucian classics. The ideal of a peasant boy studying second-hand books while working in the fields was uncommon. More likely were villages or lineage groups sponsoring children.

Another common form of social mobility was movement out of the merchant class and into the gentry. Merchants, despite their necessary function, were not respected in traditional China because they were not of the producing class and therefore tended to be considered parasitic. Wealthy merchants often invested considerable resources in the education of their sons with the hope that they would pass the exams. The desires of the merchants to escape their class may account for the lack of a bourgeoisie in early modern China. Although China was a meritocracy, social mobility was not available to all. The large numbers of highly qualified individuals who failed the exams year after year attests to this.

Bookselling was big business in Imperial China but this did not mean that books were available to everyone. They were expensive enough to remain a luxury for most Chinese. However, during the Ming and Qing periods, the number of books in China exploded, as did the number of publishers and published writers. Collecting rare books was a pastime of many gentry. The Ming-era scholar Ge Jian held ten thousand volumes in his personal library. The availability of printed texts only increased in the Qing era. At the turn of the eighteenth century, the city of Chengdu had ten major publishers. Beijing had over one hundred publishing houses. In order to sustain business empire-wide, publishers created elaborate networks involving trained block cutters (Chinese publishers used printing long before their European counterparts), distributors, local booksellers, and printing operations. The local elite sometimes established public libraries that existed alongside the growing private collections.

Women in late Imperial China could not become officials and were not allowed to participate in the civil service examination system. This removed much of the possible justification for educating Chinese women. This did not mean that Chinese women were universally illiterate or were not influenced by writing. Many elite women in China not only gained literacy but also participated in literary culture as readers or writers. Furthermore, much of the moral literature of the Late Imperial period was directed at women, who, if illiterate, could still receive lessons through the men in their lives. One example of this was the Ming and Qing adoration of chaste widows. It is not fair to say that remarriage by widows was discouraged or punished. Still, widow chastity was considered the ideal, and women who remained chaste or committed suicide to avoid remarriage were elevated as heroines of Confucian morality. The most extreme examples of chaste widows were unmarried women who killed themselves after the death of a fiancé. Sometimes, the local elite would honor these women with monuments or literature retelling and honoring their stories.

Imperial China was highly literate due in part to the respect afforded the educated by the imperial state and society. This also produced an amazing intellectual homogeneity among the elite across a huge empire of striking cultural, linguistic, and social diversity. Alongside this official orthodoxy was a significant body of popular learning, represented by people such as Li Yu. This popular learning was never strong enough to challenge the official creed. In fact, both traditions existed in relative harmony. In the nineteenth century, the Western tradition would pose a much more serious threat to the Confucian orthodoxy.

CREATIVE TEXTS

The Book of Poetry was a collection of 305 songs anthologized by Confucius, sup-posedly representing the courtly and popular verse of his home state of Lu. The songs most likely originated in the early Zhou period. Confucian scholars and students would read these poems as part of the canon, and they were required reading for the civil service exams, throughout most of late Imperial China. They have diverse themes, including courtly love, religious beliefs, and warfare. These poems remain one of the most important sources we have on early Chinese social history.

Quan Tang Shi (Complete Poems of the Tang) was not anthologized until the eighteenth century. The survival of these almost fifty thousand poems suggests not only the prolific nature of Tang poetry, but also the continued interest in poetry by Chinese intellectuals. Poetry in the Tang, as well as in the late imperial period, was an art form of particular interest to the intellectual class. Almost all officials, schol-ars, and writers were also poets and avid consumers of poetry. Poetry was evaluat-ed as part of the civil service examinations and was thus an indispensable skill for anyone eager to become an official. Despite this, poets were not confined to themes related to official business. Chinese poets fully explored the natural world, emo-tions, and the noumenal. The standard form was a four line stanza, each line hav-ing four characters. By the Tang, Chinese poets often broke free of this rigid for-mat, giving Imperial Chinese poetry a great diversity of styles. Because the educat-ed read and wrote poetry daily, readers encountered poetry in many places: as parts of longer works, on paintings, or in letters from friends and colleagues.

The Chinese form of the novel matured during the Ming Empire and has remained a popular form among readers ever since. The following six novels do not represent the entirety of Imperial Chinese novel writing, but they are the most important historically and have remained in the mind of the reading public since their creation. Two things that they have in common are that their authors pre-sented their stories in the vernacular style, and they were all intensely popular when published. If not for the vibrant and competitive publishing market in Imperial China, many of these novels would have been lost. Their survival is less a virtue of their literary merits than a testimony to their popularity among China's large reading public.

The Romance of the Three Kingdoms by Lo Guanzhong (d. 1400) is a historical novel of the "Three Kingdoms" period, which followed the collapse of the Han Empire. The novel was first published in 1522. This was the first historical novel and achieved a unification of vernacular traditions recalling the history of this period. The novel focuses on competition between two kings of the era, Cao Cao and Liu Bei. The narrative reads more like history than fiction, with each charac-ter fitting into the larger designs of heaven. It is also the least vernacular of the famous Ming novels. It is certainly one of the least fanciful of the later Imperial Chinese novels.

The Water Margin was an extremely popular novel emerging around the same time as *Romance of the Three Kingdoms*. Its popularity was due to its theme and its full vernacular style. *The Water Margin* tells the story of a group of bandits living in a mountain under the leadership of Sung Jiang, a historical bandit from the Song period. The stories suggest the realities of life for lower-class Chinese, and readers enjoyed seeing the elite outsmarted by the bandits. The novel is far from historical, instead placing the characters in fantastic, humorous, or violent situa-tions for the pleasure of the reader. It has existed in several versions, some with chapters added by editors hoping to profit from the novel's popularity. The modern version was finalized in 1641.

The Journey to the West by Wu Chengen (d. 1582) is a fantastic episodic account of the pilgrimage of Xuanzang to India in search of Buddhist texts. He is accompanied by two protectors, Monkey and Pigsy. Monkey has been sent as a bodyguard as punishment for assaulting heaven itself. Pigsy is easily seduced by sensual pleasures and is the source of much of the commentary on human nature in the novel. Wu was not unlike many educated Chinese, who, despite long years of training, failed the civil service examinations and had to find a living outside official circles. His professional frustrations probably account for some of the social critique apparent in the novel. The novel was published in 1592. But Wu did not gain recognition for *The Journey to the West* until the twentieth century, because no one knew who wrote the text until literary scholars solved the mystery. Up until the twentieth century, *The Journey to the West* was published without attribution.

The Golden Lotus was written by an unknown scholar in the sixteenth century. In some sense it would foreshadow the great Qing novel, *The Dream of the Red Chamber,* because of its intimate examination of the life of one family. It has been unfairly identified as pornography due to its unapologetic look at the sex lives of the family members. In the novel, Golden Lotus kills her husband and becomes a concubine of her lover, Ximen. Much of the novel explores the sexual relations between Ximen and his numerous wives. What is striking about this novel is its affectionate focus on women. At a time when women were playing a more important role in China's literary culture as writers and readers, it is not entirely surprising that women would gain this attention. Like the other novels, however, it maintains a moral message; Ximen becomes a victim of Golden Lotus's insatiable sexual needs, and dies. The novel also critiques elite society and religious hypocrisy.

Unlike *The Golden Lotus*'s sexual interest, *Carnal Prayer Mat,* by Li Yu, is unabashed pornography and appeared in the late 1650s. As with all of these novels, the audience was not the gentry, but rather China's large literate audience (although the gentry no doubt enjoyed these novels as well). Li Yu was the single bestselling writer in the late Ming and could enjoy a life of luxury due to the success of his stories. This is in contrast to the other novelists of the time, who often achieved fame long after they died. The protagonist, "Before Midnight Scholar," decides to seek out a life of sexual pleasures. He does this only with great difficulty—his natural assets are embarrassingly inadequate—and eventually joins a monastic order. This does not end his erotic desires, and he is forced to castrate himself. There is no doubt of the moral message in this novel, but readers did not approach *Carnal Prayer Mat* with this in mind. They were certainly more interested in the explicit and often humorous descriptions of Before Midnight Scholar's sex life.

The Dream of the Red Chamber by Cao Xueqin, published in the 1790s, was left incomplete when the author died in 1763. It is the greatest of the Qing novels and the most highly respected by Chinese readers. Cao was a part of elite society but failed to maintain his family's legacy. *The Dream of the Red Chamber* is an unvarnished examination of late imperial elite culture. The novel follows the Jia family, particularly the son Jia Baoyu. The family is in decline and much of the novel focuses on Baoyu's failures to live up to the expectations placed on him by the women in the family—the men are mostly absent. Baoyu eventually renounces the world of his family and becomes a monk. The plot is less important than the fascinating representation of elite family life and the intense characterization Cao Xueqin achieved.

Fictional prose had a very humble origin in China. Most of our extant texts from pre-Imperial China are history, poetry, and philosophy. The first fiction (*xiaoshou,* literally "small talk") did not appear until the Han period, and did not receive very much respect among educated Chinese. Short fiction represented creative fiction's first, small steps in the field of inventive literature, and much of this early short fiction fed into Chinese popular culture.

Tales of Wonder (*Lieyi zhuan*) is an early collection of short stories from the late Han era. Most of the stories tell about the encounters between human beings and ghosts or other elements of the spirit world. *Strange Stories from a Chinese Studio* (*Liaozhai Zhiyi*) written by Pu Songling (d. 1715) and published by his son in 1740, is a high point in Imperial Chinese short-story writing. As with *Tales of Wonder, Liaozhai Zhiyi* is a collection of almost five hundred ghost stories that appealed to, and derived from, popular beliefs. Prominent in *Liaozhai Zhiyi* are stories about "fox spirits," who were almost always disguised as beautiful women. Fox spirits live off the vital essence (*qi*) of men, which the Chinese believed was released and transported to women in sexual intercourse. The encounter with a fox spirit often left men impoverished, ill, or dead.

Another popular example of the genre is "Mulian Rescues His Mother," a Buddhist short story that was later developed into a popular opera. In this story, Mulian descends into hell to rescue his sinful mother. His efforts eventually convince the Buddha to restore his mother to the cycle of life and death. This tale combines Buddhist metaphysics with Confucian filial piety. Mulian's actions were not contingent on his mother's actions in life. Such a mixing of tradition was common in Chinese popular culture, and many stories did not maintain a sharp divide between Buddhism, Confucianism, Daoism, and other popular beliefs.

The period of Mongol rule in China, during the end of the thirteenth and first half of the fourteenth century, is also known for the production of the great Chinese dramas. Chinese dramas, many of them musical dramas, matured in Yuan with a format that combined spoken and sung portions. Drama, including opera, was an important way for illiterate Chinese to take part in literary culture. Although many of the dramas explored issues that would have been offensive to hard-minded Confucian scholars (love and the spiritual realm), scholars nevertheless used drama to connect to the people in various ways. For instance, when the Mulian story was performed as opera in the Ming era, the gentry could look on the story as a prime example of filial piety, although it took place within the context of Buddhist metaphysics.

Romance of the West Chamber is a thirteenth-century play by Wang Shifu about the troubled romance of a young scholar and a daughter of a strong-willed widow. Another play with a romantic theme, *Peony Pavilion* (*Mudan Ting*) by Tang Xianzu (1550–1616), is one of China's most popular dramas from the Late Imperial period. The main theme is love (*qing*) reflected in the fantastic love affair between the girl, Du Liniang, and a young scholar, Liu Mengmei. Du Liniang first encounters her lover in a dream. She awakes and experiences such heartbreak that she soon dies. Liu Mengmei soon encounters the ghost of the young girl, who is eventually resurrected, allowing them to resume a corporeal relationship after some challenges. *Peony Pavilion* is also one of the longest of China's dramas, with fifty-five scenes. As an opera, *Peony Pavilion* includes hundreds of arias. Like other writers from the late Ming period, Tang Xianzu was highly influenced by idealist philosophy and explorations of the incorporeal world. *Peony Pavilion* was created to be performed, not read. Like other drama, however, *Peony Pavilion* shows that participation in the culture of the written word in Imperial China was not limited to the literate. *Peony Pavilion* is also important because it is the inspiration for the first published literacy commentary by women in Imperial China, *The Peony Pavilion: Commentary Edition by Wu Wushan's Three Wives.* As the title suggests,

Confucius, the legendary and-much quoted Chinese Philosopher.

all three of Wu's wives were intensely interested in the *Peony Pavilion* and read the text often and with great passion.

PHILOSOPHY TEXTS

More than any other genre, China's secular philosophy was produced for an elite audience. In Confucius's day the intended audience included the numerous kings ruling over a divided China. The emergence of Neo-Confucian philosophy in the Song era again focused on converting the scholar-elite to a new way of looking at their traditions. From this tradition emerged the foundations of China's legal system and imperial ideology.

The *Analects* of Confucius are a collection of sayings brought together by his followers sometime after his death. They do not include a systematic philosophy. Confucius preferred to bring his case directly to students and kings. At the heart of Confucius's philosophy was the *junzi* (moral man) into whose hands the well-being of the society should be delivered. The *Analects* has long remained an important part of the Confucian canon, particularly since Zhu Xi enshrined it as one of the "four books."

The *Mencius* was also placed into the Confucian canon by Zhu Xi. This book was compiled by Mencius himself sometime during his life. The philosophy presented in the *Mencius* is more apparently Confucian than much in the *Analects*. Mencius argued for an egalitarian society and benevolent government based on the common goodness of humanity. The *Mencius* was mastered by every aspiring scholar in Imperial China.

The *Hanfeizi*, written by the Legalist philosopher Han Fei, remains an important reminder that the Confucian dominance of philosophy in late Imperial China was not inevitable. The late Zhou period was a time of intense debate over political philosophy. Legalists, such as Han Fei, did not believe that humanity could be trusted to be good. Instead, it was the duty of kings to apply law (*fa*) to maintain rule.

The *Zhuangzi* is one of the core texts of early Daoist thought, and it remains an important part of the Daoist canon. Zhaung Zhou, the author, presented the major message of Daoism in a series of anecdotes. In short, Daoists believed that the best approach to problems and crises was to follow the path of nature. Although never strongly a part of the imperial orthodoxy, few learned Chinese would have been unfamiliar with the major Daoists texts.

The Significance of the Spring and Autumn Annals by Dong Zhongshu (179–104 B.C.E.) helped establish Confucianism as the imperial orthodoxy. Other schools of thoughts would contest Confucianism throughout the Han and the Tang Empires, but it would be the Confucian view of the state that would win out. Dong Zhongshu argued that the secular order was dynamic and followed certain historically observable patterns. The most important of these was the dynastic cycle. According to Dong Zhongshu, when a king, who had the undisputable "mandate of heaven," fell into disfavor with the people, his rule—along with his heavenly approval—would pass to another.

ENCYCLOPEDIAS

The *Four Treasuries* project was the most complete encyclopedic project in Chinese history. Even Denis Diderot's attempt in France to collect all knowledge, the *Encyclopedie,* cannot compare in scope and size to the *Four Treasuries.* It was not the first such project in Chinese history. In the Ming period, scholars collected all the essential texts as part of codifying the most important curriculum for the civil service exams. The *Four Treasuries* was on a different scale entirely. In 1773, the Qinglong emperor announced the project, which would require the efforts of the entire scholarly community. Its goal was the unification and classification of all knowledge and all books into four great "treasuries": history, classics, philosophy, and literature. When completed in 1783, the *Four Treasuries* contained edited versions of thirty-five hundred works and the bibliographic information for seven thousand others. It is important to note that the project also suppressed significant amounts of scholarship—outnumbering what was saved—by exclusion or outright destruction. Much of this suppressed work was overtly anti-pastoral, and therefore anti-Manchu, and appeared in the Ming or early Qing eras. The *Four Treasuries* project represents both the adoration many Chinese held for scholarship, and the pressures an official orthodoxy placed on intellectual diversity.

> ### Writing and Reading in Manchu
>
> The pastoral people of central and north Asia were largely illiterate, but when they entered China as conquers they either adopted Chinese or developed written forms of their language. The best example of this was the formal invention of the Manchu language in 1599. This had the effect of differentiating the Manchu people from the Mongols, but would also ensure the continuation of Manchu identity after the 1644 conquest of China. Manchu remained an official language of the court until the fall of the Qing dynasty in 1911.

GAZETTEERS

Gazetteers were publications produced by officials at the local-county level in the Ming and Qing periods. The author was generally the county official, who recorded all official occurrences as well as the general history of the region. They remain some of the most useful sources in Chinese social history. The gazetteers recorded local news, population estimates, and were not immune from the moralizing of the author. Local governments printed gazetteers and distributed copies to the central government, where they served the emperors as resources on diverse (and often distant) parts of the empire. Beginning in the Ming period, officials published gazetteers for local consumption as well as records of the successes and failures of their office. They also served as important tools for travelers—including officials newly arriving in regions far from their homes—by providing information on local customs, food, history, environment, and power structures. Although usually rooted deep in the local experiences, gazetteers served the larger empire by ensuring that officials from the core understood regions in the periphery.

MORAL AND RITUAL GUIDEBOOKS

The publication of moral guidebooks exploded in late Imperial China during the decline of the Ming era and the traumatic transition to the Qing era. Proper moral action was a foundation of both the Confucian and Buddhist traditions in China. The Confucian classic, the *Book of Rites,* is in some ways an early moral guide book, showing individuals how to maintain social order through proper interaction. Buddhism added to this tradition by introducing the concept of retribution for ill deeds. In Confucianism, the social order suffered when individuals acted poorly. Buddhist philosophy held that one's soul would be punished in the next life. Moral guidebooks provided individuals with a set of specific instructions that would help them in their interactions with others and avert disaster.

The Book of Rites is a compilation of three texts from the Zhou era, all describing how leaders, gentlemen, and commoners should present themselves. The book contains rules for holding a funeral, for directing government activities, for competitions, and for sacrifices. Confucians, who believed that human goodness needed to be maintained through correct ritual and respect for hierarchy, were drawn to these texts. *The Book of Rites* would remain an important part of the official canon throughout most of the imperial period.

Ledger of Merit and Demerit of the Taiwei Immortal was the first of many ledgers that taught readers how to maintain careful records of their good and evil deeds. It first appeared in the fourth century. In addition to quantifying goodness, the author was attempting to teach readers in the proper way to act in daily life, improving one's overall goodness. Numerous other ledgers would emerge in the following centuries, suggesting a public interest in proper moral action.

Family Rituals was one of the most important works by the Song philosopher Zhu Xi. It was Zhu Xi's attempt to standardize ritual practices for elite families. *Family Rituals* provides necessary details on the proper way to perform marriage ceremonies, capping—for when boys reached maturity—and the all-important ancestor worship. The audience was elite, as many of the rituals would have been impossible for impoverished peasant families.

Biographies of Exemplary Women by Liu Xiang was written in the Han period but remained popular throughout Imperial China. Instead of defining women's place in society through a series of rules, Liu elevated the lives and experiences of a handful of heroic, chaste, and virtuous women. *Biographies* greatly influenced the Qing-era writer Yin Huiyi, whose *Record of Four Mirrors* would also become a standard moral guidebook.

TRAVELOGUES

The mature Chinese imperial system kept officials on the move, primarily because of the immense size of the empire and the fact that most scholar-officials came from the Lower Yangzi region. Another reason was the rule that prevented officials from administering to their hometown or any region for very long to prevent the formation of local bases of power. The long periods of disunity in early China taught rulers the danger of local aristocrats and nepotism. This combination of factors resulted in the production of travelogues by officials who often looked at their new posts with amazement.

Small Sea Travel Diaries by Yu Yonghe records his 1697 voyage to Taiwan to acquire sulfur for the imperial arsenals. Taiwan was not incorporated into the Chinese Empire until the end of the seventeenth century and had not experienced a significant degree of Chinese settlement. Yu looked on Taiwan, and the "savage" people who lived there, in amazement, and he enthusiastically recorded their customs and society. In the following century, thousands of Chinese from the south would settle in Taiwan and eventually dislodge the indigenous people. Travel accounts such as the *Small Sea Travel Diaries* probably increased interest in the island and spurred settlement.

RELIGIOUS TEXTS

Understanding Buddhism did not require long years of study of classical texts as did the mastery of Confucianism. Proselytizers embraced versions of Buddhism that were popular to the masses and easily taught. Nevertheless, literate Chinese consumed Buddhist texts. Buddhist literature included interpretations by monks, sermons, sectarian treatises, and translations of Indic texts. The influence of Buddhism on Chinese philosophy and culture goes much deeper than explicit Buddhist texts.

"The Profound Meaning of the Three Treatises" by the half-Chinese monk Qizang (d. 623) addresses the problem of sectarianism in Chinese Buddhism that was already apparent by the seventh century. Qizang was a follower of the Indian school of Buddhism known as Mādhyamika, and played a vital role in bringing this form of Buddhism into China. Although Qizang's approach never became as popular as other forms of Chinese Mahā yāna Buddhism, its temporary acceptance by some Chinese Buddhists suggest the openness of Chinese thinkers to outside ideas. In this work, Qizang argues against two extremes in the Chinese Buddhist tradition: the radical idealist, stressing nonbeing; and the materialist, stressing the suffering of existence. In fact, both approaches fail because they are equally incomplete. Qizang believed a practitioner should pursue a continual process of questioning and synthesis. This dialectical method gave Qizang's school of thought the name "Middle Doctrine."

> ### Matteo Ricci
>
> Jesuit missionary Matteo Ricci (1552–1610) lived in China continually between 1583 and his death. During this time, Ricci introduced Western learning to Chinese readers and Chinese learning to Western readers through his translations. This was the beginning of a process of exchange that continues to this day. One of his most important translations into Chinese was Euclid's *Elements of Geometry*. He also worked continually on translating Confucian classics into Latin. Throughout his life in China, he remained a devoted missionary, introducing Christian texts to Chinese readers.

HISTORY TEXTS

The Book of History, one of the Confucian Classics from the Zhou era, tells the story of China's mythic prehistory to the rise of the Zhou kingdom. It became a major source for later political theorists trying to justify the "mandate of heaven" explanation for the dynamics of history. As part of the canon, it remained on the reading list of scholars for centuries.

The Records of the Grand Historian by Sima Qian is the first self-conscious historical work of the imperial era, emerging in the first century B.C.E. In addition to setting the standards for historical writing, Sima Qian created the model for all of the dynastic histories that would follow. His major innovation was the replacement of crude annals with a synthetic narrative history. Attached to this narrative history were biographies, histories of important families, and chronologies.

Hanshu (History of the Former Han) by Ban Ku and Ban Zhao closely follows the style and approach of Sima Qian's history. This was the first self-conscious dynastic history, although it only tells the history of the Han period until the usurper Wang Mang disrupted the imperial line in 9 C.E.

Zizhi Tongjian (Comprehensive Guide for Aid to Governance) by Sima Guang was written while the author was in political exile in the eleventh century. Sima Guang wrote a comprehensive history of Chinese history from the Zhou period to the founding of the Song era. It was less politically motivated than most dynastic histories, which were often written to help justify why the "mandate of heaven" was transferred to the new dynasty.

Local histories also became more common in late Imperial China. Along with the gazetteers, they reflect the effort of local officials to record their own history alongside that of the dynastic history.

CONCLUSION

At the turn of the nineteenth century, the Manchu ruled over the stable, expanding, economically vibrant, and internationally formidable Qing Empire. However, the Manchus do not deserve all the praise for the accomplishments of the empire. The imperial system, the civil service exam, a common written language and culture, and a well-developed philosophical tradition that serviced the ruling class had been established by the Chinese in the centuries prior to the Manchu conquest. At the heart of this stability and unity were a universally literate ruling class and a highly literate population, trained in the common Confucian tradition. Reading and writing not only shaped China's cultural history, but were also integral to China's political and social development throughout the imperial period.

This stability made reform and adaptation difficult, but not impossible. In fact, reform and adaptation became crucial after a number of internal changes and external influences converged and started to impinge on China's traditional systems. The arrival of Europeans as conquerors; unchecked and unanticipated population growth, which exposed structural weaknesses in China's agricultural economy; internal unrest; and the industrialization and expansion of neighboring Japan all required that the Chinese revise their worldview. This revision, which was highly influenced by Euro-American traditions, coincided with a transformation of Chinese perceptions of the written word. By the middle of the twentieth century, the Chinese culture of reading more closely resembled that of Europe and America in ideas (Marxism, social Darwinism, science, the Enlightenment) and formats (academic journals, magazines, newspapers). Although this transformation helped to ensure that China could adapt to and eventually prosper in a world dominated by Western global modernity, it also nearly annihilated much of the Imperial Chinese tradition.

RECOMMENDED READING

Brokaw, Cynthia J. *Commerce in Culture: The Sibao Book Trade in the Qing and Republican Periods*. Cambridge: Harvard University Press, 2007.
———. *The Ledgers of Merit and Demerit: Social Change and Moral Order in Late Imperial China*. Princeton: Princeton University Press, 1991.
Brook, Timothy. *The Confusions of Pleasure: Commerce and Culture in Ming China*. Berkeley: University of California Press, 1998.
Chang, Chun-shu and Shelley Hsueh-lun Chang. *Crisis and Transformation in Seventeenth-Century China: Society, Culture, and Modernity in Li Yu's World*. Ann Arbor: University of Michigan Press, 1998.
Furth, Charlotte. *A Flourishing Yin: Gender in China's Medical History, 960–1665*. Berkeley: University of California Press, 1999.
Goldin, Paul Rakita. *The Culture of Sex in Ancient China*. Honolulu: University of Hawaii Press, 2002.
Hsia, C. T. *The Classic Chinese Novel: A Critical Introduction*. New York and London: Columbia University Press, 1968.
Hsueh-lun Chang, Shelley. *History and Legend: Ideas and Images in Ming Historical Novels*. Ann Arbor: University of Michigan Press, 1990.
Hucker, Charles O. *China's Imperial Past: An Introduction to Chinese History and Culture*. Stanford: Stanford University Press, 1975.
Ko, Dorothy. *Teachers of the Inner Chambers: Women and Culture in Seventeenth Century China*. Stanford: Stanford University Press, 1994.
Lewis, Mark Edward. *The Early Chinese Empires: Qin and Han*. Cambridge: Harvard University Press, 2007.
Mann, Susan. *Precious Records: Women in China's Long Eighteenth Century*. Stanford: Stanford University Press, 1997.
Miyazaki, Ichisada. *China's Examination Hell: The Civil Service Examinations of Imperial China*. Translated by Conrad Schirokauer. New Haven and London: Yale University Press, 1981.
Mote, F. W. *Imperial China, 900–1800*. Cambridge: Harvard University Press, 1999.
Schwartz, Benjamin. *The World of Thought in Ancient China*. Cambridge: Harvard University Press, 1985.
Zeitlin, Judith. *Historian of the Strange: Pu Songling and the Chinese Classical Tale*. Stanford: Stanford University Press, 1991.

PRIMARY SOURCES

Ban Gu. *History of the Former Han*. 3 vols. Translated by Homer H. Dubs. 1944. *The Book of Poetry: Chinese Text with English Translation*. Translated by James Legge. Shanghai: The Chinese Book Company, 1931.
Cao Pi. *Lieyi zhuan (Tales of Wonder)*. Beijing: Beijing chubanshe, 2000.
Cao Xuechin. *The Story of the Stone: A Chinese Novel in Five Volumes*. Translated by David Hawkes. Harmondsworth: Penguin Books, 1973-1986. [Also translated as *Dream of the Red Chamber*].
Confucius. *The Analects*. Translated by Arthur Waley. New York: Alfred A. Knopf, 2000.
Dent-Young, Alex and John Dent-Young. *Marshes of Mount Liang: A New Translation of the Shuihu zhuang or Water Margin of Shi Naian and Luo Guanzhong*. 3 vols. Hong Kong: Chinese University Press, 1983–1997.

Dong Zhongshu. *Chunqui Fanlu (The Significance of the* Spring and Autumn Annals*)*. 6 vols. Beijing: Beijing tushuguan chubanshe, 2003.

Guanzhong Luo. *The Romance of the Three Kingdoms*. Currently available as *Three Kingdoms: Chinese Classics* (Classic Novel in 4 Volumes). Translated by Moss Roberts. Beijing: Foreign Languages Press, 2005.

Han Fei. *Hanfeizi*. Changsha: Yue lu shu she, 1993.

Li Chi: Book of Rites. An Encyclopedia of ancient ceremonial usages, religious creeds, and social institutions. Translated by James Legge. New Hyde Partk, N.Y.: University Books, 1967.

Liu Xiang. *Lie nuüzhuan (Biographies of Exemplary Women)*. Shanghai: Shanghai gu ji chubanshe, 1994.

Li Yü. *Carnal Prayer Mat*. Translated by Patrick Hanan. Honolulu: University of Hawai'i Press, 1996.

Luo Huanchen. *Taiwei xian jun shan guo ge (Ledge of Merit and Demerit of the Taiwei Immortal)*. Hebei: Luo shi, archival material, 1932.

Luo Zhiye and Zhou Bingjun, eds. *Shangshu (Book of History)*. Changsha: Hunan chubanshe, 1997.

Mencius. *Mengzi*. Translated by D. C. Lau. London and New York: Penguin Books, 2004.

Pu Songling. *Strange Stories from a Chinese Studio*. Translated by Herbert A. Giles. London: Thos. De la Rue, 1880.

Qizang. "The Profound Meaning of the Three Treatises" in *A Sourcebook in Chinese Philiosophy*. Edited and Translated by Wing-tsit Chan. Princeton: Princeton University Press, 1963.

Quan Tang Shi (Complete Poems of the Tang). 9 vols. Taipei: Taiwan shangwu yinshu guan, 1983.

Sima Guang. *Zizhi Tongjian (Comprehensive Guide for Aid to Governance)*. Beijing: Beijing tushuguang chubanshe, 2003.

Sima Qian. *Records of the Grand Historian*. Translated by Burton Watson. Hong Kong: Research Center for Translation, Chinese University of Hong Kong, 1993.

Tang Xianzu. *The Peony Pavilion*. Translated by Cyril Birch. Second Edition. Bloomington: Indiana University Press, 2002.

Wang Shifu. *Romance of the Western Chamber*. Edited by Gamaerkian Translated by T. C. Lai.. Hong Kong: Heinemann Educational Books, 1973.

Wu Chengen. *The Journey to the West*. 4 vols. Translated by Anthony Yu. Chicago: Chicago University Press, 1977–1983.

Xiao Xiaosheng. *The Golden Lotus: A Translation, from the Chinese Original, of the Novel Chin P'ing Mei*. Translated by Clement Egerton. London and New York: Kegan Paul International, 1995.

Yu Yonghe. *Small Sea Travel Diaries: Yu Yonghe's Record of Taiwan*. Translated by Macabe Keliher. Taipei: SMC Publisher, 2004.

Zhuangzi. Translated by Hyun Höchsman. New York: Pearson Longman, 2007.

Zhu Xi. *Chu Hsi's Family Rituals: A Twelfth-Century Chinese Manual for the Performance of Cappings, Weddings, Funerals, and Ancestral Rites*. Translated by Patricia Buckley Ebrey. Princeton: Princeton University Press, 1991.

CHAPTER 14

Modern China

Evan Lampe

TIMELINE

1938	Guomindang moves capital to Chongqing
1941	Pacific War begins
1945	End of World War II
1949	Chinese Civil War ends; establishment of the People's Republic of China
1950	Chinese enter Korean War
1953	First Five Year Plan begins
1955	Bandung Conference in Indonesia
1957	Hundred Flowers movement
1958	Great Leap Forward begins
1960–63	Lin Biao begins Radicalization of the People's Liberation Army
1966	Cultural Revolution begins
1967	People's Liberation Army used to defeat Red Guards
1972	Nixon visits China
1976	Mao Zedong dies
1980	"Gang of Four" tried
1983	Deng Xiaoping institutes market-driven Economic Reforms
1989	Tiananmen Square Protests
1997	Hong Kong returned to China

INTRODUCTION TO THE PERIOD

Great Britain's victory over China in the Opium War (1839–1841) did not bring down two millennia of imperial Chinese tradition, but it did initiate a long process of self-examination that would eventually challenge much of China's traditional philosophy and society. The first manifestations of this critical self-examination appeared with Lin Zexu (1785–1850), whose attempt to put down the opium trade in Canton sparked a war with Great Britain, and who encouraged the Chinese royal court to appreciate the West's technological advantages and to adopt some of them. A little later, the scholar Wei Yuan (1794–1856) urged his readers to reexamine their country's relationship with the outside world and begin paying attention to the "sea kingdoms" abroad.

The quasi-Christian Taiping Rebellion (1850–1871) almost defeated the Qing Empire (1644–1912). Its leader, the failed scholar Hong Xiuquan (1814–1864), was introduced to Christianity by an American missionary. Even if the scholar-officials of the Qing were not reading Western texts, others, such as Hong, were exposed to Western writings due to the diligent efforts of missionaries. After an exam-induced nervous breakdown, Hong came to believe he was Jesus' brother, and that the Christian God had given him a mission to purge China of its philosophical errors, along with all foreign conquerors. He cultivated his religious—and eventually military—movement among the Hakka people of South China. His movement of "God Worshippers" established an empire in the lower Yangzi Delta, where they questioned many aspects of both Chinese tradition and foreign Manchu rule (for example, in opposition to ancient tradition, women in the Taiping armies did not bind their feet). Hong Xiuquan promised, but never fully implemented, a radical land reform. It would take a decade for the disheveled Qing armies to finally defeat the Taiping. The rebellion not only exposed the weaknesses in the Qing but also the power of imported ideas.

During the rebellion, China fought another unsuccessful war with Great Britain, ending in what would be a series of unequal treaties with Western powers. These unequal treaties gave the imperialist powers access to Chinese ports farther inland, opened much of the country to missionary activities, and ensured legal protection for foreign citizens from the Chinese judicial system. In response to these ill-advised shifts in policy, the official and military commander Zeng Guofan (1811–1872), who was instrumental in defeating the Taiping, defined the concept of "self-strengthening." According to Zeng Guofan, China needed to adopt Western military technology to empower the Qing. By adopting the technology of the West—but not the philosophies, political structures, or worldview—Chinese civilization would remain intact but be empowered to defend itself. Part of this movement was the establishment of a new foreign office, the Zongli Yamen, which helped translate Western technological texts. A later theorist of self-strengthening, Zhang Zhidong (1837–1909), suggested that China could maintain its essence (yong) even while incorporating a Western body (ti). However, the next generation of Chinese intellectuals would reveal the folly of this position, as they came to believe through their exposure to Western ideas that there were structural weaknesses in the Chinese essence.

The edifice of self-strengthening collapsed in 1895 with China's defeat by Japan, a newly industrialized nation that had once been under China's influence. Chinese scholars such as Yan Fu (1854–1921) and Liang Qichao (1873–1929), began to question the roots of Chinese tradition and offered more radical reforms. Yan Fu, who had lived in England and spent much of his life translating Western political and scientific thought into Chinese, believed that it was the West's desire for gaining wealth and power that made them successful. The implication of this idea was that the Chinese mind was in part to blame for China's failures. Therefore, the Chinese mind could benefit from improved educational facilities. Radical reformers gained the emperor's support for a reform movement in the summer of 1898. A central part of this reform movement was the establishment of a modern university in Beijing. One hundred days after it began, this reform movement was crushed by a reactionary coup, leading to the dispersal or execution of the reform leaders.

In 1912 Chinese leaders, many from Sun Yat-sen's organization of overseas radicals, reformed the Chinese state into a republic based in Beijing. It would not take long for this republic to disintegrate and power to flow to regional military leaders, known as warlords. Hopes for change after the 1911 Revolution were also undermined by the expansion of Japanese power in East Asia after the First World War (1914–1918). Both Japan and China fought on the allied side, but it was the imperial Japanese state that won the most concessions at the end of the war: Pacific islands and German holdings in China. Chinese students in Beijing University resisted the Treaty of Versailles in public demonstrations on May 4, 1919. This student activism coincided with a cultural revolution that would have significant ramifications for Chinese reading patterns.

The popular resistance to the Treaty of Versailles ended in a minor victory: the Chinese government refused to sign the treaty. But the Western powers ignored Chinese demands. Therefore, China's major problems—political disunity, imperialism, and rural poverty—became more acute after the First World War. Out of the frustration of many Chinese, including illiterate or semiliterate workers, came an explosion of political activism driven by two major forces: the Nationalist Party (Guomindang) and the Chinese Communist Party. These opposing forces achieved some degree of national unification in 1927, during a military campaign known as the Northern Expedition, in which the armies of the Communists and the Guomindang struck out from the southern city of Canton—their base of operations—and defeated the southern warlords. During the wake of this victory, the Guomindang, under the military and political leadership of Jiang Jieshi, launched a coup against the left wing of the Guomindang, including the Communists. From 1927 until the Japanese invasion of East China in 1937, the Communists and Guomindang remained at war. The Guomindang, which mostly operated from urban centers, developed a strategy of largely unfulfilled urban modernization through a close alliance with the Chinese bourgeoisie, while the Communists advanced a strategy of peasant mobilization through the formation of rural soviets. In 1934, Guomindang assaults undermined the Communist efforts in Jiangxi province and forced the Communists to abandon their base areas in an exodus westward known as the Long March.

Expanding Japanese imperialism in east China led to a fleeting alliance between the Guomindang and the Communists in 1936. Jiang Jieshi faced increasing pressure from students and warlords to deal with the Japanese instead of sustaining his wars against the Communists. The Communists, now solidly under the leadership of the brilliant Mao Zedong (1893–1976), were too weakened by the Long March to challenge the Guomindang. Despite occasional conflicts, a cold alliance between the Guomindang and the Communists survived the Second World War. Nevertheless, the war undermined Guomindang support in China and expanded popular support for the Communists. First, the Guomindang lost their base of support in the east and were forced to relocate the capital to Chongqing, in Sichuan province. Their wartime policies also alienated much of the Chinese countryside. On the other hand, the Communists used the war to expand base areas in much of west, central, and north China. By the end of the war, much of rural China was organized by the Communists, who attracted the peasants by fighting the Japanese and implementing land reform. From this strong base, the Communists won a civil war that broke out in 1947. In October 1949, Mao Zedong declared the formation of the People's Republic of China.

As the Communists pursued soviet-style industrialization in the cities under the Five Year Plans, the countryside followed two contradictory trends: land reform and collectivization. Land reform was a direct result of the revolution and gave tenant and landless farmers land that was seized from the rural ruling class. Starting in 1953, with the encouragement of Mao Zedong, peasants—first in some areas, then gradually throughout the country—redefined the land reform to mean collective and communal farms. The Communists believed that collectivization would expand production and push China along the road to socialism. Optimism about the rapid movement toward rural collectivization encouraged the Communists, under the inspiration of Mao, to support the Great Leap Forward, an attempt to rapidly industrialize China using the power of the masses and to resolve the contradictions between the countryside and the city through the mobilization of rural energies toward industrial endeavors. The Great Leap Forward was built on agricultural utopianism and faulty industrial planning, reflected in the formation of unproductive and wasteful rural steel plants. The Great Leap Forward broke from the soviet central plan and the use of a technocratic class by calling for all people to be both "red"—working-class—and "expert." Certainly, the Great Leap Forward itself did nothing to expand educational opportunities for the peasant class. Instead, it turned into a major setback for the Chinese economy and caused a famine estimated to have killed twenty million people.

The Cultural Revolution originated in the contentious political culture of the 1950s and 1960s. The first battles of what would become in many parts of China an armed confrontation began over the proper role of culture in a classless society. Rooted in the Yan'an period of the late 1930s, the role of culture was expected to be subservient to the goals of Communist revolution. The Hundred Flowers movement allowed a degree of free expression for intellectuals, but the larger objective of national modernization remained the goal. Thus the ability of party members to fight political battles through culture remained. However, it would not be literary interpretation that would bring China to civil war. The true cause of the Cultural Revolution was the continuing political struggle between Mao and his followers and the established Communist party leadership. Even when Mao retreated from active political life after the debacle of the Great Leap Forward, his fame and status continued to grow. A close ally, Lin Biao (1907–1971?), helped cultivate the so-called Cult of Mao among the People's Liberation Army and among young urban students. Thus, a growing number of people adored Mao and studied his principles of mass mobilization, revolutionary volunteerism, and continuing revolutionary struggle. While the party leadership was in full reactionary mode, still reeling from the Great Leap Forward, Mao collected a power base in key areas.

The Cultural Revolution began in 1966 during discussions over the proper role of art in a Communist society. In this case the key text was Wu Han's *Hai Rui Dismissed from Office,* an allegory of the purging of Peng Dehuai (1898–1974) posing as a historical play. The result of these conflicts was the purging of party members associated with culture, but the purges quickly spread across the nation at all levels of power. Key to these developments were Maoist students, known as Red Guards. In the late summer of 1966, Maoist leaders directed the nation, in particular the Red Guards, to defend the revolution from reactionaries. Students, as well as workers, took on Mao's call to rebellion against the party leadership. The Red Guards established a workers commune in Shanghai by throwing out the conservative party leadership. As China quickly descended into civil war, Mao ended the most radical phase of the Cultural Revolution by using the army to crush the Red Guards and worker movements, such as the one that emerged in Shanghai. The Cultural Revolution would endure in various forms until Mao's death, largely in political culture and rhetoric. The most radical supporters of the Cultural Revolution failed in their vision of continuing the revolution and Mao made peace with the party he contested, which had recovered by the late 1960s.

The Cultural Revolution discredited Maoist radicalism for many Chinese, but it would not be until Mao's death in 1976 that the door was opened to new leadership. The future leader of China, Deng Xiaoping (1904–1997), was a loyal Communist who was active in the early days of the revolutionary movements prior to the Second World War. Deng continued the process of opening China to the West that was begun by the regularization of diplomatic relations between the People's Republic and the United States. He also adopted economic and social reforms that moved China away from communism but held the promise of modernization. Deng's political actions centered on the marginalization of the Maoists, who remained in power even after Mao's death, and the relaxation of some of the lingering effects of the Cultural Revolution. Although Deng refused to accept any substantial political reforms, he did encourage the modernization of science and technology through the "four modernizations" program. Under Deng, China established new research centers that would train a new generation of scientists and engineers. The reforms also relaxed economic policies in the countryside, thus allowing a partial market system to flourish there. Throughout much of the 1980s, the industrial sphere remained closely controlled, but the reformers established special economic zones in the coastal south that could attract foreign capital and allowed capitalist practices and labor arrangements to flourish.

These reforms produced real economic growth in the countryside, helped spur a growing consumer economy and consumer culture, expanded the rule of law, and depoliticized university admissions, which increased access to higher education.

In this context, a democracy movement flourished in Chinese universities. The physicist, Fang Lizhi (1936–), became a spokesperson for young Chinese eager to voice their support for a more democratic political structure. For the most part, these students worked from within Communist Chinese political culture, but many actively rejected Chinese Marxism in preference to liberal Western political thought. This put them in line with late Qing intellectuals and May Fourth student protestors. The State attempted to repress the growing student voice, but could not put an end to China's democracy movement.

The climax and subsequent decline of China's democracy movement came in 1989 with the Tiananmen Square protests. Hu Yaobang (1915–1989), a Communist Party leader and a favorite of student activists because of his support for political reforms, died in April, 1989. Beijing University students used Hu's death to stage peaceful protests in Tiananmen Square. The students called for political reforms, an end to corruption, and a greater voice for the younger generation. The students benefited from international attention because the reformist soviet secretary, Mikhail Gorbachev, was visiting Beijing at the same time. However, Communist party leaders refused to negotiate with the students. On May 20, when support for the students expanded to the citizens and workers, and it became clear the government was losing control over the Beijing streets, Deng Xiaoping declared martial law. A tense state of affairs existed until June 3 and June 4, when the People's Liberation Army received and carried out orders to clear the Beijing streets and Tiananmen Square of protestors. This crackdown seriously hindered the democracy movement. Many student leaders, and their allies, were jailed or left China. The massacre of June 4, 1989 confirmed that, despite economic reforms, the Chinese Communist Party leaders, remembering the Cultural Revolution, would not relax their monopoly on power.

READING TRENDS AND PRACTICES

When Xie Bingying (1906–2000) was fifteen, she enjoyed spending her time reading. At her girls' middle school, she, along with her fellow students, managed a small library that had both classical Chinese literature and translations of works of great foreign writers. Her favorite work was Johann Wolfgang von Goethe's *The Sorrows of Young Werther,* which she once read five times in one sitting. She also enjoyed Oscar Wilde's *Salome.* Her interests also took her to Chinese literature, including *Water Margin* and the *Dream of the Red Chamber.* She expressed joy at reading the heroic stories of bandits and disgust at the trivial complaints and interests of the characters in *Dream of the Red Chamber.* These literary interests led her to a life of writing and political activism.

The foundation for this life was provided by the chance to attend school in her youth. She first attended the Datong Girls School in her hometown. While at this school, she unbound her feet and began reading popular publications, such as *Youth Magazine* and the writings of famous Chinese intellectuals of the day. She later attended the Xinyi Girls School and Hunan's First Provincial Girls Normal School. After completing her education, Xie Bingying lived a dramatic and eventful life, serving in the military, operating at the center of the public discourse, and eventually settling in the United States.

Xie Bingying's life reveals how much had changed in Chinese reading patterns in the years since the Opium War (1839). The most striking element is what she was reading. In Imperial China, only a very few people had any access to Western texts. The Jesuit, Matteo Ricci, was one of the few to introduce Western learning into China. A handful of merchants in Canton, where westerners were allowed to trade, may also have had access to Western learning. While Xie Bingying was growing up, she could choose from thousands of texts from the Western literary and philosophical canon, translated into Chinese.

The second striking factor is Xie Bingying herself. Although her family was not from the impoverished peasant class, it is unlikely that she would have had access to literacy without some of the developments in nineteenth- and early-twentieth-century Chinese history. She learned to read while attending a school for girls. Moreover, she received considerable support for her literary endeavors from her brother and other men in her life. Despite the existence of a small minority of literate women, such a story would have been impossible in the eighteenth century or in an earlier period.

Throughout the modern period, changes in literacy, reading, and scholarship in general were shaped by a concern for imperial or national salvation. The introduction of Western learning, the education of more people, the use of vernacular language, and the explosion in new genres, such as newspapers and journals, were all tied to the Chinese response to imperialism.

Western influence shaped reading patterns directly. One provision in the unequal treaties was the greater access for foreign missionaries to China's interior. In addition to spreading the Christian message to people such as Hong Xiuquan, the missionaries established schools for poor Chinese. Many of these schools catered to the needs of peasant girls, who lacked other means of education. Missionaries required girls entering their schools to unbind their feet, which was often a painful process. Foreign teachers or Chinese teachers recruited by the missionaries taught girls how to read, basic mathematics, and other necessary skills. Many Chinese women, such as Xie Bingying, owe their literacy to the establishment of girls' schools begun by these missionaries. Missionaries provided a needed educational service, because self-strengthening provided few means for Chinese women to gain literacy or the skills needed for modernity.

Chinese intellectuals did not passively accept Western writings and ideas, but rather questioned what westerners brought with them and filtered those ideas. The central idea of self-strengthening maintained that only the West's technological knowledge had any practical application for China. Even the more radical thinkers, who thought the Chinese should change their worldview based on an exposure to Western ideas, chose carefully. For example, Yan Fu accepted English theories of social Darwinism but became more attracted to the ideas of "reformed" social Darwinism, which advocated social interference to mitigate the cruel laws of natural selection. Yan Fu made this choice because he read Western texts through a Chinese lens; his classical training, which stressed the importance of social cohesion and the benevolence of rulers, made a full acceptance of social Darwinism impossible. Similarly, when Chinese students in Japan and France returned to China in the first decade of the twentieth century, they brought socialism with them. The socialism they brought was not that of German trade unionism or Marxism, but rather French and Russian anarchism. Possibly anarchism engaged the Chinese tradition of Daoism, or perhaps social anarchism's emphasis on cooperation made it an easier fit for Chinese students.

The Qing was eventually brought down by an anti-Manchu revolution in 1911, but even the Qing leaders had realized that more significant changes were necessary to save their empire. After the disastrous Boxer Rebellion of 1900, which brought Western troops into the capital of Beijing, the Qing court instituted a series of reforms that would undermine the foundations of traditional Chinese learning. These reforms dismantled the basis of Chinese education and official recruitment of the previous one thousand years: the civil service examination system based on Confucianism. The government sent more students abroad, mostly to Japan, to acquire new skills. The reforms of the late Qing also established local schools, paid for with onerous taxes on the peasant class. The Qing also dismantled the Manchu army and replaced it with a modern army. Many disgruntled students, now lacking an outlet for their intellectual endeavors and a career, turned to the army for employment. Looking at the new schools and taxes with distrust, peasants turned away from the Manchu in greater numbers. The 1911 Revolution was the result of these late Qing reforms, which alienated more groups than they directly aided and sacrificed much of the basis of traditional Qing rule: the examination system, the Manchu military, and cultural influence over the peasant class.

The New Culture Movement (1917–1923), which emerged from the revolution and was led by Chinese urban intellectuals, had three major components. First, writers argued that China should dispense with classical Chinese writing and use the vernacular. To this end, more and more intellectuals wrote and published in the vernacular. In a relatively short period, classical Chinese became a dead language, useful only for scholars studying the Chinese past. Second, New Culture Movement intellectuals argued strongly against the self-strengthening view that Chinese tradition was superior to that of the West. Instead, they questioned the Confucian family's impact on Chinese character and gender relations as well as the role of tradition in weakening the Chinese nation. Much of the writing of the New Culture Movement, most notably the short stories of Lu Xun, savagely assaulted Chinese tradition. Third, the New Culture Movement borrowed heavily from Western intellectual traditions, finding in them the solutions to China's problems. At the heart of the New Culture Movement were two important figures: "Mr. Science" and "Mr. Democracy." In short, the New Culture Movement transformed reading patterns in three fundamental ways: an increased use of the vernacular, the criticism of Confucian family traditions that often kept women uneducated and illiterate, and the centering of Chinese intellectual life in modern universities, which laid the foundation for a gradually expanding literacy in twentieth-century China. By directly engaging Western ideas and texts, the intellectuals of the New Culture Movement incorporated European intellectual traditions such as Marxism, anarchism, liberalism, and science as well as European intellectual institutions such as academic journals, politically oriented newspapers, and academic departments focused on modern scholarship.

Once the Communists established complete rule over China, their immediate concern was to complete the land reform that made them so popular with the peasantry. They also hoped to woo urbanites, including intellectuals. Mao Zedong and the Chinese Communists had an ambivalent relationship with intellectuals that dated back to the early days of the party's resurgent development in Yan'an. Although many early supporters of communism in China were intellectuals, Mao Zedong's rural strategy drew the party to the largely uneducated, illiterate peasant class. In his essay "On Practice," Mao encouraged party members to listen to the peasant class and draw wisdom from them. His populist message did not delegitimize education, but rather cast suspicion on "book learning." Furthermore, Mao criticized the tendency of the educated classes to impose theory on society. For this reason, intellectuals who came to Yan'an were expected to mobilize their skills and their arts for the purpose of revolution. After 1949, reflecting their pursuit of a more urban, soviet model, the Communists worked hard to expand access to primary and higher education, with the goals of creating a class of educated people who could work in socialist development projects. For this reason, the Communist education system maintained, rather than displaced, the inequalities in access and opportunity that were implicit in republican education. Most importantly, education remained an urban phenomenon. Still, the relationship between the Communists and the intellectuals was never without tension. In 1956, Mao Zedong called for intellectuals to critique aspects of Communist policy under the Hundred Flowers Movement. When this criticism turned out to be sharper than Mao had anticipated, the Hundred Flowers Movement morphed into an anti-right campaign that served to silence intellectual critics of the Communist Party.

After the disaster of the Great Leap Forward, the Chinese economy and political structure went into recovery. Out of this would come some positive developments that could continue until Mao's death and beyond. The Chinese Communist Party (CCP) reevaluated their strategy for rural development. No longer believing in the possibility of a quick fix, they focused on what could work well in the countryside. To this end, villages were encouraged to establish schools that would teach, among other things, literacy. Central to this movement was an understanding that anyone literate could teach literacy. Similarly, the "barefoot doctor" movement, in which people with practical medical training worked in the countryside, resulted in concrete benefits in public health. Even during the Cultural Revolution—when university-level education suffered a severe setback as students left the classroom to direct political action—primary education (and therefore literacy) expanded in the countryside.

After the crackdown on the 1989 democracy movement, Communist leaders pursued economic reforms at many levels of Chinese society. As a result, astounding and seemingly inexorable economic growth, as well as social and economic inequality, emerged. Although expanding education and literacy remained important to the economic modernization, the vibrant political culture seen in the universities in the 1980s was not restored. Despite fifty years of Communist rule in China and twenty-five years of relative isolation from the West, the reading culture of China remains a product of the debates and developments in the first decades of the twentieth century. It was the introduction of outside ideas and forms of writing, as well as the expansion of literacy, that shaped much of the development of modern China.

CREATIVE TEXTS

The Chinese novel was not a foreign import, but the form of it underwent significant developments in the early part of the twentieth century. The most significant developments were the expansion and standardization of the use of vernacular Chinese in fiction writing and the more overtly political nature of many of the writers. This section will begin with three novels produced in the 1930s that reflected these changes.

Camel Xiangzi, by the Manchu writer Lao She, was published on the eve of the Second World War, but it looked back on the social conditions that the author experienced in urban north China during his youth. *Camel Xiangzi* tells the story of Beijing life through the experiences of a common rickshaw puller. The Beijing rickshaw pullers, although on the bottom of urban China's social hierarchy, played an important role in keeping the city functioning. Their position also gave them access to the entire city and ensured their awareness of the life of the rich and powerful. This is reflected in the novel through a series of interlocking plotlines, tied together through the rickshaw. Their awareness did not provide them with real power to affect a change in their condition as a rickshaw puller, as

Kinhyōshi yōrin (Yang Lin), the hero of the *Suikoden* (*The Water Margin*), one of the so-called Four Great Classical Novels of Chinese literature. The novel depicts the adventures of 108 outlaws in the Song Dynasty.

the protagonist of *Camel Xiangzi* remained dependent on forces outside of his control.

Zhang Henshui also wrote about urban life and social divisions but did it through the genre of popular fiction. His *Shanghai Express*, written in the 1930s, explores the social divisions and social anxiety of modern China through a detailed exploration of a train ride from Beijing to Shanghai. Zhang's novels were extremely popular in Republican China due to their accessible nature and scandalous plotlines. In *Shanghai Express*, the protagonist, and many other characters, take advantage of the anonymity of modern life. The train, divided into three classes, also becomes a tool for exploring the changing and contentious class realities emerging in urban China. Those with means pretended to be poor, while some humble characters lived beyond their means. The climax, in which a young, beautiful woman seduces and robs the protagonist, reflects the anxieties about rapid social change Zhang and his readers felt.

Lao She's novel *Cat Country* moved away from the realism of *Camel Xiangzi* but remained a political work. It is also an example of early Chinese science fiction. Speculative and fantastic literature existed even in ancient China, but *Cat Country* drew on conventions and plot schemes common in European and American science fiction. Lao She spent much of the late 1920s in England where he would have been exposed to this emerging genre. In *Cat Country,* the narrator is marooned on Mars and finds the local feline population petty, divided, and self-centered. They are oblivious to the dangers around them and their own corruptions. The novel was an allegory for the infighting and weakness Lao She saw in China, despite the growing threat of Japanese imperialism.

Short fiction existed in pre-modern China and was consumed by a popular audience. The development of vernacular literature in the early twentieth century influenced the development of the short story. The highly charged political milieu of that era made short fiction highly polemical. Lu Xun wrote numerous political short stories, including the three represented here. Not all short fiction was so highly politicized, however much of it spoke to the social and political conditions of the day. Readers of short fiction in modern China did not read for escapism but were confronted with the realities of imperialism, inequality, and national failure. Lu Xun was an important figure in the May Fourth Movement, and he has remained popular, in part due to the canonization of his works by the Communists.

"The True Story of Ah Q" (1922) tells the story of a ridiculous man on the bottom of the social hierarchy in his town. Despite his numerous failures and humiliations, Ah Q remained arrogantly confident and continually interprets defeat as victory. Near the end of the story, Ah Q supports the 1911 Revolution not as a leader but as a follower. The local authorities arrest him and execute him for theft. Lu Xun presented Ah Q as an allegorical figure, representing China and the failure of its people to confront their weaknesses honestly. In the end, Lu Xun suggests to his readers that China would experience the same fate as Ah Q.

These same pessimistic politics emerge from "The Diary of a Madman" (1918). In this story, Lu Xun confronts the burden tradition placed on the Chinese people. As with many of his generation, Lu Xun reached maturity in a world that was still bound by Confucian tradition. Few intellectuals escaped the question of what to do with tradition. Lu Xun completely rejected the position that tradition had a place in the modern world. In "The Diary of a Madman" the insane narrator believes that has discovered a hidden message about cannibalism in the Confucian classics that dominated education and official thought for centuries.

In "The New Year's Sacrifice" (1924) Lu Xun narrows his criticism of tradition by looking at the role it played in the lives of women. In this story the woman, who is referred to as "Xiang Lin's Wife," is used as a pawn by her dead husband's family. They marry her off, against her will, in hope of benefiting financially from the transaction. She achieves some happiness in this second marriage, but even that is ended by forces outside of her control; her husband and son die tragically. At this point, Xiang Lin's Wife becomes ostracized from society and is financially exploited by those promising religious escape from her sorrows. In the end, she is reduced to servitude and begging and finally dies tragically herself. By presenting a woman shackled by tradition and superstition, Lu Xun presented one of the most powerful calls for women's liberation in the May Fourth period.

NEWSPAPERS, MAGAZINES, AND JOURNALS

Pre-modern China lacked an independent press. Local officials produced gazetteers recording local events and imperial policies. These publications were the official voice of the empire at the local level. Missionaries and merchants created the first independent newspapers for consumption of resident foreigners or congregants of Christian missions. Many of these were written in Chinese for a Chinese audience. In the late Qing, Chinese intellectuals created the modern press, which gave them an independent voice and a venue to express their political positions at a time when there were few political institutions independent of the Qing Empire.

Shenbao (*Shanghai Journal*) was started in 1872 by foreign merchants in Shanghai. The newspaper was not typical of British and American merchant newspapers because it was written in Chinese and had a Chinese readership. It advocated the modernization of the Chinese economy along Western lines and consequently was closely aligned with the perspective of the Chinese self-strengtheners. Much of the newspaper provided those involved in the growing trade between China and the West with updated commercial news.

Shiwubao (*The Chinese Progress*) was started in 1896 under the intense direction of the political reformer Liang Qichao, who served as the newspaper's chief editor and wrote many of the articles that appeared in the journal. During the ill-fated 1898 reform movement, the Guangxu emperor established *Shiwubao* as the official organ of the Chinese state. In the context of the national crisis facing China after the 1895 victory of Japan in the Sino-Japanese War, the ideas expressed by Liang Qichao in *Shiwubao* were extremely radical, although they did not go so far as to call for the total destruction of the Imperial system. Instead, *Shiwubao* looked forward to a Chinese nation-state. Liang, through the pages of *Shiwubao,* called for a vitalized citizenry, the development of the "yellow race," and the creation of a unified Chinese nation. *Shiwubao* was independent, but its contributors did not see themselves as intermediaries between society and the state. This would emerge with the publication of *Shibao.*

Shibao emerged before the failed 1898 reforms when reformist and radical intellectuals had greater faith in the imperial system and the emperor. After the reform failed and the major players were executed or exiled, the journalists who wrote for the newly created *Shibao* refused to be dependent on the Qing state or the message of exiled reformers. *Shibao* adopted many important reforms, such as the relaxation of style, the use of shorter articles instead of longer and scholarly polemics, and the use of correspondents from throughout China. The writers and editors of *Shibao* called for the modernization of the Chinese nation and the creation of citizens, but they believed the way to accomplish this was through the empowerment of citizens through information. *Shibao* was economically self-sufficient and a true reflection of the Western ideal of a free and independent press.

The Chinese press did not remain independent of the state. After 1949 the official organ of the Chinese Communist Party, *Renmin ribao* (*The People's Daily,* established one year earlier), became the dominant newspaper for the nation. During the Mao years, editorial power remained tightly in the hands of central party members. Because politics were highly contentious in this era, the *People's Daily* also became a forum for political conflict. Editorials often reflected the decisions of particular factions in the government or the final resolution of a political conflict. Although the role of the *People's Daily* has declined in recent years, it is still the official voice of China's ruling party and the major source of news for millions of readers in China. One of the demands of the students during the 1989 Democracy Movement was a free press. This goal has remained elusive despite two decades of cultural, economic, and intellectual exchange between China and the Western democracies.

Linglong (*The Ladies Journal*) was a magazine published between 1931 and 1937 for urban women readers. *Linglong*'s main purpose was to help its readers interact with urban life by providing advice on clothing, child rearing, and popular culture. *Linglong* also was involved indirectly in gender politics, encouraging its readers to embrace their role as China's modern girls even though the Chinese government and other women's magazines saw the "modern girl" as a corrupting influence on Chinese society.

Liangyou Huabao (*The Young Companion*), which began publication in the mid-1920s, was another magazine catering to young urban women. It was groundbreaking in its use of pictures, which often overshadowed the printed texts. Dominating these images were "modern girls." Through these images, *Liangyou* advertised modern life, modern dress, and modern gender norms. Magazines such as *Linglong* and *Liangyou* reflected urban realities but also helped codify the meaning of modernity.

At the center of modern China's political debates were journals published in support of particular political movements. As universities in China created academic departments and disciplinary studies, in emulation of European and American education, academic journals associated with particular fields emerged. The major readers of these journals were intellectuals, although some had significant readership and influenced politics. Many of these journals were short-lived, but collectively their influence on Chinese politics and science is unmistakable.

Anarchism, the political philosophy that holds that all hierarchies and states should be abolished, entered China during the intellectually vibrant late Qing. The first Chinese anarchists were students who studied abroad in Paris and Tokyo. *Xin Shiji* (*The New Era*) was an anarchist journal established by the so-called Paris anarchists. They believed in a slower progressive form of anarchism reflecting the ideas of the Russian anarchist, Peter Kropotkin. They believed anarchism to be desirable but placed its implementation in the distant future when industrialization and prosperity would eliminate inequality and want. *The New Era* began publication in 1907 and was the journal of New World Society. Never widely read, *The New Era* nonetheless helped introduce anarchism to Chinese intellectuals seeking routes for social change, and until the rise of communism in China, anarchism was the dominant form of socialism in China.

Political journals proliferated in China during the May Fourth era. The most important of these was *Xin Qingnian* (*New Youth*), established in 1915 by the future founder of the Chinese Communist Party, Chen Duxiu. *New Youth* would become the major organ of the infant Communist Party, but not before existing for a long period at the center of China's intellectual culture. Chen envisioned the journal as a weapon against the forces of stagnation and reaction, the very forces that controlled the fate of China during the fragile early years of the republic. The title he chose reflected his goals. He wanted to mobilize the spirit of youth against the endurance of tradition. *New Youth* published the writings of Lu Xun and the liberal Hu Shi. The journal also translated some of the first Marxist texts into Chinese, advocated for women's liberation, and called for a cultural revolution in China.

PHILOSOPHY TEXTS

Modern Chinese philosophy was heavily influenced by the introduction of Western ideas. Many major thinkers lived in the West or were otherwise exposed to European and American political thought, science, or philosophy. Traditional—including Confucian—thought did not die out; it remained influential, particularly in the early twentieth century, as thinkers made the transition from following their classical education to embracing new thought.

Kang Youwei's *Datongshu* (*The Book of the Great Unity*) showed how a very traditional, although not conservative, thinker could propose radical ideas while remaining deep in Chinese tradition. Written in 1885, *Datongshu* presented a utopian world where human suffering is eliminated, war is found only in the past, and the national divisions are replaced by a unitary world government. *Datongshu* was not a replication of European and American utopian writings. It rather developed from Buddhist views of the inevitability of suffering and Confucian beliefs in the perfectibility of humanity. What made *Datongshu* radical was its progressive message that looked forward, while much of the Chinese tradition looked backward to a utopia in the past.

Tianyanlun (Translation of *Evolution and Ethics* by Thomas Huxley) by Yan Fu is only one of many translations of Western texts produced during the turn of the twentieth century. Huxley, a critical follower of Herbert Spencer, accepted the truth of social Darwinism, the belief that natural selection applied to human societies, but refused to accept its morality. Yan Fu chose to introduce social Darwinism to China through the writings of a reformer of social Darwinian thought. Although Yan wanted China to learn a lesson from the European quest

During Mao's life, every citizen was expected to own and carry a copy of *The Thoughts of Chairman Mao*. In the West, the book was nicknamed "The Little Red Book."

for "wealth and power," his moral concerns reflected those of the Chinese intellectual class that would have consumed his translations.

After the May Fourth era, the introduction of Marxist socialism transformed the Chinese political discourse, culminating in the Chinese Revolution of 1949. Marxism was a latecomer to China, as it was not until well into the twentieth century that Marxist texts were translated into Chinese. Even Marxism, however, was transformed as it interacted with Chinese readers and thinkers. Maoism, the Marxism of Mao Zedong and his followers, presented a reformation of Marxism to make it more suitable to a peasant society, such as China. In seeing peasants as the root of the revolution, Mao Zedong broke free of not only classical Marxism but also Leninism. Although the development of Maoism was important to the early development of Chinese communism, it was not popularized across the country until after the establishment of the People's Republic of China. "The Little Red Book," officially known as *Quotations from Chairman Mao Zedong*, was a collection of Mao's sayings, taken from his collected works. It was first printed in 1964 under the direction of Mao's close supporter, Lin Biao. During the Cultural Revolution "The Little Red Book" was required reading, and in the 1960s almost a billion copies were printed and distributed, making it one of the most widely read texts in human history. The main components of Maoist thought are represented in "The Little Red Book," including self-reliance and volunteerism, populism and service to the people, the proper role of artists and intellectuals in the revolutionary struggle, people's war, and the nature of class struggle in China. Mao's thought would reach beyond China to influence the development of rural revolutionary movements in other parts of the world.

POLEMICS

Short political treatises published for broad consumption through newspapers and journals or as pamphlets were a new phenomenon in modern China. Significant political debates took place in earlier times but they often took place within the imperial court or among a small group of scholar-officials. When the center of politics shifted to the nation and intellectuals started to question if revolution was absolutely essential, broader involvement was necessary. The five polemical works examined below were of particular significance in three periods of social and political transformation in China: the 1911 Revolution, the May Fourth Movement, and the Cultural Revolution.

"The Revolutionary Army" by Zou Rong was published in 1903 and helped to shift Chinese radical opinion toward an anti-Manchu position prior to the 1911 Revolution. In this pamphlet, the nineteen-year-old Zou Rong labeled Chinese who worked with Manchus as traitors and oppressors. He believed that China— by which he meant the homeland of Han Chinese—had a destiny that had been suppressed by the 1644 invasion and subsequent conquest by the Manchus. Zou drew on the European and American political tradition and was influenced by both the American and the French Revolutions, which not only asserted national self-determination and independence but also called for democratic politics. Zou Rong was arrested by the Qing authorities for this pamphlet and died in jail before being executed.

Published in *New Youth* in 1917, Hu Shi's "Some Tentative Suggestions for the Reform of Chinese Literature" was one of the earliest calls for the promotion of vernacular Chinese in all writing. The goal of using vernacular language was to help mobilize the nation by expanding access to literacy. According to Hu, traditional written Chinese was accessible only to the privileged elite and the aristocracy. He also argued that the form of classical Chinese writing confined people's thinking to tradition themes and questions.

Mao Zedong wrote a series of articles about the death of Zhao Wuzhen, who committed suicide on her wedding day when faced with the inevitability of entering into a loveless and unwanted marriage. In traditional China, particularly in the Qing, the suicide of women to maintain virtue was honored. Suicides as a means to resist marriage were probably not uncommon, but in the vibrant May Fourth era, "Miss Zhao's" suicide, and the effort by intellectuals to make the public aware, began a debate about the role of women in a modern society. According to Mao, Miss Zhao's death was the direct result of inequality and the oppression of women. In "The Evils of Society and Miss Zhao," published in *Public Interest* in late 1919, Mao argued that society held an equal share of the blame with her parents and her fiancé's family. It was society—by which Mao meant Chinese society as tainted by Confucian gender relations—that limited Miss Zhao's ability to resist the marriage. Without education for women, a social standing for single women, Miss Zhao had no choice but suicide.

"What Happens after Nora Leaves Home," by Lu Xun, also reflected the growing concerns about women and their role in society during the early twentieth century. It also suggests the deep awareness Chinese writers had of Western literature and philosophy. Lu Xun and others had read Henrik Ibsen's play, *A Doll's House,* with great interest after it was translated into Chinese. The play tells the story of Nora, a domestically oppressed woman who leaves her husband. The ever-pessimistic Lu Xun inquired about her fate and suggested that her choices were remarriage or

Wei Jingsheng

The life of Wei Jingsheng (1950–) suggests just how powerful and dangerous writing had become for Chinese leaders after the Cultural Revolution. Wei was a Red Guard and had developed a disdain for the Communist Party leaders during his youth. After the death of Mao Zedong, Wei became active in the Chinese Democracy Movement, editing the political journal *Explorations*. During the Democracy Wall Movement of 1979, which challenged the authoritarian government emerging under Deng Xiaoping after Mao's death, Wei authored a "big character" wall poster, calling for the "Fifth Modernization," democracy. For this action, Wei was sentenced to fifteen years in prison and would remain in prison until 1997, with a brief hiatus in 1993. Both his work as an editor of a journal and as the author of a wall poster suggested the importance of the written word in the mass politics of Communist China.

prostitution. Polemics such as "What Happens after Nora Leaves Home" expanded the importance of gender politics for the reading public.

Throughout Republican and Communist China, public polemics remained a center of political discourse. One of these polemics helped start the Cultural Revolution. In 1960, a historian wrote a play called *Hai Jui Dismissed from Office*. This play was set in the Ming dynasty and focused on an honest and forthright official who was dismissed from public service for confronting the emperor in the interests of the common people. Observers of this play would not have missed the allegorical component, viz. the purging of Peng Dehuai one year earlier for confronting Mao Zedong on the policies of the Great Leap Forward. In 1965, the Maoist Yao Wenyuan attacked this play as historically inaccurate as well as politically incorrect. Hai Jui's desire to return land to the people smelled like capitalist reaction in the context of collectivization in the countryside.

The Cultural Revolution would not have become as important as it did if not for the grassroots revolutionary activism of the Red Guards, but Yao's seemingly minor criticism sparked a wave of similar attacks and eventually a call to purge the party itself of reactionary elements. Cultural criticism affected all levels of China's literacy culture. Most at risk were local party officials, notorious for corruption and distrusted by the populist Maoists, and university professors, who found their works examined in the new light of cultural and political sensitivity. Although this occurred at many levels, few articles reflected how politicized the written word has become in modern China as Yao's criticism of Wu Han.

CONCLUSION

The 1989 destruction of the Chinese democracy movement marked the end of a phase in China's political history. The crackdown left the old guard, many of them reactionary and fearful survivors of the Cultural Revolution, in charge of the Chinese state. The major sources of resistance to the limited public sphere of the Communist era, the radical Maoists and the pro-Western democracy movement, were both crushed. At the same time, the economic policies that were transforming China from an egalitarian agrarian society to an increasingly class-ridden industrial and urban society continued without a significant challenge from the leaders of the Communist Party or the society at large. By the twenty-first century these economic policies would mean double-digit annual economic growth, rapid and irreversible ecological degradation, the rise of a new ruling capitalist class, unparalleled urbanization, the emergence of an increasingly weakened working class, and increased interaction between Chinese rulers and Western capitalists. What has not occurred has been significant political change or a revival of a democracy movement capable of challenging the Communist Party.

Reading culture in China, in contrast, has remained vibrant and has experienced significant developments, including the borrowing of new texts and literary formats from outside of China and the expansion of literacy. Currently, China's adult literacy rate is at ninety percent with universal primary education. The goal of the May Fourth intellectuals of creating a literate population through literary reform and education has been successful. Increasing numbers of Chinese are learning to read English. The availability of Western texts available in translation has also increased, allowing the easy exchange of ideas.

There are several new trends in Chinese reading since 1989 that contributed to the post-Tiananmen settlement, including authoritarianism in politics and state-supported capitalism in economics. Many writers looked back on the Maoist years with horror or critical fascination, often producing memoirs emphasizing the political instability of the period. Others drifted from Marxist analyses of society and politics and explored postmodernism, rejecting much of twentieth-century Chinese social realism, materialism, and political urgency. Some continued to identify the continuing problems of corruption and the emerging social problems of inequality. Without a political movement to actualize their social criticism, as in the 1930s and 1940s, realism has lost much of its potency, if not its sharpness. For many Chinese readers, the best-seller novel and mass-produced fiction, reflecting the increasingly consumer society and an economy depending on mass production, have replaced the political novels, literacy journals, and political discussions that their parents and grandparents would have identified with the written word.

The transformation in who and what was read took place during the turn of the twentieth century, during what historian Vera Schwartz has called the "Chinese Enlightenment." It was during this period that four important transformations took place. First, the rise of vernacular writing brought the written word closer to how most Chinese spoke, making writing more accessible to Chinese in both the expansion of literacy and in the grounding of words into their experiences. Second, the debate over the place of women in the nation, the creation of modern universities such as the one established in Beijing in 1898, and consciousness about the need for a mobilized, active, and aware citizenry planted the seeds for almost universal literacy that would be achieved by the end of the century. Third, by incorporating ideas from European and American intellectuals such as Marxism, social Darwinism, anarchism, science, and democracy, Chinese intellectuals almost destroyed the Confucian tradition and introduced China's growing literate public to new ways of looking at the world and their place in it. Finally, along with new ideas, intellectuals borrowed new formats for public discourse such as magazines, newspapers, academic or political journals, and the Internet. These formats would endure throughout the twentieth century and largely replace traditional venues for ideas. By transforming the culture of reading, the Chinese Enlightenment can be said to have been successful. In another important way, the Chinese Enlightenment failed on its promises.

Today, much of the political vibrancy that characterized China since the crackdown of the Democracy movement in 1989 has evaporated in the face of political repression, state capitalism, and expanding inequality. These outcomes are nowhere more evident than in the explosion of Internet use in China. Although the Chinese government has limited its citizens' access to the Internet, China still boasts 210 million Internet users, according to a 2008 report in *The Economist* magazine. Analysis of the Chinese Internet client group reveals that their use of the Internet is motivated less by ideological or political interests and more by individual, commercial, and consumer desires. There is citizen opposition to the government's restriction of access to information (Chinese Internet users cannot access Wikipedia, and the Chinese version of Google filters out politically sensitive information), but *The Economist* reports that most of the country's Internet users are under thirty, and are primarily interested in pirated movies, television shows, online games, music, and social "chat"-type sites. Moreover, *The Economist* points out that social contact sites have become popular among Chinese Internet users because the country's persistent one-child policy has left generations of people without siblings or significant family networks. They therefore place great emphasis on creating social networks of their own. This inadvertent effect of the one-child policy may have another consequence for Chinese culture: the desire to build social connections may result in a drop in solitary practices, such as reading.

RECOMMENDED READING

Chow Tse-tsung. *The May Fourth Movement: Intellectual Revolution in China*. Cambridge: Harvard University Press, 1960.

Dirlik, Arif. *Anarchism in the Chinese Revolution*. Berkeley: University of California Press, 1991.

———. *The Origins of Chinese Communism*. New York: Oxford University Press, 1989.

Judge, Joan. *Print and Politics: 'Shibao' and the Culture of Reform in Late Qing China*. Stanford: Stanford University Press, 1996.

Lan, Hua R. and Vanessa L. Fong, eds. *Women in Republican China: A Sourcebook*. Armonk: M. E. Sharpe, 1999.

Leo Ou-fan Lee. *Shanghai Modern: The Flowering of a New Urban Culture in China, 1930–1945*. Cambridge: Harvard University Press, 1999.

Liu, Lydia H. *The Clash of Empires: The Invention of China in Modern World Making*. Cambridge: Harvard University Press, 2004.

Meisner, Maurice. *Mao's China and After: A History of the People's Republic*. New York: Free Press, 1999.

Pusey, James Reeve. *China and Charles Darwin*. Cambridge: Harvard University Press, 1983.

Rankin, Mary Backus. *Early Chinese Revolutionaries: Radical Intellectuals in Shanghai and Chekiang, 1902–1911*. Cambridge: Harvard University Press, 1971.

Schwartz, Benjamin. *In Search of Wealth and Power: Yen Fu and the West*. Cambridge: Harvard University Press, 1964.

Schwartz, Vera. *The Chinese Enlightenment: Intellectuals and the Legacy of the May Fourth Movement of 1919*. Berkeley: University of California Press, 1986.

Strand, David. *Rickshaw Beijing: City People and Politics in the 1920s*. Berkeley: University of California Press, 1989.

Yingjin Zhang, ed. *Cinema and Urban Culture in Shanghai, 1922–1943*. Stanford: Stanford University Press, 1999.

PRIMARY SOURCES

Cao Xuegin and Gao E. *The Story of the Stone* [*The Dream of the Red Chamber*]. 5 vols. Translated by David Hawkes and John Minford. New York: Penguin, 1974–1986. (Cao Xuegin completed the first three volumes; Gao E completed the last two, based on Cao's notes. Some translations list Gao E as editor of vols. 4 & 5.)

Dent-Young, Alex and John Dent-Young. *Marshes of Mount Liang: A New Translation of the Shuihu zhuang or Water Margin of Shi Naian and Luo Guanzhong*. 3 vols. Hong Kong: Chinese University Press, 1983–1997.

Hu Shi. "Some Tentative Suggestions for the Reform of Chinese Literature" *Xin Chao* [New Tide], January 1917.

Kang Youwei. *Datongshu* [*The Book of the Great Unity*]. Shanghai: Shanghai guji chubanshe, 2005.

Lao She. *Camel Xiangzi*. Translated by Shi Xiaoqing. Beijing: Foreign Languages Press, 1981.

———. *Cat Country: A Satirical Novel of China in the 1930s*. Translated by William A. Lyell. Honolulu: University of Hawai'i Press, 1970.

Liangyou Huabao [*The Young Companion*], Shanghai, mid-1920s.

Linglong [*The Ladies Journal*]. Shanghai, 1931–1937.

Lu Xun, "Diary of a Madman" in *Diary of a Madman and Other Stories*. Translated by William A. Lyell. Honolulu: Hawai'i University Press, 1990.

———. "The New Year's Sacrifice" in *Women in Republican China: A Sourcebook*. Edited by Hua R. Lan and Vanessa L. Fong. Armonk and London: M. E. Sharpe, 1999.

———. *The True Story of Ah Q*. Translated by George Kin Leung. Shanghai: The Commercial Press, 1926.

———. "What Happens after Nora Leaves Home" in *Women in Republican China: A Sourcebook*. Edited by Hua R. Lan and Vanessa L. Fong. Armonk: M. E. Sharpe, 1999.

Mao Zedong. "The Evils of Society and Miss Zhao" in *Women in Republican China: A Sourcebook*. Edited by Hua R. Lan and Vanessa L. Fong. Armonk: M. E. Sharpe, 1999.

———. *On Practice and Contradiction*. Edited by Slavoj Zizek. Brooklyn, NY: Verso, 2007.

———. *Quotations from Chairman Mao Tse-tung*. Beijing: Foreign Languages Press, 1966.

Qingnian ren [*Youth Magazine*]. n.d.

Renmin ribao [*The People's Daily*]. Beijing, 1948–.

Shenbao [*Shanghai Journal*]. Shanghai, 1872–1949.

Shibao [*The Eastern Times*]. Shanghai, 1898–1937.

Shiwubao [*The Chinese Progress*]. Shanghai, 1896–1898.

Xin Shiji [*The New Era*]. 1907–1910.

Xin Qingnian [*New Youth*]. 1915–1926.

Yan Fu. *Tianyanlun* [Translation of *Evolution and Ethics* by Thomas Huxley]. Taipei, 1967.

Yao Wenyuan. "Ping xin bian li shi ju 'Hai Rui ba guan'" ["Criticism of *Hai Jui Dismissed from Office*"] in *Yao Wenyuan wen ji* (1965–1968). Edited by Liu Cunshi. Hong Kong: Lishi ziliao chubanshe, 1971.

Zhang Henshui. *Shanghai Express: A Thirties Novel*. Translated by William A. Lyell. Honolulu: University of Hawai'i Press, 1997.

Zou Rong. *The Revolutionary Army: A Chinese Nationalist Tract of 1903*. Translated by John Lust. The Hague: Mouton, 1968.

SECONDARY SOURCES

"The Internet in China: Alternative Reality." *The Economist* Jan. 31, 2008. http://www.economist.com/displaystory.cfm?story_id=10608655 (accessed February 13, 2008).

CHAPTER 15

Japan

Samaya L. S. Chanthaphavong

TIMELINE

300 B.C.E.	**(Jomon era)** Believed to be mostly hunter/gatherers
300 B.C.E.–300 C.E.	**(Yayoi era)** Agricultural production; development of social structure (hierarchy, communities, etc.)
300–538	**(Kofun era)** Burial chambers (*Kofun*—"Old Tombs") for deceased ruling classes appear; Yamato Japan (some parts of Japan unified under Yamato Emperor)
538–710	**(Asuka era)** Capital of Japan in Asuka district; Buddhism is introduced via Korean Peninsula; Chinese form of bureaucratic rule instigated, designed to entrench Emperor's power
710–94	**(Nara period)** First permanent capital at Nara established, later moved to Nagaoka; establishment of Japanese literature by Imperial household with the publication of *Kojiki* and *Nihon Shoki;* written language flourishes and Japanese poetry gains popularity; Emperor Shomu embraces Buddhism
794–1185	**(Heian period)** Movement of Capital to Kyoto, beginning one thousand years of Imperial Rule from the area; development and explosion of new literary genres such as court diaries and novels; rise of the powerful clans such as Fujiwara and Minamoto and of the Samurai, which continued into Kamakura/Muromachi period (consolidation)
1185–1573	**(Kamakura/Muromachi period)** Zen Buddhism introduced; Bakufu system introduced; military system of rule; first printing press; Mongolian invasions unsuccessful; Muromachi district becomes ruling center of Shogun Ashikaga Takauji's government; Onin War (1467–1477)
1573–1603	**(Azuchi-Momoyama period)** Collapse of Muromachi Shogunate; spread of Christian missionaries

1603–1868	**(Edo period)** Early-modern literature; rise of cities; *Treaty of Kanagawa*
1868–1912	**(Meiji period)** Onset of rapid industrialization
1912–26	**(Taishō period)** Influence of western culture; also referred to as "liberal" era of Japanese history.
1926–89	**(Shōwa period)** Reign of Emperor Shōwa (Hirohito) the longest reign of any Japanese emperor; World War II—hostile expansion of empire throughout East and Southeast Asia; Atomic bombs dropped on Nagasaki and Hiroshima; U.S. occupation
1989–current	**(Heisei period)** Rebuilding of psyche, rise of modern and futuristic Japan

INTRODUCTION TO THE NATION

Japan is located in East Asia, off the eastern coast of the Korean peninsula, and is made up of a collection of four main islands (Honsu, Hokkaido, Kyushu, Shikoku) and several smaller islands whose collective size equals 145,883 square miles. Despite its relatively small size and mountainous terrain, the islands sustain a population of over 127 million, with an indigenous Ainu population fewer than twenty thousand. The majority of Japanese identify as belonging to the ethnic Yamato group, the name taken from the Yamato court. The Yamato are often seen as the people responsible for the establishment of the first Japanese nation-state.

Japan has a unique socioeconomic and political landscape in that it has been ruled by shogunates, a constitutional monarchy, and western-style government that has created a unique microcosm of literary and cultural texts. Archeologists and anthropologists believe that Japan has been continuously inhabited since the Paleolithic period, moving from a predominately hunting and gathering society in the Yayoi era, to Imperialism during the Nara era. Historians generally refer to Japanese history in specific eras that encapsulate a period of time, such as the Heian period, which stretched from 794 to 1185. These eras or periods take their names from shogunates, such as the "Kamakura" period, and from emperors, such as the "Taisho" period from 1912 to 1926. As such, it is common to refer to an event in Japanese history as originating from the period, then to proceed with a date.

The Asuka period (538 to 710) witnessed the rise of the Yamato state that traced its beginnings to the earlier Kofun period (300 to 538), when the unification of separate clans started. During the Asukha period, Japan underwent some important social, political, and religious changes that forever changed the nation. Buddhism was introduced to the region, and Japan strengthened her relationship with China through convoys; this resulted in the adoption of the Chinese date system (calendar) and some aspects of the Chinese sociopolitical system, in particular the administration of the country under the law codes called *ritsuryō* (Batten, 103).

Reverence to Chinese high culture continued into the Nara period (710 to 794), even going so far as to model the new capital after Chang'an, the Chinese imperial capital in central China. Court-compiled histories became a focal point of the Nara period, and two great works of historical literature were produced during this era: *Kojiki* (*Records of Ancient Matters*, thought to have been completed sometime before 680) and *Nihon Shoki* (*Chronicles of Japan*, completed in 720).

Reading for pleasure became more widespread among upper-class Japanese during the Heian period. The capital at Heian-Kyō (Kyoto) became the seat of power for the dominating Fujiwara clan, whose rule lasted throughout the Heian period in all matters of state and political life. The use of Kana resulted in the birth of the novel—a new accessible genre (albeit only to the privileged of society). It also allowed for the production of intimate narratives, the effects of which can still be seen on the literary landscape of Japan.

The Kamakura period, the era of the shogunate, immediately altered the type of texts that were considered popular reading. The emphasis shifted toward tales of military prowess rather then the subtleties of a courtly existence. Religion also became a focal point, with the appearance of Buddhist values and characters. The Edo era (1603–1868) was characterized by the relocation of the capital to Edo, and a rise in the numbers of literate citizens. Literature flourished as people became interested in the world around them—no doubt due to the opening up of Japan with the signing of the Treaty of Kanagawa in 1854.

READING TRENDS AND PRACTICES

Literature in Japan has generally been divided into six overlapping periods. These are made up of ancient literature (up to the eighth century), classical literature (ninth–twelfth centuries), medieval literature (thirteenth–sixteenth centuries), early-modern literature (mid-seventeenth–nineteenth century), Meiji literature (late-nineteenth–mid-twentieth century and World War II), and finally the post-war literary period.

Writing and reading came to Japan via the Korean Peninsula. Japanese scholars had been in contact with Chinese Buddhist teachers who provided examples of Buddhist *sutra* (scriptures) and text to Japan from before 500 C.E. The dissemination of Buddhism via its religious texts was a major influence on the creation of a Japanese system of writing and reading. In order to read, it was essential to learn the Chinese character system of writing. Therefore scholarly learning was generally limited to the wealthy classes. Chinese (and Korean) religious and political influence was felt in Japan from its early historical periods and certainly influenced sociopolitical observations and literary form. Buddhist texts accounted for the majority of literature available to readers; however, as textual content varied from social observations and personal memoirs to strict Buddhist teachings, the Buddhist texts provided a cross-section of interests. Japan, like many other writing and printing cultures, progressed from using woodcuts to using various paper materials and printing styles to communicate. Chinese and Korean modes of textual production (i.e. *sutras* on various materials and purpose-made woodcuts) heavily influenced Japanese print. A movable printing press is believed to have entered Japan in the late sixteenth century, brought by soldiers returning from Korea and China.

From around the seventh century, the Japanese began to adapt the Chinese writing system so that it became more representative of Japanese linguistics and writing, thus allowing for the creation of Japanese literary forms. This adaptation (*kanji*) was still rather limited, so during the eighth century, Japan devised a new way of writing (*kana*) that utilized kanji and allowed for expressions that were impossible using only kanji. The use of kana (which includes *hirigana* and *katakana* and whose literal meaning is "borrowed words") became popular during the Heian periods (794–1185), when Japan became particularly proactive in the production of new forms of literature and prose. *Hiragana* was adopted enthusiastically by female writers, resulting in what is widely perceived as the world's first novel, *Genji monogatari* (*Tale of Genji*).

This ema at Nonomiya Shrine in Kyoto illustrates a scene from *The Tale of Genji* (源氏物語 *Genji Monogatari*), the classic early Japanese novel associated with the noblewoman, Murasaki Shikibu, in the early 11th century. *Genji* has been called "the world's first novel."

The keeping of journals (alternatively referred to as diaries depending on the type of writing and content employed) is considered an important and integral part of Japan's continued evolution as a literary society. Thought to have first been conceptualized in the pre-Heian period and becoming common during the Heian era, the journal offers a glimpse into the daily life and practices of individuals and society long since passed. The importance of the journal was evident within the more educated echelons of society, with the application of different terminology (usually the terms *Nikki bungaku* and *Kiroku*) to describe the different styles and content forms. The keeping of private journals has remained more or less continuous throughout Japan's long literary tradition and, as such, the tradition offers an alternative and intimate personal perspective that can provide a unique point of view on the historiography of Japan.

Nikki bungaku (diaries with literary merit) was essentially a female kana-driven genre of literature that coincided with the rise of female courtly writers during the Heian period. They provided a unique female perspective on court life in a highly regimented and patriarchal society, and they also created a unique sense of cultural unity (Morton and Olenik 101). The literary style employed by the female writers was regarded as autobiographical. Interspersed with prose often attentive to their immediate relationships within the court's household, the nikki was shared and often read in groups that might have resulted in the exaggeration of aspects of one's involvement or influence in a particular event, or the changing of certain elements of events to maintain confidence or anonymity. Journals have helped to shape the historical understanding of the cultural and sociopolitical make-up of traditional Japanese society by offering an intimate glimpse into the past that is often overlooked by conventional cultural readings. In essence, the nikki genre encouraged the blossoming of literature driven by personal narratives.

Important cultural texts include Sei Shōnagon's *Makura no soshi* (*The Pillow Book*), a journal containing insights into courtly life under Empress Sadako, thought to have been started sometime after the year 990, when she became

> **The Yasukuni Shrine**
>
> The Yasukuni shrine is a military shrine that commemorates Japanese citizens who have fought on behalf of the emperor (the enshrined are known as *kami*). One criterion for inclusion is that the kami must have been on duty at the time of death. This means that some of the enshrined soldiers were not killed in battle, but died as prisoners of war (i.e. prisoners of the Allied Forces after the end of World War II), and were executed for war crimes. The head of Japan's wartime military operations, Hideki Tojo, who was feared throughout the Pacific and hanged by an allied military court, was quietly enshrined at Yasukuni as a martyr to the emperor's cause in 1978.

a royal attendant. Another famous nikki is Murasaki Shikibu's self-titled *Murasaki Shikibu nikki* (*Diary of Lady Murasaki*), written in 1008 during the time of Princess Akiko's late pregnancy and the impending birth of a royal heir, an extremely important time in Japanese history. Other notable nikki include Michitsuna no Haha's *Kagerō nikki* (*The Gossamer Years: Diary of a Noblewoman in Heian Japan*), Lady Sarashina's *Sarashina nikki* (*Sarashina diary*), and Izumi Shikibu's *Izumi Shikibu nikki* (*Izumi Shikibu Diary*). Izumi Shikibu was also a prolific poet.

Contemporary journal offerings have also helped shape cultural and historical attitudes toward Japan, and political journals have had a significant cultural impact upon Japanese society, especially those belonging to important political figures such as Emperor Showa (Emperor Hirohito), the twenty-fourth Emperor of Japan. *Kiroku* (aristocratic kanbun journals) can also be traced back to the Heian era and were mostly created by male writers as factual memoirs. An important contemporary kiroku is Grand Steward Tomohiko Tomita's *Hirohito Diaries*. These meticulous diaries were kept by Tomohiko Tomita over decades, and they are believed to be among the only publicly released, private diaries about Emperor Showa's feelings on the much-disputed Yasukuni shrine.

Intense periods of isolation have contributed to Japan's unique literary and cultural landscape. The self-imposed isolation that lasted from around 1635 (with almost full isolation experienced in 1639) to 1854 meant that Japan was resistant to foreign cultural and social influences and thus became self-reflective. The signing of the *Treaty of Kanagawa* with the United States in 1854 resulted in the opening of ports for trade; with it came the availability of new texts and, of course, new influences. With fewer restrictions placed upon foreign texts, Japan witnessed a boom in translated western literature. Not surprisingly, the texts that became widely popular were mostly those devoted to the customs and cultures of the world. Although educational, socio-anthropological texts were widely popular, niche markets evolved and were immediately adapted for a Japanese audience. In a relatively short period of time, texts became expressions of popular culture rather than expressions of one's status or religious and political affiliation. The popularity of *Kuchi-e* (mouth pictures) books pointed toward the acceptance of popular literature. Initially Kuchi-e were used as visual illustrations or signage within bookstores to promote a particular tome. However this practice created a demand for the Kuchi-e themselves. The new literary explosion saw the development of innovative literary forms, which had a much wider appeal than their predecessors.

The introduction of a new wave of texts in Japan during the late nineteenth century was again mirrored within the twentieth century, with new forms of graphic novels (*manga*) appealing to the growing youth market. The rise of the graphic novel heralded a new literary format that appealed to the mass youth market, whose topics were as diverse as princess vampires to traditional (albeit with a modern twist) Edo period story lines. The first comic strip appeared in *Asahi Graph*, a newspaper popular in the 1920s. Suzuki Bunshiro, the editor of the magazine, took his inspiration from strips he had seen on recent travels around Europe and the United States, which he believed would become a hit with his readers. After World War II, *Asahi Graph* became a culturally important magazine, as it published photos of the bombed cities of Nagasaki and Hiroshima and captured the suffering of those caught in the two cities.

World War II changed the psyche of Japan, as the nation sought to redefine its national and international identity. Experiencing rapid industrialization and modernization, Japan sought new philosophies and approaches in understanding and representing itself—an important step to ensure a successful post-war phase of rebuilding (in the literary, sociopolitical, and architectural senses). Along with a renewed sense of cultural identity, Japan sought to rewrite some parts of history that conflicted with the projected image. Many schools were issued with text books that provided a state-sanctioned "official" perspective of an event—an alternative history.

As well as redefining the national identity, the post-war period arguably witnessed a shift toward recognition of the writer, as opposed to a style of literature, and such post-war writers became renowned, world literary greats. Important Japanese literary writers such as Yukio Mishima, Yasunari Kawabata, and Kenzaburo Oe were awarded a variety of prestigious literary titles. Oe received the Nobel Prize for Literature in 1994. The new authors' various writing styles and topics were considered to be much more diverse than traditional Japanese literature, and they ranged from heart-wrenching biographies on the effect of the atomic bomb in Hiroshima to royal histories, the latter experiencing more popularity as Japan became engaged in the wider sociocultural and political sphere. Genres were reinvented and explored—especially those that are thought to have been heavily influenced and informed by western literature, such as crime and detective fiction.

Although popular, detective fiction in Japan is thought to have been heavily influenced and informed by western literature and ideas, and it first drew inspiration from real-life Chinese legal cases. The first popular detective and crime fiction is widely thought to be a collection of short stories by Saikaku Ihara in 1689, called *Japanese Trials under the Shade of a Cherry Tree*, which drew inspiration from Chinese legal sources. As Japanese translations of western fiction became more widespread and popular, it was possible to take domestic scenarios and characters and create a Japanese genre of detective and crime fiction. (Keene) This was appealing to Japanese readers as it provided a new and exciting genre that transcended the usual gender and social boundaries of an often rigid and highly structured society. The popularity of detective fiction increased dramatically during the Meiji restoration period (usually between 1868 and 1912), in which Japan underwent major social and political restructuring. The air of uncertainty regarding the future, rapid urbanization and modernization, and displacement and social upheaval provided a ripe environment for the new genre of writing, the detective story. Social problems such as gambling, prostitution, alcoholism, corruption, and general social deviance could be addressed (or at the least highlighted) in an entertaining way, thus allowing authors (and their readers) to critique society without directly attacking authority. The fictional characters and storylines allowed for the exploration of difficult issues within a preexisting social context.

As well as providing a highly interpretative outlet for commenting on Japanese social issues, the surprising popularity of the genre with female readers created new opportunities for female writers to explore female-orientated narratives. Themes such as identity and community were explored more readily, and female protagonists appeared to readers as strong, modern, and decisive—masculine traits that were traditionally shunned in women. Female sexuality is evident in more contemporary texts; however, the image of a sexually confident female was/is often at odds with the traditional projected image of Japanese woman-hood. Famous female writers include Miyabi Miyuki (who won the prestigious Yamamoto Shūgorō Prize for *All She Was Worth* [*Kasha*]), Shibata Yoshiki (*Riko-Forever Venus*), and *Out* novelist Kirino Natsuo, who became the first Japanese writer to be nominated for the 2004 MWA Edgar Allan Poe Award in the best novel category.

Literary developments among the indigenous Ainu of Japan have been less spectacular due, in part, to discrimination and forced cultural and linguistic assim-ilation. The explosion of the dominant "Japanese cultural identity" and "Japanese-centric" texts often eradicated indigenous culture in favor of a more mainstream approach to literary representations (i.e. the promotion of high Japanese culture). Unfortunately, the Ainu find themselves on the brink of cultural alienation and annihilation. Despite this threat, the Ainu's strong oral tradition has continued throughout Japan's history and is able to provide a unique, oral, cultural reading of the country and its often-forgotten people.

Modern, twenty-first century Japan is a highly developed and literate society that has continued to push toward new literary forms and conventions. Japan has been increasingly open to new communication technologies as a way of furthering literary influence within all levels of society. The advent of multimedia, Internet-enabled phones and other new information communication technologies (such as mobile, multi-format devices) has resulted in the rise of mobile texts that can be downloaded and accessed anywhere and at any time. Japanese consumers have access to everything from traditional *haiku* poetry to the local newspaper at the touch of a button, and the alternative formatting of the texts invariably lends itself to new avenues of appreciation. It appears that the twenty-first century will see Japan usher in yet another period of literary change that will, in all likelihood, have an impact upon the wider world. Japan's example indicates that the world is expe-riencing a definite shift toward alternative methods of reading.

CREATIVE TEXTS

There is a strong correlation between the natural and cultural environment and the self in Japan, and this relationship is manifested in creative texts that use, as their grounding, historical and important events that shape both the environment of the nation and the psyche of its people. Contemporary texts move away from this style somewhat, yet the majority of creative texts have, at their heart, a tale or situation that has been lifted from daily life.

The creative textual style in Japan is highly diverse, and it is usually evocative of the sociopolitical climate in which it is produced. Historical novels reconnect the reader with tales that offer a foundation upon which to build an image of Japan from ancient to contemporary times; poetry evokes a sense of timelessness and can transport the reader directly back to the Edo period; and novels and diaries can provide a glimpse into the past that brings to life characters and customs long since passed.

Heike Monogatari (*The Tales of the Taira Clan*) tells the story of the struggle between the Taira and the Minamoto clans for control of Japan during the Genpei War of 1180–1185. The Taira were defeated by the Minamotos in 1185 after a protracted battle. The Taira had overthrown the Minamoto clan in 1161. The story was originally recited by traveling monks, who used it to teach the Buddhist principles of impermanence and cause and effect to their listeners. The story became immensely popular in social settings and was depicted in Noh plays, eventually becoming a popular literary text, the most famous by Japanese prose writer Eiji Yoshikawa.

The popularity of heavier historical novels was often counter-balanced by readers' interest in lighter literary endeavors. *Oku no Hosomichi* (*Narrow Road through the Deep North/Narrow Road to Oku*) by Matsu Bashō is considered to be equal part travelogue and poetry. It is a mixture of prose and verse written by Matsu Bashō (considered to be one of Japan's great poets) five years after traveling to Oku in northern Japan in 1689. Bashō and his traveling companion Sora are believed to have spent between one hundred and fifty-five to two hundred days traveling to the inner-northern section of Japan, in part to pay homage to the late Heian poet Saigyō, whom Bashō revered. This was considered to be extremely dangerous as travel during that time generally consisted of endless walking and hiding from bandits. However, their wanderings inspired Bashō to write, and though reworked numerous times since the journey, *Oku no Hosomichi* is considered to be one of the great travel prose narratives of historical Japan.

A highly stylized form of written expression has long existed in Japan, with various forms of poetry consistently conveyed in both formal and informal occasions and settings. Haiku poetry is a relatively modern poetic form in Japan as it traces its birth only to the nineteenth century, and was devised by Masaoka Shiki in response to the rigid stylized forms of traditional Japanese poetry. The form (as *hokku* and *haikai*) had been in circulation for centuries beforehand as a teaching tool for Buddhist and Taoist monks and then as a pastime for great Japanese poets such as Matsuo Bashō, Izumi Shikibu, Yosa Buson, and Kobayashi Issa. However, Shiki aimed to release the poem from its religious connotations that, he believed, had created a stagnant poetic form over centuries. The literary worth of haikai had also been damaged in the public sphere in the early nineteenth century with the advent of monthly meetings by popularly versed but often raucous popular writers. Haiku usually consist of three lines of text made up of seventeen syllables in lines measuring five-seven-five that are evocative, while remaining minimalist in nature. Shiki wrote over twenty-five thousand haiku poems, one of the most famous of which captures a pair of ducks on an ancient lake while evening snow falls. Haiku gained steady popularity, but mostly as a social form. That is, practitioners would gather around their favorite poets and compete to produce haiku that was wittier, more delicate, or more profound than those of other members of the group.

Haiku

Haiku has become something of a "high culture" symbol in the West, making appearances in popular film, television programs, and novels. The inclusion of haiku in contemporary popular cultural forms is usually intended to ironize the subject. That is, given that haiku is associated with elevated sensibilities, the inclusion of haiku in an episode of *South Park* forces high culture into an unlikely relationship with low culture.

During the Heian period female writers were often viewed as a threat to the established social order, and as such there was a general ambivalence toward literature created by women (Shirane and Suzuki, 9–10). Thus it is testimony to the writing skill of Murasaki Shikibu that one of Japan's greatest literary productions still in publication today was created by a female. Shikibu's *Genji Monogatari* (*Tale of Genji*) is widely professed to be the world's first novel. Shikibu wrote the novel sometime during her time at the court of Empress Shoshi (Akiko) in the Heian era (estimated to be anywhere from 1005 to 1006 C.E.). The story revolves around the son of an Emperor and his romantic life within the aristocratic society to which he belonged. The book describes in great detail intricate social customs and provides a glimpse into the privileged circle of the Japanese aristocracy. The tale follows Genji as he grows into a man amid the intricate and sometimes dangerous sociopolitical backdrop of royalty. *Genji Monogatari* offers a glimpse into history that remains as vivid today as when it was written, and the work is applauded as one of the world's greatest literary achievements.

This classic text has been continuously read since its first appearance, but its original language is now all but indecipherable to most Japanese. Today, therefore, the tale is usually read in translation or in heavily annotated form. The most common contemporary manifestations of Genji's tale are in manga (or comic book) form. Young Japanese readers are more likely to know *Genji Monogatari* in its manga format, or from excerpts, translated and reproduced for classroom purposes. Interestingly, Japanese novelists have also participated in the Genji "industry," publishing their own annotations and translations of the classic text. Not surprisingly, *Genji Monogatari* has also been adapted for film and television for Japanese viewers.

Japanese fiction and narrative often borrow from history and/or actual events. In keeping with the use of historical fact around which to weave a storyline, Yukio Mishima's 1959 serial, *The Temple of the Golden Pavilion*, was inspired by the true story of a monk who, in 1950, burned down one of Japan's greatest Buddhist temples, the *Kinkaku-ji* (Golden Pavilion Temple), due to his growing obsession with beauty. The story was immensely popular with Japanese readers, who were in shock over the destruction of a national treasure that survived both World War II and the long American occupation that followed it. Mishima was able to harness public interest in the event and created a novel that became a domestic and international success. Mishima used the novel to make a statement about the cultural and social shift in Japan as it moved toward the twenty-first century. The dual obsession with beauty and destruction within the narrative is potent, and the text communicates a sense that Japanese society was under threat. Mishima committed seppuku (ritual suicide) in 1970 after a failed *coup d'etat* to restore power to the emperor (Varley, 343) and *Kinkaku-ji* became a contemporary classic of Japanese literature.

The twentieth century witnessed a depth and breadth of global social change that previous centuries had not experienced. Japan, as a microcosm of that social change, experienced periods of isolation, of western influence, and of changes in social stability, gender roles, class position, and moral culture. These profound shifts were echoed in reading tastes and in readership demographics. No genre revealed more about social change in twentieth- and twenty-first-century Japan than that of detective and crime fiction. The crime fiction genre appeals to both male and female readers, yet the majority of successful writers are male despite the high incidence of female readership. The sometimes erotic and gritty nature of detective fiction was often deemed inappropriate for the socially constructed ideal of the female and her place within Japanese society, but the female audience for this genre has never waned (Kawana, 209). During the late 1920s, magazines such as *Shinseinen* held contests looking for detec-

A reader in a Japanese manga shop. [Courtesy of David Henderson]

tive and crime fiction written by female authors. The response was overwhelming and magazines were inundated with submissions. Many of these were published as hugely popular short stories (Kawana, 213). Publishers started to realize that readers were not necessarily concerned with maintaining the domestic status quo in terms of fiction, and that female writers didn't necessarily have to conform to a female-driven narrative to write successfully.

One of Japan's most successful domestic and international female writers in the detective and crime genre is Natsuo Kirino, who became the first Japanese writer to be nominated for the 2004 MWA (Mystery Writers of America) Edgar Allan Poe Award in the best novel category. Her novel, *Out*, focuses on a group of female factory workers who inadvertently become involved in covering up the murder of one of their husbands. The novel was an international as well as a domestic success. The bleak urban setting of an outer Tokyo suburb, coupled with the unique strong female characters, propelled Kirino into the world of detective and crime fiction. The book garnered many prestigious awards such as the Grand Prix for Crime Fiction, which invariably helped to reinvigorate Japanese detective and crime fiction both within Japan and also outside of its national boundaries. Much was made of the fact that Kirino challenged societal norms via the strong, female-driven narratives. Her graphic depiction of the dismembering of one character's husband was reported widely within the Japanese media and produced enough shock value that the novel became a contemporary best-seller in Japan. Riding the success of her first novel, Kirino released *Grotesque*, an equally gritty tale centered on prostitution and societal expectations of femininity.

JOURNALS AND DIARIES

From the Heian era to the Edo era—a period of roughly one thousand years, from the eighth to the eighteenth century—one could argue that literature resided firmly within the domain of the courtly classes and the administrative classes (religious and/or political). It was rare for the lay person to be literate, and as such, the keeping of journals and diaries was reserved for those with both the time and the resources to undertake such an activity. To be able to write and document one's feelings and record events was a sign of one's socioeconomic status within society. The learned delighted in prose and the writing of novels, diaries, and journals was seen as a cultured way to pass time (as well as record one's own observations and surroundings).

As well as writing *Genji Monogatari*, Murasaki Shikibu kept a diary describing her life within the court of Empress Shoshi (Akiko). The diary itself covers the period from 1008 to 1010 and the New Year celebration. Murasaki kept a meticulous record of events and described in great detail such things as the facial expressions of certain ministers or other ladies-in-waiting, to the style of coat worn or the practice of meeting men during the Heian era. Murasaki's diary is of particular importance to Japanese literature and the cultural history of reading as it provides an alternative view of history—it is a personal collection of historical events and customs to which only a select few were privy. However, the publication of these diaries opened that world to a broader audience, and Japanese readers have helped to maintain the importance of this genre for the nation's reading tradition.

There can be no denying the popularity of writing personal memoirs or diaries for those holding courtly ranks, or for the privileged who resided within palace walls. Sei Shōnagon's *Makura no soshi* (*The Pillow Book*) was started sometime after the year 990, when the writer became a royal attendant for Empress Sadako. Interestingly, Shōnagon and Shikibu were considered rivals, and their works would have been read by those moving within their shared social circle. The work, made up of three hundred and twenty sections, is considered to be more of a collection of often random thoughts and ideas than a defined novel or book in the contemporary sense. *Makura no soshi* is considered an important piece of Japanese literature as Shōnagon expressed her thoughts and observations through elegant prose even when writing about mundane topics such as house inventories. The work offers a unique glimpse into the life of a royal attendant at a time when Japanese artistic and literature flourished.

NEWSPAPERS AND POPULAR MAGAZINES

Magazines and journals have enjoyed immense popularity in Japan for their ability to converse with a diverse cross-section of readers. The first contemporary-style magazine (as opposed to a paper insert) is thought to have been *Seiyo Zasshi* (*Journal of Western Affairs*) in 1867; however mass media magazines such as *Shokan Asahi* and *Chuo Koron* didn't appear until the early-twentieth century (1912), and these were geared toward the political and business sectors (Kreiner, Möjwald and Ölschleger, 455). Boutique magazines, readily identified by their specialized content, such as travel and leisure, appeared relatively early in the Japanese marketplace. Despite the enormous amount of business- and politics-driven consumerism, the development of travel and leisure magazines pointed toward an early need to cater toward the expanding niche leisure market.

In 1865, Hamada Hikozo (also called Joseph Hiko) launched *Kaigai Shimbun* (*Overseas News*), a newspaper that provided foreign affairs translations and is often widely credited as the first mass-produced newspaper in Japan. Newspapers that superficially targeted a domestic Japanese readership appeared during the latter half of the nineteenth century (around the year 1868), and they were immediately regarded as highly politicized vehicles of propaganda by the Meiji government, who sought, first in 1869 and then continuously throughout the years, to restrict the flow of information by the elite owners of the papers. Despite governmental and political interference, the development of newspapers within Japan resulted in mass media becoming a focal point for political discussion. The proliferation of newspapers resulted in the public being privy to a new system of information dissemination never experienced before within Japanese society. Traditionally, newspapers were used to instigate or expunge social and political reformations and as such played an important part in the development of a political public psyche. Popular opinions were informed (correctly or not) by that which they read within the papers, hence the government became wary of the newspapers' potential for the promotion of dissent.

Although newspapers were a popular medium for the masses, it became apparent that a niche market was developing around magazines and collectible texts. The aptly titled *Bungei Kurabu* (*Literary Club*) was considered to be one of Japan's most popular magazines for women and created a whole new genre of collectible texts. The magazine attracted a high readership due, in part, to its appealing format that included Kuchi-e (woodblock frontispiece) prints from 1895 to 1914. The inclusion of Kuchi-e front covers and inserts featuring additions by well-known artists such as Ogata Gekko and Mizuno Toshikata was novel, as their insertions were originally intended to provide a visual cue to the accompanying story. However, as their popularity increased, they were elevated to the magazine's frontispiece, thereby creating a highly stylized and popular text.

The popularity of collectable and stylized text occurs in contemporary Japan just as readily as in the past. The most popular serialized work in Japan is the graphic novel known by western readers as manga, but typically referred to as *Komikku* (comics) by Japanese readers. The magazines' depiction of the past, present, and future is informed through the pictorial representation of a unique Japanese identity. Manga transcends all sociocultural demographics in that it depicts a great number of topics ranging from teenage angst to violent sexual stories to historical drama. Subsets exist within manga; *Shojo Manga* typically targets female readers between the ages of late childhood to early adulthood (i.e. ten to eighteen). The comics are typically black and white and are designed to be read quickly. The more popular and collectible manga tend to be in color and have more substantial story lines. Stand-alone manga magazines are also highly collectible and have resulted in a crossover from magazine to film. These magazines typically consist of collated materials from newspapers, which are bound and printed on high-quality paper.

The origins of manga are believed to lie in the post-war era directly after the American occupation of Japan, and after the inauguration in 1947 of the Japanese Constitution in which censorship was expressly forbidden. Where once the Japanese people had been forbidden to express artistic freedoms (militaristic and political artworks) they were now able to comment on social and political injustices through the childlike artistic conventions that made manga so unique. This is why Osamu Tezuka's *Atom Boy* (*Astro Boy*) became extremely popular. The manga industry is a worldwide, billion-dollar industry that not only transcends Japan's socioeconomic boundaries but also appeals to a global audience.

POLITICAL TEXTS

Political texts in Japan are often not thought of as significant contributions to the literary landscape, yet their importance cannot be overlooked as they alter the fabric of society—for better or worse. One of the most important political texts in modern Japanese history effectively paved the way for Japan to become a major power in the industrialized and modernized world. The *Treaty of Kanagawa* is popularly known as the Perry Convention due to Commodore Matthew Perry's involvement in opening Japan up to foreign trade via the March 31 treaty. The treaty was important in that, as well as being the first treaty between Japan and the United States, it also guaranteed rights for American whalers and provided for coal ports in Shimoda and Hakodade to facilitate movement of commerce between the two nations and nations within the vicinity. The treaty also helped to establish a permanent American consulate in Japan, a move that made many Japanese unhappy due to the perceived notion that the treaty was unfairly forced upon them to the detriment of the nation. In succeeding in getting the Shogun Tokugawa to sign the treaty, Commodore Perry was often accused of "gunboat diplomacy," a term reserved for those who resort to military tactics to force a diplomatic relationship.

Censorship surrounding the American occupation of Japan became a pertinent issue for both the Japanese and Allies. Eager to establish freedom

> **Manga**
>
> Manga account for forty percent of all book and magazine sales in Japan (Cassidy, www.hollywoodreporter.com). And although manga is associated with Japan, non-Japanese manga are starting to appear all over the world. Manga forms can be found in South Korea, Hong Kong, China, the United States, and France. Moreover, manga versions of Hollywood classics can be found among the "traditional" Japanese manga. Titles include *Star Wars* and *Spiderman*. Nonfiction titles, including topics such as golf and cooking, also appear in manga format.

of the press in Japan after World War II during the time of American occupation of the country, a *Code for Japanese Press* was issued on September 21, 1945. The aim of the code was the elimination of what was perceived to be anti-Allied political and military propaganda in newspapers at that time. The code became a tool of control for the Allies as it severely restricted the Japanese press. The ten commands within the *Code for Japanese Press* summarily required that editorials be devoid of opinion and that no criticism of the Allies could occur. The code severely and effectively curtailed the creative and professional output of an entire industry. Japanese readers not only endured censorship from their own government, they were also forced to accept American-imposed censorship with the issuing of the *Code for Japanese Press*.

CONCLUSION

Japan has contributed markedly toward the global literary landscape. Manuscripts by Japanese writers are viewed as works of great literary worth that have helped to create, define, and shape literary endeavors. Despite a period of self-imposed isolation, Japan has managed to participate in all levels of literary creation covering all genres. Isolation may have contributed to the strong notion of the Japanese identity that winds its way though each piece of work; however, this identity is readily identifiable with the global citizen who devours Japanese works enthusiastically. A vast majority of Japanese literature positions itself between traditions of the past and modern ideas, concepts, and trends, much like the impression of Japan itself with its cityscape and Buddhist temples. As both creators and consumers of literature, the Japanese will continue to support their rich literary tradition, and they will continue to export their unique literary forms to the global reading public.

RECOMMENDED READING

Altman, Albert. "The Press and Social Cohesion during a Period of Change: The Case for Early Meiji Japan." *Modern Asian Studies* 15.4 (1981): 865–876.

Brewster, Jennifer. *Sanuki no Suke Nikki: A Translation of the Emperor Horikawa Diary.* Canberra, Australia: Australian National University Press, 1977.

Gravett, Paul. *Manga: Sixty Years of Japanese Comics.* London: Lawrence King Publications, 2004

Hein, Laura and Mark Selden. "The Lessons of War, Global Power, and Social Change." In *Censoring History: Citizenship and Memory in Japan, Germany and the United States*, 3–50. Edited by Laura Hein and Mark Selden. Armonk, NY: M. E. Sharpe, 2000.

Ito, Hirobumi. *Commentaries on the Constitution of the Empire of Japan.* Translated by Miyoji Ito. Tokyo: Igirisu-horitsu gakko, 22nd year of Meiji, 1889. Also published by Greenwood Press, 1978.

Ito, Kinko. "A History of Manga in the Context of Japanese Culture and Society." *Journal of Popular Culture* 38.3 (Feb. 2005): 456–475

Kawana, Sari. "The Price of Pulp: Women, Detective Fiction, and the Profession of Writing in Inter-War Japan." *Japan Forum* 16.2 (July, 2004): 207–229.

Keene, Donald. *World within Walls: Japanese Literature of the Pre-Modern Era, 1600 to 1867.* New York: Columbia University Press, 1999.

Kern, Adam. *Manga from the Floating World: Comic Book Culture and the Kibyoshi of Edo Japan.* Cambridge: Harvard University Press, 2006.

Kornicki, Peter. *The Book in Japan: A Cultural History from the Beginnings to the Nineteenth Century.* Honolulu, HI: University of Hawaii Press, 2000.

Kreiner, Josef, Ulrich Mohwald, and Hans-Dieter Olschleger, eds. *Modern Japanese Society.* Leiden: Brill, 2004.

McCullough, Helen, ed. *Classical Japanese Prose: An Anthology.* Stanford, CA: Stanford University Press, 1990.

Merritt, Helen and Nanako Yamada. *Woodblock Kuchi-e Prints: Reflections of Meji Culture.* Honolulu: University of Hawaii Press, 2000.

Morton, W. Scott and J. Kenneth Olenik. *Japan, Its History and Culture.* New York: McGraw-Hill, 2005.

Seaman, Amanda C. *Bodies of Evidence: Women, Society and Detective Fiction in 1990s Japan.* Honolulu: University of Hawaii Press, 2004.

Shirane, Haruo, and Tomi Suzuki. *Inventing the Classics: Modernity, National Identity and Literature.* Stanford, CA: Stanford University Press, 2000.

Tokita, Alison. "Performed Narratives and Music in Japan." *Oral Tradition,* 18.1 (March, 2003). 26–29.

Varley, Paul. *Japanese Culture.* Honolulu: University of Hawaii Press, 2000.

PRIMARY SOURCES

Astro Boy (鉄腕アトム, *Tetsuwan Atomu,* lit. "Mighty Atom"). Mushi Productions, Fuji TV. 1963–1966.

Bungei Kurabu (*Literary Club*), Hakubunkan, 1895–1914. *Bungei Kurabu* was a journal, popular with women readers and prized for its beautiful wood-block covers.

Code for Japanese Press, 1945. The *Code* was issued on September 21, 1945, and governed what could be published in post-War Japan. For more information, see http://www.lib.umd.edu/prange/pdf/japanese_presscode.pdf

The Gossamer Years: The Diary of a Noblewoman of Heian Japan. Translated by Edward Seidensticker. Rutland, VT: Charles E. Tuttle, 1975.

Heike Monogatari (*The Tales of the Taira Clan*). Translated by Helen McCulloch. Stanford, CA: Stanford University Press, 1990.

Kaigai Shimbun (*Overseas News*), 1864–? *Kaigai Shimbun* was the first newspaper ever published in Japan.

Matsuo Bashō. *Narrow Road to Oku.* Translated by Donald Keene. New York: Kodansha International, 1996.

———. *Genji monogatari.* Translated by Edward Seidensticker. New York: Knopf, 1978.

Natsuo Kirino. *Grotesque.* Translated by Rebecca Copeland. New York: Knopf Publishing, 2007.

———. *Out.* Translated by Stephen Snyder. Tokyo: Kodansha International, 2005.

Ono no Komachi and Izumi Shikibu. *The Ink Dark Moon: Love Poems by Ono no Komachi and Izumi Shikibu.* Translated by Jane Hirschfield and Mariko Aratani. New York: Random House, 1990.

Sei Shonagon. *The Pillow Book of Sei Shonagon.* Translated by Arthur Waley. Whitefish, MT: Kessinger Publishing, 2005.

Shiki, Masaoka. *Masaoka Shiki: Selected Poems.* Translated by Burton Watson. New York: Columbia University Press, 1998.

Shikibu, Murasaki. *Diary of Lady Murasaki.* Translated by Richard Bowring. New York: Penguin Classics, 1999.

Treaty of Kanagawa. March 31, 1854 (in English). Also available at General Records of the United States Government: http://www.archives.gov/exhibits/featured_documents/treaty_of_kanagawa/treaty_images.html

Yukio Mishima. *The Temple of the Golden Pavilion.* Translated by Ivan Morris. New York: Vintage Books, 2004.

SECONDARY SOURCES

Batten, Bruce. "Provincial Administration in Early Japan: From Ritsuryo kokka to Ocho Kokka." *Harvard Journal of Asiatic Studies* 53.1 (1993): 103–134.

Cassidy, Kevin. "Manga mania: Comic-book Franchises." *The Hollywood Reporter.com.* 15 July, 2003. 19 Feb. 2008. http://www.hollywoodreporter.com/hr/search/article_display.jsp?vnu_content_id=1933444

Higginson, William. *The Haiku Seasons: Poetry of the Natural World.* Japan: Kodansha International (JPN), 1996.

Kawana, Sari. "The Price of Pulp: Women, Detective Fiction, and the Profession of Writing in Inter-war Japan." *Japan Forum* 16.2 (July, 2004). 207–229.

Masaoki Shiki. *Masaoka Shiki: His Life and Works.* Translated by Janine Beichman. Boston: Cheng and Tsui, 2002.

Pandey, Rajyashree. "Poetry, Sex and Salvation: The 'Courtesan' and the Noblewoman in Medieval Japanese Narratives." *Japanese Studies* 24.1 (May 2004): 61–79.

Seaman, A. *Bodies of Evidence: Women, Society and Detective Fiction in 1990s Japan.* Honolulu: University of Hawai'i Press, 2004.

CHAPTER 16

Korea

Jihee Han

TIMELINE

2333 B.C.E.	The foundation of Gojoseon kingdom
57 B.C.E.	The foundation of Shilla kingdom
37 B.C.E.	The foundation of Goguryo kingdom
18 B.C.E.	The foundation of Baikjeh kingdom
668 C.E.	The foundation of the United Shilla kingdom
c. 682 C.E.	The invention of Idu, the Korean transcription system by Seol Chong
918 C.E.	The foundation of Goryo
1392 C.E.	The foundation of Joseon kingdom
1443–46	The invention of "Hunminjeongeum," the first Korean language, by King Sehjong
1592	The publication of wooden typesetting edition of *Keumohshinhwa*, the first narrative written in a mixed style of Chinese and Korean by Kim Shie-seup
1592–98	Imjin Oyran War, Japan's invasion of Joseon kingdom
c. 1600	*Hongkildong-Jeon*, the first novel written in Korean by Huh Kyun
1636–37	Byongja Horan War, Ch'ing-China's invasion of Josoen kingdom
1681–1763	Cultural Movement of the Practical Knowledge School led by Yee Ik
1860–1919	Donghak Farmers' Uprising
1882	The publication of the first Korean-translated Bible
1883	The establishment of Pakmunguk, state printing house; *Hansungsunbo*, the first newspaper printed in metal typesetting
1910–45	Japanese occupation of Joseon kingdom
1918	*Mu-jeong*, the first modern novel by Yee Kwang-su
1945–48	The Emancipation and the foundation of the Republic of Korea
1950–53	The Korean War and the partition of two Koreas; publication of Kim Ku's *Baekbeom Ilzy*
1960–92	The era of military dictatorship of Park Jung-hee, Chun Doo-hwan, Roh Tae-woo; the rise of various forms of Civil Disobedience demonstrations and movements; the publication of Kim Ji-ha's *With a Burning Thirst*

2000   South Korea begins the Engagement Policy toward North Korea;
               President Kim Dae-Joong's announcement of the "Sunshine Policy"
2005–06   The Korean Wave Phenomenon in Asia-Pacific region triggered by
               Korean TV dramas, "Autumn Tale" and "Winter Sonata"

INTRODUCTION TO THE PERIOD

Despite the lack of historical records, it is generally recognized that Gojoseon is the oldest of Korea's kingdoms (2333 B.C.E.). Chinese historian Sima Qian's *Record of a Grand Historian* (110–91 B.C.E.) indicates the kingdom's existence by describing cultural exchanges between Yin-China, Zhou-China, and Gojoseon. Historical records of later kingdoms have been fairly well preserved. Il Yeon's *Samgukyusah* (1281–85), and *Yuki*—a one-hundred-volume historical record compiled during the Goguryo period—describe Korea's ancient kingdoms, commonly recognized as Goguryo (37 B.C.E.–668 C.E.), Baikjeh (18 B.C.E.–660 C.E.), and Shilla (57 B.C.E.–668 B.C.E.). Later kingdoms such as the United Shilla (668–935), Goryo (918–1392), and Joseon (1392–1910) are described in other historical records, such as Kim Bu-shik's histories of three kingdoms and the United Shilla kingdom, *Samguksaki* (A.D. 1145). *Goryo History* (A.D. 1392–1451) and *Record of Joseon Kings* (A.D. 1392–1863) are precious historical records that provide detailed knowledge of both kingdoms.

What is noticeable in the period of Korea's kingdoms is that Korea had played the role of a cultural hub that mediated between China and Japan. For instance, according to the *Korean Printing Institute's* report, after Ts'ai Lun invented paper-making in 105 C.E., the technique was imported by Goguryo in 593 and further developed by the Baikjeh and Shilla kingdoms. The technological level and the size of the printing sector in those three kingdoms are not exactly known. Yet Dahm Jing, a Goguryo native monk, transferred Buddhist texts to the Japanese along with both methods of paper-making—hammering mulberry fibers instead of stone grinding them as Chinese technicians had done—and techniques for making stick-type black ink in 610 C.E. Wahng In, a Baikjeh-native scholar, also handed over ten copies of Confucius texts and one volume of the one thousand Chinese letter learning book to the Japanese in 608 C.E. Later, Goryo's high-quality Dahk-paper and Songyeon stick-type black ink were exported to T'ang-China and became prized products among Chinese intellectuals.

Along with its role as a cultural bridge, Korea has often been a battleground due to its geopolitical importance in the Asia-Pacific region. Chinese dynasties continuously tried to expand their territories toward the Pacific Ocean, while Japanese shoguns invaded the Korean peninsula when they got a chance. For instance, Goguryo won the battles against Sui-China in 612 and T'ang-China in 645. Shilla also fought a battle with T'ang-China and expanded its northern territory in 676. Later, Goryo protected its sovereignty against six Mongolian invasions between 1231 and 1259. Joseon also defended its kingdom against Japanese attacks in the late-sixteenth century (Imjin Oyran) and Ch'ing-China's attack in the early-seventeenth century (Byongja Horan). Then Joseon became the battleground of the Sino-Japanese War from 1894–1895 and the Russia-Japanese War from 1904–1905. At last, Joseon was divested of its sovereignty by Japan in 1910. After the Emancipation in 1945, the Republic of Korea was finally founded in 1948. Yet once more Korea became a battleground during the Korean War in 1950, and it was divided into two Koreas, South and North, in 1953. After the iron reign of three consecutive military dictators between 1960 and 1992, South

Korea is now enjoying an Information Age and progress in new computer technology. It is also replaying the role of a cultural hub in the Asia-Pacific region, cooperating with China, Japan and South Asian countries.

Culturally, Korea has maintained fairly good relationships with both Chinese and Japanese dynasties, and it has enjoyed steady progress in terms of developing a writing system. The United Shilla kingdom, which unified three ancient kingdoms after a long period of war, set out to assimilate the ex-Goguryo and ex-Baikjeh people together with the Shilla people by adopting a common language. Seol Chong, a renowned aristocrat, and one of the ten most prominent Shilla scholars, was commissioned to invent a new transcription system. He experimented with various ways of putting sounds or meanings of Chinese letters together as a way to fill the linguistic gaps and to complement the cultural sensibilities of the Korean people. He finally invented the "Idu" writing system, which reorders Chinese grammar in line with Korean ways of speaking. The "Idu" system was widely employed in official documents and historical records and also in Hyang-gah song lyrics, of which one of the most famous is *Jehmahngmae-gah*.

Eventually, the "Idu" system disappeared with the fall of the United Shilla kingdom. At that point, those who could understand the Chinese language began to feel the need to reflect their own ways of speaking while keeping Chinese letters as linguistic symbols. In the period of the Goryo kingdom, therefore, *Ku-kyeol-mun* was widely adopted. Ku-kyeol-mun is a kind of transcription system in which Chinese letters with sounds similar to the spoken language of Korean become simplified and were written in the right upper corner of the original Chinese words. This way the Koreans could break Chinese grammar and write the sentences in the same way that they spoke and understood their language.

Finally, in 1436 the great King Sehjong, of the Joseon kingdom, commissioned his scholars to develop original Korean letters and grammar and announced the invention of *Hunminjeongeum*, the first Korean language. Hunminjeongeum had twenty-eight Korean letters that enabled the Koreans to materialize virtually all sounds and meanings. In the early days, however, the aristocrats and intelligentsia of Joseon discredited Hunminjeongeum because they had long been accustomed to reading and writing in Chinese. They condescendingly called the new language "Eonmun," meaning that it was an inferior language invented for ignorant commoners and women. They even petitioned to ban Humninjeongeum in official documents, and in 1504 King Yonsahn-kun was forced to accept their petition. Nevertheless, Hunminjeongeum spread quickly among the Joseon people. In 1592, Kim Shie-seup wrote a story entitled *Keumohshinhwa* in a mixed style of Chinese and Korean languages. In 1600, Huh Kyun wrote a satiric novel entitled *Hongkildong-jeon* in Korean only, which became quite popular among literate Joseon readers. Finally, in 1894 King Koh-jong renamed Hunminjeongeum *Kuk-mun* (the national language) and announced that it would become the official language of the Joseon kingdom. Later, Zhu Shi-kyoung (1876–1914), renowned scholar of the Korean language, renamed Kuk-mun *Hangeul* (the Korean race's language), and the name is still used to designate the Korean language.

READING TRENDS AND PRACTICES

When speaking of Korean reading trends and practices, it is impossible not to mention the impact that Buddhism had on the minds of Korean readers. Buddhist monks, who were mostly from aristocratic families and had a liberal education, shaped Buddhist reading culture and developed it throughout Korea's dynasties.

The fact that all three ancient kingdoms—Goguryo, Baikjeh, and Shilla—had had Buddhism as their state religion, and that they had run higher-education centers that included Buddhist sutras as main course works, suggests that the blossoming of the Buddhist reading and publishing market was inevitable during the classical period of Korea.

Buddhist monks and scholars published transcripts of Chinese texts or their own texts with annotated interpretations of Buddhist sutras over a relatively short period, thanks to the development of wood carving technology. In particular, Baikjeh, which was located near the Sandong region of China, and therefore had easy access to Chinese cultural trends, led the Chinese wave, modernizing news and reading materials on Buddhism. In 542 Baikjeh monks also transmitted Buddhism to the Japanese and gave them literary works that contained Buddhist songs of praise. Shilla was a bit late in importing Chinese culture. Yet according to old Korean historical records, such as *Samgukyusah* and *Samguksahki*, Shilla imported as many books from Chinese dynasties as Goguryo and Baikjeh did, and also encouraged publishing, producing more books than those two kingdoms. Among the prominent Shilla monks, Won Hyo (617–686) started a new sect of Korean Buddhism for common people by simplifying Buddhist rituals and teachings into an easy-to-memorize chant—"Nah-mu-ah-mi-tah-bul-kwan-seh-um-bo-sahl." His creative interpretation of Chinese Buddhism is well-preserved in many of his writings. Won Hyo reportedly wrote at least 180 books on Buddhism, the most famous two of which are *Daeseung Kyshinron* and *Keumgahng Sahmmaekyoungron*.

> **National Treasure Number 126**
>
> *Mugu Jeongkwang Dae Darani-gyeong* is designated as National Treasure No. 126. It is a six-meter-long roll of paper imprint, which has twelve 6.7 cm×54 cm sheets. It was found inside a stone pagoda named Seokgah-tahp in Kyongju in 1966. Arguably, it was published earlier than "Keumgahng Banyabaramil" of China (868 A.D.). Recently, however, some historians have speculated on the possibility that it was imported.

In the period of the United Shilla kingdom, the Buddhist religion reached its peak in terms of philosophical and political influence. Many Buddhist temples and pagodas were built, and various annotated interpretations of Buddhist sutras were actively published by using carved wooden plates. Among the famous publications are Euy-sahng Daesah's annotated reading of the *Avatamska Sutra* and Hye Cho's *Wangoh Chonchukguk Jeon* (727), the first travelogue that recorded his trip to India along the Silk Road. *Mugu Jeongkwang Dae Darani-gyoung* (704–751) is the oldest imprint of the Dharani (or Sharani) Sutra, which was published thanks to the great efforts of a number of Buddhist monks, who carved the sutra on wooden plates for forty-seven years.

In the period of the Goryo kingdom, Buddhism could not monopolize culture but had to share it with Confuciansim. Although Goryo declared Buddhism to be its state religion, at the same time it encouraged its nobles to learn Confucius School classics as well. In those days, Chu His's Neo-Confucianism, which emphasized logic, consistency, and the conscientious observance of the classical authority of Confucius and Mencius, began to wield power among the intellectuals of Sung-China. Goryo's aristocrats and scholars actively imported a newly rising discipline and included Neo-Confucian texts, as well as traditional Confucian classics, as required reading materials for both state examinations and liberal education. Consequently, many upper- and upper-middle-class people began to read transcriptions and annotated interpretations of Neo-Confucianism. Even monk-scholars, who had mostly studied Buddhist sutras, started to read more Neo-Confucian texts in order to provide aristocrats, bureaucrats, and students with intellectual training. Little by little these intellectuals, who benefited from Neo-Confucianism and Chu His's vision of ideal politics, came to form a distinctive intelligentsia, and in the end they became the core dissident force that would over-throw Goryo to found the new Confucian kingdom, Joseon.

It was during the Goryo period that two of the most significant events in Korean printing history occurred. The first was the publication of *The Tripitaka Koreana* (1236 A.D.). Goryo monks carved about eighty thousand wooden plates, on which they transcribed Buddhist sutras. About sixty copies of paper imprints of *The Tripitaka Koreana* were given to the Japanese from the late Goryo period to the middle of the Joseon period. The second event was the publication of *Jikjishimchehyojeol* (1377) by a Buddhist monk named Kyoung-han. *Jikji* has great significance not only because it was the first metal typeset imprint, but also because it shows the technological advancement of Korea in the Asia-Pacific region and in the world. Generally, metal typeset printing technology requires mass-production of paper and proper black ink as well as metal welding technology. According to his-torians, these prerequisites had been met in King Munjong's reign (1047–1084): there had already been nationwide paper and ink producers in King Seongjong's reign (981–997), and King Seongjong introduced metal coins, which the Goryo people had used as their main currency. Thus, despite few historical records, it is generally presumed that Goryo, while improving wood carving skills by degrees, finally succeeded in inventing metal typesetting printing technology in about the eleventh century. The *Jikji* imprint, which is currently displayed at the National Library of France, is the second volume of a two-volume *Jikji*; it is known world wide as the oldest specimen of metal typeset printing, being officially older than the first imprint of the Gutenberg Bible.

With the foundation of the Joseon kingdom, Korean reading trends and prac-tices went through a drastic change. King Taejo, the founder of the Joseon king-dom, declared Chu His's Neo-Confucianism to be its state religion and repressed Buddhism, criticizing it as a devious religion that corrupted people's minds. He drove Buddhist monks out to deep mountain temples and refurbished all Goryo rules and regulations on the basis of Confucian principles. However, thanks to Goryo printing technology, Joseon made great strides in the publishing sector by applying wooden typesetting technologies to the printing process. In 1395 Taejo could read various documents printed by wooden typesetting technology. The suc-cessive kings of Joseon could expand royal libraries and establish research-oriented ministries such as Jiphyon-jeon and Hongmun-kwan. Kyujang-kak was founded in order to publish state-funded collections and anthologies and to manage a great number of books and precious imprints and typesets. Furthermore, in 1436 the great King Sehjong announced the invention of the Korean language Hunminjeoneum, which has twenty-eight Korean letters, and published a written speech *Hunminjeongeum*, which explains the ways in which the Korean language would be utilized. He also let the royal printers publish the ten-volume *Yongbiuhchon-gah*, *Wolinchongangjigok*, and *Seokbosangjeol* (the first metal typeset imprint in only Korean) in 1447. With the invention of the Korean language, the reading market enjoyed a huge boom. New readers, including high-class women and middle- and lower-middle-class people who had long been banned from learn-ing Chinese letters, could easily learn to read Korean letters and started to read romance and adventure stories written in only Korean. The most popular adven-ture story was *Hongkildong-jeon*, written by Huh Kyun in 1600, and the most widely read stories among women were *Kuwoonmong* and *Sahssinamjeongki* by Kim Mahn-joong in 1687. Also, female writers such as Huh Nahn-seol-huhn and Shin Sahimdang appeared and attracted many female readers.

In the Joseon period, the "Seonbi" intelligentsia group replaced Buddhist monks as the leaders in shaping reading trends and influencing the reading market. Mostly, they aimed to internalize Confucian virtues and cultivate the Confucian outlook on life through devoted reading and studying of Neo-Confucian texts. Yet their ultimate goal was to pass state examinations and become court officials so that they could apply their Confucian political ideals to the management of the real world. Keeping the Confucian motto, "Su-ki-Chi-In" (control yourself first and then rule others) in mind, they pursued a step-by-step reading process. They would first read four fundamental texts (Dae-hak, Confucius, Mencius, Jung-yong) followed by five books of practical knowledge (Shie-kyong, Suh-kyong, Ju-yeok, Yeh-ky, Chun-chu), and then the important Neo-Confucian classics (Yee-jeong Jeonsuh, Ju-jah Daejeon, Seong-lee Daejeon), and finally, the four history books (Sah-ki, Ja-chi Tongkahm, Yeok-dae Jeongsa, Dong-kook Jehsa). Once the Seonbi become court officials, they would read books of foreign policy and administration in order to rule the state effectively and efficiently.

However, many Seonbi of the late Joseon period began to open their minds to western practical knowledge, which was being transmitted via China. They even founded a new school of practical knowledge and tried to prepare common people as well as themselves for rapidly changing domestic and international environments. Pak Ji-won, Hong Dae-yong, Yi Duk-moo, and Jeong Yahk-yong were representatives of that school. Most were upper-class officials from good families and expanded their readings to western-style logic and astrology. They even read technology and engineering texts, which were regarded as unsuitable for the higher class in those days. In addition, in the 1890s, state-owned and state-subsidized printing houses, which had long been using both wooden and metal typesetting, started publishing newspapers such as *Han-sung Sunbo*, *Dok-lip Shinmun*, and *Hwang-sung Shinmun*.

In 1910 Japan, which had opened its trade to western countries and refurbished itself as a modern nation, seized control of the Korean peninsula over other competing countries, including China, Russia, the United States, Britain, and France, and began its thirty-five year occupation of Korea. During this period the Japanese colonial government deployed its repressive colonial policies and implemented strict restrictions on speech. Nonetheless, it is interesting to note that the size of the reading market grew during this occupation period, despite harsh regulations. For instance, newspapers became diversified, recruiting many new readers. Certainly in the Joseon period there had been *Bo*s (newspapers), but advances in mass communications in this period are really noteworthy. For instance, *Mae-il Shinbo*, subsidized by the Japanese colonial government, was published, and three nationwide Korean newspapers—*Dong-a Ilbo*, *Chosun Ilbo*, and *Chosun Joong-ang Ilbo*—were also published. As well, regional newspapers such as *Kyong-nam Ilbo* and *Dae-gu Ilbo*, along with numerous bulletins and newsletters were operated by Koreans on condition that they would cooperate with the Japanese colonial government.

With the rise of newspapers, serialized newspaper novels also came to draw readers' attention. Yee Kwang-su's *Mu-jeong*, which was very popular in 1917, explored western-style romantic relationships between modern men and women in a ground-breaking literary style. The novel really signaled the coming of a new generation of Korean writers in the 1920s and the 1930s. Influenced by Japanese socialist views and western philosophy and literature, novelists produced a broad spectrum of literary works filled with experimental spirit and artistic vision, ranging from socialist, to realist, to naturalist, to romanticist views of Korean life under the occupation. Most of their works were published in newspapers or newly launched literary magazines such as *Baek Zoh*, *Pyeh Huh*, and *Chang Zoh*.

In the late period of the occupation, Japan began to oppress the nationalist fervor of Korean newspapers and magazines more severely. It forced Korean journalists to publish editorials, essays, and columns that encouraged Koreans to actively defend the Japanese imperialistic cause. In this situation, many famous writers, artists, and intellectuals were divided into pro-Japanese and anti-Japanese camps that tapped the minds and spirits of the reading public in various ways. On the one hand, pro-Japanese intellectuals published propagandistic editorials, arguing that Japan only *helped* the modernization of Korea through colonization. Even beloved writer Yee Kwang-su published the infamous column in which he urged young Koreans to volunteer for the Japanese army and fight as proud servants of the Japanese Empire. Along with him, many famous writers, artists, and scholars succumbed to the threat of the Japanese authorities and contributed to the loss of Korean lives. On the other hand, anti-Japanese intellectuals continued to inspire the spirit of Korean independence. Shin Chae-ho's essay "A View on the Reformation of a Nation" resonated through the underworld resistance groups, and his nationalist historical view served as a torch for Koreans who tried to continue their efforts to restore the nation's sovereignty. In addition, representative poets such as Yun Dong-ju and Han Yong-un described the inner landscape of Korean intellectuals, going through conflicting emotions and feelings such as helplessness, resistance, frustration, and hope in their poetry.

The period from the Emancipation (1945) to the Korean War (1953) to the establishment of the Republic of Korea was an era of darkness in terms of reading culture. During this period, which was marked by three separate waves of ideological cleansing, ferocious political struggles, and drastic social upheavals, the once-burgeoning literary market of the 1920s and the 1930s was forced into submission, along with other cultural facilities such as schools, libraries, and presses.

After the Korean War, the Korean people put their energy into the reconstruction of the collapsed economy and the building of cultural confidence. However, this was not an easy task because Korea had suffered years of fear and social oppression. Freedom of speech had disappeared, and the influence of three consecutive military dictators had discouraged open inquiry and public trust. However, despite the ruthless military dictatorship of almost three decades, the dormant literary market started returning to life. A wide range of intellectuals and writers began to defend human rights and publish essays, articles, and books, championing democratic ideals. Kim Ji-ha brought political activism into his poetry and published the famous poem "With a Burning Thirst," which has become the anthem for ordinary people with social consciousness. Mr. Kim, after frequent imprisonment and a death sentence for his political activism during the Park regime, has become a cultural icon who manifested the spirit of resistance in the 1960s and 1970s. Cho Seh-hee's *A Little Ball Launched by a Dwarf* became an instant hit, with its heart-wrenching description of the hard lives of poor, down-trodden urban laborers. Still, it maintains its iconic status among other bestsellers. Choi In-hoon published a novel about the tragic ramifications of the Korean War and the partition of two Koreas in *The Plaza*.

When the tragic Kwang-ju Massacre occurred under the Chun regime in 1980 and many citizens and students lost their lives, intellectuals, artists, and writers published essays, editorials, columns, and poetry to condemn the use of armed force against the Korean public. Paik Nak-chung and other intellectuals founded a literary magazine, *Changbi* (*Creative Writing and Criticism*), and voiced conscientious intellectuals' acerbic social criticism of Korean life under political duress. Shin Kyong-nim and other nationalist writers proposed new *Min-jung* literature that aimed to represent the common people's voices. Ko Eun, a Buddhist-turned-famous poet, represented the public's wish for the reunification of two Koreas in his poetry. Park Noh-hae, a daily laborer-turned-activist poet, severely criticized the capitalist-oriented, depersonalized society that does not care about human rights for the working classes in his collection of poems, *The Dawn of a Laborer*. Cho Jung-rae embodied the tragic ramifications of the Korean War in *The Tae-baek Mountain Range*. Also, Yee Young-hee, a renowned historian, reassured many Koreans of the necessity for the reunification of two Koreas in *The Logics in a Transitional Period* and *Overcoming the Partition* and encouraged them to stay awake, watching out for the unpredictable shifts of geopolitical interests concerning the two Koreas.

During the period of military dictatorship (1960–1992), there occurred an interesting cultural shift in terms of international influence on Korean reading culture. Japanese cultural power receded and American culture started to influence virtually all aspects of Korean society and culture. The news articles, editorials, and columns of *The New York Times*, *The Wall Street Journal*, and *The Washington Post* were quoted and revered as reliable sources of news almost every day in various forms of Korean mass media. As curiosity about the United States rose, reading materials concerning American culture and lifestyles were in high demand. While traditional magazines dealing with current affairs such as *Time* and *Newsweek* maintained their power, women's magazines, such as *Vogue* and *Cosmopolitan*, became popular among middle-class women who wanted to satisfy their curiosity about American women's affluent and fashionable lifestyles. The children's book market also benefited from the fascination with all things American. Most of popular western children's literature, which had already been translated into Korean, was now being more actively sought, and even original English texts are imported and sold in the big city bookstores.

Further, there also appeared sophisticated writers with artistic vision and philosophical depth who led the reading trend. Park Kyong-ni started writing *The Land*, the saga of a family who goes through ups and downs during socio-politico-economic turmoil of the last period of Joseon, the Japanese occupation, and the Emancipation. Park Wan-suh recollects the turbulent period surrounding the Korean War, representing her own experience of leaving her hometown in Gae-sung, North Korea and resettling in Seoul, South Korea in *Who Ate All Those Sing-ahs?*

In the 1990s the birth of Internet news services, of which *On My News* is the most visible example, opened a new era of Korean reading culture. Because the content of the service is not determined by journalists, editors, or corporate interest, but by ordinary citizens, *Oh My News* christened a two-way, news-making era in Korean mass media history: ordinary Internet users publish a wide variety of articles, essays, and investigative reports on the Web site, which later become "news" on the basis of the numbers of Internet reader "hits" on the material. By connecting all the Koreans in the world through one network and allowing them to communicate with one another domestically and internationally, *Oh My News* (and, later, similar Internet-based news portals) gave rise to the so-called Internet revolution that has completely changed the reading habits of Korean people. In the meantime, the once-powerful traditional newspapers have been losing subscribers and, consequently, have begun to position themselves among right-wing conservative voices, defining the Internet up-starts as leftist, progressive news media. Nowadays, thanks to the rapid growth of various news-service portals, younger Korean people rarely read paper-based newspapers but instead log on to the Internet and select the news they want to read.

Currently, Korean readers are fascinated by the "teen journal" genre. Guiyoni, now one of the leading teen journal writers, initially published *The Boy Was Cool*, *A Seduction of a Wolf*, and *To My Boy-Friend* on the Internet and attracted so much interest that she eventually published them in paperback. This shift in the direction of Korean reading tastes has translated into a drop in sales and interest in traditional "literary" novels and poetry books. Now more high-brow forms of literature have given way to Internet-based teen romances and light novels. Moreover, the shift in reading interest toward American literary products and ideas has meant that domestic writers have difficulty getting their novels read or translated. According to the Korean Publisher's Bulletin (2003–2006), Korean readers prefer American popular novels and self-help books, English language and learning books, or children's books. Not surprisingly, Dan Brown's *The Da Vinci Code*, John Gray's *Men Are from Mars, Women are from Venus*, Peter Drucker's series on leadership, Stephen Covey's *The Seven Habits of Highly Effective People*, and Spencer Johnson's *Who Moved My Cheese?* are all on the bestseller lists. The *Harry Potter* series and Dr. Seuss books are also popular sellers. Virtually every English reading, writing, and speaking book is selling strongly both online and in hard copy sales. However, unlike western readers, Korean readers do not read biography, gardening, cookery, or sports books in significant numbers. They prefer to get such information on the Internet rather than finding it in paper-based books.

PERSONAL TEXTS: JOURNALS AND DIARIES

This genre has maintained its readers due to Korean readers' preference for light reading. The Korean sensibility that emphasizes a communal sense and "Jeong" (affection) within inter- and intrapersonal relationships, as opposed to a rational, logical, and calculating outlook, might be a factor, too. Koreans seem to prefer humble, vulnerable subjects to long, high-brow narratives and challenging intellectual types.

Nanjung Ilky (*A Diary*) is a diary written in calligraphy by commander-in-chief Yee Soon-shin of Joseon kingdom at Aasan naval base between 1592 and 1598. This seven volume, two hundred fifty page diary contains detailed descriptions of naval military conflicts that occurred between King Seonjo of Joseon and Toyotomi Hideyoshi and Tokugawa Ieyasu of Edo Japan from the year of Imjin Oyran (January 1, 1592) to the year he died at Noh-ryahng Haejeon (November 17, 1598). Originally, commander Yee had not entitled his diary in any way, but it was later named when King Jeongjo ordered historians to write commander Yee's biography to honor his great naval achievements and patriotism. Now it is designated as National Treasure No. 76 and preserved at Hyunchung-sa in Aasan.

Nanjung Ilky is significant first as a personal diary whose entries reveal the reflections and anguishes of a commander-in-chief facing a series of difficult naval battles. Commander Yee describes how he was accused by his rival Won Kyun and divested of his rank and how he was restored to his rank by distinguishing himself in a war. Yet his diary does not mention any grudge or rage toward his rival, and only concentrates on preparing for the next naval battle. He also takes great care of refugees in distress and orders his soldiers to cultivate farmlands for the poor. Moreover, he had such strong ethics as a commander that, even though he was ill with high fever, he insisted that "A commander would never lie down" and sat up straight at the camp for twelve days fighting his illness. At the same time, he reveals a soft spot for his mother. During the battles, his aged mother took refuge in a nearby village of Yeo-su, where the military base was located. Although he was in a position to do virtually whatever he wished, he wrote a higher court official a petition letter asking for a three-day leave in order to celebrate his mother's eightieth birthday. Soon after, his mother died, and the entry for that sad occasion is entitled "a guilty son."

Nanjung Ilky is also significant as a historical record that describes the complicated domestic and international situations surrounding Tokugawa Ieyasu's continuous military provocations, Ming-China's imperial arrogance in naming Edo Japan as a servant country, and King Seonjo's awkward position in court disputes over Joseon's political position between China and Japan. In addition, it records how Yee built *Guhbukson*, the first turtle-shaped, metal-spike-covered battleship in the world, and also how he invented a variety of firearms. The diary further reveals commander Yee's maritime knowledge and military strategy when he describes two of the most famous battles in Korean naval history, the Myeong-rahng Daechop and the No-rahng Haejeon. In both battles, commander Yee made the most of the tidal change in the Myeong-rahng channel and the Noh-ryahng inshore current and defeated 133 and two hundred Japanese battleships in each battle with only a small number of Guhbuksons. With Noh-ryahng Haejeon, the long-continued naval battles between Joseon and Edo Japan ended, and commander Yee also faced a brave death. Yet to his last breath, commander Yee did not lose his sense of obligation to Joseon. Even though he was critically wounded by an arrow, he sat up straight and forbade his lieutenants to inform his soldiers about his wound. He was more concerned for the life of his beloved kingdom than he was for himself.

Because of his strong patriotism and ethical responsibility, commander Yee is still revered as one of the great Korean heroes. His statue has been built; his famous battleship, the *Guhbukson*, appears on a Korean coin (100 Won); in Yeo-su people commemorate his military merits by offering "the Guhbukson Festival" every year; the Hyunchung temple has been built to pay respect to him in Aasan; and his *Nanjung Ilky* is on the elementary and middle school reading lists. Four hundred years later, he still watches over the Korean people, standing right in the middle of Chongro, the busiest avenue in Seoul. In 2001 his *Nanjung Ilky* was rewritten in novel form, entitled *A Song of a Sword* by Kim Hoon, and it attracted a great number of readers. A TV mini-series drama, "National Hero Yee Soon-shin," premiered in 2006 to the delight of many Koreans, who will continue his popularity.

Baekbum Ilzy (*A Diary of Baekbum*) is another diary, written by Kim Ku (also known as Baekbum) and first published in 1947. He played a critical role in a series of resistance activities; for that reason, he was on the Japanese detectives' black list during the occupation period. He also participated in the March 1 protest and served as a secretary of state and attorney general to the Provisional Government of Korea (PGK), whose headquarters were located in Shanghai. He founded the Korean Independence Party in 1928 and later became the elected president of PGK. However, when his administration did not win U.S. recognition as the legitimate government of Korea, he led the anti-trusteeship movement and deployed a conservative nationalist agenda. Finally, in 1948, his right-wing rival Lee Seung-mahn, who had earned U.S. recognition in return for U.S. trusteeship of Korea, suggested a general election that would be restricted to South Korea. Kim disagreed with Lee and went to North Korea in order to bring its leader Kim Il-sung to the discussion table for the unification of two Koreas. Yet to his misfortune Kim was assassinated by Ahn Du-hee in 1949, and his great plan for Korea's future melted away.

Baekbum Ilzy is impor-
tant in that it records
major historical events
and the key players dur-
ing the chaotic period of
modern Korean history.
Furthermore, it is an
engaging autobiography
of a dedicated leader who

The Working-class Butcher in Korean Literature

Kim Ku took Baekbum as his nickname because *Baek* means "butcher," and *bum* means "low, working-class people." Kim identified himself as a representative of farmers, day-by-day laborers, and even butchers. He wished them to be educated as much as middle-class people in order to resist Japan's occupation and achieve national liberation.

---

had a great vision for a newly emancipated country as well as a passion that transcended a personal desire for distinction. It is strongly recommended to teenagers as extra-curricula reading material and considered a "must-read" among general Korean readers who have historical consciousness.

The Postcards is a photographic edition, first published in 1993, as an accompanying volume to *Meditation in the Prison House* (1988), a hugely popular journal written by Shin Young-bok. Mr. Shin was accused of participating in the Revolutionary Party for Unification, an underground cell organization managed by a North Korean spy named Kim Jong-tae in 1968. At the time of his arrest, he was a lieutenant in service, teaching at the Military Academy. He was instantly tried by court-martial and sentenced to death by shooting in 1969. However, he was soon revealed to be just an idealist with a revolutionary mind who resisted President Park's dictatorial regime. Thus, on condition that he would not file an appeal to the Supreme Court but fill out the conversion form, his sentence was reduced to life in prison in 1970. *The Postcards* consists of a collection of 230 postcards and fragmentary notes that Shin sent to friends and family while serving twenty years in prison (1968–1988). When he began to write *Meditation in the Prison House*, an essay on his prison experiences, he says he had to resort to postcards and notes as his reference materials. The significance of *The Postcards* therefore lies in the fact that the photographs of Shin's handwriting and little drawings decorating the corners of postcards reveal the real moments when he missed his family and friends, when he struggled to maintain his sanity in a small prison cell, and when he was determined to translate a series of simple but profound awakenings into a philosophical discourse for humanity.

In some postcards, he records that in prison he faced another world where so-called outcasts and political offenders would struggle to survive their prison time. Such an awakening led him to revise his ideology-driven lifestyle and develop a new epistemological paradigm. In others, he recollects it was fortunate for him to have met Yee Ku-young, a renowned scholar of eastern philosophy, who was also arrested for being a dissident. Influenced by Yee's comprehensive knowledge of eastern philosophy and progressive socialist ideals, called *Daedong*, Shin finally formed his own philosophical discourse of interdependency and insisted on restoring the Asian frame of mind as an alternative to western individualism. Through postcards, he strove to urge the ethical duty of intellectuals by arguing that, just as water flows toward the lowest point and meets with the ocean, so intellectual leaders (high) should connect with working-class people (low) and create an ocean of social justice and political equality.

Deeply impressed by Mr. Shin's thoughts and wisdom, a wide range of readers came to revere him as a great teacher and spiritual leader. Some of them have formed a reading group called "Shinchulguimo" and read his writings religiously. Along with *The Postcards* and *Meditation*, virtually all of Shin's books have become bestsellers. This phenomenon, which is nicknamed the "Shin Young-bok Effect," is very rare in the Korean reading market. One of the visible products of this phenomenon is the publication of a book entitled *Reading Shin Young-bok Together*, to which sixty writers of various backgrounds contributed, sharing their interpretations of Shin's philosophy. In Korean lore, he is renowned for turning a twenty-year prison sentence into a blessing by unlearning abstract bookish knowledge and relearning a more profound understanding of life.

NEWSPAPERS AND MAGAZINES

Most Koreans read some type of newspaper or magazine everyday to get information. Therefore, Korean journalists are very influential opinion leaders, shaping and reshuffling public consensus. *A Cry of a Seed* was a religious monthly magazine which was founded by Hahm Suhk-heon in April 1970. The "seed" of the title symbolizes *Min-jung* (the people). Dedicating itself to the education of the masses and bringing up healthy citizens fit for a modern democratic society, the magazine featured religious essays, cultural criticism, historical reviews, and political commentaries written in an easy-to-understand vernacular style. It was cancelled after the second issue due to its critical editorial tone, but received permission to reissue in 1971. In 1980, it was again cancelled for the same reason and again resumed, voicing its radical opinions once more in 1988. When Hahm, the editor-in-chief, died in 1989, the magazine welcomed Kim Yong-jun as a new chief editor. It was cancelled and reinstated once more and published its 193rd volume in 2006.

A Cry of a Seed has political significance in that it led the enlightenment movement in the time of military dictatorship and supported the average person's right to know about the nation's political workings, encouraging them to speak out against sociopolitical injustices. It mainly circulated among the Catholics because Hahm was a Catholic priest, and yet it was also widely available to the general public at nationwide bookstores. Even though the magazine lost its power after its spiritual leader died, it carries Hahm's legacy and distinctive liberal Catholic voice.

Oh My News, an Internet-based newspaper, was founded in February 2000 by Oh Yeon-ho with a small sum of start-up money, four full-time journalists, and 727 "netizens" ("Internet citizens"). Oh, a journalist with progressive values and ideals, took "every citizen is a journalist" as the motto for his newspaper and set out to "change the world" through his innovative approach to the circulation and dissemination of news. Thus, ordinary Internet clickers who had long been passively consuming news written by professional journalists were transformed into active writers who observe all aspects of Korean society, politics, economy, culture, and living, and produce lively news, which is updated virtually on a real-time basis while an event is happening. The power of *Oh My News*, although initially doubted and then trivialized by "traditional" news organizations, astounded most Koreans, especially during the most recent Korean presidential and general elections.

Oh My News revealed that netizen-journalists, though amateurs, are patriots with a passion for democracy, who are able to produce analytical essays, investigative reports, articles, data, translations and so on whenever they notice political bias in the mainstream media news bulletins. As a result, the political propaganda that the former dictatorial regimes so successfully procured in alliance with the major newspaper organizations is no longer effective for Korean readers. The number of traditional newspaper subscribers has dropped and, consequently, the traditional concepts concerning media reporting, such as who makes and shapes news, what is news, who are journalists, and what is the standard of journalistic writing, are all undergoing radical popular change. The success of *Oh My News* has been called a "netizen revolution" and has been appreciated all the more because Korea has had such a long history of restricted speech and public discourse. Moreover, internationally prestigious news organizations such as *The New York Times, News Week, The Guardian, The Washington Post, Le Monde*, and so on have shown great interest in the interactive process and the emergence of "participatory democracy" on which *Oh My News* is based. *Oh My News* is significant not only in the history of Korean democracy but also world history, because it has created a virtual space where technology meets with civic duty and has shown how ordinary people can change their societies. Oh, the site's founder, is confident about the future of his Internet-based newspaper, believing that it will someday lead the

> **Oh My News**
>
> Doesn't "Oh My News" sound like "Oh my God"? Mr. Oh came up with that name to parody the right-wing conservative news organizations that have been posing as if they were reporting only the truth.

standard of world-wide interactive news reporting and consumption.

Changbi, which is a literary magazine, is an abbreviation of *Changjahk and Bipyong* (*Creative Writing and Criticism*). Korean-born but U.S.-educated Paik Nak-chung issued the first volume in 1966. He recalls that he felt oppressed by the conservative atmosphere of American society and academia during his stay in the United States and wanted to make some contribution to Korean literary and intellectual circles. Corresponding with his friends, he formed an idea of founding a liberal quarterly magazine for sophisticated readers. Fortunately, he had some rich, liberal-minded friends, and with their financial support he began issuing *Changbi* and remapped Korean intellectual geography.

Considering the political period in which *Changbi* was launched, the magazine had a huge impact on literature, journalism, and contemporary history in Korea. Under the leadership of Paik, Yom Mu-woong, and Kim Yun-su, the journal inherited the beloved poet Han Yong-un's nationalist spirit and introduced new novelists, poets, and scholars who would disseminate liberal or even radical ideas and expand cultural boundaries. Yet, the magazine's most important achievement is its support of Korean history professor Lee Young-hee's *Logic in a Transitional Period* (1974), which became a huge bestseller and instantly earned him the title "the father of dissidents." Lee's rational criticism of the Park regime's Cold War mentality, and his objective description of communist regimes such as China and North Korea, not only shocked college students and politically oriented readers but also awakened them to a new approach to the political tensions surrounding the Korean peninsula.

In 1975, *Changbi* was forced to close down due to political pressure but its publishing company, Changi, managed to survive the military dictatorship by publishing separate volumes of academic and cultural reading. Finally, in 1988 *Chanbi* magazine was reissued and resumed voicing its liberal ideals. In 2006 it celebrated its fortieth birthday. It is now extending its edgy criticism, exploring the urgent issues of environmentalism, neo-liberalism, the future of leftist discourses, and the possibility of global civilization. Since its first appearance, *Changbi* has maintained its influential position, introducing new literature and raising readers' awareness of right-wing conservative agendas in all forms.

POLITICAL TEXTS: SPEECHES AND LECTURES

Due to the country's turbulent political history, political speeches and lectures are regarded very highly in Korea. They have inspired Koreans to fight for freedom, democracy, and world peace. The March 1 Declaration of Independence was drafted by Choi Nam-seon in the name of thirty-three representatives of Korea, including Sohn Byung-hee, Han Yong-un, and Oh Seh-chang, during the Japanese occupation. The political situation surrounding the declaration was urgent: U.S. president Woodrow Wilson's declaration of the principle of self-determination of peoples in 1918 and the Paris Peace Conference in 1919 encouraged Korea's leaders to revive their hopes for independence. In the meantime, on February 8, 1919 about six hundred Korean students, who were studying in various Japanese educational institutions, announced the February 8 Declaration of Independence. Hearing that many of them had been wounded and arrested, Korea's leaders, moved by the students' patriotism, decided to make a formal declaration of independence, announcing the justness of the Korean people's petition to the world. Thus Mr. Choi, while maintaining the basic logic and argument of the February 8 declaration, softened the aggressive tone somewhat and emphasized a peaceful process for the independence of Korea.

Specifically, the March 1 Declaration of Independence states four logical reasons that fueled the demand for Korea's freedom. First, the declaration asserts that the Korean people had strong pride for their long history of maintaining Korean racial identity. Second, it indicates that the Korean people did not intend to insult the Japanese race but would only ask for their inalienable rights to establish a free, independent nation that would secure their happiness. Third, it appeals to the world that Korea's independence was necessary not just for Korean people but for all Asian people. It also points out that Korea's independence would secure peace in the Asian region and make a significant contribution to the development of world civilization. Fourth, it declares that the Korean people's resistance activities were not temporary outbursts but would continue until Korea was secured as a free, independent state.

Mr. Choi's draft was then signed by thirty-three representatives and sent to Yee Jong-il, who printed twenty-one thousand copies. These copies were distributed nationwide to activists and declared simultaneously in the major cities of Korea. In Seoul, Han Yong-un, one of the thirty-three representatives, solemnly read the Declaration of Independence in the main office and those who were gathering there gave three cheers for Korea's freedom. At the Pagoda Park, Jeong Jae-yong read the declaration in front of five thousand ordinary Korean people. The Declaration of Independence clearly had a major impact on the systematic deployment of subsequent resistance activities. It is such an important speech that it is included in Korean literature and history curricula for middle and high school students. Students in some schools are required to memorize the entire speech.

The Sunshine Policy was an engagement policy toward North Korea, recognizing it as a legitimate nation for the first time in South Korean history and promising to continue South Korea's humanitarian help for North Korea in terms of economic aid and sports and cultural exchanges. This move is the result not only of President Kim's long-cherished vision of the reunification of two Koreas but also of South Koreans' long-held wish for reunion with their family members and relatives still living in North Korea. President Kim was awarded a Nobel Peace Prize for his humanitarian effort.

Major Korean mass media covered President Kim's Nobel-prize-winning "Sunshine Policy" lecture and broadcast it in real time as well as in a taped format.

Most Korean people welcomed President Kim's Nobel Peace Prize award and were very proud of Korea's honor, but some right-wing conservative politicians and newspaper editorials

President Kim's Sunshine Policy

Do you know why President Kim came up with the name "sunshine"? He wanted to emphasize that geopolitical issues surrounding the Korean peninsula should be approached from a viewpoint of not the cold, ideological war but the sunshiny, warm, humanistic engagement.

tried to defame him. Even though his speech hasn't made the reading list, his "Sunshine Policy" is regarded as one of the major, historic, political decisions that have drastically changed the destiny of Korea and the mindset of the Koreans. President Kim still exerts a great political influence in the time of presidential election, and his words are still quoted in high school curricula on Korean history and in political magazines.

CREATIVE TEXTS: NOVELS

Though the reading market has been declining, some writers have always made it to the bestseller lists and have continued to attract readers. When these writers publish new works, they attract media attention that also boosts their sales. Choi In-hoon's 1961 novel *The Plaza* tells the story of a young intellectual, Yee Myong-joon, who goes through radical changes from the emancipation in 1945 through to the end of the Korean War in 1953. The novel depicts the reality of partition in the Korean peninsula and its tragic ramifications for individual lives, using the stream of consciousness technique. The story of Myong-joon's passage through one of Korea's most difficult social and political periods represents Korean history in a symbolic way: he loses both parents as a result of the ideological cleansing of South Korea and later becomes disillusioned and disenchanted with the authoritarianism of North Korea, which he once thought to be an ideal socialist country. He then meets his South Korean friend face-to-face in the Korean War as an enemy, becomes a POW, and finally commits suicide. It is a charismatic book about a personal quest for truce in the battle of life, loaded with philosophical speculation about the nature of ideology and deep meditation on the relationship between what is private and what is public.

After it was published in 1960, *The Plaza* is said to have been corrected by the author five times. It became a permanent best seller in the Korean book market, and it is on junior high and high school reading lists. *The Plaza* is significant in the literary history of Korea because it was the first long novel to deal with the subject of partition, the frenzy of the Korean War, and its aftermath. Digging deep in the closed system of ideological thinking and yet excavating the individual life suffocated and squeezed in the mannerist, authoritarian, power-oriented society, the novel skillfully maintains the balance between high-brow intellectualism and public appeal. In *The Plaza* readers can feel empathy with the intensity of the hero's inner struggle and his choice to find peace in death.

The theme of social injustice is continued in Cho Seh-hee's 1984 novel *A Little Ball Launched by a Dwarf*, which combines twelve stories in one volume, of which the fourth is the most popular and widely read. It tells a story of a low-class family's anger and frustration, living in an urban slum named "Haengbok (Happiness)-dong, Nahkwon (Paradise)-ku" of Seoul in the 1970s. Written in three parts, this story is narrated by three siblings, Young-su, Young-ho, and Young-hee, each of whom brings a social charge against inhumane, capital-oriented wealthy developers and speculators. The story revolves around a single family. The father is a dwarf, who has been trying to make a living through manual labor. He finally falls off the roof of a brick-making factory, while flying a paper plane and shooting a small iron ball toward the Moon. The mother replaces her husband and repeats the cycle of poverty and suffering. The elder son works at a printing house and joins the labor union, while a second son works at a small electrical shop. The family's daughter is sexually abused by a rich land-speculator but manages to retrieve the ballot to an apartment flat that her family once sold to the speculator.

All these socially alienated characters' stories suggest the author's insight into the irony of modern democratic society, in whose capitalist economic system the have-nots are structurally destined to be defeated, ruled, and exploited. This story of urban laborers still resonates not only for Korean society, but also for other capitalist societies around the world. Since its first publication in 1978, Cho Seh-hee's book has sold more than eight hundred and seventy thousand copies and was made into a film in 1981. It is reported that it is due to be remade and also dramatized on TV sometime in the near future. At a banquet in honor of his novel, Mr. Cho commented that contemporary Korean society still has a long road ahead in order to solve social conflicts between the haves and the have-nots. His novel has clearly reached classic status for Korean readers, and the main character, a forty-six-inch, seventy-pound dwarf named Kim Bool-yee has became a cultural

> **Literary Injuries**
>
> It is reported that many people who read *A Little Ball Launched by a Dwarf* got hurt by falling from their roofs. Why? They were trying to shoot the iron ball just as the dwarf did.

icon who still speaks to countless poor urban laborers, standing on the roof with a paper plane in one hand and an iron ball in the other.

Historical novels are also popular among Korean readers. Cho Jung-rae's ten-volume epic, *The Tae-baek Mountain Range*, was written over a four-year period, from 1986 to 1989. *The Tae-baek Mountain Range* illuminates the five-year time period from 1948 to 1953, during which the seemingly temporary partition of the Korean peninsula was turned into a permanent reality. It also spotlights the "Yeosoon Rebellion" that occurred in October 1948. The Rebellion broke out when a lieutenant colonel of the 14th brigade disobeyed the military command to quell the Jeju Civilian Insurrection on April 3, 1948. The "rebels" were suppressed within a week, but the core members, forming an alliance with regional members of Namroh-dang (the South Korean Communist Party) and angry farming civilians, retreated deep into the mountain range and kept up a series of guerilla attacks. *The Tae-baek Mountain Range* begins at this point of retreat, and Cho Jung-rae conducts a literary investigation into the nature of the Yeosoon Rebellion and its ramifications, the ensuing Korean War, and the eventual partition of the Korean peninsula. The main characters represent the political position of the ideological groups to which each belongs, such as the pro-North Korean communist group, pro-U.S. militias, a right-wing youth group, pro-Japanese landowners, nationalist landowners, and the conscientious intelligentsia. Some minor characters also play memorable roles, adding humor and romance to the tragic story line of the novel.

Just as the Tae-baek Mountain Range forms the spine of South Korea with many small ranges extending westwards from it, Cho observes how Korean history extends from the "spine" of the Yeosoon Rebellion. He explains how the initial idea of a "temporary" division of the Korean peninsula exceeded the imagination of international trustee members: the trusteeship of two Koreas elicited a wide range of ideological struggles, class conflicts, and political entanglements, which eventually affected the national psychology of the Korean people and made the division of the Korean peninsula an irreversible reality. Since its publication, *The Tae-baek Mountain Range* has been hugely popular among Korean readers, selling more than four million copies and making the must-read list. It is also critically acclaimed and greatly appreciated by fellow writers and academic scholars, who consider Mr. Cho a potential recipient of the Nobel Prize for Literature.

As a result of his dedication to the portrayal of Korea's unique political reality, Mr. Cho has produced a testimony to how deeply the Korean psyche has been scarred over time. *Arirang* (1990), anoth-

> **A Literary "Giant"**
>
> When all of Cho's manuscripts are stacked up, the tower is higher than Mr. Cho himself. He even took a photograph of himself next to his stack. Furthermore, Mr. Cho wrote all his manuscripts by hand, and is justifiably proud of his output.

er historical saga, also became a bestseller, selling about three million copies. In 2003, all twelve volumes of *Arirang* were translated into French. Evidently, this is the first time a Korean novelist has had two epic narratives reach a one hundredth printing in the country's publishing history.

The personal and the historical are combined in Park Wan-suh's 1992 autobiographical novel, *Who Ate All Those Sing-ahs?* The book describes the dissolution of a happy family as a result of Korea's turbulent history. Park recalls the blissful days of her childhood in a hamlet named Pakjuhk-gol, which is located in the current North Korean province. She depicts how her dignified, patrician mother had to endure the losses of not only her intelligent son, the pride and joy of her life, but also her wealth during the Korean War. Park describes how she survived her mother's snubbing and the indifference and ingratitude of her neighbors while working at the PX in the Yong-sahn U.S. army base. It is a story of family love, human decency, and individual empowerment, written in a simple, unpretentious, and yet heart-felt style with concrete, lively images and ordinary analogies familiar to its readers. Since its publication in 1992, it has consistently made the bestseller list, selling 1.5 million copies so far. It is currently on the middle school reading list. Park has always been a prolific

> **Park Wan-suh**
>
> Mrs. Park, one of the representative Korean writers, became a novelist by chance. At the age of forty, Park sent her manuscript to a contest sponsored by a woman's monthly magazine for a monetary prize. She won first prize, and the rest is history.

writer and is considered one of the top novelists, with strong selling power even in a fairly flat literary market. Most of her works have made the best seller list, impressing readers with humor, wit, and a seasoned wisdom on life.

POETRY

Poetry in Korea tends toward the political and nationalistic. Given that the peninsula has endured almost continual political upheaval over the last two centuries, it is not surprising that Korean readers have embraced poetry that reflects their nationalistic and ideological passions. Kim Ji-ha's *With a Burning Thirst* is one such collection of poems. "With a Burning Thirst" is also the title poem of Kim Ji-ha's second collection. This collection was published in 1982, after Kim was finally released from prison. The collection rails against presidents Park and Chun's military dictatorship and cries out passionately for democracy. Both dictators acquired their power through a *coup d'état* and ran their military dictatorship with brutal firmness. Many intellectuals, who had been hoping for a democratic government after the death of President Park, were stunned and stupefied at military dictator Chun's brutal suppression of the Kwangju students' demonstration in 1980. Many students and citizens were killed by national guards, and a hope for the new democracy evaporated as South Korea was once again under the control of a more oppressive military dictator. Kim had publicly announced his position on Korean democracy, saying, "What I ask and fight for is absolute democracy, complete freedom of speech—nothing less, nothing more," and he used his poems to further inspire the public to hold out hope for permanent democracy in their time. Kim repeatedly called for freedom from dictatorship, literally "with a burning thirst." This poem reveals Kim's unwavering determination to stay strong in the face of national pain. Readers instantly responded to his call by adding a melody

> **A Literary Family**
>
> Mr. Kim is the son-in-law of Mrs. Park Kyong-ni, who is one of the representative novelists of Korea. If asked, his wife might feel hard to answer which work she likes more, her mother's novels or her husband's poems.

to his poem and singing it in various political meetings and demonstrations. This poem occupies a significant place in the history of the Korean democratic struggle.

The Dawn of a Laborer is a collection of poems written by a laborer turned poet, Park Noh-hae, and published in 1984. The poet's first name "Noh-hae" is a penname made by using the two initials of "Noh-dong-Hae-bahng" (Laborers' Freedom from Exploitation). His poems harshly criticize the working conditions in factories and the exploitative attitudes of the owners and capitalists. His cry for human rights for laborers is in a way the extension of another laborer activist, Jeon Tae-il, who burnt himself to death in November 1970, crying out "We are not machines. Apply the labor standard law to us. Do not brush off my death." This incident—a man choosing an excruciating death over unjust working conditions—shocked many Koreans and awakened them to the depths of labor exploitation that were being exercised under, but overlooked by, the dictatorial Park regime. Fourteen years later the situation hadn't changed, as Park suggests in his poems: the laborers still worked from dawn until late at night and often all night without extra compensation; they were often hurt by the machines or made sick from inhaling dangerous chemicals; they often worked without medical assistance, and had no breaks except for a single meal time. Nonetheless, they were still afraid of filing complaints because of the risk of being fired. They therefore accepted their circumstances and continued living their hard lives, numbing their anger and frustration by drinking hard liquor called So-ju.

As a result of his public stand and the radical content of his poems, Mr. Park was put on the black list of the dictatorial government of Chun Doo-hwan and was finally imprisoned for his activities as the leader of the Socialist Labor Association. His poetry is significant in that it represented the lived reality of laborers from a laborer's point of view. His poetic imagination was as refined as that of a professional poet, and for that reason his poetry astounded even many intellectuals and writers. After he became a renowned poet, his spirit of resistance and raw outcry mellowed somewhat. Nonetheless, those hard-working factory laborers who have to work from dawn till night still identify with the first line of "The Dawn of a Laborer,"

> **Park Noh-hae**
>
> Mr. Park was once a bus driver. It is reported that he quit the job when he began to identify customers' faces with bus coins. He later said that he had been disgusted at himself for turning into a part of a capitalist machine.

which describes the despair surrounding endless work and great poverty. He is still widely read and respected, and his books of poetry are still in print and available at nationwide bookstores.

CONCLUSION

In conclusion, the cultural history of Korean reading cannot be explained without understanding the five-thousand-year history of Korea. In particular, it should be noted that, after surviving their own turbulent political history, most Koreans have become accustomed to investing their energy and time more on building economic foundations than in reading serious books and magazines. Actually, according to a Gallop Poll in 2000, more than fifty percent of Korean readers said that they prefer light novels or personal essays, and about sixteen percent liked to read historical narratives. Since 2000, this reading trend has been strengthened by the rapid development of Internet technology in Korea. However, despite the decline of the traditional reading market, the future of the Korean reading culture seems bright. As some say, a desire for reading is as strong as a desire for food, and Korean readers will continue to develop their own reading practices. Already, promising news is reported that a number of serious readers meet at Internet reading cafes or specified Internet reading clubs; they share their readings and debates by tagging blogs or doing "Cy." Furthermore, TV programs such as *Neukimpyo*, *TV Speaks for Books, Recovering the Way of Reading Aloud*, and *A Woman Who Reads Books* are playing a role, encouraging TV watchers to stop by neighborhood bookstores or to log on to Internet bookstores. In the coming year, Internet bloggers and "cyers" will emerge as leaders, shaping Korean reading trends and supporting a new generation of writers.

> **Cy World**
>
> "Cy" is an abbreviation of "Cy World," the most popular Korean Internet service portal in terms of homepage management. Cy World offers Internet users an easy-to-create mini-homepage service. Reportedly, cyers (people who avidly manage their homepages) make pseudo-kinship with other cyers and form Internet communities based upon the traditional notion of family.

RECOMMENDED READING

Choi Sun-yeol. *Modern Korean Poetry*. Seoul: Mineum, 1989.

Jang Hoh-sun. *There Is Hope for Small-Scale Medias*. Seoul: Gaema-Gohwon, 2001.

Jung Jin-suhk. *The Media and Modern Korean History*. Seoul: Communications, 2002.

Juhn Kwang-yong et al. *The History of Modern Korean Novels*. Seoul: Mineum, 1984.

Kang Jun-mahn. *Lee Young-hee, Torch Bearer of Modern Korean History*. Seoul: Gaema-Gohwon, 2004.

Korean Printing Institute. *Report on the History of Korean Printing and Publishing*. http://www.kpri.or.kr/.

Nam Tae-woo and Kim Joong-kwon. *The History of Reading in Korea: From Three Kingdoms to Joseon*. Daegu: Tae-il, 2004.

Yun Hyeong-du, ed. *The Photographic History of Books*. Seoul: Beomwoo, 1997.

PRIMARY SOURCES

Cho Jung-are. *Arirang*. 12 vols. Seoul: Haenaem, 1994–95.

———. *The Tae-baek Mountain Range*. 10 vols. Seoul: Haenaem, 1986–89.

Cho Seh-hee. *A Little Ball Launched by a Dwarf*. Seoul: Munjie, 1984.

Choi In-hoon. *The Plaza*. Seoul: Munjie, 1961.

Choi Namseon. "The March 1 Declaration of Independence." *Best Writings of Korea*. Seoul: Wolganchosun, 2001.

Hahm Suhk-heon. *A Cry of a Seed*. Seoul: Sshial, 1970–present.

Huh Kyun. *Hongkildong-jeon*. Translated by Jeong Jong-muk. Seoul: Changbi, 2003.

Il Yeon. *Samgukyusah*. Translated by Kim Won-joong. Seoul: Euleu, 2002.

Kim Bu-shik. *Samguksaki*. Translated by Yee Kang-rae. 2 vols. Seoul: Hankil, 1998.

Kim Dae-jung. "2006 Nobel Lecture on the Sunshine Policy." *Towards the Peaceful Reunification of Koreas: Major Speeches and Lectures of President Kim Dae-jung*. Seoul: Kimdaejung Peace Foundation, 2007.

Kim Gwang-chol et al., trans. & ed. *Goryo History*. 30 vols. Pusan: Donga UP, 2007.

Kim Hoon. *A Song of a Sword*. Seoul: Saenggakeuynamu, 2001.

Kim Ji-ha. *With a Burning Thirst*. Seoul: Changbi, 1982.

Kim Ku. *Baekbum Ilzy*. Seoul: Seomundang, 2000.

Kim Mahn-joong. *Kuwoonmong*. Translated by Song Seong-wuk. Seoul: Mineum, 2003.

———. *Sahssinamjeongki*. Translated by Hah Seong-ran. Seoul: Changbi, 2006.

King Sehjong. "Hunminjeongeum." *Study of Hunminjeongeum*. Translated by Kim Suhk-hwan. Seoul: Hanshin, 1997.

King Sehjong Memorial Foundation & Minjok Munhwa Association, trans. & ed. *Record of Joseon Kings*. 413 vols. www.chosunsillok.org, www.minchu.or.kr.

Kim Shie-seup. *Keumohshinhwa*. Translated by Shim Kyong-hoh. Seoul: Hongik, 2000.

———. *Seokbosangjeol*. Translated by Kim Young-bae. Seoul: Iljogak, 1972.

———. *Wolinchongangjigok*. Translated by Jeong Chan-ju. Seoul: Booktopia, 2003.

Lee Young-hee. *Logic in a Transitional Period*. Seoul: Changbi, 1974.

Oh Yeon-ho. *Oh My News*. http://www.ohmynews.com.

Paik Nak-chung. *Chanbi: A Quarterly Literary Magazine*. Seoul: Chanbi, 1960–present.

Park Noh-hae. *The Dawn of a Laborer*. Seoul: Pulbit, 1984.

Park Wan-suh. *Who Ate All the Sing-ahs?* Seoul: Woongjin, 1992.

Shin Young-bok. *Meditation in the Prison House*. Seoul: Dolbaegae, 1998.

———. *The Postcards*. Seoul: Dolbaegae, 2003.

Won Hyo. *Daeseung Kyshinron*. Translated by Yee Hong-woo. Seoul: Kimyoungsa, 2006.

———. *Keumgahng Sahmmaekyongron*. Translated by Eun Jeong-hee. Seoul: Ilzy, 2000.

Yee Soon-shin. *Nanjung Ilky*. Translated by Noh Seung-suhk. Seoul: Dongah Ilbo, 2005.

SECONDARY SOURCES

Choi Sun-yeol. *Modern Korean Poetry*. Seoul: Mineum, 1989.

Jang Hoh-sun. *There Is Hope for Small-Scale Medias*. Seoul: Gaema-Gohwon, 2001.

Jeong Euy-haeng. *Understanding Korean Buddhism through Renowned Monks*. Seoul: Milal, 2001.

Juhn Kwang-yong et al. *The History of Modern Korean Novels*. Seoul: Mineum, 1984.

Jung Jin-suhk. *The Media and Modern Korean History*. Seoul: Communications, 2002.

Kang Jun-mahn. *Lee Young-hee, Torch Bearer of Modern Korean History*. Seoul: Gaema-Gohwon, 2004.

———. *Walking Through Contemporary Korean History*. 3 vols. Seoul: Inmul & Sasang, 2002.

Kang Mahn-kil. *Correction of Modern Korean History*. Seoul: Changbi, 1994.

Keum Jang-tae. *The History of Confucianism in Korea*. Seoul: Hangukhaksuljeongbo, 2003.

Kim Young-min. *The Critical History of Modern Korean Literature*. Seoul: Somyong, 1999.

———. *The Critical History of Contemporary Korean Literature*. Seoul: Somyong, 2000.

Kim Yun-shik. *The History of Korean Novels*. Seoul: Munhakdongneh, 2000.

Korean Printing Institute. *Report on the History of Korean Printing and Publishing*. http://www.kpri.or.kr/.

Nam Tae-woo and Kim Joong-kwon. *The History of Reading in Korea: From Three Kingdoms to Joseon*. Daegu: Tae-il, 2004.

Oh She-young. *A Study of Modern and Contemporary Korean Poets*. Seoul: Wolin, 2003.

Park Jong-ki. *Goryo History: Five Hundred Years*. Seoul: Pureunyuksa, 1999.

Park Kie-heon. *Magazine and Publishing in Korea*. Seoul: Neulpureunsonamu, 2003.

Yee Duk-il. *Real Korean History*. Seoul: Humanist, 2003.

Yee Sang-tae. *Understanding Joseon History*. Seoul: Garam, 2000.

Yun Hyeong-du, ed. *The Photographic History of Books*. Seoul: Beomwoo, 1997.

CHAPTER 17

Australia and New Zealand

Alison Bartlett

TIMELINE

1788	"First Fleet" of British convicts lands at Sydney Cove, Australia
1840	*Treaty of Waitangi*, British annexation of New Zealand/*Aoreatoa*
1841	New Zealand officially declared a crown colony
1868	New Zealand becomes first country in the world to give indigenous peoples the vote; the last convicts are transported to Australia
1876	The last full-blooded Tasmanian Aboriginal, Truganini, dies
1890s	Economic depression, unionization, flourishing nationalism
1893	New Zealand becomes first country in the world to give women the vote
1901	Australian Federation begins
1907	New Zealand independence from Britain
1914	World War I: Australian and New Zealand troops suffer heavy losses at ANZAC (Australia, New Zealand Army Corps) Cove in Turkey
1939–45	World War II: Australian troops in Europe, North Africa, and the Pacific
1947	Post-war immigration from Europe to Australia begins
1951	ANZUS Pact established between New Zealand, Australia, and the United States
1965	Australia supports United States with troops in Vietnam War
1971	Neville Bonner becomes the first Aboriginal to be a member of Parliament
1975	The Treaty of Waitangi Act (New Zealand); Australian Prime Minister Gough Whitlam was fired from his post by Governor General John Kerr
1981	Asian immigration to Australia increases
1985	New Zealand refuses port entry to a U.S. nuclear warship, breaking the ANZUS Pact, and establishing itself as the world's first antinuclear country

1988	Australia's bicentenary: the new Parliament House opens in Canberra
2002	Bombing of Sari Nightclub in Bali—eighty-eight Australians killed
2004	Car bomb explodes outside of the Australian Embassy in Jakarta, Indonesia, killing nine people

INTRODUCTION TO THE REGION

Situated in the Southern Hemisphere, the islands comprising Australia and New Zealand supported indigenous oral cultures who, until the nineteenth century, read the land and sea for their histories and stories, accompanied by complex song, dance, and ceremonials. Although both Australia and New Zealand were sited and marked on maps by the Portuguese, Spanish, French, and Dutch, they were claimed for King George III as part of the British Empire by Captain James Cook. Australia was used as a penal colony to alleviate the overflowing British prisons full of petty thieves from the underclass, with the First Fleet of ships sailing into Sydney Cove to establish settlement in 1788.

"Transportation," as the practice of sending convicts from Britain to Australia was known, continued until 1848. The penal system, and the convicts who characterized it, dominated early Australian life. The island colony operated as a jail, surrounded by ocean and dominated by the island's massive internal desert. Regardless of their efforts to escape, the convicts were prisoners of the landscape; "liberty" was no safer than incarceration for those who failed to understand the rugged Australian bush. Some free settlers had arrived along with the convict ships, but every feature of the country was alien to British experience and sensibilities: the soil would not grow English vegetables; the trees would not respond to British felling and carpentry techniques; and the animals would not respond to English cooking practices. Life was extremely hard for convict and settler alike, and was made more difficult by incompetent administration and ambiguous social class lines.

The new arrivals were also mystified by the indigenous peoples. The "savages" of "New South Wales" were widely thought to be uncivilized and little separated from the island's strange animals. But it was the settlers and convicts who were struggling to survive, while the despised "aborigines" had a perfect grasp of the land and its possibilities. Often, European explorers perished precisely because they refused to accept Aboriginal help or learn from Aboriginal practices.

When the British Parliament voted to stop the practice of transportation in 1848, Australia ceased to be a penal colony and instead began to operate as a new nation colony, which continued to be controlled and administered by Britain until 1901. At this point, administrative responsibility shifted to the newly formed Australian Parliament, and the nation became a member of the British Commonwealth. The country developed into a mature nation, supported by rich agricultural, pastoral, and mining industries, as well as extensive administrative systems.

Throughout its development, however, Australia remained ideologically and culturally very close to Britain. Australia followed Britain's political lead and declared war on Germany just hours after the beginning of both the First and Second World Wars. Sixty-one thousand Australian troops perished in World War I, and forty thousand troops were lost during World War II. Culturally, Australia adopted very British traditions and customs. For example, despite celebrating Christmas at the height of the Australian summer, Australians persist with the northern tradition of the full, hot "baked dinner," complete with plum pudding and hot custard.

In the 1950s, Australia accepted hundreds of thousands of post-War European immigrants. Many of these immigrants came from Britain on "assisted passage" tickets, but many came from Greece, Italy, and Yugoslavia—three of the most battle-scarred European nations. The influx of non-English speaking families helped to broaden Australia's cultural outlook. "Australians" were no longer only people with Anglo-Irish ancestry. By the time of the country's bicentenary in 1988, Australians were as likely to eat pizza as they were to eat roast beef, drink wine instead of beer or tea, and read books by Aboriginal author Sally Morgan in place of books by Charles Dickens or Agatha Christie.

The "Britishness" of Australia and Australians became the focus of national soul-searching. At about the time of the bicentenary, Australians collectively adopted the idea of "multiculturalism" and thought of themselves as a nation within the Asian sphere, rather than as an outpost of British culture and influence. In fact, after World War II, Australians began to identify just as closely with the United States, especially given the U.S. presence in the Pacific during the war.

In the twenty-first century, Australia has been coming to terms with another national issue: the responsibility of white Australians for the history (and continuation) of violence against indigenous Aboriginal peoples. Aboriginal peoples were actively persecuted and their voices drowned out for most of Australia's post-colonial history, but the building of a politically aware and active Aboriginal lobby since the bicentenary has resulted in the raising of white awareness and acceptance of responsibility for the treatment of Aboriginals.

Two events consolidated this change in public opinion. The first was Eddie Mabo's successful application to overturn the colonial title law of *terra nullius* ("empty land") on which Britain's colonization of Australia rested. In 1992, the High Court of Australia agreed with Mabo's claim that the indigenous people of Murray Island (in the Torres Strait) should have "Native Title" to their traditional land. The "Mabo decision," as it came to be known, reshaped Australian culture and influenced the rewriting, rethinking, and reteaching of Australian history.

The Mabo decision occurred during the long Labor Party administration, which began in 1983 and lasted until 1996. When the more conservative Liberal Party took office in 1996, parliamentary concern for Aboriginal issues was once again pushed to the political margins. However, in 2006 Labor was re-elected, and the new prime minister, Kevin Rudd, vowed that Australia would officially apologize to the Aboriginal peoples for over two hundred years of prejudice and injustice. The combination of the Aboriginal people's perseverance and sustained demand that their history and legitimacy be recognized, and white political and social efforts to understand and work with Aboriginal groups, has characterized Australia's most recent cultural transformation toward true multicultural self-recognition.

In contrast to the Australian colonial experience, white whalers, sealers, traders, and missionaries set up on New Zealand (*Aotearoa*) from the late 1700s onward, and various deals were made to "purchase" tracts of land from the indigenous inhabitants. The local Maori were warriors, and in the South Island the trading of flax for guns manifested something of an arms race, with some groups relocating as a result of inter-tribal "musket wars" in the early decades of the nineteenth century. Although some efforts were made by the colonizers (or *pakeha*) to assuage Maori chiefs about their ongoing sovereignty (*rangatiratanga*), the *Treaty of Waitangi*, which was drawn up in 1840, finally assured British annexation of land despite assurances to the five hundred chiefs who signed that their authority as chiefs was uninterrupted. The New Zealand Company, formed by Edward Wakefield the year before, began promoting land ownership to potential immigrants, and a system of colonization was implemented through which Pakeha gained increased authority. A settler parliament was established through the New Zealand Constitution Act of 1852, and Maori land and cultural sovereignty was gradually eroded despite attempts at alternative authority systems such as the King movement and the Maori parliament.

New Zealand has therefore experienced its own history of colonial push and pull between the descendants of the first white settlers and the indigenous Maori people. The resulting tensions have often flared into outright confrontation, as the Maori representatives feel that the proper and legal settling of the Waitangi Treaty promises is long overdue. In the meantime, New Zealand has emerged as a modern nation with strong tourism and wool and sheep industries. Recently, the country's move into the fields of cinema and cinema operations have also brought the region international attention.

READING TRENDS AND PRACTICES

An account of convict life in Australia was first written almost a century after the "First Fleet" of convicts arrived there: the novel *For the Term of His Natural Life*, by Marcus Clarke (1874). However, biblical texts were the main source of reading for the first generations of colonizers. Christian missionaries not only brought texts with them but also played a key role in circulating and producing texts. The Maori are reputed to have been enthusiastic about written literacy after British explorer Captain James Cook began writing down their words in 1769. Following the practices of other colonized islands across the Pacific (such as Tahiti and Hawaii), New Zealand missionaries collected lists of native words, which were published as books in London and Sydney as early as 1814. Translations of parts of the Bible, hymns, and prayers into Maori were then published and distributed, and the first local printing press was installed in 1834. The consumption of Maori texts far outweighed the contemporary corollary consumption of newspapers by pakeha at this time.

The indigenous Australian population was not so lucky. There was little effort to record any of the hundreds of indigenous languages before the twentieth century, when many had already died from introduced disease, maltreatment, and massacre. Government efforts at "protectionism" during the early twentieth century meant collecting Aboriginal people from their homelands and imprisoning them in missions and reserves, where language groups became mixed or indigenous languages were forbidden. As a result, hundreds of indigenous languages have been lost or fallen into disuse.

Although a printing press did arrive with the First Fleet in Sydney, nobody could use it until some time later when a convict, George Howe, began to print government ordinances. When he was pardoned, he set up his own newspaper in 1803, the *Sydney Gazette*. Local reading content was largely restricted to newspapers, and Australia is noted as an avid consumer of newspapers, many of which included local poetry and creative writing. Australian and New Zealand printers had to import paper and then produce copy, so it was cheaper to import the more familiar periodicals and books from England, which were thought to be superior in quality anyway. *Punch* and the *Illustrated London News* were represented as sought-after reading, and ladies' journals were established and imported later in the century. "Free settler" colonies (in contrast to penal colonies) were established in Western Australia in 1829 and South Australia in 1836 (by Edward Wakefield, who then capitalized on selling New Zealand to immigrants). The cultural status attached to private libraries meant that wealthy British families who moved to the colonies brought with them the established icons of their culture: the complete works of Shakespeare, Tennyson, the Romantic poets, Robert Burns, and of course the family Bible was particularly common in Protestant families. Later, Dickens, Walter Scott, and Thackeray were added to the library shelves as they became available, as were *Pilgrim's Progress* and *Uncle Tom's Cabin* from the United States. Book clubs were formed among white settlers as early as 1824 in Australia as a method of circulating texts, and by the end of that century there were hundreds of circulating libraries operating by subscription in schools of art, mechanics' institutes, athenaeums, and literary institutes in Australia and New Zealand. Free lending libraries, the harbingers of municipally run and state libraries, began to emerge in the Australian capital cities from the 1850s and in New Zealand soon after. These were inspired by the British Museum model and were supported by the colonial governments, which often provided boxes of books to the circulating libraries.

Although there had been a steady market in England for books *about* the Australian and New Zealand experience, they were regarded—and written—as curiosities about romanticized and exotic antipodean colonies of the British Empire. It wasn't until the 1880s that nationalist fervor began popularizing more authentic, home-grown products. The Sydney-based *Bulletin* newspaper is remembered for being instrumental in promoting a "typical" Australian genre of reading, encouraging contributors of poetry, sketches, and short stories and serializing novels in its pages. It even published books, as it did for Steele Rudd's comical stories of pioneering life, *On Our Selection*. This was a concerted effort to shake off the derivative English culture imported to the colonies and to create a distinctly local cultural identity, including New Zealand contributions, which comprised an estimated 10 percent of items published between 1890 and 1900. Combining the bookselling and publishing businesses, the firm of Angus & Robertson began in 1888 to capitalize on the call for Australian-content books for the local market. Along with school textbooks, histories, and the enormously popular cookbooks, they published writers and works that had been popularized by the *Bulletin*, including A. B. "Banjo" Paterson's poetry collection, *The Man from Snowy River* (1895), and Henry Lawson's short stories in *While the Billy Boils* (1896). School textbooks also began to appear in New Zealand at this time, becoming the backbone of local publishers such as George Whitcombe.

The nationalism of the 1890s was in part due to the social unrest of the period. Suffering from economic downturn and the depression of the 1890s, the decade was marked by the formation of unions, massive strikes, poverty, and an entire generation of men leaving the city and their families to look for itinerant work in the country. This was accompanied by a wave of idealism emerging in the form of radical socialist and feminist ideas: Australia and New Zealand were among the first nations to recognize (white) women's suffrage, although this is thought to have been linked to the current scientific ideas and social anxiety about racial purity extrapolated from Charles Darwin's work. The decade also led to the Federation of Australia in 1901, whereby all the six states and two territories joined to form a federal government. New Zealand became independent of Britain in 1907. Both countries maintain the ruling English monarch as their head of state, represented in each country by an appointed governor general.

During the early twentieth century, a great deal of reading matter is still remembered as having been imported from overseas: Walter Scott, H. G. Wells, and Rudyard Kipling are remembered as being available, as are Jules Verne, Jane Austen, Anthony Trollope, Thomas Hardy, the Brontës, and P. G. Wodehouse.

Libraries were set up in workplaces to improve workers' education in the early twentieth century, especially in big companies such as mining firms, banks, department stores, and railways. This phenomenon coincided with the introduction of the forty-hour week and expectations of increased leisure time. Although the company libraries were supposed to help "improve" workers' knowledge and education through nonfiction and literature, many readers used them to acquire the latest westerns, adventures, and romances instead. The spread of suburbia in the 1930s and 1940s, the growth of an urban middle class, and the development of a mass market was accompanied by a surge of rental libraries in shopping centers that had no welfare mandate but were purely commercial. The introduction of the *Australian Woman's Weekly* in 1933 and its New Zealand counterpart were also associated with this demographic shift and a concern with domestic science, a feature of modernization the nations were keen to adopt. In Australia and New Zealand, this concern with domesticity is evident in the best sellers being cookery books (such as *Edmonds Cookery Book* or the *Country Women's Association Cookbook*), and *Yates Garden Guide*, which have proved popular for a century. Maybe it was these entrenched national preoccupations with land ownership and beautiful homes that made the moment ripe for Germaine Greer's savage critique of women's confined lives in 1970, when *The Female Eunuch* became an international best seller and a feminist classic.

Like their parents, children's reading tastes in the early twentieth century were largely shaped by overseas books, such as *Little Women, Treasure Island, Anne of Green Gables, Pollyanna*, and *Biggles*, as well as nursery-rhyme books and Christmas annuals. Very few children's books had any local content, although there are some noteworthy exceptions: Ethel Turner's *Seven Little Australians* (1894), May Gibbs' *Snugglepot and Cuddlepie* (1918), Norman Lindsay's *The Magic Pudding* (1918), and the *Billabong* series (1910–1942) by the remarkably prolific Mary Grant Bruce. Children's books that emerged in New Zealand in the late 1800s sought to combine a European heritage of fairy/fantasy stories with local Maori legend. Although this was often a somewhat clumsy enterprise, it illustrates the continuing engagement with Maori culture that is a feature of New Zealand colonization.

The predominant "bush" theme was what marked books as Australian for local and London readers alike, in both children's and adult's reading. Mrs. Aeneas Gunn's remarkably popular account of life as a white woman on a remote rural property, *We of the Never Never*, published in London in 1908, is a trend continued by Sara Henderson's bestselling autobiography *From Strength to Strength* in 1993. In New Zealand, too, the character of rural work features to legitimize property ownership, as in Blanche E. Baughan's collection of short stories in *Brown Bread from a Colonial Oven* (1912). Many bush themes managed to avoid the difficult topic of race relations, or else reflected dominant racist or patronizing attitudes of the day. Sally Morgan's novel *My Place* (1987) marked an inversion of this perspective, as it traced the effects of dislocation from the perspective of a young Aboriginal girl growing up as "white" and being told that her unusual looks were a result of Indian ancestry. *My Place* is still probably the most widely read book by an indigenous Australian writer, despite a concerted effort since its popularity to publish more black writers. Its appeal to readers still lies in its wondrous discovery of Aboriginality in a seemingly "normal" white family, and of the emotional effects this discovery has on individuals, rather than on other people and the nation. The history of colonial occupation and Maori dislocation continues to emerge in New Zealand as a compelling social issue and reading topic, especially since publishing boomed after World War II. Keri Hulme's *the bone people* and Alan

Duff's *Once Were Warriors* are two of the most widely read and acclaimed products of New Zealand, and both are concerned with the heritage of colonialism on contemporary Maori lives.

Although historical revision is always going on, the late twentieth century has been marked by a renewed interest and urgency in addressing race relations. Henry Reynolds's prolific histories since his 1981 book, *The Other Side of the Frontier*, have sought to make indigenous history understandable to white readers and have been highly influential. Another critical moment was the publication of a report from the Human Rights and Equal Opportunity Commission's inquiry into what has become known as the stolen generations. Entitled *Bringing Them Home*, the report records the emotionally wrenching stories of generations of indigenous Australians who were taken from their families and homeland to be brought up as white, in the hope of assimilating them into the dominant culture. Despite the emotional power of those stories, anxiety over the rights of indigenous people continues to disturb white Australians since the High Court's Mabo ruling in 1993, in which Eddie Mabo was declared the traditional owner with native title to Murray Island in the Torres Strait. New Zealand has been reexamining its relation and use of the Treaty of Waitangi since 1975, when the Waitangi Tribunal was established to hear Maori grievances pertaining to breaches by the Crown. This has initiated a revival of the treaty, in principle at least.

Although opportunities for local publication of children's and adult reading rapidly burgeoned in both countries in the 1960s and 1970s with government support, in the late twentieth century it was the global book distribution networks that operated to direct reading tastes, predominantly for a middle-class, largely female readership. For those who cannot afford to buy books, libraries and second-hand dealers continue to offer popular thrillers and crime and romance novels, especially international bestsellers such as Catherine Cookson, John Grisham, Stephen King, and Bryce Courtney, who are heavily promoted and read. By far the highest-selling books, however, are nonfiction: sports, gardening, cookery books, and biographies such as Andrew Morton's 1992 bestseller, *Diana, Her True Story*.

CREATIVE TEXTS

Storytelling (and receiving) history began in Australia and New Zealand with the indigenous traditions, and continued with the folktales, personal recollections, and creative stories brought to Australia and New Zealand by convicts, whalers, free settlers, and traders. As the colonies developed and the new inhabitants recorded their unusual experiences in the alien landscapes of the Southern Hemisphere, unique approaches to creative literature were developed. Furthermore, Australian and New Zealand readers looked to the stories and verses of their countries to help verify their experiences and provide new moral and ideological structures for lives lived so far from the European model.

In Australia, the tradition of reading creative literature became intertwined with folk memory and nationalist recitation. The circulation of literary texts was limited to whatever could be produced from the available resources, whatever could be transported to the isolated communities in the Australian bush, and whatever could be maintained in readable form, given the harsh climatic conditions. Therefore, "readers" were often those who had not read the text first hand (if they could read at all), but those who had learned lengthy verse stories by rote. The recitation of long narrative poems by the so-called bush poets arguably became Australia's first literary tradition.

"Waltzing Matilda"

"Waltzing Matilda" is Australia's unofficial national anthem. The "bush poet" Banjo Paterson wrote its lyrics, and the tune is a traditional Scottish melody. It tells the story of a wandering bushman who steals a sheep to eat for his dinner but is interrupted by three mounted police. Rather than be caught, the man throws himself into a waterhole and drowns, haunting the area forever singing "Waltzing Matilda." The song celebrates resistance to authority and the Australian pride in siding with the underdog, or the "little Aussie battler," which has its origins in its convict heritage. A similar sentiment lies at the base of the so-called tall poppy syndrome, which describes the Australian national tendency to cut down high achievers.

Probably the best-known of these Australian poets is A. B. "Banjo" Paterson, who wrote *The Man from Snowy River and Other Verses* (1895). This collection of poems is written mostly in ballad form and glorifies bush life, lionizing the bushman as an archetypal figure in the Australian imagination. It takes its title from the immensely popular bush ballad, "The Man from Snowy River," first published in the *Bulletin* newspaper in 1890. This title poem tells the story of a wild horse chase in the Snowy Mountains after a valuable colt from Old Regret station has escaped to join the mob of horses. An extraordinarily able and daring horseman—the man from Snowy River—riding a mixed-breed mountain horse becomes the hero of the day, and shows up the elite riders on their thoroughbreds by bringing in the mob single-handedly. The poem's galloping beat contributes to the excitement of the ride, and also lends it to recitation and memorizing. Other famous poems in the collection include "Clancy of the Overflow," "The Man from Ironbark," and "A Bush Christening." Heralded as the most successful volume of poetry ever published in Australia—it sold out in the first week, and still outsells any poetry in Australia—Patterson's poems contribute much to Australian legend in promoting the pioneering spirit of endurance under harsh conditions. Growing up in rural New South Wales and then working as a lawyer's clerk in Sydney when he began publishing, Paterson (1865–1941) is often accused of romanticizing the outback as an arcadia, but his popularity as the poet of the people never ceases. He also wrote the poem touted as the people's national anthem, "Waltzing Matilda."

At around the same time, Henry Lawson's poems, sketches, and short stories were prolific in the *Bulletin* newspaper, and *While the Billy Boils* (1896) is his first collection of prose. It is still considered to be his most popular volume. It contains his most anthologized stories, including the Mitchell stories, "The Drover's Wife," and "The Union Buries Its Dead." Although Lawson's stories are about life in the bush and so conform to the *Bulletin* school of writing, they are also unexpectedly and un-euphemistically realistic about its brutalities and anonymity. "The Union Buries Its Dead," for example, tells the story of a funeral for a stranger who had appeared in a rural township the day before. His burial is ceremonial because he apparently belonged to the union, but the mourners regard it as a brief interlude from—and reason for—drinking at the pub, and the preacher resents the heat and the flies. The hypocrisy and exclusivity of the celebrated Australian "mateship" are subtly undermined by Lawson in the resolutely masculine world of the outback where women, children, and indigenous or ethnic minorities (such as the Chinese) often end up dead, maimed, or silenced. The unrelenting heat and barren land is often shown to impact the humanity of its white occupants.

Henry Lawson (1867–1922) was raised on the goldfields of rural New South Wales and experienced poverty throughout his life, as well as deafness from aged nine, but his stories are thought to be heavily influenced by a trip he took from Sydney to outback Bourke as an itinerant worker during the 1890s depression, which was funded by *Bulletin* editor J. F. Archibald. His mother, Louisa Lawson, published a Sydney feminist journal, the *Dawn*, and Henry also held strong socialist and republican (i.e., antimonarchical) views. He contributed to many periodicals and edited the labor journal the *Worker* at one stage. Although his bush ballads confirm his reputation as a popular folk-poet, his prose is often regarded as richer and more enduring, with characters such as Mitchell, Joe Wilson, and Steelman populating stories that are deceptively simple but detailed, dramatic, and understated in their empathy and irony.

Another popular text generated by 1890s nationalism is *On Our Selection* by Steele Rudd, a series of sketches, or small stories, published as a collection in 1899 by the *Bulletin* after appearing in its newspaper. Each sketch handles an event in the grim pioneering bush life of the Rudd family on a "selection" on the Darling Downs, and the pieces came to star Dad and Dave Rudd, the father and second son. A selection is a piece of land selected from blocks offered by the government from the 1860s. The selection scheme was an attempt to encourage more small-scale farming, and to break the monopoly held by the wealthy "squatters," who had commandeered millions of acres of the most fertile land for miniscule leasing or licensing arrangements. The scheme's success was doubtful, as the best land (with water and fertile soil) had generally already been procured. Selectors were left to barely scrape a living, especially as they expected to use European farming techniques in a desert climate. The ongoing and irreconcilable disputes between squatters and selectors represent rural class divisions, but provide much of the content of Steele Rudd's stories and champion the underclass in popular Australian fashion. The book was highly successful and sequels followed quickly, with Dad and Dave becoming stereotypes of outback hicks.

The sketches offer a particular kind of slapdash humor, which may account for their popular dramatization for radio, stage (1912), and screen in both silent film (1920) and four sound films between 1932 and 1940. The author, Arthur Hoey Davis (1868–1935), grew up on a selection on the Darling Downs and worked in the public service in Brisbane when he began submitting sketches for publication under the pseudonym of Steele Rudd. He believes his identification with Steele Rudd led to his dismissal from his government job, and while he continued his writing career on the back of the popularity of Dad and Dave, he barely profited from it.

Short prose lent itself to initial publication in newspapers and magazines, and this was also the case for novels exemplified by Marcus Clarke's *For the Term of His Natural Life*. First serialized in the *Australian Journal* between 1870 and 1872 (and several times thereafter), *His Natural Life* was published as a book in 1874, and the full title by which we now know it was used from 1882 onward. It is regularly republished, and many readers encounter it as part of the school curriculum. Its pessimism and suffering does not entreat it to many readers, but it remains one of the most-recognized nineteenth-century Australian novels. Its author, Marcus Clarke (1846–1881), was a prolific writer of journalism, theatricals, and novels after he arrived in Melbourne from London. *Natural Life* was prompted by a newspaper commission to research Australia's convict history.

Natural Life is the saga of Richard Devine, who takes the alias Rufus Dawes after he is misapprehended for the robbery of murdered Lord Bellasis in England.

Dawes is convicted and sent to Australia. En route he prevents a mutiny, but he is nevertheless tried as one of the mutineers, beginning a saga of injustices against transported convicts. The novel's chapters take place in three famous locales of convict internment: Macquarie Harbour, Port Arthur, and Norfolk Island. Dawes makes several attempts at escape, and the horrors of penal servitude are emphasized, especially at the infamous Port Arthur where a young convict, Kirkland, is raped and flogged to death. The plot is complicated by a series of misidentifications and misplaced allegiances. It has been criticized for its melodrama, but nevertheless remains a powerful portrayal of the hardships of the era.

In New Zealand publishing, which boomed only after World War II, the heritage of Maori dispossession makes compelling creative reading. Alan Duff's best-selling book, *Once Were Warriors* (1990), was made into a film in 1995, massively increasing its readership from an educated middle class to a younger, and significantly larger, Maori population. Written in a gritty realist style replete with crude and colloquial language, the story confronts contemporary New Zealand social issues through the characters of Beth and Jake Heke, married for eighteen years in a volatile relationship that swings from loving good times to violent beatings and rape. Their children continue the cycle of violence once associated with their warrior ancestors but now translated into ritualized destruction. The eldest son, Nig, joins a gang renowned for tattooing and violent initiations; Boogie is committed to a delinquent boys' home after minor criminal activities; and twelve-year-old Grace takes care of the younger siblings and writes gentle fantasy fairytales that she shares with Toot, a boy living in an abandoned car-shell under the highway. After Nig is killed in a gang fight and Grace commits suicide after being raped (possibly by her father, who cannot remember his drunken acts), Beth takes action with chief Te Tupaea to remedy the community through a return to Maori tradition and values. After grueling depictions of domestic violence and cultural disintegration, this simple answer to complex social conditions proved dramatically effective but met with criticism. Alan Duff (1950–) frequently espouses his controversial ideas that Maoridom has failed, and that the Maori are the only ones who can relieve their social disadvantage, as the narrator of the book vocalizes:

> Nor was Chief into blamin people, the Pakeha, the system, the anything for the obvious Maori problems; you know, our drop in standards just in general. He didn't care bout no damn white people ta blame, no damn systems meant to be stacked against a people, he just toldem: Work! We work our way out. (185)

A rather different philosophy is espoused by Keri Hulme (1947–) in her novel *the bone people*. Originally published in 1983 by Spiral, a feminist publishing collective, the first edition of *the bone people* quickly sold out, won several awards, and was reprinted by Hodder & Stoughton in 1984, and then by Louisiana State University Press in 1985 for the American market when it was awarded the prestigious Booker Prize (now the Mann Booker Prize). The story takes its center from the character of Kerewin Holmes, a stalled woman artist of both European and Maori descent, whose sexuality is ambiguous, and who chooses to live alone in a self-built circular stone tower on a remote part of the South Island's west coast. Her aloofness from contemporary and social life is disturbed by the boy Simon Peter, a shipwreck survivor who sings but never speaks. Simon has been adopted by Joe Gillayley, a Maori laborer whose wife and son died of influenza, but Joe's violent beating of Simon lands him a jail term. These three damaged characters are tentatively drawn together and then separated through violence and suffering before a resolution of sorts is optimistically posed through a new form of mutual living arrangements that do not rely on traditional notions of family or sexuality. The pain and the generational violence is powerfully linked to the historic suffering of contemporary Maori who have survived spiritual loss that continues to impact their physical and material existence. Healing is tentatively suggested through the novel's form, which weaves together a hybrid culture of Celtic, Norse, and Maori mythology; Christianity; and simple restorative pleasures such as cooking, eating, drinking, fishing, music, and solitude. Highly poetic and evocative, the spiral is an important symbol of the novel as it continually challenges dichotomies (such as Maori/pakeha, male/female, mute/speaking, and life/death). The Maori and English languages are also combined, resulting in a work that rejects either language as being authoritative or complete for expressing post-colonial experience. *The bone people*'s popular and critical success has not been extended to the other poetry and short stories of Keri Hulme.

PERSONAL TEXTS

Personal memoir often features the outstanding ordinary lives of "characters" in extraordinary situations. Memoir, in the Australian tradition, mostly represents lives of courage and hardship in the Australian bush. And, given that the majority of Australians live on the narrow coastal strip that runs around the country, and have never lived in or even visited the "outback," memoirs of "bush life" have always been particularly popular for the Australian readership. *We of the Never Never* (1908) by Mrs. Aeneas Gunn, for example, is an account of the thirteen months Jeannie Gunn and her husband Aeneas spent on the isolated Elsey cattle station in the Northern Territory, where Aeneas was employed as manager. Jeannie travels by horseback from Darwin through the tropical wet season to reach the property, which is assumed to be quite large, as the front gate is forty miles from the homestead. Encountering resistance to the idea of a woman interfering in the male world of station life, Mrs. Gunn nevertheless maintains spirited dynamism and becomes known as the Little Missus. While detailing the vicissitudes of station life, Gunn also writes nostalgically of the characters that pass through Elsey, which becomes a kind of idyll. Chinese cooks, strappers, Aboriginal girl servants, and stockman and drovers are all given nicknames and assume dramatic dimensions in a world of oddballs and eccentrics.

Jeannie Gunn, née Taylor, (1870–1961) established a private school in Melbourne, where she was born, before marrying Aeneas Gunn in 1901 and going to Elsey station with him. When Aeneas died suddenly of malarial dysentery in 1903, she returned to the city to write this memoir and *The Little Black Princess* (1905), a novel that uses the innocence of a child as a medium for contact with indigenous culture and people. Her books were very popular and adopted as school texts but are now regarded as outdated in their treatment of Aboriginal characters.

A somewhat different relation to the outback, however, is represented by Sally Morgan's *My Place* (1987). *My Place* tells a family story about Sally, her "mum" (mother) Gladys, her "Nan" (grandmother) Daisy, and her great-uncle Arthur living in Perth, Western Australia, in the 1950s and 1960s. *My Place* is the story of Sally's discovery that she isn't really an Indian princess, as she had been told by her family, but is really Aboriginal. The book is written in the form of a quest, or mystery to uncover the story of her family's indigenous history and why it remained hidden for so long. The stories of sexual exploitation, discrimination, and abuse are finally shared and validated in the book, which marks a return to and reclaiming of Sally's indigenous identity. It is a charming book of family loyalty and conflict, written simply and without pretension. Selling over half a million copies in Australia and more overseas, it was also on the senior school curriculum for many years, representing an outstanding success for the small, regional, independent publisher, Fremantle Arts Centre Press.

Morgan continues to publish children's stories and is widely known as an artist, her work being the subject of the book *The Art of Sally Morgan*. Morgan's book was particularly potent as it was read around the time of Australia's bicentenary, which prompted much reviewing of Australia's history, especially its indigenous history. Perhaps the most widely read book by an indigenous writer, and one of the first books by an indigenous writer that was widely read, its appeal may lie in the fact that it charts an Aboriginal protagonist confronting her past, rather than white Australia being confronted with the wrongs of their past. In *My Place* the white reader can "discover" Australia's indigenous history with Sally, and empathize with the way individuals respond to it rather than with how a nation might make reparations for the same.

In an echo of *We of the Never Never*, the popularity of "station life" continued to draw readers in the late twentieth century, as attested by Sara Henderson's memoir, *From Strength to Strength* (1993). This autobiography of Sara Henderson (1936–2005) tells the story of a city woman who fell in love and followed her husband in 1964 to live on Bullo River station, a remote property of thirty-five hundred square kilometers in the Northern Territory. Conditions were difficult and isolated, the only communication being by VHF radio, and food supplies were delivered in bulk periodically when the weather permitted. The marriage was stressful as Charles was a philanderer, and when he died in 1985, the property was rundown and a million dollars in debt. Henderson physically remade the station, put it on the stock market and turned it around into a financial success, earning her the Qantas Bulletin Businesswoman of the Year award in 1991. Some of this is attributed to luck: she sold her shares just one month before the stock market crashed in 1987. However, she continued to endure personal hardship when one of her three daughters took her to court in an acrimonious public battle over the property.

The book demonstrates stock Australian bush values of practicality, horsemanship, resilience, and resourcefulness in the character of the Aussie battler, which obviously still has strong appeal as it became a best seller, bringing Henderson into demand as a celebrity speaker. She went on to write five other books, three of which ranked in the top twenty most-borrowed books from libraries in 2000/2001. Henderson became an ambassador of BreastScreen Australia, urging Australian women over fifty to have regular mammograms, but in 2000 she was diagnosed with breast cancer herself, and she died in 2005.

CHILDREN'S BOOKS

Although in New Zealand, local children's books often promoted indigenous Maori stories, in Australia indigenous Aboriginal stories are rarely featured in children's books, which have traditionally concentrated instead on ideas of an Anglo national identity. *Seven Little Australians* (1894) by Ethel Turner is an Australian children's novel about the life of the Woolcot family, which lives on a large estate called Misrule on the Parramatta River in colonial Sydney. This novel is unusual in its urban domestic focus in a period when the outback was being idealized for

Australian and English readers alike. Captain Woolcot is a military man who is strict, authoritative, and largely absent. His young second wife, Esther, is kind and loving, but she struggles to ensure the captain's high behavioral expectations of his lively and mischievous children. The seven children range in age from Meg, in early adulthood, through Pip, Judy, Nell, Bunty, and Baby, to Esther's baby, who is called the General. It is their daily life of picnics, illness, romance, naughtiness, and general pranks that provides the substance of the story (and its sequels), but it also suggests an analogy between a lively, young, antiauthoritarian national culture in conflict with a stifling British militant parent. In perhaps the most memorable event of the saga, the extrovert teenager Judy dies in the bush while saving her youngest sibling from a falling tree. Ethel Turner (1872–1958) was a prolific writer of adult and children's books. *Seven Little Australians* is frequently reprinted and was televized for Australian television in 1975.

Snugglepot and Cuddlepie (1918) is another classic children's story. Snugglepot and Cuddlepie are two "gumnut babies," creatures of the imagination of May Gibbs, who have Australian eucalypt seed pod hats as defining features, along with gum-blossom eyelashes. The creatures are part of an array of characteristically Australian "bush" creatures, which also include Little Ragged Blossom, Lilly Pilly, and the big bad Banksia men. A host of anthropomorphic animals from land and sea join with the bush creatures to undertake dangerous adventures and save the natural world from evil. The most evil creatures, however, are humans, and the moral of the story encourages children to identify with the Australia flora and fauna and protect it from harm. May Gibbs (1876–1969) spent her childhood in England, then Western Australia, before returning to London to study graphic art. She then settled in Sydney to write and illustrate children's books with this distinctly Australian theme. She published many such books, and a comic strip that ran for almost thirty-five years in various newspapers. Her books are comparable with those of Beatrix Potter, and are still widely available.

A children's story published by a more widely known artist, Norman Lindsay, *The Magic Pudding* (1918) tells the irreverent slapstick comedy of three animal friends—Bunyip Bluegum (a koala), Bill Barnacle (a sailor), and Sam Sawnoff (a penguin)— and their adventures with Albert, the magic pudding. The three owners belong to the Noble Society of Pudding Owners, whose "members are required to wander along the roads, indulgin' in conversation, song and story, and eatin' at regular intervals from the Pudding" (44). Albert has a variety of flavors, including steak, jam doughnut, and apple dumpling, and is self-replicating so it can never be finished. The pudding is also animated: it walks, talks, and gives attitude freely and crankily. It is also sought by the equally befuddled pudding thieves,

The endearing character "Little Ragged Blossom," from the Australian children's classic *Snugglepot and Cuddlepie*. [Courtesy of Monica Morgan]

Watkin Wombat and Possum. The adventures comprise the pudding being frequently stolen and then regained.

Often compared to Lewis Carroll's children's adventure books, *The Magic Pudding* is written in verse and prose and illustrated by Lindsay (1879–1969), who had a fifty-year association with the *Bulletin* as artist, writer, reviewer, cartoonist, and book illustrator. He was a charismatic and formidable force in Australian bohemia, with strong views on uninhibited sexual and creative expression as life-affirming requisites. A film of Lindsay's bacchanalian contribution to Australian artistic culture was released in 1994 as *Sirens*, and an animated movie of *The Magic Pudding* came out in 2000.

Between 1910 and 1942, Mary Grant Bruce wrote the Billabong series of outdoor adventure in the idyllic pastoral setting of Billabong station. (A billabong is a waterhole that fills with rain, and a station is a large tract of land, often hundreds of square miles, that is used for grazing animals to sell.) The first book, *A Little Bush Maid* (1910), establishes the family of Norah, who is eleven years old, Jim, who is fifteen, their father David Linton, and Jim's best friend Wally from boarding school, who spends holidays with them. The mother died after Norah's birth, and there is an assortment of housekeepers, governesses, and station-hands, as well as relatives, who appear in the stories. Although the children stay that age for the first few books, World War I ushers in change when Jim and Wally decide to sign up for military service, and later in the series Wally marries Norah and they have a child, in *Bill of Billabong* (1931). Despite the crises that need resolving in each adventure and the changes wrought by war and romance, Billabong station represents a kind of utopian stability and timelessness, promoting typical Australian outback values of hard work, honesty, mateship, ingenuity, and resourcefulness. This bush mythos, established by the Bulletin school of writers, was venerated in the production of Australian reading content, as indicated by this 1913 recommendation of *Norah of Billabong* by the Victorian Railways Institute: "the book is Australian in character, spirit and location. The characters are of our own soil . . . good, healthy reading, especially when the theme is Australian and the writer Australian too" (quoted in Lyons and Arnold, eds., *A History of the Book in Australia 1891–1945: A National Culture in a Colonised Market*). Mary Grant Bruce (1878–1958) grew up in rural Victoria, Australia, and her writing for children draws nostalgically on that childhood. She published thirty-seven children's books alone, as well as adult novels, nonfiction, and copious journalism. The Billabong series sold two million copies, establishing her as a best-selling children's author.

The Wiggles

Although Australia is renowned as a major exporter of primary industry products such as wool, wheat, gold, steel, and uranium, one of its more recent successful exports is a children's entertainment group known as The Wiggles. Aimed at two- to five-year-olds, this group of four men in colored turtlenecks, accompanied by Dorothy the Dinosaur, Captain Feathersword, Henry the Octopus, and Wags the Dog, received the Australian Exporter of the Year award in 2005, having topped $17 million in DVD/video sales as well as a host of other promotional merchandise. Now known as the "biggest children's act in the world," The Wiggles began in the late 1980s as a group project for their early childhood teacher training. Several of the group had already played in bands, most notably the Cockroaches, and sensibly decided they could earn more money doing children's shows than as preschool teachers. They are reputedly responsible for the explosion in young children's television programming in the 1990s, and have been touring internationally since the mid-1990s, playing at Madison Square Garden and Radio City Music Hall.

DOMESTIC TEXTS

Domestic texts focus on settler survival—food and gardening—and remain the most popular of books. The *Country Women's Association Cookbook* is ubiquitous in Australia. Country Women's Associations were established all over Australia from 1922 onward to provide support and companionship for rural women. CWA Cookbooks were published as early as 1932, with each state or region compiling their own as a community activity and a source of revenue to help needy rural families. New South Wales published a *CWA Coronation Cookbook* in 1937, for example, to celebrate the coronation of King George VI of England; the Northern Territory had a *CWA Buffalo Cookbook* with recipes for buffalo meat; and Western Australia extended the function of their *CWA Cookery Book and Household Hints* (1936) to include practical advice on how to prepare everything from old hens to kangaroo, and is now in its fifty-first edition.

The *CWA Cookbooks* are prized for their no-nonsense basic cookery, although recipes and tastes have changed with revised editions over time: a 1919 edition apparently includ-

> **Recipe for "ANZAC biscuits."**
>
> Melt 125 g butter and add two tabs golden syrup, one cup rolled oats, one cup coconut, one cup self-raising flour, and a half-cup of sugar. Roll into balls, flatten, and bake in a moderate oven until golden.

ed "Possum Terrine." Early cookbooks were still largely influenced by British food cooked in lard, but desserts and sweets are favorites in the books, with standards such as Pineapple Banana Muffins, Golden Dumplings, Baked Quince, or Apple Sponge. A perennial is ANZAC biscuits (cookies): a derivation of Scottish oatcakes made without egg so they wouldn't spoil on their way to the Australian and New Zealand Army Corps (ANZAC) fighting in World War I.

Similarly, no New Zealand household was without its *Edmonds Cookery Book: Sure to Rise*. *Edmonds* was the brainchild of Thomas J. Edmonds, who developed and sold his own brand of baking powder in Canterbury, New Zealand, in 1879. Living up to its motto—"sure to rise"—made it a household name, and in 1907 a book of recipes and cookery hints was published as part of its merchandising. It boasts sensible, basic recipes that are easy to follow and that work, even for beginners, and is also a guide to basic nutrition and the art of baking.

Edmonds is now the biggest-selling book, of any genre, ever published in New Zealand: it has sold over 3.5 million copies and is now in its forty-fifth edition, which had a print run of thirty-five thousand in a country where a successful book is given a print run of five thousand. But more than this, it has come to occupy a nostalgic place in New Zealand culture through its values of down-to-earth practicality and domestic comfort. Its recipes are now proudly claimed to be part of a New Zealand cooking tradition, and the book is marketed (not that it needs to be marketed) as a must-have part of Kiwi culture for overseas expatriates or as an opportunity to replace a well-worn copy.

Alongside cookery books, gardening is a major preoccupation in Australia and New Zealand, perhaps in response to their white ancestors' penchant for clearing the landscape and replacing it with European crops and trees, and *Yates Garden Guide* has been the gardening bible since 1895. Arthur Yates, the asthmatic son of an English seed and grocery merchant who was sent to the colonies to improve his health, arrived in New Zealand in 1879, opened his first seed shop in Auckland in 1883, and then began distributing in Australia, moving there in 1887. The first packets of domestic seed for home gardens were sold in 1893, opening up a market among bourgeois homeowners that had previously been confined to estates. While recovering from illness in 1895 Yates wrote the first *Yates Gardening Guide for Australia and New Zealand*, a small publication of specifically local advice and information at a time when only European guide-books were available. *Yates Garden Guide* has since divided into separate New Zealand and Australian editions, respectively in their seventy-sixth and fortieth issue, having sold over one million copies in New Zealand and seven million copies in Australia. It is still regarded as the most comprehensive gardening bible for both countries.

NEWSPAPERS AND MAGAZINES

Australians and New Zealanders have always been loyal newspaper and maga-zine readers, dating back to the colonial period when news from Britain in any form was highly prized. As the island nations' own national cultures formed how-ever, the need to break away from Britain's influence and experiment with regional identity models required native forums for speech, ideas, and expression. Therefore, the *Bulletin* and the *Women's Weekly* have experienced peak readership levels and played formidable roles in the shaping of nations in Australia and New Zealand.

The *Bulletin* (1880–present) played a formative role in the development of a national readership for Australian content through its famous Red Pages (some-times remembered as the pink pages). Founded in 1880, the paper achieved fame under the editorship of its cofounder, J. F. Archibald. In the 1890s its circulation was eighty thousand, and stories abound of lonely "swaggies" (itinerant men look-ing for work during the depression with only their swag, or bedding role, in their possession) and remote rural workers passing on poetry and yarns (tall stories) from the *Bulletin* around the campfire. Its contents were reputedly learned by heart and recited until the next available copy appeared for consumption. The *Bulletin* first published what are now regarded as iconic Australian writers, among them Henry Lawson and A. B. "Banjo" Paterson, who wrote short stories, sketch-es, and poetry, often in the form of 'bush' ballads. These two writers were respon-sible for initiating a poetry battle in 1892–1893 extolling the virtues of the city and the bush: initially a strategy to engage readers and boost sales, it took on a life of its own and became known as the *Bulletin* debate. Lawson's childhood in rural poverty is sometimes attributed to his more realist perspective of the bush as a place of hardship, anonymity, and brutality, whereas Paterson delivered a roman-ticized view of the bush as a place of natural beauty and promise where Australian values were lived and revered. The debate between the city and the bush contin-ues to pervade Australian political and national rhetoric, even though ninety per-cent of Australians have always lived in the major coastal cities.

The motto of the *Bulletin* at this time was "temper: democratic; bias: offensively Australian," but it was a particular kind of Australia that was selected, published, and read to become mythic: an Australia of heroism in hard times, of white, working-class bushmen who stood by each other, drank and gambled, avoided commitment and family, and were shy around women and laconic in the face of adversity (the lat-ter two aspects often regarded as one and the same). In retrospect, the newspaper often promoted racism, parochialism, and conservatism alongside its questioning of authority and anti-British and antielitist stance. Readership gradually fell off over the twentieth century as its national policies became increasingly anachronistic, as indi-cated by the mast-head "Australia for the White Man," which appeared in 1908 and only disappeared in 1960 when the paper changed ownership. Since then its format radically changed to become a news magazine, which it continues to be, and has since revived its flagging readership to match its circulation of the 1890s.

In contrast to the changing fortunes of the *Bulletin*, the *Australian Women's Weekly* has been the most widely read magazine in Australia since its inception in 1933 in quarto newspaper format. With a current circulation of three quarters of a million and a readership of three million, it is the flagship of its publisher, Australian Consolidated Press. During the 1950s and 1960s it was read in one out of every four Australian homes, and was the highest-circulating women's magazine per capita in the world. It has been deemed a national media institution, but there is also a New Zealand edition produced that tops sales of monthly news-stand magazines, although it is not to be confused with the more popular *New Zealand Woman's Weekly*, which began in 1932 and is published by New Zealand Newspapers. The reasons for the popularity of such magazines are various. In addition to fashion, beauty, house and garden, cooking, social issues, celebrities, readers' stories, and fiction, the *Weekly* claims to have maintained high quality production but at a low price so it can be afforded by all levels of income-earners. In the 1930s it offered something new for women, with the motto, "There is no one in the world so important as the women in the home," and yet it has always been read by other members of the family, including men. In its early days there was a strong emphasis on news events (including the Olympic Games and important visitors, such as the Pope, royalty, and presidents). It introduced children's and teenagers' pages in the 1950s when they became a new market, and because of its constantly improving production techniques the *Weekly* attracted and maintained its corporate advertisers even after television was introduced in 1956. Advertisers played an important role in the social impact of the magazine, teaching women how to spend rather than save money, and locating women as the principal agents of domestic science and home management in the post-war period. Criticized by the women's liberation movement in the early seventies for its reliance on stories of female fulfillment through traditional housewifery and motherhood, the magazine briefly tried features on rape and incest but lost readers so quickly it returned to its traditional format of optimistic, feel-good stories of success in the face of adversity. The *Weekly* changed to monthly publication in 1983, and it also publishes cookery books under its insignia as well as an endorsement program through its Women's Weekly Book Club.

HISTORY TEXTS

When *The Other Side of the Frontier* was published in 1981, its author, Henry Reynolds, presented white Australians for the first time with a version of their nation's history that considered the viewpoint of its indigenous inhabitants (Reynolds is a white historian). It suggests that the place called the "frontier" at the forefront of white settlement in Australia has historically been recorded from only one side—that of the aggressors—and that the other side deserves documenting, which he begins to do. Using oral and

Australia vs. New Zealand

Australians and New Zealanders often ridicule each other with jokes. Passport holders share reciprocal rights to work and live in each other's countries, so New Zealanders good-naturedly tolerate jokes about how many move to Australia and how many sheep are left in New Zealand. Robert Muldoon, a New Zealand Prime Minister from the 1980s, commented that "Kiwi" immigration to Australia increased the IQ levels of both countries!

documentary evidence, Reynolds argues that Aboriginal people were not the passive "dying race" stereotype that ameliorates the genocidal policies of successive colonial governors and state governments, but that they actively resisted the armed occupation of their land. The subtitle of the book, *Aboriginal Resistance to the European Invasion of Australia*, initiated the substitution of "settlement" with "invasion" in some quarters, Australia Day now being marked by some as Invasion Day. Since this book, Reynolds (1938–) has published prolifically and become one of Australia's most influential and widely read historians, in demand as a speaker and committed to writing history to be read by the people. His research has played a major role in the Mabo and Wik judgments, considered to be political and historical milestones, and his work prompted a public national debate in the mid-1990s (and ongoing) known as the history wars. Some historians believed that Reynolds' work exaggerates the effects of Australia's racial policies, claiming that he and others write a "black armband" version of history, meaning that it is sympathetic to indigenous interests. Despite being controversial in some quarters, the impact of his work was immense at a time when Australia's history was being reconsidered anyway prior to the country's bicentenary.

POLITICAL TEXTS

Although *The Female Eunuch* was published in London in 1970, it achieved notoriety and fame for Australian writer Germaine Greer after its American publication in 1971, and it had a profound effect on its (mainly women) readers. Its central claim is that women have been castrated (like eunuchs) due to social conditioning, which has taught them to see themselves as passive, timid, fragile, and private beings rather than as powerful, intelligent, and significant figures of public life. The book examines the way women have been encouraged to focus on their bodies, mindless consumerism, romance, love, marriage, and family, and the way this supports a powerless and inequitable relationship with men. Greer advocates sexual commune with men, but also claims a socialized male hatred of women, and concludes by calling for a revolution from within, whereby women readers take responsibility for their world and change it.

Greer's book was highly controversial and probably inseparable from her irrepressibly extroverted and flirtatious public persona, which appeared on television, radio, and public events in the United States, Britain, and Australia. Published at the beginning of the women's liberation movement, it was savagely critiqued by some feminists and taken up as a foundational text by others. Greer (1939–) has had an extraordinary public life as a writer, public intellectual, and academic living mostly in Britain, and continues to have an ambivalent relationship with Australia and its readers.

GENERAL POLITICAL DOCUMENTS

The most significant political documents are about colonial-indigenous relations. The Treaty of Waitangi (*tiriti*) is an important symbolic document in New Zealand history, suggestive now of both the preparedness of Maori to be active in the colonization of New Zealand (Aotearoa) and also their betrayal. When it was drafted in 1840 there were one hundred thousand Maori and two thousand European settlers, most of the latter being whalers, traders, and missionaries accumulating since the late 1700s. Maori had been actively involved in European activities: trading food and labor; taking up tenets of Christianity and dairy farming; some traveling to England and Australia; and forging a direct relation to the British Crown. In 1820, Maori chiefs met with King George IV, and in 1831 they formally petitioned King William IV for protection of their land and authority. Despite this collective action, Britain did not particularly favor settlement in New Zealand, although it did benefit from trade. The 1835 Declaration of Independence of New Zealand, organized by the resident representative of the Crown, James Busby, was written in Maori and sought to preserve Maori sovereignty over the land through the collective of chiefs, fifty-two of whom signed the declaration between 1835 and 1839. This agreement was revoked by the 1840 Treaty of Waitaingi.

The reasons for this document are various, some suggesting the British were keen to prevent French claims, and others implicating Edward Wakefield's New Zealand Company, which, having already successfully established a colony in South Australia (1834), sought to sell New Zealand land to immigrants. Others suggest that missionaries conscientiously believed the treaty had the welfare of Maori at its heart, and that the British government needed some way to exercise legal authority over their subjects in New Zealand.

A fragment of the Treaty of Waitangi, which was first signed by British colonists and Maori chieftains in 1840. The Treaty guaranteed rights for New Zealand's Maori people.

The English and Maori versions of the treaty have discrepancies in wording, which may have been a difficulty in translation, a deliberate betrayal, or an ambiguity that ensured approval from (and anticipated benefits for) Maori. What was at stake was Maori ownership of land and their rights to sell to whomever they chose (Article One), as well as the retention of the chieftain system of authority—their *rangatiratanga*—in Article Two. Article Three assured Maori of the same rights accorded British subjects. There is also suspicion about the explanation of the treaty and its implications given to the chiefs, but after seven months of debate and traveling around the country the treaty was signed by more than five hundred chiefs, agreeing to the annexation of New Zealand by the British while at the same time retaining Maori authority through chiefs. As a result, New Zealand briefly became part of the colony of New South Wales in Australia. In 1841 it became a separate Crown colony, securing a New Zealand constitution and parliament in 1852. These legal forms of governance and land acquisition increasingly ignored, excluded, alienated, and dispossessed Maori, who set up their own systems of law in response. The King movement (*Kingitanga*) installed Potatau Te Wherowhero as the first Maori King in 1858 to administer the affairs of Maori under the protection of Queen Victoria, and in 1892 a Maori parliament was established in opposition to pakeha legislation and governance, which continued to confiscate land and violate Maori citizenship and community. Despite its prominence in New Zealand history, the treaty has no legal status unless specifically mentioned in ensuing legislation.

Maori student activism of the 1970s, following other liberatory movements of the time, demanded reparation for Maori and honoring of the Treaty of Waitangi as the formative relation with the Crown. Some argued for the return of rangitiratanga as outlined in Article Two, an aspiration that seemed compromised by the urbanization and impending loss of much Maori culture and language. The *Treaty of Waitangi Act* of 1975 set up the Waitangi Tribunal to hear grievances against the Crown for breaches of the treaty, making recommendations to the government. An amendment in 1985 extended the tribunal's jurisdiction, to investigate land claims dating back to 1840, but it was then restricted in 1993 from making recommendations about privately owned land. Since then, mention of the treaty has been incorporated into new legislation, making it necessary to examine the principles of the treaty and whether they are being applied to governance. This effectively revives the potential impact of the treaty at national and local levels of governance.

Although the Treaty of Waitaingi has played a significant part in New Zealand history and is still legally respected, Australia's reparations to its indigenous people gained political impact much more recently. In June 1992, the High Court of Australia (the highest level of judicial ruling) declared that the annexation of the Torres Strait Islands in 1879 had not extinguished the customary ownership of parts of Murray Island by Eddie Mabo, the complainant who spent a decade in court arguing that his entitlement had been passed on through his family since before British settlement. This was a groundbreaking ruling, as it legally articulated for the first time that the grounds on which Australia had been colonized in the eighteenth century were false and, essentially, immoral. Those grounds were that Australia was *terra nullius*, an empty land, unpeopled, and so available for claiming by the British. This doctrine had operated legally to support the colonial government and constitute the Federation of Australia, deliberately discounting the existence of its indigenous population. By legally validating Mabo's traditional ownership, a *prima faci* case was established for the claiming of native title over the rest of the country, and white landowners everywhere became very nervous. The Native Title Act was passed in 1993 (and then amended in 1998) to deal with these implications and to regulate procedures for native title claims, but has proved to be so limiting that claims are rarely suc-

The New Zealand Haka

The *haka* is a Maori performance that has come to specifically represent a demonstration of New Zealand national pride and prowess, although the word generically means "dance." Hakas became popular about a century ago after the New Zealand All Blacks Rugby team ritualized the practice prior to rugby matches. It is performed without weapons but uses the entire body as instrumentation: hands slapped against thighs, chests puffed out, knees bent, feet stamped, eyes dilated, tongues protruded, or eyes closed and words spat in staccato with passion. Said to have originated two hundred years ago, the haka takes on a power of its own when dancers spontaneously improvise between group chants.

cessful, except in some remote areas. Another groundbreaking case in 1996, known as the Wik judgment, manifested a radical new model in which native title was legally found to coexist alongside pastoralist lease. This model of mutual land use, despite providing positive outcomes for all, has been slow to be taken up.

It was not until the following year, however, that the full extent of Australia's indigenous policies and their generational impact on indigenous communities became known in the public sphere. Beginning in 1995, the Australian Federal Government's Human Rights and Equal Opportunity Commission conducted a national inquiry into the separation of Aboriginal and Torres Strait Islander children from their families, which came to be known as the Stolen Generation Inquiry, and *Bringing Them Home* is the official report of that Inquiry. The "stolen generation" refers to the indigenous children who were forcibly separated from their parents and homelands to be placed in missions, reserves, foster homes, or with white foster families, so that they might "grow up white" and relieve "the Aboriginal problem." This was government policy during the assimilation era in the twentieth century, but has been practiced virtually since first contact, and many argue that it still continues through the operations of welfare agencies today. The dramatic effect of being "stolen" is powerfully recounted in intensely moving personal stories, which are collected in *Bringing Them Home*. Although not many would have read the entire report (which is available online), few Australians could have avoided the heart-wrenching personal stories included in the massive press coverage. The effect of this public inquiry was to bring to public, white attention for possibly the first time the depth of trauma involved in the nation's racial politics. Despite the optimistic title, it is only the stories that have hit home: many people still do not know their families, and feel socially and spiritually dispossessed as a result of this practice.

CONCLUSION

Surprisingly, most of these texts are still widely available in print. Henry Lawson and Banjo Paterson are still popular texts and are always being republished in various forms, and they are now widely available on the Internet. Steele Rudd and Marcus Clarke are often taught in high schools and universities, and are available as e-books. The New Zealand novels by Duff and Hulme are widely available in print in English and other languages, whereas the memoirs of Henderson and Morgan had such a massive print run that they are easily found in second-hand book marts, markets, or libraries if not on bookshop shelves. *We of the Never Never* is not seen so frequently, and probably not much sought-after as reading material. In the children's book area, May Gibbs' gumnut babies saturated the global market after the HarperCollins Corporation rewrote, re-illustrated, and repackaged the stories, much to the chagrin of some but to the benefit of two Australian charities who share copyright proceeds. *The Magic Pudding* had a splurge of marketing after its animated filming in 2000, and is available in a number of languages. *Seven Little Australians* is readily available, as is the DVD of the television series; however, the *Billabong* series is rarely seen except in antique bookstores in Australia. Of the domestic texts, some of the CWA cookbooks are now rarities lying on cookbook shelves in aging houses, although some are still for sale on the Internet and through local branches of the organization. Edmonds's and Yates's books are available at every bookstore chain in Australia and New Zealand, and the magazines mentioned are still mass-produced each month. Greer's feminist manifesto has been translated into at least twelve languages and enjoys repeated printing, with a twenty-first-anniversary edition published in 1991, and a revisiting of the material in her book *The Whole Woman* in 1999. The political documents mentioned are available through government printing shops and online through parliamentary web pages, and Henry Reynolds's prolific history books are widely available in English. The *Bulletin*, perhaps the most iconic Australian magazine, ceased publication in January 2008.

RECOMMENDED READING

Bennett, Tony, Michael Emmison, and John Frow. *Accounting for Tastes: Australian Everyday Cultures.* Cambridge: Cambridge University Press, 1999.

Bibliographic Society of Australian and New Zealand Bulletin, 1970–present.

Hergenhan, Laurie, ed. *The Penguin New Literary History of Australia.* Melbourne: Penguin, 1988.

Lyons, Martyn, and Lucy Taksa. *Australian Readers Remember.* Oxford: Oxford University Press, 1992.

Robinson, Roger, and Nelson Wattie, eds. *The Oxford Companion to New Zealand Literature.* Oxford: OUP, 1998.

Sheridan, Susan, with Barbara Baird, Kate Borrett, and Lyndall Ryan. *Who Was That Woman? The Australian Woman's Weekly in the Post-War Years.* Sydney: University of New South Wales Press, 2002.

Sturm, Terry, ed. *The Oxford History of New Zealand Literature in English.* Oxford: OUP, 1991.

Treaty of Waitangi Information Programme booklets, New Zealand Government. http://www.nzhistory.net.nz/politics/treaty/read-the-treaty/english-text

Wilde, William H., Joy Hooton, and Barry Andrews. *The Oxford Companion to Australian Literature.* Melbourne: Oxford University Press, 1985.

PRIMARY SOURCES

The Australian Women's Weekly. Australian Consolidated Press, 1933–.

Bringing Them Home 1997. Reconciliation and Social Justice Library, 1997. http://www. austlii.edu.au/au/special/rsjproject/rsjlibrary/hreoc/stolen/ *The Bulletin.* ninemsn, 1880–2008.

Clarke, Marcus. *For the Term of His Natural Life.* First published in the *Australian Journal,* 1870–72. First published in novel form, 1874. South Yarra, Vic.: Claremont Books, 1990.

Country Women's Association Cookbook. Australian Country Women's Association. 1932–.

Duff, Alan. *Once Were Warriors.* London: Vintage, 1995.

Edmonds Cookery Book. Aukland, NZ: Bluebird Foods Ltd. 1907–present.

Gibbs, May. *Snugglepot and Cuddlepie.* First published, 1918. Sydney: HarperCollins, 2007.

Greer, Germaine. *The Female Eunuch.* First published, 1970. New York: Farrar, Straus and Giroux, 2002.

Grant Bruce, Mary. *Billabong* series. 1910–1942. Sydney: HarperCollins, 1992.

Gunn, Mrs. Aeneas (Jeannie). *We of the Never Never.* First published, 1908. Sydney: Random House, 1990.

Henderson, Sara. *From Strength to Strength.* Sydney: Pan Macmillan, 1993.

Hulme, Keri. *the bone people.* Baton Rouge: Louisiana State U. Press, 2005.

Lawson, Henry. *While the Billy Boils.* First published, 1896. Sydney: ETT Imprint, 2004.

Lindsay, Norman. *The Magic Pudding.* First published, 1918. Sydney: HarperCollins, 1995.

Mabo Ruling, 1992. http://www.austlii.edu.au/au/cases/cth/HCA/1988/69.html.

Morgan, Sally. *My Place.* Fremantle: Fremantle Arts Centre Press, 1988.

Paterson, A. B. "Banjo." *The Man from Snowy River*. First published, 1895. Sydney: Scholastic Australia, 2005.

Reynolds, Henry. *The Other Side of the Frontier*. First published, 1981. Sydney: University of New South Wales, 2006.

Rudd, Steele. *On Our Selection*. First published, 1899. Melbourne: Penguin, 1990.

Treaty of Waitangi. 1840. Archives NZ.

Turner, Ethel. *Seven Little Australians*. First published, 1894. Canberra: National Library of Australia, 2005.

Yates Gardening Guide. Sydney: HarperCollins, 1895–.

SECONDARY SOURCES

Lyons, Martyn, and John Arnold, eds. *A History of the Book in Australia 1891–1945: A National Culture in a Colonised Market*. Brisbane: University of Queensland Press, 2001.

CHAPTER 18

The South Pacific and Melanesia

Andrew Peek

TIMELINE

40,000 B.C.E.	Human settlement in New Guinea
1300 B.C.E.	Austronesians settle Fiji, Samoa, and Tonga
100–300 C.E.	Voyage to the Marquesas, initiating wider settlement of Oceania
1526	Main island of New Guinea accidentally discovered by Don Jorge de Menezes
1766	Louis-Antoine de Bougainville departs on three-year voyage across the Pacific
1768	James Cook departs on the first of three voyages to the Pacific
1820	Christian missionaries in Tonga
1860	Beginning of transportation of people from Vanuatu, Solomons, and New Guinea to work in plantations in Australia and Fiji
1878	Pomare dynasty cedes Tahiti to France
1888	Beginning of colonial administration of New Guinea
1901	Consolidation of French Polynesia
1941	Japanese invade and occupy Territories of Papua and New Guinea
1946	American nuclear tests commence in Marshall Islands
1962	Western Samoa independent
1965	Establishment, University of Papua New Guinea
1968	Foundation, University of South Pacific, Fiji
1970	Fiji independent
1971	South Pacific Forum
1975	Papua New Guinea independent
1978	Solomon Islands independent
1980	Foundation, Republic of Vanuatu
1987	Two coups by Sitaveni Rabuka; Fiji subsequently declared a republic
1989	Bougainville conflict begins (lasts nine years)
1995	Final French nuclear tests at Muraroa atoll
1998	Noumea Accord sets timetable for self-governance of New Caledonia

2000	Malaitan militants stage coup attempt in Solomon Islands; first of two further coups in Fiji
2003	Regional Assistance Mission sent to maintain security in Solomon Islands
2005	Bougainville elects autonomous government

INTRODUCTION TO THE REGION

The South Pacific islands of Melanesia and Polynesia were settled by successive waves of migration from Southeast Asia. The islands known collectively as Melanesia are Papua New Guinea, the Bismark Archipelago, Bougainville, Vanuatu, New Caledonia, the Solomon Islands, Maluku Islands, Palau Islands, Torres Strait Islands, and Fiji. Polynesia consists of a vast triangle of islands south of the equator including the Samoas, Tonga, Niue, Tuvalu, the Cook Islands, Pitcairn Island, and Easter Island. Tahiti and the Marquesas are the main groups of islands in French Polynesia. Each island developed oral cultures with shared key-words, place names, and local spirit narratives. The concept of individual creativity and authorship, always recognized in these cultures, has carried over into written forms as they evolved. Although the decades since independence have seen wide-spread rises in standards of education and formation of urban elites, traditional oral forms survive; in place of the order of priest-poets, wandering artists collect and recreate traditional narratives coexistent with written text read in schools, libraries, and universities.

Cross-cultural contact with Europeans began in New Guinea (named because of perceived similarities with the coast of West Africa) early in the sixteenth century. However, little more happened for two hundred years. In the eighteenth century, France and England mounted expeditions to islands in Melanesia and Polynesia led by Louis-Antoine Bougainville and James Cook. Beside the dissemination of Christianity, vigorous trade began in copra, sugar, artefacts, and the supply of the whaling vessels. Missionaries began introducing literacy on a widespread basis in the nineteenth century. Printing presses began publishing indigenous text in Tahiti from 1817. Europeans and Americans living on the fringe of indige-

> **Herman Melville in the South Pacific**
>
> Herman Melville's semi-fictitious record of jumping ship in Nuku Hiva in the Marquesas, published as *Typee* (1846), remained his best-selling title while he was alive.

nous communities, including white sailors who jumped ship and established themselves as translators and negotiators with the crews of passing vessels, wrote records and took their stories back when they returned to their own countries. As a key point of transition, the beach was a focus in the Pacific Islands for indigenous and nonindigenous inhabitants.

From the late-nineteenth century, nations in the South Pacific were governed from Europe, Australia, New Zealand, and America as colonies and dependent territories. During World War II, many became caught up in the "War in the Pacific" between their colonial masters and the Axis forces of Imperial Japan. After the war, the South Pacific became the object of American popular culture in idyllic films such as *Return to Paradise* (1952) and *South Pacific* (1958). These films left a legacy with which local tourist operators and writers continue to engage. Ironically, however, from this period right up to 1995, atolls in the Marshall Islands and French Polynesia were also used as nuclear test sites, necessitating the relocation of local inhabitants and causing destruction and irradiation of topography, flora, and fauna.

The colonial era lasted up to eighty years in Anglophone Melanesia and Polynesia. Western Samoa achieved independence from New Zealand in 1962, Papua New Guinea from Australia in 1975. French Polynesia and New Caledonia opted for long, semi-autonomous transitions because of the French economic support that accompanies them. American Samoa remains an American territory and Tonga is the only permanently independent nation, still ruled by the dynasty founded by King George Tupou I (1845–1893). Fiji became independent in 1970.

Missionaries addressing a group of New Guinean students in the late nineteenth century. [Courtesy of the Library of Congress]

READING TRENDS AND PRACTICES

To meet the needs of nationhood, the University of Papua New Guinea was founded in 1965 and the University of the South Pacific three years later; the two institutions between them teach in excess of thirty thousand students at campuses throughout the western Pacific. The University of Papua New Guinea's Institute of PNG Studies became a focus for young writers, as did the National Arts School, National Broadcasting Commission, and theater companies such as Raun Raun and the National Theatre Company. Universities and polytechnics subsequently opened in Tahiti, Samoa, and Papua New Guinea, where an ecumenical institution, Divine Word University, became the country's newest university in 1996. Whether or not universities have actively supported local writers, their role in greatly expanding potential and actual audiences is unquestionable.

Twelve hundred indigenous languages are spoken in this region, many Polynesian in origin. English is spoken in conjunction with the main

Languages

There are approximately twelve hundred languages spoken across the South Pacific region and, as they write, authors translate or simply incorporate words and phrases from them. A country like Papua New Guinea has over eight hundred languages, a fact that raises extraordinary challenges for translators. A recent anthology of folk tales, published initially in the Wantok newspaper *One Thousand Papua New Guinea Nights*, includes stories from writers in 273 language groups.

local languages throughout Anglophone Polynesia, and French is spoken in French Polynesia. Pidgin is widely used in Papua New Guinea (where it is called Tok Pisin), in the Solomon Islands (where it is called Pijin), and in Vanuatu (where it is called Bislama). The Indian community in Fiji (who make up approximately half the population) speak Hindi. Literacy rates in the South Pacific average more than 90 percent, and English is accessible to readers across the region and round the English-speaking world. Because of its international standing, English is the language preferred for modern education and used almost exclusively at the tertiary level in Anglophone states. It is important to note, though, that stylistic inflections and the inclusion of indigenous words and phrases result in a hybridized and localized version of English. In French Polynesia, French is the writers' preferred language, with stimulus provided by publications imported from metropolitan France. Literacy rates are lower in Papua New Guinea, with a majority literate in Tok Pisin, closely followed by English and a small minority in Motu.

Firms in Australia and New Zealand began to publish titles by writers in Papua New Guinea and Polynesia from 1970. They established series devoted to Pacific Writing and titles were sometimes taken up by presses elsewhere. *The Crocodile* by Vincent Eri, the first published novel by a writer from Papua New Guinea, was released by Jacaranda Press in Brisbane in 1970; it was subsequently republished in the Drumbeat series by the British company Longman in 1981. Because their lists are well-resourced, promoted, and distributed, multinational publishing companies in Australasia, Europe, and the United States offer valuable support for writers in the South Pacific and have increased readership inside and outside the region. Local publishers and organizations supporting them have also played a vital role. These include the South Pacific Creative Arts Society (formed after the First Pacific Arts Festival, Suva, 1972), the Institute of Pacific Studies (USP), the Pacific Writers Forum, the University of Papua New Guinea Press, and the Institute of Papua New Guinea Studies (UPNG). Presses in the Cook Islands, Solomons, Vanuatu, Tonga, and Samoa have taken on small-scale ventures unviable for larger publishers. Government printeries print regulations, reports, statistics, and school books. Churches and religious organizations distribute imported and locally produced titles, and the Bible, together with the local paper, is still the most widely read publication in many homes.

However, the publication and circulation of books faces local challenges, in relation to transportation, production, high import taxes in some cases, and the possibility of direct political interference by governments. The influence of electronic and digital media—including television, film, DVD, Internet, and computer games—presents a threat to written and oral literature. However, multinational publishers have continued to support internationally known writers such as Albert Wendt, and the fact that the Institute of Pacific Studies and associated bodies have published work by more than two thousand Pacific Islanders testifies to the resilience and demand of local readerships. Although national libraries are modestly funded by international standards, schools, university campuses, and religious and government institutions also have libraries allowing readership access in places where the cost of purchasing books can be high. Books often pass privately from hand to hand.

Institutions such as the South Pacific Forum (1970) provide scope for representation on the international stage, but the region lacks a strong political constituency and voice, which is unfortunate, because the region faces a number of real threats. For example, although French nuclear testing has ceased, some Pacific nations face the threat of inundation from global warming. Kiribati is on the verge of disappearing beneath the Pacific, and other South Pacific nations are having to relocate the populations of whole islands and archipelagos as sea levels rise. But these threats are comparatively recent. The Pacific nations are also still dealing with the impact of colonialism on the region. The West coolly uses the term "arc of instability" to describe states recuperating from disjunctions and anomalies bequeathed by colonialism. In 1987, for instance, the descendents of indentured Indian laborers, previously transported to Fiji to work in sugar plantations, elected a government under an Indo-Fijian prime minister that was subsequently overthrown by the first of a series of military coups engineered by indigenous Fijians.

Language and politics have created particularly strong crosscurrents in Fiji and Papua New Guinea. Because both nations are made up of many tribes, ethnicities, and tongues, writers trying to establish a national identity are confronted by a difficult decision. They can use local languages, available only to a minority of readers, or deploy varieties of pidgin with their own limitations. A third possibility is English, which is incapable of indigenous nuance, freighted with colonial connotation, and inaccessible to much of its local readership. Alternatively, publication in the form of multiple translations is possible, but this is dependent on the skill and accuracy of translation and raises the cost of production.

However, traditional oral literatures continue to assert their presence beneath written forms, and in differing ways, all indigenous writers of the region draw on them. This effect is magnified by the fact that, despite the limited size of local audiences, migration to New Zealand/Aotearoa, Australia, and the United States has increased islander audiences and given rise to an evolving community around the Pacific Rim. Epeli Hau'ofa, one of the region's best-known prose writers, points to the enduring commonality of the ocean. Instead of colonial constructions that divided people into nations and fractured individual psyches, he prefers to focus on the ocean as a force for unity, a shared highway, an area of transition, and a common source of livelihood. Hau'ofa would free readers and writers alike from parochialism and taxonomy, evoking the free spirit of navigators who settled the South Pacific.

CREATIVE TEXTS: NOVELS AND NOVELLAS

The depiction of the South Pacific (previously the South Seas) as a version of earthly paradise-cum-adventure playground in romance fiction, published in the late-nineteenth and early-twentieth centuries in America and Europe, contrasts with the experience of contemporary readers and writers in the region. The latter has included

The Cultural Practice of Tattooing

Besides being decorative, the Polynesian practice of tattooing signifies group identity, status, or acceptance of a group's norms. Albert Wendt has described just how painful tattooing is in his fiction. He has evoked the process of tattooing through his graphic art in a book of poems called *Book of the Black Star*. In the Marquesas, tattoos signify either belonging to a certain group or having undergone a special event, such as rite of passage.

migration, alienation, and racism. *The Beach of Falesa* (1893) by Robert Louis Stevenson offers a more thoughtful account of life than was usual of colonial Samoa, the island he made his adopted home. His presence lingers in the work of Albert Wendt. Wendt has exercised an enduring influence as writer, teacher, editor, and supporter of literature in the region. His first novel, *Sons for the Return*

Robert Louis Stevenson's tomb on Mount Vaea, Samoa.

Home (1973) describes the migrant experience of a young Samoan studying in New Zealand and includes a love affair with a pakeha, or white woman. A large population of Samoans reside in New Zealand, many of them familiar with the experience of racism, loss, and alienation the novel evokes. Like the later collection, *Flying Fox in a Freedom Tree* (1974), *Sons for the Return Home* was made into a film supported by the New Zealand Film Commission and both films are still regularly screened. *Leaves of the Banyan Tree* (1979) follows three generations of a Samoan family transformed by colonial forces of capitalism and Christianity. As with earlier books, this novel was published in New Zealand by a multinational press. It was awarded the country's premier literary prize, the Wattie, in 1980. Although its author, Albert Wendt, left Samoa in the mid-1970s and only returns on short visits, he is still claimed as its own by the country about which he continues to write. *Book of the Black Star* (2002) marries poems with his own graphic art technique that grounds the text in the traditionally important practice of tattooing.

The granting of independence in the region from the early 1960s generated a sense of nationalistic pride and established an audience for fledgling novelists. It is easy to see how Vincent Eri's short novel *The Crocodile* caught the zeitgeist of Papua New Guinea, a country impatient for self-rule at the beginning of the 1970s. It describes the plight of Houri, a man caught in-between, subject to predatory traditions and beliefs on one hand, and exploited by cruel colonial policy on the other. In the final sentences, Houri is led off, manacled, by a policeman. Its author's political standing, culminating in a brief appointment as Governor General (1990–1991), gives additional meaning to his readership in Papua New Guinea, and the novel's status as the first published novel by an indigenous writer in Papua New Guinea ensures continued inclusion on school and university reading lists. However, it is both a product as well as a critique of a colonizing system, and as such, its continued relevance to the country's project of nation-building has been questioned by academic commentators concerned that Eri was too conditioned by colonialism to generate a genuinely new national consciousness.

The novel as a literary form has been established only recently among writers in Anglophone Polynesia. The first novel published was *Makutu* (1960) by Cook Islanders Tom and Lydia Davis. Alistair Te Ariki Campbell's later novels *Frigate Bird* (1989) and *Sidewinder* (1991) draw on his Cook Island and Scottish heritage to create an innovative hybrid rich in indigenous myth and oral culture. Campbell's novels move between Cook Island and New Zealand. They are presented by the same unnamed narrator struggling with private demons. The focus is on the humor and angst of individual subjectivity. It is in the work of figures such as Campbell and Wendt that fiction's future directions and bases for a genuinely new regional identity are being laid.

Many novelists in the South Pacific occupy university posts, allowing them to share their knowledge and extend research skills that feed back into their own writing. Although tertiary institutions play a vital role in expanding levels of education, the artificial environments they create can lead writers to write for specialized audiences. Russell Soaba's *Wanpis* (1977) recognizes the writer's duty in Papua New Guinea to engage in the formation of an indigenous national consciousness. At the same time, it argues that an existential individualism derived from European philosophy is the only realistic response to life in Papua New Guinea in the face of the complex, often chaotic nature of the country's social development. *Wanpis* signifies "outside" in Tok Pisin, a term reminiscent of French writers Albert Camus and Jean-Paul Sartre. Though Soaba sees the writer's role as that of unofficial social ombudsman, his work is not widely read outside academia. Epeli Hau'ofa, also born in Papua New Guinea (of Tonga missionary parents) was one-time Keeper of Palace Records for the King of Tonga, and has occupied a number of posts in the University of the South Pacific. Unlike Soaba, Hau'ofa's *Kisses in the Nederends* (1987) is comic, populist, and subversive. Incorporating scatological and carnivalesque elements, it satirizes ideas imposed by a globalized, post-colonial world. Its bawdiness is universal enough to find connections with a similar tradition in Japan, and a translation of Hau'ofa's novel has recently been released by one of Japan's premier publishing houses.

In twenty-first-century Apia, the capital of Western Samoa, architecture and the city center are rapidly changing—a multicultural yet distinctive blend of past, present, and future. Sia Figiel's novel *Where We Once Belonged* (1999) encapsulates the energies of her birthplace in narrative form. Her work appeals to Samoan readers for whom traditional style and community values are often best preserved by reinterpretation in contemporary artistic idiom. In interview, Figiel talks of contradiction and paradox, providing images of Samoans sitting cross-legged, praying on the floor in Nike shoes, and then watching CNN. Her novel is characterized by the heterogeneity this suggests. There is also an assertive engagement with colonial vestiges—for instance, in joyfully ironic ripostes to anthropologists Margaret Mead and Mead's critic and fellow anthropologist, Derek Freeman. Like Wendt, Figiel has an international education and profile. Unlike him, she has chosen to keep returning to the Samoan Islands after periods in the United States and Europe, and through a remarkable range of artistic skills, including painting, oral performance, written poetry, and prose narrative, educates a younger generation, many of them female.

A similar creative energy emerges from the interaction of language in the South Pacific. Although English has had a unifying effect and generated a body of fiction that can be read across the Pacific, it remains an imported language in many respects, removed from the experience of the place and its peoples. In contrast, the seamless flow of island languages in the region could lead to a different, more authentic kind of literature. Indo-Fijian novelist and academic Subramani argues that, as more people write in local vernaculars, a new and distinctively Oceanic intellectual life will be created, something borne out for him by the experience of writing a novel in Fiji Hindi, *Dauka Puraan* (2001). A master of English narrative, Subramani found himself able to use a new comic mode and to reach audiences in live readings with a heightened intimacy. His vision represents a homecoming to new readers and audiences throughout the South Pacific.

SHORT STORY COLLECTIONS

The confluence of creative individuals, institutional support, and urban settings made the University of Papua New Guinea at Port Moresby, and the University of South Pacific at Suva, natural foci for the dissemination of short fiction. From the late 1960s, though on a smaller scale, the same was beginning to happen in centers in Samoa, the Solomons, and elsewhere. Albert Wendt has demonstrated a readiness to move back and forth between novel and short story and, like Epeli Hau'ofa and Sia Figiel, his work explores the space where short story, oral narrative in performance, and longer discontinuous narrative intersect from *Flying Fox in a Freedom Tree* (1974) onward. In forty years, forms of prose narrative have negotiated new territory and growing audiences have followed them, though strong continuities between writers have also been established. Thus Sia Figiel, creator of what she calls the "novel in performance," has acknowledged that Hau'ofa, Wendt, and (Maori) Witi Ihimaera "are part of what makes me possible" (quoted in "Sia Figiel: Writing with Mana," Scott Whitney, *Pacific Magazine*, December 1, 2002). Because it can be written quickly for periodical publication, the short story has helped novelists begin their careers and helped to build audiences interested in the longer fiction they went on to write later.

After its foundation, the University of Papua New Guinea was the center of great literary creativity, including short fiction in English, Tok Pisin, and Motu. Literary works were widely published in periodicals and newspapers in the years around 1970 as the first graduates emerged. Writers such as Russell Soaba and John Kolia went on to publish in a variety of genres. From 1975, however, there was a perception that impetus was being lost. An article in 1980 by Bernard Minol attributed the "Death of Papua New Guinean Writing" to a scarcity of publishing outlets and lack of interested audiences. Short stories have continued to appear by new writers though, because the form is nimble and adaptable. Short stories published in Papua New Guinea during the 1980s allow prompt engagement with issues such as corruption among political leaders, the shock of moving from country to city, and the impact of materialistic values on personal relationships. Though they may not reach the same number of readers, they represent a counterpoint to commentaries and letters to the editor in newspapers of the period like the weekly *Times of Papua New Guinea* (which closed down in 1995).

Short stories connecting past and present, by Raymond Pilla and other Indo-Fijian writers, examine what has been called Girmit ideology. The Girmit, or Agreement, refers to the period of indenture originally signed by nineteenth-century migrants from India. Though it has a broadly political context, such fiction is concerned with possibilities for reconstruction on personal and psychic levels.

Just as Albert Wendt's short fiction marries tradition to modern form through art and poetry, innovative connections have been established between traditional and contemporary forms by communities in Western Samoa. Between the 1960s and 1980s, short stories in English published by local writers have followed on from the traditional story-telling style, known as *fagogo*. Subsequently, new stories in vernacular Samoan have been supported by national competitions, magazine publication, and, most significantly, by regular radio broadcasts that took narrative performance—"the fagogo of the air"—directly back into people's homes. Stories marketed through newspapers and street vending created a nascent narrative form rather than something obviously renovated. Writers like Agafili demonstrate in *Rhyanapoinciana: Tusi Tala faa Samoa* that, although art may not survive trapped in amber, it can flourish when it takes on different forms.

Short stories from the Solomon Islands were featured in a special issue of the periodical *Mana* in 1979. This was followed by more stories in the April 1980 edition of *Pacific Quarterly Moana*, and, subsequently, publication of the first book of Solomons' short stories titled *Houra'a*. The local Extension Centre of USP supported the project's publication and a group of secondary school teachers prepared a support booklet with activities so the collection could be used in schools. The popularity of a collection of eight stories by local writer Julian Maka'a, called *The Confession and Other Stories* (1985), was confirmed by reprints in 1987 and 1999.

The region's writers also use humor to engage with the destructive impact of colonial and post-colonial regimes. Epeli Hau'ofa's *Tales of the Tikongs* (1983), set on a fictitious island called Tiko, reminiscent of Tonga, satirizes Tongan appropriation of colonial practices and the administration of foreign aid. This writer is presently interested in writing modern oral narratives—for example, deriving from childhood experiences in Papua New Guinea during World War II. The aim is to perform them before an audience. Sia Figiel demonstrates how effective this can be in her second book *The Girl in the Moon Circle* (1996), variously described as short stories, prose poems, a novel, and a collection of performance pieces. Hau'ofa and Figiel want to stay in touch with live audiences and oral forms, a reciprocal process that nourishes the oral and the written. In dynamic environments, short stories, oral performances, radio broadcasts, and indigenous films all play an important role in cultural continuity and recreation.

PLAYS

Music and dance are at the heart of traditional performance and figure at local, national, and international levels, notably at regular South Pacific Arts Festivals. The National Dance Theatres of Fiji and the Cook Islands have adapted ancient forms for stage performance around the world. Traditional drama used oral, rather than written script; following on from this, improvisation has been the basis of traveling and community theater companies like Raun Raun Theatre (performing in Goroka, Papua New Guinea, in the 1970s), and the Wan Smolbag group (founded in the late 80s in Vanuatu). Raun Raun chose pidgin to communicate with village audiences, using schools as performance spaces. Wan Smolbag is a theater company that combines oral and text-based techniques to address pressing social issues and educational needs. These include domestic violence, AIDS, and natural disasters. The company also produces videos in English and Bislama for distribution throughout the South Pacific. This is an evolving artistic response to local needs, and it is an instrument of change for those it reaches.

The founding of the National Theatre Company of Papua New Guinea in 1976 was a bold assertion of cultural identity. National theater companies frequently attract government funding because of their iconic status, but of all literary forms, theater is also the most immediate point of connection between audience and text, often confronting contentious social issues. While Papua New Guinea's National Theatre quickly established a market for local dramatists, including Albert Toro and Nora Vagi Brash, writing has proliferated and diversified for performance in other venues. Two decades later, Brash herself was talking about the cost of literary production as a lifelong commitment, remarking that "there have been writers who've been thrown into jail, or tortured, or banned. That's a commitment they make. It's a commitment we are making" (1992: quoted by Gilian Gorle in *Pacific Studies* 19 (1), p. 75). Subjects that playwrights like Brash and Adam Vai Delaney tackle include the discrepancy between services offered to city and country dwellers (Brash, *Pick the Bone Dry*, 1986), psychological violence among apparently successful urban professionals (Delaney, *When Two Tribes Go to War*, 1991), and tribal warfare and cargo cults (Delaney, *Chant of the Witchdoctor*, 1991).

In addition to such "grassroots" origins, dramatic script is also published by writers in academic institutions. Rotuman islander Vilsoni Hereniko, from Fiji, is a professor at the Centre for Pacific Islands Studies at the University of Hawai'i. As well as poems and short fiction, he is a script-writer. *Don't Cry, Mama* (1977) was the first of seven plays he has completed. His move to films, including *Just Dancing* (1998) and *The Land has Eyes* (2004), serves to export his native culture to international audiences, at the same time promoting Oceanic consciousness at home.

POETRY

In terms of an enduring readership, poetry in English can arguably be regarded as the most fragile of literary forms in the South Pacific, because it uses an exotic language at its most compressed for a coterie audience. This is beginning to change as contemporary writers blur genres and reconnect with indigenous rhythms and feelings.

The Papua Pocket Poets series was a part of the early flowering of cultural nationalism accompanying independence in Papua New Guinea. Small, cheap booklets featured selections of work by individual poets, including John Kasaipwalova, Kumalau Tawali, Apisai Enos, and Kama Kerpi. The project was launched by expatriate German Ulli Beier, who moved from Nigeria to run creative writing courses at UPNG, an indication of the kind of national and international expectations the country roused during this period. John Saunana was the first Solomon Islands poet to have a collection of his writing published as part of the Papua Pocket Series. Writers of the period were part of a tiny educated minority, and it is no surprise that collections such as *Twenty-Four Poems of the Solomon Islands* (1977) featured work by a future prime minister, cabinet ministers, and the country's first ambassador.

Many of these poets deal with political themes, first anticolonial and then critical of post-colonial society; but however vehemently they write, poets in the region do not have the power or readership to represent a serious political threat or even irritant to government. More recently, poets see themselves as consciences (if not legislators) of society, a responsibility they discharge through observation and personal experience. Topics for discussion include the alienation induced by an imported system of education and dead-end jobs awaiting those leaving school.

Publication in Western Samoa of early poems written by Albert Wendt, author of *Inside Us Dead: Poems 1961 to 1974* (1976), and his generous support for fellow poets, boosted support for the genre in post-independence years and led to *Some Modern Poetry from Western Samoa* (1974). Collections by individual poets followed, supported by the Samoan Writers' Association, Mana Publications, and the University of the South Pacific at Malifa, where Wendt was director. Writing groups continue to offer support to new and established writers. Anticolonial themes figured in a number of Samoan poems published after 1962 but characteristic subjects for oral literature remain common, including human relationships, love, freedom, and evocation of the islands.

Poets in the region are generally readier to write in other genres than their peers in America and Europe. Alistair Te Ariki Campbell is a novelist, in addition to forty years of writing and publishing poetry. *The Dark Lord of Savaiki* (2005), his collected poems, traces a passage from early influences among British modernists back to roots in Polynesian myth from his native Cook Islands and New Zealand. He has spent most of his life in New Zealand, where many people of Cook Island origin live. Here they are able to access his books in well-stocked libraries and listen to readings Campbell gives. John Kasaipwalova's long poem *Sail the Midnight Sun* (1980) is a passionate expression of hope for Papua New Guinea's future described by its author as a Kasewaga, a form of dance drama. Kasaipwalova wrote most of the poem in prison while serving a two-year sentence after a conviction for embezzlement of government development funds. He was subsequently released after a few months and all charges were dropped.

Over the past forty years, poets writing in English in the South Pacific have learned to adapt what they write to remain in touch with their reading public. Some have chosen subjects and social themes they feel must be commented on. Others experiment with performance and the detailed exploration of myth. In either case, writers are ready to modify genres and work toward a blend of languages, indigenous and exotic. From the point of view of academics writing in the 1970s, it was possible to despair about writing in a vacuum, poets catering for tiny, partly expatriate audiences producing work that was alien and unsustainable. Three decades later these poems, often beautiful as works of literary art, now appear part of a transition to writing for wider indigenous audiences. In the process, the poets have moved back to explore traditional notions of their art's roots and responsibilities.

Though the impact of literature on culture plays an important part in teaching at the University of the South Pacific and the University of Papua New Guinea, indigenous poetry does not figure prominently in courses currently offered by literature departments.

PERIODICALS, NEWSPAPERS, AND ANTHOLOGIES

The previously mentioned problem of limited readership that pertains to scholarly works produced by academics does not apply to day-to-day reading in the South Pacific. Daily newspapers include the *Cook Island Herald, Cook Island News, Uekera* (Kiribati), *Kiribati News Star, Fiji Sun, Fiji Times, Fiji Village, Nouvelles Calédoniennes, Solomon Star, Solomon Express, Samoa News, Matangi Tonga, Tonga Star, Vanuatu Daily Post, Port Vila Presse, TahitiPresse, Tahiti Pacifique National* (New Guinea), and *Post-Courier* (New Guinea), However, economic circumstances and competition to secure skilled journalists at times makes it hard to sustain newspaper publication. The *Independent* closed in 2003 leaving the *Post*

Courier and the *National* newspapers in circulation. The fact that local newspapers are specifically oriented toward meeting the needs of their communities, and can also be immediately distributed, gives them an advantage over international newspapers, which arrive later than their publication date. However, this will change with increased use of the Internet, allowing access to the *New York Times*, the *Australian*, and the London *Times*, to name a few. *Pacific Magazine Daily News* reports on politics and government across the entire Pacific region.

Pacific Magazine also produces speciality magazine issues called *Pacific Island Forum* and *American Samoa*. The major regional magazine, *Spasifik* magazine, which is published in hard copy and online by Oceania Media Limited, has articles on a wide range of subjects including local politics, music, film, and the arts. There are other speciality magazines such as *Pacific Economic Bulletin*, edited by the Australian National University, and *Pacific Journalism Review*, now published by the Auckland University of Technology, New Zealand, and *Tahiti-Pacifique Magazine*, a monthly francophone publication dealing with current affairs. Australian's Pacific Magazines' teen magazine, *Girlfriend*, has created a Web site where its readers can choose the layout and contents of the magazine. Likewise, *Dolly*, published by Australian Consolidated Press, also has an online interactive site and advertises available positions for its readers. Where Internet access is available, these innovations, which shift the emphasis of control toward the reader, will be available to young readers in the South Pacific.

Literary periodicals, anthologies, and little magazines, though they have often been short-lived, have generated confidence, self-awareness, and professionalism in small and scattered literary communities. In Papua New Guinea, *Kovave: A Journal of New Guinea Literature* was the first of a series of periodicals that played a critical role in getting young or unknown writers into print in the South Pacific.

Mana Review was established to do the same thing a few years later in Samoa. Ulli Beier and Albert Wendt produced retrospective anthologies that consolidate work produced in this era, in effect documenting the modern literary history of Papua New Guinea in *Black Writing from New Guinea* and *Voices of Independence: New Black Writing from Papua New Guinea* (1980), *Lali: A Pacific Anthology* (1980), and *Nuanua* (1995).

The region's small journals and periodicals were created to support and disseminate work by new generations of indigenous writers. Because they mix poetry, prose, and dramatic script, these publications resist taxonomies imposed by librarians and publishers and take part in a larger return to the mixed forms of traditional culture. They are also well-suited to record collective experience. The legacy of indentured Indian laborers among contemporary Indo-Fijians extends over many generations. An anthology—such as *Stolen Worlds: Fijiindian Fragments* (2005), edited by Kavita Ivy Nandan, with nineteen entries—brings together many voices and is therefore able to convey a sense of multiplicity and the different meanings acquired by this kind of shared process.

In an effort to preserve folk tales produced by 273 different language groups in Papua New Guinea, a remarkable collection, *One Thousand One Papua New Guinea Nights* (2001) has recently been assembled by Thomas Slone from stori tambula, or "stories of the ancestors," published by *Wantok*, the Tok Pisin newspaper of Papua New Guinea. A massive resource in its own right, it represents an extraordinary example of polyglot translation, from indigenous language to Tok Pisin and then to English, and an example of dialogue between readers and those who shared local tales.

On occasion, the selection of anthologized materials has proved problematic. In a 1994 collection of contemporary South Pacific stories, C. K. Stead, a pakeha (white) editor, sparked the ire of indigenous commentators because of its omission of writers they considered significant. Books like this become canonical, especially outside the region. Folk art and culture subsumed in books by foreign academics represents another kind of "anthologization" that Pacific Islanders also question on the basis that this represents acquisition of the region's communal intellectual property.

Regional publications, such as *Pacific Islands Monthly*, cater for the needs of a broader Pacific audience, and academic periodicals, like the *Journal of Pacific Studies*, have institutional backing and global subscription lists. They tackle social, political, economic, educational, and scientific issues in addition to providing forums for academic and literary debate.

AUTOBIOGRAPHY

The lives of political leaders of newly independent states are microcosms of their times: they create themselves, their posts, and countries. Their stories celebrate what they have sought and achieved for themselves and for their nations. Albert Maori Kiki's *Kiki: Ten Thousand Years in a Lifetime* was the first of a number of such autobiographies to be published. Its author grew up in a traditional Papuan setting before going on to prominence as a trade union leader and one of the founders of the Pangu Pati, the country's first major political party. He subsequently headed various ministries in government. The autobiography was produced in association with Ulli Beier who used tape-recordings provided by Kiki. *My Childhood in New Guinea* (1972), by Sir Paulius Matane, is clearly influenced by folk-tales he grew up listening to. Ongka's *Self-Account of a New Guinea Big-man* (1979) was translated into English by Andrew Strathern, a social anthropologist and authority on language and culture of Papua New Guinea. His translation makes the book accessible to a national audience rather than a merely tribal one.

The earliest autobiography by an indigenous writer in the country was *Erstwhile Savage: An Account of the Life of Ligeremaluoga* (1932), translated by E. Collins. In a foreword to the book, Raymond Pennington announced that the book had to be cut to make it suitable for publication. In the eyes of modern readers, Ligeremaluoga's descriptions of village life represent an impoverished record that undermines the value of his culture. It was reshaped at a time when European audiences were happy to visit museums full of artefacts bought and stolen without regard for supposedly primitive owners.

In contrast to other writing in this distinctly masculine domain, Deborah Carlyon's *Mama Kuma: One Woman, Two Cultures* (2002) and Carol Kidu's *A Remarkable Journey* (2002) both focus on family life, including occasional racial attacks, when indigenous and white family life crosses racial boundaries in Papua New Guinea. It is worth reemphasising that colonial regimes in Papua New Guinea were often draconian in practice and established racial hierarchies subjugating indigenous people. This led to outbreaks of interracial tension.

Miss Ulysses of Puka Puka (1948), by Cook Islander Johnny (Florence) Frisbie, positioned by its title page in the space between male and female authorship, has been reprinted and marketed internationally. The author was the daughter of an American writer-trader and Cook Island mother, and the book is shaped by indigenous culture. In spite of patriarchal and colonial identification as "The

Autobiography of a South Sea Trader's Daughter" in a work "Edited and translated by her father" and the fact that Frisbie was only thirteen when she wrote it, the narrative emerges as a strongly individualistic text. It employs a variety of devices deriving from oral tradition, including catalogs of genealogy; Polynesian phrases in and out of translation; use of a communal voice; and incorporation in written form of song, dance, story-telling, and other modes of performance. Nineteen years earlier, Robert Dean Frisbie, Florence's father, published *The Book of Puka Puka*. It describes the atoll he moved to, to flee an unhappy life in his native United States. Florence's book ends with her father meeting James Michener, author of *Tales of the South Pacific* (1947), a detail that reemphasizes the intertextual nature of her book. The testimony of both father and daughter is still valued by members of the Pukapuka people and acknowledgments on the Internet by contemporary members of the tribe continue to praise Ropati's (Robert's) role as a recorder of their traditional way of life.

Island Boy: An Autobiography (1992), by Cook islander Thomas Davis, Pa Tuterangi Ariki, documents individual aspiration in multicultural settings. Brought up in Rarotonga, Davis moved first to New Zealand to qualify as a doctor. He became a Harvard academic and subsequently worked with NASA as a space surgeon on the American space program. His autobiography traces an extraordinary path from a small Pacific island to metropolitan America. He later returned to the Cook Islands in 1971 to become Leader of the Opposition and then a successful prime minister from 1978 to 1987. Readers have sardonically related this book to Polynesian traditions of boastfulness in oral performance. It is certainly different from other autobiographies previously mentioned, partly because of the remarkable scope of the author's life and interests.

Indo-Fijian experience incorporates a rich cultural history shaped by the largely oral tradition of the Ramaiyana and the Mahabhhrata. A distinctive body of Indo-Fijian writing in the areas of autobiography, biography, memoir, and personal testimony over the past two decades has been additionally prompted by ethnic tensions and coups, following which large numbers of Fijian Indians departed to live in Australia. The number of Indo-Fijians in Fiji and Australia in total approaches half a million, one of the largest ethnic reading publics for South Pacific writers. Subramani's *Altering Imagination* (1995), Satendra Nandan's *Requiem for a Rainbow* (2001), Brij V. Lal's *Mr. Tulsi's Store: A Fijian Journey* (2001), and Sudesh Mishra's *Diaspora and the Difficult Art of Dying* (2002) engage with a diasporic state on many levels because Fijian Indians have been obliged to negotiate with a double alienation, both from Fiji and from their Indian heritage. Lal focuses on the need for ethnic reconciliation; Nandan recounts personal anecdotes of his political life, which he assembled after the 1987 coup in Fiji.

Robert Louis Stevenson

Robert Louis Stevenson was called Tusitala, "the teller of tales," by those he lived among in Western Samoa. The country's premier school in Apia is named after him; his famous children's novel, *Treasure Island*, has been translated into the local language; and the house he built has been made into an internationally recognized museum.

In an interview in 2001, Subramani observed his feeling at the time that writing no longer offered the kind of direct contact he urgently needed with fellow countrymen and his belief that only the spoken word would do. Over the past decade, the censorship and even intimidation of individuals have on occasion challenged freedom of expression in Fiji.

As well as being inherently important sociopolitical history, all of these autobiographies represent role models and information for South Pacific islanders dealing with the challenges of rapidly changing post-colonial societies.

EDUCATIONAL TEXTS

Reading habits are formed in primary, middle, and secondary schools, and in the South Pacific, problems have arisen in this area. Where the practice of oral literature continues to predominate, reading is seen as relatively unimportant. Throughout the South Pacific, broader problems include a lack of resources, and programs are only now becoming relevant to the local situation. Libraries are poorly stocked, there are often not enough books available to students, and where they are available they are written in English. However, the situation is changing slowly; syllabi are being modified and updated, and reading lists include texts in local languages telling local stories. To meet this need, local and multinational companies distribute books in Cook Islands Maori, Niuean, Samoan, Tokelauan, and Tongan. A government-run publishing company in New Zealand called Learning Media publishes books in Pacifika languages at the rate of one every eleven days for New Zealand schoolchildren with a Pacific Island heritage.

WOMEN'S BOOKS AND FEMINIST TEXTS

Colonial and cross-cultural experience had positive and negative effects for women in the South Pacific. Their writing consequently confronts new attitudes to marriage, educational opportunities and responsibilities, and changes in family life. Missionaries believed that Christian men should be supported by educated women. Since that time, increased educational opportunities lead women in particular to review what they ask of marriage and other relationships; this leads to deeper and more meaningful unions. However, post-colonial society has also caused considerable social disruption. Conflict arises when cultural tradition is dislocated, for instance, by relationships between white and indigenous partners. This leads to insecurity and violence by indigenous men toward wives, girlfriends, and daughters.

Urbanization has also modified both rural and urban women's lives. Rural women have to assume greater responsibility for their children's education when men are obliged to work in the city and are often unable to live at home. Women in urban settings who favor the nuclear family over the traditional extended family may find themselves too dependent on husbands and thus obliged to develop their own careers. In the wake of such changes, there is an urgent need for information and, therefore, a potential readership for affordable and accessible books across a range of subjects.

Women have responded by forming groups and engaging in projects coauthored by groups of between eight and eighteen writers to produce short, informative titles selling for less than ten U.S. dollars. *Pacific Women on the Move* (1983) deals with education, business, cooperatives, and associations between the church and family law, including divorce. *Land Rights of Pacific Women* (1986) tackles topics governments have often approached in an exclusively male context. *Literacy and Pacific Women* (1991) supplies information about distance education, libraries, and the media. *Woman Ikat Raet Long Human Raet O No?* (1996), subtitled *Women's Rights, Human Rights and Domestic Violence in Vanuatu*, outlines conventions eliminating discrimination against women and, to ensure it can be read by major language groups, is written in English, French, and Bislama

(Vanuatu Pidgin). *Breaking the Silence* (1998), published by the Women's Crisis Centre in Suva, is a collection of poems, stories, and essays on the subject of domestic violence. *"Mi Mere": Poetry and Prose by Solomon Islands Women* (1983) offers a more broadly based selection of writing from the Solomons. The majority of these are marketed through the Institute of Pacific Studies at Suva.

The Women and Fisheries Network, established following discussions in Suva in 1992, exemplifies the resourceful spirit driving self-help projects among women aware that they have not always benefited from international funding obtained in their name. The group successfully applied for assistance from the International Centre for Ocean Development and, in 1995, published *Fishing for Answers: Women and Fisheries in the Pacific Islands.* Working at local, regional, and national levels, others have built on previously established organizations such as the YWCA and Sepik Women's Development Corporation. Publications will no doubt continue to appear in hard copy, as long as computers and Internet access are expensive and not widely available for personal use. However, this situation is slowly changing, and increasing Internet publication and Web sites will increase both readership and membership without the increased investment required to distribute hard copy.

In spite of such developments, the position of many women in the region has remained little changed. Urban and rural dwellers have conflicting interests and, on the subject of post-colonial recuperation, male commentators still argue it is best for women to continue in traditional roles. City newspapers that include women's pages like the *Papua New Guinea Post-Courier*, however, generate and publish lively correspondence from female readers.

HISTORIES AND ESSAY COLLECTIONS

Until independence, the history of peoples in this region was neglected as a result of their colonial status. When independence was granted, this situation changed. Newly created countries needed to tell their stories. Precolonial situations had to be researched. Colonial eras became prologues for brand-new national entities that, in the case of countries like Papua New Guinea, had consisted of large numbers of clans and tribes living on the same island. Years leading up to, and following on from, the granting of independence involved vigorous political activity as parties formed and jockeyed for power. A number of accounts of nations in the Pacific region have been completed by academics from outside, but it is appropriate for indigenous writers to take possession of their own histories as well. John Waiko's *A Short History of Papua New Guinea* (1993) gives an account of the largest and most populated country in the South Pacific. His book appeared two decades after the first phase of writing in the region. This reflects the difference between writing text shaped by personal experience, as in the case of lyric poetry, autobiography, or the narrative focus of novelist and playwright, and the monumental task of presenting the story of a nation. Although books like Waiko's are aimed at educated audiences and are most likely to be found on the shelves of university libraries and government institutions, they fulfill the indispensable role of reappraising cultural, social, and political processes.

New nationhood induces transformation, and another task facing writers is to record and preserve what has been, before it disappears from memory. A particularly effective way to do this is by using many voices and points of view within one text. *Kiribati: Aspects of History* was subsidized in part by a UNESCO grant and written by twenty-five I-Kiribati. *The History of Tuvalu*, also supported by UNESCO, was written by eighteen Tuvaluans.

Alternatively, individual authors may research, collect, and assemble diverse material. *The Fijian Way of Life*, by Asesela Ravuvu, describes custom and behavior in contemporary Fiji. In view of the 1987 overthrow of Timoci Bavadra, the democratically elected Indo-Fijian prime minister, it is not surprising that Indo-Fijian writers write compulsively about national politics. A book such as *Fiji: Paradise in Pieces* (2000), by Satendra Nandan, appeals on a personal level to the sympathy of interested readers. It is noteworthy that this is an expatriate production, prompted and supported by members of the media in New Zealand, and edited and published in Australia. Local histories heighten ownership of place, time, and narrative and are particularly suited to small, focused publications for enthusiastic audiences in the region. *The History of Rarotonga: Up to 1853*, by Taira Rere, for example, sold out its first edition of a thousand copies within two years. Undaunted by economic constraints, the author's daughters subsequently distributed the book to its Cook Islands readership photocopied and saddle-stitched.

The essay form, which provides opportunities for authors to reflect on issues and develop positions, is well-suited to debates on nation-building. Questions about the integrity of political leaders, the potentially corrupting power of wealth, and the need for egalitarianism dominate essays by Bernard Narokabi under the title *Life and Leadership in Melanesia* (1983). Like poets, playwrights, and other commentators in Papua New Guinea, Nakarobi is concerned about control exerted by foreigners within the national economy. Where creative writers dramatize, his essays tease out and establish personal positions. Polemic and scholarship can exercise a far-reaching influence on writers' perceptions of their roles and readers' approaches to written text. In a collection of essays entitled *Solomon Islands Politics* (1983), Francis Bugotu worries about states that become what he calls "copy-cat nations," unable to think and act creatively for themselves, a theme in Hau'ofa's short fiction and, more broadly speaking, a rationale for writing in every genre. Steven Edmund Winduo emphasizes the role of what he calls the Pacific writer-scholar, working through traces to "reinstate what has been crossed out but is visible even in erasure" (600). In addition to fiction by Albert Wendt and Russell Soaba, Winduo has in mind Subramani's *South Pacific Literature: from Myth to Fabulation* (1985), a work that, as he puts it, "restored confidence in the literary culture of the Pacific" (609).

Art history in the South Pacific preserves the cultural, social, and spiritual history of artefacts. *Hohao* (1971), by Ulli Beier and Albert Maori Kiki, was published shortly before independence in Papua New Guinea. *Hohoa* are carved and painted spirit boards in the Orokolo region in the Papuan Gulf. Though Orokolo culture survived longer than others in the region, its cult houses were burned down prior to World War II, most likely by Christian converts; the culture, including initiation ceremonies and artefacts such as hohoa, disappeared until the latter were revived for commercial distribution. Any kind of preservation makes its subject static and introduces additional and complicating levels of meaning. In spite of this, such documentation and testimony play an essential role in the formation of national identity and the knitting together of past, present, and future.

CONCLUSION

Readership in the South Pacific has expanded over the years since original settlement, as traditional oral and written forms evolved into the broad sweep of reading material now available in the region. The relatively high literacy rate in the region, arising from the establishment of universities in the South Pacific, currently provides a creative environment for new writers. They can fulfill the roles of spokesman and ombudsman that are particularly important in rapidly changing societies. Colonial and post-colonial stereotypes generated by nonindigenous writers become grist to the mill of indigenous writers, who develop their own subversive accounts. Complex and hybrid heritages provide a range of formal possibilities to explore contemporary experience. Text provides a unifying vehicle to address regional issues arising out of the consequences of colonial disruption and the need for various kinds of reconciliation. Readers will continue to access ideas, whether in the form of oral literature, written text, electronically—via digital media and the Internet—or through the enduring presence of the Bible and religious institutions that originally introduced the practice of reading books to the region.

At the same time, cross-cultural interaction over the past two centuries, in conjunction with more recent patterns of migration, has endowed individuals with an evolving sense of regional identity. As Epeli Hau'ofa has pointed out, the enduring commonality of the ocean within and around the Pacific liberates readers and writers alike from parochialism. In a similar vein, Fijian Indian novelist Subramani evokes a new intellectual life arising from the interaction of the twelve hundred island languages to provide a homecoming for migrants and those who have remained living on the islands where they were born and raised. As writing in the South Pacific confirms its status as a body of world literature, so it will continue to celebrate its individuality and diversity in the process.

CURRENT AVAILABILITY

Multinational companies publish writers with international profiles, such as Albert Wendt and Epeli Hau'ofa. Among a number of local online retailers, the University Bookshop Centre markets titles online from the Institute of Pacific Studies, the South Pacific Forum, and smaller publishers in the region. Amazon and other e-commerce book companies also supply specialist and nonspecialist books published in the South Pacific Region. Availability varies, and not all titles are reprinted. E-commerce companies such as Amazon may be able to advise about forthcoming reprints and carry second-hand books.

RECOMMENDED READING

Crowl, Linda. "Book Publishing in the Pacific Islands." *Trout: Online Journal of Arts and Literature from Aotearoa/New Zealand and the Pacific Islands* 1 (1996).

Dening, Greg. *Beachcrossings: Voyaging across Times, Cultures and Self.* Melbourne: Melbourne University Publishing, 2004.

Gorle, Gilian. "The Second Decade: The Theme of Social Change in Papua New Guinea, 1979–1989." *Pacific Studies.* 19.1 (1996): 53–90.

Hanlon, David. "Beyond the English Method of "Tattooing": Decentering the Practice of History in Oceania." *The Contemporary Pacific Spring.* (2003).

Hau'ofa, Epeli, Eric Waddell, and Vijay Naidu, eds. *A New Oceania: Rediscovering Our Sea of Islands.* Suva: The University of the South Pacific, 1993.

———. "The Ocean in Us." *Dialogue.* (1998): 391–410.

Lynch, J., and F. Mugler. "English in the South Pacific." *World Englishes.* 8.1 (1989).

Sharrad, Paul. *Readings in Pacific Literature.* Wollongong: New Literatures Research Centre, 1993.

Sharrad, Paul. *Albert Wendt and Pacific Literature: Circling the Void.* Auckland: Auckland University Press, 2003.

Simms, Norman. *Writers from the South Pacific: A Bio-Bibliographical Encyclopedia.* Washington: Three Continents Press, 1991.

Smith, Bernard. *European Vision and the South Pacific: A Study in the History of Art and Ideas.* Oxford: Oxford University Press, 1960.

Smith, Vanessa. *Literary Culture and the Pacific: Nineteenth Century Textual Encounters.* Cambridge: Cambridge University Press, 1998.

Subramani. *South Pacific Literature: From Myth to Fabulation.* 2nd ed. Suva: University of the South Pacific, 1985.

PRIMARY SOURCES

Billy, Afu, Hazel Lulei, and Jully Sipolo: *"Mi Mere": Poetry and Prose by Solomon Islands Women.* Suva: Institute of Pacific Studies, 1983.

Brash, Nora Vagi. "Pick the Bone Dry." *Ondobondo.* 7 (1986): 20–30.

———. *Which Way Big Man and Five Other Plays.* Port Moresby: Oxford University Press, 1996.

Campbell, Alistair Te Ariki. *The Dark Lord of Savaiki.* Christchurch: Hazard Press, 2005.

———. *Frigate Bird.* Auckland: Reed Press, 1989.

———. *Sidewinder.* Auckland: Reed Press, 1991.

Carlyon, Deborah. *Mama Kuma: One Woman, Two Cultures.* St Lucia: University of Queensland Press, 2002.

Davis, Thomas R. A. H. *Island Boy: An Autobiography.* Suva: Institute of Pacific Studies, University of the South Pacific, 1992.

Davis, Thomas and Lydia Davis. *Makutu.* London: Michael Joseph, 1960.

Delaney, Adam Vai. *Chant of the Witchdoctor: A Dance Drama Tribal Musical.* Port Moresby: Published Privately, 1991.

———. *When Two Tribes Go to War.* Port Moresby: Department of Education, 1991.

Eri, Vincent. *The Crocodile.* Brisbane: Jacaranda Press, 1970.

Figiel, Sia. *The Girl in the Moon Circle.* Suva: Institute of Pacific Studies, 1996.

———. *Where We Once Belonged.* Kaya/Muae: Kaya Press, 1999.

Frisbie, Johnny (Florence). *Miss Ulysses of Puka Puka.* New York: Macmillan, 1948.

Frisbie, Robert Dean. *The Book of Puka Puka.* New York: Century Company, 1929.

Hau'ofa, Epeli. *Kisses in the Nederends.* Auckland: Penguin, 1987.

———. *Tales of the Tikongs.* Auckland: Longman Paul, 1983.

Hereniko, Vilsoni. *Don't Cry, Mama.* Suva: South Pacific Creative Arts Society, 1977.

Johnson, Villia, et al. *Houra'a: Solomon Islands Short Stories.* Honiara: University of the South Pacific Solomon Islands Centre, 1981.

Just Dancing. Directed by Vilsoni Hereniko. Hawaii: Te Maka Productions, 1998.

Kasaipwalova, John. *Sail the Midnight Sun: A Kesawaga.* Trobriands: Credit Melanesia, 1980.

Kidu, Carol. *A Remarkable Journey.* Melbourne, Australia: Longman, 2002.

Kiki, Albert Maori. *Kiki: Ten Thousand Years in a Lifetime.* Melbourne: F. W. Cheshire, 1968.

Lal, Brij V. *Mr Tulsi's Store: A Fijian Journey.* Canberra: Pandanus Books, 2001.

The Land Has Eyes. Written and directed by Vilsoni Hereniko. Te Maka Productions, 2004.

Laracy, Hugh, ed. *Tuvalu: A History.* Suva: Institute of Pacific Studies, 1983.

Ligeremaluoga. *Erstwhile Savage: An Account of the Life of Ligeremaluoga.* Translated by E. Collins. Melbourne: Cheshire, 1932.

Lulei, Dennis, E. J. Nash, and John Saunana, eds. *Twenty-Four Poems of the Solomon Islands.* Honiara, Solomon Islands: USP Centre, 1977.

Maka'a, Julian. *The Confession and Other Stories.* Suva: University of the South Pacific Press, 1985.

Matane, Sir Paulius. *My Childhood in New Guinea.* London: Oxford University Press, 1972.

Mishra, Sudesh. *Diaspora and the Difficult Art of Dying.* Dunedin: University of Otago Press, 2002.

Nandan, Kavita Ivy, ed. *Stolen Worlds: Fijiindian Fragments.* Canberra: Ivy Press International, 2005.

Nandan, Satendra. *Fiji: Paradise in Pieces—Writing Ethics-Politics*. Adelaide: Flinders University, 2000.

———. *Requiem for a Rainbow*. Canberra: Pacific Indian Publications, 2001.

Narokobi, Bernard. *Life and Leadership in Melanesia*. Suva: IPS, 1983.

Ongka. *Ongka: A Self-Account by a New Guinea Big-Man*. Translated by Andrew Strathern. New York: St Martins Press, 1979.

Pillai, Raymond. *The Celebration*. Suva: Mana Publications and SCPAS, 1980.

Ravuvu, Asesela. *Vaka I Taukei: The Fijian Way of Life*. Suva: IPS, 1983.

Rere, Tiara. *The History of Raratonga: Up to 1853*. Raratonga: Rangaita Taira, 1992.

Slone, Thomas. *One Thousand One Papua New Guinea Nights: Folktales from Wantok Newspaper*. 2 vols. Oakland, CA: Masalai Press, 2001.

Soaba, Russell. *Wanpis*. Madang: Kristen Press Inc., 1977.

Stevenson, Robert Louis. "The Beach of Falesa." *Island Nights' Entertainments*. London: Cassell and Co, 1893.

Subramani. *Altering Imagination*. Suva: Pacific Writers Forum, 1995.

———. *South Pacific Literature: From Myth to Fabulation*. Suva: IPS, 1985.

Talu, Sister Alaima, et al. *Kiribati: Aspects of History*. Tarawa, Kiribati: Ministry of Education, Training and Culture, 1979.

Thomas, Larry, ed. *Breaking the Silence*. Suva: Women's Crisis Centre, 1998.

Tuitolavaa, Agafili La'au. *Rhyanapoinciana: Tusi Tala Faa Samoa*. Apia: Agafili La'au Tuitolavaa, 1985.

Waiko, John. *A Short History of Papua New Guinea*. Melbourne: Oxford University Press, 1995.

Wendt, Albert. *Book of the Black Star*. Auckland: Auckland University Press, 2002.

———. *Flying Fox in a Freedom Tree*. Auckland: Longman Paul, 1974.

———. *Inside Us Dead: Poems 1961 to 1974*. Auckland, New Zealand: Longman Paul, 1976.

———, ed. *Lali: A Pacific Anthology*. Auckland: Longman Paul, 1980.

———. *Leaves of the Banyan Tree*. Auckland: Longman Paul, 1979.

———, ed. *Nuanua*. Auckland: University Press, 1995.

———. *Sons for the Return Home*. Auckland: Longman Paul Limited, 1973.

Winduo, Steven. *Lomo'ha I Am, in Spirit's Voice I Call*. Suva: South Pacific Creative Arts Society, 1991.

SECONDARY TEXTS

Beier, Ulli, ed. *Black Writing from New Guinea*. St Lucia: University of Queensland Press, 1973.

———, ed. *Kovave: A Journal of New Guinea Literature*. Brisbane: Jacaranda Press, 1969.

———, ed. *Voices of Independence: New Black Writing from Papua New Guinea*. St Lucia: University of Queensland Press, 1980.

Beier, Ulli, and Albert Maori Kiki. *Hohao*. Melbourne: Thomas Nelson, 1970.

Bolabola, Cema, Dorothy Kenneth, Henlyn Silas, Mosikaka Moengagnongo, Aiono Fana'afi, and Margaret James. *Land Rights of Pacific Women*. Pacific: IPS Publications, 1986.

Bugotu, Francis, et al. *The Pacific Way (Na I Tovo Vakapasifika)*. Suva: ISP, 1982.

Campbell, Ian, Barbara Hau'ofa, and Dawn Gibson, eds. *Journal of Pacific Studies*. Suva: University of the South Pacific.

Fong, Elizabeth Reade, Jayshree Mamtora, and Joan Teaiwa, eds. *Literacy and Pacific Women*. Pacific: Fiji Association of Women Graduates, 1991.

Jolly, Margaret. "Woman Ikat Raet Long Human Raet O No? (Women's Rights, Human Rights and Domestic Violence in Vanuatu: The World Upside Down: Feminisms in the Antipodes)." *Feminist Review*. 52. Spring (1996): 169–90.

Larmour, Peter, and Sue Tarua, eds. *Solomon Islands Politics*. Suva: IPS, 1983.

Mana: A South Pacific Journal of Language and Literature. Suva, Fiji: South Pacific Creative Arts Society.

Mana Review: A South Pacific Journal of Language and Literature. Suva, Fiji: South Pacific Creative Arts Society.

Marksbury, R., ed. *Love and Marriage among the Educated Elite in Port Moresby: Transformations in Oceanic Matrimony.* Pittsburgh, PA: University of Pittsburgh Press, 1993.

Matthews, Elizabeth. *Fishing for Answers: Women and Fisheries in the Pacific Islands.* Suva: Women and Fisheries Network, 1995.

Minol, Bernard. "The Death of PNG Writing." *Times of Papua New Guinea.* 26 September 1980: 21.

Research School of Pacific Studies. *Women in Politics in Papua New Guinea.* Working Paper No 6, Canberra Department of Political and Social Change. Canberra: Australian National University, 1985.

Thomas, Pam, et al. "Pacific Women on the Move." *Pacific Perspective.* 11.2 (1983).

Toft, S., and S. Bonnell. *Marriage and Domestic Violence in Rural Papua New Guinea.* Law Reform Commission of Papua New Guinea, 1985.

Winduo, Steven Edmund. "Unwriting Oceania." *New Literary History.* 31.3 (2000): 599–613.

CHAPTER 19

A Note on Southeast Asia

Gabrielle Watling

TIMELINE

200 B.C.E.	Jawa Dwipa Hindu Kingdom in Java and Sumatra
100s B.C.E.	Hinduism and Buddhism established in Malay Peninsula
1200s B.C.E.	Islam reaches Malay Peninsula and Indonesian archipelago via Indian traders
1293–1500 C.E.	Majapahit Empire dominates other kingdoms in the southern Malay Peninsula, Borneo, Sumatra, Bali, and southern Philippines
1519	Ferdinand Magellan leaves Spain for the "East Indies"
1521	Magellan reaches the Philippines and is killed at the Battle of Mactan
1700s	Dutch East India company established as dominant colonial power in the East Indies
1811–16	British take over control of Dutch possessions during Napoleonic Wars
1800–1942	Indonesia and Dutch colonial territories collectively known as Dutch East Indies
1932	Thailand becomes a constitutional monarchy
1939–1945	World War II—Japanese occupation throughout Southeast Asia
1945	Indonesian independence; Vietnamese independence (from France, not recognized until 1954)
1954	Vietnamese defeat French colonial forces at Dien Bien Phu
1957	Malaysian independence
1960–75	War in Vietnam
1965	Attempted overthrow of President Sukarno in Indonesia
1967	ASEAN formed (Association of South East Asian Nations)
1968	General Suharto becomes president of Indonesia
1972	U.S. troops leave Vietnam
1975	Fall of Saigon; U.S. embassy closes; East Timor declares independence from Indonesia, which Indonesia refuses to recognize
1980s	Southeast Asian nations move closer to democracy

1986	"People power" deposes Ferdinand Marcos in favor of Corazon Aquino in the Philippines
1990	Free elections are held in Burma for the first time in almost thirty years (Aung San Suu Kyi's National League for Democracy party wins 392 out of a total 489 seats, but the ruling SLORC party refuses to recognize the NLD's victory. Aung San Suu Kyi is put under house arrest, where she remains to this day)
1998	Suharto bows to political pressure and resigns as president of Indonesia
2004	East Timor finally achieves independence from Indonesia; tsunami wipes out communities in Indonesia, Malaysia, and Thailand

INTRODUCTION TO THE REGION

Southeast Asia comprises a group of independent nations that are situated to the south of China, the east of India, and the north of Australia. The region recognizes and exercises its coherence through ASEAN, the Association of South East Asian Nations, which includes Indonesia, Brunei, Myanmar (Burma), Malaysia, the Philippines, Singapore, Thailand, Vietnam, Cambodia, and Laos. East Timor, which gained full independence from Indonesia in 2002, is not yet a member of ASEAN. Southeast Asia is dominated by the populous Islamic bloc of Indonesia and Malaysia, but Buddhism is the dominant religion in Vietnam, Cambodia, Laos, and Thailand. East Timor and the Philippines are predominantly Catholic (after their Portuguese and Spanish colonizers), but with a strong emerging Islamic influence.

The history of the Southeast Asian nations is dominated by a combination of diasporic movement and, with the exception of Thailand, European colonization. This combination characterizes the region in terms of major change, movement, and cross-cultural influence. Prior to European arrival, large groups of Chinese settled throughout Southeast Asia, especially in the Malay Peninsula and Singapore, and today, the Chinese constitute the ethnic majority in Singapore. Large Chinese communities can also be found in Indonesia, Thailand, Myanmar (Burma), the Philippines, and Vietnam. Moreover, large Indian communities have become established in Malaysia, Myanmar, and Singapore.

Since the sixteenth century, the Dutch, Spanish, Portuguese, British, French, and, most recently, Americans have all exercised colonial control in the region, while during World War II the Japanese occupied and brutally suppressed most of the region's nations. American, British, and Australian troops gradually expelled the occupying Japanese forces, but the battles were protracted and hundreds of thousands of allied, native, and Japanese lives were lost between 1939 and 1945. The Philippines was at the center of Japanese hostilities, and Americans have long remembered the Bataan Death March as representative of wartime hostilities in Southeast Asia.

Southeast Asia was also the site of another of the twentieth century's wars, the Vietnam conflict of the 1960s and 1970s. After World War II, many Southeast Asian nations gained independence from their exhausted European colonizers. But the fledgling nations struggled to establish economic independence. Often, the nations' financial, commercial, and productive sectors were controlled by a few wealthy families (who had enjoyed colonial preference), while most citizens could barely feed and clothe themselves. Unrest in the poorer sectors gave rise to interest in communist philosophies and the formation of Marxist unions and organizations. Marxist influence gained momentum with the aid of soviet and Chinese support. As communist influence grew and began to emerge as a realistic alternative to

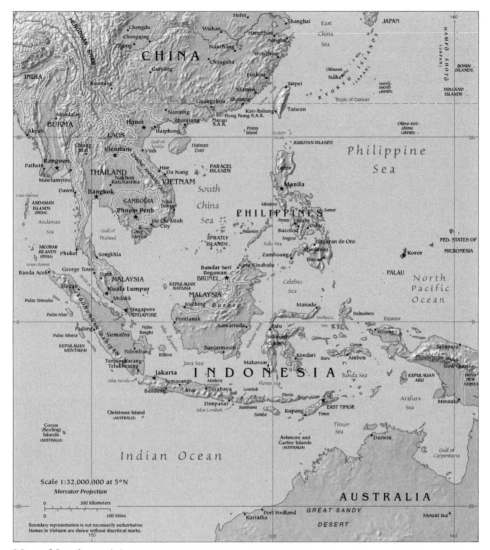

Map of Southeast Asia.

plutocratic pseudo-democracies, political instability came to characterize Southeast Asian politics. This phenomenon was nowhere more evident than in Vietnam, which U.S. government officials feared would fall to the communist "domino effect" (like North Korea before it) after the colonizing French were defeated at Dien Bien Phu in 1953. Both the conservative, commercial south and the Marxist northern sides appealed to the United States for support in the growing Indo-Chinese conflict. But the United States, in the midst of Cold War paranoia, had no interest in supporting Ho Chi Minh, the communist leader in North Vietnam. Instead, American troops (supported by their Pacific allies in Australia) were poured into Vietnam to help fight the "Viet Cong." The conflict was a disaster. Over five million Vietnamese lives were lost in the conflict according to official Vietnamese figures, along with nearly fifty thousand U.S. and Australian lives.

After the Vietnam War, many Southeast Asian nations began to modernize. Indonesia gradually turned to a more democratic political system, and the people of the Philippines famously deposed the dictator Ferdinand Marcos in 1986, and replaced him with a democratically elected president, Corazon Aquino. Vietnam eventually achieved economic stability under a communist government, ironically through western tourism and manufacturing goods for western corporations. Thailand, which has never been colonized, suffered a coup in 2006 in a reversal of the region's stabilization trend. In 2004, the region was seriously affected by a massive tsunami.

READING TRENDS AND PRACTICES

The countries and cultures of Southeast Asia were very interdependent prior to European colonization. Religions, languages, cultural practices, and literatures were freely exchanged between the peninsula and island peoples. This intermingling of cultures and ideas intensified around the tenth century, with advances in nautical technology. Islam was transported to the Indonesian archipelago by Muslim traders from India. Buddhism arrived in the mainland cultures from Sri Lanka. Hinduism was popular in the region until the establishment of Buddhism, although Hinduism remains the primary religion of Bali. These religious influences characterized early reading practices in the Southeast Asia region.

In the fifteenth century, the central Malaysian settlement of Melaka adopted Islam as its official religion; in doing so, it attracted Arabic traders who in turn strengthened the area as a commercial and cultural exchange. Cultural, linguistic, and commercial influence spread throughout the region from this central location. The Chinese also traded widely in the region, transporting ideas, goods, and practices through the Malay Peninsula and to Indonesia and the Philippines. In fact, the earliest known piece of writing from the area, the so-called Laguna Copperplate Inscription, which dates from about 900 C.E., provides evidence of a network of literate societies and the use of written language and documentation for business purposes. Anthropologists generally agree that, although written culture in Southeast Asia sprang from Indian and Chinese influences, it was given form on the Malay Peninsula.

David Smyth's 2000 book, *The Canon in Southeast Asian Literature: Literatures of Burma, Cambodia, Indonesia, Laos, Malaysia, Philippines, Thailand, and Vietnam*, is a collection of essays on the religious and cultural texts from precolonial Southeast Asia. The first contributor to the book, Yuriy M. Osipov, points out that the established "sacred scriptures" of "Buddhist hagiography" helped to develop the "national epic traditions in classical poetry, prose and drama in forming the canon of Myanmar (Burmese), Khmer, Lao, Mon and Siamese (Thai) literatures" (1). In fact, the various cultures of the region contributed to a rich literary tradition, part spiritual, part secular, which helped to shape the region's characteristic narrative format. However, the early written scriptures, and the court poetry and epics that followed them, were largely restricted to the literate: royalty, court attendants, and monks. Stories, poems, and dramas that might have been modeled on or inspired by these texts were passed through the village communities orally or through performance. This model of textual transmission—the consumption of the written document by the social elite or oral/aural or visual transmission within the common classes—was practiced throughout all human societies until relatively recently. Therefore, at the time that European colonizers arrived in Southeast Asia, reading patterns in the region were very similar to those that the colonizers had left behind in "enlightened" Europe.

Inside the Times Bookstore at the Funan Digitalife Mall in Singapore [Courtesy of Alex Daman]

However, European colonizers introduced another level of documentation. Given that their focus was profit, most available paper was used in the service of business. But as the European colonies became established and began to attract settlers, European education systems enabled the rise of a print culture. As it did throughout the world, European colonization in Southeast Asia was characterized by efforts to Europeanize the local peoples and their bureaucratic systems. To that end, missions, schools, and legal infrastructure were imposed on local customs and tribal practices. Some efforts to colonize culture were more "successful" than others: Catholicism became widespread in the Philippines, and French became the language of business and society in Vietnam.

However, one of the long-lasting effects of European communication and idea systems was the emergence of literature in print for the consumption of Southeast Asian readers. This movement had the effect of centering print material on a small group of European languages, as opposed to the thousands of dialects spoken throughout Southeast Asia. But, as European influence waned in the twentieth century, the region's nations of course took more responsibility for producing print documents themselves, and readable materials in local languages became available. However, determining patterns from the vast array of documents, languages, cultures, districts, and traditions is a daunting task. All that can be said with any certainty is that, although they had their own oral and written customs and practices, Southeast Asians probably did not become readers in the broad sense until Europeans arrived with printed devotional materials. Furthermore, as Virginia Matheson Hooker argues, "creative writer" was "not a recognised profession in traditional society" (xvi); written versions of traditional epics, fables, and myths constituted the vast majority of fictional material, even well into the twentieth century.

As print culture grew and strengthened, creative "literature" in both European and local languages started to emerge. But as Southeast Asian countries and economies merged with western cultures and economies, Southeast Asian readers added western-style publications—newspapers, magazines, and nonfiction professional advice primers—to their reading lists. These formats (the newspaper/magazine, the "how to" guide, and, to a lesser extent, the novel) appear to dominate the reading patterns of the region. For this reason, this subsection will address broad trends in reading rather than individual, textual genres.

NEWSPAPERS AND MAGAZINES

As a region of enormous political change and flux, the Southeast Asian nations have never been short of news items. Newspapers therefore top the list of reading trends in terms of publication sales. Filipinos, in particular, have long had a newspaper industry. According to Leon Comber (*Writing in Asia*), because the Philippines is the third largest English-speaking nation in the world, newspapers are mostly published in English and are mostly read by the middle and upper classes. The *Philippine Daily Inquirer* is the most widely read of the Philippine newspapers, with over 2.7 million readers and a market share of fifty percent. Moreover, Summit Media publishes a variety of popular magazines, including Philippine editions of popular American and European magazines, such as *Cosmopolitan*, *FHM*, *Men's Health*, *Seventeen*, and *Marie Claire*. Popular Philippine magazines, such as *Candy*, *Yes!*, *Preview*, and *Yummy*, dominate the reading polls, according to Summit Media, the "leading magazine publisher in the Philippines" according to its Web site (www.summitmedia.com.ph).

Sales of popular, western-themed magazines in the Philippines are not echoed in Vietnam, however, where information is still largely controlled by the government. Newspaper publishing in Vietnam *has* increased with the "*doi moi*" free-market measures adopted by the government in the mid-nineties, but the 2007 "Worldwide Press Freedom Index", compiled by the media-watch organization Reporters without Borders (Reporters Sans Frontiers) ranked Vietnam 161 out of 167 countries in terms of press freedom and transparency (http://www.rsf.org/article.php3?id_article=11715). All media in Vietnam are closely controlled by the government. The major newspapers, such as *Tuoi Tre* (published in Ho Chi Minh City), *Thanh Nien*, *Lao dong*, *Tien Phong*, *Sai Gon Giai Phong*, and *Ha noi moi*, enjoy less direct government control, but they also support government ideologies.

Large bookstores are scarce in Vietnam, and few popular magazines are available; however, the magazine supply Web site, www.allyoucanread.com, lists six magazines that appear to have circulation in the nation. They include the English language *Saigon Times* ("Your essential guide to the week's economic, business and commercial events, as well as cultural and tourist news and stories"). The remaining five magazines reflect Vietnam's major influences and suggest that reading in Vietnam is an information-gathering exercise, as opposed to a recreational pastime. *Song Manh* is a medical practices magazine that reproduces articles from western medical journals in Vietnamese. *The Vietnam Economic Times* and *The Vietnam Investment Review* indicate the growth in the business and financial sectors in recent years.

Vietnam's media offerings appear to be very slowly opening up to non-state-sanctioned ideologies. However the same cannot be said of another state-controlled nation in Southeast Asia, Myanmar (Burma). Heavy censorship and government control characterize Myanmar's literary and reading cultures, in much the same way as Vietnam's media were controlled after the end of the communist war. Since the military coup in 1962, the Burmese people have had a range of newspapers, television, and radio stations to choose from, but they are all state-controlled and deliver only state-sanctioned news and programs. And unlike other Southeast Asian countries, the Burmese cannot even rely on the Internet for outside perspectives. In September of 2007, as many as two thousand Burmese monks led protest marches through the nation's major cities, and the the government consequently cut Internet service throughout Myanmar.

According to www.allyoucanread.com, Indonesian magazine tastes spread across a variety of recognizable genres, from *Bisnis Indonesia*; to *Angkasa*, an aeronautical enthusiasts' journal; to *Bola*, a sports magazine; to *Intisari*, *Nova*, and *Hanyawanita*, all women's magazines; to *Tempo*—the Indonesian edition of *Time*; and *Warta Ekonomi*, another business magazine.

NONFICTION TEXTS

Southeast Asia is generally considered a region in development, but according to a 2007 conference, the region has a literacy rate of 91.7 percent (www.unesco.org). Literacy is highest in the most industrially developed nations, that is, Malaysia, Singapore, and, to a lesser extent, Indonesia. The appearance of major western retail book chains, such as Borders, is evidence of an upward climb in book and magazine consumption for these nations. That is, books are once more becoming a significant element of the commercial landscape in Southeast Asia. As family wealth grows, increasing numbers of children are able to attend universities, and increasingly, those universities are in western nations such as the United States, Australia, and Great Britain. Therefore, given that the young, professional classes have generally had significant exposure to western cultures and are fluent in English, book-buying patterns in the industrialized nations of Southeast Asia appear to be following general western models. So what sorts of books do Southeast Asians buy and, by extension, read?

Although evidence of reading in the region is not hard to come by, only the broadest of reading patterns emerge consistently among the area's nations. For example, the Web site that accompanied the 2007 Manila Book Fair (the twenty-eighth such book fair held in Manila) reports that the fair's primary partner organization was the Asian Catholic Communications Inc. and many of the exhibitors were Christian or religious publishers. In the Philippines at least, the evidence suggests that the region supports a significant trade in religiously themed books, which is "mainstream" enough to be housed at a major annual book fair, and not at a specialized Christian, or other religious event.

The Spanish colonizers first brought printed materials, especially devotional materials, to the Philippines. Therefore, the archipelago has a long history of Christian literature, which would have become more significant for the Filipinos as Christianity spread. Whereas we in the West make a distinction between secular and devotional literature, at least for the purposes of recreational reading, it would appear that no such distinction exists for Filipino readers.

Furthermore, although the group of nations in this region is clumped together for geographic expediency, according to the 2007 Book Development Association of the Philippines conference, books do not tend to circulate between the Southeast Asian countries (*Manila Bulletin* online). The growing Philippine trend in Christian-themed reading is not being replicated in other Southeast Asian nations, despite the area's precolonial tradition of free religious exchange. The Vietnamese, for example, generally prefer newspapers and magazines. Moreover, the Vietnamese adopted Quốc ngũ as their basic language form after French colonization, and it continues to be used for the rich oral tradition of stories, myths, and folk tales. The combination of strict government control and an established oral tradition means that Vietnamese readers do not have nearly the breadth of publications available to them as the peoples of other Southeast Asian nations.

On the other hand, Indonesia, another Southeast Asian country with a strong, ideologically based government system, has a growing book market. Not surprisingly, post-September 11 and the "Bali bombings" of 2002, which killed two hundred western tourists, the United States government has become acutely interested in what Indonesians are reading. The U.S. Department of State Web site reports that in 2005, "Bookshops did a brisk trade in fiction with Islamic themes, and Qur'anic verses were distributed via cellular phone text messages" (http://www.state.gov). However, despite the growth in Islamic texts among the Indonesian readership, more general Internet-based research indicates that Indonesian reading tastes are not limited to "Islamic themes, and Qur'anic verses." Periplus books, a major retail chain, is well-established throughout the Indonesian archipelago, with thirty-five modern bookstores. At the time of writing, the Periplus Web site listed the following titles under its "Bestsellers" heading:

- *Super Potato Design: The Complete Works of Takashi Sugimoto, Japan's Leading Interior Designer* by Mira Locher
- *Tuttle Concise Indonesian Dictionary* by Katherine Davidsen
- *25 Tropical Houses in Indonesia* by Amir Sidharta
- *The Devil Wears Prada* by Lauren Weisberger
- *25 Tropical Houses in Singapore & Malaysia* by Paul McGillick and Patrick Bingham
- *Blink: The Power of Thinking without Thinking* by Malcolm Gladwell
- *The Purpose Driven Life* by Rick Warren
- *Batavia in Nineteenth Century Photography* by Scott Merrillees
- *The Purpose Driven Church* by Rick Warren
- *The Best of Indonesian Cooking* by Yasa Boga

This list could as easily represent U.S. reading tastes in the early-twenty-first century.

CREATIVE TEXTS

As the Southeast Asian economies grow and align with western economies, media tastes become more similar. The Book Development Association of the Philippines's assertion that books do not tend to circulate between the Southeast Asian countries may well be true, but it would appear that creative litertaure—that is, novels, short stories, volumes of poetry, and drama—appear very infrequently in materials on Southeast Asian reading practices. Pramoedya Ananta Toer is one of Indonesia's most celebrated novelists, but as his many novels were mostly written while he was jailed as a dissident (the four novels of his so-called Buru Quartet were written about his imprisonment on Buru Island), and as they were therefore heavily censored by successive Indonesian governments, Pramoedya may well have more readers in the West than in his own country. In fact, the preponderance of Asian studies departments throughout the western university system is a testament to the great academic interest that the West takes in the region. The region has produced a significant number of novelists, poets, and dramatists, but to what extent do they figure in the reading habits of Southeast Asians themselves? According to its Web site, the University of Indonesia literature department, housed in the School of Humanities, lists twenty areas of literary interest. These are

1. Diaspora, migration, multiculturalism, and nationalism
2. Children's literature
3. Literature and philosophy
4. Film studies
5. Performing arts, drama, and theatre
6. Oral tradition
7. Study of hand-written manuscripts
8. Religion and cultures
9. Translation issues
10. Gender studies
11. Literary sociology and history
12. Cultural policies and cultural industries
13. Comparative literature
14. Semiotics
15. Area studies
16. Teaching of language, literature, and stylistics
17. Chinese Malay literatures and Malay literature during the colonial period
18. Poetry
19. Literary genres
20. Special interest in popular literatures (http://www.ui.ac.id/posts/en)

One could surmise from this list that regional literatures are highly valued by educated readers, at least in Indonesia. On the other hand, the largest, oldest, and most prestigious university in Malaysia, The University of Malaya, describes its undergraduate program in English in the following terms:

> The programme [sic] is comparable to those offered in universities in the United Kingdom and the United State of America. Canonical literatures in English that cover the whole period of development of English Literature, from the Medieval to the Modern, form the foundation for the Bachelor of Arts (English) programme. Due emphasis is also given to literature in English from other parts of the world such as Africa, India, Australia and USA. Apart from these, the department also offers courses reflective of current interdisciplinary developments in English Literature, such as "Literature and Popular Culture," "Language of Literature," and "Shakespeare on Screen." (http://www.um.edu.my/undergraduates/list_of_programmes)

This description suggests that European creative literatures outrank local literatures in the more westernized Malaysian education system.

Despite the low profile of creative genres in the local literature markets, Southeast Asia, as a region, supports a major literary award that has recognized and attracted some prominent names in the international literay field. The SEA Write Award (South East Asian Writers Award) has been sponsored and presented by the Thai Royal family since 1979. The Award is open to poets and writers from the ASEAN nations, although not every nation is recognized every year. Individual works are eligible for awards and these have included creative and nonfiction works in the past. The awards have a strong commercial tie-in: they are held at the Oriental Bankok hotel and sponsored by Thai Airways, along with other prominent regional corporations. However, the criteria for the award are decidedly noncommercial. The SEA is only open to living authors from the ASEAN member nations, individual literary works must be submitted in Thai (regardless of their original language), cannot be translations or adaptations of other works, must have an ISBN, and cannot previously have won any other awards. Therefore, the organizers and sponsors are promoting local literature by ensuring that popularly read western literature is not eligible for cultural recognition in Southeast Asia, despite its apparent domination of local reading markets.

However, educated readers, although a growing and influential social sector, are still a statistical minority in Southeast Asia, and in more general terms, evidence suggests that reading throughout most of the region appears to be trending strongly toward business guides, popular reference books, western-style romances, and magazines. This trend is no more apparent than in Singapore and Malaysia. These are the only two countries in which the U.S. chain Borders has opened brick and mortar retail outlets. The Borders store in Kuala Lumpur, capital of Malaysia, is located in Berjaya Times Square, a huge western-style shopping complex. According to Wikipedia, Borders Kuala Lumpur is the largest Borders store in the world. Little information on inventory is available, but anecdotal reports maintain that the store offers a huge variety of English-language business "motivational" and "how-to" manuals and business-themed biographies (such as *The 7 Habits of Highly Effective People* and quasi-biographies of Donald Trump, Warren Buffet, and Jack Welch). The next largest category is romance novels. The strength of this category is significant because it suggests that at least one sector of Southeast Asia's readership reads recreationally. Demographically, the readership would be educated (English-speaking) middle-class girls and women. Given the steady rise in tertiary education among Malaysia and Singapore's middle classes, and given the linking of English-language proficiency with education, one might conclude that the romance readership is made up of female college and university students.

CONCLUSION

Like most post-colonial regions, Southeast Asia appears to be trying to find a cultural balance between strong western influences and local cultural products. The enormous corporate machinery that ensures a constant supply of American media and media products, for example, will always present a challenge to the production and distribution of novels, poetry, and drama from the Southeast Asian region. However, the aim of this project is not to lament the overshadowing of native culture, but to take a "snap-shot," as it were, of what *is* being read around the world. The evidence suggests that reading habits in the Southeast Asian region currently resemble those of American readers. That is, recreational reading appears to be giving way to informational reading: how did America's wealthiest people become so successful in their respective fields? How can a high school student get an edge on the competition in the university entrance exams? How is the market responding to the arrival of the latest passenger jet? How does one adapt the latest make-up and beauty trends to local customs and religious ideologies? Which delicious new recipe will impress my in-laws at the next family dinner?

Furthermore, when literature is read for its intellectual properties, the literature under question may still be western, as the structure of the English program at the University of Malaya suggests. Finally, the act of reading itself is changing. Fewer people are reading recreationally, instead reading for news, information, and skill-development purposes. And, following the recent pattern in South Korea and Japan, many Southeast Asians are today getting their news from the Internet. The news sites most favored in the region are Asia Pacific News, Bangkok News, BBC Asia-Pacific, Burma Daily, CNN: Asia, and the WN Network. It would appear then that, just as the book and magazine market is gaining a commercial foothold in the region, the virtual format is poised to shift the market yet again. Therefore, given that the world's fastest growing economies are Asian-based, perhaps Americans and Europeans will be looking to Asia to guide reading trends in the future.

RECOMMENDED READING

Ieosiwong, Nithi, Christopher John Baker, Benedict R. O'G. Anderson, and Craig J. Reynolds. *Pen and Sail: Literature and History in Early Bangkok including The History of Bangkok in the Chronicles of Ayutthaya*. Chiang Mai, Thailand: Silkworm Books, 2006.

King, Victor T. *The Modern Anthropology of South-East Asia: An Introduction*. London: RoutledgeCurzon, 2003.

Kingsbury, Damien. *South-East Asia: A Political Profile*. New York: Oxford University Press, 2005.

Saunders, Graham, ed. *Tropical Interludes: European Life and Society in South-East Asia*. New York: Oxford University Press, 1998.

PRIMARY SOURCES

Boga, Yasa. *The Best of Indonesian Cooking*. Times Editions, n.d.

Covey, Stephen. *The 7 Habits of Highly Effective People*. New York: Simon and Schuster, 2004.

Gladwell, Malcolm. *Blink: The Power of Thinking Without Thinking*. Boston: Back Bay Books, 2007.

Kramer, A. L. N., Sr., Willie Koen, and Katherine Davidsen. *Tuttle Concise Indonesian Dictionary*. Tokyo: Tuttle Publishing, 2007.

Locher, Mira, and Yoshio Shiratori. *Super Potato Design: The Complete Works of Takashi Sugimoto, Japan's Leading Interior Designer*. Tokyo: Tuttle Publishing, 2007.

McGillick, Paul and Patrick Bingham. *25 Tropical Houses in Singapore & Malaysia*. Tokyo: Tuttle, 2006.

Manila Bulletin. http://www.mb.com.ph/. (The *Manilla Bulletin* is a daily newspaper, and has been operating for 108 years, according to its Web site.)

Merrillees, Scott. *Batavia in Nineteenth Century Photography*. Singapore: Editions Didier Millet, 2007.

Pramoedya Anata Toer. *Child of All Nations*. 1980. New York: Penguin, 1996.

———. *Footsteps*. 1985. New York: Penguin, 1996.

——— . *House of Glass*. 1988. New York: Penguin, 1996.

———. *This Earth of Mankind*. 1980. New York: Penguin, 1996.

Sidharta, Amir, and Masano Kawana. *25 Tropical Houses in Indonesia*. Tokyo: Tuttle Publishing, 2006.

Summit Media. www.summitmedia.com.ph. ("Summit Media: the leading magazine publisher in the Philippines" according to its Web site.)

Warren, Rick. *The Purpose Driven Church: Growth without Compromising Your Message & Mission*. Grand Rapids, MI: Zondervan Publishing Company, 1995.

———. *The Purpose Driven Life*. Grand Rapids, MI: Zondervan Publishing Company, 2007.

Weisberger, Lauren. *The Devil Wears Prada*. New York: Anchor, 2006.

SECONDARY SOURCES

28th Manila International Book Fair. http://www.manilabookfair.com/.

AllYouCanRead.com. http://www.allyoucanread.com. (An international magazine subscription Web site.)

Borders Books: Kuala Lumpur. http://www.bordersstores.com/stores/store_pg.jsp?storeID=651.

Church, Peter. *A Short History of South East Asia.* Singapore: John Wiley and Sons, 2006.

Matheson Hooker, Virginia. *Writing a New Society: Social Change through the Novel in Malay.* Honolulu: University of Hawaii Press, 2000.

Periplus Books Indonesia. http://www.periplus.co.id/browse.php.

S.E.A. Write Award. http://www.seawrite.com/SEA%20Write%20Main-E.html.

Smyth, David. *The Canon in Southeast Asian Literature: Literatures of Burma, Cambodia, Indonesia, Laos, Malaysia, Philippines, Thailand and Vietnam.* London: RoutledgeCurzon, 2000.

UNESCO. http://portal.unesco.org/en/ev.php-URL_ID=29008&URL_DO=DO_TOPIC&URL_SECTION=201.html.

University of Indonesia. http://www.ui.ac.id/posts/en.

University of Malaysia. http://www.um.edu.my/undergraduates/list_of_programmes.

U.S. State Department: Indonesia. http://www.state.gov/g/drl/rls/irf/2005/51512.htm.

PART 4
South Asia and the Indian Sub-Continent (India, Pakistan, Bangladesh, Sri Lanka)

CHAPTER 20

The Classical Period

Todd Rohman

TIMELINE

185 B.C.E.	The Mauryan dynasty ends; the last king is assassinated in a military coup
100 B.C.E.	The *Bhagavata Gita* is composed
3rd century	Pancatantra, a group of Sanskrit beast fables, is composed by Visnusarman
318 C.E.	Chandra Gupta founds the Gupta kingom in Magadha and extends its domains throughout northern India, with capital at Patna; through 470, the arts and sciences of north India expand into Southeast Asia, trade broadens
350	Samudra Gupta extends the Gupta kingdom to Assam, Deccan, Malwa; the Puranas are composed (a compendium of Hindu mythology)
375–425	*Sakuntala* is composed by Kalidasa in Sanskrit
380	Buddhist monks carve two giant Buddha statues in the rock at Bamiya, Bactria (Afghanistan)
390	Chandra Gupta II extends the Gupta kingdom to Gujarat
400	The Licchavi family unites Nepal
5th century	The *Satakatrayam* (The Anthology of Three Centuries) of Bhartrhari, a collection of Sanskrit epigrams, is produced; *Cilappatikaram*, which charts the epic exploits of Kannaki, is composed by Ilankovatikal, a Jaina monk.
400–500	*Tirukkural*, a grouping of aphorisms is written by Tiruvalluvar in the Tamil language; the *Kama Sutra*, a masterful treatise on the erotic, is composed by Vatsayana
450	The Gupta king Kumargupta builds the monastic university of Nalanda
455	The Huns raid the Gupta Empire in Punjab and Kashmir

INTRODUCTION TO THE REGION AND PERIOD

The classical, or "Gupta," period of South Asia covers the fourth and fifth centuries C.E. (320–550 C.E.). It is characterized historically by the consolidation of northern territories by Chandragupta I (318–30 C.E.), though many scholars include oral and written activity in the early "medieval" period of the seventh century. In contemporary geography, the region of South Asia includes Afghanistan, Bangladesh, Bhutan, India Nepal, Pakistan, Sri Lanka, and Tibet. Although geography provides a useful mental map of the region, it should be understood that accidents of climate, land formations, and access to rivers and lakes have bearing on oral and later literary traditions. Further, chronological divisions will always fail to capture the complexity of literary and artistic development, often only giving us a broad sense of creative activities transpiring in a given period. Such divisions are, of course, themselves transcriptions by very different cultures and during time periods much later. Geographical boundaries were permeable to outside cultural influence, and the ancient period saw influences through Greek and Arab incursions, which reminds us that cultural developments rarely occur as distinct isolates, however convenient this view may seem for scholarly inquiry.

During the classical period the Guptas' ruling dynasty, fervent supporters of art and literature, enjoyed influence that stretched throughout South, Southeast, and East Asia. Also, during this period, the now globally recognized writer Kalidasa composed works in Sanskrit, the language to which virtually all modern Indian tongues trace their origins and linguistic influence. Considering that modern India expresses four major branches of language, with these further branching into over four hundred others, the scale of classical Sanskrit influence cannot be overstated. The Indian epics were composed as text during this time (migrating from their purely oral roots), and other great works of this period include the play *Sakuntala* and the poem *Kumarasambhava* (which details the relationships and unions of great Indian gods). The *Kama Sutra*, a detailed compendium of the physical aspects of love, composed by Vatsyayana, was also written in the Gupta period. Historian and scholar John Keay remarks of this period "It was the crescendo of creativity and scholarship, as much as [that of] the Guptas, which would make their age so golden; and it was the wider use of Sanskrit and the exploration of its myriad subtleties that this awakening owed most" (132). Many of the texts set into writing in the Gupta period stemmed from much earlier works. The "classical" period also broadly refers to the period when classical Sanskrit (200 B.C.E.–1100 C.E.) developed and became defined from the preceding Vedic (1500 B.C.E.–200 B.C.E.). The separation of these languages bears some exploration. Vedic language, which contains all the sacred writing of India, was, throughout most of its usage, never a vernacular or common language. Rather, it was an "artificially archaic" form, passed among generations of priests; as versions of the Vedas become continually re-inscribed throughout their history, they come closer and closer to, and finally merge with, Sanskrit (MacDonell 20).

The pre-classical, or Vedic, period supplies important context for our understanding and appreciation of the classical period and is dominated by the works that give the period its name, the Vedas. No other scriptural text in the world is comparable in terms of its antiquity or the number of its adherents. Among the diverse range of Hindu sects, all regard the work as "Sruti," or "revealed" (literally, "heard," emphasizing the oral history of the form) and the work links all Hindus in a common spiritual bond (Gowen 8). The Vedas form the highest authority in religious and philosophic matters and are considered by Hindus to be eternal scriptures, without a beginning and without human authorship. Importantly, these works were not initially set down in writing, but rather passed orally from teacher to student. Although early scholars maintain that this oral system guaranteed a virtually "perfect" transmission of scripture, without even shifts in pronunciation over the generations, later scholars of oral traditions, such as Walter Ong, would question this assumption about oral systems. Rather than a verbatim transfer of information, Vedic teachers would more likely recite verse while responding to some degree to the exigencies of the moment of recitation (audience, occasion, etc.). Although numbers of set tropes would determine large selections of content, modern scholars contend that considerable variability could occur in such traditions. In fact, this notion of "infallible" oral transmission stems from decidedly text-based thinking, which places a premium on aspects of a written document's value based on authenticity, accuracy, and origin.

Another interesting aspect of ancient text that originally circulated through oral transmission is that commentary upon such oral performances usually predates the text itself. As the oral "texts" were seen as too sacred to be committed to corruptible material, early extant manuscripts were principally works that spoke about the sacred rites and practices. Reluctance to commit the Vedas, for example, to writing was also motivated by the desire to retain sacred texts among the priest caste. Ritual materials were often considered exclusive to Brahmans and their pupils and not for the general population. These figures regarded themselves as containers or vessels for rituals and rites, and thus setting these spoken words into written form would leave them open to the lower castes. In addition, written records were vulnerable to rot, mold, and devouring insects because the climate of South Asia is generally moist (excluding the northern regions of India). Palm leaf or even the sturdier birch-bark writing parchment did not serve well as archival material. Although these two materials are plentiful, respectively, in the northwest of India where vast forests cover the terrain of the Himalaya, and cover central, eastern, and western India, due to its perishable quality, Sanskrit manuscripts older than the fourteenth century are quite rare. The oldest known Sanskrit manuscript on birch bark dates to the fifth century, and one other (Pali) manuscript, discovered in 1897, is older yet, though the use of the material itself likely dates much further back. There is evidence that birch bark writing was also used in letter-writing correspondence in pre-classical India. Due to the discovery of a copper plate from around this period that mimics the appearance of a palm leaf in design, it is known that the palm-leaf writing was common from the first century C.E.

The use of paper appears no later than the thirteenth century and was introduced through Islamic conquest. Thereafter, in areas such as the north of India where ink was employed, writing upon palm leaves quickly fell from favor; their use, however, continued until the early-twentieth century in areas where scribes used a stylus to scratch characters into leaves, and then darkened the marks by rubbing ashes or charcoal into them. Both the palm and birch-bark manuscripts were bundled by puncturing the collection and tying with a length of cord. Interestingly, the Sanskrit word for knot, *grantha*, over time came to mean "book." *Mashi*, or ink, appears at least as early as the second century B.C.E., where evidence of its use was discovered at the site of a Buddhist relic mound. As a writing material, leather has never been used because, as an animal product, it conflicts with notions of ritual purity. The use of ink would have somewhat broadened readership; however, as Sanskrit was not a form recognizable to more common classes, its use did not result in any revolution in vernacular writing, and it remained a written language of the elite.

Classical Sanskrit literature can be organized into epic, didactic, dramatic, and narrative prose. The epic appears in *Purana* and *kavya* forms; the former is a freer composition, whereas the latter is more aesthetically contrived, though these style boundaries can be somewhat unstable. The creation of such boundaries becomes a useful tool in organizing such a wealth of historical material (much of it still untranslated). Recent scholarship salvages much of the valuable historical work that has been done within "Orientalism," or "Indology," while being cognizant of early cultural blind spots that may appear in these investigations. Early explorations into ancient literature will always be, to some degree, partial and contingent.

In fact, categorization of not only texts but the regions from which they emerge can be equally problematic. Sheldon Pollock encourages modern scholars to consider the limitations of western methods of labeling when it comes to the territory of South Asia:

> When literary history became the handmaid of nationalism in nineteenth-century Europe and in postcolonial South Asia, it was for good reason. Linguistic particularity and aesthetic difference, to say nothing of the actual stories about particular spaces and their reproduction across these spaces, produce powerful ideational effects, and have done so for a long time. But again, these effects can have histories totally different from those consecrated by nationalism and modernity. (Pollock 27)

No prior answer to the meaning (and meaningfulness) of "South Asia." "India," "Bengal," or other such notions is possible, for these have primeval and eternal meanings. They are, rather, culturally and historically constituted and intrinsically relational, which is why they can be constantly revised (Pollock 27–28). Studies progress with the notion that all such prior investigation bears the marks of colony and a history of literary appropriation refracted through a western lens. Text is never separable from its context, particularly when that context is fraught with a series of historical and cross-cultural tensions. By recognizing these realities, and by focusing more closely on auditors and readers of texts and manuscripts, we can value the way such exploration leads to understanding new literary complexities and historical relationships that are not summative or complete in themselves, but tantalizing in their demand for further attention. It must also be understood that for works such as *The Mahabharata*, *Bhagavad Gita*, *Ramayana*, as well as a great many others, sharp distinctions between "literature" and religious documents do not exist. As Dimock writes, "This is not because there has been an imposition of a system of religious values on the society; it is rather because religion in India is so interwoven with every other facet of life, including many forms of literature, that it become indistinguishable" (1). Further, not all the literature of South Asia has been accessed through scholarly inquiry; "there remains, of course, much that is not so taken up, and there is a vast body of literature, still largely unknown in the West, in the regional and tribal languages—folk songs and folktales, legends, aphoristic poetry, even epics" (Dimock 5), which are only recently being studied and considered within the broader context of the region's literary history.

SANSKRIT TEXTS IN THE GUPTA EMPIRE: FOURTH TO SIXTH CENTURY C.E.

A flourish of literature composed in Sanskrit occurs between 319–540 C.E. during the Gupta Empire. This dynasty embraced a variety of intellectual pursuits, not only in literature, but also in architecture and mathematics. Poetry and plays developed for performance at court were written in Sanskrit, which by this time had become the language of the elite and the well educated. The Guptas patronized the work of Kalidasa (400 C.E.), a dramatist whose works such as *Shakuntala* are still enjoyed today. As a result of contact with Europe through colonization, this work and others circulated in English and German translations in the late 1700s.

Kalidasa is perhaps still the most celebrated artist to produce works in Sanskrit, and many unverifiable works have been attributed to him because of his wide renown. Scholars place him at the court of Chandra Gupta II near the close of the fourth century. His work mirrors the aristocratic sophistication of the period, when, for a brief time, traditional religious practices coexisted with the more liberal values of secular Hinduism.

Kalidasa produced artful reinterpretations of popular legend. From the Ramayana, he created *Raghuvasha*, which explores the activities of Rama and his descendents. These legends may have served Kalidasa chiefly as a way to display his mastery of Sanskrit. *Shakuntala*, one of the most widely admired literary works produced in India, was inspired by an episode from the epic *Mahabharata*. His close attention to naturalistic imagery and contrasting archetypes, as well as his insights into the complexities of courtly love, have given the work broad appeal.

With the preceding context as a backdrop, it is essential to consider the most influential extant works from this period of South Asian history, the works that come to define the classical period, while focusing on what these works reveal about audience, readership, and the development of written text.

READING TRENDS AND PRACTICES

Influential works of the classical period
  1. *Astadhyayi*, "the Eight Chapters," by Panini (520–460 B.C.E.)
  2. *Mahabharata* (400 B.C.E.–400 C.E.)
  3. *Bhagavad Gita* (200 B.C.E.–200 C.E.)
  4. *Arthasastra* (third century B.C.E.)
  5. *Ramayana* (200 B.C.E.–200 C.E.)
  6. *Kathasaritsagara*, "Great Ocean of Riverlike Stories" (folktales and fairy tales), collected by Somadeva (eleventh century C.E.), Kashmiri composer
  7. Dramas of Bhasa, based on the *Ramayana* and *Mahabharata* (second century C.E.)
  8. *Kama Sutra* (fourth century C.E.)
  9. Works of Kalidasa (*Sakuntala*, *Meghaduta*), fifth century C.E.
 10. Puranas (500 C.E.)
 11. Dramas of Harsa (seventh century C.E.)
 12. Dramas of Bhavabhuti (eighth century C.E.)

Astadhyayi

The "grammar" by Panini has proved to be not only an invaluable resource for the study of the Sanskrit lexis but also a window into the literary products of this writer's contemporaries. A number of scholars point to the enormous influence grammarians had upon regulating language, enforcing and maintaining Sanskrit's more elaborate word structures (MacDonell 22). Panini's grammar, according to John Keay, is

> more comprehensive and scientific than any dreamed of by Greek grammarians. "One of the greatest literary achievements of any ancient civilization," it so refined the literary usage of the day that the language became permanently "frozen" and was ever after known as Samskrta ("perfected," hence "Sanskrit"). (61)

The power of the "Science in Eight Chapters," as it is titled, was that it forever fixed the language of Sanskrit. The name itself, Samskrta bhasa, refers to a perfected and intellectually cultivated language. Dimock elaborates on the impact of Sanskrit upon its practitioners, and upon its function as a priceless intercultural currency:

If one is to speak the language, he must speak it correctly. It is the proud possession of one whose birth predisposes him to education and whose education proceeds from, and in, Sanskrit. It was always his second language, though it was also always the language of his preference. In it he could speak to other educated Indians across the growing barriers between regionally developing dialects, and across the eternal barriers between the language families themselves, both in India and the outside, in Java as well as Tibet. He would take enormous delight in reproducing complex clusters of consonants that his regional vernacular might have lost, or might never have possessed, in tasting the rolling phrases with the fastidious tongue of the pandit, the Sanskrit specialist; and the wonder of the language, at once so rich and so neatly ordered, would perhaps inspire him to feats of complexity. (11)

Panini's grammar comprises around four thousand sayings and expressions. Although the importance of the grammar is now recognized, "Nineteenth century Western linguists did not see the significance of the context-sensitive rules of [the work]. In fact their fundamental importance was seen only when Paninian style structures were first introduced by Western linguists such as [Noam] Chomsky about thirty years ago"; also, in a gesture of historical recalibration, "According to the linguist Frits Staal: 'We can now assert, with the power of hindsight, that Indian linguists in the fifth century [B.C.E.] knew and understood more than Western linguists in the nineteenth century [C.E.]'" (Bhate 80). The language that Panini fixed or froze in his grammar is the language that appears in the earliest epic, the *Ramayana*.

Panini's work was a prized creation early on, and was quickly canonized. Though it has undergone revision, most scholars believe that the widely circulated version is quite faithful to the original, as it seems subsequent translators and transcribers have been reluctant to significantly alter the work. The standard of economy and brevity employed by Panini is now common in other contexts, such as the current invention of new technical terminology. The "sutra" (or thread) style of the work utilizes as its aesthetic a tight economy of composition. Many other works have been executed in the sutra style, but Panini's is regarded as the best example of this mode of expression and is still the foundational text for serious grammatical study of Sanskrit. His work gives indispensable insight into the language patterns of India's various language regions and gives us some guidance into movements in speech and later writing. Panini highlights, for example, distinctions he has noted among "easterners" and "northerners" (MacDonell 23). There is strong certainty that Sanskrit was spoken in the second century between the Himalaya and Vindhya ranges by Brahmans, but literary evidence suggests a broader public fluency, at least receptively, to Sanskrit. "Prakritisms," or common speech, has been found inserted into traditional texts, showing the infusion of more popular language over time, and a departure from Panini's strict conventions.

The *Mahabharata*

The longest epic in world literature (roughly one hundred thousand two-line stanzas), the work contains eighteen books and focuses on an eighteen-day war among eighteen armies. For some sense of scale, Gowen tells us that this epic is "just about seven times the length of the Iliad and the Odyssey put together" (198). The name means "the great story of the Bharatas," a name also used for the Hindu people. Though the original author of the *Mahabharata* is lost to history, and the earliest version of the story unrecorded, the tale enjoys an incredibly lengthy career, which many scholars contend began in the eighth or ninth century

B.C.E. The epic's current version appears to have been completed between the third and fifth centuries C.E., and it is perhaps more accurate to describe the work as "compiled" rather than "written" by the figure Vyasa, who is often credited as the principle author. "Vyasa," in fact, means "compiler," though he also appears as a character in the poem. The epic bears the embellishments of countless Brahmans. As opposed to the Vedas, which some have historically contended were "uncorrupted," the *Mahabharata* has undergone an endless succession of embellishments and transcriptions. Considering the work's broad historical horizon of development for the written version (perhaps from 400 B.C.E. to 400 C.E.), according to a scholar from the last quarter of the twentieth century, "it makes sense when we look upon the text not so much as one opus but as a library of opera. Then we can say that 400 B.C.E. was the founding date of that library, and that 400 C.E. was the approximate date after which no more substantial additions were made to the text" (van Buitenen xxv).

The *Mahabharata* has enjoyed enormous influence upon its readership (or its auditors) over the centuries. As van Buitenen contends, "More than any other text in Indian civilization the great epic has been the storehouse of ancient lore" (xxvi). The often-quoted epic's first section claims, "What can be found here, can be found elsewhere. What cannot be found here cannot be found elsewhere," which boldly summarizes the scope of the poem. The impact of the work has been profound, extending "to Sanskrit literature, but also to the literatures in the modern Indo-Aryan languages as well as the Dravidian languages . . . it was felt as far east as Java and Bali" (van Buitenen xxvi). Over the centuries, the *Mahabharata* has accumulated a variety of recensions, or interpolated additions.

To understand how this process occurs, one should bear in mind that, as the epic moved from a long period of oral transmission and began to be written down, the consistency and the quality of the transcription varied widely. Also, because the text was initially written on loose palm leaves that, as explained earlier, deteriorated rather quickly, constant recopying was necessary to preserve the document. Early binding of the text was accomplished by passing cord through both the pages and wooden boards that would hold the literally "loose-leaf" collection together (van Buitenen xxix). This type of binding and ongoing transcription lent itself to the addition of new material by the whim of the patron or copyist, but also to some sections simply being lost from time to time. One must also consider that the copyist himself may have been illiterate, and would easily introduce errors and create omissions or unnecessary repetitions of some sections. When such a copy would once again fall into the hands of a literate scribe, the errors would be corrected by the scribe's "best guess" as to the intended language, and new "errors," however well-intentioned, would be introduced. The result is a work that functions as an organic, layered reflection of the centuries of developing culture that ultimately produced the epic. "The character of the epic in its present form," according to Dimock, "lies more in the stories that have accreted around its basic core than in the core itself. And these stories have become so interwoven with the core that scholars can agree only on a minimum definition of what that core might have been" (50). Many of these binding practices became art forms in themselves, exemplifying the esteem readership had for bound text. Palm-leaf, birch-bark, and paper Sanskrit manuscripts were often joined between wood strips and wound in colored, sometimes embroidered, textiles. These can be found in temple libraries, monasteries, colleges, and private houses throughout India (MacDonell 20).

When one studies Sanskrit works, and in particular Sanskrit dramatic works, inspiration from the *Mahabharata* is evident. The plays of Bhasa, as well as the most well-known work of the "Indian Shakespeare," Kalidasa (though chronology

Bhishma on his deathbed of arrows with the Pandavas and Krishna, from the *Mahabharata*.

suggests that Shakespeare could more accurately be called the "English Kalidasa") draw on various *parva*, or sections of the epic (van Buitenen xxvi). Character references and expressions from the work entered the parlance of lyrical work, as well as vernacular speech, "so familiar that they in effect became proverbial" (van Buitenen xxvii). The work has been developed in virtually all of the Hindu languages, and its influence extends into the visual arts and beyond Hindu work: "the Persian translation made for the Great Mughal Akbar was illustrated by miniatures that are held to be the culmination of Mughal painting" (van Buitenen xxviii). The epic does not confine itself to influence within the "arts," as the work both reflects and informs Hindu thought, systematic philosophy, and aspects of general law: Thus there is hardly a province of Hindu culture that has not been touched by the story, and the stories, of the epic. And it does not appear that its influence is over. An endless series of movies have been based on the text, and comic books are appearing that further disseminate its messages (van Buitenen xxviii). As a national epic, it enjoys broad readership from virtually all literate levels of India's social caste system, and it circulates through oral tales among the unlettered. Even today, India holds roughly 280 million people who lack literacy, yet this work has remained vibrant and accessible.

Statue representing the discourse of Krishna and Arjuna, from the *Bhagavad Gita*.

The work continues to influence contemporary audiences. Peter Brook released an astoundingly ambitious nine-hour play based on the *Mahabharata* in 1985, and followed with a film version four years later. A television series inspired by the epic appeared on PBS, and yet another televised production is to appear in 2007. Its constellation of complex characters and its reluctance to paint clear heroes and villains (much as real life) continues to draw audiences in to reflect on its deep historical and psychological intricacies.

Bhagavad Gita

This seven-hundred-line collection of verse, although not considered sacred (*Sruti*) by Hindus, is believed to be *Smriti*, or God-inspired explanations of divine scripture. The *Bhagavad Gita* is the single most popular text in Hindu religious literature. The narrative explores the war between the Pandava clan and the Kauravas, known as the battle of Kuruksetra, which dates to approximately 1300 B.C.E. In terms of context, one must consider Hinduism's strictly hierarchical caste system: Brahmins, the ruling priest class; ksatriyas, warriors; vaisyas, including farmers, herders, and merchants; sudras, including various servants and slaves; and pariahs, the class of untouchables. One's designation within the caste system is determined by birth. Indian social custom commands obedience and performance of one's duty within the caste of one's birth.

Buddhism spread throughout India as a reaction against the inequalities imposed by traditional Hinduism. The more egalitarian Buddhism subverted the stifling caste system of Hinduism, and was of course seen as a threat to the status quo. In response, the *Bhagavad Gita* was crafted by members of the Brahmin caste in an effort to counteract the rising influence of Buddhism.

Leaning in the direction of Buddhism and the voice of the *Gita*'s Arjuna (pacifism, the sanctity of all life), Mahatma Gandhi (1869–1948) interpreted the *Bhagavad Gita* as supporting the doctrine of nonviolent resistance. It has profoundly influenced the spiritual, cultural, intellectual, and political life of the country throughout the centuries, and it continues to do so today (Prabhavananda 27). The authorship of the work is the subject of scholarly debate. The work is a complete narrative within the much larger *Mahabharata*, comprising sections 24 to 40 of this work. Whereas *The Mahabharata*, as an epic, expands on the struggles between two sides of a royal family at war, the *Gita*, as it is often called, focuses on the events of a single day on the battlefield. A dialogue among Krishna, Arjuna, King Dhiritarashtra, and Sanjaya forms the content of the *Gita*. Most scholars believe the work to be a much later addition to *The Mahabharata*, somewhere between 200 B.C.E. and 200 C.E. Though the source of its authorship and the means by which it acquired its present version are unknown, textual evidence allows many scholars to attribute the work to Vyasa. It may have developed as an addition to *The Mahabharata*, or perhaps expanded from it in the third century B.C.E. It deals with questions of social and religious duty, the nature of action, freedom of choice, routes to spiritual liberation, and the relationship of human beings to God in a period of uncertainty and transition. From early in its history the *Bhagavad Gita* was an important focus for commentators, and later it became a source text for devotional movements.

In terms of the work's reach and influence, A. L. Herman has suggested "The literary and philosophical renaissance that occurred in India in the nineteenth century would not have been as powerful as it was had it not been for the rediscovery and dissemination of the *Gita*"(6). The scripture had been translated by Indian scholars, artists, and political figures from Sanskrit into regional languages and into English. Philosopher and sage Caitanya Mahaprabhu (1486–1534), who, among his followers (regarded as an avatar of Krishna himself), popularized the Hare Krishna chanting as a form of meditation and worship, was deeply influenced by the *Gita*'s message. Notably, Ram Mohum Roy (1772–1833), who founded the reformist movement Brahmo Samaj and was a principal figure in Bengali resistance, looked to the *Gita* for guidance, inspiration, and political motivation. Mohum Roy famously worked to end sati, a Hindu custom in which widows were compelled to throw themselves on their husbands' funeral pyres. In the West, "it found warm reception among the American transcendentalists like Henry David Thoreau and Ralph Waldo Emerson in the early-nineteenth century" (Herman 6). Emerson's spiritual notion of "the over-soul" was largely informed by his exploration of the text. Further, "the poetry of Heinrich Heine (1797–1856), the writing of the German Philologist and statesman Baron William von Humboldt (1767–1835), and the life of the great German Indologist Max Muller (1823–1900)" all bear influence by the *Gita* (Herman 7). Famously, J. Robert Oppenheimer, American physicist and director of the Manhattan Project, read the *Bhagavad Gita* in the original Sanskrit, claiming it later as one of the most influential books to guide his personal philosophy of life. After witnessing the fruits of his labors during the world's first nuclear test in 1945, he stated "Now I am become Death, the destroyer of worlds" a paraphrase from chapter eleven of the *Bhagavad Gita*.

The far-reaching influence of the text is evident in the words of Mahatma Gandhi:

> [The *Gita*] is the universal mother. I find a solace in the *Bhagavad Gita* that I miss even in the Sermon on the Mount. When disappointment stares me in the face and all alone I see not one ray of light, I go back to the *Bhagavad Gita*. I find a verse here and a verse

there, and I immediately begin to smile in the midst of overwhelming tragedies—and my life has been full of external tragedies—and if they have left no visible or indelible scar on me, I owe it all to the teaching of *Bhagavad* [*Gita*]. (Harijan vol. 64, p. 256)

Arthasastra

This work is the classic Indian treatise on statecraft, written by Kautilya (though authorship is still the subject of debate) who was born in the third century B.C.E. (Keay 60). *Arthashastra* translates literally as the *Science of Wealth, Science of Material Gain*, and *Science of State*. Produced under the rulership of Chandragupta Maurya, it explores expanding the rule of law into unsettled regions of the empire. The focus of the text is economic organization and consolidation, and details the role of autocratic kingship. As a work of political philosophy, the *Arthashastra* is still relevant and often considered alongside other great works of statecraft such as Machiavelli's *The Prince* (though Kautilya's work, of course, long precedes it). The work also covers intricacies of rule such as recovering economically from famine, effective farming techniques, and plans for sustainable economic infrastructure.

Ramayana

The second great Sanskrit epic that includes teachings of ancient Hindu sages is a work more philosophical and devotional than the *Mahabharata*. The *Ramayana's* authorship has been credited to Valmiki. Written shortly before the Christian era, the content of the work focuses on war, and more generally on the battle between good and evil. Originally conceived as a morality tale, the work contains elements that transmute through time and later readings into more overtly religious implications. Much later, beginning in the fourteenth century, the growth of *bhakti*—worship of personal deities—influences reception of the text in new ways, and the poem's heroes become regarded as symbols of gods to impart salvation to humankind (a reach beyond the scope of the poem's initial interpretation—Dimock 3). The epic contains twenty-four thousand verses and details the abduction of Sita, wife of Prince Rama, by the demon Ravana, and battles among the gods. As the narrative unfolds, the demon has taken residence on earth, bringing with him a fierceness and power that threatens the positions of the gods themselves. The host of divine beings elects Vishnu to take the form of a human so that he might visit earth and destroy Ravana. Vishnu relinquishes his divine role and is born the son of a king, taking the name Rama. Reminiscent of Odysseus's challengers for the hand of Penelope, Rama proves he is able to both string a tremendous bow and to successfully strike a tiny target to both best a number of suitors and win the hand of Sita, whose virtues the poem extols. The archetypal figures of the epic are in themselves studies in Indian culture. Gowen writes of the *Ramayana's* legacy and continued presence:

> Nightly to listening millions are the stories of the *Ramayana* and *Mahabharata* told all over India. They are sung at all large assemblies of the people at marriage feasts and temple services, at village festivals and the receptions of chiefs and princes. Then, when all the gods have been duly worshipped, and the men are wearying of the meretricious posturings and grimaces of the dancing girls, and the youngsters have let off all the squibs and crackers, a reverend Brahman steps upon the scene, with the familiar bundle of inscribed palm leaves in his lap, slow and lowly begins his antique chant, and late into the starry night holds his hearers, young and old, spellbound by the story of the pure loves of Rama and Sita. (251)

Although Rama, as eldest of four brothers, should rightly inherit the king's throne, the machinations of his stepmother (who reminds the king that he promised her any two wishes) lead to his fourteen-year banishment, as well as to the emplacement of her own son, Bharata, as king. Exhibiting true "right conduct," and modeling behavior for the story's auditors to follow, Bharata meets Rama in the forest and implores his brother to return to the throne. Rama, respecting his father's wishes, refuses, and Bharata offers to serve as Rama's regent until his return.

In terms of the works influence, historian and critic John Keay views the *Ramayana*'s chief function as the legitimization of monarchical rule, particularly in Southeast Asia, whereas "Jain and Buddhist versions of the *Ramayana* story, or of episodes within it, thus show a rather different emphasis" (47) on alternative systems of state. "These alternative systems have been variously interpreted as oligarchical, republican or even democratic" (47). Indians from childhood on engage the *Ramayana* for instruction on following one's dharma, which can be understood as a concept relating to truth, duty, or correct conduct. Signs of influence abound across India; images of Rama and Sita "are everywhere, in sculptured stone about the temples, and on the carved woodwork of houses; on the graven brass and copper of domestic utensils; or painted in fresco on walls, Rama, like Vishnu, dressed in yellow, the color of joy. . . . They are the charm that has stayed the course of time in India, and they will probably continue for ages yet" (Gowen 252). The work's prominence also stems from its identity as an intentionally literary work, unlike the sprawling, less unified, eight centuries-long compendium of the *Mahabharata*. Its influence is large and long lasting:

> Various regions of India reflected the *Ramayana* according to the ways of the times. Writers of later versions added to their model lines or even full stories that changed the interpretation of the whole to one congenial to the dominant sectarian, moral, or social climate of a particular part of the subcontinent. In some places, partisans of entirely different religious traditions appropriated the story to bolster their own points of view. (Dimock 78)

Many versions of the *Ramayana* circulate and survive to this day. There are great variances among the *Ramayana* tales exchanged in North India, South India, and within Southeast Asia. Also, there is a long oral storytelling tradition based on the *Ramayana* in the countries of Thailand, Cambodia, Malaysia, Laos, Vietnam, Indonesia, and Maldives.

The most popular version, according to India's national newspaper *The Hindu*, is Ezhuthachan's *Adhyathma Ramayanam Kilippattu*. An alternate version has been lately studied that comes from the Kerala island area off the southwest coast of India. This sung version—a form called Mappilapattu—is popular among the Muslims and has included numerous episodes from the *Ramayana*. "Mappila Ramayana," have been transmitted orally through generations of listeners. This version features a sultan, conforming to the style and interest of the Muslim community, though there are no major changes in the names of characters except for that of Rama, which has become "Laman." Though the *Ramayana* as a narrative cycle has great antiquity, it appears these sung versions are more recent.

Other iterations of the *Ramayana* appeared in Nepal, such as a version composed by Siddhidas Mahaju. Another was written by Aadikavi Bhanubhakta Acharya. The version by Siddhidas Mahaju marks a great point in the development of the language called "Nepal Bhasa," whereas the one of Bhanubhakta Acharya is the first epic of the Nepali. Many other Asian cultures, such as those of Southeast Asia, have embraced the *Ramayana,* producing alternate epics with broad appeal.

A Javanese version of the Sanskrit *Ramayana* dates to ninth-century Indonesia, and adheres closely to the Hindu version. A Lao language version also appears, in which the story of Rama is presented as a previous incarnation of Buddha. In the Malaysian version, Allah bestows blessings rather than Brahma. Thailand's version develops a context that includes references to the dress, weapons, and landscape of its adapted region. Illustrations of the epic can be found in a temple in Bangkok. Other Southeast Asian adaptations include Bali (Indonesia), the Philippines, Cambodia, and Myanmar. Nor is there any sign that interest in the epic is waning. Images of key characters still appear in a variety of folk art, and contemporary explorations of the *Ramayana* include work of the modern Indian author Ashok Banker, who has written a series of six English-language novels based on the *Ramayana*. Ramayan 3392 C.E., a graphic adaptation, was published by Virgin Comics in 2006, featuring the *Ramayana* as imagined by author Deepak Chopra and filmmaker Shekhar Kapur. An anime movie called *Rama—The Prince of Light* was also released in the early 1990s, and this was preceded by numerous television versions of the epic in the 1980s.

PURANAS

The meaning of the term suggests "old narratives," or "that which lives from ancient times," (Shastri xvii). One of the main objectives of the Puranas was to make available the essence of the Vedas to the common people, and the Puranas were basically meant not for the scholars but for the ordinary reader. They bring forth the Vedic knowledge and teachings by way of parables, allegories, stories, legends, life stories of kings and other prominent persons, and chronologies of historical events. The Puranas detail the principles of Hinduism in simple, straightforward expression.

The Puranas bridge the period between the Vedic and the classical epochs. Rendered as parables, they represent the Vedas in vernacular fashion. Apart from their religious and often sectarian significance, they furnish a picture of social, political, and cultural life and comprise an astonishingly varied repertory of folklore and information regarding diverse topics including philosophy, ethics, legal institutions, popular festivals, and several arts; they deal even with subjects such as grammar, prose, rhetoric, archery, and the care of horses and elephants; many of them also describe places of pilgrimage. Many scholars have become deeply interested in the historical relevance of these works.

The Puranas are considered among the richest collections of mythology in the world. Most of them assumed their final form around 500 C.E.; however, their oral form predates the written to about 1500 B.C.E. There are eighteen major Puranas and a few minor ones. Each is a long book consisting of various stories of the gods and goddesses, hymns, an outline of ancient history, cosmology, rules of life, rituals, and instructions on spiritual knowledge. Hence the Puranas are like encyclopedias of religion and culture and contain material of different levels and degrees of difficulty.

Mahapuranas

In terms of context, readership, and influence, the pantheon represented in the "epic-Puranic" system is also that of present-day India (Bhattacharji 359). India's major epics, the *Mahabharata* and *Ramayana* are considered collectively as part of the Puranas, but beyond these major works, there are eighteen other main Puranas, in addition to many subsidiary, or *Upa-Puranas*. The term itself usually translates as "old narrative," but the Puranas develop this term as "that which lives from ancient times," or "the records of ancient events" (Shastri xvii). Relatively recently, the eighteen Puranas have come to be known as Mahapuranas. It is important to consider the characteristics that link these works. The Puranas (like the histories, such as the *Mahabharata*) are a mixture of recorded history and mythology. Shastri summarizes the five topics common to the Puranas as *sarga* (the creation of the universe), *pratisarga* (the re-formation of the universe after its destruction or 'deluge,' similar to myths of origin familiar to those in the West, *vamsa* (genealogical records, frequently of royal lineage), *manvantara* (accounts of the deeply historical past that detail the principle divinity Manu and his exploits), and *vamsanucarita* (dynastic history). Further, each of the Mahapuranas shares a more refined group of characteristics, which include: (1) subtle creation (sarga); (2) gross creation (*visgara*); (3) law and order—ensured by God (*sthana*); (4) protection—welfare of all (*posana*); (5) material lust for karmas (*uti*); (6) the periods of Manus and history of that epoch (manvantara); (7) accounts of the deeds of the Lord (*isanukatha*); (8) physical annihilation (*nirodha*); (9) liberation (*mukti*); and (10) the last resort of the universe or the ultimate reality (*asraya*) (xxii). For scholars these ten characteristics form the criteria for a Mahapurana. Upon reviewing these, one can see that these aspects are expansions of the five basic topics or characteristics of Puranas.

The fifth Purana, the *Bhagavata*, has been acclaimed by both ancient and contemporary scholars as the most significant of the group (Shastri xxi). The date of creation for the *Bharata* Purana, as well as the others, is the subject of intense speculation. Much of the dating of early Hindu texts is relative—that is, scholars have attempted to narrow the chronological field by cross-dating the particular text under scrutiny with other texts with firmer dates, usually through intertextual referencing. For example, if one prominent text A is not mentioned in text B, one could assume that text A must have been created after text B. As an example from among its many guiding lessons and models for faithful behavior, the *Bhagavata* Purana outlines multiple paths for a life of religious devotion. This "nine-fold" path includes "(1) *Sravana* (Listening), (2) *Kartana* (Chanting), (3) *Smarana* (Remembrance, meditation), (4) *Pada-sevana* (Serving the feet of the Lord), (5) *Arcana* (Worship), (6) *Vandana* (Prostration before God), (7) *Dasya* (Service), (8) *Sakya* (Friendship), and (9) *Atma-nivedana* (Self-dedication)" (Shastri lxi). According to the *Bhagavata*, these aspects are in continuous flux and point toward an ultimate union with the divine. Any devotional practitioner may reach his goal within this system by any single path or the undertaking of multiple journeys along these paths. In this context "the path to release from recurring life lay through knowledge, devotion or works" (Bhattacharji 354).

Of interest is the cultural shift represented by the popularization of Vedic themes within the Puranas:

> Pilgrimages and vows play an important role. Spread all over India are numerous pilgrimages, some grew around ancient legends and hero cults, but most were sanctified by particular epiphanies of gods and goddesses. These are usually by rivers or on mountains or hills, on the confluence of rivers or by the seaside. We are frequently told that if one fasts, bathes and offers oblations to the particular god of the pilgrimage . . . one acquires the merit of many sacrifices. . . . It indicates that the old sacrifices [of the Vedic period] were becoming obsolescent and were gradually being displaced by these new modes of religious practices. (Bhattacharji 352)
>
> The entire outlook of the age is changed, for, although man still seems to believe in the efficacy of sacrifices and does not feel satisfied unless he feels he has offered them, the sacrifices themselves are entirely different. Hence the scriptures are full of formulas of

substitutions. If one visits a pilgrimage and performs other necessary penances for two or three days, one collects the merit of this or that sacrifice. . . . Thus the merits of sacrifices (the only kind yet valid to the religious consciousness) are obtained through easier modes of religious practices. (Bhattacharji 353)

From the courses outlined in the nine-fold path of the *Bhagavata* Purana, one can see that these devotional acts are in their essential nature "portable," and often amount to mental or conceptual practices that may be enacted without the requirement of physical sacrifices. This is a tangible example of the cultural ramifications of more widely circulated and accessible texts. As Shastri contends on the continued issue of authorship,

> Whoever may be the author of the *Bharata* Purana, it is a unique work. It is not only a magnificent epic singing the great deeds of Krishna, but a scripture of the people to which the entire Hindu people from the Himalayas to the Vindhya and from Panjab to Bengal, turn for spiritual sustenance, a source of ethics constantly on the lips of all, from princes to peasants and a truly fine expression of poetic genius. (xxviii)

The Dream of Vasavdatta and Other Works, Bhasa

Before considering Bhasa specifically, a word should be said about the nature of Sanskrit drama in general and the way performances were traditionally staged. According to Dimock, "the theater itself" in Sanskrit drama "would be a simple affair: a pavilion or a raised platform with four pillars at the corners supporting a marquee, with a curtain in the rear that was split in the middle. On this simple stage all kinds of variations could be made, but the bare floor provided all that a play essentially needed" (93). With respect to viewers, the audience before whom all this unfolded was highly critical:

> Not only could one not write, but one could not adequately follow a play, unless he had undergone a classical education. There were few educated people who had not learned by heart, at the age of eight, the Eight Chapters of Panini's Sanskrit grammar [see previous entry]. . . . And all educated men would have, securely lodged in their prodigious memories, hundreds and thousands of stanzas against which the playwright's poetry could be weighed. (Dimock 93–94)

The works of Bhasa had been considered lost to history until the 1912 discovery of thirteen Sanskrit plays in Trivandrum in southern India by Pandit Ganapati Shastri. Though scholars debate whether these plays are truly the work of Bhasa, over time the works have been attributed to him. Though it is difficult to date Bhasa's work, the best evidence suggests that 350 C.E. is the latest possible date for him, because Kalidasa praises his work. "The rapidity and directness of action of Bhasa's plays is reflected in his style. More than any other dramatist, he uses the verse to further the progress of the play, in lieu of devoting it to descriptions rather poetic that directly aid the drama" (Keith 114).

> The dominating influence on Bhasa's style was clearly that of the epic and in special of Valmiki, whose great work inevitably impressed itself on the minds of all his successors. The effects are visible not merely in the dramas with epic subject matter, but extend throughout Bhasa's plays. The results of this influence are all to the good; the necessities of the drama saved Bhasa from the one great defect of the epic style, the lack of measure, which permits the *Ramayana* to illustrate by twenty-nine similes the sorrows of Sita in their captivity, while Bhasa is content with one. (Keith 115)

Kalidasa's accolades for Bhasa suggest that he may have been a major influence on his work, though the degree to which the famous poet adopted his style is difficult to definitively assess.

Kama Sutra

The *Kama Sutra* is one of the oldest written documents in existence, and is popularly regarded as a manual on the art of love. It was penned by Vatsyayana between the second and fourth centuries C.E., though elements of the work extend back much further. Portions of the work have been linked to the earliest examples of written language in the first century C.E.

The *Kama Sutra* is a compilation of works recorded by many writers now lost to history. Vatsyayana's text resonates today for its insights into social/sexual thinking of its time and for the systematic, or "thread," method of organization, which utilizes concise aphorisms to remark specifically on how one may conduct one's self in conversation, courtship, marriage, and sex. Vatsayana categorizes types of men and women in the interest of encouraging matching or equal unions. Scholars surmise that the *Kama Sutra* was written for the wealthy, male city-dweller.

Under the Guptas, around the fourth century C.E., the writer himself comments on the difficulty of collecting the work's various components, which was part of his inspiration in executing these writings. The work is organized into thirty-six chapters, further divided into seven topically related sections. Each is written by experts in various fields.

Part One—Introduction
Part Two—Amorous Advances
Part Three—Acquiring a Wife
Part Four—Duties and Privileges of the Wife
Part Five—Other Men's Wives
Part Six—About Courtesans
Part Seven—Occult Practices

The most well-known translation of the work is Sir Richard Francis Burton's, completed in 1883. Burton was a notorious Victorian "Orientalist" and frequent traveler to India. He reportedly maintained an Indian mistress during his visits, and he, with other enthusiasts, founded the London Anthropological Society and produced the journal *Anthropologia*. This periodical introduced many influential Victorians to the diversity of human sexual behavior and encouraged somewhat subversive social interests below the range of polite open society. Burton produced these translations, as well as translations of the *Perfumed Garden* and the *Priapeia*, and is also known for his unexpurgated translation of *The Arabian Nights*. Later versions reflect consultation with Indian scholars on the original texts. Interestingly, Burton's texts were printed "for private circulation only"—a disclaimer required to maintain propriety in the social climate of Victorian England.

Later, Burton cofounded the Kama Shastra Society. This secretive club or organization privately published the *Kama Sutra* in 1883, making it the first ancient Hindu text on the art of love to be translated into the English language. Amazingly they could not be "officially" published in English until the mid-1960s, following a landmark court case. Burton's translation includes a lengthy prelude that assesses various other major Hindu works on the topic of love and sexuality, even those writing long after Vatsyayana's death, that claim him as their principal influence. Further, this work was informed by the prior *Kama Shastras*

(*Rules of Love*), portions of which stretch back to the seventh century B.C.E. This work is not only still regarded as the primary Hindu manual of love, but a text read around the world and translated into dozens of languages.

The path of Vatsyayana's work into eventual English translation is of interest. When scholars translated other Hindu texts, they found various references to "Vatsya." Multiple copies of the text from the Benares, Calcutta, and Jeypoor Sanskrit libraries were obtained and compared. Hare records that along with the commentary—the *Jayamangla*—a master copy was completed, from which an English translation was created.

Meghaduta ("The Cloud Messenger") and Other Plays

The works of Kalidasa are some of the best-known classical literary works in India, though relatively little is known about the author himself. His works have earned him the reputation of being India's most renowned poet to this day. One scholar writes, "he created a glorious love poem [with "The Cloud Messenger"], surely one of the most beautiful known to man . . . [e]very image, every comparison, seems genuine, sincere" (Edgerton 2). One could argue that it is this level of emotional authenticity that has made his work so immensely popular for generations. The *Kumarashbhava* concerns events that lead to the marriage of the god Shiva; and the *Raghuvamsa* renders the life and activities of the hero, Rama.

The *Meghaduta*, a lyrical poem of 111 stanzas, is the most widely known work of Kalidasa and has been regarded as a world masterpiece. The work concerns an exiled yaksha's (a type of semi-divine being) message sent by a cloud to his wife in the Himalayas. The yaksha, for an unexplained reason, has been exiled from his wife for a year, and at the beginning of the poem four months remain before he can be reunited with her. Upon seeing a passing cloud, he confers a message upon it, hoping the cloud will carry it to his wife. The cloud signals the beginning of the monsoon season, a time when wayward travelers begin to make their way home. The image of the speaker communicating his loneliness to a cloud is, of course, a highly romantic one. The imagery mirrors a deferred passion, but also his preoccupation with his own and his wife's state of marital fidelity.

What gives the *Meghaduta* its lasting influence, and continued enjoyment by current readers, is its successful weaving of both the truth of human emotion (namely, love, loss, separation, and faith) and a cultural code of ethics relating to marriage, devotion, and fidelity. As the dialog unfolds, the work's aesthetics are infused by timeless meditations on the stresses and uncertainties of human connection.

Kalidasa is widely regarded as a master in depicting the subtleties of love, ranging from innocence to intense passion. Also, his imagery serves as a rich library of South Asian pastoral detail; his celebration of the landscape can be seen in multiple ways. In this work, as well as in *Sakuntala*, details such as "the mango, the Bimba fruit . . . the lotus" (159), and his delicate appreciation of the animal world of India set his work apart. *Sakuntala* explores the tension between public duty and the private sentiments of love. The expectations of society and the observance of intricate social codes, in this work, are at odds with the individual's desire and passions. Dimock characterizes the playwright's skills as encompassing both grand and subtle scales: "Kalidasa appealed both to the fascination that the spectacular has for the Indian mind, and to the deep awareness in the Indian heart of the simple values on which all the spectacle must eventually rest" (99).

RATNAVALI, PRIYADARCIKA, AND *NAGANANDA,* BY KING HARSA (590–647)

It is widely understood that elements of the Veda, in particular its dialogue form, carry with them the potential for dramatic expression. The ceremonial nature of ritual, including the recitation of verse, song, and various other incantations, encourages imagination, reenactment, and public presentation. Although the great epic works of India try to not describe or make specific reference to any form of drama,

> The drama owes in part its origin to the epics of India; from them throughout its history it derives largely its inspiration, far more truly so indeed than Greek tragedy as compared with the Greek epic. From the epics also developed the Kavya, the refined and polished epic, which appears at its best in . . . [the work of] Kalidasa. Harsa has generally received less praise than Kalidasa, but he is recognized for the strength of his plot development, that is, his work displays fluidity and ingenuity. (Keith 175)

Like most Sanskrit drama, Harsa's work is highly referential to tales and myths with which his audience would have been quite familiar. "The Ratnavali and the Priyadarcika are closely connected both in subject matter and form," Keith writes, "their common hero is Udayana, whom Bhasa already celebrated" (171). Harsa is not known for breaking any new ground in respect to language; his use of verse stays closely to the conventions of his day. Harsa has been described as a "clever borrower." In terms of content, the prevailing sentiments of his work explore aspects of love for a heroic nobleman. Even bearing in mind the vast historical remove from which we view Harsa, his female characters are nevertheless regarded as possessing little more than an attractive appearance and a wish to be loved by the king.

Nagananda is a departure for Harsa: "His liking for the marvelous is exhibited indeed . . . where the supernatural freely appears" (Keith 176). Keith further writes, "Harsa here rises to the task of depicting the emotions of self-sacrifice, charity, magnanimity, and resolution in the face of death" (177). Harsa's direct participation in the cultural productions of his court was more direct than that of most kings, and it is his own contribution to literary arts that makes him stand alone. In addition to the three plays, *Priyadarsika, Ratnavali,* and the *Nagananda,* he is credited with two significant poems—*Ashtamahasricaityastotra* ("Praise to Eight Grand Caityas") and *Suprabhatastotra* ("Laud to Morning")— and a treatise on grammar, the *Linganusasanam.* With Harsa's death passed an age unduplicated in Indian history. Though his rule was not the longest or even the most politically influential, his works have left the elite territory of the private court to become widely treasured literary contributions.

CONCLUSION

An exploration of the classical period of South Asia is closely tied to the language of the age, Sanskrit. The most widely read works stemming from this period were initially the most widely heard recitations and performances, long before these works were transferred to leaf, bark, and paper. Sanskrit embodies the classical period, and much work remains for scholars who wish to investigate volumes of as-yet-untranslated material. In this way, the classical period will continue to inform our notions of social and religious history into our contemporary time.

RECOMMENDED READING

Dutt, Romesh Chunder. *A History of Civilization in Ancient India, Based on Sanscrit Literature: Vol. 1 Vedic and Epic Ages*. Reprint. Calcutta-London: Thacker, Spink and Co., 1889. Adamant Media Corp. 2001.

Kagda, Falaq. *India*. "Festivals of the World" Series. Milwaukee, WI: G. Stevens, 1997.

Parry, Benita. *Delusions and discoveries; studies on India in the British imagination, 1880–1930*. Berkeley: University of California Press, 1972.

Reed, Elizabeth Armstrong. *Hindu Literature; or, The Ancient Books of India*. Chicago: S.C. Griggs and Company, 1891.

Sivaramamurti, C. *Sri Lakshmi in Indian Art and Thought*. New Delhi: Kanak P, 1982.

Snyder, Gary. "Passage Through India." Reprint, "Now India." *Caterpiller* No. 19, Vol. 3., 1972. Shoemaker and Hoard P, 2001.

PRIMARY SOURCES

Bhagavad Gita: The Songs of the Master. Translated by Charles Johnston. London : John M. Watkins, 1965.

The Bhagavadgita: A New Translation. Translated by Kees W. Bolle. Berkeley: University of California Press, 1979.

The Brahma Sutra: The Philosophy of Spiritual Life. Translated by S. Radhakrishnan. New York: Greenwood, 1968.

Edgerton, Franklin, trans. and ed. *The Bhagavad Gita*. New York: Harper and Row, 1944.

———. trans. *Kalidasa: The Cloud Messenger*. Ann Arbor: University of Michigan Press, 1968.

Hare, John B. Internet Sacred Text Archive. http://www.sacred-texts.com/sex/kama/kamaint.htm. (Accessed July 1, 2008.)

Harijan S., *The Collected Works of Mahatma Gandhi*. "Speech at Banares Hindu University." August 1, 1934. Vol. 64. 256. http://www.gandhiserve.org/cwmg/cwmg.html Accessed 8-28-2008.

Herman, A. L., trans. *The Bhagavad Gita: A Translation and Critical Commentary*. C. C. Thomas P, 1973.

Kalidasa. *The Cloud Messenger*. Translated by Franklin and Eleanor Edgerton. Ann Arbor: U of Michigan, 1968.

Prabhavananda (Swami) and Chrisopher Isherwood, trans. *The Song of God: Bhagavad-Gita*. Hollywood: Vedanta Publishing, 1973.

Shastri, J. L., ed. *Ancient Indian Tradition and Mythology*. 50 vols. Dehli: Motilal Banarsidass, 1979.

Valmiki. *The Ramayana and Mahabharata*. Edited by Romesh C. Dutt. London: Aldine, 1972.

Van Buitenen, J. A. B., trans. and ed. *The Mahabharata: The Book of the Beginning*. Chicago: U of Chicago, 1973.

SECONDARY SOURCES

Battacharji, Sukumari. *The Indian Theogony: A Comparative Study of Indian Mythology From the Vedas to the Puranas*. Cambridge: Cambridge UP, 1970, 2007

Bhate, Saroja, and Subhash Kak. "Pannini's Grammar and Computer Science." *Annals of the Bhandarkar Oriental Research Institute*, 72 (1993): 79–94.

Dimock, Edward. *The Literatures of India: An Introduction*. Chicago: U of Chicago, 1974.

Embree, Ainlie T., ed. *Sources of Indian Tradition: From Beginnings to 1800*. Vol. 1. Second ed. New York: Columbia UP, 1988.

Gowen, Herbert H. *A History of Indian Literature: From Vedic Times to the Present Day*. New York: Greenwood, 1968.

Hay, Stephen, ed. *Sources of Indian Tradition: Modern India and Pakistan*. Vol. 2. Second ed. New York: Columbia UP, 1988.

Holiday, Carl. *The Dawn of Literature*. New York: Thomas Crowell, 1931.

Keay, John. *India: A History.* New York: Grove, 2000.

Keith, A. Berriedale. *The Sanskrit Drama in its Origin, Development, Theory, and Practice.* Oxford UP, 1970.

Kirk, James. *Stories of the Hindus: An Introduction Through Texts and Interpretation.* New York: Macmillan, 1972.

MacDonell, Arthur. *A History of Sanskrit.* Reprint. New York: Appleton & Co: 1900. Ann Arbor, 1967.

Pollock, Sheldon. *Literary Cultures in History: Reconstructions from South Asia.* Berkeley: U of California, 2003.

Weber, Albrecht. *The History of Indian Literature.* Translated by John Mann and Theodore Zachariae. Honolulu: UP of the Pacific, 2002.

CHAPTER 21

European Arrival and the Colonial Period

Tom Severson

TIMELINE

1600	East India Company (EIC) given Crown Charter
1657	Cromwell's Charter revitalizes EIC
1660–1700	EIC given extended powers by Charles II; EIC established in Bengal and Bombay
1757	Battle of Plassey makes EIC dominant power in India
1767	Robert Clive leaves India in political chaos
1772	Warren Hastings appointed governor of Bengal
1773	East India Company Act provides for a governor general (Warren Hastings) and council and forbids officers to trade for themselves
1795	Warren Hastings acquitted of high treason
1820	Ram Mohun Roy writes *Precepts of Jesus*
1829	Abolition of *sati* (suttee)—in part because of Ram Mohun Roy's social journalism
1835	Macaulay's *Minute* on Indian education
1857	Indian (Sepoy) Mutiny against British rule
1858	Powers of East India Company transferred to the British Crown
1871	Michael Madhusudan Dutt writes *Is This Called Civilization*
1877	Queen Victoria proclaimed empress of India
1886	First Indian National Congress
1914–18	World War I
1926	Simon Commission recognizes failure of imperial mission

INTRODUCTION TO THE PERIOD

The period of Indian history between 1600 and 1948 was one of turbulence and rapid evolution on a number of levels. The shifting socioeconomic, political, and religious landscape of India can be attributed to a number of factors. The Mughal Empire, mostly foreign Muslim rulers over the mostly Hindu Indians, was in its decline as various successors vied for power and enacted numerous policy changes to appeal to various supporters. The Rajputs, Marathas, and Sikhs all struggled against the Mughal rule. Several European countries, including the French, Dutch, and British, were trying to establish trade and in some cases rule over certain areas in India. Christian missionaries attempted to propagate their faith, while European government officials helped spread western ideas and philosophy. Indians formed social groups to either preserve their religious and cultural identity or reform it along either more traditional or more progressive lines. While some Indians were rereading and reinterpreting the Vedas, others were reading western philosophy (such as Rousseau). As the British gained political power in the 1800s, they began educating the aristocratic Indians in English education. Famines and widespread gang activities further destabilized a troubled country. Calcutta (Kolkatta) became an economic center as well as a social and religious potpourri as Hindus, Muslims, and people of all castes lived together. Linguistic revolutions occurred as the older, established languages of the educated elite slowly yielded to the colloquial dialects of the indigenous people. Western pragmatism clashed with eastern idealism and led to social and political reform. Allegiance that had been formerly based on geography began to depend more on religious and political affiliation. This period of colonial rule caused a chain reaction of events that catapulted India from a country engrossed in waning medieval practices into a more socially progressive nation in the twentieth century.

READING TRENDS AND PRACTICES: BEFORE BRITISH/WESTERN INFLUENCE

The amount of influence that the British raj (occupation/rule) had on the Indian sub-continent is difficult to calculate. The British left evidence of their occupation in India's government, trade, social and religious views, and even linguistic development. Prior to the British occupation, much of India's literature was written in the form of verse. Only a few languages had any literature in prose form. The few examples of prose include religious commentaries and biographies that were written poorly and without form or style. The biographies were often propagandized by various sects who included myths, legends, and supernatural miracles. Depending on the faction within Hinduism, poets would write for Krishna, Kali, Shiva, or some other deity. This trend of specialization crossed literary genres. A popular verse form was the *pad*. Pads were short religious songs, often about the love of Krishna and Radha. The "Vaisnava" pad set the standard for Bengali love poetry for nearly three hundred years, even being imitated by Rabindranath Tagore and his contemporaries in the twentieth century. The pad was to India, especially Bengal, what the sonnet was to Elizabethan England. The pad was not exclusive to Vaisnavism and other Hindu sects, but was also significant in Islamic literary tradition as well. One notable pad, "Ray-mangal" by Krisnaram Das, describes the enmity between Hindus and Muslims. A battle is fought, which nearly destroys the world. The quarrel is resolved when God descends as half-Krishna and half-Muhammad to resolve the conflict. This amalgamation of Hinduism and Islam provides an important example of the seventeenth-century trend of combining denominations that occurred in Bengal.

During the 1600s, much of northern India was controlled by the Mughals who were Islamic rulers over the largely Hindu population. The Mughals used Persian for all government correspondence, official documentation, and literature, but a new dialect was evolving in areas where Persian and other Indian languages were

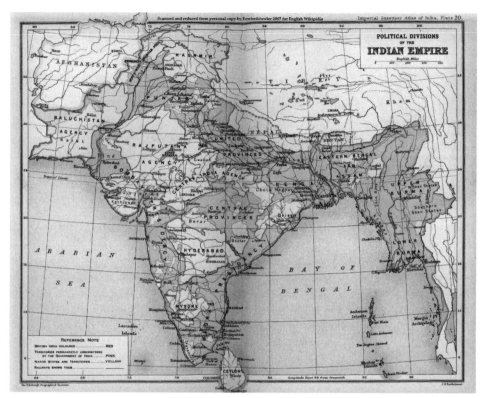

Map of the British Indian Empire, 1909.

spoken together. The result was Urdu (also called Hindustani), known as "camp language," where many of the soldiers who spoke it had come into contact with Indians speaking the local languages. In the early stages of Urdu poetry, much of the vocabulary was highly influenced by Persian, often in the form of loanwords. Outside of literature, the influence of the Persian language lasted a long time, remaining the government language until 1837 when Urdu replaced it. By 1800, works of Urdu prose were beginning to challenge the Persian monopoly on literature. Much of Urdu poetry dealt with the theme of love. Eighteenth-century lyric master Mir Taqi Mir, and seventeenth-century Tazkira a Shauq were well-known for their realistic short couplets on love and tragedy. Most of the longer poetry at this time was happier and often dealt with lovers overcoming supernatural obstacles to reunite, such as in Mir Hasan's *Sihr ul Bayan* (The Enchanted Story). Though poetry was still the standard literary form in Urdu, its prose development began earlier than many of the other Indian languages. Examples of Urdu prose are the *dastan*, which is a Persian loanword for "story" or "tale." These tales boldly paint characters as either all good or all bad. A notable example of a dastan is *Tale of Amir Hamza*, which chronicles the adventures of the uncle of the Muslim prophet Muhammad. Amir righteously battles in medieval fashion, often against infidels and witches. *Tale of Amir Hamza* is believed to have been written in Persian by Faiza around the beginning of the seventeenth century. Dastans allowed the Muslim government officials to lose themselves in the fantasy of virtuous Muslim warriors of the past fighting clearly evil opponents. However, each time they closed their books, the officials had to return to their lives in a bureaucratic world of differing shades of gray as the Mughal Empire faced domestic troubles and rebellions. Some critics have written off dastans as mere propaganda tales, which promoted a cast of heroes and their unwavering adherence to strict codes of conduct. However, these simple tales of good triumphing over evil remained popular even until the last days of the Mughal Empire.

As the Mughals pushed to expand their power in India, different rulers developed different policies on religion. This aspect of Mughal rule is extremely important, because even though the Mughal rulers were Muslims, most of their subjects were Hindu. Emperor Akbar was particularly tolerant of Hindus, but after his death in 1605, change was afoot. Several years after Akbar's rule, Emperor Shah Jahan came into power. Not forgetting the earlier rebellion of his son Khusru, who was sheltered by the Sikh Guru Arjun, Shah Jahan took an openly hostile stance toward the Sikhs in Punjab. Because of this oppressive policy, Guru Har Gobind trained the Sikhs for military defense against such aggression. The Sikh's need to militarize became especially important after the martyrdom of Guru Tegh Bahdur in 1675. However, it was not until Aurangzeb became emperor that Sikh martial maneuvers and codes became more unified and established under the organization of Guru Gobind Singh.

As a devout Muslim, Aurangzeb persecuted his non-Muslim subjects. He did this by destroying temples, converting other temples into mosques, casting down statues of Hindu deities, firing government officials who would not convert to Islam, prohibiting Hindu festivals, and reenacting *jizya*, the collection of taxes exacted on all non-Muslims. In response, Guru Gobind Singh circulated *Hakumnamas*, which were letters asking his followers to present arms and prepare for training. The most important result of Guru Singh's writings is the institution of Khalsa, which developed the blueprint for the Sikh saint-soldier. Khalsa includes five essential requirements, as follows:

> *Kes*—uncut hair, which represents the natural appearance of saintliness
> *Kanga*—a comb to maintain the hair
> *Kachha*—an undergarment that indicates chastity
> *Kara*—a steel bracelet on the wrist that symbolizes dedication to the Divine Bridegroom
> *Kirpan*—a sword for self-defense and also a symbol of dignity, power, and unconquerable spirit

Guru Singh's writings also set the standard and finalized parts of the Sikh religion. Before he died, Guru Singh pronounced himself to be the final guru and that the final authority on Sikhism would be the Sikh holy book, the Guru Granth Sahib. With Guru Singh's proclamation, the Sikh scriptures were now complete.

The Sikhs were not the only oppressed group to rebel against Aurangzeb's policies. In the second half of the 1600s, the Marathas had loosely organized several series of raids on Mughal territory. During this period, Marathi grain merchant Tukaram retired from business and began to compose verse. These songs were written to help unify the Maratha in their struggle against the Mughals. By 1680, the emperor's Hindu persecution had begun, and by 1696, Bengal had also staged a rebellion. By 1701, the Rajputs rebelled due to Aurangzeb's religious intolerance.

Before 1600, however, Europeans had begun establishing trade and settlements around India. In 1600, England granted the British East India Company the Crown Charter. By the end of Emperor Aurangzeb's reign, the Mughal Empire had been weakened by the overextension of borders and numerous rebellions. Though the Dutch, Portuguese, and French had all traded with India around this time, England had positioned itself to have the biggest impact on the sub-continent.

BRITISH/WESTERN INFLUENCE

Acting as a catalyst for cultural change in India, British colonial activity was largely responsible for the formation of modern India. Three major factors that helped induce this national development were the standardization of the rules of grammar and writing for the various Indian dialects, exposure to western political ideas, and the introduction of new literary genres and themes. These factors worked intermittently and at times interdependently of each other as India forged toward autonomy.

Historically, prose in India was considered insufficient for literary expression because it lacked aesthetic appeal. Verse had been the preferred form of expression for thousands of years for religion, love, and other aspects of life. Prose had existed in Indian languages in the form of unwieldy, artificial commentaries and records, but in general a chasm divided spoken and written language. In the late 1700s and early 1800s, British government officials and missionaries worked together with Indian scholars to begin creating prose in the various Indian languages. This collaboration of east and west would be the beginning of a new literary tradition in India.

Prose development of Indian dialects was initiated mainly by British missionaries. A notable exception is British government worker Nathaniel Brassey Halhed who wrote *A Grammar of the Bengali Language* in 1778. In Bengal, British Christian missionary William Carey was appointed professor of Bengali at Fort William College in 1801 and gathered Indian *pandits* (scholars) to work together to write the first textbooks in Bengali prose. Many of the resulting texts contained direct translations from Sanskrit, the academic language of that time. John Gilchrist, professor of Hindustani (Urdu) at Fort Williams College, collected Urdu and Hindi material. Four years later, Carey wrote a Marathi grammar book and printed a Marathi translation of the Gospel of Matthew. Due to the active missionary presence in India, most major Indian languages had a Bible—or at least a New Testament translation—between 1800 and 1819. Earlier exceptions include Tamil (1714) and Urdu (1743). Complete Bible translations had a strong developmental effect on Indian prose writing.

Despite British missionaries' primary objective of propagating the Christian religion, they also took time to print books that were nonreligious in nature. By 1815, Carey had printed three collections of Indian tales: *Simhasana-battisi*, *Pancatantra*, and *Hitopadesa*. Other western printers in India did not just print western and Christian books but also translations of Hindu scriptures, such as *Ramayana* and *Mahabharata*; popular poetry, such as Bharatchandra Ray's *Annada-mangal*; and tales, such as a translation of Aesop's fables. The introduction of the printing press by westerners had other important influences on Indian culture. Printing presses began to usurp the importance and popularity of festival recitations of *kirtan* singing and *yatra* plays (musicals about traditional religious stories). The literary patrons were being replaced by the reading public. This independence from patrons allowed the writers a chance to explore new literary ground; however, with the positive also came the negative. With this commercialization of writing and independence from the shackles of patron control, writers had to deal with the allure of the monetary rewards of appealing to the taste of readers versus their artistic conscience. Artistic integrity and financial success became important issues among writers in India's literary scene with its exposure to capitalism. Before the 1800s, many Indian writers were guided not by artistic inspiration but by *bhakti* (religious devotion). Very little literature was secular. Even stories with secular themes were fitted with a religious framework. Human love stories were often written as allegorical to spiritual love stories.

In all, Carey and Gilchrist addressed four important northern Indian languages: Bengali, Hindi, Urdu, and Marathi. William Carey and his colleagues helped to intellectually revive Bengali literature after its decline with the passing of Bharatchandra Ray. Concerning the famine in Bengal in 1769 and 1770, scholar Ghosh wrote, "Intellectual and cultural life could not thrive in a country that was literally starving" (33). In 1811, Governor General Minta said that "science and literature were in a state of decay with learning diminished and in some cases abandoned" (in Ghosh 33). Invasions and war had destroyed Indian universities, which were then not reestablished. However, British influence in helping to homogenize the rules and practices of writing in the various languages helped India to recover from this scholastic drought. The genesis of an educational revolution began with William Carey and his colleagues as they produced textbooks and books of general information, often bilingual. Though these books could hardly be classified as literature, they represented the beginning of a return to Indian intellectualism after the tumultuous eighteenth century.

Another important part of the return to learning was the Calcutta School Book Society, founded in 1817, whose purpose was the publication of textbooks. The western—and especially English—influence of the creation of prose in the Indian languages was of utmost importance. It provided an important model not only in form but also in normalizing the various written Indian languages in areas of syntax, structure, standardized spelling, and more. Despite the intrusion of the British into India, some positive results came hand in hand with this foreign rule, though they may not have been immediately recognized or appreciated.

One of the most important governmental statements made by the British about India is known as Macaulay's *Minute*. Before examining this statement, one should know about Macaulay's Indian experience—or lack thereof. After spending only one year in India, Thomas Babington Macaulay, "vehemently denounced Indian humanities as 'absurd history, absurd metaphysics, absurd physics, and absurd theology' admitting at the same time 'I have no knowledge of either Sanskrit or Arabic'" (Clark 30) Having spent only one year in India and not having bothering to learn the languages, Macaulay made a statement in 1830 that would govern the British East India Company's policies on the education of Indians. One of the most significant excerpts is as follows:

> We must at present do our best to form a class who may be interpreters between us and the millions whom we govern—a class of persons Indian in blood and colour, but English in tastes, in opinions, in morals and in intellect. To that class we may leave it to refine the vernacular dialects of the country, to enrich those dialects with terms of science borrowed from western nomenclature, and to render them by degrees fit vehicles for conveying knowledge to the great mass of the population.

Though this idea may have been pragmatic, it was also manipulative in nature. But this idea of a class of English-to-Indian language interpreters backfired in the sense that the interpreters did not want to go back to the villages to teach Indians about British culture but rather preferred to remain in the metropolises in the company of the British. Rather than solve the problems of the British ruling India, this creation of an Indian class with western education would create an even bigger problem in the future for Britain. One hundred years before India's 1947 independence, British influence on Indian education was manifested in the founding of three major universities in Calcutta, Bombay, and Madras. This was the beginning of the creation of the western-educated Indian.

After the British East India Company relinquished control of India to the British government in 1858, Indian interest in history rose, and scholars rose to the challenge as archeologists dug for evidence of India's past and authors wrote historical novels. The first wave of western influence was driven primarily by missionaries, who wrote mainly of Christianity and western philosophy. The next wave of western influence brought about the introduction of some of Britain's best literary accomplishments but also the emergence of Indian's scholars and writers. Indian authors influenced by British writers were beginning to earn nicknames based on the authors whose style they emulated. Michael Madhusudan Datta (Dutt) was known as "the Milton of Bengal." Reminiscent of John Milton's *Paradise Lost*, Datta's *Meghnad-vadh* rethinks religious doctrine by degrading the traditionally lauded Hindu heroes Rama and Lakshmana from the *Ramayana* and elevates the villains Ravanna and Meghnad, as Milton romanticizes Satan in *Paradise Lost*. *Meghnad-vadh* also imitates the canto format of *Paradise Lost*. This epic poem was European in form but Indian in character, providing an example of the amalgamation of east and west. Author of such romantic novels as *Krishna Charitra*, *Durgeshnondini*, *Kapalkundala*, *Mrinalini*, and *Vishabriksha* (*The Poison Tree*), Bankim Chandra Chatterjee was called "the Scott of Bengal." This nickname was earned because Bankim's employment of heroic men and self-sacrificing women is reminiscent of Sir Walter Scott's romantic style. The Derozian thinker, Pearychand Mitra, was known as the "Dickens of Bengal," as he exposed and criticized the social norms and pretensions of conventional society, especially in his novel *Alaler Gharer Dulal*. Not only were British authors such as Scott and Dickens popular in India, but other European authors' English translations were also read in India. As a result of Indians learning English, much of western literature was now in a form they could read. Such translated authors included Tolstoy, Dostoevsky, Romain Rolland, Maxim Gorky, and Victor Hugo. Through the 1870s, many translations of Persian and English literature continued, including Shakespeare's plays, Defoe's *Robinson Crusoe*, Scott's *Ivanhoe*, and Johnson's *Rasselas*.

English literature has given the Indian languages such prose forms as the essay, novel, short story, prose drama, travelogue, literary criticism, biography, and autobiography. With the new literary vehicle of prose came new subjects and themes, often from contemporary, everyday situations. At a time when Indian poetry was considered by some to be stale, western influence opened doors to new possibilities that led to an Indian literary renaissance. Indian poetry by the 1700s had stagnated and was characterized by cliché in phrase and image. There were, however a few exceptions, such as Bharatchandra Ray and Ramprasad Sen, who wrote Hindu devotional songs, especially to Kali. But overall, western influence opened Indian poetry to subjects formerly off-limits and introduced new formats, such as the elegy, sonnet, ode, and dramatic monologue, which were based on the works of Shelley, Keats, Browning, Wordsworth, Whitman, and Eliot. Western influence also introduced religious and political imagery to Indian poetry, including the Christian cross, the Christ figure, Adam and Eve, and the soviet hammer and sickle.

Western influence was at times welcomed by the Indian intelligentsia. An Indian who wrote in English, Michael Madhusudan Datta was strongly opposed to what he believed to be many scholars' "servile imitation of Sanskrit." Though a strong Indian nationalist, Bankim Chandra Chatterjee elevated Shakespeare over Kalidasa, an important Indian classical dramatist.

Despite the heavy influence of the British on India, the British cannot claim full responsibility for the modernization and development of Indian culture and literature.

Indians also worked toward education along with—and also independent of—westerners in the form of the School Society, the Brahmo Education Society, the Bombay Education Society, and the Pachaiyappas School. Although Indian authors were influenced by the West, they produced literature with a uniquely Indian perspective.

Though the West may have had a profound influence on India, that influence would not have been as great had it not been for Indian authors such as Rabindranath Tagore, Bankim Chandra Chatterjee, and Munshi Premchand, who were instrumental in expressing western ideas in a form that Indian readers could appreciate.

MAGAZINES, NEWSPAPERS, AND JOURNALS

Indian journalism draws much from western journalism, including the role of journalism, methods of acquiring information, editing techniques, and progressive ideology. Journalism and missionary work helped to begin newspapers in India. In 1818, John Marshman began the first Bengali newspaper. In the next four years, two more Bengali newspapers were founded. They were *Samacar Candrika*, by Bhavanicaran Banerji, and *Sambad Kaumudi*, by Ram Mohun Roy. Much of India's social progress in the 1800s is due to the work of Rom Mohun Roy. This will be explained in more detail later in this subsection.

Newspapers and journals helped to foster the growth and spread of Indian prose. By 1828, Sadasiv Kasinath Chatre began publishing *Balmitra*, which was a translation of an English version of a French children's newspaper (*L'Ami des Enfants*). This newspaper was used to teach moral lessons to young people. By 1832, Bengali newspapers founded in Calcutta led to the publication of social stories and serialized novels. In general, stories with morals and lessons were extremely popular and widespread in India during the 1800s in newspapers (and in nearly all forms of literature). This trend of didacticism was also prevalent in England during this time, and it helped set an example for Indian literature in the translations from English. Despite some newspapers' claims of pure objectivity, journalists have always been influenced by some bias toward some philosophy, religion, or ethical guidelines. In 1843, Debendranath Tagore (Rabindranath's father) founded the newspaper *Tattvabodhini Patrika* in order to disseminate the teachings of the Samaj. Tagore's father had been an associate and founding member of Ram Mohun Roy's group Brahmo Samaj.

British influence, along with traditional journalism in the form of newspapers, brought to India ideas for the publication of various journals. The journal *Tattvabodhini Patrika*, and others like it, helped educate the public on history, science, and social issues. Articles on science, only recently introduced to India, had the profound impact of establishing a viewpoint of objectivity and a genuine desire for new learning and discoveries.

Newspapers played an important role in helping to shape early prose by providing a forum for the development of structure and vocabulary. This improvement is much indebted to English, as much of the news was translated into Bengali and other Indian languages directly from English. The English example and new literary vehicle of the newspaper afforded writers a place to get a feel for their audience.

One of the most important figures in modern Indian history, Ram Mohun Roy (1772–1833), is often recognized as the figure responsible for initiating the Bengal Renaissance. Scholar Dr. D. N. Bannerjea says, "The Indian through whose courageous efforts a golden bridge was first erected uniting the progressive, practical traditions of the West with the sublime idealism of the East, I should point to Ram Mohun Roy" (Dube 54). His influences and interests were as wide-ranging and varied as his contributions were in the literary, political, social, and religious fields.

In the early 1800s, Roy translated the Vedanta (philosophy of the Vedas) and the *Upanishads* into Bengali, thus putting into the hands of the educated commoner what was formerly only available to the Sanskrit-literate *pandit* and priest. One of Roy's main tenets was monotheism, which he preached instead of the popular contemporary Orthodox Hinduism. In 1815, Ram Mohun Roy founded Atmiya Sabha, where he discussed various issues, including his group's disapproval of idol worship, the caste system, *sati* [ritual immolation of a widow on her husband's funeral pyre],

Commemorative plaque for Ram Mohun Roy in Bedford Square, London. Roy advocated for the Indian adoption of British education systems and reading materials during India's colonization.

polygamy, and his approval of allowing widows to remarry. Ram Mohun and Atmiya Sabha wrote and distributed tracts and pamphlets on these subjects to help propagate these ideas. In 1816, Ram Mohun Roy and David Hare founded the Hindu College of Calcutta, where progressive thought was taught by Derozio and students such as Pearychand Mitra studied. In 1821, Ram Mohun Roy's newspaper *Sambad Kaumudi* attacked Orthodox Hinduism and the Christian doctrine of the trinity. By 1822, a rival newspaper with opposing views was founded. Bhabanicaran Bandyopadhyay wrote in support of Orthodox Hinduism in *Samacar Candrika*. The introduction of journalism to India allowed religious and social views to be examined and debated in this emerging public forum. Mrityunjya Vidyalankar, a scholar and one of William Carey's assistants at Fort William College, held a more traditional view of Hinduism than Ram Mohun and, in reaction to Ram Mohun's attempts at religious reform, wrote "An Apology for the Present System of Hindoo Worship."

By 1823, seven years before Macaulay's *Minute on Indian Education*, Ram Mohun had already advocated English education for Indians and opposed the established, traditional Sanskrit education. He was truly convinced that a western education taught in English could benefit Indian students. In 1828, after studying the biblical Old Testament in Hebrew and the New Testament in Greek, he and Dwarkanath Tagore (grandfather of Rabindranath Tagore) founded the monotheistic social and religious reform society called Brahmo Samaj, or, the Society of Believers in Brahman, the Supreme Spirit. This group based much of its philosophy on the Isha Upanishad, which is a small portion of the *Upanishads* that speaks in a monotheistic manner of the supreme being. A few of the basic tenets of the doctrine adopted by the Brahmo Samaj are as follows: there is one God, humans are responsible for their doings, no mediator is needed between God and man (direct human-deity communion), a near universal respect of religious books and teachers so long as they do not break with certain soul revelations, and daily worship by following God's will in love. Other issues for which Ram Mohun campaigned included women's right to property and education. Scholars have noted his socially progressive views, religious influences from Christianity, and

1815 modern translation of the *Upanishads* that resulted in his persecution. However, time has reconciled Ram Mohun with history, and he now is often recognized as the father of modern India.

Ram Mohun's influence lasted long after his death. Another journalist later in the 1800s, named Vidyasagar, followed in Roy's footsteps. His articles and pamphlets opposing and condemning the ban on widow remarriage helped to initiate the Widow Remarriage Act in 1856. Like Ram Mohun, Vidyasagar courageously stood up against the social norms and criticized the pandits and others who supported polygamy and bans on widow remarriage. Vidyasagar also campaigned for women's right to education and educational reform. Because of his writing in the Bengali vernacular, as opposed to Sanskrit-influenced Bengali, Vidyasagar earned the title "father of modern Bangla (Bengali) literature." His other works include monologues arguing other political and social causes as well, such as *Bidhobabivah* (1855), on widows' rights to remarry; *Bahubivah* (1871–1873), on banning polygamy; and *Balyabivah*, on the flaws of child marriage

LANGUAGE ISSUES—THE DIVERSITY OF THE INDIAN LANGUAGE LITERATURES

When discussing the influence of literature on a culture as diverse as India, language issues must be addressed. Wars, invasions, and religion have all played both unifying and dividing roles in India. In Calcutta alone at the end of the 1700s, Bengali was only one of seven languages, along with Arabic, English, Hindustani, Portuguese, Persian, and Sanskrit. Persian and English were used for government, whereas Sanskrit and Arabic were used for religion. In the 1770s, Charles Wilkins (a British civil servant in Calcutta) made the first Bengali blocks for a printing press. This act allowed Nathaniel Brassey Halhed to print a Bengali grammar book. This is the first of many examples that demonstrate how foreigners, like British missionaries and government officials, were more interested in the local languages of India than were the scholars and educated aristocratic Indians themselves. Many Hindus still believed that the only Indian language appropriate for literature was Sanskrit. Likewise, many Muslims believed Arabic and Persian were superior to local dialects. Although many British scholars and government officials praised Bengali, most Indians did not. In fact, in the early 1800s, educated Indians were more likely to read British literature than Indian literature.

In the second half of the nineteenth century, Indians began writing more and more in their local languages, escaping the long-held grasp of Sanskrit and Persian over literary language. By the 1860s, the use of colloquial Indian languages in works such as *Hutom Pyacar Naksa*, by Kaliprasanna Simha, began to normalize the use of colloquial languages for literature, moving away from the former strictly enforced observance of using only Sanskrit, Arabic, and Persian. Another example is Nazi Ahmad's Urdu novel *The Bride's Mirror* (1869). Of course, this trend was not completely universal, as ten years later Ahmad published *Tale of Azad* (1878–79), which was more conventional and Persian-influenced. Urdu prose developed more slowly than the prose of some other Indian languages because in Urdu-speaking communities, verse was much more highly regarded than prose. This preference for verse over prose was also true for Tamil communities, who considered verse to be the only acceptable and significant form of literature.

Hindi as a literary language struggled for uniformity through conflicting dialects drawing from the different root languages of Sanskrit, Persian, and Arabic. Malayalam prose began later than many Indian languages but was not subject to the same evolutionary difficulties as other languages. Marathi literature developed under strong stylistic influences from English, in many cases imitating if not directly translating from English. French also, in an indirect way, had an effect on Marathi, in that some French literature that was translated into English was then translated into Marathi. This translation from and imitation of foreign literature was not a result of creative stagnation. Early Marathi literature favored established forms over the emerging ingenuity and imagination of new literature. A particular favorite Marathi translation was *The Arabian Nights.*

For the most part, however, most Marathi books were romance novels that remained timeless and placeless, having little or no social or political commentary. This trend continued until the turn of the twentieth century. The 1861 book *Muktamala*, by Laksman Moresvar Halbe, is described as an indigenous romance. It is a straightforward narrative about good triumphing over evil. Critics have noted of this story that the opening of each chapter begins with a description of the scene that has little applicable use to the reader in terms of explaining either the characters or the story. Of course, some authors recognized that they were writing fantastic works of fiction and defended the practice. In the introduction to his 1868 book *Manjughosa*, Naro Sadasiv Risbud states that most Hindus want to read exciting and magical tales that will take them out of their boring lives. This defense of the supernatural and reasoning for writing the fantastic tale is reminiscent of the Mughal-era dastan, as mentioned earlier in this chapter. From Marathi literature, a new type of character emerged. He was the hero's loyal servant who essentially did all the grunt work of spying on the enemy, collecting information, tricking the guards, and whatever else was necessary for the hero to enjoy smooth sailing. This character appeared in many of the works by H. N. Apte and may be based on Sanskrit *duta* characters. These characters from ancient literature were messengers who were often viewed as having the same status as a minister or prince, because they represented their nation. A duta's judgment in tough situations could affect the entire state, which meant unwavering loyalty and patriotism were necessary qualities.

Some Persian story translations with sensual elements were believed to be corrupting the young Maharashtrians. In part to combat this element, and partly because of its popularity in both Britain and India, many stories and novels were written to introduce and circulate moral lessons, which young readers were expected to learn. In 1854, Ramjee Gunnojee wrote a collection of stories, titled *Stricaritra*, imitating tales from *The Arabian Nights* but with the intention of teaching morals to women. A notable didactic and western-influenced Marathi work was Bab Padmanji's *Yamunaparyatan*. The story is about Yamuna, who is secretly a Christian. With her dying husband's blessing after his conversion to Christianity, she escapes India's usual fate for widows of that time (head shaving, jewelry stripping, abstinence, etc.) and remarries a Christian. *Yamunaparyatan* was considered quite original when compared to its contemporary Marathi works, but in retrospect critics have stated that the story's structure is too episodic to be a novel. Some consider it so didactic as to be a book of widow's rights propaganda. Also, the dialogue is actually written with each speaker's name before it, which is more in the format of a play. For these reasons, Bengalis often argue that Pearychand Mitra's 1858 novel *Alaler Gharer Dulah* is India's first novel instead.

Both novels, however, attacked what they saw as social evils of that time, though they did so from different perspectives.

Most Indian literature of the mid-nineteenth century was not yet taking as social and political a form as it would in later decades. In 1871, a work unlike most of its contemporary counterparts, titled *Vidagdha Stricaritra*, told ribald tales comparable to Boccaccio's *Decameron* or Chaucer's *Canterbury Tales*. Another genre of Marathi literature included Sanskrit and Persian adaptations of stories featuring the cleverness and witty humor of the main character. Examples include K. R. Conce's *Maharastra Bhaset Manoranjak Gosti* (1870–1873) and *Barthold* (an English translation of an Italian book). These short stories were considered primitive and anecdotal, with little character description or any real structure. Also included is Moroba Kanhoba's *Ghasiram Kotwal*, which includes humorous anecdotes with flamboyant dialogue. Over time, the Marathi literary attitude of strict adaptation and imitation changed. Under the influence of Samuel Smiles, the prolific Victorian inventor of the "self-help" genre, Marathi writers resolved to improve their knowledge of the modern world and expand their literary styles.

By the 1860s, linguistic developments included the creation of new literary terms. As a result of the mixture of languages and the debate over which languages to use in writing, distinct literary terms were created. *Sadhu bhasa* indicated literary language that relied on elements drawn from Sanskrit. *Cali bhasa* referred to literary language of a more colloquial flavor. Bhudeb Mukherji, author of *Samajik Prbandha*, which analyzed the political and social problems of India around 1892, wrote in sadhu bhasa, while Kaliprasanna Simha, describing the common people of India, wrote in cali bhasa. Pearychand Mitra saw the benefit of writing in both styles but within different contexts. Still other authors were less restricted by language and setting and combined Sanskrit and vernacular. This mixture of sadhu and cali was often looked down upon and referred to as *gurucandali* (Brahmin and outcaste). Because Indian prose did not have as long an evolutionary period as British prose had, numerous problems had to be overcome in going from verse to prose, such as vocabulary, spelling, structure, and aestheticism.

RELIGIOUS AND SOCIALLY REFORMATIVE TEXTS

Beginning with Ram Mohun Roy, India had a variety of social and religious reform groups that grew and evolved throughout the nineteenth century. These groups were often populated with writers and, therefore, influenced India either directly through campaigning or indirectly through the influence they had on the writers and their literature. In 1815, Roy formed the Atmya Sabha (Association of Friends) for weekly religious debates. A counter-group, formed in the 1820s by Professor Henry Derozio, was called Young Bengal. These thinkers based their philosophy on Bacon, Thomas Paine, the French revolutionaries, and rationalism. Those who came after Derozio's death and were influenced by his philosophy are often called Derozians. In 1828, Roy founded the Brahmo Sabha (Association of Brahma), a socio-religious reform group. Issues for which Roy fought were the abolition of sati, the abolition of child-marriages, women's rights to education and property, and public education, especially European science and technology. In 1860, the Sangat Sabha (Association of Believers) broke off from the Brahmo Sabha. Led by Keshub Chunder Sen, the Sangat worked for such social reforms as the rejection of caste, widow remarriage rights, and inter-caste marriage rights. They were successful in lobbying for the latter cause when the 1872 Brahmo

Marriage Act was passed. Other groups, such as the Sanatan Dharma Sabhas (Association of Eternal Dharma) were formed for the defense of Orthodox Hinduism. Still other groups, such as the Arya Samaj (Noble Society) and the Prarthana Samaj (Association of Prayer) were both socially progressive yet nationalistic and traditionally rooted in the Vedas.

SOCIAL AWARENESS TEXTS

Writers associated with these groups, or aware of the causes for which the groups fought, began their literary assault on what they perceived as the injustices of society. Several Bengali writers used satire to attack customs they saw as unjust, such as child marriages, selling young brides to elderly men, the ban on widow remarriage, polygamy, and banning girls from receiving an education. These problems were often associated with Kulin Brahminism. One text that denounced what it called the evils of Kulin marriage practices was Ram Narayan Tarkaratna's 1854 play, *Kulina Kula Sarvasa* (*Sarbaswa*). Poor families would often arrange for their extremely young daughters to marry the old men of the higher echelons of the Kulin Brahmin caste for dowry and racial reasons, which often resulted in child-widows. Social custom dictated that all widows, including child-widows, live together in groups apart from the rest of society, simply and humbly. But this life could better be described as one of poverty and humiliation. In 1879, M. V. Rahalkar wrote *Narayanrav ani Godavari*, which is often said to be the first Indian social novel. It also deals with the themes of polygamy and the selling of daughters to the highest-bidding suitor. In the case of this book, the highest-bidding suitor is a lecherous drunk.

Another popular theme was the dangers of western cultural influence, especially drinking and immorality. Because of this theme, a new literary character type was developed. Bengali, Marathi, Hindi, and Urdu literature all included the "new babu," who was depicted as an Indian youth aping westerners by wearing western clothes, eating foods forbidden to Indians, consuming alcohol, soliciting prostitutes, and only superficially following Indian religions to avoid complete social ostracism. In 1862, Kaliprasanna Simha wrote *Hutom Pyacar Naksa* (Sketches by Hutom the Owl), a collection of separate sketches painting literary portraits of a variety of character types found in Calcutta. The main target of these sketches was the "new babu," which Simha described as a Hindu by day and a western-influenced (i.e., drunk and lecherous) scoundrel by night. Three important features of these sketches that advanced Indian prose at that time are the organic unity of narrative and descriptive writing styles, the use of contemporary life as subject matter for fiction (a topic that was, prior to this, considered unsuitable and rarely used), and the use of colloquial language (it was one of the first prose works to do so). Under his pseudonym Tekchand Thakur, Pearychand Mitra wrote the social novel *Alaler Gharer Dulal* (1858). Often seen as a cautionary tale on the consequences of raising children improperly, this early effort at prose is often described as a set of sketches. The three main themes the book criticizes are overindulgent parents, polygamy, and the false conversions to Christianity or Islam of Indians seeking only social benefits.

In 1889, a Malayalam judge named Chandu Menon wrote an important novel called *Indulekha* advocating the synthesis of eastern and western values. As an enthusiastic reader of English novels, Menon would often tell his wife of his readings. In this way she acquired a preference for western novels, even without being able to read English. After Menon began a translation of Lord Beaconfield's

Henrietta Temple, he decided to cast aside the translation and write his own novel in Malayalam. His theme was English education, which he believed was important for Indian progress. The protagonist Indulekha was a progressive, English-educated young lady, who had also learned Sanskrit and played both the piano and the *veena* (an Indian lute). These linguistic and musical abilities helped to portray her as westernized to some degree and yet still Indian. Her eventual triumph over the old ways can be seen as a triumph for English education. Menon used this novel as a way to convince Indians of the advantages of having an English education.

Saratchandra Chatterjee's *Palli Samaj* (1916) helped the Indian city-dwellers to understand rural village life. Like Rabindranath Tagore, Chatterjee wrote with sympathy for the social condition of women, and he showcased characters from segments of society not previously explored in Bengali fiction. Like Saratchandra Chatterjee, Munshi Premchand was also concerned about the lack of attention given to the lower classes, as he was raised in extreme poverty. He wrote stories and novels about the poor with a fierce realism that brought Hindi literature out of the phase of fantasy about kings and queens and into social realism. In his colloquial style, Premchand penned numerous short stories and novels, including *Godaan*, *Gaban*, and *Nirmala*.

Born in Peshawar (now Pakistan), Mulk Raj Anand was one the most socially progressive Indian writers of the colonial period. Having lived poorly in England while working at Indian restaurants and writing his doctoral thesis, Anand associated with the left-wing literati and became committed to Marxism in the 1930s. He considered himself to be a rational humanist and believed that all art was propaganda, whether for Buddhism, Hinduism, Christianity, communism, capitalism, or some other ideology. His fiction often involves the villages, poverty, caste cruelties, and the mistreatment of women, orphans, untouchables, and urban laborers. Anand regularly utilized three classes of characters: the victims/protagonists, oppressors/antagonists (who oppose change), and the good men who tend to be social workers or labor leaders who work for positive change. Anand often wrote in an angry reformist fashion, unlike the humorous reformatory style of writers such as Dickens. In the novel *Untouchable*, accidental physical contact of an untouchable with a Hindu affects the action for the entire book. His solution for the social progress of the untouchable street sweepers (sanitation workers) was not Christ or Gandhi but sewer drainage technology. Most of Anand's writings are boldly political and written for specific reformist purposes. His works are a key example of how Indian short story writers were influenced by Maupassant, Chekhov, and Flaubert to begin challenging social standards.

POLITICAL TEXTS

Books often addressed the pros and cons of British rule, such as the educational and governmental systems set up by the British. One such writer was Dinabandhu Mitra, known as "Bengal's first great dramatist." His 1860 satire *Nil Darpan* (The Indigo Planting Mirror) deals with British indigo planter abuses against villagers. This criticism of British rule was effective and led to commission inquiries. Another writer who criticized the way the British governed was Marathi author Kesav Balavant Kelkar. In 1871 he wrote a social realist novel under the guise of a romance titled *Bodhasudha*. The basis of the story is a moral lesson, but a notable feature of *Bodhasudha* is that it is the first Marathi fictionalized critical reaction to both British rule and western ideas. The British believed the taking of bribes and corruption would end if they paid the magistrates a good salary. Kelkar thought this idea was, at best, positive thinking overreaching itself. He also criticized Christian missionaries and their work, depicting characters whose conversion was in no way sincere but rather a way of playing the system for their own benefit.

As the nineteenth century progressed, India saw an increase of patriotism and nationalism in the literary forms of historical narrative and heroic poem. Bankim Chandra Chatterjee—sometimes referred to as Chattopadhyay—(1834–1894) was an early Indian nationalist and Hindu patriot. A popular Indian national song, "Bande Mataram," originated from his novel *Ananda-math*. Bankim wrote many historical romance and social novels, often with the theme of the struggle of Hindus for political freedom. These novels helped to promote the idea of Indian nationalism. Some readers have noted a shift from a tolerant, respectful view of Muslim characters in early Bankim novels to hostility toward Muslim characters in later novels. That is, the equal treatment of Hindu and Muslim characters from the earlier novels apparently gives way to Hindu heroes and Muslim villains in Bankim's later novels. As one scholar stated of Bankim's later literature, "Patriotism was unequivocally identified with Hinduism" (Clark 76).

As the 1800s progressed, certain literary characterizations of Hindus and Muslims increasingly grew negatively biased. Arguments made by Indian scholars defending the use of Hindus versus Muslims say that this religious opposition was used as a veil to allegorize the Indian struggle against foreign rule, mainly the British. Scholars also state that earlier poets used mythological settings to allegorize the contemporary political happenings of their day. While Hindu writers were under Mughal (Islamic) rule, they often wrote using mythological settings. When Hindu writers were under British rule, they often wrote using Mughal settings.

Bankim has been criticized for anachronisms in his historical novels, writing too unrealistically, misrepresenting history, romanticizing the lives of the lower classes, being too uncritically conservative and traditional, and writing more as a moralist than a novelist. However, it is important to note that Bankim was one of the earliest pioneering novelists of the Indian languages, and he emerged from an India that was without prose but deeply steeped in religious poetry and plays for hundreds of years. Others charge him with having a pro-Hindu, anti-Muslim prejudice. Others criticize his characters' lack of free will, as they seemed resigned to the whim of fate with little ability to make choices, like the ancient Greek tragedy characters obligated to follow their *moira*.

Certainly people had a variety of ideas as to what true patriotism and nationalism meant. Some scholars believe that the nationalist movement was a moderate movement against both the uncritical acceptance and continuance of Orthodox Hinduism and also against an equally slavish and uncritical devotion to westernization. A notable example of the tempering of eastern and western tastes is seen in the works of Michael Madhusudan Datta. Later in his life, after an early devotion to western ideas, Datta grew moderate and wrote two comedic plays: one that mocked the ultra-westernized younger generation and another that explored the problems of the uncompromising Orthodox Hinduism of the older generation.

Along with criticism of religion was a renewed interest in interpreting the ancient scriptures. Ram Mohun Roy's call back to the *Upanishads* in the early 1800s eventually led to numerous colloquial translations of classics, such as the *Ramayana* and the *Mahabharata*, but also the numerous interpretational and expositional commentaries on religious texts by such scholars as Bankim, Vivekananda, Aurobindo Ghose, and Rames-chandra Datta, among others. Vivekananda echoed Roy's call back to religion and also advocated classical studies, hoping to reinvigorate India as the Renaissance reinvigorated Europe. A movement calling for universal religion started by Ram Mohun Roy was coined "the new dispensation" by playwright Keshub Chunder Sen. Sen encouraged the dramatist Trailokya to write the play *Nava Vrindavan*, which called for universal religion and featured a banner with a Christian cross, a Muslim crescent, and Buddhist and Hindu symbols.

Influenced by western education, the Bengali middle classes led the nationalist movement toward the formation of the National Congress. However, western education can be viewed both as progress and as a hindrance to progress. The spread of the English language within the Indian middle classes led to the rise of British literature's popularity. Writers such as Shakespeare, Daniel Defoe (*Robinson Crusoe*), Samuel Johnson (*Rasselas*), Charles Lamb (*Essays of Elia*, *Tales from Shakespeare*), Sir Walter Scott (*Ivanhoe*), Edward Bulwer-Lytton, Sir Richard Francis Burton (*Arabian Nights*), and G. W. M. Reynolds were widely read among Indians. Strangely enough, Reynolds was popular in India but almost unheard of in Britain. However, Victorian morality tales were as popular in India as they were in England. This trend of British literature in India created a stumbling block for the progress of the literature of the indigenous Indian languages. With readers governing what was written by supporting it with their purchasing power, Indian writers had to respond to the public's demands. Luckily for many Indian writers, not all readers wanted to read British literature or traditional Indian literature with mythological settings. Local and current political and social issues were gaining recognition. After the Sepoy Mutiny of 1857, Ram Ram Basu's *Pratapadityacaritra* was republished, which signified a renewed curiosity in Indian history. Interest in tales and heroes was not altogether repressed, as S. C. Dutt's *Times of Yore*, which was written in English, was published. Preferring English over local dialects was not just a matter of literary taste. One reason this preference occurred was due to certain social and economic benefits associated with being able to read and speak English. Jobs and business opportunities were available to Indians who spoke English and who would cooperate with the British. In opposition to this growing ideological preference for English, certain groups of Indians began rejecting English and writing literature in their own languages instead.

Despite linguistic diversity throughout India, scholars have often sought to bind Indian literature together. For example, Radhakrishnan echoed the ideas of Aurobindo when he stated, "Indian literature is one, though written in many languages" (Dube 22). Stories that reach across cultural boundaries and depict humankind in a universally recognizable way contribute greatly to national and even international solidarity. Easily one of the most recognizable names in Indian literature inside and outside of India today is Rabindranath Tagore (1861–1941). Winning the 1913 Nobel Prize for Literature for his collection of poems/songs titled *Gitanjali* (*Song Offerings*) brought him worldwide fame. But Tagore was far more than just a poet. A writer for more than sixty years, he explored a variety of forms, including writing more than one thousand poems, two dozen plays, eight novels, eight or more short story collections, over two thousand songs, and various essays and philosophical writings. His plays range from prose social comedies to verse romance. Some of his themes include humanism and internationalism. His nationalist songs called for unity despite the diversity of India, especially during the time of Indian Partition. Some of his short stories expose the evils of kulinism (corrupt upper-class Brahmin culture), caste restriction, and untouchability. In his novel *Ghare Baire* (*The Home and the World*, 1916), Tagore condemns intolerance no matter what end it may be used to seek. In *Char Adhyay*, he warns against justifying violence under the cloak of Hindu zealotry. In his 1909 novel *Gora* (*Fair-Faced*), Tagore explores the cultural identity of India concerning religion, caste, and class, and concludes that individuals are more than just members of a

Rabindranath Tagore and Mahatma Gandhi, much-read "authors" of Indian independence.

group. People do not have to be distinctly categorized as being from just one group. They can adapt some western ways but remain essentially Indian. Other issues explored in *Gora* include the religious reformist group the Brahmo Samaj, and ways to westernize Hinduism, such as doing away with certain caste and gender restrictive elements. Written in 1910, *Arup Ratan* (translated under two titles: *Formless Jewel* and *The King of the Dark Chamber*) is an allegory. Superficially, it can be seen as a beauty and the beast story, but more deeply it can be read as a "spiritual journey of man in relation to his creator." Hindu and Buddhist tenets and imagery lead the reader on a quest for the discovery of the divine. Deeply in tune with nature and humanity, Tagore wrote the following in "The Relation of the Individual to the Universe":

> [When man is] Deprived of the background of the whole, his poverty loses its one great quality, which is simplicity, and becomes squalid and shamefaced. His wealth is no longer magnanimous; it grows merely extravagant. . . . Then it is that in our self-expression we try to startle and not to attract; in art we strive for originality and lose sight of truth which is old and yet ever new; in literature we miss the complete view of man which is simple and yet great. Man appears instead as a psychological problem. (Quoted in Chakravorty 42)

Other nationalists were not as temperate as Tagore. Transformed from an English-educated academic into a political revolutionary nationalist, Aurobindo Ghose (1872–1950) "called for fire sacrifice to rid the country of foreign colonial rule"

> **Saratchandra Chatterjee**
>
> Another writer working toward equality was Saratchandra Chatterjee (1876–1938), a Bengali, whose essay "What Price Woman?" calls for women's rights. Chatterjee wrote many popular stories and novels, mostly about the role of women in Indian society. His focus was the Indian wife and her trials and difficulties in the traditional Indian household.

(Chakravorty 31) in his book *Bhavani Mandir: A Handbook for Revolutionaries* as a reaction to British use of religious separatism within India to partition Bengal in 1905. Others were even more revolutionary than Tagore. Better known by his honorary title "Mahatma" ("great soul"), Mohandas Karamchand Gandhi (1869–1948) wrote extensively in his journals *Young India* (1919–1932) and *Harijan* (1933–1942). In these publications, he extolled the virtues of overcoming opposition with love and the use of peaceful protest methods, such as *ahimsa* (nonviolence) and *asahakara* (noncooperation). Some of the political and social causes that Gandhi worked toward included women's rights, self-sacrifice, minority rights within majority rule, faith in humanity, religious tolerance, and India's independence with interdependence. Gandhi, like so many contemporary political leaders, wanted independence for India, but because of the religious and societal schisms that divided so many groups, few wanted the interdependence of a unified India.

Though Gandhi's messages were often highly respected, they were not always heeded. Violent revolutionary tactics used by other activists continued for years, as did Gandhi's form of nonviolent protest. Gandhi not only wrote and directly influenced Indian history and culture; he also became a controversial fictionalized character in numerous novels and short stories. As previously mentioned, Mulk Raj Anand's main character in *Untouchable* was inspired by Gandhi's message, but still rejected his philosophy in favor of the advancements of technology. Anand's character Lalu in *The Sword and the Sickle* returns to India after a war and, seeing the poor peasants evicted from their land, concludes that there are only two races on earth: the rich and the poor. Viewing the poor as powerless in such a political system, the character rejects Gandhi's nonviolent protest methods. In his 1938 novel *Kanthapura*, Raja Rao depicts how the philosophy of Gandhi, even when delivered secondhand, could affect a village, and how the villagers and their perceptions shaped that philosophy in return.

CONCLUSION

In many cases, the early prose writings in India were more of a reflection of the culture than an influence on it. Newspapers and journals had some of the most direct impacts on the culture, helping to start a national dialogue between readers and writers. In the early nineteenth century, the influx of foreign literature opened the door to western philosophy and social practices. This led to the social activism of Ram Mohun Roy, the Derozians, and the newly formed religious societies. One hundred years later, Gandhi and his contemporaries continued this tradition of social reform as India moved closer toward self-rule.

The nineteenth century progressed, and so too did the literary styles and quality of India's writers. Social theatre and novels brought the sufferings of the underprivileged and oppressed to the attention of both the Indian upper classes and the foreign colonists. Religious thought from various denominations, merged as pluralism, was explored by pandits and playwrights. Much Indian literature reflected the world around it, but much also began to affect and change society.

RECOMMENDED READING

Alphonso-Karkala, John B. *An Anthology of Indian Literature.* New Delhi: Indian Council for Cultural Relations, 1987.

Devi, R. Leela. *Influences of English on Malayalam Novels.* Trivandrum: College Book House, 1978.

Gowen, Herbert H. *A History of Indian Literature: From Vedic Times to the Present Day.* New York: Greenwood Press Publishers, 1968.

Ittiavira, Verghese. *Social Novels in Malayalam.* Bangalore: The Christian Institute for the Study of Religion and Society, 1968.

Lal, P. *The Concept of an Indian Literature: Six Essays.* Calcutta: Lake Gardens Press, 1968.

Machwe, Prabhakar. *Four Decades of Indian Literature: A Critical Evaluation.* New Delhi: Chetana Publications, 1976.

Raghava, Sulochana Rangeya. *Sociology of Indian Literature (A Sociological Study of Hindi Novels).* Jaipur: Rawat Publications, 1987.

Sen, S.P. *History in Modern Indian Literature.* Calcutta: Institute of Historical Studies, 1975.

Sharma, L.P. *History of Medieval India (1000–1740 A.D.).* Delhi: Konark Publishers, 1987.

Tagore, Rabindranath. *Three Plays.* Translated by Ananda Lal. New Delhi: Oxford University Press, 2001.

Terchek, Ronald J. *Gandhi: Struggling for Autonomy.* Lanham: Rowman & Littlefield Publishers, Inc., 1998.

Walsh, William. *Indian Literature in English.* Ed. David Carroll and Michael Wheeler. London: Longman, 1990.

PRIMARY SOURCES

Aesop. *Aesop's Fables.* Translated by Laura Gibbs. New York: Oxford World's Classics, 2003.

Banerji, Bhavanicaran, ed. *Samacar Candrika.* Published in Calcutta from 1830–1831.

Basu, Ram Ram. *Pratapadityacaritra.* First published in 1801. Copy held in the National Library of India.

Boccaccio. *The Decameron.* New York: Penguin Classics, 2003.

Carey, William, ed. *Hitopadesa.* Carey's specific translation of this classic Indian text is long out of print, but many newer translations are available.

———. *Pancatantra.* Carey's specific translation of this classic Indian text is long out of print, but many newer translations are available.

———. *Simhasana-battisi.* Copy in the National Library of India, Kolkata, India.

Chandra Chatterjee (Chattopadhyay), Bankim. *Ananda-math.* New York: Oxford University Press, 2005.

———. *Durgeshmondini.* Published in Bengali. Dhaka, Bangladesh: Kakoli Prokashoni, 2004.

———. *Kapalkundala.* First published in 1866. Translated by Devendra Nath Ghose. India: Ghose Press, 2007.

———. *Krishna Charitra.* Kolkota, India: M. P. Birla Foundation, 1991.

———. *Mrinalini.* First published in 1868.

———. *The Poison Tree (Vishabriksha).* Teddington, UK: Echo Library, 2007.

Chatterjee, Saratchandra. *Palli Samaj.* India: Rupa & Co, 2001.

———. "What Price Woman?" ("Narir Mulya"). First published in the journal *Jamuna,* under the pen name of Anila Devi (Chatterjee's elder sister) on 18 March 1924.

Chaucer, Geoffrey. *Canterbury Tales.* New York: Penguin Classics, 2005.

Conce, K.R. *Barthold.* First published sometime between 1870 and 1873.

———. *Mahardstra Bhdset Manoranjak Gos I.* First published sometime between 1870 and 1873.

Dutt, S. C. *Times of Yore.* With Saurindra Mohan Tagore. London: Reeve, 1885.

Defoe, Daniel. *Robinson Crusoe.* New York: Modern Library Classics, 2001.

Disraeli, Benjamin (Lord Beaconfield). *Henrietta Temple.* Charleston, SC: BiblioBazaar, 2007.

Faiza. *Tale of Amir Hamza.* Faiza's volume is no longer in print, but other editions are available.

Gandhi, Mohandas Karamchand, founding publisher. *Young India*. Published in Ahmedabad by Navajivan Publishing House, 1919–1931.

———. (ed. 1933–1942, 1946–1948). *Harijan*. 1933–1948.

Ghose, Aurobindo. *Bhavani Mandir: A Handbook for Revolutionaries*. Pamphlet originally published in 1903. Contemporary source unknown.

Halhed, Nathaniel Brassey. *A Grammar of the Bengali Language*. India: Ananda, 1980.

Hasan, Mir. *Sihr ul Bayan* (*The Enchanted Story*). In *Three Mughal Poets: Mir, Sauda, Mir Hasan*. Edited by Khurshidul Islam and Ralph Russell. New York: Oxford India Paperbacks, 2004.

Johnson, Samuel. *Rasselas*. New York: Oxford World's Classics, 1999.

Kanhoba, Moroba. *Ghasiram Kotwal*. Edited by N.R. Phatak, 1961.

Kasinath Chatre, Sadasiv, translator. *Balmitra*. Most recent edition published in 1933.

Kesav Balavant Kelkar. *Bodhasudha*. Bombay, 1871. Copy available in The Library of India, Kolkota, India.

Lamb, Charles. *Essays of Elia*. St. Asaph, UK: Hesperus, 2008.

Lamb, Charles, and Mary Lamb. *Tales from Shakespeare*. New York: Penguin Classics, 2007.

Macaulay, Thomas Babington. *Minute* [on Indian Education]. Available at http://www.columbia.edu/itc/mealac/pritchett/00generallinks/macaulay/txt_minute_education_1835.html.

Madhusudan Dutt, Michael. *Is This Called Civilization?* Published in Calcutta, 1871.

———. *Meghnad-vadh*. Published in Bombay, 1861.

Mahabharata. New York: Penguin Classics, 2001.

Menon, Chandu. *Indulekha*. New York: Oxford University Press, 2005.

Milton, John. *Paradise Lost*. New York: Penguin Classics, 2003.

Mitra, Dinabandhu. *Nil Darpan* (*The Indigo Planting Mirror*). Calcutta: Indian Publications, 1972.

Mitra, Pearychand. *Alaler Gharer Dulal*. Published under Pearychand's pseudonym, Tekchand Thakur, in 1857.

Moresvar Halbe, Laksman. *Muktamala*. Published in Bombay, 1861.

Mukhopadhyay, Bhudev. *Samajik Prbandha*. Calcutta: Paschim Banga Pustak Parshad, 1892.

Narayan Tarkaratna, Ram. *Kulina Kula Sarvaswa*. First published in 1854.

Nazir, Ahmad. *Tale of Azad*. Ahmad Nazir's specific translation of this classic Indian text is no longer in print, but many other editions are available.

———. *The Bride's Mirror*. Whitefish, MT: Kessinger Publishing, 2007.

Padmanji, Baba. *Yamunaparyatan*. First published in 1857. 4th edition, Bombay, 1937.

Premchand, Munshi. *Gaban*. New Delhi: Full Circle, 2006.

———. *Godaan*. Indianapolis: Indiana University Press, 1968.

———. *Nirmala*. New York: Oxford University Press, 2002.

Rahalkar, M. V. *Narayanrav ani Godavari*. First published in 1879.

Raj Anand, Mulk. *Untouchable*. New York: Penguin Classics, 1990.

Ramayana. New York: Penguin Classics, 2006.

Rao, Raja. *Kanthapura*. Calcutta: Oxford UP India, 1990.

Ray, Bharatchandra. *Annada-mangal*. First published in Bengal, 1752.

Roy, Ram Mohun. *Precepts of Jesus*. Calcutta: Unitarian Press, 1823.

———, ed. *Sambad Kaumudi*. Weekly newspaper published in Calcutta from 1821–1823.

Sadasiv Risbud, Naro. *Manjughosa*. First published in 1868.

Scott, Walter. *Ivanhoe*. New York: Penguin Classics, 2000.

Simha, Kaliprasanna. *Hutom Pyacar Naksa* (*Sketches by Hutom the Owl*). First published in 1862.

Tagore, Debendranath, ed. *Tattvabodhini Patrika*. Newspaper, published in Calcutta from 1843–1883.

Tagore, Rabindranath. *Arup Ratan*. In *Three Plays* (as *Formless Jewel*). Translated by Ananda Lal. New York: Oxford University Press, 2001.

———. *Char Adhyay*. India: Srishti Publishers & Distributors, 2002.

———. *Gitanjali* (*Song Offerings*). Sioux Falls, SD: NuVision Publications, 2007.

———. *Gora*. Translated by Sujit Mukherjee. New Delhi: Sahitya Akademi, 2001.

———. *The Home and the World* (*Ghare Baire*). New York: Penguin Classics, 2005.

———. "The Relation of the Individual to the Universe." Available at http://www.sacred-texts.com/hin/tagore/sadh/sadh03.htm

The Arabian Nights. Translated by Richard Francis Burton. New York: Modern Library, 2004.

Trailokya. *Nava Vrindavan.* Traditional play. No longer in print under this author's name.

Vidagdha Stricaritra. Published in 1871.

Vidyalankar, Mrityunjya. "Vedantacandrika." (Translated by W.H. Macnaghten as "An Apology for the Present System of Hindoo Worship.") First published in 1817.

Vidyasagar, Chandra Ishwar. *Bahubivah.* ("Whether polygamy should be banned.") First published in 1871.

———. *Balyabivah.* ("Flaws of child marriage.") Publication date not known.

———. *Bidhobabivah.* ("Whether widows should remarry.") First published in 1855.

SECONDARY SOURCES

Chakravorty, B. C. *Rabindranath Tagore: His Mind and Art.* New Delhi: Young India Publications, 1971.

Clark, T. W., ed. *The Novel in India: Its Birth and Development.* Berkeley: University of California Press, 1970.

Dube, S. C. *Indian Literature: Proceedings of a Seminar.* Arabinda Poddar, editor. Simla: Indian Institute of Advanced Study, 1972.

Ghosh, J. C. *Bengali Literature.* London: Oxford University Press, 1948.

Raeside, Ian. "Early Prose Fiction in Marathi, 1828–1885." *The Journal of Asian Studies* 27.4 (August, 1968). 791–808. Available at http://www.jstor.org/stable/2051580.

CHAPTER 22

Independence

Rochelle Almeida

TIMELINE

INTRODUCTION TO THE PERIOD

The phenomenon of readers desiring literature in English on the Indian subcontinent can be traced directly to the arrival of the British East India Company. Although Warren Hastings (1732–1818) and Sir William Jones (1746–1794), the "Brahmanized Britons" discouraged the introduction of western civilization and Christianity to India for fear that they would alter and/or dilute the purity of

India's native traditions, in 1813, the East India Company facilitated the arrival of foreign missionaries, whose proselytizing zeal led to the creation of printing presses for the dissemination of literature in English as well as vernacular languages. The East India Company's enthusiasm for civilizing the population through education was inspired not by Christian altruism, but because the Company's commercial expansion needed the support of a literate, English-speaking, reading, and, most importantly, writing, Indian administrative staff. The imposition of these "civilizing" systems quickly generated other manifestations of European social organization, such as India's first newspaper, *Hicky's Bengal Gazette*, which came out in 1780 and was followed closely by the establishment of missionary schools in Madras (1717), Bombay (1718), and Calcutta (1720). Higher education first came to India in 1817 when Raja Rammohan Roy (1772–1833) and his friends founded the Hindu College in Calcutta. The impetus to propagate higher education in English was propelled by the famous *Minute* of February 2, 1835, issued by Lord Thomas Babbington Macaulay (1800–1859), perhaps the single most significant British document issued in the nineteenth century. Macaulay advocated that all education dispensed in India should be in the English language, as he considered it both necessary and possible "to make natives of this country thoroughly good English scholars" (K. R. Srinivas Iyengar 27). Thus, Macaulay's ideology was completely contrary to that of Warren Hastings. It spelled the end of the pursuit of Orientalist learning in India and the beginning of a new devotion to foreign literature and reading.

By 1855 Presidency College in Calcutta, dispensing instruction in English, became the best-known institution of higher learning in India. As more colleges were created in the last quarter of the nineteenth century, education in India flourished. This period might thus be viewed as the time when Indians, fortunate enough to find education opportunities in English schools and colleges, became voracious consumers of western literature. As readers and scholars, their syllabi were based largely on the Oxbridge model and included canonical works that had long been the staple of British higher education. In the 1800s, this meant that students graduating with

---

Indian Circulating Libraries During the Colonial Regime

The emergence of Indian public libraries followed close upon the heels of English education. Of these, the most prestigious, the Calcutta Public Library, established in 1836 (and known after 1948 as the National Public Library), had paying members as well as a policy of welcoming student readers and "respectable strangers visiting the City" (Priya Joshi, *In Another Country: Colonialism, Culture and the English Novel in India*, 46) free of charge. Inspired by this success, wealthy *zamindars* (land-owners) founded libraries on their rural estates. As the number of Indian readers of British works exploded, *Thacker's India Directory* indicates proportionate increases in the number of reading rooms and libraries all over the country. For example, Calcutta went from having 49 libraries and reading rooms in 1886 to 137 in 1901, and those in Bombay increased from thirteen in 1886 to seventy in 1901. (See Priya Joshi, *In Another Country: Colonialism, Culture and the English Novel in India*.)

---

a major in English literature would have read Chaucer, Shakespeare, John Donne, Pope, and Dryden "with essays and drama following" (Priya Joshi 17). Philosophical works in the form of the treatises of Hobbes and Locke would also have been required reading; later in the twentieth century, the inclusion of Carlyle and Ruskin would have been considered mandatory. The domination of western liberal thinking influenced the mindset of the elite Indian, who was convinced that indigenous works produced in vernacular languages in India were second-rate, compared to the greatness of western thinkers and writers. Thus, as readers acquiring most of the literature they consumed from circulating libraries and "public reading rooms," Indians bought into the idea that everything western was superior to anything native—a fact that colored not only their choice of reading material but indeed the suits of clothes they switched to wearing, the use of silverware at their tables, and their general abandonment of tradition and orthodoxy for the ways of their imperial masters.

The emergence of the brown sahib is characteristic of this period. This figure, often satirized in local Indian literature, was deeply influenced by the kind of reading materials that were made available to him. Needless to say, education in India during this epoch was largely the preserve of the wealthy and exclusively the prerogative of males. Rarely were women granted entry into the world of learning and independent thinking. As the 1800s gave way to the 1900s, Indian students were instructed to believe that all forms of Indian creative literary production should not just be confined to the English language, but should imitate as closely as possible the content of their British counterparts as well as their stylistic usage of the language. Thus educated Indian readers, almost exclusively men, read epics that retold stories from Greek mythology in the conventional stanzaic patterns of the Romantic or Victorian poets. The end result of the introduction of western education through the medium of English in India was, ultimately, the emergence of a coterie of aristocratic Indian men, such as Jawaharlal Nehru and Mohamed Ali Jinnah, whose exposure to liberal humanism took them to England for university studies, made experts of them in English law, and created among them a desire and demand for complete self-government, even as it made English the *lingua franca* of the Indian sub-continent.

The Sepoy Mutiny of 1857 marked an important turning point in Indo-British cultural history. The Sepoy Mutiny in and of itself was not a major event (it largely involved a single mutineer, the famous Mangal Pandey), but it reflected growing

> ### The Sepoy Mutiny
>
> The Sepoy Mutiny brought with it fears of another uprising. This led to the 1867 Press and Registration of Books Act, which required every presidency to list the title of every book published during that year together with a general description of its contents in order to aid library accessions in Britain. This resulted in the multivolume *Catalogue of Books Printed* (sometimes called the *Appendices to the Gazette*), published quarterly in each presidency. These catalogues are invaluable for the amount of information they provide on reader profiles, title popularity, etc. Because they also list multiple vernacular translations of the same book, the modern scholar realizes that *Anandamath* was widely translated into virtually every major Indian language.

tensions between the British colonial forces and the increasingly oppressed Indian groups, which resulted in greater colonial oppression and, not surprisingly, greater native resistance. Arjun Appadurai (1936–) suggests that this development caused Indian identity to be unyoked from its regional, parochial, local, confined context and thrown into the national arena. Although it might be expected that this nationalization would create unity in India, it in fact created fragmentation. The cultural outcome of the mutiny was the widespread Indian acceptance of western education and its reading material on the one hand, and the onset of the Hindu Reformist movement on the other.

As the Industrial Revolution in Europe in the late-nineteenth century created ready markets for British goods in their colonies, the sub-continent's unemployed artisans turned to agriculture using the lowest levels of technology and producing grinding poverty among the masses. Want, coupled with the growth of nationalism, gave rise to reformist Hindu movements such as the Arya Dharm. The logic of such an institution stemmed from the belief that the downfall of Indian society was a result of the failure of its predominant religion. Thus, the nationalism of Bankim Chandra Chatterjee (1838–1894) evolved into Hindu-Bengali nationalism in Bengal, where he penned the famous patriotic song, "Vandemataram," which practically grew into India's song of independence. This song was immediately accepted by the Indian masses at the grassroots level (not just the educated elite) as the anthem for the assertion of regional pride and cultural individuality. His novel *Anandamath* (1882) was a fictional plot set during the Bengali peasants' revolt against imperialist rule in 1770, the year of the horrific famine in Bengal.

The book found great appeal among the peasants of Bengal, whose lack of exposure to formal education did not prevent them from becoming embroiled in the clamor for religious reformism.

The two decades that followed saw Indians become both fully Anglecized and contemptuous of their own native culture and heritage. The introduction of the Indian railway in 1853 and the first telegraph line in 1854 meant the rapid spread of western culture as lines of communication opened exponentially. Scholars and thinkers such as Roy, fully literate in English and deeply admiring of the British traditions of education, devoted themselves to the betterment of Hindu society. As Indian newspapers such as Roy's *Sambad Kaumudi*, founded in

---

The Typical Indian Reader in Pre-Independent India

Priya Joshi's scholarship suggests that the profile of the typical Indian reader under the colonial regime is hazy at best. According to the census of 1881, full literacy among Indian males was 6.6 percent and considerably lower for females, at only 0.3 percent. This would seem to suggest that Indian males formed the largest body of readers. James Long, a civil servant in the Bengal presidency, notes that though Indian women were unable to read themselves, they were highly intelligent, deriving a great deal of entertainment from being read to by their husbands and brothers (Joshi 42). Thus, in a limited manner, women had access to the world of print during the Raj. Indian readership of the British novel was wide-ranging, encompassing "civil servants of all rank, students of all sorts, householders and their women, minor ranks of the aristocracy, employees in the print and text industries, members of mercantile groups, and towards, the end of the nineteenth century, newly literate English readers from first and second generation rural backgrounds who had moved to cities, often for jobs in the colonial apparatus" (Joshi 44). These readers included Indians of every creed—Hindus, Muslims, Sikhs, Parsis, Jain, Buddhists, and Christians. They might be said to have belonged to the "middle class" in the widest connotations of that term. However, other Indians professionals such as moneylenders, merchants, accountants, and freeholders—also considered to be among the middle class—were rarely found among the membership roster of the circulating libraries, probably because they were not literate in English or because they were only functionally literate. Thus, there was no such thing as a "typical" Indian reader at the time, because the general reading public comprised people of both genders and every faith and professional background. Though little might be known about the demographics of this amorphous group, Joshi's scholarship has produced a great deal of valuable information about their preferences in reading.

1821, began to publish his impassioned essays, readers' minds became influenced by the need to address such issues as the abolition of child marriage and *sati*, while advocating widow remarriage. Taken collectively, the writings of these stalwart

political leaders of the time—with their impressive mastery of the king's English, acute understanding of British jurisprudence, and sensitivity toward achieving cultural ecumenism through the fusion of western and Orientalist values and ideas— had an enormous impact on India's reading public. K. R. Srinivas Iyengar refers to this outpouring of literary creativity as "The Renaissance in India."

This flowering of literary talent affected, in turn, those Indian writers whose preferred medium of expression was their own native languages. As the nineteenth century gave way to the twentieth, and as the growth of nationalism led to the ultimate demands for home rule, Indian readers found themselves able to access a wide variety of thoughts and ideas in English as well as vernacular languages, mainly through the vigorous publication of newspapers. The production of creative fiction in English, however, lagged behind, and for the first half of the 1900s, Indian writers whose talents led them toward novel-writing found themselves turning to western publication houses as India had not yet developed a base for the professional printing and dissemination of creative work in English. It is little wonder that the writers who did find publishers ready to take on the financial risk of publishing their creative offerings were based in the West themselves as Indian expatriates, or had spent a considerable amount of time in England, mostly acquiring a higher education—enough to have cultivated those invaluable contacts that led to the publication of their novels, autobiographies, and memoirs.

READING TRENDS AND PRACTICES: PRE-INDEPENDENCE SPIRITUAL LITERATURE—RABINDRANATH TAGORE AND AUROBINDO GHOSH

The work of Rabindranath Tagore (1861–1941) and the international recognition it received through the award of the Nobel Prize for Literature in 1913 catapulted Indian writing into the global arena and garnered for it many overseas readers and admirers. It is for his spiritual verses that Tagore is best remembered. Among them, *Gitanjali* is considered his crowning literary achievement. Considered the most significant epic poem in Bengali, Tagore's *Gitanjali* (later translated into English by the poet himself) is a masterpiece, not just for its exquisite lyrical verses but also for the secularist tone that he adopts throughout. Comprising several poems addressed to a spiritual power higher than himself, Tagore deliberately refrains from addressing his own Hindu god directly. There is no mention, for instance, of Ram or Krishna, or any such specific deity in his lines. Instead, Tagore refers to this entity as master, lord, and savior. This device implies a clear desire to distance himself from the politics of Hindu reformism. In asserting that he owes allegiance to a higher being whom he thinks of with respect and affection, Tagore's poetry appealed to a huge mass of readers, both in India and overseas.

Bengalis were always known to have a traditional devotion to poetry, literature, and the arts, and their embrace of this new spokesman who emerged so articulately in their midst brought immediate popularity to his writing. Tagore's own talents as a musical composer further served to popularize these works. *Rabindra Sangeet* (songs based on the lyrics of Rabindra), heard all over the British Presidency of Calcutta, where the population largely comprised native Bengali speakers, became a form of popular entertainment and a familiar pastime. Not just relegated to the gatherings of the elite, Tagore's verses were heard freely upon the lips of peasant farmers and boatmen on the Hooghly River. They served to make of this man not just a beloved poet and composer but a sage, a guru. Tagore's appearance, with

A primary school in the remote Kanji village of the Kargil district.

his flowing robes and flowing beard, only emphasized this image in the minds of the reader and made him a revered popular cultural icon.

While Tagore was based in Bengal, spiritual writing in South India became manifest in the hands of Aurobindo Ghosh, better known as Sri Aurobindo (1872–1950). Although he could not command the large fan following that Tagore was able to muster, Aurobindo's *Savitri* and *The Life Divine* are epic poems in English that incorporate religious ideology with mysticism and philosophy in order to create complex works that defy categorization. Admirers of Aurobindo's work also abandoned their worldly activities to follow his teachings—an aspect that resulted in his founding of an Ashram in Pondicherry, then a French colony in South India.

VERNACULAR POLITICAL TEXTS

Vernacular, or local, literature was produced in the form of both fiction and nonfiction. The readers of this material were middle-class Indians of the older generation, who had not been offered the opportunity to be educated in English but were perfectly literate in regional Indian languages. Although they read newspapers that kept them abreast of the growing political turmoil in the country, their appetite for fiction and nonfiction continued unabated and solidified their conviction that India's future happiness lay in an administrative system that did not include foreign rulers.

Literary endeavors in the vernacular languages flourished defiantly despite the dominant presence of English on the Indian sub-continent. In 1910, Munshi Premchand, writing in Urdu under the pseudonym Nawabrai, was charged with sedition by the district magistrate in Jamirpur for his book of short stories *Soz-e-Watan* (*Dirge of the Nation*). The volume's first story was "Duniya ka Sabse Anmol Ratan" (The Most Precious Jewel in the World), which according to Premchand, was "the last drop of blood shed in the cause of the country's freedom" (http://en.wikipedia.org/wiki/Munshi_Premchand). Every copy of *Soz-e-Watan* was destroyed. This volume is highly significant because Premchand was articulating in Urdu his dissatisfaction with British rule and his desire for independence long before the rest of the country expressed the need for complete Home Rule. It wasn't until 1929 that the Indian National Congress met in Lahore to pass a resolution for *Purna Swaraj*, or complete home rule. A devout nationalist, Premchand's work *Shatranj Ke Khiladi (The Chess Players)* also harked back to the Sepoy Mutiny and the unfair annexation of Oudh by the British after the last Nawab passed away. The banning by the British of Premchand's work in the very land of its creation makes it obvious that his stories had garnered a large native Indian reading public whose reactions the British feared. *Godaan* (1918), also written in Hindi, is considered his finest prose work. The large number of Hindi readers who were devoted to Premchand's work made him a household name. Though Premchand himself might not have intended that his work would have such a profoundly nationalistic impact upon his readers, it was influential enough to lead to the popularity of political writing in India and the eventual acceptance of the ideas reiterated in the editorials penned by Mahatma Gandhi upon his return to India from South Africa in 1915.

The political writings of Mohandas Karamchand Gandhi (1869–1948) fall almost into a category all their own, both by virtue of the gigantic stature of their author and by his sheer prolificity. Subaltern historians agree that Gandhi tried to use Hinduism as a uniting institution, acknowledging the social impact of caste division and calling for its eradication, but not granting separate electorates for untouchables—much to the anguish of Babasaheb B. R. Ambedkar (1891–1956), whose clash with Gandhi on ideological issues has been referred to as a clash of titans. This is delineated in Ambedkar's book, *What Gandhi and the Congress have done to Untouchables*. This book had a massive impact upon contemporary readers. Not only did it result in Ambedkar's symbolic conversion to Buddhism, it caused about fifteen million Hindus to follow suit within the next decade. What is further significant in terms of the impact of this seminal work upon readers is that Ambedkar was a man of lowly birth—a *Dalit* or untouchable, a caste of Hindus who had faced continuous social prejudice and injustice.

Gandhi's emphasis on secularism, a stance that was espoused by the Indian National Congress, produced two startling results: first, the growing indignation of right-wing Hindu nationalist leaders such as Vinayak Damodar Savarkar (1883–1966), better known as Veer Savarkar, who in 1923 wrote "Hindutva: Who is a Hindu?" Savarkar's imprisonment on grounds of sedition and his banishment to the cellular jail on the Andaman Islands, where he was subjected to brutal manual labor and solitary confinement, made a local martyr and regional hero of him. Today's champions of "Hindutva" regard Savarkar as their undisputed leader. The second important outcome of the insistence of the Congress on secularism at a time when religion was proving to be a divisive force among the people of India was the emergence in Cambridge, England, of Choudhary Rahmat Ali (1895–1951). His 1930 pamphlet, entitled "Now or Never: Are We to Live or Perish?" advocated a sectarian Muslim homeland in northern India as well as a "Bang-i-Islam," a separate Muslim homeland in Bengal, and Uzmanistan, a Muslim homeland in the Deccan. Thus was born the Two-Nation Theory, initially dismissed by Mohammed Ali Jinnah (1876–1948), leader of the Muslim League and later founder of Pakistan, as ludicrous, but later embraced as the only possible solution to the "Muslim Problem" in India.

The Urdu poetry of Allama Iqbal (1877–1938), and particularly his penning of one of the sub-continent's best-loved songs, "Saare Jahan Se Accha," is credited with having strengthened the Muslim demand for a separate Pakistan. The works of such patriotic Urdu writers had a powerful impact upon contemporary masses in the north. The move to set such lyrics to music further assisted in spreading ideas of cultural dignity far and wide. As in the case of Tagore, music touched far more lives than reading because education was still largely the prerogative of the wealthy. Songs, on the other hand, transcended class divisions and could be easily spread through oral transmission. In creating a sense of patriotism, they also built a sense of community among India's diverse population.

As the growing demand for Pakistan accelerated, Gandhi's *Hind Swaraj*, written in 1910 and considered his fundamental work, gained importance. This work together with his autobiography, *The Story of My Experiments with Truth*, appeared in installments in Gujarati in the weekly *Navjivan* between 1925 and 1928 and in *Young India* in English, and contains his supreme principle: realization of the truth is the purpose of human life (*Satyagraha*). To achieve this end, he used spiritual principles in practical situations (for instance, *Brahmacharya*, or celibacy, and fasting unto death). From these beliefs, also, sprang his emphasis on nonviolent noncooperation. Gandhian writing was a major influence on national politics in India, though his dissenters saw in his views a great deal to challenge. The strong impact of Gandhian writing on Indian readers all across the length and breadth of the country was evidenced by the fact that so many Indians joined forces with Gandhi, responded to his call to rid the country of British policies, donned the white Gandhi *topi*, or cap, and wore handspun loincloths with dignity. Dissemination of Gandhian ideas was carried out through publications generated through extremely modest means, at the printing presses attached to his ashram and by the rapid translation of his writings into various Indian regional languages.

In these installments, Gandhi provided the reader with philosophical discourse on a wide variety of issues. Gandhi was keener to narrate his "experiments in the

---

Gandhian Journalism

Gandhi's passion for journalism was not a new development in his life. While still a lawyer in South Africa, developing a fledgling practice among fellow South Asians, he had established a weekly paper, *Indian Opinion*. His reading of John Ruskin's *Unto This Last* affected him profoundly and led to his formation of the first of his many ashrams around the world, devoted to the idea that all labor should draw the same wage and promote the common good of the community (*sarvodaya*). At his Phoenix Settlement near Durban, and later at the Tolstoy Farm near Johannesburg, he began to develop his technique of passive resistance (*satyagraha*). His famous rebellion against the pass laws led to his being jailed in Johannesburg in 1908. *Hind Swaraj* was written while he still lived in South Africa and contains his indebtedness to such world writers as Ruskin and Tolstoy, but also Plato, Socrates, and especially Henry David Thoreau's famous essay, "On Civil Disobedience." *Hind Swaraj* was translated subsequently into English and appeared under the title *Indian Home Rule*. Covering a number of burning issues of the day such as Indo-British race relations, Swaraj (home rule), the introduction of machinery in imperial colonies, Hindu-Muslim unity, education, violence, and *ahimsa*, it contains the most essential of Gandhian ideas. It proved highly inspirational to readers all over the globe and led to his being labeled "Mahatma," or great soul.

spiritual field," which, he said, "were known only to myself and from which I have
derived such power as I possess for working in the political field" (Iyengar 249).
Gandhi's autobiography, which spoke of these "experiments" and which was titled
The Story of my Experiments with Truth, is of particular interest to the student of
his early years, delineating with a touching candor his discomfort, among other
things, with the rigors of school life both in India as well as during his legal studies in England.

Gandhi was fearless in the expression of his views, no matter how controversial.
Iyengar believes that the most explosive passage in *Hind Swaraj* relates to the doctrine of passive resistance. Gandhi wrote: "Passive resistance is a method of securing rights by personal suffering: it is the reverse of resistance by arms. When I
refuse to do a thing that is repugnant to my conscience, I use soul-force. . . . If I
do not obey the law, and accept the penalty for its breach, I use soul-force. It
involves sacrifice of self" (quoted by Iyengar 253). Readers of Gandhian philosophy became almost instant converts to his ideology. He counted among his readers other patriots like himself, of whose means for the achievement of their ends
Gandhi might have severely disapproved. In the Punjab, for instance, Bhagat
Singh, an ardent anti-imperialist, urged his fellow-prisoners to reject the consumption of food—a move that, after several days, led the British to force feed them
through their noses. Fasting unto death was rapidly adopted by Indians all over
the country as a weapon with which to fight against tough British policies.

Readers of Gandhian literature—British as well as Indian—realized rapidly,
however, that the attainment of political independence was not Gandhi's only
goal, though he is synonymous with its achievement, as his title "father of the
nation" would suggest. Gradually, Gandhi's deep commitment to the abolition of
the Hindu caste system in India, and the eradication of poverty (which he thought
was the most degrading state of human existence) and abuses such as untouchability, child marriage, and the impossibility of widow remarriage, contributed
greatly to the achievement of social change in Hinduism. Iyengar sums up
Gandhi's social preoccupations by emphasizing his belief that the cure for idleness
was work, the cure for poverty was the utilization of all existing resources and
making certain they were equitably distributed, and, finally, limiting population
growth through *brahmacharya* (moral restraint or marital celibacy) (Iyengar 158).
These thoughts also constitute what is referred to as "Gandhian economics."
Gandhi advocated personal participation in the life of a community in order to cultivate self-reliance in that community and bring dignity to all labor. This would
ensure *Sarvodaya*, a sense of self-pride and social fulfillment. Several thousand
devotees of *sarvodaya* philosophy joined Gandhi in these endeavors. The Indian
public did not just read these works and toss them aside. They became deeply
motivated to take the serious step of renouncing their worldly pursuits for the
more austere activities of communal farming and solitary spinning.

In most other areas of human endeavor, Gandhi's writings were vastly popular
and influential. Readers' responses were instant, enthusiastic, and unanimous.
Beginning with a circulation of fewer than twenty-five hundred in 1919, Gandhi's
journal *Young India* grew steadily to become a very influential mouthpiece of his
ideas with a circulation of over forty thousand at the time of his arrest in 1942.
Most appealing, perhaps, was the fact that Gandhi did not write in the bombastic
style that had been cultivated by his more literary forebears. His writing was as
simple and unpretentious in style as it was in content. He was able to reach the
common man, not just the educated elite. The old Macaulayian tradition of formal discourse, both in public speaking and in writing, ended with the advent of
Gandhian literature. His works remain important historic documents not just of

the political rebellion that marked the times, but also of the cultural revolution that readers were able to affect. No wonder Gandhi had the greatest respect for the fourth estate (as the field of journalism was known in India), used journalism unapologetically to disseminate his message, and courted the foreign press at every opportunity he received.

If Gandhi was a dominant force on the Indian sub-continent, one cannot discount the role played by his friend and fellow activist Jawaharlal Nehru insofar as the production of historic literature goes. During his incarceration in a British jail, Nehru wrote *Discovery of India* (1944). Of the last volume, most interesting is Nehru's portrait of Mohammed Ali Jinnah, his political opponent. It is his speeches, though, made to his colleagues in the Congress ("resolutions," as many of them are termed), that remain historically important. They represent a permanent contribution to political literature in India and serve to explain the pathways Nehru followed in terms of his economic and foreign policy when he eventually became the first prime minister of India and led the country toward the achievement of an individual post-colonial identity for the next seventeen years. Of his many speeches, the one he delivered upon the arrival of Independence Day in India is certainly his best-known, and it is freely quoted by Indians everywhere: "Long years ago, we made a tryst with destiny, and now the time comes when we shall redeem our pledge, not wholly or in full measure, but very substantially. At the stroke of the midnight hour, when the world sleeps, India will awake to life and freedom" (quoted by Iyengar 310). This speech is considered remarkable not just for what Nehru said in it, but for what he glaringly left out: any mention of the price that Indians had paid for the achievement of their independence—the loss of their Muslim brothers to the creation of a new country that would be called Pakistan, and the brutal slaughter of almost a million Indians.

If Nehru was active in using oratory to convince the Indian people that the country's future lay in secularism, Jinnah spent an equal amount of energy trying to convince his Muslim brethren that the creation of Pakistan was their only hope of survival on the sub-continent. In a series of speeches delivered between 1947 and 1948, Jinnah persuaded his fellow Muslims that their salvation lay only in joining forces with the Muslim League to demand an autonomous area in which Islamic culture could flourish unchallenged on the Indian sub-continent. Jinnah's *Collected Speeches*, issued by the Ministry of Information and Broadcasting in Pakistan, are indicative of his conversion from an Indian nationalist into a Muslim separatist. Delivered with passion and sustained intellectual argument, they eventually succeeded in stirring enough Muslims on the sub-continent to see the creation of a safe haven for the peaceful practice of Islam as the only solution to the centuries-long conflict with their Hindu and Sikh brothers. Eventually, Pakistan was created on two opposite sides of the map and Jinnah, referred to as "Quaid-e-Azam" by his people, became the first head of the state of Pakistan, an independent Islamic nation that came into being on August 14, 1947.

The essential difference between Gandhian writings and those of his eminent political counterparts Nehru and Jinnah, is that the former's work had a far greater mass appeal. Gandhi's appearance—his essentially Indian demeanor (as opposed to the suave Anglicized images of Nehru and Jinnah)—and his efforts to involve the masses at the lowest grassroots level in the struggle for independence, resonated with ordinary Indians in a far more dramatic and immediate fashion. The writings of Nehru and Jinnah, on the other hand, found a readership among the sub-continent's intellectual elite. Those who followed Indo-British legal proceedings and parliamentary debate were a privileged few. Access to such material was not available to the hardworking masses of India, who identified far more closely with the simplicity of the Mahatma than the spit and polish of Nehru and Jinnah.

India became independent from British rule on August 15, 1947, remaining a member of the British Commonwealth of Nations. The exit of the British resulted in the formation of Pakistan (on August 14, 1947), divided into two territories on opposite sides of the Indian sub-continent. Gandhi died a disappointed man on January 30, 1948, assassinated by Nathuram Vinayak Ghodse, a member of the right-wing Rastriya Swayam Sevak Sangh, without achieving his goals for a united India or for a peaceful Partition. Indeed, Partition created problems of identity because, for the first time, religion evolved into an identifier of where one belonged. This gave rise to the massive voluntary exodus of Hindus, Muslims, and Sikhs out of their country of birth to refugee camps on both sides of the border. The trauma that followed Partition—a mass migration of about fourteen million people, in which about one million were ruthlessly killed—has left wounds that have never healed and scabs that fester periodically.

CREATIVE TEXTS

As the second half of the twentieth century unfolded, the influence of Jawaharlal Nehru dominated India's foreign policy and her economic development. Growing emphasis on education and Nehru's single-minded devotion to scientific advancement created a new, upwardly mobile middle class determined to climb the social hierarchy by achieving not just literacy but professional training and advanced technical skills. Nehru financed the creation of the Indian Institutes of Technology, institutions of higher learning that emphasized technology and scientific education. Most Indians of this generation opted for education in English. The British colonial hangover had created the widespread belief that the road to economic prosperity lay in the acquisition of English language skills. All over India, middle-class parents hankered after "English-medium" education for their children. Schools run by missionaries and the Christian clergy continued to expand and flourish in this new ethos. Although access to higher education was still largely confined to the upper classes, the lower-middle class, who coveted education, grew at an astonishing rate as India's population burgeoned.

This wide-spread acquisition of skills in the language of imperialism resulted in the emergence by the mid-1940s of "Indo-Anglian literature," later labeled as "Indian writing in English" even as regional literatures in vernacular Indian languages remained popular. After years of using English for commercial and business purposes, Indians were ready to try their hand at writing creatively in it. For many of them, the use of English from the time of their infancy created fluency, ease, and comfort with the language that was akin to that previously only enjoyed by the native British speaker. Although most were multilingual, their preference to express themselves creatively in English spoke of their confidence. In the years immediately following India's independence, her creative writers in English would expend enormous quantities of energy in attempting to capture the new spirit of the country. In this category fall novelists such as Raja Rao (1908–2006), Mulk Raj Anand (1905–2004), R. K. Narayan (1906–2001), and Kamala Markandaya (1924–2004). India would see an outpouring of creative literary work that would draw from events in her recent history, particularly the struggle for independence through nonviolent means and the horrors of Partition. These would feature in literature from South Asia for the next fifty years and would bring international renown to its writers.

Who was the intended target audience for this new Indo-Anglian literature? Much ink has been spilled in debating the question of "audience awareness" in early Indian writing in English, including this author's book on Kamala Markandaya, which comments extensively on the detrimental effects of acute awareness of the western reader upon the themes and techniques employed by indigenous Indian novelists. Critics and scholars are of the firm opinion that most of these writers had in mind a western reading public based in the UK, the United States, and Canada. In the many interviews that these writers gave to journalists and scholars over the years, they admitted their awareness of the fact that the bulk of their readers were based overseas. However, they were also conscious of the new taste for indigenous literature in English among Indian readers. Though this readership was growing in size with every passing year, its numbers were still miniscule when compared to the total population of India. This explains why virtually no publishing houses existed in that epoch for the publication of native fiction or poetry in English. It was simply economically unfeasible for Indian presses to take on the financial burden of publishing these works. Lack of an international distribution system would have confined the audience to India and would have robbed publishers of the global reach and revenue that might have been promised by better connections with their western publishing counterparts. Knowing well that the possibility of finding publishers for their work lay only in wooing overseas agents and publishers, most Indian writers in English set their sights firmly on the foreign market. The tendency to explain certain aspects of India's traditions or the peculiarities of her culture in the body of their texts attests to their keen overseas-audience awareness. As time passed and the 1950s gave way to the 1960s, Indian novelists found favor in the West and agents were keen to represent the work of writers based in India. But the desire to cater to a foreign audience also brought with it the tendency to select themes that the West would find exotic, unfamiliar, and, therefore, fascinating, such as arranged marriage, the joint family, and Hindu orthodoxy.

With Indian creative writers turning their sights firmly on western audiences, it was not surprising that some Indian writers, such as R. K. Narayan and Raja Rao, were better known in the West than in India. Kamala Markandaya's *Nectar in a Sieve*, for instance, was so commonly prescribed on high school and university syllabi in the United States that she was a well-known name in the West while remaining virtually unknown in the country of her birth. As time passed, foreign consumers of Indian fiction in English looked upon these novels as authentic sociological documents of Indian cultural life. These

> **British Fiction and Indian Readers**
>
> Despite attempts by the colonial regime to suppress it, British fiction accounts for seventy-four percent of the total circulation, followed by poetry and drama at almost twelve percent. Among writers of fiction, most popular at the time among Indian readers was Sir Walter Scott, whose works were found in fourteen Indian library catalogues, followed by Charles Dickens, William Makepeace Thackeray, Marie Corelli, Marion F. Crawford, Alexandre Dumas (in English translation), George Eliot, Charles Kingsley, Frederick Marryat, and Philip Meadows Taylor. Among writers of nonfiction popular among Indian readers were Edward Bulwer-Lytton and Benjamin Disraeli. The mystery novels of Wilkie Collins and Sir Arthur Conan Doyle were eagerly devoured, as were the adventure tales of Robert Louis Stevenson.

writers told not just good, old-fashioned stories but "explained" India to the western reader. Although Indian critics bemoaned the role that Indian creative writers in English were expected to play—that of cultural anthropologists—it did little to stop Indian writers from continually pandering to the general ignorance about India that plagued western readers.

The mood, the milieu, and the moment spawned a vast variety of writing in the pre-independence and post-independence years in several different regional and vernacular languages as well as English on the Indian sub-continent. In Tamil Nadu, for instance, K. S. Venkatramani's *Murugan the Tiller* (1927) and *Kandan the Patriot* (1931–1932) appeared serially in *Swarajya*, a daily newspaper edited by T. Prakasam. Both were obviously inspired by the dignity that Gandhi's speeches had bequeathed upon the humblest section of India's population, its peasantry. The Assamese novelist Beena Barua's work *Senji Patar Kahni* is set in the tea gardens for which her state is famed. Iyengar refers to the work of a Marathi writer, Hari Narayan Apte (1864–1919), whose romance *Ushahkal* "tried to fuse the fighting idealism of patriots like Tilak with the liberalism of reformers like Chiplonkar and Agarkar" (323). The heroic tales of Indians fighting valiantly against the might of the British Empire offered grist for the fiction mill and became the subject of a number of literary works. Iyengar, for instance, singles out the work of K. M. Munshi, whose Gujarati novel *Tapasvini* or *The Lure of Power* (1964), his English translation, covers the period from World War I to the coming of provincial autonomy in 1937 (Iyengar 495). Similarly Venu Chitale's *In Transit* (1950) documents India's struggle for independence.

Meanwhile, in the north, the short stories in Urdu of Saadat Hasan Manto (1912–1955) spoke for the anxieties of an entire generation. His short story "Toba Tek Singh," for instance, is a fine example of the sort of identity dilemma that results when one feels dislocated. In exploring the issue of the primacy of religious identity above cultural or regional ones, Manto's stories examine the emotional trauma of loss. In India, the Urdu writer Rajinder Singh Bedi (1915–1984) produced *Ek Chaddar Maili Si*, which was translated into English in 1966 as *I Take This Woman*.

Among regional writers, of special note are K. S. Karant's Kannada work *Marali Mannige* (translated into English by A. N. Moorthy Rao as *The Return to the Soil*, 1955), Sivasankara Pillai's Malayalam *Ranti-Tangazi* (translated into English as *Two Measures of Rice* by M. A. Shakoor in 1968), the Marathi novel by Vyankatesh Madgulkar, translated into English as *The Village Has No Walls* (1959), and Thakazhi Sivasankara Pillai's *Chemmeen* (translated into English by V. K. Narayan Menon). These works take us into the heart of rural India—the India of the farmer and the fisherman—to a life that is precarious and uncertain but rife with heroism in the midst of acute adversity. In the 1960s, Jatinder Mohan Ganguly's *The Fisherman of Kerala* (1967) presented the theme of the change wrought upon traditional family structures by the onslaught of modernization, and his *Bond of Blood* (1967) is set in Calcutta during the communal bloodbath of 1946 that preempts the darkest days following India's Partition. At this time, fiction writers also turned to short stories in vernacular languages, so that Amrita Pritam's long short story in the Punjab was translated into English as *Doctor Dev*, Premchand wrote *The Chess Players*, and Parasu Balakrishna published *The Golden Bangle*.

Because most readers of these works were confined to the smaller *mofussil*, or outlying, towns of India, print orders of their works were very small, the writers earned practically no money at all, and literary scholarship in these areas remained negligible. Neither were these writers' works translated into English. Hence, they attracted no foreign audiences and remained unknown to readers outside of their local and regional communities.

Since English had emerged, by this time, as the universal language of the intelligentsia, Indian writers in English were read widely in the West. Knowing that they were bestowed the enormous privilege of influencing public opinion overseas, a few of them employed fiction to espouse their own social passions. One such writer was Mulk Raj Anand, in whose novel *Untouchable* (1935) Gandhi is actually a character. He deeply influences the determination of the protagonist Bakha, a victim of unspeakable social discrimination and caste prejudice, to keep up his spirits in a country that has succeeded in breaking him down systematically through physical, emotional, and mental abuse. Similarly, Anand's novel *Coolie* (1936) takes a close look at the lot of the impoverished, uneducated Indian masses, bent double by hunger and misfortune and forced to do rigorous manual labor to survive. These novels contain the germ of the ideas of Marxism and socialist ideology that would come to fuller fruition in independent India. Khwaja Ahmad Abbas' *Inquilab* (revolution), written in 1942–1949, appeared in 1955 and is actually filled with real-life political and socialist personalities of the era, such as Gandhi, Nehru, Subhas Chandra Bose, and Vallabhai Patel.

Among creative writers in English, G. V. Desani's (1909–2000) *All About H. Hatterr* (1948) was a milestone; not just an attempt to assert the distinctive identity of the newly-independent Indian through the ceaseless globe-trotting and hunger for multicultural experience of his protagonist, it was also a brave experiment in the unexplored possibilities of Indian-English to evoke a mood and a mindset. Liberated from imperial rule, Desani seems to suggest, Indians were finally also free to create a hybrid form of English that would be essentially their own. This kind of linguistic innovation preceded the endless attempts to twist and contort language that would form a part of the post-colonial genius of Salman Rushdie one generation later. Like his literary descendants, Desani was uninterested in complexities of plot, dealing instead in a completely refreshing way with the less-explored variances of English on the tongues of non-native speakers.

Because Anand's novels clearly did not hope to reach the toiling, illiterate coolie or untouchables—miserable figures on the Indian cultural and economic horizon—his novels were most certainly intended to be read by the educated elite in India—those caste Hindus who had tormented the lower castes for centuries—and by influential foreign readers. Desani, also, was aiming to reach the sophisticated reader both in India and abroad—one who would be familiar enough with the conventions of the British novel to appreciate his attempts to forge new forms of novel-writing through linguistic innovation.

Meanwhile, the rising middle class created a huge division between the urban elite and the rural poor—a theme that was continually exploited by the Indian novelist of this era. For example, although Kamala Markandaya's *Nectar in a Sieve* (1954) is set in an unnamed rural village somewhere in South India, her *A Handful of Rice* (1966) is set in a nameless urban venue somewhere in the same region. These two novels present a fine example of the kind of juxtaposition in terms of setting that was evident in Indian novel-writing of the era. Because novelists of this epoch seemed conscious of a "pan-Indian" readership, rarely were their fictional locales identified with geographic specificity.

Khushwant Singh's *Train to Pakistan* (1956) stands out as an example of the kind of fiction that might be produced even in the face of unspeakable trauma. The Partition of India, still merely ten years old in the public memory, proved perfectly able to evoke the horrors of dislocation and mass-migration. Choosing to write in English, a language that was rarely used by the vast population demographic that was affected by the Partition, Singh was unlikely to reach the vast numbers of Indians who had been displaced by the horror of Partition. More likely, as an eye-witness to that horrific moment in India's history, Singh wished to reach the foreign reader in order to make him or her aware of the high price that had been paid for the achievement of independence as India and Pakistan began to assert their identity as members of the British Commonwealth of Nations.

Politics and the Partition gave birth to several other novels in India: Balachandra Rajan's *The Dark Dancer* (1959), Malgoankar's *Distant Drum* (1975) and *A Bend in the Ganges* (1965), and Anita Desai's *Clear Light of Day* (1980) explore the logic of the Two-Nation Theory and the havoc that it wrought in the lives of those who were affected by the power politics of India's leaders. As far as depictions of northern India are concerned, two novels that embodied the lifestyle of the Muslims were Ahmed Ali's *Twilight in Delhi* (1940) and Attia Hosain's *Sunlight on a Broken Column* (1961). Such novels moved readers to understand that it was not just ethnic cleansing that the Partition succeeded in accomplishing, but the erasure of an ancient lifestyle based on a religion and culture that became almost extinct in India with the departure of the sub-continent's Muslims to the new haven of Pakistan. It was not merely Indian writers who were troubled enough by the suffering of Partition to turn their creative talents upon it. In Pakistan, the Zoroastrian writer Bapsi Sidhwa (1938–) also chose English as her medium for communicating the horrors of Partiton in writing *Ice-Candy Man* (which also appeared under the title *Cracking India*).

Such novels provided western-based readers of Indian fiction new insights into her recent history and explained the causes for her ethnic conflicts. As for the Indian reader, novels of this kind were read mainly on campus as part of the newly emerging syllabus that, in some more progressive universities (particularly in southern India such as in Mysore and Dharwar), created in students an awareness of these significant new Indian voices in fiction as well as an opportunity to re-examine the festering wounds of Partition's horrors. The arrival of Indian fiction on the college campus by the early 1960s led smaller presses in India to acquire the permission from their foreign counterparts to produce cheap trade paperback editions of popular novels, such as those written by R. K. Narayan, who chose to focus on the follies and foibles of small-town folk in the fictional town of Malgudi. Such works appealed to Indian students as well as sophisticated western audiences, and led to their translation into regional Indian languages.

In the 1960s, Nehru's focus shifted from agricultural refinance and development to industrialization. Because industry was city-based, a vast number of factories and mills mushroomed in the metropolis. This gave rise to rampant corruption and widened the gap between the urban rich and the rural poor. As opportunities for employment opened in India's burgeoning cities, the phenomenon of urban migration, which has not seen abatement since it first began in the 1950s, brought huge numbers of rural Indians pouring into the cities in search of work. Unable to sustain this massive influx of people, and lacking the infrastructure to provide housing, schools, food supplies, or medication, metropolitan cities saw, for the first time, the reality of homelessness as migrant workers and recent settlers literally made the streets their homes. Slum-dwellings were the most horrific immediate outcome of this mass-migration and resulted in turning once clean and well-administered cities such as Bombay, Delhi, and Calcutta into shabby shanty-towns. Urban poverty became a harsh reality of the Indian novel, and thematic treatments of such conditions proliferated during the next decade. Organized crime flourished in India's rapidly expanding cities during this era, and the mood of despair shifted from the field and the farm to the flyover, which was where the homeless frequently found shelter. Kamala Markandaya's *A Handful of Rice* (1968) is a fine exemplar of the kind of novel that can emerge when the creative writer explores the harsh conditions of urban life. Such novels were popular among readers both in India and abroad. Though they were grim and sobering in theme and tone, readers responded positively to these depictions of reality—optimistic, perhaps, that such fictional portrayals of poverty and despair would also affect social change.

By the end of the 1960s, when the political landscape underwent a transformation following the demise of Prime Minister Nehru in 1964, a new mood swept over the sub-continent. Pakistan had turned away from democracy, embracing martial law under General Ayub Khan in 1958, while India saw the arrival of her first female head of state as Nehru's daughter, Indira Gandhi, assumed power as prime minister. Within a couple of years of her arrival on the political arena, Indira Gandhi attempted to jump start the Indian economy by devaluing the Indian rupee, nationalizing banks, and abolishing the handsome privy purses that had been guaranteed to India's erstwhile royalty under agreements made with them at the time of independence. With the renewed attention paid to India's monarchs, novelists began to create fictional settings in which their lavish lifestyle was evoked as well as, in a somewhat nostalgic vein, their turbulent relationships with British officials in India. Mulk Raj Anand's *The Private Life of an Indian Prince* (1953), Malgoankar's *The Princes* (1963), and Markandaya's *The Golden Honeycomb* (1972) are good examples of the fiction about Indian royalty that was spawned by the realization that these privileged members of Indian society would soon become extinct.

Readers of such fiction had grown greatly in number by the 1960s, and the study of Indian fiction on college syllabi in India brought a new respectability to this genre of writing. By the 1960s, P. Lal of Calcutta had started a self-funded publishing house called Writers Workshop for the publication of quality Indian poetry and short fiction in English. From the mid-1960s onward, *The Illustrated Weekly of India*, under the editorship of novelist Khushwant Singh, had solicited original writing in English. Contributions poured in from all over the country, much of it mediocre but a substantial amount of impressive quality. *The P. E. N. Quarterly*, later edited by poet Nissim Ezekiel, also introduced Indian readers to a new generation of Indian writers and provided an outlet for the swiftly developing skills of Indian *litterateurs*. No longer was it necessary for Indian readers to look overseas for publishers or an audience. Though their numbers were still tiny, Indian writers had finally found a medium and a steady readership through which their work could continue to be honed. Poetry readings and fiction workshops were a direct outcome of this new readership.

PERSONAL TEXTS

The 1960s also produced a host of prose writers whose inspiration came from the large number of historical events that had recently captured the public imagination. Following in the footsteps of Gandhi and Nehru were writers of autobiography. Among them, Subhas Chandra Bose's *An Indian Pilgrim*, Prakash Tandon's *Punjabi Century*, Kamala Dongerkary's *On the Wings of Time*, Sasti Brata's *My God Died Young*, Nayantara Sahgal's *From Fear Set Free*, and Dom Moraes's *My Son's Father* are notable. However, in this genre, the most important work by Nirad Chaudhuri (1897–1999), entitled *The Autobiography of an Unknown Indian*, was published as early as 1951. Although Chaudhuri's *Autobiography* is meant to be a personal history, it emerged as a very prominent work of national history; the author attempts to prove that the young man he became was molded and shaped willy-nilly by the national upheaval that assailed his environment at the time. Because he was trained as a historian himself, Chaudhuri's *Autobiography* is an account of modern Indian history only very thinly disguised as a self-assessment.

It was inevitable that, having gone through the same trauma of Partition that Indians did, Pakistani writers would be equally prolific in recording its horrors in terms of their personal experiences even while writing narratives about the country's attempts to create an identity for itself separate from that of India's in the wake of its creation. Among autobiographies, of special interest is *Friends, Not Masters: A Political Autobiography* by General Ayub Khan (1907–1974), who became chief martial law administrator of Pakistan in 1958. Khan paints himself as a great lover and devotee of his country. By the end of the 1960s, Zulfikar Ali Bhutto (1928–1979), who subsequently became president of Pakistan, published an interesting historical work entitled *The Myth of Independence* (1969). Two years later the debacle that led to the loss of Pakistan's territory in the east and the formation of Bangladesh led him to write another historical account, called *The Great Tragedy* (1971). Pakistani readers reacted well to the literary output of their leaders, not least because it offered them insight into their authors' minds as well as justification for their political decisions. Because they were written in English, these works also found readers not just in Pakistan, but in the rest of the English-speaking world.

Although literary production in Pakistan was rather sparse and sporadic for the first two decades after its formation, the true flowering of Pakistani literature began in the 1970s, mainly through her expatriate writers, and also, in more recent years, among those still living in the country.

CONCLUSION

The immediate two decades following the departure of the British from India produced a variety of literature in a number of Indian languages. In most of them, the turmoil in the lives of ethnic minorities is a major theme. But writers also felt the need to tell their own personal stories, to record, as it were, for themselves, their families, and indeed for the fledgling nation as a whole, eye-witness accounts of what actually happened, for fear that the trauma would be deliberately repressed or forgotten or confined to oral histories alone. This is evident in creative works of fiction as well as in autobiography, where the catastrophic mood of those early days as the nation struggled to find its identity on the global stage was indeed all-pervasive. As the older generation moved on and a newer one took its place, Indian literature blossomed, producing branches of quality work in many different languages, albeit traditional in form and narration. It did serve, however, to establish a lineage to which the writers that followed in the 1970s, 1980s, 1990s, and into the early years of the new millennium would attempt to emulate but also outdo by daring to produce works that were unlike any that the country or its people had ever seen before. These innovations put India in a prominent place on the post-colonial literary scene and mapped out for her a position as one of the leading producers of quality contemporary literature.

If demographic generalizations must be made about readers on the Indian subcontinent, we might state that, during the colonial period, the majority of them were from the educated upper-middle class. After independence, readership widened as opportunities for education became far more equitable and as the numbers of middle-class readers proliferated. Both fiction and nonfiction were popular among India's readers who, on the slow road to acquiring sophisticated tastes in literature, turned often to the West. For the most part, a stamp of endorsement for a work by an Indian writer from the western reader meant instant acceptance of it on the part of his Indian counterpart. If writers slavishly imitated the modes of expression and linguistic features of the West, Indian readers were equally diffident about asserting their preferences. Few Indian critics existed, and Indian readers did not look to their opinion for guidance in directing their reading. Indian writers were equally dismissive of their critics, knowing full well that their audience lay largely overseas. Indian readers read fiction for leisure and nonfiction as part of their academic requirements. Although Nehru and Gandhi were household names, they were known far more for their contribution to politics and history than for their literary work. Few Indians would be able to recognize even India's most prominent writers of the time. All this, however, would change in the 1970s; by the time of the publication of Salman Rushdie's *Midnight's Children*, India's readers had developed the taste, the critical faculties, and the desire for quality literature that could rank with readers around the globe.

ACKNOWLEDGMENTS

The contemporary historian is indebted to many British librarians who painstakingly cataloged works in vernacular Indian languages, such as the polyglot J. F. Blumhardt, who cataloged books in Hindustani, Marathi, Gujerati, Bengali, Oriya, and Assamese, and L. D. Barnett and G. U. Pope, who cataloged books in Tamil and Telugu, respectively (Joshi 69). Many of these circulating libraries still continue to disseminate reading material to Indians today and remain a steadfast institutional symbol of Indian education under the Raj.

RECOMMENDED READING

Bhabha, Homi. *The Location of Culture*. New York: Routledge, 1994.
Brown, Judith. *Gandhi: Prisoner of Hope*. Princeton: Yale University Press, 1991.
Chakrabarty Dipesh. *Habitations of Modernity: Essays in the Wake of Sub-Altern Studies*. Chicago: University of Chicago Press, 2002.
Guha, Ramachandran. *India After Gandhi: The History of the World's Largest Democracy*. New York: Macmillan, 2007.
Jaffrelot, Christophe. *Dr. Ambedkar and Untouchability: Analyzing and Fighting Caste*. New Delhi: Purana Books, 2005.
Khilnani, Sunil. *The Idea of India*. New York: Farrar, Straus and Giroux, 1999.
Tharoor, Shashi. *From Midnight to the Millennium*. New York: Arcade Publishers, 1998.

PRIMARY SOURCES

Abbas, Khwaja Ahmad. *Inquilab (Revolution)*. Bombay: Jaico Publishing House, 1955.
Ali, Ahmed. *Twilight in Delhi*. Delhi: Oxford University Press, 1940.
Ambedkar, B. R. *What Gandhi and the Congress Have Done to the Untouchables*. 1941. Hindustan Times (1946).
Anand, Mulk Raj. *Coolie*. London: Lawrence & Wishart, 1936.
———. *Untouchable*. London: Lawrence & Wishart, 1935.
Bankim Chandra Chatterjee. *Anandamath*. Calcutta: Padmini Mohan Neogi, 1900.
———. *Vandemataram*. 1880 (no longer in print). Hind Kitabs (1948).
Bhutto, Zulfikar Ali. *The Great Tragedy*. Karachi: Pakistan People's Party, 1971.
———. *The Myth of Independence*. London: Oxford University Press, 1969.
Chaudhuri, Nirad. *The Autobiography of an Unknown Indian*. New York: Macmillan, 1951.

Choudhary, Rahmat Ali. *Now or Never: Are We to Live or Perish?* (1930). *Complete works of Rahmat Ali* (Documentary series; 2). National Commission on Historical and Cultural Research, 1978.

Desai, Anita. *Clear Light of Day*. London: Penguin, 1980.

Desani, G. V. *All about H. Hatterr*. New York: Farrar, Straus & Young, 1948.

Gandhi, M. K. *Hind Swaraj*. India: Navjivan Karyalaya, 1938.

———. *The Story of My Experiments with Truth*. Ahmedabad: Navjivan Press, 1927.

Ghosh, Sri Aurobindo. *The Life Divine*. Pondichery: Sri Aurobindo Ashram, 2006 (first published 1939).

———. *Savitri*. Twin Lakes, WI: Lotus Press, 1995 (first published 1926).

Hosain, Attia. *Sunlight on a Broken Column*. London: Chatto & Windus, 1961.

Iqbal, Allama. *Saare Jahaan Se Accha*. http://en.wikipedia.org/wiki/Saare_Jahan_Se_Achcha (first published in the weekly journal *Ittehad* on 16 August 1904).

Jinnah. Mohammed Ali. *Collected Speeches* (1930–1947). S. M. Ashraf. 5th ed. 1952.

Karant, K. S. *Marali Mannige*. New Delhi: Sahitya Akademi, 2002 (first publication date unknown).

Khan, Ayub. *Friends, Not Masters: A Political Autobiography*. London: Oxford University Press, 1967.

Macaulay, Thomas Babbington. *Minute*. 1835. http://www.geocities.com/bororissa/mac.html.

Malgoankar, Manohar. *Distant Drum*. Bombay: Asia Publishing House, 1960.

Manto, Sadat Hasan. *Toba Tek Sing*. No longer in print, n.d.

Markandaya, Kamala. *A Handful of Rice*. London: Hamish Hamilton, 1966.

———. *Nectar in a Sieve*. London: Putnam, 1954.

Moraes, Dom. *My Son's Father*. London: Secker & Warburg, 1968.

Munshi, K. M. *Tapasvani (The Lure of Power)*. 1st ed. New York: Bharatiya Vidya Bhavan, 1964.

Nehru, Jawaharlal. *Discovery of India*. New York: John Day Company, 1946.

———. *Resolutions in Congress*. (1900–1940s).

Premchand, Munshi. *Godaan*. London: Allen and Unwin, 1968.

———. *Soz-e-Watan*. 1907 (no longer in print).

Rajan, Balachandra. *The Dark Dancer*. New York: Simon & Schuster, 1959.

Sahgal, Nayantara. *From Fear Set Free*. New York: Norton, 1962.

Savarkar, Vinayak Damodar (Veer). *Hindutva: Who is a Hindu*. Bangalore: Bharti Sahitya Sadan, 1989 (first published 1923).

Sidhwa, Bapsi. *Cracking India*. Minneapolis: Milkweed Editions, 1991.

Singh, Khushwant. *Train to Pakistan*. London: Chatto & Windus, 1956.

Tagore, Rabindranath. *Gitanjali*. London: Macmillan, 1914.

Venkataramani, K. S. *Kandan the Patriot*. Madras: Svetaranya Ashrama, 1931.

———. *Murugan the Tiller*. London: Simpkin, Marshall, Hamilton, Kent, 1927.

SECONDARY SOURCES

Appadurai, Arjun. *Worship and Conflict under Colonial Rule: A South Indian Case*. Cambridge: Cambridge University Press, 1981.

Iyengar, Srinivasa K. R. *Indian Writing in English*. 5th ed. New Delhi: Sterling Publishers, 1985.

Jinnah, Mohammed Ali. *Quaid-I-Azam Speaks: Speeches of Quaid-I-Azam Mohammed Ali Jinnah*. Karachi: Ministry of Information and Broadcasting, 1950.

———. *Quaid-I-Azam Speaks: Speeches by Quaid-I-Azam Mohammed Ali Jinnah*. Karachi: Ministry of Information and Broadcasting, 1950.

Joshi, Priya. *In Another Country: Colonialism, Culture and the English Novel in India*. New York: Columbia University Press, 1995.

CHAPTER 23

Contemporary Period

Rochelle Almeida

TIMELINE

1947	Achievement of Indian independence and creation of Pakistan
1950	India adopts constitution and becomes a sovereign democratic republic
1950s	Five Year Plans give impetus to scientific education and advancement in India
1950–80	Publication of indigenous Indian poetry in English in *The Illustrated Weekly of India*
1956	India divided into states on a linguistic basis
1958	Ayub Khan becomes Chief Martial Law Administrator of Pakistan
1960s	Indian scientists seek research and educational opportunities in the West
1962	Sino-Indian War causes tension between China and India
1964	Death of India's first prime minister Jawaharlal Nehru; Lal Bahadur Shastri becomes prime minister of India
1966	Indian Sikhs secure Punjab as a separate state; Nehru's daughter, Indira Gandhi, becomes prime minster of India
1971	East Pakistan-West Pakistan Civil War and creation of Bangladesh; Zulfikar Ali Bhutto takes over as leader of Pakistan
1975	Prime minister Indira Gandhi declares state of emergency in India and suspends fundamental rights
1977	State of emergency lifted, fundamental rights restored, and Janata Party takes over government in India under the prime ministerial rule of Morarji Desai; Mohammed Zia ul-Haq seizes power from Zulfikar Ali Bhutto in Pakistan in a military *coup d'etat*
1978	Publication of Edward Said's *Orientalism* sets the tone for the emergence of Post-Colonial Critical Theory
1979	Pakistan's tenth prime minister Zulfikar Ali Bhutto executed by Chief Martial Law Administrator Zia ul-Haq
1980	Indira Gandhi's son Sanjay Gandhi dies in a plane crash

1981	Publication of Salman Rushdie's *Midnight's Children* wins UK's prestigious Booker Prize
1984	Indira Gandhi shot dead by her Sikh bodyguards; her son Rajiv Gandhi takes over as India's prime minister
1985	Penguin Publishing of the UK opens branch in New Delhi leading to the development of more international publishing houses in India
1988	Mohammed Zia Ul-Haq dies in a plane crash in Pakistan with his closest cabinet colleagues. Bhutto's daughter Benazir Bhutto returns from exile in England to become elected prime minister of Pakistan; publication of Salman Rushdie's *The Satanic Verses* causes international diplomatic crisis and leads to a *fatwa* from Iran's Ayatollah Khomeni
1990s	Rise of Post-Colonial Critical Theory and proliferation of expatriate South Asian writers who achieve international fame
1991	Pakistan awards *Sitar-e-Imtiaz,* the country highest honor for excellence in the arts, to novelist Bapsi Sidhwa; Rajiv Gandhi assassinated
1992	Michael Ondaatje of partly Sri Lankan heritage is awarded UK's Booker Prize for his novel *The English Patient*
1993	Publication of *Lajja* by Taslima Nasreen brings fatwa upon her and leads to her exile from Bangladesh
1997	Arundhati Roy's *The God of Small Things* wins UK's Booker Prize
2007	Kiran Desai's *The Inheritance of Loss* wins UK's Booker Prize

GENERAL INTRODUCTION TO THE PERIOD

Since the departure of the British in 1947, the Indian sub-continent has undergone a massive metamorphosis. Not only has the land mass been splintered into the three countries of India, Pakistan, and Bangladesh, but there has been a massive population explosion that has impacted both the publishing industry and the sales figures of all printed material. While holding on to a stable democratic form of government, India has led the region in the fields of science and technology, economics, agricultural refinance, and development and industrialization. Though Pakistan and Bangladesh are important in their own right geo-politically, it is India that is projected to become (together with China) the foremost powerhouse in Asia, and indeed in the world, in the twenty-first century.

In the past fifteen-odd years since the liberalization of the Indian economy under minister of finance Manmohan Singh (currently India's prime minister), the socialist framework upon which the new nation was conceived has given way to a quasi-capitalist form of economic growth, with the emphasis on computer engineering and software development. As the upwardly mobile middle class has reached levels of financial prosperity inconceivable under the British Raj, exposure to western culture and society through international travel has caused the *nouveau riche* to demand a body of literature that caters to their curiosity about the world and their place in it.

Literature produced in South Asian nations by their own citizens, as well as that produced overseas by their diasporic populations, has not only burgeoned but has, in a sense, revolutionized global tastes. The post-colonial global climate gave birth to a new school of critical thought and theory, and it continues to provide intellectuals with the basis for a mode of inquiry that functions as a critical tool by which to examine the impact of the Raj on the subaltern psyche. It also gave the creative writer the opportunity to create contrasts between the sanitized world of imperialist privilege and nationalist deprivation.

Disillusionment with the economic stagnancy of socialism had set in among young Indians long before steps were taken to bolster a flagging system with the implementation of economic reform in the 1990s in India. This transformation was effected under the dynamic leadership of prime minister Rajiv Gandhi, whose main credo—"to propel India into the twenty-first century"—provided the impetus to eliminate "red tapism" and the tangles of bureaucracy and to permit entrepreneurs the opportunity to strike out boldly through capitalist ventures that received government subsidies. India's software industry is the result of entrepreneurial bravado coupled with the corporate know-how and capital provided by her returning expatriates.

Inevitably, this daring new environment affected the publishing industry and led to the formation of several indigenous publication houses, as well as the creation of Indian-run branches of prestigious international publishing firms such as Penguin and Harper Collins. What gave further incentive to these start-ups was the existence and the creation of literary awards that swelled print sales figures on the Indian sub-continent and around the world. As South Asian writers competed for—and won—awards such as the Booker Prize and the Commonwealth Writer's Prize, novelists became celebrities and new generations of South Asian readers embraced them warmly. Indeed, they made their presence felt by buying books and periodicals themselves instead of relying on circulating libraries as their parents had done, and they joined in the conversation, as non-scholarly critics, on these works. To understand the vast impact of the educated middle class upon the publication industry, one has only to take a look at the large number of blogs that have originated in India, in which vigorous debates surrounding the quality of newly published works by South Asians are dissected.

Pakistan and Bangladesh have similarly large sections of the population that, being educated in English (particularly in the metropolitan cities of Karachi, Lahore, Islamabad, and Dhaka), are making a difference in terms of the commercial viability of indigenous publication. Both have been riddled in recent years by political and religious fundamentalism, which have caused upheavals in the lives of the moderate and secular middle class. The failure of democracy, and the subsequent rise and fall of a diverse number of military regimes in these nations, has led to the abandonment of these countries by some of their principal writers, who have found immigration opportunities and publication outlets overseas. This is true of Bapsi Sidhwa, Mohsin Hamid, and Taslima Nasrin. Nevertheless, a relatively free press has guaranteed the availability of foreign reading material in these countries, allowing their intelligentsia to stay abreast of international affairs. The same is true of Sri Lanka, where civil strife over the past two decades has so torn the tiny island nation apart that many of its writers have relocated to the West, where they continue to produce their most creative work.

Swelling audiences for all forms of literary endeavor have caused a rise in the number of indigenous poets and playwrights, despite the relative lack of popularity of these forms of writing. The huge influence of the Indian film industry, popularly known as Bollywood, has caused several writers to find employment writing scripts and screenplays. Nevertheless, from folk drama to sophisticated urban productions in English, theater continues to survive in India and has recently attracted new playwrights to the medium. Indeed, the insulated world of behind-the-scenes Bollywood has provided the inspiration for a great deal of novels, such as Manil Suri's *The Death of Vishnu* and Shashi Tharoor's *Show Business*. Exposure to international film-makers through the growth of Indian television and the arrival of cable TV has led to the emergence of a new breed of screen writers, who have been inspired by Hollywood's finest directors to create new genres such as the crime film and the gangster film. The growth of international terrorism, and the fact that South Asia continues to play a key role in the war on terror, has given rise to scripts that feature Kashmir as a common setting and to plots that dispel the involvement of India in destructive global conspiracies. Doubtless, fiction based on the same themes will not be long in following the lead set by the cinema.

In the sixtieth year of her independence, Indian influence spreads across the world in the form of a gigantic emerging market. Globalization has so galvanized multinational corporations to initiate business links with India that local branches of most of the world's banking and financial institutions are now a part of the social fabric of the nation. The phenomenon of outsourcing has affected Indian economic fortunes so profoundly that the middle class is now fiercely upwardly mobile. As greater exposure to the West and increased economic prosperity brings more disposable income into the hands of the educated urban metropolitan middle class, it is inevitable that the dissemination, reading, writing, and production of literature—both high-brow and popular—will be the outcome.

READING TRENDS AND PRACTICES

In the 1980s, the literary world witnessed the development of literature, written in English, emerging from the Indian sub-continent in a manner that was unpredicted and startling in its quality. Repercussions of this new flowering of creative talent from India are seen to this day, as literary agents and publishers continue to scout promising India-based writers. As literature from India acquired respectability and kudos, it also garnered a new generation of international readers. Inevitably, Indian literature's growing marketability and the demands of its new readership began to affect its themes and its forms. But where did this phenomenon begin?

As the 1960s ended, India became increasingly conscious about forging an individual national identity for herself that was removed from her colonial connections with Great Britain. No longer content with slavishly imitating western literary models, Indian writers sought to bring a distinctively pan-Indian 'flavor' to literary production. This was reflected not just in the selected themes but in the linguistic and stylistic experimentation that characterized this period. *All About H. Hatterr* by G. V. Desani (1948), appearing right after the exit of British imperialism, had set the stage for such technical innovation. Other writers followed suit using Indian settings, legends, and fables, incorporating them into story-telling techniques that had their roots in national mythology and religious stories.

Simultaneous with this desire to create a uniquely indigenous identity through the arts, Indians began traveling overseas in larger numbers than ever before. Business opportunities had opened up, and exposure to western environments had created a determination among upper-class Indians to project their country in positive terms overseas. At the same time, students eager to expand their professional knowledge sought opportunities for higher education in the booming economies of the West. Whereas previous generations of elite Indians had headed to British universities such as Oxford, Cambridge, and London, Indians in the 1970s began to look to the United States for education grants. With scholarship opportunities in the UK drying up and research possibilities opening up in North America, the numbers of Indians applying to U.S. and Canadian universities increased exponentially.

India's economic policies based on the concept of socialism also disturbed her finest scientists and engineers, who began to look toward greener pastures. Lack of funds for research activity in India caused them to feel stifled and frustrated. By this time, also, corruption and nepotism had entered Indian public life, and employment recruitment was based not on merit alone but on connections with the right people in positions of power. Governmental organizations that had employed the educated elite for the first two decades after independence found themselves bogged down by reservation policies that considered merit secondary to the need to bolster the depressed classes through schemes similar to U.S. Affirmative Action policies. These reservation policies encouraged upper-class Indian engineers and scientists, trained in the finest traditions of the Indian Institutes of Technology, to seek more lucrative positions overseas.

Upon making their way to the West, initially to acquire advanced degrees, these Indians found that they were no longer required by law to return to their home country on completion of their studies. In fact, by the mid-1960s, the United States had amended its immigration policy and, for the very first time, settlement opportunities were available to persons of non-Caucasian race. As U.S. and Canadian companies hastened to sponsor their Indian employees for permanent residence, a new class of expatriate Indians emerged in the West—a class of people that had a great impact upon the kind of literature that was produced and read both overseas and in India.

CREATIVE WRITING: POST-COLONIAL LITERATURE

In 1981, a novel entitled *Midnight's Children* won the coveted Booker Prize in the United Kingdom. Written by a virtually unknown novelist named Salman Rushdie (1947–), it created an international literary sensation and unveiled a stupendous new talent. The novel not only won global laurels but, as time went by, succeeded in creating a whole new literary genre that came to be called post-colonial literature. But post-colonial literature did not arrive from nowhere. It was the result of several sociological and economic factors that combined to create the right climate for its emergence and favorable reception. One of these factors was undoubtedly the emergence of a professional Indian community abroad.

Though it is true that for decades prior to the publication of *Midnight's Children* privileged Indians had sought education opportunities in England, few of them had made the UK their home. Most had acquired advanced degrees in law or literature but had returned home to judicial or university teaching careers in India. However, with several thousand Indians in the 1960s beginning to call the West their permanent home, a new ethnic minority began to make its presence felt. This segment of the population, born and raised in India, had arrived in the West as adults. In seeking spouses through the traditions of arranged marriage to fellow Indians, bearing and rearing children in the West, they added to the melting pot of western life and influenced literary taste and demand. Variously labeled as "ethnic," "minority," "immigrant" and "diasporic," these Indians, now in their third generation in the West, have made a huge contribution both to the production and the consumption of post-colonial literature.

Simply put, this segment of western society had a taste in literature that demanded themes and plots from cultural arenas with which they were familiar. However, their exposure to education in English had also created in them a taste for novels—for sustained literary narration—that was notable for its sophisticated language and complex chronology. Expatriate writers, such as Salman Rushdie, recognized this need and were able to cater to it because they craved the same material themselves—material set deep in the maternal roots of their origins, yet

Salman Rushdie, celebrated and controversial contemporary Indian author.

'foreign' enough to cater to the desire for a plot's gradual unraveling till it reached its denouement in the classic western style.

Enter *Midnight's Children*, a seminal novel about India, set in India and encompassing India's contemporary history. Employing every Indian technique of sustained storytelling, its Indian-born author Salman Rushdie (a self-confessed history buff himself) changed the course of contemporary Indian writing in English with this publication. Always fascinated by the complicated history of the country of his birth, Rushdie's own knowledge of contemporary India was enhanced considerably in reading modern history at Cambridge. Determined to incorporate her political history into his novels, he created the character of Saleem Sinai in *Midnight's Children*, a young man who had the good or bad fortune of being born at the exact moment when India achieved her freedom from British rule, at the stroke of the midnight hour on August 15, 1947. In that sense, then, Saleem is a personification of India itself.

Midnight's Children is about accidents—accidents of birth and accidents of history. Conceived by a poor Hindu woman after impregnation by a British property developer in India, Saleem is an Anglo-Indian in every sense of the word. Just after his Hindu mother gives birth, Saleem is placed in the care of a wealthy Muslim couple by an officious nanny. This accident echoes that of history, caused by the Partition that split the Anglo-Indian sub-continent into the two nations of independent India (a by-product of British colonialism) and Pakistan: the one secular—with a Hindu majority—the other Islamic. The novel consists of Saleem's narration of the story of his life to Padma, who, in her role of emotional listener, assists the narrator in maintaining some modicum of cohesiveness in his twisted, fragmented discourse.

Midnight's Children not only makes use of the rich thematic material available in the country's complex politics, but also experiments wildly with techniques of narration. Rushdie incorporates the entire gamut of contemporary Indian cultural life into his novel, daringly combining several languages with a massive variety of images that create a pastiche in the same manner that Bollywood movies do. To people born and raised in India, the mad series of predicted events that unfold at a dizzying pace, involving three generations, makes perfect sense. The idiosyncrasies of a plethora of characters and the huge sensual canvas against which the drama is set echoes the initial sensation that most visitors have when first arriving in India—the feeling of being assaulted by a heightened awareness of every sense organ. So enthusiastic was the response of critics and readers to this novel that it started a trend among young, educated expatriate Indians to rehash their own childhood memories of growing up in India through the medium of the novel.

The unprecedented international success of *Midnight's Children* motivated Rushdie to continue writing novels that tapped into his trans-cultural background. Rushdie employed the techniques of magical realism that he borrowed from contemporary Latin-American writers such as Gabriel Garcia Marquez. From his very first novel *Grimus* (1975), which went largely unnoticed, his work became increasingly complex, even more fractured. *Shame* (1983), for instance, a political allegory about the politics of Pakistan, introduced a character named Omar Khayyam Shakil who had three mothers. Portraying Pakistani politicians only very thinly disguised as fictional characters, Rushdie's genius was matched only by his daring, a quality that many felt he took too far in the construction of *The Satanic Verses,* a novel that offended orthodox Muslim societies and led to the declaration of a *fatwa* (official edict) from Iran's Ayatollah Khomeni that offered a large reward for Rushdie's murder. The controversy generated by this novel forced Rushdie to remain in hiding for over fifteen years, but it also brought publicity to literature about India. Though banned in some countries (including India and Pakistan), the novel was translated into innumerable foreign languages and sold millions of copies. Popular imagination was certainly captured by this courageous writer who had satirized some elements of his own Islamic background. Remaining prolific even while in hiding, Rushdie's later novels continued to do what their predecessors had done—they combined his monumental knowledge on all aspects of India's culture, history, and traditions, as well as her position vis-à-vis the West to create plots, characters, and themes that astounded readers in their brilliant craftsmanship. Such novels included *The Moor's Last Sigh* (1995) and *The Ground Beneath Her Feet* (1999). In his last novel to date, *Shalimar the Clown* (2005), Rushdie turned to the unresolved conflicts of Kashmir, the northernmost state of India whose possession has remained a bone of contention between India and Pakistan since 1947.

Midnight's Children became a best-seller in India and in the rest of the world. It was not just the high-brow reader who reacted favorably to it but "lay" readers

"The Rushdie Affair."

The "Rushdie Affair" refers to the controversy that erupted in 1988 after the publication by Penguin in England of Salman Rushdie's novel *The Satanic Verses.* Objections to the content of the novel were first voiced in the Indian parliament when member of Parliament Syed Shahabuddin brought pressure upon the weak Rajiv Gandhi-led Congress administration in India to ban the book on the grounds that it blasphemed the prophet Mohammed and Islam, the religion he founded. Despite objections from the liberal segment of the population, who insisted that the government uphold freedom of speech guaranteed by her constitution, India became the first country in the world to ban the book, followed quickly by Pakistan. This brought international attention to the novel and led, ultimately to the declaration of a fatwa, a sentence of death, against the author and publishers by the Ayatollah Khomeni of Iran. The fatwa carried with it the price of a million dollars on the head of the novelist. As a British citizen, Bombay-born Salman Rushdie came under the protection of the British Crown, which entered into a protracted diplomatic duel with Iran—to no avail—to have the fatwa lifted. Britain broke off diplomatic relations with Iran and Rushdie had no choice but to go into hiding under twenty-four-hour protection from Her Majesty's government. Meanwhile, the controversy brought global debate to such issues as freedom of expression, individual liberty, and the rapidly growing Islamic fundamentalist movement that has, since then, proven itself to have expanded far beyond Iran's shores. Rushdie's life in exile continued for almost fifteen years.

as well, people for whom modern literature had offered nothing more challenging than the possibility of passing time effortlessly. However, everything changed when the novel won Britain's prestigious Booker Prize (now called the Man Booker Prize) in 1981. This international honor earned it the legitimacy of academic acceptance as well. Since its publication, *Midnight's Children* has been frequently prescribed on university syllabi both in India and abroad for courses on post-colonial literature, and it has come to be considered the pivotal work of its genre—a work that heralded the arrival of a new kind of novel and a new kind of reader. It would not be an exaggeration to say that *Midnight's Children* spawned post-colonial critical theory, to which stalwart theorists such as Homi Bhabha, Edward Said, and Gayatri Chaktravarti-Spivak, among others, have contributed over the years. Furthermore, the novel's accumulated prestige among the world's academic readers eventually earned it the "Best of Twenty Five Years of the Booker Prize" in 1993.

The commercial success of *Midnight's Children* paved the way for a new demand in the West for stories about India written by people of Indian origin. Prior to this time expatriate Indian writers, such as Bharati Mukherjee (1940–), then based in Canada, had already begun to feel out the western market, producing novels whose themes and plots were essentially "Indian." But these did not make a huge dent in the taste of the literary mainstream. At most, it was South Asian readers based in the United States and Canada who had read Mukherjee's early novels such as *Wife* and *The Tiger's Daughter*. With *Midnight's Children* reaching such a wide international audience, both Indian and western readers began to sit up and take notice of the kind of writing talent that had become available on the Indian sub-continent.

THE BEST-SELLING TRADE PAPERBACK

Up until the early 1980s, few Indians had access to western-published novels in English. Hard-bound U.S. and British editions of contemporary novels, including those written by Indian writers, were much too expensive for the average Indian pocket. Few could afford to buy books of their own. Most Indian readers acquired reading material through public circulating libraries. Among these, the libraries of the British Council and the United States Information Services (USIS), based in major cities such as Bombay, Calcutta, Delhi, and Madras, were most popular. Some university libraries carried contemporary novels, but their budgets were rather too limited and acquisitions were generally restricted to scholarly and critical volumes. Among university and college collections, "popular" titles were avoided in the interest of academic research.

LOW-BROW POT-BOILERS VERSUS
HIGH-BROW LITERATURE

The audience for novels in English remained restricted to a very small percentage of the population—the upper-middle-class elite that had been educated in the English-medium at the college level. Even among this readership, the low-brow bestseller appearing in trade paperback format was far more popular than contemporary literature. Thrillers by James Hadley Chase and Alistair MacLean, for instance, were particular favorites. Among medical and engineering college students in India, P. G. Wodehouse ruled supreme, his Jeeves, for some inexplicable reason, finding favor in campus dorms. Similarly, American writers such as Sidney

Sheldon, Harold Robbins, and Jacqueline Susann dominated the tastes of India's reading public through the 1960s and 1970s. High school and college students and young Indian professionals had devoured such novels for years, so that a vigorous industry in the publication of pirated editions of these works emerged in India. Nobody seemed to mind as the infringement of international copyright laws allowed more reasonably priced editions to reach the Indian reader. These volumes were never sold in legitimate bookstores but could be purchased very cheaply at street corners in make-shift, unlicensed bookstalls. As such editions became more widely available, the local circulating library developed. One dog-eared copy of the same novel circulated endlessly among scores of readers in India until the copy practically fell apart.

The circulating library was also the source for a huge amount of romantic pulp fiction from Harlequin and Mills and Boon, which were read in great numbers by female students in high school and college. There was an enormous hunger for such popular fiction, but because so few readers could purchase individual copies, their interest made little commercial impact upon the international publishing industry.

It was not just paperback romances and thrillers that were devoured by the Indian reading public. Women's magazines in English also thrived from the 1960s through the 1990s. *Eve's Weekly*, a popular weekly edited for decades by a Parsee journalist named Gulshan Ewing (she derived her surname after marriage to an Englishman), vied for circulation figures with *Femina,* then edited by Vimla Patil of the Times of India Group. These magazines catered to Indian women—both housewives and professionals—and were modeled on the lines of America's *Good Housekeeping* and *Better Homes and Gardens* and the UK's *Woman and Home.* Features in these magazines pertained to female interests in cooking, decorating, sewing, embroidery, fashion, and beauty.

Bollywood-based Magazines

One of the earliest English magazines to focus on the Indian film industry that has since come to be known as Bollywood was *Filmfare,* a publication of the prestigious Times of India Group that was established in India, prior to her independence, by Bennett and Coleman Co. Ltd. As early as the 1960s, it featured full-page pin-up style portraits of popular Hindi film "heroes" and "heroines," interviews with the stars, and information about forthcoming films. Readership was restricted to the English-speaking segment of India's population that also watched Hindi films. Viewed as light entertainment, the opinions voiced in this magazine were never taken seriously. The success of *Filmfare* led to the creation in the 1960s of *Star and Style,* a magazine that appeared on a fortnightly basis. It followed the same format established by *Filmfare* and included a gossip feature from columnist Deviyani Chaubal (better known as "Devi").Then, in the mid-1970s, *Stardust* seized upon the growing popularity of Hindi films among this young and trendy teenage and twenty-something crowd. Under the editorship of Shoba De (then known as Shoba Khilachand), *Stardust* created a glossy monthly with a completely different tone and style. It offered insider views into the lives of the film stars and their work, as well as portraits of the stars— not just on the sets of their films, but in sophisticated professional studios. These portraits were created by a new host of young and dynamic photographers, who brought respectability to the profession and attained celebrity status themselves, as did a slew of film-journalists. It remains India's premier film magazine and has a vast readership in the UK, where Bollywood film fans from India and Pakistan number in the hundreds of thousands. The popularity of Hindi films and Bollywood film magazines have gone hand in hand, each industry feeding the other to the point of creating a frenzy among India's film-crazy populace at the glitzy launch of every new film (known as a premier in India).

As the 1980s marched along, the content of these magazines changed to reflect the growing intellectual involvement of this segment of the population. Stories centering on issues such as spousal abuse, sexual harassment in the work place, divorce, and family life began to make their appearance. In recent years, with *Eve's Weekly* having closed down, *Femina* has assumed a monopoly in this market, though the more recently produced *Savvy* meets the needs of the same readership. The style of these publications has had to keep up with the needs of the new emerging Indian woman who is street smart, well-traveled, well-read, well-informed and politically conscious. Her need for quality journalism means that thoroughly investigated feminist subjects form the core of these magazines, even while her typically feminine interests in celebrity gossip, gardening, and entertaining continue to be met.

Anything related to Indian cinema, particularly Hindi films, had always been popular with Indian readers. Magazines such as *Filmfare* and *Star and Style* enjoyed (and still enjoy) a faithful readership in India. Filled with pin-ups of Indian cine stars, interviews with leading actors, and information about forthcoming films, these magazines sell vigorously.

Then, in the early 1970s, *Stardust* appeared—a monthly glossy that fed the same needs for information about Hindi films, but written in a racy style that was new and exciting, and filled with not just information about films and film stars, but gossip as well. The magazine, initially edited by Shobha De (1947–), then known as Shobha Kilachand, broke all circulation records and set the trend for the publication of similar lascivious material. To keep up with the competition that *Stardust* posed, previously established film magazines changed their editorial policies and adopted the same gossip-oriented format for their feature stories and interviews.

THE DEVELOPMENT OF THE INDIGENOUS INDIAN PUBLISHER

The 1980s saw the rapid development of Indian publishing houses, due in no small part to the numbers of Indian writers who began to seek publication avenues in India. The concept of the literary agent had not yet arisen, and Indian novelists with an idea or a completed manuscript were still required to correspond with the Acquisition Editors at the Indian publishing houses directly. There was no middleman. Unable to negotiate financial returns with publishers, Indian writers found little economic profit in publishing their work in India. Among such publishers in India were Rupa and Company, Orient Longman, and Macmillan-India, which had been established as early as 1893. But they soon realized that the more astute writers had begun to study the western publishing market to look for agents in the West. There was, therefore, a time in the history of these publishing houses when, in an attempt to stay financially afloat, they brought out how-to editions on Indian cookery and yoga rather than original fiction.

Then, in 1985, Penguin Publishing of the UK opened an Indian branch in New Delhi that changed the face of Indian fiction publication forever. They began to solicit original Indian fiction in English and found themselves inundated with manuscripts from every corner of India. Although most of these lacked any measure of quality, the occasional manuscript had potential. Before long, Penguin brought out a series of original fiction in English that introduced the reading public to a new lot of Indian writers, such as Ruskin Bond (1934–) and Shashi Deshpande (1938–).Until this time, these writers had found an outlet for their creative writing only in Indian magazines in English, such as *The Illustrated Weekly of India*, which under the long editorship of novelist Khushwant Singh had published quality Indian short fiction.

Taking financial risks by publishing quality fiction and nonfiction (such as travel writing and biographies) from unknown writers with promise and talent, Penguin also used big-selling names such as that of magazine columnist Shobha De. Profits raised through the publication of such "celebrity" writing allowed the prestigious publishing house to introduce unknown writers of quality. Interestingly, it might be said that the arrival of Penguin made a novelist of De, whose writing, until that time, had been confined to magazine gossip columns and journalistic pieces. Being produced locally in India, such paperbacks, which might broadly be described as "pot-boilers," became available to Indian readers at a fraction of the cost of similar hard-bound

---

The Success of Penguin Publishers in India

The year 2007 is significant. It marks the twentieth anniversary of the founding of the Indian branch in New Delhi of the prestigious British publishing house known as Penguin. Realizing that there existed a lacuna in the availability of quality publishing houses in India for the dissemination of original Indian writing in English, the company launched its New Delhi operations from out of a modest apartment under the leadership of David Davidar, who has since gone on to publish a novel himself entitled *The House of Blue Mangoes*. The first season saw the publication of seven titles: two novels in English and one in translation from Bengali, two biographies, a travelogue, and a book of poems. Penguin never looked back. Upon realizing that the Indian market might be slow in sustaining the production of hardbound editions, the company opted to produce literature exclusively in the format of the trade paperback. Twenty years later, Penguin publishes about two hundred titles a year in every possible genre. It has published works by writers from every country on the Indian sub-continent. In 1985, it launched its original publication list in Hindi. It has also published books in other vernacular Indian languages, such as Marathi, Urdu, and Malayalam. Business connections with their British branch have permitted British editions, sometimes hardbound, to be published simultaneously in England. A number of the Indian writers whose work was first brought to the attention of the world through Penguin's imprint have won prestigious national and international literary awards, such as the Sahitya Akademi Award, the Jnanpith Award, the Booker Prize, and the Commonwealth Writer's Prize. International acclaim for such work has boosted the image of the company in India and spawned a large number of more recent competitors.

---

foreign novels. They were eagerly purchased by the rapidly growing numbers of Indian readers seeking indigenous literature in India. The commercial viability of Penguin paperbacks motivated other western publishing houses to open local Indian branches. In recent years, Harper-Collins and Random House (2005) have jumped on the Indian publication bandwagon, producing Indian fiction in other formats in addition to paperback. Tara Press followed soon after.

This boom in Indian publication was welcomed both by the authors themselves—who had hankered after hospitable publishers for years—and by readers who believed that it was about time that Indian writers were recognized for their talent, published in their own country, and rewarded accordingly. Throughout the 1980s, these Delhi-based publishers galvanized the Indian publication industry and fed the needs of India's growing reading public.

In 1996 Arundhati Roy (1961–), an unknown writer from India, found a publisher in the United States for her debut novel, *The God of Small Things*. Reportedly, the manuscript had first been handed to editor Pankaj Mishra at Harper Collins, an international publishing house with a local presence in New Delhi. Recognizing the novel's considerable promise, he sent the manuscript to the United States. The novel made history in India for having garnered the largest advance for any work of fiction—reportedly, close to a million dollars. Indian writing in English had finally come of age, with publishers overseas perceiving the potential profits that could be realized from brisk international sales of original Indian fiction and therefore beginning to take financial risks by paying staggering advances to unknown writers from the Indian sub-continent.

As predicted, *The God of Small Things* met with huge critical acclaim both in India and abroad. Set in the fictional town of Ayamennem in Kerala, a state in South India, the novel documented the cruel treatment meted out to twins Esta and Rahel, whose mother Ammu has left her abusive husband to return to her maternal home among the Syrian Christian community in Kerala, seeking shelter from the merciless judgment of the rest of the world. However, Ammu does not realize that, far from being a refuge, her home is more judgmental than the world of her husband. It is a site that brooks no tolerance of divorcees and untouchables and treats both with unmitigated cruelty. The children experience the worst side of this prejudice when they find themselves unfavorably compared to their half-white cousin, Sophie Mol, who arrives from England to usurp their Grandmother Mamachi's attention, while their mother Ammu finds solace in the arms of Velutha. Although Velutha is a Paravan, or outcast, who works as a general dogsbody for the family, he is also the "God of Small Things" of the novel's title, and the twins come to see in him an affectionate father figure. Thanks to the evil machinations of their great-aunt Baby Kochamma, Velutha is accused of raping Ammu, and of standing by and watching while Sophie Mol drowns in the nearby Meenachil river. The twins are assigned the unspeakable task of identifying him as the perpetrator of these crimes. This travesty has such a traumatic effect on Esta that he becomes a voluntary mute. Rahel is so emotionally damaged that she becomes incapable of marriage and partnership. Velutha dies a horrible death, a victim of police brutality, and Ammu eventually dies of tuberculosis, abandoned and alone. The twins, separated violently as children, are reunited as adults when an inevitably incestuous relationship between them becomes the means by which they bond and give vent to a miserable lifetime of unspoken sorrows and regrets.

It was not merely western audiences who saw the genius of this writer in the shocking ruthlessness of her plot; Indian critics too alluded to Roy's candor, her sensitivity and compassion toward the most maligned segments of India's society. By including in her plot characters such as a divorcee and an untouchable, who had long been ostracized by orthodox Indian society, the novel forced Indian readers to take stock of their age-old prejudices and to assess them afresh in the light of the new high-tech culture that the country had simultaneously begun to espouse.

As Rushdie had done a decade before her, Roy experimented fearlessly with linguistic and stylistic techniques and played tricks on the reader by deliberately complicating the chronological sequence of events. This bravery on the part of India's contemporary writers, seen in their willingness to break the mold, found favor among their readers. Critics too lauded their attempt to forge new horizons by deviating from the traditions of western novel-writing. As if to underscore Roy's achievement as a writer, her novel was awarded the Booker Prize in 1997, which helped to make the novel an international mega-hit. Fans worldwide waited with bated breath for Roy's next work of fiction, only to be informed by the author that *The God of Small Things* was her first and last novel. Admittedly autobiographical, the plot of Roy's novel drew enormously from her own childhood experiences, and, perhaps having exhausted personal sources of creative inspiration, she professed a lack of desire to write another novel. She turned instead to voicing her opinion on such public issues as nuclear proliferation, the Oil Wars, the War Against Terror, and the global dominance of the United States through a series of essays and public lectures that were published as "collections" by left-wing presses such as South End Press in Boston. Most famously, in her own country she joined the group *Narmada Bachao,* lending her voice and her fame to the controversy that had bogged down the construction of the dam over the Narmada River for decades under the leadership of Raymond Magsaysay Award winner, Medha Patkar. It would be fair to say that Roy could not have emerged in her current avatar as a public intellectual were it not for the success of her novel and for her acceptance as a keeper of public conscience by readers far and wide. Despite Rushdie's Indian origins, his British domicile and citizenship caused him to be perceived as a foreign writer, whereas Roy's birth in India, coupled with her Indian citizenship, made her a truly Indian writer. With the economic success of her novel, published coincidentally in the fiftieth anniversary year of her country's independence from British rule, western publishers were not merely willing but eager to publish creative writing that was based on material that had a wholly indigenous Indian spirit.

TRAVEL WRITING

As readers began clamoring for more novels with Indian themes and backgrounds, three writers with global experience and perspectives made their presence felt. What these writers had in common were roots in India but wings that had taken them to the West, where they had chosen to make their home. Pico Iyer (1957–), born of Indian parents in England, drew from his wide travels to create novels with interestingly varied backgrounds. In writing *The Lady and the Monk* (1991), he was inspired by the year he spent in a monastery in Kyoto, Japan. In *Cuba and the Night* (1996), he details a romantic relationship between a Cuban woman named Lourdes, desperate to escape Cuba, and an American photographer named Richard. In *Abandon* (2004) he drew upon his experiences of living in California to create the character of John MacMillan, an American student of English Literature who becomes involved with an emotionally disturbed woman named Camilla. This novel is truly trans-cultural; it involves shifting settings (Damascus, Spain, Iran, and the United States) and the commingling of diverse cultures—John is a student of the Sufi poet, Rumi, and is familiar with languages such as Persian, Arabic, and Spanish. Such fictional globe-trotting is commonplace in the recent writing of India's expatriates, and it seems to fill the need for exotic locales and perspectives among her western-based readers. A prolific travel writer, Iyer had contributed travel feature stories for years to such magazines as *Conde Nast Traveler* and *Time.* His early travel books, such as *Video Nights in Kathmandu* (1989) and *Falling off the Map* (1994), won him a large mainstream fan following. By the time his novels were published, he was already a well-known name in the West. There is no doubt that Iyer's travel writing affected the plots and settings of his novels in their essential cultural dislocation. Their exoticism seems to have appealed to readers across cultures and continents and continues to keep him marketable to this day.

Two other such writers are Vikram Seth (1952–) and Amitav Ghosh (1956–). Although the former wrote and lived in Delhi, he has spent several years in the West acquiring advanced degrees at Oxford and Stanford and traveling to China and other parts of Asia as part of his doctoral research. When he decided to write a travelogue entitled *From Heaven Lake* (1983), based on his sojourn in Sinkiang and Tibet, readers did not stop to take notice, though the book won a Thomas Cook Travel Writing award that same year. But when he published a novel in verse that was set in San Francisco and depicted exclusively American characters, he created a sensation in the literary world. *The Golden Gate* (1986) won great acclaim and made Seth a household name in India and the West. In this case, it did not seem as if it was the plot that had gained it attention, but the unusual form. Seth chose to write the entire novel in verse—in sonnets, in fact, sections of fourteen lines each with a very definite classical rhyme scheme. When his novel *A Suitable Boy* (1993) was published a few years later, set in Delhi and Calcutta, and concerning the arranged marriage traditions of North India, Indian readers took the novel to their hearts. Western readers had no difficulty at all in identifying with his characters and their follies and foibles, despite the novel's voluminous length. Readers' acceptance of such writers generated invitations to book readings and signings overseas and made "celebrities" of them in countries far from their birth. Though Seth continues to live in India, there is a remarkable desire to circumnavigate the globe in his writing. His last novel *An Equal Music* (1999) draws on his vast knowledge of western classical music, particularly German *leider*, which he sings. In this novel too, shifting settings (Venice and Vienna, for instance) lend enchantment to the romance. Multitalented Seth is a travel writer, an essayist, a poet of repute, and a novelist, in addition to being a biographer. His latest work *Two Lives* (2006), for instance, is a biography about the fascinating lives of his maternal uncle Shanti, and Shanti's wife, a German-Jewish refugee named Henny Caro, both of whom lived in England, Germany, and India through the turbulence of the twentieth century. Readers seem to respond very favorably to the various hats that such Indian writers wear, accepting them in different avatars and enthusiastically purchasing their works.

This same transnationalism is very much evident in the writings of Amitav Ghosh, a deeply talented writer whose Indian birth, Oxford education, and American domicile puts him in the same category as Iyer and Seth. His novel, *The Shadow Lines* (1990), attempts to portray the kind of tricks that memory can play when characters attempt to make sense of the fragmented nature of their lives. The genius of Ghosh's plot lies, as Rushdie's did, in his ability to incorporate contemporary history and politics into the personal lives of his protagonists. In *The Shadow Lines,* for instance, the impact of the Partition of the Indian sub-continent into India, on the one hand, and East and West Pakistan, on the other, is seen in the reminiscences of an elderly woman who nostalgically returns to Dhaka in East Pakistan, a few decades after India's independence, only to find the city changed irrevocably. The "Shadow Lines" of the novel's title reflect the borders, limitations, and blurred representations of history and selfhood that plague the main protagonists as they cross geographical borderlines in an attempt to make sense of their tangled past. In *The Circle of Reason* (1986), the plot shifts from Bengal to Bombay, from the Persian Gulf to North Africa as it follows the fortunes of Alu; and in *The Calcutta Chromosome* (1995), action moves from New York to Calcutta. Clearly, Ghosh tapped into his travel experiences to present foreign settings that deeply piqued the readers' imagination. In *The Glass Palace* (2000), he turned his attention to Burma's troubled past from precolonial to post-colonial days, and in *The Hungry Tide* (2004) he based his plot on the network of little islands near East Bengal called the Sundarbans. It is not surprising that Ghosh chose such varied settings for his novels. Like Iyer and Seth, he first made a name for himself as a travel writer; his first book, *In an Antique Land* (1994), detailed his travels in Egypt.

According to Meher Marfatia, at the core of this new popularity of Indian writing overseas lies the writer's ability to weave easily between various cultures and centuries. Marfatia writes, "Like a compound-eyed insect, this writer can be in one place but perceive and process what's going on all around with an uncommon 360-degree vision of the world" ("Words Have Wings." *Namaskar.* Air-

> **Rohinton Mistry**
>
> His appearance in 2001 on the *Oprah Winfrey Show,* when Mistry discussed *A Fine Balance* for millions of international viewers, made him a celebrity writer and turned his novel into a bestseller several years after its initial publication. This supports what journalists have been saying for ages—that readers world-wide are very easily influenced by the talk-show hostess and, regardless of the ethnic origin of the author, book sales are positively affected by an author's appearance on this show. Certainly Mistry has the distinction of being the first writer of Indian origin to have gained the attention of Winfrey and to have entered into the public's cultural imagination through an endorsement from this Grande Dame of Television.

India, Bombay, March 2006, 204–207). This is certainly true of an author like diplomat Shashi Tharoor (1956–) who, seizing upon the desire for material about India, found inspiration in India's favorite epic, *The Mahabharata.* Tharoor, like Ruskin Bond and Shashi Deshpande, cut his creative teeth by writing short stories that were published in Indian magazines. His location in the West, however, where his work was based, gave him access to western agents and publishers—something that had been denied his equally talented fellow writers based in India. Astutely combining the saga of contemporary Indian politics with the monumental wars that were fought in Indian Hindu mythology, Tharoor produced *The Great Indian Novel* (1989). In his case too, it was his Indian birth coupled with his exposure to Europe and America through his positions in the United Nations that permitted him to understand and cater to the demands of western readers and publishers. His later novels, such as *Show Business* (1992), took their cue from Bollywood cinema and its growing popularity among diasporic Indians; *Riot* (2001), a later novel, was set in India in the post-Babri Masjid climate and included Americans among the cast of characters. Such cross-cultural themes and the authors' refreshingly different treatment of them gained readers both in India and overseas and, for the first time, Indian novelists were actually able to live off their earnings as writers.

Although cross-cultural, globe-trotting, and transnational themes became popular at this time, one writer whose work was set exclusively in India, despite his own base in Canada, was Indian-born Rohinton Mistry (1952–), a Parsi novelist from Bombay who has made Toronto his home. Drawing upon his Zoroastrian background, Mistry created fiction that revealed the idiosyncrasies of this ethnic Indian minority while also mercilessly exposing the corruption and callousness of India's administrators and politicians in such novels as *Such a Long Journey* (1991) and *A Fine Balance* (1995). His distance from the land of his birth certainly did not lend enchantment to his view of it for, far from writing in fondly nostalgic terms about his childhood and adolescent experiences in India, Mistry focused on the arrogance, greed, and avarice of Indian officialdom and on the abject poverty and misery of the masses caused by national selfishness. His novels were very well received by critics and readers alike, though in India a great deal of indignation followed his exposé of corrupt Indian public life.

Interestingly, Mistry has not succumbed to the general reader's demands for exotic or shifting locales in his novels. Except for his first collection of short stories, *Tales from Firoze Shah Baag* (1987), which contains stories set in Bombay and

Canada, the rest of his novels are set exclusively in Bombay, the city of his birth, though it might not necessarily be named in the novel.

Another popular expatriate writer from India has been Chitra Banerjee-Divakaruni (1956–), Calcutta-born and U.S.-based. If Mistry drew upon his Zoroastrian ancestry in plotting and fleshing out his novels, Banerjee-Divakaruni has employed her Bengali heritage to fullest advantage. She also seems to have studied the desires of her American audience; since discovering that readers in the West have a marked fondness for stories about exploited Indian women, she has been populating her short stories and novels with confused, recent female immigrants from India, for whom the West, far from being a land of milk and honey, has turned out to be a place of disillusionment and discouragement. Her first collection of short stories entitled *Arranged Marriage* (1995) presented a number of Indian women—some new immigrants to the West, others second-generation Indians born and raised in America—who struggle with the conflicts of arranged marriage and the determination to make them work in order to avoid the social stigma of divorce. Using her dual Indian-American perspective to advantage, Banerjee-Divakaruni presents women who are repeatedly exploited—physically, emotionally, and sexually. Despite being in America for many years, they never develop the ability to assert themselves or abandon the abusive environment. Deciding to experiment with theme and technique in her later work, she turned to magical realism in the Salman Rushdie vein, so that novels like *The Mistress of Spices* (1997) present an Indian protagonist well-versed in the art of spell-weaving and potion-making. Banerjee-Divakaruni has found a firm fan following in the West, which might explain her prolificacy and her willingness to create literature in many different genres—including novels, poetry, and essays.

What international readers seem to react well to, in terms of contemporary writing from South Asia, is the wide gamut of themes that Indian writers have tapped in recent years in their quest for a universal audience. Whereas the Indian-English novel of the 1950s and 1960s focused on rural poverty, urban degradation, the abolition of royalty, and the trials of Partition, contemporary Indian novels explore such themes as immigrant angst (the writings of Bharati Mukherjee, Chitra Banerjee-Divakaruni, and Jhumpa Lahiri), spiritual quests (*The Romantics* by Pankaj Mishra), and choices of sexuality (such as *The Blue Bedspread* by Raj Kamal Jha, which deals with incest), while gay Indian writers such as Firdaus Kanga, Ashok Row Kavi, and R. Raj Rao came out of the closet themselves and wrote candidly about the dilemmas of growing up in India's homophobic environment.

Other themes that represented a clear response to the demand of the contemporary global reader for new and daring material from India were changing family equations, such as the later novels of Anita Desai (1937–) and Ruth Prawar Jhabvala (1927–), and the work of new Indian voices such as Manju Kapur, Anita Nair, and Anjana Appachana, who have written about loss and longing. These have been best expressed by the work of Vikram Chandra, especially *Love and Longing in Bombay* and *Red Earth and Pouring Rain*. Chandra's latest novel, *Sacred Games* (2007), is a voluminous work about Bombay's dreadful underworld that is meticulously researched and carefully crafted. At over nine hundred pages, it reportedly earned the author a staggering seven-figure advance and caused a bidding war among international publishers. Such facts bear out the belief that India is still "hot" as a fictional setting. Sold successfully in India and translated into innumerable foreign languages, such Indian literature has earned a place for itself right in the midst of the world's best writing.

The front and middle pages of *Anandabazar Patrika*, an Indian newspaper.

INDIAN PLAYS AND PLAYWRIGHTS

If Indian novelists have acquired international fame and fortune, the same is not true of Indian playwrights. It is interesting indeed that in a country in which the popularity of the cinema transcends all ages, classes, and education levels, dramatic writing has yet to surface as a powerful force. Within the ranks of the "Bollywood" film industry, individual screenplay writers are always in demand, but they have acquired little public prestige. This may be because the status of the film stars themselves overshadows all other forms of dramatic talent. And though India has had a vigorous tradition of oral entertainment, theater has remained largely the domain of the upper class; its audience, therefore, remains confined to urban centers, except for the folk drama that caters to lower-class audiences in the mofussil (rural) areas.

Within this rather limited world of dramatic writing, two Indian writers have acquired a modicum of success. Gurcharan Das (1946–, *Mira, Larins Sahib, 9 Jakhoo Hill*) and Partap Sharma (1939–, *A Touch of Brightness, Begun Sumroo, Sammy*), both writing in the 1960s, not only had their plays produced on the English stage, but even managed to see them in print. In more recent years the plays of Dina Mehta (1946–), such as *Brides are Not for Burning* (1993), focused on social evils such as dowry deaths, spousal and in-law harassment, and the plight of newlyweds who preferred to commit suicide rather than endure mental torture from greedy husbands. In the 1970s, poet Nissim Ezekiel (1924–2004) tried his hand at playwriting and published *Three Plays* in 1969, among which *Nalini* was produced and performed by local drama groups in Bombay. But few of these playwrights were taken seriously on the international level. Partap Sharma's *Sammy* was recently performed in some U.S. cities through a traveling troupe from India. Such original playwriting, however, has found only a limited audience in India, and even there it has failed to make a dent on the larger cultural framework of the nation.

Perhaps the biggest international success in terms of original drama from India has been the production of *Bombay Dreams* at London's West End and New York's Broadway. Produced by the legendary composer Lord Andrew Lloyd-Weber with music composed by A. R. Rahman, the extravaganza was a massive commercial success in London but did not fare as well in New York. From the fate of *Bombay Dreams* in two parts of the world, one might draw the broad conclusion that Indocentric material is much more eagerly awaited, accepted, and consumed in Great Britain than it is in India itself.

Plays in regional languages in India enjoy greater success than those in English, partly because the audience patronizing them is larger. The plays of Badal Sircar (1925–), such as *Evam Indrajit* (1967), and of Vijay Tendulkar (1928–2008), such as *Shantata* (1967), *Court Chalu Aahe* (1967), and *Ghashiram Kotwal* (1972), were performed to much public and critical acclaim in the Marathi-speaking world of the state of Maharashtra. Hundreds of performances all over India led to a few performances in New York for expatriate Indian audiences. The play went on to notch sixteen international translations. Similarly, in the Indian state of Karnataka, Girish Karnard's (1938–) popular plays are written in the local language of Kannada, which has made him a household name among members of his own community. His *Tughlaq* (1964), produced and performed by the National School of Drama in Delhi and on the Bombay stage to high acclaim, is often prescribed on Indian college syllabi, though it remains unknown to international students of post-colonial literature. His play *Hayavadana* (1972), also written in Kannada, earned him endless kudos. His success as a playwright led to screenplays and scripts for Kannada and Hindi films such as *Samskara* (1970). Needless to say, the lack of good foreign-language translations of these works limits their audiences to small groups and does not attract international attention. Indian audiences reacted very enthusiastically to Karnad's work, however, allowing him to enjoy great monetary success and public acclaim in his own country.

Although producers such as Adi Marzban and Burjor Patel spent many decades bringing Gujerati theater to Bombay audiences, in what came to be called "Parsee Theater," these producers also staged British and American plays in English for local Indian audiences. Marzban initiated the production of English comedies on the Bombay stage and was followed by Ibrahim Alkazi in Delhi and Alyque and Pearl Padamsee in Bombay, who directed Indian actors in the staging of every conceivable kind of foreign dramatic performance. These productions were eagerly awaited by urban elite audiences, for whom an evening at the theater was a major social event. Whether it was Arthur Miller or Tennessee Williams, John Osborne or Eugene Ionesco, audiences in cities such as Bombay, Bangalore, Delhi, and Madras could be sure that somewhere down the line some small amateur theater company would bring them to a neighborhood stage. Though they did not rake in massive profits, such productions were financially feasible enough for Alyque Padamsee to make Bombay his base for the staging of musical extravaganzas, which made him a star in his own right. Directing such mammoth productions as *Jesus Christ Superstar, Evita, Cabaret,* and other musicals that had been huge successes on Broadway and at London's West End, Padamsee introduced Indians to such varied talents as those of Remo Fernandes, Madhukar Chandra Das, Nandu Bhende, Alisha Chinai, Shiamak Davar, and Sharon Prabhakar. Plucking out from obscurity some of Bombay's finest musical and histrionic talent, these weekend productions enlivened the cultural life of the city enormously and played to packed houses. However, neither the producers nor the cast and crew of these shows are able to make a living from English-language theater in India. All of them are involved in alternative professions; thus, English-language theater in India has continued to be classified as "amateur" (as opposed to being "professional"). In recent years, the sons and daughters of these veteran producers and directors have made their mark. Padamsee's daughter Rael has entered the production arena in recent years, and Rahul da Cunha, son of actor Sylvester da Cunha and writer Nisha da Cunha, has taken his original theatrical material, namely *Class of '84* and *Pune Highway*, to diasporic Indian communities as far away as Muscat, Malaysia, and Dubai; in the near future, he hopes to find audiences in Germany, Poland, and the Netherlands, according to Marfatia (207).

Among young playwrights, Meher Marfatia mentions Manjula Padmanabhan, whose play *Harvest* won the 1997 Onassis Award for Theater among 1,470 entries from seventy-six countries (207), and Mahesh Dattani, whose *Dance Like A Man* and *Thirty Days in September* have gained critical attention in India and abroad. Marfatia quotes actress-director Lillette Dubey, who states that "Universally relevant writing transcends specifically rooted references, holding the attention of NRI [Non-Resident Indian] and mainstream theater-goers wherever it turns" (207).

INDIAN POETRY

As is the case in the rest of the world, poetry is considered the least marketable of literary genres in India, and Indian poets attempting to get their works into the hands of the public have had to struggle to find publishers. This is especially true of Indian poetry in English, which has a notoriously tiny readership. Even so, as early as the 1950s Nissim Ezekiel tried to create a new, distinctively Indian idiom for Indian poetry in English. Internationally acclaimed and decorated with numerous awards by the time of his death in 2004, Ezekiel attracted attention to such writing. His published work and his ceaseless attempts to publicize it through television and press interviews, and his encouragement of fledgling poets, led to other poetic writing in English from such writers as A. K. Ramanujam, Gieve Patel, Kamala Das, Jayanta Mahapatra, Arvind Krishna Mehrotra, and Adil Jussawala. Such poets achieved slow public recognition but almost no monetary rewards for their writing. Although the reading public was willing to accept novels by Indian writers with local settings and themes, they were far more reluctant to accept Indian poets. The poets were mostly thought to be a self-conscious lot, and poetry itself was considered a high-brow pursuit. Despite their dogged attempts to forge a uniquely Indian voice, diction, and idiom in their work, these poets were generally perceived as imitators of the western poetic tradition. Needless to say, they have remained virtually unknown in the rest of the world.

Contemporary Indian novel writing has become financially successful enough to have garnered media hype in recent years, both in South Asia and overseas. Though indigenous awards are nonexistent, occasional Indian writers find themselves short-listed for prestigious foreign literary awards, as was the case when Anglo-Indian novelist I. Allan Sealy's *The Everest Hotel* gained an international following after being short-listed for the Commonwealth Best Book Award in 1989. Similarly, Jhumpa Lahiri's collection of short stories entitled *Interpreter of Maladies* earned her America's Pulitzer Prize. In 2006, India-born and U.S.-based Kiran Desai, daughter of novelist Anita Desai, won the UK's Man Booker Prize for her second novel *The Inheritance of Loss*. However, unfortunately, it seems as if recognition and respect must still originate in the West for Indian writers to be considered worthwhile in the country of their birth.

PAKISTANI LITERATURE AND THE READING PUBLIC

Pakistan's literary history is rather more recent than India's, as the nation only came into being in 1947. It is as difficult to present an overview of contemporary Pakistani writing as it is to explain the literature of India. The country's multiple regions and languages have contributed a diverse mosaic to global writing. In the south, Sindhi is widely spoken, whereas Punjabi is the preferred language of communication in Lahore and other parts of the Punjab. In the north, Baluchi and Pushtu coexist among the Pathan and tribal communities. The language of literate Pakistan, however, is widely considered to be Urdu, which is also the nation's link language and official state language. Indigenous Pakistani publishing houses have long supplied the needs of non-English readers. Confined largely to the publication of religious scripture, Islamic texts, and Sufi verse, such publication reflects the taste and interest of vernacular readers in Pakistan.

Pakistan's oldest publisher, Ferozesons, set up business in 1894, when, of course, Pakistan was a part of the British colony of India. A Pakistani division of Oxford University Press is also active in the country, publishing scholarly work of high quality. Most indigenous publishing houses have focused on bringing out reasonably priced editions of Islamic scripture and Sufi poetry. In more recent times, however, Urdu translations of international literature—from Shakespeare to *Harry Potter*—have flooded the market. But indigenous publishers do not seem too keen on publishing the original work of Pakistani creative writers, for reasons of limited marketability, and indigenous writers prefer not to seek local publishers because they lack financial and distribution resources. It might be fair to say that, although most South Asia-based writers would covet a western publisher for their work, those based in India, Pakistan, Bangladesh, or Sri Lanka almost invariably end up getting their first work published by an indigenous publishing house such as Penguin or Harper-Collins. Only after a positive initial reception of a first work will they seek out western agents or publishers for their subsequent works.

Exposure to British colonial rule in Pakistan has resulted in the presence of a fairly large English-speaking segment, particularly in urban areas, for whom novels written in English (by western as well as Pakistani writers) are the preferred choice. These readers are generally educated in English medium schools and colleges in metropolitan cities such as Karachi, Lahore, Rawalpindi, and Islamabad. They have little in common when it comes to literary tastes with their Urdu-speaking rural counterparts, for whom poetry and folk tales are almost a part of daily life, being used as the basis of film songs, at wedding ceremonies, and in other cultural rituals.

Among the best-known of Pakistani writers in English are the diasporic ones who, as adults, made the West their home. Because most of the country's earliest writers in the English language lived overseas, they found a western audience for their work. Among these are Zulfikar Ghose, who was born in Sialkot in 1935, moved to Bombay where he received high school education, and then moved to London where his novels were published (*The Murder of Aziz Khan*, Macmillan, 1967, *The Triple Mirror of the Self*, Bloomsbury, 1993). He has also written poetry and essays. Ghose has described himself as a cultural exile, alien in every country in which he has lived. The themes of exclusion and marginalization that are predominant in his work would probably find echoes in the minds of his readers, most of whom are other Pakistani expatriates who have lived in the UK for generations.

Bapsi Sidhwa, a Pakistan-born, U.S.-based Zoroastrian, has used her unusual Parsee heritage as the backdrop for most of her books. Published initially through publishing houses in Pakistan with simultaneous British editions, her early novels *The Crow Eaters* and *The Pakistani Bride* found a faithful readership in the West. *Ice-Candy Man,* first published on the Indian sub-continent and in Great Britain in 1998, was republished in the United States under the title *Cracking India* in 1991, at a time when interest in South Asia was soaring in the West. This publication brought her international recognition, and her fame was augmented by the cinematic version of the novel, titled *Earth 1947,* in the hands of Indian-Canadian filmmaker Deepa Mehta. Partly autobiographical, *Cracking India* presents Sidhwa's own recollections of the uncontrolled violence that rocked Lahore, the city of her birth, in 1947 after the Partition of the sub-continent was declared. Seen through the eyes of nine-year-old Lenny, a victim of polio who frequents the company of adults through the daycare provided by her resident Hindu ayah Shanta, the Hindu-Muslim-Sikh ethnic conflict is presented in innocent, unbiased terms. More recently, Bapsi Sidhwa wrote the novel *Water,* on which she collaborated with Mehta. In a daring interdisciplinary cultural experiment, the novel was written and published after the screenplay had been written and the film shot. The movie portrayed the grim fate of India's widows prior to the Hindu Reformist Movement of the early 1900s. It gained a wide international audience and brought Sidhwa greater global readership. This unusual literary innovation seems to underscore the marketability of material with an Indian core. Clearly, publishers saw profits to be earned from a work of fiction that would have a simultaneous screen release. Wishing to cash in on the possible economic success of such a venture, they signed Sidhwa on to create such a novel. In an interview conducted several years ago, Sidhwa spoke about wanting to bring a distinctively South Asian flavor to her works by experimenting with linguistic and stylistic devices, in order to approximate the rhythm and idiom of her Pakistani characters. In doing so, she believes that she has influenced novelists such as Salman Rushdie, who followed in her wake.

More recent novelists such as Kamila Shamsie (author of *City by the Sea,* 1998, and *Salt and Saffron,* 2000), who was born in Karachi and educated in the United States, have also found publishers overseas as a result of their domicile in the West. A novelist such as Mohsin Hamid is a good case in point. Born and raised in Lahore in Pakistan, he arrived in the United States to attend Ivy League schools where his exposure to western literature resulted in the publication of his own creative work. *Moth Smoke* (2001) was very well received in the West and bagged a few prestigious literary awards. Set in upper-class Lahore in contemporary times, the novel exposed the corruption in high places that has become an endemic part of Pakistani culture. Trained as a lawyer at Harvard, Hamid now lives in London, where he has access to some of the most astute British agents and publishing houses. Many of these scout quality talent from the Indian sub-continent, as such writing has become highly marketable in the West. His recent novel *The Reluctant Fundamentalist* (2007) was short-listed for the Man Booker Prize in the UK.

Uzma Aslam Khan, who has written fearless journalistic pieces about American imperialist interests in the Middle East, found a publisher for her novel *Trespassing* in 2004. Born in Karachi, educated in the West, and having taught English in countries around the world, she ultimately made her home in Lahore, Pakistan, with her husband David Maine. Although her first novel, *The Story of Noble Rot,* was published by Penguin in India, she looked for a western publisher for

Trespassing based on the uniformly good reviews that her first novel had received locally and overseas.

Among Pakistani writers based overseas, one might include Hanif Kureishi. Born in London of mixed race and heritage (British mother, Pakistani father), he has made his culture and background an essential part of his work. His best-known novel, *My Beautiful Laundrette,* published in 1984, which was subsequently made into a film by Stephen Frears in 1985, explores the gay, mixed-race relationship in London of a Pakistani young man, Omar, and his Irish lover, Johnny. Kureishi makes no bones about exposing the seedy dealings of immigrant Pakistanis in the UK and their double standards in matters of sex and marriage. The love-hate relationship of Pakistani immigrants toward England is also insightfully delineated in this novel. Kureishi found a very eager audience for his writing in the West, and his works have garnered good reviews as well as coveted awards. Furthermore, the adaptation of Kureishi's work to television and film formats has brought him audiences from far beyond England and Pakistan. Among some of his works that have been seen on the screen are *Sammy and Rosie Get Laid* and *The Buddha of Suburbia*.

Diasporic Pakistani writing is not as common as its Indian counterpart. This makes the work of Mohsin Hamid and Hanif Kureishi particularly notable. These writers are far better known in the West than they are in Pakistan. Although Bapsi Sidhwa was honored by the Sitar-I-Imtiaz, Pakistan's highest cultural award, her novels have dealt with such things as Partition and the culture shock experienced by Pakistani women who marry and settle in the West. She has refrained from writing national exposés in the same way that Mohsin Hamid and Uzma Aslam Khan have done—a fact that might preclude them from receiving similar national honors.

PAKISTANI POETRY

Poetry is very much a part of Pakistan's culture. *Shairi* (popular rhyming couplets) in Urdu have given rise to a complex network of *ghazals*, or songs, in which audience-appreciation is vocal and frequent. No wedding reception is complete without the presence of poets or lyricists who entertain guests with their verbal virtuosity. When set to music, these rhyming couplets are transmitted far and wide and have become something of a national phenomenon, with great audience support among diasporic Pakistani communities in the West. Out of such traditions have sprung *Quawaali*, or folk songs, which are sung in unison by a group of singers with musical accompaniment. The lyrics are almost invariably taken from the works of prominent Urdu poets. Among *quawalli* artists, the late Nusrat Fateh Ali Khan was best known internationally, and his concerts brought sellout audiences in Pakistan and overseas. Known primarily for setting Sufi verse to music, he made devotional poetry a household cultural form in Pakistan. By popularizing verse in this fashion, Pakistani musicians have done a great service to their poetic counterparts, for they have removed poetry from the preserve of the intelligentsia and returned it to a grass-roots audience in the same way that Rabindra Songeet or the Bengali poetry of Rabindranath Tagore popularized poetry in India.

Among intellectual Urdu poets, Pakistan's best-known voice is that of Faiz Ahmed Faiz. A fearless critic of early Pakistani politics and an avowed communist, Faiz paid the price for his convictions by spending four years in jail in Pakistani for his alleged role in the Rawalpindi Conspiracy. These years provided him with valuable insights into life's harsh realities as well as a climate in which his poetic talents could flourish. The poems that came out of his imprisonment are collected in editions entitled *Dast-e-Saba* and *Zindan-Nama*. They have been widely translated into English in the United States by Naomi Lazard and are frequently anthologized. As a result of the widespread availability of his works in translation, Faiz is as well-known in American high schools as he is in the country of his birth. For his efforts to promote communism in Pakistan, he was awarded the Lenin Peace Prize in 1963 by the Soviet Union, an honor he has shared with such international notables as Nelson Mandela and Fidel Castro and with writers such as Pablo Neruda, Bertolt Brecht, and W. E. B. Du Bois. Though shunned by the political establishment, Faiz's poetry was popular among his own people, for most of whom the successive military dictatorships of Pakistan were hard to swallow. As a rebel with a cause who paid the price for his convictions, he was embraced warmly by his own people.

PAKISTANI POLITICAL WRITING AND SOCIAL COMMENTARY

Among Pakistani writers of nonfiction, one of the best-known names is that of Tariq Ali, a prolific London-based historian, biographer, and essayist. Another passionate communist who was raised by communist Pakistani parents in Lahore, he was sent to Oxford for a university education by his parents, who feared that he might be imprisoned in Pakistan for his political views. A fierce critic of imperialist policies, Ali's writing found an immediate readership among Britain's intelligentsia. Although the bulk of his writing has critiqued international affairs, he has probed the state of Indian politics as well. His book *The Nehrus and the Gandhis: An Indian Dynasty* (1985) was one of the first to criticize the presence of nepotism in Indian politics and the fact that the Nehru–Gandhi dynasty has run the country as they would have operated a family business. *Bush in Babylon* (2003) critiqued the invasion of Iraq by the senior President Bush, and Ali's *Conversations with Edward Said* (2005) revealed little-known facts about one of the most prominent of postcolonial critical theorists. However, it is Ali's autobiography, entitled *Street Fighting Years: An Autobiography of the Sixties* (reprinted by Verso Books in 2005), for which he is best known. He is said to have been the figure behind the famous Rolling Stones song entitled "Street Fighting Man," but this has never been confirmed.

Needless to say, the themes and the techniques that Ali has used as his medium to explore his views as a public intellectual have limited his audience to highly educated, western readers. The lack of Urdu translations of his work makes him virtually unknown in Pakistan except among the literati.

The same is true of the writings of Ayesha Jalal, considered one of Pakistan's most vocal historians. Based currently at Tufts University in Massachusetts, Jalal's book, *The Sole Spokesman* (1999), presented a daringly different perspective on Partition and the role of Mohammed Ali Jinnah, Pakistan's founder, in that development. Her perpetration of the view that Jinnah never really wanted a separate Pakistan, but was merely trying to safeguard the interests of his minority Muslim brothers, presented India's Hindu-dominated Congress in a negative light as threatened by the presence and growing influence of the sub-continent's Muslims. This view and her strident politics on campus might have cost her tenure at Columbia University, where she taught for several years. Undaunted, she accused the University of partisan politics, alleging that she had become a victim of a conspiracy initiated by the Indian faculty to get rid of her for espousing anti-Indian views in her South Asian studies courses. Her lawsuit was dismissed, however, and Jalal found a teaching position at Tufts, where she continues to espouse pro-Pakistani perspectives on Pakistan and Jinnah. *Democracy and Authoritarianism in South Asia,* her latest work coauthored with her husband Sugata Bose, argues that despite the end of colonial rule, authoritarianism flourishes on the Indian subcontinent, perhaps less overtly in India than it has done under military dictators in Pakistan.

Meanwhile, at Yale University, Sara Suleri Goodyear, professor in the English Department, has published three books that stand out in terms of clarity of vision and immaculate style. *The Rhetoric of English India* (University of Chicago Press, 1992) is considered a major work of literary scholarship on the significance of linguistic discourse and the manner in which it was employed by British imperialists to keep their colonial subjects subservient. Her autobiography, however, *Meatless Days* (University of Chicago Press, 1987), a fine piece of creative nonfiction, describes her childhood and youth in Pakistan in a large liberal Muslim household. Although the book details events in the lives of Suleri herself and those best loved by her (such as the death of her sister Iffat and her Welsh mother in a hit-and-run accident), it is the political history of Pakistan that provides the wide canvas against which the family's tragedies unfold. Reviewed in retrospect, after her emigration to the United States, critics have dismissed the perspectives of the events in the book as too cold, too distant, and too lacking in emotional energy. But this is precisely the effect that the author wished to achieve. In portraying Pakistan in a deliberately dispassionate fashion, she is able to move the reader deeply because one cannot fail but see that the turmoil in the country led to the sadness that befell the members of this elite, progressive family as they struggled to come to terms with the destruction of democracy. In 2003, Suleri published *Boys Will Be Boys: A Daughter's Elegy.* As its title suggests, it is a deeply personal account of her relationship with her journalist father, who was known as Pip.

The nature of such writing limits its accessibility to native Pakistani readers, except for those who are literate in English. Much of the critical work of such writers is geared toward overseas readers, whom they hope to reach in a desire to warn and keep informed of the political affairs in lesser-known parts of the world.

With the attacks on September 11 and the subsequent war on terrorism, sociopolitical and sociohistorical writing will undoubtedly continue to flourish as a documentation of contemporary events in Pakistan. As the world tries to make sense of the polarities that divided our planet into Islam versus the rest of the world, educated readers everywhere are seeking answers to the escalating violence that threatens our world at every turn. Unless these works are also translated into local Pakistani languages such as Sindhi, Punjabi, Baluchi, and Pushtu, their popularity will remain confined to educated, western readers alone.

BANGLADESHI WRITING

Though literature in Bengali, the national language of Bangladesh, has a long and colorful history, the literature of Bangladesh is very young. This is partly because the country (formerly known as East Pakistan) is still a fledgling state, having come into being in 1971 after a violent and bloody civil war with what was then West Pakistan.

It is interesting that Bangladesh claims as its own such writers as Rabindranath Tagore and Michael Madhusudan Dutt, who prior to Independence were thought of as Indian writers because they were born in Bengal (parts of which are now Bangladesh). Tagore has written verse in both Bengali and English, and Dutt, though writing exclusively in English, was born in that part of the Indian sub-continent that eventually became Bangladesh. Such categorization underscores the difficulties of labeling writers on the Indian sub-continent. Should they be categorized by virtue of their place of birth? By virtue of the country to which they ultimately owed allegiance? Or on the basis of the language in which they chose to express themselves creatively?

For the purpose of this essay, only literature produced in Bangladesh after it came into existence as an independent nation—that is, after 1971—will be considered and included. As with most writing on the Indian sub-continent, Bangladeshi writers are known only to their fellow Bangladeshis. The lack of translation of their work into international languages confines their fame and their readers to Bangladesh alone. Until such time as Bangladeshi publishing houses or international publishers find it economically feasible to offer indigenous Bangladeshi writing in translation, these writers will remain doomed to obscurity.

In terms of theme, recent writing from Bangladesh has encompassed historical events that have had the most traumatic effect upon the land and its people. Of these, the Partition of the Indian sub-continent in 1947, the civil war with Pakistan in 1971, and the long years of political turmoil following the assassination of Sheikh Mujib-ur-Rahman, generally regarded as the father of the nation, form the bulk of the content of such literature. Such works, like the literature of Partition in India, have underscored the impact of loss: loss of homeland and property, loss of family ties and kinsmen, loss of language and culture, and, ultimately, loss of a sense of national pride and identity.

Writers in Bangladesh have tried valiantly to restore some of these losses by writing in Bengali, publishing locally, and appealing to the common experiences of their readers. Of these writers, Rashid Karim has been the most prolific; his novels, titled *Amar Jato Glani* (1973), *Prem Ekti Lal Golap* (1978), *Ekaler Rupkatha* (1980) and *Sadharon Loker Kahini* (1982), are widely known among his own Bengali-speaking people. Syed Shamsul Haq is also highly regarded in Bangladesh. His novels *Khelaram Khele Ja* (1973), *Duratwa* (1981), *Mahashunye Paran Master* (1982), and *Ek Juboker Chhayapath* (1987) are among the most widely read. Apart from lay readers, who buy paperback editions of these novels in Bangladesh, these works are also taught on high school and college syllabi in courses on Bengali literature; canonical western writers such as Shakespeare are also widely known in academic circles among those choosing to major in English literature. The literacy level in Bangladesh, however, remains despairingly low, leaving it not only one of the world's least significant countries in terms of international publishing, but also one of the world's poorest. With education, literacy, books, and reading being exclusively the preserve of the urban-based population, indigenous publishing is almost nonexistent but for the occasional publication of novels in Bengali.

CONTROVERSIAL INTERNATIONAL BANGLADESHI LITERATURE

Those Bangladeshi novelists who have stoked controversy, however, are best known in the West. The daring Taslima Nasrin, a young woman of Bangladeshi birth, published *Lajja* (*Shame*) in 1993. The novel was written in reaction to the events that unfolded in Bangladesh following the destruction of the Babri mosque in Ayodhya, India, in 1992 by Hindu extremists. Not only were Muslims in India abused, raped, and killed after this act of violence, but in neighboring Bangladesh, Muslims turned against their Hindu neighbors to avenge the killings of their Muslim brethren in India. Nasrin was horrified by the treatment of Hindus in Bangladesh. Her novel delineates the struggles of one Bengali Hindu family in Bangladesh—the Duttas—to deal with the sudden violence that erupts against them, though they have done nothing to provoke it. Helpless in the face of such bigoted religious fervor on the part of their Muslim neighbors, who outnumber them vastly, the four members of the Dutta family face terror and disbelief, having never expected that the Muslim countrymen they loved for decades would turn so viciously against them.

In exposing the unequal treatment of religious minorities in Bangladesh in such a direct and courageous way, Nasrin incurred the wrath of the Islamic establishment in her country. A fatwa was issued for her destruction, calling to mind Salman Rushdie's treatment after the publication of *The Satanic Verses* in 1988. With a price on her head, Nasrin went into hiding and, ultimately, left her native Bangladesh. She continues to live in exile in the West, an outspoken critic of her country and the Islamic strictures that have unfairly governed the lives of Muslim women and legitimized their economic, social, and religious subordination.

In like manner, a new diasporic writer who has courted recent controversy is Monica Ali. Ali was born in Dhaka, Bangladesh, to a Bangladeshi father and a British mother. The family immigrated to Bolton, England, when Monica was three. She was raised and educated in Britain and studied at Oxford. Her debut novel, *Brick Lane* (Doubleday, 2003), met with international acclaim. In it, Ali draws attention to the cultural inadequacies of Bangladeshi immigrants in Great Britain, most of whom have congregated in the East London section of Whitechapel known as Brick Lane. Focused on the incongruous arranged marriage of Chanu with the much younger Nazneen, and the raising of their daughters in a climate that is hostile to lower-class, colored immigrants, the novel explores the frustrations and resentments of Britain's newest South Asian immigrants and the refusal of the mainstream majority to interact with them or draw them into the fold. Isolated and secluded as they are in terms of their socioeconomic levels and their linguistic barriers, these immigrants are drawn toward the fundamentalist Islamic movements currently sweeping Europe. The novel portrays, with devastating reality, the ease with which younger generation Islamic immigrants are courted by the founders of such movements, who bestow upon them a sense of national pride and individual cultural identity.

Meanwhile, action shifts simultaneously to modern-day Bangladesh, which is portrayed in equally unsavory terms as a country riddled by gender inequality, spousal abuse, and the hardships of sweatshop laborers, whom the government does nothing to protect or support. The book met with hostile reaction in Bangladesh; although it was not banned in the country in the way that Taslima Nasrin's *Lajja* was, it nevertheless earned for the author the wrath of the Islamic establishment, who see such writers as traitors to Islam. The fact that Ali lives in England with her English husband affords her the protection that was never available to Nasrin.

Although the novel garnered major international support and Ali was hailed as a major new creative voice, Bangladeshis in Great Britain, particularly those from Sylhet, were deeply offended by the portrayals of the characters in the novel. They describe them as stilted and stereotyped, and they fear that such literary depictions will only reinforce notions of racial inferiority with which they have struggled ever since their arrival in Great Britain. In fact, attempts to adapt the novel into a major motion picture, which was to have been shot on location in Brick Lane itself, have met with severe protest in the area that have earned the support of such prominent writers as Germaine Greer, who laments the fact that not only does such literary stereotyping exist in the novel, but that it is unjustified and will only cause greater problems for the inhabitants. Meanwhile, Salman Rushdie added his voice to the controversy, taking umbrage at Greer's involvement in the matter and seeing it as "philistine, sanctimonious, and disgraceful, but . . . not unexpected" (http://en.wikipedia.org/wiki/Monica_Ali). Such international furor brings attention to the work of writers from such lesser-known countries and paves the way for more spirited literary production. Though *Brick Lane* was short-listed for the prestigious Man Booker Prize in England, Ali's second novel, called *Alentejo Blue* (Doubleday, 2006), met with a lukewarm reception.

It would be false to believe that only English-speaking intellectuals are familiar with the award-winning novels of Bangladeshi ex-patriots in the West. In recent years, as is evident in the case of the publication of *The Satanic Verses, Lajja,* and *Brick Lane,* the flames of Islamic fundamentalism have fanned the wrath of segments of the populace that might have remained oblivious to such publications. Though these sections of the population might not read such literature in English, Bengali translations (either authorized or pirated) have become easily available, and strong and violent protest against them grows rapidly.

For the rest of the world, Bangladeshi writing seemed poised to gain international acceptance through the diasporic writers who have made the country the setting for their plots. Though Bengali writers remain prolific in the country, their audience is tiny, confined only to fellow Bengali speakers. As more Bangladeshis migrate across the world, their presence in the West as immigrants will call attention to their country and culture, which have struggled ever since their break with Pakistan to forge an independent identity. Still regarded as the least significant of the three countries that comprise the Indian sub-continent today, both in terms of economic prosperity and potential and in terms of geopolitical importance, the future of Bangaldeshi literature will depend very much, as it has done for Indian and Pakistani literature, on the amount of prominence it manages to gain in the international arena.

SRI LANKAN LITERATURE

The Anglophone literature of Sri Lanka, like the country itself (formerly known as Ceylon), is in its infancy, having been founded in 1948 after it gained independence from the British. Though ancient works in Pali and Sinhala exist, the readership for them is miniscule, limited to academic scholars on college campuses. The same post-colonial disparity between those educated in English-speaking schools and colleges, versus those who are barely able to afford education, as is the case in India, Pakistan, and Bangladesh, characterizes the nature of the reading public in Sri Lanka. Also multilingual, Sri Lankans in general today speak three main languages—Sinhala (found mainly in the central and southern parts of the country), Tamil (found mainly in the north), and English (found uniformly all over the island nation). Sinhalese and Tamil writing has dominated the cultural scene, whereas the production of literature in English is more recent and caters to a very small section of the population. The Sri Lankan writers in English who have gained a global readership are those who have, since independence, emigrated to the West.

Since 1983, with only a few intermittent periods of ceasefire, the country has been embroiled in a persistent civil war between the northern Tamil factions and the rest of the nation. This situation has caused large sections of the literate upper-class Tamil minority to seek emigration opportunities in the West, resulting in the growing influence of the Sri Lankan diaspora in such countries as Australia and Canada, where several writers have found publishers for their work and, subsequently, some international acclaim.

Although there are a vast number of Sri Lankan writers who have written in Sinhalese, they are unknown outside their own country. For a third-world nation, literacy levels in Sri Lanka are fairly high, and during the post-colonial period, the country has tried to make valiant strides against poverty, hunger, and disease. War born out of political conflict, however, has continued to keep the masses enslaved to age-old prejudices of race and religion and has inhibited the development of the island nation as a modern nation-state. The establishment of an indigenous press and publication network, and the regular presence of international and national book fairs in Colombo, attests to the strong marketability of foreign and indigenous authors in the country. Books in English are widely available particularly in the capital, both in original hardbound foreign editions as well as in cheap, trade paperbacks that are locally produced. However, though Wikipedia lists a lengthy number of names under the heading of "Sinhala Writers" in their section on "Sri Lankan Literature," none of the names would be familiar to readers outside the country.

SRI LANKAN LITERATURE IN ENGLISH

Inevitably, it is those writers who have emigrated to the West and who have written bravely about topics that might have been considered taboo in their own country who have gained international audiences. Of these, Michael Ondaatje (1943–), of Sinhala, Dutch, Tamil, and Portuguese ancestry, is best known and most easily recognized. Born in Sri Lanka, he immigrated to England in 1954 and to Canada in 1962, whereupon he became a Canadian citizen. His earliest recollections of his life in Sri Lanka are outlined in his autobiography, *Running in the Family* (1982). As a fiction writer, he has perfected the nonlinear style of narration, seen in his best-known novel *The English Patient* (1992), which won the Booker Prize and was made into a major motion picture. *Anil's Ghost* appeared in 2000. As in the work of most diasporic writers of South Asian origin, settings in his novels change rapidly in the most transnational sense, as the plot encompasses characters who are scattered around the globe living lives that are intertwined by history and destiny. An academic scholar, teacher, editor, and writer, Ondaatje's voice is unique and powerful. He has a wide international audience and is known for experimenting fearlessly with unconventional patterns of narration.

Also hailing from mixed racial heritage is another Canada-based Sri Lankan writer, Shyam Selvadurai. Having left Sri Lanka as an adolescent in the midst of the raging Tamil-Sinhala Civil War, where he had already begun to question his sexuality, Selvadurai made his home in Toronto, attending university in Canada. His first novel, the highly autobiographical *Funny Boy* (1994) delineates the awakening of his sexual awareness while his country erupted in chaos. Set in Colombo in the heart of an elite family that attempts to save itself from the horrific ethnic violence, the novel underscored the traditions and conventions of an upper-middle-class family of mixed race, which sought respectability and loyalty from its members. Selvadurai presents graphic images of his school life as an adolescent and of his earliest initiation into homosexual activity with a candor that is rare in South Asian writers. His novel received uniformly good reviews worldwide and led to the publication of his second work, entitled *Cinnamon Gardens* (1998). *Swimming in the Monsoon Sea* was published in 2005.

Like Ondaatje and Selvadurai, Romesh Gunasekara (1954–), also of Sri Lankan origin, immigrated to England in 1971. His books too have received a slew of awards, a fact that has brought his work to the attention of audiences in the West as well as in the country of his birth. His first book, *Monkfish Moon* (1992), is a collection of short stories that reflects the political and ethnic conflicts that have engulfed Sri Lanka in recent decades. *Reef,* his widely distributed novel, was published in 1994. It is clear that the turmoil and turbulence of modern-day Sri Lanka is of great concern to the writers who once called the country their home. It is their attempt to resolve their own losses that has resulted in literature that harks back to their past.

SRI LANKAN NONFICTION

Of nonfiction writers, the most acclaimed is Sydney-based Yasmine Gooneratne who immigrated to Australia in 1972. As a novelist and poet, her work has met with some recognition, but it is her work as a post-colonial literary critic that brought her the most international recognition. Through her scholarly writing, she has underlined the work of commonwealth writers who work within diasporic communities.

CONCLUSION

Seen as part of the mosaic of commonwealth literature, Sri Lankan writing has met with much success considering the size of the country and its small population. Until a modicum of peace returns to the nation, however, the sporadic ethnic conflicts will continue to dominate the thematic fabric of creative writers in English, most of whom are based overseas. As courses in post-colonial literature continue to attract western students, there is little doubt that writing from this part of the world will acquire greater notice and popularity.

South Asia is producing more writers in contemporary times than it has ever done, and several factors are responsible for this high output of literary work. Publishers seem eager to review multiethnic writing from the Indian sub-continent, as recent sales have proved that there is a growing international market for such literature. With more and more educated South Asians seeking immigration opportunities overseas, it is possible that more young writers will attract the attention of western agents and publishers.

The availability of mass education for the middle class is resulting in the churning out of more writers in South Asia than ever before. Literary pursuits are no longer the exclusive preserve of the educated elite. In India, for instance, Dalit Literature—that produced in vernacular languages by persons who were formerly considered "untouchable" and outcaste in society—is gaining rapid momentum. It has become an important field of post-colonial academic scholarship in both the original and translated versions. Readers are gradually becoming responsive to the work of writers from South Asia, and such writing is not only selling well around the world but earning reportedly seven figure advance payments to the writers fortunate enough to grab the attention of the international publication market. Foreign publishers with deep pockets are able to reward South Asian writers with substantial enough advances to permit them to make a living from writing. All of these factors have created a very fertile climate for the growth of Indian writing. There is little doubt that, as the demand for such literature increases through the burgeoning numbers of readers attracted to it, there will be no be dearth of quality writing from South Asia in the years to come.

RECOMMENDED READING

Appadurai, Arjun. *Modernity at Large: Cultural Dimensions of Globalization*. Minneapolis: University of Minnesota Press, 1996.

Bhagwati, Jagdish N. *India in Transition—Freeing the Economy*. New York: Oxford University Press, 1993.

Bhargava, Rajeev, ed. *Secularism and its Critics*. Delhi: Oxford University Press, 1998.

Chatterjee, Partha. *A Possible India: Essays in Political Criticism*. Delhi: Oxford University Press, 1998.

———. *The Nation and its Fragments: Colonial and Postcolonial Histories*. Princeton: Princeton University Press, 2001.

———. *Nationalist Thought and the Colonial World: A Derivative Discourse*. London: Zed Books, 1986.

Chowdhry, Prem. *Colonial India and the Making of Empire Cinema—Image, Ideology and Identity*. New Delhi: Vistaar Publications, 2001.

Cooper, Darius. *The Cinema of Satyajit Ray—Between Tradition and Modernity*. New York: Cambridge University Press, 2000.

Dissanayake, Wimal. *Colonialism and Nationalism in Asian Cinema*. Bloomington: Indiana University Press, 1994.

Dissanayake, Wimal and Moti K. Gokulsing. *Indian Popular Cinema: A Narrative of Cultural Change*. Stoke-on-Trent: Trentham Books, 1998.

Ganguli, Sumit. *Conflict Unending: India-Pakistan Tensions Since 1947*. New York: Columbia University Press, 2001.

Guha, Ramachandra. *India after Gandhi: The History of the World's Largest Democracy*. UK: Macmillan, 2007.

Hansen, Thomas. *The Saffron Wave: Democracy and Hindu Nationalism in Modern India*. Princeton: Princeton University Press, 1999.

Hasan, Mushirul. *India Partitioned: The Other Face of Freedom*. New Delhi: Lotus Collection 1995.

Hasan, Mushirul and Nariaki Nakazato, eds. *The Unfinished Agenda: Nation-Building in South Asia*. New Delhi: Manohar Publishers and Distributors, 2001.

Jaffrelot, Christophe. *India's Silent Revolution*. New York: Columbia University Press, 2002.

Jalal, Ayesha. *Self and Sovereignty: Individual and Community in South Asian Islam since 1850*. London and New York: Routledge, 2000.

Jalal, Ayesha and Sugata Bose. *Modern South Asia: History, Culture and Politics*. London and New York: Routledge, 2004.

Jayal, Neeraja Gopal. *Democracy in India*. Oxford: Oxford University Press, 2001.

Joseph, Ammu and Kalpana Sharma, eds. *Whose News? The Media and Women's Issues*. New Delhi: Sage Publications, 1994.

Khilnani, Sunil. *The Idea of India*. New York: Farrar, Straus and Giroux, 1999.

Kobayashi-Hillary, Mark. *Outsourcing to India: The Offshore Advantage*. Berlin: Springer, 2004.

Krishna, Sankaran. *Postcolonial Insecurities: India, Sri Lanka and the Question of Nationhood*. Minneapolis: University of Minnesota Press, 1999.

Ludden, David, ed. *Reading Subaltern Studies: Critical History, Contested Meaning and the Globalization of South Asia*. Delhi: Permanent Black, distributed by Orient Longman, 2001.

Mendoza, Louis and S. Shankar. *Crossing into America: The New Literature of Immigration*. New York: New Press, distributed by W.W. Norton, 2003.

Misra, Maria. *Vishnu's Crowded Temple: India since the Great Rebellion*. Penguin: New Delhi, 2007.

Mukherjee, Meenakshi. *The Perishable Empire: Essays on Indian Writing in English*. New Delhi: Oxford University Press, 2000.

Oddie, Geoffrey A., ed. *Religious Traditions in South Asia: Interaction and Change*. Richmond: Curzon, 1998.

Pandey, Gyanendra, ed. *Hindus and Others: The Question of Identity in India Today*. New Delhi: Viking, 1993.

Pattanaik, D.D. *Hindu Nationalism in India*. New Delhi: Deep & Deep Publications, 1998.

Schimmel, Annemarie. *Islam in the Indian Subcontinent*. Leiden: E.J. Brill, 1980.

Tharoor, Shashi. *The Elephant, the Tiger and the Cell Phone: India—The Emerging 21st Century*. New York: Arcade Publishers, 2007.

———. *India: From Midnight to the Millennium*. New Delhi: Viking, 1997.

Varney, Ashutosh. *Ethnic Conflict and Civic Life: Hindus and Muslims in India*. New Haven, CT: Yale University Press, 2000.

Verma, K. D. *The Indian Imagination: Critical Essays on Indian Writing in English*. New York: St. Martin's Press, 2000.

PRIMARY SOURCES

Ali, Monica. *Alentejo Blue*. London: Doubleday, 2006.

———. *Brick Lane*. London: Doubleday, 2003.

Ali, Tariq. *Bush in Babylon*. London: Verso, 2003.

———. *Conversations with Edward Said*. Kolkota: Seagull Books, 2005.

———. *The Nehrus and the Gandhis: An Indian Dynasty*. London: Chatto & Windus, 1985.

———. *Street Fighting Years: An Autobiography of the Sixties*. London: Verso, 2005.

Bond, Ruskin. *The Best of Ruskin Bond*. Delhi: Penguin, 1994.

Chandra, Vikram. *Love and Longing in Bombay*. Boston: Little Brown, 1997.

———. *Red Earth and Pouring Rain*. Boston: Little Brown, 1985.

———. *Sacred Games*. New York: Harper Collins, 2007.

Das, Gurcharan. *Three English Plays (Mira, Larins Sahib, 9 Jakhoo Hill)*. USA: Oxford University Press, 2001.

Davidar, David. *The House of Blue Mangoes*. New York: Harper Collins, 2002.

De, Shobha. *Starry Nights*. Delhi: Penguin, 1991.

Desai, Kiran. *The Inheritance of Loss*. London: Grove, 2006.

Desani, G. V. *All About H. Hatterr*. New York: NYRB Classics, 2007.

Deshpande, Shashi. *That Long Silence*. Delhi: Penguin, 1989.

Divakaruni, Chitra-Banerjee. *Arranged Marriage*. London: Trans-World, 1995.

———. *The Mistress of Spices*. New York: Anchor, 1997.

Ezekiel, Nissim. *Three Plays*. Publication details unknown. 1969.

Faiz, Ahmed Faiz. *Dast-e-Saba*. Publication details unknown.

———. *Zindan-Nama*. Publication details unknown.

Ghose, Zulfikar. *The Murder of Aziz Khan*. London: Macmillan, 1967.

———. *The Triple Mirror of the Self*. London: Bloomsbury, 1993.

Ghosh, Amitav. *The Hungry Tide*. New York: Harper-Collins, 2004.

———. *In an Antique Land*. New York: Knopf, 1993.

———. *The Shadow Lines*. New York: Viking Penguin, 1989.

Gunasekara, Romesh. *Monkfish Moon*. London: Granta, 1992.

———. *Reef*. London: Granta, 1994.

Hamid, Mohsin. *Moth Smoke*. New York: Farrar, Straus and Giroux, 2000.

———. *The Reluctant Fundamentalist*. New York: Harcourt, 2007.

Haq, Syed Shamsul. *Duratwa*. Publication details unknown. 1981.

———. *Ek Juboker Chhayapath*. Publication details unknown. 1987.

———. *Khelaram Khele Ja*. Publication details unknown. 1973.

———. *Mahashunye Paran Master*. Publication details unknown. 1982.

Iyer, Pico. *Abandon*. New York: Vintage Books, 2004.
———. *Cuba and the Night*. New York: Vintage, 1996.
———. *Falling off the Map*. New York: Vintage, 1994.
———. *The Lady and the* Monk. New York: Vintage, 1991.
———. *Video Nights in Kathmandu*. New York: Vintage, 1989.
Jalal, Ayesha. *The Sole Spokesman: Jinnah, the Muslim League and the Demand for Pakistan*. Cambridge: Cambridge University Press, 1999.
Jalal, Ayesha and Sugata Bose. *Democracy and Authoritarianism in South Asia*. Cambridge: Cambridge University Press, 1995.
Jha, Raj Kamal. *The Blue Bedspread*. London: Picador, 1999.
Karim, Rashid. *Amar Jato Glani*. Publication details unknown. 1973.
———. *Ekaler Rupkatha*. Publication details unknown. 1980.
———. *Prem Ekti Lal Golap*. Publication details unknown. 1978.
———. *Sadharon Loker Kahini*. Publication details unknown. 1982.
Karnad, Girish. *Hayavadana*. USA: Oxford University Press, 1996.
———. *Tughlaq*. USA: Oxford University Press, 1996.
Khan, Usma Aslam. *The Story of Noble Rot*. New York: Penguin, 2001.
———. *Trespassing*. Gordonsville, VA: Picador, 2005.
Kureishi, Hanif. *The Buddha of Suburbia*. New York: Penguin, 1991.
———. *My Beautiful Laundrette*. London: Faber and Faber, 1987.
———. *Sammy and Rosie Get Laid*. New York: Penguin, 1988.
Lahiri, Jhumpa. *Interpreter of Maladies*. Boston: Houghton-Mifflin, 2000.
Marfatia, Meher. "Words Have Wings." *Namaskar*. Air-India, Bombay, March 2006, 204–207.
Mehta, Dina. *Brides are Not for Burning*. Stosius Inc/Advent Books Division, 1989.
Mishra, Panjaj. *The Romantics*. New York: Random House, 2000.
Mistry, Rohinton. *A Fine Balance*. New York: Vintage, 2001.
———. *Such a Long Journey*. New York: Vintage, 1992.
———. *Tales from Firozsha Baag*. India: Penguin, 2002.
Mukherjee, Bharati. *The Tiger's Daughter*. Boston: Houghton-Mifflin, 1972.
———. *Wife*. Boston: Houghton-Mifflin, 1975.
Nasreen, Taslima. *Lajja*. New York: Penguin, 1994.
Ondaatje, Michael. *Anil's Ghost*. New York: Knopf, 1999.
———. *The English Patient*. London: Bloomsbury, 1992.
———. *Running in the Family*. Toronto: McClelland and Stewart, 1982.
Roy, Arundhati. *The God of Small Things*. London: Flamingo, 1997.
Rushdie, Salman. *The Ground beneath Her Feet*. London: Jonathan Cape, 1999.
———. *Midnight's Children*. London: Jonathan Cape, 1980.
———. *The Moor's Last Sigh*. London: Jonathan Cape, 1995.
———. *The Satanic Verses*. London: Viking Penguin, 1988.
———. *Shalimar the Clown*. London: Jonathan Cape, 2005.
Sealy, Allan I. *The Everest Hotel*. Delhi: IndiaInk, 1998.
Selvadurai, Shyam. *Cinnamon Gardens*. New York: Hyperion, 1999.
———. *Funny Boy*. Toronto: McClelland and Stewart, 1994.
———. *Swimming in the Monsoon Sea*. New York: Tundra Books, 2005.
Seth, Vikram. *An Equal Music*. London: Phoenix House, 1999.
———. *From Heaven's Lake: Travels through Sinkiang and Tibet*. New York: Vintage, 1987.
———. *The Golden Gate*. New York: Random House, 1986.
———. *A Suitable Boy*. New York: Harper Collins, 1993.
———. *Two Lives*. New York: Little Brown and Co, 2005.
Shamsie, Kamila. *City by the Sea*. London: Bloomsbury, 1998.
———. *Salt and Saffron*. New York: Bloomsbury, 2000.
Sharma, Partap. *Begum Sumroo*. India: Rupa & Co., 2004.
———. *Sammy*. India: Rupa & Co., 2006.
———. *A Touch of Brightness*. London: Grove Press, 1968.
Sidhwa, Bapsi. *Cracking India*. Minneapolis, MN: Milkweed, 1991.
———. *The Crow Eaters*. London: Jonathan Cape, 1980.

————.*The (Pakistani) Bride*. New York: St. Martin's, 1983.
Sircar, Badal. *Evam Indrajit*. Publication details unknown. 1967.
Suleri, Sara. *Boys Will Be Boys: A Daughter's Elegy*. Chicago: University of Chicago Press, 2004.
————. *Meatless Days*. Chicago: University of Chicago Press, 1987.
————. *The Rhetoric of English India*. Chicago: University of Chicago Press, 1992.
Suri, Manil. *The Death of Vishnu*. London: Bloomsbury, 2001.
Tendulkar, Vijay. *Ghashiram Kotwal*. Publication details unknown. 1972.
————. *Shantata, Court Chalu Aahe*. Publication details unknown. 1967.
Tharoor Shashi. *The Great Indian Novel*. New York: Penguin, 1989.
————. *Riot*. New Delhi: Viking-Penguin, 2001.
————. *Show Business*. New York: Viking, 1992.

SECONDARY SOURCES

Bhabha, Homi. *Nation and Narration*. New York: Routledge, 1990.
King, Bruce. *Modern Indian Poetry in English*. Delhi: Oxford University Press, 1993.
Said, Edward. *Orientalism*. New York: Pantheon, 1978.
Spivak, Gayatri Chakravorty. *A Critique of Postcolonial Reason: Towards a History of the Vanishing Present*. Cambridge: Harvard University Press, 1999.
————. *In Other Worlds: Essays in Cultural Politics*. New York: Methuen, 1987.

PART 5
Africa and the Middle East

CHAPTER 24

The Pre- and Early Islamic Period

John A. Morrow

TIMELINE

248 B.C.E.–224 C.E.	Parthian Empire
224 C.E.–651 C.E.	Sassanid Empire
570	Birth of the Prophet Muḥammad
610	The Prophet Muḥammad receives his first revelation
622	The Hijrah (migration) from Mecca to Medina
624	Battle of Badr
625	Battle of Uḥud
627	Battle of the Trench
628	Treaty of Ḥudaybiyyah; Battle of Khaybar
630	Conquest of Mecca
632	Death of the Prophet Muḥammad
632–61	The rule of the four rightly guided caliphs
661–750	Umayyad Empire controls the Middle East, Maghreb, and al-Andalus
680	Imām Ḥusayn, the grandson of the Prophet, is martyred at Karbala
700	Campaigns against the Berbers in North Africa
711	Muslim conquest of the Iberian Peninsula
725	The Muslims occupy Nimes in France
732	The Battle of Tours in France
737	The Muslims meet a reverse at Avignon in France
750–945	'Abbasid Empire
751	The Battle of Talas results in Chinese paper-making technology passing to the Muslims

762	The Bayt al-Ḥikmah, or House of Wisdom, founded in Baghdad, Iraq
763	Foundation of Baghdad; defeat of the 'Abbasids in al-Andalus
792	Muslim invasion of southern France
859	The University of al-Qarawiyyin is founded in Fez, Morocco
969	The Fatimids conquer Egypt
975	The University of al-Azhar is founded in Cairo, Egypt
1004	The Dār al-Ḥikmah, or House of Wisdom, is founded in Cairo, Egypt
1038–1194	Seljuk Empire
1082	The Almoravids conquer Algeria
1095	The first crusade
1099	The crusaders capture Jerusalem
1144	The second crusade
1147	The Almohads overthrow the Almoravids in the Maghreb
1187	Ṣalāḥ al-Dīn wrests Jerusalem from the Christians, the third crusade
1200s	Mongol invasions of the Middle East devastate the Arab-Islamic Empire
1212	Battle of Las Navas de Tolosa; the Almohads are defeated by the Christians in al-Andalus
1245	The Muslims reconquer Jerusalem.
1453–1923	Ottoman Empire controls most of the Middle East, except Persia
1492	Fall of Granada in al-Andalus
1501	Safavid Empire
1571	The Turkish fleet is destroyed in the Battle of Lepanto

INTRODUCTION TO THE PERIOD

Popularized by the British around 1900, the term "Middle East" refers to a historical and political region of Africa and Eurasia with no clear definition. From a colonial European perspective, the Middle East encompasses the Arabian Peninsula, Egypt, Sudan, the Levant, Turkey, Iran, Afghanistan, and Pakistan. Arabic speakers, however, prefer to speak in terms of the *mashriq*, the *khalīj*, and the *maghrib*. The mashriq, or East, includes the Arab countries bounded between the Mediterranean Sea and Iran, including Palestine, Lebanon, Syria, Jordan, Iraq, and Kuwait; the maghrib, or West, includes Libya, Tunisia, Algeria, Morocco, and Mauritania, as well as the Iberian Peninsula during its period of Islamic domination.

Although Egypt is geographically part of the maghrib, it has more cultural affinity with the greater mashriq with which is it usually associated. The Arabian Peninsula, including Saudi Arabia, Yemen, Oman, and the United Arab Emirates is known as the khalīj. The Arabian Peninsula in general, and the *hijāz* in particular, is considered the center of the Arabic world as it gave birth to the Islamic faith. From an Arab perspective, Turkey, Pakistan, and Afghanistan do not form a part of the mashriq, although Persia, at least during its period of Arab occupation, could be covered by the term. Because this section deals with Africa and the Middle East, the region under study would be best defined by the classical term *al-ʿālam al-ʿarabī*, or the "Arabic world," which covers all the traditional Arabic-speaking countries.

From a period of illiteracy known as *al-Jāhiliyyah* or the Days of Ignorance, when Arab cultural production was essentially limited to poetry, the Arab-Islamic world rose to represent the apex of culture and civilization and the champion of all sciences. The catalyst for this revolutionary transformation was the Qur'ān, which commanded all believers to read. As a result of the advent of Islam, the preaching of the Prophet, and the establishment of all levels of educational institutions, what had previously been an essentially illiterate society became the focal point of cultural radiation throughout the world.

The spread of Islamic civilization was further facilitated when Muslims learned the Chinese secret of paper-making. In the year 751, the ʿAbbasid caliphate confronted the Chinese Tang Dynasty for the control of the Syr Darya, a river that runs through Kyrgyzstan and Kazakhstan. After the defeat of the Chinese army at the Battle of Talas, knowledgeable Chinese prisoners of war were ordered to produce paper in Samarkand. By the year 794, paper mills were operating along the rivers around Baghdad, and paper was being shipped to all the major cities of the Islamic world. By the late-ninth century,

---

Early Islamic Literacy

During the early Islamic period, Muslims had one of the highest literacy rates in the world. In Islamic Spain, there was scarcely a boy or girl over the age of twelve who could not read or write. At present, the Islamic world has one of the lowest literacy rates on the planet, and more than fifty percent of Muslim women are illiterate. In the Arab world, some sixty-eight million people are illiterate, including thirty-eight percent of the adult population, higher than the average twenty-seven percent illiteracy rate in all developing countries.

---

one hundred book and paper shops were said to be operating in the Waddah suburb of Baghdad alone. From Iraq, paper-making technology passed to Syria, where high-quality paper was made, and thence to Egypt, North Africa, and al-Andalus. The transmission of paper-making technology contributed greatly to the rise of Islamic civilization, promoting writing, publishing, and reading. Muslim calligraphers and scribes no longer had to rely on parchment or papyrus from Egypt.

With the construction of paper mills in Baghdad, book production blossomed into a vital industry. Translators, scholars, and tradesmen soon spread throughout the Near East and the Mediterranean. Acquiring, duplicating, and locating books became a new sector of the economy, and caliphs, viziers, and deputies of various provinces competed with each other in building their book collections in an attempt to attract the brightest scholars and finest literary talents.

The cultural production of the Muslim world was staggering, with the libraries of al-Andalus alone churning out as many as sixty thousand works per year. In comparison, modern Spain publishes an average of 46,330 books per year. The Great Library of Córdoba, established by al-Ḥakam II (d. 852), contained four hundred thousand volumes, and employed some five hundred librarians, scribes, physicians, historians, geographers, and copyists. New materials were acquired without difficulty as titles moved freely from Byzantium to Baghdad and from Cairo to Córdoba by way of Venetian and Arab shipping routes. The head librarian at Córdoba employed a female Fatimid deputy named Lubna, who acted as the library's specialized acquisition expert in Cairo,

Damascus, and Baghdad. By the year 1000 C.E, the libraries in al-Andalus contained close to a million manuscripts. This number stands in sharp contrast to the cultural production coming from Christendom, where the two largest libraries, Avignon and Sorbonne, contained a mere two thousand volumes as late as 1150, a reflection of the literacy rate in the western world. By 1275, however, Mudéjar merchants had established the first paper mills in Christian Spain and Italy, and by 1325, the University of Paris alone employed some ten thousand copyists.

As a reaction to what it perceived as internal and external threats, Muslim rulers attempted to consolidate their power by imposing official orthodoxies and limiting freedoms of thought and expression. As a response to centuries of Christian crusades, Muslims became increasingly radicalized, giving rise to dogmatic literalist movements like those of the Almoravids in al-Andalus. From a period of tolerance and pluralism in which Jews, Christians, and Muslims coexisted in harmony, the Islamic world moved to a period of intolerance and antagonism. Divided, and increasingly conquered by the forces of Christendom, the Muslims lost Córdoba to the Christians in 1236, Seville in 1248, and Granada in 1492. Eventually, many Muslim territories would be irretrievably lost and many others would be colonized for centuries. As Muslims suffered losses in land and literacy, western civilization commenced its ascent, eventually becoming the most powerful culture on the planet.

> **Islamic Publishing**
>
> Islamic Spain published twice as many books per year as does modern Spain. Today, only the United Kingdom, China, the United States, Germany, and Japan publish more books per year than did the scholars of al-Andalus. At present, Canada publishes more books in one year than the entire Muslim world combined. If the cultural output of al-Andalus is combined with that of Cairo, Damascus, Baghdad, and other centers of publishing, the number of books published during the Golden Age of Islam is staggering, considering the absence of the printing press.

READING TRENDS AND PRACTICES IN THE PRE-ISLAMIC PERIOD

During the pre-Islamic period, the Arabian Peninsula was a crossroads of cultures with the Sassanid Empire to the east, the Byzantine Empire to the north, and Abyssinia to the southwest. Although the Arabs were surrounded by sophisticated cultures with long literary traditions, the pre-Islamic period in Arabia was characterized by a rich oral culture in which eloquence reigned supreme.

According to tradition, poetry had such a high status for pre-Islamic Arabs that the most famous pieces were posted in the Ka'abah in Mecca. Known as the *Mu'allaqāt*, or "Suspended Ones," these seven odes or *qaṣā'id* were the works of 'Amr ibn Kulthūm, Labīd (sixth c.), Imru' al-Qays (d. 545 C.E.), Ḥārith ibn Ḥillizah (sixth c.), Ṭarafah ibn al-'Abd, Zuhayr ibn Abī Sulmah (sixth c.), and 'Antarah ibn Shaddād al-'Absī (sixth c.). The odes enjoy a unique position in Arabic literature as the finest representations of early Arabic poetry. Besides the composers of the seven poems, there were many other great poets whose works were well-known in the pre-Islamic Arabic world. The poets Nābighah al-Dhubyānī (sixth c.), 'Abīd ibn al-Abraṣ (sixth c.), and 'Alqamah ibn 'Abādah (sixth c.) were also very popular, so much so that they were sometimes numbered among the seven. Others poets, such as al-A'shā Maymūn (sixth c.), Thābit ibn Jābir Ta'abbaṭa Sharran (d. c. 540), al-Shanfarā (sixth c.), and 'Urwah ibn al-Ward (sixth c.), were known as ṣu'lūk or vagabond poets as they would wander the land in search of work reciting poetry.

Pre-Islamic poets acted as historians, soothsayers, and propagandists, and were similar to the minstrels, bards, and troubadours of medieval Europe. Their poetry, or shi'r, contained the collective memories of their tribes, and explored many aspects of Bedouin life, from the anatomy of animals to issues of honor and pride; from themes of solitude, love, and lust, to the troubles of tribal feuds. Moreover, much like the pre-Columbian Aztecs, and the early hip-hop rappers in the United States, Arab poets would engage in lyrical battles known as zajal, which were filled with both praise of oneself and one's ancestry, and mockery of one's opponent. The city of 'Ukāẓ, a market town just outside of Mecca, would host a regular poetry festival in which poets from across Arabia would exhibit their talent.

Alongside the shā'ir, or poet, was his apprentice, known as the rāwī or reciter. The function of the rāwī was to memorize the poems and recite them, a process that ensured the preservation of the poems for posterity. These chains of transmission often continued unbroken for centuries, with one poet training a reciter to promote his poetry as well as contribute to the poetic tradition.

Although poetry was recited, it was very rarely "read" as the pre-Islamic Arabs were virtually all illiterate. Despite the fact that they did not actively employ an alphabet, the Arabs were not devoid of culture and their poets produced poems according to strict metrical rules. The few who could read and write may have been familiar with Thamudic, Lihyanic, Safaitic, Nabatean, Syriac, Greek, or Latin scripts. The first recorded text in the Arabic alphabet was written in 512 C.E. and consists of a trilingual dedication in Greek, Syriac, and Arabic. It is only one of five pre-Islamic Arabic inscriptions known for certain. The South Arabian script was used until around 600 C.E., at which time the entire Arabian Peninsula had converted to Islam giving the Arabic language and alphabet prominence.

The few surviving pre-Islamic inscriptions in the Arabic alphabet, and inscriptions in the Nabatean alphabet that show the start of Arabic-like features, include a pagan prayer and religious, business, and military matters. They include an epitaph and curse against grave-violators, words of praise to a pagan god by a man who got rich, and a couple of Christian dedicatories. They also include a long epitaph for the famous Arab poet and warrior Imru' al-Qays, describing his feats in battle; the record of a military expedition by Ibrāhīm ibn Mughīrah on behalf of the al-Ḥārith ibn Jabalah, king of the Ghassanids, who were vassals of the Byzantines; as well as various names of people.

Without an actively employed Arabic alphabet, the Arabs passed down their poetry and legends by means of oral tradition. It was only after the advent of Islam that the Arabs diligently documented their rich literary heritage, putting into print the poems and epics that had been passed down for centuries. The anthology of al-Mufaḍḍal, for example, attempted to collect all that was remembered from pre-Islamic poetry as well as some material that was produced in the eighth century. The epic poem in praise of 'Antarah ibn Shaddād and the stories of Sinbad, as well as other pre-Islamic legends, were all recorded during the early Islamic period. Widely read and recited, the Sīrat 'Antarah is believed to have influenced both Spanish and French epic poetry, namely the *Cantar de mío Cid* and the *Chanson de Roland.*

READING TRENDS AND PRACTICES IN THE EARLY ISLAMIC PERIOD

The Qur'ān and its Commentaries

Although the Arabic alphabet was used occasionally for religious and business documents, it was only with the advent of Islam, and the pressing need to preserve the Qur'ān and the Ḥadīth, that Arab culture moved from an oral tradition to a written one. The command had come from the Qur'ān itself with the imperative "Read!" (96:1) being the first word revealed to the Prophet Muhammad. The Qur'ān, which was documented during the lifetime of the Prophet, was the first book written in the Arabic language. Considered by Muslims as the actual word of God, the importance of reading the Qur'ān is emphasized in many traditions, with promises of rich rewards for those who recite it. In order to recite it, of course, people—including the Prophet himself—would be required to learn how to read.

> The first word of the Qur'ān revealed to the Prophet Muhammad was "Read!"

According to the Qur'ān, the Prophet was *ummī* (7:157–158), a term interpreted by most Sunni scholars as meaning "illiterate." Although in its modern usage ummī includes the definition of illiterate, it also means "an inhabitant of Mecca, known as *Umm al-Qurā*, the Mother of all Cities," "Gentile," in the sense of not belonging to the people of the Book, the Jews and the Christians, and "unlettered," in the sense of not having received a formal education. According to the Prophet's family, Muḥammad could read and write in seventy languages. They always insisted that the title of "ummī Prophet" referred to that fact that he was from Mecca.

According to many Orientalists, such as Maxine Rodinson, W. Montgomery Watt, and Albert Guillaume, the Prophet was indeed literate before Islam, a skill required of any businessman during the period. In some Shi'ite sources, the Prophet is said to have been literate prior to the receiving the revelation, although others argue that he became literate upon receiving the revelation. Although the literacy of the Prophet prior to the Qur'ānic revelation is subject to speculation, the fact that Muḥammad wrote and signed letters during his lifetime is sufficient proof that he practiced what he preached.

Appreciating the importance of literacy, the Prophet embarked on a campaign to alphabetize the Arabic world. The core of Muḥammad's literacy campaign was the Qur'ān, which continues to act as the primary text for alphabetization in the Muslim world to the present day. The Prophet's many sayings promoting education include: "Knowledge is worship;" "Seek knowledge from the cradle to the grave;" "The seeking of knowledge is obligatory for every Muslim, male or female;" and "Acquire knowledge and share it with the people." He also said: "Seek knowledge, even in China" stressing the lengths to which one should go in the search of science.

The Prophet encouraged his literate companions to teach his illiterate companions how to read. Due to a lack of teachers, he even enlisted prisoners of war as teachers. So long as prisoners taught two Muslims how to read, they would be set free. Although the Prophet only ruled in Medina for ten years, he created legions of literate and learned Muslims who would rise to the most sublime of scholarly ranks.

From the time of the Prophet to the present, the minimum level of literacy expected by Muslims has been the ability to read the Qur'ān. Instruction traditionally took place in grammar schools (*kuttāb*), the mosque (*masjid*), the public school (*madrasah*), or, for the privileged few, the palace school. The pedagogical approach that was employed consisted of whole reading and memorization. For most students, the ability to read the Qur'ān was the extent of their education. For others, the Qur'ān was simply a starting point leading to every other science imaginable.

While the elite continued their private education at the palace, the best and brightest students from regular society moved from the madrasah into prestigious religious seminaries and Islamic universities throughout the Muslim world. These included the Mosque of 'Amr ibn al-'Āṣ in Cairo, founded in 642; the University of Zaytuna in Tunis, founded in 732; the *Bayt al-Ḥikmah* in Baghdad, founded in 813 C.E.; and *al-Qarawiyyin* University in Fez, founded in 859 C.E. A multitude of universities were founded in al-Andalus in the eighth century, seventeen of them in the city of Córdoba alone. Other institutions of higher learning included *al-Azhar* and *Dār al-Ḥikmah* in Cairo, founded in 988 and 1004, respectively, the *Ḥawzah 'Ilmiyyah*, founded in Najaf in the mid-tenth century, as well as the Nizamiyyah University and the Mustanṣiriyyah University, founded in Baghdad in 1065–1067 and 1234. Medical education was obtained through private tutors, private medical colleges, and public hospitals, whereas most trades were learned by apprenticeship. Besides grammar schools, mosques, palace schools, public schools, and universities, higher education could also be obtained by attending bookshop schools and literary salons, where teaching was done by means of lecture, discussion, and debate. Although the level of literacy may have varied throughout the Islamic world, it was exceedingly high in its cultural centers. In al-Andalus, to cite a single example, one would have been hard-pressed to find a boy or girl over the age of twelve who could not read or write.

The Qur'ān, as the heart and soul of Islam, was the book that was most often read, and which rapidly spread throughout the Muslim world during the caliphate of 'Uthmān when it was first mass produced and distributed. Because Muslims pray five times a day, and each prayer requires the reading of short chapters from the Qur'ān, the holy book of Islam is the most read book in the world. Besides its reading during ritual prayers, the Qur'ān was read on a daily basis as an act of devotion. If there was a book in every home, that book was the Qur'ān.

Because the Qur'ān is not merely read, but chanted, many works were produced regarding the rules of recitation. As a manifestation of love for the text, large quantities of the Qur'ān were published in dozens of different scripts, including the *ḥijāzī*, *makkī*, *mashq*, *'uthmānī*, *mā'il*, *kūfī*, *thuluth*, *ta'līq*, *nasta'līq*, *dīwānī*, *bihārī*, *andalusī*, *maghribī*, and *ṣīnī* styles. Copies of the Qur'ān were calligraphed by hand on the finest paper and with the best

> **Women and Education in the Early Islamic Period**
>
> During the early Islamic period, women had free access to education. They could become scholars, scientists, medical doctors, and even religious leaders or imāms. Islamic history has left us many names of illustrious women who were surgeons, librarians, and religious scholars, among numerous other professions.

of binding. The holy book of Islam was not only read, but revered, and all the best homes guarded an ornamental copy as a precious heirloom.

As the source of so many sciences, from theology to philosophy, and from law to linguistics, the Qur'ān was not only read but interpreted, resulting in hundreds of Qur'ānic commentaries known as *tafāsīr*. In the early Islamic period, some of the most popular commentaries included *Jāmi' al-bayān fī tafsīr al-Qur'ān* by

A ninth-century copy of the Qur'ān.

Abū Ja'far Muḥammad al-Ṭabarī, the *Tafsīr* of Ibn Kathīr, and the *Tafsīr Jalalayn* by Jalāl al-Dīn al-Suyūṭī. Among Shi'ites, the most popular commentaries included *Majma' al-bayān fī tafsīr al-Qur'ān* by al-Faḍl ibn al-Ḥasan Tabarsī, *Tafsīr al-'Ayyāshī* by Muḥammad ibn Mas'ūd al-Samarqandī, and *Tafsīr tibyān* by Shaykh al-Ṭūsī. Many attempts were also made to critically compile the Qur'ān in order of revelation. The writing of Qur'ānic commentaries was limited to the learned,

> **Public Services in the Early Islamic Era**
>
> During the golden age of Islam, libraries, hospitals, schools, and universities were funded by the state treasury, with free access being provided to the public

including both legal and spiritual authorities. Although these tafāsīr were read primarily by religious scholars and students, many of them became popular among the laity. Interpreted by scholars from all schools of thought, the Qur'ān was at the center of a constant dichotomy. On the one hand were the jurists who advocated the literal and legalistic interpretation of the text. On the other hand were the mystics who advocated the spiritual sense of the text. Throughout Islamic history, Qur'ānic interpretation has swayed from the esoteric to the exoteric like the systole and diastole of the human heart.

The Sīrah, the Ḥadīth, its Commentaries, and the Science of Men

Besides the Qur'ān, educated readers from the early period of Islam were particularly interested in learning more about the Prophet, hence the proliferation of books on his life and sayings, including Ibn Isḥāq's *Sīrat Rasūl Allāh, The Life of the Messenger of Allah.* Although many ancient Islamic books were lost and many were destroyed by the Mongols after the Battle of Baghdad in 1258 and the European crusades against Islam, including the fall of Granada in 1492, the foundational books of prophetic tradition have survived the test of time, which is sufficient proof of their popularity. For the Sunni, these include *Ṣaḥīḥ Bukhārī, Ṣaḥīḥ*

An eleventh-century North African copy of the Qur'ān.

Muslim, Sunan Tirmidhī, Sunan Abū Dāwūd, Sunan Ibn Mājah, Sunan Nasā'ī, Musnad Aḥmad ibn Ḥanbal, and the *Muwaṭṭa'* of Imām Mālik, among others. For the Shī'ah, these include *Uṣūl al-Kāfī* by Kulaynī, *Man lā yaḥḍuruhu al-faqīh* by Shaykh al-Ṣadūq, as well as *Tahdhīb al-Aḥkām* and *al-Istibṣār* by Shaykh al-Ṭūsī, among others. Due to their encyclopedic size and expense, collections of prophetic sayings, their extensive commentaries, and works on narrators known as the science of men (*'ilm al-rijāl*) were not within the reach of regular readers.

Islamic Mysticism Texts

The early Islamic period produced many Muslim mystics whose works were widely read. The imāms from the household of the Prophet, who are mentioned in the initiatory chains of many Sufi orders, cultivated an Islam that balanced both its legal and spiritual aspects. One of the most popular of these works was the *Miṣbāḥ al-sharī'ah wa miftāḥ al-ḥaqīqah / The Lantern of the Path* by Imām Ja'far al-Ṣādiq, the Sixth Shi'ite imām. Other influential mystics included Abū Ḥāmid al-Ghazzālī, and the Andalusian Ibn al-'Arabī (d. 1240 C.E.), famous for his *Fuṣūṣ al-ḥikam* (*Gems of Wisdom*) and *Futūḥāt al-Makkiyyah* (*Meccan Illuminations*). Although they were relished by Sufi Muslims, many of these works were contentious and controversial, and were received with hostility by the self-proclaimed proponents of Sunni orthodoxy.

Biographical Texts

Besides books on the Prophet, early Muslims demonstrated in deep interest in the lives of pre-Islamic prophets, Muhammad's companions, the caliphs, and the imāms of Islam. Books on biblical prophets, such as the *Qiṣaṣ al-anbiyyā'* by Ibn Kathīr (d. 1373), were widely read by all Muslims. The Shi'ites, eager to learn more about their imāms, consulted the *Kitāb al-irshād* or *Book of Guidance into the Lives of the Twelve Imāms*. Unlike many traditional compilations of prophetic traditions, which focused mostly on compiling whatever sayings were circulating, many Muslim biographers were selective and attempted to separate historical fact from legend and folklore.

History Texts

Early Muslim readers were interested in both Islamic and world history. The most important history books produced during the early Islamic period include the *Tārīkh* (*History*) by Abī Ja'far Muhammad ibn Jarīr al-Ṭabarī (d. 923 C.E.). Considered the "Herodotus of the Arabs," Abū al-Ḥasan ibn al-Ḥusayn al-Mas'ūdī (d. 956) authored an influential world history titled *Murūj al-dhahab wa ma'ādin al-jawāhir* (*The Meadows of Gold and Mines of Gems*). A multitude of books were read by Muslims regarding the Battle of Ṣiffīn, the Battle of the Camel, and the Battle of Karbala, demonstrating a sense of distress over the Sunni/Shī'ah split among the early Muslims. From a single community, the Muslims had split into a multitude of schools, enriching Islam hermeneutically, but greatly debilitating it politically. Shahristānī's (d. 1153) *al-Milal wa al-niḥal* was particularly popular, as it provided a non-polemical historical study of various religious communities and philosophies with reasons for their formation.

Philosophy Texts

The early Islamic period was characterized by its intellectual curiosity and open-ness to outside ideas and influences. Founded in Baghdad during the reign of the caliph al-Manṣūr (754–775 C.E.), the *Dār al-Ḥikmah*, or House of Wisdom, engaged in the translation and preservation of Persian, Syriac, and eventually Greek works. Within a period of roughly one hundred years (1150–1250 C.E.), all of Aristotle's writings were translated and reintroduced into the West. Translated, interpreted, and appropriated, classical Greek writings were reintroduced into Europe by the Muslims, contributing to the Renaissance.

Besides the *Ikhwān al-Ṣafā'*, or Brethren of Purity, the greatest philosophers of the early Islamic age were Ya'qūb ibn Isḥāq al-Kindī (d. 873 C.E.); Abū Naṣr Muḥammad ibn al-Farakh al-Fārābī (Alpharabius / Abunaser, d. 950–951 C.E.); Ibn Rushd (1198 C.E.); Ibn Sīnā (Avicenna, d. 1037 C.E.), and Ibn Khaldūn (d. 1406 C.E.), whose masterpieces continue to marvel to this day. The *Ikhwān al-Ṣafā'*, or Brethren of Purity—a tenth-century organization of Arab philosophers in Basra, Iraq, the seat of the 'Abbasid caliphate at the time—were particularly influential.

Devotional Texts

Religiously minded readers from the early Islamic period were also interested in devotional literature, including prayer manuals and compilations of religious sermons and speeches. *Nahj al-balāghah* (*The Peak of Eloquence*) was particularly popular among Shi'ites, but also among Sunnis. Compiled by Sayyid al-Rāzī from earlier sources, the book includes famous speeches, sermons, and sayings of 'Alī ibn Abū

Ṭālib, the first imām of the Shi'ites, and the fourth caliph of the Sunnis. The cousin and son-in-law of the Prophet Muḥammad, Imām 'Alī's *Nahj al-balāghah* has been used to teach the Arabic language, eloquence, and rhetoric since the time it was published. Considered one of the oldest Islamic prayer manuals, Imām 'Alī Zayn al-'Ābidīn's *Ṣaḥīfāh al-sajjādiyyah*, translated by William Chittick as *The Psalms of Islam*, has always been popular among Shi'ite Muslims. The most popular prayer manuals in the Sunni world are the works of Sufi authors. They include the *Munājāt* (*Intimate Invocations*) of Khawājah 'Abd Allāh Anṣārī (d. 1088), the saint of Herat, and the *Dalā'il al-khayrāt* or *Waymarks of Benefits* by Muḥammad al-Jazūlī (d. 1465), the Moroccan Shādhilī Shaykh.

Theological Texts

Not unlike the analysis of any of the world's great religions, the interpretation of Islam leads to divergences of opinion in matters of belief. As various creeds were codified, Muslims divided themselves into various theological schools. Some of the Sunni attempts to systematize the fundamentals of faith include *al-'Aqīdah al-Ṭaḥāwiyyah* by Imām Abū Ja'far al-Ṭaḥāwī (d. 933 C.E.) and the *Ibānah* by Abū al-Ḥasan al-Ash'arī (d. 936 C.E.). The two most famous works on the Shi'ite beliefs include *I'tiqādātu al-Imāmiyyah* or *The Beliefs of the Imāmiyyah* by Shaykh al-Ṣadūq Abū Ja'far Muḥammad ibn 'Alī ibn Babawayh al-Qummī (d. 991 C.E.) and its correction made by his student, Shaykh al-Mufīd Abū 'Abd Allāh Muḥammad ibn Muḥammad ibn al-Nu'mān (d. 1022 C.E.), which is known as *Taṣḥīḥ al-i'tiqād* or *To Rectify the Beliefs*. Other important works on Shi'ite theology include *Tajrīd al-i'tiqād* by Nāṣir al-Dīn al-Ṭūsī and its commentary by 'Allāmah al-Ḥillī, known as *al-Bāb al-ḥādī 'ashar*. Despite some minor differences in belief, all Muslims agreed upon the fundamental aspects of their faith: the oneness of God, the prophethood, and the day of judgment.

Texts on Islamic Jurisprudence

Although all Muslims agree on fundamental aspects of faith, they are divided into various *madhāhib*, or schools of law. During the early Islamic period, Sunni Muslims followed the Ḥanafī, Shāfi'ī, Mālikī, and Ḥanbalī schools of law. They also followed schools of law that are no longer extant, including the Ẓāhirī school from al-Andalus; the Jarīrī school founded by Ṭabarī; and the schools of al-Azwā'ī, Ḥasan al-Baṣrī, Abū 'Uyaynah, Ibn Abī Dhu'ayb, Sufyān al-Thawrī, Ibn Abī Dāwūd, and Layth ibn Sa'd, among others. The Twelver Shi'ites, however, had a single school of law, known as Ja'farī, in honor of Imām Ja'far al-Ṣādiq (d. 765 C.E.), the sixth Shi'ite imām, who taught jurisprudence to Imām Mālik (d. 796 C.E.) and Imām Abū Ḥanīfah (d. 767).

In order to ensure the correct performance of their religious obligations, most Muslims referred to a treatise on Islamic jurisprudence. Among Sunnis and Sufis, books such as *Iḥyā' 'ulūm al-dīn* (*The Revival of the Islamic Sciences*) by Abū Ḥāmid al-Ghazzālī (d. 1111 C.E.), *Zād al-mī'ād* or *Provisions for the Hereafter* by Ibn Qayyim al-Jawziyyah (d. 1350 C.E.), and *'Umdat al-sālik wa 'uddat al-nāsik* (*The Reliance of the Traveller and Tools of the Worshipper*) by Ibn al-Naqīb (d.1367 C.E.) were part of a basic Islamic education. For Shi'ites during the early Islamic period, the fundamental books of *fiqh* or jurisprudence included the *Muqna'ah* of Shaykh Mufīd (d. 1022 C.E.), as well as *al-Nihāyah, Mabsūṭ*, and *Khilāf* by Shaykh Ṭūsī (d. 1067 C.E.). The basics books of the Shi'ites also included *Sharā'i' al-Islām* by

An Arabic manuscript for the *Maqamat Al-Hariri*, مقامات الحريري, during the twelfth century.

Muḥaqqiq Ḥillī (d. 1277 C.E.), *al-Rawḍah al-bahiyyah*, known also as *Sharḥ al-lumʿah*, by Shaykh Zayn al-Dīn ibn ʿAlī Shahīd al-Thānī (d. 966 C.E.), as well as many others. The Shiʿites, unlike the Sunnis, are only allowed to follow the rulings of living jurists. From the occulation of the twelfth imām in 941 C.E. to the present, Shiʿites have followed a succession of scholars in matters of jurisprudence.

CREATIVE TEXTS

Poetry

Although the pre-Islamic period was particularly prolific in its production of poetry, the genre suffered a decline during the early days of Islam, a time in which religious literature was all the rage. Although it is unclear whether pre-Islamic poetry was repressed for religious reasons, Arabic poetry definitely declined, humbled in the face of Qurʾānic eloquence or due to a lack of audience. Deeply rooted in pre-Islamic paganism, Arabic poetry represented a feudalistic worldview that had been uprooted. With its references to wine, women, and gambling, the Arabic poetry from the Days of Ignorance (*al-Jāhiliyyah*) was antithetical to Islam. It was for this reason that the

Qur'ān said: "As for poets, the erring follow them" (26:224). Muḥammad, of course, was not opposed to poetry *per se*, as he had his own personal poet, Ḥasan ibn Thābit (d. c. 674), who composed poems in praise of the Prophet.

The last of the bedouin bards is generally considered to be Ghaylan ibn 'Uqbah (c. 696–c. 735), nicknamed Dhū al-Rummāḥ, who continued to cultivate the themes and styles of the pre-Islamic poets. After the austerity of the first four caliphs, the excesses of the Ummayyad and 'Abbasid empires created an atmosphere conducive to court poetry, with its emphasis on the *ghazal*, or love poem, the master of which was Abū Nūwās (d. c. 813–815 C.E.), who cultivated a poetry that praised wine (*khamriyyāt*) and pederasty (*mudhakkarāt*). While Abū Nūwās produced pretty but polemical poems that pushed the limits of what was acceptable under Islam, and poets such as 'Abd al-Raḥmān ibn Ismā'īl Waḍḍāḥ al-Yaman (d. c. 708 C.E.) and Ṣāliḥ ibn 'Abd al-Quddūs al-Baṣrī (d. 783 C.E.) were executed on grounds of heresy, others produced more religiously themed poetry.

The courtly culture of the Ummayyad and 'Abbasid empires also contributed to the popularization of songs. Some of the famous singers included Ibrāhīm al-Mawṣilī, his son Isḥāq al-Mawṣilī, and Ibrāhīm ibn al-Mahdī. Although songs are generally viewed as an aural experience, they were so popular among a sector of society than they were actually published and read. Abū al-Faraj al-Iṣbahānī's *Kitāb al-aghānī*, or *Book of Songs* (1216–1220 C.E.), was a particularly popular collection of songs by famous singers, musicians, and poets. Although much of the material was objectionable from an Islamic point of view, people have always been eager to be entertained.

Besides profane poetry, the early Islamic period produced a wealth of pious poetry, typically penned by Sufi Muslims. Although their poetry deals with love and wine, and has been misinterpreted by most Orientalists as hedonistic, the Sufis emphasized allegorical language. They addressed issues of the flesh in an attempt to achieve transcendence with "intoxication" representing the mystic union between man and God. Rābi'ah al-'Adawiyyah, Abū Yazīd al-Bisṭāmī (d. 874), and Manṣūr al-Ḥallāj (d. 922) were some of the most significant Sufi poets. Misunderstood by many, Ḥallāj was eventually crucified for heresy.

As a result of the rise of Persian and Turkish literature, Arabic poetry declined after the thirteenth century, although it flowered a little longer in al-Andalus where the classical *muwashshah* with its colloquial *kharjah* or final strophic "envoi" were particularly popular. One of the most famous poets of al-Andalus was Muḥammad ibn 'Abd al-Malik ibn Quzmān (d. 1160 C.E.), whose rhymed colloquial Arabic verse, the zajal, is sprinkled with Romance words and resembles the later vernacular troubadour poetry of France.

The Andalusian poetic tradition, which bridged the Arabic world and the western world, abruptly found its end with the fall of Granada in 1492. Under the orders of Cisneros, the Archbishop of Granada, the corpus suffered large-scale destruction by fire in 1499 or 1500. Despite its public prohibition, Arabic literature was consulted in private by the *conversos de moros* and *conversos de judíos*, the Cryptic Muslims and Jews who had been forcibly converted to Catholicism, as well as Christian persons of culture. As a result, this suppressed Arabic-Islamic substratum continued to exert a subtle influence on Spanish literature, as can be seen in the works Sebastiano de Córdoba; San Juan de la Cruz; Santa Teresa de Ávila; and Juan Ruíz, Arcipreste de Hita.

Prose

The birth of Arabic prose, as a literary form, is attributed to the Persian secretarial class who served under the 'Abbasid caliphs in Baghdad. Popular works of the early

Islamic period include *Kalīlah wa Dimnah* by Ibn al-Muqaffaʿ (d. 757 C.E.), a series of didactic fables in which two jackals offer moral and practical advice, as well as *Kitāb al-ḥayawān*, or *The Book of Animals* by al-Jāḥiẓ (d. 869 C.E.), an anthology of animal anecdotes. These works were exceedingly popular and appealed to a wide public readership. *Kalīlah wa Dimnah* was translated into Spanish between 1251 and 1261 on the orders of Alfonso, one of the sons of King Fernando III, who would become known as King Alfonso X, the Wise. According to many critics, *Kalīlah wa Dimnah* and the *Kitāb al-ḥayawān* influenced European works such as Ramón Llull's *Llibre de les bèsties*, the *Roman de Renard*, the *Fables* of La Fontaine, and other *bestuarios*.

The *maqāmāt* or "assemblies," a genre invented by al-Hamadhānī (d. 1008 C.E.), are composed of fifty-two episodic stories about an unscrupulous rogue that poke fun at all levels of society. The genre was taken to new extremes by al-Ḥarīrī (d. 1122 C.E.). With his prowess for wordplay and his seemingly inexhaustible vocabulary, his maqāmāt are considered one of the greatest treasures of Arabic literature. These stories were highly popular among all levels of society and may have contributed to the creation of the picaresque genre in sixteenth- and seventeenth-century Spain, including such works as *Lazarillo de Tormes* and *El buscón*, among many others.

The Thousand and One Arabian Nights, known in Arabic as *Alf laylah wa laylah*, is a collection of stories compiled over thousands of years by various authors, translators, and scholars. These collections of tales can be traced back to ancient Arabia, Persia, India, and China. The oldest remnant of the work comes from a few handwritten pages from Syria dating to the early 800s. The book is also mentioned in Ibn Nadīm's *Fihrist*, which dates from the 900s. Clearly a popular work among the ruling elite, it was certainly equally popular among the common class. Although it is unlikely that lay people had personal copies, the tales were probably recited by professional story-tellers who traveled from town to town. These legends, and fables from China, India, Persia, and Arabia, were so widely read that they spread from the Islamic world into Europe, becoming part and parcel of the western literary tradition. Medieval Spanish works such as Don Juan Manuel's *El Conde Lucanor* and La Fontaine's *Fables* are filled with fictional material from the Muslim world.

One of the most influential writers from al-Andalus was Abū Muḥammad ʿAlī, known as Ibn Ḥazm of Córdoba (d. 1064 C.E.), the author of *Ṭawq al-ḥamāmah* or *The Dove's Necklace*. This was a popular work on the art of love that is considered a precursor to the *Libro de buen amor*, the *Book of Good Love* by Juan Ruíz, Arcipreste de Hita (fl. 1343). Although its Arabic original is no longer extant, the Spanish *Sendebar*, or *Libro de los engaños*, was translated from a popular Arabic book in 1253 on orders of Prince Fadrique, the brother of King Alfonso X. A misogynistic work dealing with the wicked ways of women, it was a phenomenal success in Europe. In many regards, it served as a precursor for works that protagonize "players" such as Don Juan.

The rise of popular literature as a credible genre was fostered by a rising level of literacy in the Muslim world, made possible by the paper mills in Baghdad, which dramatically decreased the cost of textual material. Prior to the introduction of paper, works were published on papyrus, which is fragile, or parchment, which is expensive. With locally produced paper, Arab publishers could produce a high-quality and durable product that was cost-efficient.

TEXTS IN THE ARTS AND SCIENCES

Scholars during the early Islamic period produced a monumental volume of works in all areas of science. As the Islamic empire expanded out of Arabia, and the Arabs encountered new language, cultures, and religions, they were eager to learn more about the ways of the world. They produced books on foreign languages and alphabets; world religions, including Hinduism, Zoroastrianism, Judaism, and Christianity; as well as studies of their scriptures. Readers had an abundance of books at their disposal, including works on zoology, ornithology, entomology, herpetology, botany, oceanography, metallurgy, physiology, agriculture, political science, sexology, psychology, architecture, apiculture, geometry, mathematics, algebra, astrology, medicine, pediatrics, gerontology, sociology, economy, mythology, weaponry, navigation, aviation, perfumery, chemistry, geology, and many more too lengthy to mention.

Some of the great scholars of the period included Muhammad ibn Mūsā al-Khawārizmī (d. 850 C.E.), a Persian mathematician, astronomer, and geographer, as well as Abū Bakr Muhammad ibn Zakariyyā al-Rāzī (d. 925 C.E.), the physician and philosopher who was possibly the first Persian doctor to write a home medical manual directed at the general public. Another celebrated scholar was Abū Rayḥān Muhammad ibn Aḥmad al-Bīrūnī (d. 1048 C.E.), the Persian genius whose experiments and discoveries were as significant and diverse as those of Leonardo da Vinci or Galileo, as well as the Andalusian Arab Abū al-Qāsim Khalaf ibn al-'Abbās al-Zahrāwī (d. 1013 C.E.). Considered the father of modern surgery, al-Zahrāwī authored *al-Taṣrīf*, a thirty-volume collection of medical practices. The works of Muslim scholars and scientists were widely read and distributed throughout the Muslim world, stimulating technological advances in all areas in a prodigious process of cultural acceleration.

LANGUAGE AND LINGUISTICS TEXTS

As a language that had emerged from obscurity to become the official language of culture, science, and civilization from al-Andalus to India, Arabic needed to be thoroughly studied and duly documented. The first Arabic dictionary ever compiled was the *Kitāb al-'ayn*, or *Book of Sources*, by Khalīl ibn Aḥmad al-Farāhidī (d. 791 C.E.). His student, the Persian Sībawayhi (d. 793 C.E.), was the first to produce an exhaustive grammatical system, which has been the point of reference for all subsequent studies to this day. Known simply as the *al-Kitāb*, or *The Book*, it falls just shy of one thousand pages, and is considered the Qur'ān of Arabic grammar. Another work of invaluable importance was *Lisān al-'arab* by Jamāl al-Dīn Muhammad ibn Mukarram ibn Manẓūr (d. 1311 C.E.), the author of the most comprehensive dictionary of classical Arabic. Many dictionaries were written for specific fields. One of the most famous books in the field of botany was the *Kitāb al-nabāt* or *Book of Plants* by Abū Ḥanīfah Aḥmad ibn Dā'ūd Dīnawārī (d. 896 C.E.).

TREATISES

The treatise, or *Risālah*, was immensely popular as it was inexpensive and easily accessible to the average reader. Considered short and sweet, these treatises, or *rasā'il*, explored every topic imaginable from religious matters, anecdotes, proverbs, moral stories, and popular recipes, to prostitution and its pleasures, alcoholic beverages, dancing, singing, gambling, instructions on making cat calls, and how to impress women, as well as epistles on thievery and witchcraft. The writers and readers of these rasā'il ranged from scholars to simpletons, from the cultured to the crass, and from the virtuous to the vile. Due to their negligible cost, treatises could be mass-produced, sold for little on the street, in markets, and in bookstores, or distributed freely. Like other publications, they could be sponsored by individuals, religious seminaries, universities, or governments. Unlike books and encyclopedias, which generally required a patron in order to publish them, treatises were much like modern-day websites or blogs, which contain material that is both cultured and uncouth, and both legal and illegal. As a result, the authors of many treatises employed pseudonyms or preferred to publish their works anonymously.

CONCLUSION

Although the rise of reading and its effects on Arabic-Islamic society serve as a model of inspiration, its decline into illiteracy and ignorance is of equal interest. Although many factors contributed to the downfall of the Arabic-Islamic world, the fundamental causes revolve around reading. For example, during the early Islamic period, Muslim scholars were open-minded and outward-looking, absorbing and adapting ideas from all over the world in what was a living, vibrant intellectual system. Following the Qur'ānic call to think and reason, an order repeated regularly in the sacred scripture, early Muslims exercised their rights to freedom of thought and expression, and Islamic civilization flourished. However, with the closing of the doors of *ijtihād*, or independent interpretation, in the tenth century, as well as the imposition of official orthodoxies, Islam moved from an open system to a closed one. Early interpretations of Islam were canonized and Islamic law, or *sharī'ah* became stagnant. Rather than looking forward, Muslims started to look backwards, becoming a people of tradition, rather than a people of progress. Muslim educational institutions moved from education to indoctrination, rejecting novel ideas as threats to established systems and wisdom. With Islamic thought frozen in time, Muslims became increasingly unable to deal with modernity and tackle new technology.

If the Muslim mastery of paper-making technology helped Islamic civilization rise to preeminence, its failure to embrace the printing press played a major role in its decline. Invented by Johannes Gutenberg around 1450, the printing press was introduced to the Ottoman Empire during the reign of Sultan Bayazid II (1481–1512), only to be virtually banned for use by Muslims in 1485. By 1510, more than one thousand printing presses in the western world had produced approximately thirty-five thousand titles, with tens of millions of copies. Using paper and pen to painstakingly reproduce books copy by copy, Muslim scribes simply could not compete with the European printing press. It was not until 1727 that Muslims started to use the printing press. By then, Muslims were three centuries behind the times; their level of literacy had plummeted, and their scholarly production had stagnated. Although the Persian, Mogul, and Ottoman Empires still controlled vast expanses of land, they no longer dominated the world of discoveries. From leaders in literacy, the Muslims had become followers. Soon, they would be subjected to western colonialism and the cultural cataclysm it would bring in its wake.

RECOMMENDED READING

Cooperson, Michael, and Shawkat M. Toorawa. *Arabic Literary Culture: 500–925*. Detroit: Thomson Gale, 2005.

Gibb, Hamilton Alexander Rosskeen, Sir. *Arabic Literature*. 2nd ed. Oxford: Oxford University Press, 1970.

Jones, Alan. *Early Arabic Poetry*. Reading: Ithaca Press, 1992.

Lewis, Bernard. *What Went Wrong? The Clash between Islam and Modernity in the Middle East*. New York: HarperCollins, 2003.

Nicholson, Reynold A. *Studies in Islamic Poetry*. Cambridge: Cambridge UP, 1921.

PRIMARY SOURCES

al-Qur'ān

―――. *The Meaning of the Holy Qur'ān*. Translated by 'Alī, 'Abdullāh Yūsuf. Beltsville, MD: Amana Publications, 1996.

Alf laylah wa laylah. Bayrūt: Dār Ṣadīr, 2003.

―――. *The Arabian Nights*. Translated by Richard Francis Burton. New York: Modern Library, 2001.

Abū Dāwūd, Sulaymān ibn al-Ash'ath al-Sijistānī. *Ṣaḥīḥ Sunan Abū Dāwūd*. Riyyāḍ: Maktab al-Tarbiyyah al-'Arabī li Duwwal al-Khalīj, 1989.

Abū Ṭarab, Ja'far, trans. *Carousing with Gazelles: Homoerotic Songs of Old Baghdad*. New York: iUniverse, 2005.

'Alī ibn Abū Ṭālib, Imām. *Nahj al-balāghah*. Edited by Muḥyī al-Dīn 'Abd al-Ḥamīd. al-Qāhirah: Maṭba'at al-Istiqāmah, n.d.

―――. *Nahj al-balāghah/Peak of Eloquence*. 3rd ed. Translated by Sayed 'Alī Reza. Elmhurst: Tahrike Tarsile, 1984.

Anṣārī al-Harawī, 'Abd Allāh ibn Muhammad. *Munājāt: The Intimate Prayers of Khawājah 'Abd Allāh Anṣārī*. Translated by Lawrence Morris and Rustam Sarfeh. New York: Khanegah and Maktab of Maleknia Naseralishah, 1975.

Arberry, Arthur John. *Arabic Poetry: A Primer for Students*. Cambridge: Cambridge UP, 1965.

―――. *The Seven Odes*. London: G. Allan and Unwin, 1957.

Ash'arī, Abū al-Ḥasan 'Alī ibn Ismā'īl al-. *al-Ibānah*. Bayrūt: Dār al-Nafā'is, 1994.

Bīrūnī, Abū Rayḥān Muḥammad ibn Aḥmad al-. *al-Bīrūnī's Book on Pharmacy and Materia Medica*. Edited by Hakim Muhammad Said. Karachi: Hamdārd National Foundation, 1973.

Bukhārī, Muḥammad ibn Ismā 'īl. *Ṣaḥīḥ al-Bukhārī*. al-Riyyāḍ: Bayt al-Afkār al-Dawliyyah lī al-Nashr, 1998.

Colville, Jim. *Poems of Wine and Revelry: The Khamriyyāt of Abū Nuwās*. London: Kegan Paul, 2005.

Dīnawārī, Abū Ḥanīfah Aḥmad ibn Dā'ūd. *Kitāb al-nabāt*. al-Qāhirah: al-Ma'had al-'Ilmī al-Faransī, 1973.

Farāhidī, Khalīl ibn Aḥmad al-. *Kitāb al-'ayn*. Qum: Dār al-Hijtat, 1985.

Fārābī, Abū Naṣr Muḥammad ibn Muhammad al-. *Kitāb iḥṣā' al-'ulūm*. al-Qāhirah: Maktabat al-Anjitu al-miṣriyyah, 1968.

―――. *al-Madīnah al-fāḍilah*. Bayrut: Maktabat al-Kāthūlīkiyyah, 1959.

Frangieh, Bassam K. *Anthology of Arabic Literature, Culture, and Thought from Pre-Islamic Times to the Present*. New Haven; London: Yale UP, 2004.

Ghazzālī, Abū Ḥāmid al-. *Iḥyā' 'ulūm al-dīn*. Bayrūt: Dār al-Kutub al-'Ilmiyyah, 2001.

―――. *Minhāj al-'ābidīn*. Bayrūt: Dawḥah, 1996.

Hamadhānī, Badi' al-Zamān al-. *al-Maqāmāt*. Bayrūt: Dār al-Āfāq al-Jadīdah, 1982.

Ḥarīrī, Abū Muḥammad al-Qāsim. *al-Maqāmāt*. Bayrūt: Dār Ṣadīr, 1965.

Ḥifnī, Maḥmūd Aḥmad, ed. *Sīrat 'Antarah*. Cairo: al-Dār al-Qawmiyyah, 1960.

Ḥillī, al-Ḥasan ibn Yūsuf ibn 'Alī ibn al-Muṭahhar al-. *al-Bāb al-ḥādī 'ashar: A Treatise on the Principles of Shī'ite Theology, with commentary by Miqdād-i-Faḍil, al-Ḥillī*. Translated by William Mcelwee Miller. London: Royal Asiatic Society, 1958.

―――. *Sharā'i' al-Islām*. Najaf: Maṭba'at al-Ādāb, 1969.

Ibn 'Abd Rabbih, Aḥmad ibn Muḥammad. *'Iqd al-farīd*. Bayrūt: Khayyūṭ, 1967.

―――. *The Unique Necklace*. Translated by Issa J. Boullata. Reading, UK: Garnet Pub., 2006.

Ibn Anas, Mālik. *al-Muwaṭṭa'*. Bayrūt: Dār al-Gharb al-Islāmī, 1999.

Ibn al-'Arabī, Muḥyī al-Dīn. *Fuṣūṣ al-ḥikam*. Ninwā: Maktabat Dār al-Thāqāfah, 1989.

―――. *Futūḥāt al-Makkiyyah*. Bayrūt: Dār Ṣadr, 2004.

―――. *The Wisdom of the Prophets/Fuṣūṣ al-ḥikam*. Translated by Titus Burckhardt, Angela Culme-Seymour. 2nd ed. Ninwā, al-Iraq: Maktabat Dār al-Thaqāfah, 1989.

Ibn Ḥanbal, Aḥmad ibn Muḥammad. *Musnad al-Imām Aḥmad ibn Ḥanbal*. Bayrūt: Mu'assasat al-Risālah, 1993–.

Ibn Ḥazm, 'Alī ibn Aḥmad. *The Ring of the Dove*. Translated by Arthur Arberry. London: Luzac, 1953.

———. *Ṭawq al-ḥamāmah*. Bayrūt: al-Mu'assasah al-'Arabiyyah, 1993.

Ibn Hishām, 'Abd al-Malik. *The Life of Muḥammad: A Translation of Isḥāq's Sīrat rasūl Allāh*. Edited and translated by Albert Guillaume. Lahore: Oxford UP, 1967.

Ibn Isḥāq, Muhammad. *Sīrah al-nabawiyyah*. Bayrūt: Dār al-Kutub al-'Ilmiyyah, 2004.

Ibn Kathīr, Ismā'īl. *Tafsīr al-Qur'ān al-'aẓīm*. Kuwait City: Dār al-Nūr, 1985.

———. *Qiṣaṣ al-anbiyyā'*. Bayrūt: Dar Nubilis, 2005.

Ibn Khaldūn, *al-Muqaddimah*. Tunis: al-Dār al-Tūnisiyyah; al-Dār al-'Arabiyyah lī al-Kitāb, 1984.

———. *The Muqaddimah: An Introduction to History*. Translated by Rosenthal. 3 vols. New York and London: Routledge and K. Paul, 1958.

Ibn Mājah, Abī 'Abd Allāh Muḥammad ibn Yazīd al-Qazwīnī. *Sunan*. Translated by Muhammad Ṭufayl Anṣārī. Lahore: Kazi Publications, 1994.

Ibn Manẓūr, Jamāl al-Dīn Muḥammad ibn Mukarram. *Lisān al-'arab*. Bayrūt: Dār Iḥyā' al-Turāth al-'Arabī, 1988.

Ibn al-Muqaffa', 'Abd Allāh. *Kalīlah wa Dimnah*. Bayrūt: Dār al-Āfāq al-Jadīdah, 1977–78.

Ibn Nadīm. *Fihrist*. Bayrūt: Dār al-Kutub al-'Ilmiyyah, 1996.

Ibn al-Naqīb, Aḥmad ibn Lu'lu. *'Umdat al-sālik wa 'uddat al-nāsik*. Bayrūt: Dār Ibn Ḥazm, 2006.

———. *The Reliance of the Traveler*. Translated by Nūh Ha Mīm Keller. Evanston, IL: Sunna Books, 1994.

Ibn Rushd. *The Incoherence of the Incoherence*. Translated by Simon van den Bergh. London: Luzac, 1954.

Ibn Sīna. *al-Qanūn fī al-ṭibb*. Bayrūt: Dār al-Kutub al-'Ilmiyyah, 1999.

———. *al-Ishārāt wa al-tanbīhāt*. al-Qāhirah: Dār al-Ma'ārif, 1960.

———. *Kitāb al-shifā'*. al-Qāhirah: al-Maṭba'ah al-Amīriyyah, 1952.

———. *Tahāfut al-tahāfut*. al-Qāhirah: Dār al-Ma'ārif, 1964–65.

Ikhwān al-Ṣafā.' *Rasā'il Ikhwān al-Ṣafā'*. Bayrūt: Dār al-Andalus, 1984.

Iṣbahānī, Abū al-Faraj al-. *Kitāb al-aghānī*. al-Qāhirah: al-Hay'ah al-Miṣriyyah, 1992.

al-Jāḥiẓ. *Kitāb al-ḥayawān*. al-Qāhirah: al-Maṭba'ah al-Ḥamīdiyyah al-Miṣriyyah, 1905.

Jawziyyah, Ibn Qayyim al-. *Zād al-Mī'ād*. Bayrūt: Dār al-Kutub al-'Ilmiyyah, 1998.

Jazūlī, Shaykh Muḥammad al-. *Dalā'il al-khayrāt*. Istanbul: Salāḥ Bilici Kitabevi, 1968.

Kindī, al-. *Rasā'il al-Kindī al-falsafiyyah*. al-Qāhirah: Dār al-Fikr al-'Arabī, 1953.

———. *al-Kindī's Metaphysics*. Albany: State University of New York Press, 1974.

Kulaynī, Muḥammad b. Ya'qūb al-. *al-Kāfī*. Karachi: n.p., 1965.

Mas'udī, 'Alī ibn al-Ḥusayn al-. *Murūj al-dhahab wa ma'ādin al-jawhar*. Bayrūt: Manshūrāt al-Lubnāniyyah, 1966–74.

Mufīd, Muhammad ibn Muhammad al-. *al-Irshād*. Ṭahrān: Intishārāt 'Ilmiyyah Islāmiyyah, 1984.

———. *The Book of Guidance into the Lives of the Twelve Imams*. London: Muhammadi Trust, 1981.

———. *Taṣḥīḥ al-i'tiqād*. Bayrūt: Dār al-Kitāb al-Islāmī, 1983.

———. *al-Muqni'ah*. Ṭahrān: Dār al-Ṭibā'ah Muḥammad Taqī al-Tabrīzī, 1857.

Muslim ibn al-Ḥajjāj al-Qushayrī al-Nīsābūrī. *Jāmi' al-ṣaḥīḥ*. al-Riyyāḍ: Bayt al-Afkār al-Dawliyyah lī al-Nashr, 1998.

Nasā'ī, Aḥmad ibn Shu'ayb. *Sunan al-Nasā'ī*. Egypt: Muṣṭafā al-Bābī al-Ḥalabī, 1964–65.

O'Grady, Desmond, trans. *The Golden Odes of Love/al-Mu'allaqāt*. Cairo: American University in Cairo Press, 1997.

Qummī, Muhammad ibn 'Alī Ibn Bābawayhi al-. *A Shi'ite Creed*. Translated by Asaf Fyzee. London: Oxford UP, 1942.

———. *Man lā yaḥḍuruhu al-faqīh*. Ṭahrān: Dar al-Kutub al-Islāmiyyah, 1970.

Rāzī, Abū Bakr Muhammad ibn Zakariyyā al-. *al-Ḥāwī fī al-ṭibb*. Hayderabad al-Dakan: Maṭba'at Majlis Dā'irat al-Ma'ārif al-Uthmāniyyah, 1955.

———. *Man lā yaḥḍuruhu al-ṭabīb*. Bayrūt: Dār al-Kutub al-'Ilmiyyah, 1999.

Ṣādiq, Imām Jaʿfar al-. *Miṣbāh al-sharīʿah wa miftāḥ al-ḥaqīqah*. Bayrūt: Muʿassasat al-ʿIlmī, 1980.

———. *The Lantern of the Path*. Shaftesbury: Element Books/Zahrā Publications, 1989.

Samarqandī, Muhammad ibn Masʿūd al-. *Tafsīr al-ʿAyyāshī*. Bayrūt: Muʾassasat al-Aʿlāmī, 1991.

Shahīd al-Thānī, Shaykh Zayn al-Dīn ibn ʿAlī. *al-Rawḍah al-bahiyyah*. Najaf: n.p., 1966.

Shahrastānī, Abū al-Fatḥ ʿAbd al-Karīm al-. *Kitāb al-milal wa al-niḥal*. al-Qāhirah: Muassasat al-Khanjī: 1903.

Sībawayhi, ʿAmr ibn ʿUthmān. *al-Kitāb*. Bayrūt: Dār al-Kutub al-ʿIlmiyyah, 1999.

Sūyūṭī, Jalāl al-Dīn al-, and Jalāl al-Dīn al-Maḥallī. *Tafsīr Jalalayn*. Bayrūt: Maktabat Lubnān, 2000.

Ṭabarī, Abū Jaʿfar Muḥammad al-. *Jāmiʿ al-bayān fī tafsīr al-Qurʾān*. Bayrūt: Muʾassasat al-Risālah, 1994.

———. *The History of al-Ṭabarī/Tārīkh al-rusul wa al-mulūk*. Albany, NY: SUNY P, 1985–.

Tabarsī, al-Faḍl ibn al-Ḥasan. *Majmaʿ al-bayān fī tafsīr al-Qurʾān*. Qūm: Maktabat Āyāt Allāh al-ʿUẓmā al-Marʿashī al-Najafī, 1983.

Ṭaḥāwī, Aḥmad ibn Muḥammad al-. *al-ʿAqīdah al-Taḥāwiyyah*. Dimashq: Dār al-Maktabī, 1997.

Tirmidhī, Muḥammad ibn ʿĪsā. *al-Jāmiʿ al-ṣaḥīḥ*. al-Qāhirah: Muṣṭafā al-Bābī al-Ḥalabī, 1937–.

Ṭūsī, Muḥammad ibn al-Ḥasan al-. *A Concise Description of Islamic Law and Legal Opinions*. Translated by A. Ezzati. Lahore: Classic, 2004.

———. *al-Istibṣār*. Najaf: Dār al-Kutub al-Islāmiyyah, 1956–57.

———. *al-Khilāf*. Ṭahrān: Maṭbaʿat Rinkīn, 1960–62.

———. *al-Mabsūṭ*. Ṭahrān: al-Maktabah al-Murtaḍawiyyah, 1967 or 1973.

———. *al-Nihāyah*. Bayrūt: Dār al-Kitāb al-ʿArabī, 1970.

———. *al-Tibyān fī tafsīr al-Qurʾān*. Najaf: al-Maṭbaʿah al-ʿilmiyyah, 1957–64.

———. *Tahdhīb al-Aḥkām*. Najaf: Dār al-Kutub al-ʾIslāmiyyah, 1959.

Ṭūsī, Naṣīr al-Dīn al-. *Tajrīd al-iʿtiqād*. al-Iskandariyyah: Dār al-Maʿaārifah al-Jāmiʿiyyah, 1996.

Zahrāwī, Abū al-Qāsim Khalaf ibn al-ʿAbbās al-. *al-Taṣrīf*. Frānkfūrt: Maʿhad Tārīkh al-ʿUlūm al al-ʿArabiyyah wa al-Islāmiyyah fī iṭār Jāmiʿat Frānkfūrt, 1986.

Zayn al-ʿĀbidīn, ʿAlī ibn al-Ḥusayn. *al-Ṣaḥīfah al-Sajjādiyyah/The Psalms of Islām*. Translated by William C. Chittick. London: Muḥammadī Trust of Great Britain of Northern Ireland, 1988.

SECONDARY SOURCES

"Arab Science: Numbers Count." *TWAS* 17:3 (2003).

Amir, Syed. "Science and the Islamic World." *Dawn* (Jan. 6, 2007).

Falagas, Matthew E., Effie A. Zarkadoulia, and George Samonis. "Arab Science in the Golden Age (750–1258 C.E.) and Today." *FASEB Journal* 20 (2006): 1581–1586.

Hamarneh, Sami K. *Health Sciences in Early Islam*. Edited by Munawar A. Anees. San Antonio: Noor Health Foundation and Zahra Publications, 1983.

Ḥamīdullāh, Muhammad. *Introduction to Islam*. Paris: Centre Culturel Islamique, 1969.

Kamal, Hassan. *Encyclopedia of Islamic Medicine*. Cairo: General Egyptian Book Organization, 1975.

López-Baralt, Luce. *San Juan de la Cruz y el Islam*. Mexico: Colegio de México, 1985.

———. *Huellas del Islam en la literatura española: de Juan Ruiz a Juan Goytisolo*. Madrid: Hiperión, 1985.

Menoscal, María Rosa. *The Arabic Role in Medieval Literary History: A Forgotten Heritage*. Philadephia: U of Pennsylvania Press, 1987.

Morrow, John A., Castleton, Barbara, and Vittor, Luis Alberto. *Arabic, Islam, and the Allah Lexicon: How Language Shapes our Conception of God*. Lewiston: Edwin Mellen Press, 2006.

Naṣr, Seyyed Hossein. *An Introduction to Islamic Cosmological Doctrines: Conceptions of nature and methods used for its study by the Ikhwān al-Ṣafā, al-Bīrūnī, and Ibn Sīnā.* Albany: University of New York Press, 1993.

Nykl. Alois Richard. *Hispano-Arabic Poetry and its Relation with the Old Provencal Troubadours.* Baltimore: J. H. Furst, 1970.

Prince, C. "The Historical Context of Arabic Translation, Learning, and The Libraries of Medieval Andalusia." *Library History* 18 (July 2002): 73–87.

Vittor, Luis Alberto. *Shi'ite Islam: Orthodoxy or Heterodoxy.* Translated and edited by John A. Morrow. Qum: Ansariyan Publications, 2006.

CHAPTER 25

The Ottoman Empire

Özgen Felek

TIMELINE

1299	Foundation of the Ottoman state
1453	Conquest of Constantinople (Istanbul) by Sultan Mehmet II, the Conqueror
1520–66	Reign of Sultan Süleyman I, Süleyman the Magnificent
1683	First major defeat of the empire at the siege of Vienna
1699	Treaty of Karlowitz, the first time that the Ottomans were decisively defeated and forced to sign a peace treaty as the clear losers.
1726	The first Ottoman printer was established by İbrahim Efendi, the *Müteferrika*
1831	*Calendar of Events* (Takvim-i Vekayi), the first official Turkish newspaper, was published by the administration, upon the command of the Sultan, Mahmud II.
1839	Announcement of the Declaration of the Reform (*Tanzimat Fermanı* or *Gülhane Hatt-ı Hümayunu*)
1856	Rescript of Reform (*Islahat Fermanı*)
1876	First written constitution was adopted and immediately suspended
1908	Restitution of the 1876 constitution
1914–18	The empire entered World War I in alliance with Germany
1923	End of the Ottoman Empire and the proclamation of the Turkish Republic by Atatürk

AUTHOR'S NOTE

Despite the existence of intense analysis and studies of the reading material from the late period of the Ottoman Empire, there is almost no detailed study on the readers of these texts. We have a great deal of first-hand material, such as letters and memoirs, from the writers and poets of the time who informed us about their own reading culture; yet these only tell us about what those "who wrote"

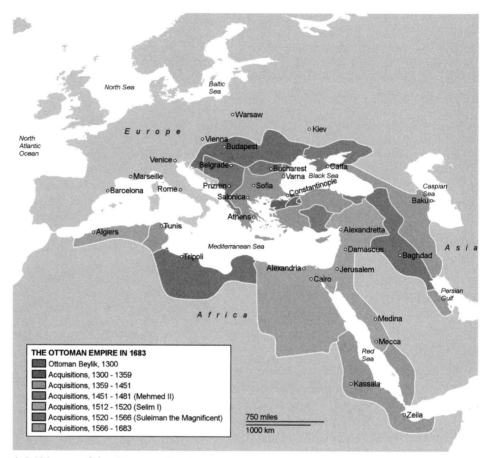

The following labels appear on the map:

North Sea

Baltic Sea

North Atlantic Ocean

Europe

○Warsaw

○Kiev

○Vienna
○Budapest

Venice○

Belgrade○
○Bucharest   ○Caffa
○Varna *Black Sea*

○Marseille

Prizren○   ○Sofia
○Constantinople

○Barcelona   Rome○
Salonica○

Caspian Sea
Baku○

Athens○

○Alexandretta

Asia

○Algiers   ○Tunis

Mediterranean Sea

○Damascus   ○Baghdad

○Tripoli

Alexandria○   ○Jerusalem
○Cairo

Persian Gulf

Africa

○Medina

○Mecca

Red Sea

○Kassala

THE OTTOMAN EMPIRE IN 1683
▨ Ottoman Beylik, 1300
▨ Acquisitions, 1300 - 1359
▨ Acquisitions, 1359 - 1451
▨ Acquisitions, 1451 - 1481 (Mehmed II)
☐ Acquisitions, 1512 - 1520 (Selim I)
▨ Acquisitions, 1520 - 1566 (Suleiman the Magnificent)
☐ Acquisitions, 1566 - 1683

750 miles
1000 km

○Zeila

A 1683 map of the Ottoman Empire.

read. Thus, although we can have a clear idea which books or journals were popular by looking at their circulation, it is difficult to determine among what type of readers these texts were popular. At this point, I am deeply grateful to Halil Hadi Bulut, a professor of Turkish Literature at Celal Bayar University, for his guidance and helpful suggestions to obtain the literature I required. I also thank Professor Jale Parla at Bilgi University and Professor Gottfried Hagen at the University of Michigan most sincerely for their review and comments on certain issues. The present study mainly looks at the reading culture and tendencies of the Turkish readers in the Ottoman Empire, presenting the most well-known "best sellers" of the late Ottoman Turkish reading culture, after the announcement of the Declaration of the Reform in 1839.

INTRODUCTION TO THE PERIOD

After its first major defeat at the siege of Vienna in 1683, the Ottoman Empire (1299–1923) gradually suffered a series of defeats and began to lose territory. In an effort to overcome these losses, the Ottomans began to view Europe more seriously as an inspiration for technological development and educational reform, and they started a series of renewal movements, which followed the developments of the post-Renaissance, western world. Reşit Paşa, the Grand Vizier, read the *Declaration of the Reform* (*Tanzimat Fermanı* or *Gülhane Hatt-ı Hümayunu*) aloud at Gülhane Park in 1839, which sparked a major turning point in the history of the Ottoman Empire. Because the sultan had signed the Declaration, this document represented the sultan's willing abnegation of some of his legislative and judicial rights. Since then, *Tanzimat* has become the term for the period between 1839 and 1876, although it is often extended to include earlier or later periods in which the empire sought cultural and social solutions for its unsuccessful military campaigns.

The proclamation of the Reform Decree was followed by several economic, cultural, educational, and military reforms aimed at establishing social and political innovation in the beginning of this westernization process. During this reformation period, Turkish literature witnessed a variety of literary movements that paralleled the region's political and social changes. This process rapidly began to influence the literary field, and the Tanzimat period gave birth to a new kind of intellectuals who distanced themselves from tradition.

The center for the transmission of knowledge was moved from the traditional school system, the *medrese*, which had been the center of the education for the Ottoman intellectuals from the fifteenth century on, to the book stores in Pera (Beyoğlu). These book stores provided foreign journals, magazines, and books to the offices of journals, publishing houses, and the Translation Bureau, where many of the leading intellectuals of Ottoman intelligentsia of the late Ottoman Empire were "trained." More importantly, London and Paris—"the land of the infidels"—against whom the Ottomans had fought for several centuries became the most significant centers for the transmission of knowledge. Unlike the earlier Ottoman intellectuals, who were the classical medrese products, well-equipped with Arabic, Persian, and Islamic sciences and under the influence of Islamic thinkers, the new intelligentsia studied western languages, particularly French, and read western thinkers.

These changes and innovations introduced the Ottoman intellectuals to a different predicament between the West and the East. Facing the powerful cultural and social structure of the West, they began questioning the problems of the Ottoman Empire, looking at everything that made them "the Ottoman," such as culture, language, literature, and religion, and compared themselves to the western world. They suggested eliminating the "chains" that they believed restricted the state and society. These post-Tanzimat intelligentsia not only engaged in literary, political, and cultural debates through magazines, newspapers, and books, but also, as Mardin states, "made use of the media of mass communication to voice extremely articulate criticism of the government" (Mardin, 4). On the other hand, despite the European influences on their political writings, their theories still had partly Islamic origins (Mardin, 404). Thus Islam, as in the past, created a new dilemma for some of the Ottoman intellectuals. Whereas the earlier intellectuals had to reconcile their Turko-Mongol heritages with Islam,[1] the new intellectuals had to reconcile Islam with the Christian West. However, the traditional intellectuals severely criticized the western-oriented intellectuals and emphasized the importance of returning to Islamic roots. This dualism not only increased the number of the western-minded intellectuals, but also strengthened Islamism; consequently, Islamic research institutions were established, such as Encümen-i Daniş (1851). Furthermore, these institutions went on to publish some of the most significant Islamic works of the modern era.

READING TRENDS AND PRACTICES BEFORE AND AFTER THE DECLARATION OF REFORM

After being conquered by Mehmet II (r. 1451–1481) in 1453, Istanbul developed into the Ottoman capital: the center of the empire and the Islamic center of literature, visual art, and music. And both during and after the reign of Sultan Süleyman I (known as Süleyman the Magnificent, r. 1520–1566), the city became the center of the Islamic civilization and embraced the great libraries and book collections that belonged to the sultan and other interested individuals. Though the written materials in these collections were not available to the public, readers could find what they needed in bookshops.

Outside of Istanbul, in addition to libraries in large towns, Sufi lodges also catered to the readers that attended them. The books listed in these collections were mostly the copies of the Qur'an, the holy book of Islam, which served as the initiation to reading for Muslim readers. Other texts included the Hadith collections, the sayings of the Prophet Muhammad; *tajweds* treaties that helped readers to learn the correct pronunciation of the Qur'an; Arabic and Persian grammar books; the *Risalas*, instructional manuals that provided information about a specific Sufi path or the spiritual journey to God (*seyr ü süluk*); and Islamic law books. In addition to these mainly educational texts, hagiographical narratives relating the biographies and the saintly miracles of Sufis were available, as well as the works of the preeminent poets of Ottoman and Persian poetry. Prominent Sufi figures, such as Rumi and Ibn Arabi, and the great Muslim theologian, Gazali, were also highly respected by the Muslim Turks in the Ottoman Empire. Rumi's *Mathnawi* and Ibn Arabi's *Futuhat-i Makkiyya* and *Fususu'-l Hikam* were among the most widely known texts. These materials provided information, anecdotes, and stories to be transmitted orally to a group or audience of listeners.

Oral stories from the Muslim tradition were also quite popular among Turkish audiences. Of these, the most well-known were the comic anecdotes of Nasreddin Hoca and İncili Çavuş; the epic of Köroğlu (son of the blind man); the heroic narratives of Ali (nephew, lieutenant, and son-in-law of the prophet Muhammad), famous for his bravery; and the romances of famous lovers and beloveds such as Kerem and Aslı, Aşık Tahir and Zühre, Leyla and Mecnun, and Şirin and Ferhad. People would come together in private houses or coffee houses to listen to the stories recounted or read aloud from books, some of which were divided into one-night reading chapters. Sometimes these books would be donated to specific foundations from where they could be borrowed by those who wanted to read them.

The narratives of *Eba Muslim Teberdari*, a heroic Muslim figure from the time of the Amawis and Abbasids, and *Hamzaname*, adventures of the Prophet Muhammad's uncle Hamza, are particularly important, as the original hard copies of these texts, complete with readers' margin notes, have survived to this day. *Eba Muslim Teberdari* is a thirty-volume story of which some volumes were recorded by Mücellit Salih, though the original author of the text is unknown. The notes on the books indicate that they were read aloud by Mehmet Emin Efendi, whose address is recorded at one of the Sufi lodges of the Mawlawiyya order in Istanbul. The other text read aloud to curious gatherings was *Hamzaname*. Although the original text is divided into twenty-four volumes, each book is further divided into fifty-three sections, each to be read in a night. These stories continued to enjoy popularity even after new genres and themes were introduced to Turkish reading culture. For example, the notes on *Hamzaname* state that, just as it was read aloud by Ebubekir Pasha at the start of the century in 1808, the text was still attractive enough to be read aloud in a coffeehouse in 1899, at the end of the century.[2]

Among these texts, the *Shah-nama*, the epic of the great Iranian kings by Firdowsi, deserves special attention, for it maintained its popularity for hundreds of years in the Ottoman territory. The stories from *Shah-nama* were narrated with great enthusiasm not only in the palaces of the sultans, but also in coffeehouses by middle-class men, for whom narrating stories from the *Shah-nama* became a prestigious activity (Köprülü, 362–375).

Although the popularity of these religious texts and "classics" persisted, with the declaration of the *Tanzimat Fermanı*, a new literary era called Tanzimat literature was launched. Tanzimat literature adopted new literary genres such as novels, theatrical plays, and short stories, as well as new themes, similes, and metaphors that were widely used by the authors and poets of the time. The classical themes of Ottoman Divan poetry, including imaginary love stories—both divine and carnal—and longing for the beloved, were replaced with more realistic themes with a social agenda such as education, snobbery, arranged marriages, household relations, slavery, freedom, justice, equality, and nationalism.

The poets and authors of these earlier days of modern Turkish literature are analyzed within two main groups regarding their approaches to literature and the subject matter that they mainly employed in their works. These two groups are commonly recognized as "the first period writers of Tanzimat," and "the second period writers of Tanzimat." The first period of Tanzimat (1860–1876) witnessed the emergence of many fresh genres and literary forms borrowed from French literature, which was particularly influential at this time, but which still struggled for attention against traditional genres and themes. Şinasi, Namık Kemal, Ziya Paşa, Ahmet Mithat Efendi, Şemsettin Sami, and Ahmet Vefik Paşa, the leading figures of Tanzimat Literature, emerged as active politicians as well as the most influential and active idealist writers of the time. Because their objective was to introduce new concepts to society, they perceived art and literature as means to reach their goals. For these authors and poets, art and literature were understood to be educative and produced for society's sake. Unlike the sophisticated language of classical Ottoman poetry, they preferred a simple, clear language, and favored topics from real life that more closely mirrored the conditions of the country. Of these intellectuals, Şinasi in particular contributed to the purification of the language with his struggle to carry the spoken language to written texts. Ziya Paşa, in his article, "Poetry and Prose" (Şiir ve İnşa), argued in support of folk poetry as the true Turkish poetry, though he later praised Divan poetry in the introduction of his *Harabat* (an anthology of classical Ottoman poetry). These authors and poets not only produced literary works that adopted western genres such as drama, plays, and novels in addition to classical genres, but also employed new themes addressing social and cultural problems as they wrote articles in favor of a language comprehensible to all.

The literary movements during the second half of the Tanzimat period (1876–1896) were mainly shaped by Recaizade Mahmut Ekrem, Abdülhak Hamit Tarhan, Sami Paşazade Sezai, and Nabizade Nazım, all of whom had different understandings of art and literature. Western-style genres were produced more successfully and more originally compared to the work produced during the first period. Because the writers of the second half of the Tanzimat period focused on the inner world rather than social and political issues, individuality came to the forefront. This move was accompanied by a more exclusive and ambiguous language and a passive, introverted, and internalized style. For example, Ottoman readers enjoyed the first psychological novel, *Eylül* (*September*), by Mehmet Rauf, during this period.

The rise in the status of literature and new forms of written communication also led to the publication of the first Ottoman newspapers and magazines, even though *News Paper* (*Ceride-i Havadis*), the first private newspaper (1840), did not receive great attention, and despite funding from the state its publication ceased in 1843. Because the Ottoman Empire consisted of different nations and peoples, newspapers in different languages emerged. Besides Turkish newspapers, the empire also boasted French, Arabic, Greek, Armenian, Hebrew, Bulgarian, Persian, Serbian, Romance, Arumonik, Albanian, Kurdish, Italian, German, and English newspapers. For example, Izmir, a city located in the Aegean province, welcomed several newspapers in Greek, Armenian, Ladino, and Bulgarian in the 1840s, though these newspapers were later moved to Istanbul, which soon became the center of publishing and media. However, because these journals addressed only the specific readerships familiar with their languages, they were not widespread. With the exception of *Calendar of Events*, almost all of these newspapers printed only a few hundreds copies and thus depended on funding from the government to survive.

One of the most important steps in the establishment and spread of journalism in Turkey was the establishment of publishing houses in almost every city. These publishing houses not only published calendars, yearbooks, and religious, literary, and scholarly works, but also "official city newspapers." Most of the essays published in these city newspapers were anonymous. Their subjects included news about laws, appointments, military successes, the speeches and essays of governors, poetry, historical research, and summaries or copies of some essays from Istanbul newspapers. These newspapers were published in Turkish, but some of them were also published in the second common language in the area. Even though their circulation was not high, they were "hung" at specific public locations and were therefore available to any public reader. Some of them were still in print until recently, although most did not last longer than a few years (Varlik, 102).

Almost as popular as the newspapers were the supplements (İlave) to the newspapers. Supplements consisted of one-page publications on different-colored paper in different sizes. As opposed to the weekend supplements of today's newspapers, the supplements of the Ottoman newspapers were published to announce late-breaking news. The first supplement was published during the Crimean War between the Ottomans and Russians (1853–1856) by *News Paper* (*Ceride-i Havadis*), and it sold out very quickly. Especially after 1908, during the Balkan wars (1912–1913), the supplements—thanks to their war news and last-minute Government announcements—became very popular. Supplements were sold by *müvezzi*, or sellers. According to Selim Nüzhet Gerçek, the müvezzis, usually middle-aged men, became fixtures on the streets, selling newspapers, supplements, and the facsimiles of novels at any time of the night or day. When people heard of the voice of the müvezzi,

> Those who were addicts [of the supplements ran] to the windows . . . [and] would dangle small baskets, and müvezzis would take the pennies from the baskets and put in the supplement. Some forgetting to put on their other coral slipper would skip the stairs two by two with one naked foot and without a slipper, hardly finding the street door, and would snatch the supplement from the müvezzi. There were also many who ran after the müvezzi, who left without waiting, although they had called him from the windows and bay windows. . . . The supplement sold very fast during the Balkan Wars. Everyone would stop by the street and would be at each other's throats just to buy a supplement. Those addicts with coifs on their heads, *hayderis* [cardigans] on their backs, in fur [coats], long cardigan or cotton, running on the humid, hazy and snowy nights of the winter months, were countless. (Selim Nüzhet Gerçek, *Türk Matbuatı*, 5)

However, not everyone welcomed the popularity of the supplements. Some daily newspapers published essays, both criticizing the supplements for including sensationalized and unnecessary news in order to sell more and asking the government to ban their publication.

Besides daily newspapers, several magazines were published by and for the elites between 1849 and 1871. In addition, until 1871, numerous magazines on military and medical issues were published addressing only professionals. The success of Ahmet Mithat Efendi's *Store of Knowledge* (*Dağarcık*) in 1872 encouraged the publication of numerous magazines, not only in Turkish, but also in other languages. For example, in 1872, thirty-two magazines were published in Istanbul, yet only three were published in Turkish. Especially after the declaration of the Second Constitutional period (II. Meşrutiyet) in 1908, an increased interest in publication outside of Istanbul, specifically in Anatolia, was noticeable. Over a thousand magazines were published on different subjects: science, art, entertainment, comics, women's issues, family, religion, music, military, and the economy. However, most did not last long, and some only published a few issues.

In addition to these magazines that addressed a broader audience, the first magazines oriented toward women and children were produced as well. One of the earliest women's magazines was *Development of Muslim Women* (*Terakki-i Muhaddarat*), which was published as a weekly edition of *Development* (*Terakki*), a mid-nineteenth-century newspaper. In 1875, *Mirror* (*Ayine*), was published in Thessaloníki (Selanik or Thessalonica/Salonica), not only for women but also for children, and *Time or Educator of Muslim Women* (*Vakit yahut Mürebbi-i Muhadderat*) emerged in Istanbul. These were followed by *Family* (*Aile*), published by Şemsettin Sami in 1880, and *Humanity* (*İnsaniyet*), published by Mahmut Celaleddin in 1882.

As Kurnaz states (1991; 1996) the earliest women's journals focused mainly on topics considered to be the responsibilities of women, such as the education and care of children, morals, marriage, and fashion. Women were perceived to be uneducated and unaware of social problems. Therefore, their education was the magazines' primary objective. With the establishment of the House of Female Teachers (Darü'l-muallimat)—the first school dedicated to female students in order to promote female teachers—a new readers' group of women emerged and a new generation of women's magazines was directed at these learned women. For example, *Şükufezar* (1886), released by a team consisting of only female authors, was aimed at this new generation of readers. Instead of the educational voice of the previous magazines, which indicated a mission to teach women how to be submissive wives and self-sacrificing mothers, *Şükufezar* preached the equality of women and men for the first time. *Journal Only for Women* (*Hanımlara Mahsus Gazete*), published between 1895 and 1908, is another noteworthy magazine whose authors were all preeminent intellectual women of the time.

After the declaration of the Second Constitution in 1908, women's magazines began depicting women who no longer conformed to the traditional Muslim image. *Beauties* (*Mahasin*), *World of Women* (*Kadınlar Dünyası*, 1913), and *Womanhood and the World of Women* (*Kadınlık ve Hanımlar Alemi*, 1914) were some of the women's magazines that emerged during this period. Of them, *World of Women* published photos of women who were members of the Ottoman Society for the Defense of Women's Rights (Osmanlı Müdafaa-i Hukuk u Nisvan Cemiyeti), which attempted to encourage equality between men and women. As the first photos of Muslim women to be published in a journal, *World of Women* is an indication of the social change in the Ottoman society.

Children's literature emerged through a set of didactic works mainly designed to teach social norms and morals. Before the 1880s, only a few texts could be considered children's literature. These included *Hayriyye* and *Lütfiye-i Vehbi*, which contained advice for children in poetic form. In addition, a rich oral collection of nursery rhymes, tales, riddles, and anecdotes served as children's literature. However, the Tanzimat period witnessed the first books written specifically for children. After Kayserili Dr. Rüştü's *Distinguished Children* (*Nuhbetü'l- Etfal*), a primer of translated short stories and fables, the 1859 magazine *Examiner* (*Mümeyyiz*), subtitled "Newspaper for Children," was published in a series of differently colored texts, all of which contained riddles and serialized novels for children.

The earliest children's books were mostly short fables and poems translated from French. Among the first translations were J. J. Rousseau's *Emile*, by Ziya Paşa; Fenelon's *Télémaque* (*Tercüme-i Telemak*) in 1862, by Yusuf Kamil Paşa; Daniel Defoe's *Robinson Crusoe*, by Vakanüvis Ahmet Lütfü (1854); Jonathan Swift's *Gulliver's Travels*, by Mahmut Nedim; and Jules Verne's *A Journey to the Center of the Earth* and *Five Weeks in a Balloon*, by Mehmet Emin. The works of Arnaud Berquin, Joachim Heinrich Campe, and Christoph von Schmid (*vide infra*) were also among the most widely known and read classical works from eighteenth- and nineteenth-century juvenile literature in the Ottoman Empire. Among the translations, the fables of Aesop, a Greek philosopher, gained special interest after their earliest Turkish version appeared in Cyrillc script in 1852. These fables were translated by several authors and translators, such as Ahmed Midhat (1870), Hafiz Refi (1874), and Osman Rasih (1877), under various titles.

Other than these translations, Ahmet Mithat's books *The First Teacher* (*Hace-i Evvel*) and *Lesson from the Tale* (*Kıssadan Hisse*) stand as the two of the earliest books written originally in Turkish exclusively for children in 1871. Meanwhile, Recaizade Ekrem wrote *Contemplation* (*Tefekkür*), and Muallim Naci wrote *The Childhood of Ömer* (*Ömer'in Çocukluğu*). Shortly thereafter, many preeminent Turkish authors, including Ahmet Rasim, Ahmet Mithat, Ziya Gökalp, Ömer Seyfettin, and Tevfik Fikret, began producing original children's books as well as books for adult readers.

The Translation Bureau

As part of the westernization process, the role of translators, especially of the Translation Bureau, cannot be ignored. The Translation Bureau was established in 1832 to train individuals to translate official correspondence, but it turned into a language school wherein the intellectuals of the time could learn French and become acquainted with French literature. Later on, Academia (Encümen-i Daniş) was established (1851) in order to provide translations of important texts from Arabic, Persian, and western languages, as well as original works for the university (Darü'l- Fünun), which were established later on. Although Academia did not last long, within its short lifetime some history, geography, biology, and economics books were translated.

Another genre that emerged after the declaration of Reform (Tanzimat) Decree that deserves special notice was comics. After the first Turkish satirical publication, *Diogenes*, was published in 1870, many other magazines in the same style emerged. However, because the sultan was unhappy with their humorous approach toward the government, the Palace announced that all the comics would be censored. Numerous comics appeared after the 1870s—particularly after the declaration of the Second Constitution (II. Meşrutiyet) in 1908—but with few exceptions, most were published only for a few issues. Some were even shut down after a single issue. Among them, *Pen* (*Kalem*) and *Cem* were the most recognized, and both were partially published in French as well. *Black Kite/Inexperienced Person* (*Çaylak*), another comic book, differed from the others in being directed toward an intellectual reading group. Although these comics were not tolerated by the Ottoman administration of the time, when Sultan Abdülhamid (r. 1876–1909) wanted to add a special article to the Press Law to ban the publication of comics, a heated debate flared among parliamentarians, and the ban was ultimately rejected by Parliament.

The freedom of the press, following the restitution of the Second Constitution, also opened a venue to a sensuous erotic literature. Most of these short novels and stories were written under a penname by the writers who were having difficulty making a living. The weekly serial entitled *Binbir Buse* (*One Thousand One Kisses*) was a striking example of the erotic literature that appeared during this period. These serials and short stories with their limited characters—usually a man and a woman—describe sexual relations experienced in an indoor space. Even though these books and serials were severely criticized and intellectuals warned parents about these dangerous materials, these texts enjoyed popularity for some time until the end of the 1920s (Karakışla; Toprak; Türe; Türkeş).

Among all these different genres, etiquette books also received attention from interested readers. As Nevin Meriç reported, about nine books published on the topic between 1894 and 1927, addressing both men and women, offered tips on the standard European etiquette of the era and aimed to teach western lifestyles and good manners. The books covered a wide range of topics including dress and appearance, how to set the table, how to behave at parties, how to entertain and receive, and how to conduct visits.

According to Nuri Akbayar, between the time that the first printing press appeared in the empire (1729), and the year of the alphabet reform (1928), about thirty thousand books were printed. Of these, 3,534 were translations from western and eastern languages into Turkish. Although different texts on diverse subjects such as religion, science, military and civil history, philosophy, and political science were published, many of the translations were of literary texts. Especially after 1880, the number of translated novels increased enormously ("Tanzimattan Cumhuriyete Çeviri" in *Tanzimattan Cumhuriyete Türkiye Ansiklopedisi*, Vol. 2, 447–451).

The following list was compiled mainly by Nuri Akbayar: The first translation of a work of western literature was the translation of *Les Aventures de Télémaque* (1859) by Yusuf Kamil Paşa, which appeared about twenty years after the declaration of the Reform Decree. *Télémaque* was followed by numerous other translations such as *Les Misérables* (1862), *Robinson Crusoe* (1864), *The Count of Monte Cristo* (1871), *Atala*, which was adapted from Chateaubriand (1872), and *Paul et Virginie* (1873). The novels translated at this time included works not only by widely known authors such as Victor Hugo, Alphonse Daudet, Lamartine, Alfred de Musset, Emile Zola, Guy de Maupassant, Pierre Loti, Alexandre Dumas fils, and George Ohnet, but also by authors such as Pierre Zaccone, Ponson de Térail, Emil Richebourg, Xavier de Montepin, Jules Mary, Pierre de Courcelle, Hector Malot, Paul de Kock, Octave Feuillet, Eugene Sue, Emile Richebourg, and Emile Gaboriau. *Taaşşuk-ı Terze ve Cozeb* (*The Love of Terze and Cozeb*), by Leonardo da Vinci, and Silvio Pellico's *Le mie Prigioni* were translated from the original Italian, while Goethe's *The Sorrows of Young Werther* was the only text translated from German into Turkish. The works of Aesop and Ksenophon from Greek and *Don Quixote* from Spanish were translated as well. As for Russian literature, though a few works by Pushkin, Turgenev, Lermontov, and Maxim Gorky were translated into Turkish, Tolstoy was the most popular Russian writer, with five translated works. Among writers whose works were translated from English were Shakespeare, Byron, and Walter Scott. The first translation of Shakespeare was *Othello*, in 1877, and translations continued with *The Merchant of Venice* (1883) and *Romeo and Juliet* (1884). Apart from Shakespeare's comedies and tragedies, his poetry also began to be translated into Turkish at this time. After 1881, realism and naturalism, and particularly Balzac and Zola, began to receive attention, which continued for a long time.

Among all these authors, the most popular western authors were Jules Verne, whose thirty-nine books were translated into Turkish from 1890 to 1900, and Victor Hugo, whose work mainly influenced the authors designated as "the first period authors" of the Tanzimat period. The translations of Jules Verne became so popular and sold so many copies that it is said that Ahmet İhsan, who first introduced Verne to Turkish readers, was able to buy a printing house. The fact that the first translations of Verne's work were completed upon the order of Sultan Abdülhamid indicates that Verne was read even by the highest level of society.

As for Victor Hugo, he became well-known particularly for his *Les Miserables* after it was translated into Turkish in 1862. Initially, its summary was published in *Calendar of News Paper* (*Ruzname-i Ceride-i Havadis*). This was followed by a detailed summary of the novel published from October 8, 1862 to November 8, 1862 under the title *The Story of Miserables* (*Mağdurin Hikayesi*). Hugo had such a following that news about his death and funeral were provided in detail by the Turkish newspapers. After his death, two eulogies were written for him; this was the first time that a foreign author had inspired a Turkish eulogy. The biographical work on Hugo prepared by Beşir Fuat became the first scholarly biographical work. Even though interest in Hugo's poetry decreased over time, his novels and dramas continued to attract many Turkish translators (Kerman, 26–32).

After the first translation of *Les Drames de Paris* (*Paris Faciaları*) by Ponson du Terrail in 1881, interest in detective and adventure novels began to rise; subsequently, numerous mystery novels were translated, mostly from French, between 1881 and 1908. Üyepazarcı states that the preferred novelists were Paul de Cock, Eugene Sue, Hector Malot, Emile Gabrieux, Emile Richbourg, Jules Mary, Pierre Zacon, Xavier de Montepin, and Michelle Zevaco. From 1908 to 1928, the works of the founders of detective novels, such as Arthur Conan Doyle, Maurice Leblanc, Gaston Leroux, and Marcel Allain-Pierre Souvestre, and dime novels that were published periodically, gained popularity among interested readers. Among the dime novels were even fake series of Sherlock Holmes and Arséne Lupin, in addition to the adventures of Nick Carter, Nick Vinter, Ethel King, Pick Vick, and Nat Pinkerton.

Among numerous readers of these mystery novels, the special interest of the sultan, Abdülhamid II, in detective novels is noteworthy. According to Üyepazarcı, the sultan established a translation bureau at the palace not only to translate news and articles from the western media, but also detective novels just for himself. Among his favorites was Carmen Silva, whose entire body of work was translated for the sultan. The sultan's focus on these types of novels was exploited by Yervant Odyan, an Armenian writer, in his 832 page detective novel *Abdülhamid and Sherlock Holmes*, which expressed his own personal hatred toward the sultan. Besides these translations, authors Ahmet Mithat Efendi and Fazlı Necip wrote original Turkish detective novels as well (Üyepazarcı, 67–71).

NEWSPAPERS, MAGAZINES, AND JOURNALS

Among numerous newspapers, magazines, and journals published after the declaration of the Reform Decree, *Calendar of Events* (*Takvim-i Vekayi*) is recognized as the first official Turkish newspaper published in 1831 by the administration, upon the command of the sultan, Mahmud II (r. 1808–1839). It provided news about administrative and governmental decisions not only to Ottoman civil servants, but also to businessmen and embassies. *Calendar of Events* also introduced the books published by the State to the people. *Calendar of Events* is also famous for its critique of Ottoman military defeats. Moreover, the military and political conflicts and arguments between Mehmet Ali Paşa, the governor of Egypt, and the sultan were conveyed through the newspapers *Calendar of Events* and *Events of Egypt*, the first Turkish-Arabic newspaper published by Mehmet Ali Paşa.

The emergence of *Interpreter of Conditions* (*Tercüman-ı Ahval*) in 1860, another noteworthy newspaper of the time, was a significant step for Turkish and Ottoman journalism. *Interpreter of Conditions* (1860–1886), which appeared as a rival to *News Paper* (*Ceride-i Havadis*), the first private newspaper that provided articles mainly on the economy and politics, was the first intellectual and literary newspaper published by the dominant nation of the Ottoman Empire. Agah Efendi (1832–1885), the owner of *Interpreter of Conditions* and also a journalist and translator by profession, began publication on October 22, 1860, quite late after the declaration of the Reform Decree (Tanzimat). The first twenty-five issues were published only on Sundays until April 22, 1861, at which point the paper was published three times a week. Later, and in order to compete with *News Paper*, its publication was increased to five issues a week. It was published by a printing house at Bahçekapı, in Istanbul, and was sold in a tobacco shop located under the printing house.

The functions and objectives of *Interpreter of Conditions* are clearly explained by İbrahim Şinasi Efendi, who led the western movement in nineteenth-century Ottoman literature and presented his progressive ideas on the adoption of western style in Turkey's first privately owned newspaper. Şinasi was also the first editorial writer in Turkey, as shown in the introductory article in the first issue. His introductory essay is widely accepted as a groundbreaking article in Turkish literature. In the article, he raised the issue of voice in the emerging newspaper format and asked if a newspaper should be written in clear colloquial language, which could be easily understood by the people, as opposed to elevated, academic language that would appeal to the nation's intelligentsia. Right from the very first issue, he stated that the newspaper was to be "a means through which people can explain their thoughts" (*Interpreter of Conditions*, Oct. 22, 1860). A newspaper should not only convey national and international events, but should also provide useful information for everyday life.

> According to newspaper legend, Sultan Mahmud II admonished the chief editor of *Calendar of Events* for using language that was not clear and understandable to a general readership. The fact that, besides Turkish, *Calendar of Events* was published in Arabic, Armenian, Persian, French, Greek, and Bulgarian indicates the newspaper's aim to reach different people and minorities of the empire.

The articles of the other western-oriented intellectuals of the time, Ahmed Vefik Paşa, Ziya Paşa, and Refik Bey, all of whom sought to better understand the reasons for the defeat and predicaments of the empire, were also published in *Interpreter of Conditions*. Besides these serious, intellectual articles, *Interpreter of Conditions* published *The Marriage of the Poet*, the first original Turkish drama, by Şinasi, bringing a fresh change to the newspaper's publication policy in 1860.

In May of 1861, the government ordered *Interpreter of Conditions* to cease its publication for two weeks, due to an article (assumed to have been) penned by Ziya Paşa, which criticized the government's approach to education. This was the first time that a newspaper's publication was halted by the government, though the paper resumed publication again and ran until March 11, 1866, after 792 issues.

MAGAZINES AND JOURNALS: SCIENTIFIC MAGAZINES

The Medical Events (Vakayi-i Tıbbiye, 1849) was the first periodical and the first Turkish medical review ever printed in Turkey. It published articles on pediatrics and gynecology. The magazine was founded on the principles of the Ottoman Association of Medicine and played an important role in education at the Imperial Medical School. The authors of the essays in the magazine were anonymous and directly addressed scholars in medical schools. It was a quite small magazine of only two to four pages (Varlık, Tanzimat ve Meşrutiyet Dergileri, 112–115).

The Magazine of Sciences (Mecmua-i Fünun, 1861) was the second magazine of the empire that contained articles on the various branches of the sciences, such as geology, biology, economy, pedagogy, and philosophy. It was published by the Society of Ottoman Science (Cemiyet-i İlmiye-i Osmaniye). In order to be a member of the Society of Ottoman Science, one had to know at least three languages—Turkish, one eastern language and one western language—to be able to translate articles and essays into Ottoman Turkish. Because the magazine addressed a broad audience from a cross-section of society, and youth in particular, it published articles and essays that were clear enough for everyone (Akünal, 117–118).

POLITICAL MAGAZINES

The Progress of Women (Terakki-i Muhaddarat) was a weekly addition to the newspaper Progress (Terakki, 1869). Although the education of women appeared to be the primary subject of the early magazines, The Progress of Women distinguished itself by being a forerunner of early feminist discourse due to its radical discussions on education and the relations and problems of family. It also conveyed news about how women's movements developed in Europe, America, and Russia, introducing western women authors to Turkish women readers for the first time.

The first humorous periodical review of the Ottoman Empire, Diogenes (Diyojen) was published by Teodor Kasap (1835–1905), a playwright and journalist, between 1870 and 1873. It was published first in Armenian, Greek, and French, and then finally in Turkish. The magazine was named after the philosopher Diogenes. A picture of Diogenes, sitting on a barrel with Alexander the Great standing across from him, with the caption: "Just get out of my sun!" illustrates the humorous tone of the magazine.

Ali Bey, the playwright for the Gedik Paşa Theater, Namık Kemal, and Ebuzziya Tevfik, the leading intellectuals of the time, were the regular writers of this review, though the articles were published anonymously. Besides the translations of Alexandre Dumas' The Count of Monte Cristo and Voltaire's Microméga, Namık Kemal's The Eulogy for Cat (Hırre-name), which addressed the grand vizier Mahmud Nedim Paşa, was published in Diogenes as well. Diogenes attracted many readers who anticipated each issue of the magazine with great enthusiasm, and it became more influential than the political magazines and newspapers of the time. Interest in Diogenes greatly increased, especially after the addition of cartoons. However, because it was criticizing problems, conflicts, and defects within the society, Diogenes was closed by the government (Çapanoğlu, 12).

After Diogenes ceased publication, the owner, Teodor Kasap, published other humorous magazines such as Rattle Tatar (Çıngıraklı Tatar) and Imagination (Hayal) in 1871. Kasap was jailed for three years for a cartoon published in Imagination of a man whose hands and feet were chained. The caption read, "The

Press is free within the limits of law" (Çapanoğlu, 12). However, *Rattle Tatar* and *Imagination* did not receive the same interest as *Diogenes* and did not last long.

LITERARY MAGAZINES

Scientific Wealth (*Servet-i Fünun*) began publication in 1891. Specializing in science articles, it covered different topics from fashion, travel notes, literature, and health issues. Around the end of 1895, when Tevfik Fikret became its literary editor, the journal changed direction and became a literary and arts magazine. *Scientific Wealth* was eventually turned into an exclusive publication of literary articles after the intellectual names of the time, including Halit Ziya, Mehmet Rauf, Hüseyin Cahit, and Cenap Şehabettin, joined the magazine as authors. The generation called "Servet-i Fünuncu" or "Edebiyat-i Cedideciler," which witnessed the second period of the Reform Decree, gathered around the magazine and created a new literary era named after it. Although they preferred a heavy language, full of metaphors and similes, and used the classical metric system of "aruz" in poetry, the genres, the topics, and the essence they used appeared to be western. Unlike the Tanzimat authors and poets, whose art was intended to connect with social issues, the Servet-i Fünun period authors and poets produced their work for the sake of art with a depressing, pessimistic, and introverted approach to life. They produced numerous poems, novels, short stories, dramas and plays, literary critiques, and memoirs. In novels, small details and analysis became important. The first examples of short stories took shape during this time. However, the western influence in *Scientific Wealth* was criticized by poets and authors who still wrote in the traditional style. Ahmet Mithat Efendi, strongly loyal to tradition, criticized the group particularly for the phrases that they made up and the themes that they borrowed from French literature.

> **"Literature and Law"**
>
> The article "Literature and Law," translated from French, was not welcomed by the sultan, Abdülhamid II, and *Scientific Wealth* was closed for six weeks until December 5, 1901. However, despite breaks in its publication, the magazine was published even after the establishment of the Turkish Republic, until 1944.

Journal Only for Children (*Çocuklara Mahsus Gazete*), published by İbnülhaki Mehmed Tahir, who also published *The Special Newspaper for Women*, enjoyed the longest publication of the children's magazines during the Ottoman period (1896–1908). It was one of the two children's magazines that reached the quality of the European magazines at the time. The magazine featured high-quality pictures that were mostly selected from European magazines, wordless picture stories, both national and foreign news, puzzles, riddles, and jokes, It also provided essays on health, literature, and theatre.

CREATIVE TEXTS

Another genre introduced to the Turkish readers was "drama." İbrahim Şinasi's *The Marriage of the Poet* (*Şair Evlenmesi*), as the first original Turkish play, marked the beginning of Turkish drama in the western style. Şinasi tried to combine the traditional and modern elements of drama in *The Marriage of the Poet*. It was written to be staged in the palace theatre, originally published serially in *Tercüman-ı*

Ahval (1859), and published as a book later in the same year. Later on, it was republished many times in small book form.

The text is based on the story of marriage of Müştak Bey, who is in love with Kumru Hanım. In the beginning, he believes that he has married Kumru Hanım, but soon realizes that he was cheated by the bride's maid of honor, the bride's family, and the imam of the neighborhood. Instead, the poet has married Sakine Hanım, the older sister. Upon realization, he rejects the marriage. The imam and the bride's maid of honor, Ziba Dudu, call the people to a coffeehouse in the neighborhood to resolve the problem, and the ensuing events turn into a comedy. Despite the criticism that *The Marriage of the Poet* was an old women's story, the play never lost its audience's interest, and it was published again in 1873 for the second time. It was even translated into German by Vambery after the death of Şinasi. Since its first publication, it has been staged several times in Turkey and is considered one of the classic works of City Theaters.

Şinasi (1826–1871) is a preeminent name in Turkish literature because of his attempts to westernize the country through publication of new genres of literature. He introduced several innovations in Turkish literature as the first journalist, the publisher of the first private newspaper, the writer of the first editorial, and one of the most prominent and influential representatives of the renovation period in Turkish literature. His own newspaper, *Description of Thoughts* (*Tasvir-i Efkar*), starting on June 28, 1862, offered what was one of the most progressive and best examples of journalism for those times, through a thorough examination of every social problem. Besides *The Marriage of the Poet*, he also translated French poets Racine, La Fontaine, Gilbert, Fénélon, and Lamartine, wrote several political and literary articles, and published a collection of Ottoman proverbs.

One of the most well-known dramas produced at the time was *The Motherland; or, Silistria* (*Vatan yahut Silistre*) by Namık Kemal (1840–1888), which is a four-scene drama. It is a patriotic play developing around the siege of Silistria in 1854. *The Motherland* is the best-known of the author's seven dramas. Although it is not considered extraordinary on the basis of its technical structure, it is important not only because it is one of the first plays staged in the empire, but also for its themes of liberty and the love of the motherland, which were unusual for the time. Structured mostly in dialogs, neither the plot nor the scenes contain any strong dramatic content. The characters in *The Motherland* are representative heroes who are all willing to die for the sake of the homeland. After the play was performed for the first time, the audience became so excited about Kemal's ideas that they began protesting against the Ottoman sultanate on the streets. The audience's excitement did not diminish, so the government closed the newspaper *Moral* and exiled the author to Magosa in Cyprus, afraid of the power of Kemal's ideas. However, the government's actions could not squelch the play's popularity or the ideas it contained. The play was staged almost six hundred times in Istanbul, İzmir, and Selanik within three years. It was translated into German, French, Serbian, Arabic, and Russian. Public interest in the play went on to encourage enthusiasm for theatre and playwriting.

Namık Kemal is known as the "freedom poet" because of his emphasis on freedom and the motherland. However, with other Young Ottomans, Namık Kemal had to flee to Europe and spent some time in London, Paris, and Vienna, where he continued his writings and translations until he returned to Istanbul in 1871. He was one of the most influential prose writers and poets of the time. He has been praised as one of the most prolific writers of the era, and his numerous works include articles on literature and politics, novels, dramas, and poetry. Among his several works are *Awakening; or, Ali Bey's Experiences* (*İntibah yahut Ali Bey'in*

Sergüzeşti, 1874), *Cezmi, the Dream* (*Rüya*), *Introduction of Celal* (1888), and *Destruction of Ruins* (*Tahrib-i Harabat*, 1886). He was also a very active journalist. In 1865, he became the editor of *Description of Thoughts* (*Tasvir-i Efkar*), owned by Şinasi. He also published the newspapers *Fink*—or *Informer*—(*Muhbir*) in Paris in 1867; *Liberty* (*Hürriyet*), with Ziya Paşa in London in 1868; and *Moral* (*İbret*) in Istanbul in 1872. In addition to these newspapers, his articles were published by several other newspapers of the time.

Zoraki Tabip (*Le Médecin Malgré Lui*—in English, *The Doctor in Spite of Himself*) is the translation and adaptation of Molière's *Le Médecin Malgré Lui* by Vefik Ahmet Paşa in Turkish. Jean-Baptiste Poquelin, known as Molière, (1622–1673) was a popular French playwright, many of whose thirty-four plays were translated or adapted in Turkish between 1859 and 1928. The majority of his plays were translated by Ahmet Vefik Paşa.

Zoraki Tabip (*Le Médecin Malgré Lui*) was staged for nine months of the year, with a three-month break. The story centers around İvaz and his wife Selime. İvaz makes his living by working as a woodcutter; yet he spends the money for his own pleasures. His wife, Selime, who works hard to make living, is not happy with his behavior, and thus they fight all the time. Eventually, after a particular fight, Selime decides to take revenge. Another character, Hamza Ağa, is looking for a physician for his daughter, Nurdil, who is ill. In order to get revenge on İvaz, Selime introduces İvaz as a disguised physician to Hamza Ağa's men, and they force him to go with them to their patron's house. When İvaz discovers that the cause of the daughter's illness is her upcoming forced marriage, he helps her flee with her true love, Daniş, but he is arrested for helping them. At the end, İvaz is released thanks to his wife Selime and Daniş. Meanwhile, because Daniş receives a big inheritance when his uncle dies, Hamza Ağa allows her daughter, Nurdil, to marry him.

Ahmet Vefik Paşa (1823–1891) was a Turkish statesman and man of letters. In addition to his translations of plays and fictions from French, English, German, Italian, Greek, Persian, and Arabic, he also penned historical and geographical manuals such as *Şecere-i Türki* (*the Genealogy of Turks*), *Fezleke-i Tarih-i Osmani* (*Ottoman History*, 1869), and dictionaries, such as *Lehçe-i Osmani* (Ottoman Dialect, 1876 and 1888) and *Atalar Sözü-Türki Durub-ı Emsal* (*the Dictionaries of Turkish Proverbs*). He is best known for his numerous translations and adaptations from Molière. His most famous adaptations from Molière are *Zor Nikahı*, from *Le Mariage Forcé*, and *Zoraki Tabip*, from *Le Médecin Malgré Lui*. He not only translated and adapted the work of

---

Ahmet Mithat Efendi

Ahmet Mithat Efendi (1844–1912) was a prolific writer of short stories, novels, and dramas, as well as memoirs, travel accounts, history, and critiques. He is celebrated as an author who taught the people of his time "to read novels" (Tanpınar, *XIX. Asır Türk Edebiyatı Tarihi*, 449). His style combined traditional storytelling with the western novel genre, and he targeted middle-class readers. Popular belief has it that, during the period when his novels were published serially in newspapers, his readers would stop him when they encountered him to ask about the rest of the story that they read on that day.

He is reported to have written 226 works, of which 208 were published. He also had articles published in several magazines and newspapers of the time. Ahmet Mithat Efendi explained that his writings were designed to enlighten people and to present their problems. Thus he occasionally provided encyclopedic information in his novels. A novel, for him, needed to be educational as well as entertaining. His novels are filled with adventure, science, travel, history, mystery, realism, and naturalism.

Molière, but also helped theatre companies to perform his translations and adaptations.

In addition to news and commentary publications, novels and short stories were also produced and translated during this era. Despite the concerns aired by noted intellectuals, such as Tevfik Fikret, and novelists, such as Mehmet Celal and Halit Ziya, about the promotion of "immorality," (Andı, 41–42) novels seem to have been avidly read by Turkish readers, especially young women. Among numerous creative texts, the translation of Alexandre Dumas' novel, *Le Comte de Monte-Cristo* (*The Count of Monte Cristo*), enjoyed a lengthy popularity among Ottoman readers. In fact, Alexandre Dumas (1802–1870) was one of the most popular French writers in the nineteenth century for Ottoman readers. Besides *Monte Cristo*, Dumas' *Anton, Queen Margot, the Queen's Necklace, Amaury*, and *One Thousand and One Ghosts* were among the numerous works translated into Turkish. *Le Comte de Monte-Cristo* was translated into Turkish by Teodor Kasap (1871). It first appeared as a serial in *Diogenes*, a popular humor magazine owned by Teodor Kasap; however, due to the intense interest of readers and curiosity about the end of the story, it was also published as a four-volume book. It was read "during the long winter nights by grandmothers and grandfathers for weeks and months" (Sevük, *Avrupa Edebiyatı ve Biz*, 237). As a result of the novel's popularity, Ahmet Mithat Efendi, the well-known journalist and novelist of the time, wrote his *Hasan Mellah*, taking *Monte Cristo* as a model.

Felatun Bey and Rakım Efendi (*Felatun Bey ve Rakım Efendi*, 1875) by Ahmet Mithat Efendi is a novel based on the two eponymous heroes who represent "ideal" and "wrong-headed" adoptions of westernization, respectively. Rakım Efendi is what he appears to be on the surface. In fact, his name, "Rakım," means "the one who writes." In his small, simple world with his limited budget, he lives happily without any philosophical or social problems. He never does anything wrong because he is always very careful. Rakım Efendi, like a machine, can work for hours without getting tired. He tutors young European girls who fall in love with him; but he marries a concubine to make his nanny happy. However, despite his self-discipline, he has an affair with a French woman. Felatun Bey, on the contrary, is the symbol of a disordered life. He is a funny character who has an affair with the cook of the house. He also does not know how to control his budget and loses money on gambling or spending on beautiful women.

Among the novels that emerged in the beginning of the nineteenth century, *The Story of a Lily* (*Bir Zanbağın Hikayesi*) is particularly interesting due to the reader attention that it received at the time. It was a pornographic novel by the novelist Mehmet Rauf (1910). The book was published twice. In each publication, the author's name and the publisher's name were not indicated. Although the book was described as "embellished with nine pictures, a merry and coquettish little story," it contains no pictures. The book is prefaced by a short introduction in which Mehmet Rauf argues that, even though this type of work is necessary, talk about it should be avoided due to considerations of honor and morality. He supports his argument with examples, such as the statement that he was the first to talk openly about pornographic fiction, which indicates that *The Story of a Lily* was the first publication of this type.

The Story of a Lily is the story of an unnamed hero. He lives with a young woman named Zanbak (Lily), but he lusts after Zanbak's lesbian friend, Naciye. In the end, Zanbak helps him reach his goal. Some blamed the book for launching "adultery literature," and it was denounced as an immoral book in Turkish publishing history. However, both the content of the book and the reactions of intellectuals to it seem to have increased its popularity, leading to its repeated copying by hand by bookstore owners who even rented it for the night. The book was even described as a text under the pillow of every young man and woman. One of the intellectuals of the time, Tahirul Mevlevi, expressed his unhappiness about the influence of the novel: "having seen the vile acclaim that the immoral Lily received, authors fed their appetite to make money without putting forth effort and hard work" (Törenek, *Hikaye ve Romanlarıyla Mehmet Rauf*, 85).

Due to detailed descriptions of sexual intercourse, the publication of *Lily* was banned, and its hard copies were gathered from the bookstores. Although Mehmet Rauf denied that he was the author for a while, eventually he was forced to confess to writing it. He was jailed and demoted from the army. Subsequently he lost his good reputation and value as an author among the intellectuals of the time and could not get a job as an author in the magazines and newspapers until one of his friends, Huseyin Cahit, allowed him to write in his newspaper, *Tanin*, under the pen name Mehmet Nafiz. But upon seeing the intense demand for his book, Mehmet Rauf (under the nickname "Süleyman") wrote another pornographic novel entitled *The Dish of Cream* (*Kaymak Tabağı*), which was published by an Iranian bookstore owner (Tarım, 35).

An Ottoman garden party, with poet, guest, and wine-bearer, from the sixteenth-century *Dîvân-ı Bâkî*.

Mehmet Rauf (1875–1931) was one of the representative authors of the Servet-i Fünun (Scientific Wealth) movement. He wrote several dramas, novels, literary criticisms, and poems, as well as producing numerous translations of western literature. Among his works, *September* (*Eylül*), is best known as the first psychological novel in Turkish Literature.

Forbidden Love (*Aşk-ı Memnu*) is considered to be the first true Turkish novel and its author, Halit Ziya Uşaklıgil (1866–1945), is considered to be the first true Turkish novelist. *Forbidden Love* was first serialized in *Servet-i Fünun*, before it was published as a book in 1900. Since then, it has become one of the best-known Turkish novels. The story is based on the interaction of two wealthy families of post-Tanzimat Istanbul. Adnan Bey is a widow with two children in his fifties. He marries Bihter, the young daughter of Firdevs Hanım. Bihter is quite young compared to Adnan Bey, but she sees this marriage as a way to reach her dreams of a luxurious lifestyle. However, their age difference soon creates problems, and a forbidden love starts between Bihter and Behlül, the nephew of Adnan Bey. But Behlül is a playboy, and he does not take this affair seriously. When he decides to

> **The Story of a Lily**
>
> *The Story of a Lily* seems to have attracted the attention of a female audience, as well as a male one. Two of the author's wives were also his readers. His second wife is said to have proposed marriage to him with a letter after having read *Lily*. However, this marriage did not last long. His third wife, a young teacher, was again one of his readers who fell in love with him after reading his works (Tarım, 10–11).

marry Nihal, Adnan Bey's daughter, Bihter tries to prevent this marriage between her lover and her step-daughter. At the end, Bihter ends her life, and Behlül leaves Istanbul.

Halit Ziya Uşaklıgil is one of the preeminent Turkish novelists. His novels vividly describe the social and cultural life and the changing face of the post-Tanzimat Ottoman society. Although he was influenced by Balzac and Paul Bourget in his early years, later he came under the influence of Stendhal, Flaubert, and Dickens. Among his best-known novels are *Nemide* (1889), *Blue and Black* (*Mai ve Siyah*, 1897), and *Broken Lives* (*Kırık Hayatlar*, 1923). In addition to novels, he penned short stories, poetry, dramas, and memoirs. With Tevfik Nevzat, he also published the newspaper *Hizmet* (*Service*) in 1886 and *Ahenk* (*Harmony*) in 1895.

Despite this demonstrated taste for highbrow culture, *Merciless Avni* (*Amanvermez Avni*), the master detective of a series of Turkish weekly dime novels, is still important in the history of Ottoman literary consumption. The series was published between 1913 and 1914, and included ten books, each with sixty-four pages, starting with *The Burned Man* (*Yanmış Adam*) and finishing with *Among the Skeletons* (*İskeletler Arasında*).

Ebussüreyya Sami, the character's creator, insisted that "Merciless Avni," whom he calls "the Sherlock Holmes of the Ottomans," was a real detective who solved crimes in Istanbul. In the beginning of each book, Sami included an affirmation of the series's authenticity that read: "This is a series that talks about incredible murder cases and the ways criminals were caught and arrested which were taken from the diary of Merciless Avni who is highly respected among Turkish Policemen." Despite his moniker, Merciless Avni is a kind and modest man, who has a non-Muslim girlfriend. The adventures of Merciless Avni signaled the start of a successful trend toward Turkish dime novels in the genre. The books demonstrated that the writer knew the police system of the time and was a good reader of detective and mystery novels. As a successful example of the genre, *Merciless Avni* influenced other dime novels such as *Merciless Sabri* (*Amanvermez Sabri*) in 1928, *Crafty Recai* (*Cingöz Recai*) in 1924, and *Merciless Ali* (*Amanvermez Ali*) in 1944.

EDUCATIONAL TEXTS

Along with novels and newspapers, some educational texts also enjoyed great popularity at the time. Of these, *The Translation of Télémaque* (*Tercüme-i Telemak*) was the first work of western fiction translated into Turkish (1859) by Yusuf Kamil Paşa. The translation of *Les Aventures de Télémaque*, by Abbe Fenelon, was circulated widely and was so popular that even the original French edition was published several times (1862, 1863, 1867, and 1869). The work of Fenelon was very popular among the Ottoman intellectuals because of its pedagogical, political, and philosophical insights; and it was also used in schools as a course reader. The book focuses on criticism of arbitrary laws and emphasizes that the rulers had to follow laws and rules as well. Though the characters and places mentioned in the book were not familiar to Turkish readers, and despite their lack of knowledge and curiosity about Greek mythology, the book was received with great interest.

On the other hand, its heavy prose language suggests that the text was addressed to elites rather than average readers. Interestingly, although the later writers were very influenced by western works, it is difficult to say that *Telemak* had the same influence on the authors of those days.

The Teaching of Literature (*Ta'lim-i Edebiyat*, 1882) by Recaizade Mahmud Ekrem (1847–1914), which was originally written as a course book for political science (mekteb-i mülkiye) students, is a significant text in the reading history of the period, and it received heavy attention in the literary world. It consisted of four main chapters. The first chapter dealt with the rules of understanding all concrete and abstract objects and issues such as thoughts, feelings, the power of imagination, delicacy, the power of memory, and pleasure. In the second chapter, Recaizade focused on the question of style, and the rules that make up a specific style such as fluency and grammar. The third chapter was dedicated to similes. The last chapter focused on the verbal arts. In the introduction, Recaizade states that he used western sources for writing his book, though he does not name these sources. The fact that the examples given in the book are mostly from western authors and Ottoman authors/poets, who used western genres and styles in their work, triggered a major debate at the time. Traditional intellectuals severely criticized the book for its western-oriented examples and blamed Recaizade for ignoring traditional Turkish authors and their works.

After its first publication in 1882, discussions about the book continued for four months. About one hundred and fifty essays and articles were written, although not all of them were about the book itself; instead, some were related to a discussion that developed around the ideas introduced in the book. When the book was republished in 1886, discussion flared again, dividing the literary world into two groups: those who were supporters of traditional literature and rejected the book, and those who were supporters of the new western literature and Recaizade's ideas. The writers and poets who favored the old literature, referring to classical Ottoman literature, gathered at the newspaper *Interpreter of the Truth* (*Tercüman-ı Hakikat*), under the leadership of Muallim Naci (Yetiş, 323–331).

Recaizade Ekrem was one of the representatives of the reformation movement in Turkish literature. As a state official and literature teacher, he joined literary circles with his friends, Namık Kemal

> ### *Les Aventures de Télémaque*
> Though he also wrote poems in prosody, Yusuf Kamil Paşa (1808–1876) is most known for the translation of *Les Aventures de Télémaque*. As a bureaucrat, he served as grand vizier, minister, member of state council, and prime minister.

and Abdülhak Hamid, both prominent writers and poets of the period. Besides the *Teaching of Literature*, he is also well-known for his poem, "Melody of Winter" (Elhan-ı şita), written as a response to another poet's work entitled *Melody* (1886), and his comic novel, *The Love for [the] Automobile* (*Araba Sevdası*), which is generally accepted as the precursor of the Servet-i Fünun novel. In addition to his plays, *The Honest Angélique* (*Afife Anjelik*, 1870) and *Atala* (1872) adapted from Chateaubriand, his poetry collections *Sweet Melody* I–II (*Zemzeme*, 1882–1883) and *Shabby* (*Pejmürde*, 1894), which includes his prose as well, are also well-known.

Another exceptional text among numerous educational works was *Method and Etiquette* (*Usul ve Adab-ı Muaşeret*), a fifty-six-page booklet prepared to introduce good manners and a European life style to the members of the army. It was published by the army in 1909. The book's introduction stated that the book had been prepared for high-level members of the army to prevent possible mistakes and embarrassing situations that might be caused due to the ignorance of the customs and traditions of foreigners at meetings and gatherings. *Method and Etiquette* differed from the other etiquette books of the time with its special sections on official greetings and introductions. The text had ten chapters on cleanliness, official greetings and official introductions, visits, feasts, tea parties, soirees, balls, compulsory visits, military social functions, jokes, and dueling (Meriç, 225–226).

CONCLUSION

During its six-hundred-year reign, the Ottoman Empire developed a rich culture that included the influence of languages, religions and customs from several different nations. The result was a rich tapestry of ideas that contributed to the literary culture of the empire. In this rich culture, though Ottoman Turks spoke in Turkish in their daily lives, Ottoman intellectuals not only read Arabic and Persian texts, but also produced their own work in Arabic and Persian, as well as in Turkish. Despite the fact that the Ottomans produced numerous prose works, it was poetry—mainly built on the topic of divine and carnal love—that was the major art form of the culture of all Ottoman Turks. It is not surprising that, in such a culture, they created an extensive corpus of highly symbolic and ritualized poetry.

From the turn of the nineteenth century on, especially after the Declaration of Tanzimat, the Ottoman intellectuals first became acquainted with the western writers, poets, and thinkers, and then began translating these works into Turkish. This process introduced new genres that had not been familiar to the Ottoman audience. The intellectuals not only translated a great number of literary texts from western languages, mainly from French and English, but also produced original works in these genres that attracted all kinds of Ottoman readers. Newspapers in particular contributed a great deal to the increase of the readership by serializing novels and dramas.

By the end of the nineteenth century, newspapers, magazines, and journals on different topics had a significant effect on the social and cultural life of the Ottomans. Authors produced numerous novels, dramas, short stories, and poetry composed in western poetic forms with worldly topics that more vividly and openly dealt with daily and social life, as well as political and intellectual issues. Although some poets and authors continued to compose poetry in its original classical form, in time they slowly began losing their attractiveness in the eyes of this new generation of readers due to the enormous changes in social and cultural life.

NOTES

1. In this regard, see Cornell Fleischer's *Bureaucrat and Intellectual in the Ottoman Empire: The Historian Mustafa Ali (1541–1600)*, (1986).
2. There are numerous copies of both *Eba Muslim* and *Hamzaname* in Turkish libraries. Information about the popularity of these specific copies can be found in Selim Nüzhet Gerçek's *Türk Matbuatı*, pp. 84–86.

RECOMMENDED READING

Andrews, Walter G. *Poetry's Voice, Society's Song*. Seattle: U. Washington Press, 1984.

Banarlı, Nihat Sami. *Resimli Türk Edebiyatı Tarihi; Destanlar Devrinden Zamanımıza Kadar*. İstanbul: Milli Eğitim Bakanlığı Devlet Kitapları, 1971.

Başlangıcından Günümüze Kadar Büyük Türk Klâsikleri: Tarih, Antoloji, Ansiklopedi. İstanbul: Ötüken-Söğüt, 1985.

Bozdogan, Sibel and Resat Kasaba, eds. *Rethinking Modernity and National Identity in Turkey*. University of Washington Press. 1997.

Evin, Ahmet O. *Origins and the Development of Turkish Novel*. Minneapolis, MN: Bibliotheca Islamica, 1983.

Faroqhi, Surayya. *Subjects of the Sultan Culture and Daily Life in the Ottoman Empire*. London, New York: I. B. Tauris, 2005.

Findley, Carter Vaughn. "An Ottoman Occidentalist in Europe: Ahmed Midhat Meets Madame Gulnar, 1889" *The American Historical Review*. 103.15 (1998). 15–49.

Finn, Robert P. *The Early Turkish Novel*. Istanbul: Isis Press, 1984.

Hanna, Nelly. *In Praise of Books: A Cultural History of Cairo's Middle Class, Sixteenth to the Eighteenth Century*. Syracuse: Syracuse University Press, 2003.

Özege, M. Seyfettin. *Eski Harflerle Basılmış Türkçe Eserler Kataloğu*. Istanbul [s.n.], 1971.

Paker, Saliha. "Turkey." In *Modern Literature in the Near and Middle East 1850–1970*, 17–32. Edited by Robin Ostle. London and New York: Routledge, 1991.

Perin, Cevdet. *Tanzimat Edebiyatında Fransız Tesiri*. İstanbul: Pulhan Matbaası, 1946.

Shaw, Stanford. *History of the Ottoman Empire and Modern Turkey, Volume I: Empire of the Gazis: The Rise and Decline of the Ottoman Empire, 1280–1808*. New York: Cambridge University Press, 1976.

Strauss, Johann. "Who Read What in the Ottoman Empire (19th–20th Centuries)?" *Arabic Middle Eastern Literatures*. 6.1 (2003). 39–65.

Tuncer, Hüseyin. *Arayışlar Devri Türk Edebiyatı*. Bornova, İzmir: Akademi Kitabevi, 1992.

Ülken, Hilmi Ziya. *Türkiye'de Çağdaş Düşünce Tarihi*. Ülken Yayınları, İstanbul: 1979.

PRIMARY SOURCES

Ahmet Mithat Efendi. *Felatun Bey ve Rakım Efendi*. Edited by Tacettin Şimşek. Istanbul: Yurttaş Kitabevi. 1960s. [Available].

Ahmet Vefik Paşa. *Zoraki Tabip; Üç Fasıllık Oyun*. Istanbul: Remzi Kitabevi, 1955 [Available].

Dumas, Alexandre. *Monte Cristo*. Translated by Ayda Duz. Istanbul: Altın Kitaplar Yayınevi, 1970 [Available].

Ebussüreyya Sami. *Osmanlı'nın Sherlock Holmes'u Amanvermez Avni'nin Serüvenleri*. Edited by Erol Üyepazarcı. Istanbul: Merkez Kitaplar, 2006 [Available].

İbrahim Şinasi. *Şair Evlenmesi: Komedi 1 Perde*. Edited by Mustafa Nihat Özön. İstanbul: Remzi Kitabevi, 1966 [Available].

———. Introductory Essay. *Interpreter of Conditions*. Issue 1, October 22, 1860. (*Tercüman-ı Ahval* nr.1, 9 Teşrin-i evvel 1277).

Mehmet Rauf. *Bir Zanbağın Hikayesi*. Istanbul: Matbaa-i Bahriye, 1326/1910. [Available in libraries].

Namık Kemal. *Vatan - yahut - Silistre;* hazırlayan Şemsettin Kutlu. İstanbul: Remzi Kitabevi, 1982 [Available].

Recaizade Mahmud Ekrem. *Ta'lim-i Edebiyat*. İstanbul: Sisçanı Yayınları, 1997 [Available].

Yusuf Kamil Paşa. *Tercüme-yi Telemak* (*The Translation of Télémaque*). Istanbul: Tasvir-i Efkar Gazetehanesi, 1286 [1869] [Available in libraries].

SECONDARY SOURCES

Akbayar, Nuri. "Tanzimattan Cumhuriyete Çeviri." In *Tanzimattan Cumhuriyete Türkiye Ansiklopedisi*, 447–451. Istanbul: İletişim Yayınları, 2 (1985).

Akünal, Dündar. "Ilk Türk Dergisi: Mecmua-i Fünun." In *Tanzimattan Cumhuriyete Türkiye Ansiklopedisi*, 117–118. Istanbul: İletişim Yayınları, 2 (1985).

Andı, M. Fatih. *İnsan Toplum Edebiyat*. İstanbul: Kitabevi, 1995.

Çapanoğlu, Münir Süleyman. *Basın Tarihimizde İlave*. İstanbul: Yeni Doğuş Matbaası, 1960.

———. *Basın Tarihimizde Mizah Dergileri*. İstanbul: Garanti Matbaası, 1970.

———. *İdeal Gazeteci, Efendi Babamız Ahmet Mithat*. İstanbul: Gazeteciler Cemiyeti Yayınları, 1964.

Enginün, İnci. *Türk Edebiyatında Shakespeare Tanzimat Devrinde Tercüme ve Tesiri*. İstanbul: Dergah Yayınları, 1976.

Ercilasun, Bilge. "Türk Edebiyatında Popülerlik Kavramı ve Başlıca Eserler." In *Yeni Türk Edebiyatı Üzerine İncelemeler 1*, 421–449. Ankara: Akçağ, 1997.

Fleischer, Cornell H. *Bureaucrat and Intellectual in the Ottoman Empire the Historian Mustafa Ali (1541–1600)*. Princeton, NJ: Princeton University Press, 1986.

Gerçek, Selim Nüzhet. *Türk Matbuatı*. Edited by Ali Birinci. Kızılay, Ankara: Gezgin Kitabevi, 2002.

Gürbilek, Nurdan. "Erkek Yazar, Kadın Okur." In *Kadınlar Dile Düşünce Edebiyat ve Toplumsal Cinsiyet*, 275–305. Edited by Sibel Irzık and Jale Parla. İstanbul: İletişim, 2004.

Karakışla, Yavuz Selim. "Osmanlı İmparatorluğu'nda Müstehecenlik Tartışmaları ve Bir Zanbağın Hikayesi." In *Tarih ve Toplum*. 208 (2001). 15–29.

Kerman, Zeynep. "1862–1910 Yılları Arasında Türk Edebiyatında Victor Hugo." In *Yeni Türk Edebiyatı İncelemeleri*, 290–341. Ankara: Akçağ Yayınları, 1998.

———. *1862–1910 Yılları Arasında Victor Hugo'dan Türkçeye Yapılan Tercümeler Üzerinde Bir Araştırma*. İstanbul: İstanbul Üniversitesi Edebiyat Fakültesi Türkoloji Bölümü, 1978.

Köprülü, Fuad. *Edebiyat Araştırmaları*. Ankara: Türk Tarih Kurumu Basımevi, 1966.

Kurnaz, Şefika. *Cumhuriyet Öncesinde Türk Kadını, 1839–1923*. Ankara: T. C. Başbakanlık Aile Araştırma Kurumu Başkanlığı, 1991.

———. *II. Meşrutiyet Döneminde Türk Kadını*. İstanbul: M. E. B. [Milli Eğitim Bakanlığı], 1996.

Mardin, Şerif. *The Genesis of Young Ottoman Thought*. Princeton, NJ: Princeton University Press, 1962.

Meriç, Nevin. *Osmanlı'da Gündelik Hayatın Değişimi: Adâb-ı Muâşeret, 1894–1927*. İstanbul: Kaknüs Yayınları, 2000.

Sevük, İsmail Habip. *Avrupa Edebiyatı ve Biz II*. Istanbul: Remzi Kitabevi, 1940.

Tanpınar, Ahmet Hamdi. *XIX, Asır Türk Edebiyatı Tarihi*. İstanbul: İbrahim Horoz Basımevi, 1956.

Tanzimattan Cumhuriyete Türkiye Ansiklopedisi. İstanbul: İletişim Yayınları, 1985.

Tarim, Rahim. *Mehmet Rauf Hayatı, Sanatı, Eserleri*. Ankara: Türkiye İş Bankası Kültür Yayınları, 1998.

Toprak, Zafer. "Meşrutiyet'ten Cumhuriyet'e Müstehcen Avam Edebiyatı." *Tarih ve Toplum*. 208 (2001). 15–29.

Törenek, Mehmet. *Hikaye ve Romanlarıyla Mehmet Rauf*. İstanbul: Kitabevi, 1999.

Türe, Fatma. "Binbir Buse'den 'En Şen En Şuh Hikayeler.'" *Tarih ve Toplum*. 208 (2001). 51–62.

Türkeş, Ömer. "Osmanlı Romanı 'Aşk ve cinsellik Ütopyası'" *Tarih ve Toplum*. 208 (2001). 63–72.

Üyepazarcı, Erol. *Korkmayınız Mr. Sherlock Holmes*. İstanbul: Göçebe Yayınları, 1997.

Varlık, Bülent. "Tanzimat ve Meşrutiyet Dergileri." In *Tanzimattan Cumhuriyete Türkiye Ansiklopedisi*, 112–125. Istanbul: İletişim Yayınları, 1 (1985).

———. "Yerel Basının Öncüsü Vilayet Gazeteleri." In *Tanzimattan Cumhuriyete Türkiye Ansiklopedisi*, 99–102. Istanbul: İletişim Yayınları, 1 (1985).

Yetiş, Kâzım. *Talim-i Edebiyat'ın Retorik ve Edebiyat Nazariyâtı Sahasında Getirdiği Yenilikler*. Ankara: Atatürk Kültür Merkezi, 1996.

CHAPTER 26

The Modern Middle East

Firat Oruc

TIMELINE

1905	Constitutional Revolution in Iran
1908	Constitutional Revolution in Turkey
1913	First National Arab Congress
1914	Ottoman Empire in World War I
1916	The Arab revolt against Ottoman rule
1917	Balfour Declaration promising a Jewish Homeland in Palestine
1919	Egyptian revolt against the British
1921	Beginning of the Pahlavi dynasty in Iran
1923	Proclamation of the Turkish Republic
1924	Abolition of the Caliphate
1925	Syrian revolt against the French
1928	The foundation of Muslim Brotherhood in Egypt
1939–45	World War II
1945	Establishment of the Arab League
1948	Creation of Israel and first Arab-Israel War
1951	Nationalization of Iranian oil
1952	Nasser's Pan-Arab revolution in Egypt
1956	The Suez Crisis
1962	Algerian Independence
1964	Founding of the Palestine Liberation Organization
1967	The Six-Day War
1973	Yom Kippur War
1975	Outbreak of the Lebanese Civil War
1979	Islamic Revolution in Iran
1980–88	Iran-Iraq War
1987	Beginning of the Palestinian *Intifada*
1990	First Gulf War

2001   September 11 attacks
2003   U.S. invasion of Iraq

INTRODUCTION TO THE REGION AND PERIOD

As a geographical location, the modern Middle East broadly refers to the area stretching from Morocco in the west to Afghanistan in the east, and from Anatolia in the north to Sudan in the south. The Middle East thus encompasses west Asia and the southeastern Mediterranean. The sense of regional unity, however, results not so much from common geographic traits as from overlapping histories and interacting cultures. Even though Islam and Arabic are considered to be major historical imprints of this region, in reality the modern Middle East is a complex synthesis of Greco-Roman, Persian, Indian, Central Asian, and African legacies. Furthermore, non-Islamic belief systems such as Christianity and Judaism, as well as non-Arabic languages such as Turkish and Persian, have continued to secure a viable place in the region's cultural landscape.

"Middle East" is a modern coinage that first appeared in the cartographic division of "the Orient" into Near, Middle, and Far as a geopolitical mark of proximity to the British Empire. This also implies the extent to which the inception of modernity in the region (as in many nonwestern territories of the world) was inseparably connected to the encounter with the European military, political, economic, and cultural hegemony. In military terms, the Napoleonic Expedition to Egypt in 1798 gave the clearest sign that the Ottoman Empire, the main political entity of the region at that time, could not resist the encroachment of the European imperialist powers. In economic terms, the Middle East found itself on the periphery of the global economic system—to be exploited for raw materials and also made dependent on importing manufactured goods from Europe. In the nineteenth century, the irreversible weakening of the Ottoman Empire began to be described as "The Eastern Question," which in essence referred to the political restructuring of the region in line with the competing European imperialist interests. The Ottoman Empire tried to delay its disintegration through a series of reforms known as the *Tanzimat*. These reforms gained momentum in the second half of the nineteenth century and were aimed at modernizing and centralizing the state apparatus, the law, and the bureaucracy. But the Ottoman Empire could not survive World War I, and it dissolved into a number of nation-states created as protectorates of the European powers. Under the League of Nations mandate, Egypt, Palestine, and Iraq fell to Britain, and Syria, Lebanon, and Morocco to France. The Modern Middle East thus arose from the collapse of traditional polities and the subsequent spread of colonial dominance.

But both of these factors led to new developments in the region. National self-determination and liberation movements quickly followed. Politicians and intellectuals across the Middle East began to explore ways of achieving full independence for their societies. In the first half of the twentieth century, nationalism became the major ideological source that inspired the Middle Eastern people in claiming their existence in the modern world. With the global weakening of the European colonial hegemony after the devastations of World War II, all the Middle Eastern countries achieved official political independence—a process that continued as late as Algeria's independence from France in 1962.

The most significant aspect of modernity in the Middle East has been secularization. Turkey, with the abolishment of the Caliphate in 1924, became the leading country in abandoning the primacy of the *shariah* (Islamic religious rules) in everyday affairs. Under the impact of secularization, most Middle Eastern nation-states adopted the European legal system, although a few others (such as Saudi Arabia) reinvented religious codes and conducts based on some form of Islamic Puritanism that still rejected historical religious practices and formations. The education system too, went through drastic changes, as a result of which religion lost its centrality. In many other venues as well, secularization became the controlling term by which the modern Middle East gauged its success of transition from tradition to modernity.

Nevertheless, the high hopes of decolonization and national independence in the Middle East suffered a number of setbacks. The powerful elite who were ruling in those countries were not immediately willing to implement popular democracy. Instead, many regimes strictly controlled and monopolized political participation. The exercise of power and authority has therefore frequently been arbitrary. Although some countries, such as Iran, were ruled by monarchical dynasties, others, such as Libya and Iraq, fell under military rule. The second significant setback, particularly for the Arab world, was the creation of Israel in 1948. The failure of the Arab world to reclaim Palestine and to confront its antagonist effectively came as the first post-colonial shock to the political and cultural aspirations of Arab nationalism. No other historical event could match the "fall" of Palestine on the collective consciousness. The third issue was the new geopolitical alignment of the international system under the Cold War. The Middle East, like other parts of the third world, became one of the intense battlegrounds of the worldwide confrontation between the United States and the former USSR. From the 1960s onward, the political gamut was further complicated with the rise of religious fundamentalism, which grew in part out of the disillusionment with the direction the Middle East had taken in modern times. In effect, the modern Middle East could not achieve continuous social and political stability throughout the twentieth century. This volatile situation has lingered into the twenty-first century, with the rise of the second Palestinian *intifada* in 2000, the September 11 attacks in 2001, and the U.S. invasion of Iraq in 2003. All these major historical events and social issues have impacted the textual production and reading culture of the modern Middle East.

READING TRENDS AND PRACTICES

The multilingual and multiethnic composition of this region remained largely intact under tributary empires of the earlier periods. Despite this plurality, however, there was a solid differentiation between "high" culture, which was mediated through manuscripts, and "low" culture, which included orally transmitted forms such as folktales, moral stories, and lay poetry. As a result, the circulation of reading materials has been traditionally limited to minority elites clustered around the royal courts. The production of these manuscripts, moreover, was itself an art form that would typically be commissioned by the nobility only. As an ornamental art, book production lacked a mass market and readership. Even so, the movement of manuscripts from one place to another, their transfer from one owner to another, and even the obsessive struggle to control and obtain them constitutes an interesting part of the cultural history of reading in the "premodern" Middle East. One could find contemporary fictionalized accounts of these earlier forms of book production and circulation in the Turkish novelist Orhan Pamuk's *My Name is Red* (1998), as well as his Lebanese colleague Amin Maalouf's *Balthasar's Odyssey* (2000).

In the nineteenth century, the decisive encounter with post-French Revolution Europe (albeit in the form of colonialism) simultaneously introduced nationalism and print culture to the Middle East. Nationalism developed as a response to both the imperialist ambitions of European powers and the dissolution of *ancien régimes* such as the Ottoman Empire. Nationalist movements made extensive use of print technology in promoting their causes through pamphlets, magazines, and newspapers. These reading materials would often be printed in major European cities such as Paris, London, or Berlin and find their readership through clandestine channels. More importantly, the modern Middle East witnessed an unparalleled interaction between the masses and cultural and artistic production. By the end of World War I, a new political cartography based on nation-states (whether totally independent or not) emerged, and the mass appeal for printed texts became a genuine concern.

A rapid increase in population accompanied the emergence of the nation-states in the modern Middle East. This was largely due to the implementation of welfare and development programs by the new states, as well as improvements in transportation and communication networks. Along with demographic growth, urbanization gained an unprecedented dominance in the region. There were, of course, centuries-old and still-vibrant cities such as Cairo, Istanbul, and Jerusalem. Nevertheless, modern urban infrastructure necessitated an irrevocable change in their traditional organization that was retained well into the twentieth century. Moreover, by the end of the 1940s, the number of people living in the cities for the first time surpassed the rural population. While at the start of the twentieth century most people lived in rural areas, urban and social mobility opportunities led people to move to the cities. The urban transformation had a considerable impact on the formation of a modern readership in the Middle East. Not only were publishing houses and intellectual circles concentrated in big cities, but city-dwellers also became the major book consumers. The urban middle class gradually displaced the aristocratic westernized elite and their privileged salons. Urban centers were also the point of origin of new literary and artistic movements, cultural expressions, and ideological and political orientations. Urban book production and readership therefore attained a central role in the modern Middle East.

Another social factor related to the formation of readership in the modern Middle East was the increase in levels of literacy. At the beginning of the twentieth century, the average rate of literacy was less than fifteen percent. As primary education became mandatory under nation-states, levels of literacy increased. This increase facilitated not only the consolidation of national cultures, but also the expansion and circulation of textual production. Without doubt, school textbooks have enjoyed the deepest impact and the widest audience. This was because, in most Middle Eastern countries, for each school subject, there would be a single "official" textbook approved by the central government. This meant that all students at a given grade read the same piece of literature, the same historical narrative, and so on. The effects of the increase in literacy naturally went beyond the confines of the schoolhouse. Mass literacy also created the conditions for the emergence of mass media. Finally, increased literacy and the advent of mass media meant that book consumption in almost every single genre increased dramatically. The publishing houses in major cities began to print affordable paperbacks in modern and simplified versions of literary Arabic, Turkish, and Persian.

In terms of influence on social and cultural change and appeal to mass readership, the novel and free verse poetry have become the most popular forms of creative writing. Both forms were introduced to the Middle East only in the early twentieth century. Despite their late arrival, their success in articulating contemporary issues secured them a viable space vis-à-vis the traditional types of prose, such as *maqama*, or metered poetry, such as *ghazal*. In fact, most of the earlier genres lost their readership from the twentieth century onward. They did not disappear completely, yet they were no longer in a competitive position with regard to reaching a wide audience. Mainstream readers were looking for texts that addressed the modern moment. They found this mode of representational capability in novels, free verse poems, and dramatic works.

In nonfiction, books promoting a particular "cause" (nationalism, feminism, or Islamism) have been in constant circulation. In particular, they attracted dissident educated youth who aspired to radical change in the social, cultural, and political tenets of their countries. Other nonfiction forms, such as autobiography and travelogue, were already well-known through earlier, classical examples such as Ibn Battuta's *Travels* (c. 1325–1354). But the so-called ideological texts, as well as published statements by political leaders explaining the reason of the state, were completely new phenomena in the cultural reading panorama of the Middle East. Nevertheless, these texts proved to be the most effective in transforming their readers' perceptions and mobilizing them in the interests of a given social goal. Due to their confrontational nature, they have also been surrounded by controversy and overwhelming debates. The readers' responses to these texts were therefore immediate.

The channels between texts and readers, however, have not always operated smoothly in the modern Middle East. Even though the civil space of readership and the new media of expression (in the form of newspapers and periodicals) have expanded to unprecedented levels, censorship, banning, and other forms of control have imposed serious constraints on the text-reader mediation. Monarchies and single-party regimes have not hesitated to remove "dangerous" books from circulation. This was due not simply to their authoritarian mentality, but also to the peculiar fact that in the modern Middle Eastern countries, a novel, poem, or manifesto could have serious destabilizing consequences because of the fragile fault lines in the social and political structure. It was, moreover, not uncommon for a particular part of the society to react furiously to the publication of certain works. The reaction of religious conservatives to feminist texts offers an example of this kind of response. Yet censorship and prohibition have not been permanently successful in controlling textual reception. "Illegal" prints continued to circulate through underground networks. In the case of Arabic-speaking countries, Beirut has become the place of refuge for books whose publication was banned in their country of origin. Before the revolution in 1979, the anti-shah groups in Iran made extensive use of the Shiite centers in Iraq as points for the printing and export of the lectures of Ayatollah Khomeini and others. Despite routine police searches, the Turkish Marxist Nazım Hikmet's poems were kept hidden in college dorms and read by an entire leftist generation in the 1960s and 1970s.

Network power has also been a determining element of the "book wars" in the modern Middle East. Books that were embraced by a certain ideological orientation fared relatively better in reaching a large audience. Sayyid Qutb's *Milestones* (1964) still ranks top in the canon of political Islam. Duygu Asena's *She Has No Name* (*Kadının Adı Yok*, 1987) is considered "the book of initiation" for Turkish feminists. In other words, the texts included here belong to a specific network of readership. This kind of network identification has to do with the fact that, with very few exceptions, neither publishing houses nor bookstores have been run by corporations. As a result, independent publishers and booksellers would typically be not so much profit-oriented as servers of their reader network. Particularly in the smaller cities, bookstores have functioned as a gathering space for like-minded readers. This is such a well-established norm in the Middle East that attacking bookstores has become one of the common symbolic ways of challenging a rival worldview.

CREATIVE TEXTS: NOVELS

Although the first indigenous novel appeared as late as 1872 in Istanbul, novel readership has acquired an unrivalled status in the cultural history of the Middle East. As a literary form, the novel's intrinsic suitability for representing the everyday made it a popular genre in the modern Middle East, as elsewhere. The reception of early novels, which would appear in weekly installments in newspapers, had didactic purposes: "learning" how to conduct a successful marriage, adopt bourgeois manners, run a household, and so on. Beginning in the 1950s, didacticism was replaced by more mature forms of social criticism. Readers were no longer content with either the "educational" novels of the literary salons or the translations of European classics (Charles Dickens, Alexander Dumas, Jules Verne, Walter Scott, and Dostoyevsky). They preferred realist depictions of the life of the nation.

The Egyptian novelist Naguib Mahfouz's (1911–) *The Cairo Trilogy* (*Al-Thulathiyyah*, 1956–7) was one of the earliest works to make a decisive impact on the imagination of the new urban class. Its secular realism has attained a prominent place in the cultural history of reading in the post-colonial Middle East and has been a model for an entire generation of Arab intelligentsia. A family saga as well as an allegory of the Arab nation in transition, *The Cairo Trilogy* was read as a chronicle of struggle for change and liberty against the pressures of religion, tradition, and politics. Despite its popularity, the reaction from the religious and conservative establishment to *The Cairo Trilogy* was negative. It questioned the stability of the traditional patriarchal family and the metaphysical certainties that informed this inherited structure. Nonetheless, for its secular readers, the novel has stood as the most important piece of fiction to grasp the turbulence of modernity in the Arab world.

In this period, the idea of "committed literature" (that is, creative texts mediating a particular social cause) aroused great interest in readers. *Her Eyes* (*Chashmhayash*, 1952), by the Iranian novelist Bozorg Alavi (1904–1997), has been an important example of this type of literature. Depicting the story of an artist who is also a key figure of the underground opposition against the monarchical rule, *Her Eyes* caused a considerable stir and was subsequently banned in Iran from 1953 to 1979. Despite the ban, the novel enjoyed wide readership through clandestine publication and circulation. In the eyes of its readers, *Her Eyes* was a manifestation of the challenges of dissidence under an oppressive regime.

Another example that appeared at roughly the same time was the Turkish novelist Yashar Kemal's (1922–) *Memed, My Hawk* (*Ince Memed*, 1955)—one of the most significant novels in Turkish literature. *Memed, My Hawk* was set in a period of belated transformation in rural Anatolia from rudimentary agrarian practices into up-to-date and socially promising structures of production. With the transition in 1950 from one-party rule to democracy in Turkey, and with the simultaneous introduction of machinery to agriculture, there emerged expectations of land reform. This expectation, however, was not easy to satisfy. For the landlords attempted to increase their power by establishing certain political alliances with conservative forces. They also sought to monopolize the use of machinery in agriculture. As a result, land reform in rural Anatolia would remain a utopia for years to come. *Memed, My Hawk* emerged in this climate. Through the story of a hero-bandit who wages a successful war against the landlords, the novel exposed the contradictions of social life in Anatolia and the urgency of a welfare society. The novel appeared in serial installments in a national newspaper and shocked its urban readers, who were unfamiliar with the feudal structure of the countryside. *Memed, My Hawk* led to a metropolitan awareness of the difficulties that the Anatolian peasantry endured on a daily basis. Moreover, it inspired the imagination of many young readers of the 1968 generation seeking a socialist revolution in Turkey.

The specters of colonialism continued to haunt the Middle East states even after independence had been achieved. The most prominent example of this preoccupation in fiction has been *Season of Migration to the North* (*Mawsim al-Hijrah ila al-Shamal*, 1966), by the Sudanese writer Tayeb Salih (1929–). This novel was not a bestseller in the manner of *The Cairo Trilogy* or *Memed, My Hawk*, but it has attained an unparalleled prominence among western-educated individuals who found themselves caught between the metropolitan north and the post-colonial south. *Season of Migration to the North* spoke directly and most emphatically to the ex-colonized, now-assimilated Arabs who felt out of place in the complicated realm of cross-cultural communication between their native cultures and those of Europe. In many ways, *Season of Migration to the North* was energized by European narratives of the "other," particularly Joseph Conrad's *Heart of Darkness* (1902). The enigma of encountering the other is analyzed through the psychological complexities of Mustafa Saeed, who "goes British" at the expense of self-destruction. *Season of Migration to the North* thus became emblematic of the predicaments of the post-colonial condition in the Arab world. For its readers, it was a symbolic way of "talking back" to ex-colonizers of their land.

Another, and more recent, novel that addresses the Orient-Occident dichotomy is *My Name is Red* (*Benim Adım Kırmızı*, 1998), by the Turkish novelist and Nobel laureate Orhan Pamuk (1952–). The novel's positive global reception was particularly due to its attempt to promote cultural dialogue, as opposed to the belligerent discourse of "the clash of civilizations." The symbolic gesture of an east-west dialogue in the novel was based on synthesizing western portrait painting with the abstract style of eastern miniature

> **Orhan Pamuk**
>
> Ferit Orhan Pamuk, who publishes as Orhan Pamuk, won the 2006 Nobel Prize for Literature. Pamuk was born in Istanbul, Turkey. His books have been widely translated, and he was the first Turkish author to win the Nobel Prize. Pamuk is widely read in his native country, throughout the Middle East, and in Europe. In a 2005 interview, he commented on the mass killings of Armenians and Kurds during the last years of the Ottoman Empire in Turkey, and was charged with insulting "Turkishness" and Turkey's armed forces. The first charge was dropped, but the second remained. Pamuk's case was widely criticized in the European Union parliament and throughout Turkey. In January 2006, all charges against Pamuk were finally dropped.

art. In contrast to the self-annihilating conclusion of Tayeb Salih's *Season of Migration to the North*, *My Name is Red* encouraged its readers to favor a hybridized modern Middle Eastern identity.

Abuse and excesses of political power and authority have been central problems in the modern political and social history of the Middle East. It is therefore no coincidence that readers have been attracted to novels that examine this issue. After the demise of the charismatic Arab leader Gamel Abdel Nasser, Egyptian citizens turned to Egyptian novelist Gamal Ghitani's (1945–) *Zayni Barakat* (*al-Zayni Barakat*, 1974) for a critical outlook on Nasser's legacy. Set

Orhan Pamuk, Nobel Prize-winning Turkish author. [Courtesy of Karin Sohlgren]

in fifteenth-century feudal Egypt, *Zayni Barakat* is a historical novel about a despotic leader who succeeded in eliminating any opposition to his rule. Writing in this genre helped the author escape imprisonment while launching a critique of the unaccountable control of Nasser's police state over its citizens. The novel was serialized in an independent weekly for two years. Its intriguing plot of political violence and its stylistic parallels with classical oriental tales made the novel all the more accessible to a large audience.

More recently, *Zaat* (*Dhat*, 1992), by Ghitani's fellow countryman Sonallah Ibrahim (1937–), develops a similar line of critique of the corruption of an authoritarian system of government backed by global corporations. In contrast to *Zayni Barakat*, *Zaat* does not pretend to be allegorical. In its direct approach, which blends excerpts from Egyptian newspapers with scenes from the daily life of the Egyptian "everyman," *Zaat* was a breakthrough welcomed by dissidents across the Arab world. More importantly, this novel warned its readers about globalization and its impacts on weaker societies.

Another important work of political dissent in the modern Arab world that attracted a young Arab readership came from the Saudi-born Turki al-Hamad's (1953–) *Adama* (*Adama*, 1998). Despite the official ban on the book and the *fatwas* (religious verdicts) issued against the author, *Adama* became a bestseller in the Middle East, selling more than twenty thousand copies of "illegal" prints through the underground book market. Especially in its own country, *Adama* invoked a scandal because it violated certain taboos on sexuality, skepticism, and authority. The novel's daring representation showed its readers possibilities for crossing the limits set by authority figures.

Historical revisionism has become a popular alternative form of breaking taboos. *Cities of Salt* (*Mudun al-Milh*, 1984) by the Jordanian novelist Abdelrahman Munif (1933–2004) offers readers an alternative history to that of the official narrative. The novel revisits the discovery and exploitation of oil, the most important natural resource in the Middle East, from the viewpoint of indigenous tribal communities of the Arabian Peninsula. By portraying the difficult transition and sudden intrusion that the native population had to endure, *Cities of Salt* led its readers to question the triumphalist narrative of prosperity and modernization through the oil industry. Munif's novel presented a powerful narrative of the rapid and shocking transformations that local Bedouin communities had to face in the name of national progress. The book attained the status of a documentary among the new generation of Arabs, who came to realize that their current comfortable life had been achieved at the cost of disruption to the social fabric of the earlier local communities whose habitat was diminished by the rise of oil economies. *Cities of Salt* caused an extraordinary controversy. Munif lost citizenship and went into exile, and the novel was immediately banned in Saudi Arabia.

NOVELLAS

The novella, or long short story, is no longer a widely practiced genre in modern Middle Eastern literatures. Despite their marginal status in recent decades, novellas had an unexpected popularity up to the late 1960s. The novella's generic conven-

> **Pan-Arabism**
>
> According to the website mideastweb.org, "Pan-Arabism is a secular Arab nationalist ideology . . . which tried to unite Arabs beyond the confines of the nation states, [and also tried] to encourage a program of modernization and secularization" in the Arab States. The movement opposes western colonization and influence in the Arab countries of the Middle East.

tions were well-suited for concentrating on a specific social issue. Equally important, the novella form was more open than the novel to the rhetorical devices and figurative constructions inherent in Arabic and Persian. This combination of social commitment and poetic/philosophical diction gave novellas an aura of authenticity that appealed to the taste of readers. Contrary to the realist novels, novellas were written from a subjective point of view and a personal tone. As a consequence, novellas have been very successful in generating an emphatic readership in the Middle East.

One of the earliest novellas written in Arabic, *The Broken Wings* (*Al-Ajnihah al-Mutakassirah*, 1912), by the Lebanese writer Kahlil Gibran (1883–1931), has had a long-lasting influence. When it was first published, *The Broken Wings* created a shock effect in Lebanon and other parts of the Arab world. It exposed the lingering effects of Arab feudalism at a time when the *nahda* (renaissance) discourse of Arab nationalism was on the rise. The novella's attack on arranged marriage, corruption of the clergy, arbitrary power of the rich over the poor, and victimization of women rang a disturbing bell in the minds of its readers.

In Iran Sadegh Hedayat's (1901–1951) *The Blind Owl* (*Buf-e Kur*, 1937) was no less controversial than *The Broken Wings*. This novella was quickly denounced as "the most dangerous piece of fiction" in modern Iranian literature. Its bitter criticism of human alienation and bleak outlook on society were found excessive. Young readers in particular were advised to refrain from its suicidal undertones. These negative reactions, however, failed to diminish *The Blind Owl*'s unprecedented fame among youth in the years following its first appearance. The novel's critique of modern institutionalized life through the narrator's demented consciousness appealed to anti-establishment individuals who were disillusioned by the tripartite monarchical regime, powerful clergy, and mercantile elite's control over every aspect of the nation.

Finally, *Men in the Sun* (*Rijal fi'l Shams*, 1963), by the Palestinian writer and activist Ghassan Kanafani (1936–1972), captures the predicaments of the dispossessed Palestinians after the creation of modern Israel, a momentum referred to as *nakbah*, or "catastrophe," in the Arabic political jargon. This novella appeared on the eve of the second defeat of the Arab countries by Israel in the 1967 war. The novella narrates the tragic journey of three Palestinians in search of work in the oil-rich Kuwait, who, after being repeatedly cheated by various middlemen, lose their lives in the water-tank in which they hide as they cross the border. *Men in the Sun* was a major blow to the promises of Pan-Arabism in regard to the question of Palestine. It indicted the Arab world as uncaring, if not entirely hypocritical, in its attitudes toward the Palestinians. The novella's implication that the Palestinians were now seen as waste bodies to be ultimately discarded found strong resonance among disillusioned Palestinians who came to realize that the Arab countries were not going to bring them independence. More than any other work of fiction, *Men in the Sun* influenced the reformulation of the question of Palestine as a specifically national one.

PLAYS

Before the twentieth century, drama readership was relatively meager. In fact, in its traditional forms, dramatic performance was based on improvisation, rather than on a written text. Dramatic texts had only gradually acquired significance in the formation of readership in the modern Middle East. The plays of the Egyptian playwright Tawfik al-Hakim (1898–1987) have been the most influential in generating a popular reception. Due to the initially negative reaction to drama, al-Hakim had to omit his last name when he wrote his first plays in the 1920s. With the publication of *The Sultan's Dilemma* (*Al-Sultan al-Hair*, 1960), readers eventually found a successful synthesis of the conventions of modern theater and the traditional narrative techniques of *The Arabian Nights*. From a political perspective, *The Sultan's Dilemma* appeared at a time when the post-colonial Arab generation began to feel frustrated by the concentration of power in the hands of a few rulers unwilling to keep their promise to abide by the rule of law. Even though the play had a historical setting, its satirical depiction of a petty king enslaved by his desire for power was welcomed as a critique of the ruling elite in the modern Arab world.

Regarded as the most popular play ever written in Iran, Bijan Mofid's (1935–1984) *City of Tales* (*Shahr-e Ghesseh*, 1969) fulfilled a parallel role to that of *The Sultan's Dilemma* in Egypt. Bijan Mofid's skillful use of the rhythmic vernacular style and folkloric art forms made *City of Tales* one of the rare pieces of modern Persian drama to reach a wide audience. In terms of its content, the play is a social commentary on the abuse of religion by the clergy, or the *mullahs*. Even though it was written ten years before the 1979 Iranian Revolution, *City of Tales* was kept alive among those segments of Iranian society who gradually lost their trust in the new theocratic regime. Recordings of the play's dialogue were broadcast from the rooftops of Tehran as a symbolic gesture of dissent. This popularity among the counter-revolutionary constituencies eventually led to the author's exile.

Dramatic texts were also instrumental in encouraging native populations to take action against their colonizers. *The Encircled Corpse* (*Le Cadavre Encerclé/ Al-Juththah al-Mutawwaqah*, 1955) by the Algerian writer Kateb Yacine (1929–1989) was the first play to center on the Algerian War of Independence. Kateb Yacine envisioned his participation in the decolonization struggle in terms of mobilizing his readership through what he called "combat theater." As a politically charged, surrealist play, *The Encircled Corpse* realized this artistic vision to the extent that its performance was prohibited both in Algeria and France. Despite the measures taken by the colonial administration, the play's trenchant attack on colonial alienation was quickly embraced by supporters of the Algerian national-liberation movement.

POETRY

As with other parts of the world, the history of poetry readership in the Middle East antedates the advent of print culture. In central cities such as Cairo and Istanbul, there was a vibrant *sahaf*, or book market, for reproduced manuscripts of poetry, called *diwan*. In the modern period, however, the place of poetry in the cultural scene underwent a peculiar transformation. For one thing, the patronage system that was instituted to financially support poetic production gradually disappeared. Poets had to rely on mass reception of their work. Further, poems were no longer read for purely aesthetic pleasure. Readers began to favor poems that embodied "the people's voice" and that were centered on the daily struggles of ordinary individuals. The poetic texts of the modern Middle East have been secular epics of turbulent times.

In Turkey, *Human Landscapes from My Country* (*Memleketimden Insan Manzaralari*, 1945), by Nazım Hikmet (1902–1963), became one of the early examples of this new poetic mission. A member of the Socialist International, Nazım Hikmet has been the most controversial and the most widely read Turkish author in the twentieth century. Written while Nazım Hikmet was in prison, and based on his encounters with convicted peasants and workers there, *Human Landscapes from My Country* is an epic poem that offers a broad panorama of the nation, its day-to-day existence, and its struggles and hopes. The poem's representation of the common people with a constant shuttling between history and present received enormous enthusiasm among university youth for successive generations. For them, Nazım Hikmet's epic was a call for the disenfranchised plebeians to gain the long-delayed emancipation promised at the outset of the new Turkish Republic. Although its full publication came after decades of confiscation and censorship, *Human Landscapes from My Country* has for many years been the canonical source for leftist politics and visions of a cultural revolution in Turkey.

The Arab readers found their counterpart to Nazım Hikmet's poem in the Egyptian poet Salah Abd al-Sabur's (1931–1981) *People in My Country* (*Al-Nass fi Biladi*, 1957). Blending the mysticism, folklore, and colloquial language of the countryside with modern artistic expressions, the poems in *People in My Country* were the first ballads to be written in modern Arabic. Their compassionate appraisal of the ways of common people, of their purity and innocence, drew sympathies from a wide spectrum of readership. This was also the heyday of Arab populism, due largely to Gamal Abdel Nasser's successful rise from modest origins to power. The volume's quest for social and existential change and a humanist future reinforced in its readers the prevalent belief in the energies of the common people.

The Iranian readership discovered a similar form of popular humanism in Ahmad Shamlu's (1925–2000) *Odes for the Earth* (*Marsiyah'ha-yi Khak*, 1969). It has been claimed that there is virtually no house where one cannot find Shamlu's poetry either in book or audiocassette format. As the leading figure in new poetry, Shamlu was critical of traditional Persian poetry's hyperbolic language and monarchical myths. Instead, he chose to compose *Odes for the Earth* in "the language of the streets." Under the harsh political conditions of the shah's regime in the 1960s and

1970s, Shamlu's *Odes for the Earth* was embraced as a book of discontent. Shamlu had to hide a master copy of his poems, because at that time it was a routine police practice to seize and burn all available copies of books labeled as "dangerous."

For the Palestinians, Mahmoud Darwish (1941–2008) has unquestionably been the foremost poetic voice of his dispossessed nation. *A Lover from Palestine* (*'Ashiq min Filastin*, 1966) had an immediate impact on the post-1948 Palestinian refugee generation. The successful synthesis of political directness and personal intimacy, liberation and love made these "poems of resistance" very popular at festivals and rallies as they galvanized support for the Palestinian cause. *A Lover from Palestine* offered to its readers a form of consolation for the losses they had to endure. As a Palestinian text, however, it had to take up the material challenges of reproduction and circulation conditions in exile. As a work of resistance to dispossession, it signaled a political commitment, and its circulation was inevitably linked to the spreading of the Palestinian cause. As a result, its movements came under close scrutiny by political authorities. Through these challenges, *A Lover from Palestine* became a foundational text in the emergence of an expatriate readership in the modern Middle East.

WOMEN'S LITERATURE

The emergence of creative writing by women has been a purely modern phenomenon in the Middle East. The early texts appeared only in the latter half of the nineteenth century, and had a very limited audience. The initial examples of women's literature came from female members of aristocratic families that, despite their patriarchal structure, were receptive to European culture. As part of their class privileges, and thanks to the cosmopolitan milieus of such urban centers as Istanbul and Cairo, these women were given access to private education by English and French tutors, as well as access to the literary salons of the time. The readership of early women's literature in the Middle East, however, remained for the most part marginal. In fact, a considerable number of texts by women writers were retained in manuscript form—to be discovered and published years later by the next generation of feminist critics.

By the 1950s, however, the isolation of women's creative writing from mainstream readership and cultural transformation in the Middle East was no longer possible. A new feminist protest literature strived resolutely for the representation of women's perspective on social issues and asked its readers to be equally receptive to these revisionist narratives. The first "novel of revolt" in the Arab world was *I Live* (*Ana Ahiya*, 1958) by the Lebanese writer Layla Baalbaki (1938–). This novel caught mainstream readers off-guard, for it was a violent attack on the patriarchy and the imprisonment of Arab women at home. The female protagonist's critique of her father as a corrupt sycophant of the French mandate was a serious blow to the unquestioned male dominance in national affairs. The decision of the protagonist to cut her hair was another scandalous gesture that was labeled "promiscuous" by conservative readers of the novel. The controversies that surrounded the publication of the novel resulted in the trial of its author. This, however, did not diminish its shocking impact. Its publication was a strong signal that women's representation of the Middle East could not be kept on the margins any more. *I Live* has thus become the first novel in Arabic language to open up a narrative space for an assertive female subjectivity.

The first feminist novel to attain a central place in the history of readership in Iran was Simin Daneshvar's (1921–) *Savushun: A Persian Requiem* (*Savushun*, 1969). This was the first novel to be written by an Iranian woman;

The library at Alexandria, Egypt. [Courtesy of Sara Eriksen]

still, it enjoyed unprecedented success among readers and became the number-one best seller in Iran during the twentieth century. Like Baalbaki's *I Live*, *Savushun* was a revisionist account of the nation's modern history from a woman's perspective. It aimed to portray the neglected role of Iranian women in difficult times, such as the Soviet-British occupation of the country during World War II. For its readers, the novel was a significant attack on the dominant narratives of a glorious nation of male heroes. It showed them the extent to which women had been the key element in sustaining the Iranian civil society during tumultuous political and social transformations. The successful reception of *Savushun* was in itself a crucial step for Iranian women eager to transform the male-dominant literary output in their country.

By the middle of the 1970s, creative texts by Middle Eastern women writers began to engage their readers in contemporary events, rather than historical revisions. One of the most important feminist creative interventions was Hanan al-Shaykh's (1945–) *The Story of Zahra* (*Hikayat Zahrah*, 1980). As a response to the devastating Lebanese Civil War that broke out in 1975, the novel narrates the dilemmas of a young woman who is caught up between an abusive patriarchal family and a destructive war among male militias. The novel's depiction of these two poles was quickly condemned as "pornographic" and "violent," which led to the refusal of publishers to accept the novel for publication. As a result, Hanan al-Shaykh published the novel at her own expense. Although *The Story of Zahra* has later been labeled by the Lebanese state authorities "unsuitable for educational curriculum," over the past decades it has enjoyed a favorable reception from both Arab and international readers.

Another feminist novel of intervention was Adalet Ağaoğlu's (1929–) *Curfew* (*Üç Beş Kişi*, 1984), published in Turkey in the aftermath of the September 1980 military coup that was supposed to put an end to political anarchy. Before the coup, in the struggle between leftist and rightist movements to gain state control, "committed literature" played an instrumental role in galvanizing support for "the cause." Similar to the Arab and Iranian contexts, however, this literature was largely male-centric in regard to its themes, writers, and consumers. *Curfew* represented not only a break with the received notions of committed literature, but also an attempt to recover the private, psychological dimensions of the ostentatiously public issues in Turkish modern life. Equally important, this novel was the first to alert its readers to the neglect of women-specific issues by the allegedly progressive leftist discourse. This criticism was quickly taken by leftist circles as a sign of betrayal. However, the post-1980 Turkish readership ultimately gave credit to *Curfew*'s narrative and responded to feminist creative writing more positively.

PERSONAL TEXTS

Autobiography has been a popular genre throughout the cultural history of the Middle East and has continued to attract readers in the modern period as well. The popularity of the genre can be gauged from the fact that almost all major contemporary presses publish an autobiography/memoir series. Despite their fashionable status, however, the impact of autobiographies and memoirs in the formation of readership in the modern Middle East has not been permanent. Even though some of them have generated polemics and controversies around their veracity, readers have tended to lose interest in them rather quickly.

All the same, one twentieth-century autobiography, *The Days* (*Al-Ayyam*, 1929), by the Egyptian man of letters Taha Hussein (1889–1973), has stood the test of time and attracted generations of readers in the Arab-speaking world and beyond. *The Days* is the chronicle of the rise of a blind child from a rural, poor background to being one of the key figures of Arab modernity. Its skillful use of the Arab oral tradition, its close affinities with Cartesian reasoning, and its witticisms in the style of Voltaire rendered this autobiography all the more palatable to mainstream Arab readership. *The Days*, moreover, offered Arab readers the ostensibly naïve yet authentic perspective of a young adolescent who experienced first-hand the cultural transformation of his country at the turn of the twentieth century. It has been argued that Hussein's blindness contributed to, rather than impeded, the vibrancy of his narrative, which captivated the imagination of its readers. Apart from its rhetorical appeal, *The Days* was also read as an account of self-enlightenment through open-minded and independent questioning of one's heritage, religion, and other received beliefs. It was this thoroughly embedded, enlightenment notion of "daring to think" that made Hussein's autobiography one of the most celebrated pieces of modern Arab writing. *The Days* has been one of the rare books that could appeal to secondary school students and high-caliber intellectuals at the same time.

BLOGS

The spread of electronic and digital media across the globe has led to an unprecedented level of synchronization of textual production and circulation. The blog has emerged as one of the successful genres in the development of alternative modes of readership in the postmodern age. Despite the relatively peripheral status of e-text consumption in the contemporary Middle East, the younger generation, in particular, has discovered new forms of expression through blog writing. This new genre has generated better conditions for the democratization of both author-ship and readership. Blogs have not only fostered freedom of expression and ways of bypassing censorship, but have also enabled the emergence of cyber-reader net-works that could overcome the limits of the territorial formats.

The popularity of blogs in the Middle Eastern countries can be gauged from the case of Iran. Even though the first Persian blog appeared in September 2001, the number of blogs in this language has reached sixty-four thousand in a few years. Blogs have created a forum through which Iranian citizens can raise their view-points on various political, social, and cultural issues concerning their country. *We Are Iran: The Persian Blogs* (2005), compiled by the Iranian activist Nasrin Alavi, has brought this widespread phenomenon to the attention of a global readership. The blog entries included in the volume communicate to their recipients the everyday concerns of common people in Iran and debunk the Manichean "funda-mentalist" versus "imperialist" binary in the foreign relations between Iran and western countries, particularly the United States. Despite increasing government surveillance, *The Persian Blogs* opened a different window on the "unknown" aspects of life in Iran and enabled the creation of a virtual network of anti-theocratic dissidents.

Another breakthrough in the global reception of blogs of Middle Eastern ori-gin came with the publication of *The Clandestine Diary of an Ordinary Iraqi* (2003), published under the pseudonym Salam Pax. These "Baghdad Blogs" appeared right after the United States embarked on the invasion of Iraq and were the single unofficial information source for readers from all over the world as to what was happening on the ground. In terms of access to the anxieties and hard-ships caused by the invasion, the blogs' immediate appeal even surpassed coverage of the war by major news agencies. It was through these blogs, written in English, that online readers were able to get a sense of the chaos in Baghdad. As the blogs became more critical of the invasion in the aftermath, they were intermittently blocked to the Arab readership. Moreover, the author had to struggle with fre-quent power outages in post-invasion Baghdad. *The Clandestine Diary of an Ordinary Iraqi* has nevertheless survived all these difficulties and has become a landmark in the readership history of the Middle East.

POLITICAL TEXTS

In the twentieth century, the Middle East has witnessed a new phenomenon in the readership scene; namely, the publication of texts by "charismatic" political leaders. In the age of classical empires, the *siyasetnames*, or political treatises on the "eternal wisdoms of good governance," were in extensive use for the purpose of tutoring the ruling elite. These texts, however, were typically written by prominent advisors to the court, rather than the rulers themselves. In modern times, states-men began to articulate their own vision of good governance and communicate it directly to the nation. Moreover, this new genre was meant to account for *raison d'état* ("reason of the state") in pragmatic and urgent ways and to draw support from the citizens.

One of the earliest "state texts," *The Speech* (*Nutuk*, 1933), came from Mustafa Kemal Atatürk (1881–1938), the founder of modern Turkey. This text presents a first-hand account of the first successful secular-nationalist revolution in the Middle East. Atatürk's discourses not only conveyed a prospective Turkey as a country fully integrated into western civilization, but they also paved the way for an ardent break with the Ottoman heritage and rapid modernization in the state apparatus, civil law, and economic and social institutions. *The Speech* has shaped the imagination of virtually all educated Turkish individuals. As the foundational text of Kemalist ideology, it has been continuously propagated through school text-books and other media.

In the post-colonial Arab world, *The Philosophy of Revolution* (*Falsafat al-Thawra*, 1955), by the Egyptian statesman and proponent of Arab national-socialism Gamal Abdel Nasser (1918–1970), has been the most influential state text. It accounts for the Egyptian Revolution in 1952 and delineates a version of third-world cultural, social, and economic nonaligned development that emerged after the Afro-Asian Bandung Conference in 1955. The urban Arab youth of the lower and middle classes heralded Nasser's philosophy of revolution as their guide to complete political and cultural emancipation. Rather than dictating a set of princi-ples, *The Philosophy of Revolution* was written in eloquent and personal language, through which Nasser the leader effectively transformed himself into the Arab "everyman," who had been dispossessed of his own destiny throughout history. The text's theatrical metaphor of Arab history as a drama "in search of its actors" moved an entire generation of idealists in the direction of this utopian vision of Arab self-realization. In more practical terms, *The Philosophy of Revolution* played a stimulating factor in Egypt's nationalization of the Suez Canal in 1956, against the will of Britain and Israel, and in the creation of the short-lived United Arab Republic in 1959.

Another significant state text that appeared in the modern Middle East is *Islamic Government* (*Velayat-i Faqih*, 1970). This political handbook consists of a famous series of lectures by Ayatollah Khomeini (1900–1989), the spiritual leader of the Iranian Revolution in 1979. It laid the principles of an Islamic theocracy in the modern world. It was a call for the replacement of the shah's regime with an Islamic government under the guidance of religious jurisprudence. The publica-tion of *Islamic Government* was a major break with the quietism of traditional Shiite theology in regard to politics. As opposed to the messianic theologians who have been "waiting for the hidden Imam" to create the ideal godly state, and thereby have been refraining from involvement in mundane politics, Khomeini ascribed to religious scholars a vicarious function of intervening with social and political issues for the good of society. This new perspective found great support among the students at the seminary schools throughout Iran as a response to the increasingly oppressive policies of the shah's regime. Because Khomeini's works were banned in Iran, *Islamic Government* had to be printed in Iraq and then smug-gled into Iran to be distributed through dissident networks. After the overthrow of the shah's regime in 1979, the political structure of the new Islamic Republic was designed on the basis of this handbook.

NATIONALIST TREATISES

In the modern Middle East, nationalism was the most influential ideology in the first half of the twentieth century. After the demise of the Ottoman Empire, nationalist movements sought to secure for their "imagined communities" an acceptable place in the international political and cultural system. The major nationalist treatises of that period tried to convince their readers that nationalism was the most feasible solution to establish a modern society while fending off western imperialism. This vision found much support from individuals who were dismayed by the disappearance of the Middle Eastern countries from "the great powers" scene. The call in these treatises for a new soul for the national body resonated strongly among those who believed in the urgency of purging foreign domination.

In Turkey, Ziya Gökalp's (1876–1924) *The Principles of Turkism* (*Türkçülüğün Esasları*, 1923) established the cultural and ideological foundations of Turkish nationalism by proposing the reconciliation of Turkish culture, Islamic religious values, and European modernity under a new national identity. *The Principles of Turkism* became a major intellectual source in the self-definition of modern Turkey. It guided the founders of the Turkish republic in their quest for a new path for the nation and offered the most convenient vocabulary for discussions about Turkish nationalism among the pre-World War II Turkish literati. It also laid the foundations for the implementation of corporatist policies in modern Turkey, as it propagated the idea that national prosperity could be achieved through economic and cultural associations controlled by the state. In many ways, Gökalp's treatise became the road map for the Turkish republic to survive its early difficult times.

In the Arab world, nationalism took the form of pan-Islamism or pan-Arabism. The main question in the collective consciousness was the Arab-Muslim belatedness and defeat in the twentieth century. The Lebanese notable Shakib Arslan's (1869–1946) *Our Decline and its Causes* (*Limadha Ta'akhkhara al-Muslimun*, 1944) gained widespread influence as a treatise on the causes of the collapse of the Ottoman Empire and the impact of European imperialism in the Middle East during the interwar period. As the work of a political activist in exile, *Our Decline and its Causes* appealed strongly to those who wanted to awaken a sense of shared history and hope for a new Islamic international order. Despite the French and British attempts to restrict its circulation in the Arab lands under their control, Shakib Arslan's treatise energized independence movements stretching from Morocco to Iraq.

The "loss" of Palestine at the end of 1948 Arab-Israel War, however, was a major blow to the Islamic national discourse. The defeat of united Arab forces by Israel exposed, among other things, the lack of a genuine solidarity among Arab countries. It was the Syrian intellectual and historian Constantine Zurayk's (1909–2000) *The Meaning of the Disaster* (*Ma'na al-Nakbah*, 1948) that marked this defeat in the minds of its Arab readers as "a catastrophic rupture" (nakbah) in the history of Arab nations. Zurayk's treatise was a bitter reminder that an Arab unity was yet to come. As opposed to the earlier nationalist treatises that relied on the "past glories" of the Arab nation, *The Meaning of the Disaster* advanced the notion that the modern Arab nation could only emerge from the present by transforming "the disaster" into a new possibility of regeneration. The first generation of Palestinian refugees, particularly the students at Beirut universities, took the call positively to the extent that they founded the Arab Nationalist Movement to struggle against political fragmentation, imperialism, and Zionism.

Another influential text that shaped modern Arab nationalism even more directly was Michel Aflaq's (1908–1989) *On the Way of Resurrection* (*Fi Sabil al-Ba'th*, 1959). As the founder of the Ba'th (Resurrection) party in Syria, Aflaq shared Zurayk's historical vision of the Arab nations recovering from disunion and heading toward a secular renaissance to regain lost greatness. Yet instead of popular nationalist movements, Aflaq regarded top-down social transformation as the surest way to create a powerful Arab world. *On the Way of Resurrection* thus became the bible of the Jacobin Arab revolutionary circles that later came to power in Syria and Iraq through military coups.

In Iran, nationalism reached its peak under the first democratic government in the early 1950s. The nationalization of oil under this government, led by the

Prime Minister Mohammed Musaddiq, was declared as a major victory against foreign domination. This optimism, however, was cut short by the removal of Musaddiq's government from power and the implementation of a hard-line westernization agenda by the shah. It was under these circumstances that the antiestablishment thinker Jalal Al-e Ahmad's (1923–1969) *Plagued by the West* (*Gharbzedegi*, 1962) gained popularity as the textual representative of both secular and religious nationalists, who accused the ruling classes of being complicit in the upsurge of western cultural hegemony in Iran. Conservatives who lamented the demise of national and religious values in Iranian universities readily embraced its criticism of the educated elite as being metaphorically intoxicated by the western educational system.

ISLAMIST MANIFESTOS

Islamism has become one of the major ideological trends in the modern Middle East. Islamist texts call particularly for de-secularization of social life in Muslim communities and recovery from backwardness and dependency by reinstating Islamic politics. Especially as the failures of modernization in secular nation-states became more visible in the second half of the twentieth century, Islamist discourse gained a stronghold in Middle Eastern countries. Through affordable paperbacks and a dispersed network of publishers and bookstores, Islamists became very efficient in spreading their canons to common readers. Even though Islamism does not by any means represent a uniform trend, the manifestos that were published in different times and spaces have attempted to convey to their readers a program for how the Islamic worldview could regain its dominance.

One of the early texts that has also retained a significant position in the cultural history of reading in the modern Middle East is *The Words* (*Risale-i Nur: Sözler*, c. 1929), by Said Nursi (c. 1876–1960). A major religious text in modern Turkey, *The Words* was written in the aftermath of the proclamation of the Turkish Republic. Said Nursi was not only dismayed by the anti-Islamic policies of the new state but also worried about "the intrusion" of positivism and materialism into the minds of Muslim youth. *The Words* thus appeared as a response to these ideological enemies and aimed to offer a rational and "scientific" explanation of the metaphysical tenets of Islam. Until it was published in printed form in 1956, only hand-written copies of *The Words* were available to readers. Because Said Nursi was followed closely by the regime, his disciples circulated the hand-written copies secretly from village to village and town to town. It is estimated that around six hundred thousand hand-written copies were produced during that time.

In the Arab world, the most influential Islamist manifesto has been *Milestones* (*Ma'alim fi'l Tariq*, 1964), by Sayyid Qutb (1906–1966), the leader of the Muslim Brotherhood movement in Egypt. This text, which has been reprinted numerous times, was written while Qutb was in prison, but his manifesto has become the major ideological source that shaped the vision of modern Islamic movements calling for a return to the early Islamic "puritan" way of life. It argued for the formation of a new Muslim community and indicted the modern age as one of ignorance and materialism. The political vision of *Milestones* resonated strongly in the minds of committed Islamists, as well as those individuals who found themselves alienated by modern secular regimes.

In Iran, the equivalent of *Milestones* in its impact on readership came from Ali Shariati (1933–1977), the major ideologue of the Iranian Revolution. His *What*

THE MODERN MIDDLE EAST

is To Be Done? (*Chih Bayad Kard?*, 1970) was an idiosyncratic blend of Shiite Islam, Marxism, existentialism, and anticolonialism. The university youth, disgruntled by the shah's pro-western regime, readily embraced Shariati's call for a new Islamic discourse that would emphasize contemporary social issues rather than obsolete theological debates. Through a visionary language, *What is To Be Done?* sought to redefine the role of Islam in social life as a revolutionary intervention, aiming for justice and lifting oppression in all its manifestations. Despite the deliberately cryptic tone of the text, the shah's regime was quick to realize the manifesto's political implications and banned it in Iran. This, however, did not stop Shariati's sympathizers from circulating his books through underground channels. Iranian students in European and North American universities played a major role in printing and then smuggling them into the country.

At the turn of the twenty-first century, no other Islamist text could rival the status of the Saudi-born Islamist Osama Bin Laden's (1957–) *Messages to the World* (c. 1994–2004). As opposed to the earlier manifestos mentioned above, these messages were initially produced on a single audiocassette or videotape to be broadcast through an affiliated website and/or an Arab news channel, particularly the Qatar-based *al-Jazeera*. The early messages that invited the *ummah*, or the Muslim community, to a wholesale *jihad* against "infidels" and their "native collaborators" were later printed in pamphlets and circulated through fundamentalist circles. These texts played a significant role in the dissemination of the al-Qaeda ideology and attracted sympathizers to its cause. One of the formal successes of these texts in addressing their Arab audience was Bin Laden's skillful use of the rhetorical energies of classical Arabic. After the September 11 attacks, Bin Laden's *Messages* became a genuinely global event. Now their primary recipients were the western countries and their citizens. Each transcript from a Bin Laden tape has been

> **Who reads Osama Bin Laden?**
>
> Osama Bin Laden's book *Messages to the World: The Statements of Osama Bin Laden* is ranked 55,346 in Amazon.com's book sales rankings, and, at the time of press, has attracted twelve reader reviews on the Amazon website. One Israeli reader asks, "Is it morally right and tactically wise to publish such a book?" while an Italian reader comments, "How can any of us put the 'war on terror' into context if we don't know what the leader of the other side is saying?"

immediately translated into all major languages across the world. The global reach of these transcripts has become an unparalleled phenomenon in the readership of Islamist manifestos. Ironically, it has shown that even the most anti-western version of Islamism could not remove itself from the intricate labyrinths of reading in the age of globalization.

FEMINIST TRACTS

The first feminist texts in the modern Middle East came from women of the educated urban class who joined the anticolonialist national liberation movements. The main reason behind this peculiar phenomenon was that, through nationalist political activism, the Middle Eastern women of the early twentieth century could legitimize their presence in the public sphere. The major feminist figures of the time then gradually began to articulate the need for improvement in women's lives as an indispensable prerequisite for complete national emancipation. The foundational texts of feminist readership in Middle Eastern countries were thus born out of women's participation in constitutional movements (in Turkey and Iran) and anticolonial struggles (in Egypt, Syria, and Lebanon). The main message that these texts tried to convey to their readers was the necessity of gender reform for a healthy national cultural life.

However, the traditional religious obligation of women to put on veil (*hijab*) in the public domain was still a symbolic as well as physical obstacle that women had to overcome before their emergence as a new social force. Even though the new nation-states were ready to banish the practice, the real issue was to convince civil society to make that move. The first feminist tract to change public opinion on the question of veiling came from a Lebanese woman activist in her early twenties. Nazira Zayn al-Din's *Unveiling and Veiling* (*al-Sufur wa al-Hijab*, 1928) argued that veiling had nothing to do with the essence of Islam, and that it was mainly a means of oppression used by males to keep women ignorant and under control. By dissociating the practice of veiling from religious life itself, *Unveiling and Veiling* immediately helped to dispel the popular belief that unveiling women were going against the will of God. *Unveiling and Veiling* also claimed that women were not in need of the clerics to read, understand, and interpret the Koran. Nobody anticipated that such an iconoclastic book would go into two editions within a month—a remarkable achievement given the low literacy rates, particularly among women. The supreme religious authorities in Damascus and Beirut declared that the book was blasphemous and ill-intentioned. Conservative circles responded to it by distributing pamphlets that accused the author of contaminating Muslim minds with Christian missionary ideas and demanded that booksellers not carry it. The controversies notwithstanding, the publication of *Unveiling and Veiling* not only prepared the grounds for the first convention of the Syrian and Lebanese Women's Union but also encouraged first-wave feminists to assert their official and public rights.

> **The Emergence of Women's Writing**
>
> By the 1950s, the isolation of women's creative writing from mainstream readership and cultural transformation in the Middle East was no longer possible. A new feminist protest literature strived resolutely for the representation of women's perspectives on social issues and asked its readers to be equally receptive to these revisionist narratives.

The text that embodied the spirit of second-wave feminism in the 1960s was the Syrian writer Ghada Samman's (1942–) manifesto, "Our Constitution—We the Liberated Women" (1961). This text was hailed as a call for political solidarity and collective action among emancipated Arab women. Rejecting the purportedly bourgeois, upper-class nature of first wave feminism, "Our Constitution" cautioned its readers against the degeneration of the so-called "liberated woman" to a figure of modern consumer culture. Amid growing concerns about the rise of consumer society and rapid westernization in the post-colonial Arab world, it reformulated the feminist agenda in Middle Eastern countries: women had to initiate a grassroots movement and oppose capitalism as well as religious conservatism.

With the decline of revolutionary fervor, the emphasis on collective identity in feminist texts began to lose its appeal. Instead, readers felt more empathy for books that developed a feminist politics out of individual singularities. The most successful texts that fulfilled this demand have been *The Hidden Face of Eve* (*Al-Wajh al-Ari lil Mar'a al-Arabiya*, 1977) by the Egyptian "maverick" Nawal El Saadawi (1931–), and *She Has No Name* (*Kadının Adı Yok*, 1987) by the Turkish writer Duygu Asena (1946–). Both texts dealt with certain taboo topics about which first- and second-wave feminists have virtually kept silent; these topics include sexuality, abuse, virginity, the equation of the female body with the honor of society, the deeply engrained metaphysical assumptions about women's inferiority to men, domestic violence, and flirting. Unprecedented in speaking out about the injustices against women in Muslim societies, both *The Hidden Face of Eve* and *She Has No Name* generated great interest as well as controversy when they first appeared. Under the "Law for the Protection of Values from Shame," *The Hidden Face of Eve* was banned for three months. Even though it was published ten years later in a different country, *She Has No Name* was also subjected to a similar law and for the entire year of 1988 it was sold in sealed bags under the category of "adult material." These measures, however, could not prevent it from going into more than sixty editions and becoming one of the best-selling non-fiction books in Turkish print history.

CONCLUSION

In the Middle East, the modern period has been as much a moment of collective exuberance and hope as one of failure and desperation. Renewal and turbulence went hand in hand. It is therefore not a coincidence that the texts that have occupied the literary and cultural space, and that have thereby attained widespread influence and readership in the modern Middle East, revolve around this paradoxical situation. Incomplete modernization, uneven development, unfulfilled national reforms, the legacy of colonialism, the question of independence, war, and conflict—these have been the major issues that the texts included here directly or symbolically deal with.

Apart from books that generated controversies, partisanships,

> **Middle Eastern Blogs**
>
> The spread of electronic/digital media across the globe has led to an unprecedented level of synchronization of textual production and circulation. The blog has emerged as one of the successful genres in the development of alternative modes of readership in the postmodern age. Despite the relatively peripheral status of e-text consumption in the contemporary Middle East, the younger generation in particular has discovered new forms of expression through blog writing.

public debates, and reading networks, there have, of course, been less visible or less durable reading trends in the Middle East. Popular history, science, and religion books, for instance, have been very popular. Certain emergent genres such as science fiction, the detective novel, travelogues, and personal development books have begun to attract a wider readership. It should also be highlighted that the reading markets of translations from foreign languages have been almost as influential as the domestic books discussed here. Especially in recent decades, the book markets in the Middle East have depended very heavily on translations; and a considerable number of these translations have made their way quickly to the national bestseller lists.

RECOMMENDED READING

Abu-Rabi', Ibrahim M. *Contemporary Arab Thought: Studies in Post-1967 Arab Intellectual History*. London: Pluto Press, 2003.

Ajami, Fouad. *Dream Palace of the Arabs: A Generation's Odyssey*. New York: Vintage, 1999.

Arabian Nights: Tales from a Thousand and One Nights. Translated by Richard Burton. New York: Modern Library, 2004.

Badran, Margot, and Miriam Cooke, eds. *Opening the Gates: A Century of Arab Feminist Writing*. Bloomington: Indiana University Press, 1990.

Battuta, Ibn. *Travels in Asia and Africa, 1325–1354.* Translated and edited by H. A. R. Gibb. London: Routledge Curzon, 2005.

Kandiyoti, Deniz, and Ayşe Saktanber, eds. *Fragments of Culture: The Everyday of Modern Turkey.* London: I. B. Tauris, 2002.

Maalouf, Amin, and Barbara Bray. *Balthasar's Odyssey.* London: Vintage, 2003.

Said, Edward W. *Orientalism.* New York: Vintage, 1979.

Shayegan, Darius. *Cultural Schizophrenia: Islamic Societies Confronting the West.* Translated by John Howe. Syracuse: Syracuse University Press, 1997.

PRIMARY SOURCES

Abd al-Sabur, Salah. *Al-Nas fi Biladi* [People in My Country]. Beirut: Manshurat Dar al-Adab, 1957. This text is not available in English, but has been translated into Spanish (*La Gente En Mi País.* Translated by Mercedes del Amo. Granada: N. O. H., 1989) and French (*Les Gens Dans Mon Pays.* Translated by Omar Saghi. Paris: Harmattan, 2005).

Aflaq, Michel. *Fi Sabil al-Baath* [On the Way of Resurrection]. Beirut: Dar al-Taliah, 1963. This text is not available in English in full. For excerpts, refer to: Haim, Sylvia G., ed. *Arab Nationalism: An Anthology.* Berkeley: University of California Press, 1962.

Ağaoğlu, Adalet. *Curfew.* Translated by John Goulden. Austin, TX: Center for Middle Eastern Studies, 1997. Original title and publication date: *Üç Beş Kişi*, 1984.

Alavi, Bozorg. *Her Eyes.* Translated by John O'Kane. Lanham, MD: University Press of America, 1989. Original title and publication date: *Chashmhayash*, 1952.

Al-e Ahmad, Jalal. *Plagued by the West.* Translated by Paul Sprachman. Delmar, NY: Caravan Books, 1982. Original title and publication date: *Gharbzedegi*, 1962.

Arslan, Shakib. *Our Decline and its Causes.* Translated by M. A. Shakoor. Lahore S. Muhammad Ashraf, 1944. Original title and publication date: *Limadha Taakhkhara al-Muslimun*, 1944.

Asena, Duygu. *Kadının Adı Yok* [She Has No Name]. Istanbul: AFA, 1987. This text is not available in English, but has been translated into German (*Die Frau Hat Keinen Namen: Eine Türkin Entdeckt Die Folgen Des Kleinen Unterschieds.* Translated by Barbara Yurtdas. München: Piper, 1992) and Dutch (*De Vrouw Heeft Geen Naam : Opgroeien in Turkije.* Translated by Melanie Deegen. Amsterdam: Muntinga, 1993).

Atatürk, Mustafa Kemal. *The Speech.* Translated by Önder Renkliyildirim. Abridged edition. Istanbul: Metro, 1987. Original title and publication date: *Nutuk*, 1933.

Baalbaki, Layla. *Ana Ahiyah* [I Live]. Tel Aviv: Deshe, 1961. Original publication date: 1958. This novel is out of print and not available in translation. English-speaking readers may refer to Baalbaki's most popular and controversial short story "A Spaceship of Tenderness to the Moon" in Arthur W. Biddle, et al. *Global Voices: Contemporary Literature from the Non-Western World.* Englewood Cliffs, NJ: Prentice Hall, 1995.

Bin Laden, Osama. *Messages to the World: The Statements of Osama Bin Laden.* Translated by James Howarth. Edited by Bruce B. Lawrence. London Verso, 2005. This book is a collection of declarations by the leader of Al-Qaeda Islamic fundamentalist network, Osama Bin Laden, between 1994 and 2004.

Danishvar, Simin. *Savushun: A Persian Requiem.* Translated by Roxane Zand. New York: G. Braziller, 1992. Original title and publication date: *Savushun*, 1969.

Darwish, Mahmoud. *A Lover from Palestine, and Other Poems: An Anthology of Palestinian Poetry.* Translated and edited by Abdelwahab M. Elmessiri. Washington, DC: Free Palestine Press, 1970. Original title and publication date: *Ashiq min Filastin*, 1966.

Ghitani, Jamal. *Zayni Barakat.* Translated by Farouk Abdel Wahab. London: Penguin, 1990. Original title and publication date: *Al-Zayni Barakat*, 1974.

Gibran, Kahlil. *The Broken Wings.* Translated by Anthony R. Ferris. New York: Citadel Press, 1957. Original title and publication date: *Al-Ajnihah al-Mutakassirah*, 1912. Also available in a new English translation by Juan Ricardo Cole from Penguin (London, 1998).

Gökalp, Ziya. *The Principles of Turkism*. Translated by Robert Devereaux. Leiden: E. J. Brill, 1968. Original title and publication date: *Türkçülüğün Esasları*, 1923.

Hakim, Tawfiq. *The Sultan's Dilemma. Fate of a Cockroach.* Translated by Denys Johnson-Davies. Colorado Springs, CO: Three Continents Press, 1994. Original title and publication date: *Al-Sultan al-Hair*, 1960.

Hamad, Turki. *Adama.* Translated by Robin Bray. London: Saqi, 2003. Original title and publication date: *Adama*, 1998.

Hedayat, Sadegh. *The Blind Owl.* Translated by D. P. Costello. New York: Grove Press, 1957. Original title and publication date: *Buf-e Kur*, 1937.

Hikmet, Nazım. *Human Landscapes from My Country.* Translated by Randy Blasing and Mutlu Konuk Blasing. New York: Persea Books, 2002. Original title and publication date: *Memleketimden Insan Manzaraları*, 1945.

Hussein, Taha. *The Days.* Translated by E. H. Paxton, et al. Cairo: The American University of Cairo Press, 1997. Original title and publication date: *Al-Ayyam*, 1929.

Ibrahim, Sonallah. *Zaat.* Translated by Anthony Calderbank. Cairo: American University in Cairo Press, 2001. Original title and publication date: *Dhat*, 1992.

Kanafani, Ghassan. *Men in the Sun, and Other Palestinian Stories.* Translated by Hilary Kilpatrick. London: Heinemann 1978. Original title and publication date: *Rijal fi al- Shams*, 1963.

Kateb, Yacine. *Le Cadavre Encerclé* [The Encircled Corpse]. *Le Cercle des Représailles, Théâtre.* Paris: Éditions du Seuil, 1959. This text originally appeared in 1955 and in French. The Arabic translation came in 1962 in Damascus under the title *Al-Juththah al-Mutawwaqah* (Translated by Malik Abyad al-Isa). No English translation is available.

Kemal, Yashar. *Memed, My Hawk.* Translated by Edouard Roditi. New York: Pantheon, 1961. Original title and publication date: *Ince Memed*, 1955.

Khomeini, Ayatollah. *Islamic Government.* Translated by George Carpozi. New York: Manor Books, 1979. Original title and publication date: *Velayat-i Faqih*, 1970.

Mahfuz, Naguib. *The Cairo Trilogy: Palace Walk, Palace of Desire, Sugar Street.* Translated by William Maynard Hutchins, et al. New York: Everyman's Library, 2001. Original title and publication date: *Al-Thulathiyyah*, 1956–7.

Mofid, Bijan. *Shahr-e Ghesseh* [City of Tales]. Tehran: 1967. This text is out of print and not available in English. The play itself is available in Persian in audio format from the following online source: http://www.iranian.com/Times/Subs/Music/April2000/Qesseh/index.html.

Munif, Abdelrahman. *Cities of Salt.* Translated by Peter Theroux. New York: Vintage International, 1989. Original title and publication date: *Mudun al-Milh*, 1984.

Nasser, Gamal Abdel. *The Philosophy of Revolution.* Translated by John S. Badeau. Buffalo: Smith, Keynes & Marshal, 1959. Original title and publication date: *Falsafat al-Thawra*, 1955.

Nazira Zayn al-Din. "Unveiling and Veiling." In *Opening the Gates: A Century of Arab Feminist Writing.* Edited by Margot Badran and Miriam Cooke. Bloomington: Indiana University Press, 1990. Original title and publication date: "Al-Sufur wa al-Hijab," 1928.

Nursi, Said. *The Words.* Translated by Huseyin Akarsu. London: Truestar, 1993. Original title and publication date: *Risale-i Nur: Sözler*, c. 1929.

Pamuk, Orhan. *My Name Is Red.* Translated by Erdag Goknar. New York: Alfred A. Knopf, 2001. Original title and publication date: *Benim Adım Kırmızı*, 1998.

Qutb, Sayyid. *Milestones.* Translated by S. Badrul Hasan. Karachi: International Islamic Publishers, 1981. Original title and publication date: *Maalim fi al- Tariq*, 1964.

Saadawi, Nawal. *The Hidden Face of Eve: Women in the Arab World.* Translated by Sherif Hetata. London: Zed Press, 1980. Original title and publication date: *Al-Wajh al-Ari lil Mara al-Arabiyya*, 1977.

Salam, Pax. *Salam Pax: The Clandestine Diary of an Ordinary Iraqi.* New York: Grove Press, 2003. The pseudonym Salam Pax wrote his blog in English.

Salih, Tayeb. *Season of Migration to the North.* Translated by Denys Johnson-Davis. London: Heinemann, 1970. Original title and publication date: *Mawsim al-Hijrah ila al-Shamal*, 1966.

Samman, Ghada. "Our Constitution—We the Liberated Women." In *Opening the Gates: A Century of Arab Feminist Writing*. Edited by Margot Badran and Miriam Cooke. Bloomington: Indiana University Press, 1990. This text, which originally appeared in 1961, is out of print in Arabic.

Shamlu, Ahmad. *Marsiyah'ha-yi Khak* [Odes for the Earth]. Tehran: Amir Kabir, 1348 [1969]. This collection of poems is not available in English in full. Several English translations of Shamlu's poems are available in *The Love Poems of Ahmad Shamlu: Selections*. (Translated by Papan-Matin Firoozeh and Lane Arthur. Edited by Papan-Matin Firoozeh. Bethesda, MD: IBEX Publishers, 2005) and *Strange Times, My Dear: The Pen Anthology of Contemporary Iranian Literature* (Edited by Nahid Mozaffari and Ahmad Karimi Hakkak. New York: Arcade, 2005).

Shariati, Ali. *What Is to Be Done?* Translated by Farhang Rajaee. Houston, TX: Institute for Research and Islamic Studies, 1986. Original title and publication date: *Chih Bayad Kard?*, 1970.

Shaykh, Hanan. *The Story of Zahra*. New York: Anchor Books, 1994. Original title and publication date: *Hikayat Zahrah*, 1980.

We Are Iran: The Persian Blogs. Translated and edited by Nasrin Alavi. Vancouver: Raincoast Books, 2005. The book form of these blogs was published in English only.

Zurayk, Constantine. *The Meaning of the Disaster*. Translated by R. Bayly Winder. Beirut: Khayat's College Book Cooperative, 1956. Original title and publication date: *Mana al-Nakbah*, 1948.

SECONDARY SOURCES

Badawi, M. M., ed. *Modern Arabic Literature*. Cambridge: Cambridge University Press, 1992.

Barakat, Halim. *The Arab World: Society, Culture, and State*. Berkeley: University of California Press, 1993.

Bowen, Donna Lee and Evelyn A. Early, eds. *Everyday Life in the Muslim Middle East*. 2nd ed. Bloomington: Indiana University Press, 2002.

Cleveland, William L. *A History of the Modern Middle East*. 3rd ed. Boulder: Westview Press, 2004.

Mattar, Philip, ed. *Encyclopedia of the Modern Middle East & North Africa*. 2nd ed. Detroit: Macmillan, 2004.

Moss, Joyce, ed. *Middle Eastern Literatures and Their Times*. Detroit: Thomson Gale, 2004.

Pappé, Ilan. *The Modern Middle East*. London: Routledge, 2005.

CHAPTER 27

Post-Colonial Africa

Walter P. Collins III

TIMELINE

1956	Congress of Black Writers and Artists in Paris; *Black Orpheus*, African Arts and Literature journal, founded in Ibadan, Nigeria
1957	Ghana gains independence
1958	South Africa gains independence
1959	Second Congress of Black Writers and Artists in Rome; United Nations condemns *apartheid*
1960	Year of Africa, declared by the United Nations; seventeen African countries gain independence from France, including Cameroon, Chad, Ivory Coast, Nigeria, Senegal, and Togo; Albert Luthuli, former president of the African National Congress, wins Nobel Peace Prize; the Mau Mau Uprising, an insurgent conflict begun in 1952, ends in Kenya
1961	Mbari Writers and Artists Club begins; later, a publishing house is established
1962	Algeria gains independence
1963	Nelson Mandela imprisoned for fight against apartheid in South Africa
1965	Commonwealth Arts Festival in London, features plays by Soyinka, Lapido, and J. P. Clark
1968	James Ngũgĩ demands the English Department at the University of Nairobi be abolished and be replaced by the Department of African Literature and Languages
1970	End of civil war in Nigeria
1976	Soweto uprising begins in South Africa
1986	Wole Soyinka wins Nobel Prize for Literature, first black writer to win the award
1988	Civil war begins in Somalia
1991	Ben Okri wins Booker Prize for Literature for *The Famished Road*
1994	Apartheid ends in South Africa

INTRODUCTION TO THE REGION/PERIOD

At the Second Congress of Black Writers and Artists in Rome in 1959, Aimé Césaire of Martinique led the rallying cry: "We must hasten the process of decolonization, that is to say, employ all means to hasten the ripening of a popular consciousness [of cultural and political freedom]" (qtd. in Ohaegbulam 294). Within a year, all West African French colonies had gained their independence, and new and creative literary, philosophical, and political energies oozed and flowed. For decades prior to Césaire's speech, a host of African nations had been colonized and occupied by European nations, most notably England and France. Strongholds in India, Kenya, South Africa, and Nigeria by the British were matched by French colonization of North and West African countries such as Algeria, Morocco, Senegal, and Ivory Coast. Soon, all-out efforts of change— affecting African education, daily routines, and religious beliefs—were in place to rescue the "primitive peoples" of the developing world. In reality, the colonial period was anything but a period of rescue or relief as Africans writhed in the oppressive and exploitative grip of western colonizers. Conditions remained this way until the mid-twentieth century.

To the surprise of many people, Africa played a considerable role in World War II. In the late 1930s and early 1940s, North Africa and Ethiopia were sites for skirmishes associated with the war. Many scholars, including Robert O. Collins, suggest that were it not for World War II then African countries may not have achieved independence as soon as they did. Collins writes:

> For over half a century Europeans had been able to dominate Africans not only because of their superior military, economic, and technical resources, but also because of the self-confidence with which they ruled. . . . Most Africans were convinced that the white man was superior. World War II shattered this illusion. . . . Despite the ultimate victory of Britain and France in World War II, events during the immediate postwar years undermined, rather than strengthened, the position of the colonial powers (139–140).

Africans sensed a change in the air concerning their one-time "superiors," and all of the "aloof and imperious colonial officials" from the prewar period no longer appeared as powerful (R. Collins 140). Ghana became independent from England and Guinea from France in 1957 and 1958, respectively. Likewise, between 1960 and 1964, other West African nations won their independence.

With independence came an increase in self-confidence for Africans. Perhaps unlike any other event in African history, decolonization triggered an individual and collective self-assurance that made Africans more aware of who they were. Africans came to understand their distinctiveness, not only in relationship to former colonizers, but also, and most importantly, in relationship to one another. This increased awareness precipitated in Africans an interest in writing about colonial and post-colonial experiences in order to share their own stories.

Although life under colonial rule was arduous on multiple levels for Africans, the early days of African independence proved difficult as well. Kwame Nkrumah, the first post-colonial leader of the first independent African country, Ghana, is the first African intellectual credited with using the term "neo-colonialism" with respect to the incidents of long-lasting and complex residual effects of colonialism after independence. Calling the post-independence period the final and worst stage of imperialism, Nkrumah penned *Neo-Colonialism: The Last Stage of Imperialism* in 1965 to lay out and analyze the traits of the neo-colonial phenomenon. Despite the continuance of socio-political troubles, Africans made strides in disseminating their ideas, thoughts, and stories. The effects of colonial and post-colonial domination prompted numerous Africans to pick up their pens and express themselves like at no other prior moment in Africa's history. One of the most revealing means for comprehending the effects of colonialism and neo-colonialism is to study the writings (both literary and nonliterary) and the reading choices of these Africans in their specific contexts.

READING TRENDS AND PRACTICES

In the Introduction to their cogent volume on post-colonial theory and literature, *The Empire Writes Back*, Bill Ashcroft, Gareth Griffiths, and Helen Tiffin remind readers of the counter-intuitive phenomenon that occurred as colonized writers were socially and historically marginalized for decades by European colonizers. They posit: "Paradoxically . . . imperial expansion has had a radically destabilizing effect on its own preoccupations and power. Marginality thus became an unprecedented source of creative energy. These notions are implicit in post-colonial texts from the imperial period to the present day" (12). However, many African readers—the immediate audiences for the resulting wave of writing—were not yet ready to ingest and process this new writing because most Africans still could not read during this period. Indeed, most African writing was destined for a western audience, as Africans either could not read the language, could not afford the texts, or could not muster the courage to pick up a written document and read it. In a lot of cases, reality was shaped by a combination of these circumstances. Charles Larson cites the situation of author Amos Tutuola as evidence:

> So widespread was illiteracy that it is possible that none of Tutuola's closest friends or members of his extended family would have been able to read his book. . . . Added to that is the likelihood that the book, an imported object, if available at stationery outlets (since there were no genuine bookshops in the country at the time) would be beyond the reach of most people's salaries. (13)

Furthermore, and with a few notable exceptions, of whom perhaps the most notable is Ngũgĩ wa Thiong'o, African writers wrote in western languages belonging to their former colonizers.

The post-colonial period of African texts, which for the purposes of this chapter begins in the early to mid-1950s and continues to the present, is characterized by a heightened consciousness of the multifarious impact European powers had on the continent of Africa. To be sure, African countries boasted dynamic literary traditions from their earliest days, even as colonizers from the West classified many African societies as illiterate, an appellation all too obviously pessimistic. Written texts existed certainly, as Oyekan Owomoyela and Bernth Lindfors note. In fact, Lindfors points out that in Anglophone areas of Africa "there had been a rich legacy of written literature in Yoruba, ranging from poetry

---

Post-Colonial Africa

Ashcroft, Griffiths, and Tiffin, in their groundbreaking 1989 work *The Empire Writes Back*, describe post-colonial Africa in these terms: "Africa is the source for the most significant and catalytic images of the first two decades of the twentieth century. In one very significant way the 'discovery' of Africa was the dominant paradigm for the self-discovery of the twentieth-century European world . . . As such, the more extreme forms of the self-critical and anarchic models of twentieth century culture which modernism ushered in can be seen to depend on the existence of the post-colonial Other which provides its condition of formation" (160).

and mythic narratives to episodic folkloric fantasies and detective novels" (*Loaded Vehicles* . . . 73–4). Likewise in Kenya, there existed before Ngũgĩ wa Thiong'o's fame "anticolonial pamphlet literature in Gikuyu and a very popular and religious literature in Kiswahili," and before South African Ezekial Mphahlele made headlines, there was "access to a full century of school storybooks published in South African Bantu languages" (Lindfors, *Loaded Vehicles* . . . 74). Literate Africans and young, school-aged Africans had access to and read these texts. But Owomoyela notes that, early on, most African societies (and European for that matter) were composed of oral cultures; more importantly, the transmission of this oral art fed a culture that thrived on the communal sharing of stories and tales (qtd. in W. Collins 31).

By the early to mid-twentieth century, Africans were disseminating written texts more regularly. *Anthologie de la nouvelle poésie nègre et malgache de langue française* (*Anthology of New Black and Madagascan Poetry in French*), published by *Négritudists* Léopold Sédar Senghor, Birago Diop, and Aimé Césaire in 1948, was preceded in 1947 by *Présence Africaine*, a journal established by Alioune Diop in Paris. Both proved to be important means for the dissemination of African literary criticism and theories, as they promulgated the positive message that all peoples of African descent (Africans, West Indians, African-Americans) should celebrate their dignity, distinctiveness, and unique aesthetic abilities. It is important to reiterate here that Africans writing at the time were by and large writing in European languages they had learned from mission schools set up by colonizers and that, according to Christopher Miller, Sub-Saharan Africans were almost wholly incapable of reading (69–70). Those who had access to education in mission schools on the African continent, and later for some in western universities, gained skills that enabled them to write about the struggles of their various countries under colonialism. Lindfors notes that "Modern African literature first became known to the outside world through the works of the elite, university-educated writers published in Europe and America . . . for they demonstrated through the force and sophistication of their art that Africa in the postwar era could speak quite eloquently for itself" (*Loaded Vehicles*, 73).

In the 1950s, novels appeared despite the many logistical challenges that African writers faced. Negotiating contracts with publishers was one difficulty, but the fact that so few Africans could read and/or procure texts also severely limited the production and circulation of books in Africa. Larson demonstrates the sheer luck Tutuola had in 1953 in eventually signing with Faber and Faber Publishing, as he had naively pursued publishing his first two novels with two unsuitable presses (27). Chinua Achebe's *Things Fall Apart* followed Amos Tutuola's *The Palm-Wine Drinkard* in 1958. Achebe, too, faced difficulties getting this masterpiece to press. Copies of his manuscript went missing for a time and Larson suggests that, had the manuscript for *Things Fall Apart* not turned up, Achebe would have given up his writing career altogether (27–8).

More writers began publishing as many African countries experienced politically charged instability, which would lead to other nonliterary African texts, addressed below. For many nations, colonialism seemed to be making its retreat. Sudan and Ghana were the first countries to gain their independence (1956 and 1957, respectively), and such liberation appeared likely within a couple of years for all colonized peoples. W. Collins suggests that "it was within such an environment that writers shared their perspectives on colonialism and that African and western readers gained perspectives on the effects of the colonial project. European colonizers had long insisted their purposes for being in Africa included helping a backward people out of the lawless, godless, and illiterate states they were in" (32). Achebe wrote, "I will be quite satisfied if my novels (especially the ones I set in the past) did no more than teach my readers that their past—with all its imperfections—was not one long night of savagery from which the first Europeans acting on God's behalf delivered them" (*Morning* . . . 72). Achebe's objective was certainly to reach Africans and teach them about their past, but he also wanted to enlighten them on the state of their post-colonial present. The use of the English language was critical in his enterprise, as it was necessary to reach western readers while reaffirming for Africans the authenticity of their past in a language that was becoming more and more ubiquitous. Later, however, post-colonial African texts tend toward more scathing and derisive remarks and commentary, sometimes subtle, sometimes overt, concerning the colonial project.

With expanding prospects for publication, African writers, from the 1960s on, added quickly to the body of African literature. In some instances however, subtle manifestations of the difficulties fledgling African publishing houses contended with are still noticeable. For instance, Miller notes that there is no chapter twenty-five in Mariama Bâ's original publication of *Une si longue lettre*, published by Les Nouvelles Éditions Africaines based in Dakar, Senegal and Abidjan, Ivory Coast. Yet when western publisher Heinemann later published the novel in English translation as *So Long a Letter*, chapter twenty-five reappeared (287). Likewise, from a business perspective, publishing is unpredictable, notes S. I. A. Kotei: "Indeed the book trade is regarded as the most risky business in the world today, after film-making (qtd in Hasan 1975: 1–8). With increasingly tough competition, the amateur publisher would be ill-advised to enter the profession without adequate training" (481). Nevertheless, African creative text publications continued in Africa and in Europe, despite ongoing difficulties. Larson acknowledges that

> African writers have not been much more successful in submitting their stories and poems to European and American publications than they were in the 1950s. Once again, the delays are enormous, the post unreliable, and many writers have little accurate knowledge about which publications might be most receptive to their works. (28)

Although these appear to be publication opportunities not to be passed up when they do materialize, Miller points out the distinct problems surrounding such seemingly positive new ventures: "Everywhere, élitism vexes intellectual life. By speaking and writing in European languages, the African intellectual makes him/herself incomprehensible to the majority of the people, who become an object in the intellectual's discourse" (70). Thus, writing in French, English, Portuguese, or any other European language extends in its own way the colonial project all the more.

Nevertheless, with only a small percentage of the native population capable of reading in any language due to feeble economic conditions, scarcity of educational opportunities, and a general overall focus on other life issues such as health, daily provision, and in some cases simple survival in the face of war and political strife, it appears that a majority of published novels were still aimed at western readers. Preeminent Nigerian novelist and critic Chinua Achebe, noting that many Africans have underdeveloped reading habits (even the elite groups such as professors, engineers, politicians, and businessmen), has asked some pointed questions: "What is the augury of the future? Will the intellectuals of tomorrow (who are at school today) read more, or is the book, already pronounced dead by some in the West, going to be stillborn in Africa?" (*Morning* . . . 63). Achebe eventually concludes that reading in Africa is poised for a positive future, and indeed with the rise in the number of libraries and publishing venues, circumstances can only improve.

That was 1972. More recently, an October 2006 entry by a Kenyan blogger, "Archer," suggests the current reality of readership in that country: "You can imagine my embarrassment when a media student asked me to recommend a few good books by acclaimed Kenyan writers. Er. . . . Name three books by Ngugi wa Thiong'o. Ok I knew a few. But that's when it hit me that I do need to read more. A lot more. A whole library more! It's embarrassing when guys from other countries know more about Kenyan authors than you do" ("Young Kenyans Just Don't Read").

Perhaps the reason "Archer" recalled Ngũgĩ's works so readily is because the author has chosen not to write in European languages, preferring instead to publish in native African languages first. Obviously, publications in Gikuyu (Kikuyu) have a limited potential audience for several reasons, yet Ngũgĩ's belief regarding the power of his native tongue to rescue Kenyans and Africans, even after independence, from lingering imperial paradigms of thought and reason propels him toward a full body of texts (literary, political, theoretical) written solely in his native language. According to Chidi

> **What Do African Intellectuals Read?**
>
> Chinua Achebe argues that "The temptation is indeed strong to answer that question in one word: nothing. But such an answer would be too simplistic—neither wholly true nor very helpful. A satisfactory answer has to be a little more complex, has to be hedged in here and there by exceptions, qualifications, even excuses" (*Morning Yet on Creation Day* 61).

Amuta, "Ngũgĩ's conviction about the crucial role of literature in creating a truly historical consciousness is born of his recognition of the instrumentality of colonialist writers in the denigration of Kenyan national identity" (162). Thus, Ngũgĩ hopes to preserve as much of his native national identity and culture as possible through the use of local language. Ngũgĩ was responsible in the early to mid-1970s for reorganizing the English Department at the University of Nairobi by changing its name to Department of Literature and placing "African oral and written languages at the heart of the curriculum" (Lindfors, *Popular Literatures . . .* 79–80). At least University students would have the opportunity to read African literature not only in English but also in African languages.

Male writers were not the only groundbreakers in African writing. In the 1970s and 1980s, women writers such as Buchi Emecheta, Bessie Head, and Mariama Bâ began to make their presence felt. Although this was a boon for writing and for women in general, most critics are quick to point out that women's fiction actually began almost a decade earlier. In 1966, Flora Nwapa and Grace Ogot published their first novels, *Efuru* and *The Promised Land*, respectively. Needless to say, their invisibility was quite simply a product of societal bias, post-colonial anxiety, and the general favoring of representative male authors who dominated the field (Achebe over Nwapa in Nigeria, and Ngũgĩ over Ogot in Kenya). Early on, women writers seemed "invisible." Florence Stratton reminds us that the first novel in Heinemann's African Writers Series is by Achebe (*Things Fall Apart*) and the twenty-sixth, the first by a woman, is *Efuru* by Nwapa. Thirty male-authored texts later, Nwapa's *Idu* appears on the list (80). However, Heinemann's series features titles that were and are available worldwide and continues to "produce a pantheon of literary greats for an international audience" (Stec 142). At Heinemann, publishing was initially based in London with limited publishing eventually taking place on the African continent. In the 1980s, notes Loretta Stec, with the onset of transcontinental economic crises, many publishing opportunities through Heinemann on African soil were sunk (142–143). It became increasingly difficult for African writers to publish unless their reputations had been well established or unless they were affiliated with a university. In 1988, Tsitsi Dangarembga faced difficulty finding a publisher for her first novel, *Nervous Conditions*. In an interview with Jane Wilkinson, Dangarembga states that at the time the manuscript was turned down she remembers wondering if "this decision from [the Zimbabwean] publishing house really reflected the fact that [she] could not write, or did it reflect perhaps the fact that [she] was writing about things that they were not ready to read about" (Wilkinson, 197). Pauline Ada Uwakweh reminds us that "patriarchal subordination of the female is reflected in the male domination of the literary arena" (75) as well, which likely accounts for the initial rejection of Dangarembga's text for publication and undoubtedly is responsible for so many distorted, male representations of females in African literature (W. Collins 72). Despite Dangarembga's troubles getting *Nervous Conditions* to press, one particular publishing house in Zimbabwe, Baobab Books, has emerged as a solid publisher that "[attempts] and sometimes [succeeds] in developing literate reading audiences. . . . Without Baobab Books, and without Irene Staunton as the publisher, the map of South African writing would look considerably different. The lesson to be learned from this? All it takes is the hard work of one publishing house, guided by integrity and quality, and the writers will appear" (Larson 109–110).

Post-colonial writers sought to communicate to their readers through fiction (often semi-autobiography) to demonstrate the degree to which the colonial project overturned traditional African societal mores, confused African values, and redirected paths to individual and community progress and development. Clearly though, nonliterary post-colonial African texts, speeches, and documents also portray the trying experiences of multiple peoples in the process of regaining recognizable and coherent identities. Many of the speeches, treatises, and documents shed light on the dire circumstances of post-colonial African societies while challenging and encouraging Africans to better themselves. In a similar manner, speeches and other intensely political documents respond to the central cultural and political events of the day. They reflect clearly the tenor of the difficulty of societies in the process of redefining themselves with no real structure or stable system of support from which to begin.

Post-colonial African texts, from the literary to the nonliterary, fully reflect the variety of cultural, social, economic, and political happenings of the period. From the benign pieces of early literary creation, wherein the countless imperial projects are lauded even by those most negatively affected in reality, to the later, most scathing condemnations of the influences of the West, African texts of this period readily confirm for readers far and wide their interconnectedness to the culture and history of these places.

SPEECHES

The push toward independence by African countries in the 1950s and 1960s engendered more freedoms for African leaders and others to assert their own influence and play critical roles in the evolutions of African countries. For many leaders, the time was ripe for declarations and proclamations concerning a future without colonial intervention. One notable speech by British Prime Minister Harold Macmillan, *Wind of Change*, became famous for its line: "The wind of change is blowing through this continent. Whether we like it or not, this growth of national consciousness is a political fact." The speech was delivered to the parliament of

South Africa in February of 1960, and brought to light several issues that South Africans were soon to face, equality and self-governance chief among them. Macmillan called for ultimate equality of all peoples of South Africa, a declaration that proved extremely contentious for the members of the mostly white, mostly ethnic European Nationalist Party. Not surprisingly, according to the British Broadcasting Corporation, the speech received a cool reception. Macmillan's speech addresses prevalent political issues of the day and is still viewed as one of the most important early moves to end apartheid. The winds continued blowing for over three decades until the racism and inequalities of apartheid were eventually put to an end in 1994.

In 1961, Kwame Nkrumah, the first post-colonial leader of Ghana—which was one of the first African countries to gain independence (in 1957) from European domination—asserted similar notions in his speeches, which often belie the realities of his time at the head of his country. However in 1966, Ghanans tired of his dictatorial style, and he lost the leadership in a *coup d'état*. Nonetheless, many ideas that came to light during Ghana's period of decolonization remained worthy goals. Nkrumah believed that unity in Africa was the key to progress toward a more promising future. The introduction to a collection of his speeches titled *I Speak of Freedom: A Statement of African Ideology*, invites fellow Africans to consider the world around them and learn from the failures and shortcomings of other nations. Nkrumah understood post-independence political and social chaos and proclaimed that future success was dependent upon cultural, ideological, and social unity achievable by individuals making the right choices daily. This speech and others were published in *I Speak of Freedom* in 1958. Subsequent editions of the book appeared in 1961, 1972, 1973, and 2001 by Heinemann, Praeger, and Mercury Presses. *I Speak of Freedom* has also been published in Japanese and in Arabic, testament to its worldwide influence.

In a courtroom in April 1964, Nelson Mandela, on trial for sabotage and high treason as well as opposing the longstanding apartheid government of South Africa, which blatantly discriminated against blacks, gave his famous speech, *I am Prepared to Die*. Mandela eloquently argued that he did not love violence and that he had never used it for its own sake. Mandela argues that all kinds of violence had for many years already been a part of South African apartheid schemes of dealing with blacks' political and social situations. He believed that blacks could justly answer with similar tactics shown them by their own government. Although he did not die in 1964, Mandela and seven others were convicted of sabotage and sentenced to life in prison. Twenty-six years later he was released from prison and in 1991 was elected president of the African National Congress. He was named the recipient of the Nobel Peace Prize in 1993, and in 1994 he was elected president of South Africa, where he served until 1999. Mandela's ideas and theories shaped not only South African culture and politics, but indeed the cultural and political issues facing the whole of post-colonial Africa. His speeches are still read and studied, as they trace very personal and human issues of equality and justice; such universal ideas resonate readily with contemporary Africans as well as individuals in all societies.

POLITICAL DOCUMENTS/TREATISES

The period of transition from colonized to independent country brought about great opportunities for concentrated analysis of the effects and ramifications of extensive and systematic colonization. What happens to the culture, social structure, and psyche of individuals who have long been oppressed by other cultures?

Martinican psychiatrist Frantz Fanon penned two of the best-known treatises of the 1950s and 1960s regarding racial alienation and the inherent oppression of colonization. *Peau noire, masques blancs* (*Black Skin, White Masks*) and *Les damnés de la terre* (*The Wretched of the Earth*) focus on racism while assessing the effects of imperialism on the colonial mind. Many of the creative texts written during the period reflect in fictional contexts the theories and tenets that underpin Fanon's observations on race and colonial interaction. Chief among Fanon's assertions was that misconception and misunderstanding, oversimplification and overgeneralization of African Diasporic peoples were at the core of much of the inequality and disparagement in colonization. The books dispense theories of racism and cultural alienation as well as observed typical psychological reactions to colonial oppression, and they are essential for readers striving to gain a true understanding of the African post-colonial period. The books are easily found in academic libraries around the world in multiple editions and a variety of translations.

On the African continent, *The Freedom Charter*, the preparation of which has been attributed to Z. K. Mathews, Lionel Bernstein, and other members of the South African Communist Party (many of whom were arrested later for their contributions), was presented and adopted during a two-day meeting of the Congress of the People in Kliptown, Soweto, South Africa, in June 1955. The document is critical to the development of the country because of the kinds of equality issues it addresses. Among the issues brought to light in the document are government by the people; equal rights for all citizens; sharing of wealth; redistribution of land; equality before the law; the right to work; security; and equal opportunities for, and access to, education, culture, and relative human comforts. Before the congress was broken up by police raids on the second day, four groups had approved the document. Many believe *The Freedom Charter* to be the primary inspiration for the African National Congress's 1994 Constitution of South Africa. Whether such is the case or not, the 1955 document gives lucid indication of the cultural, social, political, and personal difficulties certain segments of the South African population endured and clearly makes the case for change.

During this same year, similar ideologies were finding their way to publishers on the African continent. Written for *Liberation: A Journal for Democratic Discussion*, a journal published in South Africa from 1953 to 1959, *People Are Destroyed* is one of Mandela's many documents relating the circumstances of black South Africans. Mandela's reference to Belsen and Buchenwald, Nazi concentration camps during World War II, recalls the series of examples with which he begins the article, which notes that the inequalities that black South Africans faced could be viewed as stepping stones to eventual enslavement and extermination. Mandela explained how the apartheid government treated blacks unjustly to insure that there were enough mining and farm laborers. He also noted how the government squelched opportunities for education so that potential black-led uprisings could be precluded. Mandela's call for action is for "the united strength of the people of South Africa," and he pointed out that *The Freedom Charter*, calling for equality and better cultural and social conditions for black South Africans, had already been adopted. Although Mandela's appeal made its way to the public through publication in the journal and was well received, we now know that true cultural and political changes in South Africa would not be realized for another forty years.

In 1970, Kwame Nkrumah wrote *Consciencism: Philosophy and Ideology for Decolonization and Development*, which treats the opposing forces of traditional African ideology, Christian belief and ideology, and Islamic belief and ideology, which all together bombard and confound the African. Nkrumah argues that

Africans should deal with these opposing influences and arrive at some successful culmination. For him, "Consciencism [becomes] the theoretical basis for an ideology whose aim shall be to contain the African experience of Islamic and Euro-Christian presence as well as the experience of traditional African society, and, by gestation, employ them for the harmonious growth and development of that society" (Nkrumah, *Consciencism* 70). Interestingly, Nkrumah incorporates a bit of Marxist theory into the text, and although some scholars conclude that this is the work's undoing, V. Y. Mudimbe argues that Nkrumah's "theoretical legacy remains, challenging and stimulating for the new generation of African Marxists looking for paradigms of revolutionary change and cultural dynamism" (95–96). Nkrumah's ideas and perspectives undoubtedly left indelible marks on the continent of Africa, and his ideologies are still debated there and elsewhere as they remain available in collections in almost every academic library around the world.

In the late 1960s in Tanzania, President Julius Nyerere's political document *Arusha Declaration* appeared. The document is subtitled *On the Policy of Self-Reliance in Tanzania,* and the notion of self-reliance is where he indeed believes the solutions to that country's need for future development lie. The document begins with a resounding rejection of money as the solution to Tanzania's post-colonial tribulations. Additionally, he acknowledges industry as a hollow and ineffectual solution. Consequently Nyerere turns to resources to which Tanzanians do have access, namely hard work by human hands. Pointing out the country's geological and climatological advantages of fertile lands and good rains, Nyerere believes that concentrated agricultural efforts on the part of Tanzanians would yield great benefits. This call to action from the president of a newly independent country demonstrates the radical rebuilding from the ground up that many post-colonial cultures underwent. Although this was a basic message to his fellow countrymen, it effectively failed to change Tanzanians' circumstances. Problems that the declaration addresses continue to this day. It is unclear whether the Tanzanians flatly rejected the president's challenges presented in the document or whether the document was simply too idealistic. In any case, the assertions of Fanon's earlier texts, *Peau noire, masques blancs* and *Les damnés de la terre,* have been borne out in the realities of post-colonial societies across the African Diaspora.

These texts and documents remain available to the public through the Internet and in libraries worldwide. Editions of Fanon's two texts are available in over twenty-five hundred libraries in French, English, Portuguese, Dutch, Hebrew, Japanese, Chinese, Persian, and German. They remain standards in the area of post-colonial studies of the African Diaspora and are widely studied in connecting fields of anthropology of developing countries and of oppressed peoples as well.

MAGAZINES, JOURNALS, AND NEWSPAPERS

With the move toward independence for African countries, more and more publishing opportunities became available, even though publication was not without challenge. Serial publications and other literary enterprises increased in number and influence in African countries and in the West. *Présence Africaine*, established by Alioune Diop in 1947 in Paris, proved to be an important means for the dissemination of African literary criticism and theories. Diop was supported in the project by Léopold Sédar Senghor, Aimé Césaire, André Gide, and Albert Camus. The journal began as a French language publication. Beginning in 1957, however, *Présence Africaine* was published in both French and English, allowing for a more widespread circulation of ideas and theories. The readers of the journal were the educated elite of society who had found in education the ability to assert themselves and promote Africa on a global scale. The journal was extremely useful in disseminating the musings of critics involved in the *Négritude* movement begun in the 1930s.

African Drum, a literary magazine begun by Lewis Nkosi in 1951, sought contributors "to reach [Africans] for the first time in history with words that will express their thoughts, their impulses, their endeavors and, ultimately, their souls" (qtd. in Lindfors, *Loaded Vehicles . . .* 4–5). The content of the first several editions centered on what editors believed would appeal to African readers—"there were articles on tribal history, tribal music, famous chiefs, farming, religion, and sports" (Lindfors, *Loaded Vehicles . . .* 5). Ironically, the issues remained on shelves because the editors had it all wrong. Lindfors cites the outcries of African readers:

> Ag, why do you dish out that stuff, man? . . . Tribal music! Tribal history! Chiefs! We don't care about chiefs! Give us Jazz and film stars, man! We want Duke Ellington, Satchmo, and hot dames! Yes, brother, anything, American. You can cut out this junk about kraals and folktales and Basutos in blankets—forget it! You're just trying to keep us backward, that's what! (*Loaded Vehicles . . .* 5)

The message was heard loud and clear; *African Drum* soon became *Drum*, and its focus became much broader in order to deliver what its reading public desired—fewer folktales and more "stories about city life, love stories . . . detective thrillers, and true confessions" (Lindfors, *Loaded Vehicles . . .* 5). By the early 1960s, *Drum's* influence diminished, and the mission of "satisfying of appetites rather than the shaping of tastes" slowly faded (Lindfors, *Loaded Vehicles . . .* 6).

The publication of *Black Orpheus* began in 1956. Begun by a German national, Ulli Beier who lived in Nigeria, the journal was founded "to stimulate literary activity by providing an outlet for writers and by publishing outstanding works by established black writers from other parts of Africa, the West Indies, and North and South America" (Lindfors, *Loaded Vehicles . . .* 23–24). Clearly, this was a journal that sought from its beginnings to disseminate black writing to readers on multiple continents. Although its readers were still by and large the highly educated, the journal offered writers a new avenue for publication. Bernth Lindfors notes that "distribution of the journal was slow at first, because the Ministry of Education [of Nigeria] was inexperienced in this kind of work, but it improved when Longmans [Publishers] took over. Gradually, as *Black Orpheus* earned an international reputation, its circulation rose to a respectable 3,500. In Africa, writers and would-be writers read it avidly" (*Loaded Vehicles . . .* 24–25). Journals such as *Présence Africaine* and *Black Orpheus* were groundbreaking publications in their time; however, they have experienced differing levels of influence in recent years. Whereas *Présence Africaine* continues to offer regular and insightful writing dealing with interconnected social, political, and literary notions of Africa by writers from across the African Diaspora, *Black Orpheus* appears sporadically and often focuses solely on Nigerian literary and political issues instead of issues of greater interest to a wider audience (Lindfors, *Loaded Vehicles . . .* 40–41).

The Literary Market, various actual bookstalls in the commercial hub of Onitsha, a city on the banks of the Niger River in the southern part of Nigeria, also proved to be quite a force in the writing and publication arena. Although the texts began in the 1940s they did not reach their height of popularity until the early 1960s. Emmanuel Obiechina suggests that the market literature became so famous because of "increased literacy in southern Nigeria, population explosion, rural-urban migration, increased technology (including printing), and an incursion of new ideas, aspirations and desires with the return of soldiers from the Second World War" (qtd. in Bryce-Okunlola 177). Dodson adds: "the vitality of a new 'democratic' spirit . . . fostered the feeling that any man could make a name and money by writing a story" (197). Texts with titles such as *How to Speak to Girls and Win Their Love*, *Mabel the Sweet Honey That Poured Away*, and *Money Hard to Get But Easy to Spend* were top choices in the Onitsha area. It is clear that this popular literature filled an early gap in writing and publication as it served to bridge oral literature of an earlier period to the rise of written texts at independence and beyond. Additionally, the titles brought amusement to readers and addressed the "how-tos" of personal and professional life, from writing skills to money management and political analyses.

Jane Bryce-Okunlola asserts that the typical format for the literature is parody in an effort to "undermine the dominant culture by using its characteristics playfully" (178). Thus the literature provided readers with a sort of revision to their nightmarish past. Nevertheless, Lindfors notes that "they were avidly read by hundreds of students, clerks, traders, craftsmen, taxi drivers, and other semi-educated townsfolk who wanted to practice the language they had learned at school" (*Loaded Vehicles . . .* 107). Despite the fact that the language of most books was considered by some to be nonstandard, they were used as a way for African readers to practice their English and gain insights into "appropriate" cultural, social, and moral issues (Dodson 208–210). Lindfors adds that one of the more intriguing aspects of the market literature is what he terms "the transmission of fixed-phrase folklore"—a metamorphosis in wording or phrasing to some extent or other made by the author or typesetter that augments or diminishes the meaning of a well-known phrase (*Loaded Vehicles . . .* 109). Not afraid to create a new word or write in an overly adventurous manner, Onitsha authors take shock value and syrupy melodrama to a new level in their texts, an obvious source of some of the changes. Copies of various chapbooks sold at Onitsha literary markets are still available in approximately ten large university libraries in North America. Likewise, the University of Kansas has recently completed a digitized database of twenty-one of the books that makes them available on a global scale, and the University of Indiana owns over 170 actual texts that can be made available to the public but do not circulate.

PERSONAL TEXTS

Those with some education could publish their own stories. Autobiographical and memoir texts serve not only to chronicle the political and historical events of the post-colonial period, but to relay the details of personal experience—the experience of those whose personal lives were changed, many for the worse, as post-colonial history was made. From 1952 to around 1960, Kenyan rebel groups such as the Kikuyu Central Association and the Kenya Africa Union led attacks on the British colonial rulers after years of oppression and because they feared that Kenya would be consolidated under white rule like South Africa. The conflicts were often heated and dangerous. The British won the battle, so to speak, but the Kenyans eventually won the war. Over time, the British relaxed the restrictions on land regulations and coffee production and sales that had been in place, and Kenya became fully independent of British control in 1963. Josiah Kariuki's autobiography, *Mau Mau Detainee*, recounts his torment and affliction as a captive of British officials during this period of rebellion. Horrifying descriptions of life in solitary confinement reveal the degree to which rebels like Kariuki believed in their causes. Kariuki was assassinated in 1975 as he continued to oppose Kenyan government officials in the post-colonial context. He has been praised by Ngũgĩ wa Thiong'o "as an exemplar of a different kind of political education, one in direct opposition to the colonial education the novelist [Ngũgĩ,] had acquired at Makerere University College" (Gikandi 197). His personal insights during and after Mau Mau are critical, and they reveal to both African and western readers a comprehensive perspective of Kenya's post-colonial situation. According to records in both Global Books in Print and the WorldCat databases, the autobiographical account was published by Oxford University in 1963 and 1975 and is still available for purchase in the United States and the United Kingdom and for loan in over five hundred libraries around the world. In 1965, it was published in the Swahili language in Nairobi, Kenya, making it more accessible to individual readers in the country in which the rebellions actually took place.

In 1972, another critical memoir appeared. Wole Soyinka's *The Man Died* is comprised of prison journal entries written and collected by the first African to win the Nobel Prize in Literature (1986). The thoughts and observations were literally written with homemade ink on toilet tissue, gum and candy wrappings, cigarette papers, and the leaves of various books that Soyinka was allowed to read. He later smuggled them out of prison when he was released. Imprisoned because he called for a cease-fire in the civil war that Nigerians were fighting, Soyinka penned what scholars now consider the work that is at the very crossroads of his *œuvre*, as it considers themes common in the lives of searching Nigerians in the throes of independence and those common in the unjustly imprisoned of any culture. Biodun Jeyifo notes that "the particular dimension which the first person narrative voice and point of view takes in *The Man Died* is probably without any comparison in modern African literature in its completely unselfconscious and unembarrassed assertion of the indissociable identity of the author/narrator with the cause of Truth, Justice and Humanity" (179–180). In capturing the essence of the human struggle in the face of societal change and progress, the book thus appeals to African readers who have dealt with such transition and socio-cultural evolution, and it has become a part of what Charles Larson suggests is "an entire sub-genre . . . book-length accounts by writers . . . who have served time in their country's prisons" (127). The book was published three years following Soyinka's release from prison in English and in French simultaneously in both North America and Europe (Larson 129).

CREATIVE TEXTS

Creative works of post-colonial African writing are numerous and inherently thought-provoking, as the vast majority of their authors react against colonial oppression and comment on the extensive consequences of the colonial project. The contexts of many of the novels, plays, and poems rise directly from authors', playwrights', and poets' lived experiences. Although many of the texts could be categorized as fictionalized histories or veiled biographies, all connect precisely to the complex social, political, and cultural transitions many African countries faced beginning in the 1950s as independence from western nations became a reality after decades of colonization.

Chinua Achebe, number three on a list of most-read African authors in a survey of thirty African universities, published *Things Fall Apart* in 1958 (Lindfors, "The Teaching . . ." 47). The novel chronicles the misfortunes brought about by the inherent destabilizing effects of clashing cultures on a central protagonist,

10Q 1988

ПОЧТА СССР

БОРЕЦ ЗА СВОБОДУ ЮЖНОЙ АФРИКИ
НЕЛЬСОН МАНДЕЛА

Nelson Mandela was not only instrumental in bringing about an end to the system of Apartheid in South Africa, his memoir, *The Long Walk to Freedom*, was popularly read throughout the world. Mandela is pictured here on a 1988 USSR commemorative stamp.

Okonkwo, and his community. Prominent themes include cultural impact of colonialism, quality of life issues, and life legacies. Many have remarked on Achebe's successful translation of Igbo myths and legends into English. Additionally, when characters speak in the novel, they do so at a formal level of diction. The language in *Things Fall Apart* stands in stark contrast to that of previous novels where characters used broken English or Pidgin English to communicate. In *Morning Yet on Creation Day*, Achebe acknowledges his personal reasons for his use of English while suggesting the transformation involved as well: "for me there is no other choice. I have been given this language and I intend to use it. . . . I feel that the English language will be able to carry the weight of my African experience. But it will have to be a new English, still in full communion with its ancestral home but altered to suit its new African surroundings" (103).

He was successful in many ways because the English he used in telling his story triggered a reassessment of African identity. The novel is still read widely, especially in western nations, and was one of the first African novels read in anthropology, history, and literature classes at the university level. Likewise, it is read in African universities. For instance, it figures in the first year reading list for students majoring in English at Nelson Mandela Metropolitan University in South Africa. In his fairly exhaustive study of the teaching of African literature in African universities, Lindfors also notes, however, that *Things Fall Apart* figures at number twelve on a list of African texts being read in thirteen courses at ten universities in seven African nations ("The Teaching . . ." 51). Considering its status as a must-read African novel in the West, it is surprising to see *Things Fall Apart* at number twelve. Likewise, it is important to note that in African universities, two of his other works, *Arrow of God* and *Man of the People*, rank higher (numbers one and three, respectively) in terms of assigned course readings (Lindfors, "The Teaching . . ." 51). Nonetheless, Achebe notes that in 1965, eight hundred copies of *Things Fall Apart* had been sold in Britain, which contrasts greatly with the twenty thousand copies sold in Nigeria and the approximately twenty-five hundred sold in the rest of the world ("The Novelist . . ." 41). Africans were indeed reading Achebe.

Theater pieces also thrived early during the post-colonial African period. Dramatic works, because of their public performance attributes, flourished in soci-

eties where large numbers of people remained illiterate. Wole
Soyinka tops Lindfors's list as the
most widely read African writer in
African universities, as his works
are featured on reading lists for
87 courses at thirty universities in
fourteen nations ("The Teaching
. . ." 47). One of Wole Soyinka's
early plays, *A Dance of the Forests*,
was first performed by the theatrical troupe "The 1960 Masks" in
Lagos, Nigeria in 1960, the
country's year of independence.

Chinua Achebe's best-selling novel, *Things Fall Apart*.

The play, written expressly to
commemorate Nigeria's independ-
ence, won the *Encounter* independence play award shortly after its appearance.
Soyinka's *A Dance of the Forests*, according to Eldred D. Jones, transmits the best
of African myth and folklore while benefiting from the strengths of European
drama (20–21). Furthermore, Jones notes that Soyinka's writing is often inseparable from his life experience: "concern [for his society] is apparent in his poetry,
drama, and essays, but is not merely literary. It shows itself in his letters to the
Nigerian papers, which can always be relied upon to rouse enthusiastic support or
bitter opposition" [by literate Africans who read newspapers] (21). *A Dance of the
Forests* recounts the journey of the symbolic Nigerian subject over a period of
many years. Soyinka demonstrates the cyclical nature of life by drawing upon the
continuous movement, evolution, and progression of the intricacies of the human
personality. The play reflects the culture of this specific post-colonial period and
place quite clearly and demonstrates how the message might be applicable beyond
the play's temporal and physical boundaries.

During the post-colonial period, writers made a variety of efforts through writing and publication to preserve Africa's oral cultural heritage, which had been mostly stifled by western occupiers. One such effort is D. T. Niane's publication of
Soundjata ou l'Épopée Mandingue (*Soundjata or the Mandinka Epoch*) in 1960.
Guinea's Niane is credited with introducing this ancient African legend to the entire
world. He chose to do so using the French language, which is problematic for
some. However, the author believed that the story contains universal, cultural and
social truths that would benefit all of humanity. The legend chronicles the establishment of the Malian Empire as it focuses on themes of familial loyalty, exile, the
importance of recognizing and respecting prophecy and overcoming disability in
order to accomplish great things. In passing this legend along to western readers,
Niane ensured that a very important story in the storehouse of African folklore and
myth would survive in written format at a time, in 1960, when the majority of West
African countries were once again in transition. The fact that the text was written
in the French language makes it more exportable to western readers; yet Nigerian
poet Niyi Osundare acknowledges an unmistakable wariness on the part of Africans
concerning the transcription of their oral culture. He writes: "in addition to the
spoken word, the people's memory resides in the throbbing alphabet of the drum,
and the learned execution of dance steps. The people [of Africa] are not only proud
of their oral culture, they are more critical of the written lore" (17).

Another French-language text, Sembène Ousmane's 1960 novel *Les Bouts de Bois
de Dieu* (*God's Bits of Wood*), like many other novels written as African countries were

gaining independence, captures the individual and societal struggles of a transition that, on the surface at least, many expected to be straightforward. Ousmane's novel is preoccupied with themes of power between the genders, and African and western readers clearly detect that the women come to hold much more power in certain instances than do the men. For example, the female character Penda successfully leads the group of women in revolt, whereas Bakayoko, the main male character, is not able to help or assist them in any way. Ousmane's underlying message resonates clearly: the culture and traditions of colonial and post-colonial societies have for too long adversely affected women. Women now fully recognize their dire consequences and they are ready and willing to take action to change things. The novel takes up the notion of ever-evolving relationships between men and women and offers African readers a post-colonial African context in which to consider such a global issue.

Evolving relationships between men and women were but one increasingly important issue during the advent of independence in Africa. Another critical matter at this transitional time was the availability and quality of education. The 1961 novel *L'Aventure ambiguë* (*Ambiguous Adventure*) by Cheikh Hamidou Kane deals with the appeal of western education to those in Africa who have been colonized by Europeans. Many in African communities initially saw the advance of western systems of education as wholly beneficial and as social and intellectual cure-alls for the backwardness and ignorance they had been told they possessed. In reality, Africans received more than instruction: their native cultures were marginalized to make room for the foreign and strange, the empty, and ultimately the ambiguous. African readers of Kane's novel gain insight regarding the ambiguous nature of western education as Kane clarifies the ways in which the educational system both ameliorates and undermines the African experience.

Like Ousmane's *Les Bouts de Bois de Dieu* (*God's Bits of Wood*) and Cheikh Hamidou Kane's *L'Aventure ambiguë* (*Ambiguous Adventure*), Christina Ama Ata Aidoo's 1964 play *The Dilemma of a Ghost* suggests much about the status of women in Africa; the reception of female outsiders; the function, value, and ultimate role of western education in developing countries; and the acceptance of adopted foreign cultures and morés. Aidoo puts into question the real dilemmas of a post-independence Ghana where individuals still seek to leave the country, as many did during colonization, to get an education—only to come home and find that, for many reasons and because of many choices made, they now live at odds with their social and cultural background. The 1960s continued to bring up questions regarding education, as well as gender status and rank, and Aidoo's play highlights such matters for segments of the population who held jobs and could pay to see the spectacle on stage. Additionally, Lindfors notes that Aidoo is the fifteenth-most-read author among African university students (at sixteen institutions in seven countries), allowing her messages to Africans on the status of women and the value of education to be heard far and wide ("The Teaching . . ." 47).

During the 1960s, African novels increasingly resembled their western counterparts in terms of intrigue, style, and characterization. Wole Soyinka's first novel, *The Interpreters*, ranks at number seven on the list of most often assigned texts, with thirteen African universities reporting the novel on syllabi for sixteen courses (Lindfors, "The Teaching . . ." 51). It offers readers a variety of narrative acrobatics and profound characters, which prompted Gerald Moore to call the book "the first African novel that has a texture of real complexity and depth" (qtd. in Jones 159). The 1965 book includes instances of flashback and extension of thought through time, whereas brief moments of real time are often stretched over multiple pages of the *récit*. Critical themes in the novel include purposeful decision-making, navigating the world, isolation, tradition versus modernization, complacency versus action, and individual opportunity and responsibility—all issues that real Nigerians faced in 1960 when they found themselves independent from Great Britain for the first time in decades. Novels like *The Interpreters* brought personal post-colonial circumstances to the foreground in a striking manner. Readers continue to have access to the book in thousands of libraries worldwide in its original English, but also in French, Dutch, Spanish, Korean, Portuguese, and Finnish. According to the Global Books in Print database, it most recently appeared in 1996 from the presses of Andre Deutsch Publishing, which marketed it in the United Kingdom and South Africa.

In 1966, a year after Soyinka's groundbreaking novel *The Interpreters* was published, Flora Nwapa introduced her work *Efuru*. The first African novel written by a woman, *Efuru* offers a true depiction, not unlike that of Aidoo's *The Dilemma of a Ghost*, of what the lives of women were like during and after the colonial period. *Efuru* bravely tackles cultural issues of the attainment of personal dignity and fully developed selfhood that many women were never allowed to approach because of continuous oppression by neo-colonial and patriarchal power structures. *Efuru* became the first in a series of novels by female authors to chronicle the lives of female protagonists and raise awareness concerning the dilemmas women in African, post-colonial societies faced.

Notions of the attainment of personal dignity in contentious circumstances reverberate in a similar fashion through Ayi Kwei Armah's 1968 novel *The Beautiful Ones Are Not Yet Born*. This novel quite vividly reveals the squalid and debased conditions of a nameless one, "the man," trying to live his life in truth, honesty, and uprightness in a corrupted, post-independent Ghana. It ties, at number seven, Soyinka's *The Interpreters* in terms of assigned reading in African universities. The story draws on the real-life conditions of many African nationals who, after the independence of their country, were not simply returned to the precolonial calm and dignity of their traditional lives. The novel mirrors the actual corruption of societies that try to stabilize after independence, and it is full of references to the debris of society, the surrounding decay, and the greed of corruption. In the introduction to the novel, novelist Christina Ama Ata Aidoo writes: "Indeed his [Armah's] desire for writing the novel seems to have been to express with a view to destroying what he cannot take about Ghana. The contents of the book clearly delineate what his targets would be if words could kill" (introduction to *The Beautiful Ones Are Not Yet Born*). There was so much hope, optimism, and expectation at the beginning of independence, yet in the process of redefining his country, Armah observes so much sleaze from his countrymen. He reminds readers that at some future moment more promise might come, the beautiful ones who can put us on the right path might be born. Despite the dirt and corruption, hope persists. The novel remains a popular choice for readers and, according to Global Books in Print, can readily be found in its late 1980s editions published by Heinemann for markets in the United States, the United Kingdom, and South Africa. The number of instances Armah's works appear in required reading lists at thirty African universities leads him to be ranked the fourth-most-read African author out of over forty authors (Lindfors, "The Teaching . . ." 47).

Like novels that preceded it, Ahmadou Kourouma's 1968 novel, *Les soleils des indépendances* (*The Suns of Independence*) retells the story of a country at a crossroads. Kourouma masterfully captures the subtle incidents and events of cultures in transition—cultures that have been permanently altered because of colonization and for which no precolonial social and cultural stability can be reestablished. Writing in French, Kourouma nonetheless successfully captures the rhythm and images of his native Malinke, even from the first sentence of the novel. Miller notes that "Examples of linguistic 'deviance' are to be found on nearly every page. By using African-language phrases translated word for word into French, and by using African words that he teaches to the reader, Kourouma goes further than previous African writers toward closing the gap between the way French is spoken by many Africans and the way it is written" (202). The book, originally published in French by Paris publisher Éditions du Seuil, can be found at libraries worldwide. Likewise, the novel has been translated into various other languages including Dutch, Polish, and English. Although the English translation of the novel is not as commonly found in libraries (only slightly fewer than two hundred libraries own it according to the WorldCat database), it was published again in English in 2000 by Holmes and Meier of New York.

Although Senghor and David Diop became noted poets well before Christopher Okigbo, Okigbo's "collected works," *Labyrinths*, of 1971 offers something new to readers and critics. Scholars agree that his work represents the best in African poetry across several generations and speculate what that future might have been had he not died in the Nigerian civil war in 1967 when he was thirty-five years old. This real-life incident appears, perhaps, to have been in some sense forecast in "Path of Thunder," one poem in the collection, in which the narrator prophesizes that he will suffer the consequences if he continues to speak out against oppression. The poems are heavily influenced by European verse and allude to a variety of writers and musicians: Gerard Manly Hopkins, Debussy, Franck, and Ravel. Although the poems may, on first perusal at least, seem disjointed and incoherent, scholars note that various motifs appear and reappear and ultimately, in many cases, tie seemingly loose ends. Nevertheless, many have come to Okigbo's defense concerning the relative obscurity of some of his poems. Gerald Moore reminds readers that "An African poet has got just as much right to be obscure as anybody else" (qtd. in Chinwiezu, Jemie and Madubuike). However, Chinwiezu, Jemie, and Madubuike, the *bolekaja* critics who reject Eurocentrist ideology and structure in Africa's critical analysis and creative writing, also take Okigbo's style to task. Still, Okigbo's *Labyrinths* remains a collection of some of the finest poetic language by an African. It clearly offers a wellspring of symbols, images, and motifs to African readers that serve to characterize the nature and disposition of individuals in relation to their culture during the post-colonial period.

By the early to mid-1970s, despite continued gender bias in publication, it was becoming somewhat easier for women to find publishers. Although most willing publishers were outside Africa, women were able to publish some things for those who could read and who had a bit of money. Buchi Emecheta is unmistakably the best known and most widely published female African author even though she was preceded by two other African women writers, Flora Nwapa and Grace Ogot, almost a decade before she penned *In the Ditch* and *Second-Class Citizen*. Although *In the Ditch* was written in 1972, before *Second-Class Citizen* of 1974, the latter is the narrative sequel of the former. In an interview with Kirsten Holst Petersen in the 1980s, Emecheta explains her influences: "When I am in Britain I just put all my grievances [regarding how women are treated in Africa] into my books because I know that in Britain people read books, so that is how I cope with my anger in Britain; but in Nigeria I have to speak [out against such treatment] because people don't buy many books." Women's issues are only one of the concerns in Emecheta's novels. Emecheta's early novels anticipate further work she would do regarding the status of women in African societies. Her novels resonate with western female readers as clearly as they do with female African readers as they deal frankly with universal women's issues.

Women's issues across cultures is the theme as well in Mariama Bâ's 1986 *Une si longue lettre* (*So Long a Letter*). This epistolary novel features a transoceanic message from Ramatoulaye to her friend Aissatou on the occasion of the death of the former's estranged husband. Readers get the distinct impression that writing the letters that create the text of the novel are Ramatoulaye's means of finally finding a voice to communicate the silences of the five years she remained faithful to her husband when he was utterly unfaithful to her and their children. Bâ's short novel exposes themes of polygamy, spousal loyalty, exile, devotion to religious tenets while throughout expressing the varied perceptions of African culture and society to its readers. The novel responds creatively to common domestic problems experienced by many African women in the post-colonial period.

Another novel that mirrors the realities of women's existence is *Nervous Conditions* by Tsitsi Dangarembga. The story revolves around the interconnections in the lives of five women, with one of those, the young Tambu, as the central protagonist. Dangarembga examines seemingly benign notions of "Englishness"—good education, financial comfort, and independence—to demonstrate the difficulties that arise when Rhodesian women seek these things out. Pauline Uwakweh crystallizes the themes of the novel succinctly: "All the characters suffer, in a variety of ways and to a certain degree, the triple levels of entrapment that the narrator identifies: the entrapment of poverty, the weight of womanhood, and 'the Englishness' that Tambu's mother cautions against. As a veritable source of nervous conditions, it also becomes a leitmotif for the dangers of colonialism" (79). *Nervous Conditions*, Dangarembga's only novel, neatly but sadly reflects the cultural realities of colonial and post-colonial Rhodesia. Although she has focused her creative energies in other directions, the novel has come to be a staple on African university syllabi in courses from anthropology and history to world and African literatures. Ann Elizabeth Willey and Jeanette Treiber note that the novel has, since the early 1990s, been increasingly replacing Achebe's *Things Fall Apart* on reading lists for college courses [in Africa as well as the West] (ix).

A recent novel, Ben Okri's 1991 *The Famished Road* combines glimpses of Nigerian society on the brink of independence from Britain with references to and interactions with the world of the spirits. The story, though, remains a strong critical attack on the political scandals and corruption in this society. Henry Louis Gates, Jr. points out that

---

The Business of Reading in Africa

At a 2001 conference sponsored by the Southern African Book Development Education Trust, David Aduda of the Nation Media Group, Kenya, asked, *How can the Media promote reading in Africa?* He responded that "Today Africa is faced with lack of reading among its populations, be it for social, economic or political reasons. People who are illiterate cannot read. People who are the victims of river blindness cannot read. Or can they? For such groupings use of community radios for readings can be explored. Books and written material can be read over the radio and people can participate in the analysis of such readings. Plays too provide a natural flow from a basically oral inheritance. The radio can be used as a medium to persuade plays to be read. Reading can and should be encouraged by example. In South Africa where the speaker currently works and resides there is a daily one-and-a-half-hour morning radio programme, in which this speaker himself has participated, on which books are discussed. Discussions of books can also be carried on television programmes. For those who have access to the Internet, books can be downloaded and forwarded to friends and their readings can be discussed thereafter. Programmes of going to schools, reading among the students, setting up publishing initiatives are all means of reaching out." (http://www.readingafrica.com/seminarseries.htm#aduda)

"Ben Okri, by plumbing the depths of Yoruba mythology, has created a political fable about the crisis of democracy in Africa and throughout the modern world. More than that, however, he has ushered the African novel into its own post-modern era through a compelling extension of traditional oral forms that uncover the future in the past" ("Between the Living . . ." 20). Okri, like Ahmadou Kourouma, demonstrates how key concepts in African culture and tradition can make their way almost unaltered into stories told in European languages. This is to the benefit not only of readers in the West, but also African readers, offering them a critical lens through which to observe the sociopolitical atmosphere of their countries in order to act in appropriate and meaningful ways. According to the WorldCat database, *The Famished Road* is available in multiple languages in thousands of libraries around the world. Its most recent printing was completed for the New Zealand market by Random House in 1996.

J. M. Coetzee, winner of the Nobel Prize for Literature in 2003, presents readers with a startling post-apartheid scrutiny of the social realities of his own South Africa in *Disgrace*. The 1999 story of an English/communications professor, David Lurie, who falls from grace after the administration of his university learns of his affair with one of his students, Melanie, suggests the turmoil that South Africans face as their societies transition. Coetzee's analysis of social upheavals of post-apartheid society in South Africa offers revealing insight to readers around the world regarding the instability inherent in any country where social, political, and cultural change is under way. *Disgrace* was most recently published in 2005 by Penguin for U.S. markets.

CONCLUSION

African writers have always faced overwhelming difficulties in publishing their works and awkward relationships with the reading public. Publishing companies in Africa tend toward inefficiency, irregularity, and unreliability. If writers are successful at publication in spite all of the obstacles, they may then face intense scrutiny by government officials, which could in turn lead to censorship, imprisonment, exile, or death. Their African audiences, the reading public, are in many cases either illiterate, literate only in African languages, too poor to buy books, and/or utterly intimidated by reading material. Yet the last fifty years have shown that writers have been surprisingly successful in what Charles Larson calls "talking with paper." All kinds of texts, from speeches, political treatises, and biographies to journals as well as creative literary works, speak loudly for the continent. Although the use of western languages to create post-colonial African writing has been frowned on by some critics, the English, French, German, and Portuguese languages common in African texts amplify the writers' messages and make them more globally available. A writer's audience expands as a result of language choice. As educational opportunities in African nations continue to improve, one expects that illiteracy rates will decline and more Africans will have the means to access the thoughts and ideologies of writers who endeavor to capture what it means to live in post-colonial, African contexts.

RECOMMENDED READING

Booker, M. Keith. *The African Novel in English*. Portsmouth, NH: Heinemann, 1998.
Gates, Henry Louis, Jr. ed. *"Race," Writing, and Difference*. Chicago: U. of Chicago Press, 1985.
Loomba, Ania. *Colonialism/Postcolonialism*. London: Routledge, 1998.
McLeod, John. *Beginning Postcolonialism*. Manchester: Manchester UP, 2000.
Msiska, Mpalive-Hangson and Paul Hyland. *Writing and Africa*. London: Longman, 1997.
Ojaide, Tanure and Joseph Obi. *Culture, Society, and Politics in Modern African Literature*. Durham, NC: Carolina Academic Press, 2002.

PRIMARY SOURCES

Achebe, Chinua. *Arrow of God*. London: Heinemann, 1964.

———. *Man of the People*. London: Heinemann, 1966.

———. *Morning Yet on Creation Day*. New York: Anchor, 1975.

———. *Things Fall Apart*. New York: Astor-Honor, 1959. All of Achebe's works are available in most libraries.

African Drum. Johannesburg, South Africa. This journal was published from 1951 to the early 1960s, and later became *Drum;* it is available in some comprehensive academic libraries.

Aidoo, Christina Ama Ata. *The Dilemma of a Ghost*. Accra: Longmans, 1965. Text is available in most academic libraries.

Armah, Ayi Kwei. *The Beautiful Ones Are Not Yet Born*. London: Heinemann, 1969. Text is somewhat difficult to find in libraries; late 1980s edition is available for purchase online.

Bâ, Mariama. *So Long a Letter*. Oxford: Heinemann, 1989.

———. *Une si longue lettre*. Dakar: Nouvelles Éditions Africaines, 1986. English and French versions are available in academic libraries worldwide.

Black Orpheus. Ibadan, Nigeria. Journal was published from 1957 to 1967; it is available in some comprehensive academic libraries.

Coetzee, J. M. *Disgrace*. New York: Viking, 1999. Text is available in most libraries.

Dangarembga, Tsitsi. *Nervous Conditions*. New York: Seal Press, 1989. Text is available in most libraries.

Drum. Johannesburg, South Africa. Journal was published from 1951 to early 1960s, formerly *African Drum;* available in some comprehensive academic libraries.

Emecheta, Buchi. *In the Ditch*. Oxford and Portsmouth, NH: Heinemann, 1972.

———. *Second Class Citizen*. New York: George Braziller, 1974. Both of Emecheta's works are readily available in academic libraries.

Fanon, Frantz. *Les Damnés de la terre*. Paris: La Découverte, 1961.

———. *Peau noire, masques blancs*. Paris: Seuil, 1952. Both Fanon works are available in most academic libraries.

The Freedom Charter. Treatise. Adopted at the Congress of the People. Kliptown, Soweto, South Africa. 26 June 1955. Text of treatise is available at http://www.anc.org.za/ancdocs/history/charter.html.

Hasan, Abdul. "Introducing Publishing in the University Curriculum: The Delhi Experiment." Unpublished paper read at The Commonwealth African Book Development Seminar. Ibadan. 2–14 Feb., 1975.

Kane, Cheikh Hamidou. *L'Aventure ambiguë*. Paris: Julliard, 2001. Text is available in most academic libraries.

Kariuki, Josiah. *Mau Mau Detainee*. London: Oxford, 1963. Text is available in academic libraries worldwide.

Kourouma, Ahmadou. *Les soleils des indépendances*. Paris: Seuil, 1990. Text is available at most academic libraries.

Macmillan, Harold. Speech. *Wind of Change*. Cape Town, South Africa. 3 Feb. 1960. Text of speech is available at http://africanhistory.about.com/od/eraindependence/p/wind_of_change2.htm.

Mandela, Nelson. Speech. *I am Prepared to Die*. Pretoria, South Africa. 20 Apr. 1964. Text of speech is available at http://www.anc.org.za/ancdocs/history/rivonia.html.

———. "People Are Destroyed." *Liberation: A Journal for Democratic Discussion*. Johannesburg, South Africa. Oct. 1955. Text is available online at http://www.africawithin.com/mandela/people_destroyed_1055.htm; electronic archive of journal is available at http://disa.nu.ac.za/journals/jourliexpand.htm.

Niane, D. T. *Soundjata ou l'Épopée Mandingue*. Paris: Présence Africaine, 1960. Text is available in academic libraries worldwide.

Nkrumah, Kwame. *Consciencism: Philosophy and Ideology for Decolonisation*. New York: Modern Reader Paperbacks, 1970. Text is available in large academic libraries.

———. *I Speak of Freedom: A Statement of African Ideology*. London: Heinemann, 1961, xi-xiv. Text is also available online at http://www.fordham.edu/halsall/mod/1961nkrumah.html.

———. *Neo-Colonialism, the Last Stage of Imperialism.* New York: International Publishers, 1966. Text is available in libraries worldwide.

Nwapa, Flora. *Efuru.* Oxford: Heinemann, 1966. Text has been reprinted numerous times and is available in libraries worldwide.

———. *Idu.* London: Heinemann, 1970. Text is available in highly specialized library collections.

Nyerere, Julius. Treatise. *Arusha Declaration: On the Policy of Self-Tolerance in Tanzania.* Tanganyika African National Union. 5 Feb. 1967. Text is available online at http://www.marxists.org/subject/africa/nyerere/1967/arusha-declaration.htm.

Ogot, Grace. *The Promised Land.* Nairobi, Kenya: East African Publishing House, 1966. Text is available in academic libraries worldwide.

Okigbo, Christopher. *Labyrinths: with Path of Thunder.* New York: African Publishing Corporation, 1971. Text is available in most academic libraries.

Okri, Ben. *The Famished Road.* London: J. Cape, 1991. Text is available in most libraries.

Onitsha Market Literature (various titles). One hundred seventy titles published in Onitsha, Nigeria are available in the United States at the University of Indiana Library; the University of Kansas has a digitized collection of twenty-one of the books globally available online at http://onitsha.diglib.ku.edu/tdc/.

Ousmane, Sembène. *Les Bouts de Bois de Dieu.* Abidjan: Nouvelles Éditions Africaines, 1984. Text is available in academic libraries worldwide.

Présence Africaine. Paris: Seuil. Journal is available in academic libraries worldwide and electronically at http://www.presenceafricaine.com.

Senghor, Léopold Sédar. *Anthologie de la nouvelle poésie nègre et malgache de langue française.* Paris: Presses Universitaires de France, 1948. Text is available in libraries worldwide.

Soyinka, Wole. *A Dance of the Forests.* London: Oxford UP, 1963. Text is available in most academic libraries worldwide.

———. *The Interpreters.* London: A. Deutsch, 1965. Text is available in most academic libraries.

———. *The Man Died: Prison Notes of Wole Soyinka.* London: Rex Collings, 1972. Text is available at libraries worldwide.

Tutuola, Amos. *The Palm-Wine Drinkard; and My Life in the Bush of Ghosts.* New York: Grove Press, 1994. Text is available in specialized libraries.

SECONDARY SOURCES

Achebe, Chinua. "The Novelist as Teacher." In *Hopes and Impediments,* 40–46. New York: Anchor, 1990.

Amuta, Chidi. "Fanon, Cabral and Ngugi on National Liberation." In *The Post-Colonial Studies Reader,* 158–63. Edited by Bill Ashcroft, Gareth Griffiths, and Helen Tiffin. London and New York: Routledge, 1995.

"Archer." "Young Kenyans just don't read!!" *Midnight Frisco.* 19 Oct. 2006. http://midnight frisco.blogspot.com/2006/10/young-kenyans-just-dont-read.html. Accessed 19 Dec. 2006.

Ashcroft, Bill, Gareth Griffiths, and Helen Tiffin. *The Empire Writes Back.* London and New York: Routledge, 1989.

Bryce-Okunlola, Jane. "Popular Writing in Africa." In *Writing and Africa,* 174–192. Edited by Mpalive-Hangson Msiska and Paul Hyland. London and New York: Longman, 1997.

Case, Frederick Ivor. "Aesthetics, Ideology and Social Commitment in the Prose Fiction of Ousmane Sembène." In *Ousmane Sembène: Dialogues with Critics and Writers,* 3–13. Edited by Samba Gadjigo, Ralph Faulkingham, Thomas Cassirer, and Reinhard Sander. Amherst: U of Massachusetts P, 1993.

Chinweizu, Onwuchekwa Jemie and Ihechukwu Madubuike. *Toward the Decolonization of African Literature.* Vol. 1. Washington: Howard UP, 1983.

Collins, Robert O. *Europeans in Africa.* New York: Knopf, 1971.

Collins, III, Walter P. *Tracing Personal Expansion: Reading Selected Novels as Modern African Bildungsroman.* Lanham, MD: UP of America, 2006.

Dodson, Don. "The Role of the Publisher in Onitsha Market Literature." In *Critical Perspectives on Nigerian Literatures*, 195–213. Edited by Bernth Lindfors. Washington: Three Continents Press, 1976.

Gates, Jr., Henry Louis. "Between the Living and the Unborn." *New York Times Book Review* 28 June 1992: 3, 20.

Gikandi, Simon. "Traveling Theory: Ngugi's Return to English." *Research in African Literatures* 31.2 (2000): 194–209.

Global Books in Print Database. 2006. Bowker. U of South Carolina, Lancaster, Medford Lib. http://globalbooksinprint.com.

Jeyifo, Biodun. *Wole Soyinka: Politics, Poetics and Postcolonialism.* Cambridge and New York: Cambridge UP, 2004.

Jones, Eldred Durosimi. *Wole Soyinka.* New York: Twayne, 1973.

Killam, G. D. *The Writings of Chinua Achebe.* London: Heinemann, 1977.

Kotei, S. I. A. "The Book Today in Africa." In *The Post-Colonial Studies Reader*, 480–84. Edited by Bill Ashcroft, Gareth Griffiths, and Helen Tiffin. London and New York: Routledge, 1995.

Larson, Charles R. *The Ordeal of the African Writer.* London: Zed Books, 2001.

Lindfors, Bernth. *Loaded Vehicles: Studies in African Literary Media.* Trenton, NJ: Africa World Press, 1996.

———. *Popular Literatures in Africa.* Trenton, NJ: Africa World Press, 1991.

———. "The Teaching of African Literatures in Anglophone Universities: An Instructive Canon." *Matatu: Canonization and Teaching of African Literatures* 7 (1990): 41–55.

Miller, Christopher. *Theories of Africans. Francophone Literature and Anthropology in Africa.* Chicago: U of Chicago P, 1990.

Mudimbe, V. Y. *The Invention of Africa: Gnosis, Philosophy, and the Order of Knowledge.* Bloomington and Indianapolis: Indiana UP, 1988.

Nkrumah, Kwame. *Consciencism: Philosophy and Ideology for Decolonization and Development with Particular Reference to the African Revolution.* New York: Monthly Review Press, 1965.

Obiechina, Emmanuel. *An African Popular Literature: A Study of Onitsha Market Pamphlets.* Cambridge: Cambridge UP, 1973.

Ohaegbulam, Festus Ugboaja. *West African Responses to European Imperialism in the Nineteenth and Twentieth Centuries.* Lanham, MD: UP of America, 2002.

Osundare, Niyi. *Thread in the Loom: Essays on African Literature and Culture.* Trenton, NJ: Africa World Press, 2002.

Owomoyela, Oyekan. *African Literatures: An Introduction.* Waltham, MA: Crossroads Press, 1979.

Petersen, Kristen Holst. *Criticism and Ideology: Second African Writers' Conference Stockholm 1986.* Uppsala: Scandinavian Institute of African Studies, 1988.

Southern African Book Development Education Trust. "SABDET Programmes," http://www.readingafrica.com/programmes.htm.

Stec, Loretta. "Publishing and Canonicity: The Case of Heinemann's 'African Writers Series.'" *Pacific Coast Philology* 32.2 (1997): 140–149.

Stratton, Florence. "The Shallow Grave: Archetypes of Female Experience in African Fiction." *Research in African Literatures* 19.1 (1988): 143–169.

Uwakweh, Pauline Ada. "Debunking Patriarchy: The Liberational Quality of Voicing in Tsitsi Dangarembga's *Nervous Conditions.*" *Research in African Literatures* 26.1 (1995): 75–84.

Wilkinson, Jane. *Talking with African Writers: Interviews with African Poets, Playwrights & Novelists.* London: James Currey, 1992.

Willey, Ann Elizabeth and Jeanette Treiber. *Negotiating the Postcolonial: Emerging Perspectives on Tsitsi Dangarembga.* Trenton, NJ: Africa World Press, 2002.

WorldCat Database. 1992–2006. Online Computer Library Center. U of South Carolina, Lancaster, Medford Lib. http://firstsearch.oclc.org.

Appendix—Representative Bibliographies for Other Reading Areas

THE ASIAN DIASPORA

Newspapers

Rafu Shimpo: 1903–present. *Rafu Shimpo* is published daily in Los Angeles. The paper was originally only published in Japanese but is now published in both Japanese and English. Publication was suspended during World War II but resumed again in January 1946. Its current circulation is 22,000. (Alicia Benjamin-Samuels—freedomforum.org 06.18.01)

Nichi Bei Times: 1946–present. *Nichi Bei Times* is a daily newspaper published in San Francisco. It has a circulation of about 8,000 and is published in English and Japanese. (Alicia Benjamin-Samuels—freedomforum.org 06.18.01)

International Daily News: 1981–present. A Chinese-language newspaper available in the United States and Indonesia. Taiwanese-owned. Sold in Chinese communities around the United States.

Websites

http://www.panix.com/~aaww/links/asammag.html. A popular culture website that advertises Asian American youth magazines.

http://www.eastwestmagazine.com/. An online magazine aimed at a general Asian American readership. Also published in hard copy.

http://www.click2asia.com/. Large conglomeration of previously freestanding sites. The "Lounge" section is especially popular for Asian dating connections, chat, and links to specialty Asian American sites.

The gate to Montreal's Chinatown which has Chinese, Japanese, Korean, and Vietnamese restaurants inside the complex.

Individual Authors

Amy Tan (*The Kitchen God's Wife, The Joy Luck Club*)
Salman Rushdie (*Midnight's Children, The Ground Beneath Her Feet*)
Michael Ondaatje (*The English Patient*)

A Yemenite Jew at morning prayers, wearing a kippah skullcap, prayer shawl and tefillin.

THE JEWISH DIASPORA AND ISRAEL

Newspapers

Yisrael Shelanu: 1979–present. A New York paper published in Hebrew and aimed at Israelis living in the United States.

Yated Ne'nman: 1989–present. Another New York newspaper aimed at a traditional Jewish readership. It has sections on traditional lifestyle.

Haaretz ("The Land": http://www.haaretz-daily.com/).

The Jerusalem Post (http://www.jpost.com/). *Haaretz* and *The Jerusalem Post* are the two most popular newspapers in Israel, and they appear in both Hebrew and English. They are published in both print and web versions.

Tedioth Ahronoth: 1970s–present. ("Latest News") A broad-circulation, Hebrew-language newspaper published in Tel Aviv, Israel.

Websites

http://www.forward.com/. An online Jewish daily newspaper, also published as a weekly hard-copy newspaper.

http://www.jewishlivingmag.com/. A general lifestyle magazine for a Jewish readership, also published in hard copy.

http://www.nextbook.org/. A website devoted to Jewish culture in the United States: "A Jewish cultural organization that produces an on-line magazine, publishes a book series, and presents events around the country."

Elie Wiesel speaking at the World Economic Forum Annual Meeting in 2003.

Individual Authors

Elie Wiesel (*Night*)
Isaac Bashevis Singer (*The Collected Stories of Isaac Bashevis Singer*)

THE ISLAMIC DIASPORA

Newspapers

Alfazl International Weekly: Published in Pakistan and London.
Ahmadiyya Gazette: Published in Maryland, United States.
Ahmadiyya Gazette: Published in Toronto, Canada.

Websites

http://www.islamicamagazine.com/. "Opening Minds Everywhere." A U.S.-based website specializing in items of political and social interest.

http://english.aljazeera.net/. A news website based in Doha, capital of Qatar. Aljazeera ("The Peninsular") reports on world news from a Middle Eastern perspective.

http://www.azizahmagazine.com/. A U.S.-based magazine of general Islamic interest that focuses on lifestyle and is largely aimed at women.

Islamic Society of Northern Wisconsin Mosque in Altoona, Wisconsin.

Individual Authors

Orhan Pamuk (*Benim Adım Kırmızı, Snow*)
Tayeb Salih (*Mawsim al-Hijrah ila al-Shamal*)
Maulana Maududi (*Tafhim ul-Qur'an*)

EASTERN EUROPE

Newspapers

Bild: 1958–present. *Bild* ("Picture"; formerly *Bild Zeitung*, "Picture Newspaper") is the most popular tabloid in Europe. It began life as a picture-based publication, but as literacy levels rose in post-War Europe, it added more text.

Blesk: "Lightening"—a daily tabloid newspaper in the Czech Republic. It has the largest newspaper circulation in the Czech Republic.

Adevărul: "The Truth." A broad-circulation leftist newspaper in Romania.

Websites

http://aktualne.centrum.sk/. News site from Slovakia, in Slovakian.
http://www.mediapool.bg/. News site from Bulgaria, in Bulgarian.
http://www.rol.ro/. "Romania On-Line" news site from Romania, in Romanian.

Individual Authors

Vaclav Havel (*To the Castle and Back*)
Aleksandr Solzhenitsyn (*The Gulag Archipelago*)
Milan Kundera (*The Unbearable Lightness of Being*)
Heinrich Böll (*Die verlorene Ehre der Katharina Blum* or *Wie Gewalt entstehen und wohin sie führen kann*. Trans. *The Lost Honour of Katharina Blum* or *How Violence Can Develop and Where It Can Lead*)

The library of University of Bucharest, Romania.

Index

About the Contributors

Rochelle Almeida teaches South Asian studies and world Anglophone literature as master teacher of global cultures at New York University. She earned a PhD in English at the University of Bombay, India, and a Doctor of Arts degree from St. John's University, New York. She is the author of *Originality and Imitation: Indianness in the Novels of Kamala Markandaya* (2000) and *The Politics of Mourning: Grief-Management in Cross-Cultural Fiction* (2005). She is also an international freelance writer whose work has appeared in global periodicals.

Alison Bartlett is senior lecturer in English and cultural studies at the University of Western Australia, and directs the Women's Studies program. Prior to this, she spent ten years at the University of Southern Queensland in literary studies. Her PhD from James Cook University of North Queensland was in Australian literature. Her publications include *Jamming the Machinery: Contemporary Australian Women's Writing* (1998) and *Australian Literature and the Public Sphere* (coeditor 1999). Her more recent research has been on cultural discourses of maternity, pedagogy, and activism.

Samaya L. S. Chanthaphavong is a PhD candidate in the Faculty of Arts at the University of Melbourne, Australia. She has a Bachelor of Arts (Hons) with a double major in history and visual culture from Monash University (Melbourne, Australia) and a second Bachelor of Arts majoring in Asian studies from Murdoch University (Perth, Australia). She has published widely within the humanities field, focusing mainly on Southeast and East Asian history.

Diana Chlebek is associate professor of bibliography in languages and literature at the University of Akron. She has a PhD in comparative literature from Cornell University, an MA in library science from the University of Chicago, and an MA in French studies from the University of Toronto. Her research and teaching interests focus on British and European fiction, Canadian literature, children's literature, and multiculturalism in American literature. She has published extensively in these areas of specialization and is currently working on thematic studies of the nineteenth-century English novel for a scholarly reference work.

James L. Citron is an intercultural education specialist at Dartmouth College and Director of the Inter-American Partnership for Education, a program of Worldfund and the Rassias Foundation at Dartmouth College. He has taught Spanish and intercultural communication at the high school, undergraduate, and graduate levels and has served in a variety of leadership capacities in international educational exchange in the United States and Mexico. He holds a PhD in educational linguistics from the University of Pennsylvania; an EdM in administration, planning, and social policy from the Harvard University Graduate School of Education; and a BA in psychology and Spanish from Dartmouth College.

Walter P. Collins III is assistant professor of French and English at the University of South Carolina Lancaster. He completed his PhD in comparative literature with a focus on African postcolonial literature and theory at the University of South Carolina Columbia. He teaches French and English writing and grammar, world literature, and African literature courses. He is currently editing a book on literary works of emerging African writers.

Joan Curbet holds a PhD from the Universidad Autónoma de Barcelona, Spain and is currently professor of letters of the University in the Department de Filologia Anglesa I Germanística at UAB. Dr. Curbet has published a number of articles in the area of Renaissance poetry and interpretation.

Özgen Felek completed her first PhD on classical Ottoman poetry at Fırat University, Turkey, in 2007. She is currently pursuing her second PhD in Near Eastern studies at the University of Michigan with areas of emphasis in Ottoman dream culture and Islamic mysticism. With Walter G. Andrews, she coedited *Victoria Holbrook'a Armağan* (2006, in Turkish), a collection of essays in honor of Victoria Rowe Holbrook.

Carme Font Paz is an associate professor in the Department de Filologia Anglesa I Germanística at Universitat Autònoma de Barcelona, Spain, and is currently completing a PhD in early modern women writers. She has translated a number of English and German texts for publication.

Jihee Han is an assistant professor of English at Gyeongsang National University, Jinju, South Korea. She completed her PhD on modern American and Korean poetry at the University of Tulsa, Oklahoma, and teaches modern American poetry, literary theory and criticism, and English literature. She has taught in the United States and conducts research on world literature, modern Korean literature, and Korean culture and history. She is currently working on a comparative study, "William B. Yeats and Joseon-Korea's Ghangho Poetics."

Sergio Inestrosa is an associate professor of Spanish at Endicott College, Beverly, Massachusetts. He completed his PhD in modern literature at the Iberoamericana University in Mexico City, and teaches a variety of topics in the field of Latin American studies, including film, literature and culture. He has lived in Mexico and Central America and taught in the United States, Mexico, and Spain. He has published several books on the communications field, and is currently researching the U.S. electoral process and the media.

Evan Lampe is an assistant professor of history and international studies at Endicott College. His dissertation explores the place of working people in the

Pacific economy of the late-eighteenth and early-nineteenth centuries. He received his PhD from the University at Albany, State University of New York. In addition to teaching American and international history, he is researching transnational labor history and maritime history.

Malin Lidström Brock is a PhD candidate in English literature at Oxford University, United Kingdom. Her dissertation explores the relationship between women's biography and feminist theory. She teaches contemporary British and American literature, and has written on the cultural history of reading. She has also coedited *Tove Jansson Rediscovered,* a collection of critical essays on the Finnish author Tove Jansson. She has lived and worked in Sweden, France, and the United Kingdom.

Ksanna Mazhurina is a research fellow at the Institute of Asian and African Studies of Moscow State University. She concentrates on the study of contemporary women's writing in China and Russia, focusing on the problems of gender, women's consciousness, and the "self" in post-communist societies. She has taught and conducted research in Moscow University, China's Yunnan University, Taiwan, and the Five College Women's Studies Research Center at Mt. Holyoke College (USA). She is a translator of, and commentator on, the works of Zhang Jie, a prominent Chinese writer.

Molly Metherd is an assistant professor of English at Saint Mary's College and teaches courses in American literature, Latino literature, women's studies, and comparative literature. Her scholarly work is on the historical and contemporary intersections between Latin American and U.S. literatures. She has presented papers on this subject at numerous national and international conferences. She is the author of "Visions and Revisions: The Americanization of Christopher Columbus in the works of Alejo Carpentier and William Carlos Williams" (2001).

John A. Morrow is Associate Professor of Languages and Literature at Eastern New Mexico University. Dr. Morrow completed his PhD at the University of Toronto. He has authored, edited, and translated several books including *Arabic, Islam, and the Allah Lexicon; Shi'ite Islam: Orthodoxy or Heterodoxy; Humanos casi humanos;* and *Amerindian Elements in the Poetry of Rubén Darío.* He has contributed chapters to *Juan Felipe Toruño en dos mundos* and *Latino America: A State-by-State Encyclopedia.* He has also published a multitude of articles and poems in English, French, and Spanish, in academic, cultural, and literary journals.

K. Sarah-Jane Murray is assistant professor of medieval literature and French in the Baylor University Honors College, and a permanent member of the *Centre d'Etudes du Moyen Age* at the Sorbonne Nouvelle in Paris. She completed her PhD in romance languages and literatures at Princeton in 2003, is particularly interested in classical, Celtic, and biblical influences on medieval literature, and is the author of *From Plato to Lancelot: A Preface to Chrétien de Troyes* (Syracuse Univ. Press, 2008).

Firat Oruc earned his PhD from the Literature Department at Duke University, Durham, N.C. His dissertation was entitled "Plebian Fictions: Modalities of Worlding in Twentieth-Century Literature." His research interests intersect at modernist, post-Colonial, and transnational literary studies. He has presented and chaired sessions at a number of international conferences, including the annual Duke-UNC Graduate Student Conference on Islamic Studies and the American Comparative Literature Association annual meeting.

Andrew Peek recently retired as senior lecturer in English and creative writing at the University of Tasmania, having previously taught at universities in the UK, Nigeria, and New South Wales. He has a BA from the University of Cambridge, a PhD in English from Sheffield University, and a doctorate in creative writing from the University of Wollongong. He has published many articles on modernism and African and Australian literature, reviewed extensively in Australian print and electronic media, and published a volume of poetry, *The Calabar Transcript*. He is currently engaged in a study of the biography of Robert Louis Stevenson.

Hannah Platts is a lecturer in Roman history at Imperial College London, UK and a research fellow of King's College London, UK. She completed her PhD on the art, architecture, and cultural history of Roman villas in Italy from the second century B.C.E. to the second century C.E. at Bristol University, UK. She teaches a variety of topics on the history and visual culture of the Roman and Greek world including Roman History of the Republic and Empire; Greek History, Art, and Power in the Ancient World; and The Roman Villa and its Later Reception. She is currently working on a monograph that examines the villa residence in architecture and literature, as well as its role in ancient Roman society and culture.

Emily Rodgers is a university scholar at Baylor University ('08) and has been recommended for a French embassy teaching assistantship in France during 2008–2009. Her senior thesis research explores the impact of Martianus Capella's doctrines of the seven liberal arts on the development of vernacular romance narrative, in particular the works of Chrétien de Troyes.

Todd Rohman is associate professor at Governors State University IL, where he teaches American, British, and world literatures, in addition to rhetorical and critical theory. He also teaches a number of writing and grammar courses. His chapter "Hypertextualizing Thomas Pynchon's *The Crying of Lot 49*" is forthcoming in the Modern Language Association's *Approaches to Teaching* series.

Tom Severson is currently a graduate student studying at Governors State University in University Park, IL. He works as a technical editor at Goodheart-Willcox Publisher in Tinley Park, IL. By day an editor and by night a student, Tom looks forward to graduating and teaching.

Gabrielle Watling is an associate professor of English at Endicott College, Beverly, MA. She completed her PhD in post-Colonial theory and fiction at James Cook University, Queensland, Australia, in 1996. She teaches a variety of subjects, including literary theory and interpretation, British literature, gothic literature, and colonial and post-colonial literatures. She is currently researching a monograph on class negotiations in early modernism. She has lived and worked in Australia, Mexico, and the United States.

Tiffany Yecke Brooks earned her PhD from Florida State University in Tallahassee, FL, and her MA from the Department of Classics and Ancient History from the University of Bristol in Bristol, England. She has taught literature, dramatic literature, writing, and literary theory and criticism at a number of universities, including Abilene Christian University, McMurry University, and The University of South Carolina at Beaufort. She is currently a visiting instructor at Florida State, where her research interests include early Christian texts, classical heritage, Bible as literature, cultural memory studies, and performance theory.